Praise for *Many Europes*

P9-BXX-463

"I would describe this book as the book I have been waiting for."

AMANDA BAHR-EVOLA, *Southern Illinois University Edwardsville*

"I believe that this may well be the best Western civilization text so far. The book is well written, concise, and presents a picture of events that encourages readers to analyze historical events with an open mind."

MATTHEW D. SCHAFFER, *Florence-Darlington Technical College*

"I love this textbook. The writing style is descriptive, interesting and engaging, all while keeping the tone and content at a college level."

REANNE EICHELE, *Pikes Peak Community College*

"This text is a genuine rethinking, reordering and restating of the rise of Europe and, uniquely, different ways to approach the very concepts of Europe and the West."

WAYNE BOWEN, *Southeast Missouri State University*

"I would describe this book as fresh, innovative, and setting the trend for future Western civilization textbooks to acknowledge the diversity and complexity of Europe."

ANGELA L. ASH, *Owensboro Community and Technical College*

"The book takes a different approach to history, avoiding the same stagnant stories that those who have just graduated from high school already know—I do believe that it takes the boredom out of history and it brings history alive, which we should all strive to do."

MARY ANN BORDEN, *Hudson Valley Community College*

"The opening vignettes, the focus on individuals and their experiences, and the look at what historians do in the investigations section make this book better than the competition."

SUSAN G. THOMPSON, *Northern Virginia Community College*

"*Many Europes*' approach makes it more interesting and readable than other texts I have seen or used. I think that if there is a text that students might actually read and get something out of, this is it."

MICHAEL KENNEDY, *High Point University*

MANY EUROPES

CHOICE AND CHANCE IN WESTERN CIVILIZATION

VOLUME I: TO 1715

MANY EUROPES

CHOICE AND CHANCE IN WESTERN CIVILIZATION

VOLUME I: TO 1715

Paul Edward Dutton
Simon Fraser University

Suzanne Marchand
Louisiana State University

Deborah Harkness
University of Southern California

The McGraw-Hill Companies

MANY EUROPES, FIRST EDITION
Published by McGraw-Hill, a business unit of The McGraw-Hill Companies, Inc., 1221 Avenue of the Americas, New York, NY, 10020. Copyright © 2014 by The McGraw-Hill Companies, Inc. All rights reserved. Printed in the United States of America. No part of this publication may be reproduced or distributed in any form or by any means, or stored in a database or retrieval system, without the prior written consent of The McGraw-Hill Companies, Inc., including, but not limited to, in any network or other electronic storage or transmission, or broadcast for distance learning.

Some ancillaries, including electronic and print components, may not be available to customers outside the United States.

This book is printed on acid-free paper.

1 2 3 4 5 6 7 8 9 0 DOW/DOW 1 0 9 8 7 6 5 4 3

ISBN 978-0-07-333049-5
MHID 0-07-333049-3

Senior Vice President, Products & Markets: *Kurt L. Strand*
Vice President, General Manager: *Michael Ryan*
Vice President, Content Production & Technology Services: *Kimberly Meriwether David*
Managing Director: *Gina Boedeker*
Director: *Matthew Busbridge*
Director of Development: *Rhona Robbin*
Managing Development Editor: *Nancy Crochiere*
Content Development Editors: *Betty Slack, David Chodoff, Karen Dubno*
Editorial Coordinator: *Kaelyn Schulz*
Digital Development: *Meghan Campbell; Denise Wright, Southern Editorial*
Digital Product Analyst: *John Brady*
Marketing Manager: *Stacy Ruel*
Director, Content Production: *Terri Schiesl*
Senior Production Editor: *Catherine Morris*
Senior Buyer: *Laura Fuller*
Design Manager: *Debra Kubiak*
Cover and Interior Designer: *Ellen Pettengell*
Senior Content Licensing Specialist: *John Leland*
Photo Researcher: *David Tietz/Editorial Image, LLC*
Connect Media Project Manager: *Sarah Hill*
OLC Media Project Manager: *Jennifer Barrick*
Typeface: *10/12 Palatino*
Compositor: *Thompson Type*
Printer: *R.R. Donnelley & Sons*

Cover Images: *(Top to bottom, left to right)* © Archives Charmet/The Bridgeman Art Library; © Clara Amit/AFP/Getty Images/Newscom; The Gallery Collection/Corbis; © Erich Lessing/Art Resource, NY; © Bridgeman-Giraudon/Art Resource, NY; © Guido Baviera/Grand Tour/Corbis; © Digital Vision/Punchstock; © Gianni Dagli Orti/The Art Archive at Art Resource, NY; © Gianni Dagli Orti/The Art Archive at Art Resource, NY; © Bettmann/Corbis; © Werner Forman/Corbis; © Mark Harris/The Image Bank/Getty Images; © G. Nimatallah/De Agostini Picture Library/Getty Images; AP Photo/Petros Giannakouris; © Ancient Art & Architecture Collection Ltd/Alamy; © SuperStock; AP Photo/Peter Kemp; © SuperStock; Haworth Art Gallery, Accrington, Lancashire, UK/The Bridgeman Art Library; © Gideon Mendel/In Pictures/Corbis; AP Photo; © Alliance Images/Alamy

All credits appearing on page C-1 are considered to be an extension of the copyright page.

Library of Congress Cataloging-in-Publication Data
Dutton, Paul Edward, 1952–
Many Europes : choice and chance in Western civilization / Paul Dutton, Suzanne Marchand, Deborah Harkness.—1st ed.
p. cm.
(vol. 1 : alk. paper)—ISBN 0-07-333050-7 (vol. 2 : alk. paper)—ISBN 0-07-333051-5 ([special vol]. : alk. paper) 1. Europe—Civilization—Textbooks. 2. Civilization, Western—History—Textbooks. I. Marchand, Suzanne L., 1961– II. Harkness, Deborah E., 1965– III. Title.
CB203.D88 2014
940—dc23

2012036126

The Internet addresses listed in the text were accurate at the time of publication. The inclusion of a website does not indicate an endorsement by the authors or McGraw-Hill, and McGraw-Hill does not guarantee the accuracy of the information presented at these sites.

www.mhhe.com

ABOUT THE AUTHORS

PAUL EDWARD DUTTON is the Jack and Nancy Farley University Professor in History at Simon Fraser University, where he teaches the survey of Western civilization. He holds a Ph.D. from the University of Toronto and a higher doctorate from the Pontifical Institute of Mediaeval Studies. He is the author, coauthor, or editor of eight books, including *The Politics of Dreaming in the Carolingian Empire* (Nebraska, 1994) and *Charlemagne's Mustache and Other Cultural Clusters of a Dark Age* (Palgrave, 2004), which was awarded the Margaret Wade Labarge Prize for best book in medieval studies. A Fellow of the Medieval Academy of America and the Royal Society of Canada, Dutton is also the creator and editor of three series with the University of Toronto Press that seek to help students deal with the periods before 1600 CE.

SUZANNE MARCHAND received her B.A. from the University of California–Berkeley, and her M.A. and Ph.D. from the University of Chicago. She taught European intellectual history at Princeton University and in 1999 moved to Louisiana State University, where she is professor of history. Marchand is the author of two books, *Down from Olympus: Archaeology and Philhellenism in Germany, 1750–1970* (Princeton, 1996) and *German Orientalism in the Age of Empire: Religion, Race and Scholarship* (Cambridge University Press, 2009), which was awarded the George Mosse Prize of the American Historical Association for best book in cultural and intellectual history in 2009. In addition, she has been the recipient of an ACLS Burckhardt Fellowship and an Atlas Grant from the LSU Board of Regents.

DEBORAH HARKNESS received her B.A. from Mount Holyoke College, her M.A. from Northwestern University, and her Ph.D. from the University of California–Davis. An historian of science and medicine from antiquity to the present, she is professor of history at the University of Southern California. Her published works include *John Dee's Conversations with Angels: Cabala, Alchemy, and the End of Nature* (Cambridge University Press, 1999) and *The Jewel House: Elizabethan London and the Scientific Revolution* (Yale University Press, 2007) and the novel *A Discovery of Witches* (Viking, 2011). Harkness has received fellowships from the Guggenheim Foundation, the National Science Foundation, and the National Humanities Center and in 2008 was awarded both the Pfizer Prize for best book in the history of science and the John Ben Snow Prize for best book in British studies.

How *Many Europes* Guarantees Better Course Performance

Better prepared students

Imagine the dynamic class discussions you could have or lively lectures you could give if your students came to class prepared.

Enter McGraw-Hill's **LearnSmart,** the online adaptive learning system that guarantees that students come to class prepared. As part of McGraw-Hill's *Connect History* program, LearnSmart assesses students' knowledge of the chapter content and identifies gaps in understanding. Students come to class with a better grasp of the course material, resulting in more lively discussions and the freedom to lecture on what you think is important.

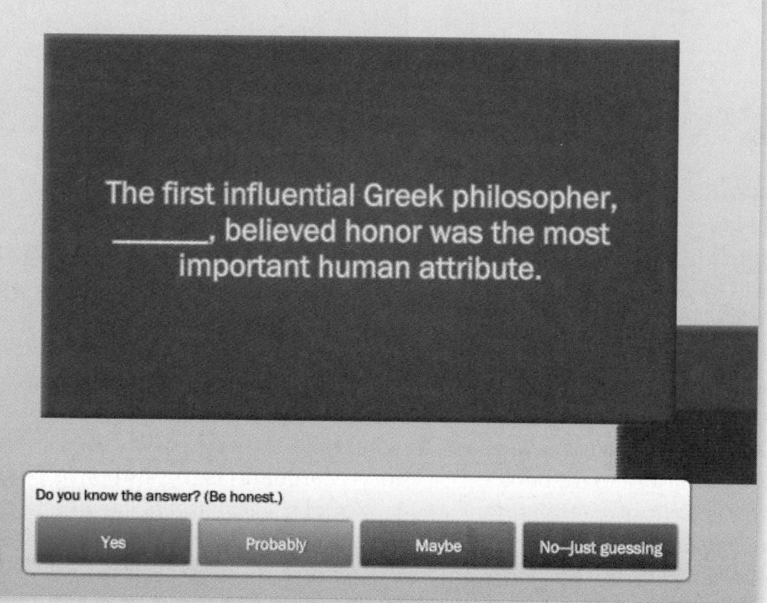
The first influential Greek philosopher, _______, believed honor was the most important human attribute.
Do you know the answer? (Be honest.)
Yes
Probably
Maybe
No—just guessing

Students tell us:

- *"I just wanted to let you know that **I love this Connect thing.** The LearnSmart modules are great and really help me to learn the material. I even downloaded their app for my phone."* —Colorado State University

And instructors say:

- *"Five weeks into the semester, students in my three [course] sections have averages of 99.93, 99.97, and 100% respectively on the LearnSmart modules. **I would NEVER get that kind of learning and accuracy if I just assigned them to 'read the chapter and take notes'** or 'read the chapter and reflect' or some other reading-based assignment."* —Florida State College at Jacksonville
- ***"LearnSmart has won my heart."*** —McLennan Community College

Better critical thinking skills

Many Europes moves students beyond memorization of names and dates and promotes critical thinking:

- **Back to the Source** is a primary source exercise that can be assigned in Connect.
- Choose from **five to eight additional primary sources per chapter** that can be assigned as activities in Connect History, or added to your print text.
- **Connecting the Sources,** an activity that compares two primary sources, is available in Connect History.
- A primer activity on **"How to Analyze a Primary Source"** can be assigned in Connect History or added to the text.
- Vibrant maps showing topographic features include critical thinking questions, while the digital program provides a wealth of **map and geography activities.**
- **"Critical Missions"** digital activities place students in a pivotal moment in time, and ask them to develop an historical argument.

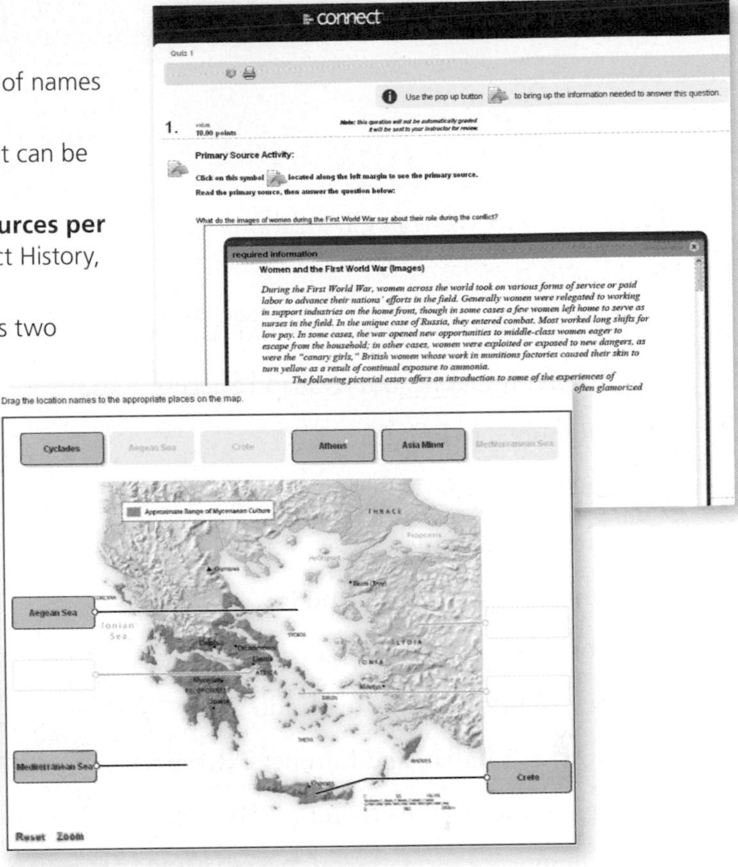

Better grades

Research shows that students' grades improve when using McGraw-Hill's Connect History and LearnSmart. Imagine being able to document this type of grade improvement through easily run reports.

Listen to instructors:

- *"My class that is **using Connect scored higher than any other class in my 25 years of teaching.**" —University of Colorado Denver*
- *"The students really love Connect. **They also got the best test scores on their first exam that I have ever seen in my teaching career.**"*
  —Georgia Southern University

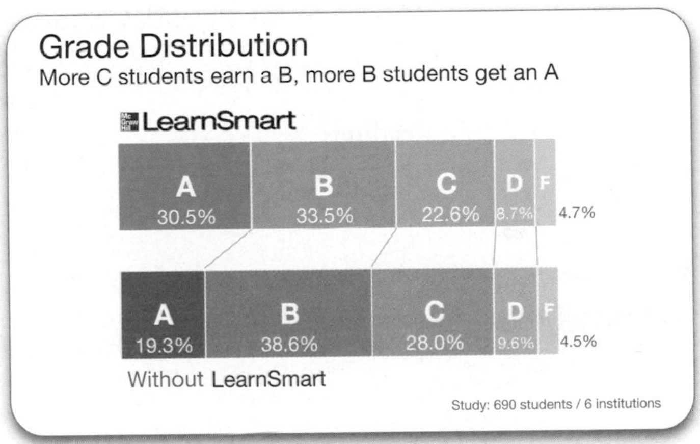

***Many Europes*: the digital and print program that Connects students to Success!**

BRIEF CONTENTS

CONTENTS

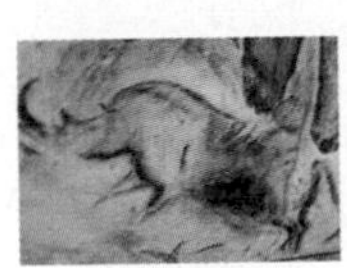

1 PRELIMINARY TO WESTERN CIVILIZATION 2

2 MANY GREECES 36

3 HELLENISTIC AGES 70
ACHIEVEMENTS AND ANXIETIES

4 THE ROMAN REPUBLIC 102
SURVIVAL AND SUCCESS

5 FROM REPUBLIC TO EMPIRE 132

6 THE SLOW TURN FROM ANCIENT TO MEDIEVAL 162

7 THE EARLY MIDDLE AGES 196

8 THE ROMANESQUE CENTRAL MIDDLE AGES 230

9 THE GOTHIC HIGH MIDDLE AGES 260

10 THE NEW WORLD OF THE LATE MIDDLE AGES 292

11 THE NORTHERN ITALIAN AND EUROPEAN RENAISSANCES 324

12 EUROPEANS TAKE TO THE OCEANS 356

13 THE RELIGIOUS RE-FORMATION OF EUROPE 386

14 ABSOLUTISM AND WAR IN THE SEVENTEENTH CENTURY 420

PREFACE

An Interview with the Authors

Q: Why "Many Europes"?

A: In historical terms, there never was a "single" Europe. The history of the European continent has always been one of many diverse peoples, languages, and regions, each seeking to survive, and striving to preserve and promote its own identity in the competitive world that was wider Europe. Diversity not unity, nations not empire, explain a great deal about the energy and dynamism of the history we study in Western civilization courses.

Q: Is this a new approach to Western civilization?

A: Absolutely. We think of it as an introduction to Western Civilization for a new generation, one that views "the West" as an important part of the world, but not the only part worth studying. With the growth of the world history course, we need to approach the history of the West in new ways and to search out what makes the many Europes different from the other great historical powers in Asia and the Middle East. One great difference is that the European continent rarely achieved the great and dominant empires that China and Islam did. Why, and is that important in accounting for the historical personality of the West? By looking at the strivings of the many Europes, its individuals and groups, we hope to present the Western civ experience in a vivid, fresh, and relevant way.

Q: You also invite students to think in terms of "Big Europe." How is that different?

A: Too many Western civilization textbooks focus almost exclusively on Britain, France, and Germany. In *Many Europes*, we made it our goal to stretch the boundaries, physical and intellectual, of Europe, integrating the vitally important, fascinating, and often blood-spattered histories of southern, central, and eastern Europe. Naturally, we also include the civilizations of Egypt, Islam, and Persia that have always been part of shaping what the many Europes could and could not be. All of them had a critical impact on the history and contours of Western civilization.

Q: Your subtitle is *Choice and Chance in Western Civilization.* Why did you choose those themes?

A: The subtitle reflects our fundamental conviction that people make history through their choices and their struggles to overcome particular problems and dilemmas. We believe that students engage best with history when they recognize that real human beings, whether in ancient Rome, medieval Byzantium, revolutionary France, or Nazi Germany, had to make difficult decisions while caught up in turbulent times, with a limited set of ideas and options available to them.

Q: That explains choice; what about chance?

A: Flesh and blood humans make history, but, as Karl Marx noted long ago, they cannot make it exactly as they wish. Chance intrudes—often in the form of external events such as dramatic or long-term weather changes, economic downturns, famines, and pandemic diseases that force people and societies to respond as best they can. Even Europe's most powerful rulers encountered unexpected forms of opposition within as well as outside their borders, and were compelled to change their plans. So, chance may matter as much as choice in shaping both individual lives and collective experiences.

Q: By "choice and chance," are you talking about the idea of contingency?

A: Exactly. Things didn't have to turn out the way they did. Surprising events, decisions, and actions of individuals and groups often turned the course of events in a new direction—for example, Constantine's unexpected embrace of Christianity and creation of a New Rome in Constantinople. We highlight the important idea of contingency with a feature in every chapter entitled "What a Difference a Year Makes." It gives students an understanding of how changeable history is, how pivotal some choices and some events were, in contrast to how inevitable it all seems when we view history backwards.

In *Many Europes*, we try to strike a balance between the micro and macro levels, choice and chance, but we seek always to emphasize *lived experience*, what it was like to be there, in a particular historical time. Context, in other words, is essential to outcomes, and we believe it a mistake to ride a wave of events without looking below the surface to the vast and sometimes ordinary forces at work generating change.

Q: Why is this idea of "lived experience" important?

A: Students can understand the choices made by individuals in the past only when we help them think themselves back into the historical and cultural contexts in which the actors lived—what it was like to be a Roman senator, an English peasant after the Norman Conquest, or a Victorian scullery maid. We can engage students in history by showing them how fascinating these stories are and why they still matter today, rather than overwhelming them with endless detail. So, we have selected illustrative and gripping human stories that reveal the past and its actors rather than offering an encyclopedic presentation of "one damned thing after another."

Q: How do primary sources fit into your program?

A: We are excited to offer instructors and students a rich portfolio of relevant and revealing primary sources to accompany the textbook. Not only have we included a primary source exercise at the end of each chapter, but we have also included a wide selection of additional primary source exercises tailored to our narrative in the associated digital program. The same choice of primary sources is available through McGraw-Hill's Create for instructors who want to customize their course materials with specific readings or even create their own reader.

Q: Is your narrative shorter than that of other "full-sized" Western civilization books?

A: Another of our departures from most other Western civilization texts involves making the narrative more concise. We have reduced the standard number of chapters from thirty to twenty-six, making it easier for instructors to cover the material in an average school year. In some cases, our chapter order reflects a compromise between chronological and thematic approaches to the subject. For the sake of student attention and a coherent presentation of historical phases, we separate early Rome and the mature Roman Republic from the collapse of the Republic and the Roman Empire, and treat the crusades as separate events and not as a single set of connected events. We also combine the material usually divided between chapters on the Industrial Revolution and on nation-building to emphasize the simultaneity of the two processes throughout most of Europe. This combination gives new punch to liberalism and nationalism, two forces that are alive in neo-versions today. But we have left room at the end of the book for a full chapter on Europe since 1989, recognizing that students today want and need to know about the developments and crises the continent has experienced since the end of the Cold War. We bring the story right up to the Eurocrisis, a development that helps us see clearly that even as economic integration, technological transformations, and cultural globalization have made life across the continent more uniform, the many-ness of Europe remains.

Q: What other unique features support student engagement?

A: Boxed features in each chapter ask students to think about the variety of ways in which history can be seen and done. In addition to "What a Difference a Year Makes," each chapter has a feature titled "Investigating the Past," which examines how historians work—how they use new evidence and approaches to throw fresh light on the past and historical mysteries.

Another feature, "Things That Remain," gives students a sense of the ways in which objects can open up the past to us and lead to valuable insights. Our explorations range from what new DNA testing can tell us about the plague that struck China, Islam, and Europe in the mid-fourteenth century, to a look at nineteenth-century Parisian department stores and the films of the great Russian director, Sergei Eisenstein.

We also include one last feature in each chapter, called "Other Voices, Other Views." It offers students other perspectives than those of the dominant voices of European history. Groups and individuals outside the main political and cultural centers of Europe had something to say about the prevailing narrative; they did not sit silently on the margins and watch it all happen without criticism and complaint. This feature seeks to hear them out, to give them back their compelling voices. Students are enriched, we believe, when they view events such as Roman imperialism, voyages of exploration, and World War II from different vantage points.

Q: Finally, why is your book different from others and do you do anything new?

A: Our emphases are certainly different. Grounding the narrative in people and their lived experience of transformative events; engaging students in a history that is not fixed but shaped by the decisions people made and the chance events that shaped their historical circumstances; and viewing Europe and the West as the special story of the competition between groups, regions, and peoples, with no one side dominating for long, make *Many Europes* a book about a history that is still unfolding, still full of tension and energy, still engaging from first to last, and its future unfixed.

And, yes, we hope to challenge instructors and students with new arguments, approaches, and ways to think about western history. We seek to engage readers in presenting to them the idea that ancient Greece drew its richness not from its unity, but from its manyness; we ask if the story of the Reformation might better be told not as one of reform but rather as one of the restructuring of religion across Europe. In the book's second half, we describe an early nineteenth century in which accelerating differences between western industrializing and eastern and southern rural regions made Europe a more diverse place than ever before. Our presentation of twentieth-century events focuses, unusually, on events in eastern and southeastern Europe where, we argue, the fates of nations and the fate of the continent as a whole were decided. Our readers need not agree with us, and we hope that they won't always do so, but we do sincerely hope that they will have stimulating discussions about the material itself by thinking about western history in new ways. The history of the many Europes and the West have earned our attention, mindfulness, and heightened engagement, for we are still living with it and within it.

Many Europes is all about CHOICE

We offer a wealth of tools to help you teach the course:

Primary Sources

Over 130 primary sources specifically tailored to this text by the authors are available through McGraw-Hill Create. You can customize the text with your own selections of primary source readings or even create your own separate reader. All sources have accompanying headnotes and critical thinking questions written by the authors.

In addition, all of these primary sources and questions are available as digitally assignable and assessable exercises in McGraw-Hill's Connect History.

How to Analyze a Primary Source Document

A brief, illustrated, five-page tutorial on how to read and analyze a primary source document can be bound into your text. Ask your sales rep for details on this Create customization.

The tutorial is also available as a video exercise in Connect. Your students watch the video and are prompted to pause and answer questions to test their understanding.

connect plus+—Online Assessment Exercises Tailored to *Many Europes*

Connect History is a highly interactive learning environment designed to help students connect to the historical tools and resources they will need to achieve success. Through engaging media and study resources, students improve their performance on exams and assignments. *Connect History* makes managing and completing assignments easier.

Connect Plus offers all this with the addition of an integrated, interactive e-book. The e-book optimized for the Web immerses students in a flexible, interactive environment. Assign e-book exercises to ensure your students are reading, or direct them to the embedded activities and multimedia for a more memorable and engaging homework assignment.

LearnSmart—Mapping Out a Personalized Study Plan for Students

LearnSmart, McGraw-Hill's adaptive learning system, helps assess student knowledge of course content and maps out a personalized study plan for success. Accessible within Connect, *LearnSmart* uses a series of adaptive questions to pinpoint the concepts students understand—and those they don't. The result is an online tool that helps students learn faster and study more efficiently and enables instructors to customize classroom lectures and activities to meet their students' needs.

Customize Your Text with Primary Sources through create

Design your ideal course materials with McGraw-Hill's Create: www.mcgrawhillcreate.com! Rearrange or omit chapters, combine material from other sources, choose your own primary sources from our Western civilization collection, and/or upload any other content you have written to make the perfect resource for your students. You can even personalize your book's appearance by selecting the cover and adding your name, school, and course information. When you order a Create book, you receive a complimentary review copy. Get a printed copy in 3 to 5 business days or an electronic copy (eComp) via e-mail in about an hour. Register today at www.mcgrawhillcreate.com, and craft your course resources to match the way you teach.

CourseSmart—an e-book version of your text

CourseSmart offers thousands of the most commonly adopted textbooks across hundreds of courses from a wide variety of higher education publishers. It is the only place for faculty to review and compare the full text of a textbook online, providing immediate access without the environmental impact of requesting a printed examination copy. At CourseSmart, students can save up to 50 percent off the cost of a printed book, reduce their impact on the environment, and gain access to powerful Web tools for learning, including full text search, notes and highlighting, and e-mail tools for sharing notes among classmates. Learn more at www.coursesmart.com.

Campus

McGraw-Hill Campus is the first-of-its-kind institutional service that provides faculty with true single sign-on access to all of McGraw-Hill's course content, digital tools, and other high-quality learning resources from any learning management system (LMS). This innovative offering allows for secure and deep integration and seamless access to any of our course solutions such as McGraw-Hill Connect, McGraw-Hill Create, McGraw-Hill LearnSmart, or Tegrity. McGraw-Hill Campus includes access to our entire content library, including e-books, assessment tools, presentation slides, and multimedia content, among other resources, providing faculty open and unlimited access to prepare for class, create tests/quizzes, develop lecture material, integrate interactive content, and much more.

PRIMARY SOURCES AND MAPS

Primary Sources

Primary Sources in the Print Text

Primary Sources in Connect History and Customizable through McGraw-Hill Create

* Indicates document is available in Connect only

Chapter 10

1. Observations of the Plague
2. The Peasants' Revolt of 1381
3. Joan of Arc's Letter to the English Invaders and Her Trial*
4. George Sphrantzes and the Fall of Constantinople

Chapter 11

1. Petrarch's Ascent of the Windy Mountain
2. Laura Cereta's Defense of Wise Women
3. Vergerio on Education as a Moral Necessity
4. Pico's Oration on the Dignity of Man
5. Three Church Responses to the Art of Printing
6. Erasmus's Sayings

Chapter 12

1. John Mandeville at Court of Great Khan
2. Columbus's First Description of the Americas, 1493
3. Bernardino de Sahagún Account of the Taking of Tenochtitlan
4. Doña Marina, La Malinche: Native Help-Mate of Cortés
5. Montaigne's American Cannibals
6. Laws and Reactions to the Americas

Chapter 13

1. The Confrontation of Luther and Charles V at Worms
2. Luther on the Good Estate of Marriage
3. The Twelve Demands of the Peasants
4. Policing Calvin's Church
5. Queen Elizabeth I's Act of Supremacy
6. Charles V's Abdication

Chapter 14

1. James I Defends Absolutism
2. Luis Granada, "Meditations for Monday Morning"
3. The Trial of Jean Williford for Witchcraft in Faversham, Kent, in 1645
4. Hugo Grotius, *The Freedom of the Seas*
5. Thomas Hobbes, *Leviathan*
6. Jacques Bénigne Bossuet, Defense of Divine Right
7. The Absolutism of Peter the Great of Russia

Maps

ACKNOWLEDGMENTS

Many Europes has been the work of many hands, so many that the authors can only mention a few here. We are grateful to all who played some part in bringing this book to completion. First we would like to thank Deborah Harkness who first conceived of this book, but withdrew midway through the project to pursue a trilogy of highly successful novels. The enthusiasm of the acquisitions editor Monica Eckman for our original proposal started us off in the right direction. Among those who have seen the project from start to finish, we would like most of all to thank our managing development editor Nancy Crochiere, who has overseen every step of the process, and done so with infinite skill, patience, and good humor over the last six years. We also owe enormous debts to the rest of the McGraw-Hill team, including the ever-inspiring Matthew Busbridge, director of products and markets; our excellent and indefatigable production team led by our senior production editor Catherine Morris; development editor Betty Slack and copyeditor Amy Marks; our extremely hardworking photo and map editors, David Chodoff, Karen Dubno, and David Tietz; and our permissions editor, Wesley Hall. Nancy's interns Melissa Henderson and Rebecca Crochiere also provided crucial assistance during the production process.

Suzanne Marchand's fabulous and beloved team of LSU grad students, Scott M. Berg, Wade Trosclair, and Jason M. Wolfe helped with many different aspects of *Many Europes'* second half, and should get credit for enhancing both the general form and the specific content of those chapters; Scott Berg and Jason Wolfe also did the lion's share of the work on the electronic primary source documents for Volume 2 that are available to instructors in both McGraw-Hill Connect and Create.

The authors would also to thank the many hardworking and meticulous reviewers of their chapters who prevented them from making a myriad of mistakes, small and large; and individually, we owe debts to the following scholars for reading chapters in their early stages: Courtney Booker, Jeffrey Herf, Anne-Marie Feenberg-Dibon, Natalie Fingerhut, Herbert L. Kessler, Christine Kooi, Paul F. Paskoff, Jonathan Sperber, and Victor Stater. The book depends heavily on the specialized scholarship of recent years; a selection of the most important of those works is listed in the bibliography and footnotes at the book's close; the authors hope that by citing this work directly that readers will be enticed to delve more deeply into those inspiring books and articles. Finally, the authors would like to thank our families, whose love and understanding has sustained us through the long process of writing and rewriting *Many Europes*, and who will, we hope, appreciate how much of their inspiration has gone into the final manuscript.

Academic Reviewers

Carl Abrams
Bob Jones University

Kathryn Amerson
Craven Community College

Stephen Andrews
Central New Mexico Community College

Angela Ash
Owensboro Community and Technical College

Amanda Bahr-Evola
Southern Illinois University Edwardsville

Thomas Behr
University of Houston

Mark Bocija
Columbus State Community College

Mary Ann Borden
Hudson Valley Community College

Wayne Bowen
Southeast Missouri State University

John Brackett
University of Cincinnati

Joy Branch
Southern Union State Community College

Bob Brennan
Cape Fear Community College

Robert Brown
Finger Lakes Community College

Harry Burgess
St. Clair County Community College

Paul Byrd
Des Moines Area Community College

Kevin Caldwell
Blue Ridge Community College

Celeste Chamberlain
Roosevelt University

Anthony Cheeseboro
Southern Illinois University Edwardsville

Karen Christianson
DePaul University

Mark Clark
University of Virginia's College at Wise

Michele Clouse
Ohio University

Lynda Coon
University of Arkansas

Eugene Cruz-Uribe
Northern Arizona University

Marion Deshmukh
George Mason University

Joanna Drell
University of Richmond

Ian Drummond
Gordon College

Eric Duchess
High Point University

Martin Ederer
Buffalo State College

Angela Edwards
Florence-Darlington Technical College

Reanne Eichele
Pikes Peak Community College

Elizabeth Elliot-Meisel
Creighton University

Paula Findlen
Stanford University

Rodger Fisher
Craven Community College

Benita Fox
Columbia Southern University

Carole Collier Frick
Southern Illinois University

Heather Fryer
Creighton University

Christopher Gehrz
Bethel University

Sylvia Gray
Portland Community College–Sylvania

Robert Greene
University of Montana

Timothy Hack
Salem Community College

Robert Harrison
Linn Benton Community College

Frances Jacobson
Tidewater Community College

Thomas Jennings
Stillman College and the *University of Alabama*

Leslie Johnson
Hudson Valley Community College

Lloyd Johnson
Campbell University

Michael Johnson
Northwest Arkansas Community College

Lars Jones
Florida Tech

Matthew Keith
The Ohio State University

John Kemp
Truckee Meadows Community College

Michael Kennedy
High Point University

Darin Kinsey
Florence-Darlington Technical College

Janilyn Kocher
Richland Community College
Tim Konhaus
Tidewater Community College
Andrew Larsen
Marquette University
Rachel Larsen
Bob Jones University
William J. Lipkin
Union County College
Wenxi Liu
Miami University–Middleton
Paul Douglas Lockhart
Wright State University
Jonathan Malmude
Saint Joseph's College of Maine
Art Marmorstein
Northern State University
Thomas Massey
Cape Fear Community College
Bruce McCord
Aiken Technical College
Edrene McKay
Northwest Arkansas Community College
Ashleigh McLean
Central New Mexico Community College
David McMahon
Kirkwood Community College
Jennifer McNabb
Western Illinois University
Elisa Miller
Rhode Island College
David Mock
Tallahassee Community College
Brandon Morgan
Central New Mexico Community College
Annette Morrow
Minnesota State University
Wyatt Moulds
Jones County Junior College
Samuel Mulberry
Bethel University
Shannon O'Bryan
Greenville Technical College
Lisa Ossian
Des Moines Area Community College
Troy Paddock
Southern Connecticut State University
Ronald Palmer
Jefferson Community College
Craig Pilant
County College of Morris
Ann Pond
Bishop State Community College
Michael Prahl
Hawkeye Community College
David Ramsey
Midlands Technical Community College
Eric Reisenauer
University of South Carolina–Sumter
William Robison
Southeastern Louisiana University
Patrice Ross
Columbus State Community College
Geri Ryder
Ocean County College
Matthew Schaffer
Florence-Darlington Technical College

Linda Breckstein Scherr
Mercer County Community College
Jessica Sheetz-Nguyen
University of Central Oklahoma
Heidi Sherman
University of Wisconsin Green Bay
Myron Silverman
Suffolk County Community College
David Stone
Kansas State University
John Taylor
Southern Illinois University
Emily Teipe
Fullerton College
Susan Thompson
Northern Virginia Community College
David Tompkins
University of Tennessee
Andrew Traver
Southeastern Louisiana University
Rebecca Woodham
Wallace Community College
Ian Worthington
University of Missouri–Columbia
Jackie Wright
Cossatot Community College of the University of Arkansas

Symposia Participants

Gisela Ables
Houston Community College
Donna Allen
Glendale Community College
Sal Anselmo
Delgado Community College
Simon Baatz
John Jay College
Mario A. J. Bennekin
Georgia Perimeter College
Manu Bhagavan
Hunter College
C. J. Bibus
Wharton County Junior College
Olwyn M. Blouet
Virginia State University
Michael Botson
Houston Community College
Patrick Brennan
Gulf Coast Community College
Cathy Briggs
Northwest Vista College
Brad Cartwright
University of Texas at El Paso
Roger Chan
Washington State University
Tamara Chaplin
University of Illinois at Urbana-Champaign
June Cheatham
Richland College
Karl Clark
Coastal Bend College
Bernard Comeau
Tacoma Community College
Charles Connell
Northern Arizona University
Kevin Davis
North Central Texas College

Michael Downs
Tarrant County College–Southeast
Laura Dunn
Brevard Community College
Arthur Durand
Metropolitan Community College
David Dzurec
University of Scranton
Amy Forss
Metropolitan Community College
Jim Good
Lone Star College–North Harris
R. David Goodman
Pratt Institute
Derrick Griffey
Gadsden State Community College
Wendy Gunderson
Colin County Community College
Debbie Hargis
Odessa College
John Hosler
Morgan State University
Lloyd Johnson
Campbell University
James Jones
Prairie View A&M University
Mark Jones
Central Connecticut State University
Sarah Jurenka
Bishop State Community College
Bill Kamil
Sinclair Community College
Philip Kaplan
University of North Florida
Stephen Katz
Philadelphia University
Carol A. Keller
San Antonio College
Greg Kelm
Dallas Baptist University
Michael Kinney
Calhoun Community College
Jessica Kovler
John Jay College
David Lansing
Ocean County College
Benjamin Lapp
Montclair State University
Lynn Lubamersky
Boise State University
Julian Madison
Southern Connecticut State University
David Marshall
Suffolk County Community College
Meredith R. Martin
Collin College
Linda McCabe
North Lake College
George Monahan
Suffolk County Community College
Michael J. Mullin
Augustana College
Tracy Musacchio
John Jay College
Mikal Nash
Essex County College
Sandy Norman
Florida Atlantic University

Michelle Novak
Houston Community College–Southeast

Veena Oldenburg
Baruch College

Troy Paddock
Southern Connecticut State University

Jessica Patton
Tarrant County College–Northwest

Edward Paulino
John Jay College

Valor Pickett
Northwest Arkansas Community College

Craig Pilant
County College of Morris

Sean Pollock
Wright State University

Michael Prahl
Hawkeye Community College

Robert Risko
Trinity Valley Community College

Esther Robinson
Lone Star College–Cyfair

Matthew Ruane
Florida Institute of Technology

Geri Ryder
Ocean County College

Linda Breckstein Scherr
Mercer County Community College

Susan Schmidt-Horning
St. John's University

Donna Scimeca
College of Staten Island

Jeffrey Smith
Lindenwood University

Rachel Standish
San Joaquin Delta College

Matthew Vaz
City College of New York

Roger Ward
Colin County Community College–Plano

Christian Warren
Brooklyn College

Don Whatley
Blinn College

Geoffrey Willbanks
Tyler Junior College

Scott M. Williams
Weatherford College

Carlton Wilson
North Carolina Central University

Chad Wooley
Tarrant County College

Connect Board of Advisors

Michael Downs
University of Texas–Arlington

Jim Halverson
Judson University

Reid Holland
Midlands Technical College

Stephen Katz
Rider University

David Komito
Eastern Oregon University

Wendy Sarti
Oakton Community College

Linda Scherr
Mercer County Community College

Eloy Zarate
Pasadena City College

Many Europes Board of Advisors

Kathryn Amerson
Craven Community College

Amanda Bahr-Evola
Southern Illinois University Edwardsville

Mary Ann Borden
Hudson Valley Community College

Wayne Bowen
Southeast Missouri State University

Joy Branch
Southern Union State Community College

Roger Fisher
Craven Community College

Frances Jacobson
Tidewater Community College

Brandon Morgan
Central New Mexico Community College

David Ramsey
Midlands Technical Community College

MANY EUROPES

CHOICE AND CHANCE IN WESTERN CIVILIZATION

VOLUME I: TO 1715

1

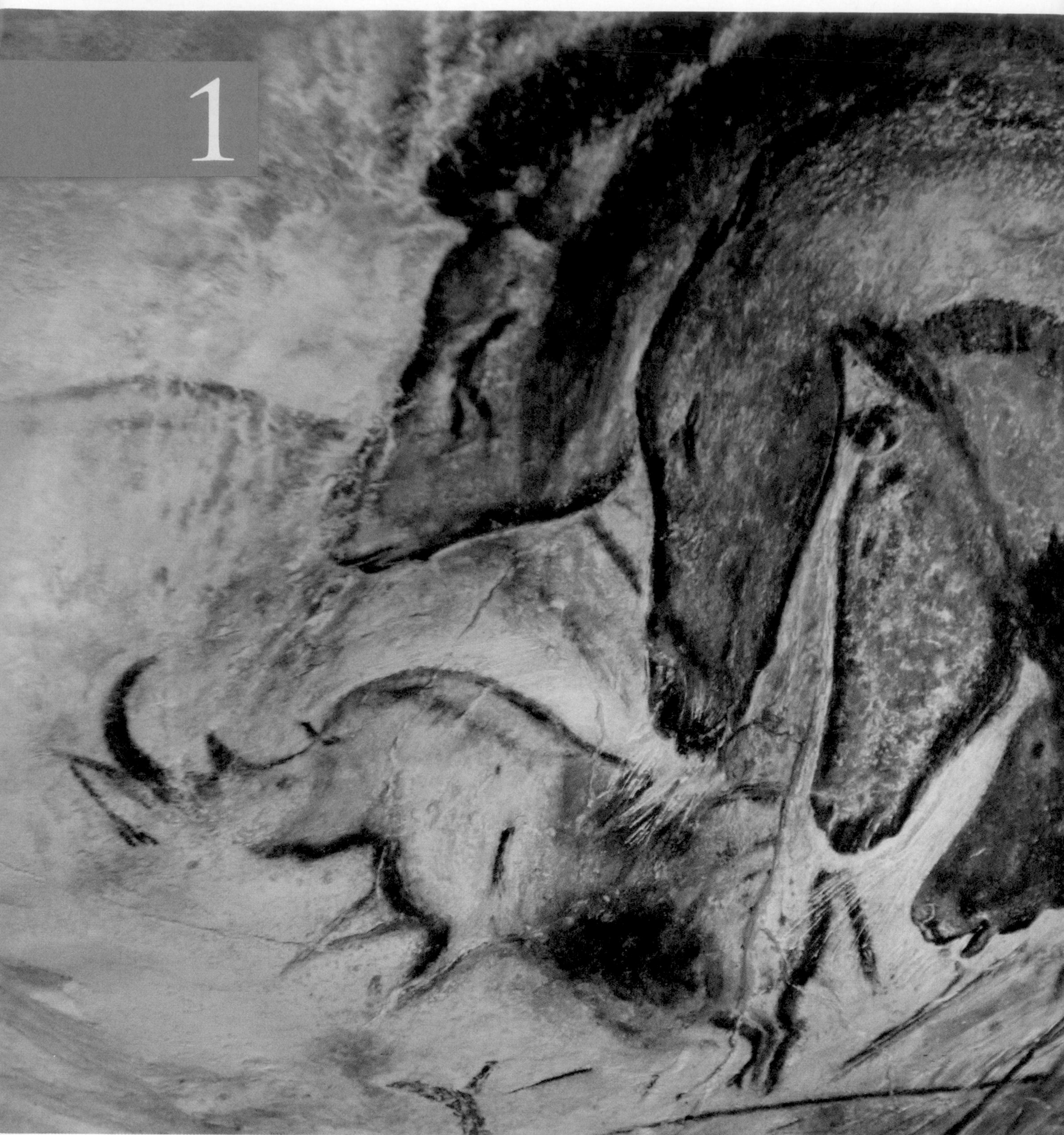

Cave Painting of Horses and Rhinoceros, Chauvet, France

PRELIMINARY TO WESTERN CIVILIZATION

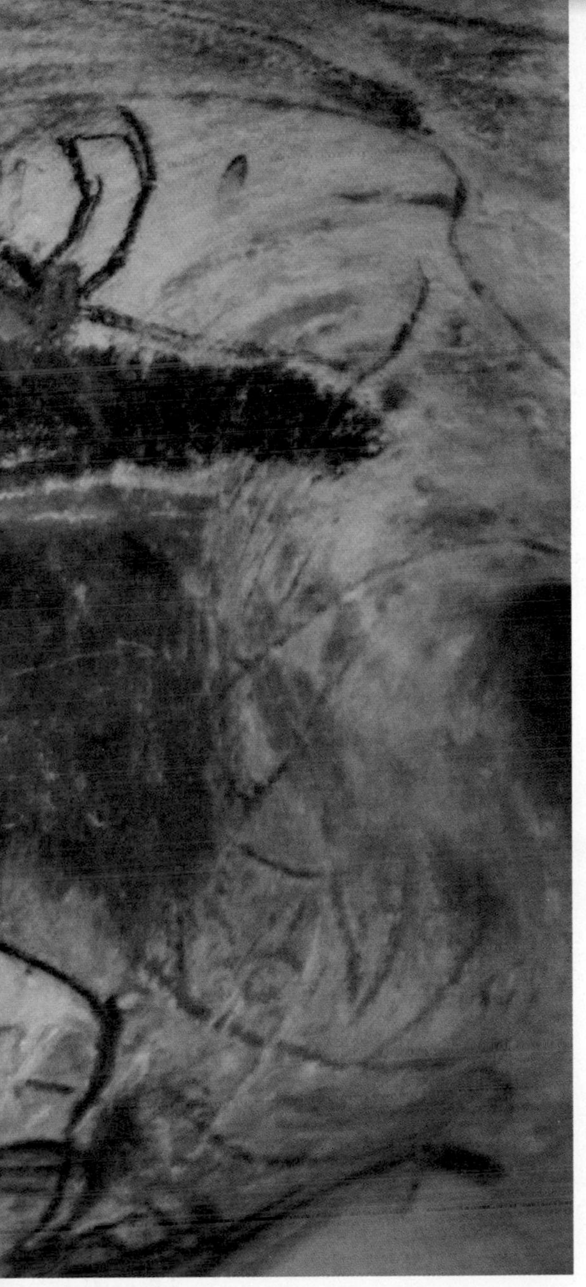

THE MURDER OF ÖTZI, THE FIRST EUROPEAN In the late summer of 1991 in the high Alps, two German hikers stumbled upon the deep-frozen, mummified remains of Ötzi (named after the place where he was found), the first European we know in detail. Thanks to melting glaciers, other bodies preserved in ice have begun to reveal themselves. The bodies of three Austro-Hungarian soldiers from the First World War found on an Italian mountain in 2004 and the Iron Age bodies found in Europe's peat bogs are impressive human remains, but they can't compare with Ötzi, who died 5,300 years ago. The dynasties of Egypt had not yet been established, writing was just emerging in faraway Mesopotamia, and the agricultural breakthroughs of prehistory were just beginning to reap results in Mesopotamia and Egypt. Ötzi's case is a good place to begin our examination of western civilization because, though he did not belong to western civilization, he did belong to its long backstory.

He was forty-five years old, small at five foot three and 110 pounds, tattooed, and suitably dressed for the mountains (bearskin cap, grass cloak, coat, loincloth, leggings, and leather shoes). He was carrying a precious copper ax, stone knife, bow, quiver with arrows (only two of them tipped), and a pack loaded with necessities (dried berries and mushrooms, and some fire-starting materials). On the day he died he had eaten some mountain goat and deer meat, as well as some wheat, dried fruit, and tubers. Ötzi had lived a hard life, but he did well enough to make it to an advanced age before his misadventure in the Alps, and he did not die a natural death. Ötzi was murdered.

Why was he in the high Alps? Ötzi had lived his life in the area around Bolzano in northern Italy (across the mountains from the area of Innsbruck, Austria) and may, as a shepherd or hunter, have been a frequent visitor to the mountains, but that autumn 5,300 years ago Ötzi had a fatal encounter. Someone shot Ötzi in the back with an arrow, severing an artery. Ötzi's head was also crushed by a rock. This was no simple mountain mugging; the perpetrator left behind the murdered man's possessions, and someone removed the arrow shaft from his back. There Ötzi lay with the Alpine snows falling on him for 5,300 years.

Ötzi A recent reconstruction of Ötzi, who died in the Alps c. 3300 BCE.

Ötzi was a continental European, but Europe as a political and cultural entity would not exist for another four thousand years. The Austrian and Italian governments wrestled over who owned the corpse of the iceman (it was eventually determined that he lay one hundred yards inside Italy), the irony being that those nations did not come into existence until five thousand years after Ötzi's death. In Ötzi's small

Paleolithic (*Homo sapiens sapiens*)
200,000–12,000 BCE

Mesolithic
12,000–c. 8000 BCE

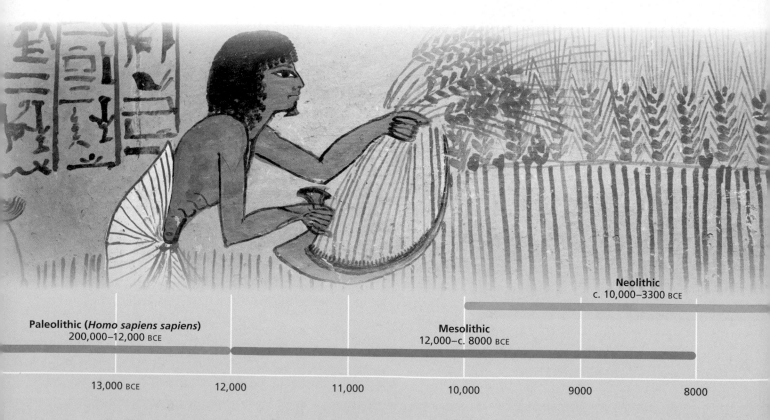

Neolithic
c. 10,000–3300 BCE

13,000 BCE | 12,000 | 11,000 | 10,000 | 9000 | 8000

Alpine world, there were no governments, no law as we know it, no settled communities of any substantial size or duration, no systematic agriculture, no writing, no higher forms of thought (philosophy, theology, mathematics). Yet Ötzi carried a copper ax and wore excellent shoes that imply the existence of cooperative communities of people who could make specialized objects. He could not have tattooed himself fifty-seven times, including on his lower back and behind his knees. Ötzi had help. His very survival suggests the existence of organized life, but we would not likely call his a civilized life.

The elements that make civilization possible are four pairs of connected things: settled life (most often in cities) and a critical mass of people, sustainable agriculture and trade, government and law, writing and abstract thought. The Mesopotamian peoples possessed all of these civilizational pairs by the third millennium BCE: cities, a large population, a working agricultural system and active trade, leaders and laws, cursive (flowing) and then **cuneiform** (wedge-shaped) writing, written laws, religious texts, and the world's first literature. The Egyptians also perfected a settled agricultural life, a prosperous economy, political rule and law, and writing. Egypt achieved steady prosperity and an enduring stability that fueled economic development in the eastern Mediterranean world over several millennia, but Egyptian life was not driven by urban growth. A different, but successful model of civilized life was at work along the Nile River. The civilizational pairs were critical to spurring a higher form of human life, far beyond what Ötzi could have imagined. These were the preliminaries upon which western or European civilization was to root and grow.

The development of **civilization** with large cities as its defining feature would not have been possible without these preliminary pairs, but we should not define civilization too narrowly. One way to look at the early ancient world would be as a series of experiments in living under specific and often confining conditions. Civilizations are more than just small, isolated communities of people. They tend to be large and encompassing, impacting entire regions and neighboring lands. Many smaller, less developed, historical communities either proved to be dead ends or were integrated, willingly or by force, into larger historical enterprises.

We need not think that the rise of civilization was a universal good. With civilization came developments that may seem less good to us: the coalescing of power into great empires, large-scale organized warfare, systematic violence, and inequalities of persons (both material and legal) and sexes. Our view of early history is distorted by the particular historical lens through which we view it. Prehistoric and early historical sources are meager and often of an unfamiliar character, and the amount of

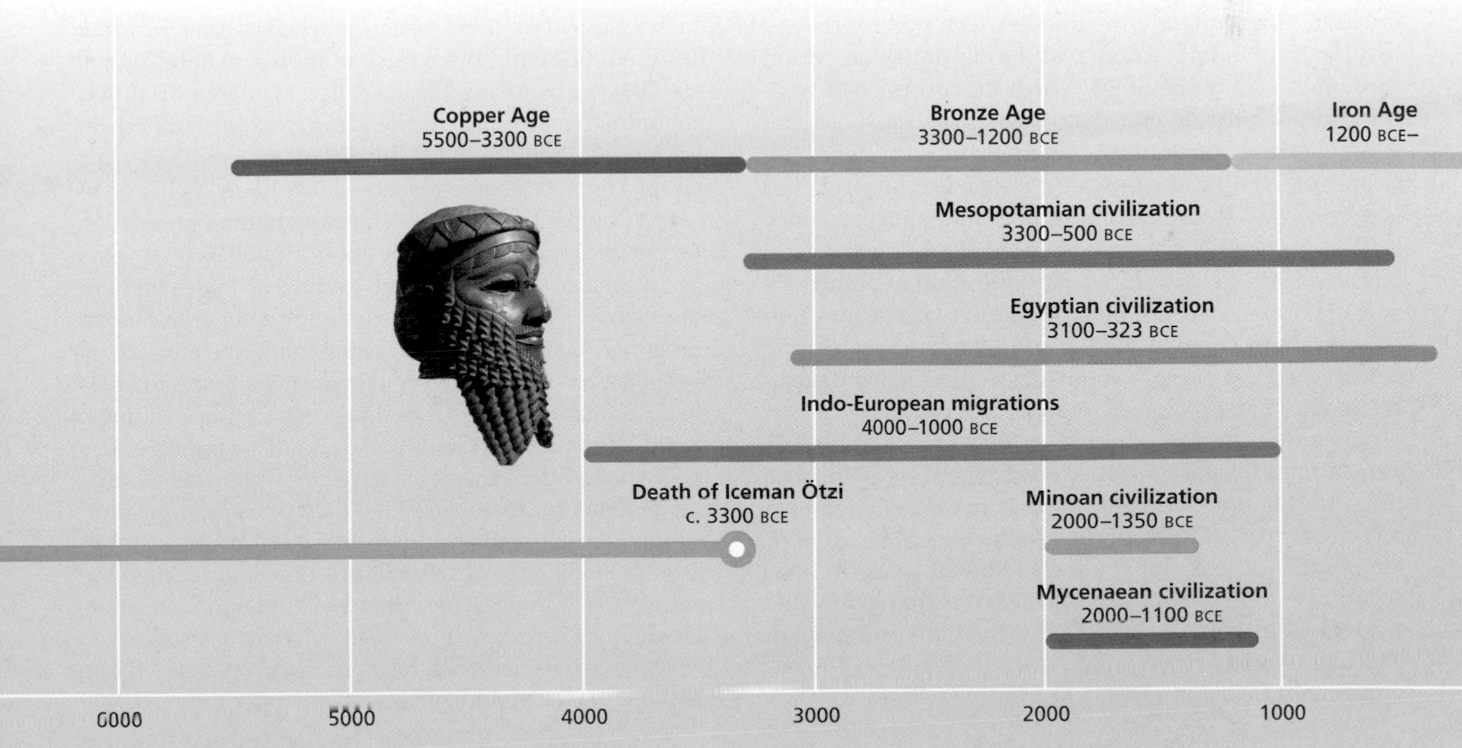

time involved is comparatively huge (almost three thousand years), which has the effect of making time seem to rush by in the telling, loading us down with names and people we cannot know, know differently, or cannot afford to spend much time with. People and places seem to dash rapidly on and off the historical stage. We can try to correct for the historical distortion, but only a lengthier dedicated narrative, particularly of three thousand years of Egyptian history, could accomplish that. Here we intend to pursue only the main contours of early history.

The Long Dawning of Prehistory

Prehistory is typically thought of as that period before the invention of writing. The nature of what we know about the past changes with writing. Written records do more than simply supply specifics about the past; they personalize it, for at last named individuals grounded in place and time step forward. Prehistory, however, is not quite as prehistoric as we once thought, as the case of Ötzi shows us. Other kinds of records have begun to fill in the prehistoric past, though they fall short of personalizing it. Yet new dating techniques have given prehistory needed contour and precision.

Why is our knowledge of prehistory limited, and are there ways to overcome those limitations? How was agriculture critical to the first stirrings of civilization?

Early writing (the critical factor in setting the prehistory-history divide) has many limitations as a historical dividing point: its spottiness, limited range, slow gradual emergence and spread, and perilous state of preservation. Consequently the line between prehistoric and historic is not sharp. There was a long transition period from one stage to the other, which the invention of writing did not entirely eliminate. Moreover, most of what goes on in daily life is never recorded and so by definition is prehistorical or ahistorical (unrelated to history). Nor is prehistory an absolute chronological distinction, since prehistoric peoples have long existed alongside historical ones, and still do. Similarly, the opposition of prehistory and history should not be a qualitative distinction into primitive and sophisticated, given that some prehistoric cultures were strikingly sophisticated and many historical peoples have been remarkably primitive.

Since our species is roughly 200,000 years old, 97.5 percent of all human existence was spent in prehistoric time. In this book, our attention is necessarily focused on only a small portion of the human experience in both temporal and geographic terms. Many of the formative, social developments of our species occurred before the time covered here. But when and how did humans, an itinerant species, settle down, learn to live in hostile environments, learn to farm, learn to live with each other, and learn to dominate others? Many of these formative changes occurred before records were kept.

Another issue we cannot afford to ignore is the pace of change (historical, social, and psychological). For almost 200,000 years, humans lived in small, scattered bands of itinerant hunters and gatherers, yet in the last 12,000 years the human population has exploded from 1–5 million humans in 10,000 BCE to perhaps 300–400 million people in 1 CE, and to 7 billion people by 2011 CE. It has been estimated that around 120 billion humans have existed, almost 6 percent of whom are alive at present. The geographic spread of humans now covers the globe, and in the past five thousand years we have gone from being the users of stone tools to a species that has landed men on the moon and unlocked the secrets of the atom. One cannot but notice that the pace of change has accelerated as we approach the present. As you go forward in this book, you will notice that the chapters treat shorter and shorter spans of time, which is itself a reflection of the increasing speed of historical change, of the expansion of the human population, and of its spatial reach. The historical record thickens not because of the passage of time, but because of the growth of the human population, the geographic spread of the species, and improved and richer record keeping. There was more change in the period from 8000 BCE to 3000 BCE than in the previous 190,000 years; more change (technological and material) between 1850 and 1950 CE than in the previous 500 years; and more change in the past six decades than in the previous century. Whether change itself at this accelerated pace is sustainable remains to be seen, but it does lead us back to our long, slow, formative beginning.

A Special Species?

Our species, *Homo sapiens sapiens,* reached its basic form (out of preceding hominid species) at approximately 200,000 (±50,000) BCE in Africa. The so-called **Mitochondrial Eve,** the common matrilineal (descending from the mother) ancestor of all living humans, lived 170,000 (±50,000) years ago in Africa. For some reason—most likely a change in the environment or climate—the early human population narrowed to a perilous point about 75,000–60,000 years ago in eastern Africa. A great cooling of the earth's climate caused by the massive eruption of a supervolcano in Sumatra 75,000 years ago probably made the survival of the species precarious. Every human male living today is the descendant (based on specific genetic traits) of a single man nicknamed the **Genetic Adam**; Mitochondrial Eve and Genetic Adam therefore never met—he was her distant descendant. About 75,000–60,000 years ago, anatomically modern humans began to move out of Africa (Map 1.1 on p. 8). By 40,000 (±10,000) BCE they had reached the continent of Europe, where they encountered a separate, older hominid species, *Homo sapiens neanderthalensis.*

Neanderthals had been resident in Europe, the Middle East, and northern Africa for a much longer time (500,000

INVESTIGATING THE PAST

The New Prehistoric Past

The division of prehistory into stone ages—Paleolithic (Old Stone, 2.5 million years ago to approximately 12,000 BCE), Mesolithic (Middle Stone, roughly 12,000–8000 BCE), and Neolithic (New Stone, 10,000–3300 BCE)—and metal ages (Copper, 5500–3300 BCE, and Bronze, 3300–1200 BCE) is convenient but deceptive. Neither the stone nor the metal ages are absolute divisions; they overlap and are only regionally meaningful. The Mesolithic and Neolithic periods arrived earlier in the Near East than they did in Europe or the Americas; so, too, did the metal ages. The old prehistoric categories housed a wide set of material, economic, and cultural traits associated with the development of human societies. These divisions were the constructions of thoughtful prehistorians and anthropologists, but they are highly subjective and somewhat contradictory. The peoples of both the late Paleolithic and Mesolithic periods were hunter-gatherers rather than farmers, but they were at different stages of development. Because no critical development in stone technology took place in the Mesolithic period, the stone (in Greek, *lithos*) element of its name may mislead. Stone technology, especially in the use and trade of polished stones such as obsidian, did improve in the Neolithic period. The Neolithic, in general, connotes the move to agricultural society along with the creation of pottery, polished axes, and new tools. The stone and metal ages are useful categories, but loaded ones lacking precision.

New dating techniques developed in the late twentieth century have revolutionized prehistoric studies. In 1947 the chemist Willard Libby discovered the basis for radiocarbon dating of organic materials. He showed that organic materials experience a steady and measurable loss of radioactive carbon-14, which is naturally present in plants because of photosynthesis, whereas carbon-12 remains in the same organic substances as an unchanging isotope and can be used as a basis for comparison. Because the half-life of radioactive carbon-14 is 5,730 years, radiocarbon testing calculates the proportion of carbon-14 against the fixed presence of carbon-12 to determine when an organic body (plant or animal) died. The technique is more complicated than it sounds and requires considerable expertise in measurement, but at last prehistorians had an objective way to determine dates in the past. The calibration of the date of each object may vary according to circumstances, but the margin of error for materials less than two thousand years old is now as little as ±40 years. Other dating techniques have since been discovered, and even human DNA contains information about the history of human bodies in relation to human populations over time.

The more exact dating of objects has revolutionized our understanding of the distant past, for the stone and metal ages were ideas shaped by theories of human development. Scientific, objective dating of the past has allowed a more reliable ordering of things and their cultures without an overlaying theory, allowing for a more exact comparative history, one not privileging literate early societies and cultural centers.

QUESTIONS | ***Why bother to date and categorize the distant past into periods? What limitations and weaknesses are there to a more exact dating of the prehistoric past?***

or more years ago) but lost out in the competition for space and resources to modern humans about 25,000 (±5,000) years ago. Interbreeding between the two species apparently occurred before Neanderthal extinction, given that an estimated 2.5 percent of the DNA of today's non-African peoples comes from a Neanderthal source.

While the last major Ice Age still held its grip on much of Europe, European hunter-gatherers of the period from about 35,000 to 15,000 years ago began to produce objects with symbolic meaning. Though their population numbers were relatively low, they made carved bone flutes and small fertility or Venus figurines (see Back to the Source at the end of this chapter). Most wondrous of all are the great cave paintings at Chauvet and Lascaux in France, though there are less spectacular examples in northern Spain and southern Germany. The cave dwellers painted representations of animals (deer, goats, horses, rhinoceroses, bears, lions), some of them now extinct, such as the auroch (a wild bull); a few humans; and abstract signs, which may be the first rudimentary attempts to communicate through written signs. The style of the paintings is naturalistic, but the scenes lack scenery—no plants, clouds, or stars—just the essential animate and symbolic objects of the cave dwellers' economic and thought worlds. The material traces of these cave visitors ceased with the end of the Ice Age 10,000 years ago (approximately 8000 BCE).

The interest of Paleolithic peoples in art was not a product of genetic makeup or an evolutionary advance of the species. The achievements of human beings over the past 20,000 years have not been caused by bigger brains or better brain wiring but by shared and cumulative cultural advances. Humans have a special capacity among animals not just to learn new things (for even dogs can learn new tricks), but to teach that learning to their communities and pass it along to future generations. This species learning curve, the basic ability to expand and preserve accumulated knowledge, may help us to understand the rapid development of human societies. We keep, communicate, and transmit cultural, economic, and political knowledge. Not all the things that we learn and pass along survive or are good, but the species as a whole gathers advantageous knowledge and conveys it over time.

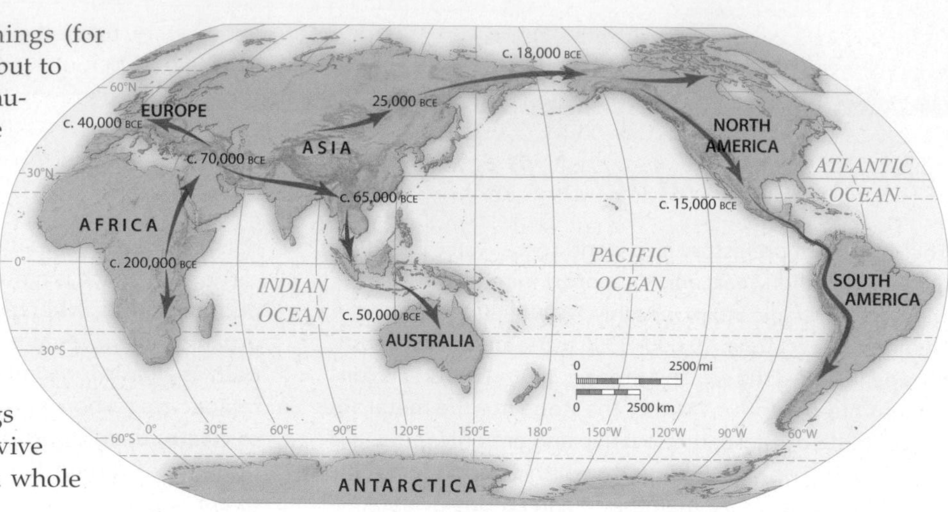

MAP 1.1 | *Homo sapiens sapiens* on the Move

Our species, *Homo sapiens sapiens,* arose in Africa about 200,000 BCE (±50,000 years). By about 75,000–60,000 BCE, groups of humans had moved out of Africa in several different waves, and by about 40,000 BCE, humans had reached Europe. ***What might explain the movement of early humans out of Africa? Where did they go? How fast or slow was the migration?***

The human imperatives to learn and convey vast amounts of information are species particular. Anatomically we are the same as people were 20,000 or 5,000 years ago. Ötzi is one of us. So how then did the dangerous, marginal human existence of the Genetic Adam or the iceman Ötzi lead to the successes of human civilization, with its vast increase in the size of the human population and its expanding pool of cultural and practical knowledge? Developments in social organization, the accumulation of useful knowledge, and success in preserving that knowledge over generations may come closest to accounting for human social, cultural, and historical development.

The engine driving evolutionary change is the external world. Unlike most species, which are products of particular environments and specially suited to their exacting demands, humans have the ability to overcome that limitation and dramatically widen their natural ecological niche by adapting themselves to survive hostile environments (with the wearing of specialized clothes, for instance) and by transforming environments (by diverting or damming a river, for instance) to suit their needs. Late Paleolithic men and women in Europe found a way with fire and clothing to survive and even thrive during an Ice Age.

The Domestication of Animals

Early human life was a constant struggle to secure food. Thus, one of the first great human transformations of the physical world was the domestication of animals and plants. Some animals were domesticated before plants, which is likely a reflection of the hunter-gatherer existence of early humans and their closeness to the animal world. Association with humans conveyed an advantage to certain animals, which were seeking their own survival.

The dog was the first domesticated animal. All dogs are descended from wolves. The DNA evidence suggests that canine descent began about 140,000 years ago and that the more complete domestication of dogs did not occur until about 15,000 years ago in the Middle East. Later, in central China, domesticated dogs interbred again with wolves. Dog remains from as early as 12,000 BCE have been discovered in graves in the Middle East. The advantages of the relationship for people are clear: dogs are teachable and they can hunt, protect, serve as guard dogs, provide companionship, and also be eaten. The advantages of the relationship for dogs are protection from predators and a more secure food supply. Sheep were domesticated around 10,000 BCE in western Asia and goats at about the same time in the area of present-day Iran and Iraq. In all these cases, domestication led to temperament and physical changes in the domesticated species: dogs became adapted to the demands made upon their activity, sheep grew longer wool, and goats developed shorter horns. The nature of the domestication process is much debated. Did humans deliberately select preferred animals that then interbred and developed in a particular direction, or was natural selection at work, with the tamable species accommodating themselves to survival with humans and the human environment? In the latter scenario, certain naturally occurring genetic mutations might have conveyed advantages to animals living with or near humans, in which case a dependent evolutionary relationship developed.

The symbiotic relationship of domesticated animals and humans has been called co-evolution, for the domestication of animals (and plants) led to a form of domestication of humans. To care for, discipline, and tend to the needs of animals regularizes human behavior. Humans, in other words, change because of their contact with and care of animals. In the transformation of hunter-gatherers into settled peoples, the domestication of animals and plants was a step in the process of managing economic resources and regularizing a wandering life.

By 2500 BCE most of the animals upon which humans depend had been domesticated: pigs in western Asia about 7000 BCE, cattle in the eastern Sahara by 7000 BCE, chickens in the area of Thailand by 6000 BCE, horses in northern Kazakhstan as early as 5500 BCE, donkeys in northern Africa by 4000 BCE, silkworms in China by 3500 BCE, camels (both Bactrian and dromedaries) in southern Russia and Arabia by 3000 BCE, and honeybees in Egypt by 3000 BCE. The cat is a special case, because its economic use is less obvious. Cats were likely attracted to human communities by the rodents (mice and rats) that lived off human food, so they were tolerated as rodent-catchers. Some evidence suggests that cats domesticated themselves, which may explain their half-wild or independent natures. Descended from Middle Eastern wild cats, early domesticated cats were much larger than today's house pets. On Cyprus, a large domesticated cat was buried beside a grave around 9500 BCE. The Egyptians later bred smaller and tamer cats than the one found on Cyprus.

Settling Down and the Birth of Agriculture

Another great challenge for early humans was to stabilize their lives by securing greater safety. A purely nomadic life would have been a perilous, exhausting life. The simplest injury or illness could lead to abandonment and death. Seasonally, hunter-gatherer groups of prehistoric humans needed to find or make more permanent and fixed habitations. The hunter-gatherer people of Chauvet and Lascaux in France could not have painted their caves so delicately and extensively if they had not regularized, to some extent, their seasonal patterns. Yet it cannot have been easy for prehistoric peoples to settle down permanently. Much depended upon the availability of local food, water, and security, but they were still hunting and gathering peoples, often following wild herds of great migratory beasts. Semi-settled and settled life came before systematic agriculture, so that agriculture may be the result of settlement rather than the reverse. By about 10,000 BCE in the Middle East various Neolithic (or New Stone Age) peoples had begun to settle at places such as Jericho. In the beginning they were not farmers.

The fact of settlements, first seasonal and then permanent, had important implications for Neolithic peoples. Economic conditions needed to be regularized. Agriculture was one way to do that, even if hunting and gathering were still necessary. Trade with other communities offered the chance for people in one place to obtain things they lacked locally. The harvesting of wild crops may have been an accidental feature of early settlements. The chronology is striking: settlements first, the domestication of plants second and at a slower pace than habitation.

Living in more or less permanent villages and towns imposed new conditions and problems on Neolithic peoples. Life in a settled community depends on cooperation between people and codes of acceptable behavior. Settled life also introduced new divisions between people, the first of these being material. Settled peoples hold, and in some sense invented, the idea of private and fixed property; nomadic peoples have only what they can carry with them. But not all houses or settlements are equal; indeed, it is their very nature to be different and unequal. Settled peoples acquire and accumulate lands and goods—some more than others—so that settled life produces differences in wealth and status between people. **Sedentism** (settling down) produced its own particular problems: greater vulnerability to attack (enemies knew where settlements were); the spread of communicable diseases, since people lived in such close quarters to each other and might suffer the same environmental stresses (from polluted water, spoiled food, poor air quality); and the exhaustion of local resources (particularly the overuse of the same soil and water resources). Though settled peoples regularized the supply of food, their diet was less varied and perhaps less healthy than that of their hunter-gatherer predecessors. The size and height of settled men and women seems, as a result, to have shrunk.

Settlement and the occupation of residences was another great leap forward in the human drive to reshape the environment from one imposed by nature to one controlled by humans. The possibilities of material culture (goods, tools, houses) expanded significantly with settlement as did new skills associated with house-building and its materials (of mud, stone, and wood). Settled humans belong to house cultures; that is, houses not only are their creations, reflecting in their materials and design particular societies and individuals, but also shape humans and their relations with the world. Settled peoples created internal or house worlds, which hastened intellectual changes unknown to wandering peoples who knew animals and food sources, the moon and stars, topography and winds, but less about themselves than they did about a demanding external world. Settled life also changed the roles of the sexes, each beginning to specialize in specific activities that were different from those of their earlier wandering existence.

As the Ice Age was drawing to a close and glaciers were retreating, as early as 10,000 BCE, a series of villages began to appear in the Near East, especially in southern Turkey (Anatolia) in the area in the north of the so-called Fertile Crescent (an area curving from the Nile to the Tigris and Euphrates Rivers). People in these communities still hunted, but they also began to construct circular homes and to farm. The domestication of sheep and goats in the same area was probably not a coincidence, but these Neolithic farmers devoted themselves chiefly to the cultivation of grain crops, which made all the difference to regularizing life.

The Domestication of Plants

The domestication of plants lagged behind the domestication of animals but was put to better advantage by settled communities. Of most importance to the Near East settlements after 10,000 BCE was the domestication of einkorn wheat, emmer wheat, bread wheat, and barley. Wheat in its wild state is of little use to humans and difficult to digest, but in the dry summers of the Middle East wheat tended to produce larger seed pods. Were these selected by Neolithic humans or was wheat another example of a domesticate that did well by accommodating itself to human needs? Perhaps it was both. Under human cultivation, possibly by women farmers tending to the nearby fields, wheat lost its toxicity and produced larger yields and more manageable germination and growth cycles.

A Neolithic Settlement A reconstruction of the settlement of Çatal Hüyük in Anatolia. Settlements such as this one occurred before the domestication of plants.

The results were significant. In the case of wheat, its cultivation and the great shift to carbohydrates in the human diet (including the focus on cultivating rice in China and maize in Mexico by 8000 BCE) allowed human beings to escape complete dependence on a nomadic gathering and hunting life. The domestication of goats and sheep made up for the protein lost from less hunting. The Near East success in farming spread west and east, to Europe, Egypt, and India. By 5000 BCE Greece, the Nile valley, and parts of Pakistan were growing the Near Eastern cereal crops. Some scholars have called this the **Agricultural Revolution of Prehistory.** Although it was a revolution in terms of radical change, it took millennia for these crops and farming skills to spread across Eurasia. Nor was this agricultural advance limited to grain crops. In the Near East fig trees were domesticated around 9000 BCE, and chickpeas, lentils, and peas by 7500 BCE. Farming led to the development of new tools, for grain crops need to be sown, harvested, and thrashed to separate the grains from their husks, and each of these stages required its own special technologies and techniques. By 6000 BCE ceramic pots were being produced at Jericho. A community of nearly a thousand rectangular houses at Çatal Hüyük in Anatolia flourished around the same time. Its residents farmed wheat, peas, and lentils; traded obsidian objects; and painted their houses with scenes of fertile women and bulls.

Mesolithic Europe

With the passing of the Ice Age, the continent of Europe entered its Mesolithic Age. As the ice retreated north, many of the migratory herd animals such as reindeer or caribou that European peoples had depended on moved north. The hunter-gatherer peoples turned to hunting smaller, solitary game and relied increasingly upon wild plants and fish. In their art they began to depict human subjects rather than herd animals. Farming came to the Mediterranean rim of southern Europe and spread slowly after 7000 BCE (on the day of his death, Ötzi had eaten some einkorn wheat), but it took three thousand years before farming spread across Europe. In Scandinavia there are nonagricultural settlement sites from 5000 BCE.

About that time, various peoples in Europe and the British Isles began erecting megaliths, giant stone and wood structures, many of them for religious reasons at grave sites. The most impressive of these is Stonehenge, erected about 2400–2200 BCE on the Salisbury Plain of southern England. Stonehenge contains a series of stand-

Stonehenge The Mesolithic stone circle on the Salisbury Plain of Wiltshire, England, was once the site of prehistoric religious rites.

ing stones called menhirs that may have been arranged to mark points in the solar calendar, particularly the summer solstice. An earlier funeral site called Bluehenge, because of its bluestones (brought from Wales), has been found nearby. Not far from Stonehenge was Woodhenge, and a causeway or marked footpath seems to have connected them. These **henges,** or earthenworks, were probably used to mark different ceremonies in the lives, health, and deaths of prehistoric Britons. On the Orkney Islands, off the coast of Scotland, the later Ring of Brodgar and other rings of stone also bear witness to related pagan belief systems and customs. These were impressive community structures, but the societies that built them were not higher civilizations. That Europe was well behind the Near East culturally and economically was a reflection of its climate; the warmer Fertile Crescent blossomed, while Europe remained chilly, its climate thawing slowly.

The Indo-European Factor

Almost three billion people today speak an Indo-European language. Linguists concluded long ago that these languages, because of their shared root-words and grammatical structures (the way their languages work), descend from a mother tongue called Proto Indo-European (Table 1.1). This language was spoken in the Pontic-Caspian area of Eurasia, in the steppes or prairie lands between and above the Black and Caspian Seas, between 4500 and 2200 BCE.

These peoples possessed a vocabulary for family members, animals, and material culture that in its root forms is common to its descendent languages. By examining the root vocabulary of Proto Indo-European, historical linguists have determined the historical and geographic setting of these peoples. For example, they had words for northern animals, but not southern ones, and for northern trees, but not for dates and palms. Their economy was pastoral, based on sheep and cattle herding in the area near the Dnieper River. The cave peoples of the late Paleolithic period had lived in matrilineal societies; the Indo-European herding cultures were patrilineal (descending from the father), perhaps as a result of the central importance of male cooperation in managing herds. As early as 5000 BCE they began to place themselves under chiefs. At about the same time, they domesticated horses, and by 4200 BCE these peoples learned to ride horses.

The vast grassland of the Eurasian steppes was not a welcoming environment for humans, but the domestication of horses gave these peoples a way to expand space. They developed wheeled carts, which allowed them to be mobile and migratory. The Indo-European peoples were thus agents of cultural penetration and engagement; they encountered others, sometimes peacefully, often violently. The steppes served as a Eurasian land bridge, allowing these peoples to move south into areas of the Fertile Crescent, east into greater Asia, and southwest into Europe (Map 1.2). Between 4000 and 3800 BCE the weather in the steppes turned colder, glaciers advanced, and spring flooding was severe. Copper and Bronze Age warriors on horseback with wagons to carry their goods brought their culture to Anatolia between 3700 and 3500 BCE. Over the next thousand years, these peoples with their horses, technology, and political and social systems moved south, east, and west. This migration was neither sudden nor constantly violent. The very fact that the Indo-European language did not join itself to native languages but generally replaced them may suggest that its adoption was voluntary rather than compulsory. Resident populations may have adopted the foreign language because of its prestige, utility, and association with power. The dependent languages that developed can be dated roughly and suggest the order of contact with Proto Indo-European: Anatolian around 4000 BCE, Tocharian (in the area of northwestern China) around 3500 BCE, Celtic and Italic around 3000 BCE, Greek closer to 2500 BCE, and early Indo-Iranian (including Sanskrit) closer to 2000 BCE.

Though the Indo-Europeans have been misrepresented for racial and nationalist reasons as Aryans by the Nazis and others, they may best be thought of as several prehistoric peoples in the Dnieper-Danube area who shared a basic language and who, because of their use of wheeled carts and horses, were able to penetrate and influence developing lands to the south, east, and west of their homeland in the steppes. They not only introduced languages that replaced indigenous languages, but also influenced the political and religious values of these lands. Patriarchal societies with chiefs, horses, and a male sky-god came to predominate.

TABLE 1.1 | Shared Indo-European Words

ENGLISH	GERMAN	SPANISH	GREEK	LATIN	SANSKRIT
father	*vater*	*padre*	*pater*	*pater*	*pitar*
one	*ein*	*uno*	*hen*	*unus*	*ekam*
Sun	*Sonne*	*sol*	*helios*	*sol*	*surya*
King	*König*	*rey*	*basileus*	*rex*	*raja*
God	*Gott*	*dios*	*theos*	*deus*	*devas*

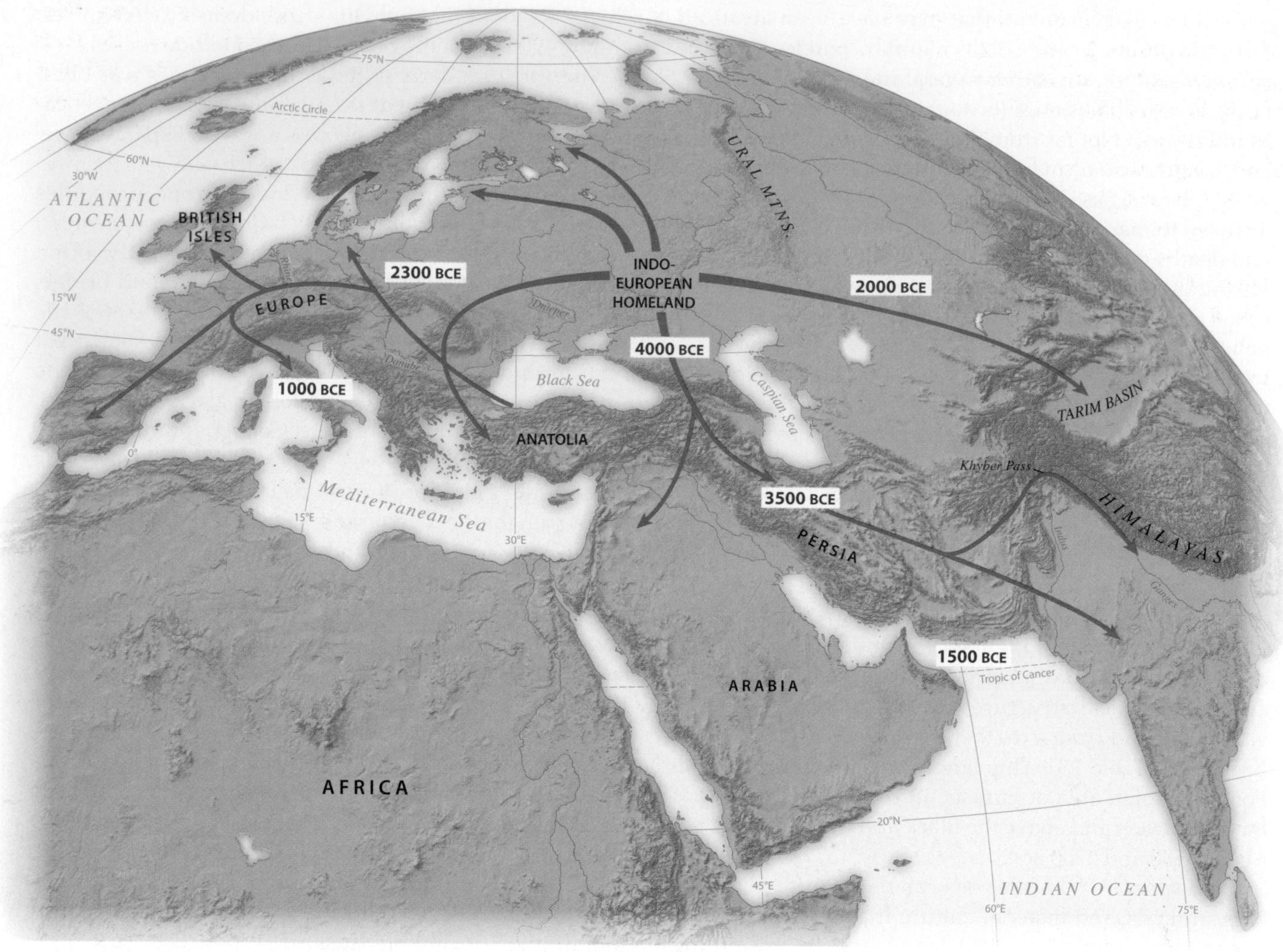

MAP 1.2 | **The Spread of the Indo-Europeans, 4000–1000 BCE**

From their original homeland in the area between the Black and Caspian Seas, groups of Indo-Europeans began, over several millennia, to spread south, east, and west, influencing the languages, cultures, political systems, and technologies of the lands they occupied. ***How might the geography and climate of the area between the Black and Caspian Seas have promoted or even forced the movement of the Indo-Europeans? How do the language and technologies of the Indo-Europeans help us to track their migration and the impact they had on the lands they entered?***

The Emergence of Cities and Writing in Mesopotamia

The word *civilization* (from the Latin word *civilis* for things referring to a city, its citizens, and society) can mislead us into thinking that without cities or substantial settlements there can be no civilization. Around 3500 BCE the important thing was the establishment of farming communities, which arose not just in the Near East, but also around the world (perhaps the effect of the waning of the Ice Age): in the Indus Valley, China, Egypt, Mexico, Peru, and parts of southern Europe. These societies were often associated with great rivers such as the Nile. In many of these places, such as the Near East and Egypt, the emergence of complex societies occurred almost simultaneously. The histories of Near Eastern peoples (Mesopotamian, Egyptian, Minoan, Mycenaean, Hittite, Hebrew, and many others) are each deserving of extended independent study, but here we examine only briefly the larger picture and direction of the civilizations that emerged at the eastern end of the Mediterranean Sea and take note of their characters and contributions to laying down the preliminaries for the emergence of western civilization.

Why was writing such an important human invention, and why did it first appear in Mesopotamia?

One of the issues we may wish to think about is why bigger was better and the predominant historical pattern of early history, which saw empires emerge from important cities and dominate and incorporate other cities and lands. This imperial impetus might be called the Mesopotamian model since it was followed by the great Mesopotamian powers—Akkadian, Babylonian, Hittite, Assyrian, and Persian. The same model did not take hold in Egypt. The particular geography of Mesopotamia may explain the pattern, but there were contributing causes for the imperial impetus: the growing complexity and expanding resources (both material and human) of Mesopotamian powers; the need to defend a vulnerable land against competitive rivals, both to overcome threats and to seize resources; the martial nature of warrior societies and their religions; and the unilateral power and dominance of all-powerful rulers who could, through an act of sheer will or individual drive, turn their societies toward singular goals such as conquest.

The historical players in the early history of the eastern Mediterranean can be divided into land empires (Akkadians, Babylonians, Hittites, Phrygians, and Assyrians) and the sea enterprises of the Minoans, Mycenaeans, and Phoenicians, which tended to be less imperial, more commercial, and somewhat remote from Mesopotamia. The particular nature of Mesopotamia, its problems and tensions, shaped the primary pattern and instabilities of early Near Eastern history.

Mesopotamia and the Appearance of Cities

In the Near East the earliest development occurred in the area the Greeks called Mesopotamia, the lands lying between the Tigris and Euphrates Rivers but stretching north into Anatolia and south to the Persian Gulf (Map 1.3). Settlements first appeared in Anatolia in the northern part of Mesopotamia between 10,000 and 7000 BCE. These urban developments coincided with the retreat of the glaciers in the northern hemisphere, leaving Mesopotamia a lusher region than it is today. In northern Mesopotamia, annual rainfall was sufficient to support crops. Southern Mesopotamia (Sumer proper) remained drier and depended on the Tigris and Euphrates Rivers to flood in the spring to moisten fields and maintain soil fertility. Sumer was at the mercy of its great rivers; sometimes they did not flood, and sometimes they overflowed at the wrong time, washing away valuable soils and crops and drowning fields. As early as 5500 BCE, farmers began to manage the great, but unpredictable rivers to irrigate their fields and protect them from seasonal flooding. Lacking rocks in that part of Mesopotamia, these peoples constructed levees of earth and used tools made of hardened clay. Large-scale irrigation projects necessitated advanced planning, organization, and cooperation between groups of people. The particular needs of southern Mesopotamia may, thus, have led farming peoples to experiment with the first forms of large-scale cooperation for the general good. Governments followed, first civic and then royal and imperial.

By 3300 BCE, while Ötzi was dying on a European mountain, Uruk on the Euphrates had grown into a recognizable city with impressive temple structures, meandering roads, and thousands of houses. Its large size (a population estimated at over 50,000) was supported by an agricultural economy producing surpluses and by satellite or dependent villages. By the third millennium most Mesopotamians resided in cities. There were twenty or so prominent cities in southern Mesopotamia (Sumer), among them Eridu, Uruk, Kish, Shuruppak, Akkad, Ur, Nippur, Sippar, Assur, Nineveh, and Babylon. The landscape of Mesopotamia—with its openness to invasion,

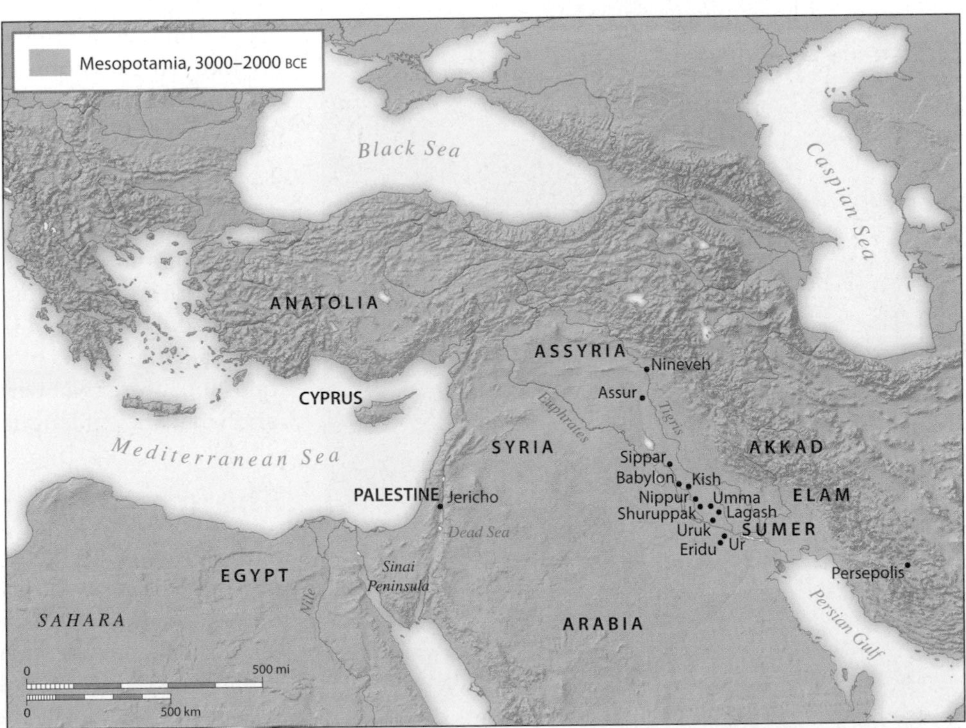

MAP 1.3 | Mesopotamia, 3000–2000 BCE
The geography of Mesopotamia was dominated by two rivers, the Tigris and Euphrates. Mesopotamia could be reached by land, particularly from the west, since the land there was unobstructed by natural barriers such as mountains. ***How did the geography of Mesopotamia shape the early history of the region? Why did so many important cities arise there, and why did they play such a critical role in the history of the region?***

rivers both dangerous and life-giving, fragile climate, and need for trade—may have made city living the best option for coping with a demanding environment. If the creation of cities and urban cultures was southern Mesopotamia's first great invention, writing was its second.

The Invention of Writing

Writing was a product of an urbanized society that wanted a way to record economic information. Not surprisingly, numbers probably came into existence before the creation of characters or word-signs. Before the full emergence of writing, early Mesopotamians had introduced marked clay tokens and stored them in round clay containers to facilitate and record transactions. At Uruk after 3300 BCE these tokens were replaced by a system employing abstract pictographs (pictures of things) with an indication of the number of objects involved. Ideographs (pictures of ideas or actions) supplemented the pictographic base. By the second millennium BCE, Mesopotamian scribes introduced signs for sounds (phonograms). They inscribed signs on wet clay, the only widely available and inexpensive surface in Mesopotamia upon which to write. These clay tablets were then dried in the sun to form a fragile, perishable surface. To make a harder, more enduring surface for important records, the Mesopotamians heated or fired the inscribed clay tablets.

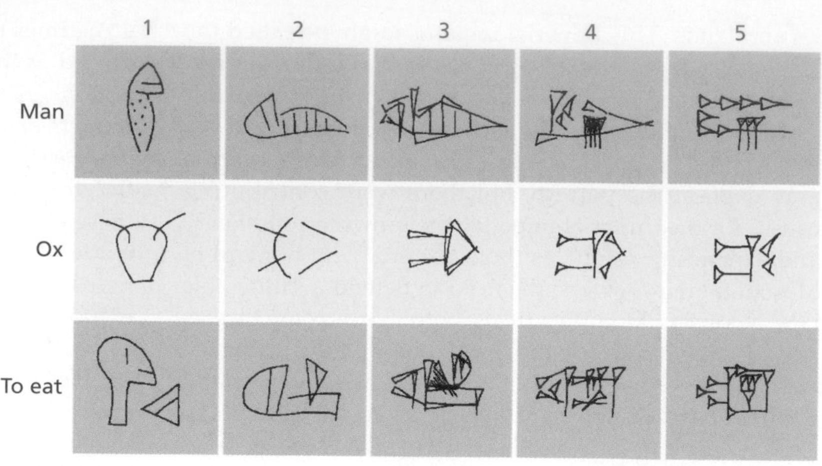

FIGURE 1.1 | **The Invention of Writing**

Mesopotamian scribes wrote in rows or columns left to right so as not to efface already inscribed signs with their right hands. After 3000 BCE, probably in order to write more quickly, scribes started to use a wedge-shaped stylus, which they pressed into the wet clay. This gave Sumerian writing an angularity and wedge-shaped look called cuneiform (from the Latin *cuneus,* or wedge). These inscriptions were more abstract in appearance and could be written and read only by trained scribes and priests (Figure 1.1).

Sumerian writing (both its original cursive form and later dominant cuneiform style) held sway for some 2,000 years in Mesopotamia and surrounding regions. Cuneiform writing was used to record a number of languages (Sumerian, old Persian, Semitic or Akkadian, and Elamite), making its modern decipherment difficult. The questions were two: what did the cuneiform signs mean, and what ancient language were they recording?

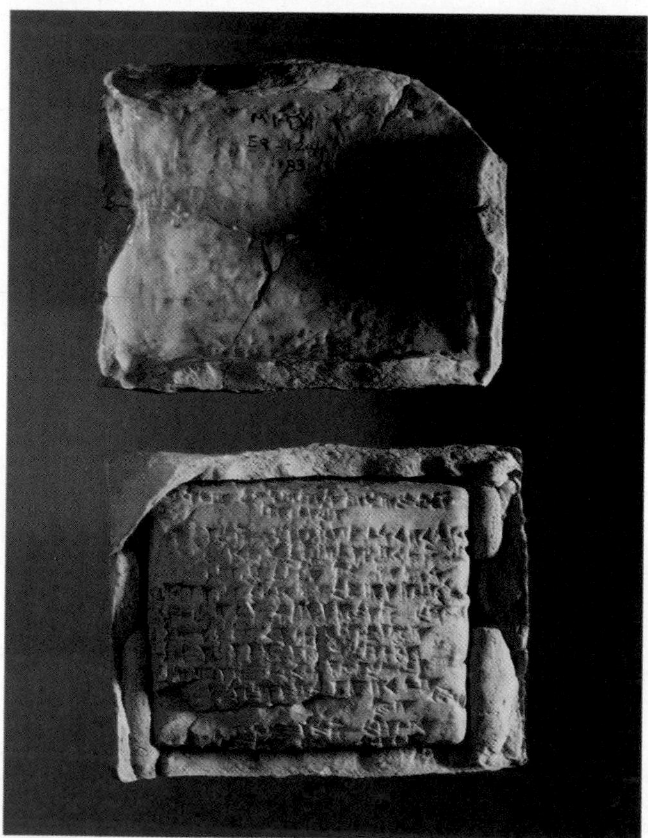

Cuneiform Clay Tablet A typical clay tablet with its clay envelope from Syria. The cuneiform or wedge-shaped writing on this clay tablet records the specifics of an inheritance.

The Importance of Writing

The slow development of writing did not change the Mesopotamian world overnight, but it was a significant step in the establishment of civilization. Mesopotamian society still remained chiefly oral (as is our own). Writing became a specialized cultural tool, known and practiced by a select few. The differences between preliterate and literate societies are, however, considerable. In oral cultures, everything of importance to a group must be remembered or it is eventually lost. Ancient oral cultures developed cultural tools such as songs and encyclopedic poems that could be remembered and passed to the next generation, but oral poems are not fixed; they change from performance to performance. Moreover, there were limits on how much information could be packed into

Cracking Cuneiform

Thousands of inscribed clay tablets from the Near East survive, some in the older cursive script (3300–2500 BCE) and an even greater number of tablets in the cuneiform script (2500 BCE–75 CE). Rulers such as Ur-Nammu, Hammurabi, and the Persian Darius the Great left extensive records in their palaces. But cuneiform was so rich in symbols and conventions that recognizing it as a script and cracking its meaning was lost until the early seventeenth century CE when the great Persian capital of Persepolis was rediscovered and copies of these strange inscriptions were first published. Initially, scholars thought that these markings were purely decorative. Only in the eighteenth century did some scholars begin to realize that they were looking at a script, whose elements could be isolated and analyzed. Georg Grotefend, a German grammar school teacher, identified divisions between recognizable words and names in the inscriptions. Among the names he recognized were Darius and Xerxes. Grotefend did not crack cuneiform, but he did at long last establish that it was a form of writing.

In Iran, one remarkable late inscription had been carved high on a mountain at Behistun (modern Bisitun). It was inscribed in three different forms of cuneiform (Old Persian, Babylonian, and Elamite) but was hard to read in its mountain setting. A nineteenth-century British adventurer, Henry Rawlinson, perched himself precariously on the mountainside to copy the inscription and hired an agile local boy to make plaster casts of the parts he could not reach. It took Rawlinson ten years to make a complete copy of the Behistun inscription, and not long afterward he was able to decode and translate Babylonian cuneiform writing. Unfortunately Rawlinson never explained how he had managed to crack one of the world's most complex scripts. He was a gifted linguist and knew many relevant old languages, which helped, but his awareness of the work of his predecessors and peers may explain both his breakthrough and his silence.[1]

QUESTIONS | ***Why did writing first emerge in Mesopotamia? Why was the knowledge of such a widespread and long-lasting script lost, and what were the consequences of that loss?***

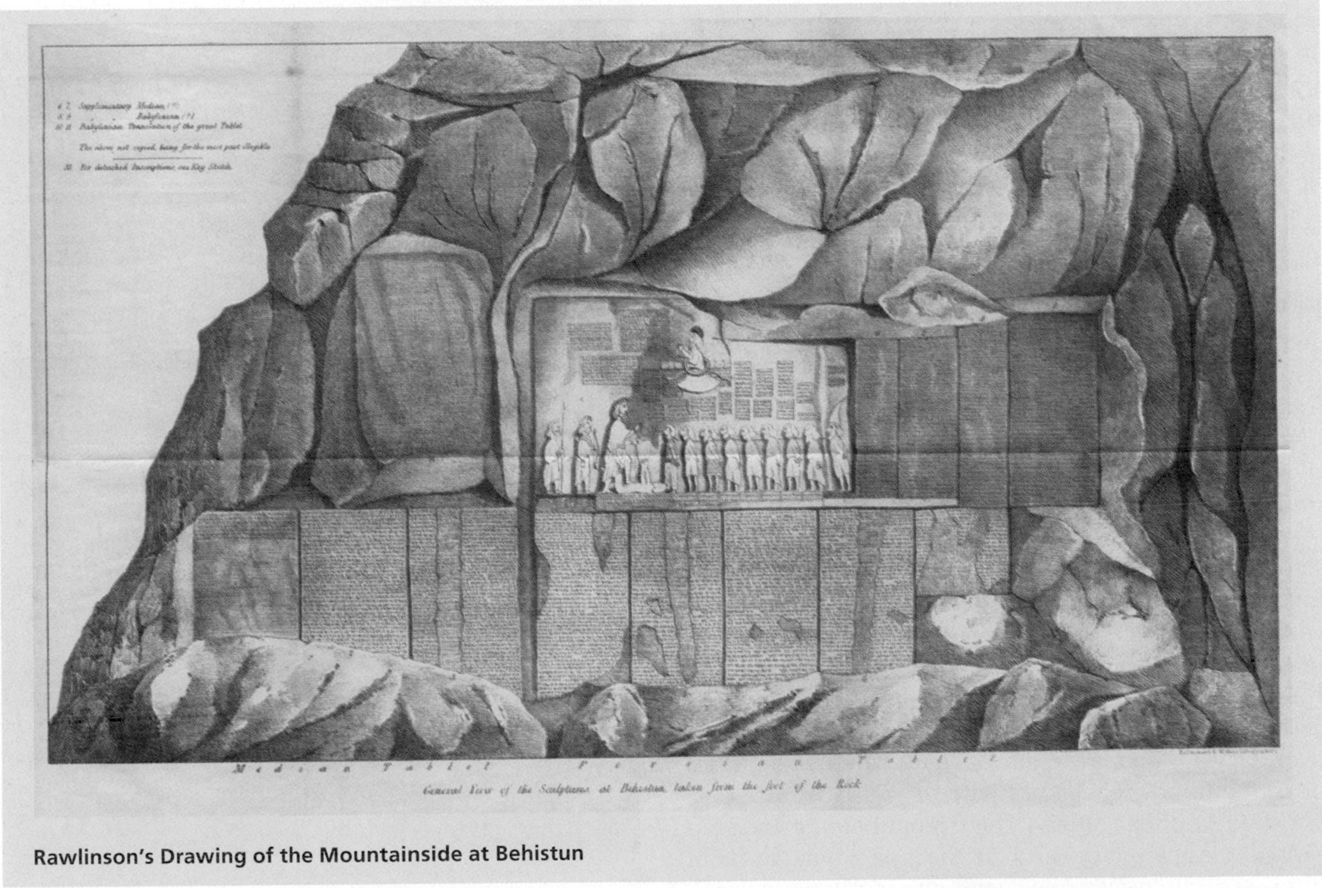

Rawlinson's Drawing of the Mountainside at Behistun

an oral song, and if the singer died before he could train an heir, the string of an oral tradition might be broken permanently.

Writing fixes information, absolving writers or their society from having to remember everything. Written records allow information to be stored and retrieved, hence, its economic and religious advantage. Writing produced, just as agriculture and permanent settlement had, new attitudes to the world and new forms of expression and behavior. Critical and rational thought depend, to some degree, on the reader's capacity to check information that lies beyond the spoken word. It is difficult in an oral and aural (hearing) world to verify what was previously said. Literacy fosters a sharper and more developed organization of thought. An awareness of different kinds of time—business, historical, and religious—depends on the existence of writing, for writing helps us to order events and transactions. The Mesopotamian merchant needed to know when and to whom he had traded his wheat and when the buyer was obliged to pay him in full. By moving away from an absolute reliance on memory, some Mesopotamians could preserve and arrange information, freeing their minds for other intellectual activities. Of course, something was lost as well, for oral societies are intimate and personal, sealed together by shared memories of events and stories. The song belongs to a community. By contrast, a written text is separable, belonging to individual readers, and can be put to a variety of selected purposes ranging from bills of sale to complex propaganda pieces such as royal inscriptions. In Mesopotamian society, writing was a tool that empowered priests and rulers. Writing was, in the beginning, concerned largely with economic information, but it proved to be just as useful in recording information about law, religion, and rulers.

Cities to Empires

By the third millennium BCE the developing cities of southern Mesopotamia established identities. Each had its own gods and rulers, often priests or priest-kings, and society was rigidly hierarchical. Kings, nobles, and priests, in that order, represented and had real power; soldiers, artisans, and farmers, in that order, represented the productive classes. Slaves stood at the bottom of society.

Southern Mesopotamian (Sumerian) cities varied in size from small (10,000 people or less) to very large (some with as many as 50,000–60,000 people). These city-states controlled a surrounding territory, including outlying villages. Their rulers were not all equal. Some were called lords, others governors, and others great ones (*lugals*). The *lugal* comes closest to being a king and ruled over the lords and governors of smaller dependent cities or communities. The *lugal*'s wife or *nin* (lady) also participated in public affairs. Their prominent partnership hints at the hereditary nature of the *lugal*'s dynastic claim to power. The *lugal*'s roles were many: religious, legal, and military. *Lugals* built complex palaces from which they governed their kingdoms with the assistance of a palace government of servants and officials. They assembled armies composed of infantry and war chariots.

Agricultural Mesopotamia was a world at war, each city always on the watch for hostile moves by its neighbors, who were often only fifty or sixty miles away. The open geography of Mesopotamia made attack inevitable and sudden. The best long-term defensive strategy for any city was to conquer nearby aggressive cities. A stable balance of power between these cities was impossible to preserve; political instability was to be the Mesopotamian condition. The first city to shatter any rough balance of power and dominate many others was Kish, just south of present-day Baghdad. Around 2650 BCE the great city-state of Uruk, south of Kish, was led by Gilgamesh, whose exploits are remembered in a famous epic. If *The Epic of Gilgamesh* is to be trusted, Gilgamesh led Uruk in its conquest of much of Mesopotamia.

Over the coming centuries a series of city-states rose to dominance (Ur, Lagash, Elam, and Umma), before the rise of Sargon the Great. Sargon spoke a Semitic language and may have begun his rise in Kish as a servant of the king. Around 2350 BCE he overthrew the king of Umma and moved to consolidate all of Mesopotamia under his control. He founded a chief city at Agade or Akkad, after

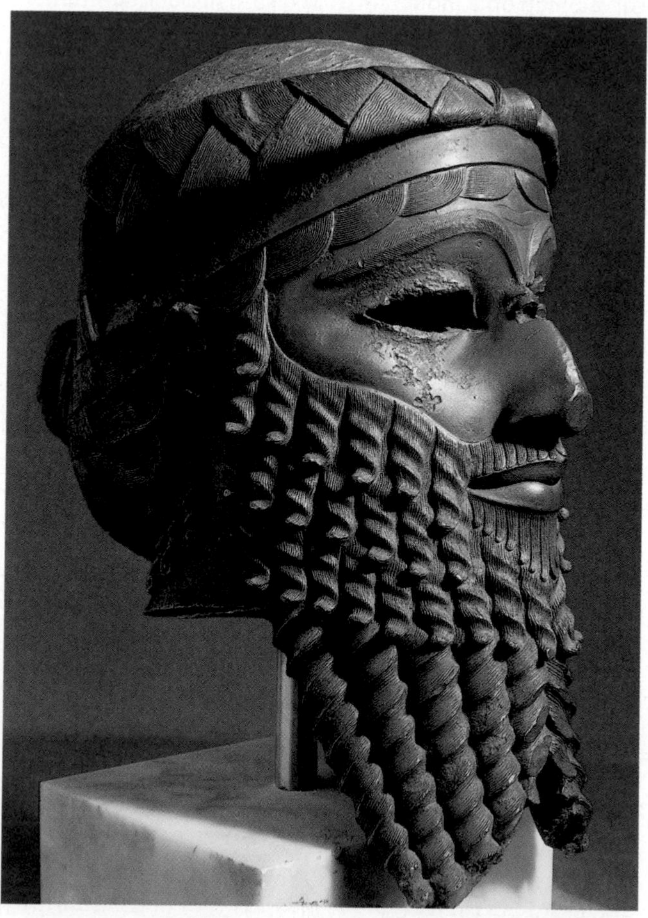

Sargon the Great A bronze bust of the founder of the Akkadian Empire of Mesopotamia.

which his Akkadian Empire is named. His was not a radical break with older southern Mesopotamian culture or governance, but in terms of its reach and prosperity Sargon and the Semitic Akkadians produced one of the first great empires of the ancient world. A century later, Sargon's grandson, Naram-Sin, declared himself and his ancestors gods and conquered territories throughout the Middle East (including Syria and Lebanon). The powerful Akkadian Empire dissolved after Naram-Sin's death.

Mesopotamia fell into a period of war between rival cities and faced a group of northern invaders known as Gutians, dragons from the mountains, as they were called in the south. By 2100 BCE, a ruler of Uruk drove the mountain men from Mesopotamia and was replaced by the famous Ur-Nammu, who created the last great southern Mesopotamian dynasty. It was Ur-Nammu who presided over the building of the famous **Ziggurat** (or temple structure) of Ur and laid down history's first law code, which survives in fragmentary form. Ur-Nammu's code specified payments rather than corporal punishments, even for many serious crimes.

By 2000 BCE the Ur dynasty had failed and Mesopotamia fell back into a period of wars between various cities that lasted almost two centuries. One of these warlike cities was Babylon on the Euphrates. Led by King Hammurabi (reigned c. 1790–1750 BCE), Babylon slowly conquered rival cities such as the fabled Mari with its immense palace of three hundred rooms and lush gardens. Hammurabi's Semitic or Akkadian language replaced Sumerian as the major language of Mesopotamia. Thousands of documents survive from Hammurabi's reign, but the most celebrated of these is his law code.

The **Code of Hammurabi** is not a set of universal laws, but rather specific decisions reached under Hammurabi's royal authority and useful to judges considering the disputes placed before them. The code was circulated on clay tablets and carved stone slabs or columns (stele). Half of the code, which contains almost three hundred legal decisions, concerns contract disputes and a third treats domestic matters. The Code of Hammurabi seems harsher than the Code of Ur-Nammu. Capital punishment was prescribed for a host of offenses, including adultery, robbery, incest, and kidnapping. If a matter could not be resolved from the evidence provided by witnesses, the accused was subjected to trial by ordeal or divine judgment. The accused was tossed into the river; the guilty sank, the innocent were able to swim to shore. Yet the presumption of innocence lies behind many of the cases in the document. The code drew sharp legal distinctions between nobles, commoners or dependents, and slaves, valuing the word and worth of nobles over the two lower orders. An individual who had physically harmed a noble was punished with the same injury, whereas an injured commoner could be paid compensation. The purpose of the code may have been less to set out a systematic law code than to demonstrate how a great ruler such as Hammurabi reached wise decisions and presided over a firm legal system.

Hammurabi Receives the Law On a stele containing his laws, the standing Hammurabi is shown receiving the laws or his authority from the sun god, thus indicating the divine origin and basis of his rulings.

After its peak under Hammurabi, Babylon prevailed until the Indo-European-speaking Hittites conquered it at the end of the sixteenth century BCE. Mesopotamia, surrounded by hostile peoples, was always susceptible to invasion because it lacked natural barriers to keep outsiders out.

Mesopotamian Religion

Prehistoric peoples doubtless had myths, legends, and religious beliefs of some complexity, but these are largely lost to us. The invention of writing in Mesopotamia marks the first sustained recording of religious belief, not its invention. Religious belief has always been part of the human condition, reflecting a desire to make sense of a mysterious world and to invest human existence with purpose.

The Mesopotamian peoples were polytheists (**polytheism** being the belief in many gods). They wanted to know about the nature of human existence and the gods, where and how humans live, what affects their lives, and how to appease the great forces that animate the world. They naturally thought of the earth as centered in Mesopotamia and ringed by its mountains and seas. Mesopotamians looked up to the sky and saw the home of heavenly bodies and looked down to the earth and imagined an underworld below it. The surface of the world, they thought, was alive with divine forces, in the water, in the air, and in living things. They conceived of a pantheon of gods, who were eternal and yet took human form. Thus, they offered their gods human food. Four principal gods, three males and a female (An, Enlil, Enki, and Ninhursag), created the world and represented the four elements: the ethereal sky, air, water, and earth. These four gods left their creation to their divine children (lesser gods, including the sun and moon) to administer. Mesopotamian religion was as hierarchical as society was. The gods were ranked and assigned numbers reflecting their importance and power.

The gods regulated human affairs. Wars, the destruction of cities, calamitous weather, and illness on earth were divine reckonings, and the lesser gods, the children of the great four, interfered with and haunted the world in which people lived. As agricultural peoples often are, the Mesopotamian peoples were convinced of the precarious and unpredictable state of the world: flooding rivers, droughts, disease, starvation, war, and early deaths seemed beyond their control, but not beyond the power of the capricious gods, whom the Mesopotamians sought to appease.

Agricultural prosperity paid for a class of priests and priestesses to serve the gods in their temples. People believed that the abundance of the land, the regular flow of the great rivers, and good weather depended on the favor of the gods, so Mesopotamian cities curried favor with the gods. Each city had its patron gods to whom it built temples and from whom it expected protection and prosperity in return. Inside these temples stood statues of the patron gods, whom the priestly class tended. Priests clothed the statues, sang hymns and prayers to the gods, and celebrated festivals in their honor. The people brought offerings for the gods, but it fell to the priests to prepare daily meals for the gods. Most Mesopotamians rarely if ever glimpsed the great statues.

Kings and powerful men allied themselves with the gods and eventually assumed a priestly function, subordinating the priestly class to state or palace needs. A southern Mesopotamian (Sumerian) king list (from the third millennium BCE) mixes divine kings, legendary kings, and real kings together as though they constituted a divinely sanctioned line. *The Epic of Gilgamesh* is not only the world's first great literary work, but also an example of the meshing of royal and religious persons. Gilgamesh, who was a real ruler of Uruk, is more god than man in the epic. He is also cruel, wanton, and tyrannical, but nevertheless a hero. Ancient heroes were not pleasant people one wanted to emulate, but rather tough superhuman figures beyond mortal reach. In the epic, Gilgamesh saves Uruk from destruction and tests the limits of human mortality. The epic gave Sumerians a look inside the divine forces that encircled their lives and determined their fates. People believed not that they would go to heaven or hell after death, but rather to an underworld. The living sent their deceased loved ones off to the lower world with the things they thought they would need there, but they interred their corpses below their houses so that the dead would not return to haunt the living world above.

The Mesopotamians shared a set of fundamental myths or religious stories. They believed that the gods were once so angry with humans that they had unleashed a great flood to drown the world, but some breakaway gods thought that the punishment was too severe, so they ordered a good man to build a boat to rescue representatives of humankind and animal life. The flood story alerts us that some portion of the Mesopotamian religious narrative became the common property of Near Eastern peoples: creation, a garden of Eden, an underworld (Hades, or Sheol for the Hebrews), the fall, a great flood, and a divinely favored people.

The Lasting Stability of Ancient Egypt

What were the chief achievements of Egyptian civilization, and what critical role did ancient Egypt play in the Mediterranean world?

Mesopotamian and Egyptian civilization emerged at almost the same time, with Mesopotamia in advance by several centuries. The two shared one essential feature: dependence on a great river complex and, thus, on agriculture. Beyond that, they had little in common. Even their rivers were different. The Nile was predictable; the Tigris and the Euphrates fluctuated wildly. Egypt's landscape and configuration made it less vulnerable to invasion than borderless Mesopotamia. Ancient Egypt had a longitudinal shape with a short hundred-mile stretch of delta open to the Mediterranean and seven hundred miles of river surrounded by forbidding deserts east and west and blocked to incursion at its southern source by dangerous rapids and waterfalls. Egypt's geography left it isolated and protected from frequent turmoil (Map 1.4). As a result, Egypt was more politically stable, confident, and self-sufficient than Mesopotamia, so much so that it became tradition bound. Why change what worked? Ancient Egypt was permanent, prosperous, and civilized; its civilization was not driven by vibrant and restless cities vying for power and domination. Ancient Egypt's stability and generation of wealth were critical elements in spurring development in the Near East.

The Nile and Egyptian Agriculture

The Nile was fed by the snows and spring rains of central Africa. Every July, like clockwork, the Nile flooded its banks, inundating the surrounding soils of Egypt and depositing a layer of fertile black mud. By November the Nile receded and farmers were able to plant crops that matured in March and April. So essential was the rhythm of the Nile that Egyptians divided their seasons into flooding, planting, and harvesting times and called Egypt "the black land," since their lives depended on the beneficial mud and 12,000 square miles of productive riverside.

Though the habitable and productive part of the Nile valley was thin (a band 5–25 miles along the river), the delta area at the mouth of the river, where the Nile broke into a fan-shaped series of rivers, supplied a different ecology that supported a larger population. Prior to 3000 BCE, Lower Egypt (the delta area from Memphis to the sea) and Upper Egypt (the rest of the river) were separate.

At the end of the Ice Age, the area of Egypt was wetter than today but climatically unstable. The warming temperatures and spread of the Sahara Desert transformed Egypt. Once various hunting and gathering peoples had moved freely across northern Africa, but the stabilization of the desert surrounding the Nile changed that. Wandering peoples settled along the thinning band of arable land along the Nile. There they built houses made of reeds on higher land beyond the reach of the annual floods. These peoples fished and hunted along the river and began to grow grain crops (emmer wheat and barley), figs, and flax.

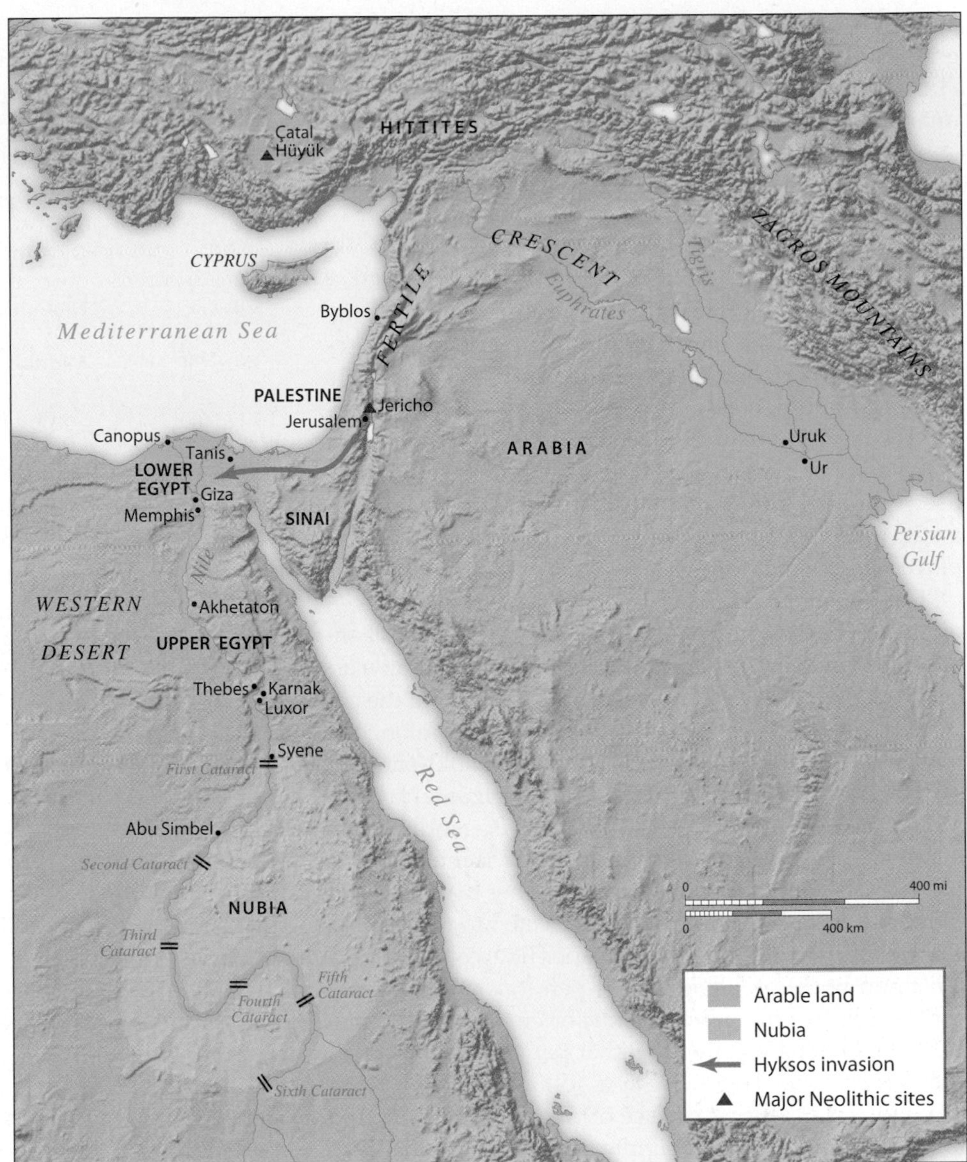

MAP 1.4 | Ancient Egypt and the Fertile Crescent

The Nile River lay at the heart of ancient Egypt. Its fertile banks stretched from Upper Egypt to Lower Egypt, ending in the fan-shaped delta where the Nile spilled into the Mediterranean Sea. The vast majority of the Egyptian population lived, farmed, and traveled along the Nile. Nubia contributed to shaping the culture of Upper Egypt, whereas Lower Egypt was early on in commercial contact with the lands along the eastern end of the Mediterranean and with Mesopotamia. ***How was Egypt, unlike Mesopotamia, sheltered by natural barriers? What effect did such geography have on the history of Egypt? How was Egypt connected to the Mediterranean world and the Near East?***

The Nile focus of Egypt shaped Egyptian civilization. The river, not roads, was Egypt's means of transport and travel. Egypt was blessed with many more natural riches than Mesopotamia: Egypt possessed stone resources (for buildings and monuments), clay (for pottery and bricks), minerals (copper and gold), and semiprecious stones (turquoise, amethyst, and garnets). To obtain the few things it needed from outside, such as hard woods, Egypt had ample resources to trade.

Hieroglyphics and Egyptian Writing

Egyptian writing appeared around 3100 BCE, several centuries after Mesopotamian writing and different in character, but it is unlikely that it was an absolutely independent development. Word of the existence of writing in Mesopotamia, carried back by travelers and traders, may have spurred Egyptians to develop their own writing system. The Greeks called the Egyptian inscriptions they saw on stone monuments "sacred carvings" or **hieroglyphics,** but the term does not do full justice to the character of Egyptian writing or to the variety of surfaces on which Egyptians wrote.

Egyptian writing started with pictographs, as had Mesopotamian writing, and retained the appearance of picture writing, but from the beginning it also possessed signs for the sounds of consonants (phonograms). There are twenty-four of these consonantal signs. Hieroglyphics, however, remained a complex system that mixed together pictographs, phonograms, logographs (whole word signs), and ideographs, to which were added determinatives, small signs that gave a specific meaning or twist to standard signs.

Hieroglyphics, the original Egyptian script, continued in use for three millennia. Its more than seven hundred signs were painted on walls, carved into stone monuments, and written on other surfaces. As Egyptian society developed, hieroglyphics became something of a formal, monumental, and prestige script. For quicker, more common writing, the Egyptians developed two cursive scripts: hieratic (c. 2000 BCE), which came to be used largely to record religious documents, and demotic, a still more popular and even more cursive script, employed for business and private writing.

There may have been a material reason for the development of cursive scripts: the Egyptians' discovery of another writing surface, this one soft and pliable. Papyrus, from which we take our word *paper*, is made from the papyrus plant, a bulrush or native reed that grew along the banks of the Nile. A longitudinal layer of split papyrus stalks was laid down and on top of it a horizontal layer of stalks; the two layers were then pressed or gently beaten together, releasing the glue-like resin of the pith of the papyrus stalks, binding the layers together to make a soft organic surface that was dried and treated to receive ink. The resulting material, soft and paper-like, could be written upon with ink using a reed pen (*calamus*). Because scribes could write more quickly, or cursively, on papyrus rolls (made by gluing together papyrus sheets), both the hieratic and demotic scripts followed. Papyrus became the chief writing surface of the ancient world, and for thousands of years its supply remained Egyptian, another special benefit of the wondrous Nile.

The meaning of ancient Egyptian writing was lost by modern times, just as the meaning of cuneiform had been. The discovery of the Rosetta Stone (now in London's British Museum) in Egypt by Napoleon's soldiers led to its decipherment. The Rosetta Stone contains an inscription written in three scripts (hieroglyphic, demotic, and Greek) and eventually allowed Thomas Young of England and Jean François Champollion of France to crack the hieroglyphic code. It was soon realized that, for much of three millennia, writing in Egypt had been an essential tool in preserving and promoting power and tradition in dynastic, religious, and economic matters.

The Dynasties Take Hold

Before 3000 BCE Egypt had evolved from several dozen village-centered regions in the delta and along the Nile to the separate kingdoms of Upper Egypt (including the older kingdom of Nubia, formed by peoples from Sudan who were famous for their use of the bow) and Lower Egypt. Egypt's long dynastic history began when the two kingdoms were united about 3000 BCE. Since writing had been introduced at about the same time, Egypt entered history literally and dynastically at the same time. Traditionally Egypt is thought to have had thirty-one dynasties over the next twenty-seven hundred years, a run that ended with Alexander the Great's conquest of Egypt in 332 BCE. Though ancient Egypt's long history is subject to many divisions and subdivisions, the most convenient is into the distinctive periods of unity achieved during the Old Kingdom (2647–2124 BCE), the Middle Kingdom (2040–1648 BCE), and the New Kingdom (1540–1069 BCE). Between the kingdoms were intermediate or transitional periods of instability and disorder.

CHRONOLOGY The Egyptian Dynasties and Kingdoms

DYNASTIES	NAME/PERIOD	APPROXIMATE DATES BCE
I–II	Early Dynastic	3050–2647
III–VI	Old Kingdom	2647–2124
VII–XIa	First Intermediate	2124–2040
XIb–XIII	Middle Kingdom	2040–1648
XIV–XVII	Second Intermediate	1648–1540
XVIII–XX	New Kingdom	1540–1069
XXI–XXV	Third Intermediate	1069–664
XXVI	Saite	664–525
XXVII–XXXI	Late Dynastic	525–332

The first transitional period is the Early Dynastic (3050–2647 BCE), and the first ruler of importance is Narmer, who is credited with uniting the two kingdoms. The first great piece of Egyptian art is the Palette of Narmer, now in Cairo's Egyptian Museum. The two-foot-high piece of slate served as a surface for the making of royal eye-paint. The two sides of the tablet show Narmer's unification of the two kingdoms. At the top on both sides, two human-faced bulls representing Hathor, goddess of love and sexual pleasure, frame a building and glyphs of Narmer's name. Narmer, wearing the White Crown of Upper Egypt, bestrides one side of the palette, his hand clutching a mace about to fall upon the head of a defeated enemy whose hair he grasps. Looking down upon the conquest of Narmer, the solar god Horus (here a falcon, but also a personification of Narmer) sits atop and so subdues a bed of papyrus reeds representing Lower Egypt. An attendant carries Narmer's sandals, while below the king's feet his enemies flee.

The obverse has four registers, the second showing Narmer, wearing the headdress of Lower Egypt, followed by his sandal-bearer and preceded by an official

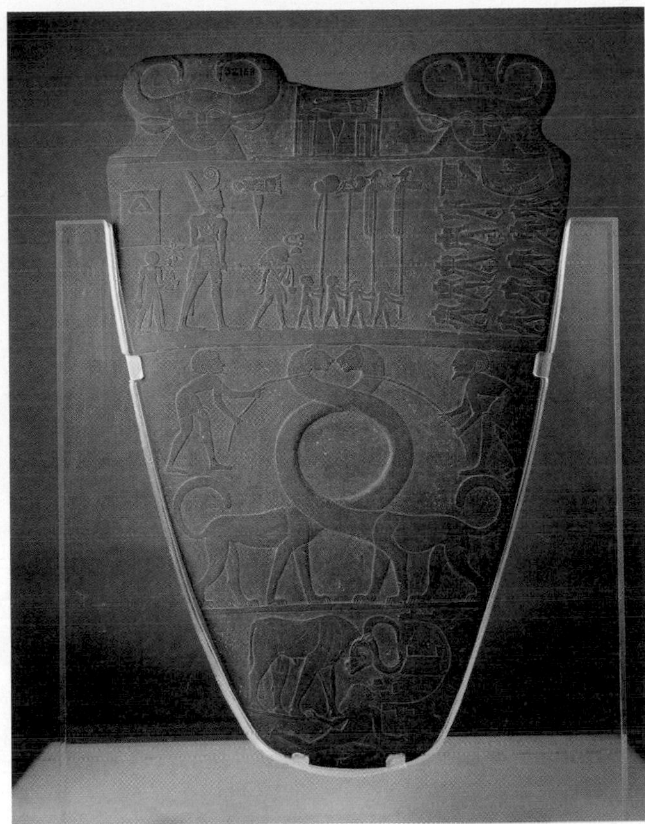

The Palette of Narmer

and standard-bearers; the group marches toward ten enemy corpses, the head of each man tucked neatly between his legs for a "head count." The third and largest register, formed of exotic beasts with their trainers, was the surface on which eye makeup was mixed. The bottom register shows Narmer as a bull trampling the enemy. By the time the palette was made, around 3000 BCE, many of the features of Egyptian history, culture, and art were already fixed and would remain constant for three thousand years. Narmer is depicted as large, godlike, symbolically powerful, and deserving of all the credit for unifying Egypt and conquering its enemies. The representation of figures on the palette is two-dimensional but highly stylized. Each segment of the human form is shown in unmistakable outline but distorted to emphasize its essential perfection: fingers of equal length, eyes full and frontal though shown in profile, and legs shown in walking position while the chest is flat and frontal. These conventions of Egyptian art would change little for thousands of years not just because they were grid based and repeatable, but also because Egyptians and their all-mighty rulers (popularly called pharaohs because they were so named in the Bible) wanted to portray stability and continuity, the virtues of Egyptian culture and of its life-giving Nile.

Written records are sparse for the predynastic period, but they increase dramatically for the stable Old Kingdom, which lasted almost five hundred years. The rulers of the Old Kingdom were extremely powerful and regarded as gods by their subjects. Old Kingdom rulers commanded the construction of pyramids in the desert to receive their bodies for the journey to the other world. Royal bodies were preserved carefully by mummification and entombed, surrounded by everything that these royal gods would need on their journey to the other world. The size of the great pyramids at Giza suggests just how prosperous and powerful kings were around 2600 BCE. A pyramid might take twenty or more years to build; involve thousands of workers, who were probably peasants (not slaves) brought to the site from their farms during flood season; and the transport of immense blocks of stone from distant places and then up earthen ramparts to their place in the pyramid. The cost of constructing huge pyramids may have weakened the Old Kingdom dynasties and empowered their nobles over the long run. The problem with a weakened dynasty was that ultimately, if the king was unable to maintain a strict control over the Nile's irrigation and agricultural production, famines and revolts followed. Smaller pyramids late in the Old Kingdom were a sign of dynastic breakdown.

The Middle Kingdom period saw a change not only of ruling families, but also of the core set of Egyptian beliefs. Ra, the chief god, was now joined by Amon, out of which a conjoint god called Amon-Ra was created. Royal culture had become so pervasive and persuasive that it moved down the social scale. During the weaker Middle Kingdom, many came to believe that all Egyptians might travel to the other world, not just their divine rulers. They gravitated to the worship of Osiris, the god of the netherworld who had been dismembered by Set, god of the desert and chaos. Osiris's wife (and sister) Isis reassembled her husband-brother's dismembered body. Thus Osiris, as a divine mummy and visitor to the other world, decided who deserved a splendid afterlife and who did not. Nobles and even common people (if wealthy) were mummified and placed inside elaborate coffins with the things they would need for their afterlife. The Egyptian *Book of the Dead* prepared the living for their encounter with Osiris at the moment of death. Though Middle Kingdom Egyptians were apparently confident that they could be taught how to pass over successfully, the netherworld's horrors made this a serious rite of passage, for if they failed Osiris's examination, they would be ripped apart by a monstrous god (a combination of a hippopotamus, a crocodile, and a lion), a death eater who consumed the unworthy dead.

Akhenaton/Amenhotep IV, Nefertiti, and the One Sun God A relief of Akhenaton, his wife, and children basking under the life-giving rays of the sun god, Aton. Note the egg-shaped skulls of the couple's children, a physical feature of their royal line.

Around 1730 BCE the Semitic Hyksos people, who possessed superior bows, horses, and chariots, invaded the weak Middle Kingdom. The Hyksos conformed to Egyptian traditions and never tried to rule all of Egypt but were finally driven out of Egypt in 1570 BCE. The dynamic rulers of the New Kingdom mastered the new technologies, hired mercenary armies, and subdued dissent within Egypt. New Kingdom rulers marched on other lands, including Mesopotamia, Nubia, and Syria. The Hyksos episode may have convinced these kings that Egypt was more secure if it attacked outsiders before they could attack Egypt; the result was an Egyptian Empire of tributary states. These new rulers built elaborate underground tombs as a strategy to avoid the grave robbers who had plundered the pyramids. The Egyptian Empire of the New Kingdom period was short lived. A radical ruler by the name of Amenhotep IV (r. 1353–1337 BCE) declared that there was only one god, Aton, the life force of the sun, and forbade all other worship. The abrupt religious change unsettled Egyptians, compelling the state to heighten its domestic military presence and to loosen control over its tributaries. By the 1250s a new line of military kings (the greatest of them the long-lived Ramses II) restored order.

Egyptian Religion

With the exception of Amenhotep IV's preference for one god, the Egyptians were thorough-going polytheists. Their complex pantheon of gods is difficult to understand. Beetles (scarabs), reptiles, mammals, plants, and stars were all regarded as divine, treated as gods, and represented in half-human forms. Thus, Anubis, a god of the underworld, is shown as a jackal or a man with a jackal's head. The Egyptians joined or fused gods to create composite gods. Some gods were greater than others. Ra (or Re) was the sun god who was particularly worshipped in the Old Kingdom, in which he was regarded as the father of the gods and humans. He was often presented as a falcon. Apis was the sacred bull who was supposed to have given birth to another creator-god, Ptah. Thoth, god of wisdom, learning, and magic, was deemed the creator of speech and writing and served as the scribe of the gods. For this reason, writing always had divine sanction in Egypt; by contrast, the Mesopotamians believed that they had invented writing, which was therefore a human or lesser art.

Egyptian rulers presented themselves as gods. On Narmer's Palette, the god Horus was not just a solar deity, but also Narmer's protector and another form of the king. When kings died their heirs identified with Horus, whereas the dead king was associated with or became Osiris, who represented the fertility of Egypt and the other world. Rulers took the names of various gods as their own, thus claiming the divine functions of the gods of the sky, earth, and netherworld. Egyptians believed that rulers were their best link to the divine and embodied **Ma'at** (justice, truth, wisdom, and harmony), principles that insured peace and prosperity for the land. Even the Nile maintained its life-giving seasonal rhythm because the king was a god and the gods were at peace with Egypt. Thus, kings were credited with Egypt's successes in good times, but they were blamed if famines and failure struck. State power flowed from the divine king;

WHAT A DIFFERENCE A YEAR MAKES

C. 1350 BCE: Follow That Name

In 1353 BCE Egypt was calm and abundant. King Amenhotep III had constructed the elaborate Temple of Luxor and added to the immense temple structure at Karnak, both in honor of Amon-Ra and his divine family. Amon-Ra, the chief creator-god of the Egyptians, stood at the center of state worship. Amenhotep III's successor, however, withdrew personal and state support from Amon-Ra, not only replacing the great god with another, but dismissing all the other gods. Radical change in ancient Egypt was so unusual that it is worth thinking about how and why this occurred.

Amenhotep IV succeeded his father and married (along with other wives) the alluring Nefertiti, who became his co-regent. Although he moved slowly at first, the new king developed a personal devotion to the god Aton, a solar deity or, rather, the life-giving energy of the sun. A few years into his reign, the king changed his name from Amenhotep (meaning, "Amon is satisfied") to Akhenaton ("devoted to Aton"). In this way he signaled to Egypt that he had transferred dynastic and state support from the cult of Amon-Ra to Aton. Some observers have suggested that he did this to undercut the traditional power of the Amon-Ra cult; its established and powerful priests; and the importance of the city of Thebes, where the old cult was enshrined. The "Great Hymn to Aton," however, makes it hard not to think that the king's worship of Aton was a deeply personal cosmic insight. Akhenaton built temples to Aton that let the sun's rays flow into his shrines and established a new capital named Akhetaton ("horizon of Aton"). If the king had stopped there, he might have met little resistance, but he soon ordered the destruction of images of, and forbade mention of, Amon-Ra and the multitude of other Egyptian gods. Akhenaton styled himself the sole earthly son of Aton, the one god, and invited Egyptians to worship Aton through him. Little of this was popular.

The transformation of Egyptian polytheism into a form of **monotheism** (the belief that there is but one god) or **henotheism** (a preference for one god while still allowing for the existence of other gods) might have taken hold and endured had it had a longer time to root and won dynastic and priestly support. But Akhenaton was succeeded by young King Tutankhaton (1336–1327 BCE), the famous King Tut, whose intact tomb was discovered by the English archaeologist Howard Carter in 1922 and whose dazzling treasures were sent on a world tour in the 1970s. King Tutankhaton was only eight or nine years old when he came to power. He was surrounded by powerful advisors who swayed the weak king back to traditional Egyptian religion. The king changed his name to Tutankhamon ("the living image of Amon"); was worshipped as a living god (or the personification of one); and relocated his court to Thebes, where the cult of Amon-Ra was restored to its former place of prestige and power. Egypt was back. Tradition had won out over dramatic change. Poor King Tutankhamon died before he was twenty, apparently of malaria and a broken leg that turned gangrenous.

QUESTIONS | ***Why was Egypt so resistant to change? Why might Akhenaton have promoted monotheism or henotheism? Was this truly monotheism or simply a radical reorganization of religion to enhance the king's power?***

his officials, including the superintendents or viziers, derived their authority from the king and through him from the gods. The viziers managed an extensive organization of bureaucrats, tax-collectors, scribes, and priests.

Living Ancient Egypt

Egyptians viewed their rulers not only as divine, but also essential to the health of the land. Nobles, who owned vast estates and were extremely wealthy, maintained their favored status by the king's pleasure. Common people were relatively poor, but because of the bounty of the Nile they survived and accepted their lot. The range of common occupations was great, with farmers dominating; but there were house-builders, painters, artisans, jewelers, and merchants. There were few slaves, and these were mostly foreign men and women captured in wars.

Commoners were, by necessity and limited resources, monogamous; marriage for them consisted of starting a new home away from their parents. Nobles, however, might maintain harems of slave girls and concubines. Royal marriages differed from those of others in one significant aspect. To keep the dynastic line pure and connected to the gods, kings wished to remain unsullied by common blood. Royal brothers and sisters could and often did marry. For this reason, Egyptian queens, sharing in royal and divine blood, were more powerful than the royal women of Mesopotamia and several of them became rulers. The most important of these was Hatshepsut (1472–1458 BCE), who ruled in her own name

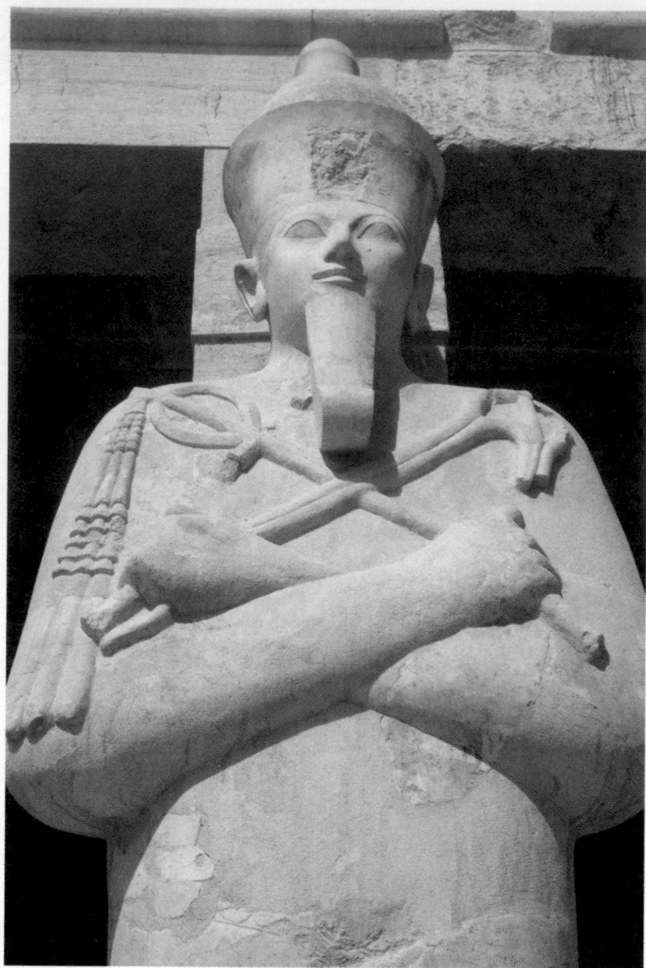

Bearded Hatshepsut On this formidable mortuary representation, the female king Hatshepsut wears, as do the other rulers in the sequence of statues, a royal beard to indicate her traditionalism, preeminence, and power as the ruler of Egypt.

Egyptian Harvesting Scene A painting of the harvesting of wheat, a tomb symbol of prosperity and the bounty of the Nile.

as the "king of Upper and Lower Egypt and daughter of Ra." Official portraits depict her with a beard. Egyptian women had the right to own property in their own name. Noble women were educated and might become scribes and priestesses. Peasant women worked on farms alongside their husbands and were kept busy at other times making clothes, bearing children, and cooking.

The farmer's diet was a sparse one, based on drinking beer and eating bread, a few vegetables, and some protein in the form of fish and eggs. The noble diet was almost limitless: fancy fruits, deer, duck, cheese, butter, and honey. Nobles, however, might for religious reasons avoid eating pork and fish. The priests, who offered up banquets of rich food and drink to the gods three times a day, ate the unconsumed food and ended up with blocked arteries, high blood pressure, and premature heart attacks. So say their mummified remains.

Upper-class men and women wore wigs (men wore them over shaved heads), applied cosmetics to their faces, and applied perfumes, customs that reveal the Egyptian preoccupation with public presentation and the surface appearance of life. The image of unchanging perfection preserved on faces, bodies, paintings, pyramids, and tombs was cultivated for the sake of maintaining tradition and easing entry to the other world, but it was also a facade that hid harsher realities. The mummified remains of Egyptians tell a story of bodies that paid a heavy price for enduring a searing climate, of diseases that terminated lives early, and of teeth worn down over a lifetime from chewing foods laced with sand. The Egyptian experiment worked because of a successful and exacting mastery of the unique bounty of the Nile, and it worked as long as the Nile's price was paid.

An Age of Bronze Turns to Iron

How can we account for the collapse of the eastern Mediterranean economy late in the second millennium BCE?

The appearance of bronze (an alloy of copper and tin) was coincident with, but not the cause of the appearance of civilization in Mesopotamia and Egypt. As a metal, bronze was used to make luxury goods and armaments, not farm implements. Bronze suited an aristocratic age, but had limited uses for agricultural economies. The so-called Bronze Age ran from 3000 to 1200 BCE, when iron first appeared. The second millennium BCE belonged not only to Mesopotamia and Egypt, but also to a series of peoples in the eastern Mediterranean: the Minoans, Mycenaeans, Hittites, Phoenicians, and mysterious **Sea Raiders** (Map 1.5 on p. 26). The appearance of iron, a more useful metal than bronze, toward

OTHER VOICES, OTHER VIEWS

The Might of Egypt Seen from Outside

In the 1880s an old woman discovered a cache of some 380 clay-tablet letters in Egypt at Tell el-Amarna, once the site of Akhenaton's capital of Akhetaton. The letters belonged to the Egyptian royal archives and had been written in the Semitic Akkadian language (not Egyptian) in cuneiform characters (not hieroglyphics) by Canaanite and Palestinian scribes. The correspondence between Egyptian kings and Near Eastern rulers and their agents dates from the 1380s to the early 1350s BCE, during the reigns of Amenhotep III and his son Akhenaton. This concentrated collection of administrative correspondence bears witness to the international reach of ancient Egypt. Near Eastern rulers from the kingdoms of Babylonia, Mitanni, and Assyria wrote to the Egyptian kings offering their deep respect and seeking favors: gold, military support, protection from Egyptian mistreatment of foreign merchants, and Egyptian princesses to marry into their families. In return, they offered loyalty, service, and gifts. The language of ancient diplomacy is ornate. For instance, the ruler of Tyre, writing to Akhenaton, begins by saying that he has prostrated himself on the ground seven times before the king, calls himself the dirt under the feet of the sun god king, and praises the royal sun god's splendor in shining on his servants and dependent lands. He promises to preserve Tyre for Akhenaton until he can bless the city with a visit. Ninety percent of the letter is devoted to praising the Egyptian king's power and humbling the sender. Only in a final small passage does the ruler of Tyre pass along some insignificant news. Petty rulers were pleased to report on rebel and criminal activity, to accuse their rivals of treachery against the Egyptian dynasty, and to defend themselves against similar accusations.

One sequence of letters informed the Egyptian king that a certain Lab'aya ("the lion-like") in Palestine was threatening to seize the city of Megiddo (south of Tyre) and to compromise Egyptian interests. Lab'aya wrote to King Akhenaton to defend himself, accusing his accusers of undermining him and Egypt's interests. The Amarna archive suggests that Egypt's power and influence, its extensive wealth and military strength, elevated it to a position as the great arbiter of Near Eastern affairs, but its relative isolation left it prey to the complaints and neediness of a turbulent Mediterranean world. Power depends not just upon a solid command of information, which in the case of Lab'aya was a difficult matter of weighing self-interested, competing reports, but also upon a willingness to intervene decisively in foreign lands. This Egypt tried not to do.

QUESTIONS | ***What cost did Egypt and the Near East bear because of Egypt's might? Was Egypt a paper tiger?***

the end of the second millennium BCE pushed eastern Mediterranean civilization in new directions.

The Minoans

Chiefly known from the palace ruins discovered on Crete by the archaeologist Arthur Evans, the Minoans were named after the legendary King Minos of Crete, the son of the god Zeus and Europa. By the start of the second millennium, Crete was enjoying the prosperity of the eastern Mediterranean world. It had few natural resources of its own, but its location in the eastern Mediterranean suited it to conduct sea trade. Aside from native olive oil, Crete chiefly supplied finished luxury goods such as ceramic pots and finished jewels to the outside world. Minoan merchants acquired metals, semiprecious stones, and raw resources from the lands ringing the Mediterranean and established trading outposts that allowed them, for a time, to dominate sea trade. The Minoans employed a writing system called Linear A that so far has not been convincingly deciphered.

Minoan rulers built great palace complexes on opposite sides of the island, at Knossos to the north and Phaistos to the south. The complexes were multipurpose centers where officials conducted the island's business, stored and distributed goods, and maintained rich palace cultures. The sites were not fortified, suggesting Crete's relative isolation and a period of relative calm in the eastern Mediterranean. We know of Minoan culture chiefly from its buildings and art, which includes ceramic pots, terracotta figurines of women, small bronze bull figures, jugs, and carved jewels. Most striking of all is the fresco from the palace of Knossos (c. 1500 BCE) of an acrobatic bull-leaping scene. Historians generally regard Cretan society at the time as remarkably sunny and peaceful, which was the way Arthur Evans wished to present the Minoans. The story of the labyrinth with its monstrous Minotaur, the product of Minos's wife coupling with a bull, which fed yearly on seven Greek maidens and seven Greek boys, undercuts that pleasant image. There is also some evidence that cannibalism was once practiced at Knossos. The Greeks remembered the Minoans as aggressive and cruel.

We have, however, only a limited and impressionistic knowledge of the Minoans. They were apparently polytheists, but their religious beliefs were more private and less state-sponsored than those of Mesopotamia and Egypt. Their cults remain largely mysterious, including their devotion to a snake priestess or goddess shown grasping a snake in each hand. Nor do we have a good sense of the social and political character of Minoan power, because it does not figure in Minoan art. Unlike the Mesopotamians and Egyptians, the Minoans did not create a cult of ruler-worship.

Events around 1400–1350 BCE brought Minoan civilization to an end. Many people, in their search for the legendary lost city of Atlantis, have wondered if an earthquake or volcanic event overwhelmed the Minoans. The island of Thera (today Santorini), a Minoan outpost north of Crete, was hard hit by a massive earthquake around 1600 BCE that produced a tsunami that crashed against the shores of Crete. But that disaster occurred well before the collapse of Minoan civilization. In the end, Minoan Crete seems to have been undone by external economic and military forces, for the eastern Mediterranean was becoming a dangerous sea by 1400 BCE. At about that time a new language and new artifacts began to appear on Crete. Linear A texts had been written in the unknown language of the Minoans, but a **Linear B** script (based on Linear A) replaced it, recording transactions in a form of archaic Greek. Certain objects such as large swords and chariots associated with the warlike Greek mainland also appeared. The Greeks had arrived.

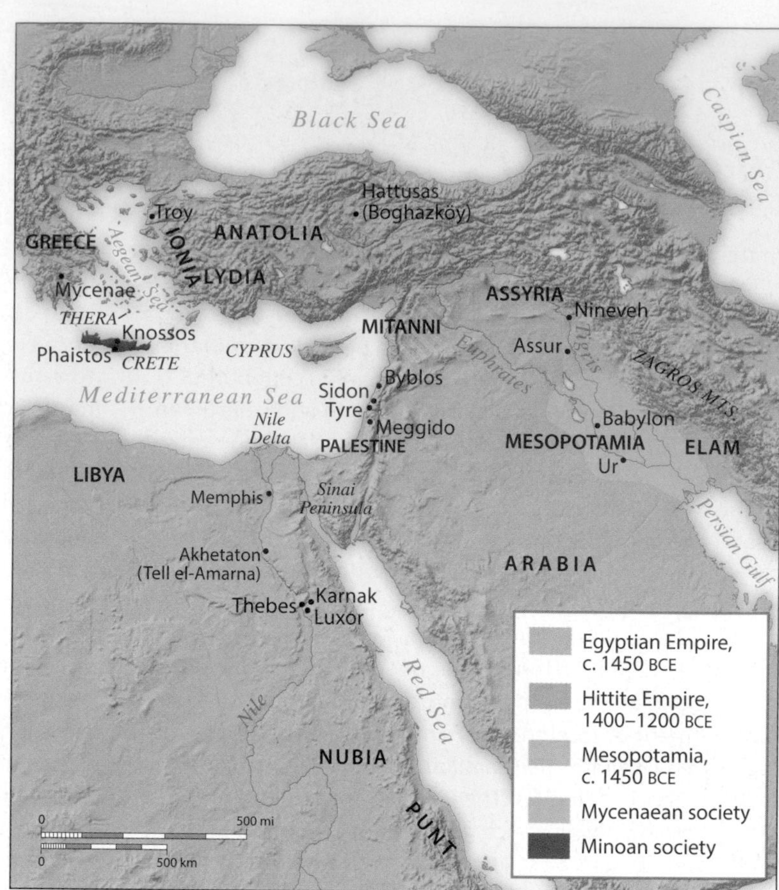

MAP 1.5 | The Near East, c. 1450 BCE
By 1450 BCE, the Near East was crowded with peoples and civilizations in competition with each other. ***How did the presence of seas and deserts shape the development of civilization in the ancient Near East? Why might Crete have played a critical role in commerce and trade? Why was the eastern Mediterranean susceptible to piracy and conflict?***

Bull-Leaping Scene from Knossos A Minoan fresco from the palace of Knossos on Crete that celebrates acrobatics and bull-leaping.

The Mycenaean Greeks

After 2000 BCE, waves of Indo-European peoples began to migrate into the area of greater Greece. Mycenaean civilization was a widespread development in Greece that has been associated with the Peloponnesian city of Mycenae because of the nineteenth-century discoveries by the archaeologist Heinrich Schliemann. He discovered graves, dating from 1600 BCE to 1300 BCE, full of aristocratic objects and instruments of war. Unlike "peaceful" Crete, mainland Greece in the Bronze Age was a land of warriors and constant conflict. Mycenaean art is filled with scenes of war, and Mycenaean palaces, unlike those on Crete, were heavily fortified. Mycenaean sites of habitation were constructed on hilltops and surrounded by great stone walls. Contact with the Minoans had a formative effect on the Mycenaean Greeks. The adaptation of the Minoan Linear A script to Greek use in the form of Linear B is evidence of that influence, as is the development of Mycenaean pottery. After invading Crete, the Mycenaeans replaced the Minoans as traders in the eastern Mediterranean and set up their own trading outposts. Trade and war, not farming, made the Mycenaeans wealthy, and that wealth can be measured by the rich grave goods found on mainland Greece.

The most memorable sequence of events of the Mycenaean Age was the so-called Trojan War, memorialized long afterward in Homer's *Iliad*. Troy, which dates from about 3000 BCE, was situated on the eastern shores of the Aegean Sea in Anatolia. The heavily fortified city of Troy, which was attacked many times, was inhabited by 5,000–10,000 Trojans, and besieged over many years by some 5,000 Mycenaeans who had crossed the Aegean in a hundred ships. Around 1200 BCE these Mycenaean Greeks destroyed the city. The Mycenaeans and their enemies took war to new levels of sophistication, in terms of both strategy and magnificent armor (bronze swords and spear tips, enclosed helmets, breast plates, body armor, and light wicker shields). Legend says that the Greeks eventually prevailed because of the clever deceit of the Trojan horse, which may have been a specially designed siege engine rather than a gift delivering Greek soldiers. The destruction of Troy was a sign of the troubles that came by sea to the eastern Mediterranean around 1200 BCE.

Reduced Mediterranean trade hurt the Mycenaean economy. But what may lie behind the unsettled conditions of mainland Greece was yet another series of Indo-European peoples penetrating Greece or moving south within Greece toward the sea. Among these Indo-European migrants were the Dorians, who preyed upon the established cities of Greece and overthrew their resident aristocratic societies. Mycenaean Greece came under attack from both land and sea after 1200 BCE. Around 1100 BCE Mycenae was sacked, and many Mycenaeans fled to Ionia, the safer shores of Asia Minor. The Mycenaean Age was over.

The Indo-European Hittites

Anatolia, at the northeastern end of the Mediterranean and lying along the northern frontier of Mesopotamia, was a hot spot of historical importance in the second millennium BCE. The Hittites, an Indo-European people from the north, moved into Anatolia around 2000 BCE and achieved political and linguistic dominance over the resident peoples. Many historians think that the Hittites dominated by inserting themselves into the area as a ruling elite with chariots, horses, superior political organization, and a richer language. The Hittites were quick to adopt local learning and cultural advances such as cuneiform writing and so have left us with thousands of written records. The Hittites established a kingdom that lasted for almost 500 years (c. 1650–1180 BCE), overcoming in time the non-Indo-European Hurrians, who controlled lands from Mesopotamia to Syria, and their Indo-European successors, the Mitanni. The Hittites also fought the Egyptians to a standstill, preventing Egypt's annexation of Syria under Ramses II (r. 1279–1213 BCE).

The Hittites were polytheists, whose religious beliefs seem more Anatolian than Indo-European. Their gods were a quibbling lot constantly at war with each other and difficult to appease. The Hittites did produce a literature, but it is an eclectic body of writing, reflecting Hurrian and Mesopotamian myths. They also produced lists of the legendary deeds of their kings.

Sea Raiders Roil the Mediterranean

The Mycenaean Greeks' violent overthrow of the Minoans and Trojans was a symptom of the instability that overwhelmed the eastern Mediterranean and strongly suggests that Greeks were one of the mysterious Sea Raiders or Sea Peoples, though there are many candidates. Among the possible, suggested, and known raiders were various Indo-European groups, the Greeks, Hebrews, Philistines, Sicilians, and various others. It is likely, given the confusion of the records, that the Sea Raiders were several different peoples who participated in raiding during the turbulent last centuries of the second millennium BCE. The identity of the Sea Raiders may remain elusive, but their impact on the Near East was real, for these peoples did not just raid the coast: they penetrated inland, leaving ruined cities behind them. The Sea Raiders attacked Egypt during the reign of Ramses III (r. 1182–1151 BCE), but the king bragged that he had fortified the Nile delta with warships and walls and crushed the invaders. Nonetheless, the Sea Raiders ended the prospect of an expansive Egyptian Empire and were one of the reasons the eastern Mediterranean was a less-than-secure body of water by the end of the second millennium BCE. The Sea Raiders limited the Hittite supply line to the Mediterranean, leaving the overextended Hittite kingdom vulnerable to various hill peoples in Anatolia. As a negative force, undermining a stable economy and curtailing the Hittites, Egyptians, and Mycenaean Greeks, the raiders had a profound impact on early Mediterranean civilization, limiting its immediate growth and economic prospects. It is no accident that the Minoans, Mycenaeans, and Hittites all fell within a 250-year span, for the Sea Raiders preyed upon prosperity.

The Advantages and Effects of Iron

The Hittites were the first to manufacture iron, sometime around 1200 BCE in Anatolia. The discovery of iron came too late to save the Hittites, in part because early iron was brittle, could not be used to make sharp-edged weapons, and was expensive to produce. At first, iron was considered a luxury good more valuable than bronze. In 1327 BCE, King Tutankhamon was entombed with gold and iron daggers, as well as sixteen iron chisels, rare objects fit for a divine king. Iron was hard to find in its pure form and required a much higher melting temperature than bronze. By 1100 BCE, techniques for handling and improving the quality of iron began to spread throughout the western world. The cost of iron dropped dramatically, making iron tools possible. Iron spread not just geographically outward, but also socially downward. Bronze had belonged to aristocratic and warrior elites; iron would become a people's metal. Moreover, iron was a common trade good, and people in the early Iron Age were looking for goods to sell beyond their home regions. By contrast, the stable Egyptian agricultural system and the less stable, but still prosperous, Mesopotamian one never had a need for such extensive trade. The Phoenicians are an example of the success of Iron Age traders and the return of some economic stability to eastern Mediterranean civilization. The great changes to the eastern Mediterranean world—the fall of the Hittites, the disorder caused by the Sea Raiders, and the collapse of the economy—occurred before ironwork had been perfected. Iron was, however, to play a critical role in the economic recovery that began by 1000 BCE (Map 1.6).

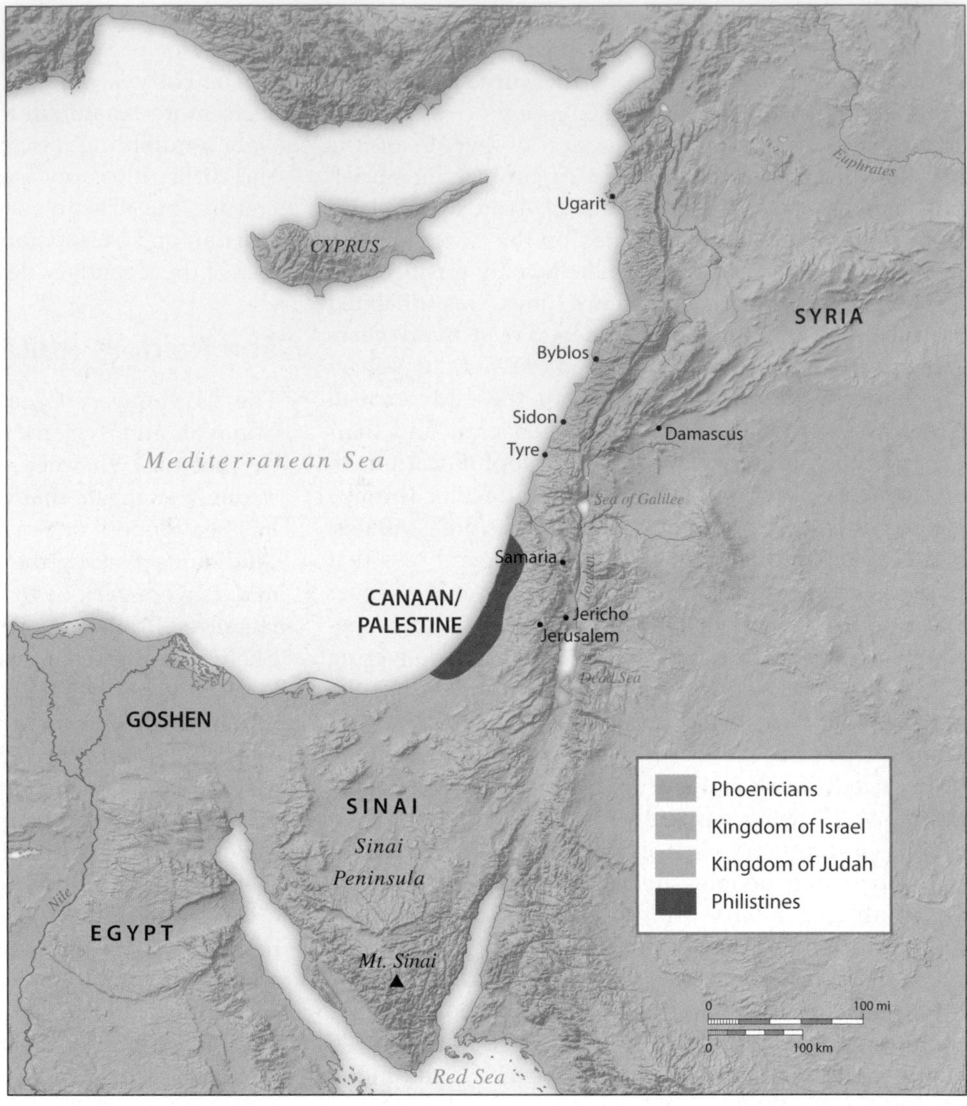

MAP 1.6 | The Eastern End of the Mediterranean in the First Millennium BCE
The kingdoms and peoples along the eastern coast of the Mediterranean were in close proximity to each other and vulnerable to attack and assimilation by each other and by the great empires of the Near East. ***Why were the lands at the eastern end of the Mediterranean so crowded and prone to conflict? Why were these commercial peoples so vulnerable to attack?***

The Semitic Phoenicians

With the sea raids subsiding and iron economies and cultures spreading by the end of the second millennium, the eastern Mediterranean was ready for the rise of great trading powers. The fall of the Hittites not only left a power vacuum in Anatolia, which was filled by the Phrygians for the next five hundred years, but also left Syria vulnerable to rising powers. In the second millennium, the eastern end of the Mediterranean (the area today of Syria, Lebanon, Israel, and Gaza) was occupied by Semitic-speaking peoples including the Amorites and Canaanites, whose chief city was Ugarit. The Phoenicians, a Canaanite people known as the purple people (from the dark red dye for which they were renowned), inhabited the area that is today Lebanon. Once the Sea Raiders ceased their banditry, the Phoenicians became the chief maritime traders on the Mediterranean. Rising to importance were prominent Phoenician cities, such as Sidon, Tyre, and Byblos (the great importer and exporter of Egyptian papyrus, from which the Greek word for book, *biblion,* derives).

Though purely mercantile peoples often have little lasting impact on civilization's major accomplishments, the Phoenicians did something critical. They adapted and spread a Canaanite writing system consisting of a Semitic alphabet of twenty-two characters, each of which represented a consonantal sound. The characters were originally pictographs; A or Aleph, for instance, represented an ox (Figure 1.2). By turning A upside down one can still see the ox's triangular head and horns: ∀.

The Phoenicians were famous for their glassware and beads. Their commercial ships were fitted with sails; their warships manned by oarsmen. The Phoenicians benefited from the growing prosperity of the eastern Mediterranean economy after 1000 BCE, but this part of the world remained a dangerous place to live and conduct business. The great empires of Assyria and Persia easily conquered Phoenicia in the first millennium. Only the Phoenician trading outpost and colony of Carthage retained its independence and vigor. Situated along the coast of northern Africa, Carthage lay just beyond the reach of the rising empires.

North Semitic			Greek		Etruscan	Latin	
Early Phoenician	Early Hebrew	Phoenician	Early	Classical	Early	Early	Classical
𐤀	𐤀	𐤀	A	A	A	A	A
𐤁	𐤁	𐤁	B	B	8		B
𐤂	𐤂	𐤂	1	Γ	)		C
𐤃	𐤃	𐤃	Δ	Δ	D	D	D

FIGURE 1.2 | Early Alphabet Characters

Source: Jerry H. Bentley, Herbert F. Ziegler, and Heather E. Streets-Salter, *Traditions and Encounters: A Brief Global History,* 2nd ed. (New York: McGraw-Hill, 2010), 22.

The Religious Breakout and Endurance of the Hebrews

Why and how did the Hebrews distinguish themselves from others and manage to endure?

They are all gone, all the civilizations, empires and kingdoms, and religions of early history—the ancient Mesopotamians, Egyptians, Minoans, Mycenaeans, Hittites, and Phoenicians—all except the Hebrew or Jewish people and their religion. They have endured in one form or another for over four thousand years, surviving one of the most dangerous regions of the world. How did they do it? One answer seems likely: that their religion and culture set them apart from the other peoples of the eastern Mediterranean world. The Hebrews abandoned the polytheism of their own early history and of all the other early civilizations of the Near East and Mediterranean world by making a pact or **covenant** with one God. That commitment prevented their complete absorption by any empire and the loss of their identity as a people.

Monotheism in its most rigorous form came slowly to the Hebrews. Their demanding beliefs bound them together as a people (ethnically, religiously, morally, and legally); politics did not. Political disunity haunted the Hebrews and left them prey to their many aggressive neighbors, but that political disunity, which is usually regarded as negative, may have played a positive role in the preservation of a culture and the endurance of a people, as did the mobility of the Hebrews. For political, economic, and religious reasons, Hebrews spread to other parts of the world, not so much to promote their religion, as to survive. They created the first great religion of a book, in their case the Hebrew Bible or Tanakh, consisting of the **Torah** (Genesis, Exodus, Leviticus, Numbers, and Deuteronomy), the Nev'im or Prophets, and Ketuvim or writings. These holy scriptures, composed over many centuries, record the sacred history of a people, although there is some question about their historical reliability. Yet Hebrew scripture remains the most detailed primary source we have of one people's experience of ancient Near Eastern history. The Hebrew Bible became the Old Testament of the Christian Bible and the monotheism of the Hebrews became the central belief of two other world religions, Christianity and Islam.

The Formative Phase: From Abraham to Moses

The Hebrew Bible supplies a detailed narrative of the history of the Jewish people, but we always need to

CHRONOLOGY The Hebrews

PERIODS AND PEOPLE	APPROXIMATE TIME BCE
Patriarchs	2000–1700
Moses and the Exodus from Egypt	1250
Judges	1200–1050
Reign of King Saul	1047–1007
Reign of King David	1000–970
Reign of King Solomon	968–922
Prophets	800
Babylonian Captivity	587

bear in mind that the Bible is not strictly speaking a historical source but rather a religious book, a sacred history. According to the Bible, Jewish history began with Abram, whose name God changed to Abraham ("father of many"). He departed from the Babylonian city of Ur sometime in the second millennium BCE. Biblical stories such as that of the great flood confirm a Mesopotamian origin for the earliest recollections of the Hebrews, who spoke a form of proto-Semitic, raised sheep, and were semi-nomadic residents of Mesopotamia. Abraham and his tribe may have begun their journey because of one of the frequent political disruptions that plagued Mesopotamia. Abraham, his son Isaac, and Isaac's son Jacob are known as patriarchs, each of whom found God and brought the Hebrews closer to fulfilling the divine plan. At this early stage not all the Hebrews were strict monotheists; it had always been possible within polytheism to prefer one god while allowing for the existence of other gods (henotheism). As late as the first millennium, Hebrews could still be found worshipping gods and goddesses such as El, Baal, and El's companion Asherah (a goddess represented as a tree). The Ten Commandments do not so much deny the existence of other gods, as place one God first in a special and direct relationship with the Hebrews. The patriarchs, however, vehemently denounced any worship of other gods by the Hebrews.

According to the Hebrew Bible, God struck a covenant or agreement with Abraham and the Hebrews, promising them that, after four centuries of tribulation and suffering, they would receive the lands between the Nile and the Euphrates as their own. For this promised land, God imposed circumcision upon his people as a sign of the special bond between them. Jacob was called an israel, a warrior for God, and to honor him the Hebrews took to calling themselves the children of Israel. Jacob's son Joseph was sold into slavery and sent to Egypt to begin a period of captivity for the Jews that may have begun as early as 1750 BCE. It was at this time that certain sources mention the existence of the Habiru or Hebrews ("the dusty ones") as a class of people performing manual labor in the great building campaigns of Ramses II. During the period of their captivity in Egypt, the Hebrews became manual laborers, farmers, and artisans, abandoning their earlier pastoralism. King Akhenaton's experiment with monotheism in Egypt and the Hebrew belief in one God were apparently unrelated.

Moses is a puzzling figure. His name seems Egyptian in origin, leading some biblical scholars to think that he was of Egyptian royal stock. The Hebrew Bible says that after his rescue as a baby from the bulrushes, Moses was reared by an Egyptian princess. After slaying an Egyptian master who was attacking a Hebrew slave, Moses fled to the Sinai Desert, where God spoke to him from a burning bush. There he learned from God that God's true name was YHWH, meaning "I am who I am." Though the Hebrew Bible generally does not give God's name fully in order to respect his mystery and sacredness, the Semitic peoples early on did not employ vowels in their consonantal writing system, so the expansion of the name has generally been rendered as Yahweh (Jehovah). The common expression *Hallelujah* thus means "Praise God" or "Praise Yah(weh)."

Moses led the Hebrews out of Egypt (the exodus) through the Land of Goshen (east of the Nile delta), across the Red Sea (the Sea of Reeds), south along the coast of the Sinai Peninsula, and then north along the Sinai coast toward Canaan. On Mount Sinai Moses received God's Law. God reinforced the covenant he had earlier made with the Hebrews, imposing upon them a special set of obligations and laws that set them apart from other peoples. There on Sinai, Moses received the Ten Commandments (the Decalogue) on two stone tablets, though the several records of these commandments vary in the number, order, and content of the commandments, perhaps suggesting later revision or interpretation.

God's renewal of the covenant with the Hebrews was a defining moment in Jewish religious history, for with it the Hebrews had their own legally based and religiously sanctioned legal and moral code, not unlike Hammurabi and the Mesopotamians before them. The Bible says that the Hebrews' exodus from Egypt took forty years, but numbers in the Bible are rarely trustworthy. Moses died before the Hebrews arrived in the promised land, a territory by then not defined as broadly as in God's original promise to his chosen people.

Led by Joshua, one of Moses's companions, the Hebrews invaded Canaan in a period known as that of the judges. The Bible provides different stories of the invasion. According to one, the invasion was a five-year military campaign by united Israelites, in which they conquered the city of Jericho, slaughtered and displaced the resident Canaanites, and laid siege to walled cities. In another account, various Hebrew tribes waged guerrilla warfare against Canaan over many years. One of the unexpected leaders of this conflict was Deborah. Dismayed by the direction of the war, she made a pact with the Hebrew general Barak to rally the Hebrews against the Canaanite forces in a battle in which the Israelites prevailed. Deborah's song (Judges 5, generally considered the oldest extant piece of the Hebrew Bible) celebrates not only the Hebrews' victory, but also the death of the Canaanite general Sisera at the hands of a Hebrew woman who, with trickery, promised to aid the fleeing general and then drove a tent peg into his skull. These were not pretty times, but the Hebrews settled Canaan, united only in their reverence for God and their sacred history. They stored the stone tablets containing the Ten Commandments in a sacred wooden box known as the Ark of the Covenant. To touch the Ark, even by accident, meant death, so sacred was the object. The Hebrew peoples took up farming and herding their flocks in Canaan and were firmly resident there by 1208 BCE, when an Egyptian king boasted that he had invaded Canaan and left Israel defeated.

Hebrew Seal from the Time of the First Temple A seal showing an archer and the inscription "for Hagab"—which dates to the time of the First Temple—was recently found in Jerusalem. Hagab is a name that appears in the Hebrew Bible.

Hebrew Singularities: The Struggle for Authority

To have survived their long exile, to have been delivered from Egypt, to have received through Moses the reconfirmation of their covenant with God, and to have been given the promised land of Israel all seemed to the Hebrews signs of God's continuing approval and protection. By this point in its history Judaism had arrived at its central beliefs: that God is singular, immaterial, and omnipotent; that God insists on the Jews' continued faithfulness; that God and the Hebrews are bound together by a covenant; and that to honor that covenant the Hebrews must scrupulously obey God's Law. The Hebrew belief that their relationship with God is singular, both religiously and historically, set them apart from other Near Eastern peoples and, at the same time, bound them together as a religious people.

Another of the singularities of the Hebrews was the scriptural basis of their religion. The Torah, the first five books of the Hebrew Bible, was a record not only of cosmic and historical origins, but one of laws, as well. The Torah was regarded as a divinely given code of instruction for living the covenant. The God the Hebrews meet there is a forbidding presence, one who delivers divine justice in the most exacting terms. Even the practical human justice of "an eye for an eye, a tooth for a tooth" may seem extreme, but the same idea of equivalent penalties was present in Hammurabi's Code and served to curtail disproportionate punishment, preventing an escalation of violent revenge beyond the concerned parties. God's justice extends beyond punishment, for it also includes compassion for the downtrodden. Widows and orphans were to be protected and slaves to be saved from ill treatment. The entire Hebrew Bible was not brought together until late in the first millennium BCE in Israel, when most of the Bible's texts were written down. Certain key Jewish ideas emerged slowly over time: the hope of God's gift of a better future for a faithful people, the immortality of the soul, and the belief that there would be future resurrection.

Canaan—or Israel after the exodus—where these beliefs were maturing, was both a blessing as the promised land and a test for the Hebrews. Theirs was a totalized religion, one that governed all aspects of their lives. It specified dietary codes of permitted and forbidden (or clean and unclean) foods, mandated morality, and regulated religious observances such as the observance of the Sabbath and the practice of circumcision. A priestly class of religious authorities oversaw strict adherence to the terms of the covenant with God. But Canaan was an alluring land of milk and honey with a powerful native culture and delights that threatened to undermine strict religious observance. In the struggle to maintain religious uniformity and authority, prophets appeared in times of tribulation. They claimed that Israel suffered because the Israelites or their leaders had fallen away from strict obedience to God. A prophet was not so much one who predicted the future as a critic of evil times and evil ways. And troubles did arise repeatedly in the ancient Near East. In the 1050s BCE the Philistines, one of the Sea Raiders, invaded Canaan and attacked the Israelites, seized the Ark of the Covenant, and carried it away as a trophy.

Kings and Kingdoms

Though the Hebrews had a religious code that bound them together, they were divided into various tribes with different regional, familial, and political interests. The attack of the Philistines exposed the vulnerability of the Hebrews on the Canaanite coast of the eastern Mediterranean. According to their scriptures, the Hebrews asked the judge Samuel to approve a king. He chose the warrior Saul to lead Israel (r. 1047–1007 BCE). Unlike the Mesopotamians and Egyptians, the Israelites did not regard their kings as divine, but rather as men who had received divine approval to rule. The Hebrews consecrated their kings by anointing them with holy oil. Saul had some small success against the Philistines but was undermined by Samuel and a young warrior named David. Saul took his own life after a defeat by the Philistines, leaving the controversial young King David (r. 1000–970 BCE) to unite the Hebrew tribes.

David was, according to the Hebrew Bible, a bit of a rascal, who was prepared to sacrifice his people's interests to personal ones. He committed adultery with Bathsheba and secured the convenient death of her husband. But he was also an inspired leader and managed to capture Canaanite Jerusalem and make it his capital. He regained the Ark of Covenant and installed it in Jerusalem. Under his leadership, the Israelites expanded their territory to the southeast, but King David pressed the Hebrews hard for taxes and labor for his extensive building program, which made him at times an unpopular ruler. His son Solomon (who began his long reign c. 968 BCE) could be brutal and had a huge harem, but the Bible reveres him as a wise man and builder. The temple erected by Solomon was of Phoenician design and part of a grand palace complex. Solomon named twelve administrative units within Israel, taxed heavily, and forced men to do military service. By the end of the reigns of David and his son, Israel had a centralized royal government, a capital at Jerusalem, a temple that was the central institutional home of Judaism, and a larger kingdom. Jewish traders were now visiting Mesopotamia and Egypt, and Israel was producing iron for the new Iron Age.

After Solomon's death, the northern kingdom of Israel revolted against his son and the Hebrews were divided between a northern (Israel) and southern kingdom (Judah, from which come *Judaea* and *Jew*). These kingdoms were disrupted by dynastic disputes, foreign cultural influences, and biting prophetic criticism. The kingdom of Judah retained Jerusalem, emphasized the importance of the temple, and was rigorously monotheistic. The kingdom of Israel, which was under the commercial influence of the Phoenicians, was more prosperous. At about this time, the Hebrews adopted the Phoenician alphabet and began to write down the books that would comprise the Hebrew Bible.

Empires and Diaspora

Even if the Hebrews had remained politically united, it is unlikely that they would have been able to resist the rising empires of Assyria and Babylon. The Assyrians were a Semitic-speaking Mesopotamian people who devoted themselves to war. Their chief gods, Ishtar and Assur (after whom they were named), were gods of war, and the Assyrians introduced standing armies, improved weapons made of iron, and mounted soldiers. By the eighth century BCE the Assyrians had conquered Damascus and began to harass the kingdoms of the Hebrews. They captured Samaria, the capital of Israel, around 722 BCE, killed or drove into exile the Hebrews who lived there, and abolished the northern kingdom. The southern kingdom capitulated, but in 701 BCE the Assyrians attacked Jerusalem, withdrawing only when paid. The Assyrians then turned their attention to Egypt and forced it into submission by the early seventh century BCE. As the overextended Assyrian Empire declined, the Hebrews resisted as best they could, but it was not until the Babylonians under Nebuchadnezzar (r. 605–562 BCE) crushed the Assyrians that the Hebrews saw their opportunity to revolt. When the plan was discovered, an angered Nebuchadnezzar marched on Jerusalem, violated the temple, and stripped it of its religious artifacts. Nebuchadnezzar transported back to Babylon many high-status Hebrews as his captives, beginning the so-called Babylonian Captivity of the Hebrews. When the Hebrews revolted again, Nebuchadnezzar destroyed the temple and displaced an even larger number of Hebrews. The prophet Jeremiah called upon the Hebrews to await the appearance of a messiah, an anointed ruler who would with justice and wisdom return Israel to its promised land.

The Assyrian and Babylonian attacks marked the beginning of the **Diaspora** or emigration of the Hebrews from Israel to other lands. The wanderings of the Jews may have strengthened rather than imperiled the Hebrews and their religion. Without the close presence of the temple to govern their lives, the exiled Hebrews turned to their sacred scriptures as a guide to preserving their special identity in lands of idolatrous and hostile others. The Hebrews had always understood suffering as something demanded of them by their God. The Book of Job tells of a man forced to lose his entire family and all his possessions and to undergo physical torment rather than forsake his God. Abraham faced the same dilemma when he was ordered by God to sacrifice his son Isaac. The overriding commitment of the Hebrews to the word of God, no matter the suffering and sacrifice asked of them, allowed the exiles to endure their condition, to preserve their unique identity, and to hope for the fulfillment and deliverance promised by their covenant with God. While the other civilizations of the early ancient world were overthrown and absorbed by greater cultural and political forces, the Hebrews because of their singular religious identity and core beliefs proved largely immune to assimilation and endured.

Conclusion

In late prehistory and early antiquity *Homo sapiens sapiens* became the dominant species of the globe. Nature played an important role, since if the weather had not changed with the retreat of the last Ice Age, it is hard to imagine the spread of the species and the change of human lifestyles that occurred in the Fertile Crescent. That these changes were climate driven and not culturally or racially specific seems evident from the fact that they occurred not just in the Near East, but across the globe, in the Indus Valley, China, and the Americas. The geographic setting of the

Tigris and the Euphrates in Mesopotamia and the Nile valley in Egypt shaped the specific economies and cultures that developed there, one unstable, the other stable; one competitively creative, the other traditional and long-lasting. These two cultures were on almost the same developmental schedule, with Mesopotamia out in front by a few centuries. Geographic proximity was an important element in the spread of higher civilization, cross-fertilizing ideas and people. The particular geography of the eastern Mediterranean Sea played a role, allowing for easy contact among the peoples of Egypt, Anatolia, Iraq and Iran, and the island of Crete.

Contact and competition—military, cultural, and religious—among these peoples made the Near East a hotbed of historical development. Those who forced advantageous change reaped rewards. Egypt's model for continued success, based on tight control of the bounty of the Nile, encouraged it to keep things the same, to emphasize tradition and regularity; its art and political system were designed to perpetuate continuity, at least on the surface. The Hebrews discovered a similar model based on the radical religious idea that as a people they had an enduring contract with one God. That all-encompassing belief allowed them to survive while all other Near Eastern peoples changed into something else or disappeared.

Humans achieved civilization through their special ability to adapt to and alter various environments, their capacity to organize into groups, and their expanding accumulation of knowledge that was preserved and conveyed to future generations. In hindsight we can see that each of these contributed to making some human societies more sophisticated and successful than others. The pairs of necessities for civilization (settled life and a critical mass of people, sustainable agriculture and trade, government and law, writing and abstract thought) came slowly in prehistory, compared to the pace of subsequent change, but they were critically important advances in the human experiment. Settlement and a sufficient mass of people were achieved in late prehistory, reaching a critical takeoff point in Mesopotamia in the fourth millennium BCE. Agriculture and trade produced the food and goods needed to support a growing and settled population. Law and government came early as well in the law codes of Ur-Nammu and Hammurabi and the religiously sanctioned laws of the Hebrews. Writing and abstract thought developed together and were spurred by the economic explosion of the same period. Writing gradually transformed the range and capacities of human thought and, perhaps more important, provided a way to break free of the limitations of individual and small-group memories and slow development, allowing human societies to preserve and convey information over generations and civilizations. Religious belief was a constant throughout early history, its dominant form being polytheism or the belief in many gods. Monotheism was at the time an outlier, but one with a future.

Government in early history took on many forms, but as eastern Mediterranean society thickened with peoples, resources, and skills, empires (Akkadian, Egyptian, Hittite, Assyrian) came to dominate, crushing, if they could, all rival powers before they were crushed. This imperial phase of early history, as brutal and sweeping as it might seem to us, contributed to the spread of ideas, peoples, and technologies around the eastern Mediterranean.

Critical Thinking Questions

1. Why are prehistory and early history particularly important to the human story?
2. Why were the Near East and the area at the eastern end of the Mediterranean Sea such early and turbulent sites for the emergence of civilizations?
3. What roles did chance and choice play in the rise and fall of various peoples and civilizations? Provide specific examples and explain why they matter.
4. What historical patterns emerged in the period 3200–1000 BCE?
5. How "civilized" was early civilization?

Key Terms

cuneiform **(p. 5)**
civilization **(p.5)**
prehistory **(p. 6)**
Mitochondrial Eve **(p. 6)**
Genetic Adam **(p. 6)**
sedentism **(p. 9)**
Agricultural Revolution of Prehistory **(p. 10)**
henge **(p. 11)**
Ziggurat **(p. 17)**
Code of Hammurabi **(p. 17)**
polytheism **(p. 17)**
hieroglyphics **(p. 19)**
Ma'at **(p. 22)**
monotheism **(p. 23)**
henotheism **(p. 23)**
Sea Raiders **(p. 24)**
Linear B **(p. 26)**
covenant **(p. 29)**
Torah **(p. 29)**
diaspora **(p. 32)**

Primary Sources in connect

For information on Connect and the online resources available, go to **http://connect.mcgraw-hill.com**.

1. **Two Early Law Codes**
2. **The Egyptian Book of the Dead**
3. **The Great Hymn to Aton**
4. **A Summary of Hebrew History and the Covenant**
5. **Two Versions of the Ten Commandments**
6. **The Song of Deborah**

The Venus of Hohle Fels

The small (2.4 inches in height) carving of a female figure, made from a woolly mammoth's tusk, discovered in 2008 in Germany, has been dated to 40,000–35,000 BCE. The figurine belongs to a group of Paleolithic Venus figurines, most of which bear similar features. Some researchers have claimed that the Venus of Hohle Fels, because of its early date, is the oldest surviving piece of western and world "art."

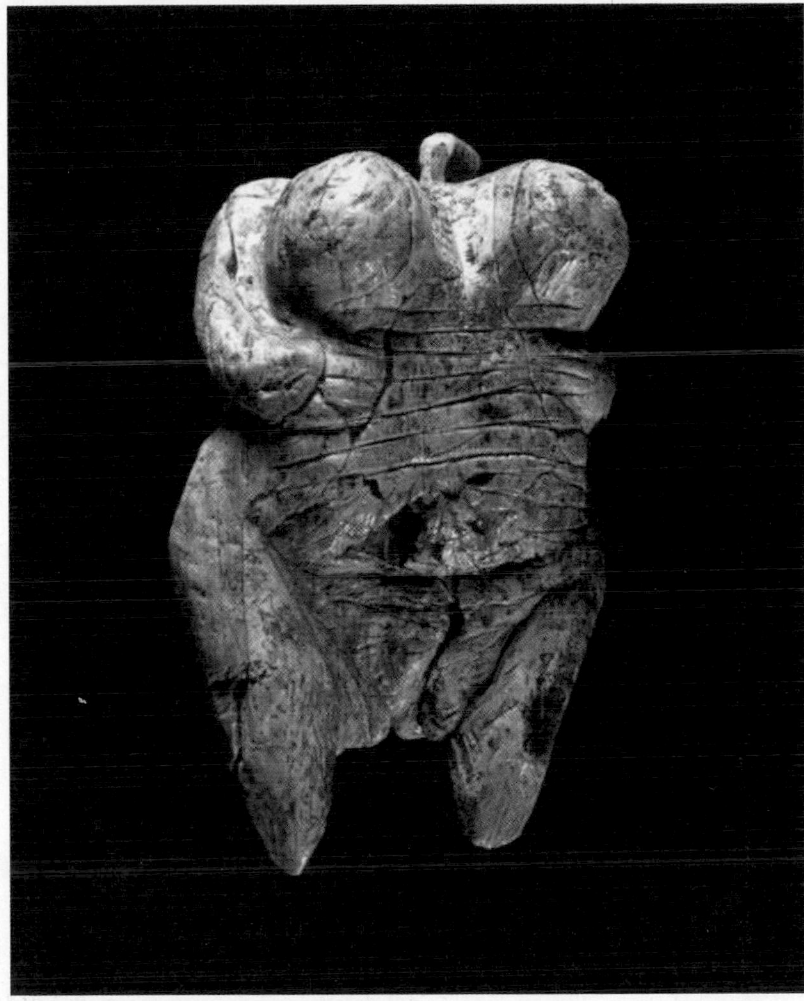

The Venus Figurine of Hohle Fels

QUESTIONS | *What does the carver emphasize and why? Is the piece best thought of as art or as a cult object, one that chiefly had religious meaning? Why? Why does the figure lack a head but have a perforated knob at the top?*

2

The God Dionysus Delivering Grapevines and thus Viniculture to Greece on an Athenian Black-Figure Drinking Cup

MANY GREECES

THE WANDERINGS AND WARNINGS OF HERODOTUS Herodotus (c. 484–425 BCE) of Halicarnassus (along the coast of Asia Minor) has been called the father of history and the father of lies. He was neither. He did write the world's first great narrative history and described his work as *historiai* or "inquiries," from which comes our term *history,* but he did not think of himself as a historian. The field of historical inquiry didn't exist at the time, and he didn't work from written records. Nor was he an especially notorious liar. He lived, after all, in the age of Pericles, the wily Athenian politician who so brilliantly and so often stretched the truth.

Herodotus was above all a marvelous storyteller. The great Greek battles of Marathon, Thermopylae, and Salamis are so vivid because of his stirring accounts of them. His histories are a strange and delightful mixture of inquiries: travelogues; ethnographies; anthropologies; and oral, religious, social, art, and sexual sketches. At times, his work has the prurient quality of a tabloid, revealing the private lives of the powerful. He tells us the story of the king of Lydia, who induced a minion to gaze secretly upon the naked body of his queen. The queen then compelled the voyeur to murder the king and assume his place since he had seen her whole.

Herodotus wrote to inform and entertain, to take the Greeks beyond the glorious imaginings of Homer into the strangeness of foreign lands and customs. Only from the outside, Herodotus may have thought, could the many Greeks see Greece whole. His history, however, constantly confirms that there was not one Greece, but many. Hundreds of city-states (**poleis;** singular, **polis**) existed within Greek lands (around 1,500 poleis have been identified in Greece and around the Mediterranean in the archaic and classical periods),[1] each with its own deep history and fiercely guarded independence. These small states had been at war with each other for centuries, and a great new war between them was building during Herodotus's stay in mid-fifth-century BCE Athens. He knew of the ancient grudges and feuds of these small states, of unforgotten slights and disgraces, and of their various plans to undermine and secure advantage over each other. The *raison d'être* of the people or nation (*ethnos*) of every city-state was to preserve its separate and autonomous existence against its many Greek enemies. In the midst of so many different Greeces, the most Herodotus could hope for was a united nations of Greece, but the many Greeces ruled the day, not the united nations.

Herodotus, the Storyteller A marble bust of the author of the *Historiae.*

Herodotus took his Greek audience on a grand tour of a world filled with peoples who lived dramatically different lives. Herodotus wanted to show the Greeks why the Persian Empire had invaded Greece and how freedom-loving Greeks had managed to thwart the imperial giant. To discover the background of Near Eastern history and the roots of the Persian invasions, Herodotus traveled to foreign lands, visited temples, saw pyramids, and questioned foreigners (through translators). He sifted stories and never hesitated to repeat a good one, even when he knew it to be untrue. His willingness not to privilege his own opinion or the truth makes him seem deceptively modern as he mixes together the real and the reported, the fanciful and the revealing.

Herodotus's style is lively, animated, and a comfortable one for us, as he digresses from the main story to explore some gripping house history, some tick in a king's life, or a bizarre local custom. He was intensely interested in people, their virtues and vices. But the reader only slowly becomes aware of Herodotus's systematic and categorical approach. He treats each foreign land in a similar way: its geography; animal life; and people and their origins, language, gods, customs, food, marital and sexual relations, and funeral rites. From Herodotus the Greeks learned fascinating things: the Egyptian devotion to cats, fantastic animals such as crocodiles, and foreign customs such as the mummification of the dead and the strange information that Egyptian women urinated standing up, men while sitting down. He reports that in Scythia (the extreme north of cultural difference from Greece, while Egypt holds the extreme south) people told stories about men with goats' feet, people who sleep for a half a year every year, and a race of one-eyed men, but he dismisses these as fanciful stories. Herodotus was not just teaching the Greeks about foreigners, but explaining the many Greeces to the many Greeks.

In writing his large, wandering, and woolly book, Herodotus seduces us with his delightful entertainments, leading us away from seeing his deeper design. Geography matters a great deal to him. The continents of Europe, Asia, and Libya (Africa) belonged in his view to their resident peoples; lands and peoples are fitted together inseparably. The fatal Persian mistake was an immoderate violation of the natural and divine order of things by stepping outside of Asia. Herodotus thinks the same of people who breach the bounds of natural justice.

Herodotus neither feared nor despised foreigners; rather, he regarded the Lydians, Scythians, Egyptians, Babylonians, and Persians as living strange, but legitimate lives that were normal for them within their appointed places of abode. A message of warning lurks ever so softly in Herodotus's great entertainment. His audience was Greek, particularly the Athenians who were then caught up in their own immoderate imperial drive, which would lead to the disastrous Peloponnesian War, and his message of moderation to them was the lesson of the Persian Wars: that unbridled imperialism was an unnatural thing that threatened the freedom and established contours of Greece and its city-states. During the build-up to the war, the Spartans and Peloponnesians had been claiming much the same, that the Athenian drive for imperial dominance violated the legitimate and traditional rights of other freestanding, long-established Greek states. The weakness lay within the Athenians, as it had within Darius and the Persians; imperialism was an external sign of the internal failings of greed, pride, and poor judgment. Athens was on its way to becoming Persia, violating the appointed limits of Greek life. As quietly as he could, Herodotus warned the Athenians that their path would lead to defeat and destruction, and so it did.

Ancient Greek history is a story of the many Greeces within Greece changing over time and space, polis by polis (or city-state by city-state), region by region, each place having a claim to be a freestanding end point of Greek history.

Classical Greek history of the fifth century BCE was the end product of the **Dark Age,** about which we know far too little, and the **Archaic Age,** which immediately preceded the **Classical Age.** The effect of Greece's geography and the depressed economic conditions of the Dark Age gave the individual city-sized areas of Greece the freedom and isolation to develop independent ways of life and governance. The broken landscape of Greece, with its many islands and rugged terrain, provided the isolated peoples of Greece the time and freedom from interference during the long Dark Age to develop autonomous traditions. The geography of Greece and the economic depression of the eastern Mediterranean world after 1200 BCE did not invite foreign occupation. The Hittites fell before they could turn their attention to Greece, and the Assyrians had richer targets in Phoenicia and Egypt.

The Greek city-states (poleis) in the Archaic and Classical Ages were fully formed and stubbornly independent. The great Greek problem was to preserve the freedom and autonomy of the poleis from those internal and external enemies who would create one Greece by conquering and uniting its separated parts. The Greek poleis faced major crises of unification twice in the fifth century BCE—first when the Persians twice invaded Greece and were resisted by an alliance of Greeks led by Athens and Sparta, and second in the Peloponnesian War when the Athenian drive for dominance provoked other poleis to resist. There were also hundreds of smaller conflicts as the poleis waged wars against each other and formed alliances of poleis to harass other poleis. The problem of cities, their freedom and independence, both made and unmade classical Greece. In the fifth century BCE in imperial Athens, in particular, one polis produced one of the most extraordinary moments of human civilization, a blossoming of the arts, of critical thought, and of a profound exploration of what it means to be human.

Darkness Descends

The Dark Age of Greece (1100–800 BCE) is the great unknown of Greek history. The age is so-called not because it was primitive (though it was that, at least in relative terms), but because the Greece of that period has left few material traces. There are no contemporary written sources and few pots or buildings to study. The period was relatively free of major conflicts, and little is known of minor local conflicts (and there were doubtless many). A lack of information should not, however, be equated with unimportance. Though we know little about the period, something significant was happening. The Greeks entered the Dark Age out of the heroic Bronze Age of Mycenaean warriors, but they emerged from it in the Archaic Age as a different Iron Age people with intense local identities and with their precious poleis in place.

How was the Dark Age of Greece primitive as well as cloaked in a fog of silence?

After the Mycenaean Collapse

After Mycenae and other cities were attacked and destroyed around 1100 BCE, Mycenaean Bronze Age culture limped along and tried to adapt for almost a century. Burned and abandoned cities were resettled, but not along the same lines. Burial practices and pottery styles changed, but life continued. Greek traders tried for a time to maintain a presence in the economically depressed eastern Mediterranean and maintained some contact with Cyprus. But the contraction of the eastern Mediterranean economy meant that the Mycenaean economy of aggressive sea trade, Greek warrior elites, and fortified palaces was no longer sustainable. The movements of peoples such as the Indo-European Dorians within Greece in the 1200s and 1100s BCE, the displacement of the Mycenaean elite (some to Ionia, some to Attica), along with the deep economic downturn, all signaled that Greece was entering a period of sharp adjustment. Linear B writing disappeared entirely, large stone buildings were no longer erected, and wars of foreign conquest ceased. Greece turned from the public (elite governance, great palaces, regional wars, heroes, and aristocratic art) to the local and personal. Each person, family, and locality was forced to cope as best they could within the restricted conditions of life in the Dark Age: Greece moved from sea trading to farming, from elite rulers to community rule—or worse, no rule—and from connected cultures to isolated local cultures. It was a great age of forgetting. Dark Age Greeks knew that they had had a glorious past, as we know from Homer, but they had forgotten the conditions that had made the Mycenaean Age work.

The Iron Age Arrives

Cyprus made the conversion to iron implements and technology sooner than did mainland Greece, but by 1000 BCE iron was in wide use in Greece. Iron replaced bronze almost entirely and better suited the coming age. Virtually all the metal objects from this period uncovered in Athens are iron ones: swords, axes, knives, and dress ornaments. One of the new economic ventures of the age was the location and mining of iron ore. The problem was that in the straitened circumstances of the age, the Greeks mined the ore locally for domestic use, not for Mediterranean trade.

After the Mycenaeans, Greece remade itself locally. The movement of the Dorians can be determined by the spread of their particular dialect of Greek. They seized much of the best land, particularly in southern Greece, and began to farm. Greece at the time had few economic outlets. Each family produced from the land what it needed to survive. Families and their productive capacities remained the core of Dark Age society. Without the existence of larger governments or recognized systems of justice, each family protected its own. Blood feuds with other families were the result. Over the next several centuries, powerful extended families established themselves, encompassing related individuals in clans and tribes, and extended their property holdings and wealth. Indo-European peoples seem generally to have had kings at their head (as had the Mycenaeans), but in the Dark Age, these kings were little more than the nominal heads of villages. Power belonged to those with productive property who soon deemed themselves the best sort of people (nobles) or aristocrats. At first they advised the king, but in many places they removed him. When the Greek poleis emerged from the Dark Age, their kings were gone or severely reduced in power.

The polis began in the Dark Age as little more than the protective wall around a village or extended area. It bound together a village or collection of villages having a common defensible high spot or hilly area (an **acropolis**) and marketplace (*agora*). The early poleis were run by aristocratic or landholding elites. There were other peo-

ples in the early poleis—slaves, workers, transients—but none of them were citizens. Property defined status and blood ties determined aristocratic standing and, consequently, citizenship. This polis development was largely absent in the Near East and may be attributed to the particular nature of the breakdown of the Greek world and its intense local isolation, community by community, in the wake of the Mycenaean collapse.

One question worth asking is why the Dark Age lasted so long in Greece, while Cyprus, Crete, and the Near East in general rebounded more quickly. Not until the ninth century BCE did Greece begin to show signs of building programs, the introduction of new death rituals, and the resumption of some forms of Mediterranean trade. Almost two centuries earlier, the Assyrians had established an empire committed to securing its borders. Assyria was uninterested in annexing Greece but slowly hemmed in the Phoenicians, who took more actively to the sea and around 800 BCE founded Carthage along the southern coast of the western Mediterranean. The Assyrians and Phoenicians created the conditions that provided Greece with the opportunity to break out of its depressed economic state. The Phoenicians, in particular, were agents of commercial and cultural contact in the late Dark Age. They brought their alphabet to Asia Minor and Greece, without which the poems of Homer could never have been recorded.

Homer, Whoever He Was

Almost everything about Homer and his poems, the *Iliad* and *Odyssey*, is controversial. The common opinion is that the blind poet of legend lived sometime between 850 BCE and 600 BCE, that he was a bard who dictated the verses about the dramatic events of the Mycenaean Age and its heroes: Hector and Achilles, Agamemnon and Helen, and lost Odysseus wandering the Mediterranean seeking a safe harbor and home. But was Homer blind? Was Homer one man or two (one poet for each poem)? Was there an author named Homer at all, and did he live around the time of the Trojan Wars or as late as the seventh century BCE?

Let us assume in the midst of these many uncertainties that someone like Homer lived around 750 BCE and was a Greek native of Ionia in Asia Minor (as detected in the diction of the poems). He was a transitional figure living at the end of the Dark Age and on the cusp of the new Archaic Age (800–500 BCE). The great epic poems, the *Iliad* and *Odyssey,* provide evidence of the cultural churning that preoccupied the Greeks during the Dark Age. Homer's stories derive from older oral ones about the preceding Mycenaean Age, and Homer was, at the very least, their recorder if he wasn't their author, though if so he was a genius at fashioning the long poetic narrative of the *Iliad* out of scattered Dark Age tales.

Homer might be thought of as the recipient, recorder, and inspired synthesizer of a long line of oral poems that had survived in changing form, from retelling to retelling, since 1200 BCE. As such the oral epic was a repository of cultural information, the living encyclopedia of a small society. Homer or the storytelling bards who repeated the poems of the Trojan War had mnemonic or remembering tricks that allowed them to perform the basic poems over and over again. Repeated lines and stock phrases such as "the wine-red sea" recur not so much for the sake of color or poetic effect as to keep the

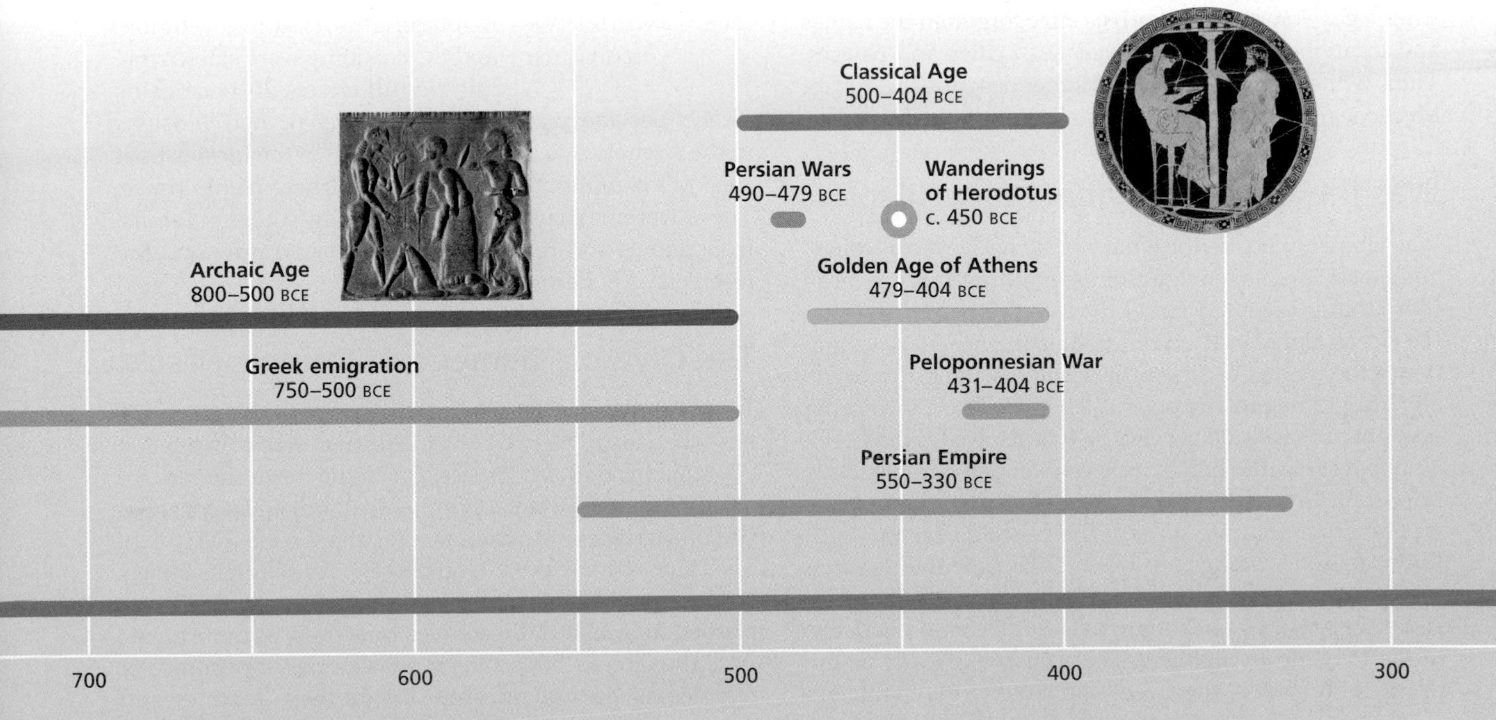

King Priam Asks for the Body of His Son The king (*center*) advised by Hermes (*right*) asks Achilles (*left*) to return the body of his son Hector, who lies at his feet, one of the events of the Trojan War recounted by Homer in the *Iliad*.

poem on track and to complete lines of verse during an active recitation.

Yet Homer's immediate predecessors were not Mycenaeans. Rather, they belonged to the Dark Age and could not avoid changing the received songs by inserting little pieces of themselves and their Dark Age values into the poems, even when they didn't square with the Mycenaean Age about which they were singing. The Mycenaean elite buried their dead in grand tombs; Homer's heroes are cremated, as people were during the Dark Age. Homer or his sources have forgotten the names and locations of the great Mycenaean cities and palaces. Thus, while the stories told by Homer describe the distant Mycenaean past, culturally they also reflect the Dark Age.

Was the Greek Alphabet an Accident?

Was Homer, whoever or whatever he was, even a writer? Some scholars have suggested something more radical: that Homer invented Greek writing, either by shaping the Greek alphabet to accommodate the needs of writing down the poems or that others had invented the Greek alphabet to record his poems. The idea is an intriguing one, but probably too good to be true. However the Greek alphabet came into being, its invention had a tremendous impact on Greece and the western world.

The Phoenicians spread their goods, some with Phoenician writing on them, around the eastern Mediterranean shoreline. The Phoenician alphabet consisted entirely of consonants. Though some exposure to the Phoenician alphabet had occurred as early as the ninth century BCE, the Greek alphabet, with characters adapted to express vowels, appeared early in the eighth century BCE. With the addition of vowels, phonetic literacy was born; now, anything spoken could be expressed more or less exactly in writing and the reverse. Did someone or some group of people introduce this adaptation to accommodate the special needs of spoken Greek, or might it have been an accident? In other words, in the late Dark Age or early Archaic Age, did the Greek alphabet come about because the Greeks didn't fully understand the Phoenician one and so assigned vowels to various characters to make the alphabet more expressive and comprehensive? The task of copying down Homer's poems might have necessitated such a breakthrough, but little evidence exists to suppose that it did. The earliest Greek writing, aside from Homer's poems, is trivial: curses, official dedications, lists.

Phonetic literacy spread no more quickly or popularly than had Mesopotamian cuneiform writing millennia earlier. It did not change the Greek world overnight or fundamentally, but it did slowly transform its possibilities. The spread and preservation of the Homeric poems is proof of that. The Mycenaean tales that Homer drew upon were fluid oral objects that could not have been preserved in fixed form. Writing them down stabilized the poems as literary texts. The *Iliad* became the bible or world history of the Greeks, a shared inheritance of stories that showed the Hellenes (the Greeks) their deep past, helped to regularize the Greek language, and pushed them toward greater self-awareness and self-knowledge.

The Archaic Age Breakout

Late in the Dark Age, there were signs that Greece was reviving. Life was being reorganized at different rates city by city; aristocratic elites were in place; and customs, religion, and the economy were stabilizing. But the full effects of those gains did not become apparent until the Archaic Age. Tensions in the Archaic Age were acute, as seen in the farmer-poet Hesiod's complaints about the unfairness of his times. There were various attempts to relieve these tensions: from games and religious authority to tyranny and the forgiveness of debts.

Why does Archaic Age Greece matter?

The Olympic Games and Delphic Oracle

Traditionally the first fixed date of ancient Greece is 776 BCE when an all or *pan*-Hellenic festival was convened at Olympia in southern Greece. Far to the north the sanctuary of Zeus on Mount Olympus had long been a special site of sacrifice and reverence for the Greeks (Map 2.1). The Dark Age did not kill off Mycenaean religious beliefs so much as refashion them locally. As the population expanded and material resources improved in the Archaic Age, the Greeks began to emphasize the importance of temples as sites of worship. Inside these temples and sanctuaries stood cult statues of the Olympian gods (Zeus and company), to which people donated gifts such as small statues, jewelry, and precious metals.

Dark Age Greeks had held funeral games to honor the dead, but they were infrequent and irregular. To honor Zeus, Olympia in the Peloponnesus mounted festival games every four years. Athletes prepared for up to ten months to qualify for the games. No prize money was given, but athletes received great prestige for winning. The results of the Olympic Games were recorded, and the champions were celebrated as heroes by their cities. The emergence and importance of the Olympic Games in the eighth century BCE was a sign of the growing confidence of the various poleis and their aristocrats who wanted to reach outside their small cities for wider Greek acclaim.

MAP 2.1 | **Archaic Age Greece, c. 800 BCE**

Greece is a mountainous land surrounded by the sea and islands, and situated not far by sea from the coast of Asia Minor. ***How did geography shape the history of Greece? Why were Crete and the islands of the Aegean Sea of such critical importance to Greece?***

The Olympic Games brought Greeks together in the shared pursuit of individual excellence (***arête***). The concept of *arête* underlined the commitment to aristocratic honor of the sort that brave heroes were expected to demonstrate in all aspects of their lives: on the field of battle, when facing the gods, and in their treatment of family and fellow aristocrats. Demonstrative outer excellence was more important than inner rightness. The other concept that defined the citizen ethos was that of **agon,** the belief that life was a constant struggle or competition. The Olympic Games made manifest the concepts of *arête* and *agon,* as the honorable outer virtue of the Greek competitor was tested publicly in competition before Zeus and the Greek world.

The sanctuary of the god Apollo at Delphi was built on a slope of Mount Parnassus just north of the Gulf of Corinth on the mainland. By the late eighth century BCE, individuals and community representatives from many parts of Greece traveled there to consult the Oracle. Greeks believed that Apollo communicated divine truths there through his priestess, the Pythia, commonly known as the Oracle. The priestess was generally a local woman of no special learning or prominence in society, but ancient stories that she was inspired by vapors and drug-induced ecstasy lack proof. Through the priestess the god delivered messages, often in a yes or no form, to specific questions. The Oracle was rarely controversial, but rather supplied divine approval for individual and community decisions already reached. On disputed matters, the Oracle's answers tended to be more elaborate and equivocal. The Oracle did not, strictly speaking, predict the future, but rather reinforced the leanings of the authority figures who sought the consultations. The petitioners came because they needed the Oracle's authority to sanction their official decisions. Since opinions on problems facing a community were often divided, the Oracle was called upon to resolve the division and offer a divine reason for moving forward.

Consulting the Oracle at Delphi Aegeus, the king of Athens, is shown consulting the Pythia, the priestess through whom the god Apollo spoke at Delphi.

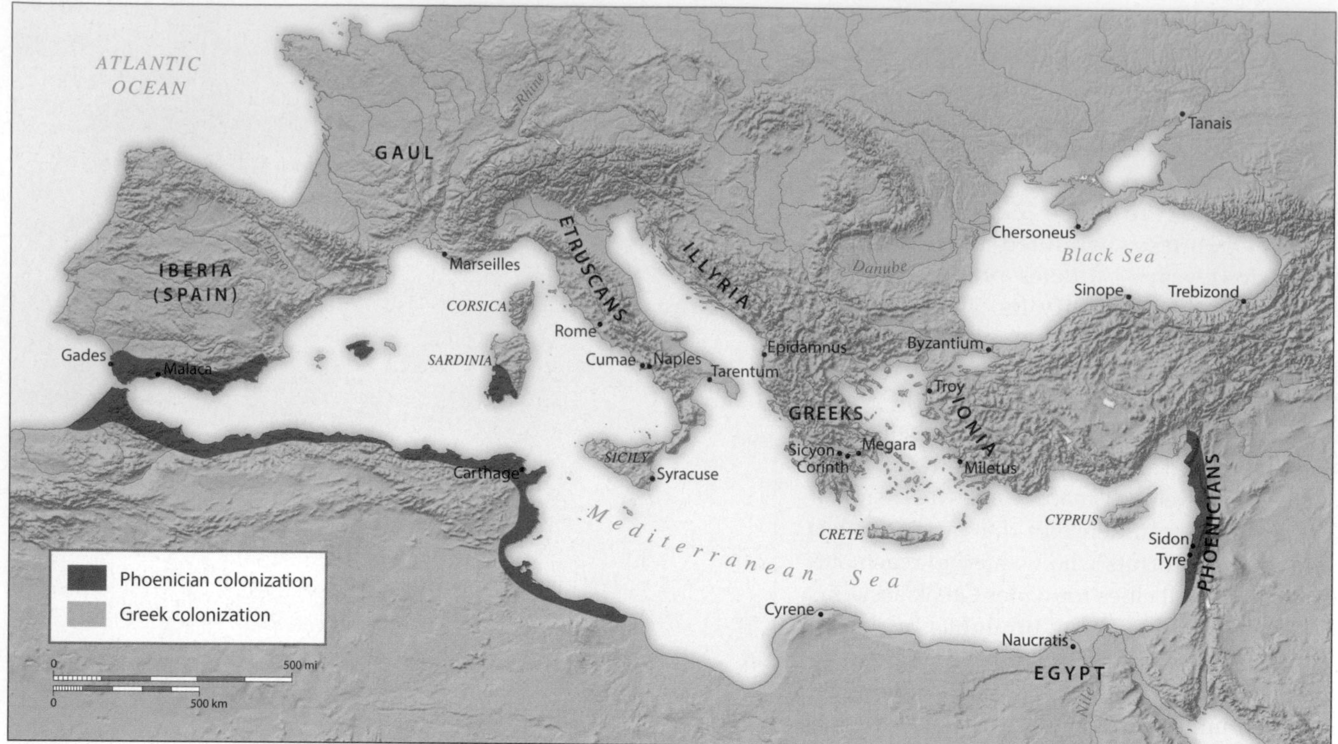

MAP 2.2 | **Greek and Phoenician Emigration, c. 500 BCE**

In the first millennium BCE, both the Greeks and the Phoenicians settled coastal lands along the Mediterranean Sea. The Greeks also established settlements along the southern Black Sea. They called their colonies "homes away from home." ***When and where did Greek emigration take place? Are there patterns to Greek and Phoenician settlements? What advantages and disadvantages, if any, did the settlements bring to mainland Greek cities?***

Delphi was, thus, like the Olympic Games, a physical and spiritual place where Greeks could step outside their small societies and local disputes to secure external approval for themselves and their communities. The important thing about these archaic Greek institutions was that they mediated local differences between rivals, for the Greeks were deeply divided, within their poleis and within greater Greece. Both Delphi and Olympia began to bind scattered and rancorous Archaic Age Greeks to a shared cultural world.

Archaic Age Emigration: Homes away from Home

The Greeks were used to migration. The Indo-European pattern was to settle and then pick up and move when necessary. There is little information, except from later self-serving classical reports, of any substantial Dark Age emigration to foreign lands. Greece was too poor at the time to support mass movements and was probably without the social pressures that forced emigration. The Archaic Age, however, witnessed widespread emigration and the establishment of Greek settlements outside Greece. The Phoenicians were also establishing settlements and outposts along the southern rim of the Mediterranean, but the Greeks tended to stick to the northern coastline.

Some observers have called this movement one of *colonization,* but that term does not perfectly describe the Greek situation. The Greeks referred to these settlements as "homes away from home." Most of the settlements (in southern France, Italy, Asia Minor, Ionia, and northern Africa) were on the coastal lands of the northern and eastern Mediterranean and the Black Sea (Map 2.2). The settlers established Greek-like cities controlling hinterlands. Though these settlements might maintain some of the traditions and customs of their home cities, they were politically independent of their original homes. Around a hundred small settlements were established, some of which later became famous cities such as Marseilles, Naples, and Byzantium.

There was no single reason for these foreign settlements, but many were caused by crises at home such as feuds, lack of land and opportunity, population pressures, economic problems including famines, and the desire to establish trading posts. The building social tensions of Archaic Age poleis may lie behind many of the settlement ventures. Land and power at home were in the hands of aristocrats not willing to share. In many cases, all-male groups of settlers voluntarily left their homes, had specific destinations in mind, and seized the new land by driving out or murdering the previous male occupants and abducting their women. Some settlements, however, seem to have occurred peacefully, based on an alliance between the settling Greeks and the indigenous population.

Not all emigrants wanted to leave their homes. Some were forced to go, as they were at Thera, which compelled families with more than one son to send one brother to the new settlement of Cyrene. Death and the loss of property were the penalties hanging over the heads of those who refused to go. The home cities had trading and economic interests to pursue in these ventures, but those seem to have been secondary considerations. The reduction of the home city's population and the opportunity for the settlers to secure new lands were more important factors. As such, the settlement movement over several centuries served as a social release valve, relieving internal civic pressures. Home cities underwrote the costs of these settlement ventures (ships, resources, arms), but that was the end of their direct investment. Each new settlement had to survive on its own and lost much of its direct contact with the home city.

A Greek Settlement on the Black Sea During the period of emigration, Greek settlers established "homes away from home" in such distant locales as Chersonesus on the shores of the Black Sea.

Each settlement experiment was different. Much depended on the character and culture of the home city, including whether the settlement was peaceful or violent, the nature of relations with the native population, the site's geography, and economic prospects. In some settlements there was a mixing of cultures (native and Greek), whereas in others Greek culture dominated. By the late Archaic Age, there was a general reinforcement in these homes away from home of Greekness or Greek values through central institutions such as temples, religious practices, language, and political customs. The new settlements were as likely to consult the Oracle at Delphi as were mainland Greek cities. War and conflict in the new lands also encouraged alliances with home cities and the aligning of political interests, often to the detriment of the settlement's autonomy. By 650 BCE, Greece had a diffuse presence on the northern and eastern rims of the Mediterranean Sea, which was a factor in the resumption of sea trade, the emergence of a greater sense of what it meant to be Greek, and the growing influence of the Greek presence in shaping the cultural character of the European continent.

Dirty Politics and Hesiod's Discontent

Hesiod lived in the eighth century BCE and wrote the *Theogony,* an account of the origins of the world of the Greek gods, and *Works and Days,* which principally concerns farming, farm labor, and the seasons. The two poems (some scholars believe that they were composed by two different poets) complement each other and constitute an Archaic Age circle of life that led from the gods on high down to human work and suffering. These were the poles of the Greek condition in the early Archaic Age.

According to Hesiod, humans had once lived in a golden age, free of strife and labor, growing fat and free of cares in a land abundant with fruit. Death came as a pleasant sleep. All was right with the upper and lower worlds, but the gods then fashioned a silver age that suited humans less, then one of bronze when men were at war, then another of frightening heroes, and finally an age of iron when men turned hard and mean. Hesiod belonged to the last age, but he wished that he had never been born or had died before entering an iron age so full of grief and suffering. Now all was ceaseless strife. His was an immoral, lying, and murdering age, in which children cheated their aged parents, and people died young from disease and want.

Works and Days is a moral poem pleading for justice in a wicked time. Hesiod begins his gloomy poem by calling upon Zeus to set right a broken world. He views Zeus and the gods as moderators, lifting up plains, lowering mountains, humbling powerful men, elevating the low. Strife and tears are the human condition, but strife is good for people, thrusting them into never-ending competition with each other, carpenter against carpenter, beggar against beggar, and brother against brother. Hesiod and his brother Perses, for whom he wrote *Works and Days,* had had a falling out over family property. They split their land, but, according to the poet, Perses with the compliance of a bribed judge had grabbed the better portion.

In the poem, Hesiod complains that the rich rule the world; in a just world the good man and his honest labor should suffice. To this end, he seeks to teach his brother and so his audience how to earn an honest living from the land: when to plow, plant, and harvest. He worries that Perses does not know how to survive except dishonestly. Hesiod longed for rulers who would render justice, and his poem cries out for fairness and for the fair resolution of disputes. *Works and Days* is not a farmer's almanac, then, but an editorial on a world that no longer valued honest labor and devotion to the land. Above all, the poem is a moral manual for a brother gone wrong; to teach him that the secret to survival is to respect the gods, to follow wise farming practices, and to dedicate himself to honest labor.

Inequalities and injustices that had been building over centuries reached a crisis point in the Archaic Age. Property may have been everything, but there was only so much land and it was held by too few people. The social tensions that permeate *Works and Days* are those also revealed by the emigration movement, the building militarism of the Archaic Age as groups of people violently seized the resources of others, and poleis that were becoming increasingly aggressive.

The Greek gods and the social and class rigor of Hesiod's age are not unconnected. With the elimination of powerful kings, Dark Age and early Archaic Age Greeks and their fledgling poleis fell under the tight control of aristocratic families. These landholders sought to justify their power and position by means other than just the possession of land. They not only claimed superior genealogy (thus allowing them to justify their families' hold on land and power), but also asserted that they were the descendants of gods and heroes.

The aristocrat's position in society, particularly as a coercive and controlling force, needed all the reinforcement he and his family could secure. It was expensive to be an aristocrat in the Archaic Age. The means of warfare were changing; horses were costly in a period when mounted warfare still mattered, and improved weapons made of iron were expensive. Helmets and body armor were necessary, but only a wealthy aristocrat could afford them. It was also costly to buy the support of subordinate groups within society and to secure the services of slaves. The needs of wealthy aristocrats sucked resources out of the economy on the backs of commoners, who tended to hold small or dependent farms. Small farmers fell perilously into recurring debt to their aristocratic patrons for seeds, tools, and land. The social tensions in Hesiod's world were real: between family members, between wealthy landowners and commoners, and between aristocrats. All the while small landholders like Hesiod complained that the prevailing distribution of resources and power was unfair.

Tyrants, Reformers, and Military Change

Hesiod's call for social justice was a symptom of a world in which the interests of the wealthy few and those who took advantage of a corrupt system predominated. Emigration, recourse to the Delphic Oracle, religious institutions, and the composition of first assemblies in poleis were all Greek innovations that somewhat helped to ease internal tensions. But matters came to a head in the late seventh and early sixth centuries BCE, when across Greece social reformers and tyrants emerged to redress internal problems. The reformers were not seeking universal equality among classes and peoples. Rather, they were attempting to deal with the disgruntled, addressing complaints that the legal system was designed to serve aristocrats and protect their interests alone.

The social reformers were trying to fix a system under siege by repairing it in the least disruptive way. The rise of tyranny in the seventh and sixth centuries BCE was a more radical and successful repair. **Tyrants** were not despots in the modern sense, but autocrats who seized power by force. They thought of themselves as kings and sought to establish lasting dynasties. They appeared when competition between aristocratic families threatened to destroy a polis or when the polis was in conflict with another polis or with foreigners. Tyrants (in places such as Corinth, Sicyon, and Athens) offered military solutions and polis superiority, and could be tremendously popular with the nonaristocratic peoples of most poleis, who saw the tyrant as someone who might release them from the excessive demands made upon them or a foreign danger threatening their polis. In general the tyrants welcomed popular support, which they maintained by distributing wealth, sponsoring religious festivals, and promoting commerce. As a group, tyrants were reluctant to engage in foreign wars or conquest. They preferred to pacify their poleis rather than to militarize them.

Unlike kings who depend upon royal blood to continue their lines, the Greek tyrants tended to be charismatic individuals such as Peisistratus (d. 527 BCE) in Athens. Successful tyrants had few successors, and tyranny proved to be but a stage in the development of the Greek polis, not its final form. In a few places tyrants did manage to break the gridlock of forces that had seized Greece since the Dark Age, overriding entrenched aristocratic interests and devoting themselves to the good of the polis and their own political success.

There were as many types of poleis as there were poleis. Each one was unique, the product of the isolation of the Dark Age, the geographic separation forced upon it by the Greek landscape, particular settlement patterns, the timing of development, and other particularizing factors. For the Greeks, the polis was three things: a built-up physical place, a territory (the city plus its outlying lands), and a political community of citizens. Scholars have long tended to translate the term *polis* as "city-state," a term that is more appropriate for some larger poleis than for smaller ones with populations of less than 1,500 people. But in all cases the polis was more than a city in our terms and less than a state by modern standards. Even a small polis was an autonomous city with its own independent traditions, identity, and foreign relations. Ancient Greeks generally described themselves as Corinthians, Spartans, Megarans, and so on. A polis was not just a place but also its individualizing character, which described who its residents were.

Greece in the Archaic Age was filled with hundreds of poleis. Many of them had similar features such as an agora and an acropolis, but there were considerable differences as well: between coastal, island, and inland poleis, between southern poleis and northern ones, between home poleis and settlement poleis. The political identities of poleis were in a state of flux in the Archaic Age. Dominant aristocratic families controlled the poleis of the Dark Age and at the start of the Archaic Age. For a time these aristocrats were the only lawful citizens of most poleis. Most commoners, all women, slaves, and foreigners were excluded from citizenship and executive decision making. The law, as Hesiod complained, served nobles and their property interests. The Athenian Draco in the seventh century BCE set out a series of harsh laws with death penalties for many minor offenses (hence Draconian refers to an arbitrary, harsh, or cruel measure), but law did not bind the Greeks together since each polis had its own laws and legal procedures.

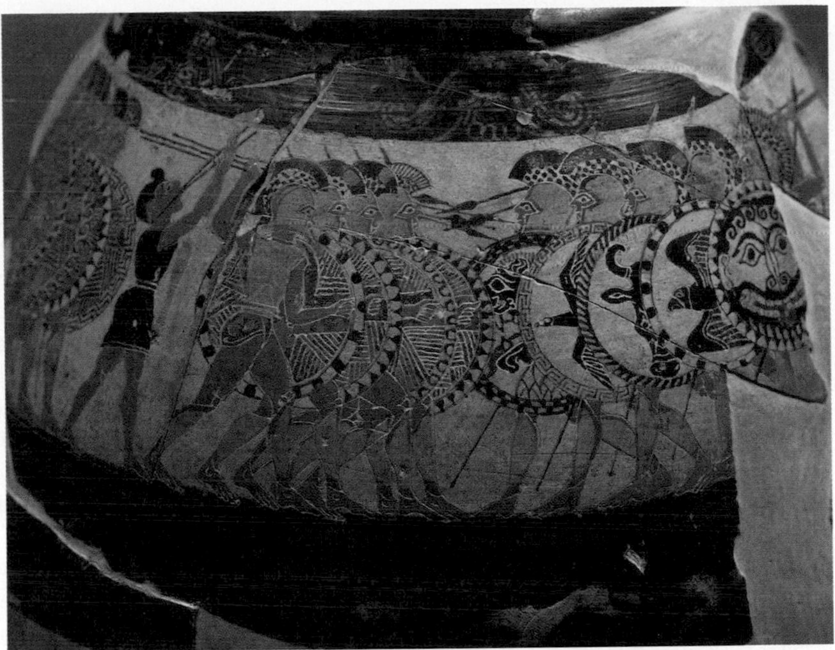

Hoplite Formation A seventh-century BCE depiction on a jug, of Greek infantry in formation. Note the importance of the wicker shields of the hoplites.

The pressure for inclusion within the political body of many poleis was building in the sixth century BCE, but there was little widespread recognition that all commoners or native-born males within a polis should be considered citizens. Some poleis (in places such as Athens, Kos, and Naxos) began to move toward more inclusive assemblies. These were not so much early democracies as they were a way to silence common complaints by allowing representatives of the lower classes to participate at some level in the political process and so to be parties to and tacit supporters of its decisions. Not just complaints about injustice, but also the changing military needs of Greece and its cities, and the growth of the population in a more prosperous Greece, began to give the non-nobles of many poleis a more prominent voice in city affairs.

The construction of the **demos** (masses, the people: free male native residents of a polis, non-noble, but of some standing and wealth) in places such as Athens paralleled the emergence of the **phalanx** as the basic fighting unit of most poleis. The soldier who stood in line with his fellows in the rectangular phalanx formation of infantry was called a **hoplite.** Hoplites were small farmers who presumably paid for their own equipment (spear, sword, shield, helmet, breastplate, and shin protectors). They were named after either the *hoplon,* the double-handled shield that was essential to the phalanx, or *hopla,* that is, all their military equipment. Shields were critical since they protected not only their bearers, but the men standing beside them in the phalanx. Great disgrace fell upon any soldier who dropped his shield during a battle, for it jeopardized the men standing beside him and the integrity of the phalanx formation. The shield and the phalanx were egalitarian in nature; the hoplites fought as a unit of equals. Although Greek battles still featured a good deal of individual hand-to-hand combat, formation warfare now became common. Gone was the heroic mounted warfare described by Homer. Yet Archaic Age battles remained messy affairs in which the phalanx did not operate as a human tank mowing down the enemy. Hoplites often ran in disarray toward or away from the enemy, there were other participants besides the hoplites, and not all the hoplites were equally equipped or disciplined.

In this new age of warfare, poleis could not afford to exclude from politics the men who fought for them. Hoplites were men with property and some stake in the survival and success of the polis. Their voice may not have become louder or more insistent in the Archaic Age, but they were better placed to speak and to be heard by the late Archaic Age.

Archaic Age Economies and Cultures

There were as many economies and cultures in Greece as there were regions and poleis. There were agricultural innovations and new crops in the Archaic Age, but they were not enough to sustain growth. The advice that Hesiod offered in *Works and Days* was designed to maximize and safeguard agricultural productivity in a relatively static economic world. The Greek farmer still relied on basic crops such as olives, grapes, and wheat, but in Greece's varied landscape different kinds of wheat were grown and at different times of year in different regions. Greek farmers knew that they needed to transport their

Harvesting Olives The economies of the many Greek poleis were based chiefly on agriculture. In this pottery depiction, we see a four-man operation: one man in the tree shakes olives loose, two use sticks to hook and shake branches out of his reach, and a fourth farmer gathers the fallen fruit.

crops for sale. Hesiod, who was reluctant to travel by ship, nevertheless advised his brother when to load his produce on ships, what size those ships should be, and what season to sail. Transport by water was critical to the diffusion of goods within Greece and abroad.

In general, Greece needed to import foodstuffs rather than to export them. For food they traded olives and wine, silver, and large vessels (*amphorae*). The Phoenicians had opened up the western Mediterranean to trade, which brought Greek settlements such as Naples into larger trading networks. On their own, the Greeks also began to trade with Etruria in northern Italy in the eighth century BCE. Corinth, in particular, sold its goods to the Etruscans.

The leading edge of economic growth for the poleis was not agricultural, but commercial. Poleis began to discover the advantages of coined money. Greeks did not invent coins (the Lydians had), but they improved their design and circulation. By the early sixth century BCE, Greek cities were issuing irregular lumps of metal (generally made of electrum, an alloy of gold and silver) stamped with a seal. By 500 BCE, most Greek poleis were producing recognizable coins made of silver with both sides marked for identification. Some of these coins were designed for local use, since they were convenient items for the collection of taxes and the payment of debts, but by the end of the Archaic Age the coins of active trading poleis such as Corinth and Athens became common coinage in Mediterranean trade. Although coinage did not revolutionize the Greek economy, it marked Greece's reentrance (or, at least, that of some of its poleis) in the sixth century BCE as a trading presence in the Mediterranean.

Just as the economy and coins were less Greek- than polis-centered, so was culture in its various forms. Greek poetry in the middle to late Archaic Age turned away from epic to choral and lyrical poetry. New meters were introduced and local poets such as Archilocus of Paros, Theogonis of Megara, and Sappho of the island of Lesbos explored new poetic voices. These poets spoke in the first person about personal crises and human emotions. Sappho's poems, in particular, are full of the subjective "I." Most of her poems are now lost, in part because of the blackening of her reputation by later periods. Sappho wrote on the labors of love between women, probably for a small audience of school girls. Her poetry in its highly refined lyric voice is not easy to unravel, but then we lack a sharp understanding of the context in which she was writing. These poems were not written for us, but for an audience in a different emotional and gendered space. Still, her poems carry universal themes. In one she writes that she would rather see the light step and lit face of Anactoria, who reminded her of Helen of Troy, than chariots and soldiers on the march.

The wise men of the Archaic Age have been much celebrated as scientists and philosophers, but they were neither. They were sages, chiefly from Ionia, who wrote few treatises but rather taught orally. They speculated on the cosmos and the place of humans in it. Many of them had been influenced by Asian work on mathematics, astronomy, and physics. Thus, another of the individualizing elements of Archaic Age culture was the intellectual differences between the overseas settlements and mainland Greece. The refined thought of the sages probably would not have been possible or been preserved without the emergence of the Greek alphabet, which had first appeared in Ionia. A new range of intellectual possibilities was emerging. Even the spread of coins may have set the sages to thinking about the problem of universals (for instance, of goodness apart from individual good things), for coins are standardized and representative items that have an abstract or universal meaning beyond the physical objects themselves.

Thales of Miletus held that water was the universal element out of which the earth originated. Anaximander of Miletus postulated that the world was generated out of an indefinite (or chaotic and boundless) space in which the contraries of hot and cold, wet and dry competed and eventually achieved balance. The important point is that Thales and Anaximander thought of the physical world as a product of physical forces with consistent physical characteristics. Pythagoras of Samos was an Ionian who lived in Italy. His comprehensive and eclectic system was based on mathematical regularities (including the Pythagorean Theorem that the square of the length of the hypotenuse of a right angle triangle equals the sum of the squares of the lengths of the other two arms). Pythagoras was also interested in politics, personal codes of behavior, morality, and ideal societies. Heraclitus of Ephesus presented himself as an oracular sage. His aphorisms, or short sayings, were designed to provoke students to deeper reflection. He sought to uncover the underlying reasons of the cosmos as opposed to the surface realities we encounter. His well-remembered saying about the river never being the same (because it is always in flux) captures the essence of his challenge to probe beyond the surface to the underlying truth of things. For Heraclitus, the *logos* (word) or divine essence was the underlying force of things. In a complex poem, Parmenides of Elea went even further in presenting this phenomenal world as deceptive, the lie told by a goddess. He advised humans to search for the truths hidden to them. These Ionian Greek thinkers speculated freely and rationally with remarkable insight, but they were content to speculate rather than to prove their propositions; they remained religiously inclined teachers whose chosen goal was to encourage Greeks to think about the nature of the world and their place in it.

Archaic Age art was innovative. Stone temples were introduced at the beginning of the seventh century BCE, chiefly of the so-called Doric design. The Archaic Age was a world without palaces, so that these temples were the most enduring buildings of the era. Dark Age Greek pottery had lacked figural representation, but by the eighth century BCE pottery began to be adorned with figures. Each region or polis tended to have its own potters, some of whom late in the period began to place their names on the pots they produced. The figural scenes grew more sophisticated as the period proceeded. The sixth century BCE (not the fifth) was the golden age of Greek pottery. At Athens, in particular, a wide variety of pots used for both personal and funereal purposes was produced. Vase painters experimented with changing the background and figure colors (chiefly black and red).

Sculpture too changed in the Archaic Age. The Greeks were deeply impressed by Egyptian sculpture and by the mid-seventh century BCE had begun to produce their own statues called *kouroi* (*kouros* being a young man or boy; *kore*, a young woman or maiden). These figures were at first as rigid and unsmiling as Egyptian sculptures, but by the sixth century BCE they assumed a Greek character. To take but one example, around 550 BCE a young woman by the name of Phrasikleia died and her parents hired the artist Aristion of Paros to make her death statue. The large statue shows the young girl in a dress pulled to one side; adorned with a necklace, belt, and elaborate hair style; and holding a lotus blossom in her raised left hand. Originally the marble statue would have been brightly painted. Phrasikleia smiles the "Archaic Smile," an expression difficult to decipher, but appropriate for one entering the other world. The statue stood on a base that bore a poem in which Phrasikleia spoke to those who chanced to see her statue. She says that she will now never marry but remain a maiden forever, bearing that name from the gods as her marker. The poem is integral to the statue, animating the young girl's claim to be remembered. By the last decades of the sixth century BCE, the freestanding nude young men of Greek statuary walk forward, one leg firmly before the other. They reveal musculature, anatomically exact bodies, and the knowing Archaic half-smile.

Statue of Phrasikleia From late in the Archaic Age, the statue by Aristion of Paros reflects the influence of Egyptian statuary but with a Greek emphasis on individuality. The base contains an inscription in which the girl addresses those who chance to see her image.

The Black Athena Controversy

The ancient Greeks were, quite rightly, proud of their cultural achievements. But how influenced were they by the ideas, religions, technologies, and art of others, the non-Greeks who inhabited the wider Mediterranean world? From the Romans to the present, many European and North American Grecophiles (people who love the Greeks) have celebrated ancient Greece's originality and creativity as though it had arisen in isolation. Some have even described the development of Greek art, democracy, philosophy, science, and history writing from the fifth and fourth centuries BCE as a "Greek Miracle," forgetting that the ancient Greeks lived in a wider world inhabited by other cultured peoples, including the Egyptians, Persians, Phoenicians, Hittites, and Hebrews. This neglect may have arisen from the European fear of Asian empires or by the belief that Greece's political and moral systems were so alien to Asian traditions that the Greeks could not have borrowed anything substantial from "the Orient" (a "baggy" term used to include all of the diverse civilizations of the Near and Middle East, and North Africa).

Egyptian Statue of Ahmes-Nefertari

In 1987, a Cornell professor of political science, Martin Bernal, unleashed a storm when he launched an attack on classicists and the Grecophile tradition in a three-volume study, *Black Athena: The Afroasiatic Roots of Classical Civilizations.* In his first volume, Bernal claimed that the amnesia about Greece's debts had begun in the early nineteenth century, as Europeans, seeking to establish "Aryan" roots for their continent, had cut off Greece from the Orient, ridiculed those who revered the Egyptians, and downplayed Greek texts such as Herodotus's *Histories* that acknowledged borrowings. In Bernal's view, the Aryanizing of Greek antiquity after 1830 influenced generations of Europeans and Americans who were taught that they were the descendants of autonomous Greeks and that their cultures had nothing whatsoever to do with the cultures of the Orient. Bernal called the book *Black Athena* not to say that all of Greek culture had its origins in Egypt and the Near East, but rather to demonstrate just how impossible it had become for Europeans to think of the founders of European civilization having black or brown faces.

Volumes 2 (1991) and 3 (2006) of Bernal's trilogy attempted to prove that Greece's debts to the Orient were more substantial than classicists and archaeologists had been willing to admit. Classicists have on the whole rejected and disproved Bernal's specific evidence of connections and interconnections, but have acknowledged that a traditional European reading of antiquity may have underestimated Greece's borrowings from Babylonian science, Egyptian art, and Assyrian literature. They have come to agree that something like a "Mediterranean cultural community" surrounded the Greeks from Homeric times forward, and that the Greeks knew more about the worlds to their east and south than was once thought. Herodotus had explored the east with great avidity, and Plato in his *Timaeus* had reflected upon Egyptian antiquity. The Greeks incorporated aspects of Egyptian cults into their religious rituals, and Homer was apparently aware of Gilgamesh's exploits. To Bernal's surprise, the primary success of his work was among readers in the African American community, many of whom have seen *Black Athena* as a means to assert ancient Africa's cultural creativity and to remind Americans and Europeans of the influence of racial thought in shaping western ideas and cultural institutions. As ancient history, Bernal's books may be flawed, but as cultural criticism, they have challenged readers to confront the nature of received history, how it is shaped, by and for whom, and for what reasons.

QUESTIONS | ***What are the dangers and advantages of radically rethinking history? What might Herodotus and Plato have said about this controversy? Can you think of other such culturally weighted and misleading characterizations of the past and the "historical other"?***

The Conflicting Pulls of Pan-Hellenism and Polis-Centrism

By the end of the Archaic Age, around 500 BCE, the Greeks were growing culturally more alike while remaining politically divided. This was to be both their curse and singular achievement. The things that united the Greeks in Greekness or Pan-Hellenism were many, but they were undercut by the ever-resilient identification of Greeks with their native poleis. Polis-centrism seems to win out, again and again, when one looks at the course of Greek history.

The Greeks spoke and wrote a common language, though local variations of dialect and pronunciation were substantial and a source of much fun for the comic poets. They shared the same polytheistic religion, with the same pantheon of gods, and a rich store of myths, but these were all subject to local emphasis and interpretation. Athens had Athena, who was not worshipped widely outside of areas of Athenian dominance. The Greeks shared religious rituals and forms of worship, specifically the common practice of sacrifice (vegetable and animal), but again subject to variation from polis to polis. The Oracle at Delphi came to be a common source of sanction for Greeks, and the Olympic Games brought the Greeks together every four years but in the individual pursuit of glory by the home athlete. The Greeks all had coins, though those were minted locally, thus reinforcing the polis-centrism of the age.

Archaic Age cultural and economic developments contributed to a new mobility. Bards and sages took their talents from city to city, thus homogenizing, cross-fertilizing, and spreading the accumulating knowledge and cultural advances of the age. Economic contact promoted economic and cultural interchange between poleis. But the lack of roads and the geographic isolation of many poleis inhibited movement within Greece. Moreover, the economic conditions of each polis were so different (with coastal poleis able to exploit sea trade opportunities, while landlocked poleis were forced to practice agriculture in traditional ways) that there was a growing disparity between poleis as the economy began to prosper in the late Archaic Age.

What the Archaic Age never overcame was the stubborn independence of each polis. Though political developments followed a similar path in many poleis, with their experiments with tyranny and the addition of citizen assemblies, each polis was different and in competition with others. The story of most of the ancient world and Greece in particular was the success of cities that stubbornly chose to cling to their independence, thus constantly raising the competitive stakes. Hesiod was right to characterize his world as an agonal or competitive place, in which every person was in competition with every other person. In Greece the polis was the engine driving this competition both internally and externally. The geography and resources of Mesopotamia had allowed its stronger cities to conquer neighboring cities and create empires. In Greece, for reasons geographic and historical, the poleis developed powerful identities, traditions, and interests that they protected fiercely against each other and imperial intrusion. The many Greeces were in constant contest, hundreds of little states at war with each other. It was unclear by 500 BCE if they could ever unite, for what reason, and what the cost of political unification would be.

The Persian Wars

The two Persian invasions of mainland Greece in 490 and 480–479 BCE were bracing experiences for the Greeks. Facing a common enemy, several Greek poleis made common cause in the defense of Greece. The odds were not good. The Persian Empire was the most powerful and aggressive power in the eastern Mediterranean at the time. The failure of the invasions may not have been all that important to Persia, but success and survival meant everything to the many Greeces.

What lessons did the many Greeces learn from the Persian Wars, and how did the invasions unbalance the many Greeces? In what ways might it have been better if the Persian Empire had triumphed?

The Persian Empire

The Persians were an Indo-European people whose homeland was in the area of present-day Iran. They were originally subject to the Assyrian Empire, but around 550 BCE King Cyrus of Persia defeated the Assyrians to create a Persian Empire. He conquered and incorporated the Lydians, Mesopotamians, and Babylonians. Since the Babylonians had controlled Syria and Palestine, the Persian Empire annexed those lands as well. The Persian model of empire was more inclusive or, at least, tolerant than the Assyrian and Babylonian empires had been. Cyrus allowed the Hebrew captives of Babylon to return home, thus initiating the Second Temple period of Hebrew history, which flowered around 515 BCE, after Cyrus's death. Persian armies under Cyrus conquered territory all the way to the edge of India, but the king died in Scythia in 531 BCE. His son Cambyses (d. 522 BCE) invaded Egypt and was named king of Egypt. Cambyses's successor, Darius (r. 521–486 BCE), launched the first invasion of Greece.

The Persian Empire was different from anything the Greeks had experienced previously. The great king, as he was called, was chosen by the gods and his subjects were all considered his slaves, there to do his bidding and to die for him. The great king's absolute power was manifest in the majesty of his person and the low station of his subjects, who prostrated themselves on the ground when in his presence. The empire was tolerant of its incorporated parts, known as satrapies, each with its own

Tribute Offered to the Persian Empire A procession of men representing subdued lands bears tribute to the Persian Empire on a relief from Persepolis. On the top level, Scythians bring cloth, bracelets, and a stallion; and on the bottom, Lydians bring objects such as vases and cups.

governor (**satrap**) who was directly subject to the great king. All was well in the empire so long as the conquered peoples and their representatives acknowledged the great king's absolute power and paid taxes. Because all regions contributed soldiers to the Persian Empire, it was able to throw huge international armies into any conflict. The king had a personal army of 10,000 Immortals (an elite force of Persian soldiers selected for their proven bravery and so called by Herodotus), who served as his imperial bodyguard.

The Persian Empire was a vast conglomerate, loosely governed and organized, but with a standard language (Aramaic), script (cuneiform), coinage, and impressive road network dominated by the Royal Road, which ran from Persia to Lydia. The Persians were devoted to the benevolent god Ahura Mazda, the god of fire, light, warmth, and purity. They also believed in the existence of malevolent gods and that all of life was a battle between the forces of good and bad, spirit and matter, light and dark. This dualistic religion was systematized by the prophet Zarathustra or Zoroaster in the eighth century BCE, and the religion was later called Zoroastrianism.

Like so many overextended empires, the Persian Empire began to experience troubles at its margins. Cyrus died fighting against the Scythians, and Darius just escaped with his life from another campaign against them. Darius led his troops into Thrace and made it a satrapy, but the problem of Greece was still pending.

Lydia and the Ionian Greeks

Herodotus begins his account of the Persian Wars with the Lydians, for that was where the conflict began for the Greeks. Lydia controlled a coastal kingdom (c. 700–550 BCE) in western Asia Minor, where there were many Greek settlements such as Melitus, Ephesus, and nearby Halicarnassus (Herodotus's home). The Ionian Greeks and the Lydians lived well together. Lydia had pioneered the use of coins, experimented with musical styles, and exposed the Greeks to Asian learning. It was no accident that Ionia, which had stimulating contacts with the wider Near East, produced the great sages of the Archaic Age, rather than isolated mainland Greece.

King Cyrus had recognized that the Persian Empire needed clear access to the Mediterranean, and so early on he targeted King Croesus of Lydia and successfully incorporated Lydia and the Ionian Greek cities into his empire (Map 2.3). Many Ionian Greeks saw the historical change not as enslavement, but as an opportunity. Greek troops campaigned for King Darius and struck agreements where necessary with his officials. But Persian Lydia was a land filled with intrigue as the Ionian Greeks tried to balance the interests of their poleis against Persian demands. Some Ionians sought advantage by working directly for the Persians. Greeks took up official and servile positions at Persepolis, the Persian capital.

The Persian incorporation of Lydia, however, upset the political stability of the Ionian poleis, which fell under the control of local Greek tyrants who supported Darius. Cities from mainland Greece also began, somewhat naively, to interfere in Persian affairs through the Ionian poleis. The Persian conquest of Thrace, north of mainland Greece, and Persian overtures to Macedonia showed how dangerous it was to irritate or even interest Darius. The Ionian Greek tyrants were in a difficult position, since they could not easily please Darius and their poleis at the same time. When Aristagoras of Melitus failed to secure Persian backing, he urged the Ionians to overthrow their Persian-backed tyrants. The result was an Ionian revolt against the Persian system. Fearing that Persia would invade Lydia again and reinstall pro-Persian Greek tyrants, the Ionians sought help from mainland poleis. The Ionians assembled an impressive navy but were outnumbered and defeated in the eastern Mediterranean by a large Persian navy. The Persians then ruthlessly suppressed the Ionians and reincorporated Lydia into the empire.

The First Persian Invasion of Greece

The poleis of Greece were divided on what the Persian suppression of the Ionian Greeks meant for each of them. Sympathetic to the overthrow of tyranny in the Ionian poleis, democratic Athens encouraged Ionian resistance to Persia. Sparta and many of the cities of the Peloponnesus avoided involving their states in the foreign conflict, though they had long been hostile to Persia. Inside Greece, poleis continued to struggle against each other over a variety of matters, most of them unconnected to the Persian business. Athens had had a long-running conflict with the wealthy island-polis of Aegina, but when Aegina, which had a large navy, symbolically submitted to Persia, Athens rallied Sparta and Corinth to attack the island. Once defeated, Aegina acknowledged the error of its ways and agreed to support the anti-Persia policy of the victors. The danger all along had been that if Persia had the naval support of Aegina, it might easily overpower Greece.

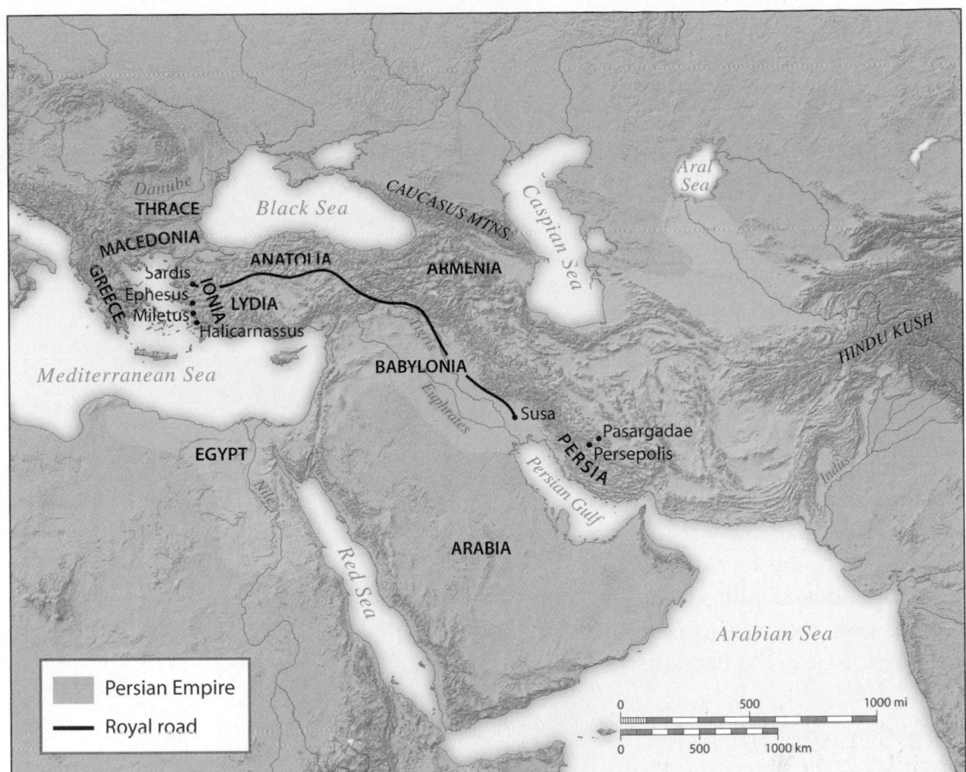

MAP 2.3 | The Persian Empire and Lydia, c. 500 BCE

The Persian Empire stretched 3,000 km (1,864 miles) from east to west and had absorbed the kingdom of Lydia directly across the Aegean Sea from the Greek mainland. Encompassing Ionia, Lydia was home to many Greeks. ***Why did the expansion of the Persian Empire threaten various Greek interests? Where was the heart of the Persian Empire? Why was Greece important to Persia's expansion? Why was Lydia a point of cultural and historical contact for Greece and Asia?***

Darius had many reasons to be infuriated by the interference of the Greek poleis in his affairs. Moreover, Greece seemed a natural territorial extension of his empire. The incorporation of Thrace in the 490s BCE was just the first step in this westward expansion. Darius may have thought Greece a particularly fragile target. His advisors told him that the Greeks foolishly and incessantly waged wars against each other. A Persian naval force was assembled and attacked Greece in 490 BCE (Map 2.4). With around 25,000 soldiers, the Persian force was extremely small by Persian standards. The Athenians asked Sparta for help, but it arrived too late to do any good. Ten thousand heavily armed Athenian hoplites engaged and defeated the lightly armed Persian force on the plains of Marathon, twenty-six miles from Athens. Several hundred Athenian soldiers died, but some six thousand Persians perished. The rest of the Persians returned to their ships and sailed home. The strange thing about the first Persian attack was how un-Persian it was. Darius did not try to overwhelm the enemy with a massive army and was not present to lead his army. Instead, the Persians fought one small battle in Greece and then retreated. Was Darius just testing the waters for a larger invasion, or had he seriously underestimated his opponents?

The Interwar Years

The battle of Marathon was of little importance to Persia but was critical to Greece, its survival, and its mood. The interwar years (489–481 BCE) were fluid ones, as poleis and politicians positioned themselves to reap the rewards of the triumph at Marathon and to take advantage of the still looming Persian threat. Athens crowed that it had saved all Greece and employed propaganda and warships against those poleis and its own citizens who had not fully supported the resistance to Persia. In these years Athens first introduced **ostracism,** a democratic technique for expelling from its midst dangerous individuals (often those accused of collaboration with the Persians). Some Athenians despised Themistocles, a prominent citizen and office-holder (a *strategos,* or popularly elected commander), who was leading a campaign to erect a powerful Athenian navy to resist any future Persian attack.

At Sparta, its nominal kings, who were Sparta's official agents for dealing with the external world, were carefully watched by citizens for any indication of Persian sympathies. Sparta led the **Peloponnesian League** (a group of poleis committed to the interests of the Peloponnesus of Greece) in pursuing a policy during the interwar years of forcing Argos (a Peloponnesian city near Mycenae) to join the League, a plan that ultimately failed. Sparta's chief worry, as always, was that its vast servile population of agricultural workers would revolt. It realized that it needed to be able to dispatch an army for foreign conflicts without leaving its home territory or its Peloponnesian allies undefended and inclined to rebel or, worse, to join the Persians.

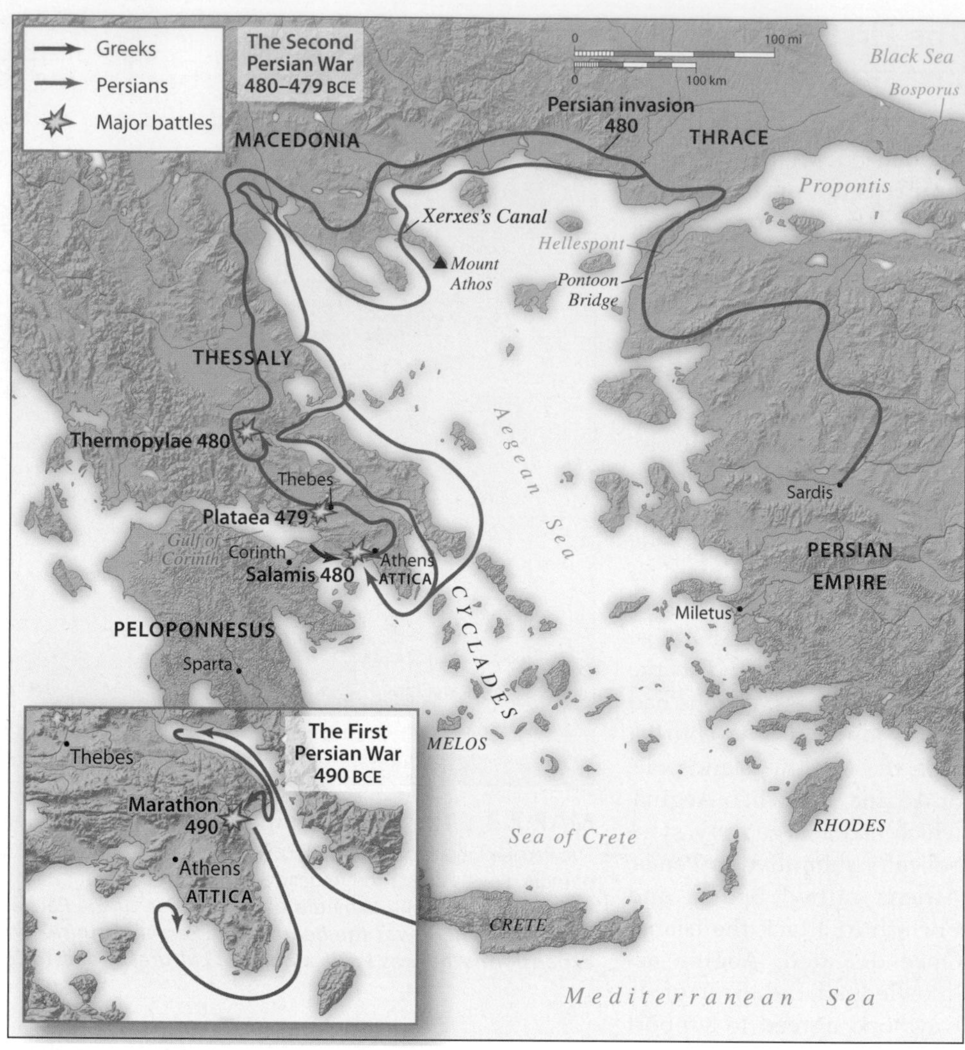

MAP 2.4 | **The Two Persian Wars, 490–479 BCE**

The First Persian War in 490 BCE was a fairly small raid that ended with the defeat of the Persians at Marathon near Athens. The Second Persian War was a major land and sea assault on Greece led by Xerxes. ***Why was the First Persian War so different from the Second? Where and why did the tide turn for the opposing Greek forces in the Second Persian War?***

The Second Invasion

Persia did not return immediately to its Greek campaign because Egypt was in revolt and the great king Darius died. His son Xerxes, however, was not one to leave business unfinished. The Persian diplomatic campaign to separate further the divisive Greek poleis heated up in the interwar years. The Persians promised gentle treatment to poleis that cooperated, and many did, often because they were more worried about hostile neighboring poleis than about the Persians. Representatives of the Greek cities and leagues met at Corinth in 481 BCE, but they were struggling as well with their various polis disputes and could not decide whether to resist the Persians or who should lead the resistance. Almost a third of the poleis decided not to resist an invasion. Using persuasion and trickery, Themistocles managed to assemble a large Athenian navy to resist the coming invasion, but only the Spartans and Athenians were firmly committed to the cause. Much of this pro-Athenian story is told by Herodotus. Many smaller poleis realized that they had as much to fear from Sparta, Athens, and hostile neighboring poleis as they did from Persia.

The Second Persian War (480–479 BCE) had two military phases, the first on land, the second at sea (see Map 2.4). In the first, Xerxes led a large army of up to 300,000 soldiers by ship and land across the Hellespont into Europe, where it won a costly battle against a vastly outnumbered Spartan force of 300 under the command of King Leonidas at Thermopylae. Xerxes invaded Athens, which had been largely abandoned by the Athenians, and ordered the destruction of the Acropolis. He left his army behind to take control of Greece, while he returned to Persia to tend to other business. The second phase of the war began after the great king departed. At sea, the Persian and the Athenian navies met indecisively several times, but the Athenians lured the Persian navy into a narrow body of water between Salamis and the mainland and defeated it decisively. In 479 BCE, the Spartans, the Athenians, and their allies defeated the remaining Persian army with its many Greek soldiers at Plataea.

The Persian Wars were over, but the aftermath proved to be more important than the wars. Herodotus's account captures the exhilaration of small but clever and determined Greece, led by Athens, overcoming a mighty foreign power that would have crushed Greece's freedom. The Athenian (and Spartan) triumph, however, reinforced the disunity of Greece, the independence of

THINGS THAT REMAIN

Stuffing the Ostracism Urn for Themistocles

In the heated interwar years of the 480s BCE, the Athenian assembly of citizens either invented or actively began to employ the institution of ostracism to expel dangerous politicians from Athens for up to ten years. The procedure was so called because citizens cast into a large urn broken pieces of pottery (shards) or prepared ceramic pieces (known as ostraka) on which had been written the name of the person they wished to ostracize. Ostracism was not a trial with the presentation of evidence and jury deliberation, but an unpopularity contest. Over ten thousand ostraka survive, a near majority of which bear the name of Themistocles. The future hero of the Persian Wars was eventually ostracized in the 470s BCE, but he was always a controversial and polarizing Athenian politician. His popularity bred animosity among those dedicated to preventing the dominance of democracy by any individual. One writer left a little verse on his vote for Themistocles's expulsion, calling it Themistocles's just "reward."

Considerable physical information can be gathered from the ostraka, including the location of the ostraka, the number and composition of the votes, the nature of the pottery shards used, and whether they came from the same shattered pots. They also contain linguistic; paleographical (old writing); and historical information, including how names are spelled, how adept the writers were, as well as what names appear, how they are related to each other, and how people are identified.

One batch of ostraka is particularly intriguing: 191 ostraka, all bearing the name of Themistocles, were found discarded in a well on the Acropolis. The shards came from the same general pottery source and bear the inscriptions of only fourteen different scribes. Was this, then, an attempt to rig the expulsion of Themistocles by stuffing the voting urns with votes? The votes, however, were discarded unused. Given the low literacy rates and pride of Athenians, not every citizen voter could or would want to inscribe a shard personally. It seems likely that scribes, perhaps commissioned by the polis, had prepared shards with Themistocles's name on them in advance so that voters could simply pick up a prepared shard. In this case, the scribes had overestimated the need and so after the vote disposed of the unused ostraka. The irony is that Themistocles himself used ostracism successfully to rid himself of opponents or to silence them by means of the threat of expulsion. That his name appears so often on legitimate ostraka may be an indication of a general if unsuccessful pushback by his enemies in the 480s BCE.

Ostrakon Inscribed with the Name of Themistocles

QUESTIONS | ***How do democracies manage dissent? Was ostracism a good or bad way to rid Athens of dangerous citizens? Why? How might such a process be abused?***

its many poleis, and the right of all poleis to continue to press for advantage within Greece by harassing their Greek neighbors, depriving them of independence just as Persia would have. Greece lacked a referee to settle disputes and enforce peace. Had Persia triumphed, it might have acted as an overriding force, preventing the poleis from attacking each other, just as it had for a time in Ionia. The outcome of the Persian Wars also left Greece with the Persian Empire as an external power to which individual poleis could appeal when seeking advantage over their Greek enemies. The Persian Wars, thus, confirmed the crippling polis-centrism of Greece. Greece had faced a similar crisis of knotted power during the Archaic Age when its aristocrats stifled progress, a crisis that was finally broken by the rise of tyrants who would be kings. Had it triumphed, Persia might have acted as a benevolent tyrant, albeit one demanding taxes and soldiers, to keep the peace in Greece and protect the poleis from one another.

The Persian Wars produced an upheaval in the Greek world, but of the wrong sort. Sparta and Athens, the leading poleis, were emboldened by their roles in fending off the Persians, but they had different visions. Sparta wanted to return to things as they were. Athens seized the opportunity to press the war against Persia even after its end because it had finally found a cause to trump the claims to independence of the other poleis. In the name of preserving the freedom of Greece, Athens was prepared to suppress the freedom of other poleis. Persia had given the Athenians the dangerous idea that only an empire could resist another empire.

Mature and Major City-States

Ancient Greek history can be divided in many ways. One way is to think that the Classical Age occupied the whole of the fifth century BCE. Another is to suppose that it lasted only from the end of the Persian Wars in 479 BCE to the end of the Peloponnesian War in 404 BCE. The latter seventy-five-year period is often associated with the Golden Age of Athens, when Athens reached its cultural and material peak. Sparta, Corinth, and Thebes were also important poleis in the fifth century BCE, but Athens outpaced them all in innovation, invention, and aggression. But Athens, because of its cultural grandeur, its ambition, and its flood of words and images, has always commanded most of the historical attention. Since historians follow the evidence and so much of it exists for Athens, it is hard to look away, but look away we should in order to restore some balance to the many Greeces of classical Greece. The fifth century BCE is not the story of a single polis, but rather of the resilience of the many Greeces (Map 2.5).

What were the strengths and weaknesses of polis-centered Greece? What joined and what divided the many poleis?

Sparta, the Radical Polis

Each polis was unique, but some were more extreme experiments than others. Sparta was an unusual polis long before the fifth century BCE. The Spartans were Dorians and thus Indo-European latecomers to Greece who had settled in the Peloponnesus. Sparta began as a series of four villages far from the coast on the west bank of the Eurotas River. Sparta was a landlocked polis without easy access to the sea. At first it controlled an area of 700 square miles in which it subdued the local population, transforming some into *perioikoi* (the nearby ones), who lived as relatively free subjects of Sparta. The *perioikoi* were called upon to fight in Spartan wars but had little influence on its foreign policy.

Spartan history took a radical turn at the start of the eighth century BCE when Sparta conquered neighboring Messenia, annexed its fertile lands, expanded its landholdings to over 3,000 square miles, and enslaved the Messenians as agricultural slaves called **helots.** From that point on the Spartans were a small minority within the region of Laconia (the southern third of the Peloponnesus) and felt forced to regiment their own society rigidly to maintain stiff control over a huge slave population. At about this time the constitution of the legendary Lycurgus was instituted. This constitution should probably be thought of as a set of working principles rather than a written document. The Lycurgan code of life militarized Spartan society. Its manifest purpose was to focus Spartan society upon the all-important need to produce perfect soldiers. Spartan men did not work but instead dedicated themselves exclusively to the art of war. Children were examined after birth and those deemed weak or deformed were left to die. Boys left their parents at an early age and were raised with their peers in common barracks, learning to fight, to sharpen their cunning by stealing from the *perioikoi* and helots, to spy on the subjugated masses, and to endure bad weather and lack of food and water. Once the boys became men and were named citizens, they were granted properties that slaves worked on their behalf. At thirty years of age, Spartan men married, but they never spent much time at home with their wives. Spartan girls were encouraged to be physically strong in order to produce strong children, to defend the homeland, and to oversee their slaves and estates while their soldier-husbands were away.

The citizen-soldiers of Sparta were a band of equals, but there were other political elements within Spartan society. Sparta retained the vestigial remains of its monarchical beginning and so still had two nominal kings, who occasionally led armies. Spartan kings were not raised in barracks to be citizen-soldiers and so were not always a respected force within Spartan society, but they were Sparta's representatives to the external world. The five annually chosen *ephors* were in charge of the Spartan citizen assembly and seem to have run the state, but the presence of occasionally dynamic kings, two royal families, and quickly changing external and internal problems meant that Sparta was less solid and stable than it seemed to other Greek states.

Sparta remained a relatively isolated regime, suspicious of the outside world, and devoted constantly to keeping a tight grip on its large slave population. The Spartan state was, thus, anxious to secure peace in the Peloponnesus and formed a Peloponnesian League of other Peloponnesian poleis to ensure the cooperation of its neighbors. The other great problem faced by Sparta was its relative lack of citizen manpower. Sparta might have produced the most impressive warriors of the ancient world, but it was never able to put many men onto the field of battle. The five thousand Spartans who fought at Plataea at the end of the second Persian invasion formed Sparta's largest army on record. More typical were the three hundred Spartans who had taken on the Persians at Thermopylae.

The polis of Sparta was a radical Greek experiment, one created to deal with its particular vulnerabilities (a vast territory, lack of easy sea access, a huge enslaved population, and small citizen-army). Sparta's cultural production was meager and that made mostly by *perioikoi*. What Sparta produced were magnificent warriors, just not enough of them. From its weaknesses flowed Sparta's dedication to land warfare, its reluctance to involve itself in wars, its slowness to act, and its vigilance and constant concern to suppress its vast, but restless slaves, who several times revolted. It must have been a wretched life to live as a Spartan slave, but it was not easy to be a Spartan.

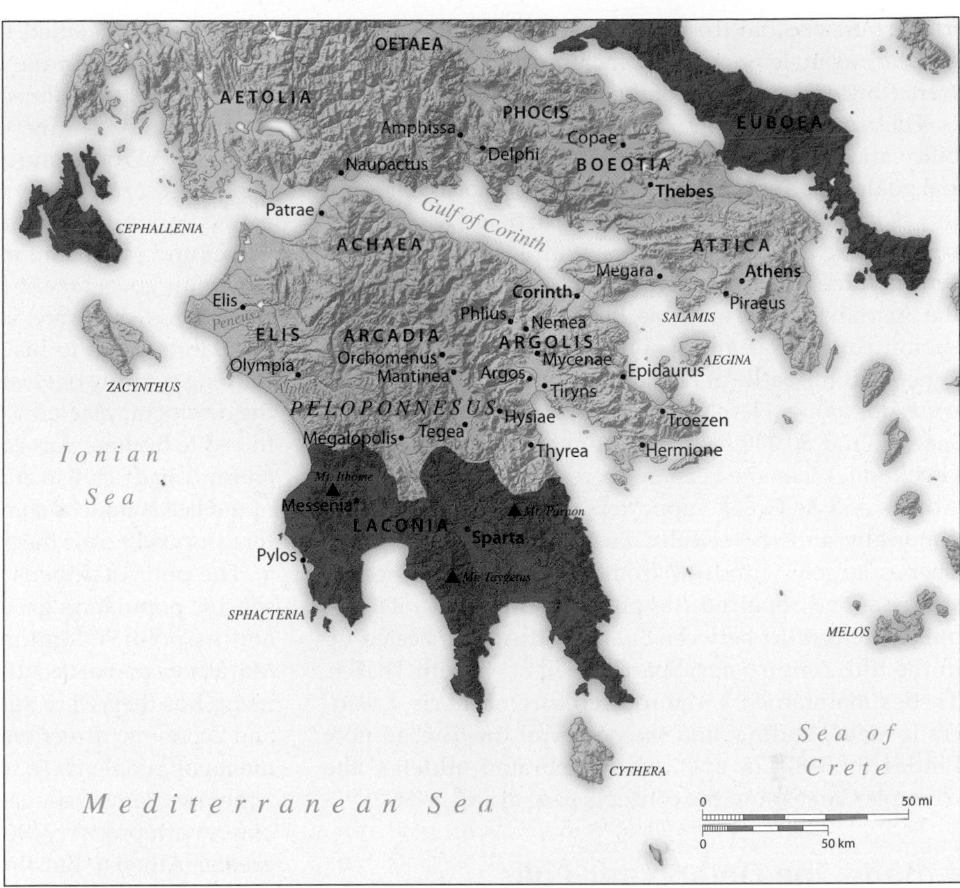

MAP 2.5 | Poleis and Regions of Southern Greece in the Fifth Century BCE

Sparta was located in the region of Laconia in the Peloponnesus; Corinth, on the isthmus that linked the Peloponnesus to mainland Greece; Athens, in the region of Attica; and Thebes, to the north in Boeotia. These important poleis played critical roles in the Peloponnesian War. ***What role did geography and circumstances play in making the poleis of Sparta, Corinth, Thebes, and Athens so different? What were the larger regional realities of Greece? Did any of the four major poleis have a distinct advantage over the others for geographic and developmental reasons? If so, why?***

Corinth, the In-Between Polis

Corinth had many advantages. Located at the eastern edge of the Peloponnesus, it controlled the isthmus that joined the Peloponnesus to mainland Greece. With its walled control of the isthmus, it could shut down land travel between the Peloponnesus and the mainland, as it did during the Persian Wars. As such, the ancients thought that Corinth handcuffed Greece. Corinth had an impressive citadel from which to defend itself and possessed harbors on both sides of the isthmus. Though Corinth had little importance during the Mycenaean Age, Homer described it as a wealthy polis during the Dark Age. As a coastal city, fronting two gulfs, it assembled an impressive navy, traded widely, and produced impressive crafts and manufactured goods for transport by sea and land. In the seventh century BCE, a family of tyrants ruled the city, but Corinth returned to an oligarchic form of government (rule by the powerful few) in the sixth century BCE.

Corinth's unique position derived from its geographic location. It was the in-between polis, almost equally distant from Sparta and Athens, but able to mediate between and communicate with both. Everything was good for Corinth so long as Sparta and Athens were dedicated to the same policies. Indeed, Corinth and the two powerful cities shared an interest in subordinating the smaller cities that lay between them and Corinth. Thus, Corinth was one of the most desired allies in the various balance-of-power struggles the poleis waged with each other. But what had worked during the Persian Wars did not work when Athens and the Peloponnesian League fell out in the fifth century BCE.

Thebes, the Federalizing Polis

Thebes was a very different sort of polis from Corinth. Located in northern Greece on fertile plains surrounded by small mountain chains, landlocked Thebes was the central polis of Boeotia. During Mycenaean times it had held a prominent place. Thebes and its twelve rival Boeotian poleis turned to agriculture in the Dark and Archaic Ages, but Thebes never conquered and suppressed surrounding peoples and poleis as the Spartans did, perhaps because the rich land of Boeotia was sufficient for all. Instead, Thebes and its Boeotian neighbors were, after many minor conflicts, forced to work toward a federation of interests. Thebes was somewhat exposed in the Boeotian plains, but by the sixth century BCE it had erected massive walls around the city. Thebes never had a tyrant but developed a stable **oligarchy** of propertied aristocrats who ran the city. Perhaps as many as a third of the city's male population, including all of its hoplites, were considered citizens of the polis.

The agricultural stability of Thebes led to political stability and freed Thebes from pursuing trade and imperial goals. The Persian invasions, however, placed Thebes in a delicate bind. Inside Thebes, a party of Persian sympathizers advocated cooperation with Persia. Thebes did send a force of five hundred soldiers to fight alongside the Spartans at Thermopylae, but after the defeat, Thebes submitted to Persia and sent troops to fight alongside the Persians at the battle of Plataea the next year. The Thebans were not alone. Herodotus estimated that Greek poleis sent around 50,000 soldiers to fight for the Persians on Greek soil. When the Persians were expelled from Greece, Athens and its Greek supporters punished Thebes both materially and rhetorically. For the next twenty years, Thebes largely withdrew from Greek affairs, licked its wounds, and repaired the physical damage to its city, but as the conflict between Sparta and Athens heated up in the fifth century BCE, Sparta allied itself with Thebes. Thebes maintained a vigorous culture of music, aristocratic male bonding, and the poetry of the Theban poet Pindar (c. 518–428 BCE), who celebrated athletes, the Olympic Games, and the concepts of *agon* and *arête.*

Athens, the Democratic Polis

The geography of Athens shaped its history, just as that of Sparta, Corinth, and Thebes had theirs. Mountains cup the city-site, providing it with a natural barrier that in ancient times was backed up by city walls. The defensible Acropolis of Athens was the organizing feature of the site and the one that made Athens a unified physical space. The hinterland of Attica, the large region around the city, was relatively fertile, producing wheat and olives, but the key economic feature of Athens was its access to the sea, not just at one harbor (the Piraeus), but over a long stretch of coastline sweeping around Attica and jutting out into the eastern Mediterranean. Attica, an area of around 1,000 square miles (the second largest territory after Sparta), contained valuable silver deposits. Athens did not suppress the farming peoples of Attica, but instead incorporated all free males of Attica as citizens. In general Athens was able to balance its moderate agricultural production with its industrial productivity (of pottery, in particular) and sea trade.

Even Athens could not surmount the economic depression of the Dark Age and emerged in the Archaic Age with the same aristocratic stranglehold that suffocated other poleis. In 630 BCE, the noble Cylon tried to impose his tyrannical rule on Athens, but failed. The statesman Solon, who was both a social and a legal reformer, became archon around 594 BCE. He attempted to deal with the mass of indebted people and the failing administration of the polis. The reforms that Solon instituted included relieving the debts of the poor. Debt relief lessened some of the social tensions that had been building in Attica. Solon also broadened the participation of the different Athenian orders in the political system, so that the hoplites and others obtained a stronger voice in politics.

Aristocratic families still held most of the power, but between 545 BCE and 510 BCE, the tyrant Peisistratus and his son ruled Athens. Peisistratus governed by placating common Athenians, buying their support with games and grain, and maintaining the outward forms of Athenian government (the assembly, the council of the Areopagus or senate, and the legal system), while manipulating them to his advantage. The general effect of the long tyranny of Peisistratus and his son was to curtail the aristocracy's claim to rule Athens. Aristocrats were forced to become part of a city governed by a wider franchise. A brief civil war occurred in Athens after the fall of the last tyrant, as some aristocrats tried to regain their former power over the state.

The polis of Athens was made up of demes (*deme,* a specific population grouping). The urban area of Athens and its politics dominated Attica. Small cities such as Marathon preserved the equivalent of a civic government, but they were subordinate to the foreign policies and economic direction of Athens. Still the local attachments of people were to their local demes. The roots of Athenian democracy lay in the recognition that all free males with property were citizens of the polis (that is, of greater Athens). But the tension between the rural and urban, coastal and inland territories within Attica made Athenian democracy a vibrant, almost electric mix of peoples with various interests.

The great compromise between these competing elements within the Athenian political system occurred after the fall of the house of Peisistratus. Two aristocratic families were locked in a struggle for dominance. Cleisthenes of the Alcmaeonid family found himself on the losing side and so took the radical step of turning to the *demos* for support. He proposed that the polis should have a council of five hundred representatives divided into ten tribes, fifty representatives from each. Each tribe would be composed of thirds made up of scattered urban, coastal, and inland demes. There were many reasons—military, economic, and political—for creating individual tribes, but it is likely that the new system favored the family and interests of Cleisthenes. Despite its complicated composition, the council of five hundred achieved some representative balance. Its power, however, was offset by that of the popular assembly, which was made up of all free Athenian males of a certain age. The *demos* remained, however, a limited group of citizens that excluded women, foreigners, slaves, and others. Athenian democracy was never universal; it was highly qualified.

Although large numbers of citizen-males (perhaps as many as 40,000) might attend the Pynx, or assembly-place, no votes were registered. Citizens voted with their raised hands or shouted their approval or disapproval of proposals. In a system of limited checks and balances, the council qualified the assembly's motions, sometimes redefining, sometimes overturning them. The coun-

OTHER VOICES, OTHER VIEWS

The Greek Bubble

There is a problem, rarely noticed, with ancient Greek history: we are trapped inside a Greek bubble, a torrent of words, seductive and persuasive, from inside Greece and virtually nothing from outside. This was partially the product of the extraordinary literary self-discovery of Greece in the fifth century BCE, but the Persians, Egyptians, Hebrews, and Lydians also wrote. Yet outsiders took little notice of Greeks or their doings. Old Persian documents for the period are choppy. There have been accidental findings at Persepolis and elsewhere of bureaucratic and administrative documents written in cuneiform from the fifth century BCE, but the Persian Empire was vast and no sustained attention was paid to Greece in its surviving records. Is this the result of the accidental nature of the survival of records or a comment on the marginality and unimportance of the Greeks? We have no right to expect a Persian Herodotus or Lydian Thucydides to spin a narrative web about the campaign failures of Darius and Xerxes, but the almost complete external neglect of the Greeks in the fifth century BCE raises questions about whether the Greeks were as important as they thought they were and about the reliability of reports from inside the bubble.

Perspective matters, but how in this case do we test the Greek narrative against other records? The historian Thucydides was pleased to report how the Athenians had almost wiped out Mytilene because it was merely contemplating revolt, but archaeological finds now confirm that the Mytileneans were planning a full-scale revolt. In this case, archaeology allows us to qualify one written account, but how do we correct or qualify the Greek record as a whole when we only have Greeks talking to or about each other? Both Pericles and Xerxes speak to us through the words of Greeks, but no Persian conveys Xerxes to us on his own terms. The story the Greeks tell is compelling and convincing, worrisomely so. Perhaps that is why the Greeks mark the beginning of western history; they constructed a captivating narrative that the Romans, when they learned to read and write, adopted without dissent, attaching their story to it as its continuation. Thus, Greece and Rome seem continuous and, as two connected points form a line, so western civilization assumed a direction and self-defining character.

QUESTIONS | ***Why are one-sided accounts dangerous to our understanding of the past? Why might the Greek (or Athenian) bubble be a problem? How might we escape from it?***

cil, whose members tended to be more aristocratic and wealthy, acted, therefore, as a senate to the assembly's congress or lower house, reserving some legal matters as its proper jurisdiction. The assembly could be swayed by popular speakers or demagogues, which made it a dangerous but fertile body of popular opinion. Athenian politics produced sophisticated politicians who appealed to the emotions of the people.

Athenian democracy was an important constitutional advance in the Greek world, but it was so complex and so different from democracy today, which has near universal suffrage (or voting rights), that it should always be qualified as *Athenian* democracy. Indeed, all forms of government in the Greek world of the time contained a mixture of elements: oligarchic, democratic, and monarchical or tyrannical, but the nature of the mix mattered, and it varied from polis to polis.

Living on the Margins of the Greek Polis

Each polis had different sets of customs, rights, and peoples, which cannot easily be generalized. The first distinction in all poleis was between the free and the not-free. To be free did not, however, guarantee full political rights in a polis. Some free men were citizens, but not all. Foreigners almost everywhere had reduced rights, if they had rights at all. In Athens, a distinction was drawn between transient and resident foreigners (**metics**).

The most unfree people in the Greek world were slaves, who can be categorized as rural slaves and city slaves. Sparta and Argos had large populations of agricultural slaves, enslaved as entire peoples when their homelands were conquered and annexed. From such slavery of place and ethnicity there was little chance of escape or improvement. City slaves in Athens, which is thought to have had around 20,000 slaves in the fifth century BCE, were generally foreigners who had been captured in wars or purchased from foreign lands; these foreigners included Greeks who had been captured in various Greek conflicts. Slaves were considered to be living property that could be bought and sold on the open market. Slaves had few if any civil rights. In Athens, slaves performed hundreds of lowly tasks from household work to street cleaning, bearing water, and prostitution. Some owners rented out their slaves for manual labor. An owner might free his slave or the slave might purchase his freedom, but this was not common. Escape

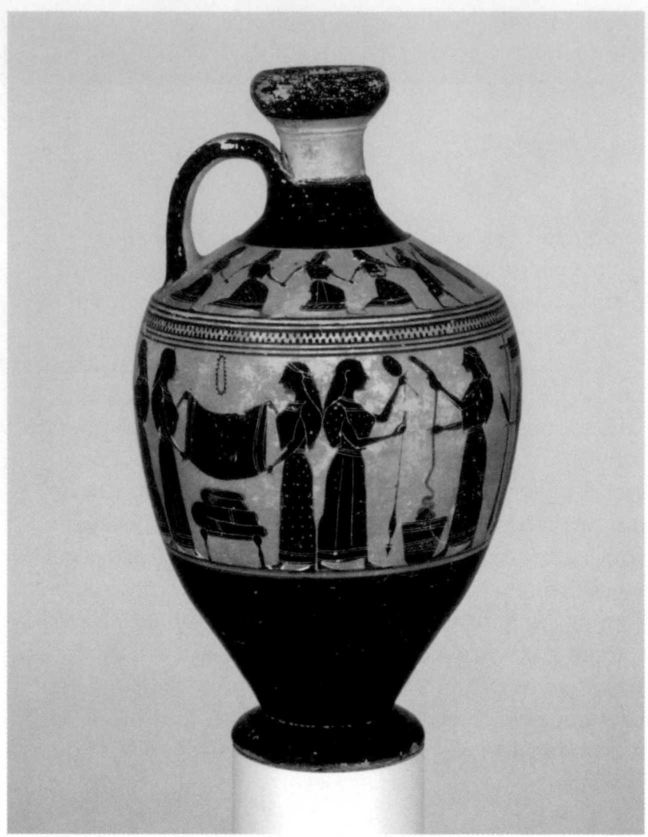

Wool Working and Weaving The oil flask shows various stages in the preparation of wool cloth by Greek women.

was a risky proposition for most slaves, but slaves who worked in the mines, where the life expectancy was extremely low, were often prepared to risk torture and execution to escape their wretched condition. The Greeks did not question the legitimacy of slavery since they believed that nature had consigned the slave to slavery because of something inferior or tainted in the slave's nature. Many owners thought of the slave as a living possession like the family cow, but some Greek thinkers came to believe that free men demonstrated their nobility by the way they treated their slaves and women.

The status of women in Greek society varied from polis to polis. At Sparta, women were honored as the mothers of citizen-soldiers and as the keepers of houses and estates while the men were away at war. At Athens, free women stayed at home out of public view; they ran the household, managed the domestic slaves, and planned and made meals. Women of the courtesan class such as Pericles's Aspasia moved more freely in the polis and occupied a more dynamic role in public life. Athenian noble women had limited property and inheritance rights. The one area in which aristocratic women might enjoy a greater public role was in religious life.

Beyond the citizen life of Athenian free-born males in the Greek polis, other groups such as merchants and traders had limited political rights, but substantial economic freedom. Networks of commercial associations arose informally since merchants needed to acquire and dispose of goods and so required suppliers and buyers, and the means to convey goods. For Athenian merchants and foreigners, the purchase of goods and their delivery in Athens could span the Mediterranean and take many weeks or months. War was not beneficial to trade, merchant travel, or the transport of goods, but by the 430s BCE it seemed more and more likely, as Herodotus had suspected, that a great war was about to break out.

The Peloponnesian War

The Persian Wars had pushed the Greek poleis toward even greater efforts to preserve their independence from and advantages over one another. Even the Athenian drive to lead Greece against the next threat from Persia may be viewed as one of those strategies, leading to an Athenian imperialism that had both economic and political elements. After a half-century of amassing power and preserving a deceptive peace, Athens threatened the city-state system of Greece. The Peloponnesian cities led by Sparta finally had had enough and fought Athens in the long and disastrous Peloponnesian War (431–404 BCE), which broke the back of the old Greek order and undid classical Greece.

How was the Peloponnesian War the natural result of ancient Greek history? Would there have been an Athenian Golden Age without Athenian imperialism?

The Delian League

The year after the retreat of the Persians after the battle of Plataea, Athens formed the **Delian League** (located on the island of Delos) of cities to continue to resist the Persians. The Spartans and the other members of the Peloponnesian League withdrew from the Persian Wars coalition, feeling that the war was over and their commitment fulfilled. The Spartans proposed that the Ionian Greeks should be brought back to Greece to avoid future conflict with Persia. The Delian League's mandate was the opposite: to liberate Ionia and its Greek settlements from Persian control. Each polis-member of the Delian League contributed ships, men, or money to the common cause. With these resources, the Delian League harassed the Persians in Asia Minor and in 448 BCE the Persian Empire was forced to free the Ionian Greeks from its direct control. In the meantime, however, the Delian League had become a vehicle for Athens to amass power and influence. Athens pressured member cities to support Athenian interests and to adopt Athenian-style democracy and values. The political and military leader of the pro-Delian, anti-Persian cause in Athens was Cimon. Under his leadership, Athens compelled the island of Euboea to join the league and conquered other Greek islands in the name of the Delian mandate. When the island of Naxos attempted to withdraw from the league, Athens attacked it.

CHRONOLOGY	Athens and Events Leading Up to and During the Peloponnesian War
DATE (BCE)	EVENT
478	Formation of the Delian League
459–456	Conflict with Corinth
456–431	Thirty Years' Peace
431–404	Peloponnesian War
Winter 431–430	Pericles's Funeral Oration
Summer 430	Plague strikes Athens
429	Death of Pericles
428–427	Revolt of Mytilene
421	Peace of Nicias
415	Males of Melos executed
415–413	Sicilian campaigns
411	Aristophanes's *Lysistrata*
405	Destruction of the Athenian fleet
404	Athens surrenders

The formation and activities of the Delian League did not sit well with the Peloponnesian League. Corinth, the in-between polis, was not at the time a member of either league, and had long had friendly relations with Athens based on their shared animosity toward the island of Aegina and the polis of Megara, which lay between them. After Athens campaigned successfully against both, Athens and Corinth were brought into direct contact without a buffer zone of shared enemies and interests. This produced what some historians have called a first Peloponnesian war between Corinth and Athens. In its drive for dominance, Athens pushed Corinth into the Peloponnesian camp. In 457 BCE, Sparta sent reinforcements to Boeotia to fend off Athenian aggression there. Thus, Thebes too was forced into the Peloponnesian camp, but Athens invaded Boeotia and subdued all its cities except Thebes. The conflict ended when the Peloponnesian and Delian Leagues signed a peace treaty in 456–455 BCE that was supposed to last for thirty years.

In 454 BCE, Athens removed any pretense that the Delian League was a company of equals by transferring its common treasury from Delos to Athens and no longer accepting men and ships as contributions, but only money dues from league members. Some of the money went toward civic improvements in Athens. To many of the Delian League members, it now seemed that they were paying tribute to Athens, not membership fees. Imperial Athens also established garrisons of soldiers in cities that contemplated secession from the league and planted representatives and spies in league cities. By the 450s BCE Athens was an empire in all but name and not a particularly pretty one at that.

Pericles and the Outbreak of the War

Pericles dominated Athenian politics for twenty years leading up to and through the first years of the Peloponnesian War. He was an aristocrat descended from two of the principal families of Athens; he opposed Cimon and his son-in-law, Thucydides, the historian of the war, who was ostracized in 443 BCE. Pericles has always seemed a charismatic politician: a powerful speaker, promoter of Athenian culture at the time of its greatest achievements, and colorful. The poets mocked him as a "squill-head" because his bulbous head resembled a sea-onion, but we cannot judge the deformity since in official portraits his head is covered by a helmet. He kept a foreign courtesan, Aspasia, as his mistress and treated her better than most Athenians treated their

Pericles, the Athenian Politician On many of the busts of Pericles, he wears a war helmet, supposedly because his head was misshapen and the subject of ridicule. The wily politician did cultivate a particular public image of himself for democratic Athens.

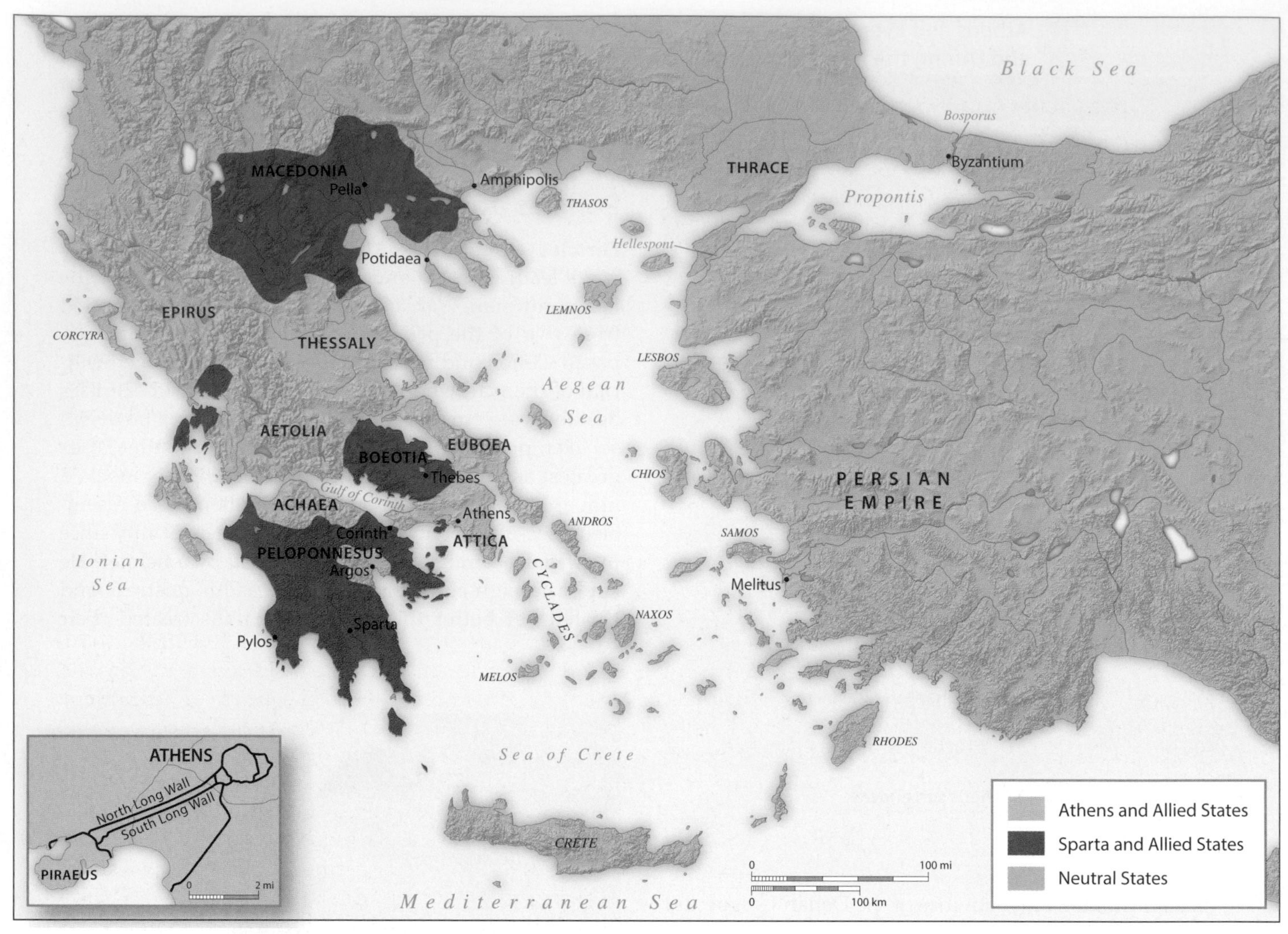

MAP 2.6 | The Peloponnesian War, 431–404 BCE

During the Peloponnesian War, many Greek cities and regions struck up alliances with either Athens or the Peloponnesian League, headed by Sparta. ***In geographic terms, where did the strength of Athens lie in the war? What of the Peloponnesian League? What role did the Aegean islands, the Greek cities in Ionia, and the Persian Empire play in the conflict, and why?***

wives. Like most successful politicians, Pericles, who regularly served as a *strategos,* pleased many audiences, but intensely irritated others. The Athenian *demos* held him in high esteem because he provided jobs, food, and diversions, and stroked their pride in their polis. Pericles served on the committees that oversaw the commissioning of Phidias's monumental statue of Athena and the completion of the Parthenon. Most Athenians cared chiefly about their prosperity and supported Pericles's active promotion of a hard-fisted, Athens-first imperialism that kept foreign monies flowing into the city. It was Pericles who moved the Delian treasury to Athens, and he opened up the treasury box for civic projects.

But could Athens afford Pericles or the drift toward war with Sparta? Pericles pursued an aggressive anti-Sparta policy, behind which lay his conviction that all the Athenian Empire had to do to triumph was to survive intact any conflict with the Peloponnesians. Pericles may have sensed how fragile Sparta was and hoped that it could not endure an extended conflict. Sparta and the Peloponnesians held the higher moral ground, for they claimed to be interested only in liberating Greeks from the imposition of aggressive Athenian imperialism; they would preserve the polis status quo against Athenian tyranny. When the war finally broke out over Athenian interference with Sparta's allies, the Periclean policy was to withdraw the peoples of Attica behind the walls of Athens while the Spartans ravaged their lands. With the Spartan land force occupied, Athens sent its navies to ravage the coastlines of the Peloponnesus and Sparta's allies (Map 2.6).

In the first phase of the war, called the Archidamian War after the Spartan king Archidamus, Athens suffered minor setbacks. Pericles's famous *Funeral Oration,* as reconstructed by Thucydides, was occasioned by one such setback. Pericles's speech conjures up an image of Athenian civic perfection to the neglect of the bloodied war dead, men who had died violent and gruesome deaths. He laid out how Athens was superior to Sparta, but not everyone even in Athens trusted his message. (See Back to the Source at the end of this chapter.)

In 430 BCE, the people gathered inside the walls of Athens by the circumstances of the war suffered a horrendous outbreak of disease (most likely typhus, though some scholars have argued that it was an outbreak of bubonic plague), described in excruciating detail by Thucydides. Pericles died the next year, perhaps from the lingering effects of the disease. The Periclean strategy of sheltering the people of Attica inside defensible Athens created the crowded conditions that contributed to the outbreak and spread of the disease.

Sparta's allies, especially the Thebans and Corinthians, continued to hamper Athenian ambitions and weaken the resolve of Delian League member-states. In 427 BCE, when the Mytileneans of Lesbos contemplated revolt against the burden of being an Athenian ally, Athens ordered the slaughter of every male Mytilenean but had a change of heart, as related by Thucydides, and killed only one thousand, expelling the rest of the community from Lesbos and turning their land over to Athenians. Athens opened up another theater of war in Sicily, with mixed success. Neither side achieved a clear victory, and in 421 BCE they struck the Peace of Nicias, which was favorable to Athens inasmuch as the agreement seemed to recognize the Athenian Empire. Sparta asked for a promise that Athens would help defend it against its slaves, which was a sign of Sparta's continuing preoccupation with its domestic problems, but of little real value to the Peloponnesian League or its preservation of the polis system of Greece.

The Long Second Phase of the War

The Nicias accord did not produce a comfortable peace. Corinth and Thebes with its Boeotian neighbors refused to sign the treaty, and many of Sparta's Peloponnesian allies were unhappy with the terms of the peace. Various poleis jockeyed for power and position. Democratic Argos reemerged as a powerful rival of Athens and pursued its own dream of Greek dominance. Corinth joined an alliance with Argos, which made its own deal with Athens and then waged a war against Epidaurus. Sparta had lost the peace, and the Greek world was drifting again into petty polis conflicts that benefited the superior scheming of Athens. At last, in 418 BCE, Sparta reached a breaking point and marched against Argos, defeated it soundly, and forced it back under the Peloponnesian umbrella.

Stirring the pot in these affairs was the dynamic young Athenian politician and commander Alcibiades. Full of intrigue and complex schemes, he seemed to be everywhere. These were suspicious and dangerous times, and Athenian imperialism was at its most brutal, an indication that Athens could not tolerate the loss of any ally lest it lose them all. In 416 BCE, the island of Melos, an ally of Sparta, was seeking to remain neutral in the war, but Athens conquered the island, killed all the men, enslaved the women and children, and sent Athenian colonists to reoccupy the island. With actions such as the Melos murders, Athens won little respect or trust from its enemies and allies. At Alcibiades's prompting, Athens decided to take the war to Sicily, whose politics was dominated by Syracuse, a Spartan ally. Alcibiades was named one of the commanders of the fleet and set sail, but just as the war began Alcibiades was recalled to Athens to stand trial on charges of sacrilege and impiety. To avoid a sentence of death, Alcibiades deserted to Sparta and for several years served as an advisor to the Spartan campaign. The Athenian attack on Sicily was a disaster. The Athenian navy was destroyed, the Athenian commanders were executed, and as many as 40,000 Athenian soldiers were thrown into the quarries of Syracuse to die horrible deaths.

Despite the Sicilian disaster, Athens hung on, just barely. Its allies revolted whenever they could. Within Athens, an oligarchic faction vied for power and control of the war. The Spartans realized that to defeat Athens, it would need a naval force of its own. Lacking the funds to build a navy, Sparta turned to Persia. Sparta agreed to cease any interference in Ionia, thus recognizing Persia's claims on Lydia. The king of Persia lent naval support and financed the continuing Spartan war effort. In 405 BCE, the Spartan navy caught the Athenian fleet off the coast of Asia Minor and destroyed it. By autumn, Spartan troops were besieging Athens; the people of Attica were dying from starvation when Athens sued for peace.

The Peloponnesian League met in 404 BCE to decide the fate of Athens. Bitter Corinth and Thebes called for the complete destruction of the city. Sparta asked for much less: the removal of Athenian fortifications at the Piraeus or port of the city, the destruction of the long walls (north and south) that led from the port to the city, and the leveling of the great protective walls that surrounded the city. Athens agreed to remove its walls and defenses, to join the Peloponnesian League, to follow Sparta's decisions, to abandon democracy, to destroy all but twelve of its ships, to release its hold on dependent cities, and to confine its activities to Attica. The Athenian Empire was dead, but polis Athens survived.

The Brief Golden Age of Athens

The Persian Wars largely created and the Peloponnesian War killed the Golden Age of Athens (479–404 BCE), a short seventy-five years that produced one of the most splendid periods of human achievement. The Classical Age was not confined to Athens or to its Golden Age, but Athenian culture led the way, influenced wider Greek tastes, and set the standards. Athens was able to achieve so much culturally because of its democracy, imperial wealth, exposure to the wider world, and critical mass of people and ideas. A good part of its cultural achievement came from its imperial success, but with imperial failure came cultural decline.

All Athenian culture was, in one light, political. Athens produced gorgeous pottery, ceramics, bronze objects, and household items such as furniture that may seem apolitical, but even these cultural products reflected

The Acropolis of Athens with the Parthenon The Parthenon was erected on the highest point of the Acropolis and stood as a symbol of Athenian religious and civic virtue, and as a symbol of imperial might.

the bounty of imperial prosperity. Athenian ships and traders covered the Mediterranean, dependent poleis and bound allies were compelled to trade with Athens, and the tributary monies that poured into Athens fueled its economy. The same could be said, to a lesser degree, of Corinth, whose exquisite culture of fine buildings and sculptures was a product of its vigorous trading economy, but its culture was proudly Corinthian rather than aggressively imperial.

Athenian culture is infected with political issues. Its public building projects were a source of civic pride. The Temple of Athena (or Parthenon) on the Acropolis had originally been a public statement of the regime of Peisistratus, but in 480 BCE the Persians had set fire to the Acropolis. When Pericles took high office, he promoted the restoration of the Acropolis and financed it with silver taken from the treasury of the Delian League. The sculptor Phidias supervised the restoration, including the building of the large entranceway (the Propylaea), the construction of the temples of Erichtheus (an early king of Athens) and Athena Nike (or Victorious Athena), and the marvelous sculpted frieze of the Parthenon. The Panathenaea frieze ran for 175 yards around the Parthenon, showing a procession of hundreds of figures (gods, civic leaders, citizens, and musicians) coming to honor Athena Polias (Athena of the city) in a striking expression of the confident mood of democratic imperial Athens. Phidias also sculpted a massive ivory and gold-plated statue of the Virgin (*Parthenos*) Athena that could be seen by ships approaching the harbor. The temple complex of the Acropolis was a demonstration to the world of Athenian preeminence. The Parthenon was a graceful and exquisite statement of civic pride and Athenian stature; it was also propaganda paid for with imperial tribute.

Golden Age sculpture sought a perfection of form based on theories of almost mathematical precision about the symmetry, proportion, and balance of the human body in motion. The Athenian sculptor Myron's original works are lost, but later copies of his sculptures survive. His Discus Thrower captures the athlete in a convincing naturalistic pose at the moment of greatest back-

The Discus Thrower A Roman copy of the famous sculpture by Myron that is remarkable for its expression of classical ideals in both art and life.

WHAT A DIFFERENCE A YEAR MAKES

405/404 BCE: The Unmaking of Imperial Athens

In 405 BCE, people were starving to death in Athens. The Spartans were at the city walls; the Athenian navy had been crushed and could no longer bring shipments of food to Athens. Although Thucydides seems to have survived the war, the surviving parts of his history do not extend to 404 BCE. He was, in any event, in exile in Thrace and would not have been able to supply personal details of the final fall of Athens. Thus, we lack a direct description of the changes that overtook Athens at the end, but we can infer them. The great walls and harbor fortifications that protected the city were torn down, which must have left Athenians feeling utterly exposed to their many enemies. Ships no longer pulled into the harbor with tribute and food from Athens's far-flung economic empire, which was dismantled quickly. The abundance of money that had funded Athenian culture dried up. Plays were no longer being mounted because there was no one, private or public, to pay for them. Employable artists and architects soon began leaving Athens for greener lands. The erection of great buildings, the mounting of plays, and the wickedness of Aristophanic comedies all stopped.

For the people crowded into Athens, the end of the war meant that the residents of Attica could now return to their homes, and the residents of Athens could reclaim their city. The population of greater Athens had been reduced by half during the war. Life in general and for some time to come was difficult in Athens, as it adjusted economically and politically to the new realities. Gone was the democratic constitution that had long governed Athens and the robust citizen debates of the war years. It was better to keep one's mouth shut in these years. A Spartan-backed faction, the Thirty Tyrants, ran the polis harshly. Yet it may have been the deprivations and extreme conditions of life in 404 BCE that made the Athenians so anxious to return to a better life. By 403 BCE, they were already plotting the removal of the tyrants and the restoration of their prosperity and democracy.

QUESTIONS | *Why was Athens unable to stop the disastrous Peloponnesian War that it had provoked? How disastrous was the Peloponnesian War on Athens, given its rather rapid recovery? Did the Peloponnesian War kill the Golden Age, or were other factors at work?*

ward tension and stillness as he prepares to swing his arm forward to release the discus. The athlete is not individualized, he is a perfected type; not a person, but an ideal. Classical art strove in Periclean Athens for elevated models of perfection. The discus thrower does not wince and is not bandaged. Sculpture was most often official or public art, as was Phidias's colossal gold and ivory statue of Zeus at Olympia, one of the Seven Wonders of the Ancient World, which was paid for by the poleis.

For introspection, Athenians went to the theater. Greek cities organized religious festivals, among them ones devoted to the non-Olympian, wine-god Dionysus. In Athens, at the festival of the Great Dionysia, competitions were held between a small number of comedies, tragedies, satyr plays, and poetry readings selected by the city officials for presentation. The plays, performed by men wearing masks, took place in a theater not only before an audience, but before a statue of the god Dionysus. At Athens, the festival became another opportunity for civic and political discourse. Though most of the tragedies were based on well-known myths about the gods, the great playwrights could turn these myths into opportunities to probe universal human problems and, under their guise, contemporary Athenian crises.

Aeschylus (525–456 BCE), the first great tragic playwright, fought in the Second Persian War and in 472 BCE presented the *Persians,* a drama about the recent invasion. His *Oresteia* trilogy (*Agamemnon, Choephori, Eumenides*) examined not only the Trojan War, but also the triumph of civic justice over blood feuds. Aeschylus wrote seventy-three plays, only seven of which survive. Sophocles (497–405 BCE) is reputed to have written 123 plays, only 7 of which survive, among them the famous *Oedipus Rex.* His *Antigone* is a product of Periclean Athens at its height, and an open-ended exploration of civic power. In it the ruler Creon has, in the interests of civic justice, commanded that the body of Antigone's executed brother should be left unburied in defiance of the rites due to the dead. Antigone, driven by family pride and a sense of human dignity, risks all to bury her brother's body and, for her act, is condemned to be buried alive. Sophocles uses the story to explore individual and collective rights, the dangers of pride (***hubris***), and the nature of power. The play refuses to reveal which side is right, instead provoking the audience to think about the issues at stake. The last great, but least popular playwright was Euripides (c. 484–406 BCE), who wrote ninety-two plays, nineteen of which survive intact. His *Medea* may be the most famous and shocking of these, as to punish her husband Jason, Medea slaughters their children.

Though he was far from being the only comic poet, Aristophanes (c. 450–385 BCE), because eleven of his forty-four comedies have survived, dominates our view of Athenian comedy. Tragedy had its feet firmly placed in ancient myth and universal themes; comedy was current and not myth bound. Most of Aristophanes's surviving plays were written and presented during the Peloponnesian War. The outrageous *Lysistrata* concerns a congress of Greek women who decide to put an end to the war perpetrated by their husbands by withdrawing from sexual relations with them. With wicked asides, mock accents, jabs at recognizable politicians and current affairs, Aristophanes set his comedies at the center of the Athenian civic discourse as it whipped back and forth during the swings of the destructive war.

Athenian philosophy and science belong to the fourth century BCE and the Hellenistic Ages, but the writing of history asserted itself powerfully in the Golden Age. Alongside Herodotus's long and digressive account of the Persian Wars stands Thucydides's impressive account of the Peloponnesian War. Thucydides, the exiled aristocrat and general, more analytically, but no less subjectively, probed the progress of the great war between the many Greeces. Unlike Herodotus, Thucydides used written sources and his personal observations of the war. He re-created the speeches of Pericles and others and wrote with seductive precision about events. Thucydides was not an admirer of the war, of Athens for causing it, or of the way Athens conducted it. For Thucydides, history was a contest for power and the calamitous Peloponnesian conflict a case study of its abuse and the dire consequences of bad policies.

Conclusion

The Peloponnesian War was not all bad news. It did push Athenians to ponder their place in the Greek world, the meaning of being citizens and human beings in times pushed to the extreme edges of experience, and the importance of history. Thucydides framed the war as one of bad human decisions, not as the playground of impish gods toying with errant humans. His account of the peoples of Attica fleeing their homes and fields for the safety of Athens and his heartrending description of the plague in Athens are studies in the war's profound impact on Athenians. Thucydides was rethinking the costs and benefits of Athenian imperialism or, as he framed it, the moral dilemma of the strong acting willfully and the weak being acted upon in ways they could not avoid. He showed his readers the stark underbelly of brute Athenian power but knew that the other actors—Sparta, Thebes, Corinth, and Argos—were just as bad.

Doubts about democracy were already spreading during the war. The Athenians had made democracy the issue by fusing it with their imperial policy and forcing their way of life upon others. In the Funeral Oration, Pericles stood at the center of proud and defiant Athens, but Socrates (469–399 BCE), the Athenian philosopher, and his circle of students doubted the wisdom of the Athenians. Indeed, some Athenians welcomed the oligarchy that Sparta imposed on them.

The Persians were for a time satisfied by the results of the war. Sparta returned to Persia what it had lost during the Persian Wars, thus sacrificing the future of the Ionian Greeks. The readiness of both sides in the conflict to entice the help of Persia to break the deadlock of power between them proved once again that the poleis of Greece thought mostly of advancing their own interests. Pan-Hellenism mattered much less than protecting one's own polis, and so Sparta turned to Persia to win the war.

Not all the victors prospered. More than ever, Sparta lacked soldiers and was spread too thin to control the conquered Athenian Empire for long. Corinth lost much of its navy and was forced to subordinate its interests to those of Argos. Only Thebes and the Boeotians seem to have prospered after the war by feeding on the carrion of the Athenian Empire, looting Athenian dependencies and annexing neighboring poleis. The Peloponnesian War was not the triumph of the polis system that Sparta had promised; the Greek poleis were weaker after the war and never recovered their earlier dynamism and stubborn autonomy.

Herodotus had been right. He had warned Athens indirectly about the dangers of straying beyond its home and native land, just as the Persians had when they sought to conquer European Greece. Athenian imperialism was built on hubris, that fatal pride in its moral, intellectual, and military superiority so evident in Pericles's Funeral Oration. One might argue that the many Greeces could not have continued as they had for five hundred years, with hundreds of fiercely independent poleis scheming incessantly to weaken and dominate other poleis. The Greek poleis did not believe in the autonomy and independence of the polis; they believed in the autonomy and independence of their own.

The Persian Wars upset the delicate balance of independent poleis, transforming Sparta and Athens into super-poleis prepared to risk all. Sparta risked all to preserve its dominance over its Messenian helots and its traditional way of life; Athens risked all to create an empire and its culture flourished as a result. Ultimately the checks and balances of the Greek polis system were too great to be overcome by any one polis, for the poleis all existed within the limitations created by the Dark and Archaic Ages. Each polis had a fixed geographic environment, a deeply ingrained culture, and traditional adaptations to its circumstances or it could not have survived into the fifth century BCE. The great Athenian mistake was to think that it could rise above the stubborn balance of entrenched powers that had produced the polis system of the many Greeces. The Athenian Empire was the first of many empires that would fail in the West, most of them unable to overcome the intense cultural and political identities of the many regions of the continent of Europe. The failure of Athenian imperialism to dominate the many Greeces and the steep cost of the Peloponnesian War permanently weakened the polis system and the great poleis, leaving them vulnerable to higher orders of power. Something had to give and it did during the Hellenistic Ages that followed.

Critical Thinking Questions

1. Why and how did ancient Greece remain a history of the many Greeces rather than of one Greece?
2. What choices did individuals and their poleis make in events such as the Persian Wars and the Peloponnesian War that pushed their histories in one direction rather than another? Consider the cases of Sparta, Corinth, Thebes, and Athens.
3. How did the distant Dark Age shape the ages that followed and the essential character and limitations of ancient Greek history?
4. What role did chance or contingency play in shaping ancient Greek history? Consider such cases as the death of Darius after the brief First Persian War, the plague in Athens during the Peloponnesian War, and the recall of Alcibiades from the Sicilian campaign.

Key Terms

polis (plural, poleis) **(p. 38)**
Dark Age **(p. 39)**
Archaic Age **(p. 39)**
Classical Age **(p. 39)**
acropolis **(p. 40)**
agora **(p. 40)**
arête **(p. 43)**
agon **(p. 43)**
tyrants **(p. 46)**
demos **(p. 47)**
phalanx **(p. 47)**
hoplite **(p. 47)**
satrap **(p. 52)**
ostracism **(p. 53)**
Peloponnesian League **(p. 54)**
helots **(p. 56)**
oligarchy **(p. 57)**
metic **(p. 59)**
Delian League **(p. 60)**
hubris **(p. 65)**

Primary Sources in connect

For information on Connect and the online resources available, go to **http://connect.mcgraw-hill.com**.

1. **The Shield of Achilles**
2. **Hesiod's Complaint**
3. **Herodotus on the 300 at Thermopylae**
4. **Plutarch on Lycurgus and His Reform of Spartan Life**
5. **Thucydides, The Melian Dialogue**

The Perfect Athens of Pericles

The Peloponnesian War had barely begun when Pericles, the leading Athenian politician and architect of the war, spoke to the Athenians about their early losses and the excellence of their city and way of life. The *Funeral Oration* of Pericles is not a verbatim account of that address, but the reconstruction of it made by the Athenian historian Thucydides, who says that Pericles stood on a high platform at the gravesite and "spoke like this."

My first words shall be for our ancestors; for it is both just to them and seemly that on an occasion such as this our tribute of memory should be paid to them. For, dwelling always in this country, generation after generation in unchanging and unbroken succession, they have handed it down to us free by their exertions. So they are worthy of our praises; and still more are our fathers. For they enlarged the ancestral patrimony by the empire which we hold today and delivered it, not without labor, into the hands of our own generation; while it is we ourselves, those of us who are now in middle life, who consolidated our power throughout the greater part of the empire and secured the city's complete independence both in war and peace.

Of the battles which we and our fathers fought, whether in the winning of our power abroad or in bravely withstanding the warfare of the barbarians or Greeks at home, I do not wish to say more: they are too familiar to you all. I wish rather to set forth the spirit in which we faced them, and the constitution and manners with which we rose to greatness, and to pass from them to the dead; for I think it not unfitting that these things should be called to mind at today's solemnity, and expedient too that the whole gathering of citizens and strangers should listen to them.

For our government is not copied from those of our neighbors: we are an example to them rather than they to us. Our constitution is named a democracy, because it is not in the hands of the few but of the many. Our laws secure equal justice for all in their private disputes, and our public opinion welcomes and honors talent in every branch of achievement, not as a matter of privilege but on the grounds of excellence alone. And as we give free play to all in our public life, so we carry the same spirit into our daily relations with one another. We have no black looks or angry words for our neighbor if he enjoys himself in his own way, and we abstain from the little acts of pettiness which, though they leave no mark, yet cause annoyance to whoever notes them. Open and friendly in our private exchanges, in our public acts we keep strictly within the control of the law. We acknowledge the restraint of reverence; we are obedient to whoever is set in authority, and to the laws, more especially to those which offer protection to the oppressed and those unwritten ordinances whose transgression brings shame.

Yet ours is no work-a-day city only. No other city provides so many recreations for the spirit—contests and sacrifices all the year round, and beauty in our public buildings to cheer the heart and delight the eye day by day. Moreover, the city is so large and powerful that all the wealth of all the world flows in to her, so that our own Attic products seem no more homelike to us than the fruits of the labors of other nations.

Our military training too is different from our opponents'. The gates of our city are flung open to the world. We practice no periodic deportations, nor do we prevent our visitors from observing or discovering what an enemy might usefully apply to his own purposes. For our trust is placed not in the devices of material equipment, but in our own good spirits for battle.

So too with education. They toil from early boyhood in a laborious pursuit after courage, while we, free to live and wander as we please, march out none the less ready to face the same dangers. Here is the proof of my words. When the Spartans advance into our land, they do not come alone but with all their allies; but when we invade our neighbors we have little difficulty as a rule, even on foreign soil, in defeating men who are fighting for their own homes. Moreover, no enemy has ever met us at full strength, for we have our navy to attend to, and our soldiers are sent on service to many scattered possessions; but if they chance to encounter some portion of our forces and defeat a few of us, they boast that they have driven back our whole army, or, if they are defeated, that the victors were at full strength. Indeed, if we choose to face danger with an easy mind rather than with vigorous training, and to trust rather in native manliness than in state-made courage, the advantage lies with us; for we are spared all the weariness of practicing for future hardships, and when we find ourselves among them we are as brave as our plodding rivals. Here as elsewhere, then, the city sets an example which is deserving of admiration.

We are lovers of beauty without extravagance, and lovers of wisdom without unmanliness. Wealth to us is not mere material for vainglory but an opportunity for achievement; and poverty we think it no disgrace to acknowledge but a real degradation to make no effort to overcome. Our citizens attend to both public and private duties, and do not allow absorption in their own affairs to interfere with their knowledge of the city's. We differ from other states in regarding the man who holds aloof from public life not as "quiet" but as useless; we decide or debate, carefully and in person, all matters of policy, holding not that words and deeds go ill together, but that acts are foredoomed to failure when undertaken undiscussed. For we are noted for being at once adventurous in action and most reflective beforehand. Other men are bold in ignorance, while reflection will stop their onset. But the bravest are surely those who have the clearest vision of what is before them, glory and danger alike, and yet still go out to meet it.

In doing good, too, we are the exact opposite of the rest of mankind. We secure our friends not by accepting favors but by doing them. And so we are naturally more firm in our attachments: for we are anxious, as creditors, to cement by kind offices our relations with our friends. If they do not respond with the same warmness it is because they feel that their services will not be given spontaneously but only as the repayment of a debt. We are alone among mankind in doing men benefits, not from a consideration of self-interest, but in the fearless confidence of freedom. In a word I claim that our city as a whole is an education to Greece, and that her members yield to none, man by man, in independence of spirit, many-sidedness of attainment, and complete self-reliance in limbs and brain.

QUESTIONS | *How reliable is the Funeral Oration, given the re-creation of it by Thucydides? Why is Pericles so proud of Athenian imperialism? Is the speech fair to the Spartans and their Peloponnesian League allies? Why or why not?*

Source: Thucydides, *History of the Peloponnesian War* 2.36-41, trans. Alfred Zimmern, *The Greek Commonwealth* (Oxford: Clarendon Press, 1911), 196–200; revised.

3

The Hellenistic Theater at Epiduarus

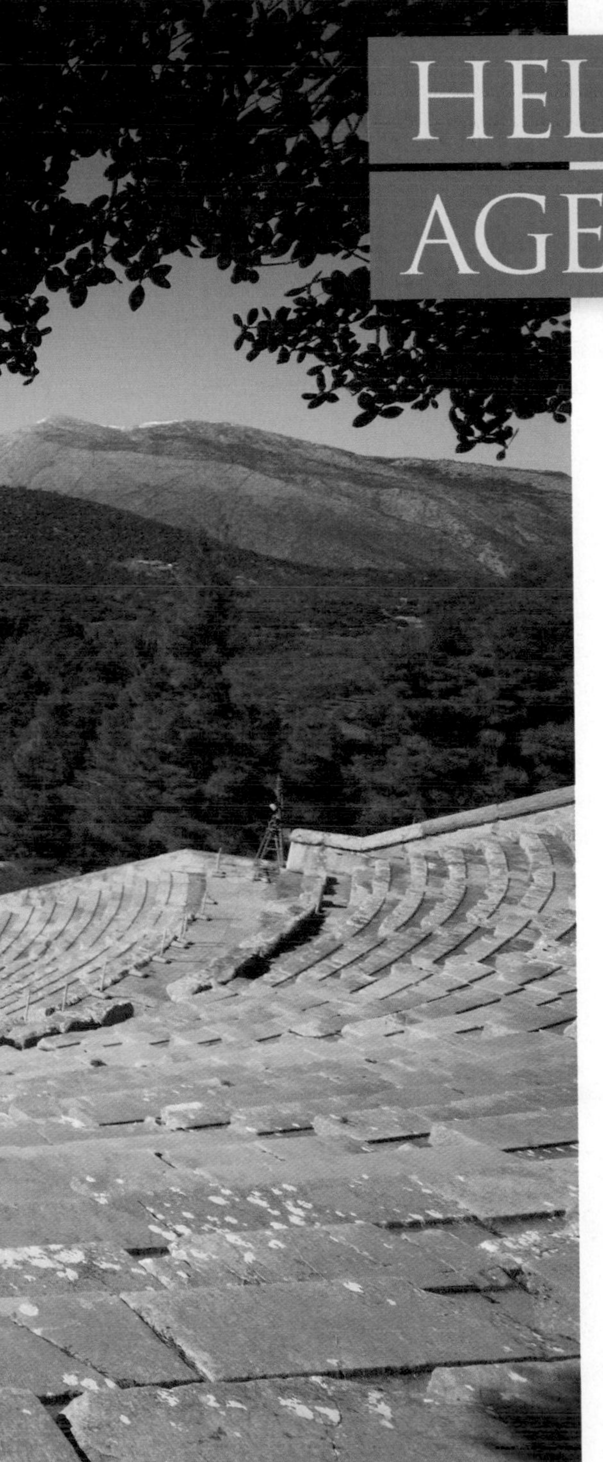

HELLENISTIC AGES

ACHIEVEMENTS AND ANXIETIES

ALEXANDER'S ENTOMBMENT IN ALEXANDRIA Two years after Alexander the Great's death in 323 BCE, his mummified body was ready to be returned to Macedonia for entombment. Sixty-four mules transported the elaborately decorated and domed carriage that housed the doubled golden sarcophagus, draped in purple, containing the king's body. The procession traveled as far as Damascus where Ptolemy I intercepted it and stole Alexander's body. Alexander's former general justified his theft by claiming that Alexander had expressly wished to be buried near the temple of Zeus Ammon at Siwah in Libya, though in fact Ptolemy redirected Alexander's coffin to Memphis in Egypt for entombment. Ptolemy probably planned all along for Alexander to be housed in Alexandria, but the city was still undergoing construction and Ptolemy was engaged in a deadly twenty-year struggle with the other claimants to Alexander's empire.

Finally it fell to Ptolemy's heirs to move Alexander's body to Alexandria, for Alexander was almost as important in death as he had been in life. Legitimacy and authority flowed from his physical presence, and Ptolemaic kings were entombed near Alexander. Over the centuries Roman emperors and tourists visited the tomb, whose gold was, for financial reasons, removed and replaced by glass (purportedly to better display Alexander). The Roman emperor Augustus is said to have asked for a private viewing, but when he bent down to kiss the emperor, he slipped and broke Alexander's nose. Since the third century CE, the site of Alexander's tomb has been lost, though many have searched for it, and still do.

The magnet of this show of a movable corpse, visiting emperors, and the royal pursuit of legitimacy was less Alexander's body than the city of Alexandria, the greatest of all Hellenistic cities, a hotbed of peoples, ideas, and religions for nearly a thousand years. Alexandria could boast of having one of the Seven Wonders of the Ancient World, the lighthouse at Pharos with a mirror at its summit to reflect the light of a fire some thirty miles out to sea and guide sailors safely to the harbor. The city also held the great temple of Sarapis (the Sarapeion); the Museum of Alexandria, with its legendary library; a theater; a gymnasium; a forum; and the royal palace complex. The plan of the city, laid out by Alexander, was realized by Dinocrates of Rhodes. He established a Greek rectilinear grid-pattern of streets blocking out the residential areas and great public buildings that shaped the urban character of Alexandria. The most distinctive feature of the city was its two harbors, which the architect created by ordering the construction of a causeway, 600 feet wide, that ran almost a mile from the mainland to the island of Pharos, thus dividing the bay in two. A brackish lake on the southern side of Alexandria left the city nearly surrounded by water. Fresh water was piped to the city from the Nile.

Alexandria became a great commercial city and symbol of the vibrant cosmopolitanism of the **Hellenistic** or Greek-like Ages of the Near East. The Hellenic period that preceded them had been more narrowly Greek (not Greek-like) and grounded in the poleis of Greece and their defining natures. Alexandria was dramatically different. Throngs of traders, scholars, Jews, Syrians, royal officials, Greeks from all over the Hellenistic world, and natives brought the city alive, crowded its wide boulevards, and carried stories of the fabled city around the Mediterranean. In 271–270 BCE, a new Ptolemaic king processed through Alexandria in a magnificent parade. In advance of statues of the gods Dionysus and Priapus and of the divine kings Alexander and Ptolemy I, hundreds of exotic animals were driven: Asian sheep, Indian oxen, a white bear, panthers and leopards, a giraffe, and a rhinoceros. Behind the carts marched women personifying various Hellenistic cities. Next came a golden Bacchic staff 135 feet long, a silver lance 60 feet long, and a golden phallus 180 feet long topped with a gold star nine feet in circumference. If those symbols of fecundity and phallic

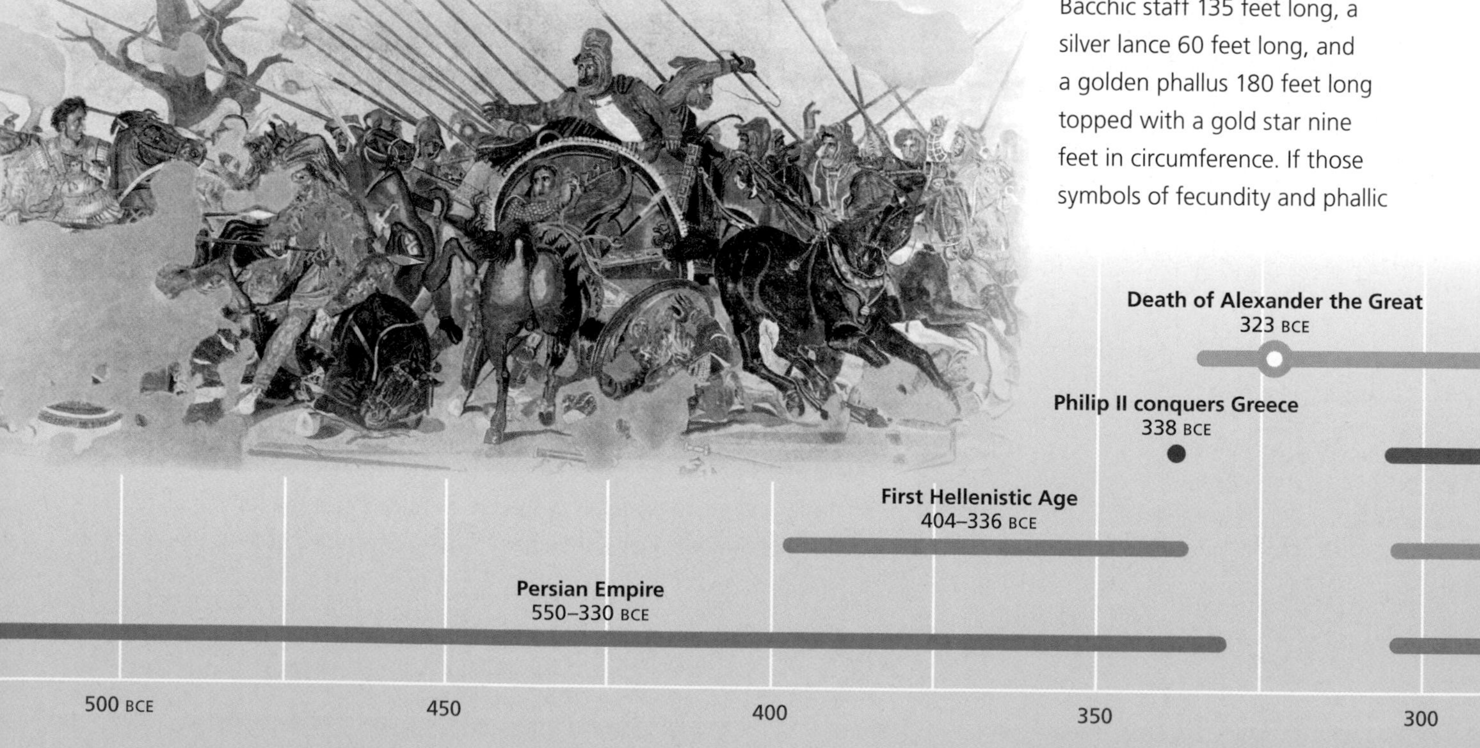

The Harbor of Ancient Alexandria In this re-creation of the city of Alexandria as it might have looked late in Ptolemaic history, we see the two harbors of the city, separated by a causeway that runs to the island of Pharos. Just off the island stood the famous lighthouse and beyond it on the coastline of the city the royal quarter, with its own docks, and Alexandria's main port.

vigor were not enough to demonstrate Ptolemaic power, the 57,600 infantry and 23,200 cavalry who followed surely did. The Ptolemaic kingdom of Egypt, rich, proud, and Greek, achieved its luxury and cultural dynamism in a productive and pacified kingdom within a century after Alexander's death.

Alexandria was hardly typical of the Hellenistic Ages, but it did embody its central characteristics: maritime, urban, commercial, cosmopolitan, culturally Greek, and royal. Alexandria was also like the Hellenistic world in its newness; nothing quite like it had existed prior to the meteoric rise of the Macedonian kings. After the Peloponnesian War, Greece was forced to unite and to abandon its older commitment to independent poleis. The passing of the Classical Age came quickly in the fourth century BCE in what can be thought of as a transitional period of the Late Classical or, as here, First Hellenistic Age (404–336 BCE), which ended with Philip of Macedon's death. The Second Hellenistic Age (335–30 BCE) began with Alexander's succession and march into Asia and ended when the Romans annexed the last of the Hellenistic kingdoms, Ptolemaic Egypt. The Greek

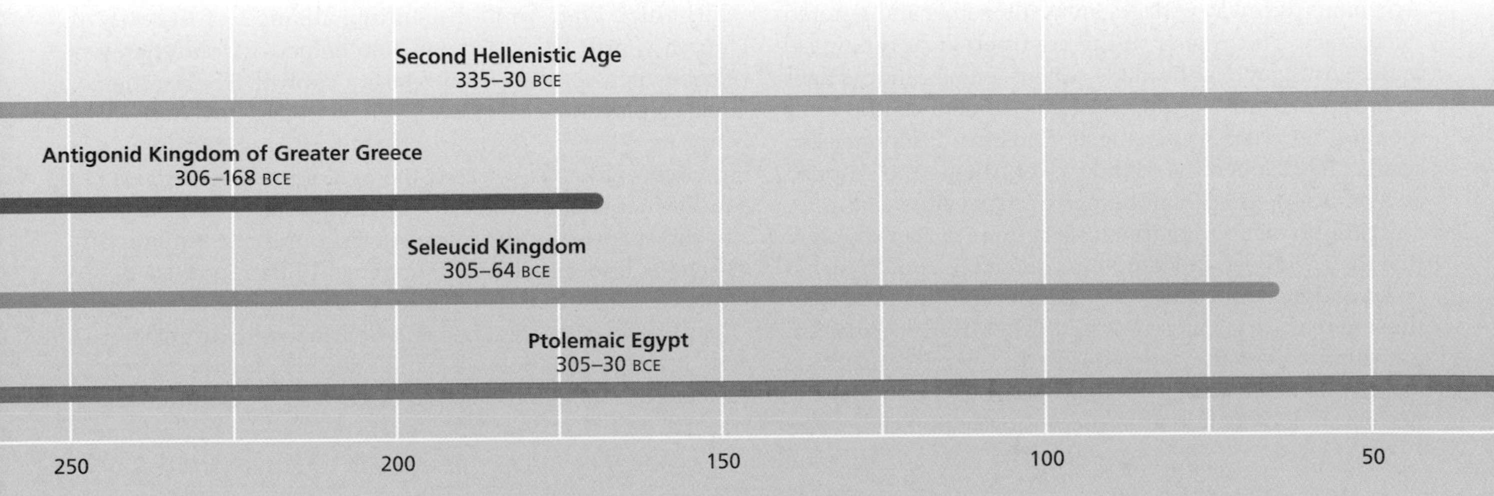

presence in and control of the eastern Mediterranean and large parts of the Near East and Asia would define the Hellenistic world. Alexander took Persia, Babylonia, Egypt, Phoenicia, and lands all the way to the western margins of India (today Pakistan). The Hellenistic kingdoms that arose after Alexander's early death consolidated Alexander's conquests and officially Hellenized or made them Greek-like. Yet the Greeks neither assimilated with the native populations and civilizations they conquered nor encouraged a deeper integration of peoples and cultures that might have permanently transformed the ancient world and so the West.

The First Hellenistic Age

After the fall of Athens at the end of the Peloponnesian War and end of the Classical Age in 404 BCE, the Greeks moved gradually into the first Hellenistic Age in the fourth century BCE. The Peloponnesian War had reconfirmed the fierce independence of the Greek city-states and, ironically, the necessity of imperial unity. The struggle between independence and empire continued but further destabilized the Greek poleis. In the first half of the fourth century BCE, the city-states of Sparta and Thebes competed to dominate Greece and the Persian Empire reemerged as a threat. Athens resumed some of its former glory and restored its battered democracy, but the emergence of the Macedonians under the inventive and determined Philip of Macedon brought the Athenian revival to an end. Philip took all of Greece before his own premature death at the hands of an assassin.

Why did Philip of Macedon succeed where so many others had failed in uniting Greece?

The Many Greeces Stumble

As a consequence of its calamitous loss in the Peloponnesian War, Athens was ruled briefly by a tyranny of thirty men, supported by a small garrison of Spartan troops. The Thirty Tyrants, who ruled harshly, were then replaced by a group of Ten Oligarchs, but in September 403 BCE the Athenians did away with oligarchy altogether and restored democracy. The cruelty of the brief period of tyrannical and then oligarchic rule made Athens long for the old days of prosperity and for a form of government central to its identity. Yet much had changed. The great Peloponnesian conflict had sapped the confidence of Athens and stripped away much of its economic empire and wealth.

Triumphant Sparta fared little better. Spartans thought that they had been called upon to defend not only Spartan independence, but also the freedom and autonomy of those Greek city-states that had fallen under Athenian dominance. Yet the outcome of the war led Sparta—against its best interests, which lay in isolation and the preservation of its limited resources of manpower—to attempt to dominate the peace of Greece. Because of its lack of experience at imperial domination, victorious Sparta made a heavy-handed attempt to "pacify" Greece and imposed cruel tyrannies and oligarchies upon its defeated rivals. The deal that Sparta struck with Persia during the Peloponnesian War (financial resources to construct a navy in exchange for recognition of the Persian Empire's claim to Ionia) proved costly in the long run to both the Spartans and the Persians.

Greeks continued to be involved in Persian affairs. Cyrus the Younger, seeking to overthrow his brother Artaxerxes II, the great king of Persia, hired Greek hoplite mercenaries to help him make his claim for power. Among these Greek mercenaries was Xenophon, who wrote the *Anabasis,* an eyewitness account of the campaign and the retreat of 10,000 Greek mercenaries after Cyrus led them deep into Babylonia against his brother. When Cyrus was slain by his brother's forces, the Greeks were left leaderless deep inside Persia, but they rallied and made a daring return to Greece.

Sparta soon found itself at war with Persia. The march of the 10,000 may have wrongly convinced Sparta that Persia was weak and ripe for the taking. Sparta's war with Persia strained its resources and produced little. Moreover, Sparta's entanglements in Greece and Asia heightened tensions within Spartan society. A few Spartans had grown rich from Sparta's imperial ventures, but many citizens had become poorer and lost their citizenship rights. The anger of the newly disenfranchised led to a conspiracy against the established order in 397 BCE, but it was detected and suppressed. Three years later a naval venture of the Spartans at Cnidus off the coast of Asia Minor failed and the Spartans abandoned their Asian interests. Back in Greece, an alliance of Corinth, Thebes, Athens, and Argos allied against Sparta in the Corinthian War (395–387 BCE). Sparta won all the battles, but was unable to maintain its authority and slowly withdrew to its Peloponnesian homeland, where its power was now largely to be confined.

Following Sparta's retreat, the Athenians rebuilt the walls of their city, restored their navy, and re-established their maritime interests. Athens then allied with Persia against the Spartans, but it was Persia that imposed a peace of sorts upon Greece in 387 BCE at the end of the Corinthian War. Amid the shifting alliances of the early fourth century BCE, Athens also helped its old enemy Thebes to free itself from Spartan control. Thebes then made a play of its own over the next decade to assert not only its freedom from Sparta, but also its dominance in Greece. Thebes rejected the age-old claim of Sparta and Athens to be the two chief city-states of Greece. To the surprise of the ancient world, the outnumbered Thebans under their brilliant general Epaminondas defeated the Spartans at Leuctra in 371 BCE. The next year Epaminondas invaded Laconia. Sparta was in dire straits. Its citizen population was small and its older economic system of small land holdings was weak. Forced to relax its traditional way of life, Sparta continued to decline.

By the 360s BCE Thebes was in conflict with Athens, Sparta, and other Greek city-states. At the Battle of Mantinea in 362 BCE, Thebes prevailed, but Epaminondas was killed. With the great general dead, Theban dominance passed.

The Rise of Philip of Macedon

Watching the unfolding chaos in Greece was Philip of Macedon. Macedonia was a rough and fairly uncivilized part of greater Greece where blood feuds still destabilized society and the people spoke a dialect of Greek almost unrecognizable to the sophisticated Athenian ear. The Macedonians worshipped the wine god Dionysus and the royal dynasty claimed to be descended from the legendary heroes Achilles and Herakles (Hercules). Macedonian kings ruled both the civilized coastal areas of the Macedonian Sea north of Thessaly and the less civilized hill country of Illyria.

Philip was a member of the royal house but had spent his youth as a hostage in Thebes. There he had learned Theban military tactics and befriended Epaminondas. In 359 BCE, only twenty-four years old and back in Macedonia, Philip became the guardian of his nephew, the young Macedonian king. Philip moved quickly to remove his rivals and foreign threats. He refashioned the Macedonian army and moved against Thrace, whose great attraction was its gold mines. Before long Philip replaced his nephew, took the title of king, and set about subduing Macedonia.

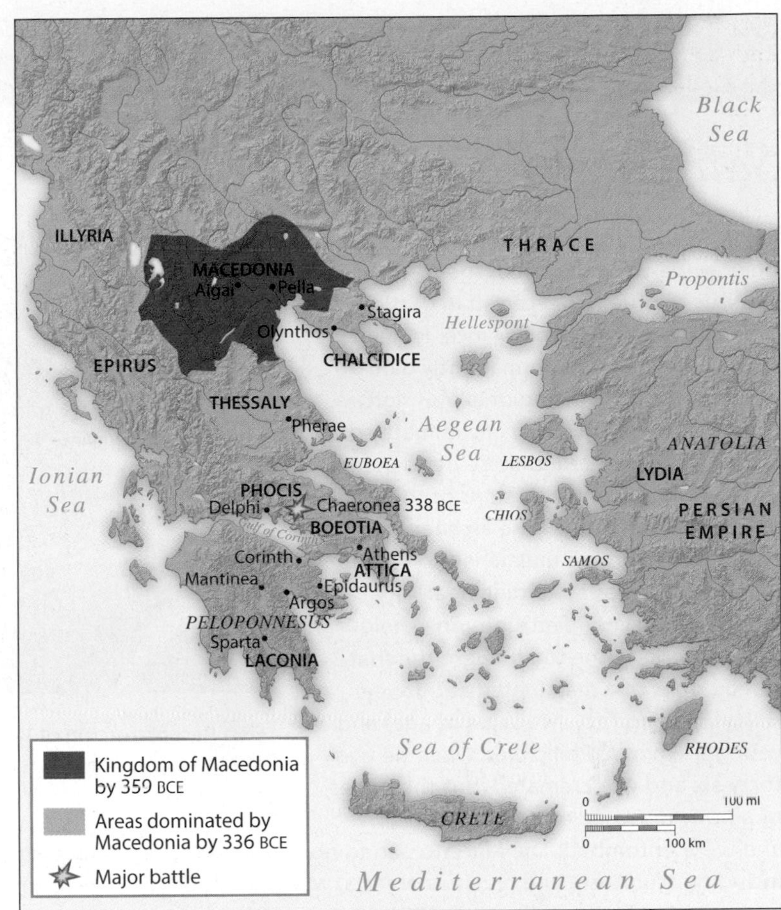

MAP 3.1 | Macedonian Expansion, 359–336 BCE
Philip II consolidated Macedonia and then moved south into Greece, defeating the combined forces of those resisting his invasion at the Battle of Chaeronea. ***What geographic and historical advantages and disadvantages did the kingdom of Macedonia have? Why was Philip's natural direction of Macedonian expansion south? Why was southern Greece such a prized possession for Philip?***

Philip sought the impossible: to unite all of Greece under his control. Against him stood a resurgent Athens, again with a powerful navy, the prospect of internal problems at home in Macedonia, and the abiding threat posed by Persia. Philip, however, had cunning and immense ambition on his side. He professionalized the Macedonian army into a formidable force, tapping into the large manpower resources of the Macedonian tribes he had subdued. He perfected the Macedonian phalanx, a rectangular body of infantry armed with eighteen-foot-long pikes (called *sarissa*), rather than short spears, and flanked by an impressive cavalry that helped to turn the tide in battles. Philip waged an ancient version of total war. He was prepared to fight summer and winter, night and day, to surprise the enemy when he could, to chase down and kill fleeing enemies, and to employ siege engines to demolish city walls. With gold from his Thracian conquests, Philip had the financial resources to support extensive war. Of greatest advantage to him, however, was the continuing disunity of the Greek city-states to the south. Philip moved against his southern neighbors, and by 352 BCE the Macedonians were engaged in conflict in the Peloponnesus (Map 3.1).

The Great Orators Demosthenes and Isocrates Part Ways

One of the first Athenians to become alarmed by Philip's aggression was the orator Demosthenes. His father, a prosperous Athenian furniture maker, died when Demosthenes was young. Inheriting little, he took up the study of oratory and the law. Since he had a weak voice, he reputedly trained his voice by filling his mouth with pebbles and made speeches in front of mirrors to perfect a rather flashy style of presentation. In time, he became a powerful orator in the Athenian assembly. Before other Athenians noticed, he labeled Philip an enemy of Athens, who must be stopped before it was too late. To this end, he wrote a series of speeches called the *Philippics* against the king of Macedonia. The Athenians admired the speeches but ignored the warning.

The orator Isocrates was older than Demosthenes and had seen the continuing chaos of Greek affairs and the failure of the autonomous city-state model of Greece.

INVESTIGATING THE PAST

Searching for Philip's Face

To his contemporaries, Philip of Macedon's body was a visual record of the many wounds that he had received in battle: his collarbone shattered by a lance, lame in his right leg, an arm permanently damaged, and, most striking of all, his right eye lost to an arrow. His consummate critic Demosthenes regarded these permanent disfigurements as visible signs of the king's lust for power. In 1977 the archaeologist Manolis Andronikos unearthed some unplundered tombs at Vergina near Aigai, where the Macedonian kings once held court. In one of the tombs were the shattered bones of a man (dated as between thirty-five and fifty-five years of age) and a younger woman. Philip died when he was forty-six and was cremated, but the bones of a body disposed of in that way survived and were entombed. The Macedonian tomb treasures, including sculptures and precious objects, were exhibited in the United States in the early 1980s. But were the skeletal remains of Tomb II Philip's? Circumstantial evidence suggested that they were. A Manchester, England, team confirmed the hypothesis; the damage to the skull was consistent with the reported injury to Philip's face. Two reconstructions of the face of the man circulated, one based on the assumption that the right eye had been untreated and a later one corrected according to Pliny the Elder's ancient report that Philip's doctor had so treated Philip's face after the loss of his eye that he was not disfigured. In the tomb a small ivory head of a bearded man bearing some similarity to known coin portraits of Philip seemed to match the reconstructed face of the king. So far, so good. The world at long last had a "real" image of King Philip that made the past visible.

First Reconstruction of Philip of Macedon's Head

Investigating the past, however, is never quite that easy. Paleoanthropologist Antonis Bartsiokas pointed out that the male skull showed no dramatic damage and that the skeleton lacked evidence of Philip's other reported injuries. Other scholars argued that the objects found in Tomb II came from a period well after Philip's death. Who then was the man whose face was reconstructed? The current thinking is that it belongs to a son of Philip, Philip III Arrhidaeus, who was reportedly poisoned to death by the mother of Alexander the Great in 317 BCE. In the search for Philip's face, the interplay of bones and written records has been revealing. The identification and reconstruction of Philip's face were guided not by bones alone, but by reading the bones in the light of the information contained in written records. Making the distant dead more immediate to us is an admirable but elusive goal. In the end, however, words may win out, if we know how to read them.

QUESTIONS | ***What is to be gained by knowing what celebrated historical figures looked like? What are the dangers? How should a truly scientific approach to historical facial reconstruction proceed?***

When Philip arrived in Greece, Isocrates wrote him a letter that circulated widely. In it, he called upon Philip to unite Greece and lead it against Persia. For Isocrates, the greatest threat to the future well-being of Greece came not from Philip, but from Persia. Demosthenes harkened back to the glories of the Golden Age and Athenian independence. Isocrates looked beyond Greece to the wider world and the rightful place of Greeks in it. In the two orators, we can dimly see the division into the old Greece and the new, Pericles and Alexander, the Hellenic and the Hellenistic.

Philip and the Macedonians Take Greece

By 352 BCE, Philip had amassed his forces in Thrace, just outside of Greece, and Athens was alarmed. Philip presented himself as a Greek and a friend of Athens, but few Athenians were reassured. The democrats of Athens had finally realized that absolute monarchs of Philip's kind should be regarded with suspicion. They formed alliances with other Greek peoples against Philip, but these ended in disaster. Philip took the city of Olynthus, destroyed it, and reduced its people to slavery. Athens opened negotiations with Philip and finally in 346 BCE struck a peace accord with him that lasted for five years. During those years, Philip insinuated himself into Greek affairs, becoming president of the great festival at Delphi, an archon of Thessaly, and a member of the great Greek council. Athens, however, remained wary and, after many intrigues against Philip's interests and the continual defamation of his claims and character by Demosthenes, provoked a war. The dispute was decided at the Battle of

Chaeronea in August 338 BCE. The Athenians, Thebans, Corinthians, and Phocians assembled a considerable army, but Philip had some 30,000 infantry and several thousand cavalry under the command of his son Alexander. Reports suggest that it was the cavalry that defeated the Theban line, which was critical to the Greek formation, and turned the battle into a Macedonian victory. Thousands of Athenians either died or were captured. Demosthenes was among those who fled.

Power over Greece now passed to the Macedonians. Philip punished Thebes for its treachery but still sought to pacify Athens. He returned the bodies of the fallen Athenians to their city, promised to free captured Athenians, and granted the city some of its traditional territories. Athens erected a statue to Philip, and even Demosthenes had to concede that Philip had treated Athens leniently. Philip established a Hellenic Confederacy that Athens and the other city-states were compelled to join. Sparta resisted, but Philip attacked Laconia and further reduced Sparta's already diminished territory. The Macedonians controlled the Confederacy and Philip soon announced his grand agenda to invade Persia, a plan that inspired few of the Confederacy's members. Philip allowed the Greek cities to remain relatively autonomous but positioned three Macedonian garrisons in Greece to keep the peace.

The Assassination of Philip

By 336 BCE, Philip had already sent an advance party into Asia Minor as a prelude to his Persian campaign. He had also married again, this time to a young noblewoman who might supply him with more heirs. He had married six times previously, including to Olympias, the dynamic mother of Alexander. Olympias and her son seem to have been worried by the implications of the new marriage and the prospect of more heirs to the throne, for they withdrew from the Macedonian court.

Philip's assassination, as with so many similar events in history, is a muddle of competing conspiracy theories, often created by contemporaries for their own advantage (to blame a rival, divert attention away from themselves, and so on). What we do know is that in October 336 BCE, Philip was killed by one of his bodyguards. The philosopher Aristotle claimed that the assassin was working out a personal grudge against the king, but the assassin killed the king at a wedding party and may not have acted alone. Several horses were waiting to carry the assassin(s) away. During his escape the assassin tripped before reaching his horse and was slain on the spot; the other bodyguards were cleared of involvement. A diviner was crucified for having identified good omens for a day that turned out so disastrously.

Philip's death pleased many. The Athenians awarded a crown to the assassin and Demosthenes rejoiced. The Persians, who knew of the planned invasion, doubtless thought that they had been spared the trouble of resisting Philip. Even Alexander and Olympias probably felt that their futures were more secure after Philip's death. Yet none of these reactions necessarily make any of these players party to the plot to assassinate Philip. His death may simply have been the result of a personal grievance, as Aristotle thought.

Philip has had the sad historical fate of being overshadowed by a brilliant son and dogged by the defamation of Demosthenes. Yet Philip shaped the Macedonian and Hellenistic future. After centuries of squabbling, the Greek city-states were finally forced to unite under his authority. Philip had fashioned the most powerful and dynamic army in Greece and pointed it toward Asia.

The Cultural Turn from Classical to Hellenistic

Before Alexander entered Asia, the culture of Greece was already turning away from the classical values of order, due proportion, perfection, and civic identity admired in the Athenian Golden Age. People began to doubt that answers could be found or that essential questions were worth asking. In the transition from classical Greek (Hellenic) to Hellenistic culture, particularism and individualism replaced the concentration on collective or universal human values that had characterized the culture of Golden Age Athens. In drama and comedy, philosophy, religion, and medicine, the thinkers of the post–Peloponnesian War era began to look in new directions, which better reflected the concerns of the new age.

Was Socrates a fish out of water or part of a great cultural turn and, if so, how and why?

From Poetry to Prose

The Peloponnesian War had undermined the confident certainties of the Athenians and the polis-centrism of the Greeks. The tragedy of classical Greek tragedy was that it did not outlive the great war. The complex social and historical conditions that had fostered tragedy and a rich civic life had changed. After the war, there was little surplus money or time to mount elaborate tragic plays, but the real reason may have been a lack of Athenian interest in examining themselves or their troubled times, as Socrates foresaw.

The last of the great tragic playwrights was Euripides (c. 485–406 BCE). He had rarely won the outright approval of the Athenian audiences that saw his plays. Late in his life, threatened with prosecution for impiety, Euripides abandoned Athens for the safer and more remunerative confines of the Macedonian court. There he wrote the *Bacchants*, in which the young rationalist Pentheus, who does not believe in the gods, is ripped limb from limb and eaten by his mother and the other bacchants (revelers and worshippers of the wine god) in ecstatic devotion to Dionysus. There is no escape for Pentheus; gods will be gods and will do as they wish. The *Bacchants* was not presented until after Euripides's death and would have disturbed an Athenian audience. The *Bacchants* led Athenians to a brutal place beyond civilization, the home of a non-Olympian, wine-soaked god, who was nonrational and willful. Euripides and the Athenians, battered by unending war, had come to doubt the underlying beliefs and structures of civilized life. Athens and its poets soon gave up on tragedy entirely.

Scene of a Farce A fourth-century BCE image of a theater scene on a wine vessel. Hellenistic audiences loved these comedies of absurd domestic situations.

Comedy faced the same dilemma. There were fewer resources available to costume the actors and little interest or courage under either an oligarchic regime or its fledgling democratic successor to poke fun at politicians on the great issues of the day. Like tragedy, Old Comedy disappeared, but it survived in the new forms of Middle and New Comedy. Aristophanes (c. 445–c. 385 BCE), the great wit of Old Comedy, was a transitional figure in the emergence of the new comedic art. He wrote only two plays over the last twenty years of his life after the fall of Athens. The *Parliament of Women* (*Ecclesiazusae*) from 392 BCE takes up a theme similar to that of his famous *Lysistrata*, rule by women and the common holding of property. The new play, however, lacked Aristophanes's former sparkle and wicked wit: there is no chorus and little that is bawdy or politically pointed in the play. His last play, *Plutus* (the god of riches), continued the playwright's late preoccupation with money. In this play about fickle fate and life's fundamental unfairness, wealth falls to the wrong people. Aristophanes reduced the characters to familiar types: an honest man, an old woman, her young lover, a funny god. In *Plutus* the outlines of New Comedy were emerging: absurd situations, stock characters, and harmless apolitical fun. It was this New Comedy that Menander (342–c. 291 BCE) would perfect. Though only one of his many plays, *The Grouch* (*Dyskolos*), survives intact, he was the acknowledged master of the form. Said one Byzantine critic, "Oh Menander, Oh life, which imitated which?" Hellenistic men and women found in New Comedy a domestic mirror to reflect their ordinary lives and the new realities and anxieties of the Hellenistic Ages in which they lived.

Socrates the Charismatic Individualist

He was plain to the point of ugliness—pug nosed, balding, squat—and proud of it. His background was undistinguished: his father was a stonemason and his mother, a midwife. Yet by force of personality and intellect Socrates (c. 470–399 BCE) became the western world's first great individualist. His individualism types him, as it did Euripides, as a transitional figure, one who lived in the Golden Age but died in and partly fashioned and reflected the newly forming Hellenistic one.

Socrates was a character so memorable that few could forget him. In a city-state dominated by collective civic values and sameness, Socrates stood out as different. He was a charismatic figure for many, a controversial one for most. He wrote nothing himself, though others talked about him a great deal. We learn about him through the writings of his students Xenophon and Plato, who recorded their subjective memories of him. In fact, we know more about him than we do about Plato. He fought with distinction on behalf of Athens in the Peloponnesian War, served as president of the Athenian assembly, and refused to carry out the order of the Thirty Tyrants to lead a just man to his execution.

He was already a controversial figure in 423 BCE when Aristophanes lampooned him in *The Clouds*. The Socrates of the play presides over a school, the Thinkery, that teaches students how to win arguments. In the play, Socrates is concerned chiefly with the natural world and cosmology, as the real Socrates once was, and descends from the heavens (or roof beams) in a basket. He doubts the gods and the certitude of any truth. In the play, an aged Athenian father wants his lay-about son to train at the school so that he can successfully argue his case against pressing creditors. The son, instead, turns his argument-twisting skills against his father, physically throttles him, fully justifies it, and offers to assault his mother in the same way. The alarmed father responds by burning down the Thinkery, sending Socrates fleeing in disgrace through the streets of Athens. Aristophanes's caricature presents Socrates as a clever teacher who believed in little, practiced a relativism whereby weaker arguments can defeat stronger ones, cast his spell over the impressionable young, overthrew family order, and disrespected the gods.

Socrates Socrates as portrayed in the third century BCE in Alexandria. He is squat, bald, and every inch an unforgettable character.

The real Socrates had street presence. Students and those who wished to discuss important ideas knew where to find him. He did not charge to impart wisdom and stoutly maintained that he had none or rather that his wisdom consisted in knowing how little he knew. Instead, he questioned those who claimed to know something, challenging their core assumptions and claims to expertise. The irony of studying Socrates is that we cannot put questions to the great questioner since we have only the reports of others about him, and we can be none too sure about those. There can be little doubt that he was a great individualist and openly questioned conventional thinking. He doubted the value of democracy, associated with rich young men, and trusted his own personal god (*daimon*) or inner voice. His critics and a public who had only heard of him thought, as did Aristophanes, that Socrates was a dangerous nuisance in Athens.

Little wonder that he was put on trial in 399 BCE. Athenian democracy had just been restored a few years earlier, and Socrates was charged with impiety for introducing new gods and for corrupting young minds. All Athens knew that some of his students had turned against Athens: Alcibiades had led the Sicilian misadventure and turned traitor, and Charmides and Critias had been among the Thirty Tyrants and had been executed when their tyranny failed and democracy was restored. No friend of Athenian democracy, Socrates had the annoying habit of questioning all accepted truths in his pursuit of abstract moral truths: what is the "good" once all the things to which goodness is attached (such as a good meal, a good man, or a good idea) have been stripped away? The **Socratic method** of teaching consisted of asking questions and drawing forth answers from students and others. The method produced no positive answers but cleared away false assumptions. The technique was hard on those questioned, since it exposed their core convictions as unsound. At his trial, Socrates tried to use his method of close questioning to expose false Athenian assumptions about him and themselves. But his questions only further angered the jurors, who found him guilty. Even then the jury was prepared to let him escape into exile, as others had, but Socrates chose to drink poison and die, wishing until the end, as he said, to be a great gadfly pestering Athens. (See Back to the Source at the end of this chapter.)

Philosophy and science had not been native Athenian strengths during the Golden Age of the fifth century. They were, however, central to the Hellenistic Age. Socrates was shaped by the Golden Age, but in the difficult days at the end of the Peloponnesian War he had refused to act against his conscience when called upon to do so by the state. His radical individualism belonged not to the collective civic values of classical Athens, which he challenged, but to the emerging First Hellenistic Age. The relentless force of his method of examining and undermining accepted truths was hard for the average Athenian to bear, for in the end Socrates left them with less certainty—he stripped away their comfortable beliefs, leaving little in their place except a method leading to truth that few were brave enough to take up.

Plato as Hellenistic Thinker and Hellenizer

Plato (c. 429–347 BCE) was in many respects the exact opposite of his master Socrates: he was an aristocrat, wealthy, a voluminous writer, and founder of a school. His method and training, however, came from Socrates, but with one great difference. Although Socrates rigorously questioned accepted truths, he rarely if ever arrived at a satisfactory definition of the truth. Plato, as he aged and moved beyond his master, became a great synthesizer. In the logical sequence of the syllogism, consisting of a thesis, antithesis (its opposite), and synthesis (the resolution), Plato often arrived at the final step.

What we may not always fully appreciate in our study of his ideas is just how fine and supple a writer Plato was. It is he who brought Socrates alive for us. His re-creation of the trial, life, and thought of his master is utterly engaging, whereas Xenophon's description fails to reveal the epic dimension of Socrates's thought or personality. Most of Plato's twenty-six dialogues are not just philosophical discussions, but moving works of art filled with unforgettable characters and believable scenes of interaction between real people, with Socrates almost always at the center of the discourse.

Plato belonged primarily to the First Hellenistic Age, even though he may not seem to. His dialogues are set in the Golden Age of fifth-century BCE Athens, but he composed them in the fourth century BCE, well after the Peloponnesian War. Plato died not long before the Battle of Chaeronea in 338, when Philip of Macedon took control of Greece. Not only did Plato work in the new world being shaped by Greek instability and the rise of Philip and the Macedonians, but he had a more cosmopolitan focus than Socrates, who had preferred to remain in the streets of Athens. Though doubts linger about the so-called Letters of Plato, which claim that Plato visited places as distant as Egypt, he did visit Sicily several times to advise its Hellenistic tyrants.

Around 385 BCE, Plato established an Academy outside the walls of Athens. Though philosophical issues were discussed at the Academy, his school's primary mission was to train statesmen. Plato was much concerned with politics, with good rule and good rulers, topics taken up in the *Republic* and the *Laws,* two of his most famous works. His notion of the philosopher-king or wise ruler reveals something of Plato's concern with the problems of the transitional age in which he lived. Like Socrates, he was no lover of democracy. Plato believed that the state would be best ruled by a wise man. As such, the events in Sicily probably disappointed him since the tyrants he advised there were hardly paragons of wisdom and order; they stole, assassinated, and acted rashly in the pursuit of power. Plato's focus remained primarily fixed on the poleis of Greece, but his thought and actions were moving in new directions, as he does in the *Timaeus,* which includes a report on Egypt and its long history and treats the cosmos and natural history, employing mathematics to reveal the symphonic structure of the universe.

Though Plato's philosophy of the Ideas or Forms derived from Socrates's search for ethical abstractions such as the Good, it fitted the search for order and absolutes in the emerging Hellenistic Ages. In the *Republic,* he explained through the fable of the Cave the essence of his notion, one grounded in the Socratic search for the underlying truth of things. A man in a cave sees images cast on the wall and assumes that he is seeing real things when, in fact, all that he is seeing are images of the real things, not the things themselves. Similarly, in our daily lives, he thought, we mistake the things we sense (both material and conceptual) for realities. For Plato the Forms or Ideas are the real things: invisible to the senses but perceived by the mind as perfect, eternal, and divine. The material world obstructs our knowledge of truth, goodness, justice, and beauty. Thus Plato moves readers from the perceptible world to an unseen and imperceptible world that is perfect and true. That world lies beyond mere conjecture and opinion in the realm of knowledge and the mind.

Several attributes mark Plato as an early Hellenistic thinker: his interest in the wider Mediterranean, his preoccupation with the politics of rule by a single man rather than the people, and his drive to achieve resolution or synthesis in the pursuit of truth. He was an influential agent of Hellenization and had a formative impact on shaping the thought of the Hellenistic Age. Virtually everything he wrote has survived, which is a testament to the popularity of his dialogues and the importance accorded them in Alexandria. Even the stories of his travels, whether created or real, reinforce the image of him as a Hellenizer. Hebrews found in Plato's teachings a vehicle for explaining the theology of their Bible, notions of the soul, the divine, and the eternal beyond a material present. Cynics, Stoics, and the Romans received their impression of Socrates and their philosophical outlook from Plato, whose Academy lasted for almost a thousand years. Plato's writings became a touchstone not only of Hellenistic thought but of all western thought.

Aristotle the Great Particularist

Aristotle (384–322 BCE), born in the northern Greek city of Stagira, was the son of a physician who served the Macedonian king (Philip of Macedon's father) at Pella. Aristotle was orphaned early but apparently was reared at the Macedonian court and probably knew the young Philip. Amid the succession battles that disturbed that court, the seventeen-year-old Aristotle was sent to study at Plato's Academy, where he remained almost until the death of his master. The Macedonian invasion of Greece made Aristotle's presence in Athens difficult; he had Macedonian connections and sympathies not shared by Demosthenes and many Athenians. In 343 BCE, Philip invited Aristotle to tutor his son Alexander. As Plato had with the Sicilian tyrants, Aristotle accepted the challenge of shaping a young prince in the hope of producing a wise ruler. Full engagement in the politics of the mid-fourth century was, however, dangerous. One of Aristotle's patrons and mentors, Hermeias, who had married his sister, was captured, tortured to reveal the secrets of Philip, and crucified by the Persians. Throughout the war years, Aristotle remained in Macedonia. After Philip's triumph at Chaeronea, Aristotle returned to Athens and opened his own school at the Lyceum, where he remained until Alexander's death. At that time, Athens, venting its anti-Macedonian resentments, charged the philosopher with impiety. Aristotle left the city and died the next year.

Aristotle was more interested in natural philosophy or science than were Socrates and Plato. He had arrived at the Academy when Plato was away in Sicily for three years and gravitated toward the scientists studying there. Aristotle's family was originally connected with Ionia, the home of Greek science, and his father was a physician. Aristotle wrote dialogues early in his career, but they are now lost and he later abandoned the form and wrote purely expository treatises. Aristotle revered Plato but never slavishly followed his teachings. He seems never to have accepted the concept of the Ideas or Forms and urged Platonists to abandon the Cave and to settle down to the contemplation of the natural world.

Aristotle's early works such as the *Categories* and *Topics* take up the dialectical issue of how best to distinguish and describe things. He wrote on a wide range of topics: nature, physics, cosmology, animals (including their generation, movement, and respiration), meteorology, metaphysics, ethics, the soul, and literature. Unlike Plato, Aristotle sought to be comprehensive, systematically ordering a topic in all its details. His thought was primarily logical and analytical. In his orderly classification of particulars, Aristotle was the chief thinker of the First Hellenistic Age.

Aristotle was also a Hellenistic political thinker. He leaned toward Isocrates's view of a greater Greece. He was suspicious of Persia, supported the ambitions of Philip and Alexander, and looked to the triumph of Greek values throughout the wider world. His late work, the *Politics,* systematically examines the different constitutions of the city-states of Greece. Aristotle's political views changed with the times and, as an old man, he was hard pressed to keep up with the world Alexander was making. He may have been particularly perplexed by Alexander's blurring of the distinction between Greeks and barbarians. The latter he regarded as naturally suited to slavery. According to Aristotle, slaves were either slaves by convention (those forced into slavery by war and seizure) or by nature (those whose intellects lacked the capacity for human deliberation and so required a master to supply direction). He viewed human beings as social creatures who gather together in families and city-states based on complementary contributions to unified and useful human units. Although Aristotle believed that both men and women contributed as active and deliberative agents of the greater social good, he thought that men were more virtuous and contributed more to society because they could transform their deliberations into action. Aristotle died before finishing his great political treatise, but Alexander's career and premature death made all political thinking speculative by the 320s BCE.

Together Socrates, Plato, and Aristotle shaped the basics of Hellenistic Greek thought, including its promise and limitations. But Aristotle's practical concern with the particulars of the material world, with the single-man rule of kings and tyrants, and with analytical thought may have made him the one most representative of the thought of the emerging Hellenistic world.

Early Hellenistic Anxieties: Asclepius and Hippocrates

The Hellenistic Ages were a great period of religious belief, but one driven by individual needs. If the polis had once protected and defined a sense of community among city-state dwellers in Greece, Hellenistic men and women now needed to look after themselves, both materially and spiritually. The polis was not there to provide them with the same protection and sense of belonging. Kings and tyrants ruled huge territories and had their own compelling interests. Almost overnight the world had become vast and overwhelming for the Greeks. Hellenistic men and women often suffered from a feeling of alienation and loss, and so turned not just to philosophy, but to religion and medicine for individual relief and comfort.

At the end of Plato's *Phaedo,* Socrates asks his friend Crito to sacrifice a rooster to the god Asclepius on his behalf. They were Socrates's final words. Asclepius was a god of healing, whose cult became extremely popular in the Hellenistic Ages. Hundreds of shrines to him were erected, the most prominent ones at Epidaurus and Pergamum. Individuals sought to forge personal connections with the divine Asclepius. In times of personal crisis, the sick and needy slept in his temples in the hope that they would be visited by the god in their dreams and receive advice about how to cure their physical ailments and solve their spiritual crises. Believers paid tribute to the god and his healing gift with inscriptions placed on stele (standing stone tablets) outside the shrines. The remarkable testimonies left at Epidaurus tell of five-year pregnancies, children born walking and talking, and miraculous cures of the blind. These stories may surprise

Hippocrates or Asclepius Treating a Woman Both Hippocrates and Asclepius were legendary healers of the sick, so there should be little surprise that we can't be sure just which one is shown healing an ill woman on this Hellenistic relief. Both were heroes and exemplary physicians to the people of an age concerned about illness and physical well-being.

modern readers, who too often think of the ancient Greeks as supreme rationalists and their religion as one of harmless myths. But, despite the rise of sophisticated philosophies, the Greeks continued to hold irrational beliefs in their daily and religious lives that may have assumed increased importance and provided greater comfort in a searching and anxious age. The devotion to Asclepius may suggest just how needy and worried about themselves some Hellenistic men and women were.

The Hellenistic Ages were also a golden age of Greek medicine, but falling into two phases, an early one best represented by Hippocrates and a later one located in Alexandria. Hippocrates (c. 460 BCE–c. 377 BCE) and Socrates were contemporaries. Little is known about the most famous of ancient doctors. Though it is difficult to distinguish the genuine works of Hippocrates from those of his disciples and the various reworkings of his treatises at Alexandria, it seems beyond dispute that Hippocrates was the first scientific physician in that he looked for physical causes for physical ailments. He was, however, interested in the whole body as opposed to its particular problems. The followers of Hippocrates, however, found the Hellenistic Ages fertile ground for an active physical medicine to address the many physical complaints people had.

CHRONOLOGY Alexander's March into History

DATE (BCE)	EVENT
336	The Assassination of Philip II
335	Destroys Thebes
334	Crosses Hellespont
334	Battle of Granicus River
Early 333	Visits Gordium
October 333	Battle of Issus
332	Takes Tyre in Phoenicia
Late 332	Reaches Egypt
331	Founds Alexandria
October 331	Battle of Gaugamela
330	Burning of Persepolis
330–325	Travels east
326	Crosses Indus River
324	Returns to Babylon
323	Dies after a royal banquet

The Opening of the Second Hellenistic Age: Alexander's Wider World

The Greeks were not unfamiliar with Asia, the Middle East, and Africa, as the experiences of Herodotus and Xenophon prove. Contact with the Persian Empire had played a part in shaping the identities of the Greek poleis in territorial, cultural, and ethnic terms. Barbarians were, for the many Greeces, peoples who spoke a language that was not Greek and sounded like nonsense (*bar-bar-bar*). At the time of Philip of Macedon, the Persian Empire remained the one great threat to Greece's survival. Whereas the Greeks had exhausted themselves in the Peloponnesian War, the Persians had regained much of what they had lost in the Persian Wars. Yet there was still something fragile about the vast Persian Empire, as the Spartans had suspected. Alexander the Great would go to Persia to settle old scores but ended by conquering a great part of the Near East and Asia and created a new and wider world for the Greeks to inhabit.

How was the invasion of the eastern Mediterranean world, the Near East, and Asia more a reflection of Alexander's dynamism and drive than a Greek mission to conquer and civilize the "barbarian other"?

Greece after Philip's Assassination

Only twenty years old when his father Philip died, Alexander was already an accomplished soldier, having distinguished himself at the Battle of Chaeronea, but his future was uncertain. If Philip had lived another decade or two, the importance of Alexander and his scheming mother would probably have passed. Persia would still have been invaded, but by Philip, who might well have limited his campaign to more achievable, short-term goals. Within Macedonian circles there were other claims to the Macedonian throne than just Alexander's. Invoking his right to avenge the death of his father, Alexander purged his enemies, and his mother Olympias arranged the murder of Philip's last wife and her child—they were roasted alive.

When Philip was assassinated, Greece thought that its Macedonian problem was over. Athens celebrated Philip's death but took little notice of young Alexander, repeating the mistake it had made earlier when it had ignored Philip's rise. Demosthenes, despite mourning the recent death of his wife, put on his finest clothes to parade through the streets of Athens in celebration of Philip's fall, but he should have known better. Neither the orator nor Greece had taken the measure of the ambitious young king who, within two years, suppressed a revolt against his rule by Thessaly, reasserted Macedonian control over Greece, and announced his intention to carry out his father's plan to invade Persia. Alexander first led

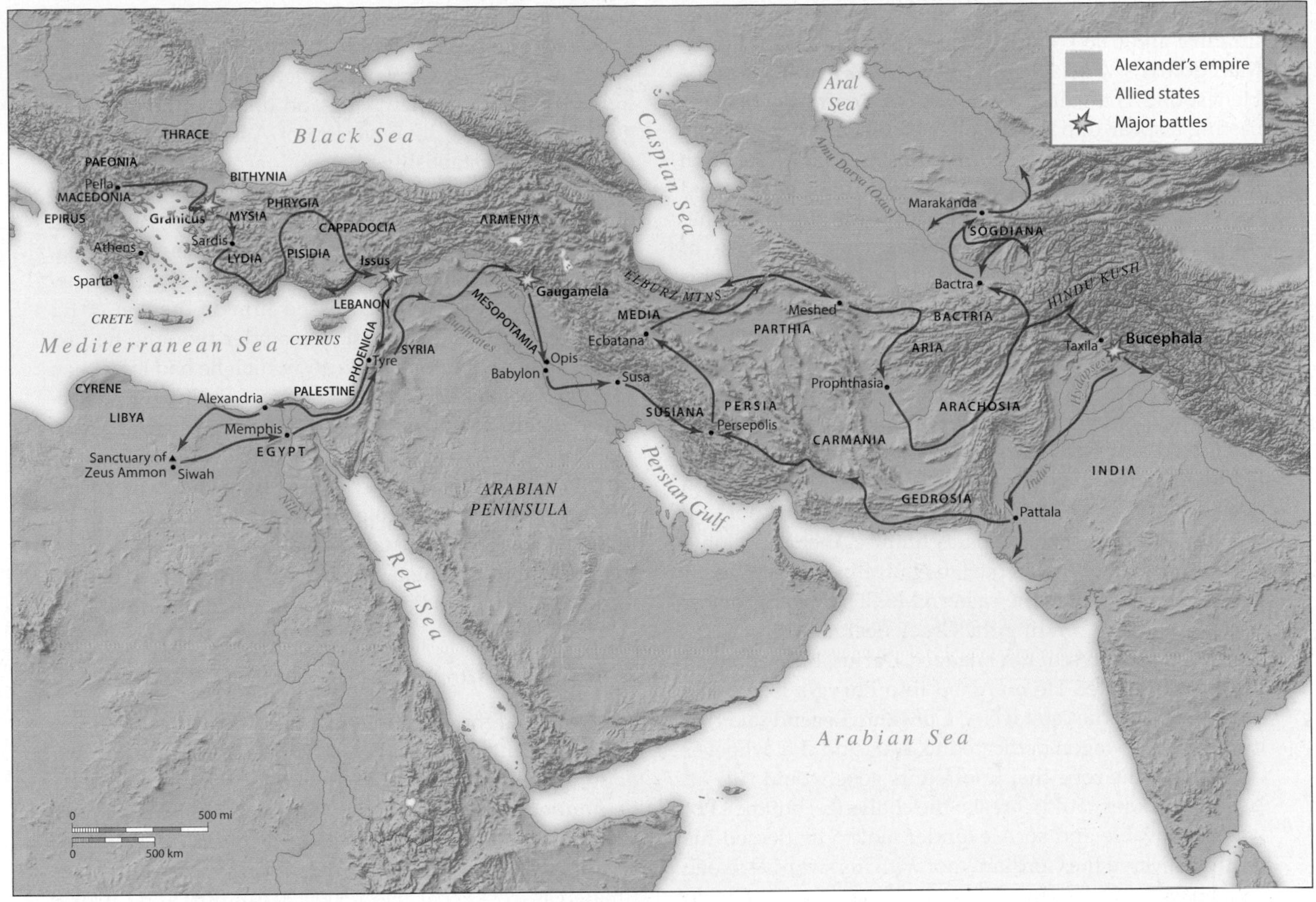

MAP 3.2 | Alexander's Empire and March into Asia, 334–323 BCE

In 334 BCE, with Greece secure, Alexander set out with his army for Persia, Egypt, and, finally, India. ***How far did Alexander and his troops travel over a decade? What explains the chronology and direction of his conquests? Where did he stop his eastward march and why? Why was Arabia the next land he wished to conquer?***

a campaign against the Tribali near the Danube to avenge an attack that they had once made upon his father. The campaign was unnecessary, but it served as a training exercise for his troops and a demonstration of Alexander's leadership. Hardly was the little war over when Thebes, with the moral support of Athens and the financial support of the Persians, revolted against Alexander's rule. Alexander rushed to the scene, defeated the Thebans, and enslaved most of its population. He then utterly destroyed the polis, preserving only the poet Pindar's ancestral home. The example made of Thebes was a powerful deterrent to any future Greek resistance to Alexander's power. Greece was now subdued, and Persia awaited his arrival.

Into Persia

A more prudent man than Alexander might have delayed his march into Persia, might have married and produced an heir before leaving on a perilous campaign, and might have more firmly secured his political control of Greece. But Alexander was Alexander, a twenty-two-year-old world winner who reputedly slept at night with a copy of Homer and a dagger beneath his pillow. Neither prudent politics nor ponderous reflection would deter him. He had a world to conquer, and his father had pointed him toward Persia.

Why Persia? The plan was Philip's, but both he and Alexander liked to claim that they were avenging Persia's assaults on Greece and the looting and burning of Athens during the Persian Wars. Alexander and his father were Hellenizing kings who saw the political advantages of placing themselves at the forefront of the Greek historical mission. Isocrates and others had maintained that Greece could never breathe easily as long as Persia, with its immense resources of men and money, threatened. Yet Alexander, like his father before him, was anxious to invade Persia for another, less noble reason. Alexander needed gold. The conquest of Greece had been costly for Philip, and his son had been forced to spend a great deal of money to keep his armies in the field and to buy support. Alexander needed not just glory, but gold from his Asian campaign (Map 3.2).

In 334 BCE, he assembled an army of almost 50,000 infantry and 6,000 cavalry, fewer than a quarter of them Macedonians. A sizable navy carried his army across the Hellespont. The young king was the first to step ashore, casting a spear into Asian soil, announcing symbolically that he intended to take Asia by force. Alexander's march into Asia also had a mythic dimension, since he repeated the symbolic deeds and religious dedications of the heroes and gods of the Greek past, particularly those of Herakles, as he went. His first battle was not with Darius III, the great king of Persia, but with one of his satraps (the governor of a region). The Persian army, which was slightly smaller than Alexander's, was divided almost equally between Persians and Greek mercenaries. On the day of the Battle of Granicus River, however, Alexander assembled only part of his army, less than 20,000 men. He led them across the river and into a battle that they won decisively. Then he turned to consolidating his hold on the coastal areas of the Persian Empire, including Ionia and Lydia. He did this in part to neutralize landing bases for the Persian fleet in the eastern Mediterranean, but lost his advantage by sending the Greek fleet home.

Alexander had still not engaged Darius, but he longed for that encounter. He marched into Phrygia in 333 BCE and headed for the capital city, Gordium. Legend said that it contained a wagon dedicated to Zeus and that whoever could untie the rope that knotted its yoke would rule all Asia. Alexander couldn't resist the challenge, but the knot was unmovable and so Alexander, not to be denied his destiny, severed the Gordian knot with his sword. Anyone could have done the same, but only Alexander dared to do so. Darius led a large army from Babylonia and engaged Alexander's forces at Issus in Cilicia. Though his army was outnumbered, Alexander concentrated his attack on Darius himself, which, as luck would have it, worked. Darius fled when the assault came too close and his huge army retreated in chaos. The Macedonians chased down thousands of Persian soldiers but failed to capture Darius. Alexander did seize Darius's rich baggage train and his family, which had been abandoned as the great king fled. Alexander treated them kindly, in essence replacing Darius as their protector and patron, and is supposed to have ordered them to learn Greek.

To Egypt and Godhood

Instead of pursuing Darius, Alexander moved along the coast westward to Syria, Lebanon, and the great prize of Egypt. He conquered Phoenicia out of fear that the Persians might attack him from behind, using Phoenicia as a base of operations. To avenge a grudge against the port city of Tyre, Alexander spent six months laying siege to the city. In the end, he destroyed much of the city, enslaved its population, and crucified thousands as a warning against resistance to his rule. He did much the same when Gaza refused to submit to him.

By 332 BCE, Alexander had reached Egypt, a land of endless fascination for the Greeks. Egypt was ancient, rich, and a home of the gods; it was also a distant and loose part of the greater Persian Empire. Egypt, pleased to be rid of Persian control, welcomed Alexander without a fight. He became its new king and honored the Egyptian gods. Throughout his invasion of Asia, Alexander was committed to establishing the evidence of his own divinity by exceeding what mere men could do and testing his own superhuman capacities. For this reason, he visited Siwah in Libya to consult the oracle of Zeus Ammon. There, at the famous oasis, Alexander entered the sanctuary where the priest addressed him as the son of Ra (Zeus to the Greeks). At last, Alexander thought, he had the proof of his personal divinity, which he had long been seeking. He was not merely the son of Philip, but the acknowledged son of the great god Zeus; ergo, he was a god. The god-king returned to the site of Alexandria, laid out the city, and set his architects and engineers to work. He also set about reorganizing the administration of Egypt, left garrisons in place, stationed a fleet of ships to guard the coast, and instituted a tax collection scheme. Then he retraced his steps to Persia and unfinished business.

Lord of Asia

Darius apparently made overtures toward Alexander, offering him territories west of the Euphrates and a daughter in marriage. But Alexander wanted more; he demanded Darius's outright surrender. Darius now knew that the impending battle was one for his empire and his life. He assembled a massive army, variously estimated as from 250,000 to 1,500,000 infantry and cavalry. Alexander's army consisted of 70,000 men. Moreover, this time Darius had no need for Greek mercenaries, but collected troops from his eastern lands. The battle took place at Gaugamela near a tributary of the Tigris River in 331 BCE. So large was Darius's army and so evident its formation that Alexander was able to plan his line of attack well in advance of the battle. His men withstood the charge of the Persian chariots, and eventually Alexander and the phalanx punched through the Persian front line and once again targeted Darius, who fled with Alexander in pursuit. Eventually Alexander halted the chase and led his men to Babylonia. Overjoyed to be free of Persian control, the Babylonians welcomed Alexander. The new lord of Asia retained the old Persian form of administrative control and moved on.

By the end of 331 BCE, Alexander and his troops were marching toward Susa and Persia proper. There he dined in Xerxes's palace, recovered ancient art removed from Greece during the Persian Wars, and took possession of the Persian treasury. But what Alexander wanted was Persepolis (Parsa), the great Persian capital, and so once again, after establishing a garrison of troops in Susa, he took to the road. Though the royal city surrendered to him, Alexander and his men had come for revenge and to settle the unfinished business of the Persian Wars of the previous century. They looted the city, assembling a vast array of riches. Alexander sent his gold on some seven

Alexander Turns the Great King of Persia A Pompeii mosaic captures the critical moment in the battle of Gaugamela in 331 BCE when Alexander, rushing forward on horseback on the left, forces the great king Darius to begin to turn his chariot around and to flee.

thousand camels to Susa for safekeeping. But the issue remained: what to do with the palace of Persepolis, now looted, but still a symbol of Persian greatness? Alexander was committed to two contradictory policies: the old commitment to avenge the burning of the Athenian Acropolis by destroying the symbol of Persian might and the new commitment to rule Asia with the support of the conquered Persians. The "accidental" destruction of the palace after a night of heavy Macedonian drinking satisfied both: the palace was destroyed, but Alexander, the lord of Asia, had not ordered its destruction and was said to have regretted the fire.

With the destruction of Persepolis, Alexander and his troops could have gone home with their goal achieved, but Darius was still on the run and plotting his return. In 330 BCE, Alexander's army set out to track him down. Darius was assembling a new army and hoped to reclaim his empire, but his support was weak in the far east of his empire and his reputation had suffered after the two defeats. With Alexander in hot pursuit, Darius's men overthrew the king and stabbed him to death. Alexander sent the body of the once great king back to Persepolis for a high state burial.

The Macedonians and Greeks may have thought that their daring adventure was now over, but Alexander wasn't finished just yet. Some troops did leave at that point, but the lord of Asia had the financial resources from his conquests to hire mercenaries to replace them and the foresight and practical need to begin training Asians for his army. The Greek and Macedonian troops forced to remain with him tried to persuade him to halt his eastward march, but Alexander argued that the murderers of Darius were still at large, that the new empire needed protecting, and that the campaign would be conducted quickly.

To the Indus

Alexander wanted to extend his empire to the far east, to India, which Greek geographers had convinced him could form a natural eastern border for his empire. To rule his new lands with more authority and native acceptance, Alexander was already adopting Asian customs. He wore both Greek and Asian dress, donned an Asian crown, employed Asian bodyguards, and allowed his new subjects to bow or prostrate themselves before him. His Macedonian men thought that Alexander had gone native, and they resented the transformation of their king. At a banquet, a general named Cleitus insulted Alexander for his oriental leanings and praised Philip. The inebriated lord of all Asia ran the defenseless man through with a pike. Several plots against Alexander's life by his Macedonian men and once loyal supporters surfaced. He could no longer trust even his old guard, but still Alexander pushed forward.

Alexander pursued the men who had betrayed Darius into Afghanistan and there established yet another city named after himself, Kandahar. He marched his troops through the Hindu Kush into Bactria, crossed the Oxus River, and entered Sogdiana. The Macedonians were forced to fight their way forward and then to deal with resistance behind them. By the summer of 328 BCE, Alexander was preparing to march to India (to lands today a part of Pakistan). After conquering Bactria, he married the Bactrian princess Roxane, the daughter of one of the princes he had defeated. Alexander's men grumbled that the marriage to a conquered foreign woman was beneath him.

Of more irritation to the Greco-Macedonians was prostration before Alexander. As the lord of Asia, Alexander permitted ritual bowing and groveling at his feet as a standard Asian custom, but soon expected it of his Macedonian troops, probably because he thought that, for the good of his army, his soldiers should be treated equally. He also believed that prostration before him constituted public acceptance of his divinity. His Macedonian old guard declined to perform prostration and there the matter rested; the Asians treated him as a supreme lord, the Greeks as a Greek king. By late 326 BCE, Alexander had marched into India, heading toward the Indus River, fighting native peoples along the way. At a tributary of the Indus, the ruler of Taxila, Porus, amassed a considerable army containing hundreds of elephants to resist the invaders. The Battle of Hydaspes River was a monumental contest, but again Alexander prevailed. Alexander made Porus his subordinate and left him in control of most of his land. Bucephala, Alexander's favorite horse, died after the campaign and Alexander founded a new city there and named it after the horse. Alexander led his men farther east, but the monsoon season was upon them and local resistance was mounting.

At the Hyphasis River, his generals advised him that it was time to end the campaign. Facing a mutiny, Alexander relented, erected monuments to the gods to mark the end of his eastward advance, and ordered the construction of a fleet. Even in retreat, Alexander wanted to explore India to the sea and so he proposed that part of his army should sail south on the Hydaspes to the Indus and thence to the Indian Ocean. A great part of the army under General Nearchus took to boats. They saw whales; were attacked by hippopotamuses, which are fiercely territorial; and sailed west to rejoin Alexander.

Alexander and the rest of his army crossed the deadly Gedrosian Desert on their return to Persia. Back in Babylonia he found that his appointed governors had become corrupt and abusive in his absence; most of them had probably doubted that Alexander would ever return from his eastern adventure. He executed some, reprimanded others, and ordered all to disband their private armies. The lord of Asia returned to Persepolis and Susa, where he married almost a hundred of his Macedonian officers to Iranian noble women. He also recognized the older relationships of 10,000 of his men to Asian women as legal marriages. There too he married two Persian princesses, the daughters of the defeated Darius and the previous great king. All of these marriages were less idealistic (the joining of the races) than pragmatic political moves on Alexander's part. He did not need to unite the races (and no Asians were sent to Greece to marry Greeks); however, he did need to rule Asia with the support of the native population, did need Asians in his army, and did want to discourage native resentment to his rule. Alexander wanted Persia to remain subservient while he contemplated his next campaign.

Arabia and Death

In early 324 BCE, Alexander was planning a new campaign, this one against Arabia, whose riches and spices attracted him. Moreover, Arabia had not submitted, even symbolically, to Alexander, which served as a pretext for the campaign. His troops, however, were not enthusiastic about the venture and mutinied at Opis. He executed the principal plotters, made a speech, and sought omens but could not rally his men. When he began promoting Persian officers to replace the Macedonian resisters, his men relented. Still they had never embraced Alexander's Asian customs in dress or ritual or the integration of native peoples in his empire and army.

By 323 BCE, Alexander was back in Babylonia, tending to his empire and small outbreaks of disorder. He was also waiting on the preparation of the fleet that would support the invasion of Arabia and later Carthage. Alexander was also beset by problems back in Greece. Demosthenes was stirring up trouble once again but was put on trial and exiled from Athens. By May, Alexander's invasion of Arabia was ready, with all that that would mean for the subsequent history of the Mediterranean world. He held a banquet in June 323 BCE, at which he drank an inordinate amount of wine, collapsed, and died at only thirty-two years of age. The most likely cause of his death was alcohol poisoning complicated by malaria; a modern coroner might rule it a death by misadventure.

In a short thirteen years, Alexander had transformed the ancient world. He was not simply a conqueror who had marched almost 11,000 miles with his troops through some of the most hostile lands imaginable. Alexander deliberately set about carving out an empire. He overthrew old dynasties and empires, took new titles, and led the Greeks into lands, such as India, that they had not previously entered. He traveled with merchants because he was aware of the trading possibilities, founded Greek cities (dozens of them) as military outposts, and established Greek rule over the lands he conquered either with his own men and garrisons or through the subordination of local rulers who were willing to rule in his name. He was not, however, always a good manager of people or money. Had he lived longer, he would have expanded his conquests, but it is also likely that his empire, particularly at its distant margins, would have been difficult to hold.

What one can never avoid is Alexander's personality. It infects all our sources and was a product, in large part, of the man himself and the subsequent Roman portrayal of him. He drank too much, acted recklessly in moments

WHAT A DIFFERENCE A YEAR MAKES

323 BCE and the Death of Alexander the Great

The effect of Alexander's death was immediate. The invasion of Arabia that he was on the verge of conducting was aborted. The more distant plan to attack Carthage and conquer all of the Mediterranean lands was forgotten, and resistance to Macedonian rule broke out in Greece. The wars of succession had begun. Had Alexander lived longer, he would most likely have conquered new lands. It is impossible to know whether the new campaigns he was planning would have lasted days or years; whether he would have been successful; and whether he could have held already conquered lands. Contemplating the *what ifs* of history can be stimulating but is ultimately a profitless pursuit. What can be said with some certainty is that Alexander's untimely death changed the course of ancient history. The year 322 BCE was very different from 323 BCE. The Macedonians went from conquering new lands to consolidating lands already conquered. They moved from the rule of one man over a vast empire to the rule of many Greek kings over discrete territories within that empire. These lesser Greek rulers turned away from many of Alexander's practical policies such as integrating native peoples into the army. They did pursue Alexander's policies of co-opting native religions to support their reigns, but they ultimately grounded their legitimacy in Alexander whereas he had claimed a divine right to rule. His claim to rule rested ultimately on his conquest of foreign lands, whereas theirs rested on Alexander's conquests rather than their own. While Alexander pursued the new, his Hellenistic heirs settled down in established kingdoms and held on to the old. All of that came about when it did because Alexander one night decided to drink more than he should have.

Alexander the Great

QUESTIONS | ***What impact does the "great man" or "great woman" have on history? Did Alexander change history or simply achieve what would have been achieved anyway?***

of drunkenness, and was vain and arbitrary to a fault. He was not just convinced of his divinity; he lived it, seeking out proofs such as breaking the Gordian knot to fulfill his divine destiny, retracing the steps of Herakles, and seeking out the oracle of Zeus Ammon in Libya. These actions were important not just to Alexander, but, at some level, to his men, who saw them as proofs of the specialness of their king. They never believed that Alexander was a god but accepted that he thought he was. Alexander was a brilliant general, motivated his men to do what seemed impossible, moved with determination and blinding speed against his enemies, was courageous to a fault, and inspired in executing battles. His greed for more land, money, and honor was a powerful force in driving his men beyond the limits of human endurance. None of this would have been possible had his father, Philip, not created the preconditions and possibilities that Alexander built upon. But Alexander was driven by the need to surpass Philip, to test himself against all that his father had accomplished, and to claim divinity in order to remake his origins. Philip conquered Greece; Alexander, a world.

Like Socrates, Alexander was one of a kind. He belonged to the Hellenistic Ages precisely because of his extreme individuality; his desire to explore new lands and to know new things; his cosmopolitan and international interests; his engagement with Asian realities; his belief in rule by one divinely inspired man; and his commitment to trade, commerce, and a wider Greek world. He was also, of course, a dangerous megalomaniac who made hundreds of thousands suffer as a consequence. Alexander the Great may not be knowable, so exceptional were his ideas and person, so extraordinary were his accomplishments, and so mythologized and opaque the surviving sources, but it is hard to believe that any other person could have transformed a world as dramatically as he did and in so short a time. But in 323 BCE he was suddenly dead and the fate of his empire hung in the balance.

The Hellenistic Kingdoms

Why were the Hellenistic kingdoms and the retreat from Alexander's grandiose scheme of conquest necessary?

Alexander's legacy was a land mass, its future fuzzy and undetermined; an idea of a governable Greek civilization of the wider world, not yet tested or proved; and an image of himself, the great, golden boy-king and self-declared god. The realization of the Hellenistic world would not have been possible without his superhuman drive, but his ill-defined dream of an enduring empire was not achievable, at least not by any less driven, mere mortal. Those who followed him were realists who established viable dynastic kingdoms. Their Hellenistic kingdoms retreated from Alexander's boundless striving, but they endured for centuries.

Back to Earth

Despite the constant dangers in his life, Alexander had not planned to die. He was probably more surprised than anyone to realize that he could. He had made few if any plans for his succession, and there was no one who could succeed Alexander as another Alexander. His Macedonian soldiers had different ideas. Some wanted to choose a new leader, to take their fair share of the treasure on hand, and then to return to Greece. The great men closest to Alexander were not ready to abandon the empire that they had helped to create. These powerful men could not agree on who should be named king, though they did concede that Alexander's half-brother should take the title, at least temporarily, until Roxane, who was pregnant when her husband died, gave birth. Roxane delivered a boy who was named Alexander, but he and his mother were murdered in 311 BCE to end any prospect of the boy's elevation. In the world after Alexander the Great, the last thing any of the chief players wanted was the return of another Alexander.

The generals and established powers divided up Alexander's territory. They founded dynasties that took their legitimacy from Alexander and his conquests, for they were his warriors and had marched with him or had been granted power by him. A week after Alexander's death, the great men had decided upon the lands each would receive and immediately departed for them, accompanied by their share of the available army and treasure. For the next twenty years, these successors (*diadochi*) to Alexander fought a series of battles with one another to test their claims to Alexander's inheritance and to establish kingdoms: in greater Greece, Ptolemaic Egypt, and the Seleucid east (Map 3.3).

The Kingdom of Greater Greece

The most problematic of the three great Hellenistic blocks was Greece and Macedonia. It was the slowest of the royal areas to achieve stability and was always a difficult area to hold. Part of the problem was that it was the homeland of the Greeks and Macedonians and so a much desired kingdom; part, that it was as historically and geographically divided as ever. The main players in this contest were the Macedonians, lords of Greece since Philip's conquest. First there was Perdiccas, who had led Alexander's cavalry and who was with him at his death; then Cassander, whose father, Antipater, Alexander had appointed to run Macedonia in his absence; and finally, Antigonus the One-Eyed, who had been the governor of Phrygia at the time of Alexander's death.

Perdiccas tried to achieve supremacy early on, but things did not turn out well. How was he to achieve legitimacy? He thought of marrying the daughter of Alexander's mother Olympias, who was trying to hold onto some vestige of power and influence after her son's death. Perdiccas permitted Alexander's half-brother to be king but only as long as he wielded the power behind the throne. The Macedonians expected Perdiccas to secure Alexander's body for royal burial in Macedonia. Unfortunately for him, he lost Alexander's body and his own life in 320 BCE.

After the death of Antipater in 319 BCE, his son Cassander tried to take Macedonia, but he was opposed by Antigonus the One-Eyed. Alexander's infant son was nominally ruler, but Cassander had Roxane and the boy killed. There were a host of other claimants and players, but Antigonus finally rose above all of them. He and his son Demetrius, who are called the Antigonids, had wanted an Asian kingdom but settled for holding Greece and Macedonia, though not without considerable and continuing difficulty.

The Ptolemaic Kingdom of Egypt

Egypt fell to Ptolemy I, one of Alexander's generals. He was fortunate, for Egypt was a governable kingdom and one that was, if well managed, extremely wealthy. Egypt produced grain and papyrus, which the Mediterranean world wanted. Alexandria became the Hellenistic world's most important commercial and cultural city. Thus, the Ptolemies were able to attract the mercenary soldiers from Macedonia and Greece that they needed to oversee Egypt and protect it from the other kingdoms, particularly the powerful Seleucid kingdom.

Ptolemaic Egypt was royalist, highly bureaucratic, and aggressively commercial. The Ptolemies taxed almost all the activities and resources of their native subjects (land and agricultural production) and kept under their direct control considerable property, which was worked by Egyptians who held leases to the land. The king also maintained monopolies over mining ventures and salt-beds. Although the Ptolemies held lands outside Egypt and tried at various points to expand their portion of Alexander's wider empire, they succeeded in Egypt because they consolidated and secured their firm possession of a defined and productive kingdom. Steady wealth permitted Ptolemaic Egypt to remain militarily strong. It lasted the longest of the Hellenistic kingdoms, enduring for three centuries.

The Seleucid Kingdom

Seleucus I had been one of Alexander's commanders, and his kingdom was the largest of the successor kingdoms. In 312 BCE, Seleucus seized Babylonia, and by 303 BCE he controlled the eastern reaches of Alexander's empire and later still Syria. In theory, then, the Seleucid dynasty held an area from Damascus all the way to the Indus

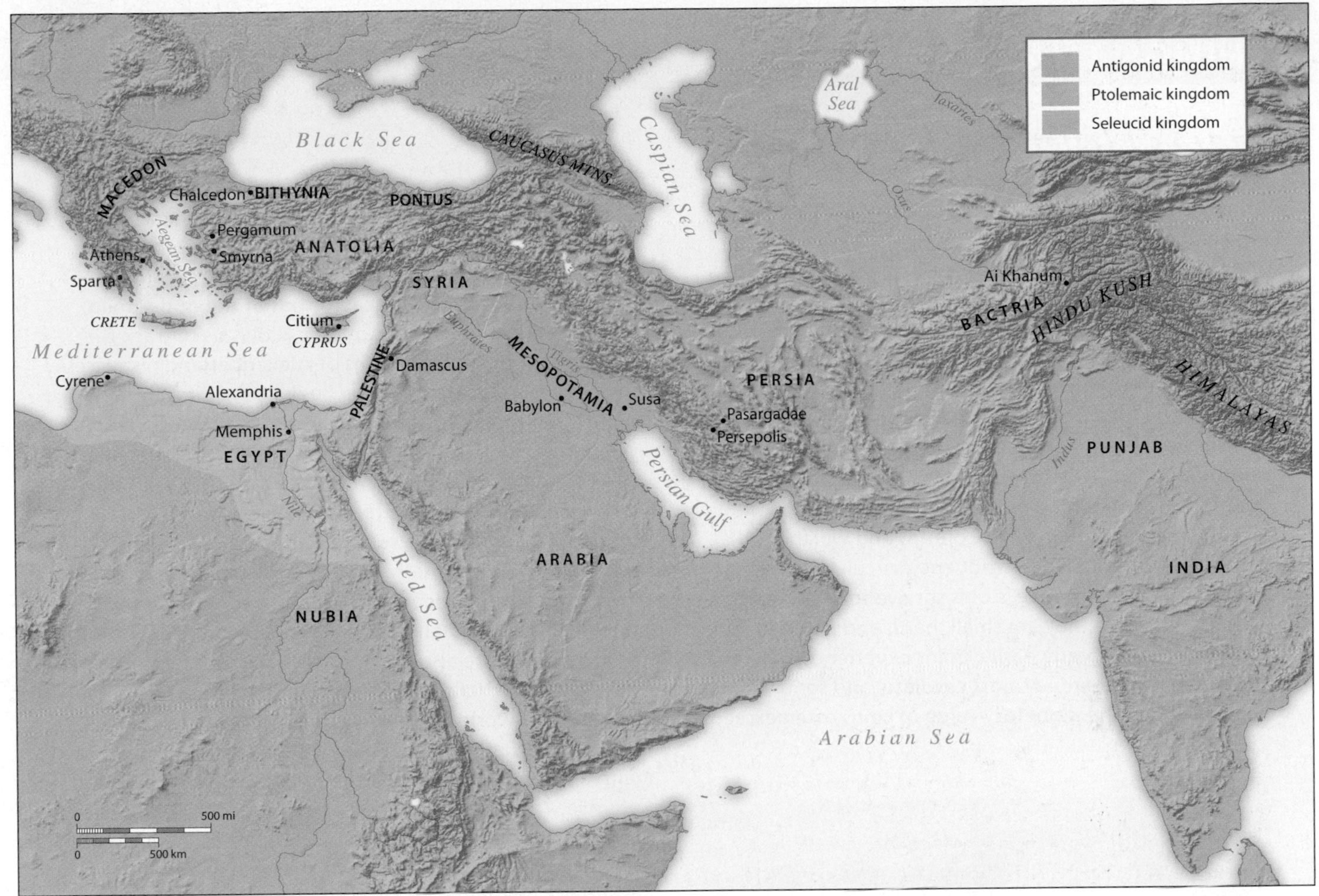

MAP 3.3 | The Hellenistic Kingdoms in the Third Century BCE

After Alexander's death in 323 BCE, his empire gradually coalesced into three major kingdoms: the Antigonid kingdom of greater Greece, Ptolemaic Egypt, and the Seleucid kingdom of the Near East and western Asia. ***How did geography determine the relative strengths and weaknesses of the three kingdoms? Which kingdom was likely to encounter the most problems and why? What lands did not fall easily into the three large kingdoms? Why did some lands quickly fall out of direct Greek control?***

River in India that contained well over 50 million people and dozens of important cities. The Seleucid kingdom was at its strongest at the start under Seleucus, but its size and complexity made it unsustainable. Distant parts of it began to fall away in the third century BCE. India could not be held, and everything east of the Caspian Sea fell to the Parthians in the mid-third century BCE. Moreover, the Seleucids were hard pressed by their Hellenistic rivals. The Ptolemies and Antigonids nibbled constantly at the Seleucid control of Asia Minor. The Seleucids were forced to pay their mercenaries with land, which over the long run left the dynasty pressed for cash. Yet the Seleucids had an impressive military machine, ambitious warrior rulers, and an army that employed elephants with impressive effect.

Alexander's eastern holdings proved, in cultural and logistical terms, to be too distant from the Macedonian heartland to maintain securely. Unlike Egypt with its one people and long tradition of being governed, the Seleucid kingdom was composed of many peoples: Babylonians, Persians, Bactrians, Arabs, Syrians, and Jews. The one constant was Seleucid rule aided by its Greco-Macedonian ruling elite, but the centrifugal and ethnic forces pulling at the Seleucid center were too great to contain.

The Outliers

The three great Hellenistic kingdoms were not the whole of the Hellenistic political world. Various outlying regions and cities achieved some independence and viability, even if they had fallen away from Alexander's empire. Greek kings ruled in Bactria and parts of India on and off for several centuries. We know about them chiefly from coins and popular tales, for they had been cut off from the greater Greek narrative. Evidence of Greek cities with grid plans and Greek ornamentation in Afghanistan and Pakistan, however, suggest the continuing presence of Greek rulers in the east. Occasionally a Seleucid king such as Antiochus the Great raided Bactria and India, thus renewing efforts to reincorporate these outlying territories into the larger Hellenistic kingdoms. Demetrius I

THINGS THAT REMAIN

India's Hellenistic Royal Coins

Coins are a remarkably enduring and useful historical resource. They carry information of several kinds: physical (the metals, their relative value, and quantity and dispersion), inscriptional (the names of rulers, their attributes, and occasionally a date), and iconographic (images of the ruler and various symbols). The range of information provided by coins is, however, limited. The images, postures, symbols, and inscriptions are often repeated, and the form is conservative and nondescriptive. Yet numismatics (the study of coins and medals) can supply, within its limits, a wealth of information. Some of it is quantitative in nature, for example, regarding metal content and worth, or the distribution of coins, their frequency, circulation, transport, and economic importance. Coins survive for a number of reasons. Physically they are small, hard, and made of metals that do not degrade easily. Coins experience different fates: many are hoarded, most circulate, and some are lost along the way. The monetary value of coins often exceeds their metallic value, so that there is often little incentive to melt them down en masse.

The coins of Alexander the Great are extraordinary. His bust profile is nearly identical to that of the god Apollo. They also occur in a sequence that allows us to track the territorial and mythical claims of Alexander and his successors. The Hellenistic kingdoms, seeking legitimacy, early on favored coins depicting Alexander, his head covered by the skin of the Nemean lion (as in the Labors of Herakles) as a conqueror of eastern lands. One rare coin from the last years of Alexander's life shows him on horseback hurling a spear at King Porus of Taxila, who is fleeing on an elephant. Occasionally the Hellenistic kings portrayed Alexander with an elephant's skin draped over his head, since like the god Dionysus he was deemed the conqueror of India. Coins are also an invaluable source of information about the Hellenistic kings of India. Cut off from the wider Greek world, these kings are chiefly known by the coins they issued. One coin shows Demetrius I (r. 200–185 BCE) with an elephant-head headdress, signaling his possession of India. The reverse sides of these coins contain Greek inscriptions and the depiction of Greek gods. A large silver coin of Amyntas (r. c. 100–75 BCE) shows a king of India, otherwise unknown, wearing a helmet, while the reverse depicts Zeus and an inscription naming Amyntas as emperor and conqueror. The last coin of these lost Greek kings of India depicts Alexander the conqueror on the reverse. Alexander remained, as he had begun, the reason for a Hellenistic presence in India.

Silver Coin of Demetrius I with Elephant-Head Headdress

QUESTIONS | ***How are coins, even now, both symbols of economic value and propaganda pieces? What are the strengths and weaknesses of coins as a historical source?***

(r. 200–185 BCE), the Greek ruler of Bactria, retook part of the Punjab region of present-day Pakistan. Demetrius was forced to recognize satraps and local kings who could rule in his name. Menander (c. 165–130 BCE) became a hero and philosopher-king of Indian legend in which he converts to Buddhism and controls lands as far away as the Ganges (well beyond Alexander's Greek footprint). Greeks ruled areas of western India and Afghanistan down until 55 BCE, but little is known about them.

Pergamum in Asia Minor near Smyrna was a fortress kingdom that soon shed Seleucid control. While the three major kingdoms dominated the Hellenistic world, Pergamum thrived by being small and defensible and by playing the great kingdoms off against each other. Under the control of the Attalid kings, it became the richest of the minor kingdoms of Asia Minor. It produced silver, a range of luxury goods, and parchment (named after Pergamum), perhaps so that it did not have to rely on Ptolemaic Egypt's monopoly on papyrus production. In the second century BCE, Republican Rome annexed Pergamum and made it the control-center of its Asia Minor holdings.

Bithynia, another petty kingdom of Asia Minor, had been under the control of Persia until Alexander's conquest. Its Greek kings variously fell under the influence of the great Hellenistic blocks, but by the second century it was a viable kingdom and survived Roman annexation longer than Pergamum did. It was, however, pressed on two sides: to the east by Pontus and to the west by Rome. The kings of Pontus were also Greek and ruled there throughout the second century BCE. Pontus mounted a major resistance to Rome, but Republican Rome eventually prevailed after three sustained conflicts against the eastern territory. Bithynia became a Roman client-state and in 74 BCE a Roman province.

The outliers in the Hellenistic world testify to several things: the extent of Greek control of the rim of the eastern Mediterranean and the Near East and the inability of the great Hellenistic kingdoms to hold on to marginal areas. Rome eventually put an end to both the large and the small but should have been pleased that Alexander and his heirs had done so much to tame foreign lands and establish governments over a vast land mass. The process involved phases: the first, Alexander's conquests; the second, the practical Greek administration of these territories in discrete units, some of them huge, some of them small, by Hellenistic kings; and the third, Rome's eventual conquest of already packaged units fitted for foreign control.

Living in the Hellenistic Age

The nature and quality of life in the Hellenistic Age depended on when you lived, where, and who you were. To be a member of a royal family or to be associated closely with one brought riches and power. It was better to be Greek than native, better to live in a large city than a village, better to be a man than a woman, better to be an aristocrat than a merchant or sailor, better to be free than a slave, and so on. An urban life in a city such as Alexandria could be rich and rewarding. There were public entertainments, ample food, and economic prospects. But in Egypt, as we have seen, most people still worked on the land and dealt with greedy and rapacious landlords, who were often Greek. In principle, the Hellenistic king owned all the land by right of conquest, but in practice his friends and the rich held it outright and paid him taxes.

Even within the rigid hierarchy of the various groups in society, there were degrees of difference. Royal and aristocratic women were much better off, obviously, than lower-class women and slaves. Some royal women achieved positions of great prominence as benefactresses, as some inscriptions record. But, at the lower levels of society, infant girls were still abandoned and left to die or sold into slavery. Female infanticide and the always lower life expectancies of women in preindustrial societies kept the size of the female population below that of the males. A tomb inscription from the second century BCE describes Sokratea of Paros as a reputable woman, whom the goddess of childbirth (Erinys) had carried off during delivery, along with her unborn child. She had bled to death. This was a man's world, for the most part. In the fourth century BCE, a Greek rhetorician smugly said that the Greek male had mistresses to serve his pleasure, concubines to serve his person, and wives to supply legitimate offspring. In Egypt at least, marriage contracts granted couples common possession of their joint property and enjoined them to live in a faithful monogamous relationship. Since some Egyptian women could own property, they could and did become businesswomen, a privilege women did not share throughout the Hellenistic world.

Wealth was not spread evenly (it never is), but the divide between the rich and the poor in the Hellenistic kingdoms was immense. Complaint was common, but there were few revolts probably because the powerful were sensitive to any sign of unrest and found ways to pacify the lower classes with free wheat, games, and public entertainment. Some poor men drifted into the army, which exacerbated the recurrent problem of depopulation in many regions. So desperate for manpower were the Ptolemaic rulers of Egypt that by the second century BCE, they were recruiting Egyptian soldiers into their armies.

Slavery was a fact of this world. A fourth-century BCE treatise said that the most important possession was the human being and that the life of the slave had three aspects: work, punishment, and food. Food was necessary to produce work and punishment to keep slaves from becoming insolent and rebellious. The slave owner needed to balance carefully the three aspects to maximize and properly manage his property. Hellenistic aristocrats thought of slavery in economic rather than moral terms. The island of Delos had a large slave market that saw thousands of slaves bought and sold daily. Egypt did not require agricultural slaves, since it had its own native farm population and had relatively few domestic slaves, but it did need slaves for its gold mines in Nubia. A Greek historian described the scene at one such mine. The slaves were kept chained and worked day and night (since it was always night underground). Escape was nearly impossible and the care and feeding of the slaves minimal. These slaves were worked until they dropped dead and were replaced, all for the glittering gold that would adorn royal costumes, precious objects, and pay for mercenary soldiers. To enjoy the bounty of the Hellenistic Age, it always mattered who you were and where and when you were. That was, as we shall see, the camel trader's complaint about his lot in life.

Hellenistic Civilization

What were the key features and achievements of the Hellenistic Ages, and how did they differ from those of Golden Age Athens? What were the roles and fates of the native populations of the Hellenistic world?

The spread of Greek culture (language, economy, art, religion, and thought) in the world carved out by Alexander had a profound effect on Roman and so western civilization. The critical sites for the diffusion of Greek culture were Hellenistic cities. Trade and taxes made up the principal language of interaction between the rulers and the native population of the conquered lands. Although there was some synthesis of Greek and foreign elements, Hellenistic culture at its leading edges was thoroughly

Greek. In philosophy, science, religion, and art, the Hellenistic Greeks achieved remarkable things, but the limited nature of the Greek penetration of foreign lands and native cultures also set cultural, linguistic, and political limits upon the western future.

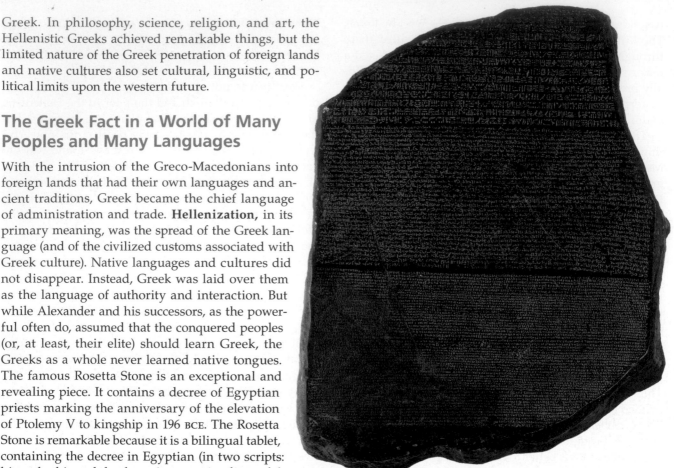

The Rosetta Stone Recovered from a wall in Egypt by Napoleon's soldiers, the stone provides parallel texts of an official Hellenistic proclamation in three scripts and two languages, from top to bottom: Egyptian hieroglyphics, Egyptian cursive or demotic, and Greek.

The Greek Fact in a World of Many Peoples and Many Languages

With the intrusion of the Greco-Macedonians into foreign lands that had their own languages and ancient traditions, Greek became the chief language of administration and trade. **Hellenization,** in its primary meaning, was the spread of the Greek language (and of the civilized customs associated with Greek culture). Native languages and cultures did not disappear. Instead, Greek was laid over them as the language of authority and interaction. But while Alexander and his successors, as the powerful often do, assumed that the conquered peoples (or, at least, their elite) should learn Greek, the Greeks as a whole never learned native tongues. The famous Rosetta Stone is an exceptional and revealing piece. It contains a decree of Egyptian priests marking the anniversary of the elevation of Ptolemy V to kingship in 196 BCE. The Rosetta Stone is remarkable because it is a bilingual tablet, containing the decree in Egyptian (in two scripts: hieroglyphic and the demotic or cursive form of the same language) and Greek. The Egyptian text is above the Greek, probably because the decree was written by Egyptians for Egyptians. Bilingualism was a native necessity, a Greek rarity, perhaps explaining why there aren't other Rosetta Stones. Since Greek was the learned and paramount language of the new world made by Alexander, native things might be translated into Greek, but Greek works were rarely translated into native languages. The Hebrew Bible (the Old Testament) was translated into Greek in a version called the Septuagint, not the *Iliad* into Hebrew.

The Greek language was changing, perhaps hastened by the Hellenistic world. Attic or Athenian Greek, which had dominated the Golden Age, was replaced by ***koine,*** the grammatically simpler form that became the common Greek of the Hellenistic Ages. *Koine* standardized Greek, eliminating regional variations, but picked up little from the native languages of the occupied lands aside from some local pronunciations and words for native objects not previously known to the Greeks. The Greek language may have remained relatively free from external influence, but Greek had a large impact on native languages such as Coptic, Syriac, and in time Latin. These native languages absorbed new vocabulary from Greek, testifying to the powerful presence of Greek in their worlds. Hebrew, in particular, absorbed a host of terms from Greek that rabbis employed to explain their sacred scriptures.

The agents of the diffusion of the Greek language were many: kings who established royal courts and distributed royal privileges; royal officials; Greek and Macedonian soldiers established in garrisons in the cities and distant regions of the kingdoms; and Greek traders. Yet the Hellenization (in the sense of learning Greek) of the native population was not promoted actively by the Greeks. Instead, it seems to have been more of a natural need for ambitious and commercially savvy natives. Positions of high power belonged to the Greco-Macedonians, and they did not need to learn native languages. Syrians and Egyptians complained that they were discriminated against because they were unable to Hellenize. Many Greeks looked down on natives. A woman in a Hellenistic poem dismissed the Egyptians as so many ants, and a Greek epigram circulating in the Hellenistic world said that one should thank the gods for being born a human not an animal, a man not a woman, and a Greek not a barbarian. Very few natives ever rose to positions of power and responsibility in the kingdoms. In the Seleucid kingdom of the third century, less than

OTHER VOICES, OTHER VIEWS

The Camel Trader's Complaint

In regimes of foreign autocratic power, taxation, and economic exploitation, there are intermediaries between the ruling powers and the natives at the lower end of the scale. Such a world is revealed by the archives of officials at work in Ptolemaic Egypt. Apollonius was a financial officer serving Ptolemy II (Philadelphus) in the mid-third century BCE in Egypt. Zenon, an agent of Apollonius, preserved on papyrus the correspondence sent to his master by people requesting privileges, permissions, and assistance. In one case, Egyptian farmers wrote to complain that a Greek named Damis had taken away lands that Apollonius had leased to them. When they protested, Damis arrested three elders and forced them to renounce their rights. In their petition to Apollonius, the farmers complained about Damis, a wicked Egyptian scribe, and newcomers (Greek migrants), who knew nothing of Egyptian agriculture. The farmers traveled to Alexandria to submit their petition, but after waiting for twenty days they had exhausted their resources and become desperate; hence, their plea to Apollonius.

Even more plaintive is the letter that an unnamed camel merchant sent to Zenon in 256 or 255 BCE. He reminded Zenon that he had been left in Syria with Crotus, another of Apollonius's agents, to complete a transaction for some camels. He reported that Crotus had repeatedly refused to pay him, even though Zenon had ordered him to do so. The camel dealer, after waiting in vain for Zenon to return, finally left Syria and followed Zenon's order to travel to Philadelphia in Egypt and to report to one Jason. This Jason refused to pay the camel trader for nine months' work, though he did give him a clothing allowance and offered to pay him in cheap wine. The camel merchant complained that Crotus and Jason had disrespected him because he was a barbarian. He asked Zenon to order Crotus and Jason to pay him what he was owed and to stop using the fact that he didn't know Greek as an excuse for abusing him. The camel trader's plight was that of many natives in the Hellenistic kingdoms. They suffered from real discrimination, attributing it chiefly to their inability to speak Greek. Their view of the Hellenistic world was less than rosy; to them it seemed economically exploitative, linguistically divided, and culturally arrogant. The camel merchant's resentment against the established Greek order and its fundamental unfairness was probably common.

QUESTIONS | ***What problems do obvious social and cultural inequities lead to? How might Zenon's role as intermediary and supervisor have softened the cultural and economic solitudes?***

The High Life of the Hellenistic Elite A master reclining on a couch is waited on by a slave. The relationship between masters and slaves was not always as comfortable as this Ptolemaic relief would suggest. There were reports from the baths in Alexandria of incidents in which masters were doused with scalding water by their slaves. It is unlikely that all these incidents were accidents.

2 percent of the native population held positions of power and prominence. Over time some of these barriers broke down and natives rose to positions of greater power, but such natives were completely Hellenized.

The Hellenistic Age was an age of movement and dislocation, which is reflected in its new comedies, which tell stories of shipwrecks and long-lost family members. The Greeks had left the smaller confined quarters of Greece for a wider world, but so did Phoenicians, Arabs, Ethiopians, and Etruscans. In this world on the move, travel on the Mediterranean Sea became more common, if no less dangerous. Many of the shipwrecks identified in the Mediterranean date from Hellenistic times. Traders moved from port to port, seeking spices from India and China, lumber from Europe, and ivory from Africa. Even peoples outside the Hellenistic world such as the Romans and Etruscans were forced to begin dealing in the Greek language if they were to play a part in the Hellenistic Age and its robust economy.

Greek Cities in Asia

The site of cultural diffusion was typically the Hellenistic city, where Greeks and other peoples mixed and interacted. Alexander founded dozens of cities (almost all of them named after him), though probably not as many as the seventy with which he was credited. He intended these cities to be military, strategic, and administrative centers for the control of the conquered lands. When he died, there were, however, relatively few Greeks and Macedonians in Asia. His Greco-Macedonian soldiers had not come to stay. They did their time, expected to be paid, and then hoped to return home. Mercenaries from Greece and Macedonia, Greek traders, royal officials, and learned men were attracted to Hellenistic cities over the next several centuries. Without this mix of peoples, Hellenistic rule and civilization would not have been sustainable.

Hellenistic cities varied in style and function from region to region. Some were centrally planned from the ground up; some developed alongside previously existing towns. Greco-Macedonians formed the ruling elite, but natives and slaves served the economic needs of the cities. A few cities such as Seleucia remained closed societies of Greeks. Few Greek women were among the original settlers of the Asian cities; soldiers took Asian wives, though in the later Hellenistic period, upper-class Greek citizens brought their wives and families with them. The central Greek institution of the Hellenistic city was the **gymnasium,** which was a place of recreation, exercise, education, and cultural exchange; gymnasia were generally exclusive institutions—all the Greek citizens of a city were expected to belong, but few others were allowed in. Other institutions such as assemblies and courts followed, depending on the size and function of the city. Egypt was unusual in not having been a land of many cities before the arrival of the Greeks. Alexandria was special; it became not only the chief city of Greek Egypt, but also the most dazzling city of the Hellenistic Age.

Hellenistic Economies

Hellenistic thinkers tended to divide economies into four types: royal, regional, urban, and domestic (the household). Yet throughout the fourth century BCE, the Hellenistic economy was a haphazard one that remains difficult to analyze. The circulation of silver coins, objects such as vessels (*amphorae*), and building campaigns provide evidence of the size and fluidity of various Hellenistic economies. By the third century BCE, for Egypt, there are enough written records for us to see roughly how one Hellenistic economy functioned.

Hellenistic economies were predominantly agricultural, but the landscape of this vast world was extremely variable. Terrain, soil quality, rainfall, and rivers varied from place to place. Whereas grain was the chief product, even in Greece, other crops such as olives, grapes, and beans were important foodstuffs. Some regions were more successful than others in growing things, and over the centuries these relative capabilities mattered. Egypt flourished economically, but Greece did less well. Land tenure was so variable within the Hellenistic kingdoms that it is hard to generalize, but at its core was the idea, as in Egypt, that the land belonged to the king by right of conquest.

No matter what was produced, if there was a surplus, it required transport: from rural areas to cities, from region to region, and from kingdom to kingdom. In the Hellenistic world, roads were less reliable than water transport and so camels in Egypt and Asia Minor were more common conveyors of goods than were wheeled carts, but they took their loads of surplus produce to rivers where they could be shipped to markets. Whereas roads were never a priority of Hellenistic development, harbors, docks, and warehouses were. Most goods of the macroeconomy passed through ports at some point. The volume of Mediterranean sea trade in the Second Hellenistic Age can be judged in relative terms by the number of Mediterranean sea wrecks that archaeologists have identified. The early Hellenistic period doubled the classical rates, but those rates almost tripled in the late Hellenistic period once the Carthaginians and Romans joined in. One of the great strengths of Hellenistic sea trade was its considerable reach, all the way to the Indian Ocean. The Hellenistic world was a conduit and market for the flow of luxury items, from Indian elephants and ivory to precious spices and gems.

The Hellenistic economies were money economies. Soldiers needed to be paid, and after Alexander, mints were established in most regions. Much of the gold that Alexander had seized from the Persian treasury at Persepolis later circulated as coin. In general, silver coins were the common currency. Kings taxed their subjects at rates as high as 35–40 percent; this excessive taxation allowed royal regimes to survive in a militaristic world in which they needed to employ and pay mercenary soldiers.

The Ptolemaic dynasty of Egypt was the most centralized and economically successful regime of the Hellenistic kingdoms. The Ptolemies took advantage of Egypt's fertile agricultural lands and of a native farming population that knew how to keep these lands productive. Egypt's surplus could be converted into cash with which to support the royal operation, obtain resources from outside Egypt, and hire mercenaries. By the third century BCE, however, lands were increasingly being turned over to Greeks in exchange for military service.

One of the casualties of the Hellenistic Age was the older polis ideal of the equality of citizens. The hoplite citizens

Pergamum A reconstruction of the dramatic setting of Pergamum with its Acropolis and extensive set of buildings neatly molded to the terrain of the site.

of Athens had fought for Athens and demanded a say in its politics and economy; Hellenistic kings hired their soldiers and controlled the dispensation of wealth. This encouraged men and women to think of their financial well-being not in civic terms, but personal ones. Some Hellenistic men and women grew fantastically wealthy. They became patrons of cities and people, acting like minor kings in dispensing wealth. The poor farmer and camel trader saw the polarization of wealth in the third century BCE as their lot, a condition from which they could rarely break free.

Later Hellenistic Philosophy

The schools of Plato and Aristotle continued in Athens throughout the Hellenistic Ages, but new movements appeared in Greece that concentrated on moral matters. The **Skeptics** doubted all knowledge, since they thought that humans simply lacked the ability to know reality or to determine truth—their doubtfulness was the doubtfulness of the Hellenistic Ages, a time when large geographic, ethnic, economic, and political realities seemed beyond comprehension.

The **Cynics** rejected the conventional Hellenistic world and dropped out of society. They spurned religious piety, reverence for kings and kingdoms, and all hypocrisy. In their place they taught doctrines of simplicity and self-sufficiency; theirs was an ancient form of a back-to-nature movement. People likened them to dogs (hence the name *Cynic,* from the Greek for dog) for their praise of simple and natural pleasures. The most famous Cynic was Diogenes, who was reputed to have lived in a barrel in fourth-century BCE Athens. Diogenes and his successors taught Hellenistic men and women how to cope with the travails of life by denying the complexity, hypocrisy, and material exuberance of the day. The Cynics even avoided the conventions of philosophy and created no school of their own.

The **Stoics** appeared late in the fourth century BCE, in Athens. Their intellectual forebears were Socrates and the Cynics, but Zeno of Citium, the founder of Stoicism (from the Stoa, or porch, where he taught), advocated a philosophy of individual responsibility, individual action, and the pursuit of virtue. Though the Stoics thought that the material world and possessions were worthless, they thought that all men, from emperors down to slaves, should strive to do their best in all the things that they did or were forced to do. It was in virtuous activity, not achievement that individuals pursued the Stoic ideal. Stoics believed in living in harmony with Nature, which they thought had been established by divine wisdom and goodness. Whereas the Cynics had withdrawn from the civilized world, the Stoics believed in living in the world with all of its troubles and public responsibilities.

The **Epicureans**—named after Epicurus of Athens, who lived in the fourth century BCE—established a school in Athens that viewed the world quite differently from the Stoics. Epicurus thought that the world was a product of random combinations of atoms, and so a purely physical or material reality. For Epicurus and his followers, the universe lacked any underlying purpose or goodness. If morality was not divinely imbedded in the universe, as the Stoics believed, then humans were free to act for their own individual and material ends. At the same time, Epicurus sought to free humans from their physical chains by teaching them that the highest good was freedom from emotional turmoil. His school renounced

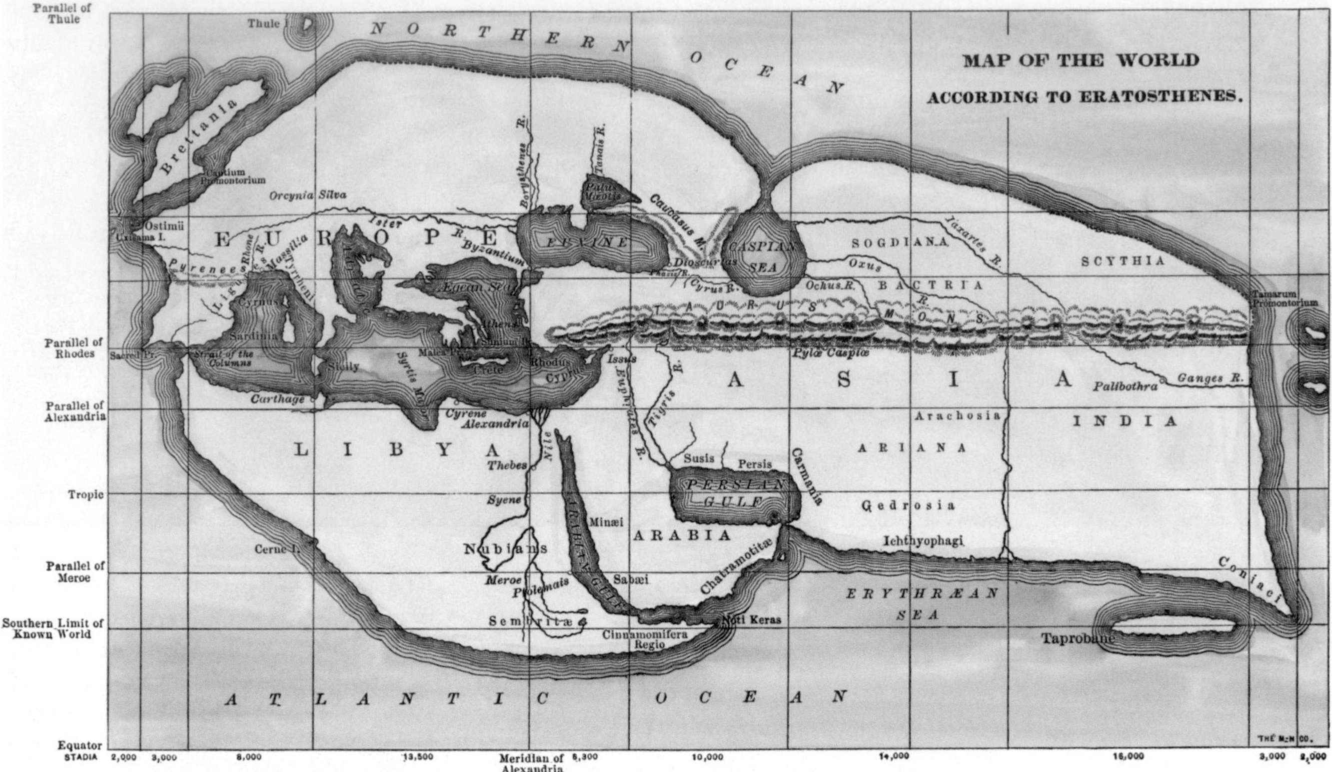

The World According to Eratosthenes A re-creation of the world map as proposed by the Alexandrian geographer.

simple hedonism, treasured friendship, and sought emotional equanimity. In its own way, Epicureanism was another response to the Hellenistic condition. The vast, alienating, material world was a fact, but the mind could free humans from the anguish it caused by recognizing it for what it was and seeking true happiness in being free of illusions about the world, living a quiet life, and treasuring friends and simple human pleasures.

Each of the distinctive philosophies that arose in the shadow cast by the philosophies of Socrates, Plato, and Aristotle were responses to the new Hellenistic world, its size and sheer complexity. The Skeptics denied its comprehensibility; the Cynics rejected its basic conventions and dropped out; and the Epicureans, recognizing the purposeless nature of the universe, withdrew from it to seek simpler human pleasures. Only the Stoics crafted a philosophy of engagement with the world based on individual virtuous action, but even they refused to embrace the pure energy and exuberance of the Hellenistic world.

Later Hellenistic Technology, Science, and Medicine

Greek technology, science, and medicine attained its greatest achievements in the Hellenistic world, chiefly in Ptolemaic Alexandria. The Second Hellenistic Age was one of great technological invention and advance: siege engines, water-powered machines such as organs and clocks, and automated devices that could move dolls, theaters, and calculating machines. Archimedes of Syracuse (287–212 BCE) was not just a brilliant mathematician, but a brilliant engineer. He is credited, for instance, with inventing a large screw-like device for conveying water from a river or pond onto fields for the irrigation of crops. His home city of Syracuse was defended by his machines.

In astronomy, Hellenistic advances were impressive. For example, at Alexandria, the third-century BCE geographer Eratosthenes of Cyrene calculated the circumference of the earth to within a reasonable margin of error. Whereas the *Geographika* of Eratosthenes approached the problem of the earth's land masses as a mathematical question, Theophrastus preferred a descriptive geography in his study of winds.

Aristarchus of Samos, another third-century BCE Alexandrian thinker, determined that the earth completes one rotation per day on an axis and circles the sun once a year. He proposed a **heliocentric** (sun-centered) **theory** of the relationship of the earth and planets, but, as so often in Hellenistic thought, the implications of such a daring idea were not followed up, partly because Hellenistic astronomers could not reconcile Aristarchus's theory with the observable progress of the constellations against the night sky. Nor did the radical implications of a heliocentric theory, which threatened to displace the earth from its central position in the universe, seem to worry Hellenistic men and women, since they probably never learned of the theory. It remained but another scientific speculation, and Alexandria produced many of those.

The mathematical concerns of the age reflected its preoccupation with space. Euclid's *Elements* of geometry, which was written around 300 BCE, concentrated on solids such as cones and spheres. Archimedes discovered calculus, and Heron of Alexandria, who worked in the first century BCE, introduced trigonometry.

The most important of the Hellenistic scientific advances were in medicine. In Egypt, with its long expertise in mummification, Ptolemaic scholars were permitted to dissect cadavers and so to explore the internal workings of the human body. In the third century BCE, Herophilus of Chalcedon and his students investigated the anatomical details of the nervous system, pulsation, the heart, and blood circulation. A contemporary said that Herophilus even dissected still living criminals, who had been condemned to death, to observe organs at work. Still, despite these daring investigations, the prevailing medical theory remained the older one of Hippocrates, that the body was subject to the four humors and that doctors were chiefly charged with restoring balance to the body.

Hellenistic Religious Ferment

When Alexander marched into Asia, he assumed that his gods were universal ones and that he would encounter and honor familiar gods wherever he went. What Alexander found, of course, were native religious beliefs that did not quite match Greek norms. Still, he and his advisors were ready to assume that, given the universal presence of the gods, the natives of Persia, India, and Egypt had the same gods as the Greeks but called them by different names and honored them in different ways. At Tyre, for instance, Alexander thought that the Phoenician god Melgart (or Melkart) was a form of Herakles. At Siwah, he regarded the Egyptian divinity Ammon as a manifestation of Zeus. Underlying polytheism was the idea that the divine was universal and omnipresent but that its manifestations (in place and form) were variable. Hellenistic kings were keen to claim some measure of religious authority by promoting and honoring local religious beliefs that in turn recognized their divinely sanctioned royal lines. Hence in Egypt, Alexander and his successors were recognized as kings and honored as gods.

What Alexander and the creation of a wider Hellenistic world had actually done was to set religion on the move. Not only did cultures collide when the Greco-Macedonians invaded foreign lands, but religions as well. Greek soldiers and traders became powerful agents of cross-fertilization in spreading religions that had previously been restricted regionally. The **mystery religions,** which had secret practices and rites of initiation, spread in this way. At the same time, the beliefs, practices, forms, and divinities of these religions often combined—a process called **syncreticism.** In this way, the Egyptian goddess Isis became an all-encompassing divinity: a great mother goddess, with many names and powers, and the ruler of the entire earth. She offered believers immortality and revealed to them the mysteries of the world. Ptolemy I wanted a central religious figure who could answer the needs of both the Greeks and Egyptians and so invented the god Sarapis (or Serapis). Associated with Memphis and the Egyptian god Osiris, Sarapis was seen as a native form of Helios (the sun) and Zeus—in statues he was bearded like Zeus and was regarded as the supreme god. The Hellenistic era thus forced on ancient religions, west and east, a period of intense fluidity of form and meaning; the top of traditional belief had been set spinning.

Alexandrian Literature

In the Hellenistic Age, Greek literature was an important cultural touchstone for the Greek minority set down in the midst of the vast native population of foreign lands. Hellenistic Greeks venerated Greek literature of the Classical Age. It reminded them of their connection to their Greek homeland and its golden past. Hellenistic kings were pleased to solidify that cultural connection and to outdo their rivals in proving who the better Greek was. Hence, Pergamum started its own library of parchment manuscripts as a way to rival the Ptolemies, but Alexandria outpaced all others. Ptolemy I and his successors were so anxious to collect texts that they insisted that all ships docking in Alexandria had to submit whatever books they had on board, which were then copied. The copy was given to the original owner; the original book entered the Ptolemaic collection. The royal library of Alexandria was probably confined at first to a portion of the Museum. The collection consisted of a half-million papyrus rolls (though probably closer to 100,000 books since each roll might contain only a small portion of a long work such as the *Iliad*), but before too long it exceeded the available space and an annex of texts was opened at the Sarapeion. Ptolemaic kings had probably been persuaded that knowledge was power and that books were the best way to acquire and retain knowledge and to preserve Greek culture. Indeed, some of the Ptolemies became writers, and one of the Seleucid kings wrote a poem about snake bites.

The mission of Alexandria's librarians was to collect and codify the masterpieces of Greek literature. Their tastes shaped some of what has survived of classical Greek literature. It was they who worked to collect the complete corpus of Plato's works, as well as those of Aristotle and the chief tragic playwrights (Aeschylus, Sophocles, and Euripides). Alexandria served as a funnel through which ancient Greek literature was channeled, defined, and preserved.

Alexandrian poets, under the weight of the classical Greek literary monuments collected and read at the library, became learned and allusive (referring by allusion to older literature). They were also brief, preferring epigrams to lengthy poems; their brevity was a product of living in the shadow of the massive collection of words in the library. What was left to be said needed to be said well, and said in few words. The librarian Callimachus is famous for his motto, much beloved by students: "Big Book, Big Evil." He wrote, however, many books and lists of his own, including a lengthy catalogue of the library's books, a list of abstruse words, a poem on the waterways and rivers of Europe, a volume on myths, and another on the habits of barbarians. He also invented different forms of verse, another recognition that the Greek greats of the past could not be equaled and so the Alexandrian poets needed to find new ways and means to say things.

Hellenistic Art

Hellenistic art departed from the earlier concerns of classical Greek art. It embraced the particular and the realistic, not the ideal and the perfect. The famous sculptures of the Venus de Milo and winged Victory of Samothrace, housed today at the Louvre in Paris, are Hellenistic pieces. Those two works are twisting, expressive, vibrant pieces that speak to the energy and dynamism of the Hellenistic Age. There had been a change in the nature of patronage, from classical civic commissions to art produced for Hellenistic kings and rich patrons. Not surprisingly, portraiture lay at the heart of Hellenistic art: on coins and tombs, in paintings and mosaics. The many busts of the philosophers Socrates, Plato, and Aristotle all come from the Hellenistic period. In keeping with Aristotle's drive for natural truths, Hellenistic art sought realizable and recognizable portraits of individuals. The mummy paintings from Fayoum in Egypt in the late Hellenistic period are portraits of real individuals, warts and all. Or take the example of the sculpture of the old market woman or courtesan on her way to a wine festival from the second century BCE. She is a stock type, as suited the concerns and conventions of Menander and New Comedy, but nonetheless a specific, highly realized example of a type and subject that would not have attracted sculptors or patrons of the Classical Age.

The Old Courtesan Hellenistic artists and patrons were interested in detailed character studies. This sculpture, with its emphasis on a particular type of person, an aged courtesan on her way to a wine festival, would have found no place in classical Greece, which wanted to see idealized, perfected human beings.

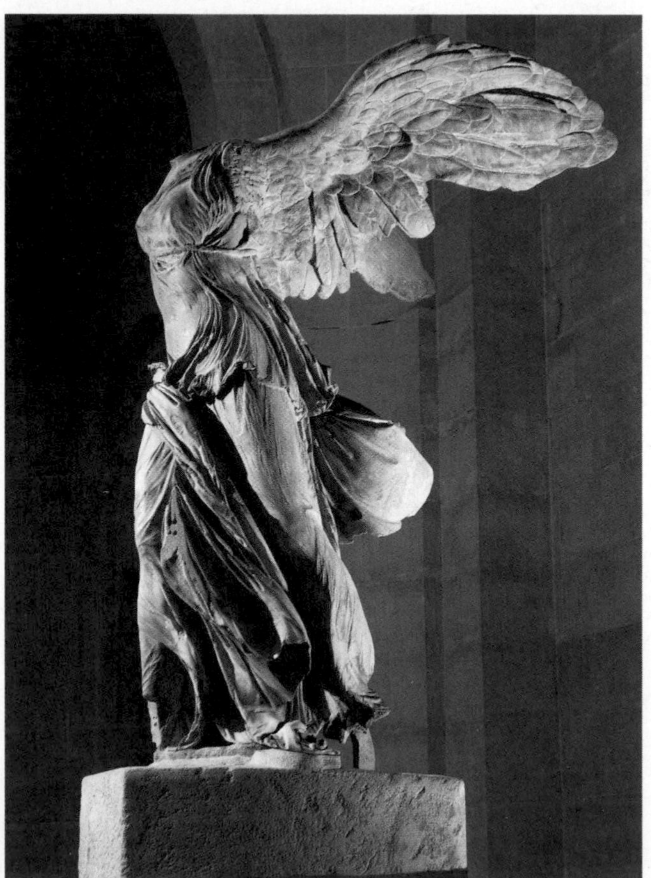

The Winged Victory of Samothrace The Winged Victory captures the dynamic energy and motion that Hellenistic artists emphasized.

Hellenistic architecture and art, including religious statues, had a propagandistic feature and left a Greek impress upon occupied lands. Native art did not disappear—Egyptian temples continued to be erected in a native style—but it was overridden by Greek art. Hellenistic architecture makes a Greek statement. Though it was eclectic, employing different types of classical columns, its geographic dispersion, regional variation, and massiveness impressed itself upon the Asian and Mediterranean landscape. The extensive complex of buildings at Pergamum (a theater spilling down the hillside, a market place, temples, porticoes, and vaulted passages), neatly molded to the landscape of an Acropolis, reinforced the Hellenistic values of the Attalid royal dynasty that sponsored the building campaign. Alexander may have shown the Greeks a wider world, but it fell to rival Greek dynasties to give it shape and character.

Conclusion

The rise of the Macedonians and their conquest of Greece may seem, in hindsight, to have been destined to occur, but Philip and Alexander were extraordinary individuals whose like were not seen before or afterward. They subdued a Greece that still had bite, as Demosthenes demonstrated, and planned the invasion of Persia. Alexander conquered a vast world stretching from the Nile to the Indus, but it fell to his Greco-Macedonian successors to shape and govern it. Some of the Hellenistic kingdoms were more successful than others, but all participated in and promoted the Hellenization of the eastern Mediterranean, Asia Minor, and lands farther east. For almost three hundred years, Greek culture, Greek officials, and Greek kings dominated this vast territory. These Greek kingdoms were shrinking by the third century BCE and were not able to withstand the rise of more aggressive peoples, but their cultural imprint was long-lasting. Greek coins were being produced in western India in the first century BCE, and Etruscan traders and Roman Republicans learned Greek as the common language of the civilized peoples of the Mediterranean world. Yet Hellenistic civilization did not so much domesticate Asia as bring it under an umbrella of Greek government and culture.

Philip, Alexander, and the Hellenistic kings paved the way for Rome's rule of the greater Mediterranean world. Yet, by not penetrating deeply or integrating native cultures, the Hellenistic Age might be viewed as a lost opportunity to create a common Greco-Asian civilization, one that might have incorporated Egyptians and Syrians, Indians and Greeks in a shared world. The only way up and out of the conditions of ethnicity, language, and culture for most natives was to Hellenize, to become Greek, and even then it was hard to rise. Egyptians and Greeks possessed their own law codes and courts. Syrians who could not speak Greek were doomed to second-class status. Even those who did learn the language had a difficult time escaping their race.

The one people who did move in the Greek direction were the Jews, but Hellenization, which meant assimilation, proved to be both a blessing and a curse. Hellenization enriched Jewish culture and gave Jews a permanent foothold in western culture, but it divided the Jewish community over its divine mission and loss of identity. The pull in different directions of the Jewish temple and Greek gymnasium became an existential drama for Jews in the Hellenistic Ages and long afterward. The Seleucid king Antioch IV went so far as to suppress the temple in Jerusalem and to attempt to demolish Jewish identity, but the backlash was a Jewish war of resistance (described in Maccabees 1–2 of the Hebrew Bible) and a period of independence from Greek interference in the mid-second century BCE. The experience of the Jews may suggest that Hellenization, as one sided and limited as it was, might not have been able to accomplish much more than it did.

The Greeks had come to rule Alexander's empire as efficiently and successfully as they could, not to absorb, reform, or destroy native realities. Egypt remained Egypt and long outlived its Greek rulers. The Hellenistic legacy of cosmopolitanism, profound philosophies, religious ferment, scientific speculation, economic specialization, and worldly alienation had a lasting effect on the Romans and so upon western civilization. But it was Islam that would inherit most of the Hellenistic territories and much of the Hellenistic emphasis on city life, science, and mercantile enterprise.

Critical Thinking Questions

1. How were the two Hellenistic Ages different, and in what ways were they different from the preceding Classical Age?
2. What did Alexander want, and what choices did he make to achieve those ends?
3. How did the chance event of Alexander's premature death change the ancient world?
4. Why did the creation of the Hellenistic worlds produce among the many peoples it affected, particularly the Greeks, feelings of dislocation, alienation, and anxiety?
5. Why did Hellenistic culture and Hellenistic Greeks not assimilate with the cultures and peoples they governed? What was the ultimate cost of the Greek failure to integrate the Hellenistic world?

Key Terms

Hellenistic **(p. 72)**
Socratic method **(p. 79)**
Hellenization **(p. 92)**
koine **(p. 92)**
gymnasium **(p. 94)**
Skeptics **(p. 95)**
Cynics **(p. 95)**
Stoics **(p. 95)**
Epicureans **(p. 95)**
heliocentric theory **(p. 96)**
mystery religions **(p. 97)**
syncretism **(p. 97)**

Primary Sources in connect

For information on Connect and the online resources available, go to **http://connect.mcgraw-hill.com**.

1. **Demosthenes and Isocrates on Philip of Macedon**
2. **Xenophon, The Apology of Socrates to the Jury**
3. **Late-Fourth-Century BCE Witnesses to the Divine Curses of Asclepius at Epidaurus**
4. **Alexander's Hellenization of Asia according to Plutarch**
5. **An Egyptian Scribe Working for the Greeks**

BACK TO THE SOURCE

The Trial of Socrates

In 399 BCE, three years after the restoration of democracy in Athens, Socrates was put on trial for allegedly not believing in the state gods, introducing his own god (or personal *daimon*), and for corrupting the young. Behind the prosecution may have been the worry by the democratic leaders of Athens that Socrates was antidemocratic and that some of his students, such as Critias and Alcibiades, emboldened by Socrates's teaching, had willfully harmed Athens. The young aristocrat Plato attended the trial and skillfully re-created Socrates's speech, much, we may suppose, as Thucydides had reconstructed Pericles's *Funeral Oration.* The jury of 501 Athenians first voted by a small majority of sixty to condemn the philosopher, but after Socrates, as was his right, again addressed the jury and advised them either to let him pay a small fine or to support him at public expense, the jury overwhelmingly condemned him to death.

How you, O Athenians, have been affected by my accusers, I cannot tell; but I know that they almost made me forget who I was—so persuasively did they speak; and yet they have hardly uttered a word of truth. . . .

I will begin at the beginning and ask what is the accusation which has given rise to the slander of me, and in fact has encouraged Meletus to prefer this charge against me. Well, what do the slanderers say? They shall be my prosecutors, and I will sum up their words in the affidavit: "Socrates is an evildoer, and strange person, who searches into things under the earth and in heaven, and he makes the worse appear the better cause; and he teaches the aforesaid doctrines to others." Such is the nature of the accusation: it is just what you have yourselves seen in the comedy of Aristophanes, who has introduced a man whom he calls Socrates, going about and saying that he walks in air, and talking a deal of nonsense concerning matters of which I do not pretend to know either much or little about, not that I mean to speak disparagingly of anyone who is a student of natural philosophy. I should be very sorry if Meletus could bring so grave a charge against me. But the simple truth is, Athenians, that I have nothing to do with physical speculations. . . .

There is another thing: young men of the richer classes, who have not much to do, come to me of their own accord; they like to hear the pretenders [those who claim to know something] examined, and they often imitate me, and proceed to examine others; there are plenty of persons, as they quickly discover, who think that they know something, but really know little or nothing; and then those who are examined by them instead of being angry with themselves are angry with me. That confounded Socrates, they say; that villainous misleader of youth! Then if somebody asks them why, what evil does he practice or teach, they do not know, and cannot tell. But in order that they may not appear to be at a loss, they repeat the ready-made charges that are used against all philosophers, about teaching things up in the clouds and under the earth, and having no gods, and making the worse appear the better cause. They do not like to confess that their pretense of knowledge has been detected, which is the truth; and as they are numerous and ambitious and energetic, and are drawn up in battle array and have persuasive tongues, they have filled your ears with their loud and inveterate calumnies. And this is the reason why my three accusers, Meletus and Anytus and Lycon, have set upon me. . . .

Men of Athens, I honor and love you, but I shall obey god rather than you, and while I have strength I shall never cease from the practice and teaching of philosophy, exhorting anyone whom I meet and saying to him after my manner: You, my friend, a citizen of the great and mighty and wise city of Athens, are you not ashamed of heaping up the greatest amount of money and honor and reputation, and caring so little about wisdom and truth and the greatest improvement of the soul, which you never regard or heed at all? And if the person with whom I am arguing, says Yes, but I do care, then I do not leave him or let him go at once, but I proceed to interrogate and examine him, and if I think that he has no virtue in him, but only says that he has, I reproach him with undervaluing the greater and overvaluing the lesser. . . . This is my teaching, and if this is the doctrine which corrupts youth, then I am a mischievous person. . . .

And now Athenians, I am not going to argue for my own sake, as you may think, but for yours, that you may not sin against god by condemning me, who am his gift to you. For if you kill me you will not easily find a successor to me, who, if I may use such a ludicrous figure of speech, am a sort of gadfly, given to the state by god; and the state is a great and noble steed who is tardy in his motions owing to his great size, and requires to be stirred into life. I am that gadfly which god has attached to the state, and all day long and in all places am always fastening upon you, arousing and persuading and reproaching you. You will not easily find another like me, and therefore I would advise you to spare me. I dare say that you may feel irritable (like a person who is suddenly awakened from sleep), and you may think that you might easily strike me dead as Anytus advises, and you would sleep on for the remainder of your lives, unless god in his care for you sent you another gadfly. . . .

QUESTIONS | *Why does Socrates think that he is being tried? Did he die a scapegoat for Athenian irritation at the end of the Peloponnesian War and its aftermath, a martyr to philosophical freedom and truth, or a stubborn old man who refused to placate his accusers? Explain. In what ways had Socrates here already stepped into the First Hellenistic Age?*

Source: B. Jowett, ed., *The Dialogues of Plato,* Vol. 1 (Oxford: Oxford University Press, 1920), 401–403, 406, 413–414; revised.

The Ruins of the Forum in Rome

THE ROMAN REPUBLIC

Survival and Success

POLYBIUS AND THE ROMANS In 167 BCE, Polybius (c. 200–c. 118 BCE) was one of a thousand Greek hostages loaded onto ships for transport to Rome. He said that the experience left him on the edge of mental collapse. His fall from high places had been steep, for he had been a politician, diplomat, and officeholder in the Achaean League, of which his native city Megalopolis was a member. Rome accused Polybius and the other prisoners of committing treachery. None of them was ever brought to trial; instead, most of the captured Greeks languished unhappily for fifteen long years in Roman detention.

The Historian Polybius One of the few representations of the historian Polybius.

Polybius made the best of a bad situation. He made powerful friends and worked his way into the highest social circles. His forty-book history of the Republic of Rome, written in Greek, investigates how a single city conquered and brought under its power the Mediterranean world. Polybius was an eyewitness to great events. He saw the city of Carthage razed to the ground and its population sold into slavery at the end of the Third Punic War, and he visited the city of Corinth not long after Rome had destroyed it in 146 BCE.

Polybius committed himself to recording events and people as accurately as he could. "Truth," he wrote, "is to history what sight is to the living," for without truth history is only a meaningless distraction for fools, and Polybius was no fool. He was, however, an unabashed and amazed admirer of what Rome had accomplished. The historical question that drove him was how Rome did it. How did a single city subdue an entire world?

❋❋❋❋

The Romans were geniuses at organization (both political and military) and survival. Surrounded by hostile peoples and cities, Rome found the means to match its times and circumstances. Guided by its **Senate,** Rome survived and prospered, perfecting the most successful of all forms of ancient government, the Roman Republic. The great challenges to its survival from the Etruscan, Latin, and Greek cities in Italy, and from Carthage and

Etruscan civilization
750–350 BCE

800 BCE | 700 | 600 | 500

the Hellenistic kingdoms, led Rome along a path to the domination first of central Italy, then all of Italy, and finally the western Mediterranean and ancient world.

In this chapter, we examine the Roman Republic's rise to power prior to the middle of the second century BCE, when things began to fall apart. In religion, government, and war, the Roman Republic before 146 BCE achieved unparalleled stability and success. Like Polybius, we need to ask how and why the Romans succeeded when so many rival powers in Italy and the wider Mediterranean world wanted to crush it. What made Rome special?

Early Stories, Early Days

The earliest history of Rome is wrapped in legend. Later Romans knew little definite about it, and Polybius even less. The simple stories the Romans told about their beginnings are both charming and chilling. Horatius fighting nobly at the Bridge, Cincinnatus laying down his arms and returning to the plow he had dropped when Rome called him to war, and the geese that warned the Romans that Gallic invaders were violating the sacred precincts of their city are legends that describe a humble agricultural people and their core virtues.

Why were the Etruscans important to Mediterranean and Roman history?

Yet, according to a darker set of legends, the city of Rome began its history with rape (of a Vestal Virgin by a god), regicide (the murder of King Amulius), fratricide (of Remus by his brother Romulus), and mass abduction and violation (of the Sabine women). Such stories did not make for the most glorious of foundation myths. In compensation, imperial Romans would overlay this bumpy narrative with the story of Trojan warriors led by the gods to found Latin Italy and to lead Rome toward its divine destiny. To elevate their past, imperial Romans joined their history to that of the Greeks, fashioning a story of Greco-Roman continuity and the westward passage of civilization.

The Etruscans and Prehistoric Italy

Italy went through a series of stages—Neolithic, copper, and bronze. Evidence of the richness of Italy's prehistoric past is abundant: cave paintings in the south, Neolithic fertility idols, thousands of small stone structures on Sardinia, and rich gold and bronze objects from graves in the north in the area around Bologna. After 1000 BCE, northern Italy began to receive waves of immigrants coming from the north and east by land and sea. The invaders, including Indo-European Italic peoples such as the Samnites and Latins, slowly displaced the previous residents.

The Etruscans, one of these early peoples in northern Italy, were not Indo-Europeans, which we can tell from their language. Although the Etruscans (unlike the Italic peoples at the time) had a written language, it is still not fully understood. It falls into that class of written languages in which the script is known, but the language is not. Because the Etruscan script consists, with some modifications, of Greek capital letters, its more than 10,000 surviving inscriptions can be deciphered, if not read for precise and full meaning. Most Etruscan inscriptions are short and do not reveal the grammatical structure and specific workings of the language. Even several bilingual texts, the most famous being the gold Pyrgi Tablets with Phoenician and Etruscan parallel texts, are relatively short and have not yet led to the unraveling of the Etruscan language.

The problem of understanding the Etruscan language and culture is compounded by uncertainty about where the Etruscans came from. In the ancient world, opinion was divided about the origins of the Etruscans. Some believed that they were natives of Italy, others that they came from Mesopotamia, yet others that they were Lydians who fled their homeland during a famine. Some modern scholars suspected that they came from the island of Lemnos in Asia Minor. Recent DNA studies, though contested, point to Lydia (or western Turkey), as Herodotus had claimed, as the original home of the Etruscans.

What little we do know about the Etruscans confirms their historical importance. Tombs, gravesites,

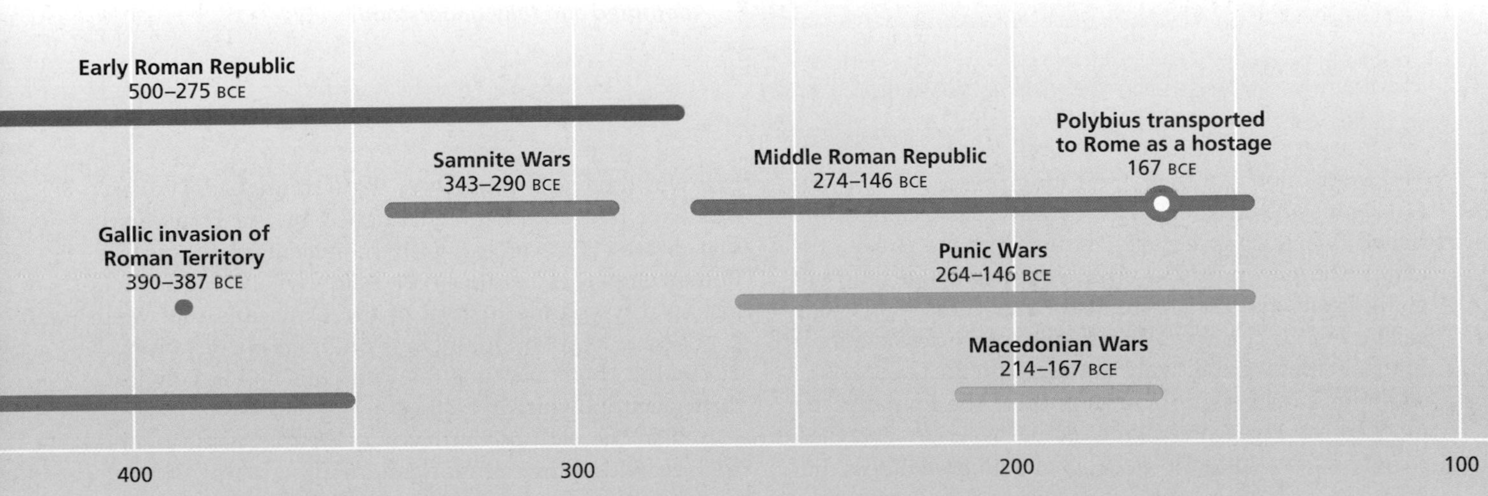

THINGS THAT REMAIN

The Pyrgi Tablets

In 1964, three thin sheets of pressed gold, rolled up like a scroll, were unearthed during the excavation of a temple site at Pyrgi on the coast twenty-five miles northwest of Rome. Pyrgi served as a port for the Etruscan city of Cerveteri. The find immediately excited interest since the gold sheets were inscribed and two of them formed a pair, one sheet written in Etruscan, the other in Phoenician. The third sheet, containing a longer text than the other two, was also written in Etruscan. Found with the sheets were the nails with which they were once affixed to a surface in the temple. The nails are bronze but have golden heads to match the tablets, suggesting that the tablets were precious display objects.

Discovery of the tablets gave scholars the hope that at long last the Etruscan language had its Rosetta Stone, a parallel text in a known language (in this case Phoenician) that would allow philologists to break the Etruscan code. Sadly the situations are not the same. The Rosetta Stone contains a long text reproduced in two different languages and three different scripts. The Pyrgi Tablets have a relatively short text in only two scripts and languages. Compounding the problem of deciphering Etruscan, the Phoenician and Etruscan texts are parallel and not literal translations of each other. Translation in the ancient world was rarely literal, a word-for-word reproduction in another language, but rather an adaptation of the spirit of the original, conveying its general meaning.

The Pyrgi Tablets honor, celebrate, and date a gift made by the Etruscan king of Caisra to a goddess. The hope that the Pyrgi Tablets would supply evidence of Etruscan-Carthaginian relations now also seems shaky. The Carthaginians and Etruscans did have formal dealings and entered into treaties with each other. Parallel texts of such a treaty might well prove to be a Rosetta Stone, but the Pyrgi Tablets are not that and they now seem not even to provide firm evidence of contact between the Etruscans and Carthaginians. After careful examination of the Phoenician text, the classical philologist Philip C. Schmitz concluded that the texts were not written in Carthaginian, but a Mediterranean dialect of Phoenician connected more closely to a form of the language used on Cyprus.

History is often a matter of small steps. Big breakthroughs such as the bonanza of a Rosetta Stone are rare. Still, one never knows what the ground might cough up tomorrow. In 1999, a bronze tablet with a long Etruscan inscription surfaced in Cortona, though it too has not as yet led to the long desired breakthrough.

The Pyrgi Tablets

QUESTIONS | ***How is our view of the past shaped (or distorted) by knowing or not knowing a civilization's language? Why has the Etruscan language not been identified and fully understood?***

and inscriptions attest to their long presence in Etruria (Tuscany) and farther north in Italy. Etruscans established twelve chief city-states that, like the Greek city-states, shared linguistic, ethnic, cultural, and religious connections, but they were also fierce competitors with each other. By the seventh and sixth centuries BCE, some of these cities were actively trading with the Greeks, who sometimes dismissed them as pirates. The Romans later mocked the Etruscans as ineffectual warriors and their society as one given to debauchery and weakness, but that was the condemnation of the winning side, whose existence had once been threatened by the Etruscans. The greatest Etruscan expert in the ancient world was the Roman emperor Claudius (r. 41–54 CE), who wrote a now-lost twenty-volume history of the Etruscans that was kept and read out annually in the Library of Alexandria. But by the emperor's time the Etruscans had largely lost their place and voice in history.

Yet, in the eighth century BCE, Etruscan cities were trading widely in minerals and artifacts. By 700 BCE,

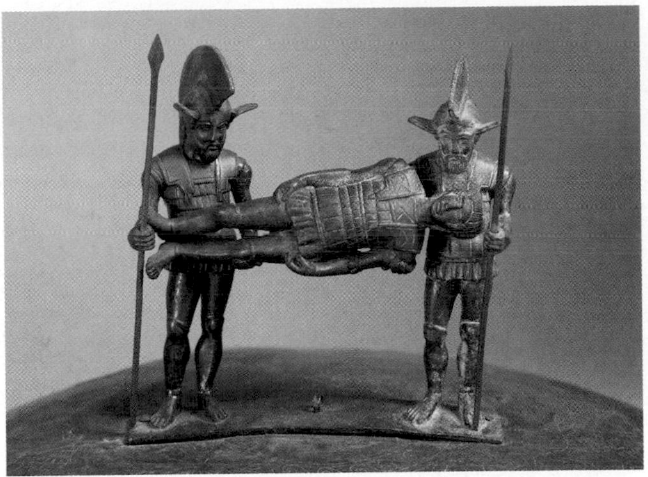

Etruscan Warriors Bearing a Wounded Comrade The Etruscans were famous not only for their far-reaching trading networks and cultural sophistication, but also for being fierce warriors. Note in particular the fringed helmets with cats' ears, spears, and leather body armor.

Etruscan Women in Funeral Procession Here Etruscan women do a funeral dance around a corpse.

they had begun to colonize the middle parts of Italy, and the islands of Elba, Corsica, and Sardinia fell under their sway. Etruscan cities established trading and diplomatic contacts with the great Mediterranean powers, particularly with the Greeks and Carthaginians. Etruscan art reveals the influence of Greek art in both subject matter and style.

The Etruscan cities of early Italy played a critical role in exposing northern Italy to the cultural influences of the Mediterranean east, particularly to Greek art and the Greek alphabet. It was the Etruscans who transformed Rome into a city.

Early Rome

The Latins, an Indo-European people like the Greeks, migrated to central Italy and settled on the plains of Latium around 1000 BCE. The people who settled the seven hills of Rome around 900 BCE were one or several offshoots of these Latin peoples. Romans later fixed 753 BCE as the foundation date of their city, but archaeology suggests that nothing like a city existed on the site that early (Map 4.1).

Rome was located fifteen miles from the Mediterranean on the Tiber River. Located on the western side of Italy, Rome lay far from the Adriatic Sea and easy access by Greek and Phoenician ships. Tributaries of the Tiber River cut through the Latin plains and reach across much of the peninsula. A series of paths and later roads joined Rome to the rest of Italy. The site of Rome was a midpoint in Italy. To the north lay the Etruscans of Etruria and to the south other Latin peoples; beyond them were the Samnites of central Italy and farther south, various Greek settlements.

MAP 4.1 | Early Italy and Its Peoples, c. 500 BCE
Early Italy was crowded with different peoples. Rome was surrounded by powerful Etruscan cities; various tribes such as the Latins, Marsi, and Samnites; and farther south, Greek cities and the Carthaginian trading outposts in Sicily. ***What advantages and disadvantages were there to Rome's location in Italy? How did the geographic setting of Rome dictate its development?***

Around 900 BCE, shepherds who grazed their flocks on the seven hills of Rome began building huts. By the mid-seventh century BCE, these settlements began to spread down the hills. The inhabitants of the area organized themselves by tribal or family groups called clans, which became a law unto themselves, protecting family members and assaulting others. Bands of mounted warriors raided other clans and neighboring territories, rustled cattle and livestock, and pursued private justice, seeking revenge for violence done to them. By controlling the means of force (a populous clan, weapons, and horses) and religious sanction, some families gained control over wide areas of the extended site and established their claims to priority and prominence. Rome was still not a city with a defined space, public laws, public spaces, or institutions. The Roman Forum (the central meeting place) began as a cattle market where people met to swap cows.

Legends speak of Roman kings, the first of whom was the legendary Romulus, whose name seems to be Etruscan in origin, but these early kings may have had a largely religious role. Only with the Etruscan phase of its early history in the sixth century BCE did Rome become what we would recognize as a city. The last three of Rome's legendary kings were Etruscans, and they transformed the site of Rome. It was not by accident that the name of the city of Rome (Ruma) comes from Etruscan. These kings encouraged migration (probably of their own people) to the new city, drained the marshes in the area of the Forum, and promoted religion by building temples to the gods. The first Roman art style is called Etrusco-Italic, one famous example being the statue of the she-wolf of Rome. Another effect of Rome's Etruscan period was that some basic political unity was forced on the scattered villages of the hillsides. The second of the three Etruscan kings, Servius Tullius, is credited with building a wall to outline a single urban space and mounting games and religious festivals to unite the dispersed population.

The economic impact of the sixth century BCE on Rome was considerable. One crude measure of Etruscan Rome's contact with the wider Mediterranean economy can be found in surviving pottery shards. Few Athenian pottery fragments have been found on the site of Rome before the Etruscans took control, but hundreds after they arrived. The economy of Rome and its hinterland remained primarily agricultural, but the Etruscans had extensive economic links with the Mediterranean world to which Etruscan Rome was exposed. Rome still lacked a money economy (that is, it had no coinage). Goods were paid for with cattle and sheep or chunks of copper.

The Etruscan contribution to Rome's political and religious formation was equally significant. The Etruscan kings introduced the Romans to **augury** (reading the will of the gods and signs of the future by studying the flight of birds) and **haruspicy** (reading entrails, particularly the livers, of animals). Even some central political symbols such as the **curule** or official chair of the **magistrate** (a representative of the people given the right to hold executive power), **fasces** (an ax and rods joined together to signify the magistrate's right to enforce physical punishment), purple toga, golden wreath, and ivory rod date from the Etruscan period. The Etruscans left Rome with an inheritance of religious, artistic, and political symbols and, above all, with a rudimentary city. Cities were not common in prehistoric Italy. Most of the peoples of central Italy lived in scattered clan-based societies, but the Etruscans, like the Greeks, organized their societies around cities.

The Etruscan rule of Rome ended around 500 BCE, though the legendary date of 510 or 509 BCE was the one given by the Romans. Roman aristocrats called on the help of another Etruscan chieftain or mercenary war lord to aid them in expelling their last Etruscan king, Tarquin the Proud. The Etruscans did not take their expulsion from Rome happily and, with the assistance of the king of the Etruscan city of Clevsin, they marched on Rome, whose weakest point of entry was the Sublician Bridge. The crossing was guarded, according to legend, by Horatius Cocles, who rallied the fleeing Romans to destroy the bridge. Soldiers dismantled the bridge behind him while Horatius fought on alone against the oncoming Etruscans. He then swam across the river to his grateful city. The story of Horatius at the Bridge was remembered by Romans as a model of the daring and dedication that good Romans owed to their city.

Though the Etruscan cities shared a language and general culture, they had little success in achieving

The She-Wolf of Rome Roman legend told how the she-wolf nursed Romulus and Remus. The Etrusco-Roman statue of the wolf dates from around 500 BCE, but the bouncing baby boys were added later in the Italian Renaissance to complete the scene.

greater Etruscan unity. Rome was on its way to becoming a fiercely independent city-state. Yet it escaped the Greek and Etruscan dilemma of failing to unite many rival independent city-states by becoming a city that dominated and incorporated surrounding lands and peoples; it found a way to become the power city without equal in the ancient world.

Archaic Roman Religion

Religion was central to Roman history and culture. As an Indo-European people, the Romans carried with them into Italy the rudiments of the polytheistic religion known to the Greeks. They possessed triads of great gods (Jupiter, Juno, and Mars—the Capitoline gods—and Jupiter, Mars, and Quirinus, a god of the early settlement of one of Rome's hills), but during Rome's earliest history no paintings, temples, or statues dotted the seven hills. Instead, Iron-Age Romans believed that vague divine forces (***numina***) animated their world. Driven by a need to survive a daunting physical world of huge boulders, disease-bearing marshes, and marauding wolves, the early Romans sought to appease the divine forces at work in their world. They turned to little gods of small things.

The *numina* attended everyday Roman life in all its mundane activities; separate gods were credited with overseeing birth, weaning, pubescence, and so on until death. Early Romans believed that, if they did not call on the right god at the right time and in the right way, they would not receive critical assistance from the gods. In a world of low life expectancies, crippling disease, violent neighbors, and sudden death, divine help was thought necessary. Rituals, as tried-and-true ways of invoking the gods, became customary.

The Etruscan kings in the sixth century BCE exposed the Romans to a more mature form of polytheism, one informed by Greek religious notions. Temples were built in Rome to great gods such as Jupiter who made the little divine forces of daily life seem puny. During the period of the Etruscan kings, Rome adopted some of the most Roman of its religious practices. The Etruscans were particularly alert to prodigies and portents, whether by reading lightning bolts or the livers of sacrificed animals.

At Rome under the kings there were two chief religious rites, the *inauguratio* and *auspicatus*. In the inauguration ceremony, the augur—a priest imbued with supernatural power—touched the king's head and so transmitted divine power. In the taking of the auspices (from which we derive the word *auspicious*), the flight of birds was studied for signs of the divine will. Romans recalled that, at the foundation of Rome, Romulus and Remus climbed their respective hills to look for birds in the sky to reveal which twin had the favor of the gods. Later the Roman Senate supervised the taking of the auspices since the rite foretold the fortune of the state.

The state also fixed the calendar and sanctioned the institutionalization of archaic religious practices presided over by **pontiffs** (high priests), colleges of priests, and the Vestal Virgins. An older Roman religion of ritual purification and forbidding taboos was modified and institutionalized as the Republic matured.

The Haruspex Reads a Liver The winged god Calchas studies an animal liver to see what it portends for the future on the back of this Etruscan bronze mirror. Each section of the liver was divided into regions, and the haruspex examined them for any unusual signs or deformities.

The Early Roman Republic: Conflict and Stability

How and why did the Early Roman Republic develop? How was its development different from that of other city-states in the ancient world?

Polybius thought that the Roman Republic had a perfectly balanced form of mixed government, for the **consuls** (chief magistrates) represented the despotic or monarchic principle, the Senate the oligarchic or aristocratic, and the assembly of the people the democratic (see Back to the Source at the end of this chapter). But Polybius, writing late in the history of the Republic, did not realize how much the Early Republic (510–275 BCE) and its constitution had changed over the centuries. There never was a written constitution, and the Republic's rules and practices had evolved over time. For that reason, even terms such as *assembly*, *senate*, and *council* defy simple definition.

The Beginnings of Republican Government

The Roman historian Livy (59 BCE–17 CE) thought that after the expulsion of its last king, Rome had developed a fully formed government designed to prevent the return of kingship. Royal power passed to a pair of consuls who held office for a single year. To choose magistrates to guide the state was a rejection of kingship. To divide power between the two guardians of the Republic, each of whom could veto the actions of the other, was designed to introduce a system of checks to prevent the omnipotence and willfulness of a single ruler. To limit the consuls' terms to a single year was intended to prevent the perpetuation of power in a single set of hands. The Romans granted their consuls extensive power (*imperium* or supreme power in both conducting wars and carrying out the law) as the military, religious, and judicial leaders of the city, but they sought to limit consular power.

Consuls, however, did not assume their high Republican roles until the middle of the fourth century BCE, long after the monarchy had been overthrown and following a critical transition to a new style of warfare and a shift in the social fabric of Rome. In the fifth century BCE, after the expulsion of its kings, aristocrats had first placed military power in the hands of horsemen (masters of the cavalry), supreme commanders, and **tribunes** of the people. For much of the fifth century BCE, Romans on horseback continued to carry out raids on their enemies.

What chiefly changed after 400 BCE was the emergence of the phalanx, whose use had been pioneered by the Greeks and Etruscans, as the chief body of warriors Rome put onto the field of battle. The phalanx was a rectangular formation of infantry in rows that moved as a unit against the enemy. The lower classes of Rome (*plebs*), who fought as infantry, came to play an increasingly important role in Roman affairs. Their representatives, the tribunes, had veto powers over Roman affairs. The Curiate Assembly, which had begun in royal times, was made up of thirty units that were supposed to represent all Roman citizens. Its function was to approve (or disapprove) by unit votes or acclamations all important decisions. The Centuriate Assembly came in Republican times to speak for soldiers and was organized like the army itself, by units of one hundred. To this early assembly fell the tasks of selecting consuls and approving wars.

The Roman constitution as such was a living set of unwritten practices and procedures, traditions and laws, always undergoing change as circumstances and customs warranted. The sheer complexity of Roman politics was the result of its various assemblies, the unfixed character of its unwritten constitution, its several classes of citizens, and its underlying conservative nature. Without a Senate to bind things together and steer a straight course, it is hard to imagine the Roman Republic becoming as successful as it proved to be. Rome's success belonged as much to its government as it did to its army and war.

The Senate

The Senate was technically a body of seniors (*senes*, meaning "old ones" in Latin) or **patricians,** men from the oldest, most well-established, and most distinguished Roman families. In royal times the Senate advised the king or sought to affect his will; in the mature Republic it became Rome's central institution. The early Senate was composed of patricians; they represented powerful families and lineages that had established themselves early on and found a way to monopolize power and prestige through an aristocratic code. The number of senators fluctuated over the centuries, but there were typically 300 for much of Republican history.

The Senate met irregularly and was called into session by the tribunes, who served as the chief operating officers of the Assembly of the People (Figure 4.1). Senate meetings were private, but representatives of the various assemblies were allowed to listen from outside the hall. The other assemblies soon found it best to follow the advice and direction of the Senate. The Senate's areas of particular concern were foreign affairs, domestic peace and order, state finance, and religion. During war and crises the Senate's power was enhanced since it made critical appointments, chose or approved a dictator (an official appointed during a time of crisis) for a fixed period of time, and controlled the purse. The Senate's institutional importance grew in the Early and Middle Republics precisely because of the increasing importance to Rome of war and conquest.

Rome was an oligarchy (rule by the privileged few) in which power was shared by a few men who were, theoretically, equals, but distinguishable by family ancestry, wealth, and achievement. In Rome, political power came to those from distinguished families who secured the support of their peers. Important decisions were supposed to be made by and within this closed group, and any aristocrat who appealed to the population at large for political support broke the code of aristocratic conduct and could be charged with rabble-rousing and executed.

The Orders of Roman Society

Roman society was divided into two chief citizen orders: the patricians (aristocrats) and **plebeians** (lower classes). The division was the result of timing and success. The aristocratic families had secured property and social stature, the means of violence (mounted raids), and the control of power and resources. The plebeians were divisible into two sorts, farmers and merchants, both of whom held a subordinate position within the Roman Republic. Before 450 BCE, plebeians were not even permitted to marry patricians.

The plebeians were always an essential part of the Roman state and had early on pressed for legal protection and political rights. Not only did they have their own assemblies and spokesmen, the tribunes, but when the consulship took on its full form in the fourth century BCE, one of the two consuls for each year was supposed to be a

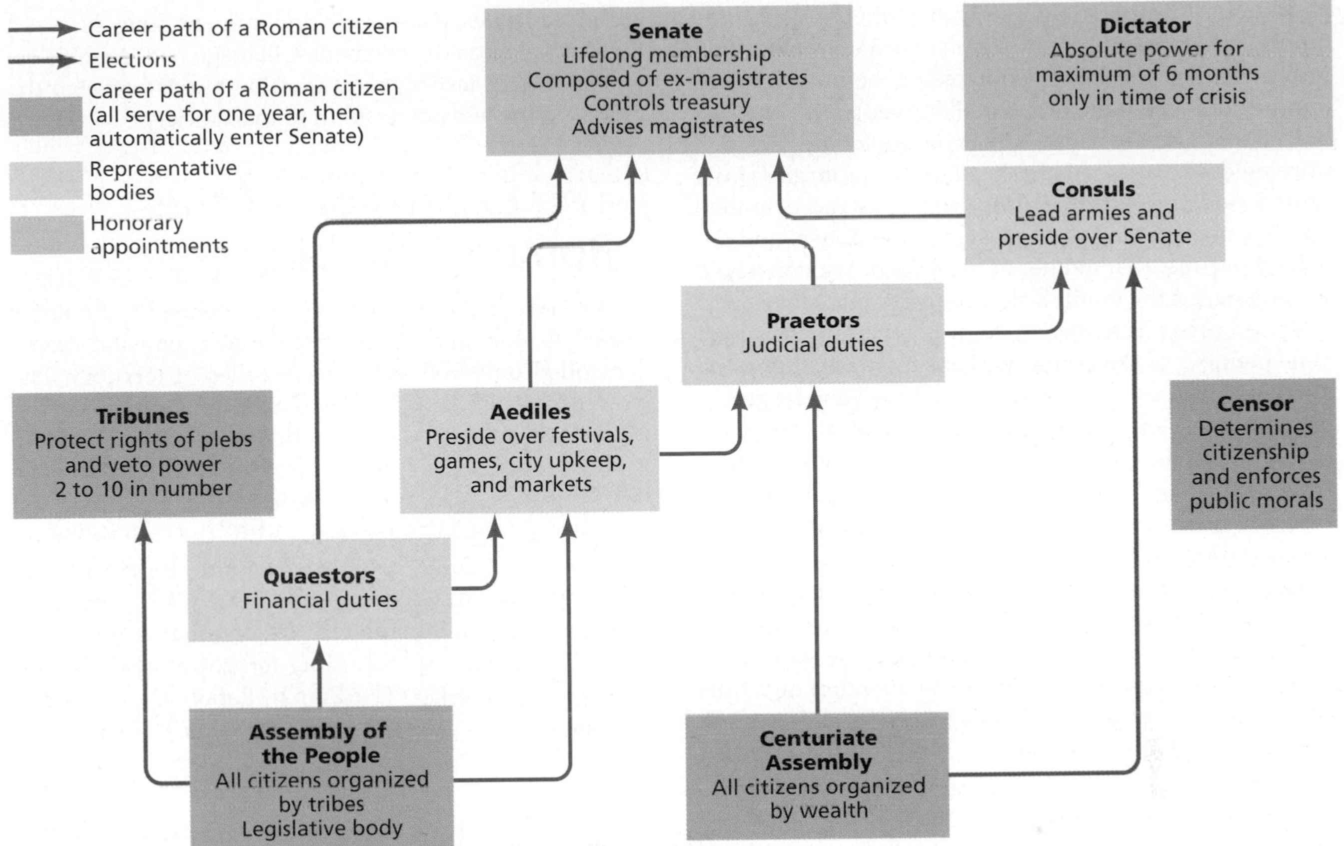

FIGURE 4.1 | Officers and Assemblies of the Roman Republic

The upward path of the Roman aristocrat toward the Senate and a consulship led through a number of offices and long years of service in the representative assemblies and high offices of the Republic.

plebeian. What has often been seen as a desperate struggle between the orders in the Republic (with the people on occasion threatening to withdraw their services, particularly as soldiers, from the state) may just have been politics as normally practiced by Roman citizens. Livy's famous statement that the *plebs* became a state within a state attests to how powerful and necessary lower-class citizens were to the success of Republican affairs.

The shift to infantry warfare made the common plebeian soldier the core military resource of the Republic and knocked the aristocracy off its high horse. As a result, aristocrats sought other ways to maintain preeminence within the state: by supervising religious rites, leading armies in conquest, using the Senate as a decision-making body, by **clientage** (by which an inferior citizen became the dependent or client of a superior), and by keeping plebeians in debt.

Although the plebeians were often unhappy with the way in which patrician power was exercised, they benefited from the material prosperity of an expanding Rome and that may have lessened social tensions in the Early Republic. Plebeians were prepared to fight for Rome because they profited materially from Rome's successes. The important thing for most common citizens was simple survival, and increased prosperity made for contented citizens. The early patrician order was to a great extent a closed group, but ambitious plebeians placed considerable pressure on the aristocracy in general and the Senate in particular to address their concerns. Since plebeians could never be patricians, the social climbers among them were attracted by a newer concept of ranking, nobility, which recognized merit as well as wealth and birth. A noble was typically someone from a family who could count several consuls among his ancestors. This made the Senate and high office the goal of both aristocrats and ambitious plebeians and ensured that there was some fluidity within Roman society. War was one of the best places to demonstrate meritorious service to the state.

The Roman Patriarchy: Fathers, Patricians, and Patrons

The main operating unit of the Roman world was the extended family. The Romans had no simple word for a nuclear family but called their larger family units a *gens* or clan. The importance of birth and background is reflected in aristocratic names. In the Early Republic these names had two parts: a personal name such as Gaius (also written as Caius) and the family name. By the later republican period, aristocratic names often had three parts, such as Marcus (the personal or given name), Tullius (the family or clan name), and Cicero (a surname that might indicate either another given name or the branch of the family from which the individual derived).

The word *familia* referred to a household and included unrelated servants. At the head of these large family units stood the ***paterfamilias,*** who was the extended family's nominal father or master of the house, and the ***materfamilias,*** that mother or mistress of the household who managed the family's children, servants, slaves, and daily resources. The *paterfamilias* was generally the senior male member of the family, perhaps a grandfather or an uncle, and his powers and responsibilities were far reaching. In matters of politics and religion, he represented the family in public. On domestic matters, he might take the advice of the family as a whole in a quasi-counsel, but he alone had the power over whether family members lived or died and to whom they could be married. He could dissolve marriages, even ones between happy couples, whenever he chose. He could also divorce his own wife at will and compel her death if he so wished. If he chose to sell a son into slavery or to abandon and thus kill a newborn child, he had the legal right to do so. His ***patria potestas*** or paternal power was almost unfettered in law, if not carried to extremes all that often.

Male power, a legacy of Rome's Indo-European background, was rooted in the Roman family and extended throughout Roman society. In the Early Republic, patricians established rules or primitive laws, laying out what was permissible and what was forbidden for all. Plebeian families seem to have shared the same male model of organization but lobbied to reduce the right of their powerful superiors to render arbitrary decisions and sought to lessen the penalties for such things as debt. In the fifth century BCE they gained a codification of Roman laws on *Twelve Tables,* so called because the laws were posted in the Roman Forum on tablets made of wood or bronze. Although the fragments of the law code that survive may seem harsh to us, a fixed set of laws was less whimsical and biased in favor of arbitrary decisions by powerful patrician magistrates. The *Tables* treat predictable matters: rules for trials, debt and property, rights of the Roman father over family members, and crime.

A person who lacked a family or membership in one of the better families was forced by circumstances to seek out a patron for protection and support. The individual seeking the protection of a patron was called a client and the network of these extra-familial associations was called the institution of clientage. The relationship between patron and client involved an exchange of assistance for loyal service, the patron giving land, gifts, and money for the client's allegiance, service, and dependence. Clientage operated as an influential ordering force throughout most of Roman history. As an institution, it helped the disadvantaged and those without powerful families to bridge the divide that lay between them and the patricians and nobles, whose help and influence they required for survival and advancement. Clientage relationships established long-lasting extra-familial bonds between the more and the less powerful in Roman society.

The Expansion of the Roman Republic

At the start of the fifth century BCE, when the Republic began its slow and steady territorial expansion, Rome controlled only 300–400 square miles of territory. The city was surrounded by hostile and ambitious peoples. After a series of military and diplomatic conflicts, it dominated and signed treaties with the neighboring peoples of Latium. Together Rome and these nearby Latin peoples moved to conquer other surrounding territories and peoples. The Roman Republic was aggressive and expansionary by both nature and need (Map 4.2).

Why was Rome so dedicated to war, conquest, and incorporating conquered territory? How did the commitment to conquest affect Roman institutions and the Roman population?

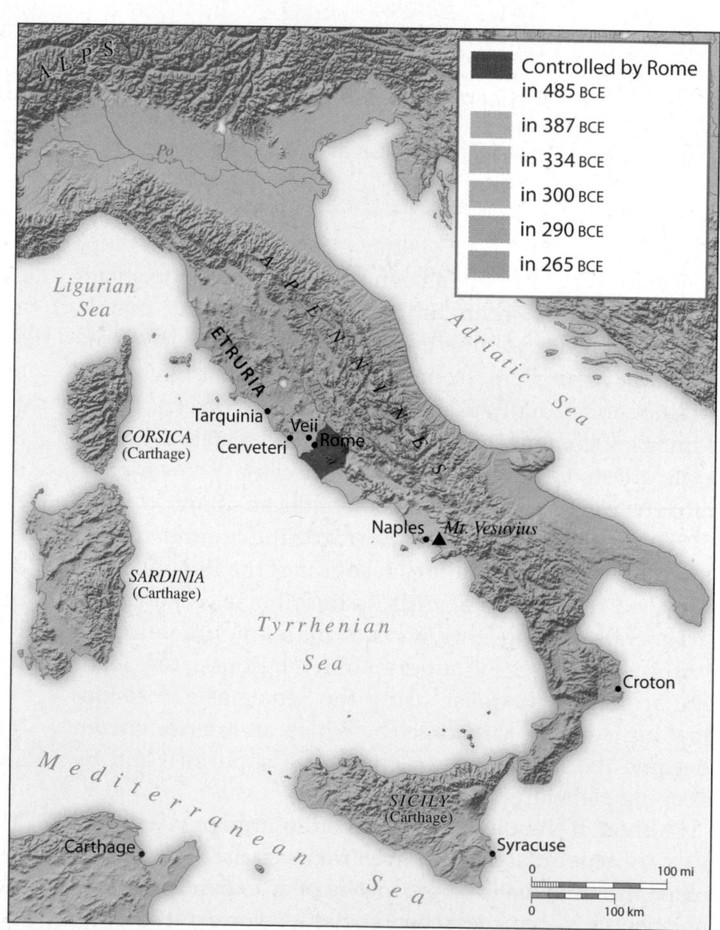

MAP 4.2 | **Rome Takes Italy, 485–265 BCE**
Over two centuries, Rome slowly but steadily took control of Italy. ***What was the pattern of Rome's expansion in the Early Republic? What was left to do by 265 BCE?***

386 BCE: Rome or Roman Veii?

The invasion of the Gauls in 390 BCE and the capture and sack of Rome in 387 BCE struck the Roman people hard. So damaging was the assault that some Romans proposed abandoning their city and moving permanently to the recently conquered Etruscan city of Veii. Tribunes pushed for the move to Veii as early as 390 BCE, when the Gauls invaded Roman territory, and they increased their campaign after the sack. They argued that Rome was so destroyed that it could not be rebuilt. Much of the population favored the move. Many had already migrated to Veii and others were pouring in daily, hoping to find a new political and social beginning in Veii.

Apollo of Etruscan Veii, One of the Gods Supposed to Protect the City

The critical issue for the Roman people was religious. They worried that the gods had deserted their city by permitting its violation. The conqueror of Veii, Marcus Furius Camillus, who served as consul and then dictator at the time of the Gallic crisis, was dead set against the move. Why, he said, should victorious Rome change places with vanquished Veii? Why should Romans abandon their gods and become exiles from their true home? In 390 BCE, the Senate rallied behind Camillus's call to stand by Rome, but he did grant the plebeians some of Veii's land. When the Gauls seized Rome in 387 BCE, the migration issue heated up again. Camillus drove out the last Gauls and immediately began to restore Rome's religious integrity. All the temples that had been polluted by the presence of the Gauls were purified, and Camillus called for games to honor Jupiter, who had permitted Rome's restoration. Tribunes, however, held mass meetings to urge the Roman people to abandon the city. At this juncture Camillus, surrounded by senators, addressed the people. Yes, he said, we ignored the dire warnings of the gods and neglected our religious duties and so suffered defeat and the capture of Rome, but we soon remembered our religious obligations, restored proper worship, and won back the favor of Jupiter. Why would we now in the midst of victory abandon our city? If we move to Veii and it is destroyed, will we move again and become forever wandering exiles? Rome's very success was connected to its urban place, to the beloved Tiber and hills of Rome, their ancestral traditions, and to the gods of the city. When Camillus finished his speech, the Senate voted to stay, rebuild the city, and rededicate itself to Rome's gods.

Had Camillus lost the argument, would there be a Roman history to write? Would the displacement of the population have cost Rome critical time in its territorial expansion and given one of its hostile neighbors an edge in the next war? If they had moved, would the Roman people have lost their conviction that they were superior to other peoples and that they were the darlings of the gods? Would the delicate and successful mix of political forces in Rome have become so unbalanced by a move to Veii that Rome would no longer have possessed the dynamism and determination that characterized its conquest of Italy? Rome's very future hung in the balance in 386 BCE, and it could have gone either way.

QUESTIONS | ***Consider the case of Rome or Roman Veii. What role does contingency, or chance, play in history? If the Romans had abandoned their city in 386 BCE, what would have been their fate and historical importance? Would Rome's history have been essentially the same?***

Cleaning Up the Neighborhood

The chief threat to the Republic at the outset came from those Etruscans whose cities were located near Rome. Etruscan power was in decline by the end of the sixth century, and the expulsion of the last Etruscan king of Rome was a symptom of that decline. Etruscan interests were also suffering in the western Mediterranean. Both the Greeks and the Carthaginians were in stiff trading competition with them. The Greeks also had holdings in northern Africa, Sicily, southern Italy, and Spain. Etruscans and Carthaginians joined together to resist them but lost a sea battle to the Greeks around 535 BCE. In 474 BCE, Greek forces destroyed an Etruscan fleet. With Etruscan power waning, the Romans were able, in the fourth century BCE, to pick off the disunited Etruscan cities one by one.

The Etruscan city of Veii lay only twelve miles from Rome along the Tiber. It was richer and more defensible than Rome. After a century of periodic hostility, diplomatic

CHRONOLOGY Two Centuries of Roman Territorial Expansion

DATE (BCE)	VICTORIES OVER . . .
340–338	The Latin League
343–290	The Samnites
282–272	Greek settlements of southern Italy
264–241	Carthage in the First Punic War
218–201	Carthage in the Second Punic War
212–211	Syracuse, Sicily
215–146	Macedonia and Greece
212–133	Spain
196–163	The Seleucid kingdom
149–146	Carthage in the Third Punic War

maneuvering, and a decade-long blockade, Rome finally conquered it around 396 BCE and annexed its territory. Roman soldiers stripped the city of its gods (that is, its statues and cult objects) and carried them back to Rome.

In 390–387 BCE, disaster struck Rome. A large band of Gauls (Celts) invaded northern Italy and defeated a Roman force fifteen miles from the city. In 387 BCE, the Gauls took the city of Rome and set fire to much of it, though some young Romans stayed behind to protect the citadel and a few patricians remained to protect their own properties. It was then that Juno's geese are supposed to have alerted the defenders to a creeping assault on the citadel of the city. Eventually the invaders were paid off and departed after sacking the city.

The Romans returned and repaired their city. Although many historians have downplayed the Gallic crisis, the Romans did not. The sack of Rome was a blow, however temporary, to Roman confidence. The incident does testify to the underlying resilience and determination of the city; Rome redoubled its efforts to remove by force its enemies from the neighborhood. Romans constructed a wall almost six miles long around the city and continued to take over nearby cities. In 351 BCE, Rome defeated the city of Tarchna, from which its own Etruscan kings had originally come, and the city of Caisra submitted to Rome's domination not long afterward. The Etruscan peoples to the north had also been hammered hard by the raiding Gauls, which left Rome the strongest city in northern Italy.

Taking on the Latin League and the Samnites

The Republic's next conflict was with the so-called Latin League, of which Rome had once been a part. Comprised of several dozen villages and tribes in the area of Latium near Rome, the league and Rome separated ways after the Gallic invasion. In 340–338 BCE, Rome successfully fought a brief war against these peoples and then disbanded the league. Rome's conquest of the Latin peoples and lands brought it into new conflicts in central Italy, particularly with the Samnites, a mountain tribe. In a series of three wars with the Samnites, fought between 343 and 290 BCE, Rome gained a measure of control over central Italy. It also gained a steady supply of Samnite slaves. The south of the Italian peninsula, however, remained a center of Greek influence and resistance to Roman hegemony.

One of Rome's advantages during these early wars was that its subordinate allies, the nearer Latin peoples, remained loyal. Rome struck treaties with its allies, stipulating what percentage of the war spoils each ally was to receive. During the Samnite wars and because of its continuing conflicts with the remaining Etruscan cities and the still dangerous Gauls, Rome restructured its army into mobile and efficient legions.

The Roman Army in the Early and Middle Republics

Rome's army and manner of conducting war was evolving constantly: from equestrian warfare to phalanxes and then legions. In the fourth century BCE, the Republic replaced the phalanx with the legion and doubled the size of its basic fighting unit to 5,000–6,000 men. The legion was broken into lines of maniples or rectangular blocks of unit formations that were spread across the field of action in thirty maniples, each containing about 150–200 soldiers. These units were under the command of a centurion and each possessed its own standard. Within the maniples the soldiers were sorted in horizontal lines according to their skill and experience.

To the enemy the legion seemed a solid and yet mobile fighting force. The maniples were assembled so that there were gaps between them, staggered so that the gaps in the front unit were filled in by the soldiers of the second line standing behind it. This open order assembly (unlike the solid phalanx) allowed a legion to cover more space and yet ensured that all its gaps were plugged.

As a battle was engaged, the javelin throwers at the front hurled their light spears at the enemy but then moved through the gaps between the maniples to be replaced by the front line of spearmen who hurled heavy spears when the enemy was within range. Once the spearmen had reached the enemy's front line, they tried to finish them off with short swords. At any stage of a battle, if the soldiers at the front were exhausted or making no progress, they could, on command, slip as a unit between the gaps between the maniples to be replaced by the fresh troops behind them. If the first and second lines both failed to win the skirmish, they would retreat through the gaps to a position behind the third line, which would then close ranks to fill all the remaining gaps, and the legion as a whole would retreat. The standards of the legion were kept with the third line, both to protect them and as a point of reference during any retreat.

The early Romans were skilled at laying siege to cities, but it was the legion that predominated during the period of expansion. Though the legion was a highly organized, hierarchically arranged, and successful fighting force, the Republic still lost many battles. Its legions had problems fighting under certain conditions: bad weather that might obscure sightlines, night battles, and charging elephants that threw the legionary formation into disarray. But Rome learned from its mistakes and was constantly adjusting its army formation and style of fighting to meet the changing conditions of war. The individual Roman legionary may not have been a better fighter than an Etruscan or Samnite soldier, but the Roman army was better disciplined and organized. Credit for its preparedness lay with the Roman Senate and its commitment to producing regular, rational warfare; to putting large numbers of men in the field under successful and ambitious generals; and to adjusting its military strategies according to need. Without a successful military machine, Republican Rome might not have survived.

Conflict with the Greeks in Southern Italy

In 280 BCE, Rome stood on the brink of ruling all Italy. The Greek colonies in southern Italy were all that stood in its way. After the conquest of the Samnites, Rome came into direct conflict with the powerful coastal city of Tarentum, a Greek foundation at the instep of the Italian boot. Tarentum, irked by Roman interference in its affairs and trade, asked the Hellenistic king Pyrrhus of Epirus (319–272 BCE) to come to its aid. In 280 BCE, the king arrived at Tarentum with 25,000 mercenary troops and some twenty elephants. Pyrrhus was an exceptional general and decisively defeated several Roman armies, in part because of his clever use of elephants to disrupt the front lines of the Roman legions he faced. The Roman Senate was reportedly on the verge of accepting his terms of settlement when the Carthaginians, eager to limit Greek influence in southern Italy, offered the Romans assistance. The conflict moved to Sicily where the Carthaginians had mercantile and political interests. Pyrrhus successfully invaded Sicily and came close to eliminating the Carthaginian presence on the island, but when he turned his troops back against the Romans his campaign stalled and he withdrew. For all his military success against the Romans, Pyrrhus could not afford to sustain the war; for this reason a **Pyrrhic Victory** is one that comes at too great a cost. The king's withdrawal left Rome in control of the south, where it now compelled the Greek cities to accept the presence of Roman troops.

At the end of the Early Republican period in 275 BCE, the Roman Republic controlled the entire Italian peninsula. Conquered peoples were enlisted either as Roman citizens or, more commonly, as allies (*foederati*). The Republic did not initially demand heavy taxes or tribute from its allies, but rather loyalty and troops, both necessary to keep the Roman war machine running. The invasions by the Gauls and Pyrrhus reveal something else about Rome's success. Rome lost battles, but not wars. It was generally reluctant to settle with invaders except to buy time for their expulsion. By treating allied lands and people as part of its expanding territory, Rome gradually integrated Italy into a greater Roman cultural and historical entity. Roman roads, often built for military purposes, began to bind Italy together. Wider Rome became the condition of all Italy and the city of Rome its center of power. Economically, Italy was becoming an interdependent unit.

By 275 BCE, Rome controlled nearly 47,000 square miles of territory, an area larger than all of the Hellenistic kingdoms except the shrinking Seleucid kingdom. It is estimated that Italy had a population of around three million people, while the city of Rome had a male population of 300,000. Yet Rome had found the means and determination to dominate the whole peninsula.

Territorial Expansion and a Religion of War

How can we account for Rome's dramatic territorial expansion? It was not dramatic in terms of speed. It took the Romans two and a half centuries to conquer an area much smaller than Alexander the Great conquered in thirteen years. But Rome's expansion was dramatic in terms of the incorporation and integration of its conquests. Rome slowly made Italy Roman in a way that Alexander never made Asia Greek. A number of reasons might help to explain Rome's successful territorial expansion.

What role did religion play in Roman life and the Roman state?

Reasons for the Republic's Territorial Expansion

HISTORICAL AND GEOGRAPHIC. The first reason for Rome's success lay in the historical and geographic nature of Italy. In 500 BCE, Rome had no master plan for subduing the ancient world. Indeed, in 387 BCE, whatever building confidence Romans had that they were a race pleasing to the gods was shaken by the Gallic invasion and sack of their city. Romans were motivated from their perilous early days by a basic drive to survive, which was a product of the unstable conditions of early Italy. Rome's geographic setting in Italy was of critical importance. It was to Rome's advantage not to be on the sea, but to have near access to it, and to be on the western side of Italy away from the hotter action in the Balkans and eastern Mediterranean.

Rome's location lay on a historical fault line in early Italy. Rome was located near the middle of Italy with powerful Etruscan cities around it and to the north and the fiercely independent Samnites and Greek cities to the south. Situated on a vulnerable, hilly site that was difficult to defend, Rome was surrounded by hostile peoples at a time when the most elemental conflicts were between tribes holding mountainous terrain and those dwelling on plains. Rome was forced to confront these various ethnic and linguistic groups that were each seeking to preserve their own way of life.

Rome's response was the obvious one: conquer or be conquered by the other aggressive peoples of Italy. The Republic of Rome realized that only by steadily defeating and incorporating its defeated enemies could it endure and thrive. Thus, it was the drive to survive in a hostile land that drove Rome to succeed.

TIMING. Chronology and chance also contributed to Rome's success. In the sixth century BCE, the city of Rome emerged and prospered under its Etruscan kings, but over the next two centuries it caught the various Etruscan cities in decline and disunity. The Latins and the other peoples of central Italy were in their own formative stages of development when they encountered Rome, while the city-states of Greece had more important business with the Persians in the east and with one another in Greece. The Greek settlements in southern Italy were at some distance from Rome. It was fortunate for Rome that Alexander the Great marched east, not west, and died young. While Carthage had the upper hand in the Mediterranean, it was a maritime power at a time when Rome's interests were land based. If an ill-favored wind had risen in the sixth or fifth centuries BCE, it might have blown Rome away, but aside from the Gallic gale of 390–387 BCE, that wind never blew.

STRUCTURAL. Another reason for Rome's success was structural. In a hostile environment, the Roman government institutionalized war. The Senate and Centuriate Assembly determined what the greatest threats to the city were and decided which wars to fight the next year and over the long term. It is striking that the Gauls, whose wanderings could not easily be predicted, were the one people to catch Rome by surprise and to do the greatest damage. Fixed and established powers with cities and territories to defend could be handled. In a world with city-states similar to its own and more decentralized clan-based powers, Rome's Senate proved a superior institution for managing external affairs and making war. In foreign affairs, Rome was opportunistic, signing treaties with some peoples while attacking others and then, in the coming years, turning the tables on its enemies. The Senate supplied justifications for these wars against its neighbors, often claiming that its motives were purely defensive, that Rome was threatened or that its rightful interests had been damaged by the enemy. Rome's centralization of power and decision making were simply superior to those of the decentralized and often disorganized peoples of Italy.

Moreover, in the fourth century, Rome improved its military techniques and restructured its army into the more efficient legion. Rome's system of war was tested on the field of battle and improved over several centuries. In short, the institutional structure of Rome led to a deliberate, rational commitment to warfare. Making war was Rome's chief function, yet Rome did not become a military state during the Republican period.

INCORPORATION. Another advantage to the Roman system, born of necessity, was the flexibility of its dealings with the other peoples of Italy. In the early days of the Republic, those peoples closest to the city of Rome were incorporated as full citizens. Other peoples farther away lacked full citizenship rights, unless they relocated to Rome, but could operate as Roman cities. They were thus reduced to the status of self-governing municipalities. Other Italian peoples agreed by way of treaties to submit to Rome as allies and to supply troops to Rome, but each of these peoples struck a different agreement with Rome and those agreements changed over time. The Samnites in the Apennine mountains of central Italy had resisted Rome so fiercely that many of them were enslaved and had their lands seized. But the Roman road system built for military reasons brought about the increasing circulation of peoples and goods, and led to further economic and social integration within Italy. Allied and conquered peoples supplied troops to Rome when so ordered and subordinated their external affairs to Rome and its central planning.

By 225 BCE, a million subordinate Italians had gained full Roman citizenship and, thus, enjoyed the benefits and protection of Roman law, though most were not given votes in Rome. One of the reasons Rome could not afford to surrender in war was that it would risk the collapse of its ally system, which depended on Rome continuing to hold the whole of its territory under the umbrella of its power. But Rome's flexible treatment of the Italian peoples also meant that not all of the Italian peoples or regions were equal, that resentments grew in some places, and that Rome would eventually have to resolve the uneven set of relationships it had with the peoples of Italy.

WEALTH GENERATION. Although survival may have been the earliest reason for Rome's wars of expansion, the conquerors' desire for material gain was always a factor. Land was the chief gain during expansion in Italy. Losing to Rome was not particularly pleasant and came at a cost not only to a territory's independence and cultural identity, but also to its real estate. Romans obtained and maintained vast and fertile villas throughout Italy. Often they took the best of any newly conquered land. Typically Rome expropriated something like a third of the land it conquered, unless it had made a treaty with the conquered that stipulated what land would be surrendered. Conquering armies also seized movable goods or riches during campaigns. By the Middle Republic, the enslavement of conquered peoples also generated immense wealth for Romans. Rome struck agreements with its allies to share the spoils of war.

ETHOS. The virtues that aristocratic Romans prized may also help to explain some part of the dynamics of Roman military success. Rome was always on a war footing and the Senate's chief business was foreign affairs or, to put it more bluntly, making war and dominating territory. In the whole of the fourth and third centuries BCE, there was hardly a year when Rome was not at war with some territory. Behind the generation of war there was a central ethos, or set of guiding beliefs.

Polybius believed that it was not by accident or without planning that the Romans sought and achieved dominion over the Mediterranean world. He thought that it was Rome's destiny. But, if we were able to ask a common Roman soldier or senator from 400 BCE whether he believed in the inevitability of Rome's conquest of the known world, he would probably have been astounded by the idea. There were too many enemies in the neighborhood and too many problems at home for them to take such a prospect seriously. Yet Rome slowly but surely swallowed a world. There was, at the time, no systematic ideology of conquest, no notion of Rome's responsibility to lift up a troubled and uncivilized world. That would come later, after the fact of expansion and the achievement of an effective empire. For much of the period of Republican expansion, Romans sought land, resources, and territorial integrity.

No abstract idea drove Rome to expand, but rather a set of immediate goals and Republican ideals. The reasons for Rome's expansion are complex, but the virtues that Republican patricians and nobles admired may have supplied the energy and competitive drive behind conquest.

Roman Virtue and the Pursuit of Glory

The Latin word ***virtus,*** from which English derives the word *virtue,* suggests the moral core of Rome's aristocratic elite. For Romans the word meant something closer to "manliness" since its root is *vir* or "man." A small constellation of virtues guided Roman males, both aristocrats and those wishing to secure noble standing. Among these were seriousness (*gravitas*), firmness of purpose (*constantia*), training (*disciplina*), hard work (*industria*), pious reverence toward the gods (*pietas*), simplicity of life (*frugalitas*), and fair dealing or trustworthiness (*fides*). The opposite of these virtues was exemplified by a man who was flippant and flighty, lazy and lacking a goal in life, self-indulgent, given to luxury, and untrustworthy.

The approval of the aristocratic group was all-important, for from it flowed stature and preeminence. But just as a group approved an individual's merits, it was another group—the individual's extended family—that benefited in terms of prestige and social standing. The Roman virtues were a set of ideal behaviors that were rewarded with "glory" or "glorious fame" (*gloria*). By battling nobly and even dying for the state on the field of battle, a man achieved a reputation of enduring magnificence that lifted him above others. He would be able to achieve such glorious renown, Romans believed, only if his life was well ordered and if he possessed in his very nature the core virtues that the Romans prized. Sallust, the Late Republican historian, said that there was an intense competition for glory among Republican Romans. Each man wanted to achieve a military victory that would bring fame, respect, and wealth to his family and himself. The competition for glory fueled the Republican war machine as aristocrats lined up to lead armies into battle.

Immortality was the ultimate prize. Polybius describes in fascinating detail the honor paid to aristocrats who died gloriously in battle. Their bodies were carried into the Forum and propped up by the speaker's platform in the Senate as though they were about to listen to their praises being sung by a senator. The man's accomplishments and virtues were then described. The ritual created the impression that the man or his spirit was watching over the proceedings, enjoying the praise for his efforts on behalf of the Republic. When aristocratic males died, wax images of their faces were made. Great Roman families stored these death masks in cupboard shrines. On important occasions, such as the death of a noble Roman in battle, aristocrats donned the death masks of their relatives, dressed themselves in rank-appropriate togas, and marched in solemn procession to the Senate to listen to a speech in the dead man's praise. On such occasions the Senate was filled with the ghostly images of the gloriously deceased of the Republic, who were its real guardians. This was the company Roman nobles and aristocrats

A Roman Patrician Cradles the Busts of His Ancestors Ancient Romans worshipped their glorious ancestors and kept images and death masks of their glorious dead.

hoped to keep. Death masks reproduced the likeness of the dead with remarkable fidelity, which may help to explain the startling realism of Roman bust portraits.

Ancestor worship animated aristocratic Rome. A noble Roman's sense of place was grounded in his family's reputation and the chance that his own glorious deeds would contribute to the family's growing repute. The Roman military machine operated so successfully because it was driven by the individual's desire to excel inside a system of collective values. These men fought not just for money and land, and not for something as elusive and abstract as power, but for immortality. Glory overcame death. What invigorated Roman expansion, then, was a complex set of factors, not the least of which was a dynamic competition to achieve glory inside an aristocratic ethos that welcomed war.

A Religion of War

Religious beliefs and a warrior ethic meshed in the Republic. When waging war, Romans paid particular attention to pleasing the gods. They thought of war as a religious rite. In 340 BCE, a consul fighting the Latins encamped near Mount Vesuvius "devoted" himself. He had, in other words, decided to sacrifice himself to the gods so that Rome might win the battle. After dressing himself in a special toga for the occasion, he veiled his head and, while standing on a javelin, invoked a prayer and offered himself and the enemy to the gods. Trusting that death awaited him, he rode out alone against the enemy.

A counter-example is the case of the Roman general Publius Claudius Pulcher (consul in 249 BCE), who was insufficiently reverent during a naval battle in the Punic wars. On the eve of the battle, he called for the ritual feeding of the chickens, a traditional test of augury that would determine if the gods favored Rome. When the birds refused to cooperate, he had them thrown into the sea, saying that if they would not eat, they should drink. His fleet was destroyed and Romans understood why. The gods had been angered by an impious general who spurned their counsel.

The point was to get war right and, to do so, the gods needed to be on the Romans' side. The historian Livy said that the (legendary) king Ancus Marcius set down the religious rites of war. An envoy should first be sent to the frontier with his head covered in a veil. He would then proclaim aloud that he was the religiously commissioned herald of Rome, declare himself to the god Jupiter, and proclaim the righteousness of the Roman cause. He would then read out a list of Rome's demands, after which he was to step across the frontier boundary, proceed to the enemy's central square, and restate the demands. If satisfaction was not forthcoming within the sacred number of thirty-three days, the envoy would declare war and return to Rome to report to the Senate. Then the herald would return to the border carrying a spear bloodied from an animal sacrifice and hurl it into the enemy territory after singing another ritual prayer. It is unlikely that Philip of Macedon or his son Alexander would have worried quite so much about religious rituals, but the Romans wanted not just to win wars but to enlist the gods, both their own and the enemy's, in their wars.

The *evocatio* or "calling out" was the religious rite by which the Romans summoned forth the gods of another city to their side. They were convinced that each city had its own protective deities. If those gods could not be persuaded to join them, it would not be possible to take the city. But first they needed to know the names of the gods they had to win over. Romans were careful not to publicize the secret name of Rome or the secret names of its protective gods. Once the names of the gods of a besieged city were known, the Romans would invoke them, promising to respect them and their temples, to offer sacrifices to them, and to treat them better than their besieged rulers had. When the Romans decided to destroy a city, a different ritual was performed. In those cases, the city was stripped of its gods and the people and properties were sacrificed to the gods. Such were the fates of Veii, Carthage, and Corinth.

Triumphs or triumphal processions through the streets of Rome by victorious generals were religious festivals. The Senate and people of Rome honored a general who had achieved a victory in which the enemy lost five thousand men or more. The general rode in a chariot through the streets of Rome, preceded by the spoils, animals, and people seized from the conquered land. At the end of the triumph the general dedicated a trophy of the armor and weapons of the defeated people to the temple of Jupiter Feretrius. With his face painted red, the victorious general wore a purple toga, sported a wreath on his head, and carried a scepter. The purpose of the triumph was to treat the successful general as if he were god for a day. The parade itself was as raucous and exuberant as urban parades for victorious sports teams today. In Rome virtually everything had a religious tinge and nothing more so than the conduct and success of war.

Living the Religious Life: The Roman Calendar and Vestal Virgins

As the Republic reaped success in war and the city of Rome grew, its religion matured and its old beliefs and practices were institutionalized. The older household gods and *numina* retained their force in the daily lives of most Romans, but the state itself increasingly sanctioned, systematized, and formalized religious practices, especially those that belonged to the public realm.

The old pre-Julian calendar may be the best witness to traditional Roman religion. On it the days of feasts, games, deities, and public business are intermeshed, suggesting how central religion was to public life. The Romans of the Middle Republic (274–146 BCE) paid scrupulous attention to the religious spheres of life, which may be what Polybius had in mind when he said that the Roman genius lay in its scrupulous attention to religion. Strict devotion to religious rites secured the approval of the gods and reinforced the Roman belief that its success came from satisfied gods. There were a variety of colleges and priests at work in Rome, the chief of whom was the **Pontifex Maximus,** who controlled the calendar and also exercised authority over the other priesthoods, including the Vestal Virgins.

The cult of Vesta may serve as an example of how religion functioned to integrate religion in daily life, and also of how Roman religion had evolved. The six Vestal Virgins were women of patrician stock of different ages, chosen by the Pontifex Maximus as young girls to serve a term of thirty years. They did not marry, and the penalty for not preserving their chastity was to be buried alive. They tended the holy fire and cult of Vesta, the goddess of the hearth. Vesta did not just represent the warmth of the hearth, but was the guardian of fire. Her cult stretched back to the distant hut age of Rome of the ninth to seventh centuries BCE, when keeping a fire alive could have made the difference between living and dying for the early shepherds and farmers of the Roman hills. As Vesta was the hearth, her cult in Rome was observed in a round building that was not a temple but a round hut. There was no statue of Vesta in the building, only an eternal fire tended constantly by the Vestal Virgins. If it died out, it was assumed that the goddess was angry because one of the Virgins had broken her vow of chastity. If identified, the unchaste woman was killed. At the very least, the Virgins were beaten and then they ritually rekindled the fire by rubbing sticks together as archaic Romans once had.

The religious festival of Vesta, the *Vestalia,* began on June 9 when the Virgins left their house in solemn procession to collect water from a holy spring. They were not allowed to set the water down as they returned to their ceremonial hut since the water would be polluted if it touched the earth. The Virgins used the sacred water to make holy cakes that were offered to Vesta. The *Vestalia* became a special festival day for the millers and bakers of Rome. On June 11 the Festival of Mothers or *Matralia* took place, when barefooted women entered the hut to visit the goddess. By June 15 the celebration of Vesta drew to a close. The Vestal Virgins swept the floor of their building and returned to their regular task of tending the flame.

The Virgins participated throughout the year in various other religious rites, many of them of special significance to women. The women's feast of the *Bona Dea* (the Good Goddess) was observed in December. On February 13, at the opening of the feast of the *Parentalia* to honor parents and ancestors, the senior Vestal Virgin gave a public libation to the ghosts of dead parents. The Vestal Virgins also processed with the other priesthoods of Rome in February as the city was purified. On March 1, the first day of the New Year in the old calendar, the Virgins offered some of their hair to the temple of Juno Lucina, goddess of women and childbirth. So that nothing would hinder the delivery of babies, Roman women loosened the knots on their garments and unbound their hair when giving birth. To assist in the unbinding, the Virgins placed strands of their own hair on two old lotus trees in a sacred grove. On May 14 the Virgins proceeded with other priests to the Sublician Bridge over the Tiber where they cast thirty straw dolls into the river. This ceremony has been colorfully called the Drowning of the Dummies. Even the Romans were not sure what the ceremony signified, but it may have been a rite of purification that stretched back to archaic times and represented a symbolic form of human sacrifice.

The Vestal Virgins held an office that endured for over a thousand years until it was abolished by the emperor Gratian in 375 CE. They were at the peak of their importance during the Middle Republic. By then the agricultural rites of expiation and purification made less and less sense to urban Romans, but they were retained as a revered feature of traditional Rome, helping to bind together the archaic agricultural religion of traditional Rome and its complex calendar. What Romans and the state wanted from a cult was constant, rigorous attention; piety; and respect. Individuals need not worry about upsetting Vesta when the state ensured that the goddess was appeased by ritual observance. The Roman calendar was filled with dozens of such religious observances that gently governed their daily lives.

The Carthaginian Contest and the Middle Republic

Rome's spreading lines of conquest had brought it into conflict with a widening frontier of others who had their own lands, cultures, languages, and economic interests. By the Middle Republic, Rome was bumping up against the interests of the great Mediterranean powers, particularly the Carthaginians and Hellenistic Greeks. Over several centuries Rome had perfected a style of fighting that had proven successful on land, but not yet at sea.

Why did Hannibal and the Carthaginians lose to Rome?

By 275 BCE, Roman Italy had taken solid shape. Pyrrhus had abandoned the Greek territories of Italy to Roman control, the Samnites had been suppressed, and the Etruscan cities had been incorporated. Internal tensions within the city of Rome were not pressing in the third century BCE because so many Roman citizens now profited from Rome's expansion, enjoying the resources and riches that came with conquest. Rome was on its way to becoming an imperial power. Each successful conquest increased the desire and need for more land and power. Moreover, because of its ally system, the manpower available to conduct wars increased with each conquest. Over the next two centuries, Rome engulfed a host of lands fronting the Mediterranean: Sicily, Sardinia, Corsica, Spain, Greece, northern Africa, and Asia Minor (Map 4.3). So quickly were the lands lying around the Mediterranean rim taken that Rome would have some difficulty managing its conquests and for a time it was

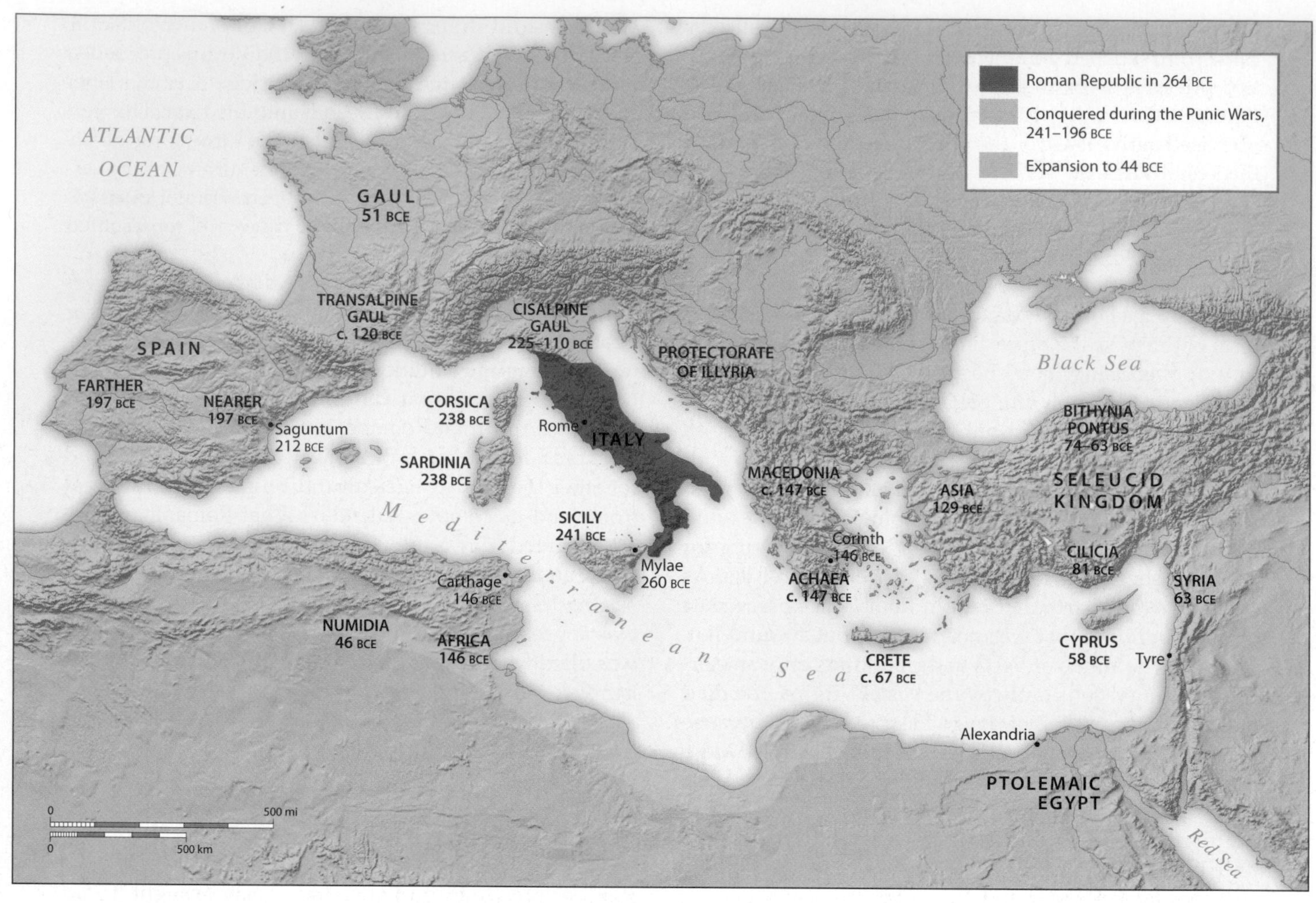

MAP 4.3 | **The Expanding Roman Republic, 264–44 BCE**

By the middle of the third century BCE, Rome was at war with its Mediterranean neighbors, first Carthage and then the Hellenistic kingdoms. ***Why did Rome's conquest of Carthage lead naturally to conflict with the Hellenistic kingdoms? What advantages did controlling the Mediterranean Sea have for Rome's military and economic interests?***

not sure that it wanted to or needed to manage the wider Mediterranean world.

Rome's contest with Carthage played out over a century, but it was a fork in the road for western civilization. One way led to a Mediterranean world dominated by a combination of eastern Mediterranean civilizations (Phoenician, Semitic, and Hellenistic), and the other to the Roman Empire, the Middle Ages, and the West as we know it. At the outset it was far from clear which side would prevail and the consequences that would follow from Roman domination.

The First Punic War

Rome's first and most dramatic Mediterranean conflict was with Carthage, a city located just across from Sicily in northern Africa (near present-day Tunis in Tunisia). The Carthaginians were Phoenicians or red-skins. The traditional foundation date for Carthage was 814 BCE, when some colonists from Tyre sought to establish a port closer to Spain. The city had remained in the shadow of its mother city until the seventh century BCE when Tyre had fallen under the control of a series of empires. Carthage, lying outside the reach of those powers, built a trading empire in the western Mediterranean that stretched from modern-day Libya to Gibraltar. Throughout the sixth and fifth centuries BCE, it continued to trade with and struggle against the economic interests of various Greek and Etruscan cities. For its part, Rome agreed not to impinge on Carthaginian trading zones, which included Sardinia, southern Italy, and Sicily. The power of Carthage reached its pinnacle in the third century BCE, when it took possession of Ptolemaic holdings along the coast of northern Africa and subdued outlying Berber tribes.

Carthage and Rome had different ways of dealing with conquered territories. Like most other ancient empires, Carthage subjugated conquered peoples and forced them to pay tribute, while Rome offered them allied status and asked for troops and participation in Roman wars. Consequently in its conflict with Rome, Carthage seldom had loyal allies, foreign friends, or permanently secure territories. Revolts within its own lands aggravated its contest with Rome. Although Carthage was primarily a sea power, it did practice agriculture on a large scale on vast plantations worked by slaves. The economic prosperity of Carthage came chiefly from the success of its maritime trade; few foreign ships dared to trade in the western Mediterranean or, indeed, ply its waters. Carthage had an effective trading monopoly, particularly once the Etruscans and Greeks ceased to compete with it. Its maritime enterprise was impressive and the harbor of Carthage had a great round house for docking and sheltering ships. The city was particularly proud of its navy, which was made up of citizen crews under veteran commanders.

The Carthaginian army was a different matter. It was largely comprised of mercenaries hired from neighboring conquered peoples such as the Numidians and Libyans. These troops fought under Carthaginian commanders who were hardened professionals. What favored Rome in the coming conflict with Carthage was the stability of its government and its greater financial and personnel resources; what worked against Rome was its lack of maritime experience.

As late as 279 BCE, Rome and Carthage had struck an agreement of mutual cooperation against Pyrrhus, whose invasion of southern Italy and Sicily threatened both their interests. Once Pyrrhus withdrew, the two cities clashed over Sicily. The city of Messina had fallen to a band of mercenaries known as Mamertines (named after Mars, the god of war), who had taken the city, killed all its men, seized its women, and carried out sporadic raids on the rest of the island. Both the Mamertines and King Hieron II of Syracuse (r. 270–215 BCE) sought to win the support of Rome to counterbalance Carthage's claim to trading rights and special political privileges on the island. In 264 BCE, two Roman legions took Messina, precipitating the First Punic (or Phoenician) War (264–241 BCE) with Carthage (Map 4.4).

Rome had a problem at the outset of the war. It had no navy. Polybius found it amazing that Rome dared to challenge the greatest of Mediterranean sea powers. If Rome had been content with its ground strength, it might have remained a second-rate power in the Mediterranean world and never have formed a Mediterranean empire. But by chance the Romans captured a Carthaginian ship and used it as a model to build its own navy. Within two months it had built sixty quinqueremes (single-decked ships with 50–60 oars, five men per oar) and twenty triremes (ships having three banks of oars, one rower per oar).

In its first naval action, Rome lost seventeen of its new ships, but it soon found a way to fight land battles at sea. Rome developed a grappling device called the *corvus* (that is, like the beak of a raven) that was lowered onto the deck of an enemy ship to form a bridge over which soldiers could pass. At Mylae in 260 BCE the Roman navy surprised the Carthaginians, boarded their ships, and destroyed fifty of them. The Roman commander was given Rome's first naval triumph; Carthage crucified its commander for his failure to counter the new strategy. For three years Rome waged a series of successful sea battles against Carthage and then decided to take the fight to northern Africa, transporting 100,000 men there. By 255 BCE, Carthage had figured out how to deal with Rome's boarding tactic, but its navy was already a largely spent force in the war, and soon afterward Rome abandoned the use of its grappling hook. Rarely do new military inventions supply more than temporary advantage, though at the time that advantage may be decisive.

Ironically, although Carthage was a sea power, in this war it did better on land. It hired a Spartan strategist named Xanthippus, who put elephants in the front line of the Battle of Carthage in 255 BCE. They wreaked havoc with Rome's legions of disciplined soldiers. Rome also lost two fleets of ships to storms at sea. For the next thirteen years, the war was confined chiefly to Sicily. In 249 BCE, the two sides fought a great sea battle in which Rome lost 93 of its 120 ships. By 247 BCE, Rome's fortunes stood very low, but Rome refused to capitulate. Carthage sent its most capable general, Hamilcar Barca (the Blitz), to Sicily but failed to give him the men and money he needed to win the war. Rome built another navy, which in 242 BCE destroyed the merchant fleet of Carthage and threatened to starve the Carthaginian forces in western Sicily.

Carthage sued for peace in 241 BCE. The terms agreed to were at first moderate, but Rome soon broke that treaty, seized the Carthaginian islands of Corsica and Sardinia, and demanded an indemnity of 3,200 talents (the rough equivalent in daily wages of 75,000 years of

A Roman Warship A relief showing a Roman battleship with armed soldiers ready to engage in conflict.

labor). If the mercantile interests of Carthage suffered a severe setback, its pride was even more deeply wounded.

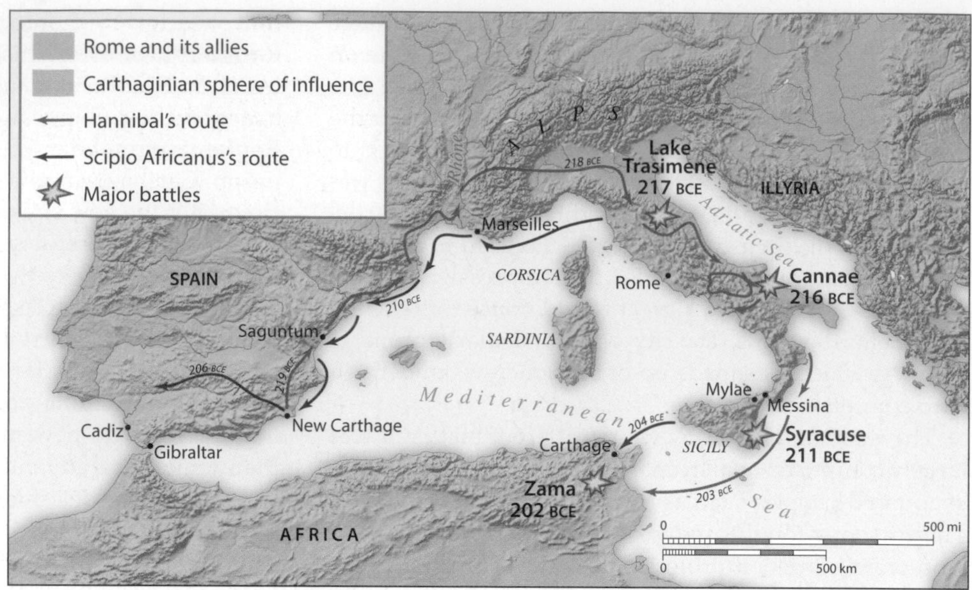

MAP 4.4 | The Campaigns of Hannibal and Scipio Africanus, 219–202 BCE
The Second Punic War played out in Spain, Italy, and North Africa, with Hannibal winning in Italy and losing at Zama in northern Africa. ***How did Rome respond to Hannibal's successful invasion of Italy? Where did Scipio campaign and why? Why did Hannibal fail and Rome prevail in the war?***

The Second Punic War

The Second Punic War (218–201 BCE) was in many ways the direct result of the first. Having lost a valuable part of its trading empire and been forced to pay a large sum of money to Rome, Carthage had trouble hiring mercenaries for its army. For three years it was forced to wage a campaign against its own disgruntled mercenaries and rebellious subjects in northern Africa. Rome seized the opportunity to invade other Carthaginian lands. Hamilcar Barca brought the war with the mercenaries to an end and then concentrated on expanding Carthaginian holdings in Spain. Rome, with its eye on Spain's mineral resources, grew suspicious of its enemy's activities there.

Hamilcar's eldest son, Hannibal (247–183/182 BCE), seized Saguntum, a Spanish city allied with Rome, in 218 BCE after an eight-month siege. Hannibal's plan was not just to irritate Rome, but to strike at its very heart. He conceived of an almost impossible scheme: to invade Italy. The Carthaginian navy had not yet fully recovered after the first war, and Rome controlled the waters around Italy. Thus, Hannibal set out to invade Italy by land. Behind his plan stood the hope that he could win over Rome's allies, leaving Rome to stand on its own.

In May 218 BCE, with about 50,000 infantry, some 9,000 cavalry, and 37 elephants, Hannibal began his expedition. There was some urgency to his march since Roman forces were rushing to cut off Hannibal's access to Italy, but his army arrived at the Rhône River a few days before the full Roman force and he managed to make the crossing. Behind him the Romans cut off the Carthaginian supply lines, so that Hannibal and his troops now had to live off the land. The lack of both land and sea support were to be important factors in the outcome of the war. By the time Hannibal's forces reached the Alps, the September snows had already begun to fall. The pass they took was treacherous, and they were assailed by Gallic mountain peoples who rolled rocks down on them. Many horses and men could not manage the narrow mountain ledges and plummeted to their deaths. Hannibal crossed the Alps in fifteen days, but he seems to have lost almost half his troops during the crossing (whether through reassignment, death, or desertion is not clear), though he arrived with most of his elephants.

For the next fourteen years, Hannibal and his army ran loose in Italy, winning battle after battle and gaining effective control over the Po Valley. At the Battle of Lake Trasimene in 217 BCE, he surprised and destroyed a Roman army that thought that he had already departed for a march on Rome. At the Battle of Cannae the next year, some 70,000 Roman soldiers fell to Hannibal's forces. The Romans came to realize that they were not going to defeat Hannibal in open warfare and so the dictator Fabius, counting on Rome's substantial resources and Hannibal's lack of them, developed a strategy of delay (hence, the term *fabianism* refers to a delaying or gradualist approach). The tactic did buy Rome the time it needed to develop a bolder plan for inducing Hannibal to leave Italy, but it unnerved the people and Senate of Rome. Much of southern Italy and Sicily went over to Hannibal's side, as did some Italian peoples such as the Samnites, but in general Rome's allies held fast. For the next four years the Carthaginians roamed the countryside south of Rome.

Hannibal's plan to win over the Italian allies was not in the long run successful. He lacked the resources to buy support and protect his sympathizers, and living off the land meant that he antagonized many of the peoples he was seeking to separate from Rome. The Second Punic War was chiefly a contest over different systems of territorial expansion and the treatment of subjected peoples. The Carthaginians imposed; the Romans, particularly in Italy, partnered up. Rome's federation of Italian peoples prevailed in the Second Punic War because the Italian peoples feared not only Carthaginian oppression, but also the wrath of Rome for any evident disloyalty. Ultimately Hannibal, for all his brilliance as a general, discovered, as Pyrrhus had, that he could win battle after battle and still not win the war against Rome and its Italian allies.

Rome Takes the War to Africa

As the war continued and there seemed little chance of defeating Hannibal in Italy, Rome decided, as it had in the first war, to attack Carthage and its territories. In 212–211 BCE, it laid siege to Syracuse and, despite the defenses of Archimedes (c. 287–c. 212 BCE), the city fell. The Roman general ordered his soldiers not to kill the famous inventor, but something went wrong and—the pen not always being stronger than the sword—the old man was killed in his study.

Rome took Spain in 207 BCE and drove Hannibal's brother Hasdrubal into retreat. He attempted to join his brother in Italy, but his army was cut down. The Romans later hurled Hasdrubal's head as a hostile greeting into Hannibal's camp in southern Italy. Rome's ultimate strategy for removing Hannibal from Italy was to take the war to Carthage, so in 204 BCE it invaded northern Africa. Hannibal was recalled, abandoning his troops in Italy. At the Battle of Zama in 202 BCE, Hannibal's weak army was largely wiped out by the Roman force led by Scipio Africanus, who earned the title of The African for his success in the campaign. Carthage could no longer continue to resist and sued for peace. It agreed to restrict its territory to Africa, to destroy its fleet, and to pay the crushing indemnity of 10,000 talents. Hannibal escaped and found refuge and employment in the Hellenistic kingdoms, which still lay outside of Rome's control.

The lines of Rome's eventual defeat of Carthage were consistent: never to surrender to an occupying force, no matter how many battles were lost, and to employ its greater resources to outlast and outflank the enemy. Of critical importance was the fact that Rome's allies had by and large stuck with it; they were now part of the expanding Roman world and cannot have been comfortable with the idea of knuckling under to a foreign power as potentially oppressive as Carthage.

Rolling Up the Mediterranean Rim

At the end of the Second Carthaginian War, Rome did not annex Carthage, but it was now fully engaged in the Mediterranean world. Over the next fifty years it would move from policing part of it to controlling most of it. The strains on the Republic of such a large imperial expansion were never hidden to Rome. One day in 180 BCE, Cato the Elder rose in the Senate and lamented the state of Rome's Mediterranean enterprise. He noted that a three-man team was being sent to Bithynia (eastern Turkey) to check on Rome's eastern Mediterranean interests, but one of the men limped with gout, the second had had a roof tile fall on his head and was permanently dizzy, and the third was widely thought to be the stupidest man in all of Rome. Cato wondered what would become of a legation that lacked feet, head, and intelligence. Cato was trying to alert the Senate to bow out of its familiar depths it now was in. Rome slowly realized that it was one thing to conquer a world, quite another to administer it.

The Senate had not been established to control other Mediterranean lands. Tensions between those who favored Roman isolationism and those who promoted expansion and imperialism often divided the Senate, but Rome found that it could no longer divorce itself from the world it had entered so forcefully. The logical conclusion to Roman expansion for purposes of survival was to keep on expanding in order to stabilize the world around its heartland. But every expansion brought new problems and the need for yet further expansion, and a widening set of problems. Prior to its wars with Carthage, Rome had had relatively little to do with the Mediterranean east. In between the two Punic wars, Rome waged a successful war against the Illyrians who lived in the Balkans along the Adriatic coast facing Italy. The Illyrian queen, Teuta, was forced to submit most of her territory to Rome.

By the start of the second century BCE, Rome was regularly receiving foreign diplomats, each seeking something from the powerful new player: protection, favor, or peaceful distance. The Senate, which controlled foreign affairs, considered it its prerogative to interfere in the name of Roman interests in the internal affairs of independent states. Underlying Rome's sense of superiority was its conviction that its people, government, and way of life were superior to those of these foreigners, almost all of whom lived under monarchs. Rome's old hatred of kings, its confidence in its own noble virtues, and its belief that the gods favored Rome continued to underlie its actions.

When Rome encountered the Hellenistic kingdoms, they were for the most part in a state of steady decline. The three great kingdoms of the period were that of Macedonia ruled by Philip V (r. 221–179 BCE), the Seleucid kingdom ruled by Antiochus III (r. 223–187 BCE), and the Ptolemaic kingdom of Egypt under Ptolemy V (r. 203–181 BCE). Philip and Antiochus were among the strongest sovereigns of their respective lines, but Ptolemy was a mere boy. When he came to power, Philip and Antiochus seized the Ptolemaic possessions lying outside of Egypt proper. Philip even struck a treaty with Hannibal when he was still roaming Italy. Rome could not forgive or forget such interference in its internal affairs during its time of crisis.

Despite the isolationists in the Senate, Rome declared war against Philip in 200 BCE. On the pretext of liberating the cities of Greece, Rome fought the so-called Second Macedonian War (200–196 BCE). The Roman general Flaminius led his legions to victory over the famed Macedonian phalanx at the Battle of Cynoscephalae in 197 BCE. Philip was allowed to retain Macedonia but had to surrender mainland Greece, where the Romans now stationed three garrisons of troops. Greece was nominally free but was to be "protected" by Rome for its own good.

OTHER VOICES, OTHER VIEWS

The Pleading of Perseus

The list of Republican Rome's victims is long, but few of them speak directly to us in the sources. Slaves, lower-class women, eunuchs, jugglers, children, farm workers, sewer men, and water carriers all pass by us in silence. Yet it would not be right to assume that these people lacked an opinion about Rome just because it was not captured by our limited sources. What of the thoughts of the long line of peoples conquered by Rome? All of them had had their own histories, traditions, languages, and identities.

Perseus of Macedon

In the Roman histories of Livy, we do encounter the protests of the defeated. He occasionally gives "voice" to their complaints, but we need to be careful about these re-created speeches. Although some of the words were based on written sources, none of them should be thought of as direct speeches. Livy's historical art demanded that he make his narrative gripping, but the speeches he presents belong to rhetoric, not to verbatim records. Rome's victims seldom speak to us in their own uncensored words. Moreover, even Livy's speeches of the defeated belong to a discourse with the Romans and are not what the victims might have said if the Romans were not in the room.

Take the case of King Perseus of Macedonia as told by Livy. In 171 BCE, as his relations with Rome were deteriorating, Perseus met with a Roman commission sent to investigate his role in stirring up trouble. First he complained that his case was a good one, but that it was fundamentally unfair for him to have to plead it before men who were both his accusers and his judges. Moreover, he pointed out that since he was not a Roman citizen he was not protected by Roman law. It was unfair, he argued, for Rome to prosecute a king for behaving as a king and ruling his kingdom as he saw fit. Rome was interfering with his royal rule and questioning his every action when in fact he was acting within his royal rights and for the good of his kingdom. Should he have to account for all his actions to a foreign power? As he finished his defense, he said that he realized that the commission would hear what it wanted to hear.

The commission carried his plea back to the Senate, where the majority still viewed Macedonia as its last great Mediterranean threat. Rome had so hedged in Perseus that he had little to lose by resistance. The king spoke to his army, reminding them of all the wrongs that Rome had done to him, his father, and Macedonia. Even now, he told them, the Romans were preparing an army to invade and enslave their land. The Romans would destroy kingship, disarm Macedonia, and lord it over an independent people. The army rallied to his cause with a roar of approval. By 168 BCE, Roman legions had defeated the vaunted Macedonian phalanx and King Perseus was on the run. He surrendered at Samothrace and was brought before the Roman general in such a state of shock that he was unable to utter a single word. All pleading was now past. Perseus was sent as a prisoner to Rome where he was forced to march in chains in the victorious general's triumphal parade. Perseus was imprisoned and died not long afterward.

All Perseus's pleading and maneuvering had not saved him from overthrow or the kingdom of Macedonia from Roman occupation, but his argument was a sound one. By what right did Rome interfere in Macedonian affairs, by what right did the Roman Senate undermine his kingship, and why did he have to play by Rome's rules? The Roman army answered, but that does not make Perseus's perspective as an outsider and humbled king any less valid.

QUESTIONS | ***How can the historical record be balanced so that history's "losers" obtain a fair hearing? Was Perseus's complaint a legitimate one or just sour grapes? Why?***

Philip's defeat led Antiochus to try to put his own kingdom in order. In 196 BCE, he invaded Thrace and in 192 BCE crossed over into Greece, claiming, as had the Romans, to be liberating it. At Thermopylae the next year Antiochus was defeated in a battle in which Philip and the Macedonians fought on the Roman side. By 188 BCE, Antiochus met Rome's terms and abandoned his hopes of controlling Greece. He left the ruin of the Seleucid kingdom to his son and marched east where he was killed by a rebellious mob as his troops sacked a temple.

Thus, by 190 BCE Philip had become a Roman client and collaborator, and by 188 BCE Antiochus had surrendered the last Seleucid hope of restoring Alexander's vast domain. Rome had subordinated two of the three great Hellenistic kingdoms, leaving only Ptolemaic Egypt unconquered, but in a state of semi-clientage. Yet it was probably not the

Roman Senate's intention to annex and absorb these lands, and its original idea was not to leave behind permanent garrisons. What turned Rome from the protector of Greece into its master was Greece's incessant squabbling.

Philip's heir, Perseus (r. 179–168 BCE), attempted to negotiate a perilous middle course; he sought to retain his kingdom's semi-independence while swearing loyalty to Rome. It was an approach destined to fail. The Third Macedonian War (171–167 BCE) broke out when Perseus's supporters rolled rocks down on a king friendly to Rome who was consulting the Oracle at Delphi. Whether it was the sacrilege or the diplomatic insult that irritated the Roman Senate, we do not know, but Rome was angry enough to approve another invasion. Perseus was captured and dragged back to Rome.

When Perseus died in 168 BCE, he was the last of the heirs of Alexander's successors to be king of Macedonia. Rome put an end to the line and partitioned the kingdom into four republics, each of which was to be separate from the others. After a failed Greek attempt to reunite the kingdom in 148 BCE, Rome turned Macedonia, Thessaly, and Epirus into a single Roman province under the rule of a Roman governor appointed by the Senate. Soon Illyria, Rhodes, and Pergamum were all brought under direct Roman rule.

The decisive showdown between the Romans and the Seleucid kingdom took place in 168 BCE. Antiochus IV (r. 215–163 BCE) invaded Egypt, which was partially protected by Rome, and the Roman Senate sent him an ultimatum to withdraw at once. He asked for time to consider his options, but the Roman general Popillius drew a line with his walking stick around the king and demanded to receive his answer before he left the circle. Antiochus capitulated to Rome, which now controlled Seleucid affairs just as it did those of Greece. Rome had rolled up the Mediterranean rim, though the nature of its control of various lands varied from place to place.

The Mature Republic

By the start of the second century BCE, Roman Italy was at peace and prosperous. With territorial expansion, Rome's economy achieved Mediterranean reach. Another reflection of Rome's growing sophistication was the emergence of Latin literature, though in its first flowering it developed under the influence of Greek literature. Below the impressive military, economic, and cultural successes of the mature Republic, tensions were building as Rome attempted to adapt to the full flush of imperial power and prosperity. The destruction of the ancient cities of Corinth and Carthage in 146 BCE was a symptom not only of Rome's excessive power, but also of the Republic's failure to cope with its expanded role in the Mediterranean world and its growing inability to balance the political and social strains at home.

What problems faced the Roman Republic in 146 BCE, after 350 years of expansion? Had it kept pace with the many changes it had brought about?

Toward a Mediterranean Roman Economy

By the middle of the second century BCE, the Mediterranean was effectively a Roman sea. As Rome expanded its territory, so had its economy expanded; from a local agricultural economy with a small hinterland in 500 BCE to trade with the Etruscans and Latins by 350 BCE, from a regionalized Italian economy in 250 BCE to a western Mediterranean economy by 200 BCE, and finally by 150 BCE to a Mediterranean economy operating with provincial centers connected to the city of Rome. Long-distance trade along the Mediterranean was in full flow. Grain came to Rome from Sicily and northern Africa, minerals from Spain, and new slaves from the east. After the wars with the Macedonians, Greece supplied the best and most learned slaves, the ones most desired by rich Roman households.

Italian traders had been in the east before the Roman army. Roman merchants began to trade at Epirus and Pergamum in the third century BCE, long before those cities were conquered. By then Rome had its own formal and state-approved coinage. In 289 BCE, the Senate approved the establishment of a Roman mint. The encounter with Pyrrhus and the Carthaginians pushed Rome away from bronze coins to silver ones, the most important of these being the silver denarius, the basic coin of the Roman world. The shift occurred while Hannibal was occupying parts of Italy. As with so much else in Roman life, it may have been war rather than commerce that moved Rome in a new direction. Merchants benefited from the change, for the denarius was on par with the Attic drachma, which had long been the basic currency of the Greek world. The Carthaginians had provided the only currency resistance to the Greek standard and that was effectively removed after the first two Punic wars. By the late third century BCE, Roman merchants were trading in Alexandria and spurred the transport of goods along the Nile and across the Mediterranean to Italy. The city of Rome was an attractive market for both precious and bulk goods.

The Roman merchant had not just come to the east to trade; he often settled down, married a Greek woman, and achieved a prominent role in a Hellenistic city. Many served as representatives for commercial houses based in Rome. Although they lived nominally under local law, Italian traders could plead their cases under Roman law and often cultivated the local Roman governor to win privileged concessions. For this reason, Roman traders often remained in areas controlled by Rome and may not have been as adventurous as Hellenistic merchants. Greek traders tended to be more aggressive in the long-distance trade routes that connected the Mediterranean economy to India and China.

Rome's Mediterranean conquests may have been designed as much to eliminate economic rivals such as

Carthage as to eliminate territorial threats. The Senate was filled with men who had a keen eye for their families' economic gain. Provincial governors were particularly gifted at putting the pinch on local populations, whether by squeezing taxes out of them or by granting special commercial rights in exchange for a bribe. Governors liked to brag that they governed without accepting bribes, but their boasts suggest just how common bribery was.

The Roman Senate's control of economic policy was relatively unsophisticated. In 166 BCE, it did declare the Greek island of Delos a free port, one in which no taxes were levied on goods arriving or exiting the port. Delos thus became a funnel for goods moving east and west. After Rome took control of most of the Mediterranean rim, trade flourished. Romans, Greeks, Syrians, Jews, and Egyptians gathered in thriving cosmopolitan centers such as Delos to barter with one another and move goods.

Taxes were another measure of economic control. In the mature Republic the Romans generally taxed lightly immediately after conquests outside Italy, but then slowly brought conquered territories under the full weight of normal taxation. Cities longed for special exemptions and tax immunities, and all lived in fear of a new round of taxation. Rome operated a tax farming system, which was subject to excess. The Senate put the taxes for cities and regions up for bid, with the highest bidder winning the right to squeeze as much as he could from the designated area. The tax collector (or publican) became a hated figure, and, when riots broke out in the east against Roman authority, tax collectors, Roman merchants, and administrators were often the first to be slaughtered.

By the first century BCE, Rome depended on its eastern revenues. Roman senators knew that the eastern territories needed particular protection and attention since together they produced more revenue for Rome than all of its other holdings put together. Back in Italy, things were changing rapidly with the seizure of the Mediterranean rim. The importation of the people seized as slaves in the conquests destabilized the Italian countryside where large estates began to practice farming on a massive scale. Italy and certainly Rome had left behind its once humble agricultural origins to become the chief consumer of the precious goods and foodstuffs of a subject world. One of the things Rome consumed was culture.

Roman Literature of the Middle Republic

Latin literature had a surprisingly slow beginning even though Rome was surrounded by writing cultures. To the north and south were literate Etruscans and Greeks. Latin, like Greek, is an Indo-European language. Many early Italian peoples spoke related Italic languages; Latin was but one of these. The language of classical Latin written by the poets was, however, not the people's Latin of daily speech, the one scribbled on street and brothel walls. Latin, whether in its literary or popular forms, is an inflected language, which means that word endings convey the function of the words in the sentence and not word order as in English and German. One must often wait until hearing or reading the final word of a Latin sentence to understand the sentence's essential meaning.

Latin has not been important to the West because of any intrinsic superiority of the language itself, but because it was long the language of power and the powerful. Its influence was immense because it became the language of the lands that Rome conquered. From it evolved the Romance languages (Italian, Spanish, and French). As languages go, Latin is easily learned and has a moderately sized vocabulary. The Latin alphabet is based on the Etruscan (that is, the Greek) alphabet, with some adaptations. Roman numerals began as finger signs.

Few genuine inscriptions of archaic Latin remain, and no literature to speak of emerged until the third century BCE, when poets such as Livius Andronicus and Ennius began writing. Livius was a Greek captured in Tarentum around 272 BCE. In Rome he wrote in Latin, producing an adaptation of Homer's *Odyssey* and various plays. Sadly the work of these first poets survives only in fragments, but later Romans do not seem to have felt the loss deeply. Cicero claimed that much of it was unbearable beyond a single encounter.

Rome's first surviving literature is unmistakably Greek in inspiration, and that may have been its problem. The curmudgeonly Cato the Elder demeaned many Republican poets as mere vulgarizers and said that Rome had not conquered Greece in order to be infected by its culture. A certain culture shock did strike Rome in the third century BCE, after the capture of the Greek south and the importation of learned Greek slaves. But Greek comedy, in particular the new Hellenistic comedy of the fourth and third centuries BCE, met the Romans where

Roman Comedy on Stage A relief from Pompeii showing a Roman comedy. A boy provides musical accompaniment with pipes, the figures wear masks, their gestures are exaggerated, and the comedy is broad and cutting.

INVESTIGATING THE PAST

Fakes and Their Outings

Not everything is as it seems, particularly when we study the evidence of the past. For almost a century, the oldest Latin inscription was believed to be the one found on a golden pin called the Praeneste Fibula from the seventh century BCE. The inscription runs backward from right to left, contains a mixture of Greek and Latin characters, has continuous letters with midpoints to divide words, and possesses archaic-looking features such as "fhefhaked" for "fecit" ("made"). The inscription reads: "Manius made me for Numerius." When the pin surfaced around 1900 near Rome, many classical scholars, including the great Theodor Mommsen, thought it was genuine. We now know that the piece is a fake. In 1980, Margherita Guarducci, an Italian scholar, proved convincingly that virtually everything about the piece—its clumsy incision, acid-aged surface, metal composition, and "archaic" Latin—is wrong. Her work, along with that of the American historian Arthur E. Gordon, revealed the dodgy history of the piece. There were whispers early on that the Fibula was not genuine, but no one said so publicly or could prove it. Guarducci thinks that the Fibula was concocted by a shady Roman antiquities dealer and a failed German archaeologist. The motive of the former was probably to make money; that of the latter, a longing for professional respectability as the discoverer of the oldest piece of Latin yet known.

An even more complex cache of fakes was put together in the seventeenth century by a Tuscan boy named Curzio Inghirami, who was in his late teens at the time. Catering to an Italian desire to know more about their ancient ancestors, Etruscan objects, and the Etruscan language, Curzio supplied a treasure trove. Since the Etruscan language was and remains mysterious, few dared to question forged documents that they could not read. To antique his forgeries, Curzio placed them in capsules made of mud, hair, and his own spit. Then, as an adult, he wrote elaborate books to explain the importance of the discoveries and to decode the texts. As happens so often in fraud cases, people found ways to give Curzio and the objects the benefit of doubt, arguing that he had been too young to have pulled off such a daring deception. Even the controversy that surrounded the forgeries enhanced their importance and Curzio's career as a philologist. Though not everyone believed in his discoveries, it was not until 1924 that forgery was proved.[1]

Forgeries haunt historians, who need always to question the legitimacy of the materials on which they work. Like all good confidence swindles, forged documents and objects appeal to the expectations, desires, and greed of buyers and true believers who expect that just such a thing should exist, must exist, and therefore, does exist. The fakers have many motives, among them the mercenary and the desire to trick the scholarly world. The damage done is substantial: the wasted years of scholars trying to make sense of a fake, the duping of the innocent, and the distortion of the past. Historians need to think critically and to be alert, for there are those who would rewrite the past by faking it.

The Praeneste Fibula

QUESTIONS | ***In our digital age, with its mass of unchecked information and blurring of the line between opinion and fact, how should we proceed to weigh the truthfulness of things? How do historians and others detect fakes and frauds? What real damage did the fibula fakers and Curzio do?***

they lived and became immensely popular in its adapted form. The plays of the Greek Menander (c. 342–290 BCE) and his imitators, with their powerful sense of Hellenistic dislocation, were reworked for Roman audiences by Plautus and Terence, the two greatest Roman comic writers. Their plays are essentially situation comedies of the sort that audiences still enjoy.

Plautus (d. c. 184 BCE), whose full name means the "flat-footed clown," wrote 130 plays, 21 of which survive. His critics accused him of writing only for money, but he, ever the comedian, considered the criticism a compliment. His plays are filled with quick-witted, sly slaves; mistaken identities; twins; shipwrecks; angry fathers; wayward sons; and gorgeous girls as the love interests around whom his plays often circle. Plautus was a lively social critic, often mocking Rome's citizens: "Want to find a liar, go to the Assembly; a nasty braggart, show up at Venus's temple by the sewer; a fallen husband, try the basilica next door." Much of the delight to be found in his plays comes from their exaggeration and earthy humor. The situations are ridiculous and may have seemed strange and foreign to Romans. That strangeness, however, may have allowed Romans to laugh at Plautus's plays without feeling the sting too deeply. In Rome slaves did not dare to talk back to their masters, women strayed at their own peril, and boys who mocked their senile fathers risked death. But Romans could see all the improbabilities of an upside-down world on view in Plautus's comedies.

Terence (190–159 BCE) may not have been as much simple fun as Plautus, but he was the darling of the humanist circle that formed around Scipio Aemilianus, the grandson (by adoption) of Scipio Africanus. He too adapted the plays of Menander and his followers, but his Latin is more sophisticated and more quotable than Plautus's. Lines of Terence, such as "He whom the gods wish to destroy, they first drive mad" (which he adapted from Euripides's *Medea*) or "I am human; nothing human is foreign to me," cut off from their context and their Roman setting, may seem more universal to us than they did at the time. Behind Terence and Plautus one senses the wider and more cosmopolitan world that the Romans had come to occupy. Its immensity was such that a man might be separated from a brother in a shipwreck, twins might be separated at birth, and a father and a son in a large city might have their eyes on the same woman. Rome was maturing and its literature was growing up, rapidly.

The Year of Reckoning: 146 BCE

The year 146 BCE was a watershed, at least symbolically, in the transition of Rome from the Republic it had been for three and a half centuries to the quasi-empire it was becoming. Rome's exercise of imperial power had by 146 BCE become one of absolute military might, of impatience with resistance, and of fractured politics at home.

In that year, Rome utterly destroyed two famous ancient cities. In Greece the Achaean League under the leadership of Corinth rebelled. Rome responded by reducing Corinth, one of the ancient world's great cities, to ruins. Polybius claimed that he had seen the results with his own eyes: the smashed city with its great works of art torn off its walls and its statues toppled. He saw soldiers playing dice on paintings thrown onto the ground. One general seized art for his own collection, giving the rather stupid order to his soldiers that if they destroyed these unique works they would have to replace them.

In the same year, Rome also destroyed Carthage. The Third Punic War (149–146 BCE) was Hannibal's bitter legacy to his homeland. So formidable an opponent had Carthage and its great general been, that Rome could not face the thought of another threat from its old enemy. The peace after the second war had been so designed that Carthage was not even permitted the resources to defend itself against its northern African enemies. Its debt to Rome had been paid off, but some Roman senators had commercial interests that would benefit from the destruction of the city once and for all. Others for political reasons whipped up hysteria in Rome against the continued existence of Carthage. Cato the Elder liked to conclude his speeches to the Senate, no matter the topic, with the line *Delenda est Carthago,* "Carthage must be destroyed." On the pretext that Carthage had broken its treaty, Rome declared war.

The city of Carthage fell after a battle of six days. Its citizens were sold into slavery and the city razed to the ground. The old story about Rome salting the site of Carthage so that nothing would grow there would seem to be untrue since it was not long before Rome rebuilt a city on the same spot. As Carthage fell, the general Scipio Aemilianus told Polybius that, though it was a wondrous thing to see Carthage burn, he feared that someday someone might give the same order for Rome to be torched. Scipio should have been more worried about the Republic's present perils: the immorality and needlessness of the decisions that led to the destruction of Corinth and Carthage, the deep divisions and disorder within the Republic itself, and the very real prospect of imperial overreach.

Conclusion

The Roman Republic had a great run in its early and middle periods. In three and a half centuries it had gone from being an insignificant village of Iron-Age huts to the dominant power of the lands that rimmed the Mediterranean. Behind it in 146 BCE lay a long line of crushed enemies: the Sabines, the Latins, the Etruscans, the Samnites, the Greek cities of Italy, Carthage, and two of the three great Hellenistic kingdoms. None of this had happened by pure chance, but what drove Rome to conquer had changed and conquest had in turn changed Rome. What had begun as a matter of necessity and the need to survive in a hostile historical environment had become habit and finally license, the freedom to do as it pleased, the brutal might of Rome that Corinth and Carthage experienced at the moment of their destructions.

The Roman Republic, with its stiff, war-hungry Senate and supportive people, was the most successful government of its kind in all of ancient history. Other Italian cities of the Latins, Etruscans, and Greeks, and Mediterranean powers such as Carthage and the Hellenistic kingdoms were just as violent and ambitious, but Rome planned and fought more successfully than they did. Romans may have thought that it was their devotion to the gods or their noble virtues that were responsible for their string of successes, but it was more likely due to a complex set of factors, at the center of which stood its unusual government. The Romans waged war better than the others, made it a way of life and a way of religion.

Yet, at its end, the Middle Republic was faced with the consequences of its world-shaking success. The challenge that faced it was to see if its government could carry it to the next level, to the administrative control of an empire of vast holdings, to the curtailment of excess and corruption, and to the transformation of a city of expansion into one that fairly and confidently governed an incorporated whole. That challenge would fall to the Late Republic and other generations of Romans. The destruction of Corinth and Carthage did not bode well for the immediate future.

Even Polybius, so impressed by the Roman Republic's many accomplishments, knew that the goddess Fortune, who had for so long smiled on Rome, might turn against it. He was not, however, a historian of decline, but of success and the reasons for it. Unable or unwilling to analyze the symptoms of the Republic's growing disorder and corruption, Polybius failed to see that the wheel of Fortune had already begun her slow turn against the Republic he so admired.

Critical Thinking Questions

1. Looking back at their history, Romans were convinced that it was their destiny to dominate the Mediterranean world. What do the facts and patterns of Rome's expansion tell us?
2. Why was the Roman Republic so committed to conquest, and how did it balance its own internal division of peoples and interests?
3. How was Rome fortunate in the Early and Middle Republics, and what choices did the Romans make to achieve success? What did they sacrifice to succeed?
4. What might have stopped Rome's rise?
5. Why did the Senate become the preeminent Roman institution, and why was it so successful?

Key Terms

Senate **(p. 104)**
augury **(p. 108)**
haruspicy **(p. 108)**
curule **(p. 108)**
magistrate **(p. 108)**
fasces **(p. 108)**
numina **(p. 109)**
pontiffs **(p. 109)**
consuls **(p. 109)**
tribunes **(p. 110)**
patricians **(p. 110)**
plebeians **(p. 110)**
clientage **(p. 111)**
paterfamilias **(p. 112)**
materfamilias **(p. 112)**
patria potestas **(p. 112)**
Pyrrhic Victory **(p. 115)**
virtus **(p. 117)**
Pontifex Maximus **(p. 119)**

Primary Sources in connect

For information on Connect and the online resources available, go to **http://connect.mcgraw-hill.com**.

1. **The Legend of the Foundation of Rome by Romulus and Remus**
2. **Twelve Tables: Laws on Offenses and Damages**
3. **Polybius on the Destruction of Carthage in 146 BCE**

BACK TO THE SOURCE

Polybius on Roman Exceptionalism

Polybius (c. 200–c. 118 BCE) belongs to the rich line of ancient Greek historians that included Herodotus and Thucydides, but he has rarely been regarded as highly. Despite his commitment to honesty and to telling the historical truth, his literary style has not always appealed to readers. But his chief problem has probably been that in his greatest work he was a Greek writing admiringly about the Romans. As such, he applied Greek values and categories of analysis to a foreign land and its people. Whether his historical approach suited the Roman case or whether Polybius understood the essence of Rome, its people, and history are open questions.

Can anyone be so indifferent or idle as not to care to know by what means, and under what kind of polity, almost the whole inhabited world was conquered and brought under the dominion of the single city of Rome, and that, too, within a period of not quite fifty-three years (219–167 BCE)? Or who again can be so completely absorbed in other subjects of contemplation or study, as to think any of them superior in importance to the accurate understanding of an event for which the past affords no precedent?

We shall best show how marvelous and vast our subject is by comparing the most famous empires which preceded and which have been the favorite themes of historians, and measuring them against the superior greatness of Rome. . . .

As for the Roman constitution, it had three elements, each of them possessing sovereign powers; and their respective share of power in the whole state had been regulated with such a scrupulous regard to equality and equilibrium that no one could say for certain, not even a native, whether the constitution as a whole were an aristocracy or democracy or despotism. And no wonder, for if we confine our observation to the power of the consuls, we should be inclined to regard it as despotic; if on that of the Senate, as aristocratic; and if finally one looks at the power possessed by the people, it would seem a clear case of a democracy. . . .

The result of this power of the several estates for mutual help or harm is a union sufficiently firm for all emergencies, and a constitution than which it is impossible to find a better. For whenever any danger from without compels them to unite and work together, the strength which is developed by the state is so extraordinary that everything required is unfailingly carried out by the eager rivalry shown by all classes to devote their whole minds to the need of the hour and to secure that any determination come to should not fail for want of promptitude; while each individual works, privately and publicly alike, for the accomplishment of the business at hand. Accordingly, the peculiar constitution of the [Roman] state makes it irresistible and certain of obtaining whatever it determines to attempt. Nay, even when these external alarms are past, and the people are enjoying their good fortune and the fruits of their victories and, as usually happens, growing corrupted by flattery and idleness, show a tendency to violence and arrogance—it is in these circumstances, more than ever, that the constitution is seen to possess within itself the power of correcting abuses. For when any one of the three classes becomes puffed up and manifests an inclination to be contentious and unduly encroaching, the mutual interdependency of all three and the possibility of the pretensions of anyone being checked and thwarted by the others, must plainly check this tendency. And so the proper equilibrium is maintained by the impulsiveness of the one part being checked by its fear of the other. . . .

Again the Roman customs and principles regarding money transactions are better than those of the Carthaginians. In the view of the latter nothing is disgraceful that makes for gain. With the former nothing is more disgraceful than to receive bribes and to make profit by improper means. For they regard wealth obtained from unlawful transactions to be as much a subject of reproach as a fair profit from the most unquestioned source is one of commendation. A proof of the fact is this. The Carthaginians obtain office by open bribery, but among the Romans the penalty for it is death. With such a radical difference, therefore, between the rewards offered to virtue among the two peoples, it is natural that the ways adopted for obtaining them should be different also.

But the most important difference for the better which the Roman commonwealth appears to me to display is in their religious beliefs. For I conceive that what in other nations is looked upon as a reproach, I mean a scrupulous fear of the gods, is the very thing which keeps the Roman commonwealth together. To such an extraordinary height is this carried among them, both in private and public business, that nothing could exceed it. Many people might think this unaccountable, but in my opinion their object is to use it as a check upon the common people. If it were possible to form a state wholly of philosophers, such a custom would perhaps be unnecessary. But seeing that every multitude is fickle and full of lawless desires, unreasoning anger, and violent passion, the only resource is to keep them in check by mysterious terrors and scenic effects of this sort.

QUESTIONS | *Why was Polybius such an unabashed admirer of the Roman Republic? How does he account for Roman exceptionalism? How might his view of the Roman constitution be criticized? What proof does he supply of the moral and religious superiority of Rome?*

Source: *The Histories of Polybius,* trans. from the text of F. Hultsch by Evelyn S. Shuckburgh (London and New York: MacMillan and Co., 1889), Vol. 1, 1, 356, 360–361, 384–385; revised.

5

The Roman Aqueduct, the Pont du Gard, France

FROM REPUBLIC TO EMPIRE

CICERO DIES, AUGUSTUS THRIVES On a chilly December day in 43 BCE, Roman soldiers finally ran Cicero (106–43 BCE) to ground. He had been fleeing to the sea, carried on a litter by loyal slaves. His head was chopped off as he poked it through the drapes of his portable couch, and then his hands. The soldiers gathered up the bloody body parts and bore them back to the Roman Senate where the great orator had spent so much of his adult life defending the Republic. There they placed his remains above the speaker's platform as a reminder to all of the mortal danger of speaking and writing against those who were determined to overthrow the Senate's power to control Roman affairs. Cicero's plan to preserve the Roman Republic had failed. It was to be the last such attempt.

A half-century later, thanks to the political genius of Augustus (formerly Octavian), the empire was established and at peace. The once dominant and deliberative Senate was reduced to a body that chiefly executed the emperor's wishes. Outside his Mausoleum in Rome stood two bronze pillars inscribed with a long list of what Augustus called his "Accomplishments" (*Res Gestae*). He had, he said, liberated the Republic from tyranny, avenged the murder of his father, Julius Caesar, successfully waged domestic and foreign wars, restored religion, and brought peace to the Roman world (see Back to the Source at the end of the chapter). His résumé was boastful propaganda, but it was not untrue. Augustus did transform the Roman world, moving the massive weight of the Roman state under house control, the house being his own. After a century of Republican disorder and instability, Rome was now an empire, but the road there had been bumpy and bloody.

The apparent peace and glory of Augustan Rome should not obscure the difficulties of the first century CE, when some emperors were still waging a campaign against the Senate and a reactionary Republican old guard that refused to accept its loss of power. The violent struggle that continued between the Julio-Claudian emperors and Rome's aristocrats is not just the story of evil emperors such as Caligula and Nero, but the more profound transformation of one world into another, one form of government into another. Only in the second century CE would the imperial government established by Augustus truly take hold, but that imperial stability would not outlive the second century.

Cicero, whose fame endures, would not have been surprised by the brutal turn that imperial power took, but Augustus might have been disappointed that he had not once and for all solved Rome's problems and created a stable and lasting empire.

Cicero

Historians have often told three stories of the transformation of the Republic into the Empire. The first is that of the dramatic end of the Late Republic (145–27 BCE); the second tells of the empire of Augustus and its awkward first century (27 BCE–96 CE); the third, that of the good emperors (96–180 CE). This transformation, however, may also be viewed, as we shall see in this chapter, as the single history of the transition from one form of stable

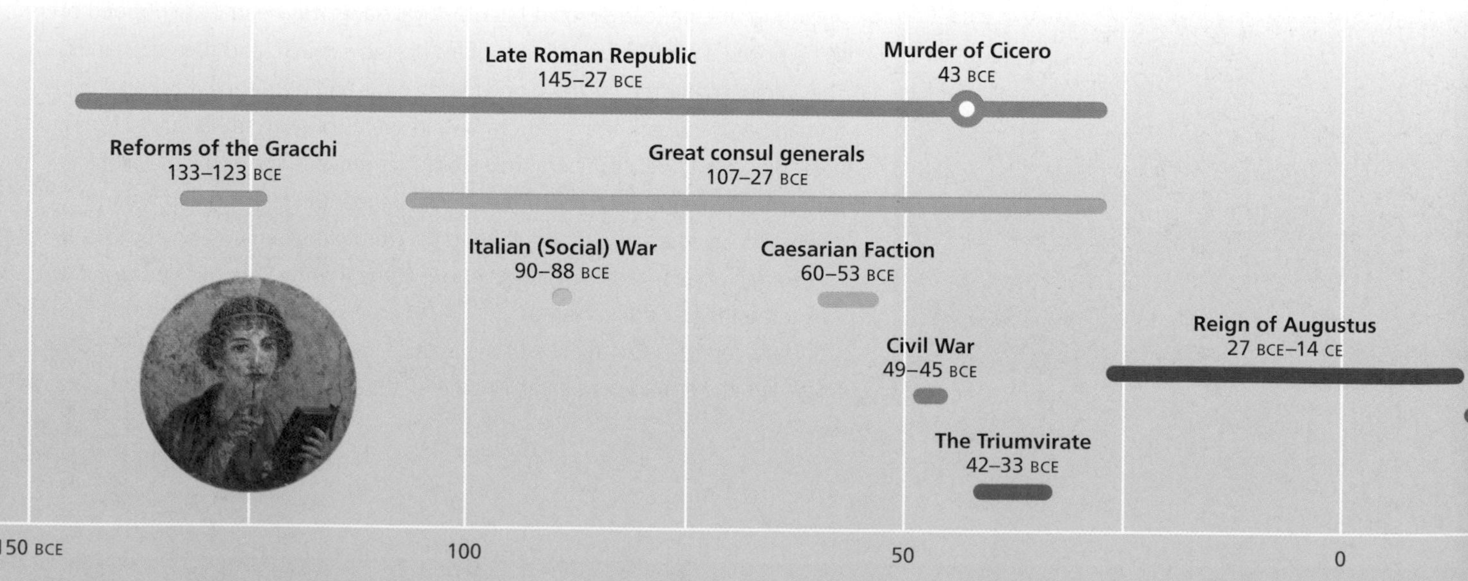

government at the end of the Middle Republic to another in the successful Roman Empire of the second century CE. To transform a form of government that had worked so well for so long was not done easily or quickly—hence, the violence and disorder, the intense rivalries, and the extreme rhetoric that characterize much of the period as the forces of conservatism and change struggled against each other.

The Late Republic in Disarray

In the Late Roman Republic the agreements and shared interests of the Roman peoples were breaking down. The Roman Republic was now three and a half centuries old and had been as successful as any government in the Mediterranean world. Yet what had worked for a city-state, surrounded by hostile forces in Italy and the western Mediterranean, worked less well for a Rome struggling to govern a vast territory. The Republic may have been too successful for its own good. Its form of government was still that of a single city with an intricate distribution of power among members of various privileged groups.

How did the Late Republic become unhinged?

By the middle of the second century BCE, many Roman citizens had begun to realize that Rome was already an empire in fact if not yet in name. Following the conquest of the Hellenistic kingdoms and the dramatic destruction of Corinth and Carthage in 146 BCE, Rome now needed to govern far-flung and foreign provinces with permanent armies. Conquest brought to the surface the underlying tensions of the Republic. Rome's government had been geared to conducting annual warfare close to home and the state had depended on war to reinforce a core set of virtues and rankings within society. Prolonged peace proved to be bad for the republican system, but so was maintaining a quasi-empire. The historian Polybius said that after Rome had been at peace for several years the population grew restless and so in 156 BCE the Senate manufactured a war "to refresh the martial way of life of its people."

Symptoms of Dysfunction

Like many governments and economies, then and now, Republican Rome depended on continual growth to thrive. It had neutralized internal tensions within society by externalizing them, encouraging the ambitious and disgruntled to seek their fortune and fame outside of Italy. By the middle of the second century BCE, Rome had transformed all of Italy and much of the Mediterranean world into relatively peaceful Roman territory. But contemporaries worried that the success of its conquests was corrupting Rome. Too much money, too many slaves, and too many exotic ideas were making their way to Rome.

There was also too much competition for too few political posts. To ascend the ladder of offices in Republican Rome was a laborious venture: the first rung on that ladder was the office of **quaestor** (magistrates and investigators: twenty positions), then **tribune** (representatives of the people: ten), **aedile** (magistrates of the people, guardians of public property: four), **praetor** (magistrates dealing with military and foreign affairs: eight), and finally, the

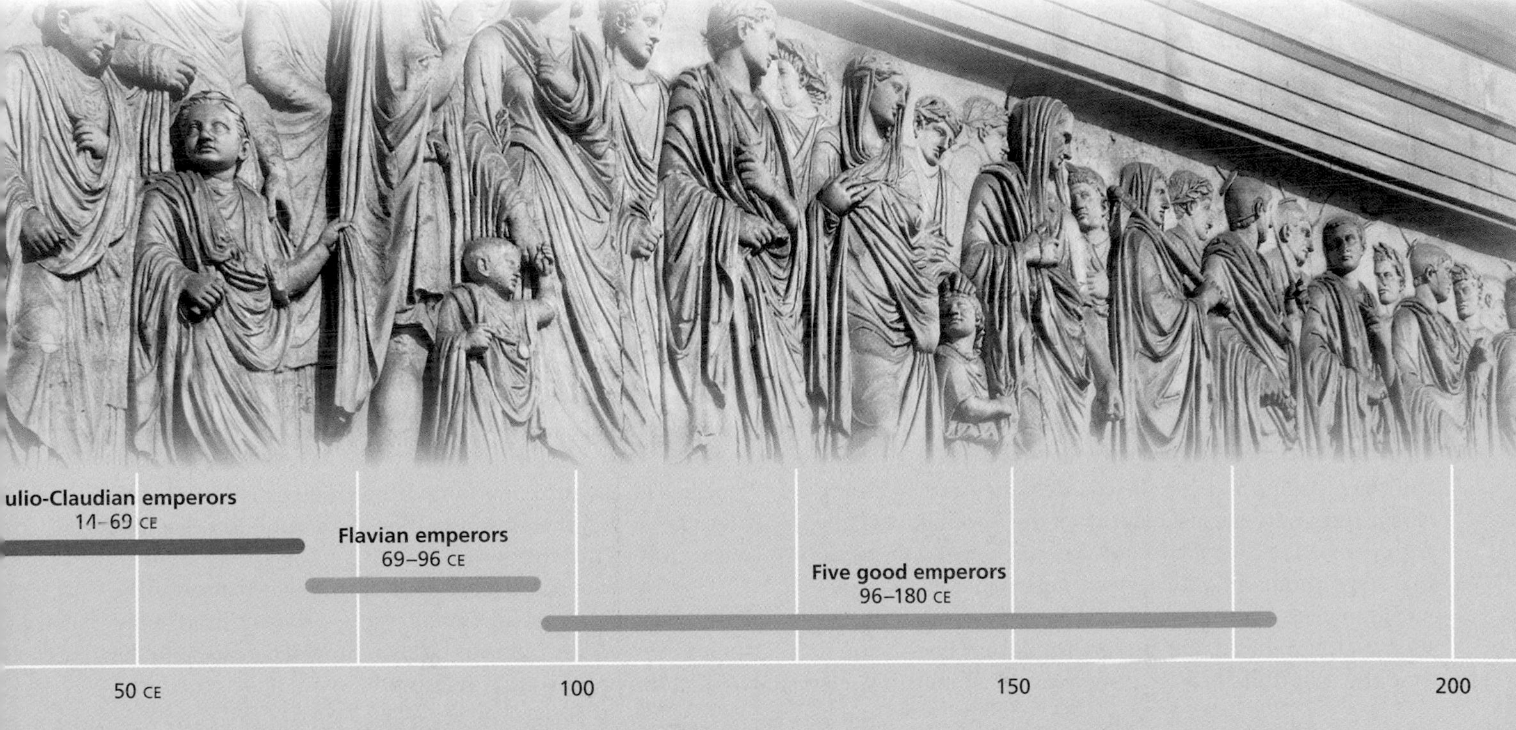

highest office of all, **consul** (two). Each of these offices had an entry age, so that men of roughly the same age moved up the ladder together, always in competition, developing complicated political alliances and lingering resentments along the way. To attain the highest ranks of the state was becoming next to impossible for most aristocrats. Only two consuls were chosen each year, and the competition for those and lesser offices bred intense and often violent rivalries between individuals and their factions.

Another problem with the system was that it offered no pay. Although officeholders worked free for the state, they found ways to benefit personally from their appointments. The system of clientage, whereby powerful men or patrons protected and provided for their clients and dependents, reinforced factional loyalties. To be the client of a great man was to side with his political interests. Powerful aristocrats used their extensive wealth to fashion vast networks of influence and to manipulate the political process. This Roman oligarchy was the greatest of old boy networks. Blood, ancestry, and personal connections mattered in ways that we can barely grasp today.

So too did money, and there was too much of it as the Republic expanded to control all of Italy and most of the Mediterranean rim. Conquest brought tens of thousands of slaves into Italy, and their sale produced fantastic riches for the conquerors and altered social and economic affairs in the Republic. With more money came bribery, influence peddling, and extreme displays of wealth. The government tried to curtail corruption and extravagance, passing laws against conspicuous consumption by soldiers and provincial governors and restricting the number and frequency of triumphs for victorious generals. Senators condemned corruption and ostentation, but they could stop neither.

With the conquest of the eastern Mediterranean, new ideas and cultural influences—Athenian democracy, Greek learning, eastern mystery religions, Carthaginian agricultural practices—came to Italy, unsettling Rome's ancestral values. Foreign peoples were exposed to Roman values, but their own customs slowly influenced their conquerors. The most obvious case was that of the Greeks, but just as important was Spain, which would supply soldiers and emperors to the empire and eventually revitalize Rome in the second century CE.

Since Rome's success prior to 275 BCE had been a product of its core virtues and traditional means of governance, success in the wider Mediterranean world unbalanced those virtues and the government that was supposed to embody them. Because the Republic, like most governments, was built to endure and designed to eliminate attempts to change its fundamental nature, conflict was inevitable, particularly since the Roman Republic was stubbornly conservative. It was designed not to change. Not surprisingly the last century of the Republic was filled with turmoil and civil discord. The violence of the period was a symptom of political dysfunction, not its root cause.

Surveying their disordered world, contemporaries such as Cicero and the historian Sallust could not see that the Republic was giving way to something else. They thought that they were witnessing the fall of Rome. Instead, the turmoil and dysfunction of the Senate and state produced a political genius in Augustus and an imperial form of government.

The Reforming Gracchi Brothers

There were early signs of trouble in the Late Republic. Military success had had a vast impact on Rome's economy, and not everyone benefited from the changes. Small free farmers in Italy found that they could no longer compete against large plantation-like estates (later called *latifundia*) worked by imported slaves. These small landholders often quit farming and drifted with their families to the city of Rome, whose size was increasing dramatically. The politics of the capital was changed by the presence of a mass of landless citizens always in need of food and entertainment. Soldiers returning home after long service discovered that their land had been seized. As well, some of the Italian peoples, who had been conquered by the expanding Republic, felt that they were getting a raw deal; they no longer wished to be merely Rome's allies and subordinates, but its citizens.

The story of the Gracchi brothers is the opening chapter of the final phase of the Republic. These two reformers may also have represented the last best chance for Rome to undertake the political changes necessary to preserve the Republic. Tiberius Gracchus (163–133 BCE) and Gaius Gracchus (154–121 BCE) were descendants of a distinguished aristocratic family that included Scipio Africanus, the conqueror of Hannibal.

Tiberius knew that something was wrong with Rome. Along with other Romans he had been shocked by a major slave revolt in Sicily in 135–132 BCE. Roman society had not yet learned how to manage its slave population, which was cruelly mistreated. Slaves who worked in mines and farms were beaten, chained, and held in pens at night. Cato the Elder, senator and landowner, thought it better to work slaves to death and replace them than to treat them humanely. The economic implications of slave labor were vast. With Italy's economy becoming more specialized, the slave revolt in Sicily cut off the secure flow of wheat to Rome.

As the supply and nature of labor changed, the citizen landholder who had once been the backbone of the Roman army was cut loose. These men still served in the army as conscripted troops, but now often lost the small parcels of land they held while they were away for long stretches of military service. Rome's military needs were changing as it was now necessary to station permanent garrisons of troops in distant places such as Greece. Tiberius Gracchus complained that the poor Roman soldier was styled the master of the world but had not a foot of ground to call his own.

Tiberius was not a rebel bent on the overthrow of the Republic. He did not advocate freeing slaves or improving their miserable lot. Nor was he an anarchist threatening the aristocratic order of Rome. Some scholars have wondered

INVESTIGATING THE PAST

Roman Slavery by the Numbers

How many slaves were there in Roman society, where did they come from, and did the economics and history of Roman slavery change over time? Historians such as Keith Bradley and Walter Scheidel have begun to break down the numbers of the Roman slave population. A quantitative approach to ancient slave demography (the statistical breakdown of population numbers) is not easy and involves the careful collection of scattered figures and a comparative extrapolation of them to obtain probable results. Unlike the African slave trade of the eighteenth and nineteenth centuries, with its detailed record of the slave traffic preserved in ship logs, sales accounts, and censuses, ancient sources are inconsistent and unsystematic. Ancient numbers are culled from narrative sources, legal records, and slave markets, but they are often large and suspiciously round. Nor do they always supply answers to basic questions: was the number of male and female slaves roughly equal, what percentage of slaves lived their entire lives enslaved, and what was the turnover of slaves in various regions and occupations?

Scheidel has drawn some conclusions based on the numbers that we do have. He estimates that over the millennium of Roman history, 100 million or more people were captured and sold as slaves. The circumstances of enslavement changed over time. During the territorial expansion of the Republic, Rome enslaved large numbers of conquered peoples: as many as 77,000 in the Third Samnite War (297–293 BCE), 100,000 during the First Punic War (264–241 BCE), and 150,000 from the taking of Epirus in 167 BCE. He estimates that in the space of less than a century, Republican Rome enslaved 700,000 conquered people. Ancient sources suggest that Caesar alone enslaved as many as a million people during his conquest of Gaul in the first century BCE.[1]

Roman Slave Collar The slave tag informs the finder of the slave to return him to his owner to collect a reward of one gold piece.

The enslavement of peoples was one of the chief causes of mobility, both geographic and social, within the Roman world. Italy received more slaves than other regions, with 15–25 percent of its population comprised of slaves. Areas such as Egypt had a lower figure (determined from census records) of around 7–10 percent, but only 15 percent of Egyptian households owned any slaves. The pace of enslavement by conquest slowed in the imperial period. Since Rome as an enslaving military and economic power depended on slave labor, how did it keep its slave numbers up? Scheidel reasons that if the average life expectancy of slaves was around twenty years, Rome would have needed 250–400,000 new slaves per year to replenish its slave pool. Conquest was not the only form of enslavement. Criminals were sometimes reduced to slavery, a man or woman might sell themselves or a child into slavery, and children abandoned to exposure by their parents could be recovered and enslaved. The principal source of new slaves, however, was biological. Scheidel thinks that perhaps 80 percent of the slave population in the empire was replaced by children born into slavery. The fertility of female slaves put up for sale was advertised. Although many older slaves were finally freed, female slaves were rarely freed until they passed menopause, their child-bearing years over, and their children legally fixed in servile condition.

Ancient slave numbers may be ragged and require deft handling, but they are chilling because they give us some idea of the scale of the institution of ancient slavery.

QUESTIONS | ***Why were ancient societies so dependent on slave labor? How can historians overcome gaps in their sources? What are the strengths and weaknesses of quantitative history, particularly as applied to something as complicated as slavery?***

if he was influenced by ideas of Athenian democracy, but universal suffrage and equality were neither the point nor the effect of his reforms. Instead, he wished to return Rome to its ancient social contract, one that granted common citizens and soldiers their rightful place in Roman society.

When he became tribune of the people in 133 BCE, Tiberius put forward a land reform package to limit the size of state land that any individual could hold to three hundred acres. He proposed redistributing the recovered land among landless citizens. Many senators vehemently opposed the reform and persuaded another tribune to veto the bill. In response, Tiberius persuaded the Assembly of the People to remove yet another tribune from office and to vote in favor of an even stronger land reform bill.

A commission was set up to redistribute the land, but the Senate cut off its funds. Convinced that his land reform measures would be stalled by further obstruction, Tiberius took the radical step of standing for reelection as tribune. His opponents claimed that he was pandering to the people and seeking to set himself up as king. Many of his reforms and actions were unconstitutional, but then so was the Senate's response. An aroused senatorial mob hunted down Tiberius and his supporters, bludgeoning three hundred of them to death. Later Romans saw the murder of Tiberius as a turning point in their history. Roman blood had been spilled, the law trampled, and the landless lower classes of Rome emerged as a potentially powerful player in Roman politics, one to whom aristocrats seeking advantage could appeal. Tiberius was dead, but the Senate grudgingly allowed his land reform to proceed.

Ten years after the assassination, Gaius Gracchus, an even more radical reformer and populist than his brother, was elected tribune. He proceeded with his brother's land reforms and sought ways to curtail the Senate's power. Gaius wanted soldiers to be outfitted at state expense, and he worked to ensure the free and liberal distribution of grain within the city of Rome. He also wanted to establish Italian colonies overseas at places such as Carthage. His goal was to create a popular base for himself, while undermining the power and authority of the Senate. To do so he appealed to the **equestrians** (the knightly class just below the patrician senators), who were often wealthy and jealous of patrician and senatorial privileges. His most radical proposal was to grant full citizenship to Rome's Latin allies and partial citizenship to other Italian allies, which angered many citizens who feared losing their entrenched privileges and birthright.

Once again, the Senate decided to put a stop to social and political change. When Gaius failed to secure election as tribune for a third term in 121 BCE, the Senate moved to undo some of his legislation and canceled the colonization of Carthage. Gaius's supporters turned violent, but a consul imposed martial law. As many as three thousand of Gaius's people were slaughtered, and his own head (without the body, of course) was returned to the Senate for the bounty placed upon it.

The reform program of the Gracchi did not long outlive them, and their legacy was to leave Rome more socially and politically fractured. The people were not happy because grain prices were not fixed and the supply was uneven. Few soldiers ended up with plots of land to compensate them for their long service to the state. The Italian allies did not receive the citizenship they sought and their resentment rose. Most equestrians were no closer, after Gaius, to breaking the senatorial monopoly on power. The Senate was more determined than ever to fend off attacks on its traditional power. The city of Rome, whose size was increasing daily, remained a stew of alienated peoples overseen by a Senate that had shown that it was unwilling to entertain change.

Jugurtha and Corruption

The failed reforms of the Gracchi were soon left behind as a series of crises struck the Late Republic. The city of Rome was shaken by lawlessness and mob violence, and Romans became convinced that the gods were angry at them. The year 111 BCE was particularly dire. Two Vestal Virgins were found guilty of breaking their vows of chastity and were buried alive. Theaters were suspected of undermining morality and were censored. When consulted, the Sibyl, a prophetic female, ordered a drastic remedy: two Greeks and two Gauls were to be sacrificed to the gods. Finally, a great fire struck Rome, destroying much of the city.

There was also the persistent problem of Jugurtha, who ruled Numidia, a client-kingdom of Rome in North Africa (see Map 4.3). King Jugurtha, one of history's rascals, had risen to power by deceit and murder. Realizing that his actions had irritated Rome, he sent agents to bribe key senators. In the fateful year of 111 BCE, the Senate sent troops to pacify North Africa; Jugurtha bribed the consul in charge of the army. Ordered to Rome, Jugurtha apparently bribed a tribune and escaped having to testify before the Senate. While in Rome he arranged the murder of a rival to his throne. For the next five years, Jugurtha evaded his Roman reckoning by bribing as many Romans as he could.

The case of Jugurtha shows how corrupt the Republic had become. The Numidian king exploited Rome's factionalism and self-interested aristocrats, particularly in the Roman Senate. Individual ambition now trumped the old moral order.

The Rise of the Great Consul Generals

What role did individuals such as Marius, Cicero, and Pompey play in the final phase of the Republic?

The Gracchi brothers had touched on many of the social and political strains within Rome, and the case of Jugurtha revealed how rampant corruption had become. Yet the greatest threat to the traditional Republic came, ironically, from the senators themselves. Rome elected two consuls each year, one of whom typically undertook military operations while the other remained in the Senate and city. In the old days, the consul generals had fought for family reputation and glory. By the Late Republic, powerful and ambitious men realized that the army and conquest promised more than just outstanding reputation; they brought power and profit. In seeking personal advantage, the great consul generals bent the Republic to the breaking point by subverting and bypassing the Senate.

Gaius Marius Subverts the Senate

Rome's war with Jugurtha continued until Gaius Marius (157–86 BCE), a man of middling birth and rank, and a former tribune, convinced the Senate to name him consul. His appointment was a sign of Rome's desperation to deal with the renegade Numidian king. It was highly unusual to elect a consul from outside the great families of senatorial rank. Marius sought the military advantages of the office of consul, for as consul a general gained not only a large army, but the chance to make vast wealth from the capture of slaves and loot. His aristocratic critics ridiculed him as a "new man," but he perceived more clearly than they did the new realities that were transforming the Late Republic.

His great innovation was to privatize or personalize the Roman army by binding soldiers and units to him personally through his power and wealth. He recruited soldiers from Rome's landless poor, who depended for their livelihood on his personal generosity or his ability to sway the government to grant them land or money. In this way, he established a deep source of personal power and extended the clientage system of personal patronage to the Roman army. In 105 BCE, after a series of successful battles, the Romans finally captured Jugurtha, who was handed over to Marius's representative, the young Sulla (137–78 BCE), who took credit for ending the war. The animosity between Marius and Sulla had begun. Jugurtha was chained and dragged back to Rome, where, unable to bribe the executioner, he was executed.

Marius found a more effective way than the Gracchi had to transform the Roman government, not by reforming it, but by subverting it. His populist thrust ushered in the phenomenon of the great consul generals of the Late Republic. Marius discovered that there was power in playing to the people of Rome, while manipulating and bypassing the Senate, whose standing and power were slowly slipping away. The degree and pace of change can be measured by the senatorial precedents that began to fall. Against all tradition, Marius was elected consul five straight times to deal with a series of military threats in Gaul, though in 100 BCE he was forced into exile when a riot broke out in Rome.

The Italian and Mithridatic Wars

The failure to extend citizenship to its Italian allies came back to bite Rome when the allies revolted in the Italian

The Italian Bull Gores the Roman Wolf A coin issued by Italia, the state set up by the Italian rebels in opposition to Rome during the Italian or Social War, does not disguise what the rebel state *wanted* to do to mighty Rome.

War (90–88 BCE), which is sometimes called the Social War (after the *socii* or allies). The rebellious allies were upset that they were no longer receiving their fair portion of the spoils of Rome's wars. Rome retained the allegiance of almost all its Latin allies, but the Marsi and Samnites of central Italy mounted stiff resistance. These peoples, who had never fully or willingly surrendered their identities and traditions, believed that Rome owed them for their recent loyalty. Moreover, they thought that citizenship would protect them from exploitation by corrupt Roman officials. The rebels established their own state called Italia that was to have a Senate and consuls. Italia began to mint its own coins and assembled an army of 100,000 men.

Rome recalled Marius to conduct the war but still lost a series of battles. Sulla was more successful, but what finally ended the Italian revolt was the Senate's offer of citizenship, first to those Italians who had remained loyal and then to all rebels who were prepared to rejoin Rome. The Samnites held out until the end, but eventually they too capitulated. With the end of the Italian War, the whole peninsula was integrated into the Roman state more effectively than it had been during the wars of expansion in the Middle Republic. The new Roman model permitted each region and city of Italy to retain its own identity as part of an expanding empire with the city of Rome as its capital and the Roman Senate as its great decision maker. Cicero said that there were now two fatherlands for all Romans, their natural homeland and Rome.

One of the reasons that Rome settled the Italian War so quickly was that Italia had sought help from Mithridates VI

(r. 120–63 BCE), the ruler of Pontus in Asia Minor. The king had extended his influence into the Aegean and had persuaded many Greeks, including the Athenians, to join him. Sulla was given command of an army to suppress Mithridates and set out on the campaign, but Marius had the order reversed and the command given to him. Sulla turned around his army and marched on Rome, breaking another long-standing tradition that Roman armies should not enter the city. Roman citizens were not pleased to be invaded and from their rooftops hurled stones down upon Sulla's army. The general replied by burning down their homes.

Events at this point became dizzying: Marius fled, Sulla restored order and set out again for the east, the people revolted in Rome, Marius returned and was elected consul again, and then died after first imposing, with his co-consul Cinna, a reign of terror on Rome. Sulla continued his campaign against Mithridates, retook Athens, brought Greece back into the Roman fold, and settled with the king, who surrendered the territories he had conquered.

Sulla, the Dictator

As Sulla marched home, Cinna was assassinated, the third consul to be killed in four years. In 82 BCE, Sulla reentered Rome with his army, which was illegal. He presented himself as Rome's liberator but quickly had himself named dictator and turned with a vengeance to eliminating his opponents. When one young senator pleaded with him to end the uncertainty about who was going to live or die, Sulla took him at his word and posted a list of proscriptions, a hit list. Sulla's list was both extensive and brutal; it included the names of 40 senators and 1,600 equestrians to be killed. Many of these men had been the supporters of Marius's regime, but some were murdered simply because they were wealthy and Sulla needed land and money to reward his troops.

Thousands of Romans died before Sulla felt sufficiently secure to begin restoring the Republic. He shored up the Senate's system of checks and balances so that no strong man like Marius (or, for that matter, himself) could again threaten it. He undid the last vestiges of the reforms of the Gracchi by limiting the power of tribunes and canceling the guarantee of grain to the people. Sulla was a law-and-order dictator and worked to reform the courts and to prosecute crime. Though he styled himself a conservative trying to restore Rome to its golden Republican past, Sulla was in reality one of the Republic's new military rulers, radically subverting the current Roman order. He used the Roman army to achieve power and advantage, overrode the Senate's directives, and shattered Roman traditions. Having restored the Republic, Sulla did something few expected: he retired.

Since 146 BCE a series of events had hammered Republican traditions and changed Rome forever. The Gracchi had both been murdered for attempting to reform the state; the case of Jugurtha revealed how corrupt Rome had become; Marius, a "new man," had been repeatedly elected consul; the armies of Sulla, Marius, and Cinna had invaded the city; Marius became consul for a seventh time, this time without an election; and official death squads had operated in the city of Rome. The Republic, which had had a relatively stable history between 509 and 146 BCE, was now a cesspool of corruption, mob violence, and state-sponsored terror. An increasingly dysfunctional Senate seemed unable or unwilling to curb powerful aristocrats. Only foolish and stubborn traditionalists still thought that Rome could return to its old ways. Cicero was one of those; Julius Caesar (100–44 BCE) and Octavian (63 BCE–14 CE, later to be called Augustus) were not.

The Strivers: Pompey, Cicero, and Catiline

By the end of Sulla's rule, nearly all the symptoms of Republican stress were evident. Landless Romans and generals such as Marius forged new clientage bonds that left the conservative Senate more and more irrelevant. The new world order was being worked out in the violent streets, morning parlors where patrons met their clients, and wealthy villas of Rome where aristocrats supped together. The problem of an excess of money in the system had not been corrected. Moreover, there was a change in the collective value system. In the earlier Republic, few individuals had stood out above their fellows. Indeed, even the glorious few had wanted little more than the praise of the great corporation of the Senate and citizenry of Rome. The Late Republic was dominated by famous great men, all striving for individual power and wealth: Marius, Sulla, Pompey, Caesar, Octavian, and even the marginal strivers Cicero and Catiline, who were not generals. It was an age of great individuals, which was itself an indication of the drift away from the collective values of the earlier Republic.

The next great consul general after Sulla was Pompey (106–48 BCE), the golden boy of the Late Republic. The end of his career was as sad as its beginning was spectacular. Early on he attached himself to Sulla and, during the period of the proscriptions, was popularly called "the young butcher" for his success in hunting down Sulla's enemies. As a general, his military timing was perfect, and he had an uncanny talent for arriving on the scene of a recent kill. He made himself useful to the Senate during its many crises, including showing up in time to clean up the final remnants of the slave rebellion led by Spartacus.

Spartacus was a Thracian slave who had once served as an auxiliary soldier for Rome. In 73 BCE, he and a group of seventy-eight slaves rioted at a gladiatorial training camp. They camped near Mount Vesuvius south of Rome and began to attract other slaves seeking freedom, revenge, and wealth. Spartacus and his slave soldiers defeated nine Roman armies over two years. When Spartacus began to negotiate with Mediterranean pirates for passage out of Italy, the Senate sent one of Rome's wealthiest men, Crassus, who had little military experience, to lead six legions against the slaves. The slaves divided their forces and Crassus crushed each in turn. He crucified thousands of the rebellious slaves along the Appian Way leading to Rome. Pompey mopped up the remainder of the slave army as it fled north, and both he and Crassus were named consuls for 70 BCE.

The Senate found it all too easy in times of crisis to make exceptional military appointments: of Marius against Jugurtha and the Italians, Sulla against Mithridates, and Crassus against the slaves. These appointments shifted the balance of power away from the Senate to powerful military men, undercut the older competitive dynamic of the Republic in which many aristocrats had vied for military commands, and enriched those who were undermining the Senate's preeminence. The Senate reinforced the pattern when it commissioned Pompey by terms of an old law, the *Lex Gabinia,* to rid the Mediterranean Sea of the pirates who had been preying upon ships and inhibiting trade for years. Though the pirates were reputed to have a thousand ships and to operate out of scattered ports, Pompey eliminated them in a mere forty days in 67 BCE, destroying both their bases and ships. The commission gave Pompey extraordinary license over the entire Mediterranean and lands up to fifty miles from the sea.

Next the Senate appointed Pompey to resume the campaign against Mithridates VI that Sulla had ended on terms that did not fully satisfy Rome. Trapped inside his palace, Mithridates killed his family and himself rather than surrender. On his eastern campaign, Pompey extended Roman holdings to the Euphrates River and substantially increased Rome's annual revenues. So impressive were his accomplishments that some spoke of Pompey as a new Alexander and took to calling him Pompey the Great, but when he arrived back in Rome he was snubbed. The Senate refused to allot land to his soldiers, probably because many senators feared that Pompey would become another strongman like Sulla.

In the meantime, the Senate and Republic faced another crisis at home. Cicero, whose family belonged to the equestrian class, had distinguished himself as a lawyer and an orator. He slowly moved up the ladder of offices and finally achieved his dream job as consul for 63 BCE. In a vigorous campaign for election, Cicero beat the shady patrician, Catiline, who took his loss badly and stood again for election the next year during Cicero's term. Losing again, Catiline hatched a conspiracy to murder the consuls and take control of Rome. Cicero learned of the plot from spies and alerted the Senate. Catiline and his supporters, chiefly disgruntled aristocrats, fled Rome and began to raise an army among the poor veterans living in Etruria. Cicero and the Senate moved quickly to round up and execute Catiline and his fellow conspirators. Cicero believed that the suppression of the conspiracy was the greatest political achievement of his career. He thought that he had saved the Republic.

The case of Catiline is important, not because the plot was a real danger to the state, but because the actions of Catiline and his followers were symptomatic of the troubles of the Late Republic. These aristocratic rebels were broke and believed that their only way to secure riches was for one of them to become consul. With high office, Catiline could reward his friends and supporters, expropriate money from the provinces, and command an army on a campaign that would generate wealth. Catiline appealed to many of the disenfranchised elements of Roman society—bankrupt nobles, the needy lower classes, displaced soldiers, opportunistic provincials—but his rebellion failed and Cicero claimed the credit. As consul, Cicero made stirring speeches appealing for harmony between the orders, but he did little to address the underlying tensions and inequities of the faltering Republic.

The Golden Age of Republican Literature

Despite all the turmoil, or perhaps because of it, the last phase of the Republic was one of Rome's richest literary periods. Turbulent times often produce the liveliest expressions of human thought. Cicero and Julius Caesar were the greatest prose stylists of the age. The range of Cicero's writings is impressive. His letters to and from his friends survive in great number (nearly a thousand of them); so also do many of his legal addresses. His speeches against Catiline and Mark Antony are barbed masterpieces. His philosophical works may now strike readers as poor knock-offs of the deeper Greek philosophical thought of Plato and Aristotle, but Cicero served as a useful bridge between two cultural worlds. His works were, at the time, an effective Romanization of Greek thought.

The great poets of the age were Lucretius (c. 94–55 BCE) and Catullus (84–54 BCE). Lucretius, an Epicurean, wrote *On the Nature of Things,* which presents a gloomy theory of the world's atomic and material existence, but his central purpose was to allay the fears of his contemporaries about death. Catullus is a poet more at home with us since he wrote short poems about life and love, particularly about the girlfriend he called Lesbia (Clodia), the sister of one of the Late Republic's blackguards. We suffer along with the poet as Lesbia torments him and he moves from wanting to drown her in a thousand kisses to a state of high agitation:

> I hate and I love. You ask me how I manage it.
> I don't know, but I feel it and am a wreck.

Catullus died when he was thirty; he was every inch a Late Republican and was caught up in its turmoil. For a time he had opposed Caesar, before reconciling with him. His hatreds and loves, often of the same object at the same time, are spun in a web of sublime and captivating lyrical poetry.

Catullus and Cicero captured the emotional tenor of a deeply divided and confused age. They were not alone. Sallust's histories of the war with Jugurtha and Catiline's conspiracy are angry indictments of corruption. Cicero's lament over the death of his daughter and Catullus's agony over Lesbia's inconstancy reflect a period of Roman history that rested on a knife's edge of emotion.

Waiting just beyond the red hot eruption of the Late Republic lay the cool classicism of the Augustan poets and their politically careful poems, but then they were men without the freedom to speak their minds openly and confusedly. Catullus and Cicero probably enjoyed the exquisite agony of their loves and hatreds as free citizens of Republican Rome.

The Civil War and Collapse of the Republic

The Late Roman Republic was in trouble for a century before it finally collapsed. The Senate was no longer able to control the corruption, militarism, and rampant individualism of its own members. When the Senate finally saw the danger that one of the last great consul generals, Caesar, represented, it was too late. Civil war was the result. Although Caesar won the war against the Senate, he could not survive the uneasy peace of the still turbulent Republic and ruled for too short a time to transform the Roman state into a Roman empire.

Why was Caesar assassinated?

Caesar Forms a Powerful Consular Faction

Pompey's problems with the Senate forced him to turn to Caesar and together with Crassus they formed a powerful faction, the **Caesarian (or Consular) Faction,** sometimes mistakenly called the **First Triumvirate,** of three magnates bound together for political purposes. Each man did so out of individual and political necessity. Pompey wanted prestige for himself and land for his soldiers; Crassus sought tax advantages for himself and his supporters as well as a way to offset the extensive power and reputation of Pompey; and Caesar wished, in the short term, to receive a triumph for his campaigns in Spain and to become consul and, in the long term, to possess an army and new lands to conquer. Each of the men had grievances against a Senate that would not accede to their demands and vaunting ambitions. Their alliance was a private arrangement, a faction, and had no official power or legal standing on its own. Its power came when one of its members held the consulship and could swing benefits in their direction. Their plan to use the consulship was not unlike Catiline's, but it was handled more deftly by more powerful and better connected politicians.

Caesar himself was already a smooth political operator. As a senator he had won the support of the popular classes by mounting gladiatorial combats and widely distributing money and grain. Whereas Pompey sought alliances among the upper classes, Caesar counted on popular support in Rome just as Marius had once done. It was this alliance between Caesar and the people that would further marginalize the Senate and shape Caesarian or imperial politics.

Caesar became consul in 59 BCE, but he preferred to operate without the interference of the other consul, who largely withdrew from the scene. One wit claimed that the two consuls for the year were "Julius" and "Caesar." Others asserted openly that Caesar's actions were illegal, and many of them probably were. Like Marius and Sulla before him, Caesar subverted the traditional powers of the Senate for personal gain, the greatest of which was his own five-year proconsular appointment (one having the rights of a consul outside of Rome) as commander of the Roman armies of Illyria and then Gaul. He spent the next ten years carving out and stabilizing new territories in Gaul and Belgium for Rome, making himself rich and famous in the process. His written commentaries on his wars are elegant self-promotions that kept his name and deeds before the public.

With Caesar in Gaul, Pompey and Crassus quarreled in Rome, but together they successfully sought consulships for 55 BCE and each received territories to subdue. Pompey's province was Spain, where his military successes were modest ones. Crassus took command of a campaign in Syria but waged a disastrous war in which he lost seven legions and his head.

The Civil War

With Crassus dead, the faction dissolved. The two most powerful Romans, Pompey and Caesar, now stood against each other. Senators who had resented the presumption of Caesar's consular faction worked behind the scenes to separate the two men. Severing further the ties between them, Pompey's wife, Julia, who was Caesar's daughter, died in 54 BCE. The next year the Senate elected no consuls and for 52 BCE, for the first time in Republican history, chose only one consul, Pompey. He and the Senate now acted to limit Caesar's proconsular powers in Gaul. They also rejected Caesar's bid to become consul again. A sense of emergency gripped Rome as Caesar's command approached its official end. Would he give up his army peacefully, return to Rome, and face the charge of overstepping his authority? Or would he become a renegade? Early in 49 BCE the Senate declared martial law, put the Republic in the hands of Pompey, and sent two legions against Caesar's small force camped in the north (Map 5.1).

In January Caesar took the decisive decision to cross the Rubicon River, which marked the border between Gaul and Italy and, therefore, the legal limit of his authority to command an army. He entered Italy with a small army, thus provoking a civil war (49–45 BCE). Picking up small armies, veterans, and defectors along the way, Caesar's army grew as it marched south. In a panic and seeking more time to prepare, Pompey and much of the Senate fled Rome, but in their rush they

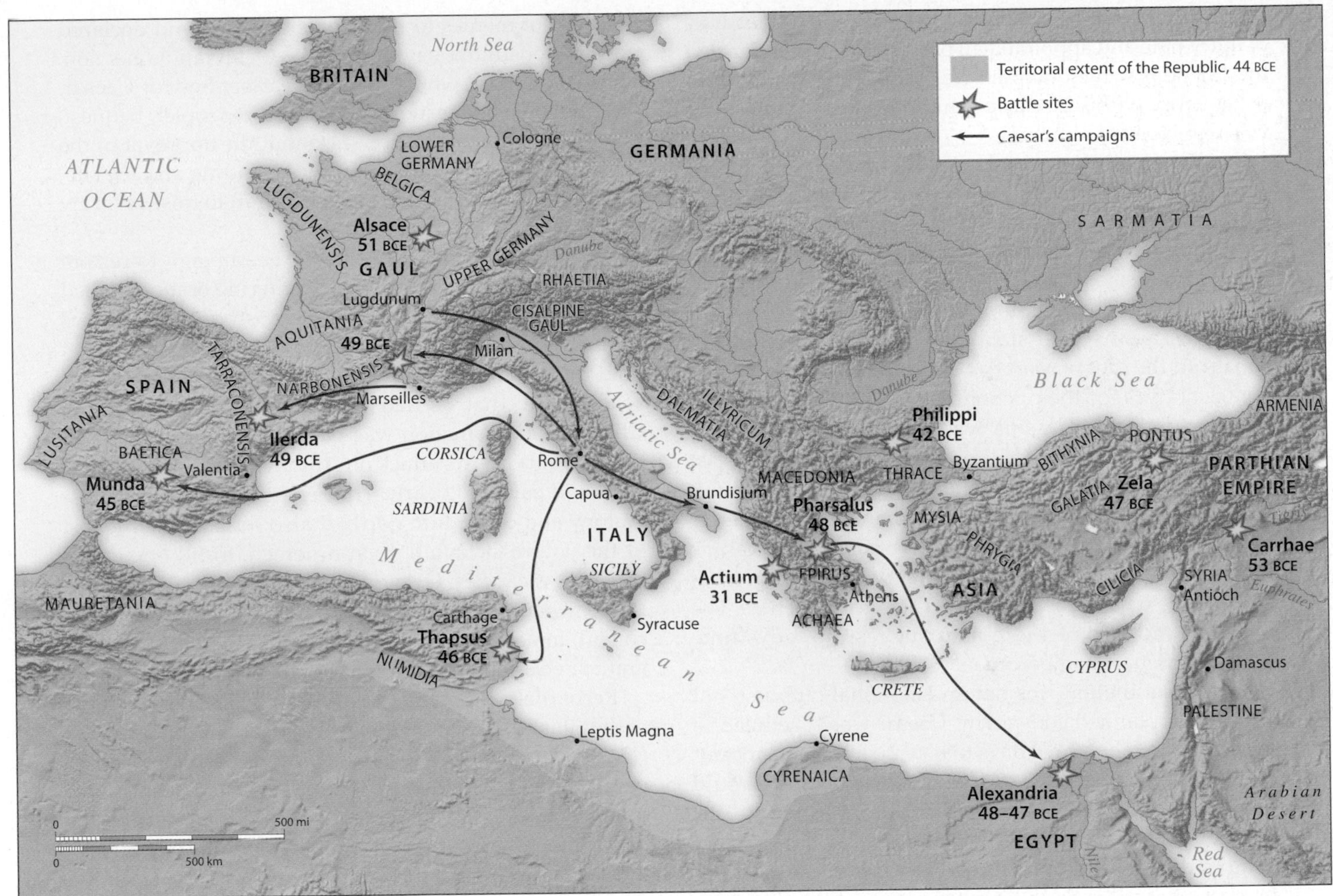

MAP 5.1 | The Civil War of the Late Roman Republic, 49–45 BCE

When Julius Caesar crossed the Rubicon River in 49 BCE, he ignited a civil war that spanned much of the Roman world. ***Why was the civil war fought outside Italy? How methodical was Caesar in conducting the war? In what ways was this war an imperial war as much as a civil war?***

neglected to empty the Roman treasury before they departed. Caesar allowed the senatorial forces to flee across the Adriatic to Greece while he concentrated on securing control of Rome, Sardinia, Sicily, and Spain. In Greece Pompey managed to assemble an army of nine legions and was preparing to return to confront Caesar, when Caesar slipped across the Adriatic with half his troops. The other half was stranded in Italy, and Caesar was left short of men and supplies.

Though outnumbered two to one and lacking the naval forces Pompey commanded, Caesar's army defeated the senatorial army at the Battle of Pharsalus in July 48 BCE. Pompey and most of the senators fled the battle. Pompey fled all the way to Egypt, with Caesar in close pursuit. The Ptolemies greeted the defeated general by cutting off his head, preserving it in brine, and presenting it to Caesar when he arrived. Caesar was, by all reports, less than pleased. Throughout the civil war he had been generous to those he defeated. He welcomed back and forgave many senators, including Cicero, and likely would have received Pompey as well, probably forcing him into retirement. Caesar spent the next three years mopping up the last of the resistance and delayed for nearly a year in Egypt where he apparently fathered a son by Cleopatra VII (69–30 BCE).

The Murder of a Dictator

Caesar returned to Rome in 45 BCE. He had already been named dictator for a ten-year term, but in 44 BCE his title was changed to dictator for life. He also held a series of other official titles: Pontifex Maximus (high priest), tribune, and consul. He fully intended to monopolize power in Rome. Indeed, he may for a moment have considered becoming a king like the Hellenistic monarchs, but in the end he came to regard his own name as its imperial equivalent: "I am not king, I am Caesar."

His legislative program was thin, but then he was only in Rome for a year and a half. During that short time, Caesar worked to improve the functioning of local government in Italy, found land for landless Romans in Gaul, and set about draining marshes to create yet more agricultural land. He replenished and expanded the ranks of the Senate and appointed all officeholders. He reformed the calendar, which by then was almost ninety days out of sequence with the seasons, and one of its months, July, was named after him.

He then made the mistake of a lifetime: he mistook official control of Rome and the Senate for absolute control, assumed that his victory at Pharsalus had decided once and for all the rightfulness and finality of his victory, and believed that those whom he had forgiven had accepted the new order. Those assumptions cost him his life.

The assassins who stabbed Caesar to death in the Senate on the Ides of March (March 15) 44 BCE had a variety of motives for their action. Some sixty senators were party to the plot. Cassius was the ringleader; Brutus, whose distant ancestor had reputedly dethroned the last Etruscan king, was its figurehead. Both had stood with Pompey and the senatorial side at Pharsalus, but Caesar had forgiven them. Some of the assassins were Caesar's own clients, officeholders, and friends, and many were "new men" whom Caesar had elevated to the Senate. The personal motives of these men suggest how dysfunctional the Senate had become.

The assassination was not an emotional outburst, but a carefully planned conspiracy. Caesar was scheduled to leave the capital in three days to take up a three-year campaign in the east and so the assassins acted before he could depart. Mark Antony (83–31 BCE), one of Caesar's loyalists, was kept in the dark about the plot. The various signs and rumors that were circulating did reach Caesar's ears, but he chose to ignore them. Someone slipped the dictator a note on his way to the Senate informing him of the plot, but he failed to read it and so was stabbed to death.

Whatever planning went into the murder, little thought was given to what to do afterward. The plotters assumed that Rome would be overjoyed to be rid of Caesar and to have its freedoms restored. They marched through the streets of Rome clutching their blood-stained daggers, proclaiming "Liberty!" When the Roman masses reacted with anger, the conspirators fled to safety. They had misjudged Caesar's popularity and the success of his patronage of the masses. They assumed that the Republic would return to its old ways without incident, and so left the dictator's body in the Senate house rather than dispose of it. The conspirators had not thought through the politics of assassination or how best to destroy Caesar's popularity.

The murder succeeded, but the Republic was already lost. It had been failing for a century.

The Official Triumvirate

Two days after the assassination, Mark Antony, who had already taken effective control of the Senate, spoke stirringly at the dictator's funeral. He reached a deal with the Senate whereby Caesar's acts were legitimized, but his murder was declared a patriotic and just deed by noble Romans. Antony deliberately obstructed the execution of Caesar's will, which called for the generous distribution of monies to the people of Rome and declared Caesar's posthumous adoption of Octavian as his son. The young man, who was the great-nephew of Caesar, sold personal properties to pay for the people's bequest; he already understood how essential the approval of the people of Rome was to his family's standing and the success of Caesarian politics. He also began to raise an army composed of Caesar's veterans.

Meanwhile Cicero began his last campaign to restore the Republic. He wrote a series of stinging orations called the Philippics (in imitation of Demosthenes's speeches against Philip of Macedon) against Antony. He did not hold back, calling Antony "a wine-soaked reprobate," so dissolute that he had once vomited in the Senate. Character assassination was part of the Senate's normal politics, but Cicero's attack on Antony was foolhardy, and he would pay for it dearly. The Senate sent a force against Antony and drove him north. It also refused the request of the young Octavian, then nineteen, to fill one of the consular vacancies. Octavian marched with his army on Rome, where the Senate felt compelled to elect Octavian consul, to acknowledge him as the legal son of Caesar, and to declare that Caesar's assassins were criminals.

Recognizing the strength of Antony and the fickleness of the Senate, Octavian established an official Triumvirate (42–33 BCE) with Antony and Lepidus, a former governor of Spain and ally of Caesar. **The Triumvirate** (sometimes mistakenly called the Second Triumvirate), unlike his father's faction, was given legal sanction by the Senate, which was aware that the Triumvirs possessed a large and threatening army. The official powers of the Triumvirate were extensive: a term of five years to straighten out the Republic and control over offices and taxation.

The Triumvirate declared Caesar a god, which enhanced its own legitimacy. It also introduced a Sulla-like list of proscriptions, with each Triumvir setting down the names of enemies to be killed. Cicero's name was high on Antony's list and so he was murdered that December day. Antony's wife at the time, Fulvia, is reputed to have pierced the dead orator's tongue with a hair pin in a fit of vengeful fury.

Antony and Octavian hunted down the assassins Cassius and Brutus, whose armies were defeated at Philippi in Macedonia in 42 BCE. After avenging Caesar's murder, the Triumvirs divided up areas of control within the empire: Lepidus took Africa, Antony the east (including Egypt), and Octavian the west (including Italy). While Antony campaigned in the east and began to court Cleopatra in Egypt, Octavian portrayed himself as the true Roman of the group. He concentrated on repairing a deeply divided and socially unstable Italy. On the surface he stood for justice, Roman religion, and Republican virtue.

Antony and Cleopatra

Like all three-legged stools the Triumvirate required all three legs to maintain its balance, and that was hard to achieve after the turmoil of Caesar's assassination. The

WHAT A DIFFERENCE A YEAR MAKES

Caesar's Big Break, 59–58 BCE

Small pivotal moments may matter as much as big and famous ones, and Julius Caesar was a man of many moments when history might have turned in a different direction. Had he not crossed the Rubicon in 49 BCE; had he lost any of the important battles he fought over the last ten years of his life in Gaul or when outnumbered and facing Pompey and the senatorial forces in Greece; had he not gone to the Senate house the day he was assassinated and instead heeded the soothsayers and stayed home with his worried wife, the Roman world might have been different.

There was a moment, barely noticed at the time, when he did little and yet a world of possibilities opened for him. In 59 BCE, as he left the office of consul, Caesar was granted the governorship of Illyricum and Cisalpine Gaul (northern Italy). The appointment gave him the legal authority to have an army, but it lacked scope for a man of Caesar's ambitions. Those regions already lay firmly under Roman control, but Transalpine Gaul was different, an uncivilized land with an unconquered people and unfixed northern border. Its conquest was to be the critical turning point in Caesar's career. Bringing Gaul under Roman power was the finest accomplishment of his career. Success there brought him wealth and a loyal army of battle-hardened soldiers, but it also provoked the events that led to civil war. In the last five years of his absence from Rome, the opposition to Caesar rose in the Senate from the likes of Cato the Younger and Pompey, who sought to strip him of his army and extraordinary legal and military powers.

A Fallen Gallic Helmet from the Site of One of Caesar's Victories in Gaul

Those developments were, however, the result of an unexpected turn of events. Caesar was not supposed to assume the governorship of greater Gaul. Metellus Celer was already the legally appointed governor and he was famously fussy about senatorial rights. Cicero saw Metellus full of vim and vigor in the Senate one day in 59 BCE; three days later he was dead. Cicero suggested that his disreputable wife Clodia (Lesbia, later the girlfriend of Catullus) may have poisoned him to death. Though her brother Clodius was a partisan of Caesar, there is no evidence that Caesar plotted to deprive Metellus of his life or his governorship. Metellus may just have died naturally as middle-aged men sometimes do.

When Metellus died, the governorship of greater Gaul was handed to Caesar and it made his career. Caesar's conquest of Gaul led him to the Rubicon and Rome to civil war. Such are the twists of history. The Republic would have fallen anyway, even without Caesar, but it would have fallen in a different way and at a different time. History is the end result of millions of little decisions, actions, accidents, and, in this case, a mysterious and opportune death. Little historical things do matter. Rome's situation in 59 BCE, when Metellus was readying himself for the governorship of Gaul, was significantly different from what it became in 58 BCE, when Caesar began his great run.

QUESTION | *How do individual historical actors and the things that alter their lives matter in the larger scheme of history?*

Triumvirate first tottered under the weight placed on it and then collapsed when Octavian forced Lepidus to retire. Even Antony's marriage to Octavian's sister could not preserve their alliance once Cleopatra entered the scene. Cleopatra proved the perfect target for Octavian to attack. Reluctant to impugn the popular Mark Antony directly, Octavian's propaganda portrayed Antony as the captive of an evil Egyptian queen. Cleopatra was, in fact, Greek, fabulously wealthy, and charismatic. Romans despised her because she was both foreign and royal. They had despised kingship ever since driving the Etruscans out of Rome, and Cleopatra was the ruler of Egypt, a land that seemed to Romans to be full of exotic mystery and deadly intrigue. As the conflict between the two sides loomed, one of Antony's greatest problems was that few Roman soldiers were willing to fight for a foreign queen.

Cleopatra VII There are few reliable portraits of Cleopatra aside from her many and varying coin portraits, but this statue, though it lacks feet, bears a hieroglyphic cartouche on the upper right arm with her name.

There is another way to view this elemental conflict. Mark Antony and Cleopatra were victims of Octavian's characterization of them. He and his propagandists depicted Antony as a boisterous boob, a big man who drank too much and was easily led astray by a wily foreigner working her foreign magic on an unsophisticated Roman. There is much to suggest that this picture is wrong. Julius Caesar himself had certainly seen Antony's many merits, among them his brilliance as a general and leader of men. Moreover, Antony had acted quickly and with skill after Caesar's assassination to win over the Roman masses and take control of Rome.

Did he fall into Cleopatra's trap, as Octavian's propaganda suggested, or was there a master plan behind his interest in her and Egypt? Antony had Hellenistic leanings. In his own religious propaganda in the east, he presented himself as Dionysus (or Osiris). After his failure to subdue Parthia in 36 BCE, Antony was even more dependent on Cleopatra and her Egyptian wealth for legitimacy and resources. In an elaborate ceremony in 34 BCE, Cleopatra, dressed as the goddess Isis, was named Queen of Kings, and Caesarion, her son by Caesar (though there were always doubts about the boy's paternity), was named King of Kings. Antony legitimized the children Cleopatra bore him, one named Alexander Helios (the Sun) and the other Cleopatra Selene (the Moon). Those names suggest Antony's Hellenistic ambitions, for he may have been attempting to graft his own line onto that of the existing Ptolemaic kingdom. Egypt was a wealthy and prosperous part of the Mediterranean world, and Antony may have hoped to establish an eastern kingdom to rival Octavian's Italy. On the other hand, Antony's Egyptian venture may just have been a colossal misjudgment. As melodramatic as the Antony and Cleopatra story may seem, its outcome mattered a great deal. If Antony had triumphed over Octavian, the Mediterranean world might have turned in a different direction.

The forces of Octavian and Antony met in a sea battle off Actium in Greece in 31 BCE. When Cleopatra fled during the fight, Antony chased after her and so lost the battle. They retreated to Egypt, where Antony committed suicide as Octavian closed in. Cleopatra did the same by the famous adder bite or, possibly, Octavian arranged for her death and made it seem self-inflicted. He ordered the execution of her son and heir Caesarion. Octavian now controlled the Roman world. He was thirty-two years old.

Augustus the Emperor

How did Augustus succeed in stabilizing Rome after Sulla and Caesar had failed?

As successful as it had been as a conquering city-state, the Roman Republic was coming apart at the seams in the Late Republic. The regions and peoples of the Roman world were unsettled, but many of them wanted precisely what Octavian delivered: an end to disorder, disunity, and violence; in a word, peace. How he accomplished the great transformation of the Roman world from a dysfunctional Republic into an official empire is a story of structural changes to the Roman state and Octavian's personal political genius. The end result was the great "peace" that washed over the Mediterranean world under Octavian's (or Augustus's) watch, displaying itself in order and economic prosperity, classical monuments and words.

The Great Transformation

Few probably believed that Octavian would be able to restore Roman order. He settled his soldiers in Italy by buying land with the money he had taken from the captured Egyptian treasury, and he established a standing army over which he was the sole ruler. In this way, Octavian returned the Roman army to state control, which was now identical to his own. He created a **Praetorian Guard** of soldiers as his own imperial bodyguard. In 27 BCE, in a false and no doubt prearranged display of give and take, he offered to turn his official powers over to the Senate, which refused them. Instead, it asked him to assume proconsular powers over the empire for the next ten years. The Senate also bestowed on him the title of Augustus because he possessed *auctoritas* or authority over the state. For that reason, the starting date of the Roman Empire is usually set at 27 BCE, though for the Romans there was no sharp line between the end of the Republic and the start of the empire. Few probably realized that a new form of government had replaced the Republic.

Augustus succeeded where Caesar had not because of his relatively slow and sensitive reordering of the Roman world. Caesar was the greater general, but Augustus by far the greater politician. The list of his "Accomplishments" indicates how deliberate and categorical his mind was. He seemed to revive the Senate and Republic, while at the same time transforming their natures. From being a deliberating and advisory body, the Senate became one that executed the emperor's will. Under Augustus, the Senate lost its power over foreign, military, and financial affairs. Moreover, he created an inner council of senators that advised him directly rather than wait for the whole Senate to advise him. To win over the Romans and Italians, he encouraged their strong sense of place and superiority: Romans ruled; others served as incorporated subjects. Unlike Caesar, who forcibly brought about the collapse of the traditional Republic, Augustus promised his empire peace and prosperity.

The political brilliance of Augustus is evident. He seemed to restore the Republic and to reinforce old Roman virtues, but kept critical powers for himself, now sanctioned by the Senate. He polished the Senate's official sheen and ancient standing by increasing its size, but was quietly transforming it into a legislative agency of imperial power. He restructured the empire by dividing it into provinces, some under the control of the Senate, others under the control of the empire (that is, of himself and his family). Wealthy Egypt became an imperial province. Italy remained under the control of the Senate, but even there Augustus and his agents influenced policy decisions and administration. He directed affairs in the city of Rome by exercising his powers as tribune or through the prefect of the city, whom he appointed. Augustus kept the masses of the huge city content with entertainment for their diversion and bread for their stomachs.

Augustus controlled the senators and aristocratic elite by in essence making them his clients, while restoring their nominal dignity. Since his approval was necessary for the elevation of men to the Senate, they were effectively his men. In the case of any sign of senatorial independence or renegade legislation he could exercise his veto power as tribune. Still he presented himself as but one of the senators, though the first among equals (*primus inter pares*) or most eminent (*princeps*).

The Augustan Ideology of Order

Augustan ideology was seductive. As the Pontifex Maximus, he restored Roman religion by building new temples and encouraging a return to traditional religion. Augustus was a moral conservative, disapproving of the moral looseness of the Late Republic and its wild times. He banished his adopted daughter Julia for committing adultery. Though Augustus tried to curb excessive displays of luxury, the times were too good for extravagance to disappear entirely.

While much of Augustus's attention was devoted to the city of Rome and Italy, his peace was good for the empire as a whole. He reduced corruption in the provinces by more strictly controlling provincial appointments and by becoming the great patron of the local nobility of the empire. He also stabilized the empire as a contiguous territory and led the Roman army in its consolidation of Spain as an imperial province. Two permanent legions were stationed in Egypt. Where he could, he allowed local client kings to hold frontier areas, but not long after Herod the Great (r. 37–4 BCE) died, he made Judaea a province. Augustus extended Roman control over Gaul and parts of Germany, but in 9 CE a disaster struck. At the Teutoburg Forest three Roman legions were wiped out and their commander Varus felt compelled to commit suicide. It was a turning point in Rome's territorial ambitions since Germania was never to be as Romanized as Gaul.

Though Augustus himself was not a brilliant general, he found men who were, particularly Agrippa, and they remained loyal to him. Augustus ordered the creation of a state navy with bases on the eastern and western shores of Italy, and in Egypt. The standing army was one of almost thirty legions (perhaps as many as 250,000 men) spread throughout the empire, but mostly paid for by each province that housed them.

As successful and sure as was Augustus's reordering of Rome, there was a worm in this polished apple: the lack of a tradition of dynastic succession. While the emperor lived, all was well. Augustus was a second Romulus, another founder of Rome, and Rome did blossom (Map 5.2).

Dressing Rome in Marble

One of the functions of great patrons was to adorn cities with monuments. Augustus claimed that when he came to power, Rome was made of bricks, but he had left it dressed in marble. He boasted that he rebuilt eighty-two temples to the gods, and erected a Temple of Mars the Avenger to fulfill a pledge made at the Battle of Philippi. On the

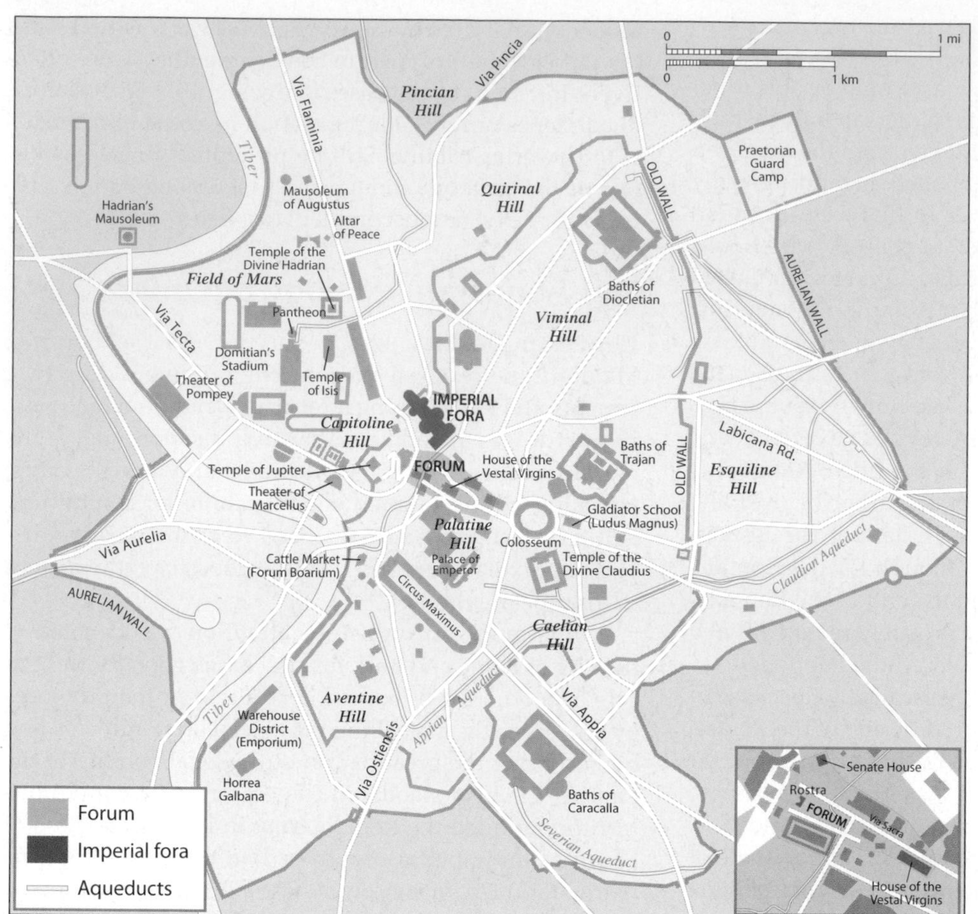

MAP 5.2 | The Imperial City of Rome in the Second Century CE

The city of Rome had changed a great deal since the Middle Republic, as the patrons of the Late Republic and early imperial period left their mark on its design, architecture, and water supply. ***How had the emperors of the first and second centuries left their mark on the city of Rome? What would a visitor to the city have been most struck by? How easy or difficult would it likely have been to move around Rome?***

roofline of the pediment (the triangular shape at the top) of the temple were statues of Venus, Mars, and Fortune. Contemporaries thought that Mars looked remarkably like Augustus. Inside the Temple were statues of Mars, Venus, and the Deified Caesar, and in a side-room a colossal statue of Augustus standing over forty feet high. In general, the architecture of Augustan Rome was classical, but an eclectic blend of classical Greek and Hellenistic forms.

The emperor's drive to rebuild Rome spread to his advisors. Agrippa planned a new complex of buildings for the Field of Mars or War, including the Pantheon. Though the Pantheon as it exists today in Rome was rebuilt in the second century CE, it still reflects the high aspirations of Augustan Rome.

After the campaigns in Spain and Gaul, Augustus vowed to honor Peace, a goddess of concord, whom he either invented or institutionalized. To honor Augustus the Senate commissioned the erection of an Altar of Peace (*Ara Pacis*). The relief sculptures of the frieze running around the walls of the altar express Augustan ideology. The bottom layer presents a pleasant pastoral imagery of twisting vines, birds, and small animals; above it moves a parade of priests and dignitaries, including the imperial family. The

The Pantheon in Rome The interior of the Pantheon, originally constructed by Agrippa and later rebuilt, reflects the monumentality and sweep of Augustan architecture.

mood is somber, the figures dignified, the procession stately.

The Prima Porta statue of Augustus is probably a marble copy of a bronze original. The carved Augustus is larger than life (at six foot eight) and youthful. He is portrayed not only as a hero, but also as a barefooted god. A little Cupid rides a dolphin at his feet, a reminder that Caesar's family claimed to have descended from Venus, the mother of Cupid. The emperor's breastplate symbolically proclaims Augustus's victory over the Parthians. A bearded Parthian surrenders to the Roman army (represented by a single soldier) the standard that they had earlier seized. Above the two figures is a symbol of the spreading sky and below them Mother Earth with her cornucopia of bounty. To the bottom left is Apollo, to the bottom right Diana; to the left of the sky figure is the Sun and to the right Dawn empties dew from a jug while elbowing aside the Moon. On the breastplate the world rejoices at the dawning of the new age of Augustus and his cosmic triumph.

The Ara Pacis of Augustus Augustus's Altar of Peace was bestowed on him by the Senate. The altar, recovered in modern times from the Tiber River, is meant to express the pastoral calm of Augustan Rome. The stately procession of Augustus, his family, and the senators conveys the stability Augustus sought to return to Rome when he took charge.

Emperor Augustus The marble Prima Porta statue of Augustus.

The imperial art of the Augustan age is rich and highly symbolic, but there is a certain sameness to much of it. The hundreds of busts of Augustus that survive all seem remarkably alike: the youthful Augustus with his head slightly tilted to his right, an aquiline nose, wavy hair, and perfectly defined ears. There may once have been over twenty thousand such busts scattered throughout the empire in cities, homes of officials, and temples. These busts were mass produced by sculptors working from models with small protuberances that the artisan could measure with compasses to replicate the image as faithfully as possible.[2]

Roman art and architecture of the time was more than just Augustan, but his period and its pronounced tendencies toward classicism and imperial imagery marked a new phase in high Roman culture. Augustus's beautification of the city of Rome set a standard that radiated throughout the empire. Even the little towns of Pompeii and Herculaneum, destroyed by the volcanic eruption of Mount Vesuvius in 79 CE, lived and were buried in the shadow of its high standards. The drive to standardize and replicate images was an imperial and high cultural moment, though there was a world of common culture beyond its reach. Still Augustus knew how to communicate in both images and words his vision of the new Rome and his place atop it.

Augustan Writers

The three great Latin poets of the Augustan age, Virgil (70–19 BCE), Horace (65–8 BCE), and Ovid (43 BCE–18 CE),

OTHER VOICES, OTHER VIEWS

Inside Out, Outside In

Empires produce both incorporation and alienation. While imperial systems tend to tolerate internal differences of language and customs as the cost of securing a unified whole, they struggle to balance a powerful imperial center and resistant marginal parts. That tension makes empires energetic and alert, but also anxious and adversarial.

Almost by definition, empires contain misfits. Among the insiders who found themselves on the outside of the Roman Empire was Ovid, the great poet of love. He had reveled in the high culture of Augustan Rome with its painted ladies, literary friends, fine dining, and imperial patrons. But in 8 CE he was exiled to Tomis, a dreary outpost on the Black Sea, at the very edge of Roman influence. Augustus was punishing him for the loose morality of his love poems and for some unspecified indiscretion. Ovid had apparently seen something he should not have. For eight long years until his death he languished in the frozen north far from the warmth of imperial Rome. Surrounded by people who knew no Latin and who lacked the basic refinements of civilization, he could not stop thinking of "Rome, home, my longing for old haunts, and that part of me that lingers in the city I have lost." The wailing poems that he wrote in exile in the hope that he would be recalled chart one distance between the center and periphery of Augustan Rome, and it was cold out there on the edge of the empire.

Ovid's complaint is deliciously literate, but many others forced unwillingly to be part of the empire did not write down their complaints. Yet their actions speak volumes. Slaves revolted and killed their masters, many poor men and women rioted when pushed or starving, and provinces waited for the opportunity to break free from Rome. No story is more eloquent or complicated than that of the Hebrews. Many Jews were pleased to see the Romans release Judaea from Hellenistic rule and so worked with their occupiers. Some Jews cooperated because in periods of toleration Rome respected their religion and way of life. But when Pompey stormed Jerusalem and desecrated the Temple in 63 BCE, Jewish resistance to Rome began in earnest. Cicero boasted that the gods had decided in Rome's favor since Jewish rites were not compatible with the great name of Rome or its ancestral customs. Jerusalem was now enslaved to Rome, he said. Few Jews saw it that way. The apocryphal Psalms of Solomon said that an alien enemy full of pride had laid waste to the land, killed women and children, and disrespected God. Portions of the Dead Sea Scrolls seem to refer to Pompey's invasion. The Jewish chronicler Josephus said that the Romans mercilessly tortured the Essenes, who probably deposited the scrolls in the caves of Quamram near the Dead Sea. The War Scroll curses Rome for bringing darkness down upon Israel. Over the next two centuries, the Jews revolted several times against their Roman occupiers, saw their Temple destroyed, and were banished from Jerusalem. The narrative of Jewish complaint against Rome provides powerful witness to what it meant for one group to be outsiders trapped under Roman rule and just how hot it was for them inside an empire of idolaters.

QUESTIONS | ***What other external views of the Roman Empire would be valuable for us to encounter? Why?***

make a splendid, if all too neat, set of complementary bards. Each wrote in a different style and each explored different topics. Of the three, only Ovid was purely a product of the Augustan age, and he did not survive it well. Virgil and Horace had known the chaos of the Late Republic but flourished in the new world of imperial patronage.

Just as Augustus had a supreme military operative in Agrippa, he possessed a sophisticated political operative and cultural advisor in Maecenas (d. 8 BCE). As a wealthy patron, Maecenas gathered together a circle of poets that included Virgil and Horace. Virgil was born near Mantua to a gentleman farmer of the equestrian class whose land was seized after the battle of Philippi and handed over to returning soldiers. Virgil drifted into the employ of Maecenas and began writing the *Bucolics* (or *Eclogues*) about the joys of pastoral life. His patron suggested to the poet that he next write about Roman agriculture, which he did in the *Georgics.* Always a slow and measured versifier, Virgil spent seven years composing the work at the rate of about one line or seven words per day, a leisurely pace that would be the envy of many students today.

Virgil's crowning achievement was the epic *Aeneid,* which tells the story of the Trojan hero Aeneas fleeing from defeated Troy (as described in Homer's *Iliad*). Aeneas sails the Mediterranean with his men and, eventually, with the aid of the gods, establishes the Roman line. By fusing Greek and Roman myth and legend, Virgil gave epic dimension to the Augustan conceit that Rome was destined by the gods to achieve a world empire: "A boundless empire has been granted" to the Romans. The *Aeneid* is a stirring work, filled with images of great and moving humanity, but Virgil had some trouble finishing

Wounded Aeneas An imperial-period fresco of Aeneas, the great hero of Virgil's *Aeneid,* attended to by a doctor.

the great work. He left orders that if he died the unfinished poem should be destroyed. The emperor, whose vision of Rome's exceptionalism the epic celebrated, overruled that order and had the book published. The *Aeneid* ended up being, as it had begun, excellent Augustan propaganda, and so much more.

Horace was a different sort of poet. The son of a freedman, Horace wrote lighter barbed verse. He had fought on the side of Brutus in the civil war but returned home after the final defeat. Like Virgil, his family's property was seized after the battle of Philippi. "Gnawing poverty," he said, forced him to write poems. He too welcomed Augustan peace and patronage, composing a choral ode (*Carmen saeculare*) for the emperor. Yet he could be a stinging critic of himself and his times: "The wise man is just less than the great Jupiter, for he is rich, free, honored, and handsome, a king among kings and particularly well off, that is, until he catches a cold." Horace never fell into the trap of taking himself or Augustan pomp all that seriously.

Ovid was born too late to be part of the circle of Maecenas and did not write epic, which was ground already plowed by Virgil. Instead, he began by writing poems on the high life of a Rome now released from the worries of war and want. He said of the age of Augustus, "I like these times. They suit my way of life." He wrote poems about love, heroic lovers, cosmetics and how to apply them, strategies for seduction or, in modern parlance, how to get girls (*Ars Amatoria*), and the remedies for love, its breakups and pains. These light-hearted poems belong to that precious moment of peace and prosperity that stole over Rome with the end of civil discord, but before Augustus's higher moral code took hold. When it did, Ovid was banished from the city. His masterpiece, the *Metamorphoses,* describes the complex and surprising nature of mythical transformation. The work is filled with dozens of stories of humans changed into trees, birds, springs, and rocks. Ovid displays a special genius for destroying innocence. The poem ends with the **apotheosis** of Caesar, the transformation of a man into a god. That final cosmic change may have been the reason he took up the theme in the first place. Among the three great poets, Ovid was the one most enlivened by the Augustan age, but in the end he paid a heavy price for his own innocence.

For all their brilliance and creativity, Augustan writers were less free to express themselves than Catullus and Cicero had been in the chaotic Late Republic. Ovid said, now "Caesar is the state." The Augustan air was rich, but confined within a watchful palace.

The Wider Culture of the Early Empire

Imperial culture was more than just the high culture of imperial patronage. It was also the religion of the common man and his family and the daily lives of workers and women, the poor and the enslaved. Great religious currents began to move through the Late Republic, transforming Rome's archaic religion into a more complex and cosmopolitan set of beliefs. Eastern mystery religions made inroads in the empire as did a new religion, Christianity. The daily lives of both common and elite Romans also changed as the city of Rome grew.

For whom was life good in the early empire? For whom was it bad?

Roman Religion in the Early Empire

By the Late Republic, traditional Roman religion was, like much else, under pressure from the ideas encountered in Rome's spreading contact with the Mediterranean world. Official Rome had been dismayed when the cult of Bacchus or Dionysus, the wine-god, made a dramatic appearance in northern Italy late in the Republic. Soldiers, traders, and travelers from the Hellenistic east were carrying new religions back to Rome. These cults stood in stark contrast to older Roman religion, which was public, sober, and state-approved. Among the new cults were those of Cybele the Great Mother from Asia Minor, Isis from Egypt, and the Greek medical god Asclepius.

The Roman pantheon of gods, stuffed with divine forces, old gods and newcomers, was growing increasingly complex. Some Romans began to doubt the entire edifice of their religion. Cicero's treatises on divination and the gods demonstrated the weaknesses and absurdities of Roman polytheism: that it possessed no rational world principle, was devoid of morality, frequently seemed silly, and was far too utilitarian. *Do ut des,* "I give [a sacrifice] that you [O god] might give [to me in return]," was the working assumption of Romans who believed that an intimate, reciprocal, and rewarding relationship existed between people and gods.

There were practical strategies for dealing with the overgrown landscape of Roman religious beliefs. Each region, city, family, social class, and individual had a tendency to worship gods special to them without denying the existence of the other gods. They were in effect customizing and individualizing polytheism. Another way to rationalize complex religious forces was syncretism, the tendency to see one god in another or to join them together. On one level, Rome was engaged in rethinking and simplifying the divine; on another, Romans of the imperial age were spiritually needy, seeking forms of personal religion that were more intense, emotionally engaging, and satisfying. The rhetorician Aelius Aristides devoted himself, hypochondriac that he was, to the curative cult of Asclepius. When he received a dream from the god that he should not bathe, he declined to take a bath for the next five years. In a world of heightened emotional strains and personalized religion, many eastern mystery religions answered deeper and individual spiritual needs.

To some it seemed that a universal empire should have a universal form of religion. Polytheism was more a mode of religion than a single set of consistent beliefs and practices. Augustus responded by restoring traditional Roman religion and insisted on the timely celebration of the religious festivals of the Roman calendar.

The cult of the emperors began under Augustus. Though Caesar may have toyed with the idea of his personal and family divinity, Augustus personally promoted the idea that Caesar had become a god and insisted on describing himself as the son of the deified Julius. As politically shrewd as ever, Augustus refused to allow Italians to worship him, but when provincials, particularly the Egyptians, asked for permission to worship his genius (or divine spirit) it was granted. He could rationalize this as a policy that pleased easterners who were accustomed to believing that their rulers were divine.

The imperial cult belonged to the patron-client network of the Roman world. Provincial bosses and aspiring politicians were happy to treat emperors as divine, to erect statues and temples to them, and to encourage emperor worship, both to please their rulers and to control their own clients and subordinate peoples. The cult was probably never a deeply or emotionally satisfying one for the average believer, but it did serve as another layer of imperial presence throughout the empire. It is unlikely that sane emperors ever took their divinity seriously. The emperor Vespasian, one of the ancient world's great jokers, is supposed to have said as he was dying, "Oh dear, I think I'm becoming a god."

Jews and Christians

In the Late Republic only one religion, Judaism, stood aside from polytheism and its root assumptions. The God of Moses and the Jews was a jealous God who would not tolerate the worship of idols and other gods. Romans generally respected the antiquity of Judaism and the fact that it did not aggressively seek converts. In an exceptional move, they even exempted Jews from the obligation to worship the Roman gods or the emperor. Jews were able to take Roman names, to pursue a variety of professions, and to travel widely in the early empire.

One underlying tension in Judeo-Roman relations was a holdover from Hellenistic times. Many Jews had long been Hellenized, which many orthodox Jews regarded as an insult to their religion. Riots occasionally broke out between Jews and Greeks in eastern cities. These conflicts were often over which institution, the gymnasium or synagogue, should lie at the heart of civic and religious life. Official Rome disliked disruption within the empire and gradually became convinced that the Jews were politically divisive. The Jews in Jerusalem rebelled in 66 CE, which led the Romans over the next few years to wage a war of suppression. When he became emperor, Vespasian sent his son Titus to end the trouble. Titus took Jerusalem in 70 CE and all of Judaea in a brutal war in which the warriors and people of the fortress town of Masada took their own lives rather than surrender to Roman rule. Much of Jerusalem was destroyed and plundered in the war. The Arch of Titus (from 81 CE) in the Roman Forum depicts Titus's soldiers carrying back to Rome the holy goods removed from the Temple: the seven-armed candelabrum or menorah, silver trumpets, and table of the shewbread (the twelve loaves offered weekly in the Temple). The emperor Hadrian would eventually do worse, ordering the expulsion of the Jews from Jerusalem itself.

Looting the Jewish Temple Detail of a relief on the Arch of Titus in the Roman Forum that shows Roman soldiers bearing back to Rome the loot taken from Jerusalem and its temple.

Little noticed in the midst of these conflicts was the emergence of a new religion. Jesus of Nazareth was, according to the New Testament, born during the reign of Augustus and died during that of Tiberius (14–37 CE). His career was spent preaching in Judaea and Galilee about the kingdom of God to come and about the need for charity or love on earth. Christ, as he was called because of his identification with the messiah, was a Jew himself and his mission was largely confined to the Jews. Before his crucifixion, few Roman citizens took notice of him or his teachings. In the midst of turbulent Jewish events, Roman authorities largely missed the first stirrings of Christianity as a separate religion.

Saul of Tarsus or Paul (c. 10–67), the name he took after his dramatic conversion on the road to Damascus, taught that Christ's message was a universal one and he worked to free Christianity from the constraints of Jewish law and custom. His letter to the Corinthians from about 55 CE is thought to be one of the oldest documents in the New Testament. The growing missionary success of Paul and the apostles and their religion's growing separation from Judaism finally brought Christianity to the attention of Roman authorities. By then Christians had already reached the city of Rome and parts of the Greek east.

The Roman historian Tacitus (55–117) describes how the emperor Nero tried to blame the great fire that struck Rome in 64 CE on the "infamously depraved Christians." Tacitus supplies a potted history of Christ's career, viewing Christianity not as a religion but as a dangerous superstition and Christians as troublemakers. The few Romans who knew of Christianity regarded it as a new superstition and, therefore, by definition, not a true religion at all.

The Roman state in general charged Christians with being antisocial, with having, in Tacitus's phrase, a "hatred of humankind." Official Romans, always concerned about the danger of social upheaval, saw that Christianity was popular with the lower classes, the have-nots of the empire. To them Christians seemed treasonous since they would not cooperate with the state or follow its normal codes of conduct. They refused to worship the emperor or to undertake military service or civil office. Moreover, Christians withdrew from standard social relations, often rejecting their pagan parents and families in order to form new spiritual families. Romans regarded this as an assault on one of their core institutions. They were also bothered by the secretiveness of Christians, for Christianity was practiced not in public, but behind closed doors and in hidden places. No wonder that wild rumors circulated about the clandestine Christians: that they were cannibals (since they ate the Host or body of Christ), that they killed and cooked infants, that they participated in orgies (because they exchanged the kiss of peace and spoke constantly of love), and that they worshipped an ass. How, Roman aristocrats asked, could they honor a man, let alone a god, whom they had executed? Christians denied the very existence of the Roman gods and rejected the Roman way of life. For most Romans, Christianity was an insulting, antisocial, and dangerous superstition.

Despite the criminalization of Christianity and bouts of limited persecution, the new religion's role in the empire was negligible in its first two centuries. There were few Christian Roman officials, no Christian generals or emperors, and little official awareness of the religion. By the time of the good emperors of the second century, relations between Christians and Romans were a matter for bureaucratic disposal.

Living the Augustan Age

The city of Rome had a population of about one million people by the time of Augustus. Knowing that political stability depended on a peaceful capital, the emperor sought to ensure the quality of life in the city. To that end the people of Rome were supplied with free grain. A list of 200,000 recipients was under the control of the prefect of the city, often a senator, whom the emperor appointed. The prefect's primary job was to maintain law and order, particularly at the games and large assemblies. The prefect also oversaw fair prices for meat and was charged with putting out fires and maintaining soldiers who would act as a police force. As the people's tribune, Augustus was the chief civic protector and patron of the people, sponsoring games and entertainment.

To appreciate the tenor of ancient life, it would be helpful to try to reconstruct what a prosperous citizen's day might have been like in the city of Rome. To do that we have to scrape away many of the things with which we associate modern life. Romans had, for instance, a less precise awareness of time than we do. Their day was composed of twenty-four hours, but their hours ("hour" comes from the Latin *hora*) were variable throughout the year according to the amount of daylight: a summer daylight hour was longer than one in the winter. Romans had no way of telling time precisely. In the early Republican period a slave posted outside the Senate house announced when the sun was directly overhead. After conquering

Butcher Shop Sign A Roman butcher, Tiberius Julius Vitale, advertises his wares.

Greece, Rome imported the Greek sundial, but its markings were latitude specific. As a consequence, Romans told the time incorrectly for more than a century. Eventually, they fixed the problem and sundials spread throughout Italy, but sundials were a tricky way to tell time given the rotation of the earth and seasonal adjustments; they were also useless on cloudy days and at night. Eventually rich Romans had water clocks, which measured time by the regular passage of a flow of water.

In the city of Rome, the day for most people began at sunrise. The Roman bedroom was sparsely furnished with a couch, chair, bed, chest, mat, and chamber pot. The poet Martial claimed that one woke to the sound of carts in the street, school boys shouting, and the hammering of coppersmiths. Most citizens spent little time washing in the morning since they were likely to visit the baths later in the day. Breakfast was often just a drink of water. A rule of thumb in Europe, even today, is that the farther south you go, the more meager the breakfast.

Males often stopped at the barber's to be shaved, which could be excruciating. The Roman razor was, by our standards, a dull piece of iron. Martial claimed that one barber left him with a battered boxer's chin and lacking a piece of ear. There were remedies for nicks, but they seem more absurd than effective: a spider's web soaked in oil and vinegar was one popular cure.

The Roman matron rose at the same time as her husband but had probably spent the night in a separate bedroom. Some women had their hair layered in elaborate constructions by slaves, who were also charged with plucking out any gray hairs spotted in the process. Cosmetics, as we know from Ovid, would then be applied. Finally she donned her clothes, which included a brightly colored and voluminous dress.

Lunch was a light meal, followed by a siesta, baths, and a visit to the games. The main meal of the day was dinner. Aristocratic Romans reclined on couches so that, as one Christian critic said, their faces nearly fell into the food. The dinner couch was a three-sided piece of low-lying furniture (*triclinium*) set around a table so that slaves could efficiently serve the diners. The Romans did not have forks but chiefly used their fingers, knives, and spoons. Eating the great meal of the day was generally a messy but extravagant affair. Unwanted bits of food were thrown onto the floor to be retrieved by slaves. In the imperial period, floors often had mosaics depicting scattered bits of seafood and other remains, the better to hide the evening's droppings.

In Augustus's time M. Gavius Apicius wrote a cookbook that includes recipes for such delicacies as boiled ostrich, Numidian chicken, and stuffed dormouse. An essential ingredient of many meals was *garum*, a fish sauce made from the entrails of fish, salted and placed in the sun to age and ripen with the heat. The Romans had an elaborate network of wine-producing regions, but Roman wine may not have been as potable as modern wine; it was generally diluted with water. Since the Romans had no refined sugar in their diet, they suffered fewer cavities than we do. The skeletons found at Herculaneum, buried after the eruption of Mount Vesuvius, reveal excellent sets of teeth, though Romans were susceptible to gum disease, given their inattention to oral hygiene. After a hearty dinner eaten late in the evening, Romans retired to bed.

The Roman Matron Aristocratic women went to great trouble to have their hair fixed in the latest styles, including this particularly elaborate bee-hive construction.

Roman Women

Roman upper-class women might be well educated, but they learned at home from tutors and did not go to a school. They could pursue rather independent social lives but were legally restricted by the male world in which they lived. Women had few independent legal rights and were legally the possessions of their fathers or husbands. Marriages were generally arranged, though women who had outlived several husbands were occasionally allowed to choose their next partner. Divorces were easy to obtain but favored the interests of the husband. The key issue was the disposition of the dowry or the goods and properties that the woman had brought with her into the marriage. Adultery was a one-way street: a guilty woman could be divorced; a man could freely indulge with women below his class without risking divorce or censure. Rape in Rome was treated in a bizarre fashion since the injured party was thought to be the woman's father or husband, whose property rights had been infringed.

A Woman Composing Her Thoughts In this painting from Pompeii, a woman, thought by some scholars to be Sappho, ponders her thoughts while holding a stylus to her lips and waxed tablets ready to be written upon.

Women were prized possessions because men outnumbered women in Rome. The average lifespan of the upper-class female was around 34.5 years; that of an upper-class man was 46 years. In preindustrial societies women tended to have low life expectancies, in part because of the primitive and unsanitary conditions of childbearing and because women unknowingly suffered from a lack of iron in their diets. Another factor in the reduced numbers of women was the selective infanticide of females, usually through exposure. Unwanted children were left at dumping sites to die or to be retrieved by strangers. Roman law mandated the rearing of all male children, except those who were deformed, but compelled families to rear only the first of any female children. This was a legacy of the agricultural past of the Early Republic.

The dynamic aristocratic women described in narrative sources lived lives of great, but exceptional privilege. The shift to dynastic rule under Augustus meant that the women of the imperial family became more politically and biologically important. Lower-class women fell into three rough categories: free born but poor, prostitutes, and slaves. The average lifespan of poor women was about 20–25 years, which means that some lived into their forties and fifties, but many died as children and young women. Female slaves could not marry but could cohabit with another slave, their children being born into slavery as the property of their master.

The Lives of the Lower Classes in Rome

Below the golden glow of early imperial Rome—and it was a more prosperous city than all others in the empire—lay the dark dirty back street where the poor lived. The poor of Italy (displaced soldiers, farmers, and their families) drifted to Rome, where they were housed in apartment blocks called islands. Only the rich could own detached homes and villas in Rome itself. Because land was at a premium, apartment buildings grew taller, reaching heights of six floors. Since there were no elevators, the higher up one went the worse the apartment. These buildings were prone to catch fire, and so it was preferable to live close to the ground. Apartments were cold and drafty. Though the Romans knew how to make glass, they did not make window panes, insulated poorly, and had not perfected venting systems that would allow inhabitants to have fires safely.

Apartments also lacked running water. Although imperial Rome had a marvelous aqueduct system that by the second century CE was bringing over 200 million gallons of water to the city each day, much of the water was poorly distributed and ran into gutters and then into the Tiber. Water had to be carried from public wells to individual apartments and was probably not used for cleaning. As a result, apartments were filthy and full of bugs. Even worse were the dank, dark streets and alleys

A Roman Apartment Building A model of a Roman apartment block, called an island, from Ostia, the port of Rome.

THINGS THAT REMAIN

The Antikythera Device

Greco-Roman technology chiefly consisted of large-scale war machines, water conveyances, construction tools, and agricultural implements. The Romans invented a harvester for collecting and threshing wheat in the field, but it did not catch on, probably because slave labor was cheaper and more efficient. War has long been an incentive to invention, and the peoples of the Mediterranean created deadly military machines: spring-loaded catapults, siege engines, tortoise rams, and Vitruvian wall drills. Archimedes is said to have built a device that could grasp the bows of enemy ships, hoist them into the air, and then release them to crash into the water.

Ancient small-scale technology did exist, but little of it has survived. In 1900, off the Greek island of Antikythera, sponge divers discovered a ship that had gone down around 85–60 BCE. The ship, likely built many years before that, may have been overloaded with precious objects, statues, and artifacts being sent to Rome. One small object was overlooked in the initial salvage operation: a mess of bronze pieces that had spilled out of a small wooden box, all much damaged by two millennia of sea currents and salt water.

The Antikythera Device Today

The object from which the pieces came was relatively thin (13″ × 6.7″ × 3.5″) and was housed in a wood casing with doors on two sides. Most remarkable, it had toothed gears (thirty of these survive) and inscriptions in Greek that arranged the calendar according to the months and Olympic games. After a century of speculation, most scholars agree that the device was a hand-operated astronomical calendar. Such mechanisms allowed the ancients to coordinate the solar and lunar calendars on a nineteen-year cycle, to plot the position of the planets, and to determine eclipses. Cicero's friend Posidonius constructed a clockwork-like sphere that would at every revolution reproduce the relative positions of the sun, moon, and planets.

Some scholars have claimed that the Antikythera device was an analog computer since, though it was hand operated, it was a device for performing calculations. Historians of science have been intrigued by the gears. It had long been assumed that no such machine with complex internal gears existed until the Middle Ages, but the small Antikythera mechanism suggests that the ancients had such devices. Why they did not have more of them, why these devices did not become widespread, and why technological advances did not follow a straight and continuous line forward are questions that belong to the study of the intellectual and social history of the ancient world. The medieval west would break through the barriers that held back all the ancient civilizations except China from making practical technological advances.

QUESTIONS | ***How might the institution of slavery have inhibited the invention of labor-saving devices or made small machines elite playthings? If the Antikythera device was a calculating machine, what other uses might such machines have been put to in the ancient world? Why weren't they?***

of Rome into which little sunlight fell. There were public toilets, but the real toilet of Rome was the street. People who lived on the top floors of apartment buildings were in the habit of emptying their chamber pots onto the streets below. The poet Juvenal referred to this as the stinking rain of Rome, which often hit those walking below. To step into the street was to step into a running stream of filth. One crossed Roman streets, as can still be seen in Pompeii today, by stepping on raised stones, set so that cart wheels could navigate between them. A little gutter ran into the streets of Rome and there refuse was dumped and chamber pots emptied. This stinking river of effluent ran into Rome's vast sewage system, which emptied at the Cloaca Maxima, or great sewer mouth, into the Tiber. The pervasive smell of ancient Rome, from body odor, smoke, stinking fish sauce, and running sewage, would overwhelm our modern noses.

The Roman masses lived in this shadowy and putrid world. Most of them were part of family units that existed on the dole of free grain. The toll of daily violence, malnutrition, and disease was great. As miserable as was the life of the poor, the lives of urban, let alone industrial, slaves were even worse. Many slaves on farms and in the mines were viciously worked until they died. In the mines of Spain, slaves died by the thousands, whipped constantly to keep them moving rock. Petty cruelty toward slaves was common. Slave labor was more than just morally objectionable, for it led the Romans to economic dependence on servile labor. As a consequence, the Romans found it easier to employ slaves to do menial work than to invent domestic labor-saving devices.

Toward an Empire That Worked

Augustus had turned failing Republican Rome around and set it on a new, more peaceful and prosperous imperial course, but we do not need to accept the exaggerated boasts of his "Accomplishments," the splendor of marbled Rome, or the poems of his client bards that he had established an enduring Roman peace, the ***Pax Romana***. Within his own family and much of the empire there was little Augustan peace.

What made the so-called good emperors good?

Augustus pacified Rome, lopped the head off of senatorial power, and replaced it with his own, but the transformation of the Republic into an empire was not finished. How was power to be passed to the next emperor? Augustus thought that his successor would come from his own family, but families are subject to unexpected twists and turns, his more than most. The four Julio-Claudian emperors who succeeded him were a mixed lot, two of them relatively competent and two others seeming disasters. After the short interregnum of the Flavian line of the emperor Vespasian, Rome saw the period of the so-called five good emperors, the most successful rulers in Roman imperial history. The long transformation of Rome from a Republic into a settled empire finally ended in the second century CE, but that successful empire lasted for a little less than a century.

The First Julio-Claudian Successors

The successors of Augustus, who sprang from his own extended family, are called the Julio-Claudians after the Julian and Claudian branches of his line and that of his wife Livia. There were four successors—Tiberius, Caligula, Claudius, and Nero—before power passed out of Augustus's family. The second century had good emperors. The first had a couple of notoriously bad ones. The paramount problem was that Augustus never solved the problem of imperial succession. His immediate successor was Tiberius (r. 14–37), the son of his wife Livia by a previous marriage. Almost all the other potential heirs had left the scene by means both fair and foul.

Tiberius was at first an efficient, if uninspired ruler, who did restore some of the Senate's powers, doing away, for instance, with Augustus's inner council of senators who reported to him rather than to the Senate. Before long he tired of the daily business of running the state and moved to the island of Capri. Tiberius still held all power in theory, but he delegated Roman affairs to a conniving soldier named Sejanus who was eventually murdered after one scandal too many.

CHRONOLOGY **Two Centuries of Imperial Rule, Bad and Good, After Augustus**

DYNASTY	EMPEROR	DATES (CE)
Julio-Claudians	Tiberius	14–37
	Caligula	37–41
	Claudius	41–54
	Nero	54–68
Flavians	Vespasian	69–79
	Titus	79–81
	Domitian	81–96
Nervan–Antonian (The Five Good Emperors)	Nerva	96–98
	Trajan	98–117
	Hadrian	117–138
	Antoninus Pius	138–161
	Marcus Aurelius	161–180

Tiberius was succeeded in turn by the "monstrous" Caligula (r. 37–41). He began well enough and was at first popular, after the disorder of Tiberius's absentee reign, but he was, according to sources, deranged. He seduced his sisters, toyed with the idea of making his favorite horse a senator, and dedicated a shrine to himself in which he was worshipped as a god. Each day the clothes on his golden statue were changed to match those that he was wearing. The Praetorian Guard eventually assassinated Caligula and replaced him with his uncle Claudius.

Claudius and Nero

Claudius (r. 41–54) was so reviled as a stammering idiot that the philosopher and statesman Seneca (c. 1–65) wrote a satire known as *The Pumpkinification of Claudius the Clod.* Claudius was, however, a fairly good emperor. He devoted himself to the fair application of justice and good administration. During his reign, Rome conquered Britain, Mauretania, and Thrace. The biographer Suetonius and others claimed that he was poisoned by his wife so that her son Nero (r. 54–68) could assume the emperorship.

Nero's early years, when he was guided by his mother and advisors, were good ones and produced a renaissance of Roman literature and arts. The period's chief writers were Seneca, the epic poet Lucan (39–65), and Petronius (d. 65), Nero's arbiter of elegance and the author of the episodic *Satyricon.* After a failed plot against his life, Nero took vengeance on his advisors and killed off his men of letters. He forced Seneca to commit suicide, and Lucan and Petronius followed.

Nero perpetrated a series of acts that defy belief. He poisoned Claudius's son Britannicus, married Claudius's daughter and then had her executed, and kicked one of his mistresses to death. He tried many times to murder his own mother before succeeding. Nero styled himself a musician and went on a concert tour in the east during which stadium doors were locked until he had finished playing. Eventually Rome and its senators tired of him, and, as Roman soldiers closed in on him, he killed himself, and so fine an artist, he is supposed to have said at the end.

The characterization of the Julio-Claudian emperors as evil and their misdeeds as monstrous derives chiefly from later Roman authors such as Suetonius and Tacitus who lived in the next century in the civilized reigns of the good emperors and who wished to show that their emperors were superior to the wickedness and incompetence of their evil predecessors. It is more important to recognize the deeper structural changes at work in the early empire. Absolute and arbitrary power unhinged young and callow rulers, which was a predictable failure of newly assumed dynastic rule. These young rulers had not been trained to be prudent, judicious rulers. Tiberius and Claudius knew the politics of surviving in a dangerous family and moved cautiously; Caligula and Nero did not or could not. Yet the arbitrary manner in which all the Julio-Claudian emperors exercised power continued the assault upon the old Republican structures of government. The senators were cowed after fifty years of unpredictable and deadly Julian-Claudian rule. They dared not protest against emperors as willful as Caligula.

The Roman Empire, however, continued to perform fairly well during this period of transition. Political disruption was largely confined to the city of Rome and did not greatly disturb the fabric of the empire as a whole. The administrative systems established by Augustus worked well even while Caligula preened and Nero fiddled.

The transition from a fully functioning Republic to a fully functioning empire ran from 146 BCE straight through to the good emperors of the second century CE. It took the Romans a century to learn the art of empire and to accept and work under the rule of a single man. The weakest points of imperial rule were apparent. Not only was normal dynastic succession a fracture point, but so was the removal of an emperor by assassination. The army and Praetorian Guard remained the chief sources of organized violence. Provincial armies were in revolt against Nero when he took his life. The year 69 saw four generals claim to be emperor. Only the last of these, Vespasian (69–79), could hold onto power and replace the Julio-Claudian line with his own Flavian house. Vespasian and his two sons were military men. They built the Amphitheater or Colosseum, which still stands today, but they did not fundamentally restructure the Roman Empire. They did, however, signal that from then on the man who controlled the army had the best claim to be emperor.

The Good Emperors

When Domitian, the last and worst of the Flavian emperors, died in 96, the Senate selected his successor, an aged senator named Nerva (96–98). The Senate wanted not only one of its members to assume the imperial title, but an old and childless man who would not rule for long and who would leave no dynastic heir. By luck as much as by design, Rome was to have five emperors in a row who were dedicated to the needs of the empire and not to their own whims or dynastic interests.

On the surface, there seemed to be an improved principle of succession, one based on merit rather than blood. Now the reigning emperor, rather than passing along the emperorship to a family member, adopted the man who seemed best suited to rule after his death. Adoption kept power within an artificial imperial family, giving legitimacy to a new ruler of already proven ability (chiefly in war) and solid political connections. The Romans thus found a way to overcome the inherent weakness of family rule by reaching outside the imperial family to recruit excellence. As rational as this development may seem, it was also partly accidental, since the next three emperors, Trajan (98–117), Hadrian (117–138), and Antoninus Pius (138–161), just happened to have no sons to succeed them and so in each case they selected a good man as their heir. Marcus Aurelius (161–180), the last of the good emperors, did, how-

Trajan at War The column in honor of Trajan's successful wars against Dacia is the greatest of Roman columns, spiraling upward with scenes of the emperor's campaigns, the daily activities of soldiers, and critical battles.

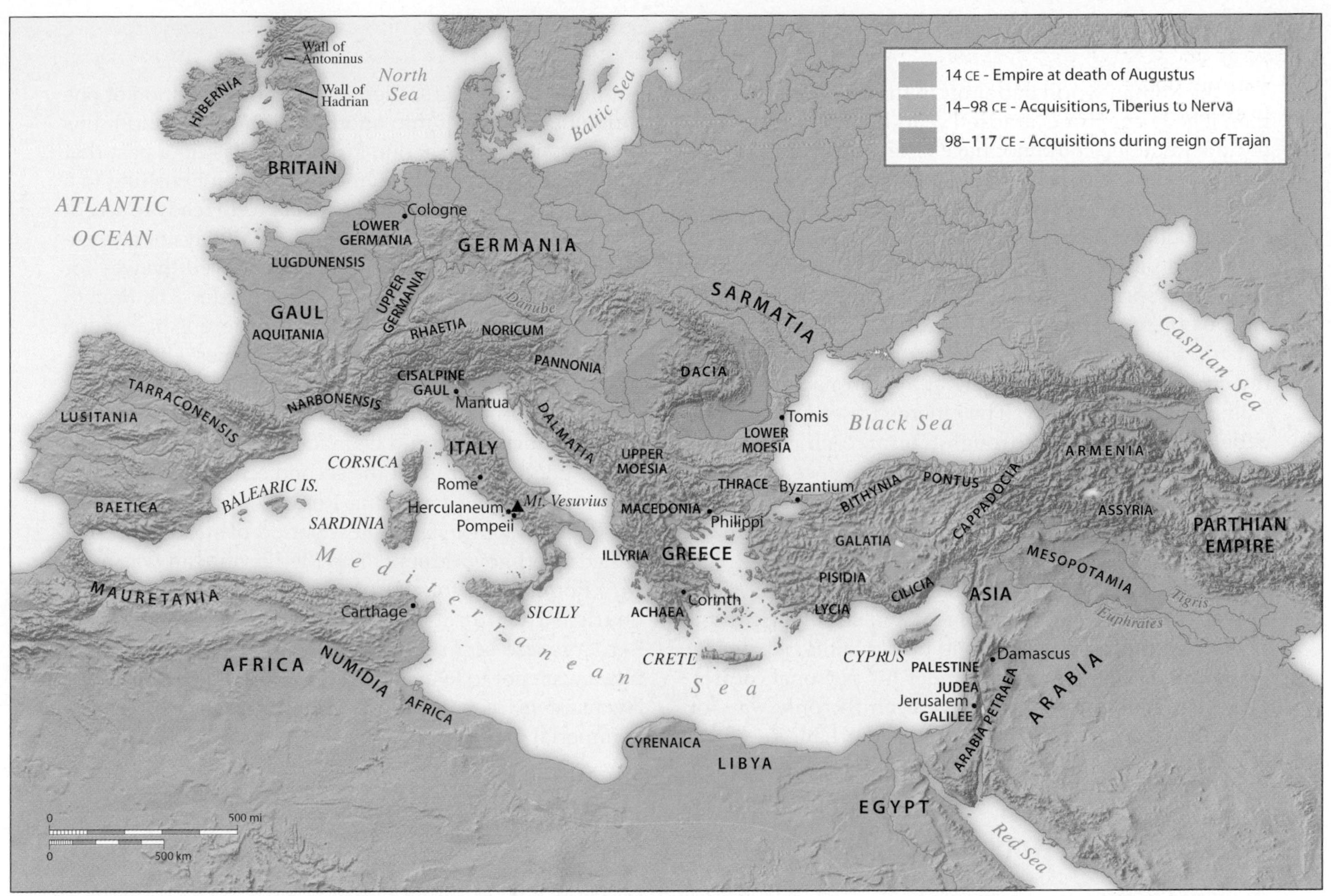

MAP 5.3 | **The Roman Empire to the Time of Trajan, 117 CE**

After Augustus defeated Antony and Cleopatra, he divided the Roman Empire into provinces. The emperor Trajan further extended the empire to its most-distant point. ***At its greatest size by 117 CE, did the Roman Empire make territorial sense? What natural and cultural boundaries prevented the Roman Empire from expanding much farther?***

ever, have a son, the dangerously incompetent Commodus, and he succeeded his father as all assumed that he would.

As a group the good emperors proved to be honest, capable, and conscientious men. All were deeply committed to dedicated service and to ruling more responsibly than their Julio-Claudian and Flavian predecessors. Trajan was, in many ways, the most successful of all the emperors. A gifted general, he expanded the Roman Empire to its greatest size, particularly by conquering territory in Dacia and Persia (Map 5.3). He was a competent administrator as his correspondence with Pliny the Younger reveals.

His successor, Hadrian, concentrated on integrating the empire and allowed some of Trajan's boundaries to collapse back inside natural borders for easier defense. He traveled to every part of the empire and promoted the standardization of Roman law, which by his time had become vast and often unworkable. He also did something unusual; he chose not only his own successor, Antoninus Pius, but also his successor's successor, Marcus Aurelius. This seemed to raise imperial succession to an even higher level of inspired planning.

Trajan and Hadrian, both born in Spain, were men of the empire, soldiers and, in Hadrian's case, an aesthete. Antoninus Pius was a bureaucrat and man of the city of Rome. His successor, Marcus Aurelius, was forced to fight a series of campaigns against the Germans along the northern borders of the empire. Marcus was also a philosopher-emperor, a dedicated Stoic, who left behind a precious, if melancholy book of *Meditations* written in Greek. Stoics believed in living in harmony with Nature, which they identified with reason itself. Roman Stoicism was concerned chiefly with ethics or the Stoic's place in the world. Stoicism prepared Marcus for a life of responsible service and clear-headed action, but he neither delighted in earthly success nor was disappointed in defeat. He did his duty. An empire ruled by a philosopher was relatively immune to corruption, excess, and indulgence at the top, but it is less obvious that a Stoic could rule with inspiration. Marcus's Stoicism was colored by his disdain for all human life, which he thought was trapped in unending flux and worldly distraction. He was a dedicated caretaker of the empire, but his view of life may not have encouraged him to rethink or renew the fragile human empire he ruled.

Conclusion

Was the Roman world better off in the second century CE than it had been three hundred years earlier? Perhaps not, but the Republic could not have lasted as it was. Built on tradition and cherished virtues, firm rules, a delicate balance of the orders of society, and a privileged aristocracy, the Republic had exerted its will upon the Mediterranean world through war and diplomacy. All the while its own house was springing leaks. It was unable to adjust to the various pressures to which it was subjected. The world outside the Senate was changing: religion was in flux, the city of Rome was growing at a rapid pace, and Italy was awash with money. The emergence of great consul generals from Marius through Caesar, each committed to using and subverting the Senate to advance their own interests, often with the support of the people of Rome, was both a cause and a symptom of the Republic's failure to adjust to new conditions.

Augustus found a way, perhaps the only one possible, to restructure Roman government and society. He did it by a sleight of hand, seeming to preserve the old Senate, while confidently slipping it under his personal control. The Augustan empire may have been the only way for Rome to survive the great crisis of the Late Republic, but much blood was spilled in the transformation of one form of government into another. Both Cicero and Julius Caesar paid the price, one for holding fast to a past that was impossible to sustain and the other for rushing to a revolutionary future before his peers were ready to accept it or him. Yet Caesar's assault on the old ways of governing Rome and its privileged oligarchy paved the way for Augustus's reformation of the Roman order. The Roman world after Augustus was a very different place, one subject to the weaknesses of all monarchies—bad rulers, troubled succession, vicious dynastic politics, arbitrary decisions, and assassination—but under Augustus and dutiful emperors it could be made to work.

The good emperors of the second century showed just how civilized and civilizing Rome could be. They gave the Roman Empire its greatest period of steady and sustained good government. The Mediterranean was a secure Roman lake for the transport of goods, urban life flourished within its limits, and prosperity was high. Borders were secure and rebellions few. But the good times were not to last, for just ahead in the third century lay disasters, economic depression, and the near collapse of imperial government.

Critical Thinking Questions

1. How might the Roman Republic have survived?
2. What larger shifts in society, culture, and history were moving the Late Republic in new directions?
3. What choices did Octavian/Augustus make in transforming Roman government? In other words, how and why did he undo the Republic?
4. Why was the Roman Empire such a seeming mess in its first century?
5. How and why was the second century CE Rome's best imperial period?
6. What was the central political or historical issue of the period 146 BCE–180 CE?

Key Terms

quaestor **(p. 135)**
tribune **(p. 135)**
aedile **(p. 135)**
praetor **(p. 135)**
consul **(p. 136)**
equestrians **(p. 138)**
Caesarian (or Consular) Faction **(p. 142)**
First Triumvirate **(p. 142)**
The Triumvirate **(p. 144)**
Praetorian Guard **(p. 147)**
apotheosis **(p. 151)**
Pax Romana **(p. 157)**
imperator **(p. 161)**

Primary Sources in connect

For information on Connect and the online resources available, go to **http://connect.mcgraw-hill.com**.

1. **Catiline's Revolution**
2. **Election Notices, Signs, and Graffiti at Pompeii**
3. **Pliny and Trajan on Christianity**
4. **Scenes of Imperial Life as Observed by a Roman Noble**
5. **Letters and Various Meditations of Marcus Aurelius**

BACK TO THE SOURCE

The Accomplishments of Augustus

The emperor Augustus wrote the *Res Gestae* or record of his "Accomplishments" and deposited it with the Vestal Virgins with an order that it be displayed in front of his Mausoleum in Rome. The bronze pillars are lost but many copies of the list survive. Although the work is factual for the most part, it is also a clever piece of memorialization and propaganda.

Below is a copy of the accomplishments of the deified Augustus by which he brought the whole world under the empire of the Roman people, and of the moneys expended by him on the state and the Roman people, as inscribed on two bronze pillars set up in Rome.

1. At the age of nineteen, on my own initiative and at my own expense, I raised an army by means of which I liberated the Republic, which was oppressed by the tyranny of a faction. For which reason the Senate, with honorific decrees, made me a member of its order in the consulship of Gaius Pansa and Aulus Hirtius, giving me at the same time consular rank in voting, and granted me the *imperium*. It ordered me as propraetor, together with the consuls, to see to it that the state suffered no harm. Moreover, in the same year, when both consuls had fallen in the war, the people elected me consul and a triumvir for the settlement of the commonwealth.

2. Those who assassinated my father I drove into exile, avenging their crime by due process of law; and afterwards when they waged war against the state, I conquered them on the battlefield.

3. I waged many wars throughout the whole world by land and by sea, both civil and foreign, and when victorious I spared all citizens who sought pardon. Foreign peoples who could safely be pardoned I preferred to spare rather than extirpate. About 500,000 Roman citizens were under military oath to me. Of these, when their terms of service were ended, I settled in colonies or sent back to their own municipalities a little more than 300,000, and to all of these I allotted lands or granted money as rewards for military service. . . .

4. Twice I celebrated ovations, three times curule triumphs, and I was acclaimed ***imperator*** twenty-one times. When the Senate decreed additional triumphs to me, I declined them on four occasions. . . . In my triumphs there were led before my chariot nine kings or the children of kings. At the time I wrote this document, I had been consul thirteen times, and I was in the thirty-seventh year of my tribunician power.

12. . . . When I returned to Rome from Spain and Gaul in the consulship of Tiberius Nero and Publius Quintilius, after successfully settling the affairs of those provinces, the Senate, to commemorate my return, ordered an altar of the Augustan Peace [the Ara Pacis] to be consecrated in the Campus Martius, on which it decreed that the magistrates, priests, and Vestal Virgins should make an annual sacrifice.

13. The temple of Janus Quirinus, which our ancestors desired to be closed whenever peace with victory was secured by sea and by land throughout the entire empire of the Roman people, and which before I was born is recorded to have been closed only twice since the founding of the city, was during my principate three times ordered by the Senate to be closed.

15. To the Roman plebs I paid 300 sesterces apiece in accordance with the will of my father; and in my fifth consulship I gave each 400 sesterces in my own name out of the spoils of war. . . .

17. Four times I came to the assistance of the treasury with my own money, transferring to those in charge of the treasury 150,000,000 sesterces. . . .

20. . . . In my sixth consulship I repaired eighty-two temples of the gods in the city, in accordance with a resolution of the Senate, neglecting none which at that time required repair. In my seventh consulship I reconstructed the Flaminian Way from the city as far as Ariminum, and also all the bridges except the Mulvian and the Minucian.

21. On my own private land I built the temple of Mars Ultor and the Augustan Forum from the spoils of war. On ground bought for the most part from private owners I built the theater adjoining the temple of Apollo which was to be inscribed with the name of my son-in-law Marcus Marcellus. In the Capitol, in the temple of the deified Julius, in the temple of Apollo, in the temple of Vesta, and in the temple of Mars Ultor I consecrated gifts from the spoils of war which cost me about 100,000,000 sesterces. . . .

22. I gave a gladiatorial show three times in my own name, and five times in the names of my sons or grandsons; at these shows about 10,000 men fought. . . .

27. I added Egypt to the empire of the Roman people. . . .

34. In my sixth and seventh consulships, after I had put an end to the civil wars, having attained supreme power by universal consent, I transferred the state from my own power to the control of the Roman Senate and people. For this service of mine I received the title of Augustus by decree of the Senate, and the doorposts of my house were publicly decked with laurels, the civic crown was affixed over my doorway, and a golden shield was set up in the Julian Senate house, which, as the inscription on this shield testifies, the Roman Senate and people gave me in recognition of my valor, clemency, justice, and devotion. After that time I excelled all in authority, but I possessed no more power than others who were my colleagues in each magistracy.

35. When I held my thirteenth consulship, the Senate, the equestrian order, and the entire Roman people gave me the title of "father of the country" and decreed that this title should be inscribed in the vestibule of my house, in the Julian Senate house, and in the Augustan Forum on the pedestal of the chariot which was set up in my honor by decree of the Senate. At the time I wrote this document I was in my seventy-sixth year.

QUESTIONS | *How did Augustus wish to be remembered after death? Was the* Res Gestae *merely commemorative, or did it have a continuing political purpose? Where does Augustus bend the record of his achievements?*

Source: Roman Civilization. Sourcebook II: The Empire, ed. Naphtali Lewis and Meyer Reinhold (New York: Columbia University Press, 1955), 9–19.

The Empress Theodora with Retinue on a Mosaic at San Vitale, Ravenna, Italy

THE SLOW TURN FROM ANCIENT TO MEDIEVAL

A Century of Imperial Anarchy
- Late Imperial Society
- Emperors Come and Go, Dozens of Them
- The Empire's External Enemies

The Romanization of Christianity
- Early Christianities: From Oral to Written
- Early Christian Thinkers and Greek Thought
- Toward Orthodoxy
- The Desert and Pillar Fathers and Mothers
- State Persecution
- Bishops and the Church Hierarchy

Diocletian's Renewal of the Roman Empire
- Diocletian Restructures the Empire
- Reforming the Economy
- Restoring Roman Religion
- Donatism and the Fallout from the Great Persecution

Constantine and the Christianization of the Roman Empire
- Constantine's Conversion
- Making a New Rome in Byzantium
- Toward a State Religion
- Julian Lapses
- Institutional Growth of the Church

German Tribes Enter the Empire
- The Visigoths Request Entrance
- Imperial Strategies for Managing the Germans
- The Sack of Rome in 410
- Attila and the Huns
- The End of the Empire in the West

Germanic Kingdoms in the West
- Vandals, Visigoths, and Ostrogoths
- King Theoderic's Troubled Last Years
- The Franks Take Control of Gaul
- The Conversion of Clovis

Justinian's Reassertion of Roman Imperial Grandeur
- The Emperor and Empress
- The Reconquest
- The Disastrous 540s: Dust-Veils and Disease
- Living a Shrinking Urban Life

Conclusion

THEODORA AND SIDONIUS CONFRONT THE OLD AND THE NEW People whispered nasty things about her—that she was the low-born daughter of the bear-keeper of the Hippodrome, an actress and a prostitute, sexually promiscuous, a murderess—but in mosaics and sculptures she is magnificent, every inch the empress of Rome. Wrapped in precious purple gowns, her head heavy with jewels, and waited on by court women and eunuchs, Theodora wears her imperial majesty. Her social agenda and political influence on her husband, the emperor Justinian, were considerable and controversial. At one critical point Theodora shamed her husband into showing some backbone, facing down their enemies, and staying put rather than fleeing a mob of raging rioters in Constantinople. She said that she would rather die than give up being empress. Theodora's tenacity and Justinian's dreams of imperial glory were proof that the Roman Empire lived on, at least in the east, in the sixth century. In a golden imperial court, one could try to forget how much had changed in the wider Roman world.

A century earlier in the west, Sidonius Apollinaris (c. 430–479), a Gallo-Roman gentleman and poet, never could; he lived in an already transformed world. One day in the streets of his hometown of Lyons he bumped into a band of Germans. He saw a Frankish prince, dressed in silk, followed by a formidable band of his men. The poet was struck by their appearance, which was so unlike that of his fellow Roman citizens. Their feet and legs were covered by boots of rough hide, their knees and thighs were bare, and they wore bright green and red garments that left their forearms bare. Around their waists they wore studded belts made of fur. From their shoulders hung Frankish swords. In their left hands they clutched magnificent shields; in their right they held barbed lances and throwing axes.

This colorful, but unnerving scene provides a glimpse of a world undergoing radical transition. Theodora's world in the east was stubbornly imperial; Sidonius's in the west was a daily encounter with the other and with change. The Germans whom Sidonius encountered were no longer merely the slaves or mercenaries of the Roman state; they were warriors, marching freely through a Roman city, their long blond hair flowing, their capacity for violence on display for all to see.

A Frankish King The replica of the seal (now lost) of Childeric, father of Clovis. His long Frankish hair flows down onto his shoulders.

Historical change may be never-ending, but some periods experience it more dramatically and discernibly than others. Around the Mediterranean Sea, political, ethnic, and religious

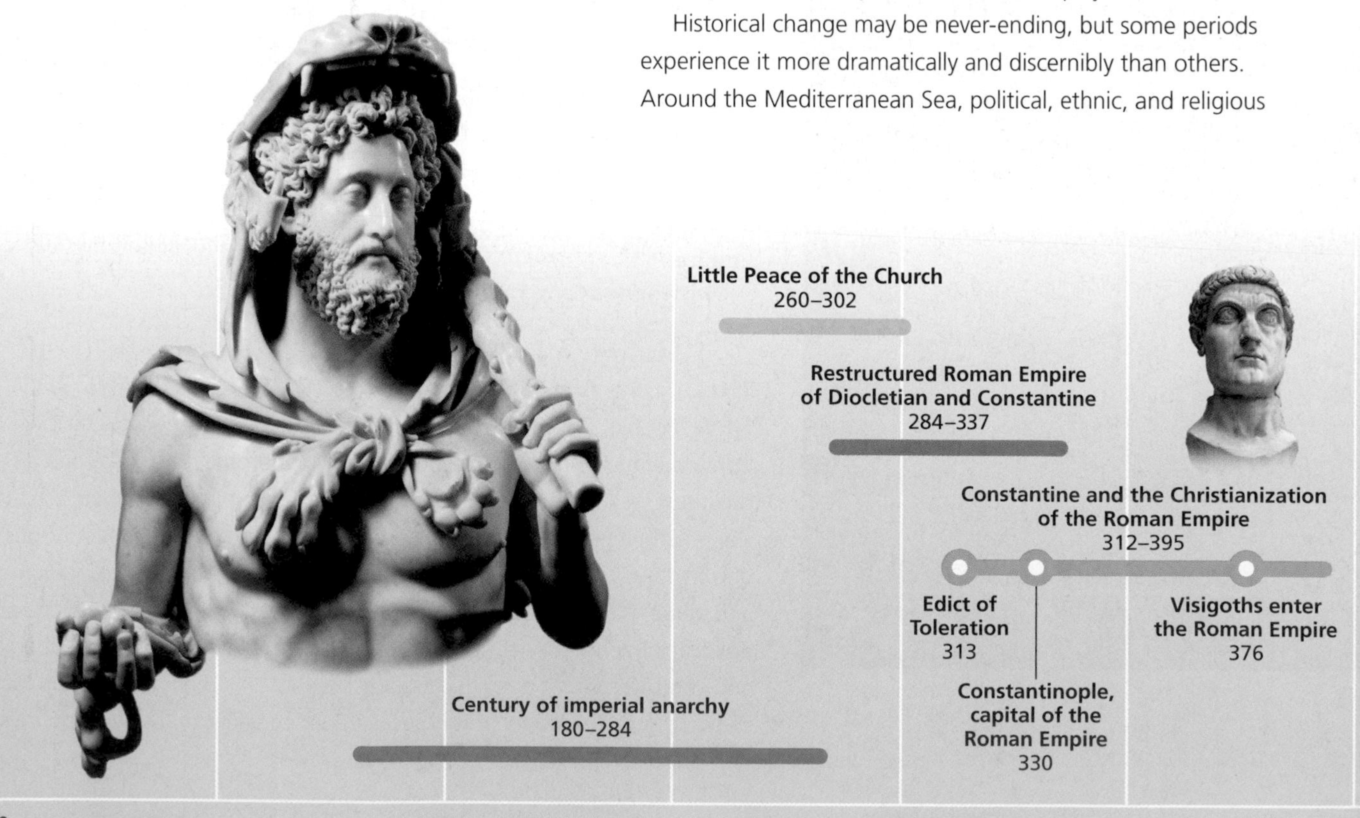

change was unmistakable. The Germans Sidonius saw were one face of change; the monks who rejected ancient civilization and retreated into the deserts of Egypt were another; farmers and laborers bound by the fixed wages set by a reforming emperor felt its new strictures; and the old city of Rome, once the lamp of the world, bore the scars of change after its sack and abandonment. Theodora and Justinian ruled the Roman Empire from the magnificent city of Constantinople, but even they dreamed of restoring the empire to its former glory by reassembling its shattered pieces.

Historians have called the period from about 180 to 565 Late Antiquity, but that label claims too much for antiquity and too little for the emerging new world of the Middle Ages. It suggests continuity when, in fact, radical change was the disorder of the day. The period from the late second century to the mid-sixth century cannot be easily typed as one thing or the other; it was the age of the great turning of the late Roman world toward the Middle Ages, and its transitional quality needs to be recognized and preserved in all its messiness.

The three central ingredients that were to make the Early Middle Ages in the west—late Roman civilization, Christianity, and the Germans—were being brought together, often violently, inside the Roman Empire. All of them sought a lasting presence and a measure of authority within the changing Roman world. In these centuries, various voices competed for place and power, and cultural clashes such as the one Sidonius experienced were common.

The political, religious, economic, and cultural changes that occurred, particularly after 300, were profound and transformative. By the late fifth century the Mediterranean world that the Romans had built was much changed, its beliefs altered profoundly, its economy downsized, its religion remade, and its political and territorial organization unlike anything anyone could have imagined in 150. The empire suffered through its worst century of political instability since the Late Roman Republic. Christianity, once an illegal religion, became the official religion of the empire. The church assumed the mantle of the institutional home and voice of all Christians. East German tribes sought entrance into the empire, set themselves up as the new representatives and replacements of Roman authority, and established Germanic kingdoms inside the empire.

The eastern Roman Empire sealed itself off from the west but mounted one last futile attempt to reconstitute the whole empire. Thus, while the eastern Roman Empire, which much later came to be called the Byzantine Empire, continued to have a centralized imperial government, the west was in near free fall through centuries of decentralization. The period from the third to sixth centuries was one of the greatest ages of radical redirection in the history of western civilization. How did a civilization as old and established as the ancient west turn directions and emerge as something as starkly different as the medieval west? The changes came about gradually, in different regions at different times, and were cumulative. Sidonius's surprise at the sight of German warriors in the streets of Lyons was the surprise of the old world meeting the new, but the empress Theodora's pride was an indication that the idea of the Roman Empire, if not its former power and reach, would not go quietly.

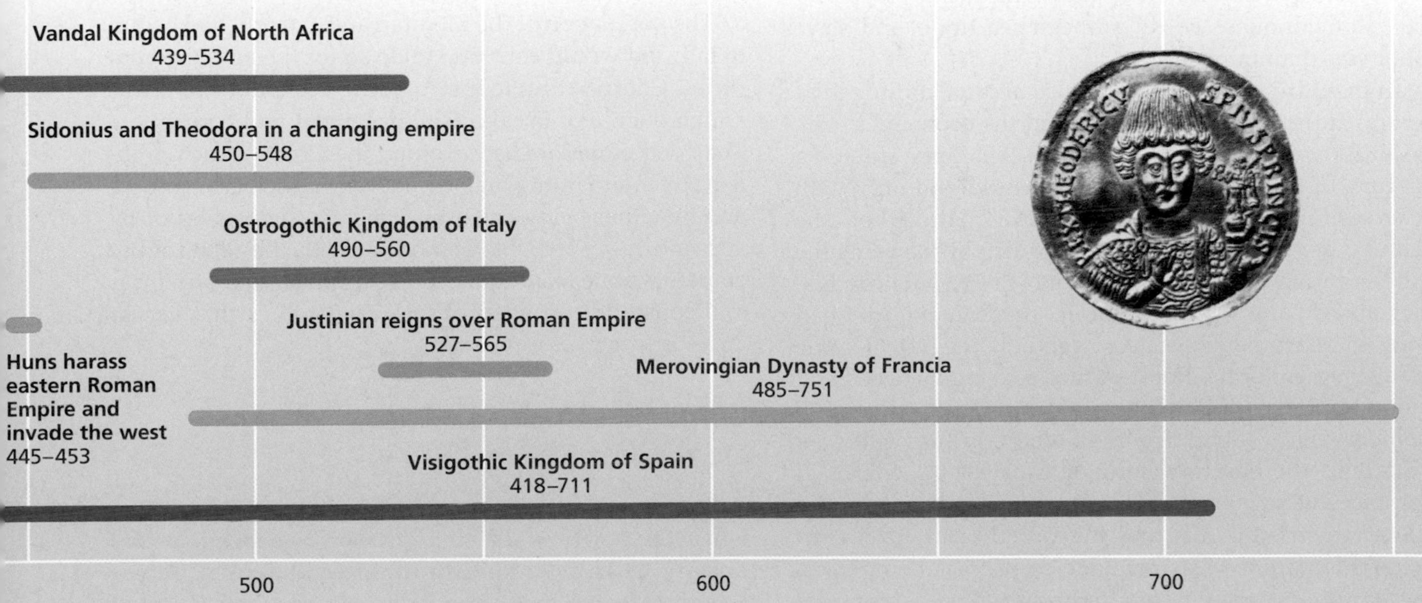

A Century of Imperial Anarchy

The events that slowly changed the Roman world began in the late second century and became apparent in the third, which was to be the first flash point of the new west. The Roman Empire underwent a century of imperial anarchy (180–284). The high Roman Empire of the second century with its good emperors and stable government could not last. That period of peace and prosperity had depended, in part, on a highly successful but partly accidental form of succession. When Marcus Aurelius died in 180, his natural son Commodus (r. 180–193) succeeded him, but Commodus was not, as imperial successors had been for almost a century, the best man for the job. Throughout the third century, an imperial system based on meritocracy gave way to a monarchical system of military tyrants.

Why did the Roman Empire experience its worst century since the Late Republic in the period 180–284?

Late Imperial Society

Maps of the Roman Empire that outline a vast mass of territory controlled by the Romans tend to mislead. The Roman Empire was more truly an empire of cities. Passing beyond the city and its hinterland with its thin layer of local temples, governors, gentry, and garrisons of soldiers, one entered a rough countryside peopled by sharp landlords, private armies, the rural poor, and bandits. The protagonist of Lucius Apuleius's dazzling novel, the *Golden Ass* (c. 180), is magically transformed into a donkey, captured by a band of robbers, and led into the brutal and uncivilized outer world that lay beyond the easy reach of urban justice and civilizing Roman order. Still this imperial world could work as long as the delicate balance of central order and widespread prosperity based on conquest, Mediterranean sea trade, and slave labor was maintained.

In the third century, that balance became unhinged as central authority began to falter and the economy to fail. With the accession of Commodus in 180, Rome entered a century of imperial disorder that would end only with the rise of the emperor Diocletian in 284. Throughout the century, new trends emerged, the principal one being the militarization of the empire. For most of Republican history and during the early empire, the Roman army had been an instrument of state power; now the state became an instrument of the Roman army, serving its needs and following its lead. Power was shifting from the city of Rome to the troubled frontiers where armies gathered to defend the empire's borders. Most of the century's emperors were generals from the provinces. Armies declared them emperors and murdered rival claimants. With this parade of army-made or barracks emperors, the empire became increasingly disunited as regional factions vied for power. The government of Rome, once the seat of senatorial power and resident emperors, fell under a military monarchy without the check of civilian law or an effective bureaucracy.

The social classes of the empire were also becoming increasingly polarized. A few aristocrats and soldiers became fabulously wealthy, but the lower classes endured hardship and the nagging threat of utter deprivation. Great landlords had incomes ten thousand times as great as those of their poor laborers. The empire underwent an economic crisis brought on by the expense of defending its borders and supporting its armies. At its edges, far from the Mediterranean, the Roman Empire was expensive to maintain. Though its roads were marvels of engineering, they were expensive to build and maintain. Moreover, it took much longer and cost more to move people and goods by road than it ever did to sail them around the Mediterranean.

The decline of the empire may well be traced back to the high cost of defending it. Excessive taxation placed pressures on an already overextended economy and began to warp economic and social relations. Roman coinage, which had maintained its value throughout the second century, was now steadily debased. A silver denarius from the time of Hadrian in the second century was a small solid silver piece; by the late third century the denarius had become a large silver-washed bronze disk with little metallic value. Debasement produced inflation and other pressures on the economy.

In more prosperous and peaceful times, Roman trade had been highly specialized, but with political disruption the flow of goods over long distances was interrupted and the Mediterranean economy was forced to downsize and localize. Regions that specialized in producing pots, sandals, or millstones suffered when they could not send their goods to distant locales and receive back salt, cloth, and olives in exchange. Regional economies shifted to the less efficient enterprise of producing most of what they needed close to home.

The population of the Mediterranean world had begun to fall, and would continue to do so for the next five centuries. Contributing to a struggling economy, there was a high degree of fiscal mismanagement and corruption. The good emperors had avoided the worst of such problems by maintaining an efficient centralized government and by either being good bureaucrats themselves or by appointing responsible stand-ins. With the new soldier emperors gone from Rome to the frontiers and provinces and constantly in need of money, much of that earlier civil vigilance disappeared.

Emperors Come and Go, Dozens of Them

Political and economic stability was hard to sustain when the turnover of emperors was so frequent and unsettling. In the half-century after Marcus Aurelius, Rome had nine emperors, only one of whom avoided

Emperor Commodus as Hercules A marble statue of Marcus Aurelius's son and heir as the mythological strongman Hercules. Commodus's flirtation with the gladiatorial life, extreme self-indulgence, and poor judgment eventually led to his assassination.

assassination. Commodus abandoned his father's defense of the Germanic frontier, put Praetorian prefects in effective control of the city of Rome, and styled himself a new Hercules. He was finally strangled to death when he offended Roman sensibilities by brazenly appearing in Rome as a gladiator-consul.

After a relatively brief spell of stability under Septimius Severus (r. 193–211), a military man who had risen to power on the arms of his soldiers, and his son Caracalla (r. 211–217), the empire slid even deeper into a long spell of disorder, at least at the top. The Severans had recognized the uneasy lie of the land. Before dying, while on a campaign against the Scots, Septimius advised his sons to make sure that they always kept their soldiers rich, and hence content, but he did not tell them how to respect each other. Caracalla had his brother Geta murdered and was himself killed while organizing an assault on the Parthians in Asia.

Over the next half-century, Roman armies advanced twenty-six imperial candidates, only one of whom died peacefully. Macrinus (r. 217–218), who conspired in the assassination of Caracalla, is a good example of how rickety the imperial house had become. He was from Africa, had a pierced ear, and was the first emperor who was not also a senator. He lost the support of the army when he canceled a pay raise and was put to death after losing a battle at Antioch. To be emperor or, worse, a claimant to the throne in the middle of the third century was a crooked path to an unhappy end. In 238 alone, six men laid claim to be emperor.

The Empire's External Enemies

Not just the political order and economy were turning against Rome; so were its many external enemies. To the east, Persia threatened and to the north Germanic tribes continued to bother the border (Map 6.1). In 251, the Roman emperor Decius (r. 249–251) died battling the Goths. His successor Valerian (r. 253–260) was captured in the east, and the city of Antioch fell to the Persians. Various peoples from the continent, among them Saxons and Angles, began to cross over to Britain on longboats and to settle. Archaeological excavations have begun to reveal the patterns of these new settlements, often erected alongside native settlements, sometimes on top of them. A sign of the weakening confidence in Roman security, even at the center of the empire, was the massive wall that the emperor Aurelian (r. 270–275) ordered to be raised around the city of Rome. Only a century earlier, a Roman rhetorician had said that the eternal city had no need of walls since the empire itself was Rome's protective wall.

Amid the crumbling confidence in Rome's strength and security, the vestiges of high Roman culture in its late and sometimes exotic form persisted. Colorful mosaics adorned villa floors, and Septimius Severus built an enormous palace in Rome. His son constructed the baths named after him that still survive in impressive ruin. The great Roman jurist Ulpian compiled extensive collections of Roman laws and the Egyptian philosopher Plotinus (c. 205–270) propounded in Rome the ideas that comprise his *Enneads*, later compiled by his students. Plotinus was

Hunting Scenes from Late Rome The lavish style of Late Roman art is evident in this mosaic depiction: colorful clothes, violence, and men and animals in agitated motion.

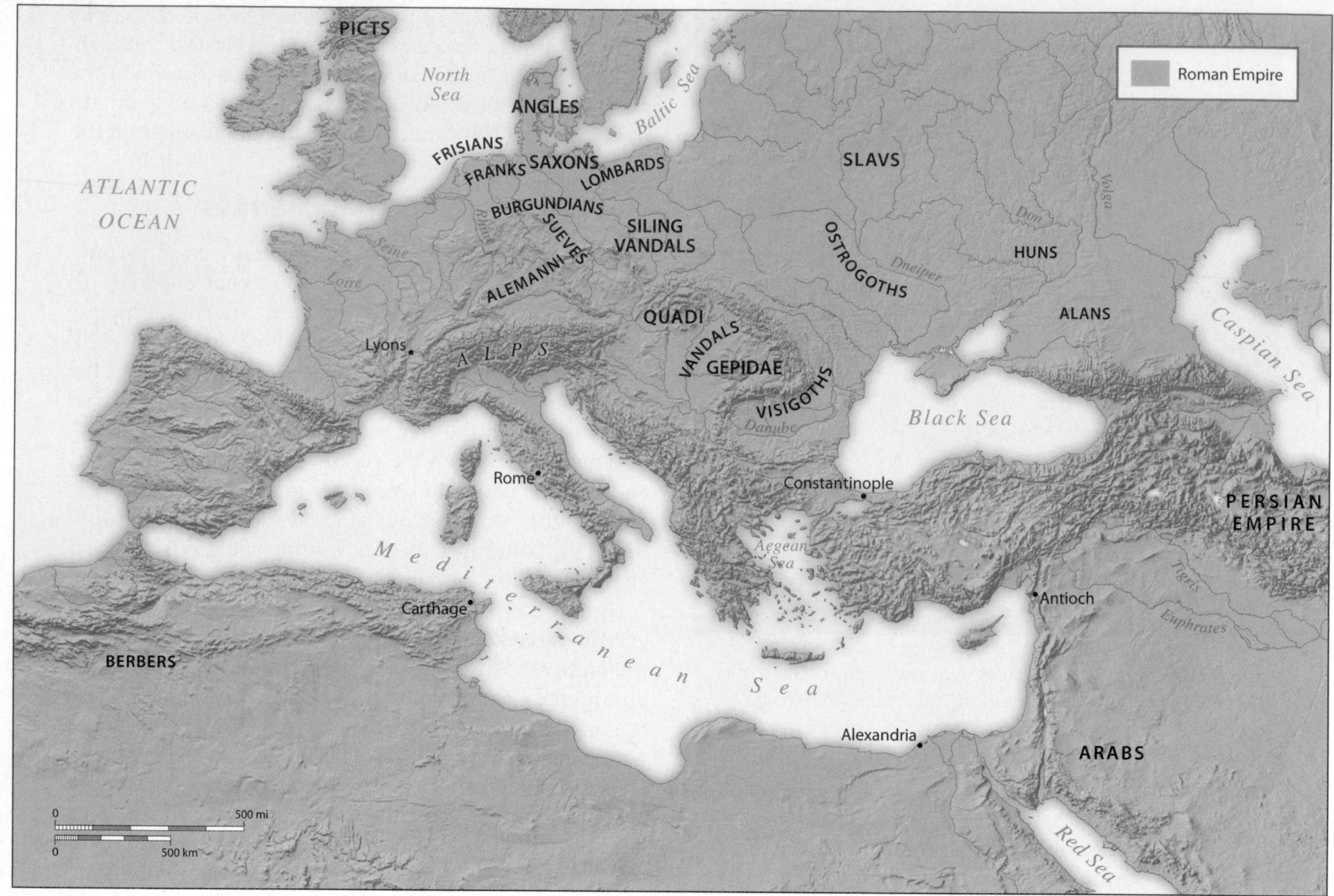

MAP 6.1 | External Enemies of the Roman Empire, c. 350

Before the late fourth century, the Roman Empire had managed to keep the Germanic and Celtic tribes and other foreign peoples outside the empire. To the east, the Persian Empire was harassing Rome's borders. ***How did the Roman Empire protect its borders? Could it keep the peoples gathering there forever outside the empire? What was the natural geographic weakness of the Late Roman Empire?***

a Neo-Platonist and believed that the One, an abstract, impersonal, immaterial, and intellectual force governed the universe.

The Romanization of Christianity

As the Roman world endured its difficult century of imperial anarchy and economic adjustment, Christians, who had not been taken seriously before, began to matter. To be a Christian was still illegal and punishable by death, but persecution was sporadic and depended on whether the emperor thought the Christians were a pressing problem. On a deeper level, a familiar pattern of the Roman encounter with alien religions was at work. In its long history, Rome had often rejected alien religions when first encountered but, after a period of prohibition and bloodshed, slowly Romanized them until they became familiar and acceptable. Some observers thought that it was Rome's genius to take in all the world's gods and remake them as its own; such was the experience of Christianity, but with one great difference. Whereas the third century saw the Romanization of Christianity, the fourth would see the Christianization of the Roman Empire.

How and why did the various Christianities develop and spread in the second and third centuries?

Early Christianities: From Oral to Written

Christianity was not in its early centuries a single set of beliefs represented by a single church. It might be more accurate to speak of christianities than Christianity during this period. As an underground religion in a world of slow travel and communication, it could not have been otherwise. Many of the books of the New Testament were circulating by the second century, including all of the Gospels (Matthew, Mark, Luke, and John), but the canon

THINGS THAT REMAIN

The Nag Hammadi Find

In December 1945 an Egyptian peasant named Muhammad and his brother were digging for nitrate to fertilize their fields near a bend in the Nile River not far from the village of Nag Hammadi when they uncovered a jar containing a collection of ancient codices written on papyrus sheets. They were afraid at first to open the jar for fear that an evil spirit might be freed but eventually smashed it open and were surprised to see a cloud of golden specks drift into the air. They were disappointed to discover that there was no gold inside, only thirteen old codices. Muhammad carried the books home and left them outside. Needing some kindling the next morning, his mother gathered up some of the papyrus sheets and some straw to start a fire. We shall never know what was lost that morning. Over the following years the surviving books found buyers, and eventually scholars realized that Muhammad's find was an extraordinary collection of suppressed religious texts copied and buried in the fourth century.

A Nag Hammadi Codex Page from the Gospel of Thomas

The fifty-two books that survived are a strange lot: among them *The Gospel of Thomas, On the Origin of the World, Thunder: the Perfect Mind, The Concept of Our Great Power, The Thought of Norea,* and *The Interpretation of Knowledge.*[1] A few of the texts were already known, but most were new or contain fuller texts than previously known. The books are written in Coptic (Egyptian) but derive from texts once written in Greek. Most of them have been roughly classified as Gnostic texts, but that hardly describes them all or precisely. As scholars have worked on the texts over the past half-century, they have begun to appreciate just how complex and precious these books are, and how dangerous they might have seemed in the past. At the center of Gnostic belief was the idea that this world, with its crimes, pain, and suffering, was not created by a good God, but by an evil one. This malevolent divinity had inserted himself between humans and the Invisible Spirit in order to work his mischief. But some humans (those who know, the Gnostics) have seen past this evil world, which most people mistake for a good creation by a good God, to the true nature of the Invisible Spirit who lies waiting beyond all the pain and suffering that the evil world visits on humans.

The collection may have been hidden because Bishop Athanasius of Alexandria sent a letter in 367 to the churches and monasteries of Egypt stipulating the contents of the New Testament and demanding that other texts lying outside the newly established canon should be purged. A monk (or group of them) at a nearby monastery may have decided that it was more prudent to hide their unorthodox library than to destroy it. The winds of orthodoxy had shifted many times; Athanasius himself was excommunicated five times. A monk may simply have hesitated to destroy books that might just be divine despite what his superiors now said. The Nag Hammadi texts open up a world of early Christian thought that was driven outside of the orthodox church's approved set of readings.

QUESTIONS | ***Why were there so many varieties of Christianity in the early centuries of the religion, and how might the existence of so many different interpretations and practices have stimulated the development of Christian thought? Why did some texts become authoritative and others apocryphal? Why bury rather than destroy texts deemed dangerous?***

of authorized texts had not yet been fixed, in part because there were so many texts of varying degrees of authority in circulation and no authoritative ruling body to select and sanction a single collection of sacred texts.

As the voices and immediate presence of the apostles and their designates as the direct heirs of Jesus's mission faded away by the end of the first century, written texts became increasingly important and circulated in portable **codex** or book form rather than in papyrus rolls. The move from oral to written authority continued throughout the third century and much of the fourth, shaping a Christian culture of texts and books.

Early Christian Thinkers and Greek Thought

While written texts were assuming greater importance, Christian thinkers began to engage their pagan critics and to work out the details of Christian theology. Many of these, including Justin Martyr (c. 100–165) and Origen of Alexandria (185–254), who was the greatest of the early Christian theologians, were heavily indebted to Greek philosophy, especially to Platonism. They tended to view problems of Christian theology in philosophical and rational terms, and their prose was shaped by their Greek rhetorical training. To refute learned pagan critics, early Christian thinkers sharpened the same dialectical skills of argumentation that their enemies employed.

This intertwining of Greek, Roman, and Christian thought was one feature of the Romanization of the Christian religion. As Christians adopted Greek ways of thinking and writing, learned pagans could begin to engage Christianity on familiar and rational terms. No matter how heated or sarcastic the debate between Christians and pagans became, they were talking.

Toward Orthodoxy

Even as they were debating their pagan critics, the great Christian apologists Irenaeus of Lyons (c. 130–c. 202) and Tertullian (169–240) were also confronting Christians who had different ideas and practices, particularly the **Gnostics.** They denounced these "others" as heretics, but it is important to recognize that orthodoxy or an established and sanctioned set of beliefs (and, therefore, its opposite, heresy) did not yet exist; the contest between the various christianities was precisely to determine which would be able to claim authoritative power and the right to define orthodox teaching, set the canon of Scripture, and specify Christian practices and customs.

There was a wide range of early Christian beliefs. The Ebionite Christians, for instance, believed that they were Jews and should hold fast to Jewish practices. Marcionite Christians maintained that they were Gentiles and should abandon Judaism and, hence, did not need the Old Testament or Hebrew Bible. In hindsight it may seem that these sects were unlikely to have created a universal religion, but at the time no one could be sure. The Gnostics (from the Greek *gnosis,* "knowledge") were elitists who held that only those few who possessed a deep and specialized understanding of the true state of the world were enlightened and so would be saved. The Gnostics set out Christianity's first systematic theologies, prompting others to reject them with systems of their own. Tertullian and Irenaeus vehemently rejected Gnostic teaching, but even they could not quite hold fast to a solid center that did not yet exist.

The total number of Christians within the Roman Empire remained relatively small throughout the third century, perhaps between 2 and 5 percent of the total population, but varying sharply between regions and between urban and rural populations (Map 6.2). The religion was stronger in the east than the west of the empire, and stronger in cities than in the countryside. Despite the small number of Christians, the sheer variety of Christian life and thought in the period is striking.

The Desert and Pillar Fathers and Mothers

Around 269 in Egypt, a well-off young man by the name of Anthony (251–356) happened to hear in a village church of Christ's injunction to rid oneself of all belongings and to follow him. Anthony was so moved by the message that he became one of the first of the desert fathers, a monk or hermit who disengaged from the urban life of the Roman world. He moved into the wilderness to battle temptation and the devil, and to concentrate exclusively on God. Women such as Mary of Egypt, a former prostitute, also retreated into the desert to cleanse themselves of earthly sin by renouncing the world and praising God.

A striking rupture in the urban life of Mediterranean civilization occurred when men and women began to abandon their homes and families to seek a closer bond with God. Since the rise of cities in the Near East and Greece, the ancients had thought of civilized life as city life with all its strengths and weaknesses. But by the third century many rich Romans were beginning to give up on cities, withdrawing to large self-sufficient estates (*latifundia*), where their security and prosperity could be ensured. While the rich withdrew from cities for material reasons, the desert fathers and mothers did so for spiritual ones; they rejected the material world of the city and instead opted for citizenship in heaven. Anthony and his fellow hermits simply walked away from urban life in pursuit of a more direct and intimate relationship with God. Theirs was not a back-to-nature movement or the pleasant pastoralism or love of rural life so admired by the ancients, but an active rejection of urban life and its state-supported structures. Cracks in the foundation of ancient civilization began to appear when Anthony and his followers came to regard the city with its shops, noise, and throngs of people as a distraction from religious life.

Pachomius (290–347) established monastic communities in Egypt that collected together hundreds of monks. This coenobitic (from *coenobium* or monastery) form of monasticism represented a commitment to organized and radical denial of the civilized world and of oneself. Less influential, but still typical of eastern monasticism, were the **stylites,** or pillar saints. Saint Simeon the Stylite (390–459) lived atop a pole in Syria for thirty-seven years. Local Christians gathered at the base of the pole seeking help and blessings from the saint. The point of living atop a pillar was so that the saint could be both among the people and apart from them at the same time. Perched between the divine and human worlds, the saint served

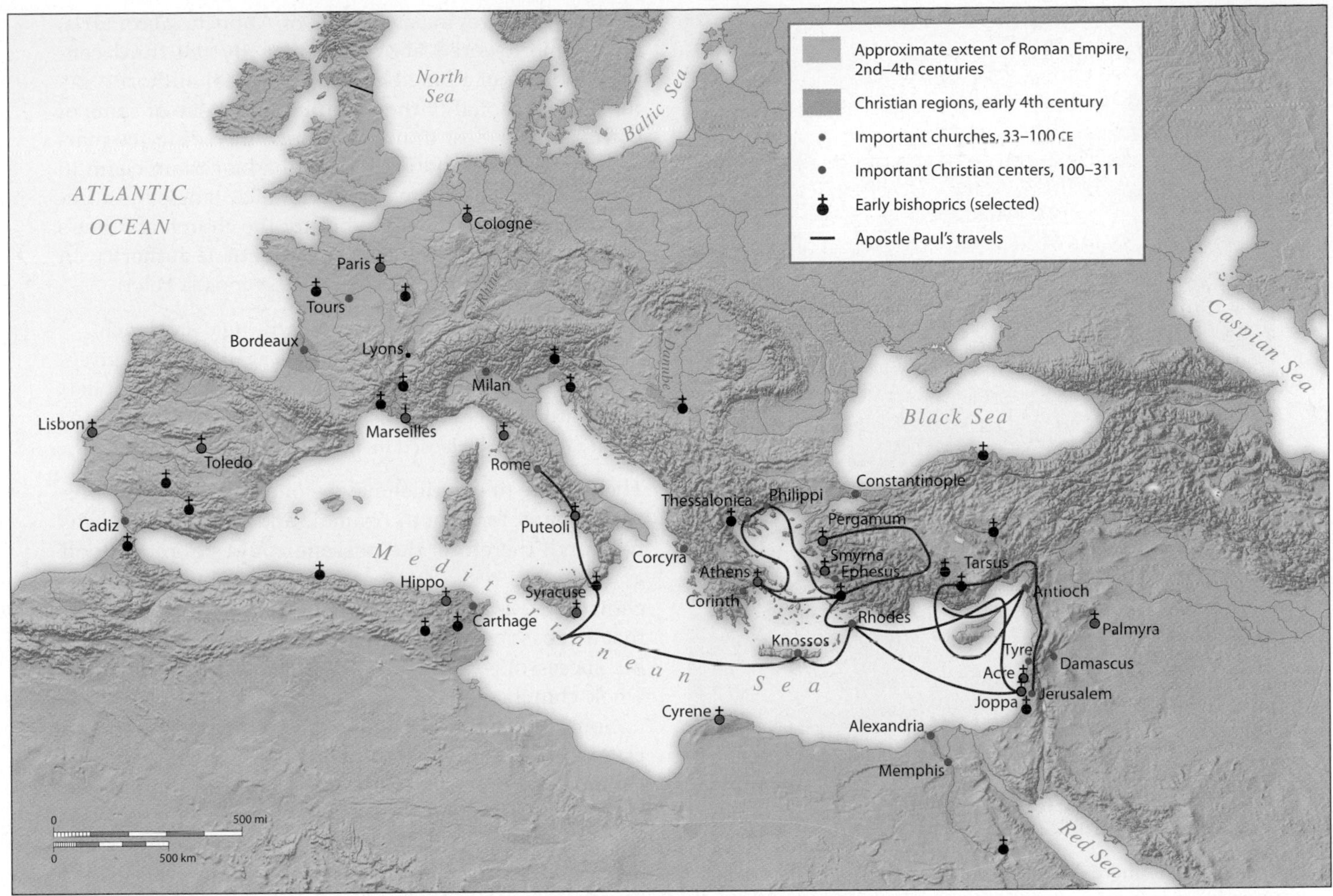

MAP 6.2 | **The Spread of Christian Communities in the Roman Empire, 33–311**

Before 311 CE, Christians tended to establish communities within large Roman cities, yet Christianity remained a minority religion within the empire until the fourth century. ***Why would Christians gather in Roman cities rather than live quietly in the countryside? Where in the empire was the concentration of Christians greatest? What do the apostle Paul's travels reveal about the way in which early Christianity spread?***

as a model of steadfast devotion to God and as an active intermediary between separated worlds.

State Persecution

The disorder of the Roman Empire late in the second century and early in the third century may have allowed the various christianities to prosper. The beleaguered Roman state was unable to focus much attention on a small religious minority, even an illegal one that did not seem to be causing trouble. By the middle of the third century, however, as Rome's difficulties mounted, many Romans concluded that Rome was being punished for abandoning its gods. The waning Roman devotion to all the gods, they thought, led to divine retribution. The gods were not happy, and so Rome suffered, but it was Christians who paid the price. As Tertullian put it, whenever a natural disaster, plague, or famine struck, the first thought of the Romans was, send "the Christians to the lion." By eliminating Christians, some Romans thought that their own devotion to the gods would once again, as in the golden past of the Republic, be pious, unanimous, and enduring. No longer would Rome be dragged down by those insulting the gods.

In 250, the emperor Decius issued an edict that established a commission to test the faith of Romans by commanding all to offer a sacrifice to the gods or to the emperor. The commission supplied certificates of pagan piety to those who passed the test of faith. Some Christians officially complied, while others found ways to avoid compliance. Some refused to hide their faith and so were executed. Decius's immediate successors continued the purge. The emperor Valerian ordered the seizure of Christian property: churches, cemeteries, and the land of rich Christians. But when Valerian died, the persecution again ceased. Without a strong imperial will, there could be no sustained persecution. The period from 260 to 302 is often called the Little Peace of the Church since,

The Good Shepherd of the Catacombs The good shepherd was a figure of Christ for early Christians as in this fresco from the catacombs of Rome.

during those forty-two years, Christianity was once again generally ignored by official Rome.

Bishops and the Church Hierarchy

By late in the third century, Christianity was a religion that had come to be represented by what we might call the Four Bs: bishop, book (the codex of Scripture, as opposed to oral culture, memory, tradition, and the papyrus roll), basilica (as opposed to the pagan temple or Jewish synagogue), and burial (as opposed to the pagan practice of cremation). The ecclesiastical structure of the universal church was being laid down. Bishops were in charge of the churches in larger cities and the areas around them. Many of these bishops claimed that their authority descended directly from the apostles. Some bishops had in the first century been in place as apostolic appointments before the New Testament was composed. By the third century that living line of direct apostolic sanction was dying out.

In its place there was a push to enhance the stature and power of all bishops by arguing that they stood in the living line of the apostles as their direct heirs. Although in principle bishops were supposed to be equal, the metropolitan bishops (later to be called archbishops) of the imperial and provincial capitals of Antioch, Alexandria, and Rome towered above the rest. By the third century the city of Rome claimed universal authority. As the ancient capital of the empire and the site of some of Christianity's most dramatic events, including the martyrdoms of Peter and Paul, Rome had a certain claim to primacy, if not absolute supremacy. The single most important piece of evidence to bolster the church of Rome's claim to primacy was the so-called **Petrine authority.** In the Gospel of Matthew, Jesus tells the apostle Peter:

> you are Peter and upon this rock I will build my church, and the gates of hell shall not prevail against it. I will give you the keys to the kingdom of heaven. Whatever you bind on earth shall be bound in heaven; and whatever you loose on earth shall be loosed in heaven. (Matt. 16:18–19)

The passage (if genuine) may be one of Christ's few preserved puns, for in both Aramaic and Greek *Peter* means rock and, therefore, the passage could be understood as "You are a rock (Peter) and upon you I will build my church." It was the official doctrine of the church of Rome that this passage gave Peter, the first bishop of Rome, and his successors, the right and obligation to govern the whole church.

Some churchmen vigorously denied the Roman claim to superiority over other bishops. Other cities also claimed apostolic foundation. Alexandria maintained that its church had been founded by the apostles Peter and Mark. Both apostolic primacy and imperial importance made Antioch, Alexandria, and Rome rivals to lead the Christian church. Constantinople would later, as the new Rome, put in its claim for primacy at a church council in 381. Its claim was based, like that of the other three great metropolitan cities, on its stature as an imperial capital. As events would prove, however, it was not just the Petrine authority that determined Rome's ultimate success but the fall of the other great metropolitan cities. Two of them were overtaken by the rise of Islam in the seventh century, and Constantinople's claim to universality was an isolated one confined to the Greek east.

Diocletian's Renewal of the Roman Empire

After a century of imperial turmoil, the Roman Empire, if it was to continue, required a new direction and a firm hand. The emperor Diocletian supplied both. He restructured the empire politically and geographically and attempted to end its economic and religious drift.

How did Diocletian restructure and in effect rescue the Roman Empire?

Diocletian Restructures the Empire

Diocletian (r. 284–305) was of undistinguished birth and from the province of Dalmatia. When the emperor whom he served was murdered, Diocletian with the support of the imperial army marched against the emperor's brother and was soon made emperor himself. His genius lay less in battle than in restructuring an empire that seemed almost ungovernable by the late third century. Realizing that the empire could no longer be ruled by one man and that the persistent problem of succession (as revealed by the fate of his many murdered predecessors) needed to be solved, Diocletian copied in the political sphere what the army had been doing to address regional disorder: he regionalized and compartmentalized imperial responsibilities and power. By so doing, he accepted and redirected the ongoing regionalization of Roman power, which had been gaining momentum throughout the third century.

By 286, Diocletian recognized that the general Maximian, whom he had earlier dispatched to Gaul to suppress a popular insurrection, was Augustus or emperor in the west as declared by his troops. Diocletian appointed two Caesars to serve under the two emperors. With this move, Diocletian created a **Tetrarchy** of four Roman rulers: two senior (Augusti) and two junior (Caesars), two in the east (one Augustus, one Caesar), and two in the west (one Augustus, one Caesar), each with his own territory to govern. Diocletian thus found a way to protect the empire from disorder by ensuring that if one emperor was assassinated, another already held the office, and his successor (the Caesar under him) was in place and ready to move against the rebels and assassins.

The Tetrarchy energized both the imperial and military systems since the new order rewarded merit (as the good emperors once had) and activism, and compartmentalized Rome's exercise of central power. Diocletian's real interest lay in the general reformation of Roman order. Seeing that the provinces were too large and bases for resistance to the emperors, he redrew the administrative map of the empire into ninety-six small provinces. Within these provinces and within the army he introduced new hierarchies of command. He also set his soldiers to work building fortifications. Diocletian held true to the Tetrarchy over which he maintained effective imperial control. When he finally decided to abdicate in 305, he forced his fellow Augustus to step down so that the junior emperors would succeed them as a matter of course.

One of the critical features of Diocletian's new empire was the recognition that its most natural dividing point was into east and west (Map 6.3). This division respected not only geography, but also the Greek and Latin cultures of the two dominant parts of the empire. Diocletian himself did not visit the city of Rome until shortly before his retirement; his own preferred center of operations was Nicomedia (today in modern Turkey). There his court adopted various eastern ceremonial features: the emperor was called Lord (*Dominus*) and revered openly as divine. Both advisors and petitioners knelt before him and kissed the hem of his robe as a sign of subservience. In Rome the Senate continued to operate under elected consuls, but in the emperor's eastern court a new set of officials was appointed, among them the count of sacred gifts and the supervisor of the lord's bedchamber, who was a eunuch. Professional spies were also appointed, as befitted the tighter, more claustrophobic court Diocletian created.

The Tetrarchs Embrace On this porphyry sculpture at St. Mark's Basilica in Venice, the four tetrarchs are shown in pairs. In each pair an Augustus embraces a Caesar to show their common purpose and the nature of their relationship. Pairs of tetrarchs also signaled that one pair governed half the empire and the other pair the other half. In this way, both the eastern and western parts of the Roman Empire were alerted that each possessed its own duo of dedicated emperors.

Reforming the Economy

Diocletian introduced new fiscal measures to repair an economy struggling with inflation and a lack of productivity. All land was now to be taxed according to its size and relative worth, and labor was assessed according to its value to society. Local farm workers (*coloni*) were now bound to the land for life. Later this provision was extended to their heirs, thus freezing both the rural

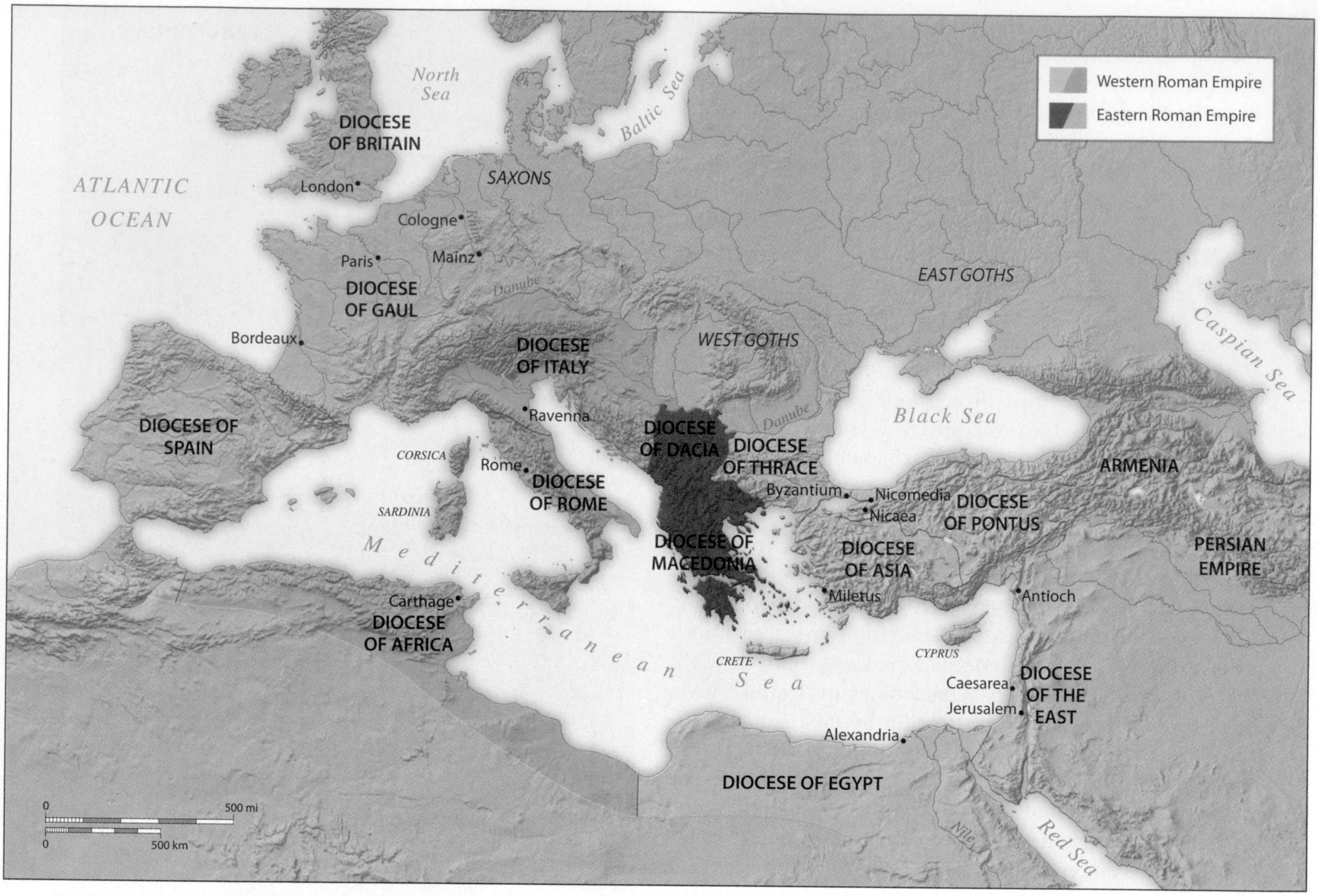

MAP 6.3 | **Diocletian's Division of the Roman Empire by 304**

In 304, the emperor Diocletian divided the empire into four territories, each ruled by either an Augustus (senior emperor) or a Caesar (junior emperor). The most striking division, however, was into the Latin west and Greek east. ***Why did Diocletian so divide the empire? Why had Ravenna in northern Italy become increasingly important? What part of the Roman Empire did the senior emperors occupy and why? What lands did the junior emperors, the Caesars, hold and why?***

Diocletian's Palace A reconstruction of Diocletian's seaside palace at Split in Croatia. The emperor Diocletian was already moving toward palace government, thus anticipating a medieval practice.

economy and its workers into place and station. In cities, workers who tried to run away to escape or improve their lot were forced both to remain and to pay the stipulated tax on their work. Little sense of freedom remained when much of the empire's population was held permanently in place with no chance of movement or advancement. Diocletian's attempt to revive a failing economy compromised the rights of Roman citizenship, including the freedom of movement and economic choice. Though restricting social mobility entirely was impossible, Diocletian's plan was an indication of the sharp needs of the state for steady income and of the stubbornness of a stagnant economy.

To combat inflation and the related problem of the falling value or depreciation of Roman coinage, Diocletian in 301 issued an edict to control wages and prices. But, given the looseness of the late Roman economy, this control of labor and goods could not succeed and was revoked eventually. The emperor also reformed the currency of the empire, in part by regulating the minting of coins. His successor, Constantine (285–337), reformed imperial currency further, introducing a new series of silver coins (*denarii*) and a gold coin (*solidus*). The efforts of both emperors to stabilize the empire's currency achieved some success.

CHRONOLOGY The Religious Fourth Century

DATE	EVENT
303–311	The Great Persecution of Christians
300–320	Saint Anthony in the Desert
312	Constantine's Christian dream
313	Religious toleration proclaimed
325	Council of Nicaea
330	City of Byzantium (Constantinople) founded
361	The Emperor Julian lapsed
367	Canon of the New Testament fixed
387	Augustine baptized
390s	The Visigoths become Arian Christians
392	Theodosius bans paganism

Restoring Roman Religion

In religion, Diocletian attempted to restore a traditional set of beliefs. He was attracted to an older Roman religion of rank, devotion, and discipline. From the start of his rule he had been intolerant of other beliefs, banning the practices of astrology, alchemy, and Manichaeism (or religious dualism). Christianity, after the long interval of the Little Peace, seemed so comfortably rooted in Roman life that Diocletian ignored it for most of his rule. Indeed, from his palace in Nicomedia he could see a large Christian basilica looming in the distance. But in 303 he and the Caesar Galerius issued the first of several edicts against Christians. Diocletian probably thought, as his predecessors had, that Christianity threatened the spiritual and political unanimity of the Roman people. Just as he tried to standardize coinage, he wanted to standardize faith. He had a tidy mind and viewed religious pluralism as a threat to his reformed state. Galerius, the less prudent of the two eastern tetrarchs, was pushing for a more extreme response to religious dissonance in the east.

As their first act, Roman authorities assaulted the church of Nicomedia and made a point of destroying its sacred books, with which Christianity, as a religion of the book, was now identified. At first the persecution targeted Roman citizens and state officials who were Christians, then moved on to the Christian clergy, and finally to all believers. Yet, even then, the persecution seems to have been uneven; worse in the east than the west, worse in cities than in the countryside. Some areas such as Gaul and Britain experienced little if any persecution. After Diocletian retired, Galerius continued the persecution until 311. Still, relatively few Christians were executed in most regions, perhaps fewer than five thousand.

But if the physical damage was relatively light, despite the horrific martyrdoms described by Eusebius of Caesarea in his history of the early church, the psychological damage ran deep. Christians had for several generations come to feel almost accepted within the empire; they had mistaken the lack of persecution for official toleration. They had begun to emerge from behind closed doors and private worship to attend church openly and to proclaim their faith publicly. Some of these Christians, not hardened by centuries of caution and an ideology that celebrated martyrdom, lapsed when put to the test. The social and ecclesiastical damage was profound.

Donatism and the Fallout from the Great Persecution

In northern Africa, **Donatism** (named after Donatus, a bishop of Carthage, who had led that region's resistance to restoring lapsed churchmen) began as a dispute over the damaged authority of churchmen, labeled as traitors, who had surrendered scriptures to their persecutors. The Donatists held that all churchmen who had committed such acts of betrayal and all the sacraments that they had administered were false. Saint Augustine (354–430) spent much of his career as a Christian bishop in northern Africa resisting the Donatists, who tried on several occasions to assassinate him. Augustine argued for a more

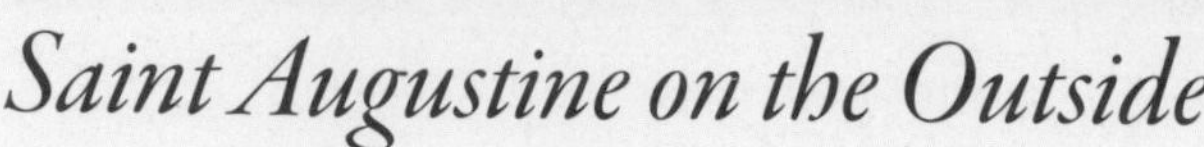

Saint Augustine on the Outside

Aurelius Augustinus, or Saint Augustine, had an immense impact on the shaping of medieval Christian thought. He wrote so much that readers have often wondered how one person could have written all that has been attributed to him. Once he became a bishop, he did have a stable of scribes to take down his thoughts. He was also an active and diligent bishop with many pastoral responsibilities and maintained an active correspondence with his many friends and sometimes enemies throughout the Roman world. Works such as *On Christian Doctrine, The Trinity,* and *The City of God* became statements of normative Christian doctrine. His episcopal concerns ranged from the good of marriage and the status of widows to the dangers of divination. He also found time to interpret Scripture, particularly in his study of the meaning of Genesis. He was also a controversialist, defending the orthodox faith against Manichaeans, Donatists, and Pelagians (who placed an emphasis on good works and free will). For all of this, he was deemed one of the doctors (teachers) of the church, whose teachings were considered orthodox and saintly.

There is another Augustine whom we think less about: Augustine the outsider and outlaw. Had he died in 385 when he was just thirty years old we might never have heard of him. From his *Confessions,* we know that, although he had been raised a Christian by his mother, Monica, he had for a time been more interested in Latin prose and poetry, the captivating sounds of Cicero, Virgil, and the pagan poets, than in Christ. When he was seventeen he went to Carthage to be educated, but as a teenager he was more excited by the alluring wickedness of the city: "I came to Carthage and there was overwhelmed by the sizzle of that frying-pan of lustful love. I was not yet in love but I wanted to love. . . ." Within a year he took a concubine and a year after that they had a son. The couple named their son Adeodatus ("given by God"), which may be an indication that his partner was a Christian, for Augustine had already begun to drift away from the faith of his mother. Like most Romans, Augustine was a materialist and he tried to understand God within the confines of Aristotle's ten categories for describing *things.* His literal reading of the Bible and his exposure to his mother's devout Christianity were failures precisely because of his material approach to them. The Bible seemed to him, at the time, to be an unreasonable book.

Instead, he turned to the banned Manichaean religion because it promised an explanation for the existence of evil in the world and the underlying reasons for things. He went so far as to become a spokesman for the secretive religion and took pleasure in mocking simple Christians. For ten outlaw years he remained a Manichaean novice, deeply offending his mother, who barred him from her house. Had he died just before he turned forty when he sailed to Rome to become a professor of rhetoric, we might know him, if at all, as just another Manichaean preacher in Carthage. Augustine's world may have accepted official Constantinian Christianity, but a seething competition of alternative teachings and religions remained. The future saint experimented with an intellectually exciting, but illegal brand before it too disappointed him. He then turned his vast and energetic intellect to making Christianity and its Scriptures reasonable and to understanding his God as immaterial and transcendent. In the *Confessions* he looks inward to his own heart to discover the memories of his past that would reform his present life and outward to a perfect and transcendent God. In *The City of God* he follows the long hard story of Rome, its misunderstandings and great spiritual mistake, but ends with the saints and the power of a living God revealed in miracles still being worked in the present.

Augustine had come a long way from outlawry and from disappointing his pious mother.

QUESTIONS | ***Why was the religious scene so unsettled in the third and fourth centuries? Why was Augustine's materialism an obstacle to his embrace of Christianity? How do Augustine's life and thought parallel the evolution of Christianity?***

inclusive and forgiving church against the rigorist, exclusive, and elitist one promoted by the Donatists.

Not only had Diocletian and Galerius powerfully reminded the Roman world that Christianity was illegal, but they had also sown seeds of dissension in Christianity that would take time to dislodge. In the early fourth century, Christianity remained a proscribed religion held by a minority of Romans. Yet the limited success of Diocletian's rigorous persecution of Christianity made it clear that the religion would not disappear from the Roman Empire. Other religions such as Mithraism, a soldier's religion, seemed, however, by the middle of the third century to have a better chance of eventual domination. But, then, something extraordinary happened.

Constantine and the Christianization of the Roman Empire

Two things make Constantine one of the west's most important historical actors: he recognized and supported Christianity, and he created a new capital for the empire in the east. Both were to be formative events in the shaping of western history for the next eleven hundred years and both turned the Roman Empire in a new, largely unexpected, medieval direction.

Why was Constantine such a powerful agent of change in Roman and western history?

Although much of the slow Romanization of Christianity occurred in the third century, the Christianization of the Roman Empire took place in the fourth. Tolerated in 313, Christianity became the state religion of the empire by the end of the century, and paganism was officially banned.

Constantine's Conversion

Despite Diocletian's plan for a stable succession after he and Maximian stepped down, the empire soon slipped into civil war. Constantine's father, one of the Caesars, died in 306, but his son was not named to replace him and so Constantine took control of his father's army in Britain. The wars of succession that followed suggest just how much the Tetrarchy had depended on Diocletian's dynamic control and not on the institution itself. In 312, at the Battle of the Milvian Bridge just outside of Rome, Constantine overcame his rival Maxentius. The next year he and another rival, Licinius, met at Milan and came to uneasy terms over their relative division of powers. Finally in 324 Constantine invaded the eastern empire and defeated and executed Licinius. Thus, after less than forty years of four-man rule, the empire once again had a single emperor.

A critical factor in Constantine's success was his religious conversion. Christians were still a fragile minority in the empire, and the events of the Great Persecution were still playing out in the east when Constantine marched on Rome. The illegal religion had been pushed underground once more, much of its property in the east had been seized, and its leaders and institutional structure had been undermined. Yet, at the Battle of the Milvian Bridge, Constantine and his troops fought under a Christian banner and called on Christ to help them achieve victory (see Back to the Source at the end of the chapter).

Constantine did not, however, proclaim Christianity the official religion of Rome in 312. In fact, he did not become a complete Christian himself, delaying baptism until he was on his deathbed twenty-five years later. The emperor, like many early Christians, believed that baptism washed away all one's sins and so was best delayed until a Christian took his last breath and so could die cleansed of all earthly sin. Constantine had much to repent since he had ordered the execution of one of his wives and his eldest son. But for much of his imperial career, Constantine was a Christian in all but name.

In 313, Constantine and Licinius did something more important, at least officially, than the famous Christian victory of the previous year. By the **Edict of Milan** the co-emperors proclaimed an edict of universal religious toleration by which Christians and others could now practice their religions openly and without state restraint. The emperors revoked all previous decrees against Christianity and ordered the return of all the property that had been seized from Christians both by the state and by private individuals.

Constantine's religious role in the western part of the empire was a delicate one. Most of the population was still pagan, and the emperor remained the chief priest of Roman religion. He allowed the cult of emperor worship to continue and sacrifices to the gods to be performed, and so fulfilled his official religious duties. Constantine presented himself as the emperor and spiritual leader of all Romans, pagan and Christian.

The general thrust of Constantine's religious beliefs, however, is evident. He and his family openly supported Christianity. His mother, Helena, built churches and promoted Christianity in Jerusalem, and Constantine financed the building of the great basilicas of Old St. Peter's and St. John Lateran in Rome. In many ways his most profound religious act was to transfer state patronage

Old St. Peter's Basilica A fresco from the sixteenth century of Old St. Peter's Basilica, which was replaced during the Italian Renaissance with the present St. Peter's.

312–313: Constantine's Big Turn

In the late summer of 312, few Christians or state officials, particularly in the eastern Roman Empire, would have predicted that Christianity was on the verge of an epochal breakthrough. Constantine's turn to Christianity on the eve of battle in October and his legalization of the religion four months later constituted one of the west's great and most unexpected turning points, and nothing about it was either inevitable or predictable. In 311, the worst of all the persecutions of the Christian cult was still proceeding in the eastern empire, and the religion was being driven underground once again. Constantine himself had had other dreams and other religious enthusiasms, some of them pagan, before the fateful one at the Milvian Bridge.

The Colossal Head of Constantine Only the head, a hand, and several body parts of the colossal statue of Constantine in Rome now survive, but they are impressive reminders of how thoroughly Constantine impressed himself upon his Roman Empire.

Roman pagans formed the vast majority of the population in 312. Their polytheism was warm and ancestral. They associated their gods with family, state, and success. For Mediterranean men and women, a true religion was never new; it was eternal and bound to the intimate passages of their personal and public lives. How could such a deep emotional attachment to a way of life and belief by millions of people change overnight? In short, it did not and need not have. Despite the rise of the great monotheisms (Judaism, Christianity, Islam) in the Middle East, Roman paganism might still have persisted openly and officially for a long time. By 312, Roman paganism was a thousand years old, and the sheer force of religious inertia might have maintained it for centuries.

But Constantine and his Christian advisors slowly moved the massive weight of old religious habits in a new direction. Imperial patronage and protection of the new religion were the sanctioning forces; church councils and local bishops were the instruments of transformation. Councils ruled against lukewarm converts who simply added Christ to the pantheon of all gods and continued to make sacrifices to pagan gods even after they had been baptized. Many of these new Christians of convenience were aware where promotion and advantage now lay. But Christian morality began to transform pagan and popular culture. Constantine outlawed gladiatorial combat, which before long disappeared throughout the empire. His officials and priests reset the calendar of the Roman world, moving it from a cycle of pagan feasts and festivals to a Christian one. The gymnasium and baths, long the institutional centers of Greek and Roman civic life, soon ceded their central place to the church, which dispensed charity and served as a public gathering place. The Sibyls and oracles who had counseled the ancient world were replaced by saints and bishops. The transformation was not entirely peaceful. At the cult site of Didyma outside Miletus, local Christians tortured Apollo's priest and prophet into silence. But, in general, the remaking of the religious worldview of antiquity was surprisingly subtle and slow.

Still one can't but wonder what it was like for millions of Romans to fall asleep one night in 312 in a familiar world of old gods and family beliefs and to wake to the realization over the coming months and years that their world was moving in a new and unexpected direction. On the very edge of the great religious turn, provincial governors were executing Christians and seizing their property, while pagan philosophers were still making rational arguments against the cult. They would not have seen the rise of Christianity as inevitable, but simply as another stroke of bad luck, this one visited on them by an errant, ill-educated, and opportunistic emperor. Yet with Constantine their world changed and they along with it.

QUESTIONS | ***Can history turn rapidly in new directions, or are large shifts in the predominant direction of a society gradual and only seem sudden? Explain. Why do we tend to associate large historical turns with spectacular events when so many complex historical factors are at work? Why was Constantine critical to the successful institutionalization of Christianity?***

from paganism to Christianity. For a thousand years, Romans had expressed their religious beliefs through inscriptions and in their worship of statues so imbued with the divine that they seemed, said Virgil, to breathe. These stones were proclamations of patronage and personal devotion to the gods. With the shift in official state support, the pagan stones of the ancient world began to fall silent and their breathing slowed.

Making a New Rome in Byzantium

The city of Rome was a problem for Constantine. It carried too much old baggage, was too pagan, and forced on him too many compromises with the old ways, both religious and political. But in the east, Constantine could create a new city of Rome and point the empire in a new religious and political direction.

The ancient city of Byzantium was located on the Bosporus Straits at the natural meeting point of Europe and Asia. It took its name from Byzas, the leader of the Greek settlers who had founded the site. The location had many defensive advantages because it could be fortified on both its land and sea sides. Merchants could travel out from it, west along the Mediterranean to Rome and east via the Black and Caspian Seas, or along land routes that led to the Silk Road and China. By the late third century the eastern part of the Roman world was also the most prosperous and Christian part of the empire.

After defeating Licinius, Constantine sent administrators and architects to the city. He had apparently concluded that the city of Rome was too difficult to defend and too pagan to serve as the administrative center of his new regime. For six years, Byzantium was fortified and redesigned and in 330 was officially proclaimed New Rome, though it quickly took on the name of Constantinople (the city of Constantine). We know it today as Istanbul in Turkey.

Constantinople was Rome with a difference. It was designed in the image of Rome and so had a Forum, a Senate house, a Hippodrome or Circus, and senatorial families transferred from Rome to the new capital. But Constantinople was to be a Christian city in which no new pagan temples were permitted. Though there was a patriarch or high churchman resident in the city and in nominal charge of the eastern church, the emperor was the effective head of the Christian religion in the east. His religious opinions and fancies mattered most of all.

Although some scholars date the start of the Byzantine Empire from the creation of Constantinople, eastern Romans still thought of themselves as citizens of the Roman Empire. Though it was Greek in nature and represented the Greek culture of the eastern Mediterranean, the eastern empire's official language for several centuries remained Latin. The people called themselves Romans and referred to their common Greek language as Romaic.

Toward a State Religion

As emperor, Constantine was called on to adjudicate disputes within the Christian church. He ruled against the Donatists and called a great church council that met at Nicaea in 325 to address the problem raised by Arius (260–336), a priest from Alexandria. Arius and his followers (called Arians) claimed that Christ was subsequent (since his human nature was created) to God the Father and his nature changeable, and therefore less divine. This doctrinal dispute roiled the church, particularly its eastern half, where there was a tendency to view God in **monophysite** or one-nature terms, that is, to view God the Father as unique and omnipotent. One could go nowhere in Constantinople, said one contemporary, without hearing shopkeepers and slaves debating the nature of Christ's person. Ask a baker for the price of bread, and he would instead tell you in no uncertain terms that the Son is subordinate to the Father.

Advising Constantine in the midst of this theological controversy were powerful churchmen, some opposed to **Arianism** (including the young Athanasius), others lukewarm to it (such as Eusebius, the emperor's biographer). The final decision of the council was the Nicene Creed. Though the Creed may sound more contractual than spiritual, the product of a committee wrestling over terminology and clauses, it became an official article of faith for the Christian church. Its central point of consensus was that Christ was "of the same substance" as the Father. But many of the fine points of Christ's nature and the Trinity (the Godhead with reference to its three persons, the Father, Son, and Holy Spirit) would continue to exercise Christian thinking for centuries to come. Still the Nicene Creed, as agreed to by the universal church, as represented by the bishops gathered together from the entire Roman Empire, set out a list of beliefs that, at a minimum, all Christians needed to hold.

Nicaea was a triumph of Constantine's religious authority. Eusebius said that the emperor had appeared before the council in a gorgeous purple robe adorned with gold and jewels and dazzled all by his presence. His costume may have sparkled, but his intellect did not. He changed his mind several times as the council wore on and did not always seem to understand the complex theological points at issue. But then Constantine's goal was to unify and govern the Roman Empire, and he may not have been all that interested in endless theological quibbling. Like others, he may just have been waiting to see which way the Christian winds were blowing. At Nicaea he finally chose the winning side. By the end of Constantine's reign, Christianity was not just tolerated; it was the preferred, patronized, protected, and defined religion of the empire and its emperors.

Julian Lapses

When Constantine died in 337 he was succeeded by his three natural sons, who murdered their rivals and had themselves declared Augusti. By 350, one of them, Constantius II (337–361), had overcome his brothers and relatives by assassination. A sarcastic contemporary said that he had only one virtue: he never wiped his nose or spat in public. In 355, Constantius raised his cousin Julian up as a new Caesar to fight against the Germans in the west.

Julian was a sensitive student of Greek philosophy and wrote a book called *The Beard-Hater,* in which he defended the long hair and beards worn by the pagan philosophers of old despite the fashion for a more clipped and clean-shaven look in his own time. Though raised a Christian, he renounced his faith in 361 and so is known as an **apostate.** Attentive to the administration of justice, property rights, and relieving the oppressed, he was a popular figure in the western empire.

Julian's popularity and military success against the Germans, however, roused suspicions about him at the imperial court. Faced with increasing imperial animosity and at the urging of his army, Julian rebelled against Constantius and marched on Constantinople. Before he arrived, the emperor died and Julian was left the sole emperor of all Rome. He now openly revealed his pagan beliefs, but he did not open a new round of persecution of Christians. Not only was Christianity too entrenched by then and his government filled with Christians too powerful to displace, but Julian's own religious beliefs belonged to an older learned polytheism that tended to be tolerant of other beliefs. Instead of persecuting Christians, he turned his energies against the Persians but was fatally wounded during a battle in 363 and died at thirty-one years of age. Julian's apostasy had not changed the Christian direction of the Roman state. By the mid-fourth century the Roman Empire was Christian and would remain so.

Institutional Growth of the Church

As the state embraced Christianity, the institution of the church was moving on a number of fronts to assume its official role in the new order. The number of bishops in Gaul increased from 26 to around 70 in the fourth century as the empire was officially Christianized. The canon of Scripture was set by late in the century; and apocryphal writings, those other gospels and secret teachings (including Gnostic writings), were labeled heretical and ordered destroyed. Throughout the empire the old aristocracy, though retaining elements of its older familial beliefs and pagan humanism, joined the Christian movement. In the west, heroic saintly figures such as Martin of Tours (316–397) took to the countryside to battle ingrained popular paganism. The church developed techniques for winning over the countryside, including a policy of accommodation. Christian churches, for instance, were erected on the sites of pagan holy places so that pagans might both see the triumph of Christianity and yet continue to associate those sites with their older aura of holiness. In battles against the entrenched paganisms of Gaul and other provinces, saints such as Martin came to represent a new set of heroic ideals based on charity, Christian compassion, and steely martyrdom. But the countryside of northern Europe was not to be completely converted for centuries. Pagan beliefs seemed to disappear from sight, but they persisted in small rituals, stubborn convictions, and village superstitions.

While Christians such as Martin were working from the bottom up converting local populations, the Roman state and church were working from the top down. The Trinity was accepted within the empire as a universal standard in 381, and in 392 the emperor Theodosius (379–395) prohibited the practice of paganism and ordered all pagan temples closed. Theodosius led the general Christian suppression of paganism in the empire. He banned older rites of divination such as the reading of entrails and the flight of birds; abolished the celebration of pagan feasts and holidays, extinguished the perpetual fire of Vesta, and disbanded the Vestal Virgins and other pagan associations; and refused to restore the Altar of Victory in the Senate of Rome. At this twilight hour for the ancient gods in the late fourth century, a few learned men still evoked older pagan sensibilities, almost as a soft reaction to the hard Christianizing of the empire around them.

By 400, pure pagan culture was a thing of the past, best remembered by learned readers but fully lived by few. The Roman Empire had an official religion with all its parts in place. Christianity was to spread relatively easily inside the Roman Empire but with considerable difficulty outside it. That compatibility was the end result of the process of the Romanization of Christianity and the Christianization of Rome; the two, empire and religion, had grown together over the previous two centuries and were now inseparable.

German Tribes Enter the Empire

Why and how did the Germanic tribes enter the Roman Empire?

The name *German* (and from it Germania or Germany as the land of the Germans) was apparently derived from a single early tribe and applied by extension to all the Teutonic peoples whom the Gauls and Romans encountered. Although some Romans thought that the word came from their own word for brother or sister (*germanus*), that derivation was farfetched; for most of their long contact the Romans had little feeling of fraternity with the Germanic peoples.

Germans had long been known to the Romans as part of the mix of peoples and cultures within the empire. Captured in wars, many had served as slaves and by the fourth century some were employed as mercenaries. What happened in the last quarter of the century, however, was something different and no longer on strictly Roman terms. Entire German tribes entered the empire as refugees, economic migrants, and invaders (Map 6.4). Those three different roles may help to explain the complexity of the German entry into the Roman Empire and to correct the common view of them as ferocious aggressors. Maps with large sweeping arrows of invading German tribes tend to mislead. So does the standard talk of a flood of **barbarians** pouring into the empire (it took half a century) and engulfing it (the German numbers were always relatively small). Such language does not do justice to the more subtle movement of peoples and the complex reasons for their entrance into the empire. Nor

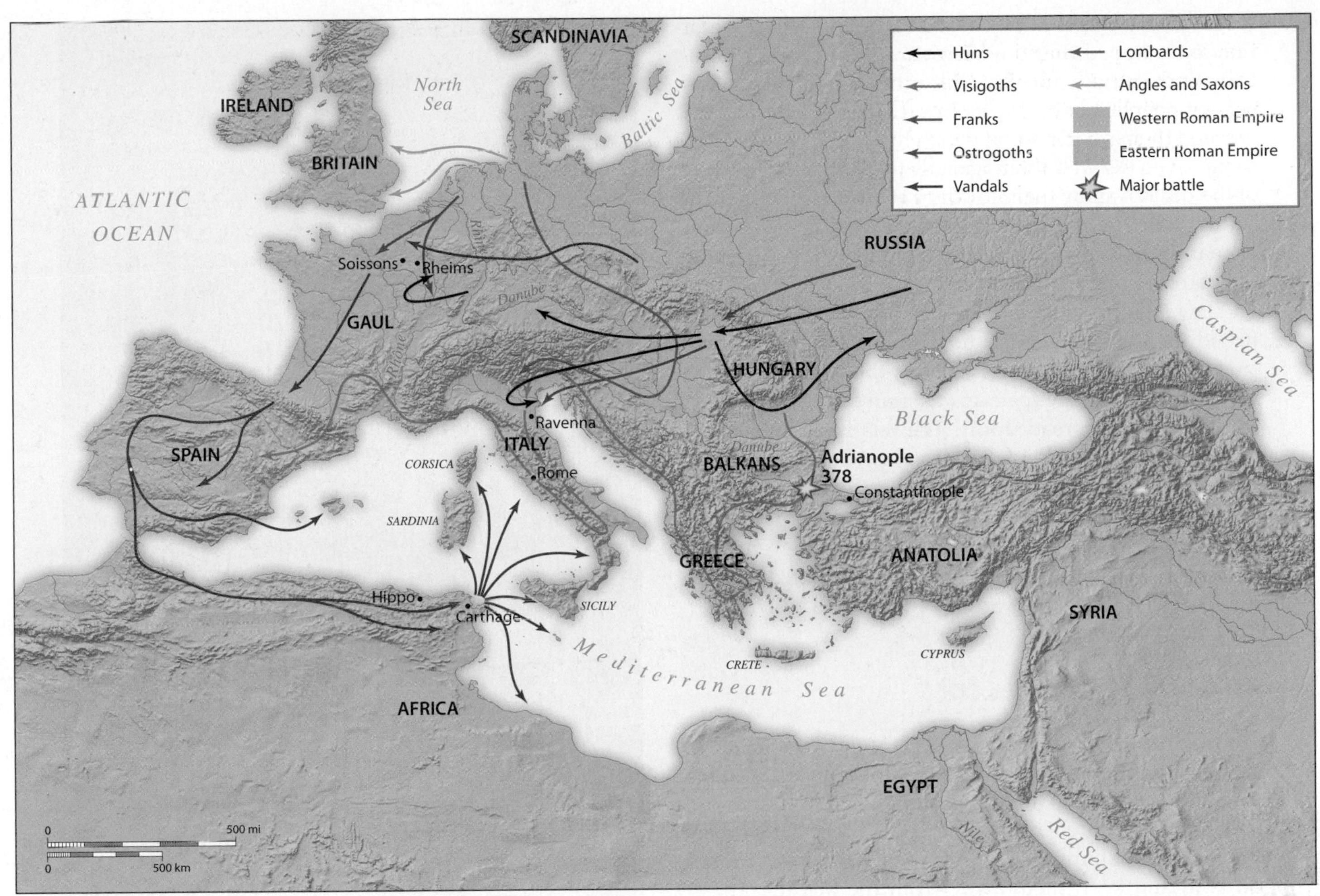

MAP 6.4 | Entry and Movement of German Tribes in the Roman Empire in the Fourth and Fifth Centuries
In the late fourth century, various Germanic tribes began to move into the Roman Empire, at first with the permission of the emperors. ***What does the route followed by the Visigoths reveal? Why and how did the Vandals end up in northern Africa? Is there a prevailing direction to these Germanic migrations? What role did the Huns play in forcing the movement of the German tribes?***

does the idea of a Germanic invasion take into account the Roman cooperation with their entrance and settlement inside the empire.

The various German peoples can be divided roughly into three basic groups: the Scandinavian peoples with whom the Romans had little contact; the west Germans comprising the Franks, Angles, and Saxons; and the east German Goths (Visigoths and Ostrogoths), Vandals, Lombards, and Burgundians. The east German tribes entered the empire; the west Germans, who would play a critical role in shaping the Middle Ages, lagged behind. Both the east and west Germans were warriors, hunters, farmers, and pastoralists, and both tended to wander as groups within the territories they occupied. Most of these tribes were small in number; even the largest do not seem to have had more than 50,000 to 100,000 men, women, and children. Still those were large numbers of people when one considers that no city in the western empire, with the exception of Rome, had that many residents.

The Germans did not want to destroy the Roman Empire; they probably never imagined that they could. They took for granted the stability and superiority of the empire and wanted to partake of its benefits. The Roman frontier had long been a magnet for the Germans. They collected near its borders to seek employment as mercenaries, to trade with the Romans, and to secure Roman protection.

The Visigoths Request Entrance

By the second and third centuries the Germans had become a persistent problem for the Romans. Even Constantine was forced to take up arms against them. But the first tribe to enter the empire did not do so until the 370s and it was with the permission of an emperor. The Visigoths were an east German group, located around the Black Sea, that began to feel pressured by the Huns who were moving southeast into China and southwest toward the eastern border of the Roman Empire. Seeking protection, the Visigoths appealed to the emperor Valens (r. 364–378) in 376 for permission to cross the Danube and settle inside the empire. Not being in a good position to refuse them, Valens allowed them to enter. The emperor may have hoped that the Visigoths would settle peacefully and, in time, integrate into the Roman world as a subject people, but he was not particularly generous. He granted them poor land on which they could not support themselves. As well their agricultural practices and way of life did not allow them to adapt at once to a permanent settled life. The Visigoths also ran up against a corrupt Roman bureaucracy that exploited them. The Visigoths felt betrayed and took up arms.

They rebelled and on August 9, 378, the Visigoths defeated the Romans at Adrianople, not far from Constantinople. Though the overall size of the Roman army in the empire was huge (perhaps as many as half a million soldiers), it was spread thinly. The relatively small army that Valens put together to confront the Germans was cut down. The wounded emperor slipped away from the battle to take refuge in a cottage, which was burned down with him inside. The emperor Theodosius eventually struck a treaty with the Visigoths that permitted them to hold land as allies.

The General Stilicho On this ivory diptych, the German general Stilicho stands on guard for Rome against the barbarian assaults on Italy. He is presented as a soldier, not as a senator or consul.

Imperial Strategies for Managing the Germans

The Romans thought that the safest barbarian (a term used by contemporaries to describe an uncivilized people who spoke an incomprehensible language) was a settled barbarian. The first imperial policy, then, was to settle them on land and keep them away from the Mediterranean Sea. Theodosius knew that as long as the Germans could be kept from the Mediterranean, the Roman way of life could continue without drastic disruption. His law code made it a capital crime to teach Germans how to build boats. As allies the Visigoths were accommodated, probably on state revenues, and so incorporated within the Roman state. This first Roman strategy of settling the German tribes inside the eastern empire proved to be disastrous. The Visigoths, though supposedly settled, turned to raiding. War had been one of their chief activities for centuries. Moreover, the German tribes knew that violence or just the threat of it was the surest way to win advantages from the Roman state.

The second imperial strategy was to deflect the Germans away from the eastern empire and to use them as a quasi-mercenary force to handle problems in the western empire, particularly to dislodge other Germans with whom the eastern empire was at odds. Thus, when Theodosius died in 395, his successor employed Alaric (d. 410) and the Visigoths to remove Stilicho, the Vandal general in charge of the Roman army of northern Italy, who was in imperial disfavor. For a decade Stilicho protected Italy against the Visigoths who attacked annually, but he was assassinated on imperial orders in 408.

The eastern Roman Empire had hit on what it thought was a winning strategy for managing the Germans inside the empire. The eastern empire decided that it would be best to have no resident Germanic tribes in the east and so encouraged or ordered them to go west, often to displace other Germans who were out of favor with the empire. The civilian population of Italy had long ago surrendered its military duties, thinking it better to let German mercenaries such as Stilicho fight on its behalf. Thus, independent east German tribes who had settled uncomfortably in the east were used as military and political instruments in the great Roman game to preserve the eastern empire and quiet the western front. Even if the result further destabilized the west, it was deemed a necessary, if desperate measure, to sacrifice the western empire to the greater good of maintaining a mostly German-free eastern empire. The cost of this scheme, however, was to accelerate the division of the empire into a relatively solid east and an increasingly fragile west.

The Sack of Rome in 410

The eastern imperial policy was a dangerous one since the east German tribes could be neither controlled nor contained once let loose in the west. Alaric and his Visigoths marched into Italy. They besieged Ravenna, by then the effective western imperial capital. Located on the Adriatic and therefore closer to Constantinople, Ravenna's rise also marked the final eclipse of the city of Rome as a center of imperial power. Alaric and the Visigoths next turned on Rome and attempted to starve it into submission. On August 23, 410, a gate was opened (reportedly by a slave) and for the next three days the Visigoths and many Roman slaves plundered the city, seizing what they could, overturning monuments, and setting fires.

On hearing of the sack of Rome, the old and weary Saint Jerome said that the very lamp of the world had gone out. Saint Augustine began writing the *City of God* in response to those pagans who claimed that the city had fallen because Rome had abandoned its gods. He argued instead that the fortune of the earthly city had always been variable and that the city of God (or better still "the state of God"), the kingdom of heaven, was the true home of the righteous. He was also apparently worried by the charge that it was *Christian* Germans who had sacked Rome and that it was Christianity itself that was bent on destroying Rome. Augustine countered that Christianity had limited the amount of damage done during the sack since the attackers had respected churches, nuns, and holy things.

The Visigoths were Christians. They had converted as a tribe to Christianity in the 390s at a time when Arianism was still in some vogue in the east. When the empire firmly returned to Nicaean orthodoxy, the Visigoths and the other east German tribes persisted in their Arianism even though by then it was deemed heretical. The east Germans may at some level have preferred Arian theology with its omnipotent God and human Christ over the intellectual complexities of the orthodox Trinity.

Everyone, including the Germans, knew that northern Africa was the grain basket of the empire, feeding the city of Rome and generating immense wealth. To take it was to control the supply lines of Rome's richest provinces. After sacking Rome, Alaric and his people headed south, but before securing ships and fair seas to carry them to Africa, Alaric died. A river in southern Italy was diverted from its course and the chief was buried in the river bed along with his treasure and the slaves who had dug his grave.

Another east German tribe, the Vandals, then crossed over the Rhine River into Gaul since the borders now had fewer Roman soldiers standing guard. For twenty years the Vandals settled in Aquitaine and Spain as Roman allies, but in 429 they captured an imperial fleet and sailed to northern Africa. They took control of the region and its wheat trade and impeded the flow of trade around the western Mediterranean. They also gained an infamous reputation as persecutors of orthodox Christians. In 455, a band of them sailed to Rome and sacked the eternal city.

Attila and the Huns

After putting pressure on the Visigoths and the area beyond the eastern empire in 375, the Huns, who were magnificent horsemen, dispersed back to their ancestral lands in the Asian steppes. In 434, Rua, the chief of the Huns, died and was succeeded by his two nephews, Bleda and Attila, who ruled together until 445, when Attila apparently murdered his brother. A Roman historian who saw Attila described him as short, broad shouldered, and flat nosed; his face was beardless, but he had angry, sunken eyes. So formidable a warrior was he that the emperor paid Attila 700 pounds of gold not to attack the eastern empire. Still, Attila and his Huns twice invaded Byzantine territories before turning west. In 452, the Huns invaded Gaul and Italy. They sacked Aquileia so thoroughly that poets hundreds of years later still sang of its unending ruin. After that the Huns attacked Milan, Pavia, and Rome.

Outside the walls of Rome, the pope is reputed to have urged Attila for the love of God to spare the city. Attila did withdraw, but some portion of the Roman church's treasury may have left with him. At the time Attila had his own problems: a famine and virulent disease (probably malaria) in northern Italy were making it difficult to continue the campaign. Attila died the next year after celebrating his wedding; contemporaries claimed that he had choked on his own drunken vomit, though it is more likely that Romans had arranged his assassination. The Roman state had plotted to assassinate him before, and failed. With Attila's death, the raids of the Huns on the Roman Empire ceased.

The End of the Empire in the West

The east German tribes soon drove out any remaining Huns and stood in effective control of the western empire. The Roman Senate in October 475 elected young Romulus Augustulus as emperor of the west, but the German mercenaries in Italy had other plans. They deposed the new emperor and chose as their king Odovacar, who, like Stilicho before him, was the German general of the imperial army in Italy. Odovacar asked the Senate to notify the eastern emperor that the west no longer needed an emperor. The eastern emperor would suffice and the Germans in Italy would serve in his place and in his name. This sequence of events effectively made Odovacar the first German king to rule Italy, but Italy officially remained part of the empire.

By 476, the Roman Empire was very different from what it had been even a century earlier. It had dwindled in size as distant provinces such as Britain had fallen out of Roman control. The city of Rome had been sacked twice, and other Roman cities in Gaul and northern Africa had suffered assaults. Even the Mediterranean was no longer a secure Roman sea. The empire continued in name in the west and in fact in the east, but various German peoples now controlled large parts of it in the west. Odovacar and his troops held northern Italy;

The Decline and Fall of the Roman Empire

One of the most enduring historical problems has been why the Roman Empire failed? It does no good to turn the question upside down and to ask the better question of why the Roman Republic and Empire lasted so long, for that still leaves the end problem unaddressed. Edward Gibbon was the first modern historian to pose the problem. The very title of his great work, *The History of the Decline and Fall of the Roman Empire* (published in three units in 1776, 1781, and 1788), contains a descriptive hypothesis as though it were a fact, that is, that the Roman Empire experienced a long slow decline and finally ended when Constantinople fell to the Ottoman Turks in 1453.

Gibbon thought he knew why: "the decline of Rome was the natural and inevitable effect of immoderate greatness. Prosperity ripened the principle of decay; the causes of destruction multiplied with the extent of conquest; and, as soon as time or accident had removed artificial supports, the stupendous fabric yielded to the pressure of its own weight." Roman historians themselves thought that the loss of Roman virtue was to blame. Greed, rampant vice, and angry gods undid the empire, but ancient historians were moralists whose goal was to reform the present and instruct the future. Modern historians have offered a variety of causes: territorial (an overextended empire, the rise of dynamic peoples on the margins, the militarization of the empire); economic (excessive taxation, the failure of the economy, inflation); material (lead poisoning, changing climate); structural (corruption and loss of power by the centralized state, the separation of civil and martial offices under Emperor Hadrian, the rise of soldier emperors), and many others.

The sheer complexity of the changing nature of the Roman state over eight hundred years defies any single or simple explanation. Important events or sequences of events can unbalance systems of government and life and lead to changes that produce yet other changes that ripple through time and space. The seeming solidity of large and complex historical phenomena such as empires may be deceptive since complexity produces interdependence and structural delicacy. A complicated machine can make intricate objects, but with a dropped gear, an interruption of power, or a wayward bolt, the thing can stop working altogether. Rome was not a machine, but there was something fragile about its greatness even in the second century. Multiple crises and underlying social and political changes produced responses that pushed Rome in new directions. But Rome did not so much fall as change. Historians can quantify some of those changes (how many books were being written, how many soldiers in the army, how many shiploads of grain, the worth of currency and goods), but historical decline remains a matter of perspective. Some people suffered, some prospered. Were outsiders (Persians, Germans, Africans), and subordinate insiders (conquered Greeks, Jews, slaves), better off or worse off as Rome changed?

What does Rome's historical fate mean for us? Are there lessons to be learned from Rome's end history? Gibbon's readers wanted to know just that and so at the end of Chapter 38 of the *Decline and Fall,* he inserted his "General Observations on the Fall of the Roman Empire in the West." He assured his contemporaries that all was well in their own world: "We may therefore acquiesce in the pleasing conclusion that every age of the world has increased, and still increases, the real wealth, the happiness, the knowledge, and perhaps the virtue, of the human race." His confidence in progress and his conviction that Rome's history was a specific case and not a universal pattern for the decline and fall of advanced societies was encouraging, but Gibbon and his contemporaries could not have anticipated the French Revolution and the rise of Napoleon, which lay only a few years in the future and shook the pleasing stability of the Europe that Gibbon had surveyed with such confidence.

QUESTIONS | ***Why, in your opinion, did the Roman Empire decline or change for the worse, or did it? Does the case of Rome throw any light on current history, or are all histories unique?***

the Vandals occupied northern Africa; the Visigoths had drifted to and now controlled much of Spain; and the Burgundians took the Rhône Valley and controlled access to the western Alps.

The fourth century had seen the Christianization of the Roman Empire; the period between 376 and 476 saw the political Germanization of the western empire and northern Africa. As jarring as these changes seemed, even to contemporaries, there was something managed and still half-Roman about them. The east German tribes had entered the empire to benefit from its protection and prosperity, and they worked within the general contours of the existing imperial system. Not only had both the Visigoths and the Vandals negotiated their entrances into the empire, but they struck treaties with the state and extorted advantages from it just as powerful Roman citizens always had. The east Germans were Christians, but Arian Christians, which was a critical point of cultural difference.

By the end of the fifth century, the Roman Empire had changed, but it had not ended. Its center had shifted

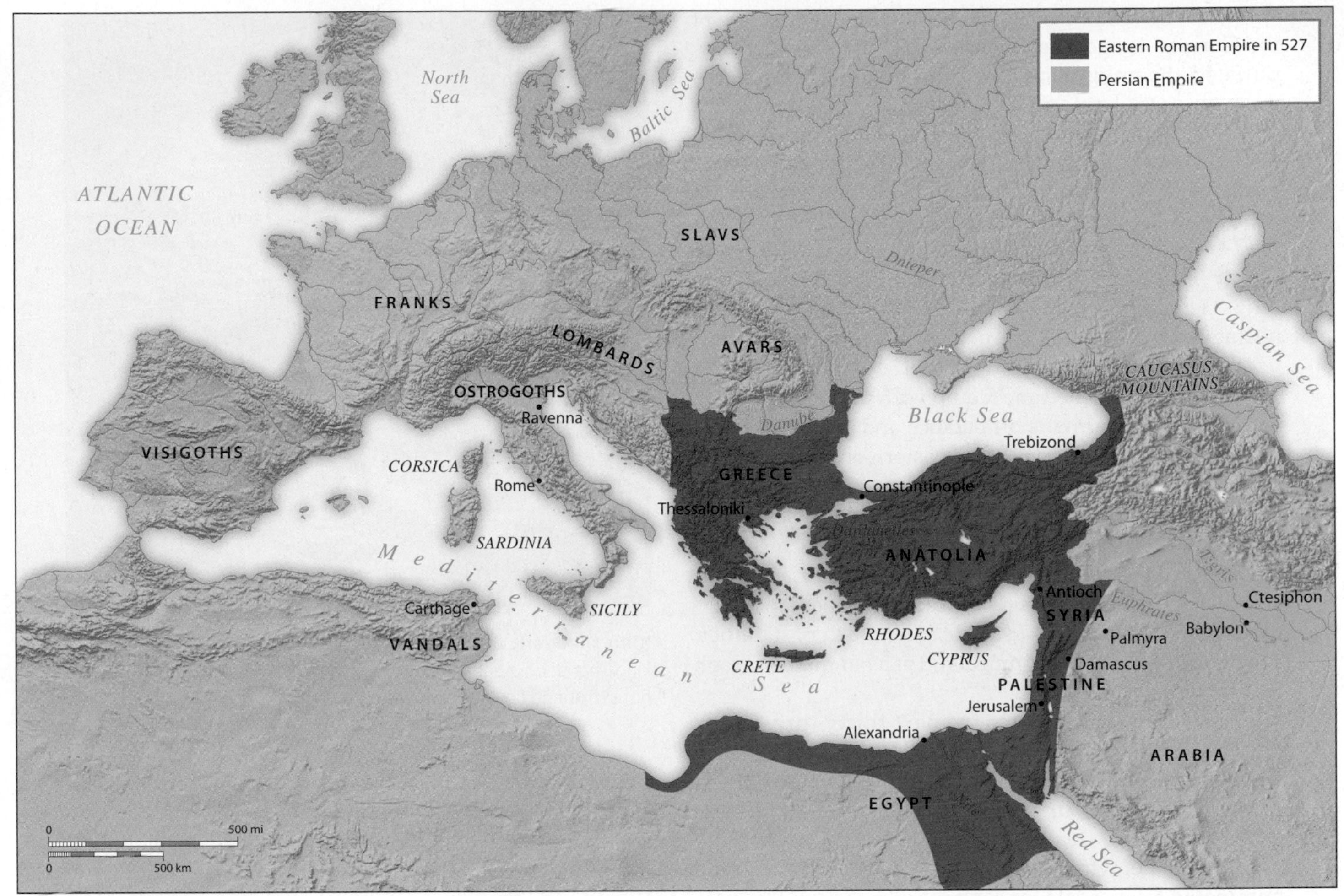

MAP 6.5 | The Roman Empire by the Early Sixth Century

Although Constantinople was the capital, after Constantine, of the Roman Empire, by the early sixth century it exercised direct control chiefly over the eastern or Greek part. By 526, various Germanic tribes had established kingdoms inside the Roman Empire. ***Where and why did the Germans establish kingdoms? Who controlled the Roman Empire by the early sixth century?***

east to Constantinople, and a case could be made that the Germans inside the empire were acting within the framework of the shrinking Roman state. Living on Roman taxes and governing in the name of the emperor, they had been co-opted into the decaying Roman order.

Germanic Kingdoms in the West

With the end of the western empire and various German peoples settled inside the empire, the future of both the eastern and western parts of the Roman world was yet to be decided. The eastern empire had made the decision to save itself, even if it meant sacrificing effective power over the west. Each of the east German tribes inside the empire approached the problem of its survival in a different way, though they all shared similar problems and a similar final fate. One west German tribe, however, found a way to move forward.

What did the German peoples inside the Roman Empire want, and how well did they play the great Roman game?

Vandals, Visigoths, and Ostrogoths

The Vandals in northern Africa forced the Romans to recognize them as allies and were able to exert some control over parts of the western Mediterranean, but their hostility to orthodox Christianity meant that they never won over the local population. They were overthrown by imperial forces in the sixth century.

After the death of Alaric, the Roman emperor Honorius (r. 395–423) employed the Visigoths to attack other Germanic tribes. The Visigoths eventually set up a successful kingdom in Spain that survived until the early eighth century (Map 6.5). They persisted in their Arian faith until 589, when King Reccared converted to orthodox Christianity. The Visigoths lasted longer than the other east German kingdoms because they seem to have worked better with the Roman state and church, moved when necessary, and eventually joined the established Christian order.

The story of the Ostrogoths may be the most tragic of the German kingdoms, for under a dynamic ruler they pursued the enlightened rule of Italy. The Ostrogoths were an east German tribe of about 100,000 people, a quarter of whom were warriors. The emperor Zeno (474–491) was eager to remove Odovacar and his arrogant dominion over Italy and so, just as another emperor had sent Alaric and the Visigoths west to dislodge Stilicho, he sent the Ostrogoths west to overthrow Odovacar. They were led by Theoderic (453–526), the son of an Ostrogothic king. He had been sent as a boy to Constantinople as a hostage, was educated there, and became the first civilized barbarian king.

After Theoderic became fed up with the Roman policy of keeping the Germans off balance and poor, he led his men on several raids inside the eastern empire. The emperor Zeno decided that it was time to remove the dangerous Theoderic and the Ostrogoths and so sent them west in 489. For three years, Odovacar and his men held out in Ravenna against Theoderic's forces. When both sides were exhausted, the two leaders reached an agreement to share power, which didn't last much past dinner. Theoderic had Odovacar murdered at a banquet and took control of Italy.

King Theoderic the Great On a gold medallion, the Ostrogothic king Theoderic is depicted as a German with long hair and mustache, but surrounded by Roman symbols.

Theoderic ruled Italy for the next thirty-three years. He was called *rex* or king but never clarified what he claimed to be king of, whether of the Romans in Italy or of his own people. He reigned in the name of the eastern emperor and dealt fairly and respectfully with the Roman Senate, which continued to meet. Each year, he nominated a candidate for consul. Since the right to issue laws still belonged to the Roman state, he only promulgated edicts. In the late imperial tradition of Diocletian he did wear purple, the imperial color, and permitted petitioners to prostrate themselves before him.

The Roman senator Cassiodorus worked for the Ostrogoths and wrote a series of letters for Theoderic that portray the king's dealings with the Romans in noble terms. Cassiodorus Romanized and idealized the king, but that may have been a reflection of Theoderic's own view of his role as a German king in Italy. He reminded the Romans that, though he was a barbarian, he was their protector against other barbarians, a role that Germans had by then long performed. He acted to protect the interests of Italy and the city of Rome, in particular. He secured a steady supply of food to the city and ordered the repair of the damage done by the Visigoths and Vandals.

Theoderic's policy was one of peaceful coexistence, not assimilation. Because the Ostrogoths and Romans were for the most part isolated from each other, the tensions between the occupiers and occupied were reduced. The only point on which Theoderic abandoned Ostrogothic tradition dramatically was by embracing Roman civil or property law over Ostrogothic law, which was based on a Germanic law code that specified fixed payments according to the worth of things damaged for both civil and criminal offenses. As a consequence of Theoderic's decision, the Ostrogothic law code is one of the few Germanic law codes that is now lost. The Ostrogoths, as an occupying military people, had their own military courts. The Romans, as a resident civilian population, were subject to civil courts.

Despite the cooperative regime, the divide between the Romans and the Germans was large. The Ostrogoths spoke a different language than the native population, and their appearance and dress were different. They wore their hair long and Theoderic sported a mustache. The Romans still generally despised Germans. The poet Sidonius claimed that they stank of garlic and greased their hair with butter.

In addition to the ethnic, linguistic, and cultural differences that separated the Ostrogoths and the Romans, so too did religion. Like other east Germanic peoples inside the empire, the Ostrogoths were Arian Christians. Although their religious beliefs were viewed as heretical in orthodox Italy, the Ostrogoths probably found that those beliefs and practices served as a useful hedge against assimilation. But, unlike the Vandals, Theoderic publicly promoted religious toleration. People, he thought, could not be compelled to believe against their will. As a consequence, he did not seize orthodox churches but began building his own Arian churches, several of which survive in Ravenna today. Despite his immersion in Italian affairs, the king had plans for a wider German world. He sought to influence parts of Gaul and Burgundy through a series of marriage alliances with other German tribes.

King Theoderic's Troubled Last Years

After the year 500, things began to go awry for Theoderic and the Ostrogoths. When Clovis, the king of the Franks, became an orthodox and not Arian Christian, the balance of power and authority in the west began to shift against the Arian Ostrogoths. Theoderic's dealings with the Romans became strained. In 523, worried that the Senate and emperor were conspiring against him and his people, he commanded the Romans not to bear arms. Next he ordered the arrest of the senator Boethius for colluding with the emperor. While in prison, Boethius wrote *The Consolation of Philosophy*, a dialogue in both prose and verse with Lady Philosophy on the nature of fortune. In 524, Boethius was executed.

The previous emperor, Zeno, may have been sympathetic to the Arians, but the new emperor, Justin (r. 518–527), viewed them as heretics and persecuted them openly. Theoderic ordered the pope to Constantinople to try to negotiate with the emperor and to put an end to the hostility. When the pope failed, he was arrested on his return to Italy. Theoderic's actions grew more desperate. He was planning a war against the orthodox Franks to the north and on August 30, 526, ordered that all orthodox churches in Italy should be surrendered to him. The next day he died of dysentery.

The future of the Early Middle Ages was not to lie with the east German tribes, but with the west Germans. Although religion had been a useful point of distinction for the Ostrogoths and the other east Germans as they tried to maintain their tribal identity in a sea of Romans, those religious differences also prevented the east Germans from becoming full members of the Roman world they occupied. Though the Visigoths, Vandals, and Ostrogoths had pursued different strategies for survival and success, each was unsuccessful in the end.

The Franks Take Control of Gaul

The Franks were a west German tribe that had received rights as Roman allies as early as the fourth century. There were two basic groups of Franks: the Salian Franks, who were located in the area around what is today Belgium, and the Ripuarian Franks farther north around the Rhine. The Franks were not attracted to the Mediterranean, as the east German tribes had been, and consequently received less attention from the Romans. The first Frankish leader of historical importance was Childeric (d. 481/482), a Salian Frank. Like other Frankish kings, his hair was uncut and flowed down onto his shoulders. This line of long-haired kings is known as the Merovingians, after Merovech, a legendary ancestor of the family.

When Clovis became king of the Franks on the death of his father, Childeric, he was only fifteen years old and in a precarious position. Frankish chiefs were the kings of a people, not a kingdom or territory, and they needed to win the support of their men by conducting successful raids and through the generous distribution of the spoils of war. Germanic kings were known as ring-givers since they bestowed on their men riches of gold and baubles. It was not royal blood so much as military success that kept a king in power.

The Salian Franks operated in Roman Gaul, where orthodox bishops had assumed active authority over the administration of their *civitates* (cities and their outlying areas). The Franks and the church maintained a cooperative relationship based on particular spheres of interest. The Franks conducted war, provided security of a sort, and controlled land and royal appointments. The church through its bishops supervised the faith and addressed the social needs of their communities with charity. Clovis began to take control of Christian Gaul and some of its most venerated Christian communities. In 486, when he was only twenty, Clovis moved against the old Roman and Christian cities of Soissons and Rheims. These conquests made it imperative for him to have good relations with the bishops of Gaul. The bishop of Rheims advised King Clovis to defer to his bishops and to heed their advice, for if he was on good terms with them, his province would remain strong.

The Conversion of Clovis

To orthodox Christians the Arians were heretics stubbornly clinging to falsehoods, lies that would lead both them and all whom they influenced to damnation. There was little point in talking to them. Pagans were a different matter; they were simply deluded and naive, polytheistic children who did not know better. For Christians, a pagan (*paganus*) was a rustic, uneducated and superstitious. Since, for their own historical and tribal reasons, the east Germanic tribes all remained faithful to Arianism, it became increasingly apparent to the Romans by the late fifth century that one of the pagan west German tribes would need to break the religious logjam.

The Franks, Angles, and Saxons were all pagans. None of the west German tribes had entered the Roman Empire during the time of Alaric or had encountered Arian missionaries in the eastern empire. The bishops of Gaul not only wanted good relations with Clovis, they also wanted to convert him to their faith, but Clovis was not an easy target. As a young prince, Clovis liked nothing better than to plunder churches and he was notoriously violent. In a dispute with one of his soldiers over who owned a piece of stolen church property, he ordered his men to line up before him. As he inspected the troops, Clovis singled out the man for having a dirty ax, hurled it to the ground, and when the man bent over to pick it up the king brought his own battle ax down on the man's skull, splitting him in two.

Clovis was under intense pressure from both Arians and orthodox Christians to convert to their form of faith. The young king had married an orthodox Christian named Clotild, a sincere believer who was pressured by bishops to persuade her husband to convert. It was a strategy employed by other bishops in the sixth century, but Clovis continued to waver, unsure where his advantage lay. Like Constantine, he finally converted on the eve of a battle sometime between 496 and 498. He too was looking for victory through religion, and the Roman church was pleased to support him, for their interest lay in having an orthodox king spread the faith through conquest, particularly over heretical lands and peoples. One bishop told the king that where he conquered, so did they.

The church's policy of converting the Germans depended on converting the king first. This was not popular, grassroots conversion, but top-down conversion. The tribe collectively converted with its leader. Three thousand of Clovis's men were baptized with him in Rheims. Clovis's conversion should not be thought of as insincere; rather, his religious beliefs were primitive or untrained. Even after conversion, Clovis's Christianity remained an amalgam of paganism and primitive Christianity. The Frankish people, without Clovis's fuller exposure to episcopal teaching, knew even less about their new religion. They were now nominally Christian, but their full conversion to Christianity would take centuries to achieve.

The political impact of Clovis's conversion was vast. By force of arms and with the sanction of the church, he defeated the Burgundians and Visigoths in Gaul and by 507 had united the cities of Gaul under his rule. In so doing, he changed the fundamental direction of the west. The various east German tribes felt the ground shift under them as they looked north and saw the success of Clovis, their orthodox Christian cousin. It was no wonder that Theoderic was planning to attack the Franks just before he died.

Clovis's triumph was not the end of Roman Gaul, but its last great flourish. The Salian Franks now controlled old Gallo-Roman territory. Agriculture based on grapes and olives still dominated in the south, huge villas remained, Roman amphitheaters in places such as Arles and Nîmes were still in use, and merchants from as far away as Syria and as near as Spain followed old trade routes into Gaul. Gallo-Roman civilization persisted, if in diminished form. The Salian Franks even continued Roman chancery or bureaucratic practices, and their documents were written on papyrus until the seventh century. Some historians believe that the Merovingians belong to the final phase of the ancient world since they still operated within the contours of the decaying empire, much as their east German cousins did.

Justinian's Reassertion of Roman Imperial Grandeur

In the eastern Roman Empire, events were unfolding that would remind the Mediterranean world that the empire still retained considerable power, even in the west. The emperor Justinian with his empress Theodora attempted to return the Roman Empire to its glory days by undoing the Germanic intrusion into northern Africa and the western empire, wiping out the Arian heresy, and making their reign a magnificent reassertion of imperial grandeur. Their bold attempt, however misguided and damaging, was to be critical to shaping the direction that the Middle Ages took.

What impact, good or bad, did Justinian's drive to restore and reassert the greatness of the Roman Empire have on Mediterranean and European civilization?

The Emperor and Empress

Justinian (r. 527–565) was the last native Latin-speaking emperor of Constantine's Roman Empire and the last to dream of restoring it to its earlier glory. In 527, he was named co-emperor alongside his uncle Justin, an illiterate soldier and persecutor of Arians. Justinian had by that time already married Theodora (r. 527–548), a

The Emperor Justinian and Attendants On this mosaic, which faces the mosaic of Theodora in San Vitale, Ravenna, Justinian is accompanied by the Archbishop Maximianus and two priests to his left and two nobles and a group of soldiers, one with a Chi-Rho shield to Justinian's right. The general Belisarius may be the grizzled noble over his left shoulder. Neither Justinian nor Theodora ever visited Ravenna.

controversial and dynamic figure in her own right. As a lower-class woman, she was roundly despised by segments of the Roman nobility. Procopius of Caesarea, the secretary of General Belisarius and the chronicler of Justinian's many accomplishments, wrote a *Secret History (Anecdota)* in which he condemned Justinian and Theodora as rapacious monsters and murderers.

Regardless of her reputation, Theodora had courage and determination. In 532, a riot broke out in Constantinople between the Green and Blue racing supporters (Circus and political factions at the Hippodrome), the rough equivalent (with knives) of a modern soccer riot. Violence spilled over into the streets of the city and for three days the mob rampaged, setting buildings on fire and calling for a new emperor. Justinian was about to flee the city, according to Procopius, when Theodora shamed him into staying and fighting back. The generals Belisarius and Mundus attacked the mob and killed thousands. The emperor survived the crisis.

Theodora was also a social reformer, seeking basic rights for women in the empire. She worked against the trumped-up adultery charges that many men used to divorce their wives and to seize the property that these women had brought into their marriages. She campaigned for the prohibition of the sale of young girls for prostitution and purchased a palace where these abused children might be housed; she called it her House of Repentance. Procopius ignored her good deeds in his portrait, concentrating instead on the seedier side of her reputation.

After the riot, Justinian set about making fundamental changes to eastern Roman society. He ordered a great codification of Roman law. The quaestor Trebonian was assigned the task of sorting centuries of Roman legal precedents and imperial laws into a rational code of civil law. The *Corpus Juris Civilis* or Body of Civil Law consists of the Code, which contains imperial laws; the Digest (or examples) of Roman laws; and the Institutes, which is a textbook of Roman law. The New Laws (*Novellae*) contains laws from Justinian's own reign.

Justinian also ordered the repair of Constantinople and the construction of new buildings. The most famous of these is the church of Hagia Sophia ("holy wisdom"), which was dedicated in 537. Its interior was gilded, by one estimate, with over 300,000 pounds of gold. Its massive dome, which seems to float on air, was supported by new engineering techniques that allowed a round dome to be placed on top of a roughly square building, allowing light to pour into the massive space below from the rim of the dome.

Hagia Sophia Justinian erected Hagia Sophia in Constantinople after the Nike rebellion. The huge church with its novel architectural features was covered with gold and decoration, but in 1453 was converted into a mosque.

The Reconquest

While Justinian's predecessors had been preoccupied with the eastern Roman frontier and the threat from Persia, Justinian dreamed instead of restoring the empire and retaking the west (Map 6.6). In 532, he struck an "endless peace" with the Persian ruler Chosroes I, which cost him 11,000 pounds of gold. That left him free to turn his attention to the western empire, where he hoped to remove the Germans and stamp out their Arian heresy. He dispatched his young general, Belisarius, along with 20,000 troops to northern Africa to overthrow the Vandals, which happened relatively quickly. The persecuted orthodox Christian population, which had suffered under the harsh Vandal occupation, rallied to their Roman rescuers.

That easy victory convinced Justinian that he could reclaim control over the rest of the imperial rim of the Mediterranean. But wars drain treasuries, and Justinian was always in need of money to pay his mercenary armies. Behind Procopius's complaints about the greed of the emperor and empress lay the emperor's need to finance his expensive wars and extensive building campaigns. Justinian taxed heavily, imposing a heavy burden on the nobility and cities of the eastern empire.

In Italy the Ostrogothic succession was in dispute. To hold on to power, Theoderic's daughter, Amalasuntha,

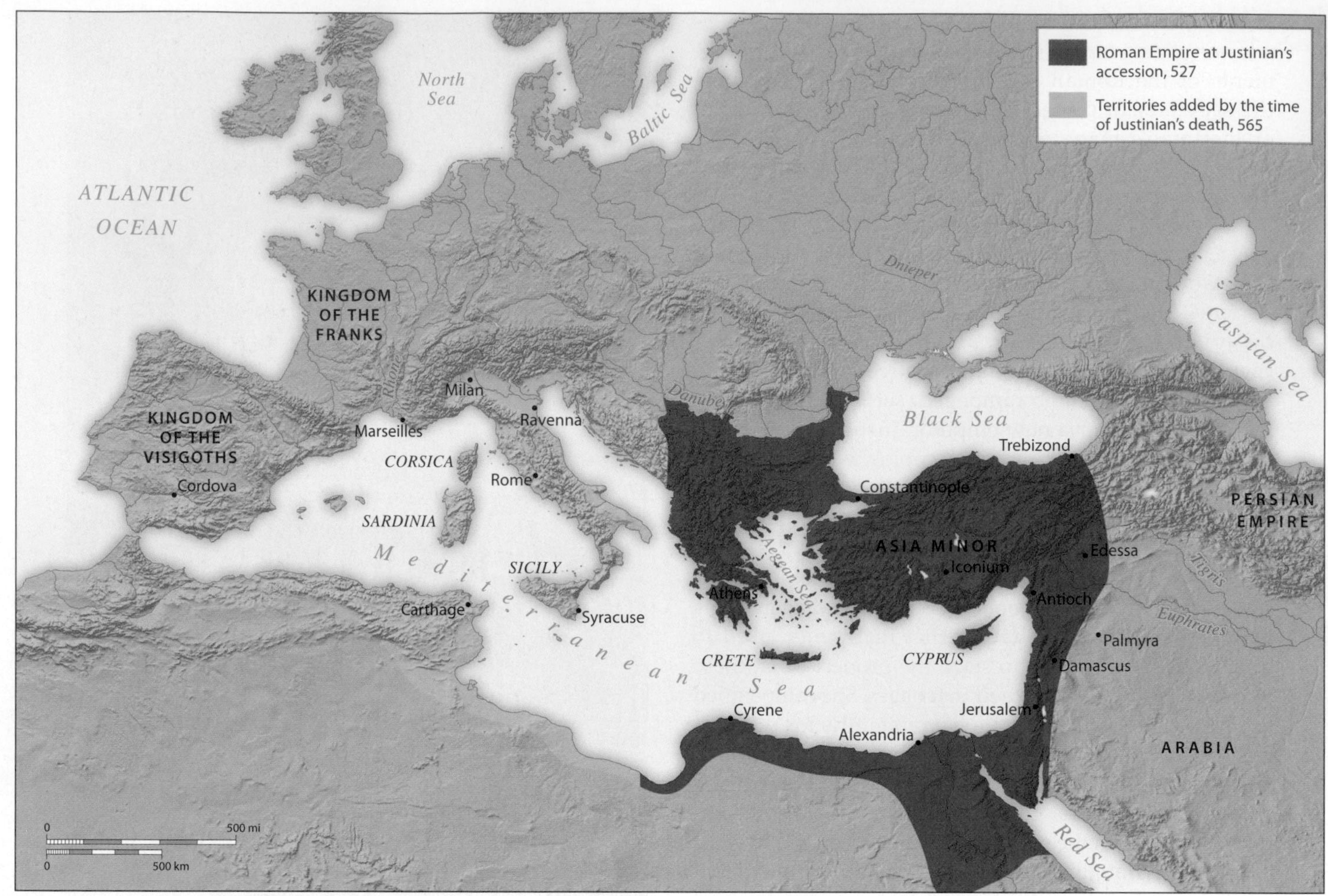

MAP 6.6 | **The Roman Empire of Justinian, 527–565**

Over his long reign, the emperor Justinian attempted to restore the Roman Empire. ***Whom did Justinian seek to displace, why, and when? Why was his restoration of the old Roman Empire both a success and a failure?***

married her cousin Theodahad, but in 534 her husband had her strangled to death while she was taking a bath and declared himself king. Justinian used this event as a pretext for sending troops to Italy to reclaim his imperial rights. The Italian campaign was as difficult as the African one had been easy. General Belisarius was given fewer troops and the native population, for the most part content with the regime of the Ostrogoths, proved less cooperative. At one point, Belisarius and five thousand imperial soldiers were cooped up in Rome for a year as the Ostrogoths laid siege to it. From there the war descended into chaos and Belisarius was recalled.

Later Justinian managed to reassert his authority over Italy, and the adornment of Ravenna reflects that conquest. Justinian's representatives attempted to erase all traces of the presence of the Ostrogothic king from Ravenna and the west. Justinian's artisans even removed the mosaic images of Theoderic and his courtiers standing under arches of his palace, but their disembodied hands can still be seen in the mosaic as though grasping pillars, unwilling to leave.

The Disastrous 540s: Dust-Veils and Disease

The cost of Justinian's campaigns was considerable, and the reassertion of imperial authority over the west would not last. Despite Justinian's endless peace with Chosroes of Persia, by 540 the Persians had sacked Roman cities, including Antioch. The Ostrogoths under a new leader rallied. They took Milan, slaughtering all males and selling the women to the Burgundians. King Totila (r. 541–552) decided to level the city of Rome and began to tear down its walls and to burn the city. For one month the eternal city was virtually without inhabitants. Late in Justinian's reign, his Slavic frontier also began to crumble.

The natural world also seemed to turn against Justinian. In 535–536, a dust-veil, most likely caused by volcanic ash, shrouded the northern hemisphere, blocking solar radiation from reaching the earth. Procopius said that the sun shone weakly in 536, its rays dull. Another Roman contemporary said the sun dimmed for eighteen months and crops failed and the wine was bitter. The effect of the dust-veil was to cool not only Europe, but global temperatures in general, perhaps by as much as 4.5 degrees Fahrenheit (3 degrees Centigrade) between 535 and 555. Whether this climate event also made the population of Europe more susceptible to disease or set into motion a complex chain of factors contributing to the transmission of a particular bacillus is not known, but a deadly disease did strike the west a few years after the dust-veil first obscured the sun.

The Clinging Hands of Theoderic and His Court After the conquest of Ravenna by Justinian's army, the mosaic decoration of Theoderic's church of San Apollinare Nuovo was reworked. Originally images of Theoderic and his courtiers had stood between the arches of the depicted palace, but they were removed, leaving only some of their hands clinging to columns as though unwilling to depart.

In 542, a pandemic known as Justinian's Plague struck Constantinople and the rest of the Roman Empire. The evidence so far suggests that the disease was the bubonic plague. At its height, Justinian's Plague was killing between 5,000 and 15,000 people a day in Constantinople alone, and it may have killed as many as 300,000 people in the city. The emperor himself fell ill but survived. The disease also reached Italy and recurred there and in various spots throughout the empire for several centuries before dying out.

The economic impact of the dust-veil and disease on the empire, which had already been experiencing a sharp decline in population, was significant. Justinian still needed money to finance his wars and soldiers to fill his armies, but manpower became scarcer and more expensive to employ. Labor costs increased, while consumer demand for goods dropped. Whatever else the dust-veil and plague meant in terms of extensive human suffering and economic hardship, they did not enhance Justinian's already faltering scheme to restore the Roman Empire to its former integrity and glory.

Despite these setbacks, Justinian remained in power and worked to restabilize his empire. Italy was relatively secure by the mid-550s, the coastal regions of southern Spain were subdued, and northern Africa was in line by the end of the decade.

Living a Shrinking Urban Life

While Constantinople rebounded from the disastrous 540s, urban life throughout the rest of the empire entered a period of dramatic decline. Smaller cities supplied men and taxes to the Roman state, but did not thrive under a stagnant economy and incessant imperial demand. The once highly specialized economy of the Roman Empire, which had remained vigorous through the fourth century, was breaking down. Even the production of items as simple as shoes, cloth, and pots to hold wine and oil had depended on a combination of regional production, transportation, and distribution within a secure empire, and an extensive series of urban markets. To impede even one of those links was to jeopardize an economic chain, and by 500 in the western empire all three were in a state of crisis. There were fewer consumers and producers, and the transportation and distribution of goods, whether across the Mediterranean or within regions occupied by the Germans, had been compromised. In the eastern empire, the economy, because of imperial security and its greater urban economic scale, was able to overcome many of these problems and remained relatively prosperous.

The east, however, was not without serious economic problems, one of those being caused by Constantinople itself. It seemed at times as though the very purpose of the eastern empire was to feed Constantinople, which sucked resources but supplied little in return. Taxation and religion, petty violence and bullying patrons were the constants of provincial life in the sixth century. Justinian's expensive imperial projects did more to distort than to stimulate the Roman economy.

Around the Mediterranean the population continued to fall as supply lines broke down and long-distance trade dried up. The maritime city of Ephesus, after fire and destruction in the early seventh century, was never rebuilt and its once vigorous harbor became clogged with silt. In Italy many towns and cities were abandoned in the fifth and sixth centuries and people moved to hilltop settlements that could be better defended. Even the city of Rome was not spared. For much of imperial history it had had a population of as many as a million people; by the mid-fifth century it probably had less than half that number. After Justinian's reconquest, the Ostrogothic ravages, the dust-veil, and the plague, the population of Rome fell to around 50,000 people. Other cities shrank inside their old Roman walls. The city life of the ancient Mediterranean, particularly in the west, was ebbing away in the century before the rise of Islam.

Conclusion

The restored Roman Empire that Justinian's heirs inherited was overcommitted and too dominated by one great city and its needs; it could not endure. Within seventy years, northern Africa and large portions of the Roman Middle East fell to Islam and the west broke away again. It might be argued that the effect of Justinian's reconquest and of the natural events that occurred during his reign left a blighted northern Africa and Middle East ready and waiting for the emergence of the dynamic new element that Islam proved to be. In the west, Justinian's legacy was just as disastrous. The new Germanic kingdoms of the Vandals, Visigoths, and Ostrogoths were enfeebled before they had fully developed. Justinian's drive to restore the old Roman Empire, which had been broken and drifting for centuries, only worked to destroy the incipient and dynamic new cultures stirring in the west and northern Africa. The west would have to wait several centuries for the appearance of a German leader as civilized and constructive as Theoderic had been. Justinian's western distraction and diffusion of resources had not materially benefited the east, which would soon see the rise of a new challenge to the surviving Roman Empire.

In many ways Rome lived on, though much diminished and deformed, throughout the sixth century. The east Germanic peoples had seen themselves as working within the Roman imperial system onto which they had grafted themselves. Even the Franks throughout the sixth century occupied a Gallo-Roman territory and by becoming orthodox Christians further integrated themselves into an existing order, one that still looked to the Mediterranean and to an underlying Roman economy of long-distance trade and international merchants.

The period from 180 to 565 marked the slow turn of the ancient world toward the medieval world it was becoming. The three main elements of the Early Middle Ages—late Roman civilization, Christianity, and the Germans—were all in place by its end, but their order of importance had shifted discernibly since Commodus's accession. Christianity, because of Constantine and his successors, moved in the fourth century from being a marginal and persecuted religion to the official belief system of the western world. The Germans, for so long a slave and mercenary element within the empire, now ran much of it. From a centralized Roman Empire with a single ruler (or four of them under the Tetrarchy), the west by 400 consisted of a centralized Roman Empire in the east and a decentralized or localized German west.

If there was one centralizing element in the whole of the old empire, it was Christianity, which had consolidated its presence in the empire, established an official church with a hierarchy of officers, and suppressed voices of difference and dissent. If religion defined the Middle Ages, giving it its distinctive character, then the Middle Ages officially arrived with Constantine. The Roman economy had lost much of its imperial fluidity as goods and people no longer moved across it with ease. There were fewer goods to trade and fewer markets to attract trade. In the west, the economy was already more medieval (highly localized and agricultural) than ancient (with an extensive sea trade and dispersion of goods). The Mediterranean Sea still remained a critical feature of the late Roman world; it was just no longer the dominant one. The Middle Ages didn't arrive everywhere at the same time; it came sooner to the west than the east. The presence of medieval ways was already evident in the west before the Roman Empire finally lost its great middle sea. When it did, western Europe turned inland and to a north bounded by the Atlantic. But the eastern Roman Empire was hardly static. It too was becoming more medieval, as its cities shrank, and its economy became more regionalized. The late Roman, proto-medieval world that stretched from the late second through to the sixth century was neither fish nor fowl, neither wholly Roman nor entirely medieval. It was a world in bumpy transition from one way of organizing and viewing the world to another. Much remained to be done before the Middle Ages overtook the west.

Critical Thinking Questions

1. What choices did late Roman emperors make to preserve the Roman Empire?
2. What roles did economics and outsiders play in the transformation of the late Roman world?

3. Why was religion such an important force in shaping change in the period 180 to 565?
4. What medieval traits were present in the period, where did they predominate, and why did they prevail?
5. What should we call the period from 180 to 565?

Key Terms

codex **(p. 169)**
Gnostics **(p. 170)**
stylites **(p. 170)**
Petrine authority **(p. 172)**
Tetrarchy **(p. 173)**
Donatism **(p. 175)**
Edict of Milan **(p. 177)**
monophysite **(p. 179)**
Arianism **(p. 179)**
apostate **(p. 180)**
barbarian **(p. 180)**

Primary Sources in connect

For information on Connect and the online resources available, go to **http://connect.mcgraw-hill.com.**

1. **Diocletian's Wage and Price Controls**
2. **The Edict of Milan, 313**
3. **The Nicene Creed**
4. **Cassiodorus, King Theoderic's Letters**
5. **The Demons Justinian and Theodora**

BACK TO THE SOURCE

Constantine's Dream

The fourth-century ecclesiastical historian Eusebius presents Constantine as a ruler who received a critical dream in his rise to power. Eusebius does not clearly set the dream on the eve of Constantine's breakthrough battle at the Milvian Bridge in 312 against the rival imperial claimant Maxentius, but others were quick to associate the dream and the pivotal battle. Eusebius informs his readers that the report he is relaying came directly from Constantine's sworn and personal testimony, which he wholeheartedly accepted and made the pivotal event in Constantine's conversion and victory.

Knowing well that he would need more powerful aid than an army can supply because of the mischievous magical devices practised by the tyrant, he sought a god to aid him. He regarded the resources of soldiers and military numbers as secondary, for he thought that without the aid of a god these could achieve nothing; and he said that what comes from a god's assistance is irresistible and invincible. He therefore considered what kind of god he should adopt to aid him and, while he thought, a clear impression came to him, that of the many who had in the past aspired to government, those who had attached their personal hopes to many gods, and had cultivated them with drink-offerings, sacrifices, and dedications, had first been deceived by favorable predictions and oracles which promised welcome things, but then met an unwelcome end, nor did any god stand at their side to protect them from divinely directed disaster; only his own father had taken the opposite course to theirs by condemning their error, while he himself had throughout his life honored the God who transcends the universe, and had found him a savior and guardian of his empire and a provider of everything good. He judiciously considered these things for himself, and weighed well how those who had confided in a multitude of gods had run into multiple destruction, so that neither offspring nor shoot was left in them, no root, neither name nor memorial among mankind, whereas his father's god had bestowed on his father manifest and numerous tokens of his power. He also pondered carefully those who had already campaigned against the tyrant. They had assembled their forces with a multitude of gods and had come to a dismal end: one of them had retreated in disgrace without striking a blow, while the other had met a casual death by assassination in his own camp. He marshaled these arguments in his mind, and concluded that it was folly to go on with the vanity of the gods which do not exist, and to persist in error in the face of so much evidence, and he decided he should venerate his father's God alone.

This God he began to invoke in prayer, beseeching and imploring him to show him who he was, and to stretch out his right hand to assist him in his plans. As he made these prayers and earnest supplications there appeared to the emperor a most remarkable divine sign. If someone else had reported it, it would perhaps not be easy to accept; but since the victorious emperor himself told the story to the present writer a long while after, when I was privileged with his acquaintance and company, and confirmed it with oaths, who could hesitate to believe the account, especially when the time which followed provided the evidence for what he said?

About the time of the midday sun, when day was just turning, he said he saw with his own eyes, up in the sky and resting over the sun, a cross-shaped trophy formed from light, and a text attached to it which said, "By this conquer." Amazement at the spectacle seized both him and the whole company of soldiers which was then accompanying him on a campaign he was conducting somewhere, and witnessed the miracle.

He was, he said, wondering to himself what the manifestation might mean; then, while he meditated, and thought long and hard, night overtook him. Thereupon, as he slept, the Christ of God appeared to him with the sign which had appeared in the sky, and urged him to make himself a copy of the sign which had appeared in the sky, and to use this as protection against the attacks of the enemy. When the day came he arose and recounted the mysterious communication to his friends. Then he summoned goldsmiths and jewelers, sat down among them, and explained the shape of the sign, and gave them instructions about copying it in gold and precious stones.

This was something which the emperor himself once saw fit to let me also set my eyes on, God vouchsafing even this. It was constructed to the following design. A tall pole plated with gold had a transverse bar forming the shape of a cross. Up at the extreme top a wreath woven of precious stones and gold had been fastened. On it two letters, intimating by its first characters the name "Christ," formed the monogram of the savior's title, *rho* being intersected in the middle by *chi*. These letters the emperor also used to wear upon his helmet in later times. From the transverse bar, which was bisected by the pole, hung suspended a cloth, an imperial tapestry covered with a pattern of precious stones fastened together, which glittered with shafts of light, and interwoven with much gold, producing an impression of indescribable beauty on those who saw it. This banner then, attached to the bar, was given equal dimensions of length and breadth. But the upright pole, which extended upwards a long way from its lower end, below the trophy of the cross and near the top of the tapestry delineated, carried the golden head-and-shoulders portrait of the God-beloved emperor, and likewise of his sons. This saving sign was always used by the emperor for protection against every opposing and hostile force, and he commanded replicas of it to lead all his armies.

That was, however, somewhat later. At the time in question, stunned by the amazing vision, and determined to worship no other god than the one who had appeared, he summoned those expert in his words, and inquired who this god was, and what was the explanation of the vision which had appeared of the sign. They said that the god was the only begotten son of the one and only God, and that the sign which appeared was a token of immortality, and was an abiding trophy of the victory over death, which he had once won when he was present on earth. They began to teach him the reasons for his coming, explaining to him in detail the story of his self-accommodation to human conditions. He listened attentively to these accounts too, while he marveled at the divine manifestation which had been granted to his eyes; comparing the heavenly vision with the meaning of what was being said, he made up his mind, convinced that it was

God's own teaching that the knowledge of these things had come to him. He now decided personally to apply himself to the divinely inspired writings. Taking priests of God as his advisors, he also deemed it right to honor the God who had appeared to him with all due rights. Thereafter, fortified by good hopes in him, he finally set about extinguishing the menacing flames of tyranny.

QUESTIONS | *What did Constantine want in the midst of a campaign against his enemies? How had the roots of his conversion been laid? How did he verify and then proclaim his conversion? How might Romans have reacted to this conversion story?*

Source: Eusebius, Vita Constantini 1.27–32, ed. F. Winkelmann, trans. Averil Cameron and Stuart G. Hall, *Eusebius: Life of Constantine* (Oxford: Clarendon Press, 1999), 79–82. © Averil Cameron and Stuart G. Hall 1999. By permission of Oxford University Press.

7

ET SYRIAM SOBAL· ET CONVERTIT
IOAB· ET PERCUSSIT EDOM IN VAL
LE SALINARUM· XII MILIA·

Cavalry Riding to War, Golden Psalter, c. 875

THE EARLY MIDDLE AGES

CHARLEMAGNE'S CORONATION The year was 800, the day Christmas, the place Rome. Old St. Peter's basilica was dressed in its finest array and filled with a throng of worshippers. The men of the moment were a pope and a Frankish king; their marriage of interests was convenient, complex, and dangerous.

When Charlemagne (Charles the Great), a tall man with a sizable paunch, short hair, and mustache, entered St. Peter's, he fulfilled the aspirations of his courtiers, who thought that the time had come for the restoration of the Roman Empire under their illustrious king. Three long centuries had passed since Romulus Augustulus had been deposed as the last emperor of the west. Charlemagne embodied the hope of a new Christian imperial order.

The king traveled to Rome to render justice and restore a pope accused of corruption. Pope Leo III had been physically assaulted by his enemies and driven from Rome. Charlemagne's idea of right order was a practical one; his family had long committed itself to the Roman church and would not now abandon it to disorder, but something went wrong in Rome. Expecting to be rewarded with the largely honorific title of emperor, Charlemagne had dressed in an elegant Greek gown for the occasion. But Pope Leo had other ideas. He took charge of the proceedings and personally placed the imperial crown on Charlemagne's head. To some it seemed that the pope was making the king an emperor. No wonder that Charlemagne later regretted the event. He probably thought that his royal use of force in subduing hostile lands, conquering vast territories, delivering justice, and promoting Christendom made the imperial title a fitting recognition for his many achievements. Leo, as the living representative of Saint Peter and the chosen agent of God on earth, apparently believed that it was by papal intervention and his choice that Charlemagne was made the Roman emperor.

Charlemagne as Roman Emperor, Silver Denarius Image

Whatever happened that day in Rome, Charlemagne's elevation to emperor marked the highest expression of restored order in a world that had long been without lasting stability. The conversion to orthodox Christianity of the Frankish king Clovis had begun the final process of integrating Rome and the Germans, southern and northern Europe, but the Merovingian kings squandered their power in family squabbles and fratricidal wars.

The Early Middle Ages in the west experienced the radical decentralization and disappearance of Roman power. The west returned to being a simpler agricultural society. When western Europe reached its point of greatest disorganization in the sixth century, it was religion, not royalty, that first began to reorder this chaotic world. Monks led the way. Monasticism, one of the great institutional creations of the Middle Ages, provided the Early Middle Ages with a form of religious stability that set a high example for society and helped it begin to reorder religious, economic, and even political life. By retreating from the world, monks grounded the external world in regularity and rationality. Saint Benedict's *Rule* for monks schooled the Early Middle Ages in the advantages of order, work, and economic and religious rationality.

Along with Saint Benedict, the other great religious man of the half millennium was Muhammad, the messenger of a set of divine mandates that inspired and

directed the peoples of the Middle East, Near East, and northern Africa, that part of the Roman Empire that had been adrift in the late Roman world, devastated by the Vandals and Justinian's costly reconquest. The territorial spread of Islam undid once and for all the Roman hold on the Mediterranean as a secure body of water for the transport of goods and peoples. Islam reshaped the territorial outline of Europe, pushing the Roman Empire in the east to become a Byzantine Empire and the Roman Empire in the west away from the Mediterranean and north toward the Germanic kingdoms.

The Carolingians, after overthrowing the Merovingians, came closest to imposing on Europe an effective new order. The very idea of Europe as a territorial, cultural, and political whole took on its first rough form under Charlemagne and his court; and when Charlemagne became the Roman emperor in 800, he and the pope with their German-Christian alliance achieved a new vision of what the West might be.

The real genius of Charlemagne's reign lay in territorial conquest, the conversion of conquered peoples, and the educational and ecclesiastical reformation of Europe. Though his heirs would squander his hard-won stabilization of Europe and the empire would be lost, the Carolingian age proved to be a turning point in the fortunes of Europe, particularly its religious renewal, material prosperity, and intellectual drive. A working synthesis of the three main elements of the Early Middle Ages—Roman civilization, Christianity, and the Germans—was achieved in the Carolingian Empire.

The mid-ninth century, however, saw the breakdown of central authority, and Vikings began to harass the shores and riverways of Europe. By 900, disorder once again became the prevailing condition of European political and social life. Although it seemed on the surface that little had changed in four hundred years, almost everything had changed inside. An ancient way of viewing and acting in the world was gone and a medieval way had taken its place.

The Making of a New Western World

The first agents of the transformation and stabilization of the west were religious, and monks led the way. The *Rule of Saint Benedict* was a response and antidote to the disorder of the Early Middle Ages. High churchmen, particularly powerful, saint-loving bishops, mediated between various quarreling powers, while the popes of Rome, particularly Gregory the Great, attempted to set their own house in order; and the cult of the saints and their relics came to occupy a central place in popular religion.

Why and how did religion play such a large role in the restructuring of western Europe after the decline of central Roman authority?

Monasticism Makes a Difference

Monasticism had its Christian beginnings in Egypt and Syria, but there hermits, desert fathers, and pole-sitters practiced forms of extreme denial of the world that relegated monasticism to the fringes of late Roman society. Early medieval monasticism in the west was a richly varied experiment in spiritual living and came in many forms, all of them committed to lasting as long as this world did and to finding ways to endure. Even the rugged monks of Ireland and northern England, who pursued solitary lives on isolated rocks washed by the cold waters of the north Atlantic, fashioned rules for living. Across

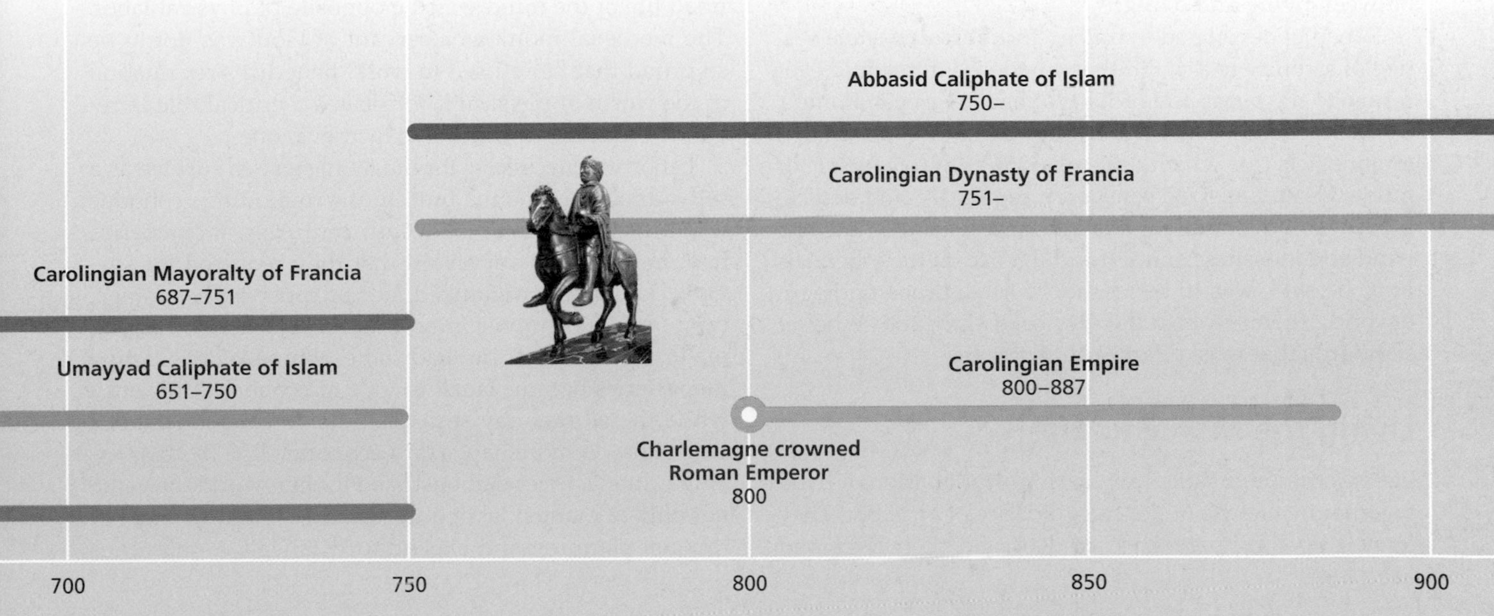

Europe, monks set out to save the world and themselves by dedicating themselves to God and to prayer, but they differed about how best to live a solitary, prayerful life.

In the midst of these many monasticisms, Benedict of Nursia (c. 480–543) supplied what became the normative form of monasticism for the western Middle Ages. When he was fourteen, Benedict renounced the world and set out to become a hermit. Although Theoderic and the Ostrogoths had temporarily reclaimed some political peace for Italy, Benedict's homeland, ravaged by war and economic collapse, was decentralizing rapidly. The population was in free fall and people were abandoning established cities in favor of hilltop settlements. Their world was shockingly poor and exposed.

Benedict settled in a cave south of Rome and there, alone, set out to test his devotion to God against the elements and the snares of the devil. It was a difficult life, both physically and emotionally. Benedict was a Roman with one foot already planted firmly in a Middle Ages of fragmented economic and political conditions and an overriding religious purpose. When the thought of a beautiful woman popped into his head, he hurled himself naked into a thicket of nettles and thorns to extinguish an interior fire with the blood of self-inflicted exterior pain.

As his reputation for extraordinary renunciation spread, Benedict attracted others seeking to abandon a wicked and distracting world. To them Benedict and his manner of life seemed the cure for what ailed the world. Benedict had powers that matched the needs of his disfigured society. In an age of material want and gnawing poverty, he was gifted at miraculously fixing things that to us would seem hardly worth the bother. He mended broken pots, located lost keys, dredged up iron tool heads from deep lakes, and moved huge boulders by prayer. His powers may have been heavenly, but they were applied to earthly ends, for Benedict and his monks lived not in golden imperial Rome, but in an Italy that had returned to a mostly metal-less age. The simplest things mattered once again, for they might make the difference between living and dying.

Benedict developed a strategy for returning some vestige of stability to a world that wondered if it would ever return to the peace and order that had once been Rome's. By 528, Benedict moved to Monte Cassino and founded a monastery for which (around 535) he wrote a *Rule* or guide. He emphasized constancy, regularity, and dedication to God over extreme forms of asceticism on the one hand and looseness and self-indulgence on the other. His *Rule,* he said, was to be a school for beginners to begin devoting themselves to the service of God, and so he set standards that most monks could satisfy.

Living the Monastic Life

Benedictine monastic life was communal. Monks lived together in a house under the guidance of an abbot. They owned nothing personally and turned their lives and bodies over to God. The monk's chief virtue was humility. He kept his hooded head down, not even looking other monks in the eye; and he dedicated himself to a regular round of daily prayer, chanting the Psalms during the seven holy services of each day. Monks swore obedience to their abbot, for they were spiritual brothers and the abbot was their father. The officials of the monastery included a porter or door-keeper, a sacristan or treasurer, a cellarer who kept the stores of food and wine, and later a prior who served as the abbot's chief assistant in administering the monastery. Hierarchy among the monks (indicated by the order in which they processed into church) was determined by the date on which each of them had entered the monastic life. Seniority of membership reinforced the idea that monasticism was a work of endurance, lasting until one was spiritually reborn in Christ at the moment of physical death.

A portion of the *Rule* was read out daily at mealtime, and for much of the day Benedictine monks observed a rule of silence; idle chatter would distract them from their steadfast devotion to God. So paramount was silence and attention to the holy words being read by one of the brothers that the Benedictines developed a set of hand-signs for communicating at the supper table in the refectory. To ask a brother for the plate of fish, the monk signed the fluttering motion of a fish's tail. Monks did speak at communal meetings called by the abbot to decide matters of importance to the monastery, but once the abbot had received their advice, his decisions were binding.

The divine work of the monk was the daily round of prayer, but manual labor was considered necessary and beneficial. Early medieval monks plowed fields, planted and reaped crops, built buildings, and made manuscripts. Benedict believed that idleness was an enemy of the soul and that physical labor was its remedy and a good thing in itself. In the ancient world, few had thought of manual labor as positive. It was servile, something done under compulsion by slaves and the working classes, and not performed at all by the leisured classes for whom a refined life of the mind was the opposite of physical labor. The medieval monk as a servant of God was not to be so proud that he refused to work. Benedict's revaluation of the worth of physical labor played a critical role in remaking ancient attitudes into medieval ones.

Labor was necessary for the monastery to survive as a self-sufficient economic unit. In the imploding economic world of the sixth and seventh centuries, monasteries had, in theory, to supply all that they required for survival. Labor was organized and purposive; the storage, rationing, and provisioning of food and drink, heating materials, and clothing had to be planned. Benedictine monasteries became small islands of economic efficiency while the work-a-day societies outside the monastery's walls knew a more haphazard economic life. By their example, monasteries demonstrated to their world the value not only of manual labor and collective enterprise, but of rational planning and expenditure as well. Monasteries became economic exemplars for surrounding communities. Despite being self-contained economic units, monasteries needed commodities such as salt and wine that they often could not supply from their own lands. They did not always acquire these on the open market, but through trade with other monasteries. Over time, monasteries acquired (generally as gifts) extensive properties, often geographically dispersed, from which they received income and resources. Monastic isolation from the world may have been a spiritual goal but was never economically or socially achievable. Important monasteries attracted the poor and the sick, who would gather at their gates in the hope of receiving charity, food, and miraculous cures.

Monasticism was the first great success story of the Early Middle Ages in the west—over three hundred new monasteries were founded in Francia (Frankish lands) alone in the seventh century—but its triumph was one of extreme localization, each monastery being a well-ordered and self-sufficient local organization. Not just the early medieval economy, but also learning benefited from the spread of monasticism. The emphasis in Benedict's *Rule* on daily reading and chanting meant that each monastery needed to train monks to read and write Latin and to supply them with books and scribal training. To learn Latin, particularly in northern Europe, monks used grammar books that were filled with classical citations as examples of good Latin, even though monks felt guilty about reading profane poetry and prose.

Early medieval monks copied their books on parchment (made from the skin of animals), a more durable surface than either the papyrus rolls of antiquity or modern paper. They chiefly reproduced the Bible and holy books, but they also made copies of the works of pagan antiquity. Without that copying, many of those texts (often written on perishable papyrus rolls) would have been lost. Benedictine monasticism institutionalized reading, writing, and the copying of books in a world that had lost much of its educational footing. To be learned or lettered in the Early Middle Ages became synonymous with being a monk.

The Benedictine monk was supposed to pray for four hours a day, to read for four hours a day, and to perform manual labor for five to six hours a day. This reading culture and the education of monks in Latin was one reason ancient culture and learning survived in the Middle Ages. It meant that the Middle Ages did not begin from scratch, but with a formal language of learning, books both religious and classical, and an educational anchor. That meant much to the survival and character of western civilization.

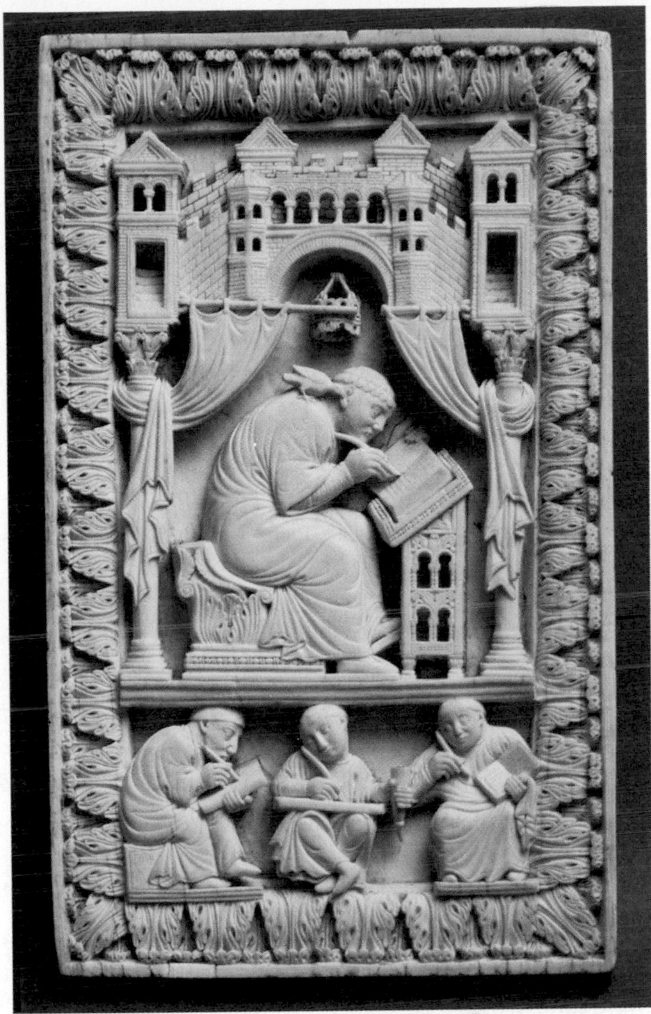

Gregory the Great and His Scribes The Holy Spirit, in the form of a dove, whispers divine words into the ear of Pope Gregory, who records the holy message and feeds off the divine inspiration. Below him, three monastic scribes copy down the saint's dictation. A ninth-century ivory book cover.

Gregory the Great and the Papacy

The early medieval papacy, at least prior to 750, was not the powerful institution that it would later become. With the breakdown of Roman order and the impoverishment of Italy, the pope in Rome was hardly more powerful than most other metropolitan bishops. The Lombards, a Germanic people originally from Pannonia, moved into northern Italy in the late sixth century and waged war against the eastern Roman outposts of Justinian's reconquest. The Italian peoples were not particularly fond of the eastern imperial presence, which taxed heavily and held a set of eastern theological beliefs (on such things as the nature of Christ) that were at odds with the theology of the Roman church.

The Lombards, like other German tribes, entered Italy as Arian Christians, but in 680 they became orthodox Christians, a conversion that still did not lead the papacy to accept their presence in Italy. The popes claimed territory throughout Italy and so were often in conflict with the Lombard kings and their nobles, who controlled territories both north and south of Rome. The long-term policy of the papacy was to try to dislodge the Lombards from Italy. With its territorial problems, doctrinal conflicts with the eastern church, and local power struggles with powerful noble families in Rome, the papacy remained as fragile as Italy was.

Pope Gregory the Great (590–604), the most dynamic and influential of early medieval popes, straddled several worlds. He was a propertied Roman aristocrat, one of whose ancestors had been pope. In his mid-thirties, when he was both a senator and the prefect of the city, he defended Rome against a Lombard assault. After that he abandoned the secular world to become a monk and founded a series of monasteries. He was soon recruited by the pope to serve as an emissary to the court of the Roman emperor. For six years he resided in Constantinople, accomplishing little, before returning to Rome and his monastic career. Gregory was elected pope in 590. His concerns and powers were chiefly those of a late Roman aristocrat. He used his own wealth to pay for the army that defended the city, and he bought the food that sustained the refugees and poor dribbling into Rome. His power over the various kings and peoples of Europe was almost nonexistent, and the distant eastern emperor was of little help in defending or provisioning the west.

Gregory was an effective aristocrat and bishop of his immediate lands and people, but he also labored to make the papacy a moral force in the west, emphasizing humility and charity as papal ideals. He actively promoted monasticism, even supplying an account in his *Dialogues* of the life of Saint Benedict. He also wrote a *Pastoral Rule* that detailed how bishops should tend their flocks. His pen (as much as his service as pope) worked to shape the Early Middle Ages. He was an avid protector of papal property, striving to preserve Rome's claim to central Italy as a papal kingdom called the Patrimony of Saint Peter. He tried with limited success to exercise power over western bishops, but though they might defer to him on general and spiritual issues, they resisted his intervention in their local affairs.

Like other great administrators, Gregory seized on new opportunities when he saw them. He placed the papacy at the head of the continuing conversion of Europe. One day in the marketplace of Rome he saw some blond-haired boys being sold as slaves. On discovering that they were from Britain, he organized a mission to the island led by one of his own monks, Augustine (not the famous writer and northern African bishop), who knew little about England, including its languages. Augustine established his Roman mission at Canterbury and set about slowly Christianizing Britain.

Augustine of Canterbury took his orders from Rome. Pope Gregory ordered the division of England into two chief provinces with one metropolitan bishop in Canterbury and the other in the north at York. Each metropolitan bishop was to receive his appointment and authority in the form of the *pallium* (a mantle of white wool) directly from the pope. By the pope's authority, each metropolitan bishop consecrated twelve ordinary bishops. Thus, unlike the disorganized episcopal arrangements of continental Europe, the tighter ecclesiastical organization of England under Gregory the Great hints at a plan for organizing the church under tighter papal supervision.

Bishops as the Great Mediators

Bishops, rather than popes, were the essential ecclesiastical actors of the Early Middle Ages, mediating between the powerful, the church, and ordinary people. Given the intense localization of early medieval life, it could hardly have been otherwise. There were no capital cities, no centralized governments, and no effective means of quick and reliable communication. As Roman imperial government first shriveled and then disappeared from much of the west, bishops stepped in to act as the chief administrators of the shrinking and insecure cities of Europe. The extreme localization of life enhanced the power and standing of bishops.

One example is Gregory of Tours, who became the bishop of Tours in 573. Like most early medieval bishops, he was born into a rich, landed, aristocratic family. Thirteen previous bishops of Tours belonged to his family; only five did not. Episcopal dynasties were common in the west, but, although they worked to stabilize older aristocratic power, they threatened the independence of the church by placing it under the control of family monopolies.

A bishop's appointment was for life. Whereas the local count with whom he shared authority over a region might be replaced or transferred to another area, the bishop stayed put. The count's interests were those of the king and his own family, particularly the desire to profit from the land. The bishop had a higher, Christian calling as well as the duty of a late Roman patron to dispense charity and grant jobs and promotions. He was the center of what remained of the urban traditions of the west; his church organized religious festivals and so governed the rhythms of local life.

Gregory of Tours promoted justice and peace within his **diocese** (the area of the bishop's jurisdiction) and city. When two men in Tours were engaged in a blood feud, it was Gregory who gave one of the men the money needed to end the dispute. The interests of the Merovingian count, who was the official arbiter of justice, were largely mercenary and private; he would not have paid a thin denarius to settle a private dispute. What remained of any higher notion of the public good came to rest with the bishop, not the king or his count. The bishop and not the count looked after public works (the repair of cities and civic improvement projects). The count lived outside the city in a great villa and had little interest in maintaining a city if it cost him.

Gregory of Tours sought to be a good bishop. He oversaw the rebuilding of churches, including the cathedral of Tours, which had burned down before he took office. He tended to his flock as best he could, but when disease struck in 580, killing many children in his diocese, he confessed that he could do little more than weep. One wonders if the local count did even that. As bishop,

Gregory visited the various monasteries of his diocese and investigated their way of life and faith. He also acted on behalf of the church in Gaul. When a nun at the monastery of Saint Radegund in Poitiers planned, with a motley crew of cutthroats and fornicators (Bishop Gregory's characterization of them), to murder the abbess and assume her position, Gregory intervened to restore peace and order. He also carefully supervised the vast properties of his church and their hundreds of workers.

Gregory of Tours also resisted heresy, writing powerfully against Arians and other dissenters. Like Pope Gregory the Great, Gregory of Tours influenced the Middle Ages chiefly through his many writings, the most famous being the *History of the Franks,* which laid out the history of Merovingian Gaul during its first century. As the most learned men in Gaul, Gallo-Roman bishops served as advisors to the king and local nobles. Bishops bridged the divide between the German rulers of the land and the Gallo-Roman people, running interference between them, counseling the king on justice, and urging the Franks to live Christian lives.

The Saints Come Marching In

The role of Gregory of Tours and his fellow bishops as the keepers of the saints meant something to King Clovis and his quarrelsome clan. One indication of that royal respect is that kings and counts honored the right of sanctuary. No matter the crime, if men and women made their way to a church and were granted sanctuary, they were generally safe from forcible removal by secular authorities. In keeping with their relatively primitive conception of Christianity and their recognition of the necessity of the church and its bishops, Merovingian rulers were reluctant to anger the saints whose remains rested in churches. As an avid promoter of the saints, Gregory of Tours wrote several books about their lives and miracles. He and his fellow bishops promoted the cult of the saints because they saw the saints as a way to harness the energy of their people and to humble arrogant and aggressive rulers.

To understand the early medieval mind and the power of religion, we need to appreciate how important and alive the saints were to the Early Middle Ages. Saints (from the Latin *sancti,* "holy ones") and saintliness do not have the particular institutional presence and character in the Bible that they assumed in the Middle Ages. In a world of untreatable disease, looming starvation, greedy German nobles who were a law unto themselves, and lawlessness in the countryside of Europe, men and women wanted someone, anyone, to look out for them. Saints seemed to offer supernatural protection, a power of first and last resort for the anxious and suffering. In the Early Middle Ages, saintly status was conferred not by a papal commission, but by the general consensus of a community. If enough people thought that Christopher was a saint and were devoted to him, then Christopher was a saint, no matter that he was reputed to have been either a giant or a dog-headed man. Such cults were promoted by institutions and influential people for whom the saint was a celebrated wonder-worker.

Medieval Christians believed that the saints had risen into heaven to stand beside Christ, where they received prayers from the faithful and interceded on their behalf with God. Since the saints had done holy works and the martyrs had died for Christ, they had built up a repository of holy credits to draw on in heaven. People in Gregory of Tours's time thought of Christ as omnipotent, too distant and austere for the average person to reach directly. They did not yet think of his mother, the Virgin Mary, as a great intercessory figure, so the saint was a closer, more approachable, and more persuasive advocate for their needs. The power to intercede in the world was Christ's, but the saint had his ear.

The cult of the saints and their **relics** did not arise spontaneously. It was a belief cultivated and channeled by bishops. Ambrose, the bishop of Milan (374–397), was one of the first to promote the cult of the saints' relics. Relics are the remains left behind by the saints, generally their bones, but also objects such as clothes and books with which they had come into contact. Although Jesus, according to the Gospels, had wholly risen to heaven at the Ascension, the things he had touched such as the

The Remains of the Saints The skeleton of Saint Ambrose—with those of Saints Gervasius and Protasius flanking his—are on display in his cathedral in Milan. The architect of the cult of relics thus became a revered relic himself.

cross of the crucifixion were considered contact relics. In 386, Ambrose discovered the remains of the saints Gervasius and Protasius and duly installed them in his church in Milan, where they still rest. Later he sent relics to bishops in the north so that they might dedicate their churches to the saints; altars were consecrated with relics of the saints.

The cult of the saints and their relics emerged after the legalization of Christianity and the Christianization of the empire. Without the ideology of martyrdom, which had sustained the church during periods of persecution, the Christian faith, particularly in the west, seemed less purpose driven, the claims of holiness less obvious. The church promoted the saints as athletes of God and the west's new heroes, but the sanctity of living humans was difficult to determine. In an age of cooling faith, Bishop Ambrose found another way to refresh the passion of the faithful. By enshrining the remains of saints in his church, he localized and renewed holiness. People from near and far knew where they could find the divine and they could witness holiness in action.

Ambrose and the churchmen were convinced that the saints had not really died, but had been reborn in heaven. The saints were thought to be entirely present and powerful in their earthly remains, no matter how small the fragment. Thus early medieval men and women thought of dead saints as still alive and active in the world. The saints could, through their appeals to Christ, bring about the healing of the sick, the exorcism of the possessed, and the granting of grace to the remorseful. The miracles brought about through the saints were small signs for them that the miracle of Christ's resurrection was still at work in the world.

Promoting the cult of the saints and their relics gave bishops not just symbolic, but real power. By managing the cult, Ambrose, Gregory of Tours, and other bishops were able to bring the scattered holiness of the saints inside their cathedrals where they could present, guard, and direct it. The Merovingian kings knew where Saint Martin was; he was in Tours, and Bishop Gregory served as the intercessor to a saint who could intercede with God. Cathedrals that enshrined famous saints reaped financial gains from the pilgrims who sought out the saints, but profit may not have been the primary motive for promoting the cult of the saints. Rather, the bishops' goal was to bring a source of tangible divine power under their immediate control to enhance their own prestige and that of their cathedrals. Bishops were not always saintly men themselves. Gregory of Tours said that one of his predecessors had drunk himself into a state of dementia and death. Personal holiness was too great an aspiration for living men, even the two Gregories, pope and bishop, who managed properties and granted and sought earthly favors. It was much better for them to stand next to the holy, to offer themselves as the guardians and earthly representatives of the saints, than to claim saintliness for themselves.

In the fragmented and localized west, the cult of the saints, like monasticism and the power of bishops, was another indication of how the west was remaking itself institutionally and intellectually in the Early Middle Ages.

Power at the Start of the Middle Ages

Germanic kingship was very different from Roman imperial government. Built on different assumptions and actions, Germanic kingship met the needs of its time, supplying a simplified world with a simple form of military might and local power. Events in the Middle East, however, directly and indirectly transformed the lands and legacy of the Roman Empire. The rapid religious and territorial rise of Islam in the seventh century pushed the Roman Empire to become a Byzantine Empire in the east and fully medieval in the west, determining what those two parts of the old Roman Empire could be and could no longer be. By its territorial, cultural, and religious impact, Islam shaped the contours of the Middle Ages.

How did the organization and exercise of power differ in western Europe, the eastern Roman Empire, and Islam in the Early Middle Ages?

Germanic Kingship: Long Hair and the Privatization of Power

With the withering of Roman imperial power in the west, notions of the public good and public citizenship disappeared from the administration and countryside of Europe. In the ancient world, men and women had lived in a world of public streets, public baths, public games, and temples that opened onto public squares. As cities shrank in the fifth and sixth centuries, private villas and rural conditions reclaimed the medieval west. As the public person disappeared, so too did sophisticated notions of a state government operating with a senate, a bureaucracy, and a standing army; indeed, the state as such ceased to exist in the west.

The disappearance of the state did not mean that the Franks ruled without operating principles. Those principles just were no longer based on Roman law or the good of the people and Roman elite as they once had been. Every age may get not only the government that it deserves, but also the one that it needs under the prevailing conditions that it faces. In this case, that government had a mobile, not fixed, base of power commanded by a dominant source of authority, the most accomplished leader available, whose chief interest was in self-preservation and the control of whatever force he could assemble. Germanic kingship fulfilled the need for a specific form of control in the disordered fifth and sixth centuries.

The fundamental source of all authority was the king (*rex*), the chief who most successfully commanded a warband of men by winning its obedience through the careful exercise of brute force and timely reward. Around

500, the title of king carried fewer ideas of blood inheritance and divine sanction than it would later, connoting instead the successful general of an army. To maintain his dominance, the king needed to carry out successful military campaigns, seize territory, and distribute lands and wealth to his men. The members of a war-band were not interested in the public good or responsible government, but rather in the private interests of themselves and their families. Such self-interest may sound like a recipe for disaster, but instead it produced the most successful and realistic form of rule possible. The Germanic war-band was a dynamic, though unstable, unit driven to succeed in the subjugation of lands and peoples.

Early medieval Germanic kings were itinerant; they moved within their kingdoms and set up many palaces. Their mobility was not just a continuation of the older restless wanderings of the Germanic tribes, but a necessity in an age in which no single villa could long support the king and his retinue. The king's retinue would soon exhaust the resources of a place if it stayed too long. The essence of the palace was not a building but its resident king. Merovingian government was palace government, and its officials took titles that originally derived from their domestic functions in that palace operation: butlers, cup-bearers, stewards, constables, and grooms.

Germanic kings might hold kingdoms, but they had only a weak idea of a territorially defined kingdom with fixed borders. The king was more truly the king of a people than of a land. The Merovingian king was *rex Francorum,* the king of the Franks, not the king of Francia. These kings and their nobles thought of their property, both fixed (land) and movable (gold and wealth), as divisible among their heirs. When a king died, his kingdom was divided equally among his heirs. Armed conflict and assassinations often followed, leading Gallo-Romans to associate disorder and violence with their Frankish kings. Gregory of Tours did not understand that these wars were dynamic tests of merit that ensured that the strongest, cleverest, and most violent rulers rose to the top and imposed their will on the Frankish nobles and kingdom.

An example of the different cultural world of the Germans is the matter of their hair. Gregory of Tours says that when the Franks occupied Francia, they set up long-haired kings in every *civitas* (a district having a major city). Both male and female Germans prided themselves on keeping their hair long as a sign of their free status and ethnicity. Slaves were shorn and Roman free males generally kept their hair short. What was typical for the average free-born Frank was extreme in the case of their kings and members of the royal line. Scissors never touched their hair from the time of birth. When a king was overthrown, his hair was cut to humiliate him and to signal his reduced status. Gregory of Tours tells the heartrending story of two Merovingian kings who wished to remove two nephews from any chance of succeeding to power. The uncles sent a messenger to their own mother, the boys' grandmother and guardian. In one hand the agent carried a pair of scissors, in the other a sword. The grandmother was forced to choose between having her grandchildren shorn or killed; she chose death for them since she preferred to see them dead rather than denied the chance to rule as kings. Such was the world of Frankish kingship, which Gregory of Tours, with his Gallo-Roman values and Roman sense of justice, could not completely comprehend.

Living and Dying the Merovingian Way

The Franks comprised a relatively small portion of the total population of Gaul, perhaps as many as 200,000 people in the midst of a Gallo-Roman population of about seven million. Noble Franks were buried with rich treasures of grave goods: belt buckles, purses, daggers, and jeweled swords. These burial plots were organized according to kin groups. The early Franks practiced polygyny (one man, several wives). Merovingian lords sought to exercise a monopoly over the available wombs, for this was a world in which, no matter how rich and powerful one was, wives frequently died in childbirth and few infants lived to adulthood. Infant mortality hovered around 50 to 60 percent.

The economy of early medieval Francia was almost exclusively agricultural. Farmers grew grain crops such as barley and raised domestic animals. Most tools were made of wood, as were most buildings. Artisans made luxury goods for the Frankish and Gallo-Roman elites, but there were few other markets for precious goods.

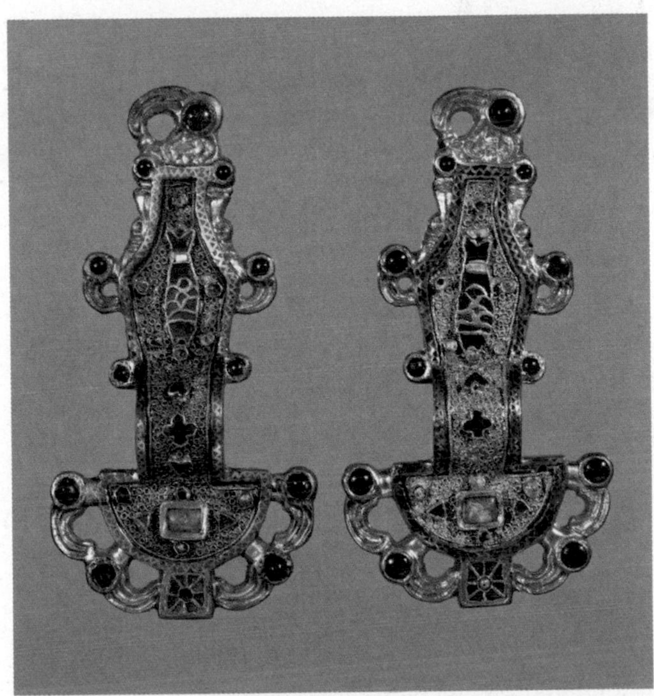

Frankish Ornament A jewel-encrusted Frankish brooch or clasp found in the tomb of a Merovingian woman who died in the mid-sixth century. The combination of animal imagery, rich decoration, gold, and cloisonné (poured enamel) was typical of Frankish ornament.

Some long-distance trade in bulk items such as slaves, salt, and spices still took place, and some prosperity did exist. Gregory of Tours reports that the merchants of Verdun were able to stand behind a loan of seven thousand gold pieces made by the Frankish king to their bishop.

Early medieval Francia was dominated by villages that were little more than a series of thatched huts marked off from the outside world by walls and hedge fences. The houses in these villages were small (6 × 6–12 feet), with approximately 50–60 square feet of floor space, but people were also relatively small, the average height for both sexes being around five feet.

Merovingian Power at the Political Turn

When Clovis died in 511, his four sons almost immediately began trying to kill one another. One of them, Theuderic, invited his brother Clothar to a meeting in order to assassinate him, but Clothar spotted the feet of assassins below a curtain and fled. Another of the sons died while fighting the Burgundians, who mounted his head on a pole. By 558, Clothar had by luck and design outlived his brothers and reunited the kingdom. King Clothar was ambitious, invading parts of Germany, but he died three years later. The kingdom was then divided between his four sons and the wars began again. Over the long run, these wars of succession shifted power to the nobles on whom the kings increasingly relied for support.

By the early seventh century, the strongest men in the land, Bishop Arnulf of Metz and Pepin of Landen, the mayor (or chief official) of the Merovingian palace (or government) of Austrasia (the eastern kingdom), became the founders of the Carolingian line. The marriage of their children joined their two lines. Arnulf and Pepin placed the Merovingian Clothar II (r. 613–629) on the throne. Thus, Clothar II and his son Dagobert (r. 629–639) were made kings by two nobles of the Carolingian house of Ripuarian (or Rhineland) Franks. Clothar and Dagobert were the last Merovingian kings to hold real power, and yet even they were already the creatures of their nobles. The year 613, thus, marked the great turn of the Merovingian house from independence and autonomy toward dependent status; the balance of power had swung in favor of their powerful nobles.

The case of Dagobert is revealing. Mocked in a French nursery rhyme as a feeble king who couldn't put on his own pants and was afraid of rabbits, he was, in fact, a warrior king, but his power and success were limited. He lost an important battle to the Slavs in 631 whereupon, with his nobles in Austrasia in revolt, he ceded effective control of the region to his mayor, Pepin of Landen. But though Dagobert was a less than dominant ruler of Francia, he was a better Christian than most of his predecessors. He was pious, heeded his bishops, and established the great royal monastery of St. Denis outside Paris, where he was buried in 639.

With the mayors of the palace, particularly the Pippinids or Arnulfings (both early names for the line that became the Carolingians), on the rise and Merovingian royal power in decline, the fate of Clovis's line was not promising by the mid-seventh century. At that very moment in the Middle East, a movement was stirring that would dramatically affect the shape and conditions of the Early Middle Ages east and west.

Islam Ascendant

In 610 a forty-year-old merchant of Mecca in Arabia began to receive messages from God, which the archangel Gabriel commanded him to recite in the name of God. Muhammad did not claim to be divine, but rather understood himself to be a prophet or messenger like Moses. Although Muhammad respected both Christians and Jews as peoples who knew God and had a great book of revealed (or divine) truth, he rejected the Christian conviction that Jesus was the son of God and thought that the Jews had forsaken God's message. A community (***Ummah***) of believers, the people of God, took shape around Muhammad and submitted itself to the will of

CHRONOLOGY The Rise and Spread of Islam

DATE	EVENT
570	Birth of Muhammad in Mecca
622	Hejira
632	Death of Muhammad in Medina
632–634	Caliph Abu Bakr
634–644	Caliph Umar
636	Islam conquers Syria
638	Jerusalem conquered
641–642	Egypt conquered
644–656	Caliph Uthman
651	Persia conquered
656–661	Caliph Ali, son-in-law of the prophet
661–750	Umayyad Caliphate rules from Damascus
698	Carthage conquered
712	Samarkand and Sogdiana conquered
711–720	Most of Spain conquered
750–1258	Abbasid Caliphate rules from Baghdad

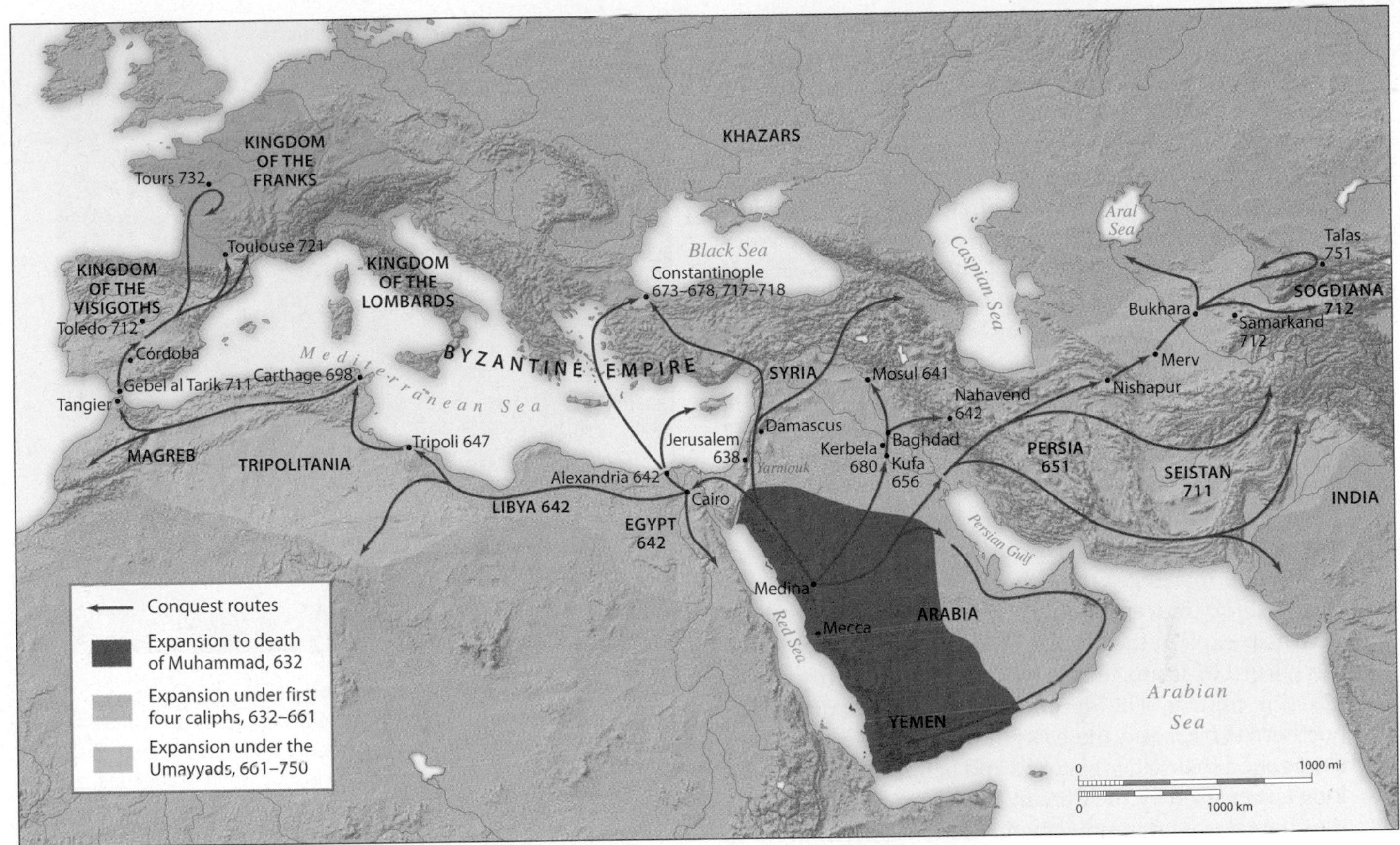

MAP 7.1 | **Spread of Islam to 750**
Within two centuries after Muhammad's death in 632, Islam had conquered the Near East, lands along the southern Mediterranean Sea, and parts of Asia. ***What did the expansion of Islam mean for lands previously part of the Roman Empire? Why were the Byzantine Empire and Spain the doorways for Islam into continental Europe? What impact did the territorial dominance of the Mediterranean by Muslims have on the western economy? How might Islam have provided a critical link for the flow of goods east and west?***

God. The word *Islam* means submission to the will of God, and a *Muslim* is one who has submitted to the will of God.

For twelve years, Muhammad preached with limited success to the people of Mecca. Their paganism and stubbornness made Muhammad's revelations a tough sell in the dusty streets of the old city. In 622 Muhammad fled to Medina, an event called the ***Hejira*** that marks the beginning of Islamic chronology. Muhammad's messages from God were collected and written down in Arabic in the Qur'an (Koran) within twenty years after Muhammad's death in 632. Other testimonies and narratives about the prophet Muhammad, his life and sayings (called *hadiths*), that survive outside the Qur'an have been sifted for their trustworthiness and importance.

The basic teachings of Islam as found in the Qur'an are straightforward. The Five Pillars of Islam are as follows: (1) there is only one God and his name is Allah and he must be obeyed; (2) Muslims are obliged to pray five times a days (facing Mecca); (3) give charity; (4) fast during daylight hours of the (lunar) month of Ramadan each year; and (5) undergo a pilgrimage (*Hajj*) to Mecca once in a lifetime. Islam has implications for the state since it teaches that there is only one society under the will of God (theocracy, or rule by God, is the result), and it follows a code of sacred law (***shari'ah***) determined by legal scholars based on the Qur'an, the traditions of Muhammad, community standards, and precedents. Thus, whereas Christian religious thought turned chiefly to matters of theology, Islamic thought would center primarily on God's law.

Islam's rapid spread shook the Middle East and the Mediterranean world (Map 7.1). By the time of Muhammad's death, Muslims dominated much of the Arabian Peninsula. The message of Islam overrode traditional tribal customs, directing not just the spiritual lives of Muslims, but most aspects of their interior and exterior lives. Tribal culture had been shame culture in which public honor and public shame were the chief elements of social reward and control. Islam subordinated human activity instead to God's judgment or law and the promise of rewards or punishment in the afterlife. In the shift from one to the other, Islam united diverse Arabian peoples under a common cause and shared set of beliefs. The Qur'an, as a book of law and rules, mediated cultural differences and divisions. Of the Qur'an's 114 suras (or individual chapters, organized from longest to shortest), some speak of the holy war (**jihad**) that Muhammad eventually led against the unbelievers, but jihad can also refer to an individual's personal calling to conform to God's will.

By uniting the Arabs and many of the Bedouin tribes of Arabia against the unbelievers inside the Arabian Peninsula and then against unbelievers outside, Muhammad not only spread the faith but pacified Arabia. After Muhammad's death, the first target of expansionary Islam was Syria, which was overrun in 636, when a Roman force was defeated at the Battle of Yarmouk. Jerusalem fell in 638; and most of Egypt, by 641. By 651, Persia was conquered; and northern Africa, all the way to Carthage, was taken by 698. Samarkand and Sogdiana had fallen by 712; and most of Spain, by 720. Thus, within a century of Muhammad's death, the southern part of the Mediterranean rim was in Muslim hands, and Islam had spread east into Asia and west into Europe. The big Europe of the old Roman Empire was shrinking fast.

Just as surprising as the relatively rapid spread of Islam was the permanence of the change to the western world. New military movements and the mobilization of peoples may help explain the success of the conquests, but it was the nature of Islam that fixed these lands firmly under Muslim control. The decadent old Roman cultures of northern Africa and the eastern Mediterranean quickly abandoned their older histories and beliefs. Many peoples long suppressed by the Roman Empire may have felt that the change was an improvement. Islam was tolerant of the other peoples of the book. Christians and Jews could continue to practice their own faith and retain their property. What Christians could not do was to convert Muslims, speak ill of Islam, or display the Christian cross. The effect of these regulations was to render churches such as the Christian church in Egypt (the Coptic Church) respected, but prevented from expanding. Non-Muslims had to accept an inferior or marginal status within Islam and pay tribute in place of the military service that Muslims rendered. Conversion to Islam offered some financial and social advantages to Christians and Jews, as well as the chance to assume public offices otherwise denied to them.

Not all went smoothly for Islam, however, since neither the Qur'an nor Muhammad had specified who should succeed him. Three rival factions emerged: those who wanted Ali, Muhammad's son-in-law and cousin, to assume control; the merchants of Mecca, who longed to see one of their number named; and Muhammad's early converts, who had supported him in Mecca and marched with him on Medina, and had their own candidate, Abu Bakr. The last group prevailed, and so for two years Abu Bakr (r. 632–634), called the caliph (successor), was the leader of Islam, and was succeeded by three other Rashidun ("rightly guided caliphs"), the companions of the prophet: Umar (r. 634–644), Uthman (r. 644–656), and Ali (r. 656–661).

Uthman's murder and disputed succession produced a schism within Islam that still endures. Although Ali was the revered son-in-law of the prophet, he was not supported by the whole Islamic community. A group known as the **Kharijites** withdrew their support from Ali and accused him of lacking an absolute trust in God's judgment.

The Great Mosque of Damascus Erected c. 700, the Great Mosque stands as a pinnacle of the cultural richness of Islam and the Umayyad Caliphate. In 750, the Abbasid Caliphate displaced the Umayyads and moved the capital of the Islamic world to Baghdad.

Theirs was an elitist view of Islam, in which only the purest and deeply committed believers should be counted within the Islamic community. As caliph, Ali labored under the charge of illegitimacy and was assassinated by a Kharijite follower in 661. For the Shi'a (or partisans of Ali), this was a dividing point in history. They maintain that Muhammad's authority flowed through Ali, the first imam (ruler), to his successor imams who possess divine inspiration and an inner or hidden knowledge of the Qur'an. They also believe that the twelfth or hidden imam, Muhammad al-Mahdi, did not die, but disappeared in 874 and is expected to return to render justice. Shi'as take the murder of Ali as a model of martyrdom and of the suffering that believers and rulers can expect in this life.

Shi'ism was and remains a prominent minority sect within Islam. The majority of Muslims are Sunnis who adhere to tradition (*sunnah*), and reject the elitism of the Kharijites and the exclusivity of descent followed by the Shi'as. Sunnis recognize the dominant caliphate tradition and tend to think of their rulers as human and temporal leaders with no particular divine connection, but who are supposed to act as defenders of the faith and caretakers of the law. Thus, Sunnis embrace the primacy of the Islamic community as a whole.

After Ali, the Umayyad Caliphate (661–750) moved the capital of the Islamic world from Medina to Damascus. The Umayyads were little interested in converting peoples within Islamic lands because the unconverted paid higher taxes. During this brilliant Arabic phase of Islamic culture, Muslims erected magnificent buildings in Damascus and Jerusalem.

MAP 7.2 | Byzantine Empire, 8th Century

By the eighth century, the Byzantine Empire was confined largely to southern Italy, Sicily, a scattering of lands in the eastern Mediterranean, and a large block of territory to the east of Constantinople. Those lands were divided into administrative units called themes. ***What were the territorial strengths and weaknesses of the Byzantine Empire? Had the empire any room for expansion?***

The Eastern Roman Empire Becomes Byzantine

Seventy-five years after Justinian's death, Roman imperial fortunes were in eclipse. The Persians, Avars, and Muslims whittled away imperial territory. In the process, the eastern Roman Empire lost control of the Mediterranean, suffered a great military defeat to the Muslims, lost the rich lands of Syria and Egypt, and looked far across the Bosporus Straits to a world dominated by a new and dynamic religion with superior resources and manpower. The Romans resisted as best they could under the emperor Heraclius (r. 610–641), but he found that Constantinople had so neglected its provinces during its resistance to the Persians and Avars that few of its residents were willing to resist Muslim forces.

By the early eighth century, Muslim armies were attacking Asia Minor regularly, but failed to take Constantinople in 717–718. Following that successful resistance, the Roman east underwent a period of recovery and transformation. In effect, the eastern Roman Empire became what we think of as Byzantine because of the rise of Islam. The Byzantine identity was shaped and fixed by the events of the seventh and eighth centuries: it embraced a specific eastern orthodox form of Christianity, was thoroughly Greek with little Latin influence, and concentrated on Constantinople and the Greek northeast of the Mediterranean world without any realistic prospect of restoring the old Roman Empire (Map 7.2).

The emperor Leo III (r. 717–741) reorganized the empire so that it could defend itself against internal and external enemies. He taxed heavily, reorganized the army, and strengthened the walls of Constantinople. Leo also forced the Byzantines to rethink their religion. He was displeased by the importance that monasticism held in the Byzantine east and jealous of the tax privileges granted to its monasteries. He worked to bring the eastern church more firmly under his control, even overthrowing one patriarch of the eastern church.

During the difficult years of contraction, the Byzantine peoples had turned for reassurance to holy images, particularly of the Virgin Mary. Byzantine soldiers, to whom Leo looked for the defense of the empire, however, had their doubts. They suspected that they were so often defeated by their Muslim opponents because they worshipped graven images against God's law. The Byzantine peoples believed that the icon or image was a tangible connection to the divine, much as saints' relics functioned in the west. Leo, however, believed that the worship of icons diverted people from the true faith; he and his advisors knew that both the Old Testament and Islam spurned idols and graven images. In 726, Leo banned icons and declared that they should be destroyed. People revolted, and in the west the pope and a church council condemned the iconoclasts (image-breakers), excommunicating them. Yet Leo and his son, Constantine V (r. 740–745), persisted in their official policy of **iconoclasm.** Constantine persecuted the image worshippers with greater relish and more violence than his father had, but he was also a successful military leader, ordering regular attacks on the Muslims and conducting war against the Bulgarians and Slavs.

The Iconoclasm Dispute The Byzantine Empire swung hard from official iconoclasm and the destruction of images to iconodulism or the veneration of images. In the ninth-century Chludov Psalter, an illustrator takes his revenge against the iconoclasts by mocking the crudity of the iconoclasts, one of whom is shown erasing a picture of Christ.

Byzantium survived its first great conflict with Islam, but the cost was great. With a reduced and still threatened territory, Byzantium was forced to militarize the state. Its official theological turn not only confounded the Byzantine peoples but drove a theological wedge between the east and west. Islam thus played a critical role in forcing Byzantium to redefine itself and forced the entire western world in directions it might not otherwise have gone.

Carolingian House Building

The Carolingians went from being a successful Frankish family in the sixth century to the noble house that managed the Merovingian dynasty in the seventh and then pushed it aside in the mid-eighth century to set up its own royal dynasty. Fifty years later the Carolingians controlled an empire that dominated the medieval west. Their success and ultimate failure determined much of the territorial and cultural character of the Middle Ages: royal and Christian, papal and Germanic, learned and Latinate, multiregional and European.

How and why did the Carolingians replace the Merovingian royal line?

The Carolingian Mayors

Merovingian Gaul was divided into three rough areas: Austrasia (the east land of German speakers), Neustria (the new land of Vulgar or late Latin speakers), and Burgundy (stretching from Langres to the Mediterranean). Each area had its own mayor of the palace (*maior domo*) or chief executive officer acting on behalf of the king of that territory. In theory the difference between a king and his mayor was that the king possessed a legitimacy confirmed by his nobles or people and the mayor was a royal operative whose office derived its legitimacy from the king; in practice the question became who had effective power and could command the loyalty and service of the nobles of a kingdom. The mayors found that, as the Merovingian dynasty experienced periodic bouts of civil war, turmoil, and the reigns of young kings, their own importance as king-makers and power-brokers increased. Not only did the Merovingian kings need them more, but lesser nobles came to associate their own standing and privileges with the mayor rather than the king. Mayoral power grew in the late seventh and early eighth centuries under the so-called Do-Nothing (Merovingian) Kings of France whom historians once mocked as lazy, powerless, and nameless. The Merovingian royal condition may not have been fatal, but the Merovingian kings slowly lost power and property until little was left and their dynasty was overthrown.

The Carolingian family was nothing if not ambitious. Around 656 one of its mayors, Grimoald, tried to graft his own family onto the Merovingian family tree by banishing the rightful Merovingian prince and naming his own son as king. Other Frankish nobles rejected the rash move and put the mayor to death. Had Grimoald succeeded, the Merovingian line would have continued, but with a Carolingian intruder as the sitting Merovingian king. Grimoald's failure did not put a stop to the Carolingian rise. In 687, Pepin of Heristal defeated the non-Carolingian mayors of the other two palaces (of Neustria and Burgundy) and united the mayoralty, thus becoming the effective ruler of all Francia.

INVESTIGATING THE PAST

Henri Pirenne and His Thesis

If the recent past is difficult to unscramble, the distant past may seem at times largely unknowable. Whereas the historian studying modern history often has too many primary sources, the ancient and medieval historian frequently has too few. Professional historians are by nature cautious creatures, couching their statements about the past in "perhapses" and "maybes." They know all too well that a single new piece of evidence may lead to the radical revision of today's confident conclusions.

The last book of the Belgian historian Henri Pirenne makes a powerful case for direct speaking and bold thinking. Toward the end of a long life of careful, qualified scholarship on Belgian, urban, and medieval economic history, Pirenne laid down a daring new explanation for how the ancient world became the Middle Ages. He had just completed a draft of the book that became *Mohammed and Charlemagne* when he died. It was his habit, said his son, to write the first draft of a work just for himself; there he put down his ideas in their boldest form. It was that version of *Mohammed and Charlemagne* that his son and a former student, the medievalist F. Vercauteren, published in 1937.

The book put forward a daring thesis: that it was the rise of Islam that essentially made the medieval west. Pirenne observed that the effective loss of the Mediterranean Sea had brought an end to the ancient world, forcing western civilization northward and inland, and that Charlemagne with his northern capital in Aachen and his land-based empire was the end result. As Pirenne famously put it, "Charlemagne, without Mohammed, would be inconceivable." Pirenne's argument was based on economic evidence such as the lack of Byzantine coins in the west after 629 and the dramatic shift in the nature of European trade and settlement.

The beauty of Pirenne's thesis is its concision; its great weakness that the events and evidence it seeks to explain so simply are frustratingly complex. Almost from the day the book appeared, it aroused denial, qualification, and support from different quarters. Archaeologists such as Richard Hodges have wondered if the thesis actually fits the available evidence. Moreover, Michael McCormick, in his monumental *Origins of the European Economy: Communications and Commerce, AD 300–900* (2001), demonstrated that throughout the late Roman and early medieval periods both people and goods continued to travel east and west, south and north.

Still it is hard to deny Pirenne's essential observation that the Early Middle Ages moved away from the Mediterranean toward northern Europe or that the rise of Islam had irrevocably broken the hegemony of the classical world, whose ghost had lingered for so long and so grandly.

QUESTIONS | ***How did the rise of Islam impact the West? Did it do so immediately or gradually? What are the advantages and disadvantages of making sweeping historical generalizations of the sort that Pirenne made in his last book?***

Pepin of Heristal's illegitimate son was Charles Martel, Charles "the Hammer" (d. 741), after whom the Carolingians (derived from *Carolus*) are named. With Charles Martel, the Carolingians entered on the road to kingship. He convened his own court of royal justice, issued decrees and laws, and assembled and led the royal army of nobles. He was as vigorous a warrior as his nickname suggests. In 732 (or 733) between Tours and Poitiers he stopped the forward advance into Francia of Muslims from Spain who were making their farthest northern incursion into Europe. That victory has probably been overrated as a turning point in European and Muslim fortunes since it coincided with changes in Spain and the Islamic world, but it did mark an end to Muslim expansion in the early medieval west. Charles Martel also led victorious campaigns into Bavaria and large parts of Germania, and made inroads into Saxony. He ruled with such confidence and relative autonomy that for a time he left the kingship vacant and ruled alone. Contemporaries called him a prince or petty king.

Pepin the Short Unmakes the Merovingian Line

When Charles Martel died in 741, Francia was divided between his two sons: Carloman became mayor of the palace of Austrasia; and Pepin the Short, mayor of the palace of Neustria. The division of Francia was now determined not by the heirs of the Merovingians, but by the interests of the Carolingian house. Although Charles Martel may not have needed a figurehead Merovingian ruler to buttress his power, his sons as fledgling mayors did, and so they elevated the obscure Merovingian Childeric III to be king (r. 743–751). Carloman and Pepin ruled in relative harmony, but in 747 Carloman retired to become a monk. Contemporaries claimed that his withdrawal was voluntary, but it was also convenient as it removed a key impediment to Pepin's drive to royal power.

But how could a new royal line be made or an old one unmade? Medieval theory maintained that God, not men, makes kings. As real Merovingian power and property were being stripped away by the mayors in the seventh century, the mayors had enhanced the religious prestige and divine standing of the Merovingian king as a way to enhance their own power as the representatives of royal authority. The title of king, which had held less real importance to the warrior Clovis, came to matter a great deal, and the long hair of the Merovingian kings took on an almost magical significance. The aura of the divine could be replaced only with another powerful set of royal symbols, this one more thoroughly Christian.

Why the Carolingians decided to take the final step of overthrowing and replacing a royal line with their own may not be a great mystery. Pepin took the final step because he could; he had the power and saw how it could be done. His father, Charles Martel, had shown him that the real ruler of Francia did not need a symbolic figurehead through whom to rule. Indeed, there was a certain danger in continuing to rule under a weak king since other nobles might seek to use the king or prop up a pretender as their own vehicle to power. To be king, rather than acting in the king's name, would bring Pepin additional protection and power, justifying his exercise of power and lifting his family above the other noble families of Francia with whom it had been competing. Kingship did not put an end to the struggle between the king and his nobles, but it gave the Carolingians a more direct way than the mayoralty to control the powerful nobles of Europe. It also gave them, if they managed it right, some protection against a dip in family fortunes.

The religious significance of the change was great. Kingship brought divine approval and divine protection. The church wanted more from its kings than the Merovingians had supplied. That the Carolingians had for so long been able to make and unmake kings suggested that they could unmake and make royal lines. By 751 a particular set of conditions and careful Carolingian engineering of the circumstances made it possible for Pepin the Short to justify overthrowing the old royal line. What chiefly distinguished the Carolingians from the Merovingians was their attitude toward the church and Christianity. As Clovis had outmaneuvered the other Germanic tribes by becoming an orthodox Christian, the Carolingians outmaneuvered the Merovingians by becoming better Christians. The education of Pepin's sons at St. Denis and Carloman's abandonment of the world for the monastery were examples of the Christian commitment of the Carolingians. Nor did the Carolingians assassinate each other, as the Merovingians had.

The piety and political interests of the Carolingians were not at odds, for they saw the advantages of Christianizing Europe. Charles Martel used the church in Francia, dispensed church offices, and treated church property as though it were his own. The Carolingians viewed the Christian church as a legitimate instrument of royal power. Believing that the kingdom should be uniformly Christian, they actively promoted missionary work inside the kingdom. With the sanction of the papacy, Carolingian rulers sponsored the English monk Boniface's mission to outlying areas of the kingdom. In the intersection of papal and Carolingian interests in converting northern Europe to Christianity, the Carolingian family and the papacy forged a supportive and codependent relationship.

Why did the papacy need the Carolingians? The papacy was still relatively weak and recognized that it needed a temporal protector. The popes hoped that with the right cultivation the distant Carolingians would thwart the Lombards and yet not directly threaten papal interests in Italy. Hence, the papacy and the Carolingians entered into an understanding about their complementary interests: kingship for the Carolingians, protection against its enemies for the papacy.

To overthrow the Merovingians, Pepin and his advisors moved on several fronts. Pepin reputedly sent the pope an official question: who should rule, the man who merely bore the name of king or the man who actually held the power? The pope answered in Pepin's favor. Yet the Merovingians were born royal; the Carolingians had to become royal. The Carolingians supplied what they lacked in royal blood by external sanction and signs: papal approval, public election, royal symbol, and religious rite.

In November 751 a Frankish assembly gathered at Soissons. Childeric III was deposed, his hair was shaved off, and he was confined to a monastery. In a parallel rite, Pepin was elected king by the Franks (that is, he was acclaimed by his nobles), anointed by Bishop Boniface, and raised to the throne by his nobles. Thus, with words and symbols the church and the Frankish aristocracy sanctioned Pepin's elevation. He was now king of the Franks. Clovis had not needed extraordinary signs and supports of divine and earthly approval; Pepin did. Pepin honored his commitment to the papacy when he crossed the Alps and attacked the Lombards in 755 and, with the **Donation of Pepin,** returned lands in central Italy to the pope's control. The new alliance freed the papacy from its nominal dependence on the Byzantine Empire for assistance and protection that it could no longer supply.

The overthrow and replacement of a royal line was a delicate moment in the early medieval west. Around 757 a papal cleric in Rome produced a document known as the Donation of Constantine, in which the emperor Constantine granted the popes control over the lands and peoples of the west. The appearance of this false document, which was not shown to be a forgery until the fifteenth century, hints at the jockeying for position that was taking place in the 750s as the Merovingians disappeared, the Carolingians took their place, the Byzantines were preoccupied with eastern problems, and the popes were plotting the fall of the Lombards and their absolute territorial control of central Italy. The Donation presented the papacy's claim to western territorial control and its rejection of any Byzantine imperial claims to the same since Constantine had surrendered them to the pope. In 754, Pope Stephen came north to visit King Pepin, and at St. Denis he blessed and anointed not only Pepin as king, but also his sons Charlemagne and Carloman. The ceremony of 751 had been about Pepin, but the one in 754 was about the sanctification of his entire dynasty. Pope Stephen blessed Bertrada, Pepin's wife and the mother of his sons, and proclaimed that the Frankish people should never, on pain of interdict and excommunication, presume to choose any king from outside of Pepin's family. Thus, Pepin secured papal approval for the permanent elevation of his dynasty to royal standing. The Carolingians were Christian kings approved and anointed by God through his earthly representative, the pope; their line was now sacred. A measure of stability had returned to Europe.

Equestrian Statue of a Carolingian King The small bronze statue was made during the time of King Charles the Bald, though it was probably a cult object meant to represent Charlemagne. The crowned king, dressed in Frankish clothes, holds a globe in his left hand and once held a sword or lance in his right.

Charlemagne as Conqueror and King

Despite all their planning, the Carolingians could not escape the Germanic custom and curse of dividing up the kingdom among heirs on the death of the king. When Pepin the Short died in 768, his sons Charlemagne and Carloman succeeded to different parts of the kingdom, but there were persistent strains between the two. When Carloman died of natural causes in 771, Charlemagne became the sole ruler of all Francia.

Charlemagne conquered neighboring peoples to acquire their lands and wealth and to make them Christian. Between 768 and his death in 814, Charlemagne's armies fought a constant series of wars against the peoples of Europe. Each spring when there was enough grass on the ground for horses to graze, his army set out for war. Their destination was determined at an assembly called by the king during the winter or early spring. Carolingian armies fought throughout the summer months, often on several fronts, and returned home in the fall. Charlemagne conducted wars in this way for forty years. In that time he expanded the Carolingian kingdom into Aquitaine, Italy, Brittany, Hungary (the Avar lands), and Saxony. He also worked to secure buffer zones called Marches between Francia and the lands of the Slavs, Bretons, Danes, and Muslim Spain (Map 7.3).

Despite all this military activity, Charlemagne himself was not known as a great warrior; he led his army in only two battles of importance against the Saxons. The nature of Carolingian warfare was such that there were few open battles. Particularly gifted at organization, Charlemagne would put more men into the field than his enemy, who then most often chose to retreat, whereupon the Carolingian army would burn down their crops and homes. The enemy would then sue for peace, agree to pay tribute, and accept conversion to Christianity. Charlemagne's genius lay in planning wars and the enforcement of the military obligations of his nobles and the Frankish peoples. Every free Frank who possessed 120 acres of land was obligated to fight in these wars, to appear when summoned by the king with the necessary arms and provisions to go to war for the length of the annual summer campaign. His vassals (dependents) and their vassals or men fought because they owed the king service for the land that they had received from him (a subject treated in Chapter 8).

Carolingian armies were smaller than ancient armies, used both infantry and a cavalry of knights who, unlike the ancients, used stirrups and thus could sit more firmly on their horses when running the enemy through with lances. Not particularly good at siege warfare, the Carolingian army was otherwise a formidable fighting force. One Byzantine observer spoke of the sheer pandemonium of fighting the Franks, for with reckless bravery the Franks thundered forth into battle seated on their heavy horses, the sound and confusion alone intimidating the enemy. Charlemagne's campaigns suggest just how deliberate he was in seeking to pacify the areas that bordered the Frankish kingdom and how stubborn he was in pursuing a goal. The campaign against the pagan Saxons lasted for thirty-two years, but in the end Saxony became part of the Carolingian Empire, Christian, and a critical part of medieval Europe.

Charlemagne was not content to take land; he sought to incorporate it within his Christian kingdom. The war against the Saxons was difficult because after each year's successful foray into Saxony, the Saxons would agree to accept religious conversion, Christian priests, and Carolingian outposts. When the Carolingian army returned to Francia, the Saxons would slaughter the Carolingians and priests left behind, and the Frankish army would be forced to return the next year. Charlemagne integrated conquered lands into the Carolingian territory by granting parcels of land to his men, who occupied it and whose presence stabilized a region; by subjecting conquered areas to Carolingian royal law; and by promoting the establishment of Christian churches and the Christianization of the population, by force if necessary.

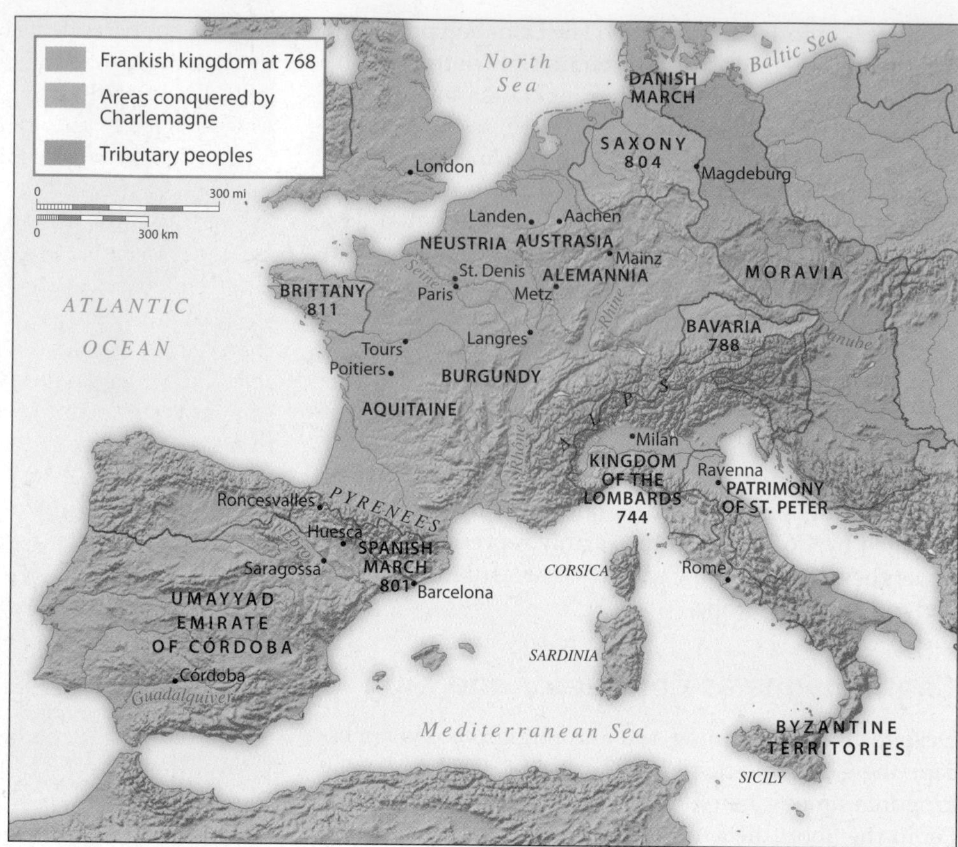

MAP 7.3 | Charlemagne's Empire by 814

Pepin the Short, before 768, and Charlemagne, before 814, expanded the size of the Carolingian kingdoms considerably and sealed their territory with Marches, or borderlands, and tributary peoples. ***What advantages and disadvantages did this land mass present to any potential rulers? How did Charlemagne try to administer such a large territory? What troubles did he and his heirs encounter?***

Within his kingdom, Charlemagne was the effective head of the church, which he treated as an arm of government. He approved the appointments of bishops and regarded monasteries as an institutional part of his government. Since his kingdom was vast, controlling areas at the periphery was difficult. Charlemagne was an itinerant king, visiting various parts of the kingdom to administer justice. At its core, his government remained a palace operation, but by the late 790s he had established a permanent capital at Aachen in southern Germany. He employed royal officials called ***missi dominici*** (the lord's agents), who were sent out in pairs, one secular and one ecclesiastical agent, as traveling judges to administer justice in the name of the king. They often carried with them **capitularies,** royal laws issued in chapters (*capitula*) or itemized form by the king. These laws supplemented the various Germanic law codes that continued to hold force in most regions.

Charlemagne, Father of Europe and Roman Emperor

The idea of Europe, its character and territorial reality, took on its first rough form during Charlemagne's reign. Europa was a figure from Greek mythology, a Phoenician woman or moon goddess who was seduced by Zeus in the form of a bull. Greek geographers had named the continent after her, but as a political reality Europe had had little force before the Carolingians. A Spanish chronicler in 754 called the troops of Charles Martel, who had defeated the Muslims at Tours/Poitiers, "Europeans" (*europenses*), the first known use of the term. A German annalist later identified Europe and the kingdom of Charlemagne as one and the same thing. Charlemagne's poets called him the "Father of Europe," "the glory of Europe," and the "shining light of Europe." The Europe that Charlemagne shaped was Christian, Latinate in learning and official language, universal in aspiration, and territorially complete (though having only a marginal presence in Spain, Poland, Hungary, and the Slavic lands, and no control over Scandinavia or the British Isles).

Charlemagne's courtiers, men like Alcuin (c. 732–804), the Anglo-Saxon teacher and deacon, came to the conclusion that a universal dominion with one faith and one king should be called an empire and its ruler an emperor. Just as Pepin the Short had looked to the papacy to "royalize" his family, Charlemagne looked south to Rome and the papacy to imperialize his preeminence. Such recognition depended on events and relative vulnerabilities. Just as one pope had wanted help against the Lombards when he agreed to recognize Pepin as king, so another pope needed help to remain on his papal throne when he crowned an emperor.

Charlemagne may have viewed the imperial title as an honorific, but it brought him more trouble than he had expected. The pope so engineered the actual ceremony that it looked to some, particularly in Rome, as if the pope had made an emperor and that it was his exclusive right to do so. Back home Charlemagne had to have his people swear their oaths to him again, now that he was emperor, lest there be some technical dispute about the legality of their earlier oaths to him as king. He may also not have fully foreseen the anger of the Greeks at the existence of another Roman emperor, for they already possessed a universal Roman emperor of their own. Not until 812 would Charlemagne secure their recognition of his new title, and even then the Byzantines qualified their recognition by calling Charlemagne the emperor of the Franks.

Still, for the first time in over three centuries, the west once again had its own emperor, but the idea of a western emperor and western empire would both frustrate and inspire Europe throughout the Middle Ages. The imperial title brought Charlemagne few additional powers. His courtiers and the church were pleased, for *empire* and *emperor* belonged to the realm of ideas, not to the realities of medieval politics. Yet Charlemagne's imperial title was a fitting symbol of the partnership of the Carolingians and the papacy and marked a new stage in the elevation of both partners. Thus, within fifty years, the Carolingians had moved from being a powerful noble family to the height of imperial majesty, and the papacy had inserted itself at the center of the medieval European identity and politics as the sanctioners of empire.

Al-Andalus, a Hot Corner of European-Islamic Conflict

When Charlemagne was delaying in Italy after becoming emperor, he received the gift of an elephant from the caliph Harun al-Rashid (r. 786–809). Harun (whose exotic court is the setting for *The Thousand and One Nights*) was the fifth caliph of the Abbasid Caliphate that overthrew the Umayyads in 750 and moved the capital of the Islamic world from Damascus to Baghdad. The Umayyads had provoked resistance in the widening Muslim world by their Arab-first policy. The Abbasid focus was more cosmopolitan, integrating Persians and other Muslims in its government, and the move to Baghdad symbolized the eastward shift of Islam away from its original Arabian heartland. The move east also compelled the Abbasids to accept, reluctantly, that hereditary Muslim rulers controlled distant regions such as Egypt, Syria, and Spain. It was probably that irritant that explains Harun's extraordinary coronation gift to Charlemagne. Harun and the Abbasids longed for the overthrow of the Umayyad emirs (commanders) who held al-Andalus (Spain), and they hoped that their "friend" Charlemagne might rid them of that line of imposters.

Charlemagne and his father tried. Pepin the Short drove the Umayyads south of the Pyrenees; and in 778, at the invitation of the disgruntled emirs and provincial governors of Barcelona, Saragossa, and Huesca, Charlemagne invaded northern Spain. Finding little success, Charlemagne withdrew. As he and his troops, forced into a long line by the mountainous terrain, reached Roncesvalles, Christian Basques attacked the rear guard of the army and seized its baggage train, which carried some portion of Charlemagne's movable wealth. The embarrassing defeat, no matter how unimportant, passed before long from history into legend. The Carolingians remained committed to establishing a firm border or March in northern Spain to protect Europe from any further incursions from Muslim Spain and to offer some assistance to the Christians of northern Spain.

In 711–712, Umayyad armies had invaded Spain from northern Africa and over the next decade dislodged the Visigoths from the Iberian Peninsula and established al-Andalus, a Muslim province with its capital at Córdoba in the south on the Guadalquivir River. By the 720s, Muslim armies were making raids on Aquitaine, though Christians in northern Spain set up their own kingdom of Asturias north of the Ebro River. Even then, during this first phase of conquest, northern Spain was under Muslim control and Muslims made ambitious raids farther north, including the attack on Tours/Poitiers, where they were turned back by Charles Martel.

Andalusian society was made up of Muslims, Jews, and Christians; and its Muslim rulers were tolerant of the various faiths in Spain, in part because Muslims remained a minority population within Spain. Moreover, Spain's Muslim governors were trying to contain not provoke internal dissension, since they were under constant pressure from rival tribal and dynastic claims. In 755, the Umayyad Abd al-Rahman I was fleeing Abbasid Caliphate forces when he led his Berber troops across the Mediterranean to Granada and set himself up as the emir of al-Andalus. He slaughtered the reigning Abbasid emir and his men, and sent their body parts to Abbasid Baghdad as proof of his victory. Abd al-Rahman established a dynasty that successfully managed the various populations and powers in Spain for over a century.

The Carolingians, always concerned about their borderlands, slowly pushed the frontier between Francia and al-Andalus back to the Ebro River, and established a March between the two. At the very time Charlemagne was in communication with the caliph Harun al-Rashid, he commanded his son Louis the Pious to free Barcelona from Umayyad control, which happened in 801—not a bad reason for Harun's gift of an elephant, though the Carolingians made little further progress into the Iberian Peninsula.

Abd al-Rahman and his descendants transformed Córdoba into a cosmopolitan jewel of bazaars, bookshops, and magnificent architecture. In the 780s, the emir began the construction of the Great Mosque of Córdoba, which has hundreds of columns, horseshoe arches, and a surrounding orchard of orange trees. Al-Andalus was the last great holdout of the Umayyads against the Abbasid Caliphate, and Córdoba was designed to rival Abbasid Baghdad. Its libraries, institutions of higher learning, and vibrant cosmopolitan population surpassed in many areas Charlemagne's own cultural achievements and may have indirectly inspired a few of them.

The Great Mosque of Córdoba Córdoba was the jewel of al-Andalus (Muslim Spain), and its great mosque, with its hundreds of columns, was a magnificent architectural achievement. Some of its features may have made their way into Carolingian churches.

Carolingian Cultures: High, Low, and In-Between

The intersection point of the many Carolingian cultures—ecclesiastical, court, noble, ethnic, regional, and popular—was the church, in which all groups participated to varying degrees. Charlemagne and his advisors were the architects of an early medieval movement that has sometimes been called a renaissance, but that may be more appropriately thought of as a reformation of western Christian culture. Charlemagne emphasized the reform of church practices and education. To inform and enliven his kingship he established a vibrant court culture, while at the same time raising the standards of education among the clergy and monks throughout the realm. His investment in education paid dividends in subsequent generations as the Carolingian church achieved high standards of clerical practice and a thriving written culture of monks and clerics who wrote hundreds of books that laid down essential dogma and raised profound poetic, theological, and philosophical ideas. The Carolingians also created the basic print script that we still employ.

What were the chief characteristics and achievements of Carolingian culture?

Court Culture and Education

Charlemagne began collecting foreign scholars for his court in the 780s. English, Italian, Irish, and Spanish scholars came to the king's court, creating an intimate international circle of learned men around their patron, the king. The Anglo-Saxon scholar Alcuin, whose interests included arithmetic, theology, poetry, letters, and Christian doctrine, became both the headmaster of the Carolingian court school and an advisor to the king. Court poets gave each other playful nicknames and called their king David after the Old Testament king. They circulated poems that poked fun at one another, ridiculed buffoonish nobles and drunken monks, and achieved moments of transporting warmth and spirituality. "Give sweet sleep to the brothers in this royal court for a dark power sends terrors that worry our sleep," wrote Alcuin. Royal poets spawned intense rivalries while trying to attract the attention of the king. Some of their controversies may amuse us today, particularly the one over whether darkness and nothingness are something or nothing and Ratramnus's later letter on the dog-headed people, but they do suggest the lively intellectual atmosphere of the royal court and Carolingian thought.

Almost all these learned men were churchmen; they served not just for the amusement of the king, but were his counselors and took on important church postings and state offices such as that of traveling judges or *missi dominici*. One who was not a churchman was Einhard, a Frank who was educated at the monastery of Fulda and later wrote the famous biography of Charlemagne (see Back to the Source at the end of the chapter). Einhard seems to have taken on the job of supervising the construction of Charlemagne's chapel complex. By the late 790s the king had a capital and chief palace at Aachen, and he was building an impressive church to adorn it. Like so much else, Charlemagne's chapel, which is octagonal in shape and furnished with materials removed from Ravenna, is an impressively solid building with a late Roman feel to it, yet its arches of alternating black

The Palace Chapel of Aachen In the 790s, Charlemagne began to erect a church at his capital in Aachen. The chapel is an impressively sturdy building with an octagonal shape, dome, central space, and heavy round arches. Charlemagne's throne is set on the second level, from which he could observe the service below.

and white stones remind one of the same feature in the Great Mosque of Córdoba.

The king was convinced that many monks and churchmen in Francia were poorly educated, for his advisors had noticed that the letters these churchmen sent to court were often poorly written and ungrammatical. Since such faults might lead to errors of religious expression and dangerous misunderstandings, Charlemagne ordered his abbots and bishops to establish schools to provide education to repair such deficiencies. This education of boys in the basics of Latin was far from universal, leaving out most of the poor and most women. Carolingian education was designed primarily to serve the needs of the church and government; still, some local village boys were educated in schools housed outside the precincts of the monastery. Charlemagne's emphasis on basic education led to several generations of highly literate churchmen and a few educated laymen and women. Charlemagne's educational reform reached few women since its primary goal was to train boys for the church and state.

Charlemagne, his courtiers, and monks were aware that the different scripts used in writing contributed to miscommunication and error. By the 790s a new or reformed script called **Caroline Minuscule** began to appear in Tours and other monasteries and to radiate out from the court itself. Caroline Minuscule is a small, regular script that maintains space between its simply shaped letters and emphasizes legibility; it is the basic print script found on this textbook page (the only real differences being the use of the tall *s* [ſ] and the lack of the dot over the letter *i* in Caroline Minuscule).

At the same time, Carolingian scholars, for whom Latin was a learned language and not the language spoken in their birth homes, began to reform early medieval Latin, returning it closer to the classical standards of

Caroline Minuscule As seen in this manuscript with its amusing portrait of the evangelist Matthew, Caroline Minuscule was the new script of small, regular, evenly spaced letters that was promoted by Charlemagne and his court. Caroline Minuscule became the main script used by medieval Europe until the twelfth century and was reintroduced as the standard Roman font in the Italian Renaissance.

writers such as Cicero. This Carolingian reform marked an important dividing point in the linguistic history of Europe. The medieval version of classical Latin became the official literary language of government, learning, and the written word, whereas the Romance languages (French, Italian, and Spanish) began as Latin but developed their own characteristics as popular, regional, spoken languages. Under Charlemagne, Carolingian humanists began to correct many ancient texts such as the Vulgate or Latin Bible and classical texts such as the works of Terence, Lucan, and Cicero, which had over the centuries of copying and recopying accumulated textual errors. The Carolingians also began to place primitive musical notations called neumes in the manuscripts of their prayers, a practice that assisted them in standardizing the singing of Gregorian Chant, which despite its name dates from after the time of Pope Gregory the Great.

The Carolingians also created some of the most splendid illuminated manuscripts of the Middle Ages. At Charlemagne's court, different groups of painters began to make deluxe Gospel books for the king. The differences between these manuscripts in style, use of color, and representation underline both the influence of antique models on court painters as well as the new and experimental nature of Charlemagne's court culture. After Charlemagne, manuscript illumination, like learned culture in general, was associated less with the royal court than with individual monasteries. Both the Ebo Gospels, with its painterly depictions of the evangelists and marginal scenes of everyday life, and the willowy line drawings of the famous Utrecht Psalter (a manuscript of the Psalms) were made near Rheims in the 830s. By the mid-ninth century the scriptorium (the place where scribes worked) of St. Martin of Tours was producing stunning one-volume Bibles called pandects for royal and noble patrons. In the First Bible of Charles the Bald, the painting of King David set in a blue cosmic egg, dancing nude beneath a light linen wrap to demonstrate his lack of pride before God, is a triumph of early medieval book art.

David Dances Naked before God One of the masterpieces of Carolingian book art, this image from the First Bible of Charles the Bald called on King Charles to be as humble and respectful to God and his priests as was the Old Testament king. The four virtues are personified as women in the corners of the painting, and the king is surrounded by his four musicians and two guards.

Learned Carolingian culture moved in phases: from the intense and intimate court culture of Charlemagne, to the brilliant writerly culture of Louis the Pious's reign, the mid-ninth century when dozens of writers associated with individual monasteries and cathedrals were at work, and finally to the slow tailing off of written culture in the last decades of the century, interrupted by the late brilliance of Charles the Bald's royal court. Ninth-century high culture was the result of Carolingian royal patronage but was dominated by churchmen. We know of very few lay writers and the three most prominent of these—Einhard, Nithard, and Dhuoda—all moved within the orbit of royal politics and Christian culture.

The Carolingian Church: Royal, Monastic, and Militant

Charlemagne's drive to reform Christian culture reflected his conviction that he was the guardian of the church in his empire. Bishops were the principal ecclesiastics in the Frankish church, but the king approved their appointments, employed them to serve the needs of his government, and sought their advice on the state of the kingdom, religion, and the Frankish people. He often appeared at church councils, and his capitularies frequently concerned ecclesiastical matters that would then work their way down to local parish priests and villages.

Despite the worldly authority of bishops, monasticism held spiritual primacy in the Carolingian world. The so-called three orders of Carolingian society were monks, priests, and laypeople. Monks, because of their closeness to God, stood first in the spiritual hierarchy. Charlemagne and his son Louis were particularly concerned to ensure that monasteries were regularly ordered and governed, for a corrupt monastery threatened to poison Carolingian relations with God since it was the monk who prayed for all. Under Charlemagne and Louis there was a drive to standardize Benedictine monasticism as the norm for the realm; Louis even sponsored a new and improved edition of the *Rule of Saint Benedict.*

THINGS THAT REMAIN

The Past Preserved in Ice

Everything that exists exists in the present; the past itself is entirely gone. All that we know about the past we know from the slight record of it (for it is never the whole) that has somehow survived into the present. All historical evidence, whether the thoughts of Plato recorded in a dialogue, a monument such as Constantine's Arch, or the lyrics of a medieval drinking song, have survived in some concrete form, however altered, into the material present.

That does not mean that we will not find new records of the world's past of which we had been unaware. Such is the ice of Greenland. For thousands of years the snows that fell annually on Greenland captured and deposited atmospheric particles containing chemical traces of human and climate events. Between 1987 and 1993, scientists from the United States and Europe extracted a three-kilometer-long ice core from Greenland containing a record of 110,000 years of atmospheric activity. They analyzed the chemistry of the core's layers at 2.5-year intervals. Known events, such as the volcanic eruptions of Mount Vesuvius in 79 CE and Krakatoa in 1883, left physical traces in the form of sulfate deposits.

The volcanic record revealed in the ice has begun to produce striking results. Europe's weather during the first millennium CE was warmer and more stable than that of the second. The Early Middle Ages, particularly around 800, benefited from warmer temperatures and longer growing seasons, but was still hit by eight multiyear severe winters between 750 and 950 that correspond to major volcanic deposits in the Greenland ice core. Particles ejected by violent volcanic eruptions were carried into the jet stream and blocked the sun's rays from reaching the earth, producing colder weather and agricultural failure. In 763–764, volcanic activity produced a particularly cold winter in Europe: crops failed, people died from lack of bread, portions of the Black Sea froze solid, and a gigantic iceberg taller than its city walls struck the port of Constantinople. In 821–824, Carolingian Europe was hit by cold, wet summers and a harsh winter—again caused by some distant volcano—that killed animals, froze humans, and devastated the agricultural economy. The emperor Louis the Pious asked his people to pray for God's forgiveness.[1]

The vagaries of unseen volcanoes, darkened skies, cold weather, and poor harvests remind us that humans are not in complete control of their historical environment and, more positively, that there are still new records for us to find in our search to understand the human past in the physical present.

QUESTIONS | ***What role does climate change play in history? What are the dangers of using climate explanations to account for specific historical phenomena such as the rise of Islam or the Viking raids?***

Carolingian kings demanded military service from their abbots and bishops, for the higher Carolingian clergy was a church militant. These men were almost always of noble stock. In promoting a candidate for the office of abbot, a bishop of Mainz listed the man's noble lineage and wide connections to the nobility, as though he needed to say little else to make the case for the candidate's suitability for high office. These noble prelates were raised as warriors, went to war, and fought in battles; simple monks and priests were forbidden to do so.

Frankish nobles shared a medieval aristocratic culture of manor management, control of their workers (serfs), disdain for the lower classes, and celebration of war and feats of bravery. They also shared a love of banquets, song, and drink, but Charlemagne and the church tried to curb the worst excesses of noble life. Charlemagne disapproved of public drunkenness, and his son frowned on the courtly amusements of jugglers and mimes and refused to smile in public. Since the abbots, bishops, and archbishops of Francia generally came from noble families, the nobility was well connected to the Frankish church and its basic mission; nobles often turned to churchmen to approve questionable marriages or to grant forgiveness when scandals surfaced.

Despite the integration of church and state, each preserved its own spheres of jurisdiction. Both belonged to the same general enterprise, yet the Carolingian state was not theocratic in the way that Islam was. The corporate or bodily character of medieval society meant that, in theory, each order had its own separate goals, duties, and areas of action, all pointing toward the common goal of pleasing God in the perfection of a Christian society. Yet, in reality, these orders constantly rubbed against each other, producing friction and frequent ruptures. Late in his life, as the abbot of St. Martin of Tours, Alcuin once found himself at one of these friction points when a criminal fled to his church and sought sanctuary. The emperor demanded that he surrender the man, which Alcuin, with some embarrassment, reluctantly did. But the common people of Tours rioted over the insult shown to their saint by men ready to invade his sacred precinct to retrieve the criminal. The complex interplay of groups in the Carolingian world meant that the various Carolingian societies rarely achieved lasting stability.

An Economy of Trade and a Shift to Silver

Carolingian civilization was for the most part river-valley civilization. Because northern Europe was covered by old and dense forests, Carolingian towns and cities lay along the natural clearings and available water supplied by rivers. The Roman road network still existed in parts of Gaul, but was often in a state of disrepair. Thus merchants found it easier to transport wheat and bulk goods along rivers than to travel over land. Towns and cities situated along rivers were, however, vulnerable to spring flooding and, by the mid-ninth century, to raids by the Vikings.

Carolingian trade was chiefly local, along rivers from town to town, although some evidence indicates that Carolingian Europe sent bulk goods such as wood, grain, and even slaves into the Mediterranean to Byzantine and Islamic lands in exchange for spices and precious metals. Primarily agricultural, the Carolingian economy was by the late eighth and early ninth centuries surprisingly successful. Carolingian agriculture benefited from the warmest temperatures in Europe for many centuries, giving it longer growing seasons and generally good harvests.

The wealth of the church, revealed by extensive church building and the creation and collection of precious religious objects, suggests just how successful the Carolingian economy was. The relative prosperity of the Carolingian Empire, both from its own agricultural economy and from the conquest of peoples such as the Avars, was a factor in attracting Viking raids.

Charlemagne moved Francia from a gold standard of coins to a silver one. Gold was hard to acquire in Europe, whereas the Carolingians possessed silver mines. Charlemagne and his successors established mints that regulated the production of coins. Whereas earlier Germans had once made payments in cattle, the Carolingians established a partial money economy with exact monetary amounts paid for many transactions. The fluctuating price of bread during times of scarcity, for instance, was recorded.

Living Off the Land

The Carolingian economy remained chiefly agricultural, with each area, village, and farm producing the crops and animals that grew best on its terrain. The rural economy was a **subsistence economy,** one producing just enough to meet its own needs, but it seems to have operated on a three-year scale of subsistence so that even if a village or region experienced crop failures over several years, it might still avoid starvation conditions.

Manorialism was a system in which the holder of the land, who had probably received the parcel of land from the king, lived in a manor house overlooking the land, which was farmed by dependent laborers with different rights and obligations (Figure 7.1). These workers came with the land as part of its fixed resources. They lived in a village and farmed plots of land allotted to them.

The Labors of the Months This Carolingian picture shows the activities of the months arranged over four panels left to right: January, a peasant warms his hands; February and March, lords practice falconry and the collection of small animals; April, a peasant collects the winter wheat and first fruits; May, a lord prepares the land for planting; June, plowing begins; July, hay is gathered; August and September, summer wheat is harvested, threshed, and winnowed; October, grapes are gathered; November and December, pigs are slaughtered.

These farm workers (sometimes called serfs or peasants) received a portion of the produce of their work, but owed the lord of the manor work on his property, other service, and dues. Depending on his legal status, a man might have to spend so many days of the week working on the lord's land and an extra amount of time planting and harvesting the lord's crops. His wife and children might owe the lord work in the manor house, time spent weaving cloth, and eggs from the family's chickens. The lord of the manor took on the roles of judge, mayor, and *paterfamilias* of the village.

Despite the rudimentary nature of the Carolingian rural economy, it was more rational than the Merovingian economy had been. Since the demands of kings and the church upon the land were heavy, the Carolingians kept inventories of properties and of the people who worked them. They knew how much each farm and worker should produce from the land. Carolingian innovations to farming benefited the Middle Ages and may explain the slow increase in the medieval population that started in the eighth century. The Carolingians used a heavier plow that was better suited than the light Mediterranean plow (or scratch stick) to turning over the heavy, moist soils of northern Europe. To pull this plow, they employed oxen or the heavy Carolingian horse. They introduced the so-called three-course system of agriculture in which they planted some strips of land in the fall with winter wheat that would ripen in the late spring, planted nearby strips in the spring with summer or fall wheat, and every third year left the strips of land in which the winter wheat had been harvested the previous year fallow for a full year. The next year they rotated their use of the land. The system increased the amount of land producing crops each year; spread the labor needed to farm the land over several seasons; ensured that crops were planted and harvested at different times of the year, thus safeguarding against calamitous crop failures caused by poor weather; and better preserved the fertility of the soil. Finally, the Carolingians promoted the use of water mills for grinding wheat to make bread, thus making integral use of machines as labor-saving devices.

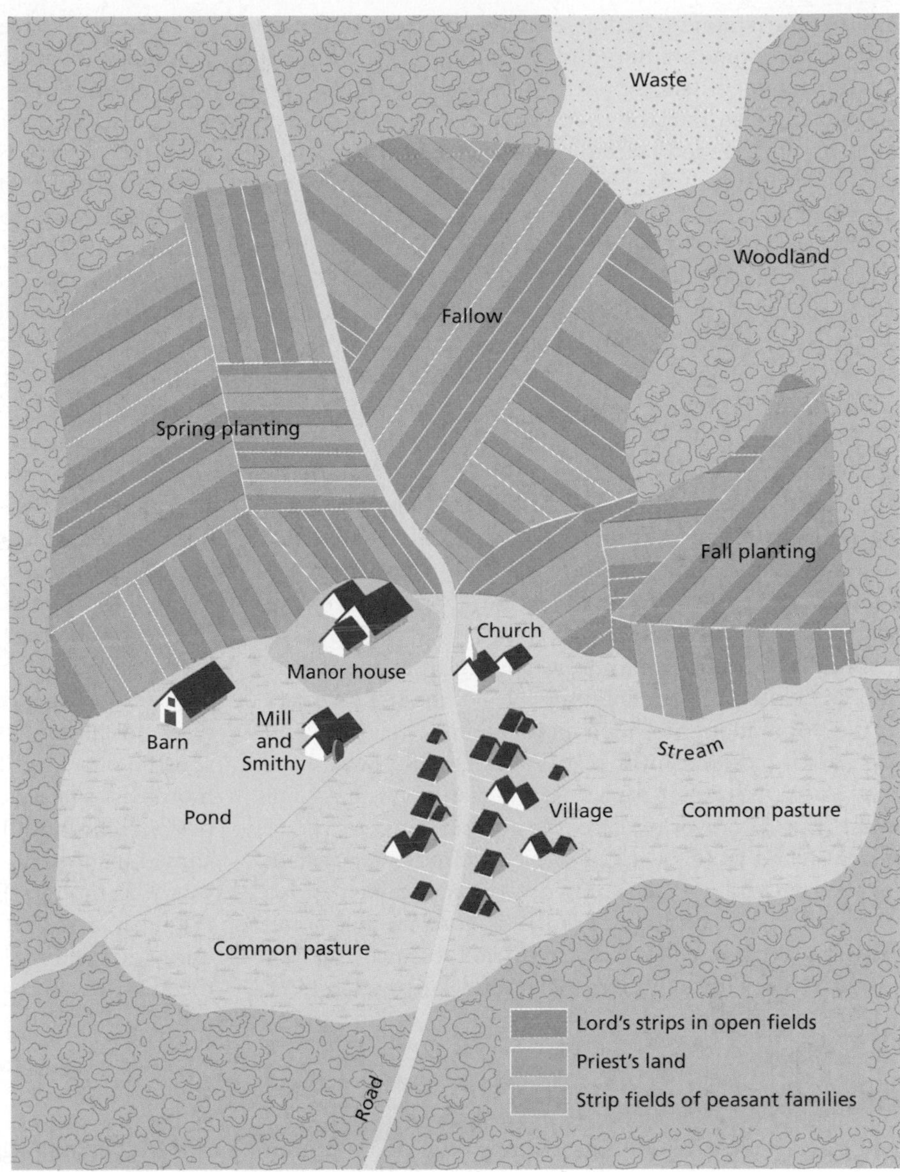

FIGURE 7.1 | **An Early Medieval Manor**

Medieval peasants or farm workers lived in villages on the lord's land. They went out each day to work the nearby fields for the lord; some peasants were allotted several strips of land for their own use, as were the miller and the blacksmith.

Source: Dennis Sherman and Joyce Salisbury, *The West in the World*, 4th ed. (New York: McGraw-Hill, 2011), 235.

These improvements contributed to the success of the Carolingian economy, but it remained an economy susceptible to shortages and famine. Monastic records report that some twenty-five years between 764 and 874 suffered serious shortages or short hungry seasons, generally in the late winter or early spring when, after a paltry harvest the previous fall, the surplus of grain had run out and the spring crop had not yet come up. Even then, Carolingian men and women knew how to forage for nuts and berries in the forest, kill a domestic animal (though that was not a good economic choice in most cases), kill one of the many half-domesticated pigs that roamed the forests, buy bread at inflated prices if they had the means, or turn to a local church or monastery for charity. During this 110-year period, deaths by starvation were reported in only 3 years. The real problem was that the Carolingian diet was excessively dependent on bread. The average monk may have eaten as much as three and a half to four pounds of bread per day. The heavy reliance on cereal crops had the effect of distending Carolingian stomachs so that when bread was unavailable, Carolingian men and women became extremely hungry. It was a hard life, but a sustainable one; life expectancies were low, but the population was growing.

Popular Beliefs

We know something about the activities of the common people of the Carolingian Empire, but their thoughts largely escape us. Though these people do not speak directly to us, learned churchmen did occasionally report what the people thought, often to censure them. One night in the middle of the ninth century, a bishop was hard at work writing a sermon in his study when he heard a commotion outside. The moon was in eclipse and his parishioners had assembled to bring the moon back to life; some shattered plates, others shouted at the moon, and yet others shot arrows at it. They were apparently convinced that the moon was being attacked by a monster and needed help to rouse and defend itself. The next day in church the bishop explained the nature of a lunar eclipse and chided his flock for their superstition.

Many superstitions did exist in the Carolingian countryside. A bishop of Lyons said that everyone in his region, high and low, young and old, believed in weather wizards who could send hailstorms to destroy crops. He had also heard that people believed that in 810, when animals were dying in the kingdom, enemies of Charlemagne had come from southern Italy to poison the fields and waters of the empire. In these two cases, people were chiefly worried about two key elements of the Carolingian economy: crops and cattle. In a subsistence economy without crop insurance or protection from setbacks, Carolingian farmers worried about the weather and looming calamity.

Popular Carolingian culture sprang from the village and its fields, which defined the lives of the vast majority of the population. These people seldom traveled beyond the narrow confines of their villages, learned what little they knew from their parish priest, drank with him, suffered from aggravating diseases and farming accidents, and watched as their children died young and harvests failed. They did not lack shrewdness; survival demanded it. They had a practical knowledge of others in their small communities, knew the land, and tried to survive physically and mentally a difficult and often relatively short life.

Disorder Returns to Europe

After Charlemagne's impressive reign, the Carolingian dynasty quickly returned to the root Germanic problem of succession. Charlemagne's luck had been spectacular; he had outlived all his heirs but one and so escaped the problem of passing down a divided kingdom. His surviving son, Louis the Pious, was neither as fortunate nor as powerful as his father, and his commitment to an indivisible empire worsened the problem. Civil war ripped apart the realm, and by the end of the century the Carolingian line had self-destructed.

Why did the Carolingian Empire fail, or did it?

The Woes of Louis the Pious

In 813 Charlemagne summoned his only living legitimate son, Louis the Pious, from Aquitaine to Aachen where a great council was held. After days of discussion his advisors persuaded him to make Louis co-emperor. Charlemagne may not originally have intended to bequeath the imperial title, but with only Louis left he may have decided that no harm would be done. Louis has often been criticized for not measuring up to his father's accomplishments, but the last years of Charlemagne's rule were already difficult ones for the empire. Charlemagne was in his sixties and no longer the active ruler he had been for much of his energetic career. He now remained in Aachen much of the time, soaking in hot springs and making the occasional hunting trip. In 810 when a Danish king threatened to invade Francia, Charlemagne personally assembled his army and set out on his last campaign, but his elephant died along the way and the old emperor suffered a dramatic fall from his horse.

Louis was a different ruler from his father, more attentive to the advice of his churchmen, more pious as his name suggests, and less committed to war and decisive command. The Carolingian church flourished during his reign with Benedictine monasticism leading the way, successful and learned churchmen advising him, and a supportive papacy. But in 817 Emperor Louis decided to name the eldest of his three living sons co-emperor and to make the other two kings, but subordinate to their brother. Only in this way, he believed, could the empire endure and remain united in faith. His younger sons were not happy. In 830 and then again in 833, all three sons revolted and tried to force their father to become a monk, a form of forced retirement and permanent imprisonment. Both times he sought restoration and reassumed his throne. The real problem behind these revolts was that many self-interested nobles believed that the Frankish kingdom should be divided equally among all the legitimate male heirs, but that notion clashed with the idea of an indivisible empire.

Three Brothers and a Civil War

When Louis died in 840, his eldest son, Lothar, immediately tried to impose his imperial will on his two younger surviving brothers, Louis the German and Charles the Bald, who was only seventeen at the time. A civil war broke out that pitted the younger brothers against their older brother. The Carolingians found themselves in a difficult moral and religious dilemma. It was one thing to kill pagan or heretical outsiders, quite another to wage war against Frankish Christians and your own blood. In a great battle at Fontenoy in 841, the younger brothers defeated Lothar. Two years later the three brothers agreed by the Treaty of Verdun to divide the Frankish territories into three parts (Map 7.4, p. 224).

The geography of the division was as much human as physical since the treaty framers were charged not just with dividing Europe into three viable kingdoms, but also with preserving the landholdings of the three brothers' men. Some European nations mark their beginning from the treaty because the rough outlines of France and Germany can be seen in the divided kingdom, but those national boundaries seem largely coincidental. Lothar's middle kingdom with its strangely elongated shape could not last, but the division allowed Lothar to separate his

WHAT A DIFFERENCE A YEAR MAKES

817: An Imperial Watershed

Several sources describe the occasion in 813 when Charlemagne made his son, Louis the Pious, co-emperor. In one version, the father crowns his son; in another, Charlemagne invites Louis to retrieve the crown resting on an altar and to crown himself. There is a small world of difference between the two acts. What is certain in both is that the pope was not present and did not crown Louis co-emperor. The ceremony was a strictly Carolingian affair, not a papal production. The shadows of 800 and the papacy's claim to the right to make emperors may have worried Charlemagne to the end of his life.

Whatever doubts the old emperor had in transferring imperial power, his pious son had few. In 816 Louis arranged for the new pope, Stephen IV, to re-crown him emperor in Rheims. That act reinforced the papal prerogative. What Louis did the next year proved to be a turning point in Carolingian fortunes. Louis was only thirty-nine years old at the time, but he had had a serious scare that spring. The wooden arcade that ran from the palace to the church in Aachen collapsed on him and his retinue, killing some nobles and leaving the emperor injured. Not long after the accident, Louis crowned his eldest son Lothar co-emperor, made his younger two sons kings, but subordinate to and dependent on their older brother, and marginalized his nephew, Bernard of Italy, on whom Charlemagne himself had bestowed the kingdom of Italy. Bernard and his supporters, who were still loyal to the deceased Charlemagne and his earlier territorial arrangements, revolted. Bernard surrendered, was blinded, and died, an event for which Louis later did penance. Worse was to follow. Louis's younger sons never accepted their subordination to Lothar. Louis himself remarried in 821 and bore a fourth legitimate son, Charles the Bald, and so tried to undo the provisions of 817 in order to find a fitting place for his youngest son in the realm. His first three sons revolted twice and deposed their father.

Louis the Pious in Letters The image of Louis the Pious set in Hrabanus Maurus's work on the Holy Cross is an example of "figured poetry." The letters make up an acrostic poem that can be read across or down and, to add yet more complexity, Louis's image (including the halo, headdress, shield, and cross) contains lines of verse that can be read separately. Louis, the most religious of Carolingian kings, has literally become a lettered man and something of a holy cipher.

The year 817 was a watershed both for Louis's reign and for the fortunes of his house. Louis had abandoned his father's imperial caution, probably for religious reasons. A universal Christian faith, he believed, should be contained within a united and enduring empire. But the idea of an indivisible empire clashed with the Germanic tradition of dividing lands equally among legitimate heirs. Louis's embrace of a primitive form of primogeniture (succession by the first-born male heir) also undercut older Frankish notions of the equality of heirs. Louis's plan in 817 was bold and radical. Had it succeeded it might have produced a stable and united imperial line and a different fate for the Carolingian Empire, but it did not work and perhaps never could have. From it came political turmoil, revolt, and civil war. By 818 the Carolingian world had political turbulence and failure in front of it. Stability lay in the past, and the memory of Charlemagne's golden reign cast a lengthening shadow over his heirs.

QUESTIONS | ***What is the difference between the two reports of Louis's coronation in 813? What was the essential Carolingian constitutional issue? How had the Roman Empire for a brief time overcome the problem of imperial and dynastic succession? Why was Louis the Pious's commitment to empire either a bold or a foolish idea?***

brothers and to hold the two imperial capitals of Rome and Aachen within his middle kingdom. Lothar clung tenaciously to his preeminence as emperor, even if the civil war had shown that he could not dominate his brothers by right of imperial title. The end result was that Europe was left with a nominal emperor whose power was scarcely more than that of his brother kings, all three of them operating in their territories as kings with relative autonomy.

The Vikings Raid Francia

Civil war and the general political confusion in northern Europe encouraged the **Northmen** (as the Carolingians called them) or **Vikings** (as we know them, from *vik,* meaning a bay or creek, from which their ships set out) to increase their raids on the continent. The Viking raiders were opportunists who seemed to know which areas of Europe and the Middle East were easiest and most profitable to strike. From late in Charlemagne's reign, various Scandinavian warriors, mostly Danes and Norwegians, began conducting raids on Ireland, northern England, and the western parts of the Carolingian Empire. The nature of these raids, which were often acts of piracy not supported by the pagan kings of Scandinavia, shifted over time.

The Scandinavians were Germanic peoples doing what the east and west Germans had done four centuries earlier, raiding more powerful and richer lands to the south. They could do so because of their superior sailing skills and ever larger ships. The Carolingian Empire was a land-based power without a navy. The early Viking raids were relatively small affairs. As violent and disruptive as these piratical raids were, they probably did little substantial physical damage to the overall Carolingian agricultural economy.

In the first four decades of the ninth century, the Vikings attacked along the coastline of Francia and sailed up rivers, targeting monasteries and churches that were conveniently located along waterways. The pagan Vikings knew that churches held the greatest repositories of movable wealth in the form of gold and silver objects (chalices, plates, crosses). The Viking raids may actually have done the western European economy some good by recirculating wealth that had dead-ended in churches or that the Vikings had stolen from Islamic and Byzantine cities. Some Carolingian ports and trading centers such as Dorestad in northern Francia were struck repeatedly.

Carolingian accounts of the raids are often exaggerated. Churches and monasteries were the prime targets

MAP 7.4 | The Division of Carolingian Lands by the Treaty of Verdun, 843
After the civil war of 840–843, the three living legitimate sons of Louis the Pious agreed to divide the Carolingian lands into three kingdoms. ***Why did the emperor Lothar I take the middle kingdom? What problems was such an elongated kingdom likely to experience? Which of the three kingdoms was the most vulnerable in the disturbed conditions of the mid-ninth century? With what limitations were the treaty makers working?***

A Viking Dragon-Head Found with the Viking ship buried at Oseberg c. 825, this post with its dragon-head was like those mounted on the prows of the Viking ships that raided the continent.

OTHER VOICES, OTHER VIEWS

Dhuoda Inside Out

Dhuoda was a pious mother, a noble woman, and the wife of one of the ninth century's great rascals. She proudly recalled that she had married the noble Bernard of Septimania in Charlemagne's chapel at Aachen. Her world began to fall apart not long after that day, for her husband, Louis the Pious's chamberlain (or chief of staff), was accused of committing adultery with Empress Judith, the emperor's young second wife, and was driven from court. During the civil war between the sons of Louis the Pious, Bernard hid out in Aquitaine and Dhuoda, left behind near the Spanish March, raised money to aid him. Then came the greatest emotional crisis of her life. In 841 her fifteen-year-old son William was turned over to King Charles the Bald to ensure Bernard's good behavior and to regain some of the family's lost lands and privileges. The resourceful Dhuoda began to write a manual to help her son survive at the court of a hostile king and to teach him how to be a good Christian.

Her emotional pain was doubled since she had recently given birth to a second son, whose name she did not yet know. Bernard had sent the child into hiding before he was even baptized. Dhuoda urged William to share the manual with his baby brother when he was old enough to read. Beyond merely setting out the forms of proper Christian and noble behavior for William, she also pondered the state of her own soul and life. "Returning to Myself, I Mourn" is the title of one of the last chapters of her book. She feared that she would soon die and begged William to pray for her and their entire noble family, to pay off the debts she had incurred on Bernard's behalf, and to protect his brother. With her little book she hoped, from a distance, to bind together her dissolving and wounded family.

Dhuoda supplies us with a special perspective on Carolingian life and politics. She was, so far as we know, the only laywoman of the ninth century to write a book, and she speaks as a mother caught up in the great events of her time. Her view is unique since virtually all other Carolingian literature was shaped by royal patronage and interests, by the center not the edge. But Dhuoda speaks from the margins—of a distant territory, of an embattled family, and of her gender. She placed her noble family ahead of all other considerations except Christian ones. We do not know when she died, but if she lived long after finishing her manual she would have been devastated by the storm of destruction that swept over her family, for the king executed her husband and her son William when he was only twenty-four, after he had tried to assassinate the king. He had not, after all, heeded his mother's instructions on how to survive in a dangerous world and to do the impossible: to please God, his noble family, and the king, all at the same time.

QUESTIONS | ***What role did women, both noble and common, play in the Frankish world? Make a case that Dhuoda was either an insider or an outsider. What is most remarkable about her situation?***

of the raiders, thus bringing the attackers and the people reporting on those attacks (monks and priests) into direct contact. No wonder that church reports of the raids are often hyperbolic and apocalyptic. Since these church reporters were convinced that nothing happened outside of God's will, they interpreted the Viking raiders as "the rod of God's wrath" and thought that the Carolingian kingdom and its leaders were being punished for their sins. A Carolingian farmer might have been somewhat less worried that the Vikings would attack him and his family since there was little reason for the Vikings to burn down fields of wheat. The Vikings lacked the manpower to wreak widespread devastation.

The Vikings did not bring down the Carolingian Empire; the Carolingians themselves did that with civil war and political division. But it would be wrong either to glorify the Vikings as blond-haired warriors sailing south in search of high-minded wars to test their manhood or to dismiss them as harmless visitors adventurously opening up a closed world. They were many things—farmers, fishers, traders—and not all Scandinavians were Vikings raiding the Carolingian Empire, the Byzantine Empire, or Islamic lands. But those who did were pirates and, in the medieval context, terrorists. Their attacks, which were hard to anticipate and thwart, sapped the confidence of Carolingian society and inflicted psychological damage, just as they were intended to. The raids were brutally violent, and the Vikings went out of their way to convince their victims that they were bloodthirsty and vicious. They were prepared to assassinate bishops in front of their congregations, to steal saints' relics and drop them into the Atlantic, to murder women and children, and to enslave victims, all to remove present and future resistance to their raids.

By the 840s various Viking groups realized that they could make better use of their time if they wintered over in Francia, often on an island, so that they could begin raiding early the next spring. By the 880s some had decided to seize territory in places such as Normandy (the land of the Northmen) and eventually to become Christians.

Other Viking groups had entered the Mediterranean, where they encountered and attacked Muslim lands; twice they attacked Constantinople. Another group of Vikings called the Rus made it to Russia and established settlements at Novgorod and Kiev. In England, the city of York fell to the Vikings; and the Danes occupied much of southwestern England.

Two other groups of raiders attacked the large Carolingian Empire. Saracens (Muslims) made sporadic raids on Italy and southern Francia in the ninth century, and late in the century the Magyars (Hungarians) began to attack along the empire's eastern frontier. None of these raids amounted to much. While churchmen moralized about the Viking attacks, Carolingian kings took a more practical view, striking deals with the Vikings to attack their Frankish rivals, granting them land when necessary, and paying them off when possible. These arrangements were part of a longer-term process of accommodation and integration. As well, Louis the Pious sent missionaries north to begin converting the Scandinavian peoples.

The Viking experience was not all bad for Europe: it shook the Carolingian Empire out of its comfortable complacency, introduced a dynamic force into a settled world, and forced various rulers to become more efficient in their handling and distribution of power. Eventually, in the tenth and eleventh centuries, the Vikings would be fully assimilated into Europe, becoming Christians and an energetic presence within medieval European society.

An Audience with Charles the Bald The monks of the monastery of St. Martin of Tours are shown presenting the First Bible of Charles the Bald to the king c. 845. The scene is a complex court scene with the king seated on his throne and accompanied by his retainers as the monks present him with the Bible. The image is an active one as the monks move into position and different stages of the ceremony are depicted.

The Imperial End Game: Two Charleses, One Bald, One Fat

The last two emperors of the Carolingian Empire were Charles the Bald and Charles the Fat. The bald one survived the civil war of the early 840s and went on to establish a viable kingdom in west Francia. Once the troubles with his brothers had settled down, he mounted a spirited resistance to the Viking raiders, establishing island outposts and barricades to prevent the Vikings from having free access to the river highways into his kingdom. He dreamed of reuniting his grandfather's empire, though it never happened. Yet on Christmas Day 875 the pope crowned him emperor.

Like his grandfather, Charles the Bald established a viable court school, his under the Irish master Eriugena (c. 810–c. 877; also known as John the Scot, *Scot* meaning "Irish" in the ninth century). Eriugena was the greatest thinker of the Carolingian age. He taught the liberal arts, including grammar and music; and wrote amusing poems, including drinking songs and a funeral epitaph for a despised bishop who was still very much alive: "the best thing he ever did was die." He also knew Greek and immersed himself in Neo-Platonic Christian books. From these he created a comprehensive Christian cosmology in his masterwork, the *Periphyseon* (meaning "about nature"). For Eriugena, Nature encompasses all, including God, and can be divided into four parts: (1) that which creates and is not created (God); (2) that which creates and is created (the ideas or first thoughts of God); (3) that which is created and does not create (creation, including humans); and (4) that which does not create and is not created (God as the point of return of all things). Eriugena's work may have reassured Charles the Bald and his contemporaries that beyond the chaos of the political present there was a cosmic plan sweeping humans toward a reunification with God at the end of time. Eriugena did not believe that a hell of physical punishment awaited sinners. All would return to God, even the pagan Vikings.

Despite the Irishman's enfolding view of history, human and divine, Charles the Bald's difficulties did not end when he became emperor. He invaded the eastern Frankish kingdom of his nephews and was beaten soundly. In 877 he marched into Italy to aid a beleaguered pope and died while retreating through the Alps.

One of his nephews, Charles the Fat, became emperor in 881, but he had few resources and little power in an overextended empire. Once again powerful nobles held the upper hand. The Vikings were besieging Paris in 887 when some east Frankish nobles deposed him. Charles the Fat was the last legitimate Carolingian emperor.

Thus, although the Carolingian hold on power in much of Europe lasted for two hundred years (687–887), the Carolingian Empire (800–887) came to an end after a mere eighty-eight years. The royal line itself would not be completely extinguished for some years, but the last Carolingian kings were hardly towers of strength. What is surprising is not that the Carolingian Empire had such a short run, but that the Carolingians were successful for so long. The difficult conditions of Europe (the vast and varied geography, lack of roads, poor communications, rural economy, and absence of a vibrant urban element) and the lack of reliable resources (no standing armies, few fortifications, no direct taxation, and a rather primitive form of government) make their accomplishments, particularly those of Charles Martel, Pepin the Short, and Charlemagne, seem all that much more remarkable. During the following centuries, Europe would turn away out of necessity from Charlemagne's model of a united European whole, but the Carolingian experiment in power and culture would ripple through the Middle Ages. Its achievements in learning, language, script, and agricultural innovation formed the basis on which the culture and economy of the Middle Ages would be built.

Conclusion

Some historians have called the period from 565 to 900 the crucible of the Middle Ages, an age in which the basic elements of the Middle Ages were being mixed and ground together to form a more stable amalgam. The Early Middle Ages was a formative period for western civilization; out of it came the basic contour and character of the Middle Ages. Religion and, in particular, monasticism were the early agents of that transformation. The Carolingian dynasty temporarily straightened out the politics of the age, transforming Germanic kingship into a royal rule based on Christian teaching and the institution of the church. The Carolingians hitched their fortune to the papacy, notions of a universal church and universal empire, and the value of Latin learning and the classical ideal. That Charlemagne's empire did not last long mattered less than its reformation of European society. The work of these proto-Europeans had a subterranean effect. Below the surface, Europe was being transformed into a defined space with a set of shared cultural traits and ideals.

Little of that transformation would have been possible without the parallel rise of Islam and the Carolingians. It would be wrong to say that Islam created the medieval west and Byzantium, but not by much. Islam removed from the west a great deal that had belonged to the Roman legacy, effectively forcing a form of redefinition on the eastern Roman Empire, which now became a Byzantine Empire, and leaving the rural west to find its way in a world without the Mediterranean Sea in play and without Byzantine interference. Charlemagne and the Carolingian Empire took up the challenge, forcing on continental Europe a set of cultural and religious standards and a loose political model of many Europes or regional realities inside a relatively weak imperial system. The long political and cultural redirection and identification of Europe had finished only its first phase when the Early Middle Ages came to a close.

Critical Thinking Questions

1. What events, cultural and political changes, and people are important to determining when the Middle Ages began?
2. Who were the most influential figures and what were the most influential forces at work in the Early Middle Ages?
3. Was religion the defining feature of the Early Middle Ages? If so, why? If not, what was?
4. How did the rise of Islam affect the many Europes, east and west, their contours and natures?
5. Was the Carolingian Empire an exceptional or a natural development of the post-Roman world? Why?

Key Terms

diocese **(p. 202)**
relics **(p. 203)**
Ummah **(p. 206)**
Hejira **(p. 207)**
shari'ah **(p. 207)**
jihad **(p. 207)**
Kharijites **(p. 208)**
iconoclasm **(p. 210)**
Donation of Pepin **(p. 212)**
missi dominici **(p. 214)**
capitularies **(p. 214)**
Caroline Minuscule **(p. 217)**
subsistence economy **(p. 220)**
manorialism **(p. 220)**
Vikings (Northmen) **(p. 224)**

Primary Sources in connect

For information on Connect and the online resources available, go to **http://connect.mcgraw-hill.com**.

1. **The Rule of Saint Benedict: A School for Monks**
2. **The Salic Law: A Compensatory Code for Living**
3. **The Donation of Constantine**
4. **Charlemagne as an International Figure**
5. **Are the Dogheads Human?**
6. **Dhuoda's Lament**

BACK TO THE SOURCE

Charlemagne as Family Man

Einhard, long a presence at Charlemagne's court, wrote a biography of the king about 826–827, just over a decade after Charlemagne's death. One of the things he claimed to know most about was the inner workings of Charlemagne's domestic life: his troubles with his brother and how he treated his mother, loved his children, and disregarded the scandalous behavior of his many daughters.

18. . . . [Charles] protected, increased the size of, and beautified his kingdom. Now I should begin at this point to speak of the character of his mind, his supreme steadfastness in good times and bad, and those other things that belong to his spiritual and domestic life.

After the death of his father [in 768], when he was sharing the kingdom with his brother [Carloman], he endured the pettiness and jealousy of his brother with such great patience that it seemed remarkable to all that he could not be provoked to anger by him. Then [in 770], at the urging of his mother [Bertrada], he married a daughter of Desiderius, the king of the Lombards, but for some unknown reason he sent her away after a year and took Hildegard [758–783], a Swabian woman of distinct nobility. She bore him three sons, namely Charles, Pepin, and Louis, and the same number of daughters, Rotrude, Bertha, and Gisela. He had three other daughters, Theoderada, Hiltrude, and Rothaide, two by his wife Fastrada, who was an eastern Frank [that is to say, German], and a third by some concubine, whose name now escapes me. When Fastrada died [in 794], [Charles] married Liutgard, an Alemannian woman, who bore no children. After her death [in 800], he took four concubines: Madelgard, who gave birth to a daughter by the name of Ruothilde; Gersvinda, a Saxon, by whom a daughter by the name of Adaltrude was born; Regina, who bore Drogo and Hugh; and Adallinda who gave him Theoderic.

[Charles's] mother, Bertrada, also spent her old age in great honor with him. He treated her with the greatest respect, to the point that there was never any trouble between them, except over the divorce of King Desiderius's daughter, whom he had married at her urging. She died [in 783], not long after Hildegard's death, but [had lived long enough] to have seen three grandsons and the same number of granddaughters in her son's house. [Charles] saw to it that she was buried with great honor in St. Denis, the same church where his father lay.

He had only one sister, whose name was Gisela. She had devoted herself to the religious life from the time she was a girl. As he had with his mother, he treated her with the greatest affection. She died a few years before him [in 810] in the monastery [of Chelles where she was abbess] in which she had spent her life.

19. [Charles] believed that his children, both his daughters and his sons, should be educated, first in the liberal arts, which he himself had studied. Then, he saw to it that when the boys had reached the right age they were trained to ride in the Frankish fashion, to fight, and to hunt. But he ordered his daughters to learn how to work with wool, how to spin and weave it, so that they might not grow dull from inactivity and [instead might] learn to value work and virtuous activity.

Out of all these children he lost only two sons and one daughter before he himself died: Charles, his eldest son [who died in 811], Pepin, whom he had set up as king of Italy [died in 810], and Rotrude, his eldest daughter, who [in 781] was engaged to Constantine, emperor of the Greeks [she died in 810]. Pepin left behind only one surviving son, Bernard [who died in 818], but five daughters: Adelhaid, Atula, Gundrada, Berthaid, and Theoderada. The king displayed a special token of affection toward his [grandchildren], since when his son [Pepin] died he saw to it that his grandson [Bernard] succeeded his father [as king of Italy] and he arranged for his granddaughters to be raised alongside his own daughters. Despite the surpassing greatness [of his spirit], he was deeply disturbed by the deaths of his sons and daughter, and his affection [toward his children], which was just as strong [a part of his character], drove him to tears.

When he was informed [in 796] of the death of Hadrian, the Roman pontiff, he cried so much that it was as if he had lost a brother or a deeply loved son, for he had thought of him as a special friend. [Charles] was, by nature, a good friend, for he made friends easily and firmly held on to them. Indeed, he treated with the greatest respect those he had bound closely to himself in a relationship of this sort.

He was so attentive to raising his sons and daughters, that when he was home he always ate his meals with them and when he traveled he always took them with him, his sons riding beside him, while his daughters followed behind. A special rearguard of his men was appointed to watch over them. Although his daughters were extremely beautiful women and were deeply loved by him, it is strange to have to report that he never wanted to give any of them away in marriage to anyone, whether it be to a Frankish noble or to a foreigner. Instead he kept them close beside him at home until his death, saying that he could not stand to be parted from their company. Although he was otherwise happy, this situation [that is, the affairs of his daughters] caused him no end of trouble. But he always acted as if there was no suspicion of any sexual scandal on their part or that any such rumor had already spread far and wide.

QUESTIONS | *What strengths and flaws does Einhard identify in the character of Charlemagne? Why does Einhard's account include so much about the children and so little about the wives? Why would Charlemagne not allow his daughters to marry? Why should any of that matter to Einhard or to history?*

Source: Einhard, *The Life of Charlemagne* 18–19, trans. Paul Edward Dutton, *Charlemagne's Courtier: The Complete Einhard* (Toronto: University of Toronto Press, 1998), 27–29.

8

"Gislebertus Made This." The Tympanum Sculpture of the Last Judgment, St. Lazare, Autun

THE ROMANESQUE CENTRAL MIDDLE AGES

THE LAST JUDGMENT OF GISLEBERTUS Anyone wishing to see the Romanesque Central Middle Ages (900–1100) could not do better than to spend some time with Gislebertus, a sculptor who worked in a number of churches in Burgundy at the start of the twelfth century. His finest work is to be seen in the cathedral of St. Lazare of Autun south of Paris. There he and a team of sculptors carved a series of stunning capitals. Some scenes are shocking: a demon hurtling at breakneck speed toward the ground; Judas being hung by howling demons who tug on the rope. Some are touchingly tender: Joseph leading a funny little donkey on which sits a perfectly peaceful Mary cradling her divine child; an angel reaching out delicately to wake the Magi (Wise Men) beatifically asleep below a blanket of dramatic swirling lines.

There are dozens of such capitals, many of them masterpieces, but the great **tympanum** sculptures placed above the doors of the church take us even closer to the Romanesque imagination. On the north portal, Gislebertus sculpted one of the first female nudes of the Middle Ages, a languorous Eve just before the Fall, casually reaching out to pluck the apple that will undo her and all of humankind. Above the west portal entrance to the church, Gislebertus mounted a monumental depiction of the Last Judgment. An inscription on the lintel (the horizontal piece above the door) tells us that Gislebertus made (or, perhaps, that someone of that name sponsored or supervised) the piece. Christ as the final judge occupies the middle of the semicircular space, his arms stretched wide to encompass all. To his right are the saved, some already entering paradise where Mary holds court, others gazing with reverence upon Christ. To Christ's left, sinners are weighed on scales, while Satan and agitated demons herd the damned together for never-ending torment. Below Christ runs a carved frieze also divided right and left into the elect and the damned. There, with chilling effect, a pair of giant disembodied hands grasps the head of one sinner to haul him off to hell.

The Temptation of Eve

Gislebertus's genius lay in capturing the extremes of the Romanesque worldview: of light and dark, spirit and body, joy and horror. The Romanesque age was one that knew and experienced such extremes: the rough times around the year 1000 and the pursuit of peace, the slaughter of innocents in the temple at Jerusalem at the end of the First Crusade and the hushed silence of great monasteries, the resolute conquest of England and a flowering economy. In stone and on parchment, artists captured the dynamic energy of the age. Romanesque figures are rarely static. They move, twisting and writhing in punishment, or elegantly bend upward to gaze upon the blessed. The uncertainties and charged energy of the tenth and eleventh centuries can be sensed in its agitated art.

Romanesque churches are stately if slightly dour constructions; hence, the need for lively adornment, sculptures and objects to enliven stern spaces. These were massive stone basilicas with round Roman arches (from which the name *Romanesque* derives), heavy walls, and

Romanesque Interior of St. Foy of Conques, Eleventh Century

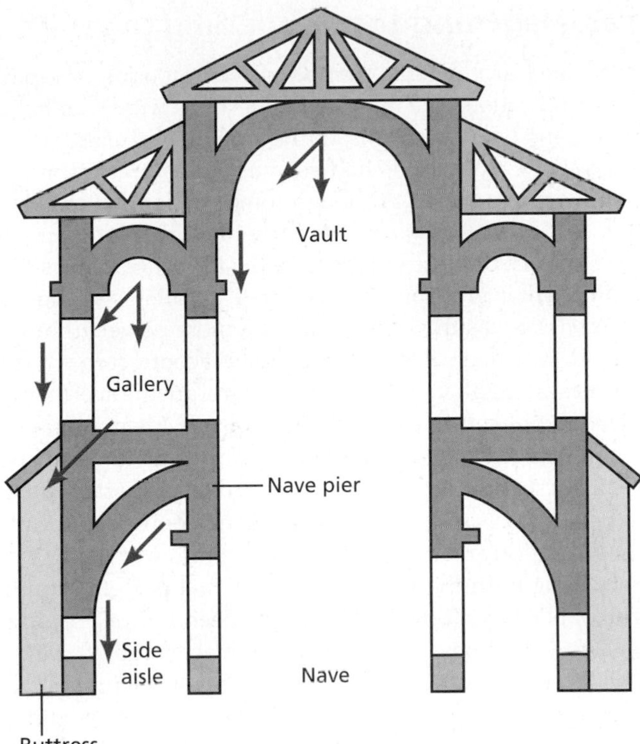

FIGURE 8.1 | Cross-section of a Romanesque Cathedral

The vertical thrust of the vaults and narrow width of the nave give the Romanesque cathedral its stately and imposing presence.

Source: Adapted from *Romanesque: Architecture, Sculpture, Painting*, ed. Rolf Toman (Cologne: Koenemann, 1997), 27.

small windows. The main aisle of a Romanesque **nave** (the central longitudinal space, from the Latin *navis* for ship, so named because it resembles the upside-down hull of a ship) has two or three vertical levels: the first fixed by the arches, which create a tubular effect that draws believers toward the choir in the east end and the main altar, and move sideways through the side arches into parallel side aisles; the second is the gallery level above the arches; and the third, a clerestory level of windows above the gallery (Figure 8.1). These immense buildings, whose physical footprint might occupy an entire city block, dwarfed the small wooden houses of townspeople that lay in their shadows. With bold lines and towers that seem to scratch the sky, Romanesque basilicas dominated their world. In northern Europe, Romanesque churches are often dark and gloomy inside, but in the south, awash with sunlight, their interiors are filled with light. The Romanesque style, which grew out of the rich range of Carolingian architectural experiments, was the first great pan-European style of architecture.

Architectural description fails to encompass what these churches meant to the people of the Middle Ages or how relatively poor farming communities could have erected such massive buildings. Romanesque **basilicas** served as the institutional, religious, and social centers of their communities and of western Europe as a whole. In them communities met, people were married, babies baptized, and funeral rites read. The decoration of these churches shaped the average person's visual understanding of the world. At Autun, Gislebertus and his team greeted Christians at the door of the cathedral with re-creations of the unseen world lying behind the flat and impoverished facade of the real world. By the eleventh century, Romanesque churches sported stained glass windows, trumeaus (the central columns of the portal) decorated with twisting saints and back-biting beasts, and delightfully strange capitals. Approaching the entranceway of an imposing cathedral such as Autun, people entered a world of stark opposites. It was almost as if a visual contract was being laid down before they entered. To set foot in a cathedral like Autun and to participate in the medieval Christian community was to accept a view of the world as one of sharp opposites. The life one lived would soon be examined by the great judge Christ and a final reckoning would be made: sinners would suffer for all eternity, gnawed by fiends, while the righteous would enter paradise and join the restful company of Mary and the saints. There was no avenue of escape, no other options on display.

The great story of the Central Middle Ages was how Europe once again transformed itself, turning away from the failed Carolingian imperial model (of a single family of strong kings and a universal emperor, court culture, dependent church, and rural economic realities) to the Europe that was emerging by the late eleventh century (with weaker kings, vibrant regional and national cultures, a formidable papal church claiming to lead all Christendom, burgeoning cities, and a resurgent European economy). The first great problem was how, in the aftermath of the Carolingian collapse, to redistribute power. In a world in which central power had been shattered, power went to ground, becoming local and often brutal in vast **vassalage** networks. How would power that was so segmented and localized be re-collected by centralizing forces, or would it? What would bring about that centralization, and who would give Christendom a set of uniform values and purpose? Emperors and popes each thought that they should supply Christian Europe with the needed leadership and direction. By 1100, some answers were becoming evident. The popular First Crusade had been fought, a medieval Christian culture was in place, an imperial papacy had emerged, the economy was vibrant and growing, and Europe was ready to wrestle with the wider world.

In the Aftermath of the Collapse of Carolingian Order

At the end of the ninth century, Europe seemed to be falling back into political disorder and a new dark age, the name so long and so inappropriately applied to the Early Middle Ages. The collapse of the Carolingian Empire meant that authority and legitimacy were once again uncertain. Throughout Europe self-made, petty kings stepped into the political vacuum left by the Carolingians, but they exercised little power and could claim even less legitimacy.

Why was vassalage a natural vehicle for the reorganization of power in a decentralizing world?

Charlemagne's great cultural enterprise died with his house. His had been a royally sponsored court culture and educational enterprise, but when his dynasty failed, so did its cultural model. Writing fell off, dramatically. The tenth century had a fifth of the literary output of the ninth. Church building slowed or stopped altogether. The institutional church, which had benefited from royal supervision and resources, began a slow drift into disorganization and the corruption of standards, irregular practices, and spotty devotion. The papacy seemed a long way away in Italy, and it had its own problems now that its great protector, the Carolingian house, was gone. The economy of Europe, however, may not have suffered to the same degree since the population of Europe continued to creep upward. There were signs that a fundamental restructuring of Europe was taking place in the troubled tenth century.

Vassalage and the Grounding of Power

After the Carolingians, Europe entered a period of rapid decentralization. The most basic questions were who held power and by what means. In the seventh and eighth centuries the Carolingians had established contractual relations with lesser men. Although some scholars have called this institution *feudalism* (an early-modern term coined from the fief, or piece of land, that the lord gave to his subordinate), it is probably more accurate to call it vassalage.

A vassal was the sworn man of a more powerful individual. Vassalage was sealed by an oral contract in which the vassal publicly and orally swore allegiance (commended himself to the lord), did homage (demonstrated his subservience), and committed himself to perform military service on behalf of the lord. The vassal swore to be the lord's man. The lord in turn promised the vassal protection and granted or invested him with land (the fief) along with the people bound to that parcel of land. The public ceremony was formal, indeed holy since God was its real witness and oaths were often sworn on relics. The ceremony was a whole body experience with visual, oral, aural, and tactile elements. The rite was enacted before witnesses who watched as the inferior man knelt before the lord (or, on occasion, lady) and swore homage or fealty to him, while the lord cupped his hands around the outstretched hands of the vassal. The vassal received the lord's declaration of acceptance and pledge of protection and care; the lord then offered him a piece of land, often symbolized by a clump of earth or stick. By the physical ceremony, vassals were said to have become "men of mouths and hands." They and their lords had acted out their contract and bonding by means of reciprocal gestures. The land given (the **benefice**) was the property and resource that the vassal would use to sustain his service to the lord, provide for his family, and outfit himself and his dependents for armed conflict in the lord's service.

While vassalage properly refers to a military and political arrangement that was contractual and legal in nature,

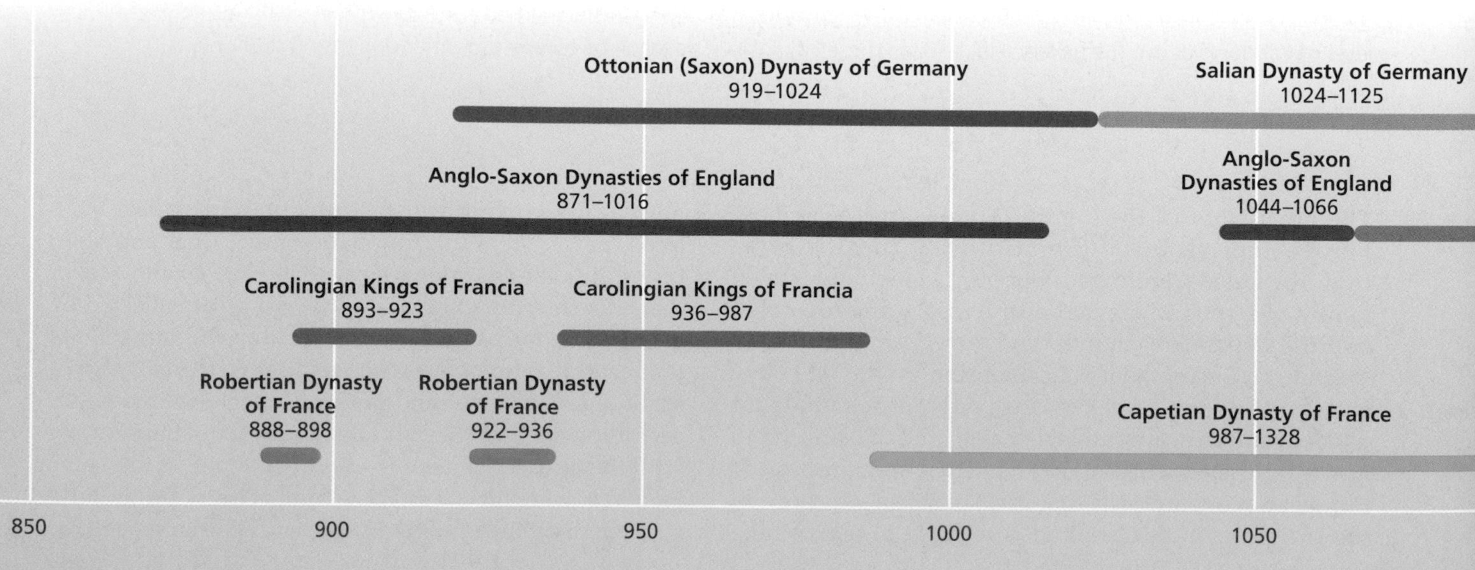

A Lord and Vassal Publicly Make a Contract In this twelfth-century depiction, the lord clasps the hands of a standing man to make him his vassal. Typically the man would have knelt before the lord to demonstrate his subservience and the nature of their relationship; here, the vassal bends his knees. Notice the crowd of witnesses: an oral contract required a publicly witnessed ritual. The unsmiling demeanor of all suggests the seriousness of the ceremony.

manorialism (treated in Chapter 7) refers to an economic and social one that was not contractual in nature (that is, it was not formalized or witnessed), though it did involve obligations by both parties. Though ties of dependency may characterize both vassalage and manorialism (the man to his lord, and the worker or serf to the lord of the manor), the functions and purposes of the arrangements were different. Vassalage forged a contract between two free parties; manorialism was a noncontractual, already-existing set of arrangements between a propertied free man and his dependent workers to work the manor he held.

At its core vassalage concerned the alignment of power, for it sorted men into formalized power and resource relationships. Vassalage existed prior to the collapse of the Carolingian house. Before they became royal, the Carolingian family used vassalage-like contracts to bind men to them since they could not expect the allegiance of supporters and subjects that a king could command just by the fact of his sovereignty and standing. When they became a royal dynasty, the Carolingians were somewhat less supportive of vassalage because they could now command men's allegiance because all were subjects of the king. Yet they did not abolish vassalage; it still sorted power and property between men at levels below the king. Instead, the Carolingians tried to control vassalage to ensure that it did not impinge on their royal rights.

As the Carolingian dynasty began to lose power during the civil war and weakened further in the second half

Norman Dynasty of England 1066–1154

Gislebertus at work on Cathedral of Autun 1120–1135

1150 1200 1250 1300 1350

INVESTIGATING THE PAST

To Use the "Feudal" -ism or Not

All *-isms* (such as monasticism, manorialism, capitalism, humanism, and Marxism) have some value as terms, but they can easily mislead, enticing us to accept as actual wholes our own collections of often unrelated parts. Feudalism is an *-ism* to consider. The great nineteenth-century legal historian F. W. Maitland observed wryly that, should someone ask what feudalism was, one good answer would be that it was a seventeenth-century essay in comparative jurisprudence, by which he meant that feudalism was a legal invention of the early-modern era imposed by scholars on the medieval past. By the eighteenth century the idea of a medieval feudal system was used to describe the totality of medieval social and political relations.

Mid-twentieth-century medievalists tended to adopt either an exclusive or an inclusive understanding of feudalism. F. L. Ganshof confined "feudalism" to the military relationship between a lord and his vassal, who were tied together by the lord's gift of a fief (land) in exchange for military service from his vassal. Marc Bloch spoke in broader terms of a feudal society characterized by ties of dependency: lord and vassal, manor lord and serf, bishop and priest, abbot and monk, and so on. In a refreshing review of the topic in 1974, Elizabeth A. R. Brown advocated abandoning the term *feudalism* altogether since it is artificial and distorts the specifics of medieval power relationships. It is a fact that no medieval man or woman had any notion of feudalism *per se* or ever used the term. They knew oral contracts and obligations, understood what a fief was and what service was, but they doubtless also knew that these social arrangements varied widely from place to place, time to time, individual to individual. The truth for them lay in the details. Specific contractual arrangements, not some overriding institution, determined the relations between people.

Many historians (though perhaps fewer economists) have begun to drop *feudalism* as a term, recognizing that the problem with the term will never be settled by having a better definition. They have rejected the argument that the term is a necessary simplification of complex social dealings suitable for students, who can more easily grasp the ordering of medieval power if it is sorted into a pleasant feudal pyramid. The problem with all *-isms* is that they box us in, forcing us to think of abstract wholes instead of detail and difference. In a major book in 1994, Susan Reynolds reexamined the entire subject and made a case for studying feudalism on its own terms. Whether or not we decide to use the term *feudalism,* it would be good when encountering all *-isms* to think critically about what they mean and how they may direct our thought away from the actual to convenient pigeon-holes.[1]

QUESTIONS | ***What other -isms are there, and how accurate, convenient, or misleading are they? If Scotland, England before 1066, and freeholders throughout Europe were never a part of "feudalism," and if "feudal" relations were constantly changing and never the same in time or place, what case can still be made for employing the term feudalism?***

of the ninth century, Carolingian kings had increasing trouble ensuring that the vassalage arrangements their subjects were making with one another did not compromise royal power. Kings needed noble support during those difficult times and were pressured to grant their subjects special privileges, including making fiefs heritable so that the son of a vassal might under special circumstances hold his father's benefice after his father died. The danger was that once a benefice became an inheritance or a family holding, it ceased to be a freely given grant of land and position that a great lord exchanged for service, but rather was a traditional right that passed out of the king's or lord's direct dispensation.

Local Lords and Castle Building

With the disruption of the Viking attacks and the weakening of royal power, and its eventual collapse, powerful nobles assembled large numbers of dependent vassals who recognized that their futures and livelihoods were better protected by local lords than by a distant king with decreasing power. Vassals did not always welcome their contractual dependency but were forced by the rearrangement and redistribution of power taking place to accept their inferiority. Vassalage represented the localization of power, its grounding, but it did not cause that localization. Nor did it fundamentally cause disorder, though it may have seemed that way to contemporaries. In the tenth and eleventh centuries, local lords came to dominate the countryside of Europe, particularly in the area of greater France, where disorder was greatest. There men with limited local power fell to fighting each other and victimizing others by blocking roads, waylaying travelers, handing out rough justice to the people of their lands, and exacting fines and fees. That might seem to make for a brutal and disordered society, but power had in fact found a principle of organization in local expressions of force. That fragmented power would not begin to flow back up to regional and centralizing forces until the eleventh and twelfth centuries.

With most of Europe lacking effective monarchies between 880 and 950, local lords filled a power vacuum. Vassalage, then, may be viewed as a necessary reordering of power in the countryside of Europe in response to the decline of central power. Local lords had already begun erecting fortifications by late in the ninth century. Kings such as Charles the Bald ordered their destruction, but the threat of Viking raids and attacks by their own aggressive neighbors made the lords' need for protective defenses paramount. Early on these structures were made of wood and stone and were generally situated on a prominent piece of land such as a hillock or rock outcropping. The **keep** (or *donjon*, "dominant point") was a stone tower erected on an elevated site within the fortification. The keep served not only as the lord's residence, but also as a place for his family and vassals to retreat when under severe attack. Around the castle were various earthworks and walls, encircled by a ditch or water-filled moat. The Normans in the tenth century built what are called Motte-and-Bailey castles, the motte being the mound of earth on which the keep was built and the bailey being the outer wall that surrounded the motte, keep, and a small parcel of land.

Castles later evolved into grand, often stylized medieval constructions of great size, but in the tenth and eleventh centuries, smaller sturdy fortifications represented the frontline of a struggle for power and survival. The local lord was oath-bound to protect his vassals and a castle did that, since its function was largely defensive. But the right to build castles and so to control territories was hotly contested. Greater lords and kings did not want their inferiors controlling pockets of territory they considered their own, to have castles with which to protect themselves when they should be relying on superior lords, or to assemble and protect armies of vassals who should rely on a greater lord. Great counts such as Fulk Nerra in Anjou spent considerable effort ringing their territories with castles and destroying the rogue castles of lesser men. Much of the tenth and eleventh centuries was taken up with a struggle between lesser and greater lords over who had the right to build and maintain castles, many of which were attacked and leveled as the chief point of contention in local power struggles.

An Ethic of Service

As an institution built on something as fragile as an oral contract, vassalage required extraordinary social and ideological support if it was to hold firm. An ideology of vassalage that glorified service and condemned disloyalty emerged. It was a system of values aimed downward, insisting on the faithfulness of vassals. Fulbert of Chartres's injunctions about the relations of lords and vassals are negative in nature, stressing the vassal's obligation not to injure his lord's interests, but largely ignore the lord's reciprocal obligations toward his vassal. An ethic of service put pressure on vassals to be subservient and to remain utterly faithful to their lords. A Carolingian capitulary had set out the grounds on which a vassal might break his oath, but the conditions were so exceptional that under most circumstances the contract was unbreakable. A vassal could break his oath if his lord sought to enslave him, plotted against his life, committed adultery with his wife, drew a sword to kill him, or failed to protect the vassal as he had promised.

The *Song of Roland* (*Chanson de Roland*) promotes this ideology of service. The core of the story concerns the ambush of Charlemagne's baggage train at Roncesvalles in 778, but the epic poem in Old French that was written down by 1100 reflects the social and political conditions of the tenth and eleventh centuries. The poem transforms the enemy from the mountainous Christian Basques into an international army of Muslims. The two main Christian warriors of the epic are brave Roland and wise Oliver. Both are good men who ride pell-mell into battle atop mighty steeds, slashing the enemy with great glistening, fabled swords. Charlemagne's men in the *Song* are impulsive, high-spirited warriors, all bicker and bite, proud and ready to fight wherever and whenever their lord commands. Roland is the bravest of them all, the best of the vassals, not because he is prudent—indeed, he injures Charlemagne's interests—but because of his utter, doglike loyalty.

A Motte-and-Bailey Castle A reconstruction of what a typical eleventh-century castle fortification might have looked like: an outer wall (bailey), moat or ditch, inner wall, interior space, and mound (motte) with a keep or sturdy castle at its summit.

The poem is like Roland and the values he embodies. It is active, not reflective; exterior, not interior. The lines of verse are broken into short, self-contained bursts of action that belonged to an age that knew intense episodes of isolated action. The poem's very style and rhythm are combative. At the end, as the battle turns against the outnumbered men at the rear, Oliver urges Roland to blow his horn to summon help. Roland refuses. He says that men must endure such burdens, suffer searing heat and freezing cold, sharp wounds and bloodied bodies for their lord. Roland will not consider damaging his reputation and so brings destruction upon himself and his fellow warriors. Only when the cause is lost and his death certain does Roland blow his horn to alert the king. No enemy fells him. Rather, in signaling the king, the exhausted warrior blows out his own brains, the blood gushing from his temples. He dies the perfect vassal's death.

Roland Blows His Horn A thirteenth-century depiction of the vassal Roland blowing an oliphant or horn to alert King Charlemagne that he and the rear guard are under attack. In fact, in the *Song of Roland* the struggle to resist the pagan attack was already over and in blowing the horn Roland burst his temples and died.

As he dies, Roland lifts his gloved hand to the heavens, transferring his service from Charlemagne to God. In death, Roland becomes God's vassal. The *Song of Roland* puzzles modern readers. Wise Oliver would seem to us the better man; Roland is too proud, impulsive, and rash, but Roland is the hero of the poem because of his utter, unquestioning loyalty to his lord. Everything was forgiven because of his loyalty and bravery, even his stupidity and stubbornness. The *Song* sings not of kings (Charlemagne is two hundred years old, frail, and beset by bad dreams), but celebrates vassalage. But Roland, bound and restricted by the rules and obligations of being a vassal, is a prisoner of his condition and can find transcendent freedom only in action on the field of battle and in glorious death.

A second, simpler story makes the same point. Stephen of Bourbon recorded a medieval legend of a knight and his lady who left their infant son in a cradle in a castle room with a faithful greyhound as his guardian. A snake slithered into the room through an open window and was about to attack the baby. The dog leaped to the rescue, throttled the snake, spilling blood over the baby and himself in the fight, and then cast the snake out the window. Hearing the commotion, the noble couple rushed into the room. Seeing their baby covered in blood and blood around the dog's mouth, the knight killed the dog. When he later discovered the dead snake at the foot of the castle and realized that his son was uninjured, he understood that the dog had been protecting his son and deeply regretted having killed him.[2]

The death of the innocent greyhound reflects the ideals of the age, for the dog died the faithful servant of his lord, mortally wronged. Vassalage celebrated the silent, misunderstood, ever loyal, resolutely faithful servant. No matter the cause, he did his unwavering duty. An open wound of misunderstanding and victimhood belonged to vassals. It was the burden they bore for their service to a superior. The ideology of vassalage promoted the idea of self-sacrifice; Roland died and so, too, a loyal dog.

Imperial and Royal Power

Despite its weakened state, kingship remained, at least in principle, admired and sought after by many. Power in the Middle Ages may be viewed as the story of a continual contest for power between noble and royal interests. When one was up, the other was down. The struggle played out in small, gradual advances and retreats over decades. The empire and imperial title returned in the tenth century under the Ottonians (the dynasty named after Otto I the Great), but the Roman Empire of the Ottonians contained little more than parts of Germany and northern Italy. The Carolingian dream of an empire of all Europe was gone. All medieval empires after theirs were regionally restricted. The idea of empire persisted, but medieval empires were more royal than imperial in the world of real politics and power.

How did kingship find its footing again in the Romanesque Central Middle Ages?

The Ottonian Moment in the Imperial Sun

In 911, when the last Carolingian king of eastern Francia died, nobles recognized Conrad, the duke of Franconia, as king, but they gave him little support and often waged war against him. Though the Vikings had not done great damage to east Francia, the Magyars (Hungarians) continued to harass its eastern border. Conrad may not have been a strong king, but he did something remarkable as he lay dying. He lacked a son, and so in 919 he decided to pass the crown to Henry the Fowler, the duke of Saxony. As king, Henry labored to subdue his powerful German neighbors and used a nine-year truce with the Magyars to secure his own territory and build fortifications. At the Battle of Unstrut in 933 he defeated the Magyars and then turned his attention to the Danes, who soon sued for peace.

Otto I the Great (r. 936–973) succeeded his father in 936 and was crowned king at Aachen in Charlemagne's chapel. He resumed the campaign against his troublesome neighbors and in 955 at Lechfeld decisively defeated a force of Magyars, marking an end to their harassment. At the time of their defeat, the Magyars were already becoming a settled, agrarian, European people, and in the tenth century they became Christians.

Otto was drawn into Italian and papal affairs. In 960 Pope John XII begged him to rescue the papacy from the king of Italy, which Otto did, even though John was not the most admirable of medieval popes. His critics charged that Pope John had ordained a deacon in a stable; accepted money to ordain priests; committed adultery with four women (one of whom was his niece); turned the papal palace into a brothel; blinded his godfather; castrated a rival; and was an arsonist, a drunkard, and a gambler. Despite that defamation of the pope's character, Otto allowed John to crown him emperor and his wife Adelaide empress in 962, but Otto deposed the infamous pope the next year and spent several years sorting out papal affairs. Like Charlemagne, Otto considered both the safety and the integrity of the papacy and the church to be a critical part of his imperial mandate. The **Ottonian system** for managing the church extended to investing bishops and abbots with their offices, controlling the proprietary church (that is, having the lands of a church belong to a secular lord appointed by the king), and appointing secular operating officers of church lands.

Otto sought to open up relations with the Byzantines. He sent an ambassador, Liudprand of Cremona, to Constantinople to secure a Byzantine princess for his son to marry, thus hoping to further legitimize his own imperial dynasty. He eventually found a Greek bride for his son, Otto II (r. 973–983), but Otto II was forced to fight the Byzantines and Saracens in southern Italy and lost a critical battle there. Italy held other dangers for all the Germans, particularly from its malaria-infested swamps in the north. When Otto II died from malaria, he left his three-year-old son, Otto III, as his co-regent and heir (r. 983–1002). Otto III took control of the government in 994 when he was fourteen and became emperor in 996. Though Otto III ruled for only six years, his was one of the most precocious of medieval reigns. He modeled himself after Charlemagne, styling himself the restorer of the Roman Empire and placing the learned Gerbert of Aurillac on the papal throne as Pope Sylvester II (999–1003), but Otto died when he was twenty-one and was succeeded by his cousin Henry II (r. 1002–1024), who ruled the empire from Bamberg in Germany.

Emperor Otto Honored by His Empire The four chief provinces (represented as women) of the Ottonian Empire (Germania, Francia, Italia, and Alemannia) pay homage to the enthroned emperor. It is not certain which of the three Ottonian emperors is depicted.

The Ottonians showed their debt not only to the lengthening shadow of Charlemagne, but also to a firm commitment to religious rigor, the restoration of the Roman Empire, and renewed contact with the Greek east.

The First Millennium and the Delayed Second Coming

Otto III's death in 1002 was just one of a series of calamities that worried Europe around the year 1000. Apocalyptic fears had been the background noise of western civilization since the rise of the Roman Empire, though official sources always firmly reminded Christians that only God knew when and how the world would end. A monk by the name of Raoul Glaber (also known as Rodulfus Glaber and Bald Ralph) compiled a chronicle that begins with the events around the year 1000: outbreaks of heresy, strange events, disease, famine, fire, and floods. Raoul's world was wrapped in symbols and signs, prodigies and portents with which he believed God was speaking to

An Ambassador's Purple Rage

Perspective is always particular and relative. Who does the seeing, when, from what angle, of what object, and to what end? Virtually all the documents that historians employ involve matters of perspective. No better demonstration of how changeable and tricky perspective can be comes from two contacts between east and west that occurred late in the tenth century.

Liudprand of Cremona (c. 920–972) visited Constantinople twice, but the reports of his two experiences are strikingly different. In 949 he went as a young man keen to learn Greek and found all things Byzantine wondrous. The emperor Constantine VII Porphyrogenitus received him graciously; housed, fed, and entertained him exquisitely; and flattered the young man with courtly attention. Liudprand was so embarrassed by the meanness of King Berengar II of Italy for whom he was carrying a letter full (as he said) of lies for the emperor, that he gave the emperor his own gifts in Berengar's name. Liudprand had brought Constantine four child-eunuchs as slaves. He was rewarded with imperial gifts and could not stop talking about the marvels he saw at the imperial court, the glorious buildings, and his own privileged reception.

Medieval Map of Constantinople

Twenty years later, in 968, he returned to Constantinople, this time as a legate of the emperor Otto the Great. By then, Liudprand had become the bishop of Cremona and Otto entrusted him with the delicate task of arranging for a Greek imperial bride to marry his son. Everything that could go wrong on a trip did go wrong this time. He was housed in drafty lodgings far from the imperial palace; had an awful, grumbling, penny-pinching landlord; and was forced to drink wretched wine full of pitch, pine juice, and plaster. From the start, he was received rudely and treated with humiliating disrespect by the Byzantines. He dealt chiefly with the emperor Nicephorus's brother Leo, who went out of his way to insult Otto and his ambassador. Even the eastern emperor, when he finally deigned to see Liudprand, treated him insultingly. At a state dinner, the ambassador was seated far from the emperor at the end of a table where the tablecloth had run out. Nicephorus baited Liudprand, telling him that westerners regarded their bellies as their gods, were given to drunkenness, and were not true Romans. Liudprand gave as good as he got, telling the emperor that the Romans (that is, Byzantines) should remember that Romulus was born of a whore and murdered his brother. He said that when in the west they wanted to insult someone they called him a Roman. The trip was all downhill from there, and as the ambassador was leaving the city with his mission a crashing failure, officials searched his bags and seized some purple imperial robes that they said no westerner had the right to export. Liudprand was outraged by the violation of his baggage and the suggestion that he was smuggling precious goods.

Why the stark difference between the two experiences? Almost everything had changed. In 949, Liudprand had been a young unthreatening westerner received by a generous host and shown the splendors of Constantinople. In 968, he was the official representative of a western emperor whom the Greeks regarded as an imposter. In the meantime, Liudprand had aged and as his standing in society had risen, so had his pride. The memory of his glorious first visit had probably raised unrealistic expectations about what he might expect on his return. His second account (*Tit for Tat*) was written for Emperor Otto, and Liudprand wanted to explain why his mission had failed. What better way to do that than to document the cruel treatment that he had received as Otto's legate. Perspective, in short, depends on particular historical, personal, and contextual circumstances, all of which had changed dramatically for Liudprand between his two trips to Constantinople.

QUESTIONS | ***How should historians identify and handle matters of perspective when considering primary sources? Are both of Liudprand's accounts true, or in what way are they true?***

the world. Raoul was convinced that Satan would be loosed upon the world at the millennium, and so he collected evidence that the end was near as he attempted to read God's mind.

When the world didn't end, some learned men recalculated and came to the conclusion that the true millennium, the second coming of Christ, should occur around 1033, a thousand years after Christ's crucifixion. Raoul gathered the signs: the deaths of nobles, kings, emperors, and high churchmen; eclipses; and a famine with a horrific outbreak of cannibalism in 1033. Raoul was not alone in worrying about the end time. The French king had heard that it had rained blood in Aquitaine and asked the wise men of his realm to explain the event. When the world survived the 1030s, even Raoul noticed a new optimism at work in his world as it put on what he called "the white mantle of churches," that is, the freshly cut stone of the new Romanesque churches that were being erected. For some people, it was as if the western Christian world had survived some great test set by God and could now turn to new things.

Others were less sure. Raoul continued to collect signs of the times into the 1040s, trying to understand what God was telling them about the workings of divine history. The sculptor Gislebertus, at the end of the Romanesque Age, was still preoccupied by stark visions of final things.

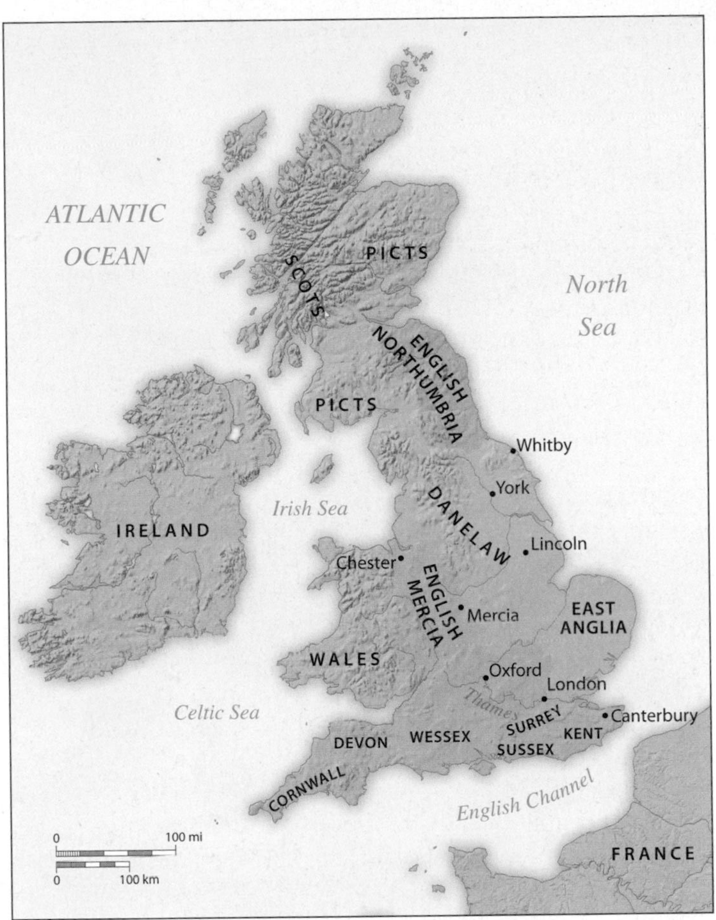

MAP 8.1 | Anglo-Saxon England, c. 900

At the end of the reign of Alfred the Great, southern England was under the control of Anglo-Saxon kings, but the rest of England was under Danish control (the Danelaw). ***Why was Alfred's reign important? Why was England so divided and the Danes such a continuing threat?***

The Stirrings of Stronger Monarchies in England and France

The Anglo-Saxon kingdoms of England were hit hard by various Viking attacks. The Danes occupied East Anglia in 869–870. Mercia fell to the invaders in 874, and Northumbria, including York, fell to Danish settlers two years later. A large portion of Wessex fell under Danish control during the same period. King Alfred the Great of Wessex (r. 871–899) and a small band of supporters were forced to travel through parts of his occupied kingdom at night. Over the next twenty years, Alfred slowly recovered his kingdom, reorganized Wessex, secured its defenses, and built a navy to resist the Danes (Map 8.1).

When Alfred died, Danes still inhabited parts of his kingdom and England, but Alfred's reign marked the beginnings of an Anglo-Saxon revival. As a learned man, patron of the church, and maker of laws, Alfred set a model for Anglo-Saxon kingship. Alfred was also an author and composed works in Old English. While continental Europe turned chiefly to Latin as its learned language for writing, Anglo-Saxon England had the earliest and most vigorous vernacular written tradition in Europe. By the reign of King Edgar (r. 959–975), much of England was under west Saxon (or Wessex) control and at relative peace.

Monarchy reasserted itself in England without a great deal of direct Carolingian or Ottonian influence. Anglo-Saxon kings established traditions for ruling that would persist until the Norman Conquest in the eleventh century. The Danish occupation forced Alfred and his successors to make their governments more efficient. Older Anglo-Saxon divisions of the land were abandoned, and in their place, Alfred and his heirs introduced the hundreds (an area of approximately one hundred families), boroughs, and shires. To build his navy, Alfred ordered each three hundred hides (a hide being enough land to support a single family of dependent farmers) to pay for the construction of a ship. He and his successors insisted that their men do garrison duty, standing ready to thwart invaders.

The prestige and claims of Alfred and his royal line rested on their successful resistance to foreign occupation. There were fewer noble challenges to monarchy in England than on the continent. Nobles assembled at the Witenagemot or Witan (the supreme council), but it was filled with the king's advisors and its function was to carry out his will. Moreover, Alfred and his heirs had the support and sanction of the church. Anglo-Saxon kings did seek oaths of fealty from their subjects, but the institution of vassalage was absent. Royal law was enforced by thegns (king's agents) and shire reeves (sheriffs). The instrument of command was the royal writ,

MAP 8.2 | **Medieval Europe, c. 1000**

By the year 1000, Europe contained a number of weak kingdoms, a territorially limited empire, and lands held by Islamic powers. Even within these seemingly solid blocks, power remained fragmented. France was a fiction in that the area of royal control was limited to a small territory around Paris. ***What are the geographic and historical reasons for Europe's fragmentation?***

short documents written in Anglo-Saxon (Old English), which began to appear in the early tenth century. Despite all the Anglo-Saxon successes, England experienced another round of Viking attacks starting about 980, and Cnut (d. 1035), the king of Denmark and Norway, became king of England. Thus Anglo-Saxon control of most of England lasted for just over a century before England was ruled by a foreign magnate.

The situation in France was almost the opposite of what occurred in Germany, in part because the Carolingian dynasty had held on longer in west Francia, despite having experienced more severe Viking invasions than other areas of the continent. Late in the ninth century, after Charles the Fat's fall, Odo, the count of Paris, declared himself king and Odo's son Robert held the title briefly before it returned to a Carolingian claimant. Between 936 and 987, the Robertians waited for their opportunity to reassert their claim to kingship. The Robertian Hugh the Great (d. 956) and other French nobles slowly whittled away at late Carolingian royal rights, lands, and offices. By the tenth century, the monarchy of Francia was impotent; these kings made no laws and could hardly rule. King Louis IV (r. 936–954) held only one fortified town, Laon. His vassals held far more property and power than he did. To travel outside his small royal realm, the king had to secure the permission of his nobles.

In 987, the last of the Carolingian kings of France died. Hugh Capet (r. 987–996), one of the sons of Hugh the Great, was elected and crowned king of France at Rheims, where he enjoyed the support of the archbishop, Adalberon. Hugh's power lay not in the royal title that his family (called the Capetians) now held, but in his might as lord (or suzerain) with an extensive network of vassals at his command. He dominated the territory between Paris and Orléans. Like most successful lords, Hugh and his line knew how limited their power was and how small the area of royal France was at the time. Throughout the eleventh century, the Capetians continued to lose land to the powerful dukes of Champagne and Burgundy. Hence, the Capetians moved slowly and cautiously in pressing their new royal claims, but kingship had time on its side (Map 8.2).

King Henry I's Dream King Henry late in his reign is supposed to have dreamed of being attacked by peasants, knights, and bishops, which were the three orders of medieval society (those who work, those who fight, and those who pray). The nightmare suggested how greatly the king had upset the balance of the three orders in England.

The Royal Ideology of the Three Orders

Whereas the institution of vassalage and the noble-military complex laid its ideological emphasis on faithful service, kings had their own persuasive ideology in the scheme of the three orders, which appeared when monarchy was at its weakest. In his Old English translation of Boethius (the Roman senator and philosopher executed by Theoderic), King Alfred asserted that, to rule, a king needed priests (*gebedmen*), warriors (*fyrdmen*), and workers (*weorcmen*). A century later, an Anglo-Saxon abbot explained that royalty rests on three supports: workers (*laboratores*), warriors (*bellatores*), and priests (*oratores*). All were necessary—the workers to provide sustenance for the kingdom, the warriors to protect it against invasion, and the priests to intercede with God—for the kingdom to function. The division into the three orders of those who work, those who fight, and those who pray lays out an interdependent trifunctional society, one that effectively limited women to two of the categories and included a class of people, the workers or farm laborers, who were not free. The king stands outside the orders, surmounting them.

In Francia, when royalty reached its lowest point, Adalberon, the archbishop of Rheims, who oversaw the elevation of Hugh Capet to kingship, advocated the same: a well-ordered society of those who work, those who fight, and those who pray. The assumption behind this ideology was not only that each order produced something good and necessary for society as a whole, but also that kingship was necessary to govern the parts of a harmonious whole. The thrust of the ideology from the king's perspective was to equalize the orders, each being necessary to the kingdom. Here the warriors did not dominate as they had seemed to in the *Song of Roland*.

Royal ideology could, however, produce nightmares. According to his physician, King Henry I of England in the early twelfth century had a bad dream one night late in his life while visiting Normandy. He first envisioned a mob of peasants with their rustic tools rioting around him. The king awoke in a start as his guards fled. In a second sequence, the king dreamed that a host of soldiers dressed for war was threatening his life. He awoke screaming, grabbed his sword, and slashed at the air. In a third dream sequence, archbishops, bishops, and abbots approached the king with their staffs, complaining bitterly over his seizure of church property. The dream-story suggested that an aggressive king had upset the balance of the three orders and so a smoothly functioning kingdom.

The scheme of the three orders, which was later transformed into the idea of the Three Estates, was never descriptive of medieval society, which was infinitely more complex and varied. There were merchants, sailors, Jews, children, lepers, popes, outsiders, and many others whom it failed to include. The point of the ideology was rather to advocate a simplified scheme of medieval society's general shape and of the necessity of having a king to reign over its complementary parts. The ideology of the three orders did not concern itself with theology or God's sanction of kingship, but with the king's natural duty to rule over society if it was ever to achieve stability and perfect harmony.

Religious Corruption and Reform

If one way to view the Middle Ages is as a struggle for power between lords and kings, another way to understand it is as sequences of church corruption and reform.

What were the strengths and weaknesses of the imperial and papal views of church-state relations?

By the tenth century, the western church was in disarray. Fewer local and regional councils were held, local lords thought of the churches and monasteries in their territories as their property and a place to employ family members, and the education of priests and monks had declined dramatically. The call for reform came from the Cluniacs, but before long the papacy took charge and steered the reform of the church from the top down. By the end of the great reform period of the eleventh century, the papacy, and so western Christendom, had been transformed. An imperial papacy was the result, and the Middle Ages was never to be the same.

Cluny Begins Reforming Monasticism

Monasteries were always prone to corruption. Over time as abbots and monks interpreted the *Rule,* little changes grew into big changes and customary habits, loosening standards of rigor and practice. Some monasteries allowed women to live with their monastic husbands and others permitted a generous daily allotment of wine. Graver charges were made: that in some monasteries sodomy was common, that abbots bought their offices, and that monks were so uneducated that they could not say the Lord's Prayer. Small reform movements sprang up in areas of Germany and France in the tenth century, but none that compared to the scope and success of Cluny.

Cluny was a Benedictine monastery founded in Burgundy in 910 by Duke William of Aquitaine (thought to be the grandson of Dhuoda) and his wife. William and Cluny's first abbot conceived of something special, a monastery that was not subject to a local bishop or lord, but nominally to the papacy. By this innovation, Cluny obtained independence and freedom from local interference, both lay and ecclesiastical. Cluny was a monastery with a central administration, a heavy regimen of daily prayer, and strict rules. Between 910 and 1109, Cluny had only six abbots, all of them dedicated reformers. When abbots, particularly laymen, wanted to reform their corrupt monasteries, they turned to Cluny to investigate and purge its vices. Odo, the second abbot of Cluny, was nicknamed the "digger" because of his ability to see into the hearts and wayward habits of the monks he visited. Many monasteries signed on to the Cluniac movement and in turn became reforming monasteries. By the twelfth century, Cluny had hundreds of dependent and associated monasteries, many of whose monks were Cluniacs who professed in person to the abbot of the mother house. By the eleventh century, Cluny was so powerful that contemporaries mocked its fourth abbot as "King Odilo."

What Cluny specialized in, aside from reform, was ritual observance, chant, and prayer. Its particular devotion to prayer struck a receptive chord with people, who had become convinced by the disordered and tumultuous times in which they lived that God's reckoning was about to fall. The best remedy they could see was to give land and wealth to Cluny, which stood closer to God than worldly sinners ever could. Cluny would not just pray for their souls, but would keep praying for them until doomsday. Cluny's rigor and steadfast attention to the eternal promised donors their best chance to reach the merciful ear and forgiveness of God. The land they gave

Cluny Re-imagined The third church of Cluny was a large Romanesque basilica erected 1088–1121. The building was almost entirely destroyed during the French Revolution. On the drawing, the principal features of the church are evident: two towers at the west end, long nave, distinct crossing with three towers to form a cross, and built-up east end (the choir) with radiating chapels around the apse.

was intended to ensure the security of Cluny, to remove it from the flux of the world so that the monks could keep on praying. Cluny's example and commitment to church reform had a powerful impact on the eleventh century and wider church reform.

An Emperor and Church Reform

In 1024, the Saxon line of the Ottonian emperors was succeeded by a line of four Salian (or Frankish) kings and emperors that also thought of the papacy and the German church as under its special care. Some scholars date the beginning of the so-called Holy Roman Empire from 1024, though others would date it from the time of Charlemagne in 800 or that of Otto I in 962. The name, however, may be no more than a convenient way to distinguish a medieval empire centered in Germany from the ancient Roman Empire. Under the Salian emperors, the Ottonian system of church control continued, though it was increasingly resented by many churchmen who thought that the church should be independent and self-governing. They pointed to corrupt practices within the church that compromised its purity and godliness, particularly clerical marriages and **simony** (the buying of ecclesiastical offices).

The emperor Henry III (r. 1046–1056) agreed that the church should be reformed, though his idea of church reform differed from the one held by most ecclesiastical reformers. Henry refused to accept gifts or favors for promoting individuals to clerical offices. Like his Ottonian predecessors, he viewed himself rather than the pope as the true guardian of the integrity of the church, especially since the popes seemed to be doing such a poor job of it.

The papacy's problems in the early eleventh century were many. Its power remained largely local. Even a learned and upright pope such as Sylvester II carried little authority outside Rome and papal lands. Many of his successors could not even claim respect for their spiritual authority. They were often the creatures of their noble families and the intense factional politics of Rome. The noble house of Tusculum had over time successfully placed three members of its family on the papal throne, but in 1045, another aristocratic family arranged the election of one of its own as pope. The problem was that Pope Benedict IX was still in office. Benedict abdicated in favor of another pope, but then withdrew his abdication. In 1046, with three men claiming to be pope, Emperor Henry intervened. He deposed all three popes and oversaw the election of a German cleric as Pope Clement II (1046–1047).

The emperor's interference angered some church reformers and the noble families of Rome, but an important group of reformers within the church applauded his efforts to save the papacy and church from itself. Peter Damian (d. 1072), a Cluniac monk and sharp critic of clerical sin, welcomed Henry's intervention. With the emperor's support, Clement's successor, Pope Leo IX (1048–1054), took charge of the movement to reform the church. In a dramatic meeting at the cathedral of Rheims in 1049, he placed the relics of Saint Remigius on the high altar and then called upon the collected bishops to swear that they had not bought their offices. The group panicked. Some slipped out of the meeting before speaking, some requested time to consider their answers, and others were reputed to have been so flustered that when they rose to speak no words issued from their lips. Pope Leo had made his point. The high church was infested with corruption, and it fell to the papacy to cleanse it.

Among the reformers gathered around Leo was Cardinal Humbert (d. 1061). Humbert wrote a treatise against simony and precipitated a crisis of relations with the eastern church. On a papal legation to Constantinople in 1054, he presented the expansive claims of the reforming papacy in favor of western ecclesiastical predominance and the supremacy of its doctrines. The eastern patriarch resisted, and each side excommunicated the other. The break of the Christian Church into a Roman Catholic western church and a Greek Orthodox eastern church created the **Great** (or **East-West**) **Schism** that was not repaired (at least formally) until 1965.

Pope Gregory VII and the Investiture Controversy

The papal reformers had just begun. Like so many revolutions, this one gained speed as it went. While the emperor Henry III lived, he was as much the patron of the reform movement as the pope. When he died in 1056 and was succeeded by his six-year-old son, who was under the supervision of his mother, the church reformers asserted their right to elect the pope without imperial interference. But, since Otto the Great, the emperors had claimed the right to nominate popes. Pope Nicholas II (1058–1061) and his reforming clergy wanted to be free not only of imperial control, but also of interference from the Roman nobility. They proposed that in the future popes should be elected by cardinal-bishops. The regent for the young king Henry IV (r. 1056–1106) reacted harshly and lobbied German bishops to reject the proposal. Thus, a few years after Henry III's death, a rupture opened between the interests of the empire and the papacy. The conflict forced the papacy to reach out to other Christian kingdoms for support against the empire and thus to become more European and to practice international politics. Pope Nicholas even began to cultivate the Normans as a vassal state and his protectors. The Normans, who had an infamous reputation and had invaded southern Italy and Sicily, had even captured Pope Leo and held him for ransom in 1053.

Into this maelstrom of shifting papal prerogatives and high ambitions came one of the most enigmatic of medieval personalities, the Italian monk Hildebrand. He had gone into exile with one of the popes deposed by Henry III, but quickly found himself working for the reforming popes. He was elected Pope Gregory VII (1073–1085), not by the cardinals as the reform agenda stipulated, but by the acclamation of the people and clergy of Rome. Gregory, after whom the reform movement is called Gregorian, was not just a dedicated reformer; he was a supremely stubborn one. Now that the papacy had more or less established its autonomy, Gregory set out to put his Catholic house in order. He pushed hard against priests being married and promoted the practice of absolute clerical celibacy. He denounced simony, as had his predecessors, but Gregory's signature reform concerned the lay investiture of ecclesiastical officeholders. For that reason, the Gregorian Reform is commonly called the **Investiture Controversy.**

The Ottonian emperors and their successors had insisted on their right to invest bishops with the symbols of their office, the ring and staff (crosier). To Christendom at large it may have seemed that by this act the emperor, king, or a local lord was granting the officeholder his position and authority, in effect making him bishop. To the emperors it was critical that they continue to reserve the right to approve, nominate, and appoint bishops. The Ottonian system of controlling the proprietary or propertied church depended on it and, indeed, at some level the emperor thought of himself as the equal of, or even superior to, the pope, both being appointed by God and both having a religious or priestly function. Throughout the empire, bishops appointed by the emperor had a vested interest in maintaining the emperor's right to choose and approve bishops. To the reformers, however, **lay investiture** seemed to represent the secular control of spiritual life.

Upon this issue rested the future of both the empire and the power of the reformed papacy and its control of the church. By pursuing church reform, the papacy became one of the first centralizing forces in Europe after the collapse of Carolingian order and the localization of power. Pope Gregory claimed that all archbishops must swear an oath of obedience to the papacy and receive their palliums (mantles) from the pope. Strictly speaking, some of Gregory's claims were not based on precedent and so were not reforms, but claims for new powers. In a document called the *Dictation of the Pope* (*Dictatus papae*) an extraordinary range of bald claims was made. The problem is that we are not entirely sure of the document's origins or purpose. One explanation might be that the *Dictation* is a set of research topics or talking points that awaited precedents and proofs from the papal archives. The document does, however, suggest just how high the revolutionary Pope Gregory aimed.

King Henry IV, not yet emperor, and Gregory struggled over the appointment of bishops. In the case of the church of Milan, each supported a different candidate. In 1075, Henry marched on Milan, drove out Gregory's candidate, and invested his own choice as archbishop. The pope threatened Henry with excommunication. Henry and his bishops responded by calling Hildebrand a false monk who was claiming unprecedented powers for himself and disturbing the peace of the church. Henry's bishops broke with the pope and no longer recognized his authority. Gregory responded by excommunicating the king and did something even more damaging; he released all Christians from the allegiance they had sworn to Henry and forbade them to serve the king. It was a brilliant stroke. Henry's German enemies almost at once began to plot against him.

King Henry realized that he had been outmaneuvered by Gregory, but he seems also to have understood that, now that the matter was a public spectacle, the contest was far from finished—it was check, not checkmate. Rebels were already waging war against Henry in Saxony when his magnates granted Henry one last chance. If he did not set things right with the pope and bring about an end to his excommunication, they would choose another king. Many of them wished Henry to fail and so tried to block any attempt he might make to communicate with Rome. Henry broke free and set out to track down Gregory to ask for forgiveness. The pope for his part tried valiantly to elude Henry and to get to Germany to attend the meeting where Henry was to be deposed. The weather intervened, however, and the pope was forced to take refuge from a snowstorm in the castle at Canossa in northern Italy. There Henry found him and for three days, dressed in sackcloth as a penitent, he stood barefoot in the snow outside the castle, begging for the pope to forgive him. Finally the pope relented and forgave Henry, readmitting him to the church and undoing his excommunication. Gregory's priestly obligation to forgive sinners had not allowed him to do otherwise, though it changed everything and was not in his political interest.

King Henry was now free to suppress his enemies in Germany. Angered that the pope had abandoned them,

Henry IV Seeks Forgiveness With Abbot Hugh of Cluny as his witness, Henry IV begs Abbess Matilda of Canossa to intercede with Pope Gregory VII to lift Henry's excommunication.

the rebels elected a new king to replace Henry. Gregory claimed that he had never restored Henry to kingship, but Henry acted as though he had. With a rebel king and Henry now both claiming royal authority, a conference was called at which the pope would decide between the two. Henry was not prepared to allow Pope Gregory to render a decision that would depose him, and so he worked to undermine the conference. Gregory, however, excommunicated the king again and this time sanctioned a replacement. Henry did the only thing he could; he declared the pope deposed and replaced him. At first no one paid much attention to that deposition, but things changed when Henry defeated the rebels in 1080 and the king appointed by the pope died in the battle. In 1084, Henry marched on Rome, and his chosen pope declared the king emperor. Gregory fled into exile to his Norman protectors and died the next year.

What Cost an Imperial Papacy?

The contest between the papacy and the German rulers was chiefly over the proper place of the church in the world: who governed it, on what basis, and to what end. Since Charlemagne and Otto the Great, German rulers had felt that they were the best and divinely sanctioned protectors of the church. The emperors had integrated the church into the operation of their governments, and they were not prepared to have a distant pope abolish their authority. Moreover, the emperors were not the source of corruption within the church, as the reformers charged, for the evidence suggests that rulers such as Charlemagne, Otto the Great, and Henry III had what they thought were the best interests of the church in mind. They rescued popes on numerous occasions, deposed bad and criminal popes, and appointed to episcopal office men who they thought were good for the church and shared an interest in the state and good government.

The controversy became a war of pamphlets and propaganda as both sides sought to justify their actions. The early church reformers had not been opposed to imperial oversight of the church because they realized that negligent popes had allowed the church to drift. By the late stages of the contest, however, the reformers were dedicated to removing all secular interference from the church. Pope Gregory tested the core of the issue: did God vest the pope with the singular responsibility of ruling the church or did he also appoint the emperor to watch over it? In the process of the Investiture Controversy and, despite Gregory's final failure to unseat an emperor, the popes claimed complete leadership over the church, but they also transformed the papacy into an international political player in Europe. The *Dictation* claimed that popes could depose emperors and that only popes had the right to wear imperial insignia (a right granted by the *Donation of Constantine*). The reforming papacy had become an imperial papacy. It sought a measure of control over the empire and kingdoms of Europe, developed an impressive bureaucracy, and called for and sanctioned wars. But popes discovered, as Gregory VII did, that while they could recognize kings and make emperors, it was less easy to remove them. Gregory's papacy showed just how unsettling and intrusive a powerful and politicized papacy could be.

Finally, at Worms in 1122, an agreement or concordat was struck whereby another emperor renounced the imperial right to invest bishops with the symbols of their holy office, but was permitted to supervise their election and to invest them with their scepters, the symbols of their worldly power. The emperor thus retained some influence over the process of choosing bishops and retained an interest in one dimension of their power, but he ceded some of his religious rights over the church. The striking thing is that the kings of Christendom were not forced to surrender their own religious claim over their bishops and churches. The same contest over a king's right to control the church in his realm and the church's interest in defending its independence was waged several times over the following centuries. Kings held fast to the notion that they held a royal and religious power over the churches in their realms. Powerful churchmen and monarchs were bound to infringe on one another's authority for the simple reason that in the medieval world the church had become politicized and monarchy sanctified since kings believed that they too were sacred guardians of the church appointed by God.

The emperor Henry IV remained cut off from the official church as one excommunicated until he died. The contest with the papacy left Germany weaker than it would otherwise have been, for the emperor was left without firm control over his church and his status within Christendom remained religiously uncertain. It may not, in the long run, have been in the best interests of medieval Europe for popes and their supporters to undermine Christian kingship and emperorship. Still, the radical reform of the church, its reordering and cleansing, spilled over into local churches and local practices throughout western Europe. The church was well on its way to becoming a central player in the history of the Middle Ages; and Gregory VII had created, as his *Dictation* suggested, an imperial papacy. Although the reformers had begun by seeking a church free from worldly corruption, they ended with one that was politically engaged, centralized, and more in the world than ever.

Power Shifts at the Edges of Europe

Important power shifts occurred in the eleventh century at the territorial margins of Europe: in Byzantium, southern Italy, and England. The rise of the Seljuk Turks and their impact on the Islamic world and on Europe introduced another dynamic element into an increasingly aggressive period that was remaking the West. The Mediterranean

What did the Norman adventurers want, and what was the effect of their various conquests?

Sea and southern Europe reentered western European history and England rejoined continental history when the Norman William the Conqueror took England.

Byzantine Troubles and the Rise of the Seljuk Turks

The Byzantine Empire had a rough mid-eleventh century. The Macedonian dynasty that had, with many ups and downs, distinguished itself in the ninth and tenth centuries in war, the cultivation of the arts, relative religious stability, the adoption of the Eastern Orthodox faith by the Kievan Rus, and a secure front against Islam, came undone after the death of the emperor Basil II (the Bulgar Slayer) in 1025. Problems of imperial succession, riots, earthquakes, and disease beset the empire. The Great Schism of the universal church occurred just when the empire was weak and almost leaderless as the Macedonian dynasty reached its end. A Russian prince crossed the Danube and invaded Byzantine territories in the 1040s, and various Byzantine generals, backed by provincial strongmen, revolted.

Worse still for the Byzantine Empire was the rise of the Seljuk Turks who set out to conquer Islamic and Byzantine lands. The Turks consolidated their control of Persia, and in 1055 the general Toghril Beg (r. 1038–1063) seized Baghdad and was named sultan. The Seljuk Turks reinvigorated Islam, bringing a new religious commitment to territorial expansion and the suppression of infidels. The late eleventh century was an age of fervent intellectual development under the Seljuks. The Persian poet Omar Khayyam wrote his famous quatrains and al-Ghazali, another Persian, was at work on *The Incoherence of the Philosophers,* his critique of Islamic philosophers who had grown too dependent on Plato and Aristotle. There were resisters to the Seljuks, particularly the so-called Assassins, an assassination cult that broke off from the Ismaili sect of Shi'a Muslims. They targeted the Seljuks, who had been persecuting them.

The sultan Alp Arslan (r. 1063–1072) waged campaigns against portions of the Byzantine Empire. At the Battle of Manzikert in 1071, the sultan demolished a Byzantine army and captured the Byzantine emperor. The Seljuks seized Armenia and regained Antioch.

Norman Adventurers Take Sicily and Southern Italy

While Byzantine lands were falling to the Seljuk Turks in the east, they were failing in the west, as well. The Byzantine Empire still claimed parts of southern Italy, particularly Calabria, but it was an unfixed territory with shifting allegiances. Opportunistic Normans first hired themselves out as mercenaries to local lords and by 1029 had been granted land as payment for their service. Other Normans infiltrated the area, and by the 1040s they were plotting to divide up the region of Apulia in southern Italy. The nastiest of the Norman chiefs, Robert Guiscard, nicknamed the "Cunning One," and Richard of Aversa, forced themselves on the area. Pope Nicholas II granted them Calabria, Apulia, Sicily, and Capua as papal fiefs. The Norman adventurers, thus, found a reforming papacy ready, for its own political reasons, to give them legal sanction.

The Norman dukes attacked Byzantine and Muslim outposts in southern Italy. Robert seized the Byzantine city of Bari in 1071 and continued his conquest of Sicily, which was subject to three quarrelsome Muslim emirs. Messina was taken in 1061 and Palermo in 1072. Sicily would not become a Norman kingdom until 1130, but the Norman presence in the south signaled a shift in the balance of power in favor of an energized and increasingly aggressive western Europe. As the Byzantine Empire withered under Muslim attack, the Norman adventurers in southern Italy showed that western-led war had reached the Mediterranean.

William Conquers England

Early in the eleventh century, Aethelred (meaning "noble counsel") II (r. 978–1016), but called the Unready (*unred* meaning "without counsel"), married Emma, the daughter of the duke of Normandy. Aethelred was all too ready to murder his Danish retainers and noble hostages, including the Danish king's sister, but less than ready to defend England when the Danish king Swein invaded and drove Aethelred into exile. Swein's son, Cnut, ruled England until 1035. After Cnut, with a civil war raging in Denmark, the Anglo-Saxons supported Edward the Confessor (r. 1042–1066), the son of Aethelred and Emma, as their new king. But Edward had no children, and in the 1050s the men wanting to succeed him began to make their preparations. Among them was Edward's cousin, William, the duke of Normandy, to whom Edward was said to have promised the crown. Godwin, the earl of Wessex, had long opposed Edward. After Godwin's death, his son Harold amassed considerable lands and powers and laid claim to the throne. Unfortunately for Harold, he became a prisoner of William when he accidentally strayed into Norman territory. To win his freedom, Harold was forced to swear homage to William and to agree to support the duke's case as the rightful successor to Edward.

Edward the Confessor died early in 1066, and the Witan crowned Harold king. The king of Norway, Harald Hardrada, threatened to invade England to press his claims and Duke William was finalizing his planned invasion. William accused his vassal Harold of betraying his oath to support his lord. William secured the support of the pope for his claim to the throne and, most important of all, he assembled some eight thousand Norman soldiers to cross the Channel and invade England. In the meantime, Harald Hardrada landed in northern England

The Many Mysteries of the Bayeux Tapestry

The first mystery of the Bayeux Tapestry is its popular name, since it is not a tapestry, but an embroidery. The work is 230 feet long and 20 inches high with a main panel of narration and running margins filled with small scenes and details, some decorative, particularly in the top band, and some, typically in the bottom margin, serving as decoration and commentary on the main narrative above. The work is named after Bayeux, where the cloth has been located since at least the Late Middle Ages.[3]

The second great mystery is how the Bayeux Tapestry has survived. Great stone churches and palaces have crumbled and disappeared, precious metalwork has been melted down, and most of the clothwork of the Middle Ages has turned to dust, but the Bayeux Tapestry survives, and in relatively good condition. There were many moments when the work might have disappeared. The first mention of the work's existence in the cathedral of Bayeux occurs in an inventory of 1476. It was not mentioned again until the eighteenth century, when it was displayed for a week each year in the religious calendar. During the French Revolution, the Bayeux Tapestry briefly served as a covering for a wagon-load of military equipment. When Napoleon was contemplating an invasion of England, he ordered the work to be publicly displayed. During World War II, the Nazis, who were planning to invade England and who identified with the Normans as a Nordic people, moved it to the basement of the Louvre. Paris fell to the Allies before the work could be transported to Berlin as Hitler had ordered, where its survival would have been endangered. If history didn't destroy the Bayeux Tapestry, moths and other natural causes easily could have, but against long odds the embroidered cloth has survived.

The other mysteries of the Bayeux Tapestry are many. For whom was it made? By whom? When? Opinion varies, but many scholars believe that the piece was commissioned by William the Conqueror's half-brother Odo, the bishop of Bayeux and a combatant at Hastings. The work was probably made in England by Anglo-Saxon women following a design. The work presents the Norman victory but shows William's troops brutally burning down buildings and pillaging, and shows the doomed King Harold nobly crowned. The Bayeux Tapestry has Latin inscriptions, which are simple labels that identify and locate scenes but do not explain events. The work announces King Harold's death, but two men are shown being killed—one with the outline of an arrow penetrating his eye and the other on the ground being hacked to death. Are both Harold? The last seven feet or so of the cloth are missing. Did these missing seven feet of cloth show William being crowned as the termination of the story? The work has little religious content and yet was preserved by a cathedral. Some of the marginal illustrations are obscene, yet the work was displayed in a church. Lastly, what are we to make of the mystery woman Ælfgyva? She stands with a cleric who is shown slapping her face while below her in the bottom border a nude man dances. Who is Ælfgyva? What part does she play in the story of the conquest? Is the marginal scene of the nude man a comment on her story or utterly unrelated? None of these questions has been answered satisfactorily. Ælfgyva is a reminder to us not to dismiss the Bayeux Tapestry as a cartoon, but rather to meet it on its many different levels: as a reflection of medieval thought, a medieval way of presenting history, and a piece of captivating medieval secular art.

Ælfgyva Slapped by Priest on the Bayeux Tapestry

QUESTIONS | ***Why are cartoons and caricatures so often political in spirit? How might the Bayeux Tapestry be medieval propaganda? If so, why is its meaning so unclear?***

but was defeated decisively by King Harold at the Battle of Stamford Bridge near York. Duke William landed in the south four days after Stamford and Harold rushed down to meet the invading force. They met at the Battle of Hastings, where Harold and his brothers died on the field of battle.

That single battle cleared away all the immediate rival claimants to the throne except William. England's future had been decided by fewer than 15,000 soldiers. William the Conqueror was crowned king at the Romanesque Westminster Abbey (since replaced) on Christmas 1066.

The Norman Restructuring of England

Hardly was the battlefield at Hastings cleared when William began to legitimize his conquest and assert his authority over his new kingdom. He founded Battle Abbey on the site of his victory to thank God for his blessing that day. It took William years to overcome resistance to his conquest, from both Anglo-Saxons in the north of England and Vikings. William respected Anglo-Saxon law as it had existed before the conquest, but he set out to rule England in Norman fashion. Thus, he built castles and imposed upon England a continental form of vassalage. He regarded all the land of England as his royal property by right of conquest and redistributed much of it upon receiving oaths of allegiance. Less than 10 percent of England remained in the hands of the old Anglo-Saxon nobility. Toward the end of his reign, he commanded a great accounting of the properties of his kingdom. A chronicler complained that the king wanted to know everything he owned, right down to the last ox, cow, and pig. William's great reckoning known as the **Domesday Book,** which is now to be seen in several volumes in the Tower of London, was modeled on continental inventories of lay and ecclesiastical property. The book remains a treasure trove of information on the social history of England at the time.

William's hostile takeover did not please most Anglo-Saxons, who thought of their country as occupied by French foreigners. Revolts broke out in reaction to William's usurpation and brutality. In 1069–1070, the king savagely suppressed a rebellion in the archdiocese of York. William imposed a ruling class of French and Norman barons and subordinated Anglo-Saxons to inferior places in his government and across the land. His continental aristocrats, for social and economic reasons, reduced the Anglo-Saxon lower classes of England to a stricter servile condition. William took control of the forests of England, as was the custom on the continent, and denied English commoners their traditional right to enter and use the forests. The king's court replaced the Witan, and local lords' courts administered justice. Below the surface, however, as the Domesday Book reveals, the underlying nature of private and public life in England remained Anglo-Saxon. The Normans retained the division of the land into shires and hundreds, continued to employ sheriffs, and issued writs.

William also regarded the English church as his church, one that was reformed as the Norman church had been. Out went clerical marriage, simony, and bad bishops. William began to replace Anglo-Saxon bishops with continental clerics and reorganized the episcopal map of England, moving some episcopal seats from small towns to more prominent places. William's spirit of church reform belonged to the ideals of the emperor Henry III, not to the radical claims of Pope Gregory VII. The Conqueror agreed to pay the papal tax called Peter's Pence, but never swore fealty to the pope as Gregory requested. With William's conquest, England for better or worse joined the main course of European history.

Europeans on the Move

The Middle Ages was never static; people, individually and collectively, traveled to and settled in new places. Servile farm workers bound to the land and service to their lords might never have traveled farther than twenty miles from their birthplaces in a lifetime, but many people did. Merchants, Jews, clerics, pilgrims, scholars, and soldiers traveled vast distances, even in the Early and Central Middle Ages. There were conditions, of course, that inhibited travel: invasions by the Vikings and Magyars, the loss of open control of the Mediterranean Sea to Muslims, local lords who did not permit travel through their lands, intermittent wars, lack of good roads, heavy forests, and the lack of an infrastructure to support travel (no hotels, instruments of credit, safety or security). In the eleventh century, many of these inhibiting conditions began to change.

Why did the First Crusade occur?

As power slowly flowed upward, the intense localisms of the tenth and early eleventh centuries began to break down. People in the west began to move about more often and more freely. The late eleventh century might be thought of as a critical takeoff point for European mobility and outreach.

A Measure of Internal Peace Returns to Europe

Even the grim chronicler Raoul Glaber noticed that, after 1035, Europe seemed a more vigorous place. Churches were being built, and people were on the move. It was not the passing of the millennium of Christ's birth or death that caused that revival, but changing political and social conditions. For one thing, the invasions had fallen off, and the Scandinavian peoples had become Christian. Although it was a great age of castle building and local lords and, therefore, of internal wars, forces both religious and political were working to stabilize Europe.

Before the papacy began to reform the church, various bishops and church councils were already acting to suppress local violence. Late in the tenth century, churchmen began to promote the **Peace of God,** a movement aimed

1066: How Much Changed?

The year 1066 may mark a great sea change in English and European political history, but the year could have turned out very differently than it did. William the Conqueror, for all his planning and industry, arrived in southern England with fewer forces than King Harold could command, didn't know the lie of the land as well as his opponent, and in fact didn't know who his enemy would be. If King Harold had lost at Stamford Bridge, William would have been forced to fight against Harald Hardrada. But King Harold won a stunning victory and set out at once to confront William. Had Harold delayed, raised more troops, or even rested the ones he brought with him, all might have turned out differently. Even then the Battle of Hastings was close. During the battle, a rumor spread that William had been killed. With his troops in retreat, William entered the fray, lured Harold's infantry off a piece of commanding land where they were prevailing, and his troops killed King Harold, thus giving William a spectacular win.

The battle was a decisive turning point. For one thing, it marked the end of any real Viking threat to the fortunes of Europe, Harald Hardrada being the last Scandinavian leader to threaten England. As well, the Norman use of horses signaled a change in the nature of medieval warfare for England. The Anglo-Saxon reliance on infantry had proven itself inferior to mounted knights. The Anglo-Saxon nobility was pushed aside and replaced by a continental nobility made up of Normans, French, and Bretons. For the rest of the Middle Ages, English kings would have continental cultural and property interests that often entangled England in continental wars that it had previously avoided.

What did all of this mean to common people? There are those who doubt that the decisions of the great affect little people at all and who believe that social history is real history and political history but a superstructure that doesn't penetrate the main fabric of society. The Norman Conquest is a test case. Imagine a common farm worker living in a village like Dorchester on Thames near Oxford. His immediate lord and his lord's greater lord were replaced by Normans who soon increased the demands they made upon him and his family. They demanded more work, more dues, and a tighter interpretation of his legal standing and relations to the manor lord. He was no longer able to venture into the forests to hunt small game. He and his wife thought of their new lords as foreigners, who spoke a foreign tongue and mangled English when they spoke it at all. The local court was now more imposing and introduced trials by ordeal for cases that could not be resolved in any other way. Moreover, Dorchester lost its bishop. The new king transferred the episcopal see to Lincoln far to the north.

Change didn't happen overnight, but 1066 represented a turning point in English life for serfs, the old nobility, the English language, justice, tenure, and religion. By the 1070s, even commoners would have begun to realize how much had changed, all because their impatient Anglo-Saxon king had fallen on the field of battle to a band of horse-riding, French-speaking, foreign nobles.

QUESTIONS | ***How and why do big events impact little or ordinary people? Why was the Battle of Hastings important?***

King Harold's Death on the Bayeux Tapestry The inscription states that Harold here dies, but is he the man to the left who seems to have received an arrow to his eye, the fallen knight being butchered on the right, both of them, or neither of them?

at curbing the violence of local lords against innocents (farmers, women, and children). The Peace of God sought to extend the church's protection to society's defenseless by threatening to excommunicate violators.

The **Truce of God** extended the same policy to cover the violence done by knights and vassals to each other. The church specified certain times of the year such as Lent and certain days of the week such as Sunday and then Friday on which warriors were not to attack each other. Cluny extended these Peace and Truce rules to all of its monastic lands.

As stronger kings and greater magnates amassed power, they sought to suppress the quarreling of lesser lords and knights in the countryside of northern Europe. Those efforts helped to bring a measure of internal peace to Europe.

Pilgrims Take to the Road

Pilgrimage to holy places has always been a feature of religious experience. In the ancient world and the modern, people have been prepared to travel great distances under difficult circumstances to experience the holy. By the late ninth century, the disruption of the Vikings in the north and Muslim raids in the south and the breakdown of central authority had made the conditions for long-distance pilgrimages to holy sites such as Jerusalem difficult. A Frankish monk by the name of Bernard undertook such a pilgrimage to the Holy Land in 867. In southern Italy, he and his two companions took passage on a ship transporting hundreds of slaves to Alexandria. When the ship docked, however, the captain extorted money from the monk before he would let him disembark. Though Bernard had secured letters of identification and security from Muslim officials in southern Italy, he found himself having to pay to proceed and once was thrown in jail until he agreed to settle accounts. Nevertheless, Bernard visited the Holy Land with relative ease and saw places (or so he believed) associated with Christ's life and death. His experience on the return trip was less than happy, and he complained about how difficult it was to pass through Christian lands with different lords and kings in dispute with each other. He wrote that it had been easier and safer to travel in Muslim territories than in Christian Europe.

Bernard's account of his trip is similar to many medieval pilgrimage records, which emphasize the hardships endured in the name of God on the outward-bound trip, the holy sites seen, and then a lightly described uneventful return. A pilgrimage was a series of physical and spiritual hardships on the way to a holy destination. Though these pilgrimages are often described as individual tests, they almost always occurred in traveling parties, often of considerable size.

Pilgrimages were not all the same or undertaken for the same reasons. There were pilgrimages of penance, pilgrimages to imitate the life of Christ and its hardships, pilgrimages to honor vows, pilgrimages for medical reasons, and, less often, pilgrimages as punishments imposed by the church. Pilgrimage changed over time according to historical circumstances. In the late ninth and tenth centuries, when conditions were disordered and dangerous, shorter-distance pilgrimages within Francia were more common. In a world with poor medical care, saints' relics were the draw. People suffered from a bewildering range of ailments: demonic possession, involuntary spasms, crippled limbs, blindness, and deafness. Some traveled by boat to visit the relics housed in Einhard's church in Germany; others rode, walked, or crawled. The sick and poor gathered in great crowds seeking cures from the saints and charity from Christians. Carolingian and Romanesque churches were designed not just to house relics, but to invoke internal pilgrimages within their interiors. Chapels, which contained relics, radiated off the nave and choir of these churches. The visitor could make a mini-pilgrimage from chapel to chapel, saint to saint within the safe confines of a church.

Pilgrims Set Out on Their Journey Two pilgrims follow Christ on their journey from Emmaus on this Romanesque stone relief that served as an emblem for the pilgrimage to St. James of Compostela.

Trips to the Holy Land became somewhat easier and safer in the late tenth and early eleventh centuries. After Stephen I, the king of Hungary (r. 997–1038), converted to Christianity and the Byzantines rewon the city of

Antioch from Muslims, the overland route to the Holy Land opened up and was considered to be safer than the sea route. The weakening of the Umayyad Caliphate in northern Spain meant that travelers could pass unmolested from southern France to Santiago of Compostela where the remains of Saint James (from *Sant* or Saint and *Iago* or James), the supposed brother of Jesus, were said to be kept. Monasteries and hospices began catering to the crowds of pilgrims on their way to Santiago along the great pilgrimage roads of France and Spain. Holy travel and pilgrim commerce not only spurred a revival of trade and monasticism, giving some monasteries a particular economic and spiritual function, but also made Europe more interconnected. Cluny and its daughter houses promoted and facilitated pilgrimage. With profound awareness of their sinful state, Christians in the tenth and eleventh centuries saw pilgrimage as a form of release. We know of one female sinner who visited Vézelay in France, entered the great Romanesque church under its forbidding tympanum sculpture, and placed a list of her sins on the high altar, whereupon they were forgiven. Some bishops advised members of their flocks to make pilgrimages to Santiago and perform penance for their sins.

Preconditions for Crusade

After 1035, European society became more aware of itself as a Christian community and of those inside and out who were "other." As the church reformed its doctrines and practices, Christians became aware of those who were different. The Great Schism between the eastern and western churches was one sign of an aggressive new definition of western doctrinal orthodoxy. In territorial terms, the Norman attack on the Byzantines and Muslim powers of southern Italy and Sicily was also an attack upon the "other." In northern Spain, a similar drive to retake lands from the Muslims was under way.

The reforming church also began to identify those whose beliefs did not meet orthodox standards. Shortly after the year 1000, a number of popular heresies sprang up in Europe. Some of these "heretics" were anti-materialists who believed in holding property in common, spurned marriage and the sacraments, and refused to eat meat. One such sect broke out at Orléans in northern France in 1028. Two of the so-called heretics maintained that they were just following a simpler understanding of God's power and rejected the "fictions of carnal men written down on the skins of dead animals [parchment]." They were tried, stripped of their clerical vestments, and burned to death. Another example is the case of the peasant Eon. When he went to mass one day, he heard the priest intone in Latin *"per eundem . . . Jesum Christum"* [through Jesus Christ himself]. Hearing these words, Eon thought that he had been named in the service and so concluded that he was Jesus. He went through the countryside preaching until the authorities silenced him. As the church formalized its doctrines, it identified those who held heterodox beliefs and sought either to reincorporate them or to remove them from the body of true believers. This stage in the doctrinal centralization of Europe was similar to the territorial centralizations occurring in the same period.

Living the Material Surge of the European Economy

Perhaps the greatest precondition for crusade was material. Both crusade and cultural revival depended on an economic surge that was transforming the material basis of European society in the eleventh and twelfth centuries, for neither war nor advanced thought can occur in a material vacuum. By the late eleventh century, Europe was an increasingly prosperous society. For one thing, Europe's climate was improving. Climatologists have identified a **Medieval Warm Period** that stretched from 775 to 1275, reaching a climatic optimum in the late eleventh and early twelfth centuries. The evidence for this warming climate is indicated by longer, warmer growing seasons as measured by tree rings and tree lines pushing farther north and farther up mountainsides. The Domesday Book records vineyards in England, and English monasteries such as Glastonbury were producing wines, which suggest the existence of higher temperatures. In a predominantly agricultural economy, warmer weather benefited areas with fertile fields such as France. The surpluses generated by the agricultural economy help to explain how the great burst of church building in the eleventh century was financed.

Improving weather and more bountiful agriculture may also have had something to do with a changing attitude toward nature. In the Early Middle Ages, men and women had tended to think of nature as dark and foreboding, a threatening presence in daily life. Now poets began to sing of gentle south winds and to speak of *Natura* (nature) as a goddess. Late in the Romanesque Central Middle Ages, the notion took hold that nature was a resource, a good given to humans by God for their benefit and exploitation. From that shift in attitudes from nature as a hostile "other" to nature as a good, God-given resource may derive many western attitudes (positive and negative) toward nature and the place of human beings in it or above it.

The eleventh and twelfth centuries were centuries of exciting invention. Anna Comnena, the Byzantine historian and daughter of the eastern emperor Alexius I, made the astute observation that the Franks (westerners) were obsessed with gadgets. Mills of different types now dotted the European countryside. By 1120, England had over five thousand watermills; windmills appeared late in the twelfth century. These mills were often controlled by lords who charged their dependent farm workers to grind their wheat. Europe was turning from an almost exclusively woodworking culture to one of ironworkers and stonecutters. The erection of massive stone buildings required complex machinery to cut and raise to great heights stones weighing as much as a ton. New developments in armor, castle building, and plumbing appeared.

Thanks to improvements in agriculture and economic production, the health of many Europeans improved, which led to an increased birth rate. The population grew dramatically. Estimates suggest that Europe's population may have risen from 40 million people in 1000 to as many as 48 million in 1100 and to 60 million in 1200, thus a roughly 50 percent growth in two centuries. By the mid-twelfth century, Paris may have had as many as 30,000 people; Rome, 35,000; and London, 40,000. Throughout the Early Middle Ages, Europe had been predominantly rural. Now it had a vigorous urban dimension as well, which spurred trade since rural areas now had markets for the sale of the foodstuffs and resources that only they could supply. Europe also saw the return of a money economy in the eleventh century. In 900, England had only ten mints, but by 1100, it had over seventy. The greater use of money and an expanding commercial base stimulated a shift toward arithmetical and rational thought among the merchant and burgher (prosperous townsmen) classes of the towns and cities of Europe.

Much of the dramatic demographic upsurge occurred in France, the Netherlands, northern Italy, and southern Germany, but marginal areas such as Hungary, northern England, Ireland, Scotland, and Poland saw only small population increases. Some internal colonization took place, and new towns were founded, often not located on rivers. New lands were being cleared and marginal agricultural lands brought into production. Monks moved into "wilderness" areas that previously had been deemed unsuitable for easy human habitation. In the Netherlands and Flanders, land was being recovered from the sea as marshes were drained and dikes built.

The production of surpluses and the return of limited peace may also help to explain the growth in population, but it may also have produced the conditions for more internal violence. The period between 1050 and 1150 witnessed the emergence of a youth culture with an excess of young men without obvious positions and employment. Young nobles were trained to fight and to seek adventure, but most were not destined to inherit land or title, at least not in greater France, where the practice of **primogeniture** (passage of land and title to the eldest son) had taken hold. So not only were there more people to go on pilgrimage to distant places, wandering scholars, and traveling merchants, but also young warriors looking for wars and a fitting place in an increasingly competitive and crowded world.

The First Crusade

Pilgrimages by land to the Holy Land were relatively easy until the 1060s, in part because of the Byzantine success in regaining part of Syria. Various Islamic groups were at war with one another in the area, so that there was for a time no general policy prohibiting travelers from reaching Jerusalem. In the late 1060s and early 1070s, however, the Seljuk Turks finally placed most of the Holy Land under their control and imposed a stricter version of Islam, one that distrusted infidels. Western Europe began to hear rumors of the persecution of Christian pilgrims in the Holy Land, and Pope Gregory VII regretted that the Holy Land had fallen into pagan (as Muslims were portrayed at the time) hands. He planned a campaign of 50,000 warriors to liberate the Holy Sepulcher (the church site of Christ's temporary tomb after the crucifixion) in Jerusalem. Thus did the idea of crusade first occur to a pope who was trying to secure his universal leadership of Christendom. His political difficulties and death denied him his dream of liberating the Holy Land, but the right to call for a crusade became a papal prerogative just as was its right to crown emperors. When popes called for and mounted crusades, a militant imperial papacy sought to demonstrate its leadership of all of Christian Europe.

CHRONOLOGY Dating the First Crusade

DATE	EVENT
1096	Failure of the Peasants' Crusade
1096	Crusaders assemble at Constantinople
1097	Crusaders cross the Bosporus Straits; take Nicaea
1098	Crusaders stall at Antioch; find the Holy Lance
1098	Crusaders capture Antioch
1099	Crusaders capture Jerusalem; Kingdom of Jerusalem established

The Byzantine Empire may not have fully appreciated the dynamics of the unfolding western crusade, but it played a critical role in the process. By the last quarter of the eleventh century, the Byzantine Empire had seen its gains in Syria rolled back by the Turks and its buffer zone against Islam once again gone. The eastern emperor Alexius I (r. 1081–1118) wanted to employ western knights, the Franks, to assist him in regaining Christian lands and cities in the east and to protect Constantinople. He sought mercenaries, but instead got western warriors with a religious mission and territorial aims of their own.

At the Council of Clermont in 1095, Pope Urban II (1088–1099) gave an inflammatory speech to a gathering of bishops, abbots, and Frankish nobles. He invited them to put away their petty squabbles with each other, to enter upon the road to the Holy Sepulcher, and to liberate the Holy Land from the wicked race polluting it. His language was harsh and unforgiving, designed to stir his knightly listeners to hatred of the enemy and to free holy places from their desecrators. An unclean nation, he said, was engaged in destroying Christian churches and desecrating altars. Pagans were enslaving and torturing

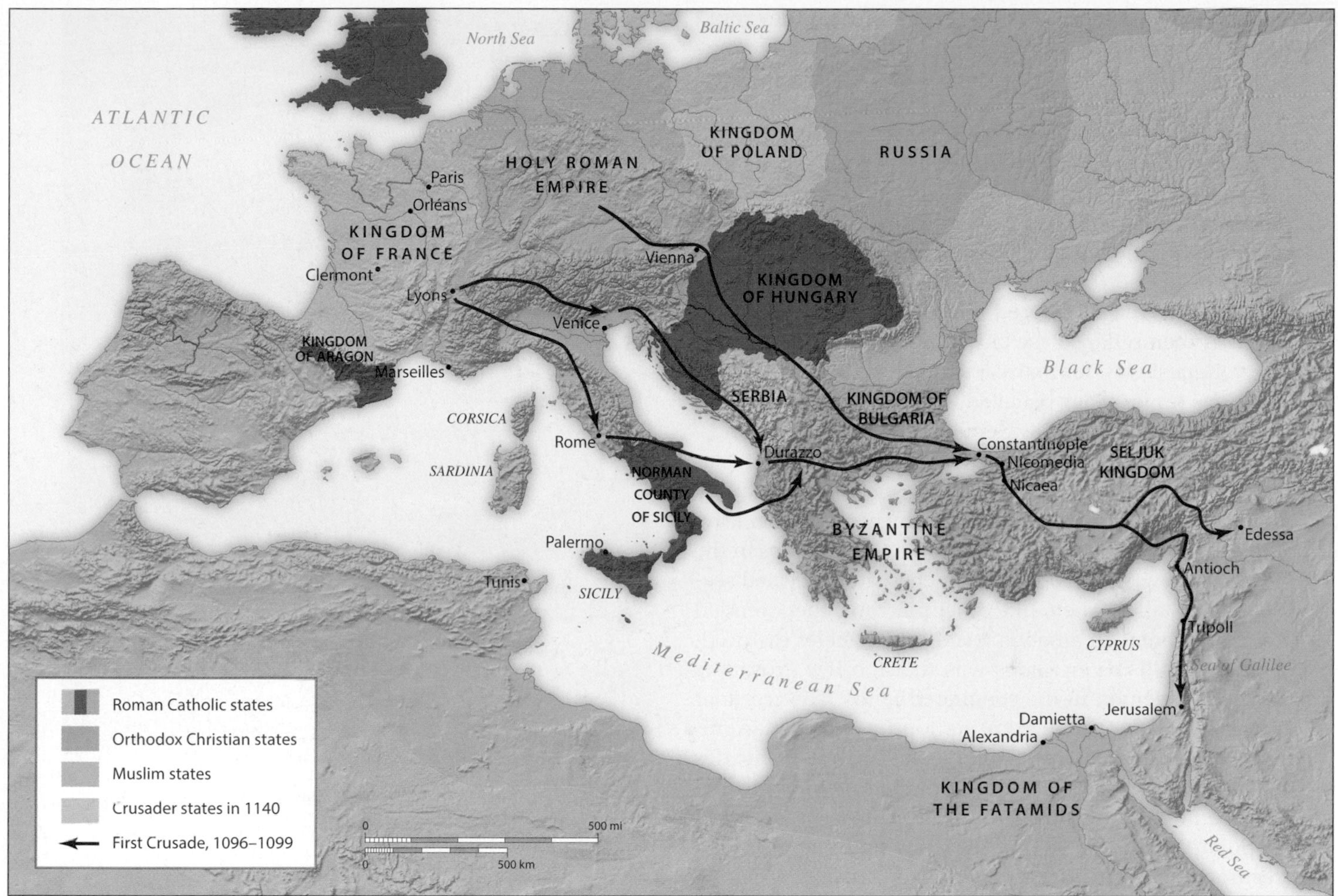

MAP 8.3 | **The First Crusade, 1095–1099**

The First Crusade began with Pope Urban II's call for a crusade to the Holy Land in 1095 at Clermont, France, and ended four years later with the conquest of Jerusalem. ***What were the staging points of the crusade? Why did the crusaders follow a land route to the Holy Land?***

Christians and raping Christian women. His appeal to Christians was religious, for he spoke of crusade (from the French word for "cross") and called on the Franks to think of their adventure as an armed pilgrimage. They were to travel with the sign of the cross on their foreheads and to return home with it on their backs as a sign of fulfillment. Crusaders were promised a plenary or full indulgence (or remission) for their sins, the right to keep the land they conquered, and the postponement of the debts they owed at home (see Back to the Source at the end of the chapter).

The pope did more than just announce a crusade to rewin the holy land; he actively promoted the idea. He went on a speaking tour in France to stir up support. Popular preachers, with colorful names such as Walter the Penniless, also began to preach crusade. One of these preachers, Peter the Hermit, led a throng of people toward the Holy Land on the so-called Peasants' Crusade, but it lacked official sanction and these common crusaders and their families were slaughtered long before they arrived. In Europe, popular movements at the time also led to the persecution of Jews as a dangerous "other" in their midst. As the rhetoric rose, **pogroms** against the Jews were carried out in various European cities. The idea of crusade immediately struck Europe as an exciting adventure. The motives of the crusaders were many and mixed. Some went for religious reasons, others for material gain, others for a military adventure, and yet others because crusade opened up possibilities for advancement that Europe denied them. By 1096, thousands of western crusaders began to assemble outside the walls of Constantinople, ready to march to Jerusalem (Map 8.3). The Byzantine emperor Alexius was surprised by the size and fervor of the mob of armed Franks and was not prepared to let them pass until they swore an oath of fealty to him. By 1097, the western crusaders had crossed over the Bosporus Straits and quickly took the city of Nicaea, which they turned over to the emperor Alexius.

As the crusaders proceeded, they established the first of four crusader states at Edessa. At Antioch, the crusade stalled when the city would not surrender and the siege became protracted. The chroniclers report that it was at this point of despair that crusaders discovered the holy lance that pierced Christ's side while he was on the cross.

It apparently did not bother the crusaders that they could have seen another holy lance in Constantinople. They expected to find physical evidence of Christ in the land that he had once walked. The miraculous discovery, no matter how convenient its finding, re-inspired the crusaders, who captured Antioch in June 1098 and slaughtered all its male inhabitants. The crusaders did not reach Jerusalem until 1099 and broke through the walls of the Holy Sepulcher on June 15. One of the historians who was present claimed that 10,000 Muslims (men, women, and children) were slaughtered inside the temple. The conquerors then pillaged the city of Jerusalem. As brutal as the conquest was, for many it was also a moment of high religious fervor. They believed that they had restored the holiest of holies (the Holy Sepulcher) to Christian hands.

A kingdom of Jerusalem was established. Most crusaders, however, had not come to stay, and gradually small groups began to make their way home. Before leaving they went on tours of the Holy Land, took dips in the Jordan River, gathered palm branches, and collected seashells in Galilee. Then, like other pilgrims, they wended their way home to anxious loved ones. One of the problems with all the crusades was that too few crusaders wished to remain in the conquered lands. The crusader kingdoms were ruled from the top by a Christian minority that built magnificent castles such as Krak des Chevaliers in Syria, but that remained distant and defensive in the conquered lands. The First Crusade was a popular crusade, reflecting the growing dynamism of a resurgent west, its internal energy and tensions. Crusade was, in part, a safety valve releasing European demographic and social pressures onto the external world. It was also a vehicle promoted by the papacy for reinforcing European and papal identity. That same burst of energy was also at work in the building of magnificent cathedrals such as the one that Gislebertus adorned at Autun, in rousing martial epics such as the *Song of Roland*, and in the revival of culture that was redefining Europe.

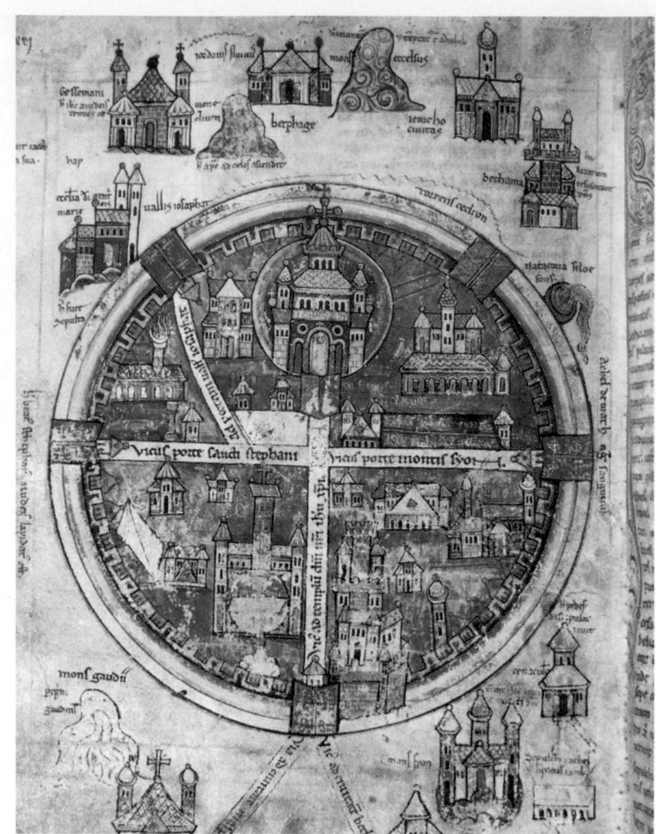

Jerusalem during the Crusades A map of Jerusalem from Robert the Monk's chronicle of the First Crusade.

Conclusion

At the end of the Romanesque Central Middle Ages of the tenth and eleventh centuries, medieval Europe stood on the brink of assuming its most refined form. Cluniac monasticism and a reformed papacy had redirected the purposes and efficiency of the medieval church, which was now more centralized, rigorous, and powerful. An imperial papacy believed that at some level it was in command of Christian Europe, even to the point of overthrowing emperors, establishing vassal states, demanding the fealty of kings and all Christians, and calling for holy war. At a popular level, religion had become the spiritual heart and motive force of Europe. Driven by religious fervor, men and women went on great pilgrimages to distant places, turned over their property as bequests to monasteries, and prayed for their eternal salvation. They visited massive new cathedrals such as the one built at Autun, and on its exterior and interior they saw high Christian art such as Gislebertus's unforgettable scenes of the life of Christ, the Last Judgment, and the horrifying figures of the demons who haunted their nightmares. The church offered them a glimpse of another and truer world.

Royal and imperial power had been relatively weak in the tenth century after the fall of the Carolingians. Local lords and their vassals stepped in to take what power they could throughout Europe in this period of decentralization. The Ottonian emperors may have shaped their power along Carolingian lines, but empire was a diminished thing after Charlemagne, since its territorial command of Europe was limited. But by the eleventh century, power was once again returning to central authorities. The Anglo-Saxon kings of England and the Capetian kings of France showed that royal power had a future beyond the ideology of the three orders, which they had emphasized when kingship was weakest. In the late eleventh century, territory and power in Europe and the Middle East was still in flux, but the state changes in southern Italy, Byzantium, Islam, and England established the territorial conditions for the High Middle Ages. The First Crusade was the product of a reinvigorated and aggressive Europe and a sign that medieval Europe was reaching its mature, most developed, and dangerous form. Gislebertus, the sculptor of the portal of the forking path to paradise and hell at Autun, would not have been surprised. He knew something of the extremes of the human condition and reflected the Romanesque Age's restless energy and its preoccupation with the light and dark sides of the European imagination.

Critical Thinking Questions

1. How and why did the Middle Ages change direction in the tenth and eleventh centuries?
2. What impact did the disordered conditions of life in the Central Middle Ages have on people and their attitudes toward the world and their place in it?
3. What were the big events of the period, and how did they change Europe?
4. Why did so much of the historical action of the Central Middle Ages occur on the edges of Europe?
5. What choices did people such as vassals, pilgrims, Otto the Great, Pope Gregory VII, King Henry IV, and William the Conqueror make, and why did they matter?

Key Terms

tympanum **(p. 232)**
nave **(p. 233)**
basilica **(p. 233)**
vassalage **(p. 233)**
benefice **(p. 234)**
keep **(p. 237)**
Ottonian system **(p. 239)**
simony **(p. 245)**
Great (East-West) Schism **(p. 245)**
Investiture Controversy **(p. 246)**
lay investiture **(p. 246)**
Domesday Book **(p. 250)**
Peace of God **(p. 250)**
Truce of God **(p. 252)**
Medieval Warm Period **(p. 253)**
primogeniture **(p. 254)**
pogrom **(p. 255)**

Primary Sources in connect

For information on Connect and the online resources available, go to **http://connect.mcgraw-hill.com**.

1. **A Vassalage Oath**
2. **Fulbert of Chartres on the Obligations of Vassals**
3. **The Deaths of Oliver and Roland**
4. **The Dictation of the Pope (*Dictatus papae*)**
5. **A Lady Sings for the Return of Her Crusader**

A Pope Calls for Crusade

In November 1095 at Clermont in France, Pope Urban II presided over a council of high churchmen and various princes from France and Germany. In a public square he addressed the assembled people. Five versions of the speech survive. The one presented below comes from the work of Robert the Monk, who wrote his account early in the twelfth century, but Robert may have been a witness to Urban's call for crusade.

Oh, race of Franks, race from across the mountains, race chosen and loved by God—as shines in many of your works—set apart from all nations by the situation of your country, as well as by your Catholic faith and the honor of the holy church! To you our discourse is addressed and for you our exhortation is intended. We wish you to know what a grievous cause has led us to your country, what peril threatening you and all the faithful has brought us here.

From the confines of Jerusalem and the city of Constantinople a horrible tale has gone forth and often been brought to our ears, namely, that a race from the kingdom of the Persians, an accursed race, a race utterly alienated from God, a generation indeed that has not directed its heart and has not entrusted its spirit to God, has invaded the lands of those Christians and has depopulated them by sword, pillage, and fire; it has led away some captives into its own country, and some it has destroyed by cruel torture; it has entirely destroyed churches of God or appropriated them for the rites of its own religion. They destroy altars after having defiled them with their uncleanness. They circumcise Christians and the blood of circumcision they either spread upon the altars or pour into the vases of the baptismal font. When they wish to torture people with a degrading death, they perforate their navels, drag forth the end of their intestines, and affix it to a stake; then with flogging they lead the victim around until their innards gush forth and the victims fall flat on the ground. Others they bind to a post and pierce with arrows. Others they compel to extend their necks and then, attacking them with naked swords, attempt to cut through their necks with a single blow. What shall I say of the abominable rape of women? To speak of it would be worse than to be silent. The kingdom of the Greeks is now dismembered by them and deprived of a territory so vast in extent that it cannot be traversed in a march of two months. On whom, therefore, falls the task of avenging these wrongs and of recovering this territory incumbent, if not you? You, upon whom above other nations God has conferred remarkable glory in arms, great courage, great energy, and strength to humble the hairy scalps of those who resist you.

Let the deeds of your ancestors move you and incite your minds to brave achievements; the glory and greatness of King Charlemagne, his son Louis, and your other kings, who have destroyed the kingdoms of the pagans, and have extended in these lands the territory of the holy church. Let the holy sepulcher of the Lord our Savior, which is possessed by unclean nations, especially incite you, and the holy places which are now treated with baseness and irreverently polluted with their filthiness. Oh, most valiant soldiers and descendants of invincible ancestors, do not be degenerate, but recall the valor of your ancestors.

But if you are hindered by love of children, parents, and wives, remember what the Lord says in the Gospel, "he that loveth father or mother more than me, is not worthy of me." "Every one that hath forsaken houses, or brethren, or sisters, or father, or mother, or wife, or children, or lands for my name's sake shall receive a hundred-fold and shall inherit everlasting life." Let none of your possessions detain you, no concern for your family affairs, since this land that you inhabit, shut in on all sides by the seas and surrounded by mountain peaks, is too narrow for your large population; nor does it abound in riches; and it furnishes scarcely food enough for its cultivators. So it is that you murder one another, that you wage war, and that frequently you perish by mutual wounds. Therefore, let hatred depart from among you, let your quarrels end, let wars cease, and let all dissensions and controversies slumber. Enter upon the road to the Holy Sepulcher; wrest that land from a wicked race and subject it to yourselves. That land which as Scripture says "floweth with milk and honey," was given by God to the children of Israel to hold.

Jerusalem is the navel of the world; the land is fruitful above others, like another paradise of delights. This the Redeemer of the human race made illustrious by his advent, beautified by residence, consecrated by his suffering, redeemed by death, and glorified by his burial. The royal city, therefore, situated at the center of the world, is now held captive by his enemies and is in subjection to those who do not know God and to the worship of the heathens. Jerusalem seeks, therefore, and desires to be liberated, and does not cease to implore you to come to her aid. From you especially she asks for relief, because as we have already said, God has conferred upon you above all nations great glory in arms. Accordingly undertake this journey for the remission of your sins, with the assurance of the imperishable glory of the kingdom of Heaven.

When Pope Urban had said these and many similar things in his polished speech, he so moved to one purpose the thoughts of all present that they cried out, "It is the will of God! It is the will of God!" When the venerable Roman pontiff heard that, with eyes uplifted to heaven, he gave thanks to God and with his hands commanding silence said:

Most beloved brethren, today is manifest in you what the Lord says in the Gospel, "Where two or three are gathered together in my name there am I in the midst of them." Unless the Lord God had been present in your spirits, all of you would not have uttered the same cry. For, although the cry issued from numerous mouths, the source of the cry was singular. Therefore I say to you that God, who implanted this in your chests, has drawn it forth from you. Let this then be your war-cry in combat, because these words were given to you by God. When you are making an armed attack upon the enemy, let this one shout be raised by all the soldiers of God: It is the will of God! It is the will of God!

And we do not command or advise that the old or feeble, or those unfit to bear arms, undertake this journey; nor should women set out at all without their husbands or brothers or legal guardians. For such [women] would be more of a hindrance than aid, more of a burden than advantage. Let the rich aid the poor; and, according to their wealth, let them take with them experienced soldiers. Priests and clerics of any order are not to go without the consent of their bishops; for this journey would profit them nothing if they went without the permission of those. Also, it is not fitting that laymen should enter upon the pilgrimage without the blessing of their priests.

Whoever, therefore, shall commit to this holy pilgrimage and make his vow to God to that effect and shall offer himself to him as a living sacrifice acceptable unto God, shall wear the sign of the cross of the Lord on his forehead or on his chest. When he has fulfilled his vow and wishes to return, let him place the cross on his back between his shoulders. By that two-fold action he will fulfill the precept of the Lord as he commands in the Gospel, "He that taketh not the cross and followeth after me, is not worthy of me.

QUESTIONS | *Why might the speech and the First Crusade be viewed as the conclusion or culmination of the Romanesque Central Middle Ages, its tensions and aspirations? Why did Pope Urban sponsor a crusade? How did he excite the passion of the crowd? How did he justify the proposed attack upon a foreign land?*

Source: "The Speech of Pope Urban II at Clermont," trans. Dana C. Munro, *American Historical Review* 11 (1906), 231–242; revised.

9

Interior of St. Denis

THE GOTHIC HIGH MIDDLE AGES

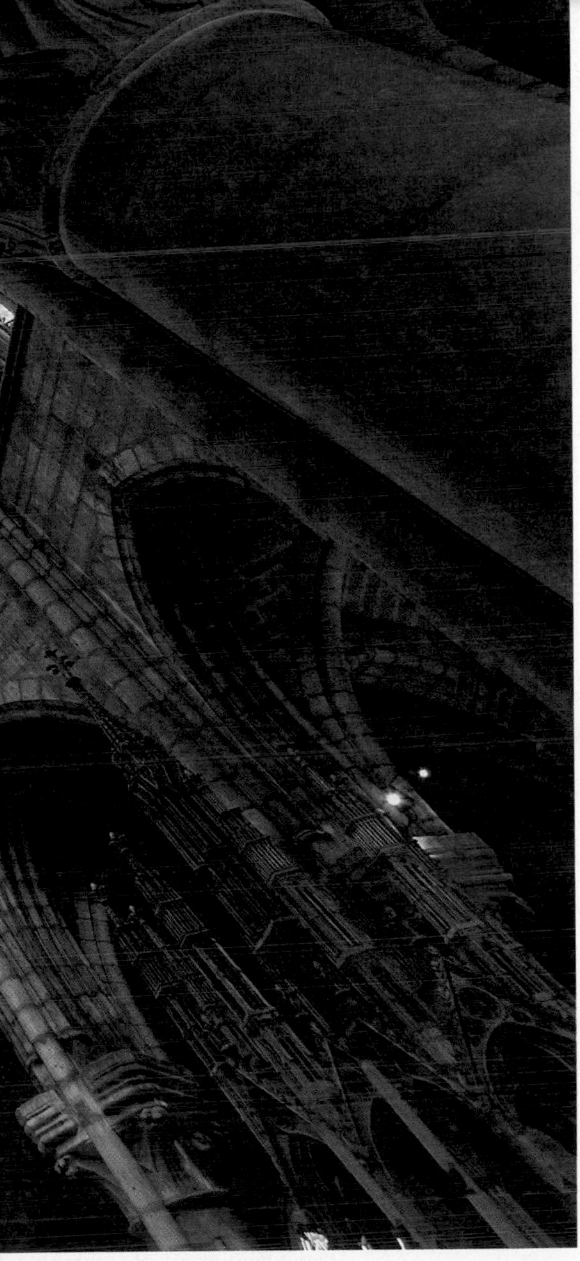

THE AFFAIR OF ABELARD AND HELOISE The affair of Abelard and Heloise was not only a great scandal; it flouted the conventions of the ordered society the High Middle Ages was laying down. Abelard was in his thirties, Heloise in her late teens or early twenties when they became lovers. He had been employed as her private tutor because of his towering reputation and sterling character. Bloated with pride, he set out to seduce his student. Intimate reading soon led to whispers of love. Eventually her uncle Fulbert caught the two of them. She may already have been pregnant. To protect himself against her enraged uncle (since to hurt him would be to endanger her), Abelard sent his lover to stay with his family in Brittany, where she gave birth to their son. With his reputation in danger of ruin, Abelard resolved to marry Heloise, but secretly so that he could continue to hold his clerical teaching post. Heloise argued vigorously against marriage, preferring "love over marriage, freedom over bondage." If the Roman emperor himself had offered her marriage, she said, she would still rather be her lover's whore than empress of the whole world. They did marry, but Fulbert remained resentful, and so Abelard spirited Heloise away to the monastery where she had been educated. Uncle Fulbert, a church deacon, furious over his public disgrace, sent henchmen to castrate Abelard, the violator of his niece. After that cruel cut and the public humiliation of it, Abelard became a monk and compelled Heloise to become a nun.

The melodrama of their passionate affair should not cause us to lose sight of what these two extraordinary individuals have to tell us about the Gothic High Middle Ages, particularly about the great intellectual and institutional achievements the age made. Education led the way and so we need to spend time in this chapter following the path that led from cathedral schools to universities, from Abelard to Aquinas, and that produced a remarkable confidence in the human capacity to know the world.

The Romanesque Central Middle Ages, after its bumpy start and troubles managing rapid growth and political and religious upheaval, had longed for reform, order, and rules. The High Middle Ages sought to perfect a form of Christian society best reflected in soaring Gothic cathedrals, rigorously rational scholastic thought, universities, representative assemblies, and powerful kings and popes. The heavy weight of authority, of centralized power and ecclesiastical bureaucracy, Aristotelian logic and synthetic thought, great wealth and a flourishing economy produced before long a backlash of popular, learned, and religious resistance.

Abelard and Heloise were among the first to test the strictures of a society striving for order and high purpose. Their unconventionality was challenge enough. They named their son Astralabe, a strange name since an astrolabe was a mechanical instrument for plotting the stars. Their careers were highly unusual. Abelard was a fiery wandering master of logic who shattered conventional forms of thinking and captured the imagination of a generation of students who flocked to Paris and wilderness retreats to hear him lecture. To his students he seemed a young prince slicing through the stale thoughts of the old masters and the dead weight of authoritative teaching. He was almost always in trouble: with his fellow masters, with church authorities, with the abbot of his monastery, and with a living saint.

Abelard's calamities continued after his affair with Heloise ended. His ecclesiastical enemies pursued him for two

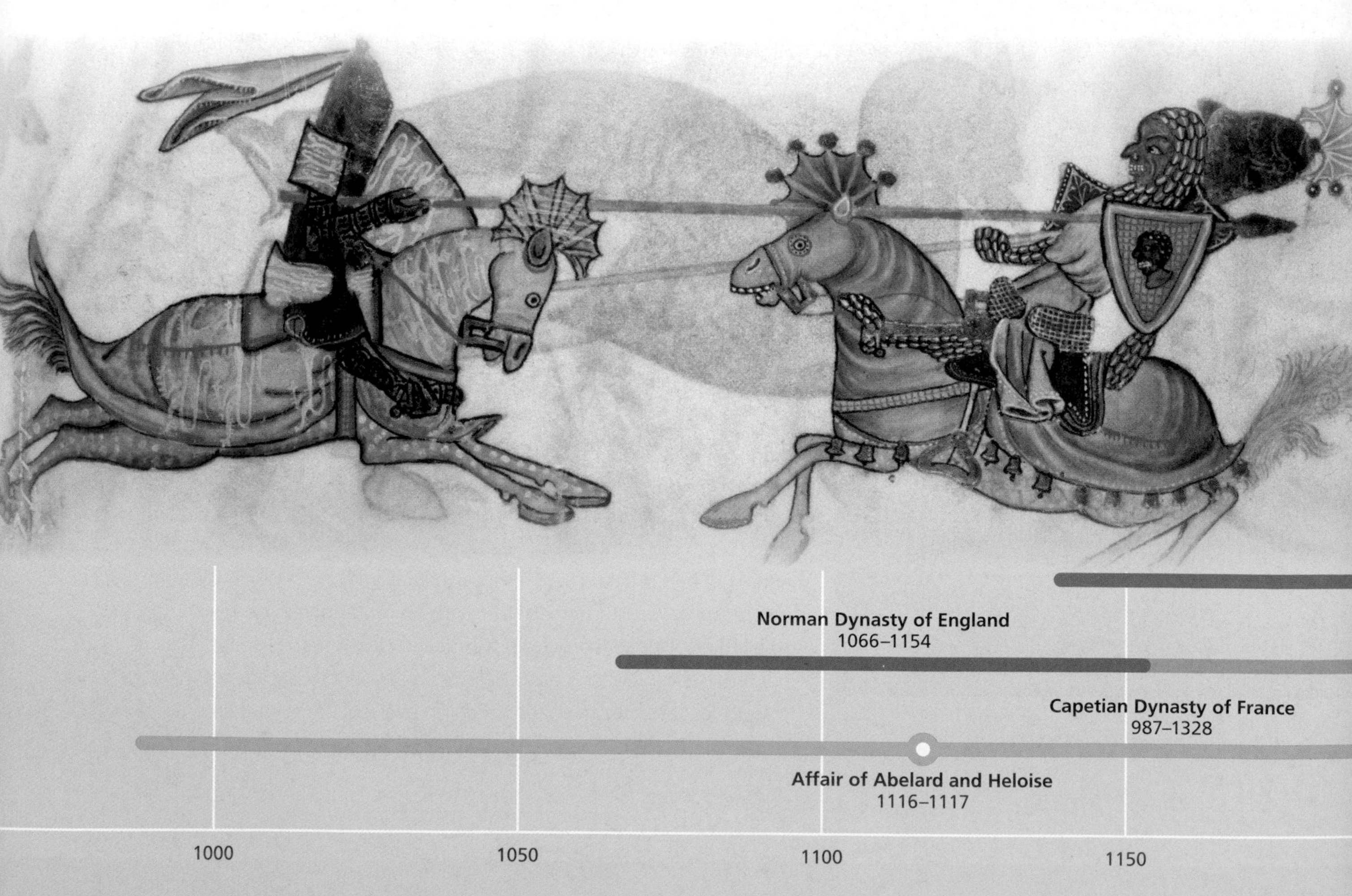

decades. To escape them, he retreated to the countryside, but students sought him out, begging him to continue to impart his new style of reasoning. In a moment of despair, he even dreamed of escaping to Islamic Spain, where he might be allowed to think in respectful peace. The core of his revolutionary method was to question received wisdom and tradition in a logical and systematic way: "Ask not who said a thing, but what is said," he advised his son. Twice the church put Abelard on trial for his teachings; at the first, a few years after the affair with Heloise had turned sour, the authorities forced Abelard to burn one of his books and confined him to a monastery. After the second, the pope excommunicated him.

Heloise was as remarkable as Abelard. Trained in a monastery school, she wanted something unheard of for a woman of her time: she wanted to be a writer and philosopher. Even as a young woman she was reputed to be the most learned woman in all of France, but Heloise had few options. She probably could not marry well for social reasons, and there were few occupations or opportunities for learned women outside of the church. Eventually she became a much admired abbess. Her letters of unrequited love and complaint to Abelard are supple and demanding. She had a gift Abelard lacked for penetrating the emotional and intellectual core of life. She never forgot Abelard, their physical and emotional bond preoccupying her thoughts about her place in the world until the day she died.

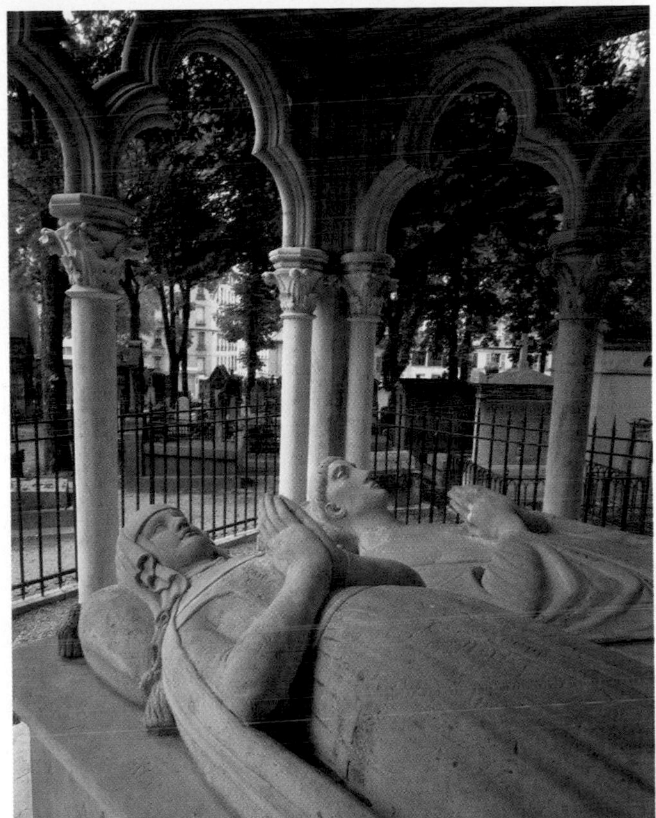

Tomb of Heloise and Abelard in Père Lachaise, Paris The remains of the controversial couple were not moved to Paris until the nineteenth century. Today there is still disagreement about where their remains are buried.

The robust intellectual searching of the early twelfth century gave way in the thirteenth century to a society that was often crowded, restrictive, and repressive. Yet its accomplishments were many: the creation of universities, scholasticism, soaring Gothic cathedrals, and the greatest systematic thinker of the Middle Ages. Thomas Aquinas became the common doctor and leading intellectual light of the Middle Ages. His life was hardly a quiet one, but his logically rigorous philosophy represented a peak of high medieval thought.

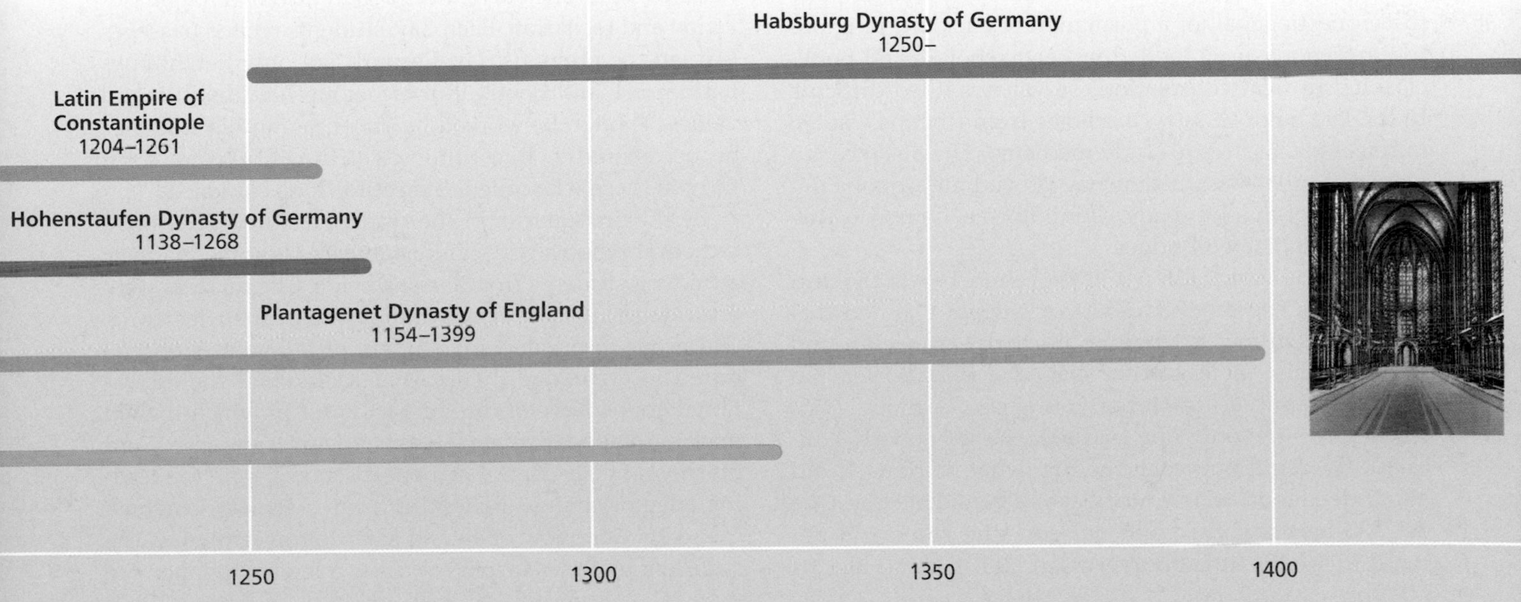

Life in Paris and other European cities was crowded by the thirteenth century. Despite disastrous crusades, strong monarchs emerged once again, and the most powerful pope of the Middle Ages, Innocent III, reformed church practice, sanctioned new religious orders, and played politics at the highest level. Enemies of the established order resisted what they deemed to be an increasingly repressive and misguided society. The thirteenth century was prosperous, urban, and intellectually vibrant, but there were signs that the medieval world (or one form of it) was reaching its limits.

A New World of Learning

Abelard was a product of the cathedral schools of greater France, which laid down the foundations of the High Middle Ages and European intellectual life. This great movement, sometimes called the Twelfth-Century Renaissance, was dynamic, humanistic, and controversial, producing at its leading edge an engagement with the world through dialectic or logic, and was succeeded by the rise of the universities and the triumph of scholasticism. The intellectual history of the age can, thus, be roughly divided into its cathedral school and university phases. Self-reflection, classicism or humanism, and a pronounced individualism characterize the first phase; limited scope but logical rigor and soaring achievement, the second.

What was the old way of learning, and what was wrong with it by the early twelfth century?

The Old Way of Learning

By the late eleventh century, stale air hung over the monastic schools that had dominated western education for six centuries. Monastic education, like life in the Early Middle Ages, was highly localized. Each monastery set its own educational standards and practices, which were chiefly religious in nature. Monastic learning and the monastic ideal (of a permanently enclosed religious life in a monastery) tended to keep scholars and books closeted in relative isolation. Travel remained difficult. In the late tenth century, a scholar from Rheims wanted to travel to Chartres to study medicine. The distance is a mere 120 miles, but the journey proved an arduous undertaking of missed roads, dying horses, injured travelers, and dilapidated bridges.

In France, things did not improve much over the next fifty years. The monk Guibert of Nogent claimed that there were so few teachers in northern France around 1060 that his noble mother bribed a tutor to leave a relative's family to teach her young son. Although this teacher was the only one available, he was poorly educated. He could not teach the boy what he himself did not understand and used to beat and berate the boy. One day Guibert's mother told her son that she could not stand to see his little body bruised all black and blue. If he wished to abandon his studies and become a knight (as the less dangerous occupation), she would support him. The plucky little boy told his mother that he would rather die on the spot than give up studying to become a cleric (or clerk). He went to a nearby monastery, where he learned Latin and began to write. His abbot, however, disapproved of young monks writing, and so Guibert was forced to write at night in secret.

Great learning still lingered in many monasteries, and outstanding monastic scholars such as Anselm of Bec (or Canterbury) wrote treatises to prove the existence of God. But too many scholar-monks were bound by a rigid older tradition of scriptural commentary and the interpretation of the symbols they saw in their texts and the world. A symbolist mode of thinking dominated the old way of learning.

Monks mumbled as they read and were said to "eat" their books, that is, they read out loud and ingested the contents of entire books as they tried to make them part of their very being. Their reading was a whole body experience of chanting and swaying that belonged to an older, primarily oral culture that knew only a few great books that needed to be learned in their entireties. It was a style of reading and thinking that was about to change, as was the large, plain, early medieval book.

The Tumult of the Schools

From 1075 to 1175, the leading educational institution of Europe was the cathedral school. Such schools had existed earlier, but they now flourished as the population grew and expanding cities surrounded their old cathedrals. The townspeople of these vibrant small cities sought places to educate their sons in Latin and the liberal arts of the **trivium** (grammar, rhetoric, and logic) and the **quadrivium** (mathematics, geometry, astronomy, and music). Bernard, the master of the cathedral school of Chartres, was reputedly so gifted a teacher that he could teach boys, even dull ones, how to read and write Latin within a year. The curriculum relied heavily on memorization and recitation. Each day, students recited passages learned the previous day. Bernard not only taught boys Latin prose and poetry, but also sought to instill moral values. Though he worked by encouraging his students, he occasionally, like other twelfth-century masters, flogged those who failed to meet his high standards.

By the first quarter of the twelfth century, prominent cathedral schools with famous masters became magnets attracting students from far and wide. The masters were formidable figures: stern, impressive in their learning, and prone to humble any student or fellow master who dared to challenge them. Abelard likened the educational atmosphere of the time to a war in which the old masters defended their citadels against new ideas and brash young rivals. But cathedral schools were the leading edge of change, benefiting from a society in which the roads were now open and safer to travel, there was a sufficient material surplus to allow a few young men the

Lost or Found? The Love Letters of Heloise and Abelard

In his account of his troubles, Abelard confesses that one of the reasons he seduced the highly educated Heloise was that she was someone with whom he could exchange letters when they were separated, writing things to each other that they dared not say in person. Some of his love songs, he recalled, became popular and were long sung by those pursuing lives of pleasure. Did the two lovers send each other love letters, and if so, what happened to them? Abelard and Heloise exchanged another set of letters called "the personal letters" twenty years after the end of their affair. The authenticity of the personal letters was a subject of some doubt in the late twentieth century, but that doubt seemed to have subsided by 2000 when a new controversy broke out. In 1999, Constant J. Mews, a leading Abelard expert, published *The Lost Love Letters of Heloise and Abelard.* Twenty-five years earlier, Ewald Könsgen had published a Latin edition of 113 love letters and poems and wondered (with a question mark in the title of the book) if these might be the lost love letters of Heloise and Abelard. Mews removed the question mark with a sustained historical, textual, and circumstantial argument that the letters were, indeed, the missing love letters of the famous couple.

The attribution is not without difficulties. There is no twelfth-century manuscript evidence of the letters. The love letters were copied by a fifteenth-century Cistercian monk who was interested in them initially because of their elaborate salutations (Man: "To his most brilliant star"; Woman: "To a shining lamp and city set upon a mountaintop"). The greater problem is that neither of the letter-writers addresses the other by name. Still the couple in the letters had as many ups and downs in their relationship as Abelard and Heloise did in theirs: breakups, hurt feelings, and solidarity against their detractors. They share events and cultural characteristics that might well fit with Abelard and Heloise. Although many prominent medievalists accepted the attribution as certain or probable, others have doubted it. Jan Ziolkowski carefully compared the Latin of the Man's letters against the known writings of Abelard and came to the conclusion, based on a comparison of verse techniques, prose rhythms, and word use, that Abelard could not be the author of the love letters. Mews observed, in response, that the special conception of "love" developed in the letters is one that Abelard alone went on to develop further in his works, as though he (or he and Heloise) owned the idea.[1] The attribution of the love letters to Heloise and Abelard still awaits consensus, but then a quarter of a century ago so did the personal letters. That dust-up seems to have died down as the leading edge of the controversial careers of Heloise and Abelard has moved forward to the new brouhaha over the love letters. In their lives and in the scholarship about them, controversy has always dogged the two lovers. Abelard, at least, might have been pleased, for he believed that it was only through the presentation of contraries, argument, and analysis that true understanding could be achieved.

QUESTIONS | ***Why was a celebrity culture, at least in modern terms, not possible in the Middle Ages? Why were Abelard and Heloise so controversial? Did Abelard just have a contrary nature, or was there something about his time that was inherently controversial? Why? How does the comparison and contrast of ideas lead to intellectual progress?***

luxury of obtaining a higher education, and larger towns and small cities that looked to cathedrals to educate boys. Part of the appeal of these schools was the star quality of upstart masters such as Abelard.

Abelard and other daring masters worked less by exposition than by questioning received wisdom. Abelard's *Sic et Non* (*Yes and No*) is an extraordinary example of the method. He collected contradictory authoritative statements by the fathers of the church and a few from the Bible and set them beside each other to demonstrate their differences. He chose not to resolve those differences but demonstrated that the authorities were in disagreement and, following the dialectical method, left it to the reader to engage and resolve the differences.

Anselm, the master of the cathedral school of Laon, with whom Abelard tangled, systematically amassed and sorted through the vast body of scriptural interpretation. In his evening meetings with senior students, Anselm also explored various issues that they might expect later as parish priests to hear from their flocks: could a man marry his longtime lover, what was to be done when a child died before receiving baptism, and how should the claims of some women that they had sexual intercourse with demons (the *incubi*) be handled? These question-and-answer sessions were one place where the higher learning of the schools touched a wider world of domestic concerns.

Around 1125, William of Conches, a young master of Chartres, produced a textbook he baldly called *Philosophy,* a summary of what could reasonably be said about the world. His approach was based not on scientific experiment or observation, but on reason and intelligent book learning. In opposing his monastic critics, who trusted in what the Bible and sacred teachings had to say about the natural world, William doubted that God was a capricious bender of the rules of nature. He cited the case of peasants who believed that God could make a calf from a tree trunk. God could do that, of course, says William, but has he ever actually done so? William's was a twelfth-century version of Albert Einstein's quip that God doesn't play dice with the universe. William's attitude, in medieval terms, was scientific, for he respected creation as a physical phenomenon and the human capacity (also given by God) to understand it. Nature, for him, was regular and followed established rules and patterns. William's book reflected a new attitude toward the material universe, its rational causes and processes. Not surprisingly, that attitude landed him in trouble with certain monks and conservative elements within the church, since he seemed to have put reason ahead of doctrinal or church authority. Like Abelard and Anselm of Laon, William of Conches belonged to the great rethinking of the medieval world that was transforming twelfth-century thought.

Hildegard Receiving a Vision Here a molten light pours into Hildegard in visionary rapture while a monk (in an adjoining space or room) takes down her description of the vision and a nun tends to her.

John of Salisbury from England was one of William's students and a **humanist** (in medieval terms, one with an interest in the classics, Latin eloquence, and human affairs). John went on to write on papal politics, the doings of kings and courtiers, and the tumultuous world of the cathedral schools. When as a young man in 1136 he had arrived in Paris, he found dozens of teachers on such subjects as logic under whom he could study. A critical mass of intellectuals had gathered there to argue with each other and collectively work toward a rational explanation of the world, one in which the created world rationally reflected the divine will. The masters were confident that their logical methods (of ordered and systematic investigations and reasoning) would make sense of the world as it was and that these methods, if applied systematically, would restore the proper place of human beings in the cosmos. The masters fought with and ridiculed each other but established a high medieval confidence in the "knowability" of the world.

The Revitalization and Renewal of Monastic Learning

In the early twelfth century, the exciting new worldview of the masters began to revitalize even the monastic schools. Heloise herself was a product of the monastic school of Argenteuil, where she had imbibed classical and medieval learning, learned Latin poetry, and become a twelfth-century humanist in her own right. Women were excluded from the cathedral schools, but many religious women continued to pursue scholarly work in monasteries. The parents of Hildegard of Bingen had surrendered her as a child to the religious life. She became a Benedictine nun in Germany and eventually an abbess. She wrote works on natural history, medicine, and theology; corresponded with popes and famous men and women; and went on speaking tours. Most startling were the visions that informed her spiritual life. Some people have speculated that Hildegard's visionary experiences, which she illustrated and which came to her while she was conscious, were caused by migraine headaches. Others claim that they should be taken as reflections of her intense and expressive personality. Hildegard believed them to be divine.

At Paris, the monk Hugh of St. Victor showed just how high a reformed monastic education could aim if informed by the new learning. In his *Didascalicon* (meaning "things instructional"), Hugh laid out the essential importance of reading and a program for learning the sum total of things. For Hugh and his contemporaries, human knowledge as well as the human image had been shattered by the Fall of humankind. Twelfth-century men and women were attempting to restore human knowledge to its original state before the Fall, reassembling and ordering all the knowledge that God had once given them. Hugh and the masters thus undertook a great project to restore the human image and human mind to their pristine state through modern learning.

Abbot Suger and the Birth of Gothic Architecture

In 1122, the monk Suger became the abbot of St. Denis, the ancient royal monastery just outside Paris. The kings of France were buried at St. Denis, which also preserved the symbols of the monarchy, including the Oriflamme or banner under which the French kings fought. Suger's goal was to enhance St. Denis's standing as the royal abbey of France and so enthusiastically supported the Capetian king, Louis VI (the Fat), and wrote an account of his deeds. Louis was reputedly so large that he required a crane to help him mount his horse. Suger zealously promoted the interests of his large king and proud abbey, no matter the cost to others. To gain more property for his monastery, he expelled the nuns of Argenteuil, including Heloise, claiming both that he had charters proving that their property originally belonged to St. Denis and that the nuns were leading immoral lives. His case had little basis on either count, but he obtained the land. With Heloise now homeless, Abelard turned over his own small and poorly funded monastery, the Paraclete, to Heloise and her displaced sisters. Suger thus changed the course of the lives of the famous lovers, bringing them back together again, for Heloise became a successful abbess and administrator and Abelard spent much of his later life devoted to the Paraclete's interests, writing a rule for Heloise's convent as well as a book of hymns.

In his account of his efforts on behalf of St. Denis, Suger describes collecting and restoring its precious objects, managing its properties, and rebuilding the church. St. Denis was old, parts of it having been constructed in the Merovingian and Carolingian periods. To restore and expand the church, Suger planned to rebuild the west facade and narthex (entranceway). He discovered that he lacked the necessary stone columns for the job. Having determined that old columns from the ancient palaces and baths of Rome might serve his purpose, he hoped to transport them from Rome to Paris. After years of planning, he found that he could obtain the same stone columns from a nearby quarry. He also required wooden beams but was told that none large enough were available. Suger personally led an excursion into a local forest, found trees of the right size, and supervised the harvesting. Suger's dynamism is an indication of the energy and purpose driving twelfth-century Europe.

The product of this determination and industry was a massive new west end for St. Denis, with heavy wall buttresses, three large portals with statues, and a central tympanum scene of the Last Judgment. The west end of St. Denis delights the eye with its organized presentation of elements, vibrant tympanum, and colorful rose window. As impressive as the exterior was, St. Denis becomes even more dramatic on the inside, for Suger's vision inspired an architectural revolution. He wanted to flood the church with colored light pouring in through large stained-glass windows. In his reading, he had been struck by the doctrines of light and transcendence in the writings of the Neo-Platonist writer now known as Pseudo-Dionysius, who was thought at the time to be the Denis the Areopagite mentioned in the New Testament and the patron saint of his church. When Abelard after his castration became a monk of St. Denis, he questioned the association of St. Denis with Denis the Areopagite, which forced him to flee the monastery and its angry monks. Suger had no such doubts about the divine origins of the abbey or his own inspiration.

To achieve Suger's spiritual goals, the masons of St. Denis were the first to introduce the basic elements of Gothic architecture: the use of buttresses (attached and later on flying buttresses), which supported the lateral or horizontal pressure on the external walls, and pointed arches, which conveyed the downward vertical pressure of the weight of the walls and roof to the earth. The Romanesque round arch was heavy and squat in order to bear the great weight of a heavy stone building, and Romanesque walls had to be heavy to support the immense load. With the pointed arch and the better flow of pressure downward, walls absorbed less downward pressure and so could be made higher and opened up with larger windows, allowing more light to enter sacred spaces. Finally, instead of Romanesque barrel vaults (essentially a series of round arches), the masons of St. Denis created ribbed vaults, which allowed the weight and stresses of a large stone building to be collected and transferred down to the ground. The interior of Suger's church pinches upward and achieves a heightened sense of verticality.

Some of these Gothic features had been pioneered in Muslim buildings and in various Norman churches, but at St. Denis they were brought together to achieve the beginnings of a new architectural style that we know as Gothic. Strangely, in his account of his administration of St. Denis, Suger says not a word about these specific developments. His attention was fixed not on the technical details, but on the end result: the desire to build a taller, light-filled building that would honor God, concentrate the divine light, and sparkle for France and its savvy, self-promoting abbot.

Romanesque remained the main architectural style of Europe, but the new Gothic style would be at first a royal Capetian or Île-de-France (Parisian) style that was refined over the next century and spread across Europe. The finest example of the high or mature Gothic style in France is to be found in the cathedral of Chartres. Its older Romanesque cathedral had caught fire in June 1193, and immediately a campaign was carried out between 1193 and 1250 to build a state-of-the-art cathedral to replace it. The finished cathedral contains the classic elements of High Gothic: rich sculptural programs at its

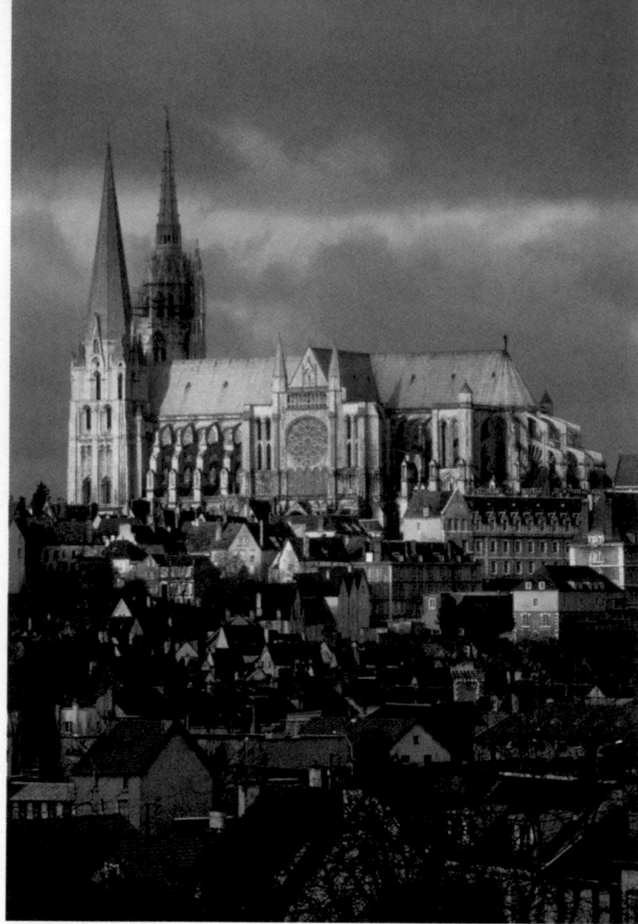

Chartres Cathedral With its asymmetrical towers, mature Gothic style, rich stained-glass windows, elongated figural statues, and dramatic natural setting, the cathedral of Chartres has often been considered the high point of Gothic architecture.

main portals, pointed arches, flying buttresses, and a complex vaulting system that allowed for greater light to shine into the cathedral through stunning stained-glass windows (Figure 9.1).

Bernard of Clairvaux and the Cistercians

By the mid-twelfth century, a chill had settled over the cathedral schools of France. The church opened up prosecutions of three masters (Abelard; William of Conches; and Gilbert of Poitiers, the bishop of Poitiers) for teachings that endangered the Catholic faith. Bernard of Clairvaux was involved in all three cases. He so stage-managed the case against Abelard in 1141 that the master didn't stand a chance; he was condemned before he could defend himself. The case against Gilbert's complex teachings collapsed and the one against William never got off the ground.

Bernard should not be judged solely on the basis of these repressions of intellectual "heretics." He was the conscience of his age, a charismatic religious leader whose career touched many of the formative events of the twelfth century. Bernard was a Cistercian, a reforming monastic movement that took shape in Burgundy at the monastery of Cîteaux at the end of the eleventh century. There a group of monks devoted themselves to a simpler form of monastic life, one not encumbered by the excessive and time-consuming prayers and rituals of the Cluniacs. The Cistercians rejected pomp and ceremony, riches and city-living. Instead, they set out for the wilderness, erecting plain monasteries in out-of-the-way places and devoting themselves to charity and manual labor. Eventually, the Cistercians would have hundreds of monastic houses throughout Europe, but in the first half of the twelfth century, the Cistercian monastic movement was finding its footing and Bernard of Clairvaux was its spiritual voice and guide.

Bernard was austere, even condemning the fancies of Romanesque decoration of the sort that Gislebertus had carved at Autun. Bernard wondered what depictions of fabulous creatures and bizarre scenes had to do with a contemplative monastic life. He asked why monasteries were decorated with sculptures of obscene monkeys, lions and tigers, warring soldiers, multiheaded creatures, fish with mammalian heads, and creatures half-horse and half-goat. He objected to the distracting quality of such fanciful art. Monks could spend the whole day gazing upon these entertainments carved in stone rather than reading the Bible. The Cistercians turned away from Romanesque decoration toward simpler unadorned churches and manuscripts.

In addition to spurning artistic fantasies and learned heresies, Bernard was dismayed by the rise of popular heresies. In the 1140s in Cologne a number of heretics claimed that they led a more apostolic life than did the representatives of the Catholic Church; they ate no meat, embraced poverty, and altered the practices of the official church. Bernard attempted to refute their teachings by restating Catholic truths as simply as he could, for he thought that the wayward should be brought back to the true faith by argument and persuasion. A mob in Cologne was less patient and burned some of the heretics to death. Bernard was moderate and forgiving, but his righteousness belonged to an increasingly repressive church. As the number and variety of unorthodox beliefs swelled in an ever more complex society—or became more apparent to increasingly vigilant religious authorities—the church turned from persuasion to coercion.

Bernard stood deep within the power structures of his age, and one of his followers became pope. As a powerful speaker and writer, Bernard was called on to preach against heresy and to defend the church. In 1144, the crusader kingdom of Edessa fell to the Seljuk Turks. At the pope's request, Bernard called for a Second Crusade (1146–1149). Though the fervor for crusade had cooled in Europe, Bernard's oratorical magic galvanized Europe to take up the cross once again. After Bernard delivered a stirring sermon in Vézelay in northern France, thousands of people assembled to retake the Holy Land. Castles emptied and women were left without husbands, said Bernard. He roused the nobility and royalty of Europe to go on crusade. In Germany, crusade fever and popular preaching

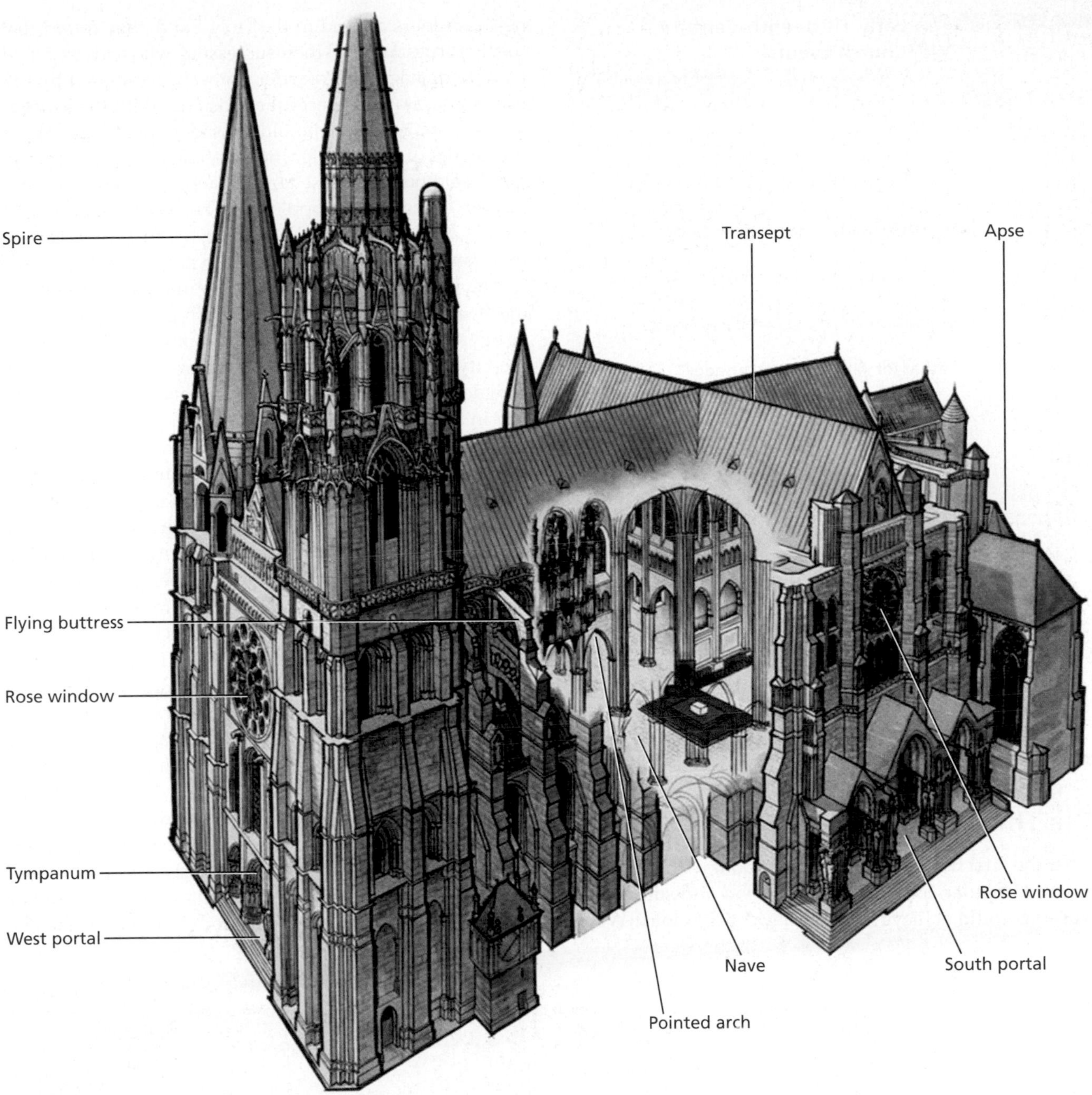

FIGURE 9.1 | **Principal Features of a Gothic Cathedral (Chartres)**

spilled over into attacks on Jews. Bernard tried to put a stop to the persecution, but many Jews were massacred. The Second Crusade was a disaster of disorganization and royal rivalries that soon failed. In the end, Bernard regretted his role in calling for so disastrous an undertaking and denounced the folly of the Second Crusade.

Despite that disaster, Bernard of Clairvaux played a critical public role in fortifying the Catholic Church by bolstering its core spiritual values (particularly by his devotion to the cult of Mary) and orthodox character in the midst of an expanding, prosperous, and contentious world.

Two Thirds and Two Fourths

The Third Crusade proved to be no more successful than the Second, but under the powerful stewardship of Pope Innocent III (1198–1216), the Catholic Church reached the summit of its political power in the Middle Ages. The range of Innocent's activity—interfering in the politics of his day, correcting

Why might Innocent III have been the most powerful and imperial of medieval popes?

CHRONOLOGY	Early-Thirteenth-Century Church Events
DATE	**EVENT**
1198	Innocent III becomes pope
1200	University of Paris receives its royal charter
1204	Fourth Crusade takes Constantinople
1208	England placed under interdict
1209	Establishment of the Franciscan Order
1209–1229	Cathar (or Albigensian) Crusade
1215	Fourth Lateran Council
1216	Establishment of the Dominican Order
1231	The beginning of the Inquisition
1244	Thomas Aquinas becomes a Dominican friar

kings and emperors, shaping Catholic doctrine in the Fourth Lateran Council, and promoting crusade—was a high water mark for the medieval church. Yet the Fourth Crusade led to the capture of Constantinople and shattered the hope of reconciling the eastern and western churches.

The Third Crusade

What the First Crusade had brought about with spontaneous and popular enthusiasm, the second and subsequent crusades could achieve only with great difficulty. When new crusaders arrived in the Holy Land, they found that the first crusaders and their successors, who had remained there to manage the crusader states, had survived by settling into a state of peaceful coexistence with the Muslim population. Many of the old crusaders had come to see the virtues of Islamic life, and all of them understood that they could not rule these foreign lands without the acquiescence of the native population. The new crusaders were almost as distant from the heirs of the first crusaders as they were from the resident Muslim population.

The Islamic world became more united by the end of the twelfth century. Saladin came to power as the ruler of Egypt and Syria in 1174. This inspired warrior retook the city of Jerusalem in 1187 and overthrew the Latin Kingdom of Jerusalem. Europe was once again called to war in a Third Crusade (1189–1192). The Holy Roman emperor, Frederick Barbarossa (so called for his red beard), set out for the east in 1189, but his army was destroyed and he died while fording a river. Richard the Lionheart, king of England, and Philip II Augustus, king of France (r. 1180–1223), had more luck and retook Acre and Jaffa, but the two warrior kings were locked in a personal contest for power and land in greater France and rarely cooperated. Complicating their relations was the fact that Richard as the duke of Normandy was the vassal of Philip. Eventually Philip withdrew from the crusade and once home attacked Richard's continental holdings. Worse for King Richard, on his way home from the crusade, he was captured by a duke of Austria and held for ransom by the emperor Henry VI.

The Third Crusade ended as had the Second, in disunity and disaster. The religious motives and popularity of the First Crusade had been replaced by grudging royal commitments to the pope to take up crusade and by stubborn European economic and territorial interests. The Christian presence in the Holy Land continued to shrink.

Richard the Lionheart and Saladin Joust In this fantasy, Richard and Saladin face each other as chivalric heroes. No wars were settled in this way, though many knights wished they could be.

Pope Innocent III

Pope Innocent III A thirteenth-century fresco portrait of the most powerful of medieval popes.

In 1198, Lothario di Segni was thirty-seven years old, a cardinal and canon lawyer, when he was elected pope and took the name Innocent III. Italy was in turmoil, and the emperor Henry VI had just died. The Investiture Controversy had succeeded in establishing not just the reform of the church, but also the doctrine of the **papal plenitude of power,** that is, that the pope had unlimited or absolute power. The imperial papacy's claim to extensive powers over Christian Europe had been exercised fitfully by Innocent's predecessors. Gregory VII's reign had ended in exile, but Urban II and his successors had marshaled Europe for three crusades. Two of those crusades failed miserably, and heresy in Europe was thought to be on the rise. Innocent moved against corruption within the church, particularly **pluralism** or the holding of several offices at once (as, for instance, when one man was bishop over several episcopal sees at the same time). Despite the difficult times, Innocent became the strongest, though not the most other-worldly of medieval popes. One of his chief goals was to secure control of central Italy and a strong papal state.

Innocent was a brilliant papal politician. He secured the succession of the four-year-old Frederick II as king of Sicily and forced several European monarchs to become papal vassals. Innocent crowned the new king of Aragon in Rome and tried to overthrow the king of Norway. When the pope and King John of England disagreed over the appointment of a new archbishop of Canterbury in 1208, Innocent placed England under **interdict,** effectively closing the church in England. Sacraments were offered only to the sick and dying. When King John seized church properties and bishops fled the kingdom, Innocent responded by excommunicating the king and invited the French king to invade England. To restore his standing, John surrendered his kingdom to the papacy and received it back as a papal fief. King John was also forced to grant the church a series of freedoms from royal interference. In this contest of wills, Pope Innocent prevailed because he was the more astute politician.

Innocent's papacy was the end result of the Investiture Controversy with its claims of extensive papal power over all Christendom and, therefore, over the monarchs and emperors who claimed to rule it. Under Innocent, the medieval imperial papacy achieved its fullest expression, but it was not to go unchallenged.

The Fourth Crusade

If the Second and Third Crusades were small disasters, the Fourth Crusade (1198–1204) was an outright crime, an international mugging in the European daylight. At the start of the First Crusade there had been a delicate moment when the Byzantine emperor was worried that the crusaders gathered outside the walls of Constantinople might attack his city rather than pass by it peacefully on their way to the Holy Land. The Fourth Crusade led to the feared conquest of Constantinople and the Byzantine Empire by western crusaders.

In the second half of the twelfth century, many Latin traders resided in Constantinople, but in 1182 many of them had been massacred by the Greeks. A succession of incompetent and often corrupt emperors reigned in the east, but Constantinople, however chaotic and dangerous, remained the most fabulous city in all of Christendom, and its wealth attracted the predatory. Early in his reign, Pope Innocent had sent legates to Constantinople to urge the eastern emperor to end the Great Schism of the church by acknowledging the supremacy of the pope in Rome. Innocent played a dangerous game, even threatening the Byzantine emperor with a forcible solution to the disunity of the church if he did not conform. In the meantime a new crusade to liberate the Holy Land, called for by Pope Innocent, was being planned in the west, financed in part by the doge (chief official) of Venice. In 1195, a claimant to the Byzantine throne named Alexius promised the crusaders that if they elevated him to the throne, he would pay off the debt owed to the Venetians, provide the crusaders with money to campaign in Egypt, and reunite the eastern and western churches.

A number of western interests thus came to focus on Constantinople early in the thirteenth century. In June 1203, western ships sailed within sight of the walls of the grand old city. An assault on the city might still have been avoided, but the religious, dynastic, and commercial disputes were too great. When a wall of the city was breached, the emperor fled the city and the crusaders waited to be paid. When the newly installed emperor Alexius and his

Christians and Moors Battle over Spain A thirteenth-century depiction of Christians and Moors (Muslims) at war in Spain. The reconquest of Spain spanned centuries but was over by 1492.

father could not find the funds needed to satisfy the assembled attackers, they were deposed and Alexius was strangled to death. At the urging of the doge of Venice, the crusaders continued the attack on Constantinople. On April 12, 1204, two ships financed by Latin bishops took two of the city's towers; a week later Constantinople fell to the wayward western crusaders. For three days they ran riot in the city, burning and looting. Many of the precious objects that Constantine and the Romans had transferred to the city centuries before were seized and sent west, among them the four ancient copper horses that were mounted on St. Mark's Basilica in Venice.

In short order, the western crusaders established a Latin Empire of Constantinople in the east that lasted until 1261. In the west, Pope Innocent publicly condemned the crusaders for their shocking seizure of Constantinople and the diversion of the Fourth Crusade from its mission to reclaim the Holy Land. He realized that the capture of Constantinople would make the reunification of the churches more difficult, but he eventually came to accept that the new Latin Empire in the east was a judgment of God and a miracle. The Byzantines lamented the fall of their city and regarded the crusaders as the agents of the Anti-Christ. Once again the dream of reuniting all of Christendom under one faith had been dashed.

The Fourth Lateran Council

In 1215, at Pope Innocent's command, a great council of the church was convened in Rome. Some thirteen hundred church officials gathered, along with spokesmen for the various monarchs of Europe. The council considered the sorry state of the crusading movement and the threat to the church posed by heretics, but it was its codification of church practices that was to have lasting significance.

Under Innocent's direct guidance, the prelates of the Fourth Lateran Council set about binding the Catholic Church to clear rules and tighter conduct. The council condemned heresy and stipulated how heretics were to be identified and prosecuted. Even though the Greek church was, after the Fourth Crusade, more compliant, the council condemned any remaining resistance to papal primacy.

Innocent's great council worried that the church was under assault from the forces of a changing world and far too loose for its own good. The council regulated standards for the high medieval church. It established tighter qualifications for the priesthood, often framed in negative terms: no irrational feasting or breaking of celibacy by priests, no drinking, no hunting, no pub crawling, no trials by ordeal overseen by churchmen, and no surgery performed by priests. The council mandated the election of bishops, set stricter monastic standards, and specified and justified papal taxes on the clergy. All Christians over eight years old were to confess once a year and receive communion, generally at Easter, or be excommunicated from the church. Marriage was confirmed as a sacrament, and restrictions were imposed on who could be married (dependent on the relatedness of the couple) and under what conditions.

The council also served as an arbiter of high politics in Christian lands, confirming the elevation of Frederick II as Holy Roman emperor and settling scores with the nobles of southern France who sympathized with heretics. In some cases, the nobles' lands were to be removed from their possession until they complied with the church; and in others, transferred to their conquerors. The Fourth Lateran Council was Innocent's attempt to establish the Catholic Church as a universal church in fact as well as theory.

High Times for the Medieval Economy

The medieval economy was working about as well as it could by the thirteenth century, at least in lands such as France, which sustained a large and growing population. By nearly every indicator—food production, population growth, urbanization, industry, and trade—the economy was flourishing. Growth, however, produces tensions and it did so in Europe, particularly between towns and villages, burghers and nobles.

How did population growth in the High Middle Ages begin to transform Europe?

WHAT A DIFFERENCE A YEAR MAKES

1215: A High Water Mark for the Middle Ages?

The year 1215 was an extraordinary one, filled with events that determined the direction the Late Middle Ages would take. King Alfonso VIII of Spain died the previous year, not long after opening the long campaign to expel the Muslims from Spain. The Latin emperor of Byzantium, Henry of Flanders, died the next year after uniting the four provinces of his eastern empire. Simon IV de Montfort was leading the crusade (backed by the pope) against the Cathars of southern France and in 1215 was named the count of Toulouse; in May he entered his city.

For Pope Innocent III the year was a busy one. He forced Frederick II to agree to go on crusade and was raising monies for a Fifth Crusade. Though he had called for a great council of Christians two years earlier, the Fourth Lateran Council did not meet until November 1215. Among those attending the council was Saint Dominic, whose order of preachers was confirmed the next year. Innocent had approved the order of the Friars Minor or Franciscans in 1209. Together these mendicant (begging) orders would transform the "street-presence" of Catholicism in Europe. Innocent III died the next year.

Gothic architecture had not yet reached its pinnacle, but many of its finest examples were under construction in 1215. The cathedral of Laon was complete; Sens was largely finished but had been damaged by a fire; much of Noyon stood, and its west facade was being erected; the west facade of Notre Dame of Paris was being erected; and Chartres was partially built by 1215, but its choir and buttresses had not yet been executed. Thus, had one visited any of the great cities of France in 1215, one would have seen massive Gothic cathedrals rising up with fresh pale stone, seen huge cranes lifting stones into place, heard the sound of hammers, and watched as hundreds of workers climbed about on scaffolding.

In 1214, Philip Augustus, the king of France, won the battle of Bouvines against English troops and forced King John of England to depart from Normandy. Philip's famous grandson, Louis IX (known to us as Saint Louis), was born that year. In defeat and disgrace, King John returned home to deal with his angry church, irritated magnates, and anxious people. On June 15, 1215, at Runnymede he capitulated to his rebellious barons and signed the Magna Carta, which restricted the king's arbitrary royal powers. At Aachen in Germany, in Charlemagne's chapel, on July 15, Frederick II was crowned emperor and a few days later oversaw the transfer of Charlemagne's corpse to a gold and silver sarcophagus, even throwing off his imperial robes and driving nails into the new tomb. The year 1215 was a remarkable one for the Middle Ages. What would the High Middle Ages have been without great Gothic cathedrals, friars, the powerful church of Innocent III and his great council, the removal of the Cathars, the continuing Christian reconquest of Spain, or King John's comeuppance?

QUESTIONS | ***What other years might be considered historically more important than others? Was the year 1215, with its remarkable events, a pinnacle and, therefore, a turning point for the High Middle Ages? Why or why not?***

The Agricultural Base

At its base, the medieval economy of the High Middle Ages remained rooted in the countryside and in agricultural production, now in its most perfected medieval form. Most of the agricultural techniques in use had been introduced in the Early Middle Ages, but now the horse rather than the ox was used in many places to increase the speed and quality of plowing. Lords and their workers, who pressed north and east in search of new arable lands, extended western Europe's unfixed borders. Inside Europe, marginal lands were brought into production as marshes were drained and tidal areas reclaimed from the sea, particularly along the coast of the Netherlands, Germany, and England. Europe was getting bigger by the day. As the forests were cut back, new villages and towns appeared. By the twelfth century, northern Europe had a clear agricultural advantage over southern Europe, which had less arable land, poorer soil, and less water. The great Medieval Warm Period (775–1275) brought higher temperatures and longer growing seasons to northern Europe but may have made agricultural conditions in the south worse.

In the great growing season of the High Middle Ages, France benefited more than any other region of Europe. Its population grew to about twenty million people, roughly six times the size of England and two and a half times the size of Italy. The population of northern France would not surpass its high medieval peak until modern industrial times. An increase in population, however, need not mean an increase in the physical well-being of individuals. The average serf or peasant was still lucky to survive into his or her late twenties, and their children continued to die in high numbers. Deforestation, expanding towns, and rivers used as the carriers of waste materials had environmental consequences, producing floods, local pollution, and disease. Many of the outlying lands brought under cultivation were marginal for a reason; they possessed poor soil that was quickly exhausted from overuse and poor land management. The population increase in Europe was a product of an agricultural system that had achieved its highest medieval form, but by 1275 the economy was beginning to experience difficulties.

Farmers remained the backbone of the economic world of the High Middle Ages and were recognized as an essential part of the social and economic fabric of society. Their legal standing, however, varied from place to place and individual to individual. Some agricultural workers were free and others servile and entirely dependent on their lords for sustenance and legal standing. The lord, or *seignior,* viewed the farmers who worked for him as his dependents. Upon them he imposed duties of labor and taxes, and even had some control over their personal lives.

The effect of such tight and exploitative overlordship in places such as northern France bound the peasantry together as a group living with common conditions, interests, and grievances. One group of farm workers held by a royal monastery of Paris resented that the king had, with a stroke of his pen in 1178, reduced them to servility. They carried their complaint to the pope in Rome, who recognized their free status. The papacy could not, however, enforce its opinion and, by 1226, the peasant community had capitulated. Its drive to achieve freedom was finally purchased twenty years later with an agreement to pay an annual tribute to the king. Peasants understood that their lot was not fixed, but negotiable. They turned to popes and kings for relief and demands for justice. Higher authorities, who were involved in building power bases of their own, helped occasionally, but their own serfs could look to few higher authorities for assistance.

The Growth of Towns

Towns and small cities flourished in the High Middle Ages. Small cities such as Bruges and Cologne reached populations of around 30,000 people. Paris grew to at least 75,000 to 100,000 residents by 1300 and may have been almost twice that size. In Italy, mercantile cities such as Venice and Florence had around 90,000 people by the early fourteenth century. Kings and magnates had an interest in promoting towns and cities in their realms since they lay outside the direct control of nobles or could be dislodged from their control. Magnates such as the duke of Poland actively promoted the foundation of new cities as engines of economic activity.

Medieval towns were mixed or complex economic centers closely connected to nearby villages. Many towns continued to operate as large villages, in which farming was still practiced on plots of land around the town and many residents went out to work on local fields just as early medieval villagers had. Towns and small cities of the High Middle Ages increasingly imported and exported goods, and served as depots for the storage and distribution of goods. Many towns, particularly those in the textile trade in Flanders, specialized in specific industries. Northern traders moved from a base of operations in some city out to other towns, villages, or into the Mediterranean Sea and Slavic lands, areas long traveled by Byzantine traders. The in-home or **cottage industries** that had existed in medieval villages moved to towns where larger enterprises could be maintained. Medieval towns and cities also offered financial services, particularly the lending and investment of money.

Guilds and Industry

In early medieval villages, women had worked not only on the land with their families, but also in cottage industries producing clothes and other local necessities. In the High Middle Ages, associations of craftsmen called **guilds** were formed to control production. These associations largely excluded women from membership or, if they were allowed in, denied them official roles. Guilds

The Blessings of Good Government Ambrogio Lorenzetti's mural (1337–1339) in Siena, Italy, of the benefits of city living, peace, and good government.

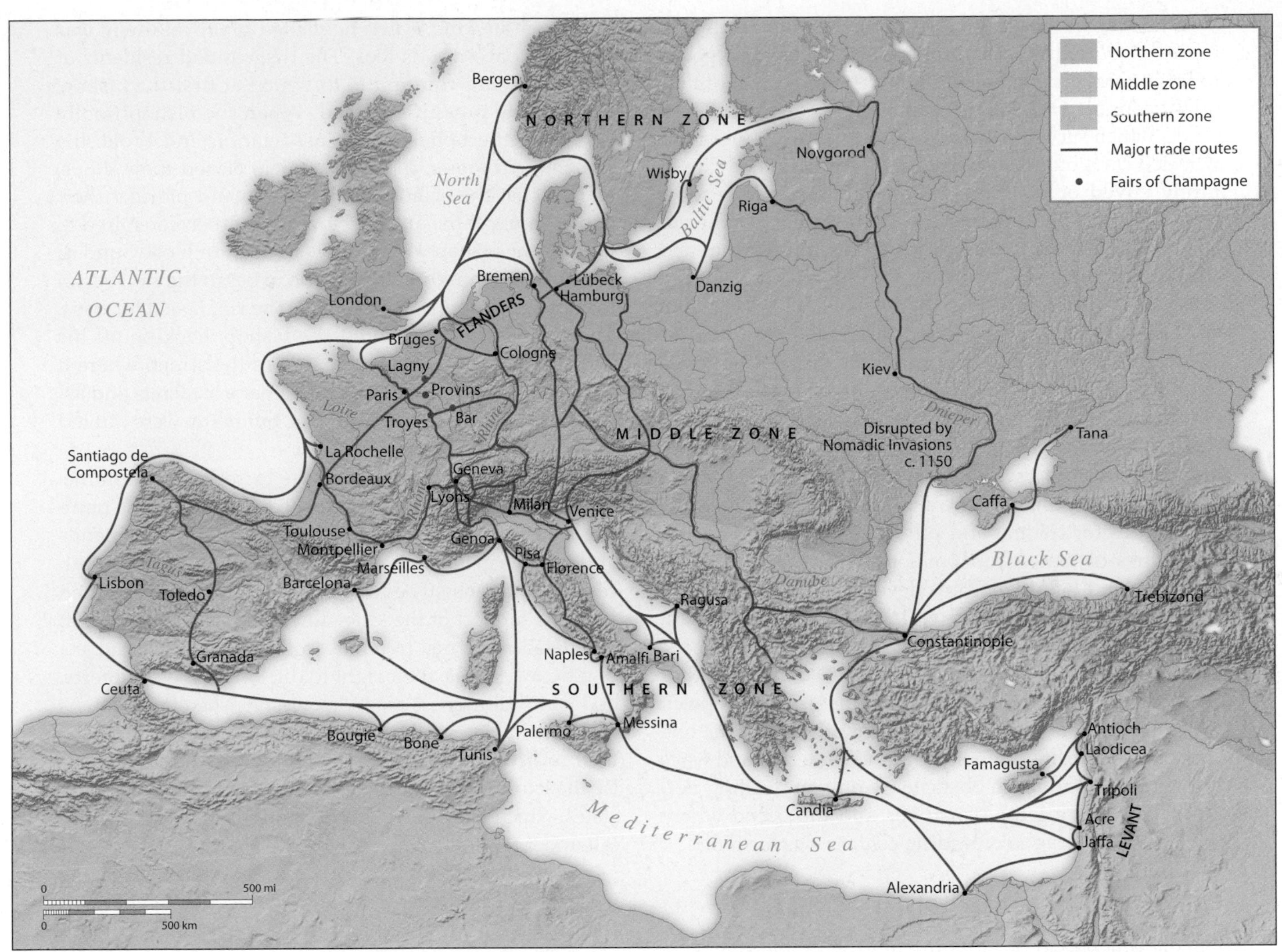

MAP 9.1 | **Trade Routes and Fairs, c. 1100–1300**

This map highlights the principal trading areas and routes for the flow of goods in the High Middle Ages. The system was more complex than shown here. ***How did trade and commerce work to integrate Europe, or did it? How was trade a point of international contact?***

controlled production, divided workers into masters and apprentices, and set prices and the terms of trade. Most large towns had guilds that made cloth, shoes, parchment, and furniture. Although the guild system guaranteed the quality of the goods produced, it was economically and socially rigid. The guild system suppressed competition. Long-serving apprentices often had little chance of becoming masters and were forced to accept low wages to sustain themselves and their families.

Not only craftsmen, but professional groups formed guild-like associations. Italian city-states established hierarchies of guilds in which professions such as the notaries were ranked higher than the craft guilds. Merchants and universities would imitate the basic system of masters and apprentices to control the terms and conditions of production within their spheres of activity.

The scale of industry in the High Middle Ages could be impressive. In Ghent, 5,200 men worked to produce cloth. In Paris, 130 different guilds looked after everything from the building trade and leather goods to making manuscript books. One could judge the size and development of a town by the number and variety of its guilds and professions and the range of goods and services supplied. Towns in which the chief guilds supplied horsemen and farmers with equipment such as stirrups, bridles, harnesses, and yokes defined an economy as local and serving the needs of farmers. Moneylenders and financial guilds tended to prevail in port cities, where traders and seamen gathered and active maritime trade networks operated.

In some sectors, Europe's agricultural production was so large that traders needed to transport their goods over great distances to find markets (Map 9.1). In good years, England exported fifteen million pounds of unprocessed wool. French vineyards supplied millions of barrels of wine to Europe. By the thirteenth century, Italian port cities were picking up bulk goods from England and Flanders for transport and trade in the wider

Mediterranean. An improved road network facilitated trade, encouraging local producers to send their goods to large markets such as Paris and London, where they might connect with long-distance trade networks. These roads, which served chiefly as surfaces for two- and four-wheeled carts pulled by horses, mules, and donkeys, were rarely paved or planked. A wheeled cart might cover only ten miles per day, and ground transport could add as much as a third to the cost of goods. It was faster and cheaper to send goods by boat.

By 1300, the European economy was operating about as well as it could, sustaining in fertile areas such as France a dense medieval population, spreading goods throughout Europe and reaching the Mediterranean, Baltic, and Slavic frontiers. Traders from Venice, Pisa, and Genoa could be found in all major ports and were helping to restore a wider world of Mediterranean trade. Annual fairs in Champagne and elsewhere provided opportunities for traders and purchasers to collect at specific times of the year. More sophisticated commercial contracts and loan structures developed. Some shipping contracts specified late fees, which were actually interest charges disguised to avoid church prohibitions against practicing **usury** (charging interest on loans). Another method for circumventing rules against making a profit was to accept payment in a currency other than the one the contract specified. Capitalists and traders found ways to overcome economic obstacles. Complex trading networks arose along the North Sea and the Baltic, where the Hanseatic League of trading centers was forming.

Communes and Urban Tensions

During this period of rapid urban growth and economic development, tensions surfaced as towns attempted to extend their control over the surrounding countryside. One point of conflict centered on transport and travel. Traders wanted free access to roads and bridges, but wherever they could local lords and villages imposed tolls on passage through their lands or across their bridges. Tolls were one of the only ways in which the countryside and local nobility could derive economic benefit from prosperous towns. Early in the thirteenth century, the town of Toulouse waged a small war against local country lords and their "excessive" tolls. Forming an integrated economy meant sorting out which was the dominant force and which the subservient one in each region; the answer varied from place to place, region to region. In Flanders, the towns won; in parts of England and France, the countryside often did.

Towns were also grappling with the tensions caused by rapid internal growth. At the start of the twelfth century, towns in northern France were hotbeds of tension between residents and the prevailing powers. A few years after Abelard went to Laon to study under Master Anselm, a murderous communal riot broke out. The burghers, merchants, and priests of the town bridled under the arbitrary rule of their bishop and local nobles, who imposed arbitrary taxes and subjected them to indignities. Even the king, when he visited his royal town, was forced to pay various fees. The disgruntled residents of Laon formed a **commune,** to which at first the bishop, under some pressure, agreed. When the bishop finally dissolved the bonds of the association and broke his previous promises, the shopkeepers closed their shops, fearing that the bishop and nobles would plunder their goods. Some of the angered townsmen then conspired to murder the bishop. When he went to church one Sunday, one of them, thinking it was time to begin the riot, began to chant, "commune, commune." The riot lasted for days. The conspirators murdered the bishop, hacking off his legs and leaving his corpse to rot in the street, where it was rescued by Master Anselm. Other aristocrats and associates of the prelate tried to flee, but many were hunted down and murdered by the mob.

Laon was not the only town to form a commune. Burghers and merchants established communes in a number of northern French towns, as well as in the Netherlands and northern Italy. During the twelfth and thirteenth centuries, towns struggled to govern themselves, often with the support of the king. Towns established laws that stipulated residents' freedom from tolls but their subjection to town taxes, their right to dispose of their property, and their willingness to abide by established laws. Towns and small cities set out their rights in charters to ensure their relative freedom from noble and church interference. By the late thirteenth century, however, some Italian city-states, which had been self-governing republics, began to fall under the control of local lords (*signori*).

As towns and small cities were asserting their rights in the High Middle Ages, villages were often left behind, their prosperity reduced and any hope of independence gone. The economic centralization of Europe produced winners and losers. The countryside of Europe, ironically, became more exclusively agricultural than it had been in the Early and Central Middle Ages because large towns monopolized nonagricultural production and cottage industries in villages could not easily compete.

Dissent and Control, Church and State

After the Investiture Controversy, the new imperial papacy sought to eradicate ideas and practices not sanctioned by the reformed church. As medieval society became more vigorous and urban and people traveled greater distances, new ideas about religious life inevitably emerged, many of them in reaction to a church that was seen as too powerful and worldly. At the same time, medieval states were becoming more centralized and controlling, but their development was uneven.

Why did the ordered society of the High Middle Ages produce so much complaint and outright resistance from common people, learned "heretics," and religious dissenters?

Dealing with Dissent

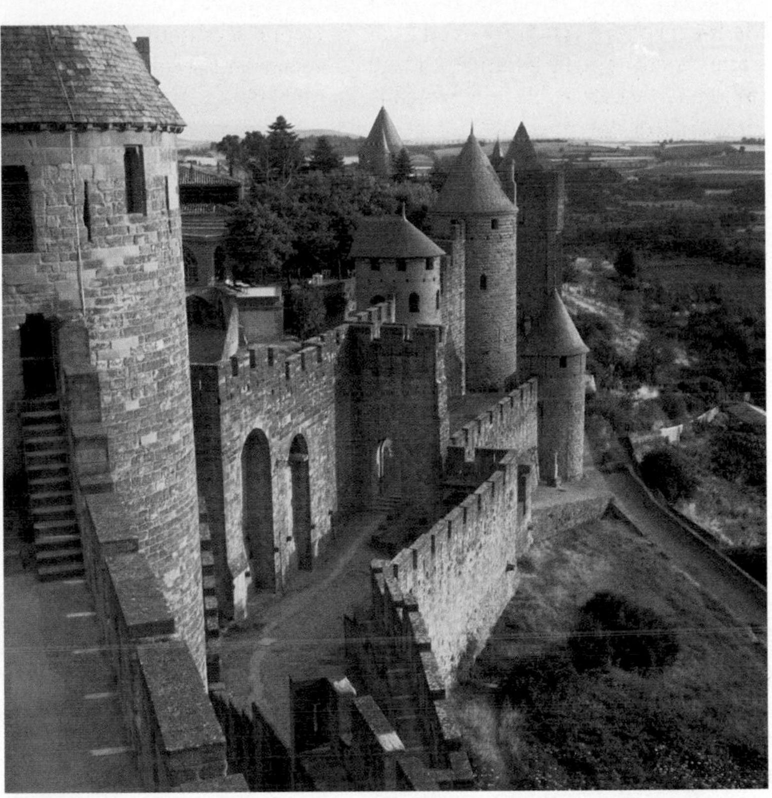

The Walled City of Carcassonne Southern France was troubled in the thirteenth century by outbreaks of heresy, frequent wars, and political disruption, which also struck the walled medieval city of Carcassonne. The small, enclosed city, which still stands, was forced at one point to expel its Cathar citizens.

Popular culture mocked an increasingly prosperous and bureaucratic church. In the Gospel of Silver Mark, a widely circulating parody, a poor man approaches the gates of the papal palace, begging for mercy, but is sent away. He was told that he could not enter until he had surrendered his last dime. When he sold his only cloak, the cardinals counted it as nothing and sent him away again. Yet a fat priest, who had committed murder and greased all the right palms with cash, was welcomed by the pope, who advised his cardinals to take from their flocks as he did from his, which was to make mock of the golden rule to do unto others as you would have them do unto you.

In the twelfth and thirteenth centuries, groups critical of the church attracted official attention. The Poor Men of Lyons or Waldensians (their leader was Peter Waldo) rejected a propertied church and corrupt clergy, and advocated the relief of the poor. They were also antipapal, which was to doom their movement. By Pope Innocent III's reign, the popes led an aggressive campaign to identify and condemn those such as the Waldensians who were critical of the church. The church labeled them heretics.

Most of the heresies that arose in the High Middle Ages were anticlerical and antipapal. The Patarines in northern Italy repudiated clerical marriages and simony, the same as the reforming popes had, but their leader, Arnold of Brescia, went further, arguing that the church should not own any property.

The strongest of the dissenting movements was the one associated with the Cathars or Albigensians (named after the city of Albi in southern France). Centered in southern France and northern Italy, Catharism flourished among the prosperous middle class in towns. Cathars were not Catholic Christians, but Manichaeans. These dualists believed that the world was divided into forces of good (light) and evil (darkness), which were at constant war with one another. They believed that all things material, including flesh and the world, were evil. In its most extreme stages, Cathars practiced total asceticism or self-denial, right down to ritual starvation. The Cathars rejected Catholic norms: the sacraments, marriage, and reproduction. They avoided all consumption of flesh, preferring to eat foods such as melons and honey, which they thought were produced asexually. The movement was structured so that only its leaders, the good men or "perfected ones," starved themselves to death.

Pope Innocent sponsored an internal crusade against the Cathars (1209–1229). He first sent missionaries into Languedoc in southern France to try to win back the faithful to the church. When that failed, he gave the noble warrior Simon IV de Montfort license to proceed against the Cathar heretics. Simon did just that, but he and his men also wanted to uproot the nobility of southern France, which was sympathetic to the good men, and to seize their lands. Ultimately, Catharism was destroyed.

The situation of Jews in Europe deteriorated in the thirteenth century. Not only had crusade fever engendered attacks on Jews, but the new theological rigor of the west meant that Jews were often thought of as "other" and enemies of Christ. After the Fourth Lateran Council, most European Jews were forced to wear signs of their faith: symbols, special hats, or particular clothes. In England there was a campaign to cancel debts owed to Jews, and in 1182 King Philip Augustus of France expelled all Jews from France, in large part to seize their European assets.

The Mendicant Orders and the Inquisition

The official church was not without its own popular religious movements and the means to resist heresies through persuasion rather than violence. In the early thirteenth century, two men emerged with new missions: Saints Francis and Dominic. They established movements of **mendicant** or begging friars (so named after the Latin, *fratres,* for brothers), who devoted themselves to the Roman Church, the papacy, the poor, and the sick (especially lepers). The mendicants preached and begged in the cities of Europe, and practiced absolute poverty. The

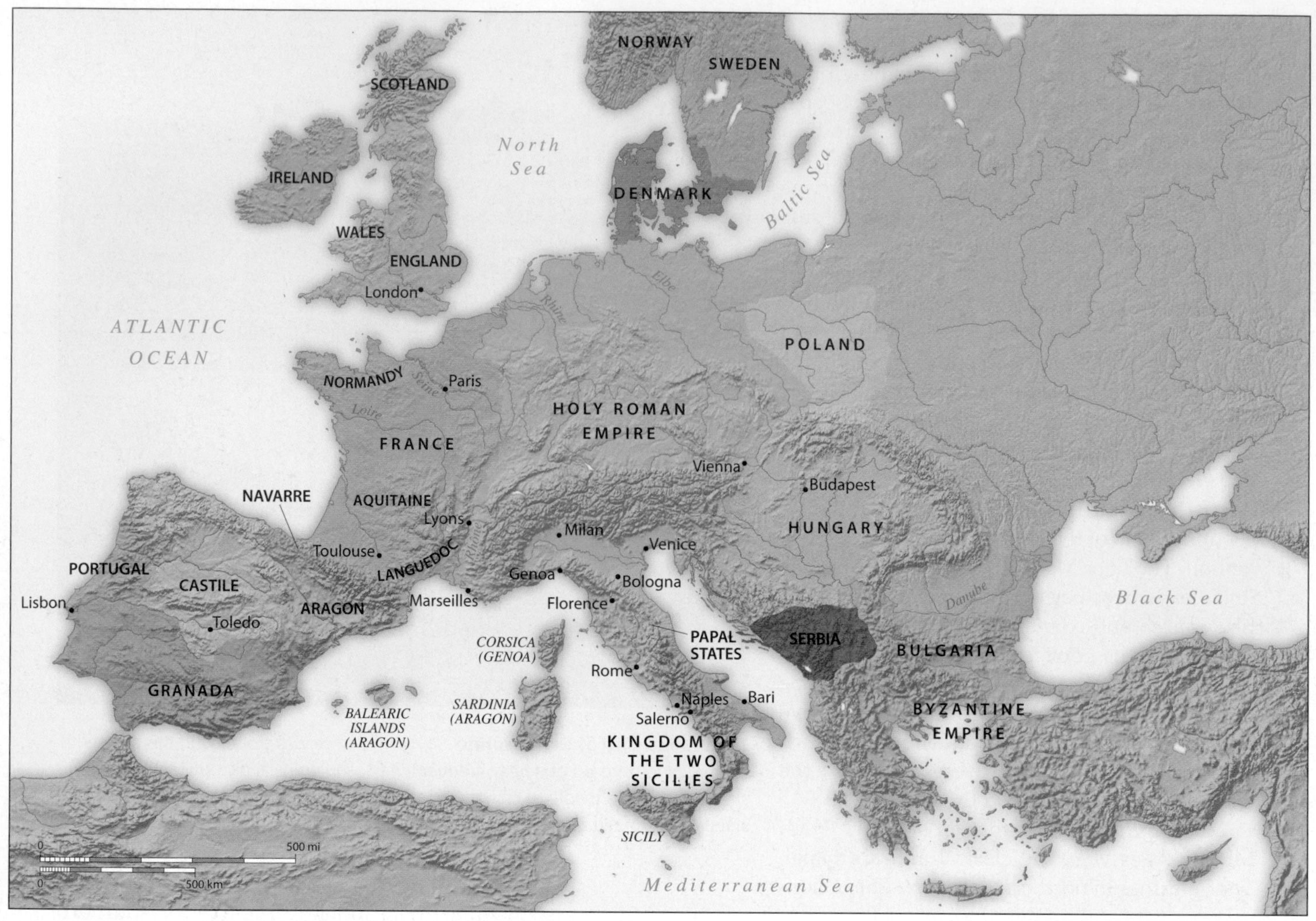

MAP 9.2 | **European State Development, c. 1100–1300**

By the High Middle Ages, Europe was filled with states that had various degrees of power and command over their regions and borders and different ways of organizing themselves. The Holy Roman Empire may seem large and dominant on this map but was in reality relatively weak and only in loose control of its vast territory. ***Why was Europe so regionally divided? Which forms of government prevailed? Where and why?***

friars fitted the needs of high medieval society. Unlike monks who were cloistered in monasteries, the mendicants were mobile and responded better to the new urban realities of the thirteenth century. They were a visible and vocal presence on the streets of European cities. Pope Innocent recognized the legitimacy of the Franciscans, and his successor recognized the Dominicans (the order of preachers). The Dominicans, in particular, devoted themselves to teaching and were to be key agents in the investigation of heresy. Their goal as educators was to bring about the end of heresy by identifying, correcting, and enlightening wayward Christians.

One papal complaint was that the investigation of heretics, which often fell to local episcopal courts, was too lax. Various rulers in France attempted to set up **inquisitions** of the Cathars, but Pope Gregory IX (1227–1241) decided to formalize the process. He appointed Dominican friars as inquisitors to examine, under the watchful eye of a papal legate, the Cathar sympathizers of southern France. At Toulouse the inquisition took on its high medieval form, including secret accusations, torture, and the keeping of meticulous records of the interviews of suspects. From the standpoint of the church, the purpose of an inquisition was to restore balance and rectitude to the Christian religious body either by reincorporating those who had strayed from the orthodox faith or by cutting them off (by death) from the faithful before they contaminated the entire body. Much blood was spilled and many lives ruined in the process.

State Development

Europe was politically and territorially segmented in the High Middle Ages (Map 9.2), and state development differed in three basic areas. In the first, England after the Conquest and France after 1100 developed strong monarchies. In the second, Germany and Italy were internally divided and power there was fragmented. In Germany the decisive factors for fragmentation were of long standing: a Holy Roman emperor with claims to extensive

OTHER VOICES, OTHER VIEWS

Mongol Relations

Before the merchant family the Polos (Marco, his father Niccolò, and uncle Maffeo) ventured to the Far East in the 1260s and 1270s, Europeans had already made official contact with the Mongol Empire. Twelfth-century stories of Prester John, a Christian king in the east, the supposed heir of the Magi, may have fueled western fascination with the mysterious East, but in the thirteenth century there were real relations brought on by war and religion. Genghis Khan and his heirs pressed not only into China, but also along the edges of eastern Europe, ravaging parts of Hungary and Russia. Pope Innocent IV was alarmed and sought to open negotiations with the Mongols. In June 1245 in Lyons, the pope called together a council that decided to send a party of Franciscans, led by Lawrence of Portugal and Giovanni di Piano Carpini, on a long and difficult journey to the Mongol court. They carried letters for the khan, whose name the pope and his emissaries did not know at the time. The papal party set out immediately after the council, reached Kiev by early 1246, and six months later were at the Mongol court to witness the elevation of the new Mongol khan (Küyük, the grandson of Genghis). They presented their letters to the khan and received a letter to take back to the pope. They arrived back in Lyons by late 1248. The letters they carried both to and from the Mongols were worlds apart.

The pope's first letter is a complex discourse on Christianity that is so layered in European thought and technical language that it may have been difficult for its recipients in Asia to understand. The letter did, however, introduce the pope's emissaries and asked for the khan to protect them and to listen to what they had to say. The pope's second letter, also written before the mission set off, was an unequivocal assertion of Catholic supremacy and judgment. In it Pope Innocent condemned the Mongol invasions of Christian and other lands and called on the khan to stop the slaughter lest he suffer in hell for the savagery his people committed on earth. Carpini, in his impersonal account of the journey, reports that after they had presented the court with the letters he was asked whether his pope understood the Russian, Saracen (Arabic), or Mongol languages. The Franciscans suggested that the khan's court should reply in Mongol and that they would translate it into Latin and supply the pope with both versions. The Mongol court's secretaries insisted on interpreting the khan's letter to them and then carefully checked the rendering of it into Latin to make sure that there were no errors that might cause trouble or misunderstanding. The khan's letter survives in both Latin and Persian (the original is in the Vatican Library). The pope was probably not pleased by the khan's letter, but then neither was the khan by the pope's two letters. The great khan demanded that the pope and his princes come and submit to him. He claimed not to have understood the pope's letters about either religion or the Mongol conquests. He had conquered peoples because of their impudence and charged the pope with the same offense. Moreover, he was the emperor of all peoples and the success of the Mongol conquests was proof of God's approval. If the pope chose not to submit to him, he should know that he would be the khan's enemy and should expect war. The religious disagreements between the pope and the khan were profound. The khan rejected propositions not found in the letters (and so, perhaps, conveyed orally by the Franciscans) that the khan be baptized, become a Nestorian Christian (an eastern form of Christianity that had reached India), or an ascetic. The khan denied the pope's claim to speak for God and convey his judgment. Instead, the great khan claimed that Genghis Khan and his successors were the ones who had been sent by God.

Küyük Khan

Long-distance disagreements, filtered through several languages and worlds of cultural difference, made the perspectives of the western pope and eastern khan sharply different, but the papacy sent other delegations of Franciscans to talk to the Mongols and to collect information. Thirty years later the Polos would, more successfully, speak a different language, the language of trade and mutual advantage, which was somewhat more accommodating.

QUESTIONS | ***Why is war in some cases a first form of communication? Was the papal mission to the Mongols a good idea or not? Why? How deep was the cultural chasm between far east and far west? Why might those cultural differences have been largely official and not societal?***

powers, strong magnates, and papal interference. In Italy the situation was different: a resident and intrusive papacy, imperial claims, and stronger urban and local traditions. The third area of special state development was the imperial papacy, which reached its apex under Innocent III but struggled after that. At the end of the thirteenth century, Pope Boniface VIII aggressively extended the claims of the papacy, but he met strong resistance from powerful secular forces. Princes were now often stronger than popes.

The mechanisms of state control improved in the High Middle Ages. A more sophisticated bureaucracy assisted the drive toward centralization and control. In France and England, noble interests were increasingly subordinated to royal ones. The concept of real boundaries to a kingdom began to emerge, at least in England and France. Systems of taxation also improved. By the thirteenth century, Europe may still not have achieved any sharp sense of state, but the conditions for that conception were emerging. Politics remained primarily dynastic, and thinking about the state (as in Thomas Aquinas's *On Kingship*) remained God centered and religious in purpose. The duty of a prince was not to achieve the practical and necessary, but to do the religiously right thing. Real rulers, as opposed to ideal ones, knew how to serve their own political interests. Pope Innocent and Frederick II with their new sense of political possibilities played the game at a more calculating level, but they had to deal with the intricate city-states, chiefly republics, that were developing in Italy. City-states such as Venice not only managed their own territories and internal urban affairs, but also operated as if they were fully autonomous European states on the international stage.

The high medieval state was still conceived of as a corporate body or incorporated entity. John of Salisbury likened the various groups of society to parts of a body: the king was the head, the priesthood the soul, soldiers the breast, tax collectors the intestines, and farmers the feet. As rudimentary as this scheme may seem, its effect was to treat the state as a living body of interdependent parts, each of which had its proper place and function. John also began to explore the limits of kingship, the most controversial being the removal of a tyrant. John granted that the king deserved the support of his subjects, but only so long as he obeyed God and his commandments. Should he wage war against God, then he would be, by definition, a tyrant who should be removed from office, by force if necessary. Thus John proposed a doctrine of tyrannicide (the murder of a tyrant) and not regicide (the murder of a king), since a ruler who attacked God no longer ruled by divine right or rightfully held the title and office of king.

By the early thirteenth century, some limitations on kingship were being formulated in England. After his capitulation to Pope Innocent III, King John faced the resistance of his barons, who resented his many attempts to raise monies and to levy demands upon them. At Runnymede in 1215, he finally relented, issuing the **Magna Carta,** or Great Charter (to distinguish it from a smaller one), which provided a series of guarantees to the magnates and people of England that delimited what the king could demand of his people and powerful lords. The document may not have been the groundbreaking constitutional charter some once thought that it was, but it did set down rules about taxation, property rights, and limits on the king's power. The king was no longer allowed to tinker with or undo legitimate inheritances, to allow his agents to seize the property or goods of any man without fair payment, or to override the law of the land in pursuit of royal interests.

The monarchies of France, England, and to a lesser degree Spain were not yet states in the modern sense of the term, but they were on their way toward statehood in having defined territories and representative assemblies of the king and the powerful of the land. Spanish kings met with their knights and lords in an assembly called the *cortes,* where they decided on united action and settled disputes. By the end of the thirteenth century, Spanish rulers accepted that they required the support of their people, as expressed in the *cortes,* to make general laws for all. What mattered was who was included in the assemblies. In England, each borough was able to send two representatives to its assembly or parliament, which had developed out of the older Anglo-Saxon Witan. France attempted to widen the franchise even further, including not only lords and church prelates, but also representatives from hundreds of villages and towns. These assemblies were limited bodies, since they met irregularly and at the will of the king. As promising as the assembly movement was across Europe in the thirteenth century, it may also be seen as just another tool for the centralization of the state under powerful monarchs. In the Late Middle Ages, these assemblies would generally weaken.

Rulers Respected, Feared, and Loved

To learn about a period and place there may be no better way to measure its ideals than to see which rulers it admired and despised, and why. The medieval Christian ideal (as found stated explicitly in early medieval political treatises) was that a ruler should be loved and feared, just as God was. The hard realities of ruling meant that few high medieval rulers could achieve both and survive.

Consider the case of Henry II, king of England (r. 1154–1189), who was respected but not loved. After the death of William the Conqueror, England had lived precariously on the edge of civil war and rebellion as the church, the great barons, and the people were upset over new taxes and royal demands. During his long reign, Henry II put down regional resistance to England in Scotland and Wales, reorganized English government by improving the quality and jurisdiction of royal officials, regularized royal revenues, and insisted on the rule of law, both royal and common. Trial by ordeal was slowly replaced by the collection and weighing of evidence by juries.

Henry was a canny and successful king, but he was not loved—not by his subjects, not by the church, and not by his family. He spent the majority of his reign outside the realm, but he had organized his kingdom so well that it could run without him being physically present. As duke of Normandy and the husband of Eleanor of Aquitaine, he was a powerful continental lord and presided over the so-called Angevin Empire. The curse hanging over the Angevin (or Plantagenet) Empire was dynastic dispute, and Eleanor and Henry were a quarrelsome couple. Their three sons—Richard (the Lionheart), Geoffrey, and John—sided with their mother and their continental land holdings. They joined with their mother in supporting the French against Henry, who overcame their rebellion and in 1174 imprisoned Eleanor.

Eleanor of Aquitaine and Her Royal Family In a damaged mural from the chapel of St. Radegonde, Chinon, France, Queen Eleanor and her daughter Joanna (in the center) ride behind King Henry II of England and in front of two retainers or guards. The meaning of the mural is uncertain. Some scholars have suggested that it shows Eleanor being led into captivity by her husband, others that she has just been released from house arrest, and yet others that it is just a magnificent procession of the royal Plantagenet family.

Henry's conflict with his old friend Thomas Beckett belonged to the final stages of the papal reform of the church, for Henry thought of the church in England as under his care and control. But Thomas, whom the king appointed archbishop of Canterbury, fought hard for church rights and resisted royal interference in church affairs. John of Salisbury was present when Thomas was murdered in his cathedral by noble supporters of the king, who thought that they were ridding their king of an impolitic and rebellious enemy. In the eyes of the church and people, Thomas Beckett was a martyr and they blamed the king for his murder, but Henry took the necessary steps to repair his reputation and his culpable soul. He performed penance, was scourged, and gained papal absolution for the murder, but the church found it hard to love and embrace Henry, who treated the church as just another player in the game of royal politics.

Though Henry achieved a united England, promoted royal justice and a more efficient government, balanced the financial books, and maintained his continental possessions, few wept when he died on the continent after an unsuccessful campaign against the king of France and his own son Richard. Henry was shrewd, competent, and better for England, but the heart of the age belonged to the swashbuckling Richard, the noble crusader, who succeeded him.

Richard the Lionheart spent less than a half year of his decade in power (r. 1189–1199) in England, preferred France, probably couldn't speak English, had rebelled against his father, and exhausted the English treasury filled by his father. But Richard was larger than life and apparently much loved by the people. It is not hard to see why. He was famously generous and charming, reputedly handsome and courageous, and every inch the ideal chivalrous king. Moreover, by treating England as an afterthought in his international career, Richard had not aroused many grievances against him within English society. Richard's popularity and neglect of active government were possible only because his father, Henry, had demanded so much and ruled England so well.

Few knew what to make of Frederick II: some were amazed by the *stupor mundi* (the wonder of the world), who stunned the High Middle Ages with his novel behavior; some were horrified. His father was the emperor Henry VI, his grandfathers Roger of Sicily and Frederick Barbarossa. When he was three years old, his father died and a year later Frederick was named the king of Sicily. When his mother died the next year, Pope Innocent III became the boy-king's guardian. Sicily was a crucible of Arabic, Christian, Italian, and Norman influences, and the young Frederick became a proto-renaissance man: he wrote a scientific book on falconry, planned castles and canals, spoke several languages, and dreamed of restoring the empire. At age fourteen, and finally free from the pope's control, he became the ruling king of Sicily. By age eighteen he was king of the Romans, and at twenty-six he became emperor of the Holy Roman Empire. What stunned Europe was his extraordinary behavior. He reclaimed Jerusalem not by war, but through negotiation and marriage, challenged a hostile papacy, started the

University of Naples, collected exotic animals, promoted science, doubted the truths of established religions, and allowed Muslims to settle and openly practice their faith in Sicily. No wonder people of the time either praised or feared him. The papacy portrayed him as an Anti-Christ and a heretic, and excommunicated him several times because of the unorthodox way in which he retook Jerusalem. Enemies of the papacy rejoiced over Frederick's resistance to Rome, believing that he would free the church from its unholy worldliness and return it to a state of apostolic poverty. Thirteenth-century men and women projected many hopes and fears onto Frederick II, for he showed them a future different from the one that the papacy had so carefully constructed for the High Middle Ages.

Frederick II occupied the dark imagination of Europe. Saint Louis, the king of France, fulfilled its Christian aspiration for a good and lovable king. Louis became king of France on his father's death in 1226 but did not take control of the kingdom until 1234. Twice he went on crusade (the Seventh and Eighth Crusades), and despite their futile outcomes, he was admired greatly for his devotion to the Christian cause. His capture by Egyptians in 1250 shocked Europe, but he was ransomed for an enormous amount of money. For four years he remained in the Holy Land, repairing castles and improving the standing and defense of the Christians there. At home, Louis ruled a Christian state at the peak of its power and wealth. He could do almost no wrong. He was a devoted servant of Christianity, buying precious relics for France and building impressive churches. Like Pope Innocent IV, Louis sent emissaries east to meet the great Mongol khan; he thought that it was his duty as a Christian king to convert pagan kings. Even his support of the inquisition and the persecution of the Jews—seizing property to pay for his crusades and ordering the destruction of Jewish holy books—seemed to his age to be the just deeds of a true son of the church. He died a "good death" in 1270 while he was on his second crusade, and his remains were returned to St. Denis for burial. While he lived, Louis was already considered to be a holy ruler. In death he became a saint.

For the Middle Ages, Louis was a perfect Christian king, loved, but not particularly feared unless you were a Jew with property or holy books, a heretic, or a Muslim in the Holy Land. Richard the Lionheart was much admired and loved, but he was an absent and irresponsible ruler. Frederick II stunned his age with his audacity and daring, but he was little loved and much feared. Yet he personified a vision of a different sort of Europe, one not dominated by religion and the high medieval papacy, but his politics brought Europe little peace and may have doomed Germany to its long division of powers and principalities. Henry II of England was respected, but little loved by his family or country, and yet he transformed England into a better kingdom, one governed by law, order, and a strong monarchy. Yet his claim to properties in greater France meant that England would continue to be dragged into continental wars that were of royal and not necessarily English concern, as his son King John discovered.

The Medieval University

Like the monastery and representative assemblies (parliaments), the university was an institution invented and shaped by the Middle Ages. Institutions should not be thought of as buildings, but as sets of rules and customs that help specialized societies preserve authoritative cultures from generation to generation. Institutions work to overcome the limitation of mortal life, ensuring continuity across time. With written and unwritten rules, linked offices and officers, the goal of institutions is to persist, carrying out specific functions for the general good of a society.

Why did the Middle Ages, and not some other period, create the institution of the university?

Neither the Greeks nor the Romans had found a suitable, broadly based institutional receptacle for higher learning. Plato's Academy was too elitist and unstructured. Roman aristocrats had largely privatized higher education in a tutorial system. Yet eight hundred years ago in Salerno, Bologna, Paris, Montpellier, Oxford, and Cambridge, masters were lecturing to university students and still do. The university had no exact moment of birth and there was no one individual who created it, but there were reasons for the university's emergence and persistence (Map 9.3).

The Passing of the Cathedral Schools

The great cathedral schools led by the likes of Bernard of Chartres and Abelard in the first half of the twelfth century could not cope with the demands of society or the reorganization of knowledge in the second. Instead of an advanced student seeking out a master, wherever he might be located, in order to learn a specific discipline, it became more efficient for students to move to educational centers that contained many masters. By the mid-twelfth century, Paris was already becoming one of those central meeting points for masters and students.

The University of Paris grew out of the school operated by the cathedral of Notre Dame. By 1200, Paris was four or five times the size of Chartres, and the older cathedral schools, no matter how distinguished, could not compete. Moreover, cathedral schools depended on the prestige of their great masters to draw students, but, as Abelard's case shows, respect for old authoritative teaching was under intense pressure. Adelard of Bath, an adventurous English scholar of the early twelfth century, quipped that authority had a wax nose that could be twisted. Students were restless for new ways to learn and new masters to learn from.

When asked by their father what they did at their cathedral school, two students at Chartres characterized their experience in less than elevated terms: "We make glosses; we owe money." Such an education was based on a master pronouncing upon a text, but there were few texts available to comment on. Bernard of Chartres apparently owned twenty-four volumes, which was a large personal library

MAP 9.3 | The Spread of Medieval Universities

The institution of the university spread throughout Europe after the rise of the original six: Salerno, Bologna, Paris, Montpellier, Oxford, and Cambridge. ***Why did universities become so popular so quickly? Which regions and periods saw the greatest growth in the number of universities and why?***

for the time. The technique of glossing (essentially making notes in the margins of a book) was the product of an educational world based on a few core texts that received intensive study. By the mid-twelfth century, students were impatient with this older style of learning. Like Abelard and William of Conches, they wanted to know the reasons for things. Part of Abelard's popularity was that he made his subjects clear, not obtuse and rarefied, and subject to reason. He was also wickedly funny. Ambitious masters began to gather where the students were, often in larger centers such as Paris, and there offered instruction for a fee.

Translating the Collected Wisdom of the West

Students and their teachers wanted new and better books. By the middle of the twelfth century, the texts that had sustained five hundred years of medieval education began to be displaced by a new generation of books, though they arrived too late for Abelard to put them to use. The vast store of ancient wisdom had been divided and localized by the breakdown of Roman order. The Latin works of Rome had fallen to western Europe; 90 percent of the ancient Latin texts that have survived had been copied and preserved by the Carolingians. The Greek works survived in the monasteries and schools of Byzantium. Between 700 and 900, Islamic and Middle Eastern scholars assiduously translated (into a variety of languages) and studied the Greek remains. By 1100, it was still unclear which of these three players (western Europe, Byzantium, or Islam) would attempt to unite the mass of ancient learning. Since Byzantine and Muslim scholars showed no abiding interest in Latin texts, it was likely, though not inevitable, that the Latin west would

THINGS THAT REMAIN

How the Middle Ages Saved and Modern Technology Recovered Archimedes and Hyperides

On April 14, 1229, with the Byzantine Empire under the control of the Latins and Jerusalem once again in Muslim hands, Ioannes Myronas closed the book he had just made, a palimpsest, or book made by writing overtop an old one. His creation may be a testimony to the hard times on which the empire had fallen, for Ioannes was desperate for parchment. To save the cost of purchasing parchment or because it was unavailable, he took several manuscripts, already several centuries old but no longer in much demand, and pulled them apart. He laboriously removed the previous writing, scraping off and erasing the old lettering, turned the large pages sideways, folded them, and began copying a series of Greek prayers. The humble little prayer book he produced ended up at the monastery of St. Sabas in the Holy Land, where it remained until the early twentieth century, when it was transported to Istanbul, then Paris, and other places. The palimpsest shows centuries of use and misuse (candle wax stains, pages missing, mold, and fire damage), but the book survived because it served a purpose and contained holy words. In making the prayer book, Ioannes had inadvertently saved some of the rarest texts of the ancient world.

The lower text (the one that was written over) of the palimpsest contains pages from the lost works of the great mathematician Archimedes and lost speeches of the ancient orator Hyperides. These ancient texts could hardly be read: portions of the lower text lay hidden under the binding and some pages had been painted over with fake illuminations by a modern forger. The modern owner of the palimpsest turned the damaged book over (for purposes of conservation and investigation) to the Walters Art Gallery in Baltimore, which organized a team of philologists, classicists, and scientists to recover the lost texts. Using multispectral analysis (essentially subjecting the surface of the parchment pages to different frequencies of light) and breaking down the information by algorithms and computer analysis, the team was slowly able to read the ancient texts lying beneath the prayers, all the while preserving both the lower text (the ancient texts) and the upper text (the Byzantine Greek prayers) of the palimpsest. A nineteenth-century German editor of Archimedes had studied the codex and made a first edition, but his eyes could only see so much; modern technology and experts finally freed the ancient texts from their damaged pages.

Yet the words of the ancients might not have survived at all if a medieval scribe had not recycled what he probably thought were useless texts written on perfectly good parchment and secured their survival by filling the palimpsest with holy words.[3]

QUESTIONS | ***In our digital age, how might we be in danger of losing the information contained on paper pages? Why would a Christian scribe have written over precious ancient texts?***

Reading the Archimedes Palimpsest with Modern Tools

stir itself to the task of understanding the surviving knowledge of the ancients.

The cultural acquisition and appropriation of the ancient library was part of the same aggressive drive that led the Christian west to wage the First Crusade, for by the twelfth century the Latin west had become militarily aggressive and culturally acquisitive. Translation centers were the cultural parallel to crusade.

In 1085, the cosmopolitan city of Toledo in Spain, with its rich Muslim and Jewish cultures, fell to Christian conquerors. By the early twelfth century, Toledo was an established center of translation, where scholars such as Adelard of Bath, Dominic Gundisalvi, and John of Spain began translating Greek and Arabic works into Latin. Gerard of Cremona translated numerous works, including those of the ancient geographer Ptolemy, Aristotle, Euclid, Hippocrates, and Galen. Another translation center opened in Palermo in Sicily.

A massive influx of new books poured into Europe between 1150 and 1250, undermining the old liberal arts curriculum of the cathedral schools and altering the fundamental character of western thought and its methods of inquiry. By 1250, the majority of Aristotle's treatises were available to the Latin west. The Middle Ages may have had an inherent bias in favor of Platonism and the idea that this world is a mere appearance behind which lie its invisible real forms and essences, but its encounter with Aristotle, with his logical methods and scientific interests, pushed higher education in a new direction. By 1255, the *Timaeus,* Plato's great work of cosmology, which had been partially available in Latin since the Early Middle Ages, was removed from the curriculum of the University of Paris. Plato's thought did not disappear, but instead went underground, finding an outlet in popular vernacular works such as Jean de Meun's *Roman de la Rose* (*Romance of the Rose*) before finally resurfacing in the Florentine Renaissance reclamation of Plato in the fifteenth century.

The creation of the university was a corporate response to the need to integrate and make sense of the mass of ancient knowledge, particularly the works of Aristotle that were flooding the west. Without the new texts, particularly those of Aristotle, Hippocrates and Galen, and Justinian's *Digest,* the thought of Thomas Aquinas, advanced medical studies at Montpellier and Salerno, and legal studies at Bologna—indeed, the very existence of **scholasticism** and the universities—would have been unlikely. The task of the university, then as now, is to systematize and synthesize information, though the modern university emphasizes the creation of new knowledge while the medieval one was tasked with understanding older book learning.

The book itself also underwent a dramatic transformation between 1150 and 1250. The large early medieval codex that monastic readers consulted in restricted libraries gradually gave way to smaller, portable books made from thinner parchment. Caroline Minuscule, the regular and highly legible script that filled medieval manuscripts from the ninth century to the twelfth, was replaced by the small, cursive, highly abbreviated Gothic script; more words could now be squeezed onto a page. The slow munching and mumbling of words by monks as they sought to ingest whole books gave way to quick, silent, and searching reading by a wider range of readers. The book became a source of information, a tool, not a part of one's being. The high medieval book became easier to use, taking on those formal characteristics with which we associate books today: title pages, tables of contents, chapters with titles, running heads, paragraphs, diagrams, and indices. Those features attest to a new scholastic way of reading in a world with many more books and a flood of information that needed sorting and easier access. The High Middle Ages invented the essential organization and properties of the modern book.[2]

Birth of the University

The institution of the medieval university was not created by any one person, country, or place. Four famous universities appeared in the years between 1175 and 1200: Salerno, Bologna, Paris, and Oxford. Cambridge University began slightly later, when some Oxford scholars left their university in protest after two students were hanged for murder. The first universities had different educational emphases. Salerno concentrated on medicine, Bologna on law, and Oxford and Paris on arts and theology. Each was a response to the mass of new information that needed to be explored.

The university at Bologna grew out of the need to make sense of Roman civil law. For most of the Middle Ages, Justinian's great *Corpus of Civil Law* had been lost, but around 1076 the *Digest* was rediscovered in Italy and studied intensively. The rapid growth of towns and trade made the need for civil law, with its emphasis on property rights, pressing. In the early twelfth century, Irnerius wrote an influential commentary on the *Corpus* that laid down the basis for the systematic study of Roman law. By the mid-twelfth century, canon (church) law at Bologna assumed a place almost equal to the study of civil law. Gratian's *Decretum* became the core textbook of canon law. Bologna supplied canon lawyers to the church for the rest of the Middle Ages.

By 1158, the emperor Frederick Barbarossa had conferred a set of special rights and privileges upon the schools of Bologna. These protections were needed to safeguard the developing university from the local town, which often preyed on the students and masters, forcing them to pay exorbitant rents for rooms and charging excessively for food and transport. As a term, *university* does not refer to universal knowledge, but rather to *"universitas societas magistrorum discipulorumque,"* that is, "the university is an association [or guild] of masters and students." They stood, in other words, as a small society of students and teaching clerics apart from the lay townspeople. At Bologna and elsewhere the university assumed a corporate identity.

Protection against exploitation by the town may have been the first reason for incorporation, but each university developed its own identity. Bologna was thought of as a students' university. There the professors were closely regulated and monitored. The town did not want its masters to leave and so enforced covenants against their free movement, including compelling masters to leave a deposit before they left Bologna to guarantee their return. As early as 1193, the students at Bologna set up a student union, which defined the nature of their contract with the masters. Instruction was a service contract setting the terms for the buying and selling of knowledge. At Bologna, professors were not permitted to miss classes without the corporation's prior approval and were fined if they failed to lecture to at least five students. The professor at Bologna was required to begin his lecture when a bell rang and to finish when the next bell sounded, and he was not allowed to skip over important subjects or squeeze them in at the end of his lecture.

Medieval masters may have needed curtailment. They could be extremely arrogant. They feigned nobility, wore elaborate gowns and gold rings, and sat on elaborate elevated thrones. Students occasionally mocked them. At one university a statute prohibited students from throwing stones at their professors during lecture, even if they missed. Since professors lacked secure employment and depended on student fees to survive, they needed to please both the corporation and their students. Many of them grumbled that their students were poor payers, eager to receive instruction, but never to pay for it. When the mendicant friars, particularly the Dominicans, began teaching in Paris, it caused considerable controversy, since the friars taught for free and thus threatened to undermine the guild-like system of the corporation.

The medieval professor was a product of the system, having obtained a teaching license, which was the first of the university degrees. A master of arts degree (the M.A.) was awarded at the end of six years of instruction and the acceptance of a masterwork. The new master joined the teachers' guild and swore to uphold the statutes of the university. He was then placed on his throne, held a book of Aristotle in his hands, was invested with a ring, and was kissed by his fellow masters. This rite of passage from student to master allowed the new master to teach the liberal arts.

The University of Paris

Unlike at Bologna, masters at the University of Paris held the upper hand. The university developed out of the cathedral school of Notre Dame, which was under the direct control of its chancellor. By the second half of the twelfth century, Paris was growing rapidly, as was its student population. By 1200, students may have formed 10 percent of the city's population; perhaps there were as many as 2,000 to 4,000 students. Tensions were inevitable, particularly in the Île de la Cité area around the cathedral. These tensions often led to town-gown fights. In 1200, a tavern brawl broke out after some German students imbibed too much wine, misbehaved in their search for more to drink, and were attacked by locals, leaving some of the students dead. In the wake of that incident, a royal charter conceded that students stood outside lay courts and lay justice. The scholars of Paris welcomed the king's recognition of their relative autonomy.

The Medieval Classroom At the University of Bologna, a master lectures from his high throne while students pay varying degrees of attention to his instruction. Although the third student in the first row may seem to our eyes to be a woman, it is highly unlikely that the artist meant to depict a female because women were excluded from the medieval university.

The faculty of arts at Paris comprised almost two-thirds of the student population in the thirteenth century. The masters of arts soon developed a corporate identity for their institution and resisted the chancellor's interference. The university was divided into four "nations" of students—French, Norman, Picard, and English-German—each with its own proctor or supervisor. These nations bandied words and blows with each other. The medieval university seethed with various tensions—between the local town and the corporation, students and teachers, church authorities and the university, and various groups of students.

By the mid-twelfth century, logic and philosophy began to displace the study of grammar (in its wider medieval meaning of philology or textual studies), which had been at the core of the cathedral school curriculum. Instruction was in Latin, which was an artificial and learned language for all. By the thirteenth century, the works of Aristotle had replaced many classical texts, including the ancient poets. At Oxford and Paris, students read and commented on the logical works of Aristotle, the grammatical works of Priscian and Donatus, and Aristotle's *Ethics* and natural treatises. Examinations were oral and tension-filled. Some study manuals with sample examination questions and pertinent topics survive. Students likened their examinations to the Last Judgment. On occasion, students simply froze, unable to respond. At Bologna, one student became so flustered during his oral exam that he reminded the gathered witnesses, who hurled abuse at him, of a bleating goat.

Living the Medieval University Life

Student life was distinctive. All the students at the medieval university were male, many of them from the lower gentry and upwardly mobile middle class. They started their university years as young as age thirteen or fourteen. They were called clerks (*clerici*), though they were not priests. They underwent a symbolic haircut (tonsure) and at some institutions were compelled to wear long black gowns. Most universities prohibited the wearing of extravagant dress by students: no pointed shoes, ballooning sleeves, or bright stockings. Students lived in residences under the supervision of a master, but strict rules were enforced. Students late for breakfast received only bread. The house kitchen was off-limits. They could not bring friends to their residence to eat and drink, nor could they have women in their rooms or assault servants. Poor students had their own residences.

Classes were held in rented rooms or a church and began as early as 5 or 6 a.m. Students sat on wooden benches or the floor and took notes on waxed tablets, from which they might later make a good or, at least, more organized record of the lecture on parchment. The greatest hindrance to learning was the limited access to books. Manuscripts were expensive to buy, and libraries were out of bounds to undergraduates. At the University of Paris, a stationer authorized by the university would rent portions of texts for students to copy.

Two themes dominated medieval university life: poverty and drink. Paris was expensive, and lecture fees needed paying. Masters realized that if their students could not convince their parents and patrons to keep the funds flowing, they would go unpaid, and so they taught their students how to write begging letters. Said one master: "Let us take as our topic today that a poor but deserving student has to write home to his mother for the funds he needs . . . ."

Most medieval university students may have been earnest and hard working, but it is often the others whom we hear about in the regulations. These wilder students apparently loved to play dice and to fence. In Bologna, one student pulled a sword on another during a lecture. In Germany, freshmen (*beani*) were hazed to rid them of their rusticity, but university regulations prohibited the tormentors from insulting, yelling at, harassing, drenching with urine, or defiling with dust and filth their fellow students.

University students, then as now, live in a transitional state, caught between the mature workaday life of the career that awaits and their younger days at home. Medieval students found themselves in relatively large cities such as Paris, which observers called a paradise of delights, but uncertain who they were or where they were headed. A profound feeling of alienation haunts the poems and drinking songs of the clerks. The most gifted of these, the Archpoet, prays in his confession to die with a tankard by his side with angels looking down upon him and singing joyously, "Let God keep company with this mighty drinker."

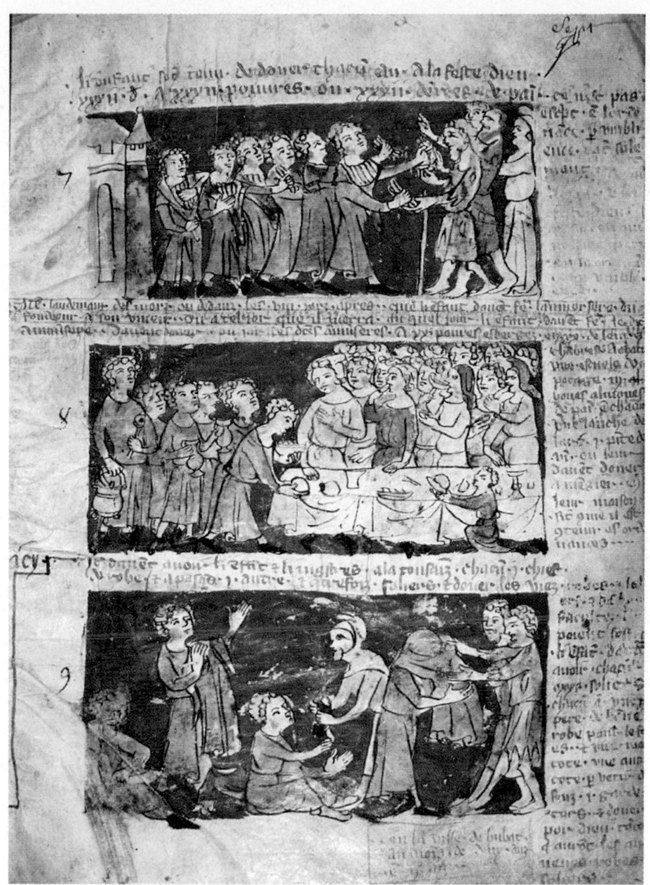

Poor Students Receiving Charity Poor university students received clothes, shoes, food, and shelter from charitable churches and religious orders so that they might pursue their education.

Scholasticism and the Dumb Ox

Scholasticism is the general term for the intellectual movement of university thinkers (the schoolmen) of the period between 1150 and 1350. They applied a highly refined form of logical reasoning or disputation to understanding revelation. Many Christian thinkers had from the beginning sought the same, but at the medieval university, especially in Paris, the pursuit took on a particular methodological and intellectual rigor. The intellectual explorations of the early-twelfth-century cathedral school masters had been individually and intellectually more daring, but they had often lacked a concentrated focus and method. Thirteenth-century scholastic thought was narrower, but a more exact synthesis of Christian thought, and the greatest of its thinkers, was the "Dumb Ox," Thomas Aquinas.

The curriculum at the University of Paris moved away from the liberal arts and its concentration on grammar, rhetoric, and the classics. Twelfth-century humanism gave way in the thirteenth century to the logical synthesis of complex doctrines. Dialectic (or logic), one of the liberal arts, took over, displacing even scientific and mathematical inquiry. As a consequence, the Latin written by the university doctors lacks the eloquence and charm of twelfth-century writers such as Bernard of Clairvaux, Suger of St. Denis, Hildegard of Bingen, and Heloise. Instead, university doctors wrote tight logical arguments without flourishes or, for the most part, personality. The beauty of scholasticism lay in the quality of its reasoning, not its prose.

Theology had always been the queen (or summit) of medieval inquiry, but she now pushed aside the subdisciplines, including philosophy. This did not happen quickly. The thought of Augustine and medieval Platonism remained strong, but the influx of Aristotelian and other ancient texts slowly changed the direction of university attention. Aristotle's texts did not arrive all in one piece or at one time. In the late twelfth and early thirteenth centuries, his works were known chiefly through translations from Arabic commentaries such as those by Persian philosopher Avicenna (Ibn Sina, 988–1037), which were colored by Neo-Platonic ideas. Thinkers of this transitional period still viewed Aristotle through a Platonist lens that allowed them to align Aristotle with Augustine, though with some difficulty. To some, Aristotle already seemed a threat and for a time his books were banned from the curriculum.

Early in the thirteenth century, medieval thinkers did not yet have a firm grasp of Aristotle's own works. It fell to the mid-thirteenth century and to the Dominicans to rediscover the genuine Aristotle. William of Moerbeke, a Dominican friar from Flanders, translated for Thomas Aquinas such works as Aristotle's *Politics* and *Economics* from Greek. Other translators such as Herman of Carinthia had translated such works as Aristotle's *Nicomachean Ethics* and *Poetics* by the mid-thirteenth century. With these texts, Thomas Aquinas could begin his great synthesis of scholastic thought, Aristotelian in method, Christian in purpose.

Thomas Aquinas was born near Aquino (between Naples and Rome). His noble family sent Thomas as a boy to be trained at Monte Cassino. His family may have hoped that he would someday obtain a high church office, but when the emperor Frederick II expelled the monks in 1239, Thomas moved to the newly established University of Naples. Mendicant friars were a vigorous presence in the city and were actively recruiting university students. In 1244, Thomas chose to become a Dominican friar, much to the shock of his brothers, who kidnapped him and, in a medieval version of deprogramming, kept him cut off from his order and profession for a year in the hope that he would renounce his Dominican vow. When he finally secured his release, Thomas went to Cologne to study under the famous scholastic thinker, Albert the Great. Thomas was teaching at Paris by the 1250s, but when the mendicants' role at the university was disputed, Thomas left for Italy, not returning until 1269. He soon found himself embroiled in controversy when he challenged the so-called Latin Averroists. The Averroists (followers of Averroës or Ibn Rushd, the Arabic interpreter of Aristotle) chose to concentrate on the study of Aristotle and generally placed reason above faith, even above Christian authority. On the other side, Thomas was attacked by conservative Augustinian theologians for granting too much scope to reason and Aristotle and not enough to faith. Thus, Thomas stood between the intellectual progressives and traditionalists or left and right of his day.

Little is known about Thomas's personal life. He was reputedly very fat and given to long silences, prompting one wit to call him "the Dumb Ox." He was apparently slow to anger and gentle in the classroom. His handwriting (the so-called *littera inintelligibilis*, "incomprehensible handwriting") was almost unreadable except by his personal scribes; Thomas wrote with his left hand and writing with a quill pen was difficult for the left-handed.

Thomas is best known for his two *Summae* (*Summa contra Gentiles* and *Summa Theologica*), the massive summaries of his thought, but he also wrote commentaries on the works of Aristotle and Pseudo-Dionysius, expositions on Scripture, short philosophical works, and hymns (see Back to the Source at the end of the chapter). Thomas Aquinas was, above all, a great synthesizer who set himself the task of applying logical reasoning to a Christian understanding of the revealed world. He resolved the vexing problem of the relationship between faith and reason that had preoccupied medieval thought. In his time, the issue was playing out in Paris. Siger of Brabant and the Latin Averroists sought primarily to understand the physical world, not God's miracles, and to treat what was natural in a natural way. Opposing this sufficiency-of-reason school of thought was the great Franciscan thinker Bonaventure, who emphasized the primacy of faith over reason. Bonaventure subordinated philosophy to divine truth. Thomas essentially synthesized these two positions, treating philosophical issues philosophically and theological ones theologically. For Thomas, there was no conflict between faith and reason. One did not intrude on the other, but rather they complemented each other.

Paris in the 1270s was a hotbed of rancorous dispute. Certain contested propositions by the Aristotelian schoolmen, among them several by Thomas, were challenged and finally condemned in 1277. Thomas had, however, already left the scene. In 1273, he had a mystical experience or, perhaps, suffered a neurological incident and wrote no more. He apparently confessed to a friend that all that he had written now seemed to him to be but straw compared to the revelation of the unseen he had experienced. He died the next year. Eventually Thomas's thought became not only the accepted standard for scholasticism, but for the Catholic Church. One reflection of that is to be found in the *Divine Comedy* of Dante Alighieri, which has a scholastic rather than humanist bent. Thomas occupies a high and glorious place in Dante's Paradise.

The Gothic Peak

The Light-Filled Interior of St. Chapelle Built by Saint Louis, the king of France, St. Chapelle is a late style of Gothic architecture known as Rayonnant. At St. Chapelle, the walls seem made of glass, the dimensions of the church intimate, and the overall effect that of a precious architectural container for the king's collection of relics.

Scholars have long seen a similarity between scholastic thought and Gothic architecture: both were perfected syntheses and rational demonstrations of elevated truths. One can easily see that high Gothic architecture makes visual sense. The eye follows ribbed columns upward until they run into ribbed vaults; on the exterior of the church, flying buttresses rise from the ground to meet and support the external stone walls of the nave and choir. Unlike most architecture, Gothic cathedrals show us how they work, displaying both the skeleton and body or, in medieval terms, form and substance. The scholastic arguments of Thomas Aquinas are demonstrations that proceed from theses, overcome objections (antitheses), and are resolved in syntheses. There is a solid structure of demonstrated connections in both Gothic architecture and scholastic thought, a systematic ordering of parts leading to a truthful summit.

Yet the likeness of scholasticism and Gothic architecture cannot strictly be true. Medieval masons were not university trained, and scholastic thinkers did not receive their education from ribbed vaults. Both were relatively closed systems, building off previous developments in their fields and extending their possibilities. They did, however, share the general desire of the Gothic High Middle Ages to perfect itself, to demonstrate its reasons or how it worked, and to bring particular forms to their logical conclusions and highest state of accomplishment. By the late thirteenth century, each had also begun to discover its limits, but this was true of the High Middle Ages as a whole.

One way to measure the progress of Gothic architecture is to follow its chronological search for height. The crown or summits of the vaults reached 81 feet at the Cathedral of Sens in the 1140s; 116 feet at the Cathedral of Chartres in the 1220s; 137 feet at the Cathedral of Amiens in the 1230s; and finally, 157 feet at Beauvais, when the choir collapsed in a windstorm in 1284, putting an end to the Gothic search for ever-higher buildings. Gothic architecture was by then already turning away from the high style of the Cathedral of Chartres. The Rayonnant (radiant) style of Gothic emphasized instead the penetration of light, with the surface walls reduced to a lattice of glass. Saint Louis sponsored the construction of St. Chapelle in Paris as the holy receptacle for his collection of precious relics. With its intimate dimensions, lacelike windows, and interior washed with colored light, St. Chapelle is a radiant reliquary.

Gothic churches were still being erected in 1300, but the Gothic high style and purpose had found their limits and were slowly losing direction or, rather, moving off in new directions. So too was medieval thought. Scholasticism was to play itself out in the fourteenth century in a set of logical extremes.

Conclusion

During the Gothic High Middle Ages, Europe achieved remarkable things in thought, religion, architecture, education, and state development. The age saw the rise of institutions such as representative (or parliamentary) assemblies and universities that have been enduring legacies of the West. The economic vigor of the period led to increased population and the growth of vibrant cities such as Paris, Venice, Florence, and London. In intellectual life, the exciting and rambunctious twelfth-century cathedral schools gave way to thirteenth-century universities, Abelard to Aquinas, pioneering thought to scholastic synthesis. The High Middle Ages perfected the codex as the most efficient means for presenting and rationally organizing information in a book form designed for the eye rather than the ear. Massive Romanesque cathedrals were succeeded by soaring Gothic cathedrals as the leading architectural style of Europe.

Yet, for all its many accomplishments, the High Middle Ages was far from placid, and its pursuit of perfection and power did not go uncontested. The centralized and bureaucratic powerhouse of the Catholic Church, best represented by Pope Innocent III, incited a stubborn resistance from sovereigns such as Frederick II, who sought to curb the church's state power and its self-proclaimed religious right to govern Christendom. Religious sects, labeled by the church as heretical, charged that the church was too worldly and material. Popes called for crusades against both external and internal enemies of the church. One of these captured the Byzantine Empire, but all of them were questionable exercises and produced little of lasting worth. For the papacy, the point was not so much to win these wars as to preserve the right to call them and, by so doing, to unite Christendom and its secular leaders under church authority.

The heavy weight of a reformed and authoritarian church and of stronger monarchs in places such as France and England produced a backlash that made Europe at its high medieval peak an aggressive and antagonistic society of rival forces. The perfection of a Christian medieval society, particularly in the thirteenth century, was a powerful illusion that could probably never have been sustained much beyond its already towering achievements. A storm was coming.

Critical Thinking Questions

1. How was the High Middle Ages different from the Early and Central Middle Ages?
2. Why were medieval crusades after the First Crusade so problematic?
3. Why did dynamic individuals and individuality become so prominent in the period, and how were they offset by powerful collective and conservative forces?
4. How did women do in the High Middle Ages? What choices did they have?
5. In what ways is the modern university an institution that still reflects its medieval origins?

Key Terms

trivium **(p. 264)**
quadrivium **(p. 264)**
humanist **(p. 266)**
papal plenitude of power **(p. 271)**
pluralism **(p. 271)**
interdict **(p. 271)**
cottage industries **(p. 274)**
guild **(p. 274)**
usury **(p. 276)**
commune **(p. 276)**
mendicants **(p. 277)**
inquisition **(p. 278)**
Magna Carta **(p. 280)**
scholasticism **(p. 285)**

Primary Sources in connect

For information on Connect and the online resources available, go to **http://connect.mcgraw-hill.com**.

1. **Heloise's Second Letter of Complaint to Abelard**
2. **Bernard of Chartres's Six Keys to Learning**
3. **Abelard's Yes and No, the Preface and Passages**
4. **The Mongol Correspondence**
5. **Magna Carta**
6. **Thomas Aquinas on the Nature and Domain of Sacred Doctrine**

BACK TO THE SOURCE

The Existence of God

In his *Summa Theologica,* the scholastic philosopher Thomas Aquinas, a Dominican friar, set out five proofs for the existence of God. Both the arguments and the method he uses owe much to Aristotle. For Aquinas, reason and Christianity were not at odds, but rather complemented each other, as we see in his presentation of the five proofs, which begin with particular antitheses or objections before moving to proofs and answers to the objections.

Third Article: Whether God Exists

Objection 1: It seems that God does not exist; because if one of two contraries be infinite, the other would be altogether destroyed. But the name God means that he is infinite goodness. If, therefore, God existed, there would be no evil discoverable; but there is evil in the world. Therefore God does not exist.

Objection 2: Further, it is superfluous to suppose that what can be accounted for by a few principles has been produced by many. But it seems that everything we see in the world can be accounted for by other principles, supposing God did not exist. For all natural things can be reduced to one principle, which is human reason or will. Therefore there is no need to suppose God's existence.

I answer that: The existence of God can be proved in five ways: The first and more manifest way is the argument from motion. It is certain and evident to our senses, that in the world some things are in motion.... [Now], whatever is moved must be moved by another. If that by which it is moved be itself moved, then this also must needs be moved by another, and that by another again. But this cannot go on to infinity, because then there would be no first mover, and, consequently, no other mover, seeing that subsequent movers move only inasmuch as they are moved by the first mover; as the staff moves only because it is moved by the hand. Therefore it is necessary to arrive at a first, moved by no other; and this everyone understands to be God.

The second way is from the nature of efficient [or productive] cause. In the world of sensible things we find there is an order of efficient causes. There is no case known (neither is it, indeed, possible) in which a thing is found to be the efficient cause of itself; for so it would be prior to itself, which is impossible. Now in efficient causes it is not possible to go on to infinity, because in all efficient causes following in order, the first is the cause of the intermediate cause and the intermediate is the cause of the ultimate cause, whether the intermediate cause can be several or one only. Now to take away the cause is to take away the effect. Therefore, if there be no first cause among efficient causes, there will be no ultimate, nor any intermediate cause.... Therefore, it is necessary to admit a first efficient cause, to which everyone gives the name of God.

The third way is taken from possibility and necessity, and runs thus. We find in nature things that are possible to be and not to be, since they are found to be born and to die, and consequently they are possible to be and not to be. But it is impossible for these always to exist, for that which is possible not to be at some time is not. Therefore, if everything is possible not to be, then at one time there could have been nothing in existence. Now, if this is true, even now there would be nothing in existence, because that which does not exist only begins to exist by something already existing. Therefore, if at one time nothing was in existence, it would have been impossible for anything to have begun to exist; and thus even now nothing would be in existence, which is clearly false. Therefore, not all beings are merely possible, but there must exist something the existence of which is necessary. But every necessary thing either has its necessity caused by another, or not. Now, it is impossible to go on to infinity in necessary things which have their necessity caused by another, as has been already proved in regard to efficient causes. Therefore, we must admit the existence of some being having of itself its own necessity, and not receiving it from another, but rather causing in others their necessity. This all men speak of as God.

The fourth way is taken from the gradation to be found in things. Among beings there are some more and some less good, true, noble, and the like. But "more" and "less" are predicated of different things, according as they resemble in their different ways something which is the maximum, as a thing is said to be hotter according as it more nearly resembles that which is hottest. There is then something which is truest, something best, something noblest, and, consequently, something which is most being; for those things that are greatest in truth are greatest in being.... Therefore, there must also be something which is to all beings the cause of their being, goodness, and every other perfection. And this we call God.

The fifth way is taken from the governance of the world. We see that things which lack knowledge, such as natural bodies, act for an end, and this is evident from their acting always, or nearly always, in the same way, so as to obtain the best result. Hence it is plain that they achieve their end, not fortuitously, but designedly. Now whatever lacks knowledge cannot move toward an end, unless it be directed by some being endowed with knowledge and intelligence; as the arrow is directed by the archer. Therefore some intelligent being exists by whom all natural things are directed to their end. And this being we call God.

Reply to Objection 1: As Augustine says: "Since God is the highest good, he would not allow any evil to exist in his works, unless his omnipotence and goodness were such as to bring good even out of evil." This is part of the infinite goodness of God; that he should allow evil to exist, and out of it produce good.

Reply to Objection 2: Since nature works for a determinate end under the direction of a higher agent, whatever is done by nature must be traced back to God, as to its first cause.... For all things that are changeable and capable of defect must be traced back to an immovable and self-necessary first principle, as was shown in the body of this Article.

QUESTIONS | *What are the five proofs for the existence of God? Can they be reduced to one argument? What is Thomas's method of argumentation? How convincing are the proofs for the existence of God?*

Source: Thomas Aquinas, *Summa Theologica,* ed. Anton C. Pegis, *Basic Writings of Saint Thomas Aquinas,* Vol. 1 (Indianapolis, IN: Hackett, 1997), 21–24.

10

Alabaster Mourners from the Tomb of John the Fearless, Burgundian, Fifteenth Century

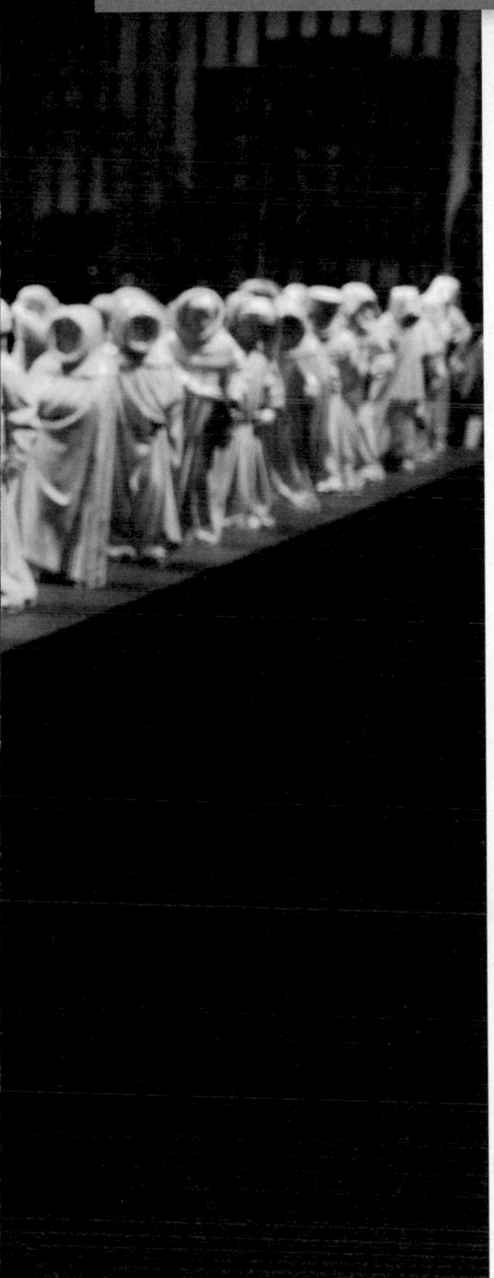

THE NEW WORLD OF THE LATE MIDDLE AGES

YERSINIA PESTIS VISITS A MONASTERY No one saw her or even knew that she existed, but they felt her effects. She was one of the dominant actors of the Late Middle Ages (1300–1500), ruining families, undermining faith, and fracturing medieval confidence that the world was knowable and perfectible. Yersinia Pestis is a strange little lady, a rod-shaped bacterium adapted to surviving in ground-squirrel populations around the globe. On occasion, she leaves her preferred host and begins a long migration through less welcoming hosts, whom she tends to kill in staggering numbers. The loss of her host means that Yersinia must soon find another or die. Tiny Yersinia began her long and strange voyage in the 1330s. Setting out from the steppes of central Asia, she traveled by flea and rodent, caravan, wagon, and boat, until she arrived in China, the Middle East, and the shores of Europe, where she wreaked such storied havoc that the very idea of plague still haunts the human imagination.

Late in 1348, Yersinia came calling at the Carthusian monastery of Montrieux in France, home to thirty-six monks, including Gherardo, the brother of Petrarch. After the woman Gherardo had loved from a distance died in Avignon, he abandoned the world and became a monk. Gherardo was lucky not to play host to little Yersinia, who has the annoying habit of killing almost everyone she comes into contact with, but his brother monks did. The prior urged the monks to flee, but only the prior himself fled. Gherardo was determined to stay where God had put him. The monks soon fell ill and started dying. Gherardo buried them one after the other, sometimes three or more a day, as they succumbed to Yersinia's deadly charm. Finally, only he and the monastery's dog were left alive. With his canine companion, Gherardo guarded the monastery by night and rested by day until summer came and he could begin making plans to restore and repopulate Montrieux.

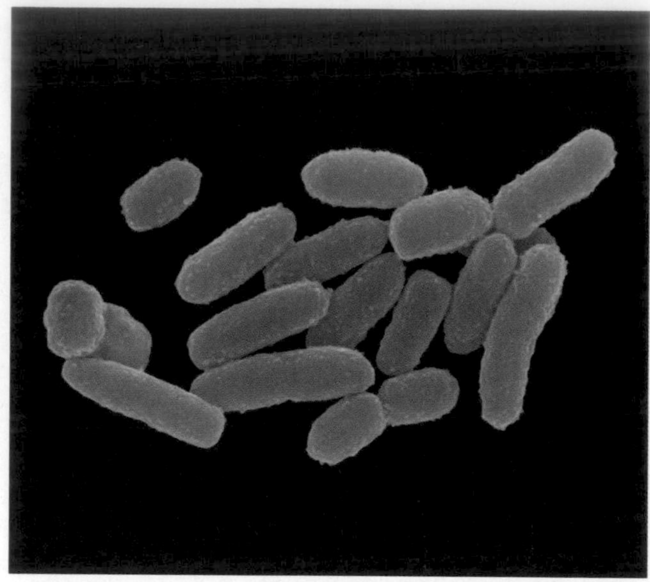

***Yersinia pestis* Bacteria**

The plague did not kill off the Middle Ages, but Yersinia played a critical role in shaping its final act. A single crisis rarely destroys a civilization, but a sequence of disasters can compromise the delicate web of a complex interconnected world. Fourteenth-century Europe was hammered by a series of calamitous events, some of its own making, most not. The weather turned bad with the onset of the Little Ice Age; a Great Famine indirectly brought about the deaths of millions of people and weakened the generation that survived; wars, including the poorly named Hundred Years' War, unnerved Europeans; the papacy confused already shaken western Christendom further when it abandoned Rome for Avignon and later split into several rival popes; and the bubonic plague devastated a once comfortable world. The impact of these calamities was quick and far-reaching: insurrection, the reordering of society, the transfer of land and the redirection of its use; the reshaping of religious beliefs; and the

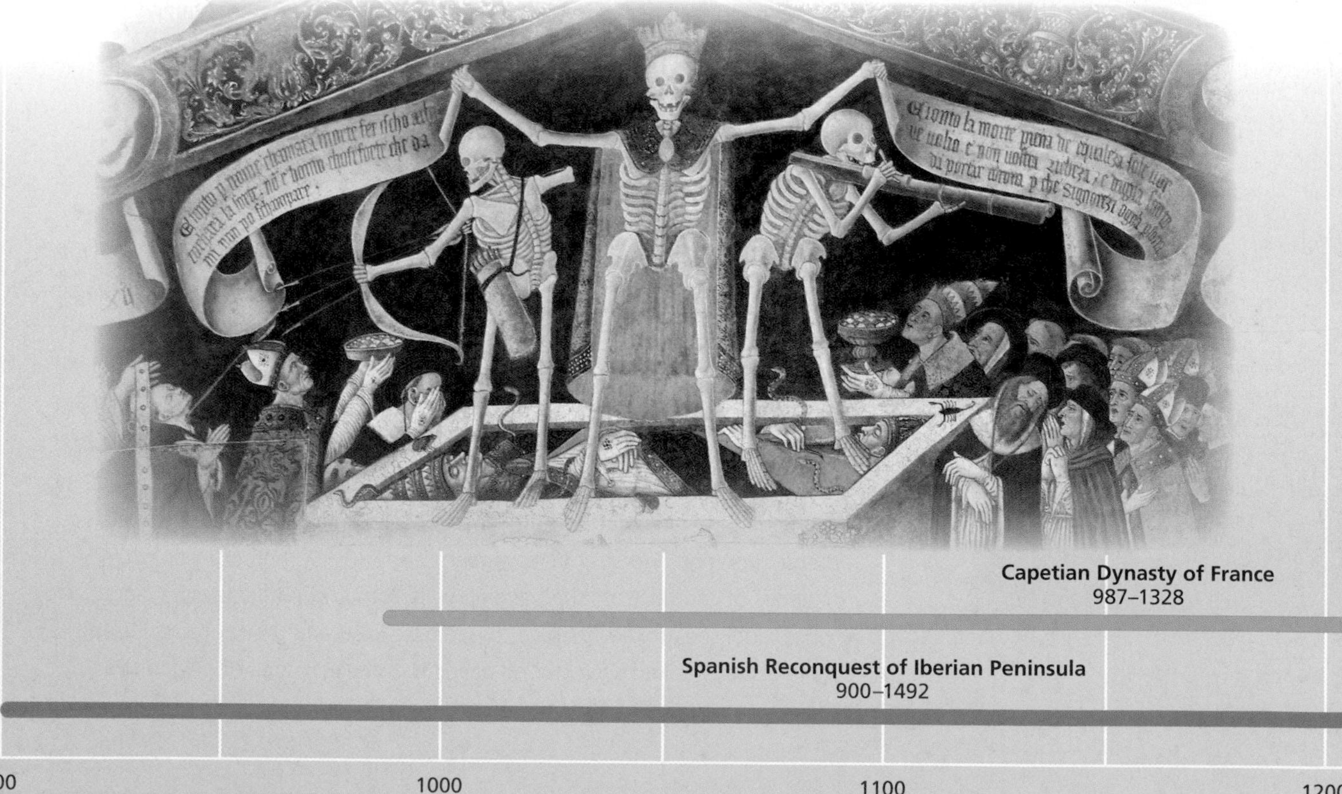

replacement of royal houses and whole political orders. The many Europes that emerged in the mid-fifteenth century were different from those of the High Middle Ages. The world of the Late Middle Ages was, in many ways, made anew, and it set the conditions for the radical developments to come in the ensuing centuries.

Winter in the Late Middle Ages The depiction of the winter month of February in *Les Très Riches Heures du Duc de Berry* does not look all that harsh, but at the time the miniature was being produced in 1416 the Little Ice Age was well under way in the northern hemisphere.

The Fourteenth Century Opens with Calamities

There were already signs late in the thirteenth century that the High Middle Ages was in trouble, but the first crisis of the fourteenth century could hardly have been foreseen: the weather turned cold and wet, and famine followed. One crisis did not necessarily cause the other, but Europe was soon shaken from the pleasant high medieval confidence and prosperity that it had enjoyed for two centuries.

Which was worse for medieval Europe, the onset of the Little Ice Age or the Great Famine? Why?

The Arrival of a New Ice Age

The Medieval Warm Period had stretched from the late eighth century to the late thirteenth, achieving its peak (the climatic optimum) in the period 1075–1125. By the second half of the thirteenth century, colder weather returned to the North Atlantic. Sediment cores taken from the coastal areas of Greenland reveal that the climate

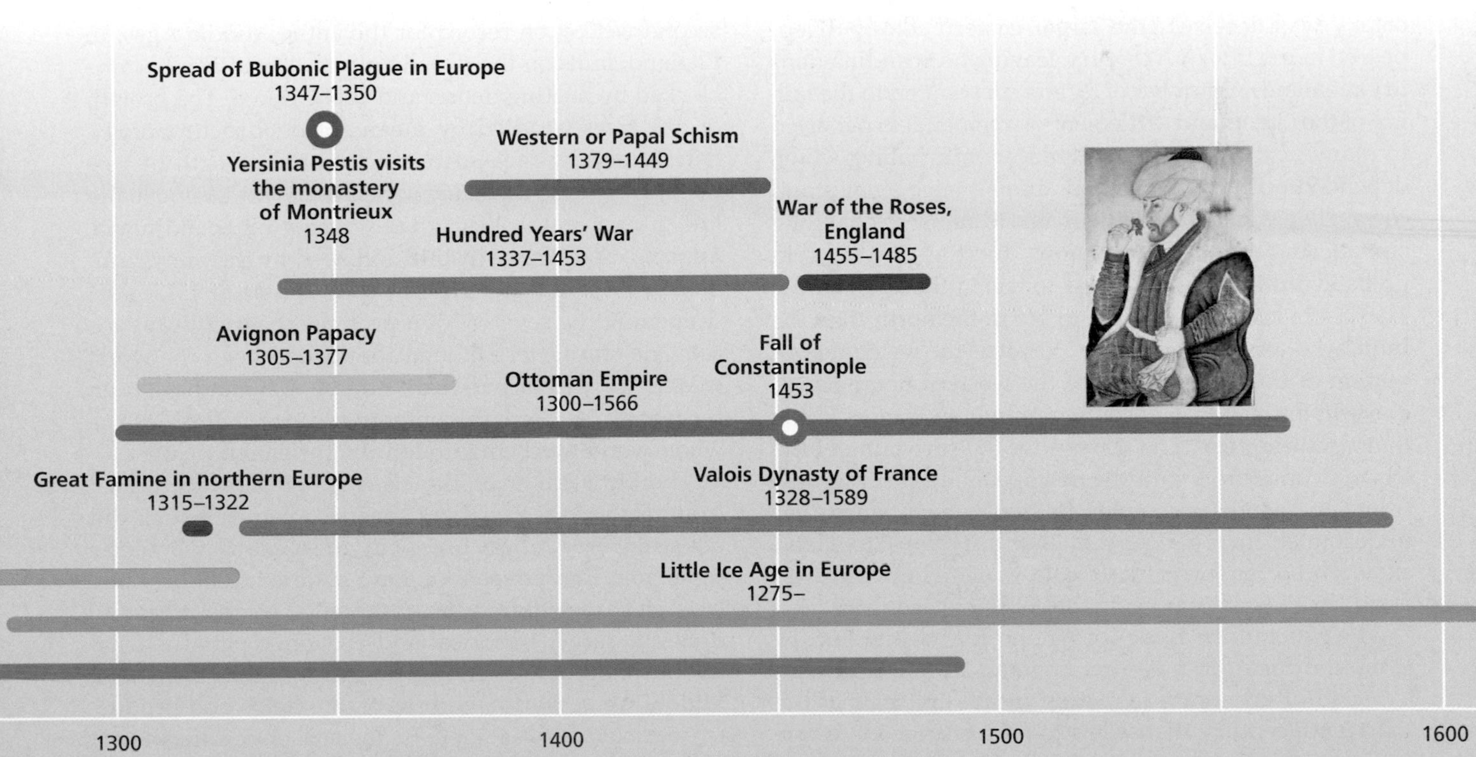

of the northern hemisphere had been relatively mild and warm between 900 and 1200, but was followed by particularly cold weather between 1270 and 1370. The fourteenth century was the coldest century of the millennium in Greenland. Climatologists call this period a **Little Ice Age,** a term based on the advance of the globe's ice. After centuries of retreat, Swiss glaciers began to move down the valleys of the Alps, and other glaciers across Europe advanced. The Little Ice Age might still be the world's prevailing climatic condition were it not for the rapid climate change or global warming that began in the twentieth century and continues to accelerate in the twenty-first (Figure 10.1).

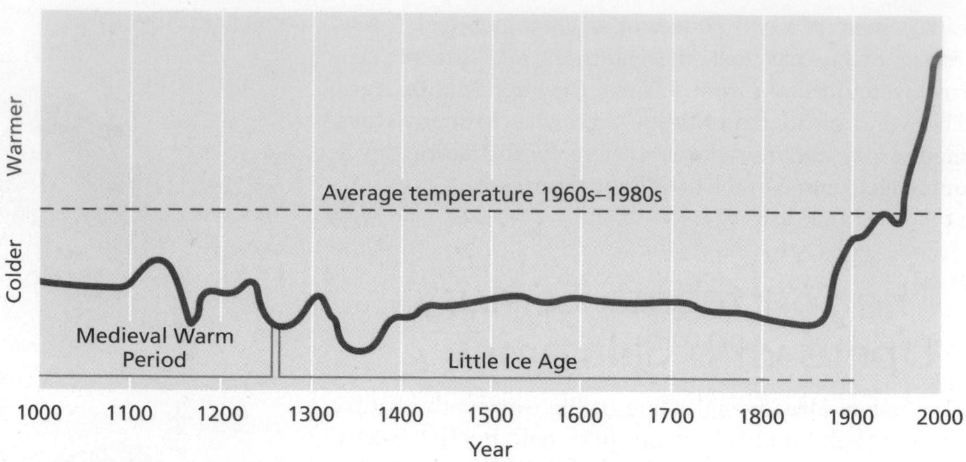

FIGURE 10.1 | Smooth Temperature Graph, 1000–2000

Source: Adapted from Eugene Linden, *The Winds of Change: Climate, Weather, and the Destruction of Civilization* (New York: Simon & Schuster, 2006), 75.

The gentler North Atlantic climate of the Medieval Warm Period had made possible the extensive travels of the Scandinavian raiders known as the Vikings. During the Warm Period, arctic ice packs were confined to the far north. By the late tenth century, Scandinavians had migrated to Iceland and from there set out for and established communities in Greenland and a temporary outpost on the tip of Newfoundland in North America. In the mid-fourteenth century, as the weather worsened, Greenland lost contact with Iceland. At the same time, Icelanders generally abandoned growing cereal crops. On the lands lying along the fjords of Greenland, the colonies suffered a general collapse. By about 1360, the western colony was deserted; the larger eastern colony disappeared in the fifteenth century, leaving no Scandinavians in Greenland. A number of factors contributed to the failure of the Greenland settlements. Greenlanders persisted in many of their Scandinavian economic habits, which depended on cereal crops and animals such as pigs and cows. They were apparently unable to adjust to changing climatic and economic conditions, and the growing cold probably inhibited their access to fish in the open ocean. They were less well adapted to life in the north than the Inuit, who were replacing the Dorset as the resident population of the arctic region of the western hemisphere, and whom the Norse encountered in open battles in the fourteenth century. The reasons for the shriveling of the Iceland community and the disappearance of the Norse from Greenland are complex, but the worsening weather undermined their marginal hold on survival. Greenland experienced ten particularly cold winters between 1343 and 1355, the last year being the coldest in centuries.

The effect of the Little Ice Age on continental Europe is more difficult to measure. England suffered through a period of economic retraction in the first half of the fourteenth century that seems to have been made worse by the turn in the weather. The arable land of Norway shrank in the Late Middle Ages and half of its farms were deserted, again something that had multiple causes, one of which was the weather. Farms in Denmark, particularly those in Jutland, were abandoned. A decrease in population may explain some of these land desertions, but it is striking that northern Europe suffered so dramatically in a time of cooling temperatures. In a subsistence agricultural system with low crop yields, even small changes in climate conditions can make marginal lands unproductive.

Europe experienced bad weather in the early fourteenth century. A series of cold winters struck between 1310 and 1330, with the second coldest winters of the entire Middle Ages occurring between 1320 and 1330. The rain-soaked summers between 1310 and 1320 were the second wettest on record for the entire Middle Ages. In England, mills on the usually placid Avon River became blocked by floating debris and broke down. The growth of oak trees (studied by means of dendrochronology, determined by measuring the annual growth of tree rings) reinforces the same conclusion, that of unusually low growth in the 1320s. Bad weather hit Scandinavia, England, and France in 1315, followed by the rainy summer of 1316, and the bitterly cold winter of 1317–1318, deepening the severity of a prolonged agricultural crisis. One chronicler claimed that it had been the worst weather in a thousand years, and he may not have been far wrong. A German contemporary thought that the whole world was being undone by inclement weather.

The Little Ice Age, like all weather patterns, varied from region to region, hemisphere to hemisphere. It did not strike everywhere in exactly the same way or at the same time. Europe seems to have suffered from the Little Ice Age earlier than other continents. Nor is it easy to draw out larger historical and economic patterns from the turn in the weather, but it is striking that in the Late Middle Ages, France, with its fertile fields and productive agriculture, was not to be the economic and cultural powerhouse that it had been during the High Middle Ages. The proto-industrial economy of Germany, which had superior mining and manufacturing capacity, gained more prominence in the Late Middle Ages, and northern Italy, which escaped some of the direst aspects of the Little Ice Age and had an economy based on short- and long-distance trade and mercantile interests, flourished. Several hypotheses are, of course, possible: that the Little Ice Age provoked a crisis in the agricultural economy of the Late Middle Ages, that it contributed to an underlying weakness in an economy that was already in crisis, that it was a marginal factor, or that it was no factor at all.

MAP 10.1 | Northern Europe, c. 1300
The Great Famine struck the heavily populated areas of northern Europe. ***Given the regional scope of the Great Famine, what sort of economic problem was it? What does the Great Famine reveal about the European economy, and how might the bout of scarcity been dealt with?***

The Great Famine

Europe north of the Alps was struck hard by famine between 1315 and 1322, perhaps contributing to the deaths of four to five million people in a population that was then in excess of thirty million people in the north (Map 10.1). Severe bouts of famine can have long-lasting effects, altering economic and social relations over space and time, but it is hard to gauge their causes and long-term impact, partly because they are so entangled with other events.

The **Great Famine** that struck northern Europe came about for a number of linked reasons. The first of these was probably the poor weather that pushed parts of Europe over the edge of successful subsistence. For the economy to fall so hard and so fast into a crisis of agricultural production suggests that it was already close to the edge by 1300. Crop yields had been falling for years in France. The high medieval population in some places such as northern France was excessive, given the new economic conditions. The population had grown to unsustainable levels partly because of the good weather of the Medieval Warm Period, which had lasted for so long and had allowed for the gradual perfection of a particular form of economic activity. Marginal lands had been brought into production when times were good and the population growing, but those same lands failed to deliver in bad times and many were abandoned in the fourteenth century. As with all medieval shortages, the slowness and inefficiency of transport meant that regions that were still fairly bountiful could not easily supply suffering areas in times of dire need. Europe was not well interconnected economically. Just as in Greenland, the farming population, long used to a form of agriculture that had worked well in good times, could not adapt immediately to an unbroken sequence of seasonal disasters, and the Great Famine was seven bad years long.

Beginning in 1315, crop failures were extensive. England experienced agricultural catastrophe over several years. Contemporaries spoke of water-logged fields and rains washing away good soils. It can take thousands of years for nature to produce (and, therefore, replace) fertile top soils. Yields were already low, rarely above ten to one (that is ten seeds produced for every one sown) and more typically five or four to one. At Winchester in England in the crisis years, productivity fell below three to one; elsewhere it fell as low as two to one. Such low rates of return left barely enough seed, after consumption needs were met, to replant the fields the next year. In East Anglia, yields in the crisis years fell 20–30 percent below the yields of previous decades. At some places in France, harvests dropped by as much as 50 percent. Not just grain crops, but viniculture also collapsed. The year 1316 was famous for producing no wine.

During the famine years, humans suffered, but so did their animals. A lack of hay and fodder left many domestic animals weak and susceptible to disease, which did break out, leading to a remarkable die-off of animals in 1317–1318. Sheep flocks in England fell by half during the crisis, and many older animals were killed (for sale, for food, or to preserve what fodder there was for younger, healthier animals). Only pigs, which had access to forests and to other marginal foods, seem to have withstood the crisis. Another result of the rainy weather was a dramatic fall in the production of salt. Salt flats require sun and heat to produce salt, and there was little solar heat during the famine years. The wet weather also left many of the dirt roads of northern Europe muddy and rutted, which made the transport of goods by wagon difficult.

The Dire Impact of the Early-Fourteenth-Century Famine

The mortality caused by the Great Famine is difficult to measure. Death rates varied over northern Europe during the Great Famine, depending on the resources and resilience of local economies, but there is no escaping how serious a crisis it was. English parish figures for 1315–1318 suggest a mortality rate of 15 percent. Flanders lost nearly 10 percent of its population in 1316 alone. In the small city of Ypres (with a population under 30,000), city officials kept a running tally of weekly mortality for the period between May and October 1316: the sequence started off with weekly deaths of 54, 173, 146, and 101, but by late summer had reached weekly rates of 158, 172, 190, and 191, before closing out October with 115, 37, 27, and 15. Close to three thousand people (or 10 percent of the population) died in Ypres that awful year. Nearby Bruges, with a slightly larger population, lost two thousand people.

The price of grain rose dramatically during the famine years, reaching its highest price since the twelfth century. Even though consumption dropped because much of the population lacked the means to pay the elevated cost, grain prices continued to rise. Some scholars have speculated that the price for cereal crops in France may have risen by as much as 800 percent during 1315–1317. A dramatic rise in prices also occurred in Flanders, Germany, and England. Grain riots broke out as people blamed grain sellers and speculators. A riot broke out in Douai in northern France in 1322 when two women harangued people in the market-square to take up arms against those hoarding grain. People pillaged granaries and burghers' homes, looking for hidden grain. For a time, the grain rioters took control of Douai.

During the worst famine years there were reports of atrocities (always difficult to confirm) such as cannibalism and the eating of corpses and children (with shades of the Hansel and Gretel fairy tale). In the countryside and towns and villages of northern Europe, vast numbers of beggars haunted the streets. By 1316–1317, the poor were dying in the streets of Europe in astonishing numbers. One witness remarked how hard it was to listen to the wailing of the poor, homeless and starving, writhing in agony in Europe's streets.

Lands were abandoned, whole villages deserted, and homesteads within villages vacated. The famine weakened local lords, especially those with small holdings, since for seven years their lands produced little and their farm workers could not render the service and dues they owed. Even great lords had problems generating much income from their extensive lands in the famine years. Centuries-old landholding patterns began to break down in the early fourteenth century as lords lost revenue and workers to death and desertion.

The attitude of the church and people to the economic calamity was moralistic, for they tended to see God's judgment in the unfolding disaster. Rains were likened to biblical floods and starvation to Old Testament punishments visited upon a sinful people. There was a good deal of blaming: of Jews, of those who hoarded, of burghers and lords. The most striking indictment came later in William Langland's long allegorical poem, *Piers Plowman* (written c. 1370), in which the character Hunger blames lords for not relieving the suffering of the poor during a time of famine; they failed to fulfill their appointed social role.

Not All Was Doom and Gloom

There are always people who prosper in times of adversity, and there are those who prevent things from becoming worse than they already are. The church responded to the breakout of famine by trying its best to relieve suffering. There are some indications, however, that by 1317 some monasteries and churches could no longer cope with the demands on their resources, which were also in crises of production. In some cases, princes, local lords, and cities responded to the lack of food by increasing their own charitable outlays, trying to control prices, and seeking to obtain foreign grain. Some places were better situated to deal with famine than others. Bruges, for instance, may have suffered less than Ypres because it was better connected to long-distance trade routes and could import what it could not produce locally.

An unexpected result of the Great Famine was the settlement of new lands. The poor were not entirely passive in the face of the disaster. Many took to the road in search of food and livelihood. Some of them, particularly from Germany, moved to Poland and Bohemia as part of a mass migration driven by hunger. It could also be argued that the Great Famine forced deeper and beneficial adjustments upon the economy as marginal lands fell out of production and agricultural efficiencies were forced on the lands that remained in production. By 1325, older and familiar crop yields returned and the medieval economy regained much of its old stride.

Areas that had not suffered from the weather crisis to the same extent as northern Europe or been struck by famine conditions—such as northern Italy, northern Spain, and southern France—may have benefited from the economic crisis to gain an advantage over the rest of Europe.

They sold or traded their grain surpluses to northern Europe at exorbitant rates. Italy's early-fourteenth-century prosperity and mercantile dynamism may not, then, have been just the product of hard work and ingenuity, but also of opportunism and good fortune.

Living the Great Famine

Most victims of the Great Famine did not die of starvation, but from diseases that overcame them in their weakened state. Lacking bread, many of the poor began to consume what contemporaries called strange diets, a miscellany of available edibles: earth, insects and worms, spoiled grains, clothing, diseased animals and birds, bark, grasses, leaves, and things that we can hardly imagine. These strange diets further weakened people and left them vulnerable to disease and severe malnutrition. Dehydration and severe diarrhea accompany slow starvation, and outbreaks of disease did follow the famine. Observers reported that pestilence broke out in Germany in 1315 and that people died quickly, another indication that they were already severely weakened by hunger.

The Great Famine was probably harder on nursing infants, young children, and the old than it was on young adults. Birth rates fell over the period 1315–1322. The young people who survived the famine were on the whole permanently weakened by the famine years of their youth. Developmentally impaired, they would have had weak immune systems, poor bone development, and smaller bodies than other generations. Thus, while the malnourishment of northern Europe between 1315 and 1322 passed and normal dietary intake returned by the mid-1320s, it was a weakened generation that made its way through time toward another rendezvous with calamity. A child born in 1315 was in his early thirties when the plague arrived. Many northern Europeans who were above the age of twenty-five when the disease hit northern Europe between 1347 and 1350 had survived the Great Famine, but many from that famine generation, wounded by the damage done to their development during the hungry years, had bodies that were less able to resist Yersinia Pestis.

Church Captivity, Imperial Indirection, and Chivalric War

The European world did not grind to a stop when the first of the fourteenth-century crises struck; it adjusted. There were still problems of church and state to address, a papal church in distress, and the code of aristocratic conduct known as chivalry reached its absurd end as it came up against the reality of actual war in the Late Middle Ages.

Why did medieval Europe seem to be flying apart and losing its central convictions in the fourteenth century?

The Babylonian Captivity of the Papacy

The powerful medieval church achieved by Pope Innocent III was in some trouble as the fourteenth century opened. Pope Boniface VIII (1294–1303) and King Philip IV (the Fair, r. 1285–1314) of France were locked in a fierce struggle over the wealth and control of the French church. Boniface sought to stop the French crown from taxing the French clergy, which he considered his own resource pool. In his papal **bull** (a public letter or proclamation) *Clericis laicos,* Boniface threatened to excommunicate any layman who taxed the clergy. The king responded by prohibiting the removal of monies from his kingdom by the church. To assert his rights and his irritation with a meddlesome cleric, Philip in 1301 arrested the bishop of Pamiers on a charge of high treason. In response, the next year, Pope Boniface issued the bull ***Unam sanctam*** in which he declared the absolute supremacy of the papacy over all Christendom. Philip decided to bring Boniface to trial on a host of charges, including his improper election as pope. In 1303, Boniface retreated to his hometown of Anagni and was composing a bull that would have excommunicated Philip and freed his subjects from their allegiance to the king. Philip's men intervened and seized the pope in Anagni on September 7, but Boniface's fellow townsmen rose up in outrage over the insult to their pope. They rescued Pope Boniface and spirited him away to Rome, where he reportedly died in a state of delirium in mid-October.

Boniface's successor tried to bring peace to the church, but served for only two years before he was succeeded by Pope Clement V (1305–1314), who moved the papacy and the governance of the church to Avignon in southern France (technically outside the royal realm), where they remained from 1305 to 1377. Popes had previously lived outside of Italy for extended periods, but the Avignon residency was exceptional for the length of the papacy's absence from Italy and the predominance of the French in papal affairs. Clement was from Gascony, an area of southwestern France above Spain. His Curia (the papal court of officials, tribunals, and assemblies), however, was divided between those who supported King Philip and those who still defended the policies of Pope Boniface. Clement and his successors chose to side with the French king.

Pope Clement even went along with the French king's campaign to dissolve the order of the Knights Templar. The order of the Poor Fellow-Soldiers of Christ and of the Temple of Solomon had been founded after the First Crusade as a military and charitable order to protect pilgrims visiting the Holy Land. The Knights Templar gained a reputation as formidable warriors but were also recognized for being particularly skilled at managing the charitable donations they received. They became the managers of a large financial and property enterprise, but that became a problem for them by the early fourteenth century. Not only did the order lose its central purpose as the crusade movement withered, but worse, King Philip was heavily in its debt and accused the order of holding secret and criminal ceremonies and perpetrating obscene and illegitimate acts such as spitting on the cross. It was whispered that the Knights practiced idolatry, held heretical beliefs, participated in sexual crimes, and were corrupt in their handling of donations. With the pope's support, Philip ordered the arrest of the Templar leaders, had them tortured, forced them to confess to false charges, and burned them at the stake. The king's assault on the Knights left him free of his debt to the order, which the pope disbanded in 1312, turning its property over to another order. In this case, the French state and the Avignon church cooperated in a two-pronged attack on an illustrious arm of the Catholic Church.

The Palace of the Popes in Avignon Despite the impressive solidity of the magnificent papal palace in southern France, the Avignon popes insisted that their residence there was temporary.

To many observers, it seemed that the Avignon papacy was an agent of the French king. Though a magnificent papal palace was erected in Avignon, the papal residence there was regarded as temporary. Public opinion was never favorable to the Avignon papacy. In Italy, people widely considered the Avignon popes to be corrupt French puppets. To call the period of the papal residence in Avignon, as critics did, the "Babylonian Captivity of the Church" was to censure the worldliness and temporal subordination of the Avignon church. Some blamed Pope Boniface for this sad state of church affairs. The poet Dante placed Boniface deep in the *Inferno* among the simoniacs (those who had paid for their offices) for sowing confusion in the church, and many Italians lamented that Rome was bereft of its rightful holy father. The Avignon period brought the fourteenth-century papacy into disrepute and undercut its claim that it commanded a universal church.

The Further Fragmentation of the Empire

The so-called Holy Roman Empire ("so-called" because, as Voltaire later observed, it was neither holy, nor Roman, nor an empire) continued in the fourteenth century to be weighed down by its many territorial claims and obligations. The emperors were dragged continually into Italian affairs and territorial disputes that lay well outside their legitimate German interests. Each emperor had to be elected. Efforts to establish a strict hereditary principle of imperial succession had failed. Frederick II (r. 1220, the date of his papal crowning, to 1250) and the emperors who followed him all had to earn acclamation, a costly and divisive waste of energy and resources. Each new imperial family also had to begin anew since there was little continuity between reigns, governmental agencies, or record keeping. When Rudolf of Habsburg (r. 1273–1291) was elected emperor in 1273, he had little more territorial reach and resources than his rival German princes. There was almost no fixed imperial land for the emperors to draw upon for funds, yet they had few other sources of revenue. Rudolf, however, successfully extended his properties to the east. When he died, the electors of Germany, anxious not to further empower his family, elected the relatively weak Adolf of Nassau, who conducted a series of unprofitable wars, as his successor.

The electors kept the empire in a constant state of weakness for much of the fourteenth century by disputing elections, choosing new imperial families to succeed to imperial power, and placing restrictions on imperial action. The popes and the French monarchy also contributed to the destabilization of the imperial system by supporting rulers they thought would support them. The great game of fourteenth-century politics was to see who could best keep the emperor and empire weak and in line. In 1313, when two men claimed to be emperor, the pope excommunicated one of them, Lewis of Bavaria, in the interests of promoting a pro-French candidate. Lewis prevailed but did not achieve much beyond establishing a lively imperial court at Munich attended by Marsilius of Padua, who challenged papal authority in his *Defender of the Peace,* and William of Ockham, the last great scholastic philosopher.

Between 1273 and 1400, the empire had ten emperors (from six different dynasties), five of them never crowned, and two of them anti-emperors or rival claimants. The election of Charles IV (Wenceslas) of Bohemia in 1346 brought some regularity to the electoral process, though not wholly in the emperor's favor. In 1356, Charles issued the **Golden Bull,** an edict meant to straighten out the constitutional complexities of the empire, particularly those governing the relations of the emperor and the seven electors, who were the archchancellors of Trier, Cologne, and Mainz, and four great regional princes. The Golden Bull (called so because of its golden seal) recognized that the right to elect an emperor belonged to the seven German prince-electors, whose own lands were fixed, their autonomy and independence acknowledged, and any offense against them deemed treason. By the Golden Bull, other powerful groups in Germany were in effect subordinated to the interests of the emperor and electors, and the pope's role in the choice and approval of an emperor was sidelined.

Charles was not just emperor, but also the king of Bohemia, and though he was ineffective as the first, he accomplished much as the second. With Prague as his capital, Charles encouraged Czech migration there and founded a university. With the consent of the pope, Charles established Prague as a metropolitan or an archiepiscopal see and rebuilt its cathedral. He established a court culture that attracted European luminaries. Charles's imperial reign, though less than successful, signaled the increasing importance of eastern territories to the empire.

The Opening Act of the Hundred Years' War

Since it lasted 116 years and was not one war, but a series of prolonged skirmishes punctuated by extended truces and periods of long inactivity, the **Hundred Years' War** (1337–1453) is poorly and misleadingly named. The underlying reason for the war was the old claim the English crown had on continental lands, but there were a host of irritants, often of long standing, between the two sides. William the Conqueror, Henry II, and their heirs had set this sad table, but by the early fourteenth century the English kings controlled little of wider France. In fact, they held only a part of Gascony, where England had commercial interests. As the century opened, King Philip IV of France and King Edward I (r. 1272–1307) of England were at war over Gascony. That conflict ended inconclusively in 1303. Both kingdoms were also seeking to control the fate of Flanders, where the English traded their wool. When King Charles IV (r. 1322–1328) of France died without leaving a son as heir, King Edward III (r. 1327–1377) of England laid claim to the French throne, since he was descended from the French royal family on his mother's side. The French responded by denying that inheritance could pass through the female line and crowned Philip VI (of Valois) king (r. 1328–1350). Edward bided his time, but in 1337 he renewed his claim to the French throne and invaded. There were, at the time, a dizzying number of irritants between France and England. Both were seeking to extend their influence and control over the Low Countries and Flanders, and both had different and competing claims to the duchy of Brittany. Ships were being attacked in the English Channel. Perhaps the greatest provocation was Edward's claim to the right to confiscate Gascony.

CHRONOLOGY **Over a Hundred Years of Ups and Downs**

DATE	EVENT
1337	King Edward III of England invades France
1346	English triumph at Crécy
1356	English forces led by the Black Prince win at Poitiers
1360	Treaty of Brétigny acknowledges English control of Aquitaine and Calais
1415	English under Henry V win at Agincourt
1420	King Henry V named heir to the French crown
1422	King Henry V dies; Henry VI becomes king of England and France
1429	Joan of Arc rescues Orléans
1431	Joan of Arc executed
1435	By Treaty of Arras, Burgundy agrees to support France
1453	English defeat in Bordeaux
1453	The Hundred Years' War ends

King Philip was a flashy, chivalrous knight, but not much of a warrior in the field. He and his barons thought that France, which had over three times the population of England and, despite the Great Famine, was still relatively rich, would have no problem handling the English invaders. But Edward had both military strategy and technological superiority on his side. He paid for support where he could and starved obstinate towns into submission (Map 10.2). By 1346, he was outside the walls of Paris, and the first decisive battle in the conflict came at Crécy in the same year. The French attempted to dislodge the English from a strong position on the field of battle at Crécy, but the English moved the wings of their army around the assaulting force and shot at them with deadly longbows from three sides. The French relied on their crossbows, but the English archers could fire their longbows three times as rapidly as the French and from farther away and, thus, safely out of the range of France's crossbow bolts. The French defeat at Crécy did not end the war, which limped lazily on for years. King Philip died in 1350.

The English invasion of France in 1356 was two pronged: one army moved against Normandy, while Edward, the prince of Wales, called the Black Prince (by chroniclers after his death because of his black sword or coat of arms), invaded Aquitaine. At Poitiers, the Black Prince was outnumbered, but the French made a rash attack

MAP 10.2 | The Hundred Years' War, 1337–1453

The Hundred Years' War between England and France had many phases and hot spots of activity over the length of the protracted conflict. ***Why did two of the critical battles in the war occur in the north in areas outside of France? Why were Orléans and Poitiers important strategic sites for the English and French? What was peculiar about Joan of Arc's geographic origins, given her prominent historical role in the war?***

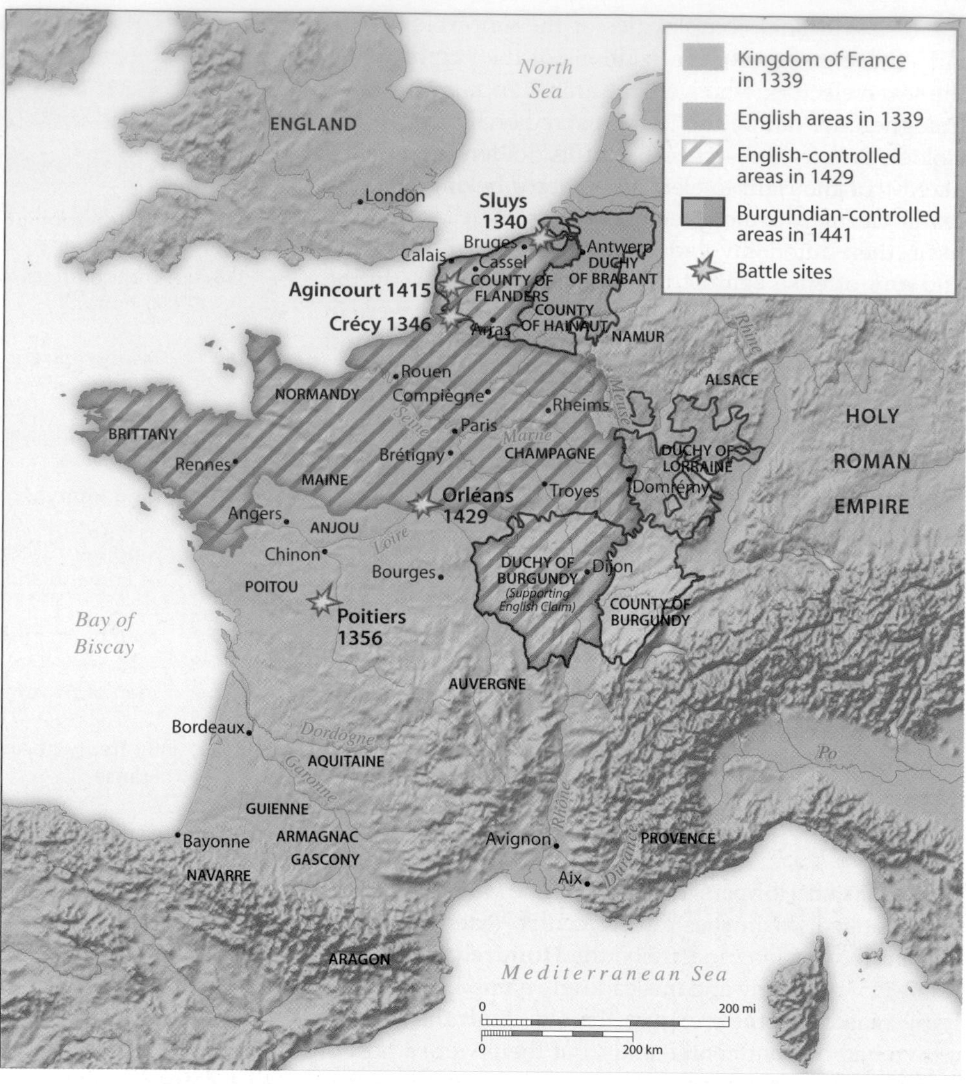

and were defeated. Worse, the French king, John II, was captured and held for ransom by the English. By the Treaty of Brétigny of 1360, the French agreed to ransom back their king and granted the English control over much of Aquitaine and the trading city of Calais. With that treaty, the Hundred Years' War turned temporarily quiet, but the underlying problem of the English claim to French lands and the French king's insistence that the English king held those lands as his vassal remained.

The Chivalric Ideal

On the evening after the Battle of Poitiers, the Black Prince wined and dined the captured French king and his knights. The Prince himself served the French at their own high table and refused to sit with King John, not because he was his prisoner, but because he was so distinguished. The Black Prince, full of courtesy and flowery French, told the king not to despair; he had acted with great skill and bravery in battle and Edward's father would surely treat him with friendship and honor, as far as circumstances

The Battle of Crécy Here the more numerous French are shown employing crossbows against the English with their longbows. In reality, the English archers fired a volley of arrows from considerable distance at an opposing army, trusting that some arrows would find their targets.

would allow. The French knights whispered to each other that the Black Prince was truly noble and destined to achieve great things. These men shared a chivalric ideal that may seem to us reckless, the very opposite of realistic politics and their own best interests. King John was taken to England and held for ransom. When the French finally raised part of the huge sum demanded, the king was released and the duke of Anjou took his place as a hostage and security for the remainder. Breaking his oath, the duke escaped from detention and returned to France. King John's chivalric pride was hurt and his family shamed by this betrayal of the chivalric code, so the French king freely returned to England, to confinement, and to his eventual death.

Chivalry is a term with many meanings, but the root of the word comes from the French *cheval* (horse), the *chevalier* being a horseman or knight. Chivalry refers in part to the code of conduct espoused by these horsemen. Elements of chivalry were already present in rituals of vassalage and the *Song of Roland,* but they were codified, transformed, and stylized in the High and Late Middle Ages into something more formalized. Knighthood had always allowed powerful men to distinguish themselves from the other classes of society, particularly the lower classes and clergy. Knightly power was essentially that of coercion—the fist, the sword, and the abrupt and arbitrary use of violence to intimidate others. The war horse with its mounted rider was an intimidating elevation of elite power; it was large, expensive, and frightening. In the Central Middle Ages, the knight was a brutal warrior with few redeeming social virtues or higher ideals. Chivalry did not so much tame the rough knight as lift him into a society of those who espoused a set of ideals that defined them as superior to others. Knights belonged to a rarefied elite of the socially superior, who had their own models, symbols, and rituals.

Of course, what distinguished these knights in the first place was their violent occupation. They were warriors who delighted in killing the enemy and not just their equals, but little people. They burned down villages and did not always think twice about running through women and children with their swords. They needed special skills to do even that. Boys began training when young for the demanding job of being a knight. Outfitted in increasingly heavy and impregnable armor (which could weigh between 40 and 150 pounds depending on the style and metal used), knights sat on rushing war steeds and wielded a variety of heavy weapons (swords, lances, battle axes).

In the Central Middle Ages (and probably throughout much of the Late Middle Ages), knights were exalted robbers on the hunt for plunder. As the conditions of life changed in the twelfth century and the great age of castle contests and crusades began to subside, knights needed a higher purpose, which their poets were pleased to supply. The vernacular poets of Provence in southern France were the first to give chivalric meaning and glory to the knight's role. In their idealized portraits, the knight was not a thug; he was a man with a pure and holy purpose. He was dubbed a knight by a superior, who in this way transmitted elevated status to his man. In chivalric times, the church even viewed dubbing as a form of sacrament, the Christianized bonding of an elite, one that included the knights' families, in a closed aristocratic circle.

The poets set other goals for this horse nobility. The knight no longer robbed, but pursued a great quest against long odds for an unobtainable, but singular object such as the Holy Grail (thought to be the cup Christ drank from at the Last Supper) or the idealized perfect woman. In moving from the *Song of Roland* to the romances of the poet Chrétien de Troyes and the troubadour (or wandering) poet-musicians, we move inside. Roland and his band lived in a world of exterior earthly action. Chrétien's knights live a more interior life in their own minds, imagining the noble deeds they will do. From these literary roots came the romantic imagination, and chivalry was its higher code.

Knights of the Late Middle Ages lived in domesticating societies that counted courtesy and manners within the group as their defining traits, hence, the Black Prince's deferential and dignified treatment of the captured French king. Both the captor and captured were defined and joined by acts of courtesy and respect. This knightly set of values was based on idealized models: King Arthur and his court, Charlemagne and his paladins, and the mythical and mythologized strivers of the past (Hercules, Alexander, and Caesar). These were exemplary heroes constructed by court literature and deemed fit to be imitated. As the chivalric code was refined, heraldic tokens such as coats of arms, colors, and symbols were invented

Siege of the Castle of Love Even love was seen in chivalric terms on this fourteenth-century ivory carving on the back of a mirror. Here women try to thwart the besieging warriors.

and highly refined distinctions and rituals within chivalric society laid down. The tournament and pageants became the place where the relative equals of this closed aristocratic society met and tested themselves in jousting against each other and in displays of pomp. Their families, particularly the ladies of the court, came to watch and test themselves against each other. The language of chivalry and courtly love was, for the most part, French. The high ideals of chivalry and courtly love may have belonged more to books than the real world, but the ennobling of a class of women may also have helped free the Middle Ages from some of its older misogynistic baggage, which had associated women with temptation, danger, and destruction.

The Chivalric Code Meets Actual War

By the fourteenth century, chivalry had begun to lose much of its luster in society and its effectiveness in war. Cannons and gunpowder, against which the mightiest knight was no match, appeared in Europe in the 1320s. But the knight was already susceptible to arrows and crossbow bolts. Common English bowmen had felled many a knight at both Crécy and Poitiers. The tactical advantage of the English at both battles was precisely the coordination of their cavalry and infantry. Knights might dream of settling contests, as they did at tournaments, with clean contests between two equals, but that was no way to settle a war. Great knights agreed upon when they would fight, where, and how, and they labored to make sure that all the conditions were fair for both sides. But the conditions of war are rarely fair and courteous. At Crécy the English had the better lie of the land and took advantage of it. Shaped by their chivalric pride and bravery, the French knights acted rashly at Crécy and Poitiers. But their military technology was no match for the longbow, and they launched their attack at the wrong time and from a poor position on the field. War, like most human activities, is a learning experience. With heavier armor and better placement of its troops, the French eventually learned to overcome the deficiencies of chivalric warfare. They developed a more systematic plan for capturing castles and fortified towns by employing explosives to undermine walls and ramparts.

Chivalric ideals were one of the causes of the opening of the Hundred Years' War, but the English had already begun to move beyond chivalry. The Black Prince, the courteous victor at Crécy, was not content with glorious combat between equals. He destroyed villages and burned crops to weaken French resistance to his campaigns. He massacred people in large numbers in French cities and leveled exorbitant taxes on conquered lands. No dreamy knight was the Black Prince, but rather a warrior committed to winning wars by means both fair and foul. Moreover, the turn to mercenary armies made war not a matter of glorious contests between knights, but one filled with companies of paid adventurers and outright murderers.

The sign that chivalry was on the wane came not so much from the field of battle as from the intrusive control of chivalry by kings. King Edward III founded the Order of the Garter (c. 1348). This order and the Order of the Golden Fleece, founded in 1430, not only collected knights into royally sanctioned societies, but also turned them away from the chivalric ideal of the solitary and individual quest toward collective patriotism for king and country.

What also began to undermine chivalry was disastrous war itself. The Hundred Years' War was not a particularly noble affair and that soured many people on the ideal of chivalric adventure. Kings banned judicial duels, the last of which were fought in the fourteenth century.[1] By the fifteenth century, chivalry was much criticized and afterward became a figure of fun for writers such as Miguel de Cervantes in his picaresque novel, *Don Quixote de la Mancha.* Yet a residue of chivalry was implanted in the western moral code in the form of gentlemanly manners, conventions of romantic love, and rules for the conduct of war.

Yersinia Pestis Comes Calling

Twenty-five years after the Great Famine, plague came to Europe. The Little Ice Age may have in some way created the conditions that disrupted the life cycle of Yersinia Pestis and its host population and set it on the move. The conjunction of climate change and plague may, in other words, be more than just coincidence. The impact of the plague on the Middle Ages was, in conjunction with the other fourteenth-century calamities, immense.

Why did the plague hit Europe so hard?

The Arrival of the Plague

Medieval Europe may have been particularly susceptible to the plague. Its cities, built of wood, were often cramped, dirty, and rat infested. Frequent wars had unnerved the population and upset social stability, and its people were malnourished and many of them in northern Europe had been developmentally disadvantaged by the effects of the Great Famine. None of those reasons, however, may have mattered as much as the fact that Europeans had not been exposed to the plague since the early eighth century, when the last small outbreaks of Justinian's Plague petered out in depopulated northern Italy. European peoples had not been exposed to the plague for six hundred years and possessed no natural resistance to it when it arrived. Europe was virgin territory for Yersinia.

The fourteenth-century plague was not an epidemic, but a more dangerous **pandemic** (an outbreak of communicable disease extending over many regions and involving high mortality) that began in the 1320s in the Asian steppes and moved east into China and west toward

OTHER VOICES, OTHER VIEWS

The Plague Strikes Others

The plague pandemic of the mid-fourteenth century struck not just Europe, but Asia, Africa, and the Middle East, as well. Some historians have speculated that it was the Mongols who spread the disease, allowing Yersinia to escape its home in the central Asian steppes. The Mongols had opened up long-distance trade routes (as explored by the Polos) that not only brought foreign peoples into closer contact, but also exposed them to alien diseases. An interconnected world is always more susceptible to all things communicable (ideas, religions, goods, economic crises, and pathogens). The plague spread across late Yüan China in the 1330s, killing 13–30 million people, yet little official attention and few records were devoted to the disease. In China the plague was not an epochal event, perhaps because the Chinese had previously been exposed to the bubonic plague and it had settled into being, as it would eventually become in Europe, an endemic, permanent disease presence, killing chiefly the young. Those who argue that the plague undid the Mongol dynasty's control of China and led to the rise of the Sung Dynasty may have been overly impressed by the impact the plague had on European society.

The plague also swept through the Islamic world, killing as many as 40 million people. A hundred people a day were dying in Damascus in June 1348. In Europe, the disease tended to intensify the religious devotion and fear of most people; but many Muslims viewed the plague as a form of martyrdom for the faithful and as punishment for the unfaithful. Yet the Muslim reaction to the swelling sickness was hardly passive. Muslim physicians supplied theories about the disease and advised practical measures for resisting it: avoid contact with those who have contracted the disease; get plenty of fresh air, good food and drink, and lots of sleep; and avoid excessive exertion. Doctors were advised to bleed people who did contract the disease and to open sores surgically once they were ready to release their poison, which seems to have been good medical advice.

Abū Hafs 'Umar Ibn al-Wardī was a Muslim scholar living in Aleppo in Palestine when the plague arrived. He had heard through the vast Islamic grapevine that the disease was coming. It had ravaged India and China, moved through Persia, and killed people in Cairo before it came to Palestine. Al-Wardī presents the plague as a frightful visitor, doing its deadly work like a silkworm, a lion, and a king swaggering upon his throne. Al-Wardī contracted the disease in 1349. His reaction to the disease in general was fatalistic, as it was for many Muslims, who refused to flee from a disease that God had sent. Muslims did not generally view the plague as a civilization-ending event, though it did tremendous damage in Islamic lands.

Arabic Medical Consultation

QUESTIONS | ***Why do new diseases often lead to irrational explanations for them among the general population? What are the typical responses to a new contagion? How and why did the plague strike Islam and Europe differently—materially, spiritually, and historically?***

Europe. It was not called the **Black Death** until the sixteenth century. Medieval men and women commonly referred to it as a plague (from the Latin *plaga,* meaning "blow"). By the late 1330s, Europe had already begun to hear rumors of a dread contagion on the loose in Asia, and over the next decade, the disease passed in a complex way from Asia to Europe. As many as thirty million people died in China alone by the late fourteenth century. The disease also hit Islamic lands as the pandemic spread westward.

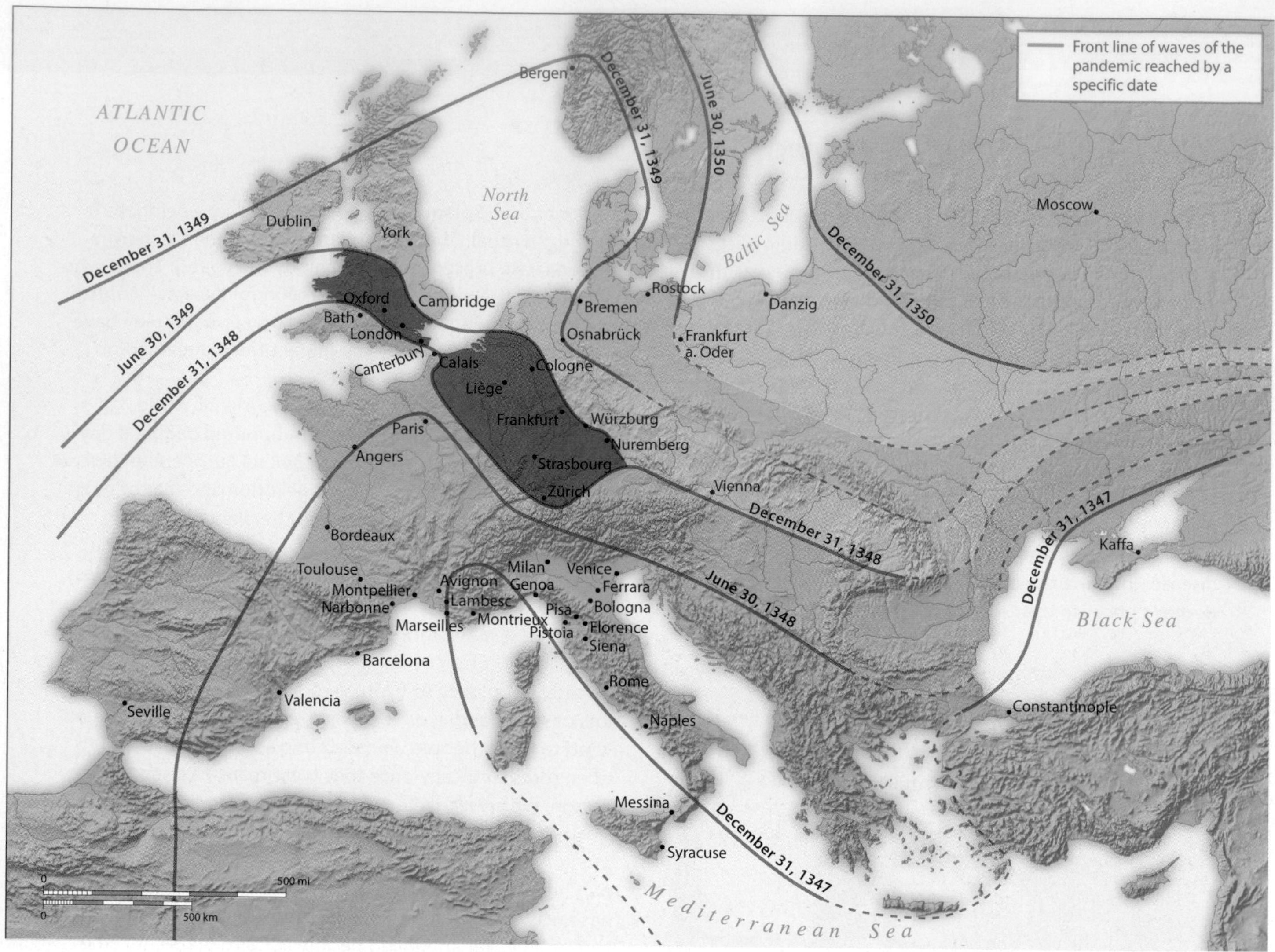

MAP 10.3 | **Spread of the Plague, 1347–1350**

The plague moved in what look like waves, south to north, to cover Europe over a four-year period, 1347–1350. ***Where and why does the wave pattern seem to break down? Why were some years and seasons more dangerous for human populations than others? What can we infer from the wave pattern about humans spreading the disease and how they were moving about?***

By the 1340s, Yersinia Pestis had reached centers where Europeans traded with Asia (Map 10.3). Here the bacterium found a new host, the Italian sea trader. Medieval chroniclers had a good story of the first European outbreak of the plague. They claimed that a Tartar (Mongol) lord, besieging some Genoese merchants at Kaffa (or Caffa) in the Crimea, ordered that the plague-infected corpses of his men should be catapulted into the enemy's encampment. When the merchants started dying, they fled to their boats and headed back to Italy, carrying the plague with them. Although the story seems too good to be true, merchant ships probably did carry the disease to Europe. By 1347, Constantinople experienced an outbreak of the plague, which then spread around the Mediterranean. A Genoese merchant fleet docked at Messina in Sicily in October 1347; port authorities recognized that these were plague ships and barred the sailors from entry into the city. Nonetheless, within a month Sicily was laid low by the plague.

Transmission and Symptoms of the Disease

How then did these ships infect Sicily, if indeed they did? Yersinia is an efficient traveler. She typically infects fleas that live on rodents, and rats such as the black rat (*Rattus rattus*) are good at surviving on boats and climbing down ropes. Hence they are sometimes called ship rats. Yersinia can travel on old clothes and lie dormant for months until awakened into activity when conditions improve. So something left these ships or arrived in Sicily by similar means.

The infecting agent is the flea, for as it becomes filled with the plague bacillus, its esophagus becomes clogged.

THINGS THAT REMAIN

Was Yersinia Pestis to Blame?

The pathogen that infected China, Islamic lands, Byzantium, and Europe in the fourteenth century has been assumed to be Yersinia Pestis since the Swiss bacteriologist Alexandre Yersin first identified the bacterium and disease in 1894, but scientific confirmation was lacking. In the past, the identification of historical diseases has depended almost entirely on contemporary descriptions of symptoms, and these can be variously interpreted. Even the swellings associated with bubonic plague, as described by medieval contemporaries, might be attributed to other diseases such as typhus. In the 1990s, a French team began to investigate whether DNA might resolve the matter. Led by Michel Drancourt, the team retrieved dental pulp from the teeth of people who were supposed to have died from the plague in the sixteenth and eighteenth centuries and to have been buried in plague pits in Lambesc and Marseilles, France. The French team believed that they had found DNA evidence of the presence of septicemic plague. A later French team, led by Didier Raoult, identified the traces of Yersinia in the DNA extracted from the dental pulp of three fourteenth-century victims of the plague in Montpellier. A German team achieved similar results working with the DNA of some sixteenth-century Bavarian plague victims, but an English team working with English "plague victims" was unable to replicate those results in their extraction and analysis of medieval DNA.

The matter of whether Yersinia was to blame for the fourteenth-century plague still lacked uncontroverted physical proof. This did not mean that Yersinia was not responsible, but that the scientific proof of her role was not yet definitively established. Other evidence still pointed to Yersinia: fourteenth-century paintings that show swellings on the necks and armpits of victims, descriptions such as the one by Agnolo the Fat of Siena that victims "swell under the armpits and in the groin area" or by Gui de Chauliac, the pope's physician, who described both the bubonic and pneumonic forms of the disease and himself contracted the disease. Finally, in 2010, a team of European paleopathologists, working with seventy-six medieval skeletons from France, Germany, Italy, and the Netherlands, announced that they had positively identified the presence of Yersinia Pestis in the DNA samples that they had gathered.

Treating Plague Victims A doctor lances a bubo on the neck of a woman while a man shows the swelling below his armpit to the doctors, and a young boy indicates that he suffers from the same ailment.

QUESTIONS | ***What are the inherent flaws of historical descriptions of diseases? Why do scientists and historians, even in an age of DNA analysis, need each other in order to resolve the diagnosis of historical diseases?***

In trying to clear itself of the infection, it bites its host and thus transmits Yersinia to a new host. When the host rodent dies, its colony of 25–30 fleas moves to another available warm body. Although neither rats nor humans are the preferred host of the fleas, an infected and hostless flea is not choosey about its next residence. It too is trying to survive.

Since the disease was finally identified in the late nineteenth century after a massive outbreak of plague in India, we know that the disease takes on three basic forms. Bubonic plague (transmitted directly by an infected flea) is the most common form and so named because of the buboes or swellings of the lymph nodes in the armpits, groins, and necks of its human victims. This form of the infection lasts about a week and 50 to 60 percent of the infected die. Pneumonic plague is transmitted from human to human by infected air and surfaces, much as a common cold is. In this less common form of the disease, the incubation period is three days, and 95 to 100 percent of all victims die. The rarest form of the disease is septicemic plague, in which Yersinia directly infects the bloodstream of its victims and kills all of them in short order.

What is still not completely understood are the microbiological details of the transmission of the disease in fourteenth-century Europe. Both bubonic and pneumonic plague probably played a part, but the death rates seem very high and the means of transmission are not perfectly clear. Did Yersinia mutate into a particularly virulent form in fourteenth-century Europe; did the pneumonic form of the disease predominate and speed transmission, overcoming the winter lethargy of the carrier fleas; or was Yersinia the same and the European population and its resistance to this specific disease just weak?

The Spread of the Disease in Europe

By early 1348, outbreaks of the disease struck the major port cities of Italy. The disease leaped from port to port and then worked its way inland and north at a rate of about five to ten miles per day. At Florence, the great banking city, the disease was particularly virulent, killing perhaps half the population, or 45,000 people out of 90,000, over its six-month run there. The disease arrived in the port city of Marseilles in February 1348, killing approximately 50,000 people. At Montpellier, 40,000 people died; at Narbonne, 25,000. In papal Avignon, four hundred people were dying each day early in the year. One graveyard in Avignon received 11,000 corpses in six weeks. One out of every three cardinals died, and seven thousand houses were abandoned. Paris was hit in the late spring of 1348, and late in the year plague reached Britain, with London being hit near the end of the year. The disease spread through late 1348 and early 1349 up the valleys of Europe, jumping from large center to large center before working its way back to infect rural districts.

The disease generally quieted down during the colder winter months, but in 1349 Yersinia again began to move north in Europe and by 1349–1350 had reached Scandinavia. In its initial four-year run, something like 35 to 40 percent of Europe's population died, probably 25–35 million people. Pope Clement VI's agents put the total death count at 23,840,000, which seems a reasonable minimal figure for the mortality caused by the plague.

What Could Europeans Have Done?

Could anything have been done? It is unlikely. Given that the disease was not identified until 1894, medieval men and women knew nothing of the transmission of the disease from bacillus to flea, rat, and human. The chain of the disease can be broken at the outset if rats and their fleas are absent and unavailable to serve as the hosts of Yersinia. Or, as the comedian Mel Brooks said, the problem with the Black Death was "Too many rats, not enough cats." Contemporaries did not note any large-scale die-off of diseased rats, which should have occurred, but their silence is hardly surprising since their attention was on dying humans, and sick animals often seek out concealed places to convalesce or die.

Some outlying regions such as Poland and Bohemia, without extensive merchant trade, were largely spared. Cities such as Milan, Liège, and Nuremberg escaped severe outbreaks of the disease, but there were probably particular reasons involving the absence of infected rats. At Milan (where the death rate was close to 15 percent), a ruthless policy of quarantine was imposed. When plague victims appeared, they and their families were walled up inside their homes, though it is unlikely that this would have effectively quarantined Yersinia, the rat flea, or the rat. It was much better for people to abandon infected areas, particularly towns. Giovanni Boccaccio's *Decameron* recounts the stories of a group of men and women who flee plague-stricken Florence for the countryside.

Medieval men and women had many theories about the origins of the disease: that it had been set loose by a meteor, an earthquake that released pestilential air from subterranean vaults, or a perverse conjunction of the stars. They were looking for a macro-explanation for a micro-event, the pernicious work of invisible Yersinia. Medieval people generally viewed the plague as caused by pestilential air and so were advised to burn special, aromatic woods and herbs to ward off the foul air. Some physicians prescribed special potions according to the wealth of their clients: drinkable gold for the rich, garlic-based concoctions for the poor. The University of Paris went further, ordering students and faculty to observe a moderate lifestyle: no exercise, bathing, or sex.

Medieval doctors could do little and were heavily blamed for their ineffectiveness. Some contemporaries accused them of gouging money from the sick for cures that did not work; others charged that doctors abandoned their patients when they fell ill. Doctors seem to have died in greater numbers than other groups in society, which suggests their greater exposure to the ill, but even so they were criticized. Many people doubted the usefulness of doctors, who in general seemed unable to save themselves.

The Immediate Consequences

As the plague moved through communities and across Europe, there were immediate consequences. In many places, the rituals accompanying dying and death broke down. How does one grieve when so many people are dying and you yourself might die? There was a general reluctance to handle diseased bodies, and often too few people were left living to bury the dead. Men of the lower classes were often hired to bury the dead, but their rates of death were likely as high as if not higher than those of the wealthy. In many places, the death bells stopped ringing altogether since death was no longer a special event to be solemnized, and the church bells would have been ringing all day and night, further disturbing the infirm.

As with the Great Famine, people blamed human agents for producing the crisis. A widespread rumor charged that Jews had poisoned wells and the air, and many Jews were massacred. It did not matter to panic-stricken people—swept up in a moment of intense fear and irrationality—that Jews were dying from the disease in the same numbers as other segments of the population. Pope Clement VI banned such persecution and tried to enforce it by excommunicating the persecutors of Jews.

In the short term, there were practical problems to deal with: abandoned houses, the collapse of family units, orphaned children, and the critical breakdown of institutions (city governments, cathedral operations, monasteries). Gherardo's experience at the Carthusian monastery at Montrieux is a stark example of how bad it could get. Not only did he bury his dead brothers, but he was forced to protect the monastery against thieves, for some people were taking advantage of the breakdown of social order for personal gain.

Couples Amusing Each Other during the Plague The depiction of a scene from Boccaccio's *Decameron,* in which people fleeing plague-infested Florence seek to distract themselves from the dead and dying of northern Italy in 1348.

The plague devastated families. Agnolo the Fat of Siena buried his five children (see Back to the Source at the end of the chapter). In Florence, where marriage ties were intricately complex and negotiated over many years and involved complex social standing and property issues, new family matches had to be made among survivors and property rights worked out. At its simplest level, new social bonds needed to be established in this contracting society.

The immediate response of many people to the plague was to live for today. Boccaccio noted that many people thought that the best response to the death-bringing plague was to treat it as a gigantic joke, to drink much, enjoy life, and to surrender to one's desires. Promiscuity was common. In fact, birth rates in the immediate aftermath of the plague were higher than normal, as though a biological response to sudden population decline. At the other extreme were those who turned antisocial, sealing themselves off from others in self-enforced social quarantine. Herein lay the roots of the reported abandonment of the sick and the unburied dead, for many medieval men and women were convinced (rightly in some cases) that this disease was a matter of person-to-person contagion. The pope was quarantined to prevent him from having contact with infected people. Others fled infected cities as quickly as they could, which was an understandable response to the plague, though a seemingly heartless one.

The impact of the plague on Europeans' psyche was immediate. Contemporaries observed that a cloud of anxiety hung over communities as they received rumors of the approaching disease. When it arrived and family units and social order broke down, the damage was worse than imagined. The ideals of Christian charity and love suffered. The plague seemed to encourage selfishness; why worry about others when you yourself might soon die? Agnolo the Fat simply said that so many died, people believed the world was coming to an end. But Dame Julian of Norwich, the English mystic, said, with the light of divine optimism, "alle shalle be wele."

The plague did engender a new spirit of energetic activism and opportunism among survivors, which some observers mistook for greed. A French friar who lived through the plague lamented that the survivors were a greedy and contentious lot, grasping for the goods freed up by the deaths of others. The plague cleared away not only people, but also physical, religious, and psychological space for the survivors to fill and exploit. The survivors were left to remake their world with a new set of attitudes and energies, and this new world did not reward passivity. The older medieval ideal of withdrawal from and contempt for the material world failed to meet the needs of a reordering society.

A Battered Society Responds

History is made by the living, not the dead, who are no longer historical actors. As tragic as the suffering and deaths of over 25 million people was, we need to examine the response of those who survived. The surprising thing is that many of them were better off once the plague subsided and society slowly began to remake itself.

How did Europe change after the great calamities?

Medical Implications

Many of those who survived the plague were actually better off, though they doubtless did not realize it at first. By successfully warding off the disease, many survivors now carried immunities against the plague. Human DNA is filled with what were once thought to be junk strands that seemed to have no immediate purpose. Many of those sequences are the remnants of previous body wars, biological battlefield adjustments of our ancestral DNA to fight off diseases encountered in the past, including the fourteenth-century plague. Europeans needed that protection since the plague was not finished with them just yet. In 1361–1362, the plague returned again, this time infecting children born after the first outbreak. After that, Yersinia Pestis became a frequent visitor, coming back uninvited almost every decade, often attacking the young. The population of Europe flat-lined for the rest of the Middle Ages and would not begin a slow upward trend until the late fifteenth century.

Even as the plague struck, some cities took measures to control the disease. In 1348 at Pistoia, not far from Florence, the people's council issued a set of statutes to deal with the disease: limiting the travel of Pistoians outside of their city, particularly to plague-stricken places; controlling the importation of cloth from outside; setting stipulations regarding the handling and transport of the dead, burials, and funerals; and imposing restrictions on the handling of meat and general assembly. The measures constituted a policy of civic quarantine that attempted to restrict Pistoia's contact with a diseased world.

Economic Adjustments

If Europe had been overpopulated in 1300, famine and plague quickly solved that problem. In the countryside, better lands became available to the reduced population of survivors. Farm workers now had more fertile lands available to them, and some became wealthy as a result. Even if they did not obtain better land, their labor was still worth more than it had been before.

With the workforce of Europe reduced by at least a third in four years, those who survived the plague were potentially better off than they had been in the crowded and competitive pre-plague world. Recognizing that their labor was more valuable, city workers sought an increase in wages or a change in the conditions of their work. Cloth workers in Flanders wanted to work fewer hours than they had before the plague and asked for fixed hours. Some scholars claim that a growing awareness of the conditions of work gave rise in western Europe to ideas of merchants' and workers' time and to more sophisticated ideas about the economic value of time and labor. Rapid adjustments in the market forces of the economy played out in the reordering of the economy across Europe in the period 1350–1375.

In the countryside of Europe, farm workers discovered quickly that the balance of power between them and their lords had shifted in their favor. Some insisted on a strict observance of their customary rights, which lords had tended to disregard, or a reduction of the dues (both of service and money) that they owed to their lords. Many took the opportunity to flee farms since towns offered them a steady wage for their work. Wage earners benefited from the plague's reduction of the population, but those with fixed resources such as lords and monks did less well. They had to pay their farm workers more for their labor and received less work from them at a time when the price and demand for agricultural goods was fluctuating. Some manor accounts in England show that a plowman in 1347 was paid 2 shillings for a week's work; in 1349, 7 shillings per week; and by 1350, 10 shillings 6 pence a week. This represented a 500 percent increase in weekly wages in just three years.

Social Insurrection Spreads

Local lords resented the inflation of labor costs. In 1351, the English Parliament passed the Statute of Laborers, which sought to restore the old economic order by fixing wages at pre-plague rates. The act had little success. Serfdom itself was fading in the face of the new economic realities. Although the European world now had fewer people, it still had the same amount of hard money at its disposal, which meant that almost overnight survivors had to pay more for goods. But the disruption of production (due to the random death of workers, lords, and owners) meant that the supply of goods was radically uneven. An inflationary spiral took hold in the 1350s. If the working people who survived had done well after the great initial die-off, by the late 1350s lords and kings were trying to return the genie of social and economic change to its bottle.

Kings still needed, on occasion, to raise extraordinary monies. In 1358, to ransom King John of France, the French royal family raised the taxes on farmers and local lords, and increased rents in the area north of Paris. Peasants revolted in an uprising called the **Jacquerie,** named after the caricature of a good peasant, Jacques Bonhomme (Jack the "good guy"). These fellows were far from good and soon began attacking their lords, pillaging, raping, and roasting them alive. French aristocrats were shocked since they believed that coercive power was their divine right, not that of their inferiors. They viewed the Jacquerie uprising as a satanic plot to overthrow God's appointed social order. Around the same time, a rich merchant in Paris led a campaign by merchants to seize the dauphin (French heir) and the royal treasury. Aristocratic armies suppressed both insurrections with great brutality.

In England, a peasants' revolt erupted in 1381. Three times between 1371 and 1381, the English king had imposed a poll or head tax on his subjects. The last imposition sparked a rebellion. In the wealthy western part of the kingdom, Wat Tyler and John Ball led the resistance, questioning the very authority of their lords. The memorable motto of the rebels was:

> When Adam delved [dug] and Eve span [spun],
> Who was then the gentleman?

The rebels questioned the arbitrary and unnatural nature of social classes, for at creation Adam and Eve had lived in a simple world without social distinctions and inequalities. The rebels had some successes, but they were almost as violent as their aristocratic oppressors, and murdered the archbishop of Canterbury. Before agreeing to return to their homes, they compelled the young king, Richard II (r. 1377–1399), to make some concessions to their demands for justice and tax relief. The king, however, broke his word and the rebellion was suppressed violently.

In Italy, a revolt by the Ciompi (wool carders or combers) broke out in 1378. Other revolts by the lower classes broke out in almost every region of Europe, all of them symptomatic of the restructuring of medieval society. None of the insurrections was successful in their immediate aims in the fourteenth century, but all were a product of the raised expectations of the lower classes, who did not want to lose the gains they had made after the plague. The lower classes were not starving; downtrodden and emaciated people rarely have the energy or resources to revolt. In the second half of the fourteenth century, prosperous peasants jealously protected their rights against the weakened authorities who were trying to reclaim their previous powers and social primacy.

Massacre of Rebellious Peasants The French soldiers of the dauphin are depicted slaughtering rebels in 1358 by throwing the dead or wounded into the Seine River, which flows through Paris.

Towns recovered more quickly from the economic impact of the plague than the countryside of Europe, in part because they could replace lost workers with farmers now ready to become wage earners. Indeed, the plague may have spurred the increased urbanization of Europe or, at least, the balance of power shifted from the rural to the urban after the plague. Yet the plague had hit towns harder than the countryside. Town councils and guilds became more restrictive and jealous of their privileges, not more open. It was an understandable reaction to all the breakages: of contracts, covenants, and economic security.

Although one element of town life became more restrictive and conservative, the plague promoted a new spirit of economic activism among most survivors. The plague broke the lock on innovation and venture economics that had kept the medieval economy conservative and sustainable. In Germany, new mining ventures opened up in the late fourteenth century. With reduced markets, some industries widened their reach to pursue the entire market, not just luxury markets. Thus, in England there was a mass production of cloth and in Flanders the production of cheaper fabric for a wider market of consumers. Europeans also began to look to innovations and inventions in shipbuilding, navigation, and armaments, as they began to reach outside the European world for other individual, economic, and national advantages.

Remaking Religion: Personal Piety, Schism, and Conciliarism

The crises of the first half of the fourteenth century hit organized religion hard. Institutional religion had been as helpless as any group in society to deal with the devastation of the plague and may have suffered more than other groups because of its emphasis on community living. All of Gherardo's brothers at the monastery of Montrieux died. In Exeter and Norwich, over half the priests succumbed to the disease; in Barcelona, over 60 percent died. Some elements of the institutional church tried to respond to the needs of believers during the plague years. Many dioceses lacked priests because so many had died, fled, or taken up safer and more rewarding posts in the private chapels of the wealthy. As a result, extraordinary measures were needed. The church responded as well as it could. The bishop of Bath and Wells permitted laymen and laywomen to hear the confessions of the dying and to administer sacraments.

Following the first outbreak of the plague in 1347–1350, various penitential groups interpreted the disease as a sign of God's anger at a sinful world. Their response was not so much anti-institutional as extra-institutional; they were still believers but sought to appease God outside the confines of institutional religion. The **Flagellants** (from *flagella*, "whip") paraded through the streets and countryside of Europe, whipping themselves to atone for their sins and those of humankind and to imitate Christ's suffering. The Flagellants were not sanctioned by religious authorities. Instead, they reflected and focused a shifting set of popular anxieties: the widespread conviction that the world was evil and God was punishing it, that the world was ending (millenarianism), and that the established church and priesthood had lost God's favor. The more immediate the plague and the more devastating its results, the more intense the Flagellant movement was. When the plague subsided, the Flagellant movement quieted down.

Many people in the Late Middle Ages began to turn away from organized religion and toward expressions of personal piety. In England, aristocrats built elaborate private chapels, both so that they would not have to practice their religion with commoners and to establish a more direct relationship with God. Rising levels of urban literacy created a market for personal Books of Hours (prayer books) and Psalters (collections of the Psalms), evidence of the growing privatization or personalization of religion. The rise of powerful spiritual women such as Catherine of Siena (1347–1380) suggests something of the intensity of later medieval spirituality. Catherine drove herself into states of spiritual ecstasy by extreme asceticism, particularly extreme fasting, for which she won the admiration of popes and common people. The unsettled conditions of the Late Middle Ages led many to want a more intense and intimate relationship with God than the established church could supply or contain.

King Death Triumphs A fifteenth-century Italian fresco shows a king, bishops, monks, and others bowing down before King Death, humbly acknowledging his victory over them, and offering him gifts. The bottom panel shows a parade of the skeletal dead leading the living to their ultimate end.

There were many collective responses to the new world of religion after the plague, but the new way preferred simplicity of faith over elaborate ritual. Lay brothers and sisters formed societies outside the formal church to live in imitation of Christ and to practice charity. Gerhard Groote's Brethren of the Common Life (founded in 1384) explored a new form of personalized devotion, the ***devotio moderna,*** that emphasized individual education, piety, and commitment to God that depended little upon the sacraments and other standards of the Catholic Church. The most famous manual of the age was Thomas à Kempis's *Imitation of Christ* (c. 1418), which sought to establish a direct and personal contact between the believer and Christ.

Religious fervor found new expression in popular culture. It was, for instance, but a short distance from the late medieval doctrine of transubstantiation (that the bread and wine of the Eucharist were transformed in all but appearance into the substance of the body and blood of Christ) to the cult of the body of Christ (*corpus Christi*) and the many medieval blood cults that entranced the Late Middle Ages.[2]

One popular enthusiasm involved reimagining and reenacting the experience of the plague. The dance of death (*danse macabre*) was first performed in 1348 to ward off the disease. By the 1370s, frenzied dancers began to appear in many parts of Europe, dancing to bagpipes and drums until they dropped and were trampled by other dancers. Their herky-jerky, rattling dance may have been meant to imitate the symptoms of dying plague victims, who were then trod upon as though to stamp out the disease. By the late fourteenth century, the dance of death had been transformed into a morality play, a reminder that the disease felled all without distinction: popes, kings, monks, women, and children. The church took up that message as a reminder to all that life was short, death random, and eternity long, but that had not been the dance's original meaning, which may instead have signaled the triumph over the plague by its anxious survivors.

Early in 1377, Pope Gregory XI brought an end to the papacy's self-enforced exile in Avignon and returned to

Rome. He died the next year and the cardinals, under pressure from the Roman people, elected Pope Urban VI (1378–1389). Of low birth and stubborn temperament, Urban ran afoul of many cardinals and, worse, of the French king, Charles V, who was unhappy to see the papacy decamp from greater France. Before long, the king's party among the cardinals declared Urban deposed and elected the bishop of Cambrai as Pope Clement VII (1379–1394); he returned to Avignon. The rival popes each appointed their own cardinals. The so-called **Western** (or **Papal) Schism** of rival claimants to be pope lasted long after the deaths of Urban and Clement. A church council held at Pisa in 1409 declared the two popes of the rival papal parties to be heretics, which led to the election of a third pope. At the Council of Constance (1414–1417), all three popes were deposed and Pope Martin V (1417–1431) was elected in an attempt to end the schism. After he died, his successor Eugenius IV (1431–1447) fell out with the conciliarists, who with support of the king of France elected an **anti-pope** (one elected in opposition to a pope duly elected by church law and custom), Felix V, who did not step down until 1449. Not until the Council of Basel (1431–1449) did the Western Schism end, with the election of Pope Nicholas V (1447–1455).

The Avignon period and the Western Schism made the Catholic Church a source of confusion to Christendom. The pope was no longer the universal representative of God, as Pope Innocent III had vigorously claimed in word and deed. Instead, for almost seventy years, rival popes and their supporters divided Christendom along political lines. The schism divided not just popes and regions of Europe, but diocese and parishes, as well. Many episcopal sees had two bishops during the schism, each appointed by a rival pope, thus forcing individual believers to pick sides. The one ray of light amidst papal division was the **conciliar movement,** which held that a general council of the church, not the pope, had the authority to set the standards for proper governance for the church and Christian behavior. The Council of Constance, in particular, elevated the claims of the powers of general councils dangerously high. The council claimed to receive its powers directly from Christ and demanded obedience from all, including the pope. It maintained that it had the right to repair schisms and to reform the church and all its members. But conciliarism also contributed to division. The Council of Basel had elected and supported the anti-pope Felix. Conciliarism finally foundered on one key issue: it remained the pope's prerogative to call universal councils of the church and, after the Western Schism ended, popes were wary of calling councils, whose principal power seemed to be to depose popes.

Critics of the Church: Wyclif, Hus, and Valla

The Roman Catholic Church was still the most powerful institutional presence in Christian Europe, but Pope Boniface VIII's misadventures, the papal retreat to Avignon, the Western Schism of the papal church, and the general questioning of the usefulness of institutional religion after the calamities of the fourteenth century left Europe religiously uncertain and the church adrift. Many critics charged that the papacy itself was the problem, though the society in which the church operated had changed and a universal church may no longer have been able to meet the needs of so many divergent European communities.

The English theorist John Wyclif (c. 1324–1384) called into question some of the fundamental tenets of the late medieval Roman Catholic Church, including the need for the seven sacraments. Before the plague hit, Wyclif had been studying scholastic philosophy at Oxford University, but scholastic philosophy had lost much of its steam by Wyclif's day. In the thirteenth and fourteenth centuries, scholasticism turned away from the drive toward synthesis of the Dominican friar Thomas Aquinas and toward **nominalism,** which holds that universals are mere names and have no real existence. The Franciscan friar Duns Scotus (1266–1308), the subtle doctor, thought that God was so remote that human reason was insufficient for understanding him. The dunce (from Duns) cap was a caricature of his obtuse students. Another Franciscan, William of Ockham (1280–1349), was a nominalist who thought that the human mind could understand only this world and should not unnecessarily multiply nonexistent entities. This principle, widely known as Ockham's Razor, argues that, all things being equal, the simplest explanation is generally the best one. Scholasticism was still the prevailing mode of academic thought in Wyclif's time, but the plague hit the universities and their thinkers hard, and Ockham may even have died from the plague. Eclecticism crept into post-plague thought. It was neither as purpose driven nor as logically rigorous as it had been in the High Middle Ages. Humanists such as Petrarch were already rejecting scholasticism as arid and moving in new directions, away from substance (truth) to form (style). Others were moving toward mysticism.

Wyclif himself was a dabbler. Heavily influenced by Ockham, he still rejected nominalism. His inclination was to study the sciences and mathematics, but he took up theology and played politics (even attending the Hundred Years' War peace council held at Bruges in 1374 as an English representative). He denied that England should have to pay the papal tax on its lands as agreed to earlier by King John. Wyclif criticized the Avignon papacy and the claim that the pope held both spiritual and worldly power. Wyclif wanted the church and clergy to be less worldly and to embrace apostolic poverty. Although some elements within the state supported him, the English church was horrified by his teaching and condemned many of his propositions. Wyclif also translated the Bible into English and turned to a strict literalism in his interpretation of the Bible. He denied, for instance, that the pope was the head of the church, since

Christ was, and he supported the mendicant friars, but attacked monasticism. He was blamed for stirring up the peasants who revolted in 1381, though he criticized them and their materialist goals. Despite a church council that condemned his teachings in 1382, King Richard II and the English Parliament would not allow Wyclif's condemnation as a heretic. His supporters, called **Lollards** (idlers) by their Catholic critics, continued to propagate his works and theological views throughout much of the fifteenth century. Wyclif's attack on the existing church was, in many ways, a fundamental rethinking of the nature and purpose of the established church.

Jan Hus Burned at the Stake The Council of Constance in 1415 revoked its pledge of safe conduct to the Bohemian reformer and ordered his execution.

In Bohemia, the conditions were more favorable for the emergence of an early national (or Bohemian) church set in resistance to Rome. The emperor Charles IV's creation of Prague as a Czech town, with its own cathedral (and, thus, free of control by the episcopal see of Mainz) and university (with a Bohemian focus) established the basis for the rise of a Czech church. Jan Hus was a student of theology at the university of Prague and there first encountered the doctrines of Wyclif. During the Western Schism, Hus, now the rector of the university, supported the conciliarists, but his archbishop excommunicated Hus and prohibited him from preaching. Hus and his followers were critics of a corrupt clergy, a temporal papacy, and a wealthy church. Hus appealed to poor Czechs, long subject to Germans and to heavy church taxation. Like Wyclif, he believed in the primacy of the Bible, even subordinating the established church to its teaching. In 1415, with the promise of safe conduct, Hus attended the Council of Constance, was put on trial, and condemned when he would not recant his teachings unless they were in opposition to the Bible. He was found guilty of heresy and burned to death. In Bohemia, a Hussite church (with married priests, services in the vernacular tongue, and unadorned churches) developed in opposition to the Roman church. The Hussite national church was not suppressed for many years.

Resistance to the papal church of Rome came not only from national religious movements, but also from princely quarters. In the 1440s, Lorenzo Valla, an Italian humanist, was in the employ of Alfonso I, the king of Aragon, Sicily, and Naples. Alfonso was waging a campaign against the pope over the possession of Italian lands, which led his employee Lorenzo to examine one of the central documents of the medieval Catholic Church. By the terms of the so-called Donation of Constantine and widely accepted in the Middle Ages as legitimate, the emperor Constantine, at the moment of his conversion to Christianity, had bestowed upon Pope Sylvester and his heirs the lands of the western empire as well as extensive rights over the west. Lorenzo made a critical (though hardly disinterested or perfectly objective) examination of the document and found that it contained anachronisms, barbaric Latin, statements that did not square with known history or geography, improper dating, and internal inconsistencies. Lorenzo dismissed the papal document as a forgery, and not a very good one at that, thus removing another prop that had supported the claims of the imperial papacy of the Middle Ages.

The Roman church as headed by the pope was much challenged by the new forces of the Late Middle Ages, at a time when there was a general crisis of confidence in institutional religion. The church, however, was not the only institution to feel the effects of the upheavals of the fourteenth century.

The Late Medieval State

The crises of the first half of the fourteenth century did not immediately alter the medieval state, but the conditions produced by those crises disrupted the delicate balance of late medieval society. The crises and accompanying social upheavals undermined the high medieval confidence in a corporate state of cooperative units.

> What signs of redirection and renewal are evident in the fifteenth century?

A New World of Political Relations

The crises struck hard at the institution of kingship, or perhaps the royal dynasties of the High Middle Ages had just naturally begun to fail, as all dynasties eventually do.

The Hundred Years' War was a product, in part, of the Capetian failure to put a dynamic heir on the throne. The English War of the Roses came about because two rival dynasties (Lancaster and York) laid claim to the throne. In France, England, Castile, Portugal, Naples, Hungary, and Poland, the monarchs by 1450 were not the direct descendants of the monarchs who had been in place in 1300.

The pressures on kingship increased as society changed. Fiscal pressures rose as a result of the many wars that states were engaged in, for wars were more expensive to wage in the Late Middle Ages. Kings found that mercenaries were more available and reliable soldiers than their nobles, but also more expensive. A settled nobility, hit hard by the economic downturn of the first half of the fourteenth century, when its landed resources were unreliable and underworked, could not be counted upon. Given the lack of manpower, lords preferred to pay the king in money rather than men (an arrangement sometimes called bastard feudalism). Kings welcomed the exchange because mercenary armies of adventurers were more professional and directly dependent on the royal purse and person. The nature of warfare was also changing as cannons and guns became more common, though costly. Castles could no longer resist battery in an age of cannon shot.

While war was becoming more expensive to wage, royal revenues were falling. Kings had previously relied on revenues from their own domains, but as with the nobles' landed resources, royal estates were producing less money after the great depopulation of 1315–1350. Kings could tax their subjects, but they found that they could do so only on an extraordinary and irregular basis. To ask for consent from representative assemblies was to admit some dependence on nobles for their approval of royal action, which kings wished to avoid. Assemblies always wanted something in exchange for their consent, most often the redress of some old grievance.

The late medieval nobility was a particularly troublesome class for the king. They were deeply dissatisfied with how their fortunes had fallen and sought the restoration of their old rights and privileges. The brutality of the suppression of the various popular insurrections across Europe suggests just how angry a class the nobles had become. One of their greatest complaints was that kings no longer needed them as they once had. Thus the corporate ideal of cooperative orders of farmers, aristocratic lords, priests, and others that had sustained the High Middle Ages had been damaged irreparably in the fourteenth century. The orders occupied a world of fluid social relations by 1400, one that had been scarcely imaginable in 1300.

The Final Phase of the Hundred Years' War

When King Edward III of England died in 1377 and was succeeded by the boy-king Richard II, it may have seemed that the war between France and England could be brought to a close, but the French monarchy was unlucky in the extreme. The French king Charles V (the Wise; r. 1364–1380) died prematurely and was succeeded by a son, Charles VI (r. 1380–1422), who was incompetent, quarrelsome, and at times incapacitated by mental illness. Complicating the French resistance to the English was a civil war (1407–1435) in greater France between the Burgundians and Armagnacs (a French faction that supported the dauphin). Both sides in that conflict sought to ally with the English in order to control the French throne. Eventually the martial king Henry V of England (r. 1413–1422) renewed the Hundred Years' War with considerable zest, and at the Battle of Agincourt in 1415 his outnumbered forces defeated the French. English archers and poor French strategy once again determined the day. Eventually the French struck a deal with Henry whereby the dauphin Charles, the son of Charles VI, was deposed. Henry was named the regent and heir to the French throne and married the French king's daughter, Catherine. In 1420, Henry set about claiming his territory, including Paris, by force.

The Maid of Orléans

Although disinherited by treaty, the dauphin Charles led the resistance to the English and Burgundians. The dauphin was popular in certain quarters, but his resources were limited, his position perilous, and his legitimacy in doubt. France, occupied by English and French opponents, was in disarray—plunder, rape, and devastation destabilized France—and people fled, if they could, to walled towns. Charles had been declared king but had not been crowned and was deeply aware of the many challenges to his royal standing. The city of Orléans was under siege by the English when Joan of Arc (c. 1412–1431) came to the rescue. Joan was a peasant girl from the village of Domrémy who had begun to receive visions commanding her to save Orléans and assist the dauphin, Charles. After an interview with Charles, in which she confirmed his rightful claims, and an examination by his theologians, she was given permission to accompany the French army to the besieged city. In March 1429, she sent a remarkable letter to the king of England and the duke of Bedford, his chief operative in France. She denied them the right to hold France and declared that she had been appointed by God to reclaim the blood royal for France. She warned that if the English did not leave France, she would have them executed. Dressed in soldier's armor, Joan successfully led the relief of Orléans in May.

The next stage of her mandate from God was to ensure that Charles VII was crowned at Rheims, which against long odds and English resistance occurred in July. She next hoped to reclaim Paris for her king, but Charles stupidly accepted a Burgundian truce and postponed the attack. Against her king's wishes, Joan went to Paris anyway, but the attempt to take the occupied city failed. At Compiègne, Joan was captured by the Burgundians and sold to the English, who put her on trial in Rouen as a

Joan of Arc the Soldier By most accounts, Joan insisted on dressing as a soldier and participating in relieving the siege of Orléans in 1429. She was later executed for heresy by the English, who cited cross-dressing as a sign of her heretical depravity and stubbornness.

heretic. Her cross-dressing was deemed particularly perverse and a sign of heretical stubbornness. She was not yet twenty years old when she was put to death at the stake on May 30, 1431. Her last word was *"Jhesu."* Her ashes were cast into the Seine, lest people collect her bones as relics.

Whatever else the strange short career of Joan of Arc means, it speaks to the emergence of a deeply patriotic and royalist sentiment in France. Joan had demonstrated that the king, no matter how weak a sovereign, was sacred. The king belonged to France and France to the king, and in Joan's thought God had appointed them for each other. Joan's mission was a religious one; she was the virgin sent by God to rescue France from foreign oppression and corruption. She became a national heroine and, much later, was declared a saint.

The Hundred Years' War wore down after Joan's death, not because of her, but because it was becoming clear that the English could not hold France. The cost was too dear and popular acceptance of foreign rule impossible. In 1435 by the Treaty of Arras, Burgundy finally moved to support the French rather than the English side, which changed the balance of power. The French may never have rallied as enthusiastically as Joan did to Charles VII, but they knew that the English were worse. King Charles finally became more decisive. He took Paris, entered a new truce with the English, and slowly began to recover French lands from the foreigners. In 1453, after an English defeat at Bordeaux, the Hundred Years' War ended fittingly without any treaty or truce. All the truces, treaties, and breathing spaces had prolonged the war, allowing the equally matched parties to recover and fight decade after decade under different actors. In 1456, a French high court annulled the original condemnation of Joan of Arc as a heretic and Charles set about repairing his exhausted kingdom.

New Medieval Monarchy

Charles VII may have started badly, but by the end he led the way for the new monarchs of Europe. Relying on good advisors, he instituted fiscal, military, and administrative reforms of the state. The king alone was permitted to call up and pay troops. He established a standing army by stationing garrisons of soldiers in provincial towns. A paid army meant that the king had to raise taxes on a regular basis, so Charles instituted a permanent tax in France. Indeed, the king let the assembly of the Estates General of France lapse. Many minor nobility now looked to the king for employment.

King Charles had limited success in kick-starting the economy, but the prosperous career of Jacques Coeur (c. 1400–1456) in Bourges shows just how much could be achieved. Coeur began as a silversmith but won royal favor and took charge of the royal mint in Bourges. He parlayed his role as a royal minter into that of a merchant-trader and assembled his own navy, which supplied France from the Mediterranean. Coeur was skilled at the new financial techniques pioneered in Italy such as double-entry bookkeeping and kept careful track of his venture capital, expenses, and income. He made himself indispensable to King Charles as a wealthy financier and advisor on both domestic and diplomatic matters, for which he and his family were ennobled. Though he was every inch the new-style official that the new monarchs promoted, Jacques Coeur in the end was undone by his success and the chicanery of Charles. The king and so many nobles owed Coeur money that the easiest solution for King Charles and his court nobles was to arrange the fall of the mighty money man. Charges of corruption and treason were laid, Coeur was imprisoned and condemned. He escaped but died in exile outside France.

Western monarchs in the mid-fifteenth century were less and less inclined to rely on their nobles. They established more rewarding relationships with towns and filled their bureaucracies with military counselors, lawyers, and merchant-traders such as Jacques Coeur. In so doing, they found a way to centralize authority under their control, and, as Jacques Coeur discovered, the king's new officials and friends were easier to use and dispense with than the old nobility ever was.

France continued its state reform under King Louis XI (the Spider King; r. 1461–1483). Louis was known to be particularly crafty, patiently waiting for his enemies to fall into the traps he had prepared for them. When Duke Charles the Bold rashly died in battle in 1477, Louis annexed the Duchy of Burgundy, thus removing a powerful thorn in the side of medieval French kings and their control of greater France. During the reign of Louis's son, Charles VIII (r. 1483–1498), France was involved in a series of Italian conflicts that pushed the French state toward a more efficient, but also more expensive bureaucracy. France could afford the cost of expanded government, being in much better economic shape by the last half of the fifteenth century. By 1400, several thousand French villages had been abandoned because of famine, war, and disease, but in the period 1450–1500, bountiful harvests returned and the Hundred Years' War was no longer a steady drain on the treasury.

Between 1455 and 1485, England was divided by the War of the Roses, the white rose representing the House of York and the red rose the House of Lancaster; those memorable designations were created later by Tudor historians. At the Battle of Bosworth Field in 1485, the Lancastrian Henry Tudor defeated the unpopular Richard III and founded the Tudor dynasty as King Henry VII (r. 1485–1509). Henry was in desperate need of money, but his subjects expected him to "live of his own." Henry set about discovering ways to amass money that did not lead through Parliament. He increased the royal domain, took charge of custom revenues, resurrected old taxes, charged fees for royal services, and assigned fines for the administration of justice. These monies went straight into the royal accounts. Henry was particularly gifted at squeezing money out of his nobles, often on some trumped-up charge of disloyalty or some manufactured scandal. To do so, he required an instrument of royal investigation and so employed the Court of the Star Chamber to examine, discipline, and break the landed gentry that opposed him. Henry loathed, as the Tudors generally would, the expense of foreign wars, which was the lesson of England's long entanglement on the continent.

In the late fifteenth century, Spain at last achieved unity. The Iberian Peninsula was composed of three basic areas: Portugal, with 1.5 million people; Castile (including Léon and Navarre), with a population of 8 million; and the area of Aragon (Catalonia, Aragon, and Valencia), with approximately 1 million people.

In October 1469, Isabella, heir to the throne of Castile, married Ferdinand, heir to the thrones of Sicily and Aragon. It was an almost impossible marriage to pull off. Because the ruling king of Castile, Henry IV (the Impotent), had no heir, he reluctantly agreed for a time to support the elevation of Isabella, his half-brother's sister, against the wishes of his own nobles. The marriage ceremony of Isabella and Ferdinand took place in Toledo under the most unlikely circumstances. King Henry had withdrawn his consent, and a forged papal document permitting the marriage mysteriously appeared. To get to Toledo, Ferdinand dressed as a mule-driver to slip by those seeking to stop the marriage. The king subsequently condemned the marriage, denied that Isabella was his legitimate heir, and chose another. Yet Isabella hung on, and after King Henry's death in 1474, she was quickly crowned queen.

Castilian nobles, fearing that the marriage would lead to the unification of the Spanish kingdoms, revolted, leading to a decade of civil war. Instead of immediately imposing unification upon Spain, Isabella and Ferdinand set about securing their borders. Between 1482 and 1492, they initiated the conquest of the Moors in Granada. This completed the long reconquest (*reconquista*) of Spain that had stretched over many centuries (Map 10.4).

As part of their campaign to purify Spain and make it entirely Christian, Ferdinand and Isabella in 1492 expelled Spain's Jewish population. By 1502, Muslims who would not convert were expelled, as well. The king and queen employed the Spanish church to bring about unity of faith in Spain and introduced the Spanish Inquisition as a national instrument of inquiry.

Isabella was a powerful sovereign in her own right and retained control of Castile. It may not be a coincidence that it was at this time in Spain that the game of chess took on its modern form. The game had long been played in European and Islamic lands, often with no queen piece or a queen with little power. During Isabella's reign, the queen piece finally became the most powerful and dominant player on the board.[3]

The Coerced Baptism of Muslim Women A wood panel decoration from an altar depicts Muslim women in Granada undergoing baptism after the success of the reconquest of Spain by Ferdinand and Isabella.

The splintered states of the Holy Roman Empire and the city-states of Italy are treated in subsequent chapters, but the late medieval monarchs of France, England, and Spain were already pointing the way toward the new methods and goals of late medieval government and increasing their intense competition with each other for resources and land. They did this by securing new forms of revenue, employing new-style officials, bureaucratizing their governments, arranging strategic marriage alliances, bypassing or subordinating their nobles, and supporting new international ventures outside of Europe.

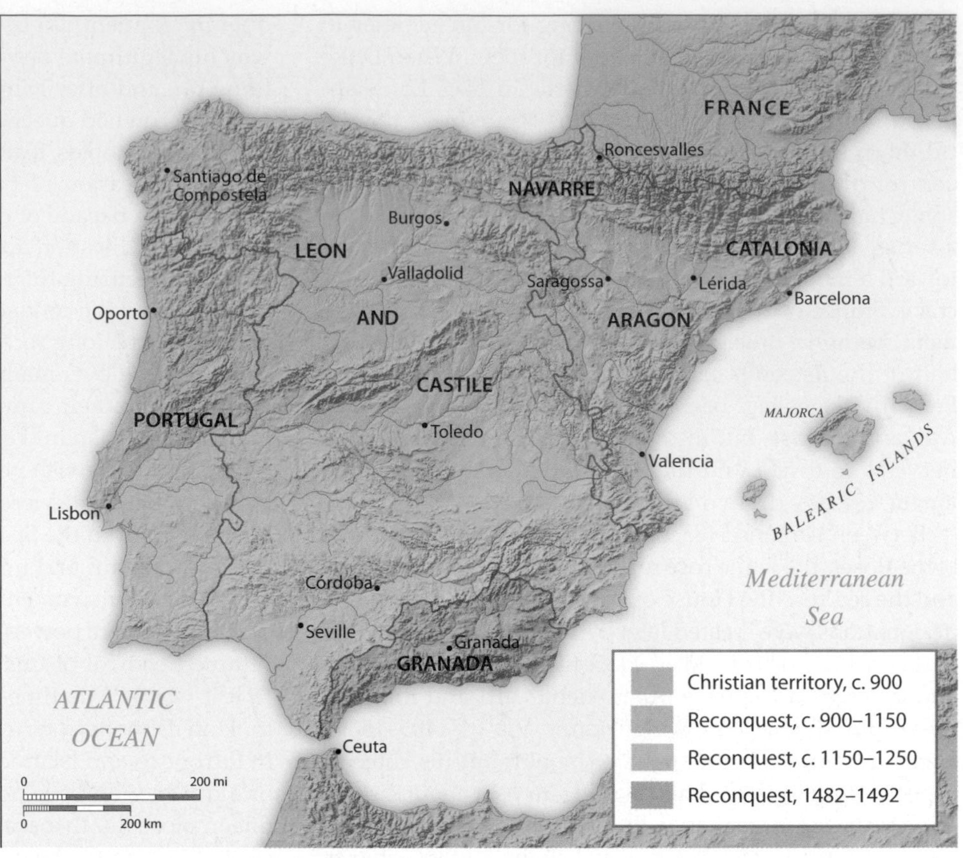

MAP 10.4 | The Reconquest of Spain, 900–1492, and Its Final Phase
The Christian reconquest of Spain spanned almost six centuries, concluding with the retaking of Granada by Ferdinand and Isabella and the expulsion in 1502 of all Muslims who would not convert to Christianity. ***Why had Muslim Granada been able to hold on so long? How was the Christianization of Spain part of a larger European movement of consolidation? Why did Ferdinand and Isabella make reconquest such a critical part of their consolidation of Spain?***

The Fall of Constantinople

The decline of the Byzantine Empire transformed Europe and the historical and geographic setting it occupied. For eleven hundred years the eastern Roman Empire had been an enduring counterpoint to western Europe, supplying it with economic, intellectual, and theological stimulation. The existence of Constantinople in the east was a hard fact during times when western Europe seemed adrift and dangerously unstable. But the emergence of the Ottoman Turks, particularly under Beyazit I Yilderim (the Lightning), had stripped Byzantium of its empire, including Greece, and left it with only Constantinople. Beyazit was on the verge of taking the city in 1402 when he was forced to withdraw his forces to engage Tamerlane (Timur the Lame), a Mongol Muslim, who had conquered Baghdad and Damascus the previous year. At the Battle of Ankara, Tamerlane defeated and captured Beyazit. Constantinople survived a little longer, then, not because of its internal resources but because of external forces beyond its control.

Early in his reign, the Turkish sultan Mahomet II (r. 1451–1481) resumed the assault on the great city. Complicating matters, the attempt of the Roman Catholic Church to enforce a union of the eastern and western churches remained unpopular in Constantinople. Many Byzantine Christians believed that the sultan would respect their orthodox beliefs in ways that the pope would not. The emperor Constantine XI was able to secure the service of few western soldiers to defend his city. In April 1453, Mahomet assembled over 80,000 soldiers and some three hundred ships outside the city's famous double walls. Constantine had only 8,000 men (3,000 of them westerners) to defend his city. Moreover, Mahomet brought an immense cannon to bear on the walls of the city, which soon crumbled, and he blocked any relief supplies from entering the city. In late May, his troops poured through the breaches and the emperor Constantine was killed in the fighting. Constantinople was ransacked and renamed Istanbul, and the famous Hagia Sophia, built by Justinian, was made a mosque. Istanbul became the capital of the Turkish or Ottoman Empire.

For westerners, the fall of Constantinople seemed a second fall of Rome, but they did not have long to lament its passing. The rise of a powerful Ottoman block to its east had the effect of enclosing, redefining, and balkanizing Europe. Europe's outlet to the east was now cut off, economically, territorially, and psychologically. Overseas exploration to the west would be the result.

1453: To Fall Asleep in Constantinople and Wake in Istanbul

There are two stories of Constantinople's fall: one Greek, the other Muslim. One is a story of death and destruction, slavery and forced dispersion, the loss of church and pride of place. The other is a story of proud achievement, of the green banners of Islam and the red banners of the sultan being unfurled in a city that had resisted the Islamic world for eight hundred years, but was now the brightest jewel in the resplendent Ottoman crown.

The city of Constantinople fell to Mahomet II Fatih (the Conqueror) on May 29, 1453, and for the Greeks of Constantine's city, everything changed overnight. Some 4,000 defenders of the city were killed, and nearly 30,000 Greek residents were captured and enslaved. Within days, long lines of chained Greeks were paraded through their former city and shipped to slave markets in Islamic lands. Among them was George Sphrantzes, an imperial official and former Byzantine governor. He was eventually ransomed in September, but his wife and children were enslaved to a Turkish family before being purchased by a high Turkish official, who eventually sold the children to the sultan. After a few years, George was able to ransom his wife, but his two captive children died in the sultan's seraglio (harem), his daughter from disease and his son John executed by the sultan because he had been plotting Mahomet's murder. The fate of George and his family was probably similar to that of many rich and powerful Byzantines—a story of broken families, dispersion, and loss. Greek officials and scholars fled to the west, seeking what employment they could find. The story of lower-class Constantinopolitans was one of a horrific fall into foreign servility, silence, and oblivion.

Sultan Mahomet II

If the world of the Christian Greek residents of Constantinople was upended overnight, so too was that of the Turks of the new Istanbul, but their half of history's hourglass was now on top. The great city was quickly "Islamicized." Churches were turned into mosques, which became the new organizing centers of the city renamed Istanbul. A minaret was erected within days at Hagia Sophia. The sultan encouraged traders, including the Italians, to set up shop in the city and sought to internationalize the city, forcing some of his subject peoples to relocate there and trying to attract others from outside to his new capital. Twenty-five years after the conquest, the city was twice as populous as it had been in 1453. Muslim Turk families now made up half the city's population, Greek households a quarter of the civilian population. In the days after the conquest not all the Greeks were sold into slavery. The sultan claimed a fifth of the captives, perhaps as many as six thousand Greeks, as his own and settled them in a part of the city that would become a Greek quarter. He also allowed those Greeks who had fled the city before it fell and, therefore, had not resisted him, to return to repossess their property. Mahomet approved a new patriarch for the Greek church and proved himself to be a benevolent ruler, who was interested in Greek and Persian poetry and was proud to establish a quasi-Byzantine court to rival those of European rulers.

QUESTIONS | ***In what ways is history merely a story of winners and losers? Constantinople fell, but how was its place in the Greek identity preserved?***

The Waning of the Middle Ages

What makes historical works classics may not make them great works of history. Historical classics share common features; they capture the imagination of readers by breaking out of the boxes that others inhabit and they create an unforgettable image and understanding of a period. They are also controversial. They endure as books read by the generations because they demand engagement, discussion, and debate. Classics are rarely definitive studies, for the fate of many definitive works is to be absorbed into the accepted interpretation of a period. Classics are books that we return to again and again; they keep kicking.

Johan Huizinga's *Waning of the Middle Ages* is one such classic. It has gone through numerous editions and translations since its initial publication in 1919. Its arresting opening (in Fritz Hopman's translation) is gripping: "To the world when it was half a thousand years younger, the outlines of all things seemed more clearly marked than to us. The contrast between suffering and joy, between adversity and happiness, appeared more striking. All experience had yet to the minds of men the directness and absoluteness of the pleasure and pain of child-life." What follows in Huizinga's book is an impressionistic study of the violent tenor of late medieval life, its pessimisms, chivalric and heroic ideals, visions of life and death, religious sensibilities, and the movement from a symbolic to realistic imagination. The tableau Huizinga lays before us is sweeping and sensuous; his Late Middle Ages in the north is overripe, reeking of the rot of final things.

Professional historians were not pleased. Huizinga's book, they thought, was too beautiful, too topical and imagistic to be historically true. They noted that Huizinga had a weak sense of historical change and chronology; that his book was actually about Burgundian society, not the whole of northern Europe in the Late Middle Ages; that he ignored politics, the economy, and the mass of people who did not participate in high culture. His was a cultural history designed to evoke the sensibility of the Late Middle Ages, not the reasons it had become that way. In North America, the book became a classic college text when Hopman's translation appeared in an Anchor paperback version in 1954, but that version reduced the number of chapters, eliminated much of the original, and was based on the French translation of the work and not the final Dutch edition. To repair those flaws and give Huizinga fuller voice, Rodney J. Payton and Ulrich Mammitzsch brought out a complete retranslation (but of the second edition of the work) in 1996 under the title *The Autumn of the Middle Ages.*

A work that continues to attract so much attention and to provoke so much discussion qualifies as a classic. It is not a book that leaves readers unmoved. Huizinga's view of the Late Middle Ages—that it had its own voice and natural ending—seemed to speak to the modern world. So did J. R. R. Tolkien's *The Lord of the Rings* (1954–1956). Tolkien saw the Middle Ages as a rejection of so much that he disliked about the modern world: mechanization, democratization, and materialization. Yet Tolkien's sprawling three novels are hardly an accurate re-creation of the Middle Ages. There is nothing like the Catholic Church in the Middle-earth of the wizard Gandalf and the Hobbits Frodo and Sam. Huizinga and Tolkien, to different degrees, present us with quasi-medieval worlds, whose very point is to make us think about the world we live in through the lens of its opposite.

QUESTIONS | ***Is the Middle Ages the opposite of the modern world? Why or why not? Why is the Middle Ages the subject of so many modern projections and fantasies in popular culture (movies, novels, and music)?***

Conclusion

Just as there is no consensus on when the Middle Ages began, there is little consensus on when it ended. The Middle Ages ended not with any single event, but rather with a series of fundamental changes: the educational changes that occurred in the fifteenth century during the Italian Renaissance, the fall of Constantinople, the invention and spread of the printed book after 1450, overseas exploration in the fifteenth and sixteenth centuries, and the religious re-formation of western Christendom in the sixteenth century. The most popular view may be that the fifteenth-century developments in northern Italy were the bridge to an early-modern age that saw the loosening of the church's stranglehold on medieval Europe. Others might look to the fall of Constantinople in 1453 as removing one of the critical features of the Middle Ages, a Christian eastern empire in place since the emperor Constantine's day. As such, the rise and fall of Constantinople might be viewed as bookends enclosing the Middle Ages. The arrival of the printing press in the 1450s removed another key feature of the Middle Ages: the parchment manuscript. Others look to 1517–1520, when Luther and his movement of protest fractured the Catholic Church's hold on Europe, but Christianity would remain the predominant religion of Europe.

Questions of periodization are never easy to resolve, but they do force us to think about what was essential to a period. The beginning and end of a period are likely to be fuzzier than its core, when it was essentially itself in its most developed form.

There can be little doubt that the crises that overtook Europe in the fourteenth century brought about change and produced a new world in the Late Middle Ages. The onset of the Little Ice age, the desperate times of the Great Famine, and the disaster of the plague undermined some of the main achievements of high medieval civilization. If the building campaign of a great Gothic cathedral was not finished by the early fourteenth century, it would not likely be completed for centuries. The loss of resources and people in the first half of the fourteenth century sapped the energy and dynamism of high medieval civilization. The survivors of the calamities, however, did not surrender; they adapted. Not all the changes happened on the same time scale. Workers in the cities and farms of Europe were sensitive to economic changes and responded quickly to new opportunities. A generation later, workers and peasants revolted against measures to claw back their gains. Royalty was relatively slow to react to the new conditions of life, but by the late fifteenth century, kings were back on top, transforming monarchy into a more dynamic and self-sufficient force. Along the way, customs and practices that had defined the medieval order were transformed or ended. The French king's move to impose permanent taxation was one of those, since the Middle Ages had begun with and had long relied on an exchange of land for service.

The church too was changing. The imperial papacy created by Gregory VII and the Investiture Controversy had its last moment of great pretense early in the fourteenth century under Pope Boniface VIII, but he died in retreat, painfully aware of the limits to his power. The Avignon papacy, the Western Schism with its rival papal claimants, and the stirrings of national churches in Bohemia and England were all symptoms of a papal church beleaguered. In the aftermath of crises of climate, sustenance, and disease came a reworking of religion that turned gradually from institutional answers to personal and private ones. Religion was, if anything, more important after the crises, even if the papal church was weaker than it had been in the High Middle Ages.

Little Yersinia and her companions Cold and Hunger cut Europe to the quick, forcing it in new directions—political, economic, and religious—that would have been inconceivable seventy-five years earlier. From this great shattering of medieval direction and confidence came the great trifurcation of European history into the Northern Italian and European Renaissances, overseas exploration, and religious re-formation, which we take up in Chapters 11–13. Those historical developments had their roots in the new world of the Late Middle Ages and would be responses and reactions to its many troubles and surprising achievements in fashioning many new Europes.

Critical Thinking Questions

1. How did the elements of chance and choice play out in the fourteenth century as people dealt with calamity and change?
2. Which groups in society were hit hardest by calamity and changing circumstances?
3. Why was the Hundred Years' War such a prolonged and fruitless set of conflicts?
4. How did religion change between 1300 and 1450?
5. How and why did the period 1300–1450 either kill off the Middle Ages or refashion it?

Key Terms

Little Ice Age **(p. 296)**
Great Famine **(p. 297)**
bull **(p. 299)**
Unam sanctam **(p. 299)**
Golden Bull **(p. 300)**
Hundred Years' War **(p. 301)**
chivalry **(p. 303)**
pandemic **(p. 304)**
Black Death **(p. 305)**
Jacquerie **(p. 310)**
Flagellants **(p. 311)**
devotio moderna **(p. 312)**
Western (Papal) Schism **(p. 313)**
anti-pope **(p. 313)**
conciliar movement **(p. 313)**
nominalism **(p. 313)**
Lollards (idlers) **(p. 314)**

Primary Sources in connect

For information on Connect and the online resources available, go to **http://connect.mcgraw-hill.com.**

1. **Observations of the Plague**
2. **The Peasants' Revolt of 1831**
3. **Joan of Arc's Letter to the English Invaders and Her Trial**
4. **George Sphrantzes and the Fall of Constantinople**

BACK TO THE SOURCE

Agnolo the Fat and the Plague

Agnolo di Tura, called the Fat, was an eyewitness to the destruction the plague visited on Siena and his own family in 1348. Agnolo was a man on the way up in Sienese society. Though his origins were in the lower classes, his wife Nicoluccia came from a higher station and never let him forget it. Together they had five children, but his wife and children died, along with some 80,000 other Sienese when the plague struck according to Agnolo. At different points in his life, Agnolo worked as a shoemaker, tax collector, and chronicler. His account of the plague's destruction is part of his larger chronicle (*Cronica Maggiore*) of Siena from 1300 to 1351, which he based partly on official documents and partly on his own observations.

The mortality began in Siena in May [1348]. It was a cruel and horrible thing; and I do not know where to begin to tell of the cruelty and the pitiless ways. It seemed to almost everyone that one became stupefied by seeing the pain. And it is impossible for the human tongue to recount the awful thing. Indeed, one who did not see such horribleness can be called blessed. And the victims died almost immediately. They would swell beneath their armpits and in their groins, and fall over dead while talking. Father abandoned child, wife husband, one brother another; for this illness seemed to strike through breath and sight. And so they died. And none could be found to bury the dead for money or friendship. Members of a household brought their dead to a ditch as best they could, without priest, without divine offices. Nor did the death bell sound. And in many places in Siena great pits were dug and piled deep with the multitude of the dead. And they died by the hundreds both day and night, and all were thrown in those ditches and covered over with earth. And as soon as those ditches were filled more were dug.

And I, Agnolo di Tura, called the Fat, buried my five children with my own hands. And there were also those who were so sparsely covered with earth that the dogs dragged them forth and devoured many bodies throughout the city. There was no one who wept for any death, for all awaited death. And so many died that all believed that it was the end of the world. And no medicine or any other defense availed. And the lords selected three citizens who received a thousand gold florins from the commune of Siena that they were to spend on the poor sick and to bury the poor dead. And it was all so horrible that I, the writer, cannot think of it and so will not continue. This situation continued until September, and it would take too long to write of it. And it is found that at this time there died in Siena 36,000 persons twenty years of age or less, and the aged and other people [died] to a total of 52,000 in all in Siena. And in the suburbs of Siena 28,000 persons died; so that in all it is found that in the city and suburbs of Siena 80,000 persons died. Thus at this time Siena and its suburbs had more than 30,000 men, and there remained in Siena [alone] less than 10,000 men. And those that survived were like persons distraught and almost without feeling. And many walls and other things were abandoned, and all the mines of silver, gold, and copper that existed in Sienese territory were abandoned as is seen; for in the countryside . . . many more people died, many lands and villages were abandoned, and no one remained there. I will not write of the cruelty that there was in the countryside, of the wolves and wild beasts that ate the poorly buried corpses, and of other cruelties that would be too painful to those who read of them. . . .

The city of Siena seemed almost uninhabited for almost no one was found in the city. And then, when the pestilence abated, all who survived gave themselves over to pleasures: monks, priests, nuns, and lay men and women all enjoyed themselves, and none worried about spending and gambling. And everyone thought himself rich because he had escaped and regained the world, and no one knew how to allow himself to do nothing. . . .

At this time in Siena the great and noble project of enlarging the cathedral of Siena that had begun a few years earlier was abandoned. . . .

After the pestilence the Sienese appointed two judges and three non-Sienese notaries whose task it was to handle the wills that had been made at that time. And so they searched them out and found them. . . .

1349: after the great pestilence of the past year each person lived according to his own caprice, and everyone tended to seek pleasure in eating and drinking, hunting, catching birds and gaming. And all money had fallen into the hands of the *nouveaux riches*.

QUESTIONS | *How is Agnolo's account enhanced or compromised by his personal experience and individual losses? What symptoms of the disease did he detect? Based on the numbers he provides, who suffered most from the disease, the young or the old, city dwellers or country folk?*

Source: Translated by William M. Bowsky, in William M. Bowsky, *The Black Death,* 1st ed., pp. 13–14. © 1971 Wadsworth, a part of Cengage Learning, Inc. Reproduced by permission. www.cengage.com/permissions

11

Gentile Bellini, *The Procession in St. Mark's Square,* Venice

THE NORTHERN ITALIAN AND EUROPEAN RENAISSANCES

PETRARCH, CASSANDRA, AND THE DYING BOY On the morning of April 26, 1336, Petrarch set out to climb Mont Ventoux ("windy mountain"), the tallest mountain in southern France. From there he could, with a sweep of his eyes, see France, Italy, and toward Spain. He wanted to imitate the ancient king who had climbed Mount Haemus. Petrarch (Francesco Petrarcha; 1304–1374) was the progenitor of humanism and the **Italian Renaissance** rethinking of Europe's past and present. He was also a complex and contradictory character. He spent his formative years and early career as a creature of the Avignon papacy, but longed for Italy and its golden past. He was a cleric and chaplain, but he idealized from a distance the sublime Laura, a young woman whom he first saw in church in 1327 and about whom he wrote elegant love poetry in Italian. He wrote often about Laura yet bore illegitimate children with women about whom we know next to nothing.

Petrarch's ascent of Mont Ventoux was also full of contradictions. He chose his brother, the monk Gherardo, as his boon companion for the climb, but they took servants with them to do the heavy lifting. Petrarch presents the climb as an allegory of the soul's ascent. The problem was that he kept losing his way, descending into valleys, while his religious brother made the easier and straighter ascent. At the summit, Petrarch opened a copy of Saint Augustine's *Confessions,* where his eye fell upon a passage criticizing those who admire tall mountains, vast seas, and the stars, but forget themselves. He descended the mountain in a blue funk, refusing to speak to the others and blaming himself for his love of the material world. Petrarch was torn between this world and a higher one, the present and the distant past, between activity (*negotium,* meaning the daily business of life) and contemplation (as the result of ease, *otium*). Convinced that his own age reeked of corruption and fallen standards, Petrarch admired the superior men of ancient Rome, the superior government of the Roman Republic, and the superior art and writing of the classical past. He had that rare gift of inspiring others to take up his cause, in this case rethinking the assumptions of his age.

If Petrarch was the father of humanism, Cassandra Fedele and Laura Cereta were his intellectual and spiritual daughters. In 1556, the Republic of Venice requested that the ninety-one-year-old humanist Cassandra Fedele (1465–1558) give a public address in honor of the visiting Queen of Poland. Cassandra was an internationally renowned scholar. From the age of twelve, she had studied philosophy and the natural

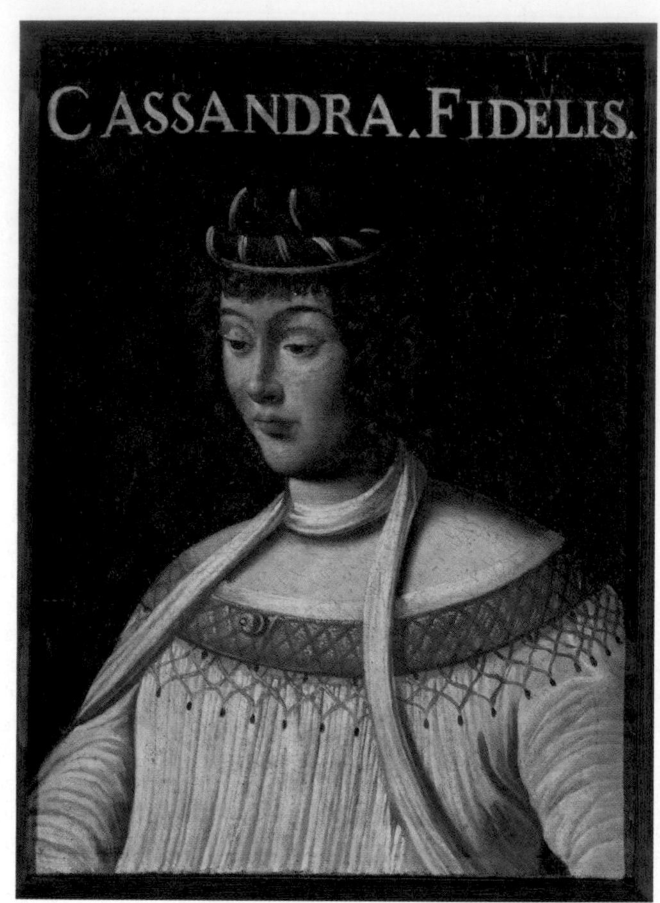

Cassandra Fedele A portrait of the humanist of Venice by an unknown artist.

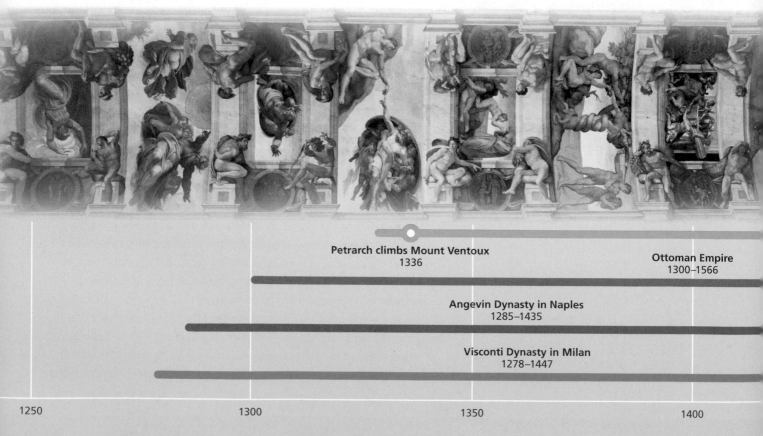

Petrarch climbs Mount Ventoux
1336

Ottoman Empire
1300–1566

Angevin Dynasty in Naples
1285–1435

Visconti Dynasty in Milan
1278–1447

1250 1300 1350 1400

sciences and knew classical literature intimately. At the age of twenty-two, though barred as a woman from attending university, Cassandra addressed her cousin's graduating class at the University of Padua on the subject of the value of the arts and sciences, a speech that was published many times during her lifetime. At a time when women were expected to either marry or become nuns, she chose to marry a physician, and moved to the island of Crete, which brought her close to the Ottoman Empire and the vestiges of Greek civilization. Angelo Poliziano, the Tuscan poet, praised her to his patron, Lorenzo de' Medici, for her great beauty and fluent command of Greek and Latin. Two years after making her address to the Polish queen, Cassandra died and was given a Venetian state funeral. Cassandra Fedele lived the Renaissance, its opportunities and limitations. She and Laura Cereta were the heirs of Petrarch's humanist movement, but they knew how hard it was to pursue advanced learning in a world that still constrained women to familiar roles. The Italian Renaissance, as lived by Petrarch and Cassandra, was not revolutionary. It was transitional, a world in-between, not quite modern, but not entirely medieval either. The Renaissance was working its own slow, cerebral, and distinctly human way toward something new.

We can visualize this world in transition in a painting by Gentile Bellini. It shows the great square outside of Saint Mark's Cathedral in Venice on April 25, 1444. At the leading edge of the painting we see a procession through the square. The previous day, a wealthy merchant had taken his son to the square, but the boy had fallen down and fractured his skull. He lingered on the edge of death. The next day the brothers of the Confraternity of Saint John, dressed in white, mounted a ritual procession for the soul and recovery of the boy. The brothers bore a relic of the True Cross, while the father, shown in the painting in a brilliant red gown, knelt down in solemn prayer to Saint Mark to save his son. Much of the scene remains medieval (the belief in relics, miraculous cures, religious orders, and prayers to saints), but other elements in the painting seem strangely new: flags fluttering with the civic pride of Venice, citizens milling about in the square oblivious to the ritual taking place in their presence, men and women in idle conversation, and the looming cathedral and ducal palace (to the right). Even to paint the drama of civic life reflected something of the new urban vigor and attitudes toward life and its cultural possibilities that were animating life in the great cities of northern Italy in the fifteenth century.

❋❋❋❋

Any mention of the Renaissance conjures up images of the fascinating notebooks of Leonardo da Vinci, of Michelangelo's gorgeous frescoes in the Sistine Chapel, and of the ruthless politics of the Medici and Borgia dynasties. The Italian Renaissance has long seemed a time of flashing genius, a rush of creativity, and shrewd decision-making. What has been less apparent is that during this glittering period poverty, famine, and disease remained pressing problems; creative men and women struggled to secure financial support from capricious

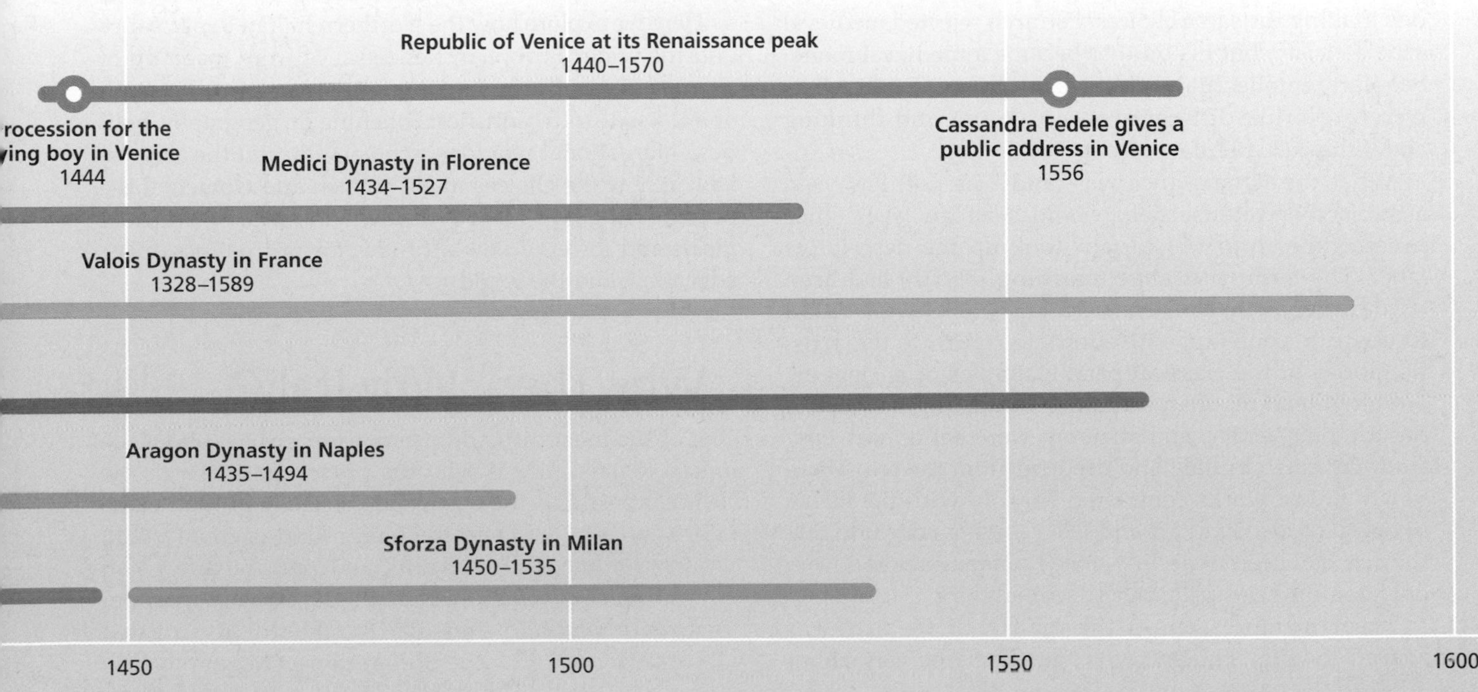

patrons; and relatively few extraordinary men (and only a handful of women) participated in the Renaissance in any meaningful way. The Italian Renaissance achieved remarkable things, but it did not represent a dramatic shift in political, social, or cultural attitudes. It took centuries before most people reaped the benefits of its emphasis on universal education, individual potential, and service to society. Among the privileged few who lived this high cultural moment, hard decisions had to be made: between old and new models of life, between family and the pursuit of individual fame, and between their Christian faith and the allure of ancient and pagan beliefs that was pulling people in different directions.

The Italian Renaissance presented some men and women with a series of choices and opportunities to reimagine the world. A new approach to scholarship and the arts was emerging, one that privileged the distant classical past as a golden age. The result was a form of scholarship known as Renaissance humanism that emphasized the study of the Latin and Greek languages and literatures. In the Renaissance, medieval Christianity as developed over a thousand years (with its emphasis on collective values, humility, and steadfast devotion) remained a powerful shaper of attitudes and actions, but alongside it was a growing emphasis on the importance of the individual in society and of human activity in the world, a drive that began after the plague and the crises of the fourteenth century had shaken the otherworldliness of the High Middle Ages. Caught between the classical and Christian pasts, and between traditional religious beliefs and a new secular emphasis on living in the moment, men and women in the Renaissance were forced to decide how best to move forward. Petrarch's confusion on Mount Ventoux was the confusion of someone torn between the competing ideas and impulses of the age, not sure which way to turn, but fully aware that there were choices, good and bad, to be made. Nor was everyone making the same choices. Petrarch rejected medieval scholasticism, but his brother became a medieval monk. Scholars, intellectuals, politicians, princes, and artists were exploring different ways of living and thinking about the past and the present.

What the Renaissance was (and was not) has been a subject of intense debate and scrutiny ever since nineteenth-century historians took up the descriptive label. The term *renaissance* (meaning rebirth) had been used earlier by the Italian artist and writer Giorgio Vasari to describe contemporary efforts to return to the artistic glories of the classical past. Examples of ancient art and architecture, often revealing a dazzling mastery of design, perspective, and anatomy, were being recovered from the earth in Italy and dredged from the sea. These newly found works contrasted sharply with the iconic imagery of medieval art and led Vasari to conclude that the arts had been in decline since Roman times and were only beginning to regain their former glory.

Vasari's impression of the rebirth of the arts was shared among scholars, who felt the same way about their rediscovery of classical literature. They knew that many works by Greek philosophers and Roman humanists had been lost sight of over the centuries, and that their knowledge of the classical Latin and Greek languages was limited. As Greek scholars and theologians fled the crumbling Byzantine Empire in advance of the Muslim armies of the expanding Ottoman Empire, they carried with them to Italy previously unknown and unstudied texts. Western scholars, like its artists, felt that they were recovering a lost golden age through these precious manuscripts. The study of ancient languages and literatures was tackled with enthusiasm as scholars began the arduous work of translating and deciphering those texts. Cassandra Fedele could speak with pride of the University of Padua as a place where the liberal arts were once again flourishing as they had in ancient Athens. For Cassandra, the past had become present.

Despite the feeling of rebirth among artists and intellectuals, it was not until the nineteenth century that the term *Renaissance* was capitalized and used by historians as a shorthand description for an entire age. The most well-known proponent of the Renaissance was the Swiss historian Jacob Burckhardt, who saw fifteenth-century Italy as a turning point between the darkness of the Middle Ages (the time between the classical past and the Renaissance) and the bright light of modernity. Today few historians see the Renaissance as a radical rupture with the Middle Ages. Nor do they see the Middle Ages as dark, backward, and superstitious. Despite the changes in the way that historians now use the term, Renaissance has remained a widely used label to designate the period from as early as 1350 to as late as 1650, with its core in fifteenth-century Italy, the so-called Quattrocento (the 1400s). The term has its problems, since the Renaissance has no firm starting or ending dates, unfurls at different moments in different parts of Europe, and was experienced fully by only a small, elite segment of the population.

Here we explore how the Northern Italian Renaissance and the wider European Renaissance were made up of a series of small developments between the fourteenth and the sixteenth centuries. Touching on geography, politics, international relations, scholarship, and the arts, we look at how the choices made by men and women of the period shaped an identity based on a return to ancient ideals and fostered new attitudes toward politics, texts, education, and the world.

Why Then, Why Italy?

Why did the Italian Renaissance occur when and where it did?

One of the most difficult questions to answer about the Italian Renaissance is why the preoccupation with the classical past and the associated sense of rebirth came to the foreground of intellectual, cultural, and political life when it did in the northern Italian peninsula? Burckhardt argued that the Renaissance began on the peninsula because "Italy began to teem with personalities," implying that a fortuitous convergence of gifted people in one place was sufficient to explain the changes. Historians are no longer satisfied with that explanation, which seems to take the effects of the Renaissance for its cause; they prefer instead to emphasize the specific and local conditions that fostered the Italian Renaissance.

Some general causes can be identified. The crises of the Late Middle Ages in the first half of the fourteenth century changed Europe, and some of those changes benefited northern Italy. Though Italy was hit hard by the plague, it escaped the poor weather and famine that struck northern Europe. Moreover, threats to the relative stability and prosperity of northern Italy were few in the period from 1350 to 1493. The papacy, which for much of the Middle Ages had constrained the freedom of development and action in Italy, was weakened by the plague, its residence outside of Italy, and the Western or Papal Schism of the Late Middle Ages. Italian cities found that they could, for a time, operate without much papal interference. The German or Holy Roman Empire was also for much of this time weak and unable to interfere in Italian affairs. French kings were busy trying to deal with English invaders, restless nobles, and their own wobbly reigns, all of which left some parts of Italy time to trade and prosper. Cities in the north flourished.

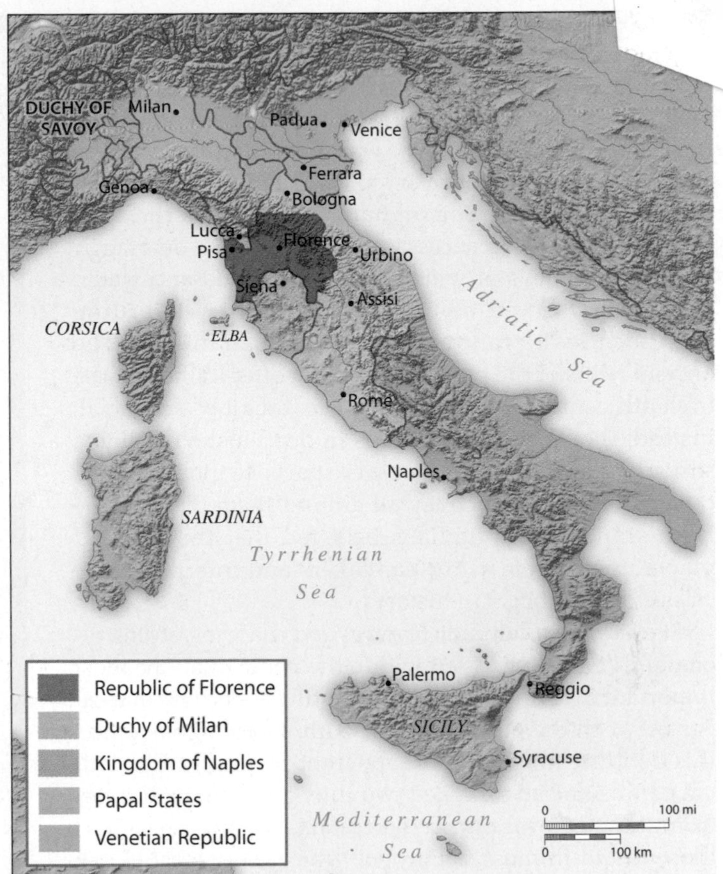

MAP 11.1 | Renaissance Italy, 1454

At the height of the Northern Italian Renaissance, Italy was divided into republics (such as Florence and Venice), a duchy (Milan), and the Papal States cutting across the peninsula. The Kingdom of Naples dominated the south. ***Why did Renaissance Italy separate into the advanced city-states of the north and the more traditional monarchy of the south? What geographic advantages did Venice have? Why was Milan vulnerable to attack and invasion? Why could this balance of powers in Italy not last?***

Geography, Politics, and Society on the Italian Peninsula

The Italy of Petrarch and Cassandra was not a single state, but a diverse region where different languages and dialects were spoken, with different calendars used and different political systems in place. The one thing that distinguished Italy from the rest of Europe in the fourteenth century was the predominance of cities (Map 11.1). Northern Italy was more urban than the rest of Europe, including southern Italy. By 1300, twenty-three northern and central Italian cities had populations over 20,000. The mid-century plague reduced the population of Europe, but left northern Italy still relatively populous. By 1550, forty Italian cities had populations in excess of 10,000 people. Rome had a population of around 45,000; Florence, 60,000; and Venice, 160,000.

Northern Renaissance Italy was dotted with independent city-states (the chief of which were Florence, Venice, Rome, and Milan) where wealth and power were increasingly in the hands of urban elites who, unlike their noble superiors, required relative peace and stability with rival states in order to foster trade and economic development. The peninsula boasted a higher rate of literacy than other parts of Europe at the time, and urban men and women increasingly viewed education as a way to achieve individual glory and to rise to greater heights of prosperity. By the fifteenth century, vernacular education in Italian dialects flourished in classrooms dedicated to educating urban boys and girls in the mathematical and linguistic skills necessary to thrive in the competitive world of business and trade. The city-states of northern Italy were known throughout Europe for their well-developed trading networks, conspicuous consumption, and craftsmen skilled in producing luxury goods such as silk, glass beads, and paintings. This combination of social, economic, and political factors was particular to the region and casts light on why Vasari believed that his age was one of transformation, fueled by intense competition between cities and between people.

Although many differences existed on the peninsula, the region shared some common geographic and historical features. Throughout the peninsula there are steep hills, deep valleys with rivers running through them, and ancient ruins. These features had long been there, of course, but were to prove critical to the developing Renaissance. The hills, for example, made Italian states easier to defend militarily. Cities and towns were almost always built on hills, which afforded a good view of advancing armies and also a clear vantage point from which to shoot at the approaching enemy. The most notable exceptions to this rule were Venice with its lagoon layout and Florence, which was built along one of the peninsula's prominent river valleys. River valleys, which offered more fertile soil and arable land than the adjacent hillsides, were necessary to towns built on craggy overlooks. Valleys provided towns with food and water; their rivers served as transportation arteries leading from the Mediterranean Sea to the Italian interior. The ancient ruins of the peninsula did not offer Italians of the fifteenth century anything that was tangibly beneficial; instead, they grounded Italians in deep history. Italians shared a conviction that they were part of a glorious past, the evidence for which lay all around them. During the Renaissance, many Italians believed that they should play a unique role as the caretakers and interpreters of classical and Christian history.

Despite these common features and concerns, strong regional differences existed within the peninsula. The most important dividing line was—and still is—the one that exists between the north and the south. In the Renaissance, this dividing line was most apparent politically. The Italian peninsula had inherited two chief governmental styles from the medieval period: hereditary kingdoms (such as those found in most of Europe), which were located primarily in the south, and communes, which were found chiefly in the north. Kingdoms were dominated by hereditary elites that provided military power in exchange for economic support in the form of tax revenues and the right to receive a portion of agricultural goods.

The Mercantile and Maritime Prosperity of Venice A ship is being loaded with grain at the port of Venice. The painting by Ambrogio Lorenzetti in the mid-fourteenth century depicts the miracles of Saint Nicholas, who was reputed to have miraculously filled the holds of ships.

Communes consisted of groups of local, powerful men who governed the northern states, many of which were based in a city. During the early medieval period, communes were relatively small, being made up of only about 200–300 individuals in a given area. Between 1198 and 1250, middling landowners, merchants, shopkeepers, and members of trade guilds began to play a larger role in the political life of communes. The growing governing class of these cities produced larger communal bureaucracies and the need to pay city officials whose full-time occupation was to run the government. Expanding communes also led to a growing sense of what is known in Italy as *campanilismo,* the love of the bell-tower of one's birthplace, which can be understood as civic pride and identity. After 1250, many communes began to fall under the influence of powerful local families. Within families and between powerful families there were frequent feuds and murders as ambitious people sought supreme power for themselves. Only one medieval commune, Venice, managed to escape this fate and transformed its commune into an enduring republican form of government.

After years of interference from foreign powers that sought to manipulate the region's political fragmentation to their own advantage, the Italian peninsula emerged in the fifteenth century as a conglomeration of strong independent states. Most Italian states of the time were anchored by flourishing cities—whether it was the Kingdom of Naples of the south; the Papal States that surrounded Rome; the republics of Siena, Florence, Genoa, Lucca, and Venice; or the duchies and counties of Ferrara, Savoy, Milan, and Mantua. Although much of the power base of western Europe still depended on landholding and an economy based on agriculture, the states of the Italian peninsula were coming to depend increasingly on urban centers and their ability to engage in commerce and trade. Italy's merchant economy meant that the states of the peninsula were wealthy by European standards. Surplus wealth was spent on ambitious building projects; on commissions for literary and artistic works; and on territorial expansion through advantageous marriages, diplomacy, and warfare.

The peninsula's dependence on trade for economic survival meant that political leaders needed to keep their desire to make war for territorial gain in balance with their interest in maintaining peace and order to facilitate mercantile activity. Because Italian political elites enjoyed the benefits of both peace and war, they cultivated civic behaviors unlike those of the traditional medieval nobility. These included reading, writing, and debating artistic merit and new ideas. One Florentine historian, Matteo Palmieri, viewed the Italian elite as participating in a new kind of army, one outfitted with pens and paintbrushes rather than swords. Palmieri was grateful that he had been born into an age that was so full of hope and already rejoicing in a greater army of gifted noble souls than the world had seen in a thousand years. Despite the fourteenth-century plague or, perhaps, because of it, Italian elites embraced the future, convinced that they had survived the worst calamity in history and were poised on the brink of a new and wonderful flowering of cultural and historical achievement.

Examining three Renaissance cities and their different styles of political leadership should help highlight what made the Italian peninsula so suited to the growth of Renaissance ideas and ideals. There were many important Italian cities (including, among others, Milan, Naples, Siena, and Urbino) in the fifteenth century, but Rome, Florence, and Venice (to be treated in the next section) stood out to contemporaries and later historians as striking examples of Renaissance politics and culture in action.

Rome: The Popes Return to Prominence

In the medieval period, the ancient city of Rome had always been considered the center of the Papal States, which sprawled diagonally across the middle of the Italian peninsula. Rome was special among the cities of the Italian Renaissance because of its defining relationship with antiquity and the institution of the Catholic Church and papacy. Medieval and Renaissance popes were temporal as well as spiritual leaders, and they depended on the income and power they drew from the Papal States to maintain their relative political autonomy. The Papal States in Italy provided Renaissance popes with agricultural crops, tenants, armies, and merchant enclaves that could be relied on to support and sustain the papacy and its centers of bureaucratic and administrative power at the Vatican and in Rome.

Though smaller than other Renaissance cities, Rome underwent enormous change during the Renaissance. The papacy's removal to Avignon in the fourteenth century had caused Rome's population to decline markedly as hundreds of clerics left the city along with their entourages. A small number of lawyers, doctors, and merchants remained to carve out lives for themselves in Rome, but otherwise there was little industry or commerce. Consequently, by the beginning of the fifteenth century, Rome had a population of only about 25,000 individuals, the majority of whom were still associated with the church.

As the schism of the papacy wound down after 1417, most Europeans probably thought that the city was beyond saving. At that time, gang warfare was rampant between the rival Orsini, Frangipani, and Colonna families; innocent people could not walk the streets for fear of being robbed or murdered; and the artists and minor clergy members who had accompanied the papacy into southern France were only beginning to trickle back to the city in search of patrons and commissions. What was needed to turn the city's fortunes around was the return to prominence of energetic and dynamic popes.

The pope was vitally important to Rome and the center of the peninsula not only as the spiritual leader of the Catholic Church, but also as the temporal ruler of the Papal States. The ideal pope, from the point of view of the city of Rome, was someone present, pragmatic, and sophisticated. The best popes were shrewd politicians who could negotiate and coexist with the Roman nobility, while handling the administrative needs of church and state. The Renaissance popes who guided Rome back to a position of prominence cut splendid, princely figures by supporting art and architecture. Such worldly popes were a boon for Rome. The church, however, often paid the price when its leaders seemed less concerned with spiritual life than with European politics and world affairs.

The first pope to return the papacy permanently to Rome was Martin V (1417–1431), whose abilities as a statesman made it possible for him to repair some of the damage done to Rome and the Papal States during the long Avignon absence and troublesome schism. A native Roman and a member of the powerful Colonna family, he was ideally suited to manage the city's difficult political climate, even though charges of nepotism threatened to bring about his ruin on more than one occasion. Martin thought that Rome could and should reestablish itself as one of Europe's premier cities by becoming a center for the arts and scholarship. His successor Pope Eugenius IV (1431–1447) was an important opponent of the Council of Basel and of conciliarism in general.

Nicholas V (1447–1455), the first post-schism pope, followed Martin's lead by focusing on the renovation of Rome. One of his pet projects was to establish a grand papal library. By 1481, the Vatican Library had one of the largest collections of books in the west with over 3,500 volumes. Pope Nicholas commissioned scribes to copy special editions of rare texts, which were then bound in distinctive red bindings closed with silver clasps. For all his interest in architecture and scholarship, Nicholas also proved to be a strong political leader. He survived an attempted coup during the Porcari Conspiracy of 1453, when native Romans tried to restore the ancient republican form of government to the Papal States. His successors were a mixed lot. Pope Pius II (1458–1464, born Aeneas Silvius Piccolomini), who while in office wrote an account of his life, was learned and committed to the good of the church. But Pope Sixtus IV (1471–1484) was plagued by charges of gross corruption and of being more interested in indulging in political intrigue than in looking after the church.

Pope Alexander VI (1492–1503) possessed elements of both predecessors. Like Pius II, he was a great promoter of education and learning. But like the pontificate of Sixtus IV, his was overshadowed by his colorful personal life and dynastic scheming. Born into the noble Spanish-Italian Borgia family, Alexander was always an outsider in Rome. His position worsened when he tried to use his church office to place members of his family in positions of power and influence throughout Europe. His publicly acknowledged mistress, Vannozza Catanei, bore him four children, including the infamous Cesare and Lucrezia. Cesare Borgia (1476–1507) made the pope's family name synonymous with greed, treachery, and murder. Cesare was rumored to have arranged more than 250 murders in the city of Rome, including those of his elder brother and his sister's second husband. Made an unlikely cardinal at the age of fourteen through his father's political maneuverings, Cesare ultimately left the church to take a more active role in family politics and was eventually assassinated.

Popes such as Martin V, Nicholas V, and Alexander VI focused new attention (both positive and negative) on Rome, and the city began to revive. Tourism, industry, trade, and banking began to thrive, bringing new economic opportunities and wealth to Romans. Pilgrims flooded into the city each spring to visit the center of western Christianity, leading to housing shortages, inflation, and epidemic disease. Despite these pressing urban problems, Pope Nicholas declared a "Jubilee Year" in 1450 to encourage still more pilgrims to visit Rome. Over 100,000 people flooded into the city, so many that the balustrades of the main bridge over the Tiber collapsed and over two hundred people were trampled to death or fell into the river and drowned.

Living the High Life in Renaissance Rome

In addition to the tourists, clergymen, and bankers, Rome had a thriving entertainment industry, and chief among it were the courtesans, who were famed for their refined tastes and great beauty. Many of these women adopted classical names and saw themselves as heirs to the ancient Roman tradition of imperial courtesans. During the pontificate of Alexander, Roman courtesans experienced their own golden age of prominence and patronage, holding elaborate salons and posing for famous artists. One of the most popular and famous courtesans of the period was Imperia, who lived like a princess. She had a palatial home filled with carpets from the east, embroidered gold tapestries, and antiquities discovered in Roman soil. Imperia was exceptionally successful, and her notoriety and that of other courtesans made them a famous or infamous feature of Roman life. Evidence suggests that in 1500 as much as a tenth of the city's population was made up of courtesans, prostitutes, and their operatives. By 1566, so large a proportion of the city's population was connected to the prostitution trade, and so much of the city's taxable wealth was tied up in the leisure industry, that it proved difficult for reform-minded popes to dislodge the courtesans without risking the collapse of the urban economy.

The Political Landscape of Florence

Rome was unique on the Italian peninsula because of its association with the classical and Christian pasts, but Florence stood out during the fifteenth century because of its vigorous mercantile activity and enormous wealth. One contemporary observed that a Florentine who was not a merchant had no standing or respect among his fellow citizens. To be rich in Florence was to be honorable and powerful, and nowhere in Renaissance Europe was the desire to acquire wealth more pronounced.

Florence's rulers tried to maintain a delicate balance between urban professionals, craftsmen, and businessmen, who brought economic power and prestige to the city, and the hereditary nobility of the region. Throughout the medieval period, Florence struggled to check the development of family factions such as those that were found among the Roman nobility, but political instability was the norm. Around 1300, Dante said that Florence was like a sick woman, tossing and turning on her plush bed, unable to find a comfortable position in which to lie. During times of crisis, Florence's government became more oligarchic as wealthy merchants and nobles worked to preserve the republic in the face of an increasingly frustrated and anxious populace. Despite the growing influence of noble families and prominent individuals on Florentine politics, the city's life was still dominated in the fifteenth century by the twenty-one guilds that oversaw all business dealings. Among them were seven major guilds (led by the lawyers, wool-makers, and bankers) and fourteen minor guilds. Although the guilds dominated political and economic life in Florence, 75 percent of the city's population did not belong to any guild at all.

Florence's oligarchic government was led by a nine-member committee called the *Signoria.* All members of the city guilds who were male and over thirty years of age were eligible to serve on the *Signoria* for a two-month term. Each person on the *Signoria* was selected at random from among guild members, their names picked out of a leather bag. During a two-month term of service, the members of the *Signoria* moved into the central Palazzo della Signoria in Florence so that they could be available at any hour for city business; they also received a paid salary to keep them from being distracted by their own business concerns and enjoyed the assistance of a dedicated staff. There were two chief problems with the *Signoria.* First, like most representative bodies, the quality of the *Signoria* and its ability to rule varied widely, depending on its members. Second, although the process seemed democratic, in reality the most prominent and wealthy Florentine families were able to keep the names of eligible men out of the bags, rigging the selection process to ensure that their own people were chosen to serve.

The Medici family rose to prominence due to its place among the urban elite and prominent role in the *Signoria*. The patriarch of the family, Giovanni di Bicci de' Medici, belonged to the powerful wool and banking guilds; he built his family's vast fortune first on the cloth trade and then on the careful management and investment of the profits. Giovanni founded the Medici bank in Florence, and it eventually had bank offices in most of the important cities of Europe, including Rome, Venice, Naples, London, Bruges, Geneva, and Paris. Giovanni de' Medici's friendship with the anti-pope John XXIII established the family as the papacy's bankers for decades. With the papacy's money in hand, the Medici were able to invest it at a profit for themselves rather than its depositor. The Medici and Florence were at the forefront of the formative development of banking. Using Arabic numerals (rather than the more clumsy Roman numerals), bankers in Florence were better able to keep track of money, profits and losses, and investments. They also were among the first to use double-entry bookkeeping (as first described by Luca Pacioli), a system that records transactions as credits and debits on different sides of the ledger or book.

The Medici Dynasty and Its Cultural Clients In Botticelli's painting *The Adoration of the Magi* (1475), the Medici and their cultural and political circle are active participants in the scene. Three Medici have taken on the roles of the magi: Cosimo de' Medici (long dead) as the old magus kneeling before Mary, Piero de' Medici as the second magus in red cloak kneeling at the center, Giovanni de' Medici as the third magus in white kneeling to his right, and Lorenzo de' Medici standing with the red and black garment. The artist may be the figure in yellow at the far right.

The Medici success in business led to its political prominence in Florence. As a non-noble family, the Medici were viewed as upstarts by Florence's hereditary elites, but the Medici proved that it was possible for people to rise above the conditions of their birth. The Medici accomplished that by amassing power based on their wealth and shrewd political deals rather than on hereditary power.

From Medici Munificence to Magnificence

In addition to advancing a new style of rule, the Medici staunchly supported Renaissance cultural and intellectual pursuits, and under their influence the city of Florence came to be one of Italy's leading centers of scholarship and the arts. The first member of the family to achieve civic prominence was Cosimo de' Medici (1389–1464), the wealthiest man in Florence. Educated at a local monastery, Cosimo was particularly adept at foreign languages, being fluent in German, French, and Latin. He also had some mastery of Hebrew, Greek, and Arabic, leading Pope Pius II to describe him condescendingly as "more lettered than merchants usually are." When Cosimo began exercising his authority in 1434, the *Signoria* was in disarray and the city was slipping into decline. Cosimo stepped into the void and began to supervise the government of Florence, using his money to exert his influence over Florentine society. He excelled in the arts of negotiation, preferring to buy support or to manipulate events behind the scenes rather than to wage showy, but expensive, wars. His support came from the loyalty of his power base among ordinary citizens, whose allegiance he cultivated by implementing a policy of upward mobility, promoting members of the lower orders into positions of power rather than relying on the hereditary nobility.

Cosimo de' Medici was the most powerful and wealthiest man in Florence, but he maintained a modest and reserved demeanor. His approach to leadership was based on munificence: he was generous with his money and influence, not only among his family, but also among Florentine society at large. His style of rule was therefore strikingly different from that of the hereditary nobility, because he preferred to work within the existing political system of Florence to achieve his objectives, rather than undermining it. No one in Florence, however, doubted who was in charge.

Cosimo's grandson, Lorenzo de' Medici (1440–1492), known as "the Magnificent," rose to power in 1469 after

CHRONOLOGY	The Fortunes and Misfortunes of the Medici Family in Florence
DATE	**EVENT**
1300s	Medici family members active in the wool-makers' guild
1396–1400	Medici involved in political plots, banned from political activity
c. 1397	Giovanni di Bicci de' Medici founds the Medici bank in Florence
1434–1464	Cosimo de' Medici, son of Giovanni, runs bank, governs Florence
1464–1469	Piero I de' Medici, son of Cosimo, an invalid often ill with gout
1469–1491	Lorenzo I de' Medici, son of Piero, neglects bank, governs Florence
1478	Pazzi Conspiracy attempts to assassinate Lorenzo, kills his brother
1490–1497	Savonarola in Florence
1492–1494	Piero II de' Medici, son of Lorenzo
1494	Medici bank goes out of business
1494	Bonfire of the Vanities in the central square of Florence
1494–1512	Medici expelled from Florence
1513	Machiavelli, in exile, writes *The Prince*
1523–1535	Giulio de' Medici, nephew of Lorenzo, becomes Pope Clement VII

his father Piero's death. As a child, Lorenzo had been intellectually precocious and showed from an early age the diplomatic and political skill for which his grandfather Cosimo had been so famous. From the age of fifteen, Lorenzo conducted diplomatic missions for his father and participated in the backroom politics of Florence. Lorenzo was not, however, as keen to respect and follow tradition as his grandfather had been, and his unusual marriage to a woman not of Florentine birth, the Roman noblewoman Clarice Orsini, proved to be a diplomatic and public relations disaster. Lorenzo had hoped that his alliance with the Orsini family would secure his family's fortunes with Rome and the papacy, hopes that were dashed when the scheming Pope Sixtus IV backed the leaders of the Pazzi Conspiracy in 1478. The Pazzi sought to overthrow the Medici family by assassinating Lorenzo, but succeeded only in assassinating his brother and unleashing Medici anger upon the conspirators and the church that had supported them. Though this sequence of events forced Florence and Rome into bitter hostility for years, it did not hurt Lorenzo's status in the city, and by the time of his death he was regarded as the virtual king of Florence.

The Bonfire of the Vanities

Lorenzo, for all his ostentation, was neither as charismatic nor as capable as Cosimo had been. He was unable to see the value of munificence as a political strategy and turned instead to showy magnificence as a way to impress Florentines and achieve greater influence over the political life of the city. Lorenzo's showiness ultimately turned the tide of public opinion against the Medici and contributed to the rise of an unlikely, but spellbinding religious adversary, Girolamo Savonarola. A physician's grandson and the son of a failed merchant, Savonarola had attended the University of Ferrara before becoming a Dominican friar. The Dominicans or "hounds of the Lord," as they were known in the Renaissance, helped Savonarola to craft an image of himself as a knight fighting in the service of Christ. Savonarola prepared for this life by studying biblical and medieval scholastic texts and preaching to growing audiences. Women, in particular, were drawn to his sermons, despite Savonarola's belief that women should play only a minor role in religious life. He also attracted intellectuals such as the young Pico della Mirandola and the artist Sandro Botticelli, who gave up painting as a result. In 1485, Savonarola revealed that he had been given the gift of prophecy and had been called upon to preach a message of penitence and reform to the people. At the suggestion of a leading humanist who was under Savonarola's intellectual and spiritual spell, Lorenzo made a critical mistake and chose to summon the friar to Florence in 1490. In Florence, Savonarola developed a loyal following called the *Piagnoni* ("the snivelers" or "big cry babies") because of their constant weeping over the fate of the world.

On a chilly winter day in December 1494, Savonarola declared that the Florentines had been chosen by God to receive salvation, but his claim came at the expense of the autocratic regime of the Medici family. Clandestine meetings between Savonarola and the land-hungry French king, Charles VIII, led to the elaborately engineered expulsion and enforced exile of the Medici family.

Savonarola's own star was already in decline when he convinced his followers to burn their books, paintings, cosmetics, and Florence's famous luxury goods in the main governmental square, the Piazza della Signoria. The event became known as the **Bonfire of the Vanities,** a vivid conflagration that consumed the idle material trappings of exuberant Florentine life. But in the spring of 1497, the youth of Florence, tired of Savonarola's efforts to stamp out the urban pleasures of drinking and gambling, rioted in the streets. Sensing that the winds were blowing against the Dominican preacher, Pope Alexander VI excommunicated Savonarola just nine days after the riot. Arrested by an angry mob, he was tortured and burned alive in the same piazza where he had presided over the bonfire. Florence, again a functioning republic, soon returned to its typical style of politics and self-promotion and the Savonarola episode seemed but a bad dream.

Machiavelli's Cold Eye

The political theorist Niccolò Machiavelli (1469–1527) served as the second chancellor (or secretary) of Florence under the Medici (of whom he could be critical) and as an ambassador to France for the restored Republic of Florence after the fall of the Medici. He also worked to improve the Florentine militia, but when the republican government of Florence was overthrown in 1512, he found himself out of work, and was arrested and tortured. In prison, he was dropped six times on a rope tied to his wrists, which were bound behind his back. Later he retreated to his country estate, where in 1513 he wrote the infamous *The Prince,* in which, with a calculating and cold eye, he describes and praises the often ruthless political style of the Medici and lauds the shrewdness of Cesare Borgia. *The Prince* so shocked contemporaries for its candor, cold-bloodedness, and seeming amorality that some people thought it a satire.

The Bonfire of Savonarola In the same square where the Bonfire of the Vanities happened, the Dominican friar Savonarola and two of his Dominican supporters were executed by the citizens of Florence in 1498. The three men were hung first and then the pyre was set aflame, both to send them to hell and to eliminate their bodies lest relics remain. The men carrying bundles of wood to the fire underline the public support for the execution.

Medieval political treatises had been devoted to teaching future princes how to be good and pleasing to God. Machiavelli wanted to teach princes how to survive and operate successfully without reference to what was right or pleasing to God. Medieval political theorists assumed the existence of evil, but preached the good and godly. Machiavelli assumed the existence of human political realities and advised princes how to manage them. His political examples are chiefly ancient and modern (with few medieval), but they do include the non-Christian Ottomans. Machiavelli was a strikingly systematic political thinker, as he proceeded logically toward provable conclusions, but he was also a man of his time: he believed that comets foretell the future, that history is cyclical, and that infantry armies composed of citizens, as in the Roman Republic, were the most effective military force. He also dreamed of the unification of Italy and dedicated his work to a younger generation of the Medici in the hope that they would emulate the family's great rulers,

Niccolò Machiavelli Diplomat, statesman, and political theorist, Machiavelli was also a politician in Florence and advocated such schemes as a republican militia made up of citizens.

WHAT A DIFFERENCE A YEAR MAKES

1527 and the Sack of Rome

For almost two hundred years, the Italian peninsula was free of direct foreign interference and invasion, which meant that its small city-states were, in relative terms, evenly matched and free to explore their commercial, cultural, and political opportunities. Ludovico Sforza, the regent of Milan, observed in early 1494 that Italy was like a duck pond, in which each duck swims in circles, unconcerned with the other ducks: the Venetians hide, the Florentines joust, the Milanese hunt, the pope makes cardinals, and the king creates counts. He feared the ruin that would fall on all if they did not awaken from their self-centered sleep. For twenty years, various cities such as Naples, Milan, and Florence had suffered from severe political instability. By destabilizing Florence and its resident rulers, the Savonarola affair was one of the events that invited foreign intrusion. Savonarola looked to the intervention of the French to tip the balance of power in Italy in his favor. In September 1494, King Charles VIII of France did just that. With an army of 32,000 men, he crossed the Alps and marched on Naples, which he took in February. Not the peoples of Italy, but other European countries rose in resistance, forming a Holy League to expel the French invader. A year later, Charles was back in France, driven out of Italy by disease and the armies of the emperor and king of Spain. But the door had been opened to foreign interference, and for the next thirty years Italy was a playground for contests between the French and Spanish. In 1499, King Louis XII of France laid claim to Milan and seized it from the Sforza dynasty and Ferdinand of Aragon took southern Italy, so that by 1500 the French dominated the north and the Spanish the south of Italy.

No wonder Machiavelli viewed politics in such coldly realistic terms. Artists deserted Florence for more peaceful and prosperous cities. Botticelli left an inscription from 1500 on his painting of the *Mystic Nativity,* which he said he had completed in Italy's time of troubles, likening the age to the one predicted by Revelation when the devil would be loosed upon the world. Italy's troubles after the foreign invasion of 1494 were ones that revealed the fundamental weakness of small states in a world of new and more powerful European monarchs, and there was no easy fix. By the early sixteenth century, Rome was the chief patron of the arts in Italy. Leonardo and Raphael had worked there under papal commission, and Michelangelo had finished painting the ceiling of the Sistine Chapel by 1512. The 1520s was a trying time for Italy: disease, famine, and the sack of cities such as Genoa, Milan, Naples, and Florence. Worse befell Rome. In 1527, in a dispute with the French king and the pope, the emperor Charles V ordered the taking of Rome. The troops that did so, poorly paid and refusing to follow orders, ransacked Rome, burned down buildings, murdered thousands, held cardinals and rich Romans for ransom, and tortured others to reveal where their money was hidden. The economy of the city collapsed, the pope fled into exile, and the brutalized population of Rome fell by half over the next several years. It was the end of Rome's cultural renaissance and, in some ways, a symbol that the Italian Renaissance was finished, since Italy could no longer manage its own affairs.

QUESTIONS | ***How did the situation of Renaissance Italy parallel that of classical Greece, in both its cultural achievements and its political vulnerabilities? Did the Italian Renaissance end in 1494 or 1527, or had it already transformed into something else?***

restore Medici power, and, perhaps, return Machiavelli to government once again (see Back to the Source at the end of the chapter).

West and East in the Renaissance

One of Cosimo de' Medici's most significant political triumphs came in 1439, when he successfully lobbied to have a General Council of the Roman Catholic and Greek or Eastern Orthodox Churches meet in Florence. Four centuries of doctrinal differences and historical friction had kept apart these two branches of the Christian church (in the Great or East-West Schism), but with the Muslim Ottoman Empire gaining strength in the eastern Mediterranean, reconciliation seemed prudent and no one was better at high and low negotiations than Cosimo.

Why was Venice special?

The eastern ambassadors and clergymen from the Byzantine Empire made a lasting impression on Florence. Emperor John Paleologus, the Eastern Orthodox patriarch Joseph II, and over seven hundred delegates with long, impressive beards, opulent clothes, and complicated headdresses walked the city's streets with their African and Mongol servants in tow. The artists Gentile da Fabriano and Benozzo Gozzoli painted images of the exotic visitors on canvases and frescoes, where they appear

Cosmopolitan Headgear Benozzo Gozzoli's painting *Procession of the Magi* (1459) shows a variety of different head coverings, including the eastern headdress of the three bearded magi. The artist is the figure wearing the turban with an inscription.

as the Magi from the east, bringing gifts to the infant Christ. When a doctrinal compromise was finally brokered between the leaders of the two Christian churches in the summer of 1439, it was trumpeted as reuniting east and west. "Let the heavens rejoice and the earth exult," Patriarch Joseph proclaimed, "for the wall that divided the western and eastern churches has fallen." The religious divide had not, of course, been repaired and the council did not prevent the fall of Constantinople in 1453, but the proclamation sounded good and awakened deeper cultural interest, east and west.

Western Europe had long been fascinated by the exotic wonders of the East. Crusaders brought back stories of Constantinople's wealth and of strange spices and aromatic foods unknown in Basel, Florence, and London. Soldiers returned to the West with silks, relics, and a taste for sugar. The fifteenth-century Italian Renaissance also recognized that the East possessed an unrivaled knowledge of ancient Greek culture, which was important to its own growing critical appreciation of classical civilization. Eastern clothing, food, and literature were fashionable in the Renaissance, so much so that Pope Alexander VI had his son and daughter painted wearing Turkish costumes. Despite the attraction of things eastern to those in the west, the relationship between east and west was tense, with deep ideological and theological divisions and memories of a troubled past, particularly the imposition of the Latin Empire of Constantinople in the thirteenth century. These tensions, however, should not obscure the strong economic ties and regular social contacts that persisted, despite struggles over belief and territory.

Venice, City of Banks, Ships, and Republican Ease

Venice played a critical role in connecting east and west, both commercially and culturally. Venice's singularity came from its geographic location and status as the only true republic in Italy. Known as *La Serenissima* ("the most serene one"), Venice steadfastly resisted the pressures of invading armies and navies, and the territorial ambitions of nearby despotic leaders, without giving in to the lure of being ruled by a single, charismatic figure. As a result of its republican ease, Venice had no popes or Medici princes to engage our historical attention.

During the High Middle Ages and the Renaissance, Venice evolved from a relatively small and remote urban enclave on a lagoon into a bustling gateway between west and east with colonies that extended across the Adriatic and into the Mediterranean (Map 11.2). The only medieval city of any significance not surrounded by walls, Venice was instead encircled by waterways that were navigable but that shielded the city from direct armed attacks by military forces on horseback or on foot. Venice's position on the northeastern edge of Italy gave it the ability to participate in and eventually dominate Adriatic and Mediterranean trade. Its geographic location made Venice a cultural and economic force in European life.

The economic power of Venice was symbolized by its relatively stable currency, which enabled Renaissance merchants to trade money for goods in distant ports. More Venetian money was in circulation during the Renaissance than that of any other western European power, and from 1400 to 1460 the republic had more of its money in circulation than the kingdoms of England and France combined. A Venetian ducat was recognized throughout the Mediterranean world because the republic's government made sure that it always contained the same amount of precious metal. Venetian currency set the standard for most other currencies, and in 1425 Cairo debased its gold currency to bring it into line with that of Venice.

With so much money on hand, Venice had to devise new methods to store and protect it. Venice and not Florence was the first state in Europe to establish banks, which at first were seen simply as secure warehouses for money. Banks in fact take their name from the benches (*banchi*) set up in the center of Venice on the Rialto Bridge over the Grand Canal, where people with surplus cash to invest went to meet with individuals who had projects in need of funds. Once deals were struck, Venetians faced another problem: how to get those funds across the European continent or across the hazardous

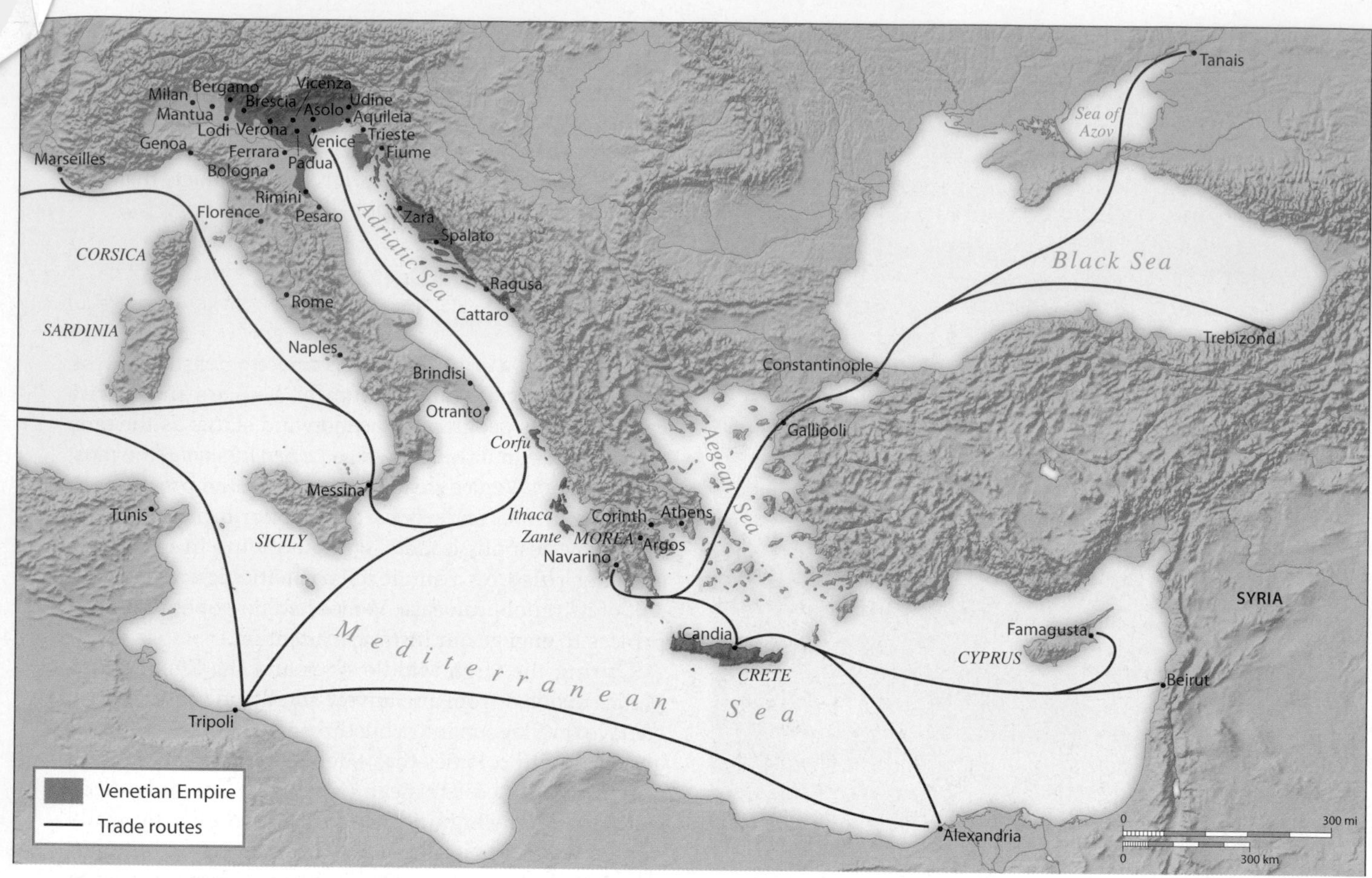

MAP 11.2 | The Commercial and Cultural Reach of Venice in the Fifteenth Century
In the fifteenth century, the Republic of Venice reached commercially across the Mediterranean, trading with centers as far east as Tanais on the Sea of Azov. ***Why did its geographic location enable Venice to dominate trade in the Mediterranean world? How did it support its trading operations? Why was Venice destined to be not just an aggressive trading state, but one that facilitated cultural exchanges?***

Mediterranean Sea. Because transporting cash was too dangerous, Venetian banks began to issue letters of credit to their clients. When Venetian merchants wished to import paper from China through middlemen in Syria without worrying about bandits or blockades, they carried letters of credit from a Venetian bank to a bank agent in Syria, who turned over the sum of money stipulated by the credit agreement.

Venice's trading success depended not only on the stability of the republic's currency, but also on its technical and military expertise as represented by another symbol of the city, the **Arsenal.** Located at the mouth of Venice's Grand Canal, the Arsenal equipped and repaired the republic's warships and its merchant vessels. During the Renaissance, the Arsenal had one of Europe's first industrial-style production lines, where hundreds of workers labored with saws, hammers, and brushes. The Arsenal featured prominently in the popular images of Venice. In the *Inferno,* Dante described it as a place of bubbling pitch and stifling heat. Inside the Arsenal, a warship could be completely built and outfitted in twenty-four hours, a remarkable achievement made possible because of the mobilization of a large number of skilled workers. Some five thousand workers were employed at the Arsenal at any given moment during the Renaissance, each one with specific skills. In one of the Arsenal's buildings, people made nothing but rope; in another, men and women made sails for the fleet.

The ships outfitted and repaired at the Arsenal were a point of Venetian pride and an example of Venetian ingenuity. The Venetians introduced the **galley** to western Europe, a unique vessel (between 120 and 150 feet long, carrying a crew of 100–200 men) employed for transporting cargo and conducting naval warfare. What made the galley special was its dual power system: it could travel under oar or sail power. When there was no wind or when the galley was leaving or entering a port, rowers propelled the ship forward. The majority of rowers on Venetian galleys were not slaves, but free men hired for the voyage. When the galley was farther out at sea and enjoying favorable winds, the oars were pulled in and the sails were raised.

The third symbol of Venice was the *Libro dell'Oro* (*Book of Gold*), a list of two hundred Venetian families compiled in 1297. The Venetians selected their political leaders from men over age twenty-five who could trace their lineage directly from one of the family names listed in the *Libro* and were therefore automatically accorded lifetime membership in Venice's Great Council. The Great Council was used as a pool for constituting governmental subcommittees such as the Senate (which instituted policies), the College (which put Senate policies into action), and the Council of Ten (which oversaw Venice's security). Presiding over all these committees was the **doge,** the chief official selected to serve the republic for the remainder of his lifetime by a system so complicated that it was difficult for one family to control the process, although many old Venetian families managed to influence it. The doge's functions were largely ceremonial: he opened buildings, presided over Venetian ceremonies, and entertained visiting ambassadors. With a governmental apparatus so wide reaching and complex, Venice's political system limited the loopholes that could be exploited by a single family, as the Medici had done in Florence.

Venice's unique position, successful trade operations, and strong republican politics made careful diplomacy essential to the maintenance of Venetian serenity. Secure peace was as important to Venice's success in the world as its currency or the ships that departed from the Arsenal. In the Middle Ages, diplomacy had been a recognized but underused form of political interaction. Most nobles preferred to go to war rather than to sit and negotiate, and most medieval diplomatic negotiations came at the tail end of warfare when agreements had to be made about the division of territory and titles, and the marriage of noble children. Renaissance Venice preferred to exhaust diplomatic channels before undertaking a war. Ambassadors from Venice were among the first resident diplomats to take up positions at courts throughout Europe and the eastern Mediterranean. By 1500, virtually every royal court in Europe, northern Africa, and Asia Minor had a resident Venetian ambassador who attempted to keep the peace between the republic and its mercantile and military rivals.

In their own ways, Rome, Florence, and Venice were each archetypal Renaissance cities. Interested in the ancient past, intent on charting a new course for their city-states in European politics and culture, devoted to the Roman Catholic faith, intrigued by the cultural traditions of other peoples, and eager to participate in the new secular possibilities of trade, finance, and exploration, these cities were vital, vibrant, and competitive urban centers during a period of cultural and political transition.

The Colonial Reach of Venice

None of the great Renaissance city-states had greater geographic reach than Venice. It achieved security and prosperity by expanding its territorial holdings along the northeastern tip of the Italian peninsula, around the Adriatic coastline, and toward Asia Minor. Venice won many of those territories from the Ottoman Turks, who had launched a campaign to extend their territories into western Europe. In 1414, Venice defeated an Ottoman army at Gallipoli and went on to conquer Morea, Cyprus, and Crete. Despite these victories, the republic of Venice was almost constantly in conflict with Ottoman forces in the fifteenth century and struggled to remain the preeminent power of the central Mediterranean and Adriatic Seas.

Renaissance Venice was also the port city through which most eastern goods, peoples, and ideas flowed west. Venice was the only European nation at the time with colonies, a string of small islands extending toward Asia Minor that, along with a block of territory at the very top of the peninsula, made up the maritime republic of Venice. Venice's colonies served important commercial and military functions, for they made it easier for the republic to protect vital sea lanes through which its goods and naval forces traveled. The colonies also made it easier to provision merchant and naval ships because they could dock at Venetian ports on their way east. Venice's early colonizing efforts, along with its long-standing relations with the Byzantine Empire and other political entities in the Adriatic, Black, and Mediterranean Seas, set the republic apart from the other states of Italy.

The Ottoman Empire as a Renaissance State

One of Venice's most important trading links was with the Ottoman Empire. The Ottomans, a frontier people, had established their power along the Aegean coast (Map 11.3). They absorbed different elements from the traditions of Islamic civilization, the Byzantine Empire based in Constantinople, and the Seljuk Empire of western Anatolia. Though officially rooted in the Muslim faith, the Ottomans tolerated other "peoples of the book"—Christians and Jews—living within their borders. They viewed the followers of Muhammad, Christ, and Moses as branches of a single family tree.

Still there were considerable differences in religious interpretation and historical mission between the West and East, and within their territories. Western Christian rulers had expelled or, in the case of Spain, were about to expel Jews and Muslims from their lands. The Ottomans had conquered Greece and imposed higher taxes on Jewish and Christian residents and barred Jews and Christians from wearing certain types of clothing and adornment. A case could be made that the Ottoman Empire was more cosmopolitan and tolerant than western Europe was at the time. The Ottomans, for instance, were willing to allow religious minorities to coexist with the Sunni Muslim majority, and they employed Jews and Christians to help them rule their multiethnic empire. It was not unusual to find Jews among the sultan's advisors, Christian merchants in Ottoman cities, or western military experts supplying tools and techniques to the Ottoman army and navy. Mahomet II hired Christians from Greece and from the Italian port cities of Venice and Genoa to build ships for his navy. A Hungarian engineer

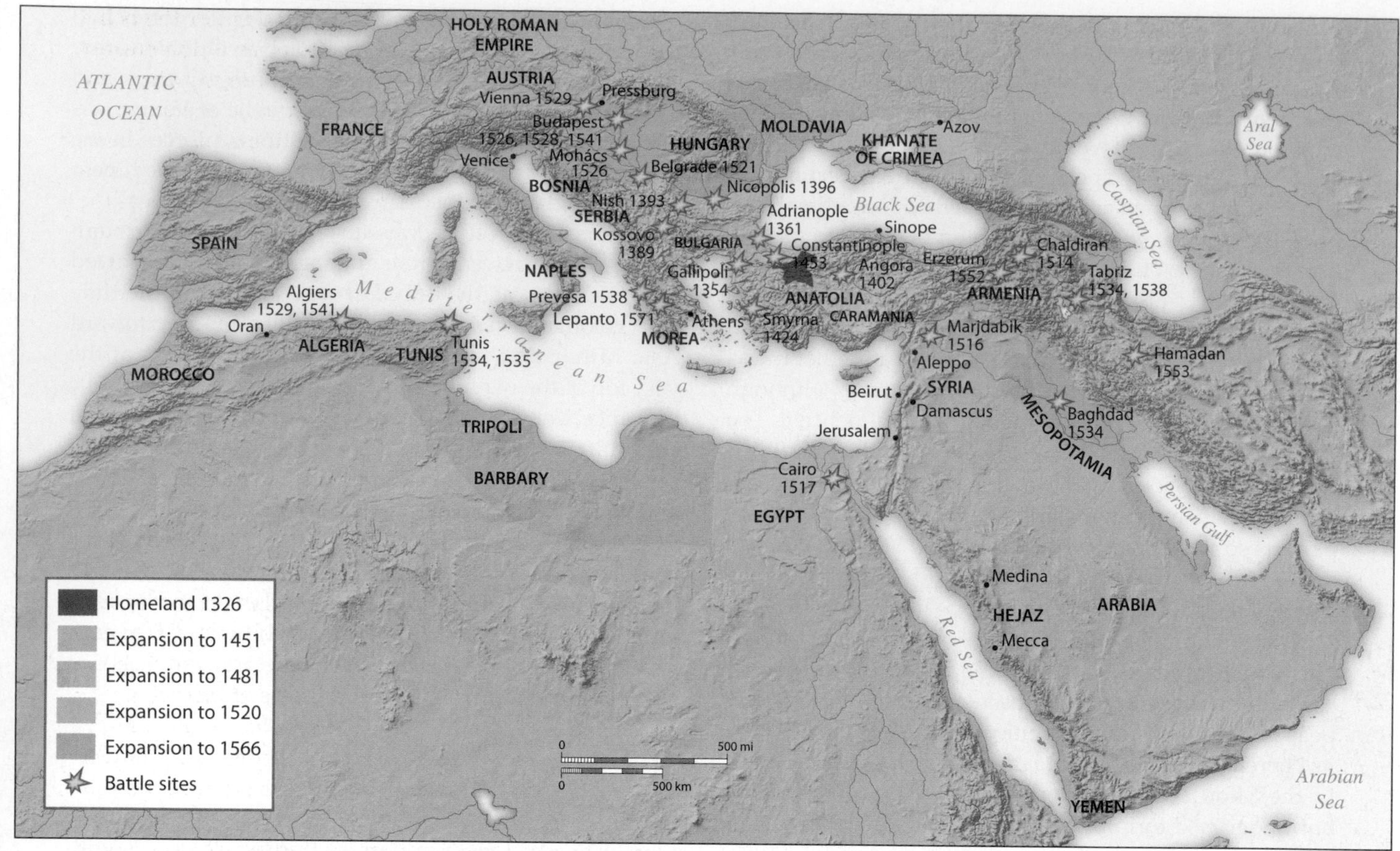

MAP 11.3 | **The Spread of the Ottoman Empire, 1326–1566**

The Ottoman Empire was a powerful presence in the Mediterranean world, controlling access to the east and managing goods from Asia moving west. The effect on western Europeans was to block their own eastward movement, essentially boxing them in. The Ottomans arose in the shadow cast by Constantinople, first conquering lands that had belonged to the Byzantine Empire, then moving into the Middle East, northern Africa, and eastern Europe. ***Why was the Byzantine Empire no match for the Ottomans, geographically or historically? How did Venice deal with the Ottoman presence? What was the likely long-term impact of the Ottoman Empire on the many Europes of the late fifteenth and early sixteenth centuries?***

provided Mahomet with the designs for the large cannon with which he took Constantinople in 1453. Mahomet, with his cosmopolitan city, foreign advisors, trade with Europe, interest in Greek culture, and ability to speak six languages, was in his own way a Renaissance prince.

Renaissance Cosmopolitanism in Big Europe

The cultural mixing and blending that was a hallmark of the Ottoman Empire affected western Europeans as well as the Turks. In the increasingly cosmopolitan world of the Mediterranean, it was not unusual for Italian princes and merchants to own slaves they had acquired through Venetian middlemen from Istanbul and other Ottoman ports. Both Cosimo de' Medici and his son, Giovanni de' Medici, purchased Circassian slaves in Venice to be their mistresses. Andrea Gritti, a Venetian nobleman who was elected doge in 1523, had a wife and son at home and four more sons in Istanbul who had been born to a faithful Turkish mistress who served as his official hostess and partner while he was conducting business and diplomatic missions in the city. Merchants often lived for significant portions of their adult lives in eastern cities. One such merchant, Lorenzo Contarini, lived in Damascus in 1437, Beirut in 1440, and Syria between 1451 and 1455. Cosmopolitan contacts of this sort brought West and East closer together, expanding the cultural footprint of Europe.

An additional connection was made by Greek and Italian intellectuals. Scholars in the Byzantine Empire and Italy believed that they shared a tradition of Greek and Latin philosophy and letters that stretched back to antiquity. When Constantinople fell to the Ottoman Turks, Byzantine scholars were quick to lament what they viewed as the final collapse of Greek civilization. Some of them fled west with their rare manuscripts and fluent command of the Greek language, and were received warmly in Italy by a growing critical mass of humanist scholars.

Venice was the most exotic city in Europe. The city's cosmopolitan residents and their enormous wealth were celebrated in works of art and scholarship. Venetian architecture is the best example of its exotic, hybrid culture since it blends western European, Muslim, and Byzantine styles. The city's buildings often included minarets, towers, and elaborate decorative details. These buildings provided an exotic backdrop for the lavish public ceremonies and celebrations that glorified Venetian life and the republic. The diversity of Venetian life and commerce was enhanced by its large population of Jews. The Jews of Venice were known for their learning, their wealth, and their language skills, all of which were important attributes in a cosmopolitan center as rich as Venice's. Venetian Jews attended beautiful synagogues in the city, and even the doges visited them to hear the rabbis speak about education and faith.

Humanism and Individualism

> **What was Italian Renaissance humanism, and how important and transformative was it?**

The city-states of northern Italy established the material and political conditions for the Italian Renaissance. Its defining feature, however, has always seemed to be the remarkable flowering of high culture that occurred as a result of prosperity. Yet Petrarch, the father of humanism, began the movement outside Italy. The Middle Ages had always had a strong humanist tradition of interest in the Latin classics, most pronounced in the ninth and twelfth centuries, though that tradition was driven underground by the rise of universities and scholasticism in the thirteenth century. It was against the aridity of scholasticism—all syllogisms and *summae*—that Petrarch reacted so strongly. The first phase of the humanist movement in Italy was concerned with the recovery of the Latin classics, the ancient Roman past, and the perfection of superior (that is, classical) forms of Latin literary expression. The second, which took over after 1430, was more concerned with the recovery of the ancient Greek language and Greek classics, thus completing the agenda to recover the Greco-Roman past and to improve living humans in the light of Europe's towering classical past.

The humanists were Renaissance scholars who prized a course of study based on the mastery of ancient languages; the close, unmediated reading of ancient texts (that is, without medieval glosses and commentaries); and the emulation of ancient literary, artistic, and philosophical models. Based on a deep and historicizing interest in the classical past, this set of interests came to be known as humanism or **Renaissance humanism.** Not only did the classical past shape Renaissance humanism, but Renaissance humanists shaped the classical past, giving it contour and definition. There was some pushback against the humanist agenda. One Franciscan friar stoutly denied that the fathers of the church had had any use for classical authors; the humanists dismissed such opponents as barbarians.

Along with **Renaissance individualism,** or the belief that human beings occupy a special place in the created world and are capable of extraordinary achievements, humanism supplied one of the foundational cornerstones of Renaissance cultural and intellectual life. While it is common to see the development of humanism and individualism in the West as a product of exchanges between the classical past and the Renaissance present, both humanism and individualism were also influenced by the interplay in the period between the West and the East and by new trends in European societies and Italian cities.

The Humanist Course of Study

Petrarch and his humanist friends hunted down copies of Latin authors such as Cicero that had long lain on the library shelves of Europe's monasteries. They plumbed the works of the great poets, Virgil, Horace, and Ovid, for stylistic leads and elevated forms of expression. Petrarch became so passionately attached to the eminent literary figures of classical Rome that he wrote a series of *Letters to the Ancient Dead* addressed to the likes of Cicero, Horace, Virgil, Homer, and other famous figures, in which he expressed his fervent wish that he had lived among them rather than in his own corrupt times. Humanism was more than just a literary agenda; it was a moral one. Petrarch and his humanist friends imitated Cicero's Latin prose, but after Cicero's *Letters to Atticus* were found and revealed Cicero to be less than perfect (crafty and equivocating politician that he was), Petrarch ceased to idolize Cicero, much to the dismay of his Ciceronian friends. Petrarch may have loved Rome's golden past, but he pushed his contemporaries toward a more critical and historically exact appreciation of that golden past.

The second (or Greek) phase of the humanist movement benefited from the arrival of Greek scholars in Italy in 1439 at the opening of the General Church Council in Florence, when learned Greeks appeared as part of the entourage surrounding the Byzantine emperor and the Eastern Orthodox patriarch. Eminent Greek scholars such as Basilius Bessarion (later a cardinal) and Georgius Gemistus Plethon became established figures in the intellectual and cultural circles of Renaissance Italy. It is hard for us to imagine the pure excitement aroused by the arrival of Greek scholars and Greek manuscripts in Italy, the intellectual ferment caused by the first lectures on Plato, or the eagerness that Italian scholars felt when they first caught a glimpse of a Greek text that had never before been seen in western Europe. Italian noblemen, politicians, scholars, and artists avidly followed each new development and responded enthusiastically to new courses of study concentrating on Greek language and literature. One young humanist in France spent three hours on his wedding day studying Greek, somewhat to the consternation of his bride. Cosimo de' Medici, after hearing Plethon lecture on Plato, was inspired to sink a considerable amount of his wealth into the foundation of a Platonic Academy in Florence. "I myself intend

OTHER VOICES, OTHER VIEWS

The Jewish Tradition in the Italian Renaissance

In 1516, Venetian leaders decided to segregate the city's Jewish residents in a specific area known as the *geto nuovo* (meaning "the new foundry," where slag or metal waste was deposited). It is from this Venetian residential and industrial district that the West derived the word ***ghetto,*** meaning an area segregated by race or religion. Jews had been expelled from England, France, and Spain at various points in the Middle Ages. The decision to segregate Venice's Jewish residents, which was a milder form of those religious expulsions, came after centuries of toleration and inclusion and marked a change in the official treatment of Jews.

During the Renaissance, Jews could be found in cities throughout the Italian peninsula. The region's political fragmentation was helpful in establishing resilient Jewish communities because, even if they were expelled temporarily from one region, they were often welcomed by the next. The largest population of Jews in western Europe during the fifteenth century was in Rome, the center of Roman Catholicism, where they played a critical role in teaching Hebrew to church figures studying the Old Testament. After 1437, when the Medici came to power, Jews were welcomed back to Florence, where they remained prominent in banking circles so long as the Medici family remained in the city. Briefly expelled while Florence was under the influence of Savonarola, they returned again to the city with the Medici in 1512. In Venice, the Jewish population increased steadily throughout the fifteenth and sixteenth centuries.

Renaissance Jews led double lives, one among Italian Christians as bankers specializing in loaning capital to princes, politicians, and merchants and the other within their Jewish communities as teachers, scholars, and neighbors. Affluent Jewish banking families like the Volterras of Florence became targets of hatred among their less prosperous Christian neighbors and faced an omnipresent risk of expulsion and resettlement. On the other hand, Renaissance Jews were avid travelers, who shuttled between Italy and the Holy Land, where they made pilgrimages to Jerusalem and visited sites of religious significance. Pilgrimages helped to balance their experiences as a disenfranchised and marginalized population within Europe, bringing them into contact with other Jews from Europe and the Middle East and with places of holy and spiritual importance to their religion.

In addition to appreciating their banking and mercantile expertise, learned Christians looked upon Renaissance Jews as a deeply learned people. Because Jews tended to know not only Hebrew, but also Latin and Arabic, they were able to communicate with both the ruling Muslim elite and the conquered Christian population in Muslim parts of Spain. Despite the Christian interest in the Jewish intellectual tradition, Jews were formally barred from attending the west's universities after the Council of Basel in 1434. These strictures were largely ignored by Italian schools. As early as 1409 a Jew, named Leone Bendiati, received his doctorate from the University of Padua. In the faculties of Italian universities, there were Jews who taught Hebrew, astronomy, medicine, and mathematics. One of the Italian Renaissance's most illustrious scholars, Giovanni Pico della Mirandola, learned Hebrew and the esoteric Jewish wisdom of the kabbalah at the University of Padua from Elia del Medigo (c. 1458–c. 1493). Del Medigo is an example of the intellectual versatility possessed by many Jewish scholars of the Renaissance. He was born on the island of Candia in the Venetian colony of Crete, and translated Greek works of Aristotle and the Arabic philosopher Averroës into Latin for Renaissance scholars. Fluent in Hebrew, Latin, Greek, and Arabic, he studied medicine along with the traditional teachings of his faith and may once have attended classes at the University of Padua. By 1480, Del Medigo had made a home in the nearby city of Venice, where he taught philosophy to the children of the Venetian elite. Del Medigo's life story exemplifies the contradictions of the Jewish experience in Renaissance Italy. Prized as an intellectual, but marginalized and vulnerable because of his faith, Del Medigo knew nobles, clerics, scholars, and poets but was never fully welcomed into Christian circles.

QUESTIONS | ***What other groups were disadvantaged by the Italian Renaissance? Why might the opportunities for Jews have been better in cosmopolitan Renaissance Italy than in the rest of Europe?***

The Jewish Ghetto in Venice

to pursue immortality through such study," Cassandra Fedele wrote. Her imagination was stirred by the promise of humanism and the brave new world of classical texts that she was encountering.

While humanism emphasized the study of classical languages and literature, it also spurred renewed interest in European vernacular tongues. Three late medieval Florentines—Dante Alighieri, Petrarch, and Giovanni Boccaccio—all believed that their native Tuscan dialect possessed as much beauty and literary potential as any ancient language. Those three writers led the way in inspiring humanists to study both vernacular and classical literature. Dante wrote on the eloquence of the vernacular language, penned courtly love lyrics and the sweeping *Divine Comedy* in Italian, and published a polemical political treatise (*Monarchia*). Boccaccio knew Petrarch and was so inspired by his passion for antiquity that he set himself the task of learning Greek and collecting as many ancient manuscripts as he could.

The followers of Dante, Petrarch, and Boccaccio were particularly interested in what Cicero (106–43 BCE) had called the *studia humanitatis*: grammar, rhetoric, poetry, literature, and moral philosophy or ethics. By the fifteenth century, many people perceived the *studia humanitatis* as standing in sharp contrast to scholasticism and the intellectual curriculum of the medieval university, which combined the mastery of Aristotelian logic with the study of theology. Although scholasticism was also based on the study of ancient texts, the approach that medieval scholars took to those texts was not as historically sensitive as the one taken by the humanists, who regarded ancient texts as textual artifacts that needed to be carefully preserved and critically studied. The Renaissance recognized the historical otherness of ancient texts.

All humanists began their training with an intensive study of classical Latin, for without Latin it was impossible to read most modern or ancient texts, to correspond with scholars in other cities, or to compose the elaborate prose that was considered the hallmark of the educated individual. Renaissance humanists did not stop their language training with Latin, but proceeded to study the other two ancient languages of the Bible and classical world: Hebrew and Greek.

Reading Classical Literature

After learning ancient languages, a humanist might spend the remainder of his life reading and explicating classical texts. Manuscript hunters such as Poggio Bracciolini scoured old European monasteries and contacted refugees from Constantinople to obtain ancient texts for Renaissance humanist readers. In 1415 at Cluny, Bracciolini found several orations of Cicero that were believed to be lost, and the following year at St. Gall in Switzerland, Bracciolini found a complete manuscript of the Roman rhetorician Quintilian's *Education of an Orator*, which became the Renaissance's most widely used rhetoric textbook. Bracciolini did more than just collect ancient manuscripts. As a humanist, he tried to determine whether they were authentic and to date them more precisely. This historical attitude toward texts became vital as more manuscripts entered into circulation and were systematically studied by humanists.

Hundreds of ancient texts were identified during the Renaissance, but none were more important than the works of the philosopher Plato, which had largely been unavailable to scholars in the medieval West. When Plethon attended the council of 1439, he reintroduced the works of the ancient philosopher to Italian audiences through his lectures. One of Plethon's most avid students was Marsilio Ficino, the small, hunch-backed son of Cosimo de' Medici's personal physician. Although his father had hoped that his son would follow in his footsteps and become a doctor, Ficino's wide-ranging intellect kept him from settling on one subject of study. When Ficino's brilliance came to Cosimo's attention, he employed Ficino in 1463 to translate all the recently recovered works of Plato from Greek into Latin in order to make them available to a wider audience. It took Ficino six years to complete the monumental task.

In recognition of Ficino's accomplishments and expertise, Cosimo put him in charge of the Platonic Academy he housed in a Medici villa outside Florence, where the humanist presided over scholarly conversations and entertained visiting philosophers, scholars, lawyers, businessmen, and poets. In 1474, Ficino published an influential synthesis of Platonic and Christian ideas, the *Platonic Theology*, in an attempt to find the hidden unity among the diverse ancient authors and opinions that were beginning to overwhelm humanist scholars. Ficino next turned from Plato to the works attributed to a legendary wise man known as Hermes Trismegistus. Hermetic texts blended ancient Egyptian, Neoplatonic, and early Christian ideas and reinforced Ficino's belief that there was a single, unified core of ideas in ancient philosophy and theology just waiting to be discovered.

Civic Humanism and a New Sense of History

Once Renaissance humanists had learned Latin, Greek, and maybe even some Hebrew and had steeped themselves in the texts that men such as Bracciolini and Ficino were making available, questions were raised about what humanists should do with their learning. Humanists were quick to respond that the *studia humanitatis* was meant to do more than just teach students more languages. The curriculum should also prepare ideal citizens, trained to be both eloquent and virtuous and to emulate the examples of heroic behavior from the classical past.

Fifteenth-century humanists applied their new learning to improving educational standards. Pier Paolo Vergerio in a series of books advocated a form of liberal education that balanced the grammatical and language skills of the teacher against the natural abilities and interests of students. He also emphasized physical education and thought about which sports or games would exercise which parts of the body. Vergerio was interested in developing the whole person and designed programs for those destined for a military life. At Mantua, Vittorino da Feltre established a school called the Casa Jocosa ("happy house") in 1423 that taught both rich and poor boys a rounded Renaissance educational program broken into three parts: religious training, classical learning, and military training. Vittorino was keen to demonstrate in a practical way that Christianity and the classics were not at odds. His was a Christian humanism.

The application of humanist thought to political and social problems is known as **civic humanism,** and it came to the fore as humanists gained confidence that ancient ideals might be used to reform and enlighten their communities. Their model for civic humanism was Cicero, who was thought to be the embodiment of virtuous dedication for the greater good. The chief civic humanist of the period was Leonardo Bruni. A Florentine from a modest family, Bruni studied at the University of Florence and became a language tutor in the Medici household. During his lifetime, he held a number of positions in the government and in each he was guided by his humanist ideas about what constituted the civic good. Bruni inspired his fellow Florentines to follow models of ancient literature to better craft their written and spoken work, pointing out that Cicero was important not only for what he said, but also for how he said it.

A new emphasis on the importance of recent history flowed from the *studia humanitatis* and civic humanism. Bruni wrote a *History of the Florentine People* (1442), modeled after the ancient histories of Livy, which explored the significance of both ancient and more recent political events. Bruni's book focuses on the machinations of actors motivated not by piety or the lack of it (as had often been the issue in medieval histories), but by their worldly pursuit of power, money, glory, and revenge. Humanist scholars of the Renaissance tended to exaggerate their distance from the Middle Ages and to disregard the debts they owed to their immediate predecessors. At the same time, they were sharply aware that a vast temporal and cultural gulf separated their world from that of the ancient Greeks and Romans. Whereas Christian scholars of the medieval period divided human history into two periods (the pagan world before the birth of Christ and the Christian era), Renaissance humanists divided history into three periods: a period of classical antiquity that ended with the sack of Rome in 410; a middle age (*medium aevum*) that stretched from the fall of the Roman Empire until the fourteenth or fifteenth century; and the present, when the legacies of classical antiquity were being rediscovered and renewed.

With the humanists' new sense of history came problems of interpretation. They discovered evidence that ancient authors and philosophers had not always agreed and had not always been admirable human beings, and other evidence indicated that some ancient texts had been altered and corrupted over the centuries. Humanists, therefore, sought to return to the purest, oldest examples of the texts they were reading. This ***ad fontes*** spirit, which means, literally, a return "to the sources," informed the work of many Renaissance humanists, including Lorenzo Valla's investigation of the *Donation of Constantine* for his patron, King Alfonso. The pen and the humanist spirit of textual criticism produced a new sense of the importance of the learned individual in society. Humanism empowered humanists.

Individualism

Individualism, like *humanism,* is a term that can have many definitions. As used in relation to the Italian Renaissance, individualism refers not just to the older sense that humans occupied a central and important place in the created world between the divine world of the angels in heaven and the mindless life of the animals on earth, but also to the dynamic potential of individuals to grow, learn, and achieve. Vasari's treatment of Renaissance artists focused on individuals in the act of creating and accomplishing great things.

The development of Renaissance individualism is linked closely to another humanist from Florence, the nobleman Giovanni Pico della Mirandola. At age fourteen, Pico began his formal university studies at the University

Three Great Lights of Florentine Humanism A fresco depiction by Cosimo Rosselli of Pico della Mirandola (the wonder boy of the late Italian Renaissance), Marsilio Ficino (the Florentine Platonist), and Angelo Poliziano (the poet and classicist), three leading lights of the Florentine Renaissance, front and center in the painting.

of Bologna. Eventually, his interests led him to the Universities of Padua and Florence, where he met and became the pupil of Marsilio Ficino. Under Ficino's guidance, Pico became convinced by his teacher's belief that there was a philosophical unity behind ancient ideas that could unite pagan and Christian beliefs. Unlike Ficino, however, Pico believed that ancient Jewish and Islamic ideas should be included along with the theology and philosophy of ancient Greece, Rome, and Christianity. He began to study Hebrew and Arabic in an effort to expand the number of ancient texts he was able to consider. In 1486, his studies resulted in a remarkable, if pretentious, set of nine hundred theses about philosophy and theology known as the *Conclusiones,* which he wanted to debate in public in Rome. Church authorities prevented the event when they realized how sympathetic Pico was toward Jewish and Muslim philosophy and theology.

Pico wrote a brief treatise to accompany his nine hundred conclusions known as the *Oration on the Dignity of Man.* In the *Oration,* Pico argues that each individual is a creature of importance and dignity because each human being stands at a midpoint between the divine heavens and the corrupt earth. But, unlike all other creatures, humans have the God-given capacity for self-invention and unlimited self-development and self-realization. We are the only free agents of creation. For Italian Renaissance humanists, individualism meant that every person—and every intellect—was a precious part of the divine plan and should be cherished and nurtured. Cassandra Fedele, who shared Pico's appreciation of the power of individualism, maintained that every individual and not just the philosophers, but even the most ignorant man, recognized and admitted that reason is what separates humans from the animals. An individual's ability to maneuver between the world of the senses and the world of the intellect was seen by Pico, Cassandra, and other humanists as a gift that would lead humanity to a more moral way of life and to a greater understanding of the natural and divine worlds.

Italian Renaissance Art

What were the chief characteristics of Italian Renaissance art?

Humanism was based on the study of languages and classical texts and individualism depended on a particular application of human reason to life. Renaissance art was not so very different in capturing the tenor of the age, its underlying principles and purposes. The moment when God reaches out from heaven to touch the finger of Adam, as depicted in Michelangelo Buonarroti's fresco on the Sistine Chapel ceiling, is in harmony with Pico's belief in the dignity and importance of the individual. But we need to remember that Michelangelo's finely modeled human forms evoke the classical sculptures he had studied. Just as humanists admired ancient works of literature, so Renaissance artists sought to learn from and emulate classical works of art. To some of these artists, medieval painting and sculpture seemed stiff and one-dimensional when compared to lifelike classical art. The ancient mosaics, frescoes, and sculptures they admired were naturalistic and infused with classical ideas of due proportion, harmony, and symmetry. But Renaissance artists were not slavish imitators of ancient things. They had new ideas and made their art in new ways and with new techniques that were alien to the ancient world. Renaissance artists introduced four new ways of achieving their artistic visions: through the use of contrasting light and shadow (**chiaroscuro**) to shade figures and give them a sense of three-dimensionality; the mastery of **linear perspective,** which gave paintings a sense of depth; the use of paints that had an oil base; and the close, almost clinical observation of both the natural world and the human body. Nor were Renaissance artists overawed by the classical past. They thought that they could both equal and even surpass ancient monuments, which reflected the confidence of their Renaissance individualism.

Living Renaissance Art

Renaissance artists were not trained in universities or libraries, but in urban workshops where knowledge was handed down from master to apprentice according to the medieval craft tradition. Most Renaissance artists were of humble background, the sons of shopkeepers and artisans. Few peasants and few nobles made art. Michelangelo, coming from patrician stock, was an exception, and his family disapproved of his occupational choice. In Renaissance Italy, manual work was less valued than military service or scholarly pursuits, but a few great artists were seen as individuals of genius and talent and commanded handsome commissions and rewards. The emperor made Gentile Bellini of Venice, the painter of the procession for the dying boy in Venice, a count; and Raphael was led by the pope to believe that he would be made a cardinal. Most artists, however, were still regarded as mere artisans engaged in degrading manual labor, and some were considered social deviants. A fair number of them were. They acted out, some committing murders and assaults, as Benvenuto Cellini in his autobiography confessed that he had; and some had eccentric social habits. Donatello kept all his money in a basket hanging from the ceiling, allowing workers, friends, and family to take what they wanted.

What connected the historical and economic worlds of the Italian Renaissance with artists and the efflorescence of culture was patronage. Who paid for art, what did they want, and what was the relationship of the artist and the patron? The Middle Ages chiefly had religious and royal art because the church and kings commanded it. In northern Italy in the fifteenth century, with its prosperous cities, ambitious rulers, wealthy merchants, and civic and religious institutions, new patrons were in play. Vasari explained that to succeed in Florence, artists needed to be clever, critical, and competitive. They were in intense competition with each other for commissions and reliable patrons. Literary humanism was not strictly a paying proposition until the sixteenth century, but visual artists and makers of music sold their services and their creations. Yet at the end of his life, Donatello was destitute, until Piero de' Medici granted him a farm. Many artists had to deal with patrons who delayed payment. Both Raphael and Michelangelo were owed large sums of money by their patron-popes. A few artists did become rich and enjoyed paid positions within their patrons' households, but most were happy to settle for regular employment in a thriving workshop. As an apprentice, Michelangelo was paid 32 lire a year, at a time when a Florentine servant made 40 lire a year, a Venetian soldier 150 lire a year, a bank manager in Florence close to 600 lire a year, and a Venetian cardinal around 140,000 lire a year. Still it was not a bad salary for a fourteen-year-old boy just starting out on his career. It was, however, held against both the rich and the poor artist that they labored for financial gain, to which Leonardo responded, so did his patrons.

Artists were sought out by powerful patrons, including rulers such as Cosimo de' Medici, by Renaissance popes and church figures, by wealthy merchants, by cities, and by religious confraternities to paint commemorative portraits, design frescoes, and sculpt statues with elaborate allegorical themes using characters from classical literature and scenes from the Bible. As the most celebrated artists traveled to princely courts and between the rich cities of Florence, Rome, Milan, and Venice to consult on art commissions, their work began to command high prices and their status rose even higher in the eyes of their contemporaries. Owning a statue by Michelangelo or a painting by Raphael was considered a symbol of cultural refinement within princely circles. In contrast, we know the names of few medieval artists before the Late Middle Ages, little about their lives or the contours of their careers. Vasari's detailed and personalized biographies of artists reflect the Renaissance's cultural celebration of great art and its makers. A few of these artists became widely known and had outsized personalities. Michelangelo was known to be particularly prickly, once leaving Rome and the pope's employ because the pope's secretary had failed to grant him an instant audience with the pope. Leonardo was not much better, causing a scene in a bank one day when the clerk tried to pay him his monthly salary in small coins; he said he was no penny painter and quit working for his current patron.[1]

The Early Renaissance: Ghiberti, Donatello, and Masaccio

Some of the earliest artistic expressions of Renaissance ideas occurred in Florence. The wealthy Florentine elites saw commissioning art as a way to express their devotion to the church and to the republic, and entered into contracts with artists to complete public art projects to be displayed in the city's churches, public squares, and government buildings. The city of Florence itself was a major patron of art, ordering works that would glorify and celebrate the city and its people.

Ghiberti's Gate of Paradise Scenes from the lives of Cain and Abel from the great bronze doors that Ghiberti made for the Baptistery of St. John, Florence.

Lorenzo Ghiberti achieved lasting fame when he won a contest to complete a massive set of decorated bronze doors for Florence's oldest building, the Baptistery of St. John. One set of doors had been completed by Andrea Pisano in 1329, but it was not until 1401 that the city announced that it was ready to commission the second set of doors. Seven artists competed for the honor, including distinguished artists with established reputations, but it was a relatively unknown twenty-one-year-old artist who received the commission. Ghiberti had impressed the judges with the vitality of his figures and the way that he made biblical stories come to dramatic life. Ghiberti established a workshop to train younger artists to help him in his work, but it still took over two decades before the twenty-eight bronze door panels were completed. Ghiberti was also a historian and an author committed to the ideals of humanism. He composed the first autobiography by an artist, a testament to his sense of the worth of the artist as an individual.

Donatello (c. 1386–1466) was one of Ghiberti's apprentices. Before going to work for Ghiberti, Donatello began as a goldsmith and excelled at low-relief carvings that were surprisingly lifelike. Donatello, like his master, was fascinated by history and traveled to Rome to engage in excavations of ancient ruins and detailed studies of surviving buildings such as the Pantheon. Donatello's most famous works are the five statues he carved for one of Florence's major landmarks, the Duomo's bell-tower. These five statues, especially those of the prophets Habacuc and Jeremiah, were modeled on statues of classical Roman orators, but have highly individualized faces and features. In 1430, Donatello was able to sculpt the first free-standing nude (a statue of the biblical hero David) since ancient times for his patron, Cosimo de' Medici.

Ghiberti and Donatello specialized in sculpture, but Florence was also home to many skilled painters. Chief among them in the early Renaissance was Masaccio, an artist famous for his frescoes. A devoted student of linear perspective, Masaccio was able to give rounded, three-dimensional forms to his human figures that made them appear strikingly realistic to early-fifteenth-century viewers. His most important commissions were religious, including the frescoes on the life of Saint Peter in the Brancacci family chapel in the church of Santa Maria del Carmine. Masaccio died a young man, his full potential unrealized, but he had a profound influence on later artists, including Leonardo, Michelangelo, and Raphael.

The High Renaissance: Leonardo, Michelangelo, and Raphael

As the fame of Florence's artists spread throughout the peninsula, along with word of their interest in classical models and their emphasis on the individual, Florentine artists were called upon by patrons outside the city who wanted to commission their work. Chief among those patrons were the popes, who commanded both resources and prestige. As a result, the next generation of Renaissance artists shuttled back and forth between Florence, Rome, and other Italian cities in search of commissions and new artistic opportunities.

Leonardo da Vinci (1452–1519) was born in a hillside town outside Florence, began his artistic career in the city, moved to Milan in 1482 to work for Ludovico Sforza, returned to Florence, worked again for the Sforza family in Milan, and then moved to Rome to work for the pope. He died in France in 1519, in service to his last patron, King Francis I. In every city, and with every patron, Leonardo showed an insatiable curiosity about the world around him. Everything from anatomy to engineering was a subject of interest to him, and his curiosity and ability to move easily between fields of study such as painting, sculpture, physiology, botany, armaments, and civic fortifications have made him the image of the archetypal "Renaissance Man." But Leonardo was far from a typical man of the Renaissance. For one thing, he did not receive a rigorous Renaissance education and never learned Latin and Greek, which hobbled his access to certain sophisticated circles of learning. Yet he has always seemed an extraordinary example of what people are capable of achieving.

Leonardo's insatiable curiosity meant that he was not always an ideal employee. Renaissance princes and popes were accustomed to having their commissions completed on time and to their specifications. Leonardo left many projects unfinished, and his experiments with painting techniques often led to disastrous final results in frescoes (as in the case of his *Last Supper in Milan,* which began to deteriorate almost before the paint had dried). His constant search for something new to stimulate his active, brilliant mind made him restless and easily distracted. Despite these difficulties, Leonardo completed some of the most important and influential works of Renaissance art, including highly individualized portraits such as the *Mona Lisa* and paintings on religious themes such as the *Virgin of the Rocks,* which employed linear perspective and chiaroscuro painting techniques to great effect. He also left thousands of pages of notes written in his backward or mirror script,

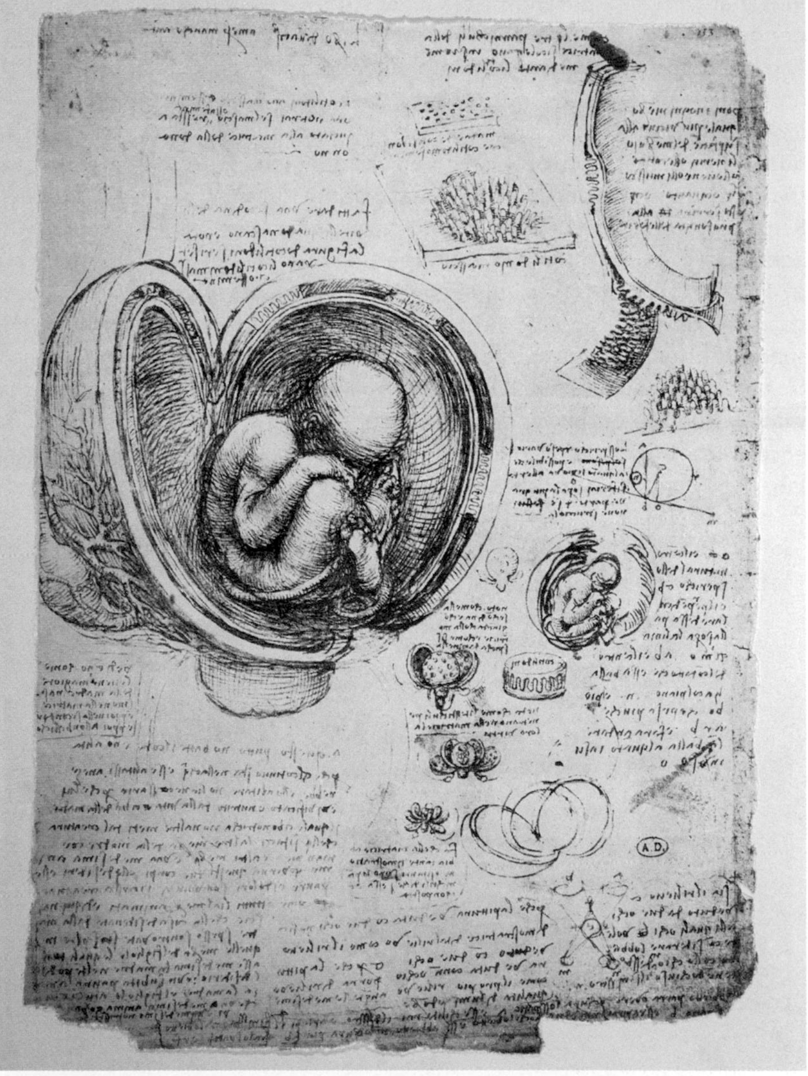

Leonardo's Womb A page from Leonardo's notebooks on which he examined a fetus in the female womb and the nature of conception. Note Leonardo's distinctive backward or mirror writing, which as a left-handed writer he found easier to execute.

INVESTIGATING THE PAST

Seeing the Renaissance in a New Light

On the last day of December 1989, as television cameras whirled and photographers clicked, the world let out a collective gasp when one of the Renaissance's most cherished works of art, the frescoes of the Sistine Chapel ceiling at the Vatican, were publicly unveiled for the first time after a restoration program that began in 1981. Though work to restore the remaining frescoes on the walls of the chapel was not yet complete, the restored ceiling showed an image of Renaissance art that was very different from the subdued colors and shadowy chiaroscuro that centuries of visitors had known and come to love as they gazed sixty-five feet above the chapel floor at the details of the painted ceiling above. Bright colors, strong lines, and an almost garish use of oranges and greens characterized paintings that were very different from what students of the period had come to know and think about Michelangelo. They were seeing the Renaissance in an entirely new light, and they were not sure that they liked the result.

Michelangelo painted the frescoes that adorn the Vatican's Sistine Chapel between 1508 and 1512, and since that time they have become emblematic of the Italian Renaissance. Every inch of the ceiling is covered with images from the Old Testament, from the very first chapter of Genesis forward. Michelangelo did not lie on his back to paint the ceiling as popularly thought, but worked from a special scaffolding system that allowed him to reach over his head and lean back while painting. Still he complained that his sight never completely recovered from the experience. Michelangelo applied pigment to wet plaster, working quickly before the plaster dried and fixed the image. Occasionally, he painted over or touched up the images that he had captured swiftly on the ceiling's surface. The pictures were large, bright, and colorful, painted to be seen by people standing far below on the chapel floor. As early as 1800, however, conditions inside the chapel had already obscured Michelangelo's masterpiece. Smoke from the candles used in religious ceremonies left a dull, sooty film on the walls and ceiling of the room. Leaky roof tiles let in water, which calcified into a hard, white crust in some places on the ceiling and stained others brown. Years of repair using varnishes and glue did damage, too, as the layers of later materials built up.

Not surprisingly, given the treasured status of the frescoes, an international team of conservation and art history experts was gathered to guide, supervise, and execute the project. They discussed and planned the restoration for three years between 1981 and 1984. Chemical analyses provided new insights into Michelangelo's fresco technique and revealed the extent of the damage. Once the work on the frescoes began, conservators worked on scaffolding that was modeled after Michelangelo's and made to fit into the support holes he had left in the walls so as to avoid further damage to the deteriorating ceiling.

The restoration of the Sistine ceiling frescoes was the subject of controversy from the moment the project was announced in 1981. One group of American art historians tried to halt the restoration process during its early stages, arguing that the layers of chiaroscuro that Michelangelo had applied to the frescoes were being removed. Others believed that Michelangelo had applied the layers of glue found on the ceiling's surface to deliberately tone down the bright pigments that he had applied to the wet plaster. Detractors hated the "ice-cream colors" revealed by the restoration and, though proponents of the restoration countered their claims by pointing out that the sophisticated coloration and brush techniques were monumental achievements, even today some people miss the older, more muted ceiling. Once the cameras had stopped rolling and the bright lights were turned off, however, the dimly lit chapel was far less garish than it had first appeared.

Michelangelo's Painting of the Sistine Chapel Ceiling

QUESTION | ***What does the case of the restoration of Michelangelo's frescoes reveal about our expectations about the past and its art?***

which suggest the range of scientific and technical questions that interested him and of his extreme individualism.

Working in Florence and Rome at the same time as Leonardo was another great Renaissance artist, Michelangelo Buonarotti (1475–1564). Like Leonardo, Michelangelo was a man of wide-ranging interests and awe-inspiring talents. He could paint and sculpt, and was a talented architect, poet, and engineer. Michelangelo was born in Arezzo in Tuscany, and was trained as an artist in Florence before his talents were noticed and brought to the attention of Lorenzo de' Medici, who oversaw his education and introduced him to prominent philosophers and intellectuals such as Pico della Mirandola and Marsilio Ficino. In the first phase of his career, he divided his time between completing projects for patrons in Florence and Rome, such as the Pietá and the statue of David. In 1505, Pope Julius II invited Michelangelo to Rome, where he embarked on an ambitious fresco cycle for the Vatican's Sistine Chapel.

Despite Michelangelo's considerable success, the most popular artist of the age was his contemporary, Raphael (1483–1520). Born in Urbino, Raphael at the age of twenty-five was commissioned by Pope Julius II to paint frescoes in the Vatican palace. Raphael's frescoes focused on both classical and religious themes, and established him as a serious painter who adhered to his patron's artistic vision and fulfilled his contracts. In 1514, he was appointed the Vatican architect, and the following year was given responsibility for cataloguing and conserving the Vatican's growing collection of ancient Roman sculpture. The high style of Italian Renaissance art faded after the political troubles of the 1520s, succeeded by Mannerism and then Baroque, which turned away from the strict rules of classical proportion, moderation, perspective, and background.

The Spread of Renaissance Ideas: The European Renaissance

The Renaissance began in Italy, but by the late fifteenth century its ideals, interests, and techniques had touched many parts of Europe and transformed the movement into a European (or, as it is sometimes misleadingly called, northern) Renaissance. Renaissance ideas traveled outward along trade routes from Florence, Rome, and Venice; they spread between artists in Italy, the Netherlands, France, and Germany; and they were adopted when European princes and patrons began to see the advantages associated with a political toolbox that included force, diplomacy, espionage, and cultural competition. The reach of Renaissance values was extensive. Matthias Corvinus, the king of Hungary (r. 1458–1490), was not only a Renaissance ruler who eventually became the king of Bohemia and duke of Austria, but he also knew Italian, assembled Renaissance humanists at his court, established a vast library, and lived in a Renaissance palace. While the Italian Renaissance and its individual civic expressions served as models for other European rulers, countries, and kingdoms, the wider European Renaissance took on its own regional and continental flavors. Just as the unique conditions of the Italian region had shaped the Renaissance's primary motivations and expressions, other areas of Europe put their own distinctive stamp on these developments. The Renaissance proved to be a set of possibilities, interpreted differently in different places and times, but sharing a new, more critical and systematic way of doing things and viewing the world.

What, where, and when was the European Renaissance? How and why did it differ from earlier cultural developments?

In general, the European Renaissance (which included significant developments in the arts, literature, and education in Germany, the Netherlands, England, France, and Spain) began to unfold at a later date than did the Italian Renaissance. Most historians detect an interest in humanism and individualism outside Italy as early as 1450, and underscore the importance that artists, church leaders, and noble patrons played in promoting Renaissance values and ideas. European artists, who traveled to Italy to study art and learn from Italian workshops, were particularly sensitive to the new changes they encountered and then carried home, where they affected and mixed with the native cultural styles of France, the Netherlands, and Germany. Despite similarities with the original Northern Italian Renaissance, the European Renaissance is often described as having a more overtly religious cast to it, as humanists outside of Italy applied the *ad fontes* spirit of humanism to the church and its texts, teachings, and doctrines. The wider European interest in commerce also made Europeans eager to explore how the beliefs in individualism and the tenets of their religious faith might work with and justify business and trade. The European Renaissance was, however, not merely an extension and adaptation of dominant Italian Renaissance ideas. It was a living and evolving expression of new ideas and tendencies that came to include Italy as one of many voices.

Commerce and Urban Life in the European Renaissance

As in Italy, much of the energy of the wider European Renaissance was associated with urban centers. In northern Europe, the chief Renaissance city was Bruges in Flanders, the capital city of the dukes of Burgundy. Bruges had become enormously wealthy through commerce and trade. The patronage opportunities provided by the Burgundian court and by the city's wealthy elites attracted artists and intellectuals from all over Europe. The traffic was in both directions. Italian artists and architects were in great demand, and Flemish artists traveled to the Italian peninsula to learn of the new artistic styles being developed there.

Bruges, like Florence, was a city associated with luxury goods, including textiles, wine, and spices. Trading companies from Genoa and Venice had long established merchant colonies that linked the Flemish port to the trade routes of the Mediterranean. From Bruges, Mediterranean goods flowed to the other cities in northern Europe, where they were traded for furs, fish, and grain. So much international trade took place in Bruges that currency exchanges and banks emerged early there and were run from its *Bourse* (exchange).

Fifteenth-century Bruges was home to the court of Philip the Good, the duke of Burgundy. An ally of King Henry V of England, Philip was known for his glittering court and chivalric ideals. Burgundian clothing styles, tapestries, metal goods, and jewelry set the standard for high fashion throughout Europe. The duke of Burgundy was known as a generous and discriminating patron who advanced the careers of important artists. He was also a scholar interested in the translation of classical texts and the production of literature in the Flemish vernacular. But the pinnacle of Bruges as a center of the European Renaissance passed after Philip's death.

Not only had the Duchy of Burgundy been annexed by France in 1477, but around 1500 the port of Bruges lost some of its navigability due to silting. As a consequence, large merchant and cargo ships looked elsewhere to dock and unload their cargoes. Antwerp and then Amsterdam became the ports of choice for ships from the Mediterranean. As money and trade went elsewhere, so too did the energy of the continuing European Renaissance.

The Arnolfini Wedding Scene Jan van Eyck's oil painting on a wooden panel (1434) is the subject of endless interpretation. Is it even a wedding portrait as popularly thought? Though the woman may seem pregnant, all indications are that she is not. The mirror on the rear wall shows the couple in reverse and two mysterious figures in a doorway. The painting abounds with symbols: cast-off shoes, lap dog, and oranges on the window sill.

European Renaissance Art

The artists of the European Renaissance absorbed stylistic elements from Italy, but they also made major new contributions to the development of western European art. The most significant of these developments was the formulation of oil-based paints. By blending pigments into linseed oil, instead of the egg white mixture used in previous centuries, Flemish artists were able to manipulate their paints over extended periods of time, adding layers of detail and subtle shading that made their works seem to shimmer with life. Oil paints were particularly revolutionary when it came to portraiture, as the new pigments were capable of capturing fine physiological details and could more effectively represent skin tones and fabrics.

Two important artists of the European Renaissance, Jan van Eyck (1395–1441) and Rogier van der Weyden (c. 1400–1464), exemplify the exchange of Renaissance ideas and demonstrate how Italian Renaissance concepts and techniques influenced and were influenced by other Europeans. Van Eyck was a court artist who served Duke Philip of Burgundy. In addition to painting important commissions for his patron, he also conducted diplomatic missions. Van Eyck traveled to the Iberian Peninsula to conduct wedding negotiations for his ruler and patron. He was a master of the use of the new Renaissance oil paints, specializing in painting religious works that included finely detailed portraits of his patrons. Van der Weyden also painted important religious commissions for patrons that included donor portraits. His work became well known in Italy after he traveled to Rome in 1450 to celebrate Pope Nicholas V's jubilee year. In Italy, he accepted the patronage of the Medici family and lectured on the use of oil paints. After Van der Weyden's death, his style influenced later Renaissance artists in the Netherlands, England, and Spain.

The portraits of Van der Weyden and Van Eyck, including the famous Arnolfini wedding portrait, with its enigmatic wall mirror, are vivid expressions of individualism. What made them so arresting was their detailed treatment of the human face and body. At the same time, Van Eyck and his successors lavished attention on the depiction of natural and manufactured objects. The juxtaposition of religious themes with individualized portraits and carefully rendered material objects became hallmarks of European Renaissance art.

The Print Revolution of the European Renaissance

Just as art and artists circulated in Renaissance Europe, so too did works of literature. Prior to 1450, these works were copied laboriously by hand onto parchment. Large books such as the Bible took hundreds of hours and hundreds of animal skins to manufacture. As a result, they were rare and expensive, and were locked away in private or church collections. Their content was also subject to variability because scribes (sometimes expert, sometimes incompetent) working for long hours were prone to make mistakes as they copied. Yet no real alternative to manual copying existed in the West.

Johann Gutenberg, a German gem-cutter and goldsmith, was not a humanist, but he had an idea that would shake the Late Middle Ages and European Renaissance. His "automatic writing" was a technique for producing medieval manuscripts more quickly and in greater number. As inventive and ambitious as Gutenberg was, he was not a particularly good businessman. In 1438, he and his partners invested their capital and industry in making 32,000 trinkets with small mirrors set in the middle to capture the holy rays of the saints' relics that would be on display the next year in Aachen. Unfortunately, Gutenberg and his partners had the year wrong. The Aachen relics would not be revealed to the public and pilgrims until 1440, and Gutenberg had invested his capital and energy a year too soon.

After the failed venture in manufacturing potential contact relics, Gutenberg returned to Mainz to work on what he called "mysterious" or "secret arts." These were techniques for printing text mechanically. Gutenberg may not have been a humanist, but he realized that there were now more readers in the cities of Europe and so a growing market for available and affordable books. His great achievement was to perfect a technology for the mass production of books. He invented little. The Chinese had already pioneered the use of rag paper (which was spread west by Islam), block printing, and the printing press. But the obstacle to printing in Europe was a character set that required a large number of small letters and signs that needed to be set, reset, and replaced when broken. Gutenberg, the metal worker, came up with a hand mold, a portable device for casting type on the spot. He and his workers also perfected the use of an olive or screw press, movable type, a suitable ink, and the alignment of characters so that they made the proper contact with the paper surface. By 1450, Gutenberg had already tried printing some small texts and a Latin grammar book for his humanist market. He then turned to the first great moment in the history of print: the production of his so-called 42-Line Bible. His majestic Bibles were large, the lettering dark and clear, and the text largely free of error. His stock of up to 180 Bibles (approximately 35–40 printed on parchment, the rest on paper) sold out almost immediately, but by 1455 Gutenberg was bankrupt, his equipment seized, and the secret of automatic writing let loose upon Europe.

What followed was a revolution in European communications. Fifty years after Gutenberg produced his great Bible, 250 cities in Europe had printing presses in operation. In 1440, there had not been a single printed book in Europe; by 1500, there were over six million. The books printed in that first fifty years are called **incunabula** (from the cradle or beginning). The industry and business of print transformed elements of the European economy. Soon gone were parchment makers and scribes (but not notaries); in their place were new trades and professions: typecasters, typesetters, book sellers, and book peddlers.

The intellectual impact was just as great. The scriptorium of the medieval monastery and stationers of the medieval university were replaced by the print shop as the center of intellectual exchange. Writers were freed from having to search out patronage since they could find printers and readers to support their work. By the late fifteenth century, people no longer needed to go to the few places where manuscripts were kept; the book traveled with them or to them. Now many readers could read the same book, and one reader could read many books. As a result of print culture, the author became a distinct individual; he or she was named on the title page, and all the readers of his book could refer to the same page and be relatively sure that they were discussing the same thing. The printed book produced a standardization of typeface, text layout, size, and format. The fixity of print made the post-Gutenberg world more intellectually exact. New forms of literature (autobiographies, advertisements, and broadsides) met people where they lived, intellectually and financially.

European Renaissance humanists such as the Dutchman Desiderius Erasmus; his English friend Thomas More, who wrote *Utopia*; and the French satirist Françoise Rabelais, who wrote the wickedly outrageous history of the giants Gargantua and Pantagruel, embraced the new printing technology to perfect their texts and to reach large European audiences. Erasmus prepared the first published edition of the Greek New Testament in 1516. Devoted to an *ad fontes* approach to reforming the Catholic Church and improving the text of the New Testament, Erasmus believed in restoring the church to its pure and spiritual foundations. His most famous work, *The Praise of Folly*, is a satire on both popular superstition and the abuses of traditional church practices. Not all of Erasmus's work was religious. He was fond of adages (even supplying some for the young man who would become King Henry VIII of England) and published a volume of sayings culled from his extensive reading of ancient, medieval, and Renaissance literature. These included phrases we still use today, such as "one step at a time" and "many hands make light work." Erasmus's interest in adages reflects the humanist preoccupation with education, as most of the sayings he collected were intended to teach children not only the classical vocabulary, but also valuable life lessons.

Humanizing Print: Aldus Manutius

Aldus Manutius came to Venice in 1490. He was a humanist and schoolteacher, but not a gifted writer. Yet he was sure that he could contribute to the humanist program. Above all, he wanted to make Greek classical texts available to an intelligent reading public and so spread humanist values. The printing press took some time to reach Italy. By 1465, a press run by German clerics was in operation in a monastery near Rome; later the printers moved their press to Rome and were printing several thousand books per year. These printers found themselves in conflict with the old scribal culture of Rome: with master scribes, stationers, and a church that wanted to retain authority over the spread of texts.

A generation later, Aldus Manutius was free of some of those concerns and was a sharper businessman than Gutenberg. He had taken careful steps in planning his intellectual and business enterprise in Venice before publishing his first book. He designed beautiful Greek and Latin typefaces for his books that were easier to read than Gutenberg's Gothic font. His Roman or Humanist typeface was designed after the model of Caroline Minuscule. He pioneered the use of a clean and clear Greek minuscule script and, most striking of all, an Italic form of Roman characters, which he had copied from the reformed book script perfected by a humanist copyist. The Italic script also saved paper because more characters could be printed on the page. Finally, in 1494 he was ready to go and began publishing, at first large handsome books of Aristotle and the Greek classics. He soon found, however, that the Greek books sold less well than the Latin classics and that large-format books sold less well than small books. Thus, he introduced small, pocket-size, portable books. His print run for most editions of the classics was between 1,000 and 4,000 copies, and he reprinted the bestsellers. His press became famous for the quality of its works and had its own logo, a dolphin curled around an anchor, meaning "hasten slowly." Authors such as Erasmus spent time in Venice working in Aldus's print shop to oversee their publications, and Thomas More praised the beauty and utility of Aldus's books. The books of his press, called Aldines, were so attractive that people thought them a good investment.

Thousands of these Aldine books survive today in the great libraries of the world, among them the British Library, Vatican Library, National Library of France in Paris, State Library in Munich, Library of Congress in Washington, and the university libraries of North America. With Aldus Manutius and his press, the age of the incunabula was over and the first age of printing, with its lightning changes and awkward moments, had passed. The book was now a modern thing and little different from the books that have been published for the past five hundred years. Aldus Manutius had spread the central texts and the new method for reading them (directly and in good editions) of the humanist agenda. He had humanized print and transformed the classics into obtainable commodities, blending together in one small package the intellectual and commercial faces of the Renaissance. The printed Aldine book was a masterpiece of art and materiality, classicism and commerce.

QUESTIONS | ***How does the history of print from Gutenberg to Aldus Manutius parallel our own awkward transition from print culture to digital media? What lessons can be learned from the print revolution? Why was Gutenberg almost destined to fail and someone like Aldus bound to perfect the art of printing? How did Aldus Manutius marry Renaissance values and the economics of publishing?***

ERASMI ROTERODAMI ADAGIORVM
CHILIADES TRES, AC CENTV-
RIAE FERE TOTIDEM.

ALD·STVDIOSIS·S·

Quia nihil aliud cupio, q̃ prodeſſe uobis Studioſi. Cum ueniſſet in manus meas Eraſmi Roterodami, hominis undecunq; doctiss. hoc adagiorũ opus eruditum. uarium. plenũ bonæ frugis,
& quod poſſit uel cum ipſa antiquitate certare, intermiſſis antiquis autorib. quos pa-
raueram excudendos, illud curauimus imprimendum, rati profuturum uobis
& multitudine ipſa adagiorũ, quæ ex plurimis autorib. tam latinis, quàm
græcis ſtudioſe collegit ſummis certe laborib. ſummis uigiliis, &
multis locis apud utriuſq; linguæ autores obiter uel correctis
acute, uel expoſitis erudite. Docet præterea quot modis
ex hiſce adagiis capere utilitatem liceat, puta quẽ-
admodum ad uarios uſus accõmodari poſ-
ſint. Adde, qđ circiter decẽ millia uer-
ſuum ex Homero. Euripide, & cæ
teris Græcis eodẽ metro in
hoc opere fideliter, &
docte tralata ha
bẽtur, præ
ter plu
rima
ex Pla-
tone, De-
moſthene, & id
genus ali
is. An
autem uerus ſim,
ἰδοὺ ῥόδος, ἰδοὺ καὶ τὸ πήδημα.
Nam, quod dicitur, αὐτὸς αὑτὸν αὐλεῖ.

AL DVS

Præponitur hiſce adagiis duplex index. Alter ſecundum literas
alphabeti noſtri. nam quæ græca ſunt, latina quoq;
habentur. Alter per capita rerum.

The Title Page of Aldus Manutius's Second Printing (1508) of *The Adages of Erasmus*

Pieter Bruegel the Elder, *Netherlandish Proverbs* (1559) Several paintings by Bruegel surveyed the popular culture of his age.

The Dutch painter Pieter Bruegel the Elder (c. 1525–1569) also had a humanist agenda that reached down the social scale. In his painting *Netherlandish Proverbs,* he depicts over a hundred common proverbs and vernacular expressions such as "she can even tie the devil to a pillow," "patient as a lamb," "he fills the well after the calf has drowned," "he stoops to get on in the world," and "he has the world spinning on his thumb" (scenes running along the front from the far left of the painting). His delightful painting *Children's Games* shows hundred of children engaged in dozens of different games, but makes deeper humanist points about the stages of childhood, about the adult world that children imitate, and about the darkness of city life and the light-filled world of nature, the world's innocent playground.

Humanism may have begun with a small group of learned men and women in Italy, but by the middle of the sixteenth century it had become a European phenomenon that reached out and into society. The Renaissance was a way of viewing the world in its messy splendor. The spreading Renaissance (with its shared belief in superior models, critical and systematic analysis, and the appreciation of cultural and linguistic particulars) made Europe more distinctly European, just as Christianity and the Middle Ages once had.

Conclusion

Between Petrarch and Cassandra Fedele, western Europe underwent a significant change of attitudes toward the ancient past, educational programs, politics and its methods (statecraft, diplomacy, espionage, and bureaucracy), and technology. Italy's cultural and intellectual preoccupations with humanism and individualism spread through much of Europe. The visual and literary arts flourished, with new styles and techniques of painting and sculpting, the rise of vigorous vernacular literatures, a critical approach to classical texts and the classical past, and the wondrous spread of printed books. The Renaissance at its humanist core was a movement for intellectual, individual, and social improvement.

Events between 1494 and 1527 meant, however, that Italy would have to surrender its centrality to the movement. The independence and vigor of the Italian city-states was fatally compromised, and Italy and its Renaissance were drawn ever deeper into European affairs. The Italian Renaissance was absorbed into an overriding European Renaissance that by 1550 was fracturing at the seams; there was too much information, too many disagreements between various schools of thought, and too many regional and religious interests for it to hold together as a coherent movement. The next two stages of European history—overseas exploration and religious re-formation—were laced with humanist aspirations but would in the end move in very different directions. For one thing, the Renaissance had trumpeted the values of travel and new experiences, the acquisition of new knowledge, and the discovery of new things. Petrarch ascended Mont Ventoux for spiritual and personal growth, but he was also climbing a tall mountain because no one had done so before (or for a long time), because the experience was worth having, and because he might learn something new about the world and himself. By the late fifteenth century, Europeans were looking beyond Europe and beyond the Ottoman imperial block to the east, which was territorially and spiritually suffocating Europe's lust for new lands, riches, and peoples to convert. Many church reformers of the sixteenth century—including Erasmus, More, and Rabelais—were humanists, intent on improving the church, just as they improved their old and corrupt texts. The European Renaissance and its Italian beginnings were not unconnected to the formative and fundamental changes that would remake and reform Europe in the sixteenth century. Above all, they drove the desire to make a better (or at least, different) world, no matter the cost to others.

Critical Thinking Questions

1. What was the Italian Renaissance a "rebirth" of? Does the label adequately cover the changes at work in fifteenth-century Italy? Why or why not?
2. What case can you make that the Italian and European Renaissances were still part of the Middle Ages?
3. Why did Renaissance art emerge and flourish? How big a departure was it from previous trends in art?
4. What did the Renaissances achieve, and what lasting effects did they have on European history?

Key Terms

Italian Renaissance **(p. 325)**
commune **(p. 330)**
Bonfire of the Vanities **(p. 334)**
Arsenal **(p. 338)**
galley **(p. 338)**
doge **(p. 339)**
Renaissance humanism **(p. 341)**
Renaissance individualism **(p. 341)**
ghetto **(p. 342)**
civic humanism **(p. 344)**
ad fontes **(p. 344)**
chiaroscuro **(p. 345)**
linear perspective **(p. 345)**
incunabula **(p. 351)**

Primary Sources in connect

For information on Connect and the online resources available, go to **http://connect.mcgraw-hill.com**.

1. **Petrarch's Ascent of the Windy Mountain**
2. **Laura Cereta's Defense of Wise Women**
3. **Vergerio on Education as a Moral Necessity**
4. **Pico's Oration on the Dignity of Man**
5. **Three Church Responses to the Art of Printing**
6. **Erasmus's Sayings**

BACK TO THE SOURCE

Machiavelli's Crafty Prince

Niccolò Machiavelli (1469–1527) was a contrary and contradictory character in his own time and has been a controversial one ever since. In 1513, he wrote the contrary and controversial *The Prince* for a junior line of the Medici.

Those Who Become Princes through Crime

. . . [I]n gaining a state by force, a conqueror must weigh carefully all the negative things he must do and then do them all at once so that he does not have to do them over and over again. By refraining from applying constant coercion, men will begin to feel safe and the prince will secure their loyalty through the rewards he bestows upon them. Any ruler who proceeds otherwise, because he is fearful or hesitant or because he follows poor counsel, will always need to have a dagger within reach. For he will never be sure of his subjects' support since their new wounds will always be fresh and they will never feel safe under him. The prince needs to impose all negative things at once, for the less often they are inflicted, the less they sting. Rewards, however, should be given in small doses, but often, so that they may be fully appreciated. And a prince needs to live alongside his subjects and in this way be aware of their thoughts so that no unexpected event, either positive or negative, should force him to alter his agenda. For when crises arise you will not have the opportunity to sway your subjects with cruelty, and any good you do to them will not help, since they will think that you were forced by circumstances and you will receive no appreciation whatsoever.

On Cruelty and Kindness

. . . A prince should always be careful not to believe too fervently or to act too openly, but he also should never seem timid or hesitant. He should moderate his actions with prudence and a human touch so that excessive trust does not lead him to take foolish risks or too little trust make him inflexible.

From this arises the question of whether it is better to be loved than feared, or the contrary. I would recommend that the prince should be both, but since it is hard to combine them, it is safer to be feared than loved, if one must choose between them. For it is true of men that they are ungrateful and fickle, full of deceit and double-dealing, absolute cowards who still remain greedy for their own advantage. While you pour rewards on them, they remain loyal and will offer you their blood, property, lives, and offspring, that is, so long as all danger is distant. But when danger draws close, they turn away from you. Any prince who relies entirely on their empty promises rather than finding his own means to protect himself will doubtless be destroyed. For any friendship that is bought rather than based on greatness and nobility of character is never true and cannot be cashed in when needed.

Moreover, men are not concerned about harming someone who seeks to be loved rather than feared, for love is bound by a voluntary obligation, which men, who are at the core rotten, are prepared to break whenever their own self-interest is in jeopardy. But fear always binds tightly because anxiety about punishment never disappears.

A prince, however, should make himself feared in such a way that, even though he may not have won the love of his subjects, he will have avoided incurring their hatred. Being feared but not hated is a good combination, so long as the prince keeps his hands off the property and the women of his subjects. If you must execute someone, insure that you do so only when there is an obvious reason and a proper justification for it. Above all, avoid seizing the property of others, for men would rather forget the deaths of their fathers than the loss of their inheritance. Indeed, there will never be any shortage of reasons for seizing people's property. . . . To return to the question of whether it is better to be loved or feared, I think that since men love by their own will but fear by the will of the prince, a prudent prince should always depend upon himself and not on the will of others. But he should, above all, seek only to avoid being hated, as I said above.

How a Prince Should Keep his Word

. . . A prince should be a fox so as to spot the traps set out for him and a lion to frighten the wolves. Those princes who only employ the lion's nature mistake their business. A prudent ruler, therefore, cannot and should not keep his promises when it is to his disadvantage or when the reasons that inclined him to make the promise have ceased to exist. If men were entirely good, this advice would be wrong, but since men are at their core rotten and will not stand by their promises to you, you similarly need not keep your promises to them. A prince never lacks legitimate reasons for breaking his promises. I could cite innumerable modern examples to show this. . . . Rulers who know how to act as foxes have always been the most successful. But the prince should also know how to disguise his character and to be a consummate hypocrite and a brazen liar, for men are so naïve and so governed by their immediate desires that the deceiver will always find a fool willing to allow himself to be duped. . . .

A prince must appear to be thoroughly merciful, faithful, honest, kind, and pious. And it is especially necessary for the prince to seem to possess the last of these, since men generally judge more by what they see than by what they touch. Everyone sees what you appear to be, few know what you really are, and those few won't contradict the opinion of most men, who are protected by the majesty of the state. Since for the actions of everyone and particularly those of princes there is no court of appeal, we need to examine their outcomes. A prince should, therefore, boldly seize and maintain his state. His means will always be judged praiseworthy and will be lauded by all, for common people are constantly deceived by appearances and by outcomes, and in the world there are none but common people.

QUESTIONS | *What makes Machiavelli a product of the Northern Italian or European Renaissance? What does Machiavelli seek to achieve by advising the prince to be crafty, insincere, and entirely self-interested? What weapons does the prince have in his political toolkit?*

Source: *The Historical, Political and Diplomatic Writings of Niccolò Machiavelli,* trans. C. E. Detmold (Boston: J. R. Osgood, 1882), 51–52, 54–59; revised.

12

EUROPEANS TAKE TO THE OCEANS

THE CHOICE AND CHANCE OF BERNAL DÍAZ Bernal Díaz del Castillo was born in the Spanish city of Medina del Campo around 1496, just a few years after Christopher Columbus landed unexpectedly on a cluster of islands in the present-day West Indies. At the age of nineteen, Díaz set sail for the Americas to make his fortune. As was so often the case among the adventurous young men who crowded onto the ships, his high hopes for the expedition were dashed by encounters with resistant native populations, mission mismanagement, and the general ignorance of local lands and customs. After making his first port-of-call in what today is Panama, Díaz tried to improve his prospects for financial success by starting over again in Cuba. In 1517, he undertook his first mission to the Yucatán coast, where he and his fellow soldiers encountered the Maya, an ancient people with a still prosperous and sophisticated culture. Dazzled by the potential riches of the Yucatán

◄ Vasco da Gama's Caravel under Sail

Peninsula, the Spanish soon organized expeditions to explore the region.

While there, prisoners and translators told the Spanish of an even richer civilization to the northwest. The lure was irresistible to the Spanish, and in 1519, under the brutal and gifted military commander Hernán Cortés, Díaz once again found himself under sail and headed to an unknown land of golden promise. Cortés's forces soon found themselves pitted against the powerful Mexica (Aztec, as the Spanish called it) Empire of Moctezuma (Montezuma). Cortés's hostile contact left the native population overcome by warfare and ravaged by disease, and brought about the collapse of the Mexica control over its far-flung territories in Mesoamerica. The Mexica Empire was effectively destroyed; the Spanish overseas empire secured.

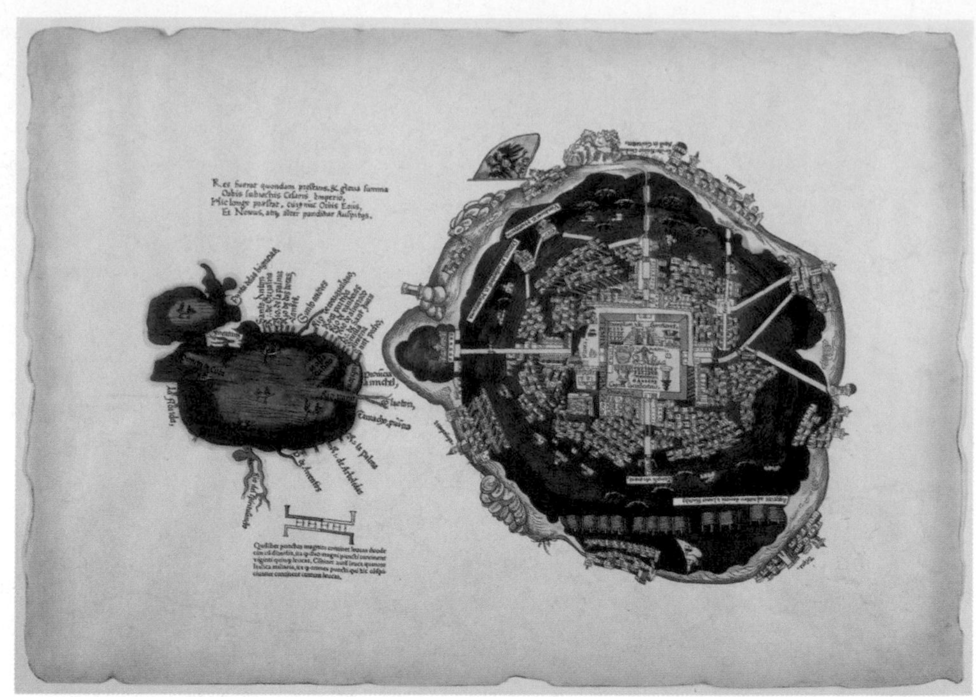

Tenochtitlán, 1524 An early map of the large capital city of the Nahua or Aztecs in Mexico as it might have looked near first contact.

Díaz's life, and those of many European men and women of the time, was shaped by the challenges and opportunities that arose in the wake of Columbus's voyage of 1492. At the end of many weeks on the open sea, with a fleet of only three ships manned by less than a hundred men, Columbus had failed to find a direct route to the fabled lands of Japan for his expedition's Spanish sponsors. Instead,

Reign of Moctezuma I Mexica Empire 1509–1520

Reign of Louis XII, France 1498–1515

Reign of Henry VII, England 1485–1509

Reign of João (John) II, Portugal 1481–1495

Reign of Manuel I 1495–1521

Bernal Díaz del Castillo sets sail for the Americas from Spain 1515

Reign of Isabella and Ferdinand, Spain 1474–1516

1470 1480 1490 1500 1510

he came to a world previously unknown to Europeans. Thanks to a skillful propaganda campaign that began the moment Columbus wrote up his report for his royal backers in Spain, European contact with the Americas soon came to dominate the imaginations and aspirations of princes, merchant sailors, and ambitious young men throughout the West.

The Americas became a promised land for young Europeans forced to find their own way in the world. Díaz's family was old and honorable, but it was not wealthy. He could hardly rely on it for land or titles to make his fame and fortune. He had received some education, but not enough to think of becoming a humanist scholar, and he had no vocation for the priesthood. Díaz instead pinned his hopes for social advancement on a career as a **conquistador,** a soldier of fortune, in the Americas. His early hopes for an easy route to wealth and glory were crushed by the harsh conditions, poorly managed military engagements, and resistant native populations of the Americas. This was to become the common fate of many who explored and colonized the Americas, but the chance for gold and glory drew them irresistibly onward.

More than thirty years after arriving in Panama and Cuba, and after receiving an administrative post in Antigua Guatemala for his service to Cortés and the Spanish monarchs, Díaz wrote an account of his life in the Americas. His *True History of the Conquest of New Spain* is not easy for us to read five centuries after the 1519 attack on the Mexica Empire. In the Americas, Europeans encountered civilizations as ancient and complex as their own, but they seldom appreciated their rich histories, deeply rooted religious beliefs, complicated economic systems, or intricate political thought. Exploration led to the conquest and subjugation of the native peoples in the Caribbean, Mesoamerica, and North and South America. After enduring centuries of unflattering comparisons between their own culture and the wealthy and sophisticated cultures of the Far East and Middle East, Europeans were ready to assert the superiority of their civilization over that of native Americans. European overseas exploration was to prove a turning point in the West's relationship with the rest of the world.

The early modern explorations and conquests of Europeans are subjects of continuing controversy, and long have been. Mark Twain captured the mixed feelings many have about this transformative episode in European history when he said: "it was wonderful to find America—but it would have been more wonderful to miss it." What we can do, at the very least, is to be aware of the bias built in to the European records and perspectives on the experience, and to guard against blindly accepting European assumptions, terms, and frames of reference. For one thing, though it was the explorers' language of description, the New World was not new and the Old World was not any older than the Americas. These terms are relative ones and have the potential to mislead. Nor were the Americas unknown. They were unknown to Europeans, just as Asia, Africa, and Europe were unknown to native Americans. Even the language of discovery seems misplaced: the Americas were not lost and so could not be found. Yet Europeans in the age of exploration were convinced that they had discovered unknown new worlds. Maps and books spoke of a *Mundus Novus* (New World) and the discovery of new

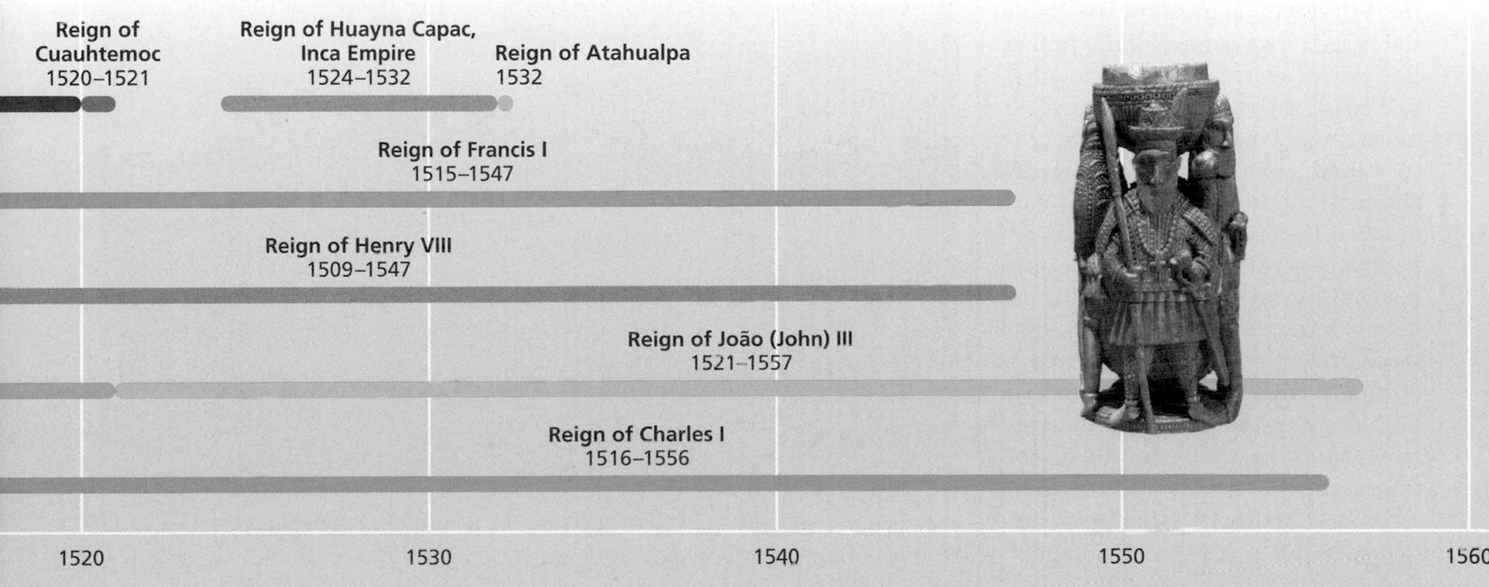

things and new peoples. Talk of newness and discovery helped Europeans to conceptualize and deal with realities beyond their existing knowledge and expectations. But it is important for us to recognize that there was not a single European exploration, conquest, and colonization, but rather a series of explorations, conquests, and colonization movements by various Europeans in competition with each other in different areas and representing different interests. Europe was no more a unified block of interests than the Americas were a unified and single thing.

Nor were early modern Europeans the first or only explorers. Human beings are a migratory species. We have already seen the spread of *Homo sapiens sapiens* out of Africa, the movement of the Indo-Europeans and Germanic tribes, and the travels of the Muslims and Vikings in the Middle Ages. Several characteristics of the European experience in the late fifteenth and sixteenth centuries, however, set it apart from those of earlier migration movements:

- The late medieval and early modern movement of Europeans overseas covered a vast distance in a relatively brief interval of time. Within fifty years, the economic and political contours of the globe were sent in new and unanticipated directions.
- This was the first great transoceanic movement of peoples in recorded history, behind which stood a series of technological transformations and particular historical circumstances in Europe.
- Europeans and native Americans came into contact with lands and peoples outside their previous experience and knowledge and, as such, theirs was a meeting of utterly alien societies.
- The impact worked in both directions, slowly transforming the European and American peoples, their societies, histories, and economies.

These distinctions may highlight the extraordinary nature of European expansion, but not why it took place. The two main reasons typically given for European expansion are material (greed for gold and land) and religious (to convert or coerce others to Christianity), but a third may be more convincing and house the other two: that is, the intensely competitive character of late medieval and early modern Europe. This dynamic competitiveness was the result of the spirit of activism and opportunism that animated Europeans after the crises of the fourteenth century, the fracturing of high medieval certainties and traditional ways of living, and the vigor of Mediterranean mercantilism. Both China and Islam had more sophisticated and technologically advanced cultures, but it was the competitive Europeans who took to the oceans in pursuit of advantage. European monarchs, rulers, merchants, and priests were locked in to contests for dominance over each other. The many Europes had taught them that lesson the hard way. Europe was **balkanized** or broken into dozens of small units of various sizes and importance (kingdoms, principalities, republics, cities, regions) in constant struggle with each other. At the personal level, individuals such as Gutenberg, Columbus, and Díaz were looking for their big break, gold and glory, by rising above their competitive contemporaries. This war of interests did not begin when Columbus set sail. It had been building throughout the fifteenth century and would continue throughout the early modern period.

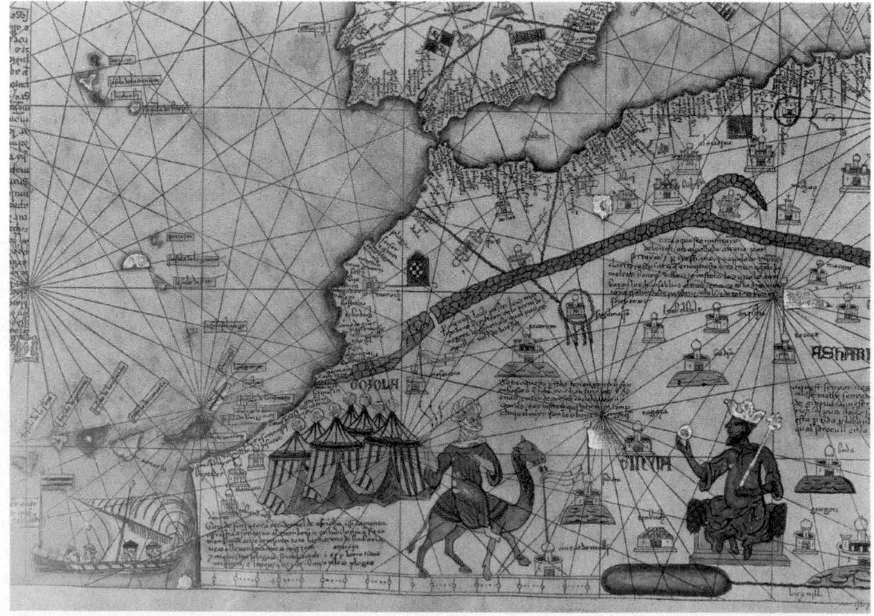

Fourteenth-Century Iberia and Africa The Catalan Atlas of 1375 set out what Europeans knew at the time of islands in the Atlantic and of northern Africa.

European Exploration before 1492

As startling as Columbus's discovery of the Americas was to Europeans, his voyages were only the latest in a series of voyages of exploration in the Late Middle Ages. Knowledge acquired over centuries of maritime experience in the Mediterranean and near the North Atlantic came together with a desire to find a way to trade with Asia that did not require Ottoman middlemen, an interest in converting others to Christianity, and a political interest in expanding the territorial holdings of European kingdoms.

Why did Portugal and Castile send their ships outward into the Atlantic rather than inward to the Mediterranean?

Europeans had been building toward their Atlantic breakout from Europe for over a century. Extraordinary developments in navigation and technology made the voyages possible. Columbus's journey across the Atlantic was preceded by decades of explorations of lands closer to Europe sponsored by princes, funded by merchants, and undertaken by adventurous mariners. For two centuries before 1492, Europeans had been undertaking voyages of exploration in the eastern Atlantic Ocean and along the coast of Africa in search of a route that would lead them to the Indian Ocean and Asia. Developments in shipbuilding technology made it possible for mariners to sail farther than ever before into uncharted seas and along unmapped coastlines. At the same time that the ideas and ideals of the two Renaissances were being developed, the knowledge and skills necessary for lengthy voyages across open seas were being developed in western Mediterranean cities such as Genoa, Lisbon, Barcelona, Valencia, and Cadiz. In the process, islands were encountered off the coast of northern Africa that provided opportunities for early colonial experiments that would shape what Columbus and his successors did in the Americas. The Canary Islands, in particular, proved to be a testing ground for European expansion and the struggle for advantage between rival powers and ambitious men.

Western Fantasies, Western Wanderlust

Europeans had long been fascinated by the exotic external world known to them through tales of strange peoples, monsters, and freaks of nature. Were they culturally (as well as historically) predisposed to explore and migrate? The Bible, with its accounts of the Near East, foreign lands, and wandering Hebrews, transported Christian Europeans to a world other than the one they inhabited. The various accounts of the adventures of the desert fathers took them into an Egyptian landscape filled with strange creatures such as crocodiles and hippopotamuses, and shape-shifting demons. Stories of this kind served as the fantasy literature of the Middle Ages. Added to this was the information about bizarre lands, pygmies, fire-breathing mountains, and stones that burned (phosphorous) that they could cull from reading Roman encyclopedias such as Pliny the Elder's *Natural History*. By the Early Middle Ages, fantastic tales of the wonders of India were in wide circulation. The Middle Ages and Northern Italian Renaissance were equally attracted to the exotic East, spawning their own stories such as the one of Prester John, the legendary Christian king in the east surrounded by hostile pagans (Muslims) and waiting to rejoin the Christian community in the west. There was a hunger in Europe for stories of distant travel to marvelous and dangerous places. Geography and history combined with myths and legends in popular chronicles and travelers' tales such as *The Travels of Sir John Mandeville.*

Genoese Trade and Travel

Beyond the eastern fantasies that fueled western wanderlust, there were real contacts with Asia in the Middle Ages. In the thirteenth century, as we saw, Franciscan friars and merchant adventurers such as the Polos had reached the Mongol court. The fall of the Mongol dynasty, the closing down of long-distance travel routes, and the fourteenth-century plague that stunned European society and its economy meant that the late fourteenth century was no longer as conducive to long-distance travel. By the mid-fifteenth century, Europeans were once again on the move. The European economy had recovered and, indeed, there was more money for urban Europeans in particular to spend. Those who had never been able to afford luxury goods found that they could afford imported cloth or a packet of Asian spices. The European appetite for luxury goods grew in the plague's aftermath. Given the competition in the Mediterranean for control over shipping lanes and ports, the European need to find new trade routes and opportunities was acute. The Genoese, who tried to fill that demand, were among the most adventurous searchers for mercantile advantage. The first recorded attempt to reach Asia by a southern sea route was made by the Vivaldi brothers of the Italian maritime republic of Genoa in 1291, when their expedition attempted to round the coast of Africa. The brothers anticipated that it would take ten years to reach Japan. Somewhere off the northwestern coast of Africa the ships disappeared, and so entered travelers' lore, but the Vivaldis had planted the idea that Europeans might one day find a southern sea-route to the Far East.

Throughout the late medieval period, the Genoese won colonial outposts closer to home on islands in the eastern Mediterranean, such as Chios, and in the Black Sea near the Crimea. While much of Genoa's military and mercantile effort was directed eastward and in direct competition with Venice, its more westerly location meant that the Genoese were also attuned to developments in the Atlantic and were in competitive trading networks with Portugal, France, the Netherlands, and England. Genoa played a critical role in these northwestern European economies because, apart from agriculture, those economies were based largely on wool and cloth production. Through its colony on Chios, Genoa controlled the European supply of alum, a mineral substance used to fix dyes in cloth and to tan hides for leather goods. The substance was in high demand in countries where significant amounts of cloth were produced.

Always in a political and economic struggle with Venice over shipping lanes and access to Mediterranean ports of call, Genoa was dealt a severe blow in 1453 when Constantinople fell to the Ottomans. Though Chios remained a Genoese colony, Ottoman forces on the seas and within the lands that surrounded it made transporting alum to Europe an increasingly difficult and expensive operation. Alum was so important to the European economy that when it was discovered north of Rome, at Tolfa in 1462, the papacy proclaimed it a miracle. The Genoese moved quickly to monopolize the supply, but they had learned a lesson in economic diversification and began looking for ways to monopolize and control other commodities in other ports.

Travelers' Tales

While preparing for his first voyage across the Atlantic, Christopher Columbus repeatedly read a strange traveler's tale by John Mandeville that he hoped would give him some idea about where he was going and what he might encounter. Jehan de Mandeville (John Mandeville, as he is known in English) is the name attached to a compilation of travelers' tales drawn together between 1357 and 1371 as *The Travels of Sir John Mandeville.* Though the tales were written in Anglo-Norman French by a man who claimed to be an English knight, there is no evidence that John Mandeville ever existed, and these "autobiographical" tales were most likely elaborate fabrications. Nevertheless, they were thought to be true and became immensely popular among late medieval readers. Such tales were translated into dozens of European languages and dialects, and hundreds of manuscript copies of them survive. After the advent of print, the tales of John Mandeville and Marco Polo circulated widely.

John Mandeville as Portrayed in a Copy of His Tales

Early travel accounts such as those ascribed to John Mandeville can give us important insights into the stories and experiences that shaped European attitudes toward different peoples and cultures, but they can be tricky to use. Some of the material in the early travel books is undoubtedly drawn from firsthand, eyewitness accounts of people, places, and events. But rumors and legends that might contain only a nugget of truth were imaginatively embellished in these books. Other tales about exotic people and faraway lands were completely fabricated to entertain listeners. Mandeville's supposed encounters with dog-headed men, Amazonian warriors, and a race of pygmies with giant slaves were based on ancient and medieval fables that had been passed down at European firesides for centuries.

As time passed and Europeans were no longer able to travel to Asia as they had under the Mongols, it became harder to sift the true from the false in various travelers' tales. Even so, the widespread interest in these stories demonstrates just how curious medieval and early modern Europeans were about the external world. As western Europeans took to the seas and explored the globe, their interest in ancient and medieval travelers' tales grew as they looked for guidance in interpreting what they saw and heard. It would be centuries before books such as *The Travels of Sir John Mandeville* were recognized as works of fiction. Until that time, they continued to shape European attitudes toward other peoples and cultures, and thus provide important clues as to why explorers and colonizers behaved as they did.

QUESTIONS | ***What literature today serves the same function as did the late medieval travelers' tales? What is that function? How did such tales both reveal and shape European attitudes?***

The Genoese pioneered a trading strategy different from their Venetian rivals. Specifically, Genoa established small trading colonies in foreign ports that oversaw the procurement of raw materials rather than the acquisition or production of finished luxury goods for trade; it would then trade those raw resources in European markets. The republic turned its attention to purchasing or leasing mercury mines in Spain, iron mines on the island of Elba, and salt manufacturing operations on Ibiza. Although the Genoese colonies were not as large or strategically important as the long chain of Venetian colonies that ringed the Adriatic and extended into the eastern Mediterranean, they helped Europeans to appreciate the importance of controlling the resource trade.

Portugal's Big Breakout

By the fifteenth century, Europe was a small continent surrounded by Muslims and water (see Map 11.3, p. 340). One was a block, sealing Europe inside Europe; the other a watery avenue to a wider world. Just as the rise of Islam had shaped the European Middle Ages, so too did its territorial dominance of the Near East play a critical role in determining the direction of European expansion. The dramatic rise of the Ottoman Empire had blocked off the eastern Mediterranean and made the Silk Road to China and the Far East largely inaccessible to Europeans. Moreover, the rise of more aggressive monarchs in Europe in the Late Middle Ages meant

CHRONOLOGY Timing Overseas Exploration

YEARS	EVENT
1405–1433	Chinese Admiral Zheng He surveys the Indian Ocean
1455–1487	Portuguese explore the African coastline from Cape Verde to the Cape of Good Hope
1492–1493	First voyage of Christopher Columbus reaches the Bahamas and Hispaniola
1493–1494	Second voyage of Columbus establishes settlement of La Isabella
1497	John Cabot reaches Newfoundland and Nova Scotia
1497–1499	Vasco da Gama rounds the Cape of Good Hope and enters the Indian Ocean
1498–1500	Third voyage of Columbus reaches Venezuela and Orinoco River
1499–1501	Amerigo Vespucci touches down in South America
1502–1504	Fourth voyage of Columbus surveys the coast of Central America
1513	Vasco de Balboa crosses Isthmus of Panama and sees the Pacific Ocean
1519	Hernán Cortés conquers the Mexica Empire
1519–1522	Ferdinand Magellan's expedition circumnavigates the globe
1531	Francisco Pizarro conquers the Inca Empire

that Europe was not an easy place in which to expand internally. The Hundred Years' War between France and England had shown how costly and destructive it was for one European country to claim territory from another. Yet European countries continued to hunger for growth and advantage, and were intensely competitive with each other. By the fifteenth century, it was becoming apparent that the only way to break out of the competitive gridlock of Europe was by seeking advantage outside of Europe by water, in effect by sailing away from Europe.

Portugal, a small land on the western shore of the Iberian Peninsula, is a revealing example of what drove European kingdoms to maritime exploration and territorial expansion (Map 12.1). Portugal was carved out of Muslim Spain when King Dom Afonso Henrique in 1147 employed western crusaders to assist him in capturing Lisbon. By the late thirteenth century, the territory of Portugal was fixed, with Muslims (Moors) and the Christian kingdoms of Léon, Castile, and Navarre as its less-than-friendly neighbors in Iberia. There was little prospect of Portuguese expansion within the Iberian Peninsula and none whatsoever in Europe. Moreover, Portugal's physical setting was such that it lacked rich agricultural land; its economy depended on fishing and trade. Portugal's big breakout from its Iberian and European limitations would, therefore, have to be by sea and by aggressive trade. While Genoa cornered the European alum market and developed merchant colonies, the kingdom of Portugal set its sights on acquiring gold. Little gold was found in European mineral deposits, and most of the gold in circulation in Europe in the fifteenth century came by way of Muslim middlemen in cities on the north coast of Africa who drew on suppliers from western Africa. Loyal to the Ottoman Empire, the gold traders dealt with Europeans on increasingly unfavorable terms. The Portuguese hatched a plan to deal directly with western Africans. To do so, they had to increase their knowledge of the African coastline, make contacts with the resident peoples, and find safe and efficient ways to move gold from the African interior to the coast.

In 1415, Portugal conquered Ceuta, a strategically important port directly across the mouth of the Mediterranean from the Straits of Gibraltar. This gave the Portuguese two mercantile and strategic advantages it had lacked: direct access to the Mediterranean Sea and a territorial foothold on the continent of Africa. They soon took Tangier and established a permanent trading presence in northern Africa. With the aid of Muslim geographers, Portugal began to expand its knowledge of Africa, breaking out of the older Greek or Ptolemaic scheme of the world centered on the Mediterranean Sea. After Ceuta, the Portuguese began to explore and map the western coastline of Africa. Leading this exploration was Prince Dom Henrique (Henry the Navigator; 1394–1460). He trained navigators, ordered maps of the African coastline, and sent ships out each year to proceed farther south down the coast of Africa. In 1455, the Portuguese sailed past Cape Verde and saw that, beyond the Sahara Desert, Africa was lush and green. After the death of Henrique, the Portuguese continued to push south, reaching Benin by 1475 and reaching the southern tip of Africa (later called the Cape of Good Hope) in 1487–1488. Ten years later, Vasco da Gama (1460–1524) rounded Africa and headed for India. We will return to the eastward voyages of the Portuguese at the end of the chapter.

As they extended their knowledge of the African coast, the Portuguese established outposts to trade with local rulers. They traded horses, saddles, cloth, wine, salt, lead, and copper in exchange for gold to fuel their economy, spices and drugs to supply the luxury market, grain to feed their people, and slaves to provide labor. The Portuguese interest in acquiring slaves began as early as 1434, when they raided the Saharan coast, capturing and enslaving native Africans. Tensions with local rulers soon convinced the Portuguese that it was politically and economically more advantageous for them to trade

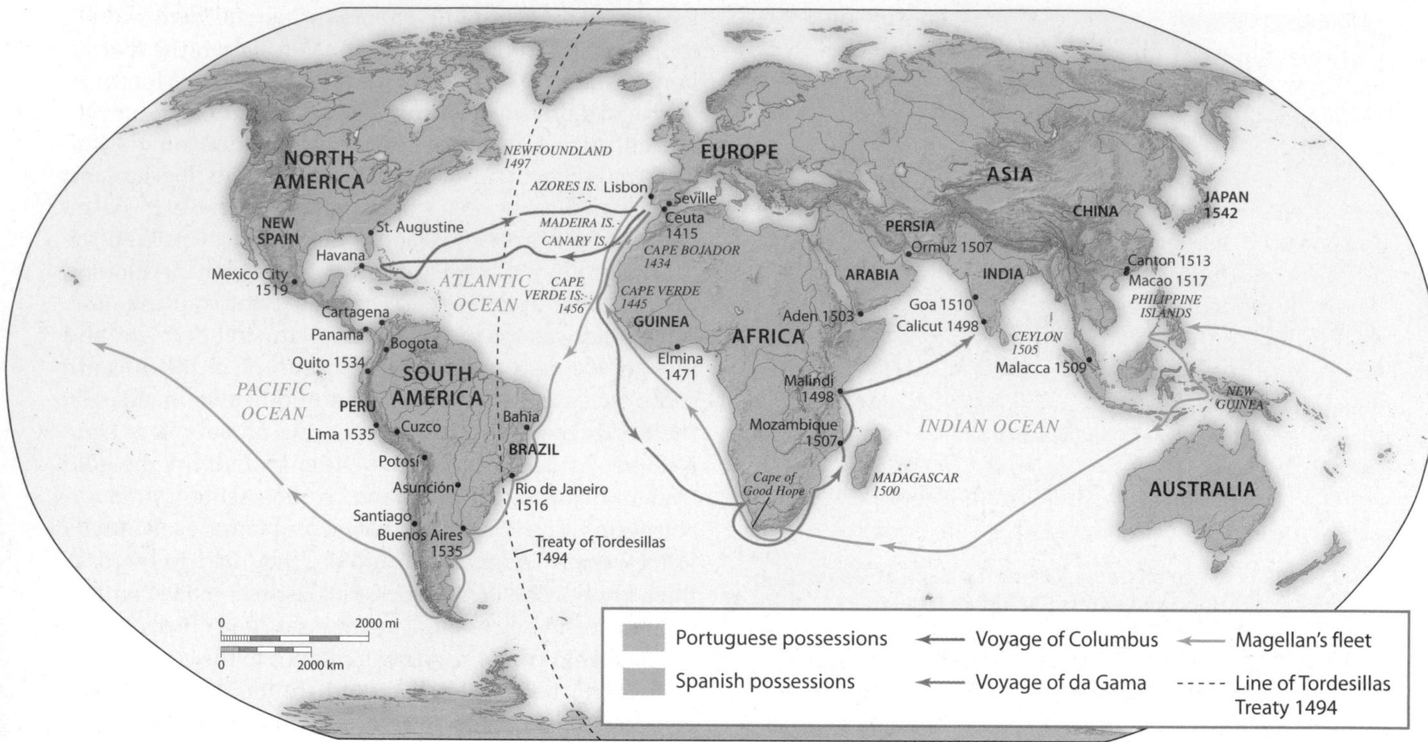

MAP 12.1 | Portuguese and Spanish Overseas Exploration, 1450–1542
This map shows only the significant "firsts" or breakthrough voyages that Europeans made to open up new territories overseas. Europeans made many other voyages overseas. ***Why did the Portuguese and Spanish go in different directions? What results did the division of Tordesillas in 1494 have? What do the different settlement patterns of the Portuguese and Spanish suggest?***

European goods for slaves through African agents than to launch their own slave raids.

The African slaves who entered the European economy through the hands of Portuguese traders did not, for the most part, end their journey in Lisbon or another European city. Instead, they were transported to the Atlantic archipelagos of the Canary and Madeira Islands off the northwestern coast of Africa to work on the plantations and farms that European colonists were developing there.

Under King João (John) I (r. 1385–1433), the Portuguese focused their colonization efforts on the Madeira Islands. In 1417, to stave off Castilian plans to occupy the Canaries and Madeiras, King João sent one hundred settlers to the chief islands of Madeira and Porto Santo under the leadership of two minor Portuguese nobles and a longtime Italian resident of Portugal, Bartolomeu Perestrelo. The crown was able to exercise greater control over the islands after 1433, when King Duarte placed them under the supervision of his brother, Prince Henrique (Henry the Navigator).

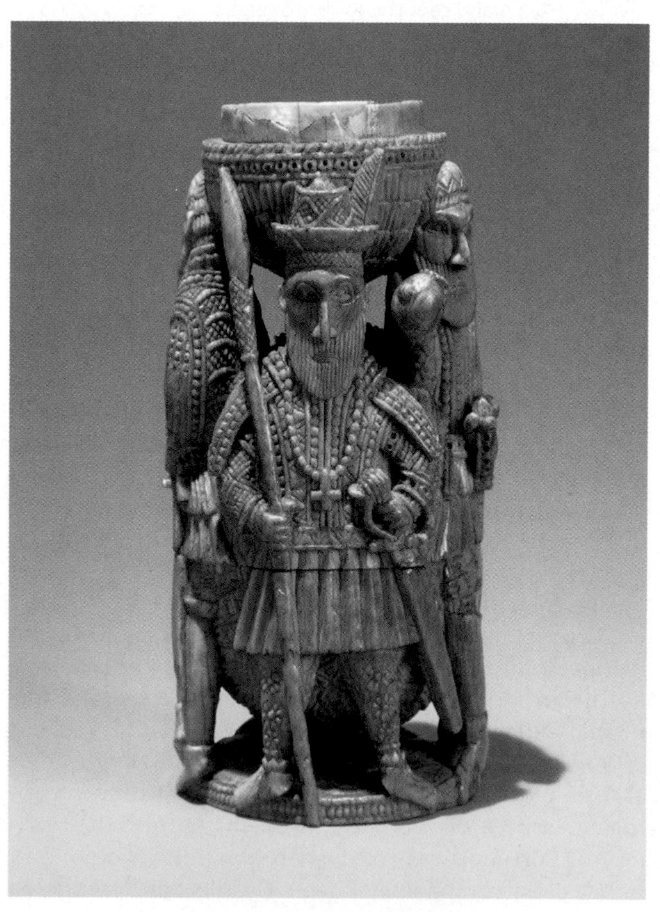

An African View of the Portuguese An Edo or Benin carver depicted four Portuguese (two wealthy traders facing out) and their assistants (in profile) on this ivory salt cellar. The sculptor paid particular attention to the elaborate dress of the Portuguese traders. The salt cellar was probably a trade item meant for the traders or the Portuguese market.

The Portuguese were able to gain control over the Madeiras relatively quickly, for though the islands were fertile, they had been uninhabited. Portuguese settlers had to clear forests and establish irrigation systems before the islands could be planted with valuable crops such as grain and sugarcane, but there was no native population to overcome or enslave. By 1450, the Madeiras were producing a profitable amount of grain and flour, and after 1452, its sugarcane crops yielded enough to make a tidy sum for the Portuguese crown and investors. Planters there never relied heavily on slave labor for their agricultural work since the influx of cheap Portuguese laborers eager for a better life kept up with the demand for plantation workers. Given the profitable enterprises that were established on the islands, it is not surprising that the population grew dramatically, from 100 settlers in 1417 to as many as 800 by 1455, and to somewhere between 15,000 and 18,000 settlers and a small number of slaves by 1600.

In the fifteenth century, the Portuguese finally broke out of the restricted confines of Iberia and Europe, brought western Africa into a European trading network, and finally found a direct sea route to Asia. By doing so, they escaped the limitations imposed on them by crowded and competitive Iberia and Europe. In the Madeira Islands, they laid down a model for the exploitation of conquered lands through plantation agriculture. They also influenced the next generation of explorers, including Columbus.

Castile and the Contest for the Canaries

Portugal's most serious rival in Africa and the Atlantic islands was the kingdom of Castile, which dominated the Iberian Peninsula both geographically and politically. Castile had coastline on the Mediterranean and the Atlantic but shared the Iberian Peninsula with the kingdoms of Portugal, Aragon, Navarre, and Muslim-held Granada. Despite their relatively landlocked position, the Castilians were eager to explore new ways to enter into maritime trade and to best their Portuguese rivals (see Map 12.1).

Their first great struggle was over the Canary Islands, a set of volcanic islands (like the Azores and Madeiras) forming an archipelago off the western coast of Africa. Berbers had attempted to take the islands in the eleventh century but met resistance from the native inhabitants. The islanders (called Guanches) were a non-Muslim people of northern African origin who herded animals and farmed. Though the islands were known in classical antiquity, serious European interest in the Canary Islands did not begin until the fourteenth century. In 1341, ships from Lisbon, with a mixed European crew, landed on the islands. The Europeans attempted to communicate with the natives by sign language but were interested chiefly in sizing up these strange people and the wealth of the islands. They were particularly struck by the Guanches' nakedness, strange diet, and lack of organized religion. The Portuguese brought back four islanders as proof of their landing.

The existence of the Canary Islands and their unknown people posed a problem for European thought. Who were these people, and why did neither the ancients nor the Bible talk about them? The Florentine writer Giovanni Boccaccio, struck by the pastoral simplicity of the Canary islanders, wrote a short treatise on the islands that was not published in his lifetime. Petrarch also wrote about the islanders, seeing them as masters of solitude because they were cut off from the rest of the world.

Portugal may have had first claim to the Canary Islands, but in 1402 Castile launched a force to conquer the islands. The Castilian efforts in the Canary Islands would set patterns of conquest, colonization, and economic organization that would shape their later practices in the Americas. Though the Portuguese established plantations on the Azores and Madeiras, those island chains were empty and open to Portuguese settlement. The residents of the Canary Islands, however, fought back and were able to use the rocky terrain of the islands to hide from and ambush any invaders. Prince Henrique had his own plans for securing control of the Canaries, but his attempts in 1422 and 1434 were futile. Not until 1479 did Portugal and Castile settle their dispute over who owned the islands; they decided to divide up the African islands. Portugal gained absolute possession of the Azores and Madeiras, and Castile took the Canaries. Castile spent much of the late fifteenth century trying to subdue the islands, but it was not until 1496, when the island of Tenerife finally fell, that the archipelago was entirely under Castilian control.

The Castilians viewed the native Guanches as a people who could be subjugated and sold into slavery or put to work on the sugarcane plantations that were being introduced on the islands. Over the fifteenth century, the relatively small population of Guanches was reduced substantially by warfare, capture, and slavery for those who resisted, and even further by the spread of the epidemic diseases carried by Europeans. As the native population shrank, slaves were brought back from Spain, from raids launched by the Castilians in northern Africa, and from Portuguese slave traders dealing in African slaves. Over time the enslaved labor force of natives was replaced by labor from the Iberian Peninsula, which was sufficient to keep the relatively small sugar plantations operational.

The Canary Islands proved to be a testing ground and template for the coming century of overseas explorations, conquests, and the establishment of settlements by Spain, Portugal, and the other exploration-sponsoring powers of Europe. Europeans may have had an intellectual interest in figuring out who these unknown peoples and places were, but their real interests were economic and competitive. There was a race to secure an advantage over their rivals by dominating territories previously unknown to Europeans and then to put them to economic use. To that end, the native population was turned into a subservient labor force and its religious well-being and security were ignored. The identity and culture of these residents was not a primary consideration in the larger scheme of exploration. Western war did some damage to the Canary islanders, but it was western diseases that destroyed them and their way of life. Native Americans would undergo much the same experience.

The Pursuit of Technological Advantage

As the Genoese, Portuguese, and Castilians were expanding their geographic knowledge of the Atlantic and the coast of Africa, they were also improving their navigational tools and skills. Changes in shipbuilding resulted in ships that were lighter, more resistant to damage, and faster. By the time Columbus set sail in 1492 for Japan, he could sail the open seas for a significant distance and period of time.

Prior to the fifteenth century, two basic kinds of ships were in use in Europe: galleys and round ships. Galleys were faster and powered primarily by oars, although they used sails when possible. They had small cargo areas, required large crews, and were heavy and slow. Round ships were short, wide, and powered by small triangular sails set on a single mast. They required only small crews but were almost entirely dependent on the prevailing wind conditions to achieve speed, and they were never very fast. Their sails were notoriously inefficient. Round ships often waited in port for months before the winds allowed them to depart.

To cross any large expanse of water, Europeans needed to blend the two styles into a single vessel that combined their strengths. First, larger, square sails replaced the smaller, triangular sails of the round ships; these were better at catching the wind. The new square sails, however, were incapable of filling completely in light winds, and by 1492, shipbuilders had developed a three-masted ship called a **carrack** that was rigged with both square and triangular sails to ensure that any hint of wind would be caught. These new ships still remained large, heavy, and hard to maneuver. Carracks were best employed as merchant vessels, since their holds could contain 100–200 tons and they required large crews to tend to the sails. The three-masted **caravel** required only a small crew, could hold 50–70 tons of cargo, and its sails could capture sufficient wind to power the light-hulled ship across the open seas with speed.

The challenge of steering vessels into unknown waters and along unknown shores demanded advanced navigational instruments and techniques. There were three essential navigational tools on fifteenth-century ships: the magnetic compass, the Portolan chart, and the astrolabe or quadrant. Pilots who knew how to use these instruments were critical to the success of any voyage. The earliest European compasses appeared in the twelfth century, following Arabic examples, and were little more than magnetized needles that pointed to true north and were mounted on a card painted with the four cardinal directions. Over time, the designs became more sophisticated, as demanded by wealthy merchants and venturesome princes.

Portolan charts showed navigable ports, landmarks, geographic features, and compass headings so that a pilot could plot his course with respect to the shoreline and his ship's position. These charts were of little use in the open seas where there were no fixed coastal reference points from which to take bearings. In the northern hemisphere, mariners used **astrolabes** (or the smaller quadrants) to steer on the open seas by the only fixed point available, the Pole Star. On clear nights, mariners used an astrolabe to calculate their latitude relative to their earlier positions on the voyage. Astrolabes measured the angle of the Pole Star relative to the horizon, but as Portuguese explorers moved south of the equator in their search for the southern tip of Africa, the Pole Star disappeared from view. Instead they used the astrolabe and the sun's position at noon relative to the horizon to approximate their position, and in 1500 they identified the southern equivalent of the Pole Star, the constellation known as the Southern Cross. This enabled more accurate calculations of position in the southern hemisphere and improved the accuracy of maps and charts.

Despite this progress, fifteenth-century mariners undertaking long voyages on unknown seas still had no easy way to calculate with accuracy their speed or to find their longitude (east-west position). Experienced mariners were adept at "dead reckoning," a method for calculating how fast a ship was traveling and in what direction based on a combination of observing the hull's progress through the water, noting each change of compass heading, and measuring the passage of time with an hourglass.

West to Asia: Columbus's Voyages

Why was Columbus both a success and a failure?

Christopher Columbus had an unlikely idea: to sail west to Asia. His passion and persistence convinced at least three patrons that he was not crazy, but might be on to something. His personal ambitions by pure luck matched the economic, territorial, and religious aspirations of Spanish monarchs who were in the full flush of success and ready to take a gamble on the Genoese mariner. Like most of the early explorers and administrators, Columbus was not a renaissance humanist, but a man of humble background and enormous ambition. His accidental landing in the Americas was an unexpected event that changed history.

Columbus's Early Years

Christopher Columbus's life prior to 1492 is shrouded in relative obscurity. Surviving evidence suggests that

Christopher Columbus Sebastiano del Piombo painted this portrait of the explorer thirteen years after Columbus's death in 1519, but it captures the majesty of the man in the full flush of his achievement.

he was born in the seafaring republic of Genoa around 1451. Columbus's father, Domenico, was a humble wool-weaver who, around 1439, opened a shop in Genoa, married Susanna Fontanarossa, and had four children.

Columbus spent his early years learning the skills that he would need to pursue his father's trade. During those years, Columbus received a rudimentary education at home and may have spent some time in a grammar school that taught the children of guild members in the city how to read and write. He was raised a Roman Catholic, though some historians have, with little evidence, argued that Columbus's family were ***conversos,*** Jews who had converted recently to Catholicism. By the time Columbus was twenty-one, he had entered the wool trade, but the pay was too poor for such an ambitious young man. To make more money, Columbus kept a tavern and picked up jobs in the harbor, serving on ships that traveled to England, Ireland, and the Genoese colony of Chios.

Around 1476, Columbus decided that he was more interested in a life at sea than a life spent in a wool shop in Genoa. He left for Portugal, determined to make his fortune and a name for himself. There he worked as an agent for a Genoese merchant; studied theories about the earth and seas; and began to learn languages, including Latin (which was essential for the study of cosmology and mathematics), the Castilian dialect spoken at the royal courts on the Iberian Peninsula (which was vital to win influential patrons), and Portuguese (the language of the mariners who worked on ships).

In 1478–1479, Columbus solidified his position in Portugal by marrying Felipa Moniz Perestrela, the daughter of Bartolomeu Perestrelo, the official from the Portuguese colony on the Madeira Islands. The marriage provided Columbus with access to the Perestrelo family's navigational papers. These included Portolan charts, wind readings taken on the open seas of the Atlantic, and detailed information about the African coastline. The Perestrelo family's court connections gave Columbus his first opportunity to put together and promote his plan for reaching Japan and China by sailing west across the Atlantic, rather than east through the Mediterranean or around Africa.

Columbus interviewed sailors, ship captains, and merchants about their experiences in the Atlantic. Much of the information he gathered was a mixture of myth and rumor, but from it he concluded that the earth was smaller than generally believed, that Asia extended thirty degrees of longitude farther east than it actually does, and that Japan was 1,500 miles east off the coast of the Asian mainland. The novelty of Columbus's theory, then, was not that the earth was round (something assumed by medieval men and women), but that the earth was smaller than generally believed and that Japan was much closer to the west coast of Europe than Europeans believed. If Columbus was right, it meant that a ship could reach Asia before it ran out of manpower and supplies. Not surprisingly, Columbus found little support for his radical and erroneous idea.

The Search for Sponsors

Despite the skepticism about his theory, Columbus stuck with it and promoted his plan tirelessly. He approached King João II (r. 1481–1495) of Portugal in search of funding for his venture, but the king's advisors warned against it. In 1485, still bitter over João's rejection, Columbus left Portugal for Spain. There he resumed interviewing mariners about their experiences in the Atlantic and sought out people who might endorse his theory about the size of the earth and the feasibility of a westward voyage to Japan. He also contacted King Henry VII of England with his idea for a westward voyage to Asia but received little encouragement at the young Tudor court. In Spain, however, Columbus gained the support of several Franciscan friars who served as middlemen between Italian merchants and the royal court of Isabella of Castile. In 1486, Isabella and Ferdinand agreed to provide Columbus with enough funds to plan his voyage, but not enough to set off across the Atlantic.

Six years later, Columbus was chafing to get under way and threatened to leave for France if he was not given the funding to outfit his ships. At that point, a combination of events and the intervention of an unlikely sponsor changed Columbus's prospects. The year was 1492 and Isabella and Ferdinand were elated by their victory over the Muslim armies at Granada. At that moment, Luis de Santangel, a Jewish *converso* and royal financial minister, offered to help finance the voyage. Luis convinced Isabella and Ferdinand that their victory over the Muslims would pale in comparison with converting the Japanese to Christianity. Buoyed by their success and relieved of the responsibility of financing the venture entirely by themselves, the monarchs released the funds and approved the voyage. Columbus hired a crew of fewer than a hundred men (all he could afford) and left the port of Palos in Spain in early August 1492 with a fleet of three ships, a carrack named the *Santa Maria* and two caravels named the *Niña* and *Pinta.* He headed first for the Canary Islands, but learned while there that the Portuguese had sent out a ship to arrest him. On September 8, he quickly left the Canaries, headed west into the Atlantic, and made landfall in the cluster of islands now known as the Bahamas on October 12, 1492. Columbus thought he had reached Japan, but he had actually entered a world unknown to western Europeans.

To the Americas

The impact of Columbus's landing would not be felt immediately, but after October 1492, the lives of Europeans and indigenous Americans were never to be quite the same. We have only Columbus's fragmentary accounts of these first encounters between Europeans and native Americans. The Taíno people whom the Spanish encountered in the Bahamas showed no hostility, and Columbus described them as beautiful, brown, naked, and poor. He thought that they had a temperament and nature that would make them ideal servants to Europeans. He also believed that it would be easy to convert them to Christianity because, in his eyes, they lacked any religion.

Today we know that the Taíno (which means "good" or "noble" in their own language) dominated the Caribbean region; five of their kingdoms stretched throughout the region. The Taíno were farmers, growing manioc (cassava), and fierce warriors who had a long-standing rivalry with the Carib peoples of South America and the Lesser Antilles. They had a complex religious and ceremonial life based on ancestral gods and a highly organized matrilineal society. None of their traditions would have been recognizable to the Europeans, who saw them as simple, childlike, and lacking in sophistication. Only two days after he made landfall, Columbus boasted that he could conquer the entire population with a force of only fifty men and govern them as he wished.

Columbus spent the next six months sailing around the Caribbean, exploring not only the Bahamas but the islands that we now call Hispaniola (the island divided today between the Dominican Republic and Haiti) and Cuba. Wherever he went, Columbus met with curious Taíno and exchanged European goods for a little gold, new foods, and other material tokens of his discovery. Columbus and his crew captured a few parrots and two dozen Taíno. All were transported back to Spain in the spring of 1493. Fewer than a dozen Taíno survived the voyage, but they were the first in a long series of native Americans unwillingly or unwittingly taken to Europe to show investors and patrons what the territories had to offer.

From the start, Columbus and his crew were sizing up the economic, territorial, and religious potential of the Caribbean. As his boats sailed from island to island, Columbus made sure to stake the Spanish crown's claim to each, gave each island a Spanish name, and planted a cross on foreign soil. Since the Europeans and Taíno had languages unfamiliar to each other, sign language served in their place, but there was considerable misunderstanding between the natives and explorers. When natives on one island resisted his authority, Columbus showed them a crossbow and sword and indicated that he could kill them if he so chose. Columbus took the next aggressive step at Christmas and established a settlement of thirty-nine of his men on Hispaniola. He also left a cannon with his men. The *Santa Maria* had been wrecked on a reef, so he could not take all his crew back to Spain.

Columbus's effort to promote his explorations in Europe was not limited to the material objects and native peoples he brought back with him, for he knew that he had to launch a publicity campaign to explain why he had not reached Japan and the Asian mainland. He remained convinced for the rest of his life that he had been just about to do so; one more voyage and he would have been there. His rationalization began in earnest with the letter he wrote to his patron, Luis de Santangel, in which he described the "New World" as a paradise inhabited by peace-loving natives who had no knowledge of weapons, little suspicion of newcomers, and no objection to him flying the Spanish royal standard in their waters. This behavior seemed to prove that the native population welcomed the Spanish and accepted their rule. Columbus also described the richness and money-making potential of the land, which had fruit, flowers, singing birds, honey, gold mines, and spices. His account not only exaggerated, but also misrepresented, the true state of things, for little gold had been found in the islands he visited.

The letter to Santangel arrived in Spain before Columbus himself did in 1493, since he sent the letter when he docked in Lisbon to make repairs to his ship. The letter was translated into Latin and printed in various cities in Europe within months. When he arrived in Barcelona, word of his triumph had spread widely. Banquets, parades, and public baptisms of the surviving Taíno were staged in his honor. Ferdinand served as godfather to Spain's new Christian citizens. Columbus received a coat of arms and was appointed the admiral and governor of all the lands that he had encountered. Plans commenced immediately for a return voyage.

There was one little territorial problem that needed sorting out first. The Portuguese claimed that Columbus's discoveries belonged to Portugal. Ferdinand and Isabella submitted the question to the pope, who in May 1493,

WHAT A DIFFERENCE A YEAR MAKES

1493–1494: The Columbian Exchange

When Columbus returned to the Americas in the fall of 1493, he led a far larger contingent than on the previous expedition. Nearly a thousand settlers returned with him, along with the animals and food needed to establish a colony. His second expedition, thus, kicked off what has become known as the **Columbian Exchange,** a long-term process of the two-way transfer of peoples, goods, diseases, and ideas between Europe and the Americas. The ecosystem and human geography of the Americas began to change, in some areas slowly, in others rapidly, after 1493.[1]

A Nahua Farmer Cultivating Maize One of many drawings in the Florentine Codex that detail the popular culture of Mexico and Central America in the sixteenth century.

One of the most striking features of the exchange is that it was far from equitable. Over the long run, Europeans introduced more animals into the Americas (including cattle, horses, sheep, pigs, cats, and dogs) than they took back to Spain. Most of these animals were domesticated, and the native American populations that received them were traditional hunting societies. The introduction of domesticated animals disrupted ancient patterns and practices associated with hunting societies and led to the establishment of permanent tribal settlements. Native Americans introduced Europeans to the alpaca, llama, and turkey.

Though the animals of the Americas had a negligible impact on Europeans, the plant and food products they discovered brought much needed diversity to European agriculture and the European diet. New varieties of beans and nuts such as the cashew and peanut provided alternative sources of protein for Europeans. Foods that were rich in vitamins and minerals (avocados, peppers, pineapples, and tomatoes) were introduced to Europe, along with foods and agricultural products such as cocoa and tobacco that would become sensationally popular. Over the long run, corn (maize) and potatoes from the Americas became important staples in Europe, serving as caloric alternatives to wheat and other grains.

The Columbian Exchange had more than one dark side, for Europeans unknowingly introduced deadly new diseases to the Americas. This biological imbalance was one of the chief **contact vulnerabilities** of native Americans when they encountered Europeans. Native American bodies had had no exposure for almost 20,000 years to European and Asian diseases. Beginning in 1492, these invisible colonizers did the work of a vast army when it came to weakening the defenses and reducing the numbers of the indigenous population. Malaria, cholera, and typhoid (diseases associated with poor hygiene) spread among native Americans. So too did viral diseases and pathogens such as influenza, the bubonic plague, and, the most deadly of all, smallpox. Native Americans had never been exposed to these diseases and that proved devastating. Though exact figures are difficult to calculate, it has been estimated that smallpox alone was responsible for hundreds of thousands of deaths during the initial decades of colonization. In exchange, the Europeans were exposed to a relatively small number of new diseases, including a tropical skin infection caused by spirochetes (yaws) and a strain of yellow fever. It was once thought that western Europeans were first exposed to syphilis in the Americas, but recent research on ancient and medieval burials has cast doubt on that assumption.

QUESTIONS | ***How might the negative impact of foreign peoples have been softened? Why was the exchange between continents so uneven? What was the ecological impact of the Columbian Exchange on both Europe and the Americas?***

mere months after Columbus's return to Europe, divided the world from the North Pole to the South, 100 leagues (about 300 miles) west of the Azores. Everything to the west was assigned to Castile, to the east to Portugal. By the Treaty of Tordesillas in June 1494, the Portuguese and Spanish reset the dividing point as 370 leagues (approximately 1,000 miles) west of the Cape Verde Islands off Africa. This left the coast of Brazil, not yet identified, lying within the Portuguese allotment, a claim they secured with force when Brazil was identified in 1500.

Later Voyages

Columbus's return to Spain in 1493 was the highpoint of his career. The final decade of his life would mire him in disappointment and controversy. He would be charged with fraud and incompetence as voyage after voyage failed to put Spain in contact with Japan. Columbus was a victim of his own grandiose promises.

Columbus returned to the Americas three times: in 1493, 1498, and 1502. The rationale for each voyage was the same and was based on Columbus's unwavering belief that he had reached the Spice Islands near Japan. He believed that it was simply a matter of time before he reached that fabled land and forged an all-important alliance with the Japanese emperor. If members of his crew suspected that they were not anywhere near Japan, they were never able to persuade Columbus.

In September 1493, Columbus left Spain with seventeen ships and over a thousand sailors and settlers. His crew this time was a more official one: with priests, friars, a physician, and an archdeacon whose royal authority rivaled Columbus's. He sailed around the Caribbean for over nine months, naming islands as he went. Columbus and his crew charted the locations of the Lesser Antilles, Greater Antilles, Virgin Islands, and Puerto Rico before returning to Hispaniola. There they returned to the settlement and fort established in 1492 and found that it had been violently demolished and his thirty-nine crewmen were all gone. As persistent as ever, Columbus established another short-lived settlement, named La Isabella after the queen. The second voyage confirmed the rumors Columbus had heard from the natives on his first visit that the Caribs were a fierce, violent people who practiced cannibalism. Modern archaeology suggests that these reports were probably true, though Europeans were quick to conclude that some of the natives that Columbus encountered were not just uncivilized, but subhuman animals. That conclusion became a further pretext for the violent conquest of native Americans, even though to natives the Spanish Inquisition might have seemed an equally barbarous ritual.

Columbus was an inspired explorer, but a poor administrator. The purpose of his second voyage was not just to find new territories, but to begin the process of the European domestication (through colonization and economic exploitation) of the Americas. The French essayist Michel de Montaigne later said that these new lands were so infantile that they needed to learn their ABCs. Spain kept close watch on its man in Hispaniola as he began to establish settlements. As governor, Columbus regarded the native population as mere labor, directed gold mining operations, and introduced taxation. As an explorer, Columbus remained disappointed that he had not yet located the Japanese islands that he had been seeking, worried about the outstanding costs of his voyages, and was driven to satisfy the demands of his sponsors and royal patrons. When he returned to Spain, complaints about his governorship of the colonies and his failure to find the Far East followed him home and kept him in Spain for four years trying to win over investors and skeptics.

Given the hesitations about Columbus's plans to return along his previous route, it is not surprising that the 1498 voyage involved only six ships. Once he reached his destination, the difficulties continued. Some of his crew mutinied. The settlers who had been left at La Isabella complained about the living conditions and the fact that this was not the land of plenty that they had been led to expect; and the indigenous population was quick to resist the Spanish once they realized that the visitors meant to stay. In spite of these problems, Columbus reached the South American mainland and began to explore the Orinoco River in what is now Venezuela. But the voyage was not judged a success, and on his return to Spain, Columbus was jailed on suspicion of fraud and mismanagement of the colony.

Columbus tried one last time, in 1502, to redeem his reputation by proving that he had found the Indies. Accompanied by his brother and son, Columbus took a fleet of four ships from Spain to Hispaniola. He narrowly avoided a hurricane that destroyed a fleet of Spanish galleons loaded down with cargo from the Americas. While looking for Japan, Columbus explored the coasts of the Honduras, Costa Rica, Nicaragua, and Panama. In Panama, natives told Columbus that gold could be found in the interior, as well as a navigable passage to another great body of water. It was the first hint that Columbus had of the Pacific Ocean, but he did not realize that this other ocean lay between him and his longed-for destination. Storms, native resistance, and an uncooperative Spanish governor on Hispaniola kept Columbus in the Caribbean until 1504, when he was rescued from the island of Jamaica, where he and his crew had been starving for months. He left the Americas that summer, never to return.

The Atlantic Space Race

Like Gutenberg, Columbus could not contain or control his breakthrough. Within a few years, European ships sponsored by European monarchs were regularly crossing the Atlantic. Columbus was convinced that he had reached the islands surrounding Japan, but his contemporaries were not. The explorers who followed in his wake also dreamed of finding territories and riches unknown to Europeans, but they, more practically, chose to exploit the existing resources of the Americas by establishing permanent settlements and profitable trading colonies for their kingdoms. This development sprang from the realization that if the lands Columbus reached in the western Atlantic were not the easternmost edge of Asia, they were still valuable, and offered a distinct territorial advantage for European kingdoms locked in intense competition with each other.

How did the nature of European overseas exploration evolve in the first half of the sixteenth century?

Exploration, conquest, and colonization of overseas lands also fulfilled the imperial aspirations of western monarchs. The Italian and European Renaissances had made them ever more aware of the greatness and dimensions of imperial Rome and that empires were greater things than the enfeebled Holy Roman Empire in their midst. Just as they were territorially blocked in Europe by their long established European neighbors, they were also imperially blocked by the existence of an ineffectual Holy Roman Empire sanctioned by the pope and Catholic Church. Most European monarchs could never be emperors of the many Europes, but they could be the emperors of vast European states that held overseas territories. Spain led the imperial way in the first phase of exploration. Its recent consolidation and unification of the Iberian Peninsula had convinced Ferdinand and Isabella that they already reigned over a multiregional and multicultural kingdom. Hence, it was not by accident that Columbus's voyage across the Atlantic was authorized only after the reconquest of Spain was complete. It was in fact the next logical step in imperial expansion to add other lands to Spain's holdings. England and France would, in Spain's immediate wake, follow the same tack, seeking to assemble empires built on the conquest and domination of overseas territories. In the process of creating empires, they would establish many Neo-Europes abroad, a New Spain here, a New France and New England there, each replicating overseas their own societies and state patterns.

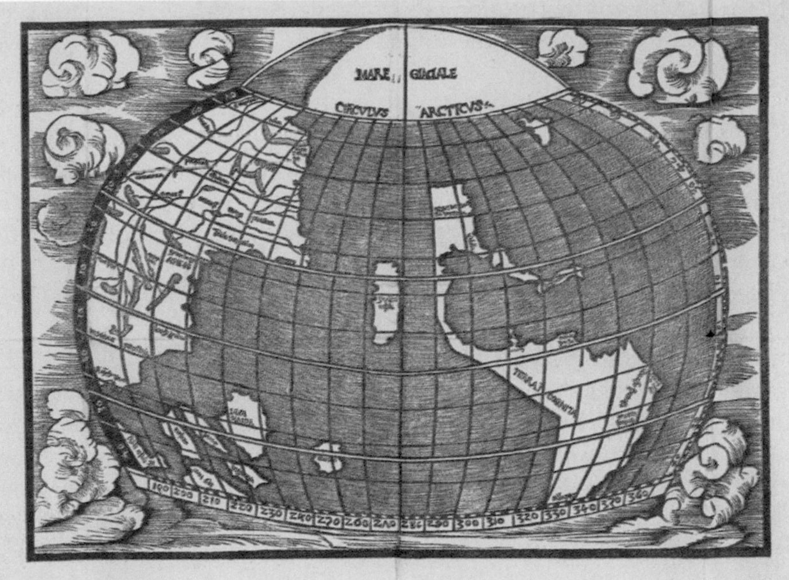

Half an America The cartographer Jan ze Stobnicy's 1512 outline of the Americas depended on Martin Walseemüller's 1507 map. In both, South America was roughly filled in, but North America was still half a continent, not yet complete in the north or west. The large island lying to the west of Central America may be Baja California, not yet recognized as a peninsula. Maps of the sixteenth century gradually filled in the rest of the continent as more information became available.

Amerigo's New Continents

The Florentine Amerigo Vespucci (1454–1512) was the first to proclaim that the lands across the Atlantic were previously unknown continents. Though other explorers of the time called the landmasses and islands they encountered "the Indies" in an effort to conjure up images of the East while remaining vague about their precise identity, Vespucci's recognized that South America (and, later, North America) were separate landmasses unconnected to Asia.

Vespucci, like many of the early explorers, was a merchant and mariner who had a substantial knowledge of navigation and geography. He entered into the service of Ferdinand of Aragon and, between 1497 and 1502, participated in voyages that crisscrossed the ocean between present-day Cuba and Florida and explored the coastline of South America. As Vespucci and his company traveled farther south, he compared their findings with maps of India and realized that they far exceeded its possible coastline.

Like Columbus, Vespucci understood the benefits of publicity and patrons. He wrote letters to various princes to describe his adventures that were the basis for the stories of Vespucci's travels that were drawn together and published between 1502 and 1504. Vespucci's travel tales proved as popular as medieval accounts of voyages to strange and unknown lands and were translated into various European languages. As a self-publicist and popularizer, Vespucci was unrivaled. He titillated Europeans with stories of naked and promiscuous natives who wished to mate with Europeans and tales of South American cannibals. Many of the details of his accounts were either fanciful or fabricated, but he did not invent the American continents; he merely recognized their existence. Yet Vespucci had inserted himself into the narrative of the Americas, and in 1507 a German mapmaker, Martin Waldseemüller, named the previously unknown southern continent as America after the Latin form of Vespucci's first name.

Vespucci's publicity campaign paid off when Ferdinand of Aragon named him "pilot major." Along with the title and office came the responsibility for training Spanish pilots and mariners about geography, navigation, and the routes across the Atlantic. From a school set up in his home, Vespucci trained the next generation of Spanish mariners and explorers, including men who would explore the Pacific Ocean and circumnavigate the globe. Most of the men under Vespucci's guidance set out on their voyages of exploration to reach the Americas—not Japan—and to find other lands unknown to Europeans, and their "discoveries" kept coming. In 1513, Juan Ponce de León, searching for the fountain of youth for his aging king, Ferdinand, made contact with the Calusa natives of Florida. The same year, Vasco Núñez de Balboa crossed the Isthmus of Panama and gazed upon the Pacific Ocean. In 1530, Spaniards reached Baja California and the Spanish began their exploration of the western coastline of what would become the United States.

Living on Board

Exploration was a business for the tough of mind and body. Crews were typically paid by the month or with a share of the booty. On Columbus's first voyage, the ships' masters and pilots earned 2,000 maravedis a month; experienced sailors, half that much; and the inexperienced, a third. It hardly seems enough for what they endured. The ships were small (barely 70–80 feet long) and, except for a couple of bunks for Columbus and the masters, all the other sailors slept wherever they could find space, often in the hold with the ship's supplies or on some protected part of the deck. The deck was often preferable since after weeks at sea, the hold stank of rotting food and was infested with rats. The crew prayed and ate twice a day. Their diet consisted of meats such as pork preserved in brine or dried, salted fish such as sardines, beans, lentils, and olives. They drank poor wine diluted with water.

The length of a voyage was always uncertain. Columbus's initial crossing took a month; Ferdinand Magellan's (1480–1521) to Brazil, seventy days. Later in the Pacific, Magellan's small fleet was at sea for over a hundred days. One of the ship's company described the hunger the sailors experienced. He said that their biscuits had been reduced to worm-infested powder soaked with rat urine. They ate sawdust and the hardened ox hides used to cover the area under the mainmast, and thus were literally eating their ship. Rats were in high demand, but expensive since there was an active trade in captured rodents. Nearly the whole crew fell sick with scurvy from lack of vitamin C. Their joints ached and gums swelled and bled, so that they couldn't eat anything at all and soon died. The death toll on these voyages was horrendous. Vasco da Gama lost most of his men in 1499 to scurvy; Magellan lost 80 percent of his crew.

Magellan left Spain in 1519 with 239 men spread over five ships; one ship finally limped back to Spain in 1522 with eighteen survivors on board. Magellan was not among them; he died fighting in the Philippines the year before. In the thirty years after Columbus's first voyage, twelve explorer-captains died on their expeditions, due to storms, disappearances at sea, misadventures on land, and sickness. Balboa was beheaded for treason. Mutinies were common. Before his death, the Portuguese Magellan had been overthrown by the Spanish captains of his fleet, who charged that he was going to betray their Spanish mission to Portugal. Once he regained his ships, Magellan had forty of the mutineers executed.

Ships were tense environments and the seamen had much to worry about: leaking ships, whales, falling overboard, fierce storms, lack of food and water, disease, and what awaited them on shore in lands said to be filled with monsters and cannibals. If the grumbling sailor was disloyal or disrespectful, he faced a variety of punishments: keelhauling (being dragged under the boat), flogging, or worse. One of Magellan's masters was executed for sodomy. The sailors' suffering was nothing compared to that of the native peoples they invaded and infected, but living on board was grim and coarsening, and it may help explain why the European invaders dealt so roughly and unsympathetically with the native Americans they encountered. The sea had not trained them to be kind.

Hernán Cortés and the Conquest of the Mexica Empire

As Vespucci's mariners and explorers undertook extensive voyages to chart the coastlines of the Americas, they brought along with them soldiers and colonists to explore and settle the interior. These individuals encountered flourishing civilizations that at first welcomed and then resisted them (Map 12.2). Native Americans found themselves up against not only mounted men, guns, and armor, but also the microbes the men carried, which proved even more deadly. The first major Mesoamerican people to succumb to Spanish conquest were the Nahua, who were called Aztecs by the Spanish.

The Aztecs were a single tribe that had established the Mexica Empire in the fifteenth century through a triple alliance between three of its principal cities: Tenochtitlán, Tlacopan, and Texcoco, with Tenochtitlán eventually dominating the alliance. By the time that Cortés and his troops arrived in 1519, the Mexica Empire centered in Tenochtitlan included much of present-day Mexico. The first Spanish force to explore the Mexica Empire was led by Diego Velázquez, the governor of Cuba. Velázquez sent expeditionary forces into the Yucatán Peninsula and the Gulf of Mexico between 1516 and 1518 to gather information. They heard of a wealthy empire just beyond the Gulf. Velázquez selected Hernán Cortés to lead an expedition of exploration.

Cortés had left Spain after growing tired of his life as a lawyer and of the threats from the husband of a woman he had seduced. As a clerk in Cuba, he impressed Velázquez and had the necessary charisma to lead such an undertaking. In the winter of 1519, Cortés left Cuba to search for the Mexica Empire. He had only a few pieces of artillery; sixteen horsemen; and roughly four hundred soldiers recruited from the poorest white residents of Cuba, including young Bernal Díaz, who would later boast that he took part in 119 battles on the expedition.

Once on the Gulf coast of present-day Mexico, Cortés abandoned his mission of exploration in favor of conquering the Mexica Empire. Fearful that his troops would mutiny, he destroyed all but one of his ships so that they could not return to Cuba and notify Velázquez. On the lone surviving ship, Cortés sent a letter to the Spanish king, Charles I, to explain that he had decided to launch a "just war" against the tyrannical ruler of the Mexica peoples and his "ungodly ways." Stories of the Mexica practice of ritual human sacrifice and other non-European ways had already reached the ears of the conquistadors. To ensure that he had the king's full attention, Cortés included enticing references to the wealth of the Mexica Empire and the excellent prospects for converting the Mexica peoples to Christianity. Without waiting for a reply, Cortés set out for the capital city of the Mexica, Tenochtitlán, and began to look for local allies, whom he found among the Cempoalans and the Tlaxcalans.

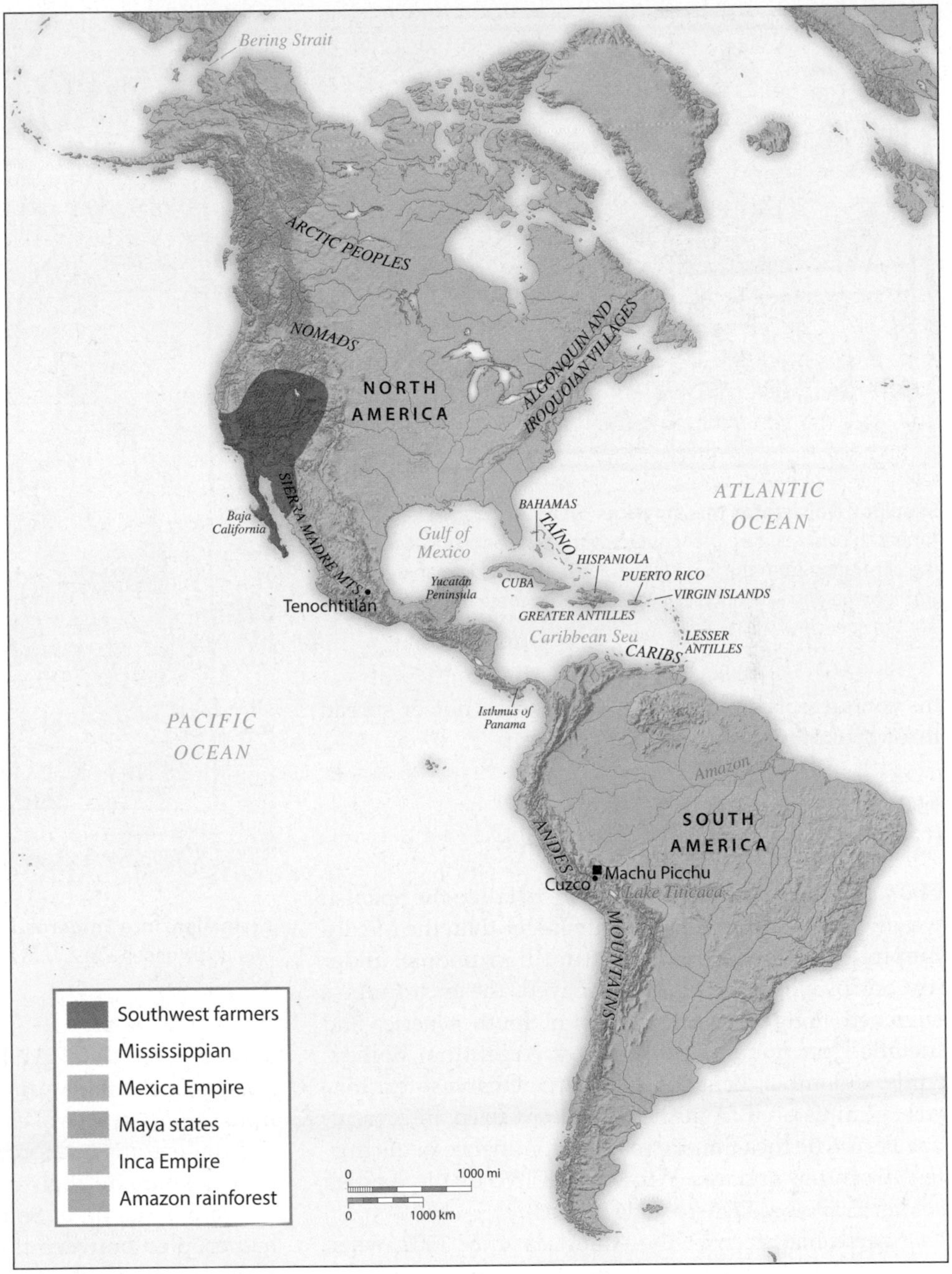

Three months later, Cortés arrived in Tenochtitlán. The city was nearly two hundred years old when the Europeans arrived. The Spanish, on first seeing the capital compared its luxuries, elaborate canal system, and spectacular bridges to those of Venice, one of Europe's most glittering cities. The city had refinements equal to any in Europe, including aqueducts to deliver fresh water, craft workshops, schools, museums, zoos, a large aquarium, gardens, palaces, and religious temples. By 1521, the Europeans had sacked the city and most of it lay in ruin. Today the remains of Tenochtitlán lie below Mexico City.

The indigenous Mexica population greeted Cortés as the long-awaited descendent of the white-skinned god Quetzalcoatl, who was reputed to have departed in the tenth century, but who was destined to return from the east. The emperor Moctezuma viewed Cortés's arrival as the fulfillment of that prophecy and lavished gifts on the Spanish forces. As with most Spanish expeditions, after a few weeks of relative courtesy, things began to fall apart. Cortés seized Moctezuma and held him as a prisoner. That act stunned the natives, who began to gather treasure throughout the empire to ransom their ruler. While still a prisoner, Moctezuma was struck on the head by a rock during a dispute between the Spanish and the indigenous population, who were protesting the massacre of hundreds of unarmed Mexica. The insurrection was so severe that Cortés retreated to collect fresh troops. Cortés and his forces returned in 1521 and laid siege to Tenochtitlán, starving its citizens, already weakened by European diseases, into surrender. When Cortés entered the city, he razed all of its buildings. By 1540, the Spanish had constructed a capital for Spanish America, Mexico City, on the ruins of Tenochtitlán. Cortés received a title, wealth, and fame from the Spanish government for

MAP 12.2 | Native Peoples of the Americas in 1500

When Columbus first reached the Bahamas, the native peoples of the Americas were geographically dispersed, spoke different languages, and had organized themselves in a variety of different ways. ***How did geography separate native Americans from each other? Why did empires develop in Mexico, Central America, and South America, but not North America? Why were native American societies so vulnerable when they made contact with Europeans?***

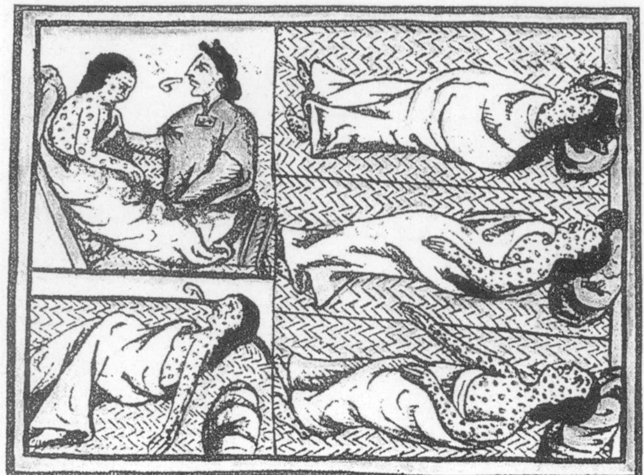

Smallpox Devastates the Americas Smallpox ravaged native American communities after contact with the Spanish invaders. In this illustration from the Florentine Codex, a medicine man treats smallpox victims. The bubbles near mouths in these drawings are signs of speech.

his conquest. From Mexico City, Spanish power spread throughout the former Mexica Empire.

Francisco Pizarro and the Conquest of the Inca Empire

The second native American empire to fall to the Spanish was the Inca Empire. Territorially larger than the Mexica Empire, with an estimated 20 million people under its control when the Spanish arrived, the Inca Empire stretched along the western coast of South America and included portions of present-day Argentina, Bolivia, Chile, Colombia, Ecuador, and Peru. This vast territory was administered from the capital of Cuzco, in present-day Peru. The Inca Empire rose to prominence in the thirteenth century and was conquered in 1533 by the Spanish soldier Francisco Pizarro (c. 1474–1541).

Pizarro had been in the Americas since 1502, when he arrived at the Spanish colony of Hispaniola to make his name and fortune. Born into a minor Spanish noble family around 1474, Pizarro was illegitimate and therefore unable to succeed to his father's titles or lands. He was a second cousin to the famous Hernán Cortés, so it is not surprising that the path he chose was that of a conquistador. In 1522, Pizarro first learned from sailors of a powerful indigenous empire to the south of Hispaniola. He immediately decided that he would find the empire, conquer it, and claim the land and people for Spain. Four years later, Pizarro arrived at his destination and began to scout out the terrain and the people under the control of the emperor in Cuzco. After talking to locals, Pizarro realized that this empire was far grander than he had imagined and he returned to Spain to seek official approval for a military undertaking to conquer it.

Pizarro received the title of viceroy or governor of the soon-to-be-conquered territories and the funds to recruit

Atahualpa, Inca Emperor, in Prison Guaman Poma's drawing of Atahualpa under arrest with a Spanish guard watching over him.

a force of less than two hundred men. After six years of strategizing and planning, he returned to the Inca Empire in 1532. Two strokes of chance enabled his relatively small and underequipped force to succeed. First, European diseases had made their destructive passage through the native population of South America. Second, a civil war had erupted between the two sons of the Inca emperor, Huayna Capac, who had split the empire between them on his death. The Inca armies, with standing forces of well over 200,000 men, had been decimated by disease by the time that Atahualpa's forces finally overcame those of his brother, Huáscar. Atahualpa had little time to enjoy his victory, since he was captured by Pizarro's troops shortly after the civil war ended and became a puppet ruler acting on Spanish instructions. About a year later, after outliving his usefulness to Pizarro, Atahualpa was strangled to death and Spain took control of the empire.

The English and the French Enter the Race

While Spain quickly took the lead in exploring and colonizing the Americas, it soon had overseas rivals anxious to create empires and overseas Neo-Europes of their own. French and English monarchs were eager to enter the race for new territories, riches, and settlements. Though none of their efforts resulted in the collapse of indigenous empires, the French and English undertook to establish their own permanent colonies in North America.

Still smarting from his failure to hire Columbus before the Spanish did so, Henry VII turned to the Cabot family to take up overseas explorations for England. John Cabot (c. 1450–1498), like Columbus, was from the Italian peninsula, most probably from the region surrounding Venice. In 1490, he led his family to England, where he hoped to put his navigational expertise at the service of the new king. Cabot believed that he could find a northwest passage to Asia. In 1496, as the Spanish were busy exploring the south Atlantic, Henry VII supplied Cabot with five ships and the funds needed to explore the north Atlantic and to look for an alternative route to the Spice Islands and Japan. The fleet left England in the late spring of 1497 and by July had made landfall on the east coast of present-day Canada. Cabot mapped the coastline from Newfoundland to Nova Scotia and believed that he had arrived at the continent of Asia. He returned to England in August, was warmly received by the king, and was promptly given the funds for another attempt to reach Japan. Five more ships left England in 1498, but after a fierce storm, one ship was damaged so badly that it had to return to England. The other four ships continued west into the Atlantic and were never heard from again. Though he sponsored Cabot's voyages, Henry's real interest lay in assembling a fleet of merchant vessels that could be quickly refitted into small warships if England ever faced an attack from its traditional rival, France. As the monarch of an island nation, King Henry was one of the first European kings to appreciate the benefits of possessing a professional navy. He never fully realized his naval hopes, but he did make a fundamental investment in ships and maritime technology and England became a maritime power.

The French joined the European space race after Spain and England, but were driven by the same desire to secure new territories and riches, and to rival their traditional enemies. Under Francis I (r. 1515–1547), France ventured into the Americas. In 1524, the Italian explorer Giovanni da Verrazzano (c. 1485–c. 1528) surveyed the North American coastline between the Carolinas and Newfoundland, claiming Newfoundland for the French crown. Jacques Cartier (1491–1557), like John Cabot, came from a family of mariners. As a young man, Cartier took part in voyages to Brazil and Newfoundland. From the king, Cartier received the funding to embark on a voyage to find a northwest passage in 1534. During his first voyage, Cartier mapped the Gulf of St. Lawrence and portions of what are today Canada's Atlantic maritime provinces, traded with members of the Mi'kmaq people, and apprehended two Iroquois boys (the sons of a chief) to take back to France. One year later he returned and reached the St. Lawrence River, where the boys were reunited with their tribe. The French remained on the St. Lawrence through the winter, but disease and starvation took their toll. Iroquois medicines likely saved the eighty-five Frenchmen who survived, but many tensions remained between the two groups. That same winter, Cartier jotted down his impressions of native American society and tried to establish better diplomatic relations with the Iroquois. By the time he returned to France in 1536, he was convinced that what he called Canada (his misunderstanding of the Iroquois-Huron word *kanata*, for village, settlement, or meeting place) was a land previously unknown to Europeans. In 1541, Francis, dreaming of a colonial empire and of creating his own Neo-France or New France overseas, ordered the young nobleman Jean-François de la Roque de Roberval (c. 1500–1560) to establish a permanent settlement in Canada. Roberval hired Cartier to serve as the chief pilot for the first voyage, but his attempts to establish a permanent colony were not successful, and the colony was dissolved in 1543.

Spanish Colonization and Its Critics

The history of the European explorations, conquests, and settlements of the Americas was told chiefly by Europeans, and they most often cast it as a story of heroic triumph over difficult conditions and hostile pagan peoples. At the distance of five hundred years, it may seem that Europeans would inevitably succeed in their efforts to control and exploit the Americas because of their superior weaponry and technology, but the case of the tiny Canary Islands suggests otherwise. There a small resident population of Guanches had successfully resisted the periodic invasions of Muslims, Portuguese, and Castilians for almost five hundred years. In the Americas, during the first half century of exploration and warfare, Europeans did not know the immense land or its many different peoples. The Europeans had guns and iron, but they also had limited knowledge of the local conditions, no dependable food supply of their own, and relatively small numbers of men to send overseas. Yet they did succeed in conquering and colonizing the Americas.

Why did the Spanish turn to the colonization and economic exploitation of the Americas?

Spain had to grapple first and most dramatically with the day-to-day problems of conquest and colonization. Facing enormous challenges and resistance from native Americans, the Spanish resorted to harsh and deadly means to conquer and then control the native populations through systematic colonization and economic exploitation. As the English and French also moved from exploration to colonization, the template established by Spain informed many of their early colonial ventures. Colonization was not without its critics in Europe and the Americas, and, as the problems mounted, Europeans began to question their treatment of native Americans.

The Problems of Colonization

The problems with colonization were many. Europeans boarded their ships with assumptions and expectations that were not well founded, but that shaped their behavior and actions in the Americas. Europeans had two models for the establishment of permanent settlements: the Italian/Portuguese and the Spanish. The Italian/Portuguese model had been pioneered by the Genoese and Venetians in the Mediterranean and the Portuguese along the coast of Africa. The Italian and Portuguese goal was primarily to locate potential markets and then to establish trading centers on the peripheries of a foreign land in order to gain access to its inland resources and trading networks. This less invasive approach led to the exploitation of local resources without making heavy investments of manpower, money, or military presence.

The Spanish method was rooted in the medieval reconquest of the Iberian Peninsula and the Spanish experience on the Canary Islands. The Spanish emphasized the systematic military takeover of a territory, followed by a division of lands and goods between the conquerors and the conquered, with the largest share going to the conquerors. This was a model of invasive or intrusive expansion that had the long-term goal of permanent settlements, rather than the short-term goals of trade and the exploitation of resources. Once the Spanish controlled most of a territory, however, they could begin the widespread and systematic exploitation of its resources, including labor and land.

These two models were applied by the Spanish, Portuguese, and Italians in the Mediterranean, Africa, and the Americas, and then adapted by the French and English. When Columbus set out for Japan in 1492, he had the Italian/Portuguese model in mind, since he was intent on reaching the court of the Japanese emperor and establishing trading and political relations. It was only after Columbus realized he had not yet reached the Japanese court that the Spanish model of conquest and colonization took over, and the desire for settlement and economic exploitation replaced that of diplomacy and trade with a partner.

The military expeditions that set out from Spain in the decades after Columbus, thus, had conquest and colonization as their primary goals. Evidence for this can be seen in the fact that the leaders of the expeditions were given the military rank of captain. The captain then put together a company of investors and participants to finance and make the voyage. As in an early modern army, the members of the company provided their own equipment and provisions in exchange for a share in the profits of conquest. Most were not military men, but came from a variety of backgrounds and social classes that included artisans, merchants, clergy, lesser nobility, urban and rural residents, and even freed blacks from Africa. During the first waves of conquest and colonization, little effort was made to ensure a diversity of skills and abilities among the company, which often led to disaster when few knew how to farm, shoe horses, or repair weapons.

First Encounters

When the Europeans met native Americans for the first time, they came into contact with the descendants of peoples who had migrated from Asia across the Bering Straits (either by an ice bridge or by boat) between 18,000 and 15,000 BCE. As they fanned out throughout the Americas, those peoples eventually formed more than 350 tribal groups speaking over 160 languages and possessing dozens of distinct cultures. The population of the Americas was isolated from Africa, Asia, and Europe, where people, diseases, goods, and technologies had been swapped back and forth for millennia. As a result, native American society prospered and developed without external continental contact or interference.

All of that began to change with the coming of the Europeans. The isolation of the native American population meant that they had no natural immunity to European diseases such as smallpox and plague. They also did not possess the iron and steel weapons that dominated warfare in Europe, Asia, and Africa. Native American encounters with Europeans set off an exchange of goods, microbes, and technologies unlike anything that either party had ever experienced. The debilitating effects of this exchange made it easier for Europeans to conquer and exploit the Americas. After the conquest of the Yucatán, the Mayan Chilam Bayam wrote that before the arrival of the Europeans there had been little sickness, no smallpox, no stomach ailments, no consumption (tuberculosis), and few headaches among the people. The arrival of the foreigners had changed everything, he said. In 1493, Columbus sent five hundred Arawak people back to Spain to serve as slaves. On the ship, disease spread rapidly in the crowded and filthy conditions in the cargo holds where the slaves were confined, and only five shivering captives arrived to be sold in the streets of Barcelona.

Once in the Americas the Spanish were usually met by a friendly and curious indigenous population that was used to treating visitors as guests, provided that there was no sign of hostility. During this first period of contact, the Spanish made careful surveys of the land and people to determine whether they represented a resource ripe for seizure. Within a few weeks or months, the Spanish would typically exhaust local food supplies and resources and begin helping themselves to food, women, and precious goods, and would soon wear out their welcome. At this point, the native people often turned against the Spanish, sometimes harshly, as on the island of Hispaniola when a coalition of tribal leaders joined forces to expel the Spaniards for a time. In most cases, however, the Spanish advantage in military technology (swords, guns, and cannons) allowed them to put down the uprisings and capture local tribal leaders, thereby compelling indigenous cooperation.

Although the Spanish approached their first encounters with native Americans with an eye to conquest and colonization, native Americans generally regarded the Europeans as visitors with whom they were prepared to trade. This was another of what might be called the contact vulnerabilities of native Americans. The tribal societies of the Americas expected that encounters with other peoples would provide opportunities for exchanging goods and ideas. Although warfare occurred between native peoples before Columbus and long after he was gone, there were also more peaceful cross-cultural exchanges.

Though the Europeans were not interested primarily in cultural exchanges with native Americans, exchanges nevertheless took place. In the first stages of European contact and conquest, few women accompanied the soldiers and administrators who traveled to the Americas. Many European men had both coerced and consensual relationships with native American women. Hernán Cortés's relationship with a Nahua woman known as La Malinche began when she helped him communicate with the Mexica people. She was fluent in a number of local languages and quickly learned Spanish. Diáz wrote with admiration of her beauty and intelligence, as well as her power and influence, and explained that La Malinche was of noble lineage but had been sold into slavery. La Malinche became Cortés's mistress and the mother of his son, Martin.

The mixing of European and native American blood happened across the Americas in the early modern period, but it was often unsettling. Europeans resorted to stereotypes and other tactics to demean natives in order to keep the two peoples and cultures distinct. Columbus, for example, believed that the indigenous population of the Caribbean spoke a form of Spanish and kept listening for familiar words, but other Europeans described native Americans as so strange that they seemed not to be human, which made it far easier to justify enslaving or murdering them. It did not help that the Caribs practiced cannibalism, which allowed some Europeans to see native Americans as less than civilized or even human. One telling example of the European struggle to cope with their encounters with native Americans is that they called all indigenous peoples "Indians," a single, familiar, and incorrect name that conveyed nothing of the diversity of peoples they encountered.

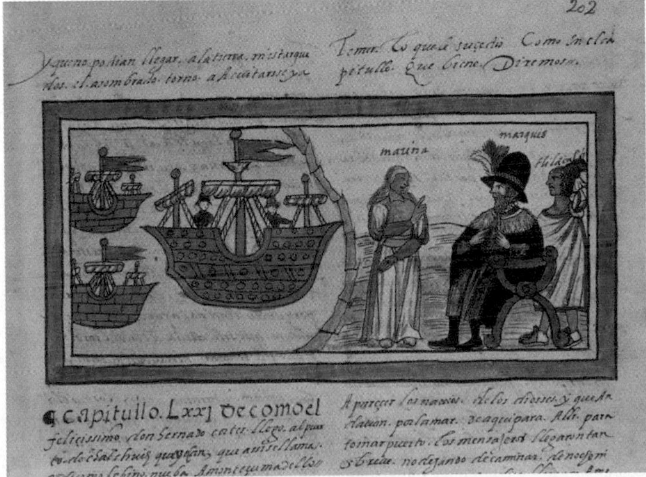

Malinche Meets Cortés Malinche became the mistress and interpreter of the conquistador Hernán Cortes, and the mother of his children.

The Economic Impact of Spanish Colonization

When Europeans realized they were not in or anywhere near Japan, their priorities shifted to outright economic exploitation and religious conversion of lands and peoples. Once local resistance was crushed through a combination of military technology and disease, Europeans found institutionalized ways to coerce the indigenous population to engage in agriculture, pay tribute, and mine for precious minerals. In the Spanish colonies, native Americans were placed under the **encomienda system,** a modified vassalage relationship in which a Spanish settler was given, in the name of the king, trusteeship over a piece of land and its residents in exchange for the military enforcement of Spanish rule and a promise that the colonist would teach the indigenous peoples in his charge about Catholicism. It fell to the Spanish *encomendero* (trustee) to determine how best to make use of the land and people to benefit the Spanish crown's coffers and his own pocketbook. Initially, the grant of an encomienda was not supposed to involve more than three hundred native Americans, but in practice few encomiendas reached that size. Spain established the first encomienda in 1493 in Hispaniola; the system was not abolished until 1791.

In the eyes of the Spanish colonists, the encomienda system was not slavery because native Americans were given a choice to convert to Catholicism and, thus, could avoid being taken under the legal protection of an encomendero. In reality, however, the lines of communication and enforcement between Spain and its possessions were stretched thin, and the encomenderos were free to do what they liked with the land and the people on it with little interference. Widespread abuse of the system led to charges that it was nothing more than slavery. These charges were often made by clerics who visited the colonies and were horrified by the working conditions of native Americans and the lack of attention paid to their religious instruction.

Because of concerns over the breakdown of proper relationships between encomenderos and the indigenous population, the crown drew up two documents "to protect" native Americans. The *Requerimiento* (Requirement) of 1510 provided soldiers and settlers with a legally binding document that had to be read aloud to native Americans before any hostilities could ensue or any encomiendas could be established. Few native Americans, especially in newly conquered lands, knew enough Spanish to understand the document, which outlined the history of the creation, the establishment of the papacy, the rights of the Spanish crown in the Americas, and the people's need to recognize the authority of the pope and Spain. If the natives failed to agree to the terms of the *Requerimiento*, the Spanish were authorized to seize their lands and claim them for Spain, extract labor, and wage war on them if they resisted.

The Laws of Burgos were drawn up at the request of Ferdinand of Aragon in 1512. Designed to define proper government and treatment of the native Americans, the laws reduced the size of encomiendas, gave tribal chiefs rights and exempted them from certain types of work, and outlawed some forms of punishment. The laws, however, were never fully enforced because of the complexities of administering far-flung territories. The Laws of Burgos were rewritten and strengthened in the New Laws of 1542, which proposed a gradual abolishment of the encomienda system. But colonists, many of whom were encomenderos and saw that the laws would mean their economic destruction, rose up in revolt in Peru and resisted their implementation. The New Laws, as a consequence, were not enforced and the encomienda system remained in place.

Under the encomienda system, the native American population was further reduced by European diseases, harsh labor conditions, and brutal mistreatment. The tragic results of the land system, however, were dwarfed by those associated with the brutality of silver mining. The Americas were associated with gold and silver in the European imagination, and the silver mines of South America fed those dreams. The most famous mine site was the *Cerro Rico* ("rich mountain") of Potosí in present-day Bolivia. Between the middle of the sixteenth century and the end of the eighteenth century, more than 45,000 tons of pure silver were extracted from the site. Long hours of bone-crushing labor with picks and shovels, combined with the adverse effects of exposure to mercury, which native Americans amalgamated with crushed silver ore using their bare feet, led to such a precipitous decline in the population of the city that African slaves had to be imported to work the mines by 1608. More than 30,000 African slaves worked the Potosí mines before 1800.

Spanish Colonization and Conversion

The economic aspects of colonization were important to all concerned, but the religious beliefs of the native American population were a matter of special concern to the Spanish crown and the Catholic Church. With their hopes of making a strategic alliance with the Japanese against the Ottoman Turks fading, the Spanish focused on the opportunity to baptize thousands of new Catholics in the Americas. Though priests had accompanied Columbus and other early explorers, by 1500 church and crown officials recognized the need for an organized approach to establishing the faith in the conquered lands. The church responded by appointing bishops and priests to oversee the newly founded churches of the Spanish colonial territories, and by sending missionaries from the church's monastic orders to convert native Americans. The missionaries, unlike bishops and priests, tended to see themselves as independent of the local encomenderos and crown officials and were, therefore, more likely to try to meet native Americans on their own terms and to communicate with them in their own languages. They established schools in the colonies and often lived among the native Americans they sought to convert. Much of what is known about the life and customs of native American peoples comes to us through treatises such as Bernardino de Sahagún's *General History of the Things of New Spain*, which was based on the richly illustrated volume of Nahua accounts and drawings copied from his original reports and known today as the Florentine Codex.

The task of converting native Americans to Catholic Christianity during the first three decades of settlement was taken up by three religious orders: the Franciscan friars, the Dominican friars, and the Augustinian monks (canons). The first to arrive overseas in any significant number were the Franciscans, who entered Brazil with the Portuguese in 1500 and were active in Venezuela by 1508, Mexico by 1524, and California slightly later. The Dominicans began their work in Haiti in 1510 and came in considerable numbers after 1525. The Augustinians were the last of the three orders to arrive, in 1533.

The work of conversion was made easier because of the tendency of native Americans to adopt the religious systems of their conquerors. This was another of the contact vulnerabilities of native Americans. The Inca and Mexica Empires had practiced this form of cultural conquest alongside their own military conquests, and native Americans did not resist participating in the worship and rituals of the Catholic Church. A lack of resistance, however, is not the same thing as complete acceptance, and traditional Nahua beliefs persisted. Catholic missionaries often emphasized similarities between cultures, such as the Mexica belief in ritual sacrifice and a mother goddess, to help native Americans accept Christian beliefs in the power of the Eucharist and the Virgin Mary. The Virgin of Guadalupe, the iconic image of the Catholic Church in the Americas, shows how the indigenous and European religious traditions might blend together. When a newly baptized native American named Juan Diego Cuauhtlatoatzin saw a vision of the Virgin Mary on a hill outside Mexico City in 1531, the Virgin appeared with brown skin, spoke to him in the native language Nahuatl, and asked him to build an abbey on the spot. In the decade following Juan Diego's vision, the missionary campaign was widely successful and most native Americans joined the Catholic Church.

Criticizing Spanish Conquests and Colonization: Las Casas

As the encomienda system became entrenched and the evangelizing efforts of the missionaries continued, critical voices began to speak out against the abuses of colonization. Bartolommeo de Las Casas (1474–1566) was one of the most vocal critics of the Spanish colonial system, and he knew it intimately. A former encomendero who had come to the Americas in 1502, Las Casas became a leading European advocate for native Americans. In 1514, he heard a sermon by the Dominican Anton Montesano, who argued that participating in the encomienda system was a mortal sin. Three years later, Las Casas gave up

Fragments of the Native Narrative of the Conquest

Beginning in 1547, the Franciscan missionary Bernardino de Sahagún began drawing together Nahua accounts of the colonization of Mexico in an effort to preserve a detailed picture of native society from just before the conquest to the present. Sahagún knew the indigenous language, Nahuatl, and in 1558 he was encouraged to make a systematic study of the Nahua people to aid in conversion efforts. Between 1558 and 1569, he spoke to the oldest men and women he could find whose memories stretched back to the earliest years of the Spanish presence. Though Sahagún wrote down all the testimony, he had his Nahua students copy the stories into a trilingual work that included Nahua, Spanish, and Latin and over 1,800 illustrations. Sahagún later edited and in some cases censored the work of his students, and several of his abbreviated versions of the work survive. In 1580, a version of the work was compiled that included only the Spanish translation.

Given Sahagún's role in the production of the text, the Florentine Codex must be seen as a collaborative work. Nevertheless, it provides our best view of native American responses to the Spanish during the first months of encounter and conquest. According to the codex, the Nahua first viewed the Spanish as gods who had come from the heavens and appeared on the waters. Questions have been raised about whether the Nahua had that view initially or were influenced by later efforts by Cortés and other crown and church officials to make the transition between Mexica and Spanish rule seem as seamless as possible.

While the Florentine Codex is the best-known text that includes Nahua reactions to the conquest, scholars have over five hundred codices or partial codices to draw on for information about indigenous life before and during the early years of the encounter. Most were written after the conquest, but a few were made shortly before. That so many codices survive and continued to be made even after the Spanish conquest is in part because of the traditional role that the *tlacuilo* or codex painter played in Mesoamerican life. Four different writing systems had developed in Mesoamerica before the conquest, though the Spanish did not recognize that fact when weighing how civilized these peoples were. Before the Spanish arrived, the *tlacuilo* created volumes that outlined the Nahua calendar and depicted important rituals and ceremonies. Later, the Spanish added captions to these works to explain their meaning for a European audience. After the conquest, many of the codices that survive were dedicated to histories of the Mexica Empire and genealogies of important native families.

Today, these Nahua texts with many additions still survive, having passed through many hands. They stand in stark contrast to the fate of the Mayan codices in the Yucatán Peninsula in the sixteenth century, when whole libraries of volumes that described the history of the Mayan people for nearly a thousand years were destroyed deliberately. The final destruction of the Mayan codices in 1697 in Guatemala left scholars with so little information about the Maya and their culture that today we know far more about the Mexica Empire before and during the conquest than we do about the great Maya Empire.

Libro.

The Florentine Codex Depiction of Nahua Women Preparing a Banquet

QUESTIONS | ***Why were the writings of and about native American societies dispensed with or destroyed? Given the circumstances under which those codices were produced and survived, can we trust them to provide useful insights into Mexica life and civilization? Why or why not?***

his land and began preaching against the enforced labor of native Americans. After his attempt at creating a new style of colonial government in northern South America failed, Las Casas went to Hispaniola and entered the Dominican order in 1522. As a Dominican, Las Casas believed that meaningful conversion was achieved through peaceful methods that respected native cultures and beliefs. His views were controversial, but they influenced the formulation of the New Laws of 1542.

Las Casas debated his views with Juan Ginés de Sepúlveda in the Spanish city of Valladolid in 1550–1551. Las Casas argued on behalf of the church and the crown that native Americans were a free and rational people who could be freely led to Christianity and that they should be treated no differently from other Catholics. Sepúlveda argued in support of the Spanish landowners of the colonies that native Americans were fitted by nature to be slaves and could be forced into dependent labor relationships by war and conquest. Enslaving them was not a sin, but in accordance with natural law, which was an early modern version of Aristotle's argument about the different conditions of peoples, some deserving to rule, some to serve. Both Las Casas and Sepúlveda later claimed victory, but no one won, certainly not the native Americans at the heart of the issue. There was no change in governmental policy or the encomienda system.

In 1552, Las Casas completed the work for which he is best known, *An Abbreviated Account of the Destruction of the Indies.* It is a far different account of the Spanish in the Americas from the one written by Bernal Díaz. For Las Casas, the Spanish perpetrated unspeakable cruelties against native Americans, who were treated not as children of God but as animals fit only for labor. He noted that by the time he arrived, Hispaniola was home to only 60,000 native Americans. He estimated that nearly three million natives had been killed by warfare or excessive labor in the encomienda system and the mines during the short period from 1492 to 1552. Who in the future, Las Casas wondered, would ever believe such a thing? Spanish arrogance and their victimization of native Americans became a theme that other colonizing powers such as France and England would embroider into the "Black Legend" of Spanish colonial excess. But England and France also found it difficult in North America to balance the needs of colonizers and the rights of the colonized.

East to Asia: The Portuguese Venture

The conquest of the Americas by Europeans was an accidental and world-changing event, but the original dream of finding a direct eastward route to Asia had, in fact, proceeded forward at the same time. The Portuguese reached the Indian Ocean in late 1497 and in the sixteenth century established a long-lasting Asian trading network. They were followed by both the Dutch and the English, who came to dominate Asian trade in the seventeenth century and paved the way for a legacy of western colonialism, mercantilism, and imperialism in Asia.

Why was the Portuguese enterprise in Asia different from the Spanish program in the Americas?

The Portuguese Reach Asia

The Portuguese never accepted that the way to Asia was west across the Atlantic. They had, instead, resolutely and patiently continued their annual progress south along the coast of Africa until in December 1497 Vasco da Gama finally sailed around the Cape of Good Hope and sailed east into the Indian Ocean. His goal was to find those Christian princes who were thought to hold lands in the east and to acquire gold, spices, and jewels. He made his way up the eastern seaboard of Africa and by May 1498 had reached India. He had not expected to find established trading networks in the Indian Ocean, many of them controlled by Muslim traders. On their first entry into the Indian Ocean, the Portuguese had brought goods (wool garments and trinkets) that Asians found inferior and not worth acquiring. Da Gama did make contacts, acquired some spices, and lost two-thirds of his crew before turning around and sailing home, reaching Lisbon in late 1499. He returned with a large flotilla of ships in 1502 and this time brought military force to bear to begin monopolizing the trade in pepper, which was shipped back to Portugal for a handsome profit.

The Portuguese proceeded to set up trading outposts (*feitoria*) and fortifications around the Indian Ocean, which allowed them to maximize trade, undermine their rivals, and force trade deals. Some of these trading outposts remained in Portuguese hands for centuries. Goa in India was set up in 1510 and not reacquired by India until 1961. The Portuguese did not reach China until 1513 and were allowed to establish a trading base at Macao in 1556 (not surrendered until 1999) so that they could barter for silk cloth. The Portuguese monarchs divided their Asian trade interests into two enterprises: the *Carreira da India* for handling trade from Asia to Portugal and the *Estado da India* for trade within Asia. In Lisbon, a large dockyard and arsenal employed thousands to manage Asian trade as loaded ships came in and new ships were sent out to India. The king issued licenses and approved monopolies over the spice trade in pepper, nutmeg, and mace. Such was Portugal's dominance of the spice trade that Venice transferred its spice operations to Lisbon.

The impact of the Portuguese in the Indian Ocean was considerable, disrupting or severing older trading routes that had supplied the Venetians and, hence, Europeans with spices through the Ottoman Empire and Egypt. There was local resistance to Portugal's intrusion into old trading lanes. Traders in India were not pleased. In 1501 at Calicut, where the Portuguese had set up a trading post, Muslim traders rioted and were met with cannon fire from Portuguese ships. At the other end of this trading network stood the Mameluke rulers of Egypt, who

INVESTIGATING THE PAST

Alternative Junk History

The claim that the Portuguese reached New Zealand and Australia long before Captain Cook did in the late eighteenth century is possible, but virtually no evidence supports the claim that the Chinese in the early fifteenth century discovered Australia, New Zealand, Antarctica, and the Americas. Yet in 2003, Hu Jintao, the president of China, claimed before the Australian Parliament that the Chinese had been the first (that is, after aboriginal settlement) to visit Australia. It is true that in the early fifteenth century, during the Ming Empire, the eunuch admiral Zheng He commanded a fleet of junks that sailed west into the Indian Ocean and supplied reports on the Indian subcontinent to the Chinese emperor. There is no evidence, however, that Ming mariners sailed farther east or west or established settlements or trading posts far outside of China.

In 2002, Gavin Menzies set off a firestorm of controversy when he published *1421: The Year China Discovered the World.* In his sensational book, Menzies claims that during the reign of the emperor Zhu Di, Zheng He's fleet, captained by four eunuchs, discovered a host of lands while circumnavigating the globe. Historians universally panned the thesis, noting not only that no solid proof existed for such a claim, but also that Menzies had misunderstood or misrepresented maps, references, and archaeological and DNA evidence. The publisher referred to the work as an alternative history; the critics claimed it was a pure fiction. Over a million copies of the work were sold and *1421* became particularly popular in China, where it seemed to satisfy a longing for an early modern history to rival that of Europe.

History depends on evidence, context, and sound judgment, all of which seem to be lacking in *1421: The Year China Discovered the World.* Alternative history may not be history at all, but it does respond to other needs, both nationalistic and financial. In the case of Menzies's book, the publisher, Transworld, supplied a team of over one hundred people to produce and package a book that addressed that audience. When pressed about the lack of evidence to support the extraordinary claims in his book, Menzies and the publisher answered, as so often is the case for alternative histories, that there had been a conspiracy to destroy the evidence; that when Emperor Zhu Di died in 1424, the next emperor decided that it would be best not to endanger the Chinese economy by pursuing the discoveries and, thus, his bureaucrats systematically removed mention of Zheng He's extensive expedition from the official records. Menzies followed up the first book with the 2008 publication of *1434: The Year a Magnificent Chinese Fleet Sailed to Italy and Ignited the Renaissance.* It seemed not to matter to the author that 1434 was a little late to ignite a renaissance movement that was already well under way by then or that not a single Italian humanist, and they were an observant and loquacious crowd, described the arrival of the Chinese fleet. Alternative history can be fun and thought provoking, but it requires correct labeling so that bookstore clerks, at least, will know where to shelve new books when they arrive, whether in the history or fiction aisles.

QUESTIONS | ***In our digital age, how can we best assess the various alternative histories that populate the Internet? What sort of evidence should we require to support new and extraordinary claims? Why is the idea of extensive Chinese exploration in the fifteenth century so appealing to some audiences?***

saw their trade with Europe drying up. They assembled a fleet of ships to evict the Portuguese from the Indian Ocean but were defeated decisively in the important naval battle of Diu Island in 1509. This event critically undermined the traditional Muslim role as the critical conveyors of jewels, spices, and gold from Asia to Europe.

Portugal defended its trade interests in the Indian Ocean but apparently never dreamed (as had the Spanish in the Americas) of conquering the old and established states that ringed the ocean. They had too few men and, perhaps more important, they lacked the military and disease advantage that the Spanish had possessed in the Americas. There simply weren't the same contact vulnerabilities between Asia and Europe that there were between the Americas and Europe. Though Asia had been cut off from easy access by Europeans for a century, Europe and Asia were effectively one military and disease pool, with no one side having a distinct advantage. That relative equality forced the Portuguese to tread more lightly, to negotiate, and to trade, much as Columbus imagined he would have done had he reached Japan. In fact, the Portuguese adapted to local conditions, often employing Muslim traders, with their local knowledge and command of different European and Asian languages, as pilots and emissaries to conduct negotiations for them. The Portuguese got to Asia first, which was a distinct advantage, but they never had the manpower or the resources to dominate Asia or to keep their European rivals out. Instead they traded, replacing the Muslim middlemen who had facilitated east-west trade in the

Indian Ocean for centuries. The Portuguese influenced but did not dominate or overwhelm the languages and cultures of the Asian peoples with whom they interacted. Asians came to call the Portuguese "hat men" because of their distinctive black head gear.

The Dutch and the English Arrive

Portugal's rivals first reached Asia by the westward or Pacific route. Ferdinand Magellan was Portuguese but worked for Spain. He sailed with five ships around the southern tip of South America in 1520 and then set out across the ocean that he named the Pacific (peaceful) Ocean. He died in a battle in 1521, but one of his ships made it back to Europe the next year. Though Portugal's European monopoly of trade with Asia was supposedly protected by terms of the world-dividing Treaty of Tordesillas of 1494, the terms of the treaty were undercut in 1580 when Philip II of Spain was also crowned king of Portugal. Instead of giving Spain the absolute right to dominate world trade, both American and Asian, Spain's many enemies seized the opportunity to establish their own trading interests in Asia.

Both England and the Dutch Republic in the early years of the seventeenth century sanctioned companies that were given monopoly trading rights to East Asia. The English and Dutch proved more aggressive and resourceful than the Portuguese in pressing their advantage in the Indian Ocean. The Dutch East India Company eventually out-hustled the English and Portuguese, took the East Indies (Indonesia), and gained a toehold in South Africa. The age of global mercantilism and imperial reach arrived in the seventeenth century.

A New Wave of Christianity Hits Asia

Asia has experienced many waves of Christian contact. In the early Christian period, India had small communities of Nestorian and Thomas Christians; and in the Middle Ages, China under the Mongols was exposed to the Franciscans and made contact with the medieval papacy and Christian traders such as the Polos. In the sixteenth century, as Europe's religious temperature rose, Catholics (not Protestants) began active missionary work in Asia. Magellan was given permission to baptize some natives in the Philippines in 1521. Later in the century, the Spanish found themselves locked in religious warfare with Muslims in the Philippines.

The Portuguese attempt to convert the peoples around the Indian Ocean was secondary to Portugal's economic interests. With the creation of the Jesuit order (see Chapter 13), however, the Christian effort by both the Spanish and the Portuguese intensified. The most famous of the missionaries was Francis Xavier (1506–1552), one of the founders of the Jesuit order. With the approval of the Portuguese king and his own appointment as a papal representative, Xavier set off for East Africa and India in 1541. Xavier worked from the top down by trying to convert kings, nobles, and powerful men, and was constantly on the move: from Mozambique to Goa, India; to the Spice Islands; and then to Indonesia. By 1549, he was in Japan where he tried to convert the emperor to Christianity. Unlike their experience in the Americas, the Christian missionaries to Asia encountered deeply entrenched and sophisticated organized religions (Islam, Buddhism, Hinduism, and Shinto) that were difficult to dislodge or replace. Xavier died of a raging fever on an island off the coast of mainland China in 1552.

Conclusion

European overseas expansion changed the world. In some ways, this was the first great moment of a connected global history, for continents previously unknown to Europeans, Africans, and Asians were brought into play. The very notion of the Earth as a globe of scattered landmasses set in two chief bodies of water was born, a change in awareness that was being worked out visibly, line by line, on sixteenth-century maps.

Deep contact between continents separated by vast oceans would have happened anyway at some point in world history, with many of the same disastrous ecological and demographic results for the Americas, but it occurred in the late fifteenth century because of the competitive tensions at work in Europe and between Europeans, and because of the strange conviction of one Genoese explorer that the world was smaller than it actually is. By the late fifteenth century, Europeans found themselves hemmed in by the sea and surrounding Ottoman Muslim lands that blocked their way east. Ambitious European countries could not find suitable outlets within Europe for their goals of expansion or their imperial aspirations. Locked into fierce struggles with each other for advantage, first Portugal and then Spain, England, and France, turned to the sea to break out of the territorial gridlock of Europe. The success of Islam in locking down the Middle East, Near East, and Asia forced Europeans to look south and west, whether along the coast of Africa or across the Atlantic. Within European society the same struggle for advancement and advantage was being played out between individuals such as Columbus, Vespucci, and Cortés, all of them looking for their chance to make their own breakthrough to wealth and fame and for royal patrons to fund their ambitious schemes. Middling men such as Bernal Díaz saw exploration as their way to move up in the world.

Once Columbus made contact with the Americas in the Caribbean and publicized the fact, others rushed to follow in his sea-steps. The pace of early exploration was furious, for within forty years of Columbus's landing, Europeans had mapped the coastline of the two Americas, circled South America, and sailed around the globe. The Portuguese at the same time had rounded Africa and sailed to India, China, and Japan. This was discovery not for the sake of new knowledge, but for economic and religious gain. Colonies with economic and religious goals began with Columbus's first voyage and were institutionalized as royal policy. In the Americas, Europeans had come not just to visit, but to stay, dominate, and exploit their possessions, to create Neo-Europes in their own image. In this, they pursued their national advantages and exported their European rivalries overseas. Spain profited more than the others in the short run, as the sixteenth century was to be its golden age, fed by South American gold and silver. The many Europes can seem the big winner of the overseas gambit, since they had extended their footprint over two more continents and escaped the narrow confines of their own small continent and their even smaller kingdoms. They had circumvented their effective containment by Islamic lands, thus gaining a huge advantage over their nearest neighbors in world domination. The European world further shifted its economic and political focus from the Mediterranean to the Atlantic and Pacific.

The balance sheet of European expansion can seem starkly unbalanced. The fall of two empires in the Americas, the disruption of patterns of existence that were thousands of years old, and the shocking loss of life in the Americas from disease, conquest, and economic enslavement make it seem that native America, with its hundreds of different peoples spread over two continents, was the passive victim of the invaders. The demographics of European expansion are shocking. When Columbus first visited Hispaniola there were about 100,000 residents; seventy-five years later, only 300 natives were left on the island. The native population of Mexico might have been as high as twenty-five million people in 1520 but had dropped precipitously to around one million people by 1600. These changes didn't happen overnight; native Americans made subtle accommodations and adaptations. Take the case of horses. Though horses had first evolved in the Americas, they had gone extinct long before the explorers arrived and the Spanish reintroduced them. Yet within a century many American peoples had made the horse the central animal of their cultures and economies.

If there were small gains for native Americans, there were large losses for some Europeans. Not every European country participated in overseas expansion. The Germans, most Italian city-states, the Dutch, and the Belgians did not enter the first rush of sixteenth-century exploration and spent much of the following centuries hankering for territorial holdings and empires of their own outside of Europe, but the big prizes in the west were already gone. Spain, the chief and most successful imperial dreamer in Europe, was, despite all the precious metals that poured into the country or, perhaps, because of them, bankrupt by the end of the sixteenth century. Even the Portuguese found that their domination of the spice trade was less lucrative than they might have hoped. The massive influx of gold and silver into Europe from the Americas distorted the European economy and led to a runaway inflationary spiral throughout most of the century. The price for goods in Spain had doubled from pre-exploration levels by 1560. Aside from the economic problems caused by expansion, the balance-of-power problems within Europe were made worse or more complicated by overseas expansion. The rivalries between European states had not been solved by expansion, just diffused to other arenas of engagement. Europeans now had more lands and conflicts to dispute and wage war over.

The most interesting impact of European expansion may have been intellectual. When Boccaccio and Petrarch wrote haltingly about the Canary Islands, they were in effect dealing with the European and Renaissance problem of authority versus firsthand experience. In its discovery and reverence for classical antiquity, the Italian Renaissance had erected a new realm of classical authority (based on ancient authors) to set beside the Christian one (based on the Bible), and these intellectual regimes threatened to inhibit Europeans from a more adventurous investigation of the world. The Americas challenged that fixity, for they needed to be dealt with on their own terms, a thing the bookish Columbus had trouble doing. In 1560, a Parisian lawyer said that it was astounding that classical authors had had no knowledge of the Americas. And in 1512 the Nuremberg geographer and humanist Johann Cochlaeus said, after reading of Vespucci's voyages, that whether his accounts were true or a lie, they had nothing to do with cosmography or history and were of no interest to geographers. Illustrious humanists such as Erasmus simply ignored the Americas. The Renaissance reinforcement of authority, albeit classical, would lead to some difficulty in certain quarters adjusting to new information not bound within familiar book covers.

The encounter with nonclassical and nonbiblical peoples in the Americas led to a category crisis. Where were these peoples to be placed on the human tree that descended from Adam and passed through Athens and Rome? A Portuguese adventurer, Antonio de Montezinos, in the seventeenth century proposed that he had located in Ecuador one of the ten lost tribes of ancient Israel, but the theory came late and was an indication that a century and a half after Columbus's contact, the peoples of the Americas were still difficult to fit into familiar European categories. Pico Mirandola's Renaissance flourish on the dignity of man meant little on the shores of the Bahamas, especially if explorers were disinclined to recognize that these others were fully human. Few explorers coped well with contact, regarding native Americans as childlike, uncivilized, promiscuous, and murderous primitives (see Back to the Source at the end of the chapter). Christian missionaries did better, for at least they saw the American peoples as human beings with souls to save and lives to reform, though they too participated in a form of exploitation, this time religious.

The Americas and their many peoples could not, however, be denied. They had to be dealt with by experience and observation. A cosmographer of the sixteenth century said that what he had to say about the Americas couldn't be learned in Salamanca, Bologna, or Paris. Christianity and Eurocentrism cushioned Europeans against the utter shock of new knowledge and new experience, layering perception with old and familiar ways of perceiving the world. But the Americas opened up the European imagination and knowledge bank to new possibilities and realities. Some boldly embraced the new. One Spaniard by midcentury proclaimed that contact with the Americas was the greatest event since the creation of the world. Another confidently claimed that the world had been opened up for the human race, by which he meant, opened up to Europeans. The very existence of the Americas and its unknown peoples expanded the European imagination. After reading of Vespucci's travels, Thomas More in his *Utopia* imagined a more perfect society existing somewhere across the sea far away from troubled Europe. But native Americans were neither primitive nor pure and did not exist in some state of innocence; they were themselves and that took longer to recognize and respect. Still, the Americas were that breath of fresh air that Europeans had long needed to extricate themselves from their old view of the world and their tired debates. The explorations that began with the Canary Islands and Columbus's first landing in the Bahamas shook Europe out of its comfortable medieval and renaissance restraints, confident and settled certainties, and territorial confinements. But Europe had another old, large, and lingering problem yet to resolve, and religion would be the great battleground of the early modern world.

Critical Thinking Questions

1. What is wrong with using unqualified terms such as *New World* and *Old World, Known World* and *Unknown World,* and *Discovery*?
2. What best explains the drive of Europeans to explore and colonize overseas?
3. What were the contact vulnerabilities of the Americas and the many Europes? Why did they exist, and what was the result?
4. Why was it so difficult for Europeans to conceptualize and deal with overseas realities?
5. How did overseas exploration and conquest change the explorers, the many Europes, and the world?

Key Terms

conquistador **(p. 359)**
balkanize **(p. 360)**
carrack **(p. 366)**
caravel **(p. 366)**
Portolan chart **(p. 366)**
astrolabe **(p. 366)**
converso **(p. 367)**
Columbian Exchange **(p. 369)**
contact vulnerabilities **(p. 369)**
encomienda system **(p. 377)**

Primary Sources in connect

For information on Connect and the online resources available, go to **http://connect.mcgraw-hill.com**.

1. **John Mandeville at the Court of the Great Khan**
2. **Columbus's First Description of the Americas, 1493**
3. **Bernardino de Sahagún's Account of the Taking of Tenochtitlán**
4. **Doña Marina, La Malinche: Native Help-Mate of Cortés**
5. **Montaigne's American Cannibals**
6. **Laws and Reactions to the Americas**

BACK TO THE SOURCE

Picturing European Fantasies of the Americas

Within a few years of Columbus's landing in the Bahamas, European illustrators were already imagining the delights and horrors of the Americas, as seen in the two woodcuts below. The first fantasy, based on Columbus's account, shows King Ferdinand of Spain extending his approval of Columbus and his three ships as they land overseas on a tropical island paradise populated by scantily clad natives. The second woodcut (Augsburg, 1505) presents more of the dark than the light side of the Caribbean islanders, who are shown as promiscuous cannibals. Even by late in the sixteenth century, the Mannerist painter Paolo Farinati (1524–1606) of Verona still expressed something of the continuing European fantasy with the Americas and their strange peoples in his allegorical painting *America* (1595).

DATI, *La lettera dell'Isole* . . . 1493. NEW YORK PUBLIC LIBRARY

QUESTIONS | *Analyze the main elements of the three images. What European assumptions do they reveal? How are the native Americans imagined and portrayed? What has changed between the imaginings of the early woodcuts and Farinati's later painting? What does the painting imply? Why did Europeans indulge in these fantasies?*

13

Jean Perrissin's Painting of the Calvinist Temple of Paradise, Lyons, France (1565)

THE RELIGIOUS RE-FORMATION OF EUROPE

ERASMUS AND KATHARINA VON BORA LEAVE MONASTICISM BEHIND Erasmus, the prince of humanists, was a self-made man. Born Herasmus Gerritszoon, he later took the first name of Desiderius and dropped the last name, which identified him as Gerard's son. As the illegitimate son of a young man who had abandoned him and his mother, Erasmus had little social standing and few worldly prospects, and so his family pushed him toward a religious life. After some training in the new devotion promoted by the Brothers of the Common Life, which was the rage in the Netherlands at the time, Erasmus was compelled to enter the monastic life. He had wanted to go to a university, but became instead an Augustinian monk (canon), and was often resentful, bored, and restless. Yet there were benefits to being a monk: conversation with other bright young monks, access to a decent library, and a superb training in Latin. His reputation as an accomplished

Portrait of Erasmus in 1517 by Quentin Metsys

Portrait of Katharina von Bora in 1528 by Lucas Cranach

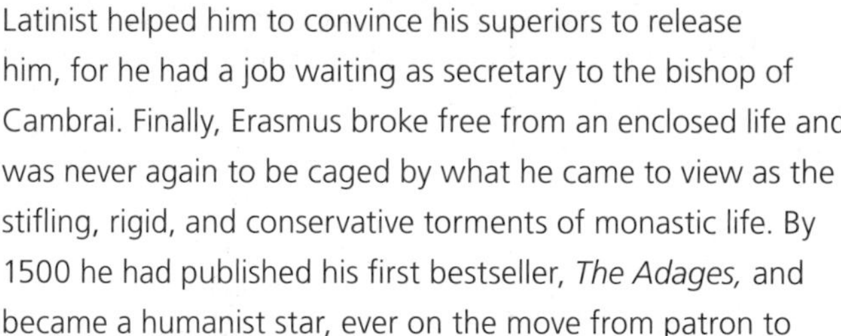

Latinist helped him to convince his superiors to release him, for he had a job waiting as secretary to the bishop of Cambrai. Finally, Erasmus broke free from an enclosed life and was never again to be caged by what he came to view as the stifling, rigid, and conservative torments of monastic life. By 1500 he had published his first bestseller, *The Adages,* and became a humanist star, ever on the move from patron to patron, always in search of a good meal, fine wine, and clever conversation with learned friends.

Erasmus was not alone in wanting to break free from the chains of monasticism. Other famous reformers of the sixteenth century abandoned the monastic life, among them both Martin Luther and his future wife, the noble Katharina von Bora. Katie, as Luther came to call her, had been raised from the age of

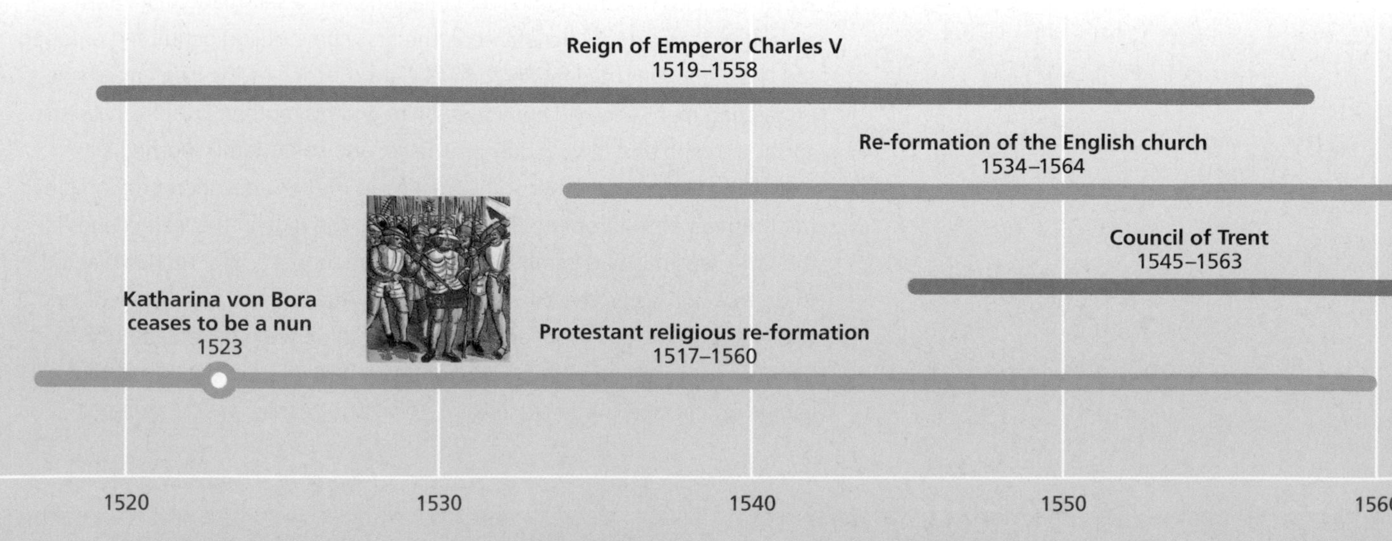

five in a convent, learning Latin and the basic teachings of the Roman Catholic Church: the need to do good works in pursuit of salvation, the spiritual necessity of celibacy, and the supremacy of the pope. But during the years of Katie's monastic confinement, people were beginning to question the nature of their religious beliefs. The Catholic monk and university professor Martin Luther was the most prominent of these, and his writings and ideas made their way into Katie's monastery. She and her sisters wrote to him about their growing doubts. With Luther's personal encouragement, Katie and eleven of her sister nuns decided that their path to salvation did not lie within the confines of a monastery or Roman Catholicism. They plotted to abandon the convent, break their monastic vows, and join Luther and his followers in the city of Wittenberg. On Easter eve 1523, under cover of darkness, the nuns crept out of their monastery. Following Luther's plan, they hid in the wagon of a fish merchant and were driven away from the monastery by a sympathetic city councilor. When the wagon pulled into the university town of Wittenberg, the students took note of the arrival of a "wagonload of vestal virgins . . . more eager for marriage than life." Two years later, after her first love match had failed, Katie married Martin Luther and became the wife of Europe's most controversial married cleric.

The abandonment of monasticism by the likes of Erasmus and Katharina von Bora was yet another sign that the Middle Ages was slipping away, just as the Fall of Constantinople and the replacement of the parchment medieval manuscript by the printed paper book had signaled its end. Ten years after Katie left the monastic life, King Henry VIII ordered the dissolution of the monasteries of England, seized monastic properties, and sent monks and nuns out into the world they had rejected. Since the Early Middle Ages, monasticism had been a central element of the Catholic Church and its claim to be in intimate and constant conversation with the divine. When nuns such as Katharina von Bora quit the monastery, broke their vows of chastity and obedience to the spiritual guidance of the Roman Catholic Church, and pinned their hopes for salvation on a radical new way of viewing and living a Christian life, their departure from the old ways was as revolutionary a social act as had been the hermit Anthony's abandonment of Roman city life for the desert in the third century. The religious life of Europe was being remade and Christianity re-formed.

Though the period has typically been called the Reformation, that familiar term has lost some of its capacity to shock us into an appreciation of the radical and transformative nature of the remaking of European religion that occurred in the sixteenth century. As a label, *the Reformation* has many problems. By 1519, Luther was no longer interested in reforming the Catholic Church, but was determined to do away with it, replacing it with a different ordering of the relations between humans and the divine. Moreover, there were several reformations, not just the Lutheran or Protestant Reformation, but also a Radical Reformation and a Catholic Reformation. Only

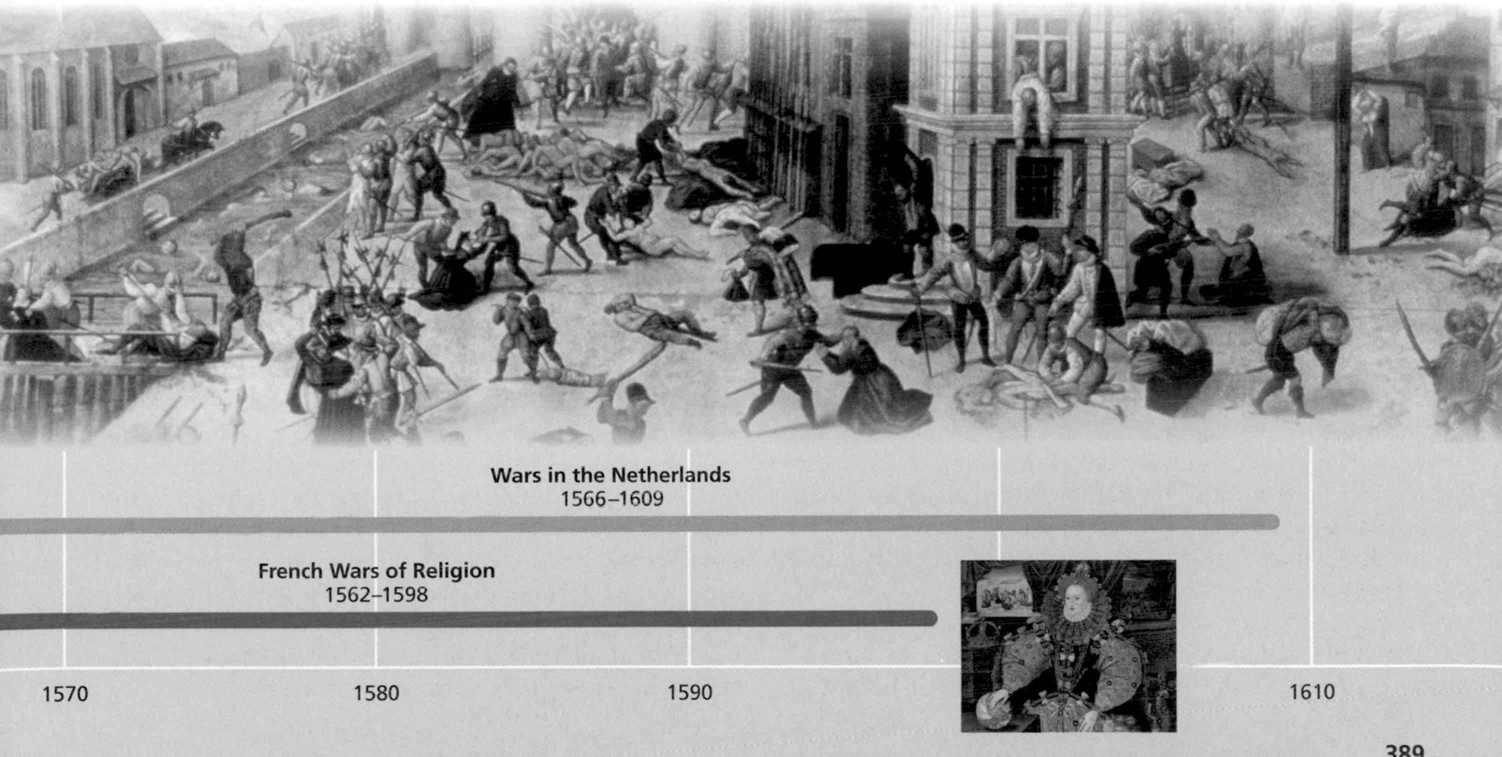

the last of these consisted of the actual reformation of an existing church and not its replacement. Some scholars have, instead, called the Catholic Reformation a Counter Reformation, for to call it a Catholic Reformation is to assert that it was a preexisting movement, generated internally, and largely independent of Protestant criticism, whereas to call it a Counter Reformation is to suppose that Catholics reformed their church only in reaction to the Protestant Reformation. Some observers have wondered if the Protestant Reformation would be better called a revolution, since the effect of the radical rethinking of Christendom by Protestants was to overthrow an old religious order that had dominated western Europe for over a thousand years.

To treat the period as a re-formation, remaking, or refounding of Christian institutions and beliefs is not, we hope, just to play with words, but an attempt to capture something of the active restructuring and fundamental reordering of Christianity that took place in the sixteenth century. For if "to reform" is to revise, correct, and improve something while leaving the thing itself still intact, "to re-form" is to shape something anew, to begin again from the ground up and put aside the old, which may legitimately be said of the Protestant approach to the establishment of new churches and new forms of Christianity based on the apostolic or early Christian church. The first formation of the church had taken place in that early period stretching from Christ's life to the emperor Diocletian's great persecution of the Christian Church. The second period began with Constantine's conversion and stretched through the Early Middle Ages, east and west. In that long period, the church took on its normative institutional and doctrinal form. The third great reform of the church, often called the Investiture Controversy or Gregorian Reform, was the restructuring of the church by the papacy in the eleventh and twelfth centuries. That reformation produced the Great Schism of the church into eastern and western churches, and was the last great reordering of the western church and of its sources of power and fundamental claims before the monumental events touched off by Martin Luther. The religious re-formation of Europe in the sixteenth century was one of the West's great turning points. It was turbulent, revolutionary, and lasting in effect.

The medieval church had rested on a set of fundamental beliefs and practices, at the heart of which lay the celebration of the Mass (as the reenactment of Christ's last supper). The Catholic faithful met in the physical and spiritual church under the supervision of a priest who acted as an essential intermediary between humans and God. The priest administered the granting of the sacraments to the faithful, for humans were regarded as deformed and sinful as a result of the Fall and so in need of sacramental remedies. Moreover, Christians required a priest to serve as an agent intervening with God to secure forgiveness and favor for them. The Catholic Church also held that **Purgatory** was a place between heaven and hell, where the sinful dead awaited the Last Judgment and welcomed the prayers of the living in the hope of securing release from everlasting torment and a prolonged period of punishment or purgatorial cleansing. On earth the pope was God's supreme representative, his archpriest, and the arbiter of all things concerning the faithful. Martin Luther and the Protestants would in time challenge each of these fundamental tenets of Catholicism, and by so doing create new churches, new sets of beliefs, and a re-formed idea of the essential meaning of Christianity. Protestants broke the back of the unity and universalism of the Roman Catholic Church.

At its most basic level, the religious re-formation of Europe was a struggle for authority that pitted individual faith against the Catholic Church's traditional and institutional monopoly over Scripture and religious practice. This crisis of authority had profound implications for religious and political life throughout the early modern period, and for the political and religious contours of the West. When the Catholic Church lost its institutional and religious monopoly, it was as though a dam had burst. Long pent-up ideas, frustrated spiritual desires, and political aspirations flooded forth, washing over the many Europes and into its many nooks and crannies.

The Protestant Religious Re-Formation Begins

Why couldn't Luther just go along with tradition and the age-old weight of church authority?

The problems of the late medieval church and the new trends in medieval religion were many, as surveyed in Chapters 10 and 11: the profound impact of the plague and other crises; the Babylonian Captivity of the papacy in Avignon; the Western or Papal Schism, when multiple popes reigned at the same time; the rise of a vigorous conciliar movement; the emergence of a deeply felt lay piety less dependent on the institutional church; the turbulent national religious movements in England under John Wyclif and in Bohemia under Jan Hus; and the rise of humanism, with its critical examination of texts, both classical and religious. None of these disturbances, however, can account for the appearance and impact of Martin Luther (1483–1546), one of history's great radicals. They were rather the background noise against which he emerged. As a university professor of theology and a member of the Catholic clergy, Luther was an unlikely candidate to bring about the re-formation of the Christian religion. But his growing conviction that the pure message of Christ and Christianity had been perverted over the centuries by the existing church led him to a radical rethinking of salvation, of the individual's relationship to the divine, and of the essential purpose of the church. By 1600, Europe was dramatically different, at least religiously, from what it had been in 1517, when Luther accidentally sparked a revolution in Christian thought and practice.

CHRONOLOGY	Thirty Years of Religious Turmoil
DATE	**EVENT**
1517	Martin Luther issues the Ninety-Five Theses
1518	Huldrych Zwingli begins to reform the Catholic Church in Zürich
1519	Charles V becomes emperor
1519–1521	Huldrych Zwingli establishes his own re-formed church in Zürich
1521	Luther refuses to recant his beliefs at the Diet of Worms
1522	The Knights' Revolt
1522	The sausage scandal in Zürich
1524–1525	Peasants' Revolt in Germany
1525	Luther marries the former nun Katharina von Bora
1525	Anabaptists publicly gather in Zürich
1529	Luther and Zwingli meet at Marburg and fail to unite their churches
1530s	Scandinavian kingdoms all join the Lutheran Church
1531	Zwingli dies in battle against the Catholics
1534	Henry VIII by the Act of Supremacy breaks from the Catholic Church
1535	Anabaptist Münster falls to Catholic forces
1540	Ignatius Loyola founds the Society of Jesus (Jesuits)
1541	John Calvin establishes his re-formed church in Geneva
1545–1547	The Council of Trent's first session
1547	Defeat of the Protestant Schmalkaldic League at the Battle of Mühlberg

Martin the Monk

Unlike the noble Katie, Martin Luther was of middle-class background. His father, Hans, the son of a successful farming family, became a prosperous miner in Saxony and married well. Hans dreamed of Martin becoming a lawyer and helping out their large family. To that end, Hans funded his son's education right through university. Like Erasmus, Luther was enrolled in schools established by the Brothers of the Common Life and distinguished himself as a student by his quickness and intelligence. In 1501, he entered Erfurt University to study secular law and thrived, earning his degree after a single year of study and continuing on to acquire his master's degree three years later.

He then began the advanced study of the law, but in July 1505 a sudden summer storm changed the direction of his life. Luther was very nearly struck by a bolt of lightning. Cold, wet, and frightened, he prayed to Saint Anne (the mother of the Virgin Mary), promising that if he lived he would dedicate his life to the church. Luther made good on his promise by entering the Augustinian monastic order. The world lost a lawyer that stormy day, but gained a religious revolutionary.

Unlike Erasmus and Katie, Luther willingly and with utter spiritual sincerity entered into the monastic life, and he proved to be a dedicated monk. He advanced to the priesthood and even traveled to Rome on behalf of his monastic order. Luther, however, was unsatisfied, for as a monk he was tormented by the worry that he was a wretched sinner who would never achieve salvation, not even by being the best monk that he could be. He did try, driving himself to religious extremes by abstaining from

The Young Martin Luther, 1520 Lucas Cranach's engraving of Luther early in his career, three years after the Ninety-Five Theses and a year before his confrontation with Emperor Charles V. Luther is still dressed as a monk, is tonsured, and has a look of righteous conviction that his supporters and opponents came to know well.

sleep and meals, and observing all-night prayer vigils. In 1511, his superiors, fearing for the health of their driven young monk, encouraged him to return to a life of scholarship and so sent him, still a monk, back to school.

Luther and the Indulgence Controversy

The Augustinians sent Luther to the new University of Wittenberg, which the elector of Saxony, Frederick the Wise, had proudly opened in 1508. There Luther became a professor of theology. Though a lifelong and devoted Catholic, Frederick was extremely proud and protective of his fledgling university and of its brilliant new professor. Luther soon established himself as the dominant voice of the university. His first target, however, was the curriculum, not religion. He led an assault on the older scholastic study of Aristotle and the schoolmen that lay at the core of the new university's curriculum. In early 1517, he released a less well-known set of Ninety-Seven Theses on curriculum reform, whose central conviction was that "Aristotle is to theology what darkness is to light." To a friend he explained that, when he was done, the study of the Bible and Augustine would have entirely displaced Aristotle. As a teacher, Luther was an inspired innovator. He stripped away medieval commentaries from the texts used by his students so that they could read Scripture afresh, unhindered by the erroneous interpretations of the past. Although Luther was indebted to humanist ideas about how to handle texts and the need to cut through textual complexities to rediscover original simple truths, he was never a humanist in spirit. His view of the world and of humankind was always too dark and pessimistic to have shared in humanist optimism about human potential and human capacities.

While he was earning a reputation at the university as a stirring teacher, Luther continued to worry about his own salvation. He discussed with his students the Catholic doctrine of salvation, which taught that faith, good works, and the confession of sins led to divine forgiveness. In an effort to answer his students' questions about the subject, Luther looked to early church teachings and the New Testament for guidance. He slowly came to believe that faith was a gift freely bestowed by God and that it might be a sign of salvation. Luther's ideas about salvation were not fully developed in 1517, but he was heading in a dangerous direction, for, according to the Catholic Church, faith alone was not sufficient for salvation. The believer also needed the Catholic Church and all that went with it (pope and priests, church and custom, sacraments and intercession). The matter soon came to a head.

One of the most popular forms of good works in Catholic Europe was the purchase of **indulgences.** Indulgences were believed to shave time off a sinner's sentence or lessen the severity of his or her punishment in Purgatory, the waiting room to heaven or hell, in exchange for a fee. Luther had been struck by the church's reliance on indulgence monies when he visited the Vatican in 1510, a year in which Michelangelo was hard at work painting the ceiling of the Sistine Chapel. Indeed, the two are not unconnected, for Luther's great doubt about the existing church was rooted in his dismay over the opulence of the papacy and its drive (first by Julius II and then Leo X) to adorn the papal palace (including the Sistine Chapel) and St. Peter's Basilica. Michelangelo and Luther thus stood at opposite ends of the same papal imperative to beautify the Vatican, one as its client-painter, the other as its critic-priest.

Within Catholic theology, the sale of indulgences made perfect sense, for the sinner by purchasing an indulgence was performing a penitential act of repentance and restitution for his crimes, and Christ as a fount of limitless power could save whomever he wished, indeed the whole world if he so chose. Even if the sinner fell short of deserving to be saved, she might appeal to the intercession of Mary and the saints, who were believed to have done so much good in the world that their merits constituted a vast treasury of credits that could be expended on behalf of the penitent.

In 1517, the church enlisted a Dominican friar named Johann Tetzel to sell indulgences in Germany. Frederick the Wise, however, was himself a great collector of relics and saw the indulgence campaign as competition to his own fundraising plans. He banned the sale of indulgences in his territory, but students and citizens from Wittenberg were soon leaving the elector of Saxony's lands to purchase indulgences across the line. The purpose of this indulgence campaign was to help the pope finish his expensive renovations of papal Rome and to assist the Hohenzollerns, an ambitious noble family from Brandenburg, to secure the important archbishopric of Mainz for one of their own, Albrecht, who was already the archbishop of Magdeburg. The archbishopric of Mainz was a great prize since Mainz occupied a critical place in the selection and election of the Holy Roman emperor. Moreover, Albrecht was already deeply in debt to the Fugger banking family that was bankrolling his bid for the Mainz see and various other enterprises. The powerful players promoting the sale of indulgences in 1517 were not, however, crass hypocrites, since they also remained confident that the purchasers of indulgences would still obtain an earlier entry to heaven through their pious act.

Luther was perturbed that the students and citizens of Wittenberg were purchasing indulgences. He had questioned the indulgence trade before, but in 1517 he was still preoccupied by the curriculum reform he was spearheading at the university and may not have fully appreciated what a storm of controversy he was about to unleash. On October 31, 1517, he issued a list of Ninety-Five Theses against the sale of indulgences and other church abuses. We can no longer be sure that he posted these statements on the door of the cathedral in Wittenberg or that he expected a debate to follow, but the theses soon spread in printed form in both German and Latin versions. He also sent a copy to Archbishop Albrecht, who sent the contentious propositions to Rome for review. Within weeks, copies of Luther's Ninety-Five Theses had reached a wide audience in Europe, sparking a pamphlet war of words

THINGS THAT REMAIN

Viewer Beware!

The satirical image of "Johann Tetzel, the Dominican Monk, with his Romish Sale of Indulgences," as the caption to the cartoon reads, has appeared in many surveys of western history. The image is a Protestant caricature of Tetzel's indulgence campaign. The pretentious friar sits on an ass, as Christ did on Palm Sunday, while a haloed dove hovers above his head and insects or small birds encircle it. Nestled in his left arm are fox-brushes (fox tails), a common symbol of deceit and double-dealing. In his right hand he rings bells to beckon penitents, who approach the heavy, locked money chest to deposit their coins in a pan and purchase forgiveness for their sins. The first approaching penitent may be a noble, since he wears boots and a sword, but the smaller figure being dragged forward is a poor barefooted peasant. The accompanying poem mocks, as Luther did in his Ninety-Five Theses, the idea that "The moment the money into the pan rings, the soul into heaven springs."

Caricature of Johann Tetzel Peddling Indulgences

The great problem with this striking cartoon is that it is a secondary (or subsequent) source, not a primary (or contemporaneous) one. It did not appear in 1517 as a piece of Protestant propaganda during the Indulgence Controversy, but a hundred years later in Wittenberg as a broadsheet commemoration of Luther's protest against indulgences and the start of Luther's revolt against the Catholic Church.[1] For generations the drawing has worked to fix an image in student heads of the Protestant complaint against the crude sale of indulgences by Tetzel and the church. Yet how accurate is it? The caption calls Tetzel a monk and the caricature shows him as tonsured or balding, but in fact Johann Tetzel was a Dominican friar. In the Ninety-Five Theses, Luther never once mentioned Tetzel by name, and though he criticizes the outlandish claims of the indulgence sellers, Luther had bigger fish to fry. His propositions were more academic and abstract in nature, not the stuff of a personal drama between him and a fiery Dominican preacher. When we encounter icons of the past, we need to maintain a critical attitude, always questioning, particularly in our own electronic and imagistic age, whether what we are looking at is what it pretends to be. It matters historically whether the image of Tetzel atop an ass was contemporary propaganda and influenced Luther's contemporaries to turn against the Catholic Church and its sale of indulgences or was a later, distorted commemoration of the past.

QUESTIONS | ***Why might historical images easily mislead us? What critical questions should we raise when examining them? Why are printed drawings and images from the early modern period particularly susceptible to misinterpretation?***

and images with the Dominicans, who felt obliged to defend their man Tetzel. Had the wider world and the religious parties simply ignored the theses of the obscure German professor from the little university, his critique of the church might have passed unnoticed, but this was the age of print, and a narrow academic argument soon became the opening sally in a religious revolution.

The strange thing about the Ninety-Five Theses is that they seem, with hindsight, not to be overly provocative (see Back to the Source at the end of the chapter). Luther did lay into the pope and the papacy as an institution, calling on the pope to pay for St. Peter's Basilica out of his own extensive riches, and not the meager resources of the poor, but he held out the possibility that the extremes of the indulgence trade were the product of extreme preachers. He charged that the pope could not remit any punishments but those that he had imposed. Though Luther doubted the theology and efficacy of indulgences, it is striking how much Catholic teaching he still accepted. He qualified some assumptions about Purgatory, but still accepted its reality, as he did that of the saints and sacraments, penance and merit, and good works. Though it may have been but satirical posturing on his part, he presented himself as someone seeking to help the pope live and act within his rightful powers and religious limitations.

Struggling with Rome

Pope Leo returned Luther's theses to the Augustinian order to sort out internally. Luther still suspected that his criticism of the sale of indulgences could be contained within the existing framework of the Catholic Church and resolved in academic debate, so he agreed to attend an Augustinian convention in Heidelberg in the spring of 1518. There Luther planned to discuss his criticisms with his fellow monks and reduced his ninety-five propositions to a more manageable list of twenty-eight, chiefly on the subject of grace. When Luther arrived and presented his ideas, his fellow Augustinians cheered him, but his Dominican critics remained sullen, resentful over the attack on one of their own, and opposed to the implications of Luther's theological impertinence.

In Rome, as reports filtered in from Germany about the slow pace of indulgence sales and the swelling impact of Luther's protest, Pope Leo X became concerned. He ordered Luther to report to Rome by August 1518 to present in person his objections to the sale of indulgences. Unsure whether to obey the order, Luther sought out Frederick the Wise for guidance. Frederick was assured by his private chaplain that the professor was not a heretic but was simply trying to bring the Catholic Church into proper alignment with Christian teachings. Concerned that the pope might not share this opinion, Frederick advised Luther to remain in Wittenberg.

In October in Augsburg, Luther did meet with the pope's representative, Cardinal Thomas Cajetan, a Dominican scholar, who found the professor brash and stubborn. At about this time, not finding a sympathetic ear within the official church, Luther came to his most critical theological insight after reading the letters of Saint Paul, that it was "by faith alone" (*sola fide*), as a pure gift of God, that believers live and are righteous. Christians can do nothing to achieve salvation by their own merit, he thought; no good work could win them their way to heaven. At this point, Luther turned away from the authority of the church and its doctrine of good works to the primacy of faith as encountered in the Bible. "By Scripture alone" (*sola scriptura*), he concluded, and not from church tradition or through its priests, was the word of God to be known. "By grace alone" (*sola gratia*), which was a pure gift of God, was the believer saved. Luther and his followers held that humankind was so fallen, so sinful, that it could do nothing to achieve salvation on its own. The human will was simply too weak to achieve salvation; only God's intervening grace could save humans. These core insights were to undermine the Catholic Church and its doctrinal foundations. Luther's radical theology made the church unnecessary and, indeed, an obstacle blocking Christians from the truth.

In 1519, with the support of the Hohenzollerns, a new Holy Roman emperor was elected. As Luther's arguments were hardening, the nineteen-year-old Habsburg Spanish king, Charles I, became the emperor Charles V. His was an unenviable lot, for he suddenly had vast and difficult territories to govern and faced in the north the stirrings of the new religious movement that was rapidly taking concrete form (Map 13.1). Charles's problem, like that of all overcommitted people, was that it was difficult to do any one thing well when you have too many things to do, and Charles was dragged from one crisis to the next over the forty years of his tumultuous reign.

Luther, who was still just an outspoken member of the Catholic clergy, was challenged by an ambitious professor named Johann Eck to a traditional academic debate in Leipzig on the idea of salvation. In the debate, Eck attacked Luther for his criticism of the papacy and forced Luther to defend Jan Hus, even though a council had executed Hus for heresy. In this way, Eck trapped Luther into revealing his animosity toward the entire Catholic Church, both to the papacy and to its councils. In the aftermath of Leipzig, Eck crafted the formal papal bull *Exsurge Domine,* in June 1520, giving Luther sixty days to recant his heretical beliefs or face excommunication. Luther publicly burned the papal bull, the treatises of his opponent Eck, and the legal documents drawn up against him.

Luther then went on the offensive, taking his case to a wider public. In short order in 1520, he produced three concise works that spread quickly in print and that constituted a frontal attack on the Catholic Church. In the first, *The Address to the Christian Nobility of the German Nation,* he presented the pope as the Anti-Christ interfering with the administration of the empire and the clergy as the destroyers of the Christian church. For Luther, all people, not just clerics, could establish a direct relationship with God. He spoke of ordinary worshippers as belonging to "a priesthood of all believers" that bore the responsibility for seeing that the church was set on the right path. In the second pamphlet, *The Babylonian Captivity of the Church,* Luther continued his assault on the papal and priestly perversion of the Christ's message and church. Here he rejected four of the Catholic Church's seven sacraments (confirmation, marriage, the taking of holy orders, and last rites), leaving only baptism, the Eucharist, and penance as sanctioned by Scripture. Finally, in his treatise *On Christian Liberty,* which was addressed to Pope Leo X, Luther returned to his argument that good works, merits, and indulgences do not lead to salvation, only faith does. With the publication of these tracts, Luther went around the established church to address Germans and Christians at large. The German monk now stood so far beyond the Catholic Church that he was unable to reenter.

Luther's pamphlets finally made it clear to the pope and emperor that something had to be done about the rogue monk. Leo X signed the orders to excommunicate Luther and passed them to Charles to enforce. The young emperor found himself in a difficult spot, caught between the pope and Frederick the Wise of Saxony, Luther's protector

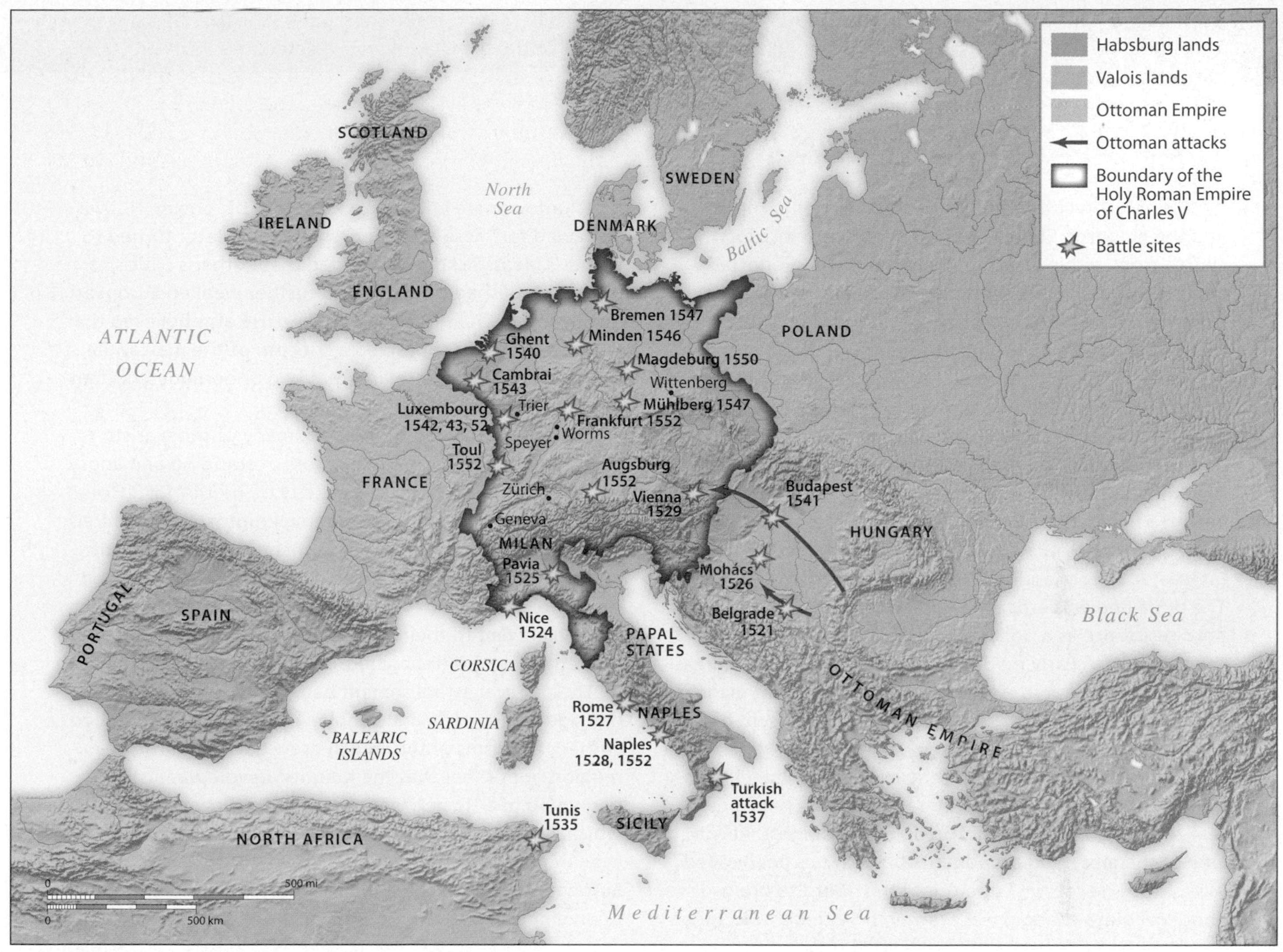

MAP 13.1 | Charles V's Europe, 1519–1558

The Holy Roman Empire and Habsburg lands were not the same, but Charles V's empire consisted of both. Together they made him the preeminent ruler in the first half of the sixteenth century, but one whose lands were scattered and troublesome, each having its own demands and interests. In addition, the Ottoman Empire was encroaching from the east and the Valois kings of France were bothersome in the west. The locations of many of the emperor's battles during his long reign are marked on the map. ***Why was Charles V's inheritance of such a vast territory a mixed blessing? What sense can be made of the timing of the various battles and areas of conflict? How did Charles's political and territorial problems affect the attention he paid to religious problems?***

and the emperor's potential military ally. Charles tried to reach a compromise by calling an imperial meeting (diet) in the city of Worms. On April 17, 1521, Luther appeared at the diet and was asked to recant his heretical beliefs. Luther asked for a recess. The next day, he refused to revoke his belief in salvation through faith alone and spoke the famous words "Here I stand. I can not do otherwise."

From Instituting to Living the Lutheran Faith

After Luther held fast to his religious principles at Worms, the emperor issued an Edict of Worms (1521) that declared Martin Luther an outlaw. Added to the pope's earlier excommunication decree, this declaration made Luther a pariah in the eyes of both church and state. The terms of the edict made it illegal for anyone within the empire to aid Luther and his followers, or to buy, sell, read, preserve, or print any of Luther's writings. If the threat of civil penalties was not enough to deter them, Luther's excommunication placed at risk the immortal soul of anyone who offered him shelter. But Charles had been as good as his word at Worms; he respected the terms of the safe conduct that he had granted to Luther and allowed him to leave Worms in peace. Frederick the Wise engineered a mock arrest of Luther and sent his controversial professor to the castle of Wartburg in Saxony, where for ten months, while northern Europe seethed with religious turmoil, Luther remained out of harm's way and beyond the emperor's reach.

While in hiding, Luther worked on a new, vernacular translation of the New Testament (the Old Testament

WHAT A DIFFERENCE A YEAR MAKES

1521–1522: The Knights Rebel

By 1521, Martin Luther had powerful enemies in the pope and the emperor. Though he had begun by criticizing the church from within as a monk and had been supported by his university, his Augustinian order, and the elector of Saxony, his position as a critical insider vanished at the Diet of Worms. By 1522, Luther's ideas were being used by others to attack the political and religious establishment. The stakes surrounding Luther's actions were high. When Luther attacked the church, he had not only explicitly questioned the pope's religious powers, but also implicitly called into doubt the secular powers of the pope and earthly princes. By standing up to the emperor at Worms, he had snubbed his nose at Europe's most powerful leader (at least in theory and symbol) and protector of the faith. The pope and emperor were forced to take Luther's stubborn resistance as a political as well as religious threat to their authority. Early modern Europeans had little awareness of the concept of a loyal opposition, and that made it imperative for political authorities to silence dissent before it spread.

Charles's worst fears about the explosive connections between political rebellion and religious criticism were realized in 1522 with the outbreak of the Knights' Revolt. One of the most avid proponents of what has been called "swash-buckle reform" (the use of the sword to bring about religious change) was Franz von Sickingen. Sickingen was a member of the traditional landed nobility of the Holy Roman Empire and had seen the fortunes of his family decline while those of the merchant classes rose. To make ends meet, Sickingen used military force to extort payments and trade agreements from those families and cities unfortunate enough to fall under his power. He was outlawed for these extortions in 1515 and later turned to Luther's ideas. Sickingen believed that Luther's criticisms of the established church would further weaken European institutions such as property holding. He also believed that Luther's doctrines contained a criticism of the mercantile culture of buying and selling that had undermined his family's traditional privileges.

Sickingen gathered supporters, many of them aristocrats also disgruntled over their loss of standing and angry at the church. They attacked the city of Trier in 1522. To defend itself against the marauding knights, the city hired Philip of Hesse, a supporter of Luther, who did not want to see Luther's religious movement linked to political and social violence. The city's forces drove Sickingen from Trier; his soldiers fled to their own estates, where they were hunted down and dispatched.

The political establishment had won the day, but the damage was done. Many people who were sympathetic to Luther's criticisms of the church drew back from the new religion out of fear that the Knights' Revolt was just the beginning of a flood of insurrection. Politics and religion, which had been uneasy bedfellows for centuries, became even more tightly connected in the minds of early modern Europeans after Martin Luther refused to bend to the wills of an emperor and a pope.

QUESTIONS | ***Why do revolutions so often take on a life of their own and soon spin out of control? Why and how did Luther's stand at the Diet of Worms encourage political and social rebellion?***

translation came later). Luther's translation of the Bible was to have a formative influence on shaping the German language. He made his version of the Bible consistent with his Augustinian and Protestant interpretation of the text. As well, Luther began to assemble the pieces that would serve as the theological foundation for the Lutheran Church. To do so, he adopted the *ad fontes,* or back to the source spirit of humanistic textual analysis, and closely examined Scripture to be sure that his new church was in agreement with the ideals practiced by Christ and the Apostles.

One of Luther's goals for his new church was to offer worshippers a greater sense of spiritual connection with God. For Luther, one of the essential ways to achieve this connection was through re-formed church services and a Bible that was in the common language. Reading and listening to the word of God in German, rather than Latin, advanced lay spirituality, Luther argued, and further diminished the Catholic distinctions between the laity and the clergy. The Lutheran Church would have ministers, who would be thought of as members of the congregation, not priests. Luther argued that all worshippers should receive both bread and wine in the Eucharistic ceremony. The new practice departed from Catholic custom, which taught that the wine, as transformed into Christ's blood, was too spiritual to give to the laity and so was offered only to the clergy. For Luther the idea of a "priesthood of all believers" meant that the faithful would not need intermediaries such as priests or saints to help them communicate with God. In Luther's new church, every worshipper was capable of speaking directly with God without an intervening agent, whether human or institutional.

While these doctrines were important to formulating the theology of the new Lutheran Church, Luther knew that he needed to address clerical and church abuses when he established the guidelines for his new religion. To reinforce the idea that a person's faith was all that was truly important to God and to achieving salvation, Luther simplified church rituals and ornamentation, removing images of saints from churches and their feast days from the official church calendar. He discouraged the collection of relics and declared that neither indulgences nor good works had any value in achieving salvation. Luther also reduced further the number of legitimate sacraments from three to two, leaving only baptism and the Eucharist in place. Luther also opposed the Catholic Church's belief that the priest, by saying the holy words of consecration in the Mass, completely transformed the bread and wine of the Lord's Supper into the body and blood of Christ. Luther replaced this Eucharistic doctrine known as transubstantiation with the idea that the substance of the bread and wine coexisted with or alongside the presence of Christ's body and blood.

Luther also doubted the value of a monastic life and a celibate clergy. He did not believe that ascetic or celibate lives were any holier than other forms of faithful living, and in fact monks and celibates were living unnecessary and unnatural lives. As a result, he argued against monastic orders like his own that had served as spiritual bedrocks of the Catholic tradition. Luther believed that the clergy should be out among the laity, teaching and preaching the word of God, not praying in isolated monastic cells. Since they were no closer to God than any other believer, monks should abandon their monasteries and rejoin the congregation of the faithful, the very argument that he made to Katie and her sister nuns. For Luther, the Catholic priests' vows of celibacy ignored God's instruction to be fruitful and multiply. Instead, Luther argued for the importance of a married clergy that could, through the example set by their households, promote Christian beliefs and principles. For him, marriage was a Christian good that established a decent, friendly, charming, and necessary relationship between man and woman.

Luther put his beliefs in a married clergy and the importance of the family into practice when he married Katharina von Bora in 1525. Their household grew over the years to include their own six children, the children of relatives, and Luther's students who boarded with the family to provide extra income. Ever the good Protestant wife, Katie treated the sick, brewed and sold beer, and involved herself in the day-to-day business of running an early modern household of considerable size.

Within Lutheran families, discipline and order were seen as the cornerstones not only of virtuous private lives, but also of virtuous public lives. Lutheran communities called for all people to live without sin within the boundaries of acceptable collective moral behavior. The best way to enforce these ideals was through the institution of the family. A strict hierarchy of father/master, mother/mistress, children, and servants was observed to help promote personal virtue and civic righteousness. Within Protestant families, age was superior to youth, masters to servants, and men to women. Despite this hierarchy of power, the mistress of a household, as the second in command, bore considerable responsibility, and many women were drawn to the Lutheran Church because of the relative autonomy and respect it promised them.

The Early Re-Formation of Church and State

By the time Luther emerged from his castle retreat, the religious revolution he had started was spinning out of control as dissidents and radicals emerged from the cracks now evident in the vast facade of the Catholic Church. In 1521, there were already incidents of idol smashing as the old tokens of the Catholic Church were being torn down and destroyed. In 1522, the so-called Zwickau prophets began to show up in Wittenberg, claiming to speak directly to God. As Wittenberg reeled from incidents of idol smashing and social riots, Frederick insisted that Luther return from his castle hideout in Wartburg to restore order. Luther returned, banished the false prophets, and worked to stabilize Wittenberg. The speed of the unfolding events brought out Luther's own social and political conservatism, alerting him to the pressing need to establish his re-formed church. Though he had unleashed the forces of religious heterodoxy and divergence, he did not intend to license the free play of religious thought and experiment in Europe.

How did the existence of many Europes and the political divisions of the early sixteenth century save Luther and Protestantism from being silenced and suppressed?

By 1522, Luther was trying as hard as he could to control and direct the religious forces he had loosed on northern Europe, giving definition to his true religion, and casting out all those ideas and people who refused to remain within its ever-tightening definition of the faith. He did not intend to test the wild world of religious ideas seething outside Saxony, except in print; he rarely left the comfortable confines of re-formed Wittenberg. His most immediate problem was how to ensure the survival and success of the Lutheran Church. For Jan Hus and the Hussites in Bohemia, that part of their religious program had turned out badly. Luther and Lutheranism needed to find a better way. Support from the elector of Saxony and deference to political authority were Luther's critical starting points in securing secular support for his religious movement.

As Lutheranism grew and gained a wider following, problems arose regarding the relationship between church and state. Nobles and other powerful people in the Holy Roman Empire began to convert to the new religion but were placing themselves on a collision course with the empire and the papacy. In addition, new religious leaders such as Huldrych Zwingli and John Calvin challenged not only Catholic Church teachings, but also Luther's ideas, and moved to establish their own churches. Finally, the interest in national churches shared by many of the new monarchs bore unexpected fruit when Henry VIII of England broke with the Catholic Church to clear his way to divorce and remarriage. By the middle of the century, the relationship between church and state was explosive.

The Peasants Protest Most copies of The Twelve Articles, which was reprinted dozens of times in the early months of the rebellion, were confiscated and destroyed. This image from a rare copy of the pamphlet depicts the peasants sympathetically, but determined and armed to the teeth.

Lutheran Princes

In the years following the Diet of Worms, Luther found a way to combine his religious radicalism with political conservatism; he never revolted against his immediate worldly masters in Germany. But princely conversions to Lutheranism in Germany were complicated by the princes' continuing commitments to Emperor Charles V. Some of Luther's earliest princely followers came, therefore, from Scandinavia. Unencumbered by political alliances with the Catholic emperor, Gustavus Vasa of Sweden (r. 1523–1560), Frederick I of Denmark (r. 1523–1533), and Christian III of Denmark (r. 1534–1559) established national Lutheran churches in the 1530s. Through Christian III's efforts, the Lutheran faith was also taken up by Norway, which made Scandinavia staunchly Lutheran by the 1540s.

The adoption of Lutheranism was more problematic in the Holy Roman Empire. One of the earliest setbacks occurred when the Peasants' War broke out in Germany in 1524. Some historians have seen the earlier Knights' Revolt as a dress rehearsal for this much lengthier and bloodier revolt. In the Peasants' War, the rebels were peasants who had been suffering under the financial burdens of paying not only local taxes, but also imperial and papal taxes. New taxes were imposed on beer and wine and even on slaughtering one's own farm animals for food.

In 1524, peasants in the Black Forest rebelled against their overlord by declaring that they would not pay tithes or taxes to him, nor would they honor their traditional obligation to work his land. The peasants stopped working and began to gather supporters. As they did, the conflict began to spread through southern Germany. A radical mystic and former follower of Luther, Thomas Müntzer, who had become frustrated with the slow pace of Lutheranism, aligned himself with the peasants and encouraged them to see themselves as God's chosen ones in a war of the godly against the godless. Müntzer was looking to the end of time and saw the peasant uprising in apocalyptic terms. The peasants' actual grievances were a complex mixture and confusion of social and religious complaints. They sought an end to serfdom and tithes, freedom from oppressive lords and their punishments, a lifting of restrictions on hunting and fishing, the right to choose their own pastors, and to have them preach to them only the Gospels, clearly and without human additions or doctrines. Luther was at first sympathetic to the peasants, but he soon realized that their goals were not ones of religious improvement, but of social revolution. In the spring of 1525, large peasant armies seized lands, burned castles, and looted churches and monasteries that stood in their path. In May 1525, Luther urged European authorities, both Catholic and Protestant, to put down the revolt by any means: "let all who can, strike, slay, and stab them, in secret or in public, remembering that nothing is more poisonous, harmful, or devilish than a rebel." Luther, the religious rebel, saw no contradiction here; his political sympathies lay on the side of order and established secular power. Some 70–80 thousand peasants were slaughtered in 1525.

Despite this unsettling incident, German princes continued to convert to Luther's church, and by 1526 the emperor Charles V once again found himself in a difficult situation. He needed the support of the German princes to fight an expensive war against the Ottoman Turks, who were threatening to invade Hungary and Austria. When the urgency of the problem required the emperor to recognize the fact of Protestantism, Charles convened an imperial diet in the town of Speyer in 1526. He intended to use the diet to reinforce the terms of the Edict of Worms, but the gathering instead called for a general church council to meet and discuss the issue of religion in the empire. The Diet of Speyer decided that until the council could meet, a degree of religious toleration and coexistence should be granted to the princes so that every state could continue to exist, govern itself, and follow its own religion if it believed that it could be justified before God and the emperor. The decree not only postponed the implementation of the Edict of Worms, but also gave many princes the opportunity to adopt the new religion. After the diet, the rulers of eight regions and eight cities in Germany quickly adopted Protestantism as their official religion.

Three years later, Charles was back at a newly convened diet in Speyer (1529). Imperial armies had failed to halt the Ottoman advance on Hungary, and the Ottomans were now threatening Vienna. This time the extreme crisis encouraged representatives of the emperor to take a harder stance against Luther's new religion. The decisions made at the first Diet of Speyer to delay the implementation of the Edict of Worms and permit religious diversity in the empire were overturned at the second in favor of a stricter enforcement of the Edict of Worms. The Lutheran princes protested against these reversals, earning themselves the name **Protestants,** which followers of all branches of the re-formed Christian faith have held ever since. The Protestant princes joined together to defend themselves against the attack on their religious beliefs and adopted the motto "The word of God remains forever" to link their protests to the authority of Scripture, on which the Lutheran Church rested.

Huldrych Zwingli

The thirteen cantons (small territorial divisions) of the Swiss Confederation fared no better than the empire did in achieving religious compromise and stability. A Catholic priest and religious radical, Huldrych Zwingli, propelled the region into religious war. Educated at the Universities of Vienna and Basel, Zwingli developed ideas of church reform that were based on the principles of Christian humanism, especially those of Erasmus. He thought that both the church and the state could and should be reformed and renewed in conformity with the Bible. His study of the Bible led him to a series of radical conclusions. The words that Christ spoke at the Last Supper ("this is my body" and "this is my blood") were, he came to believe, purely symbolic and did not connote the transubstantiation of the bread into Christ's body or the wine into his blood. He also determined that it was wrong and unnecessary to venerate the saints, to display images, to sing in church, or for priests to remain celibate.

By 1518, Zwingli had carried his message of reform to the city of Zürich. Although still a Catholic priest, Zwingli was by 1521 an increasingly vocal critic of the church, which placed him in opposition to his bishop and to the officials of the Holy Roman Empire. Matters reached a crisis point in 1522, when Zwingli's followers violated the Catholic prohibition against eating meat during Lent, the forty-day period of fasting and prayer before Easter. Since they could find no evidence in the Bible to support that Catholic custom, Zwingli's disciples divided up and ate two smoked sausages in public during Lent, though Zwingli himself refrained. In the aftermath of the sausage scandal that ensued, Zwingli provoked an even greater outcry when he revealed that he had married a young widow named Anna Reinhard earlier that year. He petitioned city officials to abolish a celibate clergy and to start down the path toward constituting a new church. Zwingli had passed quickly from Catholic reformer to church re-former. No longer content to work within the Catholic system, he was ready to establish a new church based on a different set of practices and beliefs, all of them grounded directly in the Bible. The Catholic Church responded by sending officials to Zürich to silence Zwingli. In 1523, city officials held a public debate to consider Zürich's religious future and Zwingli's fate. They decided that Zwingli should be allowed to continue preaching in the city and that all priests should confine themselves to preaching the Bible.

News of Zwingli's victory in Zürich and the city council's support of re-forming religion soon spread to the other urban cantons. Officials in Bern and Basel welcomed the precedent Zürich had set in taking control of its own religious affairs. They also approved of Zwingli's idea of a lived faith, in which believers followed in the footsteps of Christ and modeled their lives after his. Urban leaders promoted both re-formed teaching and preaching as a way to build a more cohesive and unified society.

Despite Zwingli's popularity in the Swiss cities, the countryside remained Catholic and loyal to the emperor. Concerned about the threat of religious and civil war, Zwingli reached out to Luther and his followers to form an alliance of religiously re-formed Swiss and German cities. The two men met in the city of Marburg in 1529, along with other prominent Protestants. At the Marburg Colloquy, they found that they shared a great deal in common, but their radically different beliefs concerning the Eucharist were irreconcilable. Zwingli remained convinced that Christ's words at the Last Supper were symbolic, whereas Luther maintained that the body and blood of Christ were present along with the bread and wine. Zwingli, like Luther, could hardly keep up with the moving frontline of Protestant development, and many of his supporters after Marburg charged that he had turned soft and was not ready to follow his conscience or Scripture all the way.

Without support from the Lutherans in Germany, the threat of religious war between Catholics and Protestants in the Swiss Confederation drew closer. The war broke out in October 1531, but the Protestant armies were no match for the Catholic forces supported by the emperor. Zwingli was wounded in battle, and when the Catholic army discovered him they executed, dismembered, and burned him as a heretic, scattering his ashes in the wind.

OTHER VOICES, OTHER VIEWS

Picture Wars

The experiences of both Luther and Zwingli demonstrate the important role that cities and the printing press played in the spread of new religious ideas. By 1523, almost four hundred editions of Luther's various treatises were in circulation in northern Europe. Early modern cities such as Wittenberg and Zürich were crowded and vibrant. Even though the number of residents in an early modern city may seem relatively small by modern standards, population densities were comparable. Tens of thousands of people clustered into urban spaces that were often confined to a few square miles. In such a restricted environment, new ideas spread quickly, not only in print, but also through the networks of gossip.

These cities often possessed many literate citizens. Printers were active in most European cities by the 1520s, and printing presses spread new ideas and images rapidly. Urban schools, many established by craft and trade guilds, provided basic education to the city's children, who could then take advantage of books, broadsides, and cartoons. Available for relatively small sums of money, printed works tended to be written in the vernacular. Not everyone, of course, could read even the vernacular, but religious pamphlets often relied more on pictures than words to convey their messages.

The Protestant images below seek in cartoon form to capture the differences between Catholic and Protestant worship. On the right side of the first image, a group of men and women of all ages with a few children is shown listening with some degree of distraction to a well-fed Catholic priest wearing splendid robes while many of them work their rosary beads. On the left side, people share copies of the Bible while the simply dressed Protestant minister speaks from a plain pulpit with an open Bible before him. The contrast between the two scenes was meant to inspire debate and discussion. The cartoon invites the viewer to choose the better form of worship. In the middle of the cartoon, an elderly man with outstretched arms seems by his gesture to invite the viewer to pick one side.

Although this cartoon is relatively sophisticated and understated, many were not. They were crude caricatures and lampoons of the other side. This was, after all, a contest for souls and the ultimate reward for choosing rightly was a better chance to enter heaven. In this picture war, re-formers understood the power of such images to demean the Roman Catholic Church. In the broadsheet below, the pope is depicted in the act of selling indulgences. The pope sits on a plump pillow on his throne while surrounded by bishops and a cardinal as he signs a stack of indulgences. A woman seems to be bribing a Catholic priest. Before the pope, simple Catholics count out money to purchase their chance at salvation. The line of those waiting to purchase the indulgence includes the poor and old, whose needs stand in sharp contrast to the hale and hearty clerics tending to the pope and not the faithful. The mockery of the piece is obvious in the image of the dog defecating below the pope.

QUESTIONS | ***How did the combination of visual culture and the printing press help spread Protestant ideas, and what were the dangers of using cartoons to spread the message?***

Woodcut Image of Rival Church Services, 1529, by Hans Sachs, Nuremberg

Woodcut Image of the Pope as Moneychanger and Indulgence Seller, 1521, by Lucas Cranach

Martin Luther, on hearing of Zwingli's gruesome death, was rumored to have said, "He got what he deserved." It was not the finest moment of either re-former.

Henry VIII Divorces the Catholic Church

The divisions between Catholic and Protestant and between church and state were complicated further when the pious Catholic monarch, Henry VIII of England (r. 1509–1547), decided to divorce his first wife and so the Catholic Church. Few could have foreseen that Henry would be the first prominent monarch to break with Rome. He was on record as despising the religiously rebellious Luther and had lined up behind the emperor and other princes against the new religion, but as so often before in Europe dynastic interests overrode religious ones. At the time, Henry was married to Catherine of Aragon, the daughter of the Catholic monarchs Ferdinand and Isabella of Spain. But Henry feared that, if he passed his throne to a woman (in this case, his daughter Mary), another civil war would erupt in England. He wanted a son, and so began the great Tudor melodrama that would transfix England for the rest of the century. The melodrama was created both by religious division and by the king's reckless fickleness and extreme power. By 1526, Henry had his eye on a preferred partner, Anne Boleyn, a young English woman with aristocratic connections, French manners, a sharp tongue, and Protestant leanings.

Divorce or, more commonly, the annulment of a marriage was not impossible in the early modern Catholic Church, but ending a marriage to the aunt of the Catholic emperor Charles V was next to impossible, especially since imperial armies had sacked Rome in 1527 and were still occupying the city. The pope's freedom to act was more limited than usual. Catherine herself refused to give way to her husband's demand for an annulment of their marriage. Had she but relented all might have been different, but Catherine as the last child of Ferdinand and Isabella of Spain was a woman of considerable pride and determination. Moreover, Charles and the pope were annoyed that Henry had declined to participate in the campaign against the Ottoman Turks. Thus, despite Henry's earnest pleas for the pope to annul his marriage to Catherine, Pope Clement VII refused. The English king relied on the advice of his chief religious and legal advisor, Cardinal Thomas Wolsey, and continued to press for an annulment on the grounds that he and Catherine should never have been granted a papal dispensation to marry in the first place since the Spanish princess had previously been married to the king's older brother, Prince Arthur. Not only was Pope Clement poorly placed at the time to resist Emperor Charles's wishes in the matter, but he was also reluctant to admit, given Luther's recent attack on papal authority and the institution of the papacy, that the earlier papal dispensation had been a mistake.

In 1529, Henry dismissed Cardinal Wolsey and soon turned to officials who might arrange his divorce. Thomas Cromwell (1485–1540) concerned himself with the legal and political side of the matter, and Thomas Cranmer, a Catholic cleric, with the religious side. Both men wanted to curb abuses in the English church, as well as to advance their own careers and to protect England from foreign political interference. Together, they advocated an approach to the problem of the divorce that would use English common law and the English legal system to annul the marriage, rather than relying on a Roman Catholic court or the approval of foreign powers. To make their case, they argued that England was an empire and, therefore, that its ruler could have no superior, not even the pope.

While the English Parliament heard the king's case against his marriage to Catherine, Anne Boleyn, who had been holding the king at arm's length for over five years, finally became his mistress. The couple was secretly married in January 1533 when it was clear that she was pregnant. The marriage technically made the king a bigamist, since he was now married to two women at the same time. Henry pressured Parliament to resolve the matter quickly, and in May 1533 English church courts pronounced the king's marriage to Catherine invalid. The king then married the visibly pregnant Anne Boleyn in a lavish ceremony; she was crowned queen within weeks.

In September 1533, King Henry and Queen Anne announced the birth of their daughter, Elizabeth. It was not the dynastic outcome that Henry had hoped for, but there was no going back since English law was in the process of making the Church of England (the Anglican Church) a separate religious entity with the monarch, Emperor Henry VIII, as its "supreme head." The **Act of Supremacy** that passed in 1534 established the king and succeeding monarchs as the supreme religious authorities of the English empire, with the full right to determine church doctrine and practice. In the first weeks of 1535, Parliament passed the Treason Act, which made it a capital crime punishable by death for anyone to fail to uphold the Act of Supremacy.

Even the king's closest advisors were not spared the consequences of the Treason Act. Sir Thomas More (1478–1535), who had earlier been one of Henry's chief advisors, refused to swear an oath supporting the Act of Supremacy. King Henry could not allow his notable subjects to disobey him and disrespect his new religious authority, so More was put on trial. The verdict was never in doubt. More was found guilty of treason and beheaded at the Tower of London in July 1535.

With the passage of the Act of Supremacy, it fell to the king in name and his advisors in fact to shape the new English church. Cromwell handled the political and governmental fallout. He realized that he could smooth the ruffled feathers of the nobility and wealthy merchants with money and so devised a plan to dissolve England's monasteries and friaries, and redistribute the vacated property and monastic wealth to the king and his supporters. Between 1536 and 1540, about one-third of the land in England, which previously had been held and managed by the Catholic Church, was turned over to private individuals who built great houses on it and paid taxes to the

Henry VIII and Charles V in Conference before the Pope An Italian artist created this scene of Henry VIII in discussion with the newly crowned Emperor Charles V (*seated*) under the watchful eyes of Pope Leo X. The date seems to be about 1520, when Charles and Leo were pressing Henry to support their stand against Luther. In 1521, the pope declared Henry a defender of the faith for his denunciation of Luther. Some scholars have portrayed this painting as a debate between the English king and emperor over Henry's request to annul his marriage to Queen Catherine of Aragon, but that seems unlikely if not impossible.

king rather than to the pope. Henry dissolved England's monasteries, but he did little to replace their charitable and community functions. No wonder so many Tudor beggars (often former monastic dependents) gathered in cities such as London; they now had no other place to go to seek local charitable relief. With the overthrow of old practices, traditional English religion was unsettled and believers were confused about what to believe. Cranmer responded by instituting new church doctrines and practices, but his drive to establish the new Anglican Church was compromised by the king's own religious conservatism. Henry personally disapproved of married clergy and remained for a time a great admirer of churches with statues, beautiful music, and other adornments of Catholicism. The result was an English church that was cut loose from Rome, but not fully re-formed either. Henry did agree eventually to supply parish churches with William Tyndale's English translation of the Bible, which may have done more than anything else to sever the English church from the old order, since English men and women could now read and hear the Bible in their own tongue. Not until the reign of Edward VI, the son of Henry and Jane Seymour, would the English church take a firm turn toward re-formed religion with Cranmer's *Book of Common Prayer,* the removal of images from churches, and the lifting of prohibitions against clerical marriage.

John Calvin and the Religious Re-Formation of Geneva

One of the problems facing the Protestant Re-Formation was that few religious re-formers had taken the time to think through the political implications of radical religious change until they were well on their way to overthrowing old institutions and establishing new churches. John Calvin (1509–1564) and the Swiss city of Geneva were different, but then Calvin was a second-generation re-former and subtle theorist. He was the first Protestant leader to work out ideas about the relationship of church and state in a systematic, lucid, and persuasive fashion.

Calvin was born to a family of urban merchants and professionals who placed a premium on education. He was sent to study at the University of Paris, where he was steeped in the ideas of the European Renaissance. Initially, Calvin expressed an interest in theology, but his father felt that a career in the law would better advance the family's fortunes, given the religious turbulence of the age. Like Luther, Calvin dutifully followed his father's wishes, at least until his father died in 1531. Calvin then returned to the university to embark on a humanistic program of language education and religious study. After hearing a friend lecture on Luther's doctrine of justification by faith alone, Calvin had an overwhelming religious conversion and a year later was forced to flee Paris as a recognized re-former. Paris was rocked at the time by the so-called affair of the placards, in which a group of students broke into the king's palace and scrawled Protestant slogans and cartoons on Francis I's bedroom door. Outraged by this assault on his royal dignity and authority, King Francis clamped down on Protestants and Calvin fled to the re-formed Swiss city of Basel.

In Basel, Calvin began work on his masterwork of theology, the *Institutes of the Christian Religion* (first published in 1536). Calvin was only twenty-six when the treatise appeared, but it established him as one of the leading religious thinkers in Europe and he would continue to refine and extend the work until 1559. In the *Institutes,* Calvin set out his belief in the importance of preaching and adherence to the two sacraments of baptism and the Eucharist. He believed that the body and blood of Christ were spiritually present in the bread and wine of the communion service, but that they were not physically present, as believed by Catholics. Calvin's formulation could not, however, be reconciled with Luther's formula and would keep their churches apart. As a consequence, Protestantism was never to be a single church, but then the revolt against the monolithic Catholic Church was always pluralistic in nature. Each movement against the Catholic Church had developed separately in a specific location and under the leadership of a charismatic individual. The result was not just many Europes, but many religions inside the many Europes, each having its own teachings and separate histories.

In the *Institutes,* Calvin set out his belief in the majesty and authority of God, urging his readers not to focus on feelings of their unworthiness in the face of God's total power, but instead to concentrate on God's love for all his creation. One way that God expressed this love was in a finely tuned master plan that would guide the world until the end of time. Calvin urged people to put their faith in God's plan and to accept that they could never know what was in store for them. According to Calvin, God had already determined who had been elected for salvation and who would be damned. There was no way of knowing with certainty which future awaited an individual, though possessing faith might be an indication that you were in the right camp. Thus, Calvin's followers looked to the quality and depth of their faith for signs, no matter how small, that they were among the elect. Material success (such as a thriving business) and spiritual rectitude (such as resisting temptation) were taken by some people as indications of election, even though these indications were not a specific part of Calvin's theology.

In the same year that the first edition of Calvin's *Institutes* appeared, he visited Geneva and, at the request of one of the city's ministers, began to sketch out how government and religious life could be joined into a single institutional framework that would oversee matters of faith and civic affairs. Geneva was at the time a city of some 16,000 rambunctious inhabitants who had driven out their local bishop. No wonder, then, that Calvin believed that the power to excommunicate citizens who would not follow church standards was critical to re-forming the city, but officials balked at the demand. When, in 1538, Calvin refused to administer the Eucharist during Easter services on the grounds that some Genevans were not worthy to receive it, the city expelled him. He traveled to Strasbourg, where he was impressed by the New Testament–style unification of church and government taking place there under the leadership of the Protestant Martin Bucer. While there, Calvin married, but as a second-generation re-former, his marriage did not raise even a ripple of interest. Meanwhile, without strong religious leadership, Geneva began to experience difficulties, just as Wittenberg had when Luther was hiding in his castle. Attendance at church services declined and moral infractions were on the rise. In 1541, city officials invited Calvin to return, granting him sweeping powers to establish a church that would constitute a godly society.

Living a Religiously Re-formed Life in Calvin's Geneva

With the *Ecclesiastical Ordinances,* Calvin shaped a church in Geneva with the power to discipline its members through a variety of methods, including excommunication. Calvin divided the ministry of the church into pastors, who preached and looked after the needs of the flock, doctors who taught, elders who disciplined, and deacons who oversaw charity and counseled Christian love among believers. A combination of church officials and elected members of the laity formed a court called the Consistory to hear charges and levy punishments for infractions that ranged from public lewdness to bad business deals to violent crime. Calvin's Geneva banned dancing, ribald song, and superstition. Perhaps it was for this reason that one sixteenth-century artist painted Calvin as something of a cold fish, his head assembled of skinned chickens and dead fish.

Nonetheless, Protestants from all over Europe were soon flooding into Geneva to witness "the most perfect school of Christ on earth." Geneva became a center of Protestant thought and a model of how re-formed religion and civic life could be joined together to promote law, order, and Christian principles. But all was not peaceful in Geneva. Calvin's program was demanding; he was particularly on guard against idolatry, even forbidding reverence for the Virgin Mary as a form of idolatry. Two to three witches a year were burned to death in re-formed Geneva, and in 1553, Calvin saw to it that the bold thinker Michael Servetus, who was visiting the city, was burned to death. Calvin saw Servetus as a competitor and heretic, and, like Luther, he was determined to keep a tight rein on thought that fell outside the boundaries of his re-formed church. Despite the bracing morality of Geneva, the city cared for the sick and elderly and possessed a first-rate university that spread Calvin's ideas across Europe. Geneva was clean, orderly, charitable, and worked, just as Calvin's thought did, and that may have been advertisement enough of the high standards that re-formed religion might achieve.

The Schmalkaldic League and Peace of Augsburg

With the many Europes fracturing further along religious and political fault lines, the emperor Charles V had no choice but to convene further imperial assemblies in an attempt to stem the tide of the spreading Protestant re-formation of the church and to keep the empire from disintegrating entirely. At the Diet of Augsburg in 1530, Charles assured the Lutheran princes that all men would be heard fairly. In keeping with that conciliatory overture, the Protestant prince John of Saxony asked Philip Melanchthon, one of Luther's disciples, to draw up a statement of the Lutheran faith that came to be known as the Augsburg Confession. It set out Luther's theological views clearly and concisely. But the Augsburg Confession also gave Charles and the Catholic Church a clear target. The emperor commissioned Johann Eck, the man who had first labeled Luther a heretic, to write the report now known as the *Confutation,* which supported the traditional doctrines and teachings of the Catholic Church.

Giuseppe Arcimboldo, *The Lawyer* (1566) Arcimboldo is famous for his paintings of figures constructed of familiar objects. Here he caricatures the lawyer as one with books for guts, legal documents for his neck fringe, a face made of poultry parts, the mouth of a fish, and the beard of a fish tail. Calvin, as a lawyer and disapproving Protestant, has been suggested as the subject of the painting.

After his initial attempt to be tolerant and conciliatory, Charles was exasperated by the continuing stubbornness of all parties and decided that he had no choice but to insist that Protestants in the empire accept the *Confutation.*

In response to Charles's decision, the Lutheran princes established the Schmalkaldic League in the winter of 1531 to ensure the safety and security of Protestants within the empire. The purpose of the alliance was chiefly military. Eleven Protestant cities in the empire and eight Protestant princes promised to offer military assistance to one another in the event that any one of them was attacked for religious reasons. The alliance was put to the test in the Schmalkaldic Wars (1546–1547), when the emperor led armies into the field to do battle with the League. Despite their defeat at the Battle of Mühlberg in 1547, members of the Schmalkaldic League regrouped with the unlikely assistance of the Catholic king of France, Henry II (r. 1547–1559), who had no wish to see the emperor resolve his serious problems in Germany.

By 1550, few in Europe would have thought that politics and religion or church and state were separate. Experiences in the empire and in England had demonstrated that decisions regarding religion were deeply political. In 1555, Charles returned to Augsburg to try once more to broker an agreement that would make it possible for Protestants and Catholics to live together within the empire. The resulting treaty between Protestant and Catholic powers in the empire, known as the **Peace of Augsburg,** acknowledged that there were two permissible forms of religious observance. Although the Peace of Augsburg succeeded in bringing peace to the empire for a time, two of its conditions caused further instability. First, under the terms of the treaty, it was agreed that the religion of the ruler would determine the religion of his or her state (*cuius regio, eius religio*; "his region, his religion"). But this meant that a region's religion could flip back and forth between Lutherans and Catholics in a few short years, depending on the faith and longevity of its ruler. Second, the Peace of Augsburg did not include Calvinism as a religious option, though Calvinism was by that time the most popular of the Protestant faiths. The exclusion of Calvinism from the agreement led to more warfare in the empire and beyond.

The Radical Religious Re-Formation Splinters and Spreads

What was the Radical Re-Formation, and why was it a natural consequence of the Protestant revolution?

As Luther, Zwingli, and Calvin consolidated their followers into distinct churches with carefully outlined beliefs and practices, some individuals, drawn to the exciting freedom of remaking and reorganizing their religious beliefs, continued to move forward. These radical re-formers represented the frontline of the advancing religious re-formation of the many Europes, but they soon found themselves outside both the old Catholic Church and the new Protestant churches, and spurned by all. Instead of subordinating their beliefs to the new churches, these radical re-formers formed into small Protestant sects, which were radical experiments in living and thinking.

Fundamental to the beliefs of the radical Protestant sects were notions of perfection and separation from the unbelieving, errant others. To stay true to God's word, Protestant sectarians felt the need to withdraw from what they saw as a coercive state and from church laws that forced people to accept religious beliefs and practices sanctioned by the established churches. Instead, the radical re-formers believed in an entirely voluntary church in which membership was a matter of private choice and conscience.

These radical groups believed that separatism and voluntary religion should lead to the complete separation of church and state. Only within such a framework could true religious freedom be achieved and the religious and political entanglements that had crippled Europe fade away. The beliefs of the sectarians were for the most part peaceful and unthreatening, but they offended most mainline Protestants and Catholics, who thought that the sects were anarchic, antisocial, and a refuge for dangerous fanatics and revolutionaries. The various sects drew followers from the lowest orders of society, many of whom were happy to separate from the mainstream of a society that had not been kind to them. They lived in the hope that the present religious turmoil might one day cease and leave them at peace with their God.

Anabaptism

If the chief dividing point among the major church re-formers, Luther, Zwingli, and Calvin, had been over the nature of the Eucharist, the principal disagreement between them and the radical re-formers was over baptism. In his careful review of the biblical precedents for the sacraments, Luther had realized that there was no support for infant baptism anywhere in the Bible. He nonetheless believed that, since everyone should be a Christian and a full member of the religion, it was necessary for all to be baptized as infants. Zwingli and Calvin believed the same; for mainline Protestants it was one matter where Scripture did not win out over tradition. In Wittenberg, the Zwickau prophets, having tested the sacraments against Scripture, were already speaking against the baptism of infants. For Luther, Zwingli, and Calvin, the issue smacked of runaway radicalism. For the radical re-formers, infant baptism was not justified biblically, was not a voluntary act (since infants could not make such a choice of their own free will), and was forced on all by the coercive establishment.

In 1525, in Zwingli's Zürich, a group of the most fervent re-formers collected together in public and began to baptize each other. Protestant church authorities, including Zwingli, were outraged. They labeled the radicals re-baptizers or **Anabaptists** and passed legislation against the practice of re-baptism. Four of the Anabaptists were drowned, death by water being considered a fitting punishment for their particular form of dissidence. One problem that Catholics and mainline Protestants had with re-baptism was that it seemed to insult the power of Christ, who was thought to have acted once already in the baptism of the child, which should be sufficient. God had no need of "do-overs." Another problem was that re-baptism seemed to set some individuals outside the normal congregation of Christians, as a twice-baptized elite.

One of the radical enthusiasts for adult baptism in Zürich that day in 1525 was Conrad Grebel, a well-educated humanist. As the number of Grebel's followers increased, he began to refine Anabaptist thought and practice based on a literal reading of Scripture. Grebel's group advocated a return to a simple, biblical pattern of life involving agricultural work and simple church services in private homes. They withdrew into disciplined communities that stood apart from the rest of early modern society, calling their religious fellows "Brethren" and subjecting Brethren to a policing of community behavior known as the "ban." Within Anabaptist communities, all other forms of religious discipline or governmental control were shunned, and the Brethren would not take oaths of office, swear fealty, or bear arms on behalf of the state.

Millenarians Make a Last Stand

Within Anabaptism, there were even more radical elements. The religious re-formation was, as so many revolutions do, spinning out of control and moving toward disaster. The most radical of the re-formers may have wanted just that, to bring on the very destruction that the book of Revelation had promised. Some Anabaptist sects viewed their actions and the persecutions they were suffering as signals that the end of the world was near and a new time of peace and prosperity at hand. This belief, known as **millenarianism,** was fueled by the increasingly volatile religious and political persecutions within the empire.

The center for millenarian religious belief in the mid-sixteenth century was the German city of Münster. The city had first appointed Lutheran ministers to preach in its churches in 1532. Protestants flocked to the city as a religious safe-haven. Among them were the followers of a Dutch baker named Jan Matthys, who believed that he was the reincarnation of Enoch, a biblical figure come to usher in the end of days. Matthys preached that his followers should take up the sword of righteousness against the ungodly, and he proclaimed that Münster was "the city of God" and would become the "New Jerusalem." In Münster, some of his more enthusiastic followers, on learning of his prophecy, removed their clothes in order to stand naked before God's final judgment, and ran through the streets warning people of Christ's return. Once Matthys entered the city, all those who accepted him as a prophet were re-baptized, private property was abolished, and new laws were struck. Anyone who would not follow Matthys's Anabaptist and millenarian beliefs and would not willingly leave the city was evicted forcibly.

Catholics and conservative Protestants, outraged by Matthys and the extreme radicalization of Münster, laid siege to the city as though it threatened to infect other Christian communities. Matthys's followers were so convinced that the end of days was at hand, one young woman came to believe she was called upon to imitate the biblical heroine Judith, who had saved her city by slaying the invading general Holofernes. This new Judith believed that she must assassinate the former Catholic bishop of Münster. She walked straight into the hands of the enemy, was tortured, confessed, and then beheaded.

Despite extreme incidents of this kind, the Catholic-Protestant army was unable to oust Matthys from Münster until the prophet had a vision that persuaded him to do battle with the former bishop of the city. Matthys believed that God would protect him from musket fire. He was wrong, dying in the battle, and Jan Beukels (John of Leiden), one of Matthys's men, took over. To reassure the faithful of his calling, he too ran naked through the streets, fell into a trance, and proclaimed that he was a

The Execution of Jan Beukels The Anabaptist rulers of Münster were defeated in 1536 and their leaders, including Jan Beukels, were hung in cages from the church of St. Lambert as a message to the radical reformers and millenarians of their fate.

new prophet and the king of Zion. Beukels instituted even more radical measures, including the institution of polygamy. He led the way, taking sixteen wives (including Matthys's widow), but he had one beheaded for talking back to him. Finally, after sixteen months of protracted warfare, the besieging armies conquered Münster in 1535 and tortured and executed its Anabaptist leaders, hanging their corpses in iron cages as a warning to all that Münster was not the New Jerusalem and its Anabaptist leaders were frauds and false prophets of the end of time.

Separatism and Peace: The Mennonites

Münster gave Anabaptism a bad name that was hardly fair, for sectarian movements, by their very nature, always have many different faces and group beliefs. One successful form of Anabaptism was pioneered by Menno Simons, a man of genuine faith and deep piety. Born in the Netherlands, Menno served as a Catholic parish priest for over a decade. In 1527, he heard shocking reports of the torture and execution of an Anabaptist in Holland. Menno consulted the Bible and, like Grebel, he could find no passages that supported infant baptism. Despite his conviction that there was nothing sinful about adult baptism, he was hesitant to abandon his Catholic training. When Menno heard tales about what the Catholic and Protestant armies were doing to Anabaptists, he was ashamed that so many were willing to die for their belief in adult baptism while he remained silent.

In October 1536, Menno was re-baptized and became an Anabaptist preacher, spreading the message of separatism and peace among the faithful. Menno set out his ideas about adult baptism and pacifism in two books, *Christian Baptism* (1539) and the *Foundations of Christian Doctrine* (1540). Menno also advocated the literal reading of the Bible, telling his followers, "the children of peace," that Scripture did not need interpretation, just obedience.

Anabaptism took so many forms, including the Family of Love in England, the Netherlands, and Germany, which followed eclectic spiritual and mystical practices, that it is not possible to detail them all here. Anabaptism survived not just because of enlightened leaders such as Menno Simons, Hans Huth in Germany, or Jacob Hutter in Moravia, but because its vibrant sectarianism allowed small separated groups of believers to hunker down against the violent storms blowing against them from a hostile external world. Yet, their separation from the outside world also meant that the Anabaptists would remain within relatively small, tightly bound groups that stood outside of normative society and the established religions. The events at Münster, however, became an excuse for European authorities to damn all the radical reformers as evil and deserving of destruction.

The Catholic Reformation

How did the Catholic Church fight back, and why did it take so long?

The Catholic Church dismissed Luther's early complaints as baseless criticisms that would never amount to much and viewed his refusal to recant at Worms as evidence of his stubbornness and heresy. But the church found it difficult to remain untouched by calls for reform. Indeed, Catholic figures such as Erasmus had long worked from the inside to reform the church. As more reformers (including Henry VIII, Zwingli, and Calvin) parted with the church, Catholic clerics began to worry about the church's survival. As the number of Protestants in Europe grew, deciding how to respond to the challenges of religious diversity became a pressing issue within the Catholic Church. The Peace of Augsburg presented one solution in the form of political alliances and agreements. Such measures, however, did not address demands for spiritual reform or answer calls for the reform of existing church abuses such as indulgences. When the church began to seek for ways to address these issues, it found that reformation and consolidation were its most effective responses.

An Order of Spiritual Soldiers: The Jesuits

One of the most striking Catholic developments was the founding of the Jesuit order in 1540. For the next two and a half centuries the Jesuits would be a controversial organization in western Europe, admired and feared by many. The Jesuits, as highly educated and engaged Catholics, served as the spiritual soldiers of the Catholic Reformation, seeking to convert non-Christians and always ready to resist Protestant critics.

The order's founder, Ignatius Loyola (1491–1556), was born into an aristocratic Spanish family and became a soldier. While recuperating from wounds suffered in battle in 1521, Loyola contemplated the life and sufferings of Jesus and the saints, and experienced a surge of renewed faith. His was the vision of a chivalric knight, with Mary as the lady he would seek in a Christian quest, waging war against the Devil and his minions who wanted to keep him from his divine lady. Loyola was convinced that his quest could be fulfilled only within the Catholic Church and with the support of its leader, the pope. His appointed mission in God's great plan was to convert Muslims in the Holy Land to Christianity. Loyola traveled to Jerusalem to spread his ideas among the Catholic faithful there, but he found little support in that cosmopolitan city, long exposed to the ebb and flow of religious fervor.

At the age of thirty-four, Loyola decided to educate himself. To learn Latin, he entered a class of boys to begin his language training. Within three years, Loyola knew enough to be admitted to the University of Paris, the preeminent theological university of Catholic Europe. Loyola spent seven years there, perfecting his command of Latin and reading the spiritual teachings of the Catholic tradition. He assembled a band of followers from his fellow students, all of whom were captivated by his idea of converting Muslims to Christianity and following the orders of the pope.

In 1534, Loyola and six of his friends dedicated their lives to missionary work in the Holy Land. Frustrated by their inability to get to Jerusalem, the men traveled to Rome to offer their services directly to the pope. While waiting for an audience with the pope, Loyola and his band began to work among the sick and poor in Rome. Their activities brought them to the attention of Pope Paul III, who agreed to establish them as a holy order under the name the **Society of Jesus.**

The Society of Jesus (or Jesuits as they have come to be known) was envisioned as a small brotherhood of around sixty men who would perform charitable works on behalf of the papacy. Quickly, the Jesuits became so popular and so powerful that they exceeded those modest expectations. One explanation for their success was the respect that many Catholics had for the rigor of Jesuit training. Each Jesuit "client" underwent a program of intense contemplation supervised by a single Jesuit advisor. This program of contemplation and education, which might extend over a decade or more, fostered a spiritual awakening of the sort described in Loyola's own "Spiritual Exercises." By 1550 almost all Catholic states had at least one leading figure who had been trained in the "Spiritual Exercises."

As the number of Jesuit supporters grew, Loyola and his advisors drew up a set of guidelines called the *Constitutions* that set the standards for the order. Those who wanted to join had to undergo a two-year period of probation to test their faith, during which time they did menial work for the sick and prisoners, underwent a pilgrimage, received extensive theological training to become a priest, and passed a second test of their faith. By 1556, more than a thousand men were interested in becoming Jesuits, but there were still only forty-three full members. Those forty-three men operated like a military order in their efficiency, their emphasis on obedience, and their strict adherence to the instructions of their leader (called a general) and the pope. Some Jesuits took up Loyola's initial interest in conversion and became missionaries to the distant continents of the Americas and Asia. Other Jesuits became educators and established

Jesuit Missionaries in China The Jesuits made a spirited attempt to convert Asians to Catholicism; it was one of their central mandates as set out by the founder of the Society of Jesus, Ignatius Loyola.

a Jesuit college (Collegio Romano) in Rome to promote learning and the formal study of theology.

Catholic Mysticism Connects

The logical and educated rigor of the Jesuits was one expression of the Catholic Church's reform and renewal; another was the rise of a Catholic mysticism that captured the popular imagination. In the religious confusion of the mid-sixteenth century, many people wondered amid all the religious noise what God truly wanted. The mystic cut through all uncertainty to make direct contact with the divine. Ignatius Loyola's own mystical experience was far from unique among sixteenth-century Catholics. The ecstatic visions of people such as Teresa of Ávila (1515–1582) and John of the Cross (1542–1591) inspired a popular renewal of Catholicism, for God was speaking to the world through Catholic religious men and women, approving of the Catholic life and institutions, the lives and sanctity of monks and nuns, and the holiness of a celibate life.

Teresa of Ávila had a Jewish background but was raised within the Christian church. Plagued by chronic illness after entering a Carmelite convent at the age of twenty, Teresa experienced ecstatic visions during her sufferings. When spiritual advisors suggested that her visions might be more diabolical than divine, she tested her faith by fasting and scourging her body. Gradually, she became convinced that she was receiving messages from God and, between 1559 and 1561, she experienced repeated visions of the suffering Christ. The motto associated with her, "Lord, either let me suffer or let me die," captures the close connection between pain and spirituality in Teresa's mysticism. To suffer was to be Christian and God's beloved. In 1562, she established a reformed Carmelite convent that observed strict vows of poverty and celibacy. As a symbol of their poverty and humility, the nuns wore nothing on their feet, and when church officials granted Teresa permission to found a new order of nuns in 1567 they were called Discalced Carmelites, or shoeless Carmelites.

One year later, in 1568, another Spanish mystic, John of the Cross, founded a parallel, male order of Discalced Carmelite monks in Ávila. Influenced by Teresa's example, John of the Cross was drawn to both the strictness of the order and its emphasis on suffering. In late 1577, he was jailed by senior members of the Carmelite order who did not approve of Teresa of Ávila's order. Imprisoned and tortured for a period of nearly nine months, John of the Cross experienced religious ecstasy through his suffering. During his imprisonment, he wrote one of the great works of Catholic mysticism, *The Spiritual Canticle,* on paper that was secretly passed to him by one of his jailers. Today, John of the Cross's poetry and his writings on the progress of the soul toward salvation, such as *The Dark Night of the Soul,* are considered among the finest examples of Catholic Reformation spirituality as well as landmarks of Spanish literature.

CHRONOLOGY Popes in an Age of Religious Change

DATES	POPE
1492–1503	Pope Alexander VI
1503	Pope Pius III
1503–1513	Pope Julius II
1513–1521	Pope Leo X
1522–1523	Pope Adrian VI
1523–1534	Pope Clement VII
1534–1549	Pope Paul III

Reforming Popes and the Council of Trent

Along with new religious orders and the emergence of higher educational standards and ecstatic mysticism, the vitality of the Catholic Church was evident in the reform agenda of the popes and the doctrinal decisions made by the Council of Trent (1545–1563). Though he did not live to see the council's final work, Pope Paul III led the drive to reform and consolidate the Catholic Church.

Paul was born into one of Italy's wealthiest and most aristocratic families. He experienced a spiritual awakening late in life and was ordained a priest only in his fifties. Sixty-six years old when he became pope, he turned quickly to the matter of reforming the Catholic Church. Paul's plan was to reestablish papal authority by rationalizing Catholic doctrine and fostering a healthy College of Cardinals to assist the papacy. He reestablished the Roman Inquisition in 1542 to combat the spread of heresy and gave the investigative body wide-ranging powers to act against persons suspected of heresy.

The pope's most important decision came in 1536, when he decided to call a general church council to address church discipline, administration, and spirituality. His goal, he said, was to reform the Catholic Church in both its head and its parts. After years of delicate negotiations about who should attend the meeting and where it would be held, the council finally met in 1545 to discuss clerical abuses and to draw hard and fast lines between acceptable and unacceptable religious beliefs and practices. The Council of Trent transformed Catholic doctrines (or teachings) into Catholic dogmas (sanctioned and necessary tenets), thus making any reconciliation with Protestant beliefs that much more difficult.

The council confirmed that both faith and good works were necessary for salvation, that both tradition and Scripture were valid as the sources of the Catholic faith, that Thomas Aquinas's teachings were normative, that the seven holy sacraments were the conduits of grace, that the doctrine of transubstantiation was a true description of what happened to the bread and wine in the Mass, and that the need for clerical celibacy was paramount. The council also refused to do away with indulgences and reaffirmed the authority of the Vulgate Bible as translated by Saint Jerome, despite its imperfections.

Between 1562 and 1563, under the influence of the French crown and French clerics, the Council of Trent reconvened. Efforts were made to extend the precisely defined teachings of the church to Catholic practices. The religious life of the laity became the focus of deliberations, and church discipline was strengthened by placing more emphasis on the role of bishops in Catholic reform. After the council, bishops were expected to serve as middle managers responsible for seeing that priests kept in regular contact with the laity and were better trained and more effective. Trent's resolutions had a vast impact on standardizing Catholic belief and practice. A priest now had to supervise a Christian marriage, and the confession box became standard. At Trent the Catholic Church regained its moral and institutional footing, and the inquisition worked to eliminate dissent within the church.

In 1562, the Council of Trent also began to deal with the issue of print culture and how the Catholic Church should handle the heretical religious works flooding Europe from Protestant printers and urban centers. The church had finally realized how important printed works had been in disseminating the ideas of Luther and the Protestants. In 1559, the pope had authorized the Roman Inquisition to compile an index of prohibited books (*Index Librorum Prohibitorum*, known simply as the *Index*). The *Index* banned the publication, possession, and reading of scores of books, including all vernacular Bibles and any works written by leading Protestants such as Luther, Calvin, Zwingli, and Henry VIII. Even some works of Erasmus were forbidden. The Council of Trent recognized that the 1559 *Index* had been too restrictive and reformulated the *Index* to allow for a greater degree of freedom for publishers, authors, and readers. The works of heretics such as Luther and Calvin, however, remained on the prohibited list. Published in 1564, the *Tridentine Index* served as a model for the subsequent forty editions of the *Index* and gave censors guidelines to follow in weighing orthodox and harmful publications. The final authorized version of the *Index* appeared in 1948, but in 1966 the *Index* was abolished by papal decree.

Welcome Back: The Baroque Embrace of Rome

The Council of Trent asserted that images were useful in promoting the faith, particularly to illiterate, common Christians. Protestants had gone in the other direction. Worried about idolatry and artistic distraction, Protestants had stripped their churches bare of symbol and visual delight. By the late sixteenth century, with their confident reassertion of traditionalism, Catholic churches embraced not only their old symbols and art, but also a new artistic and architectural style known as **Baroque.** The word *Baroque* originally suggested the deformed and tortured. New Catholic churches were sumptuously adorned, golden monuments that not only impressed a visually impoverished age, but also demonstrated a renewed Catholic confidence. Baroque churches were filled with thundering organ music, rich liturgy, and ceremonies that overwhelmed the senses of the faithful. Baroque art may be the most remarkable and vibrant celebration of resurgent Catholicism, standing in stark contrast to the iconoclastic spirit of plain Protestant churches devoid of images and often of transporting music.

If classical art was an art of restrained observation and simplicity, Baroque is its opposite, an overly rich feast, sensuous and expressive, full of electric energy. In Rome, Caravaggio (1573–1610) found many church patrons for his dramatic scenes of the lives of Christ and the apostles, but he also shocked them with the liberties he took with the holy. The Carmelite sisters of Santa Maria in Rome had commissioned him to paint *The Death of the Virgin*, but were shocked by what they got, a painting showing a bloated corpse in a frumpy and disheveled red dress, her feet bare, fingers fat, face a sickly greenish yellow. It was rumored to be a portrait of the drowned corpse of a

Caravaggio's *Death of the Virgin* (1605) Caravaggio's life and paintings are colorful Baroque dramas.

prostitute. Yet the painting is utterly engaging, for it is (except for the thin halo encircling Mary's head) a thoroughly human scene of a very human death. Only the stunned apostles looking on and Mary Magdalene weeping in sorrow alert us to the importance of the event, but that was Caravaggio's point: that the divine story is a human one and the Gospels live in the present. The shocked sisters did not see it that way and refused the painting.

The Roman painter Artemisia Gentileschi (1593–c. 1653) was influenced deeply by Caravaggio's sense of drama and his play of light and shadow. Her painting of *Judith and Her Maidservant with the Head of Holofernes* captures the same sense of heightened drama and high intrigue. Judith, with the sword still in her hand and a servant stuffing the assassinated man's severed head into a sack, looks off canvas at something hidden from our eyes.

Gian Lorenzo Bernini (1598–1680) worked on the exterior and interior of St. Peter's Basilica, including the shimmering Throne of St. Peter. His sculpture of the *Ecstasy of Saint Teresa of Ávila* takes us deep into the sensuous ecstasy of a woman who knew spasms of the divine. The sculpture has not a still moment, as Teresa swoons and her gown swirls in rippling waves that envelop the viewer in her transporting passion. Such art simply refuses to leave the viewer unmoved and unengaged.

Bernini's *Ecstasy of Saint Teresa of Ávila* The sensuous rippling folds of the saint's garment reflect the high energy and sheer passion of Baroque art and its drive to engage the emotions of observers.

Early Baroque captured the great drama of the Catholic view of the world as a lived experience, for both the human and the divine. By the seventeenth century, Catholicism was back and on demanding display. Opulent Catholic churches were a sensuous answer to plain reformed churches and Baroque paintings, rich, colorful, and filled with bodies in motion and unfolding dramas, answered pointed, but shallow Protestant cartoons. Protestant complaint may in the end have animated the Catholic Church, giving it the "other" against which it could rediscover its doctrinal and spiritual confidence; Baroque art and architecture embraced those already inside the church, and those returning.

The Wars of Religion

As religion and politics became ever more entwined in the first half of the sixteenth century, struggles over religious authority often became indistinguishable from struggles over political authority (Map 13.2). The Knights' Revolt of 1522 and the Peasants' War of 1525 were early, ominous signs of how religious protests could turn into political and social revolts. By the second half of the sixteenth century, with the religious situation across Europe becoming more varied and complex, religious warfare broke out in France, the Netherlands, and England. Religion had become a complicating factor in the relations of states.

Why did wars over religion dominate the second half of the sixteenth century, and what did Europe learn from them?

The French Wars of Religion

Between 1560 and 1600, France was beset by a series of conflicts known as the French Wars of Religion. These struggles brought destruction and disorder to a once prosperous kingdom, ushered in social and economic change, and pushed the French monarchy into a period of decline.

The French monarchy already had problems. The king's traditional power base had been limited to a small area around present-day Paris, while the competitive French nobility controlled the remainder of the country. A series of strong monarchs, especially Louis XII and his successor Francis I, had made strides in consolidating power and prestige. Thanks to them, France was better able to engage in an expensive military campaign in Italy, where the French army fought against both the emperor and the Spanish crown. In matters of religion, the French kings had been able to manage the growing number of French Protestants, nearly a million of them by 1560, who were largely followers of John Calvin. Called **Huguenots** (a term of derision whose etymology remains uncertain), these Protestants clustered in towns and urban centers prior to 1560, and their religious views were not seen as a serious threat to the stability or authority of France. The Huguenots, however, were never a uniform group but ranged from royal supporters to extreme Calvinists. That variability was a common feature of Protestantism. Divisions and differences existed not only between Protestant churches such as the Lutheran and Calvinist, but also within Protestant religions, wherein different groups viewed their religion and its essentials in different ways. England would experience a similar fluidity of Protestant belief and practice.

MAP 13.2 | The Religious Make-up of the Many Europes by 1600

By the end of the sixteenth century, the many religions of the many Europes were more or less fixed and immovable. Catholicism may seem to have remained territorially dominant, but Calvinism was a presence in many states, and Lutheranism prevailed in a solid block in the far north. ***What might explain the nature of the territorial spread of the re-formed religions? What areas remained free of Protestantism? Why?***

In 1559, the French king, Henry II, died during a jousting accident. The event brought home the fragility of royal authority, for while Henry had been a popular king with a string of military and political successes to his credit, when he died his eldest son, Francis, was only fifteen years old. His mother Catherine de' Medici stepped forward to take an active role in government. Tensions between the French nobility and the Italian queen mother escalated as the guardianship of her other children became a matter of dispute and rivalry. Catherine, isolated at court, complained that there was no one whom she could trust.

Her son Francis II died in 1560, after less than a year of rule, and was succeeded by his ten-year-old brother Charles IX. Catherine, determined not to be pushed aside by the nobility, managed to secure the control of her son's political actions by assuming the position of regent, giving her the power to govern in his name until he was ready to rule. From this moment on, the French Wars of Religion took shape within a shifting balance of power between the queen regent and three powerful noble families: the Montmorencies (Protestants), the Guise (Catholics), and the Bourbons (Protestants).

Amid these perfect conditions for a civil and religious war, armed hostilities broke out in 1562 and were not resolved until 1598. A series of seven wars were waged over the three and a half decades, each one a combination of family feuds, struggles for authority, and various religious conflicts. Catherine showed her preference for conciliation over war by issuing an edict in January 1562 that promoted a policy of religious coexistence between Catholics and Huguenots and gave Protestants the right to worship openly and to hold religious assemblies. Her efforts were not well received, however, and war dragged on as the Guise family opposed vigorously any move toward religious toleration.

In 1572, the growing intensity of the Wars of Religion reached a new peak when Huguenots and Catholics flooded in to Paris for the St. Bartholomew's Day celebration of the marriage that Catherine had arranged between her daughter, Margaret of Valois, and Henry, the son of King Anthony of Navarre. Following the ceremony, Admiral Coligny of the Montmorency family was shot while walking home from the royal palace. Huguenots rushed to the wounded man's side, and King Charles IX issued an official proclamation against the would-be assassins. Many people believed that the Guise family had plotted the attack, but some suspected that Catherine herself was involved. Protestants demanded retribution and Catherine, no longer willing to be conciliatory, convinced her son that the only solution was to do away with all the Huguenot leaders who remained in Paris. The king's Swiss guards were given a list of potential targets, blockaded the streets and city gates so that no one could escape, and began massacring Huguenots. Admiral Coligny was one of the estimated two thousand Protestant men, women, and children who were killed in Paris before the St. Bartholomew's Day Massacre ran its course. As news spread of the situation in Paris, Protestants in other towns in France were also massacred. Estimates are that another three thousand Protestants were killed.

The St. Bartholomew's Day Massacre was a religious, political, and diplomatic disaster for France. Protestant leaders throughout Europe were outraged by the persecution, and even Tsar Ivan IV ("Ivan the Terrible") of Russia spoke out on behalf of the murdered Huguenots. The French Wars of Religion were not resolved until Catherine de' Medici and all her sons were dead and the crown passed into the hands of her son-in-law, Henry III of Navarre. In 1589, he became King Henry IV of France. Born and raised a Protestant, Henry put aside his religious upbringing and converted to Catholicism in 1593 to bring stability and peace to his still largely Catholic country. "Paris," Henry is purported to have said, "is worth a Mass." In 1598, Henry brought the wars to a close through the **Edict of Nantes,** which set out the conditions under which Huguenots and Catholics could coexist within France. The terms of the edict differentiated between loyalty to the crown and religious faith, essentially acknowledging the existence of a loyal other within French society. It also restored certain civil rights to the French Protestants, including the right to practice their religion openly and the right to hold public offices formerly restricted to Catholics. In 1562, the enthusiasm for Catherine de' Medici's much milder edict had been lukewarm, but by 1598, after the massacre, the French people were tired of religious conflict and willing to agree to the terms of the new edict.

Saint Bartholomew's Day Massacre On the day of the saint, August 24, 1572, Swiss guards were ordered by King Charles IX to begin rounding up and murdering the Huguenots, or French Protestants, who had assembled in Paris for a royal wedding. Two thousand were slaughtered in and around Paris, and another three thousand in France in an event that shocked Europe.

The Dutch Revolt and the Spanish in the Netherlands

North of France, religious warfare broke out between Catholics and Protestants in 1566. In the Spanish Netherlands, Philip II of Spain ruled a profitable conglomeration of commercial cities that provided a stable source of income for the maintenance of his extensive empire. The seventeen distinct provinces under Philip's control, including present-day Belgium, Luxembourg, and the Netherlands, had a variety of populations with many different religious beliefs. In addition to Catholicism, the people of the Spanish Netherlands were drawn to various Anabaptist sects, Calvinism, and Lutheranism. After years of debilitating tax policies, war broke out when Philip tried to oust Calvinism from the provinces. Devout Calvinists responded by destroying statues, paintings, and other ornaments in Catholic churches. Philip sent the Spanish duke of Alva north with an army of more than ten thousand troops to put down the Dutch revolt.

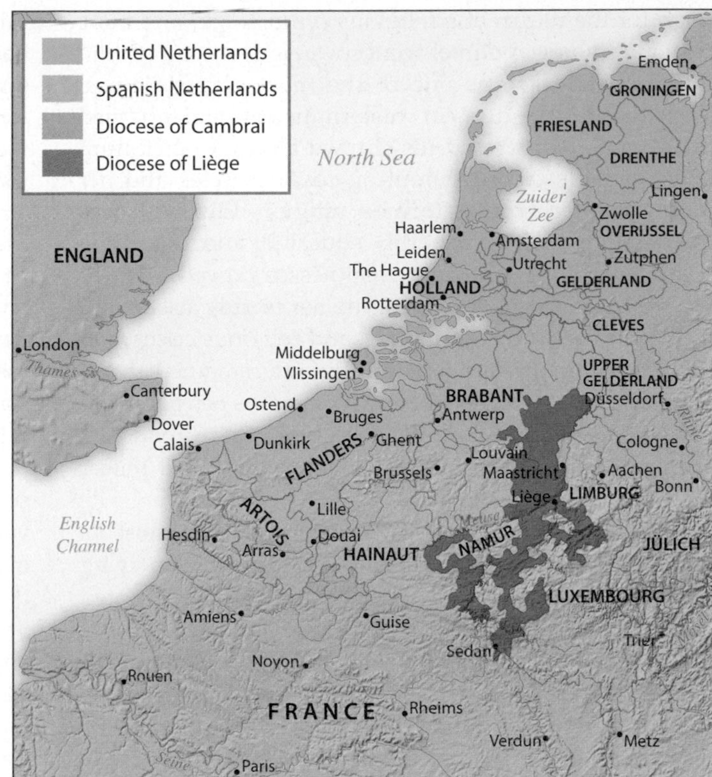

MAP 13.3 | The Netherlands in 1609

After religion, politics, and Spanish interference divided the Low Countries into a number of different interests and religions, the long conflict in the Netherlands led to their further division into a Protestant north and Catholic south, each with its own political and religious configuration. ***How were William the Silent and his supporters in the north able to fend off the mighty Spanish Empire? What made the north a more difficult area for the Spanish to control? Which area was likely to be more prosperous, at least in the short run?***

The Dutch resisted the military campaign of the Spanish to impose religious standards on the provinces. William the Silent, the prince of Orange, organized rebellious Dutch citizens in the northern provinces. In the North Sea, experienced Dutch mariners harassed the Spanish navy and laid siege to the Spanish army stationed on the coast. William's goal was to unify the Netherlands under a single Dutch ruler. After years of warfare, he seemed to have achieved his goal when Philip II agreed to the terms of the Pacification of Ghent in 1576. Philip had recalled the militaristic duke of Alva in 1573, but one of his later replacements, the duke of Parma (as much a politician as a warrior), managed to undermine William's delicate coalitions. In 1579, the northern and southern provinces split along religious lines. In the largely Catholic south, the Union of Arras was formed under Spanish rule. In the primarily Protestant north, William's Union of Utrecht was established to oppose both Catholicism and the power of Philip.

War between the Union of Utrecht and the Union of Arras went on for decades, fueled by funding and military assistance from Protestant England as well as Catholic Spain, which supplied troops and resources along the so-called Spanish Road. In 1609, the two regions of the Netherlands reached a formal truce that all but recognized the independence of the seven northern Protestant provinces as the United Provinces. With the powerful merchant cities of Amsterdam, Rotterdam, and Utrecht within its borders, the United Provinces became known as the Dutch Republic (Map 13.3).

Elizabeth I and the Spanish Armada

Philip II of Spain, not content with an empire that stretched from the west coast of South and Central America to the kingdom of Naples in the east, Sicily in the south, and the Netherlands in the north, set his sights on adding England to his possessions. England had seen its share of religious turmoil in the years following the death of Henry VIII, as the Protestant boy-king Edward VI (r. 1547–1553) tried to promote a mixture of moderate Lutheran and stricter Calvinist forms of worship among the English people. Edward's brief reign was followed by that of his Catholic half-sister, Mary I (unfairly called "Bloody Mary" by her Protestant critics; r. 1553–1558), who attempted to return England to the authority of the pope and the Catholic Church. Nearly three hundred people were executed for their religious beliefs during her reign. Philip got a taste of what it might be like to rule over England when he married Mary in 1554. Their marriage was childless, however, and on Mary's death the throne passed to her half-sister Elizabeth I (r. 1558–1603), the daughter of Henry VIII and Anne Boleyn. Yet Mary's short and somewhat abrupt reign created the conditions that set up Elizabeth's successful one. For if Mary was less than subtle in her religious maneuvers, Elizabeth was full of subtlety and sensitivity in her political and religious actions, and the Protestants of England were ready after Mary's harsh reign for the return of a religious sympathizer and more politically adept and intelligent sovereign.

Elizabeth remains one of the most enigmatic and skilled political figures in western history. She inherited her father's temper and his shrewd ability to pick ministers capable of implementing royal policies and her mother's interest in re-formed religion. Elizabeth was intellectually gifted, superbly educated, and vain. That combination of talents and weaknesses proved to be effective when it came to managing her unruly aristocrats, the country's growing financial and religious crises, and dangerous foreign diplomacy. Elizabeth remained an unmarried ruler at a time when marriage was considered to be a diplomatic and dynastic necessity, vital to good government, and critical to the peaceful transfer of power from one generation to the next.

Elizabeth's reluctance to take hard stands was most evident in her early religious policies, when she was trying to heal the deep religious divisions that had been created during the reigns of her brother and sister. She famously said "there is but one God, the rest is a mere dispute about trifles." In 1559, Elizabeth instituted a new Parliamentary Act of Supremacy (known as the Elizabethan religious settlement) that made her the "supreme governor" of the English church. The Act of Uniformity, which put the English Book of Common Prayer back in churches and restored vernacular worship, followed shortly thereafter. The growing power of Calvinism, which had proven to be disruptive in the empire and in France, undermined Elizabeth's efforts, as did the threat posed to her by her Catholic cousin Mary Stuart, queen of Scots. Mary was Elizabeth's obvious heir and when she fled Scotland after a Calvinist coup in 1568, she turned to Elizabeth for help. In the 1560s the Scottish lowlands had taken up the religious re-formation of the church as promoted by John Calvin, driven out a Catholic French occupying force, and overthrown the Catholic Church and its clergy. Mary left her young son behind in the hands of the Calvinists when she sought exile in England. Elizabeth placed Mary under castle arrest and kept her confined for more than two decades, which angered Mary's Catholic sympathizers.

In the 1580s, a cluster of problems and challenges shattered Elizabeth's careful efforts to bring about religious peace. First, Elizabeth turned a blind eye when English mariners such as Sir Francis Drake and Sir Walter Raleigh seized Philip's Spanish ships returning from the Americas loaded with treasure. Their piracy fattened their own pockets, as well as the English treasury, but the Spanish king viewed the raids as a form of warfare against Spain. Second, Elizabeth had formally agreed by the Treaty of Nonsuch in 1585 to give military assistance to the Dutch Revolt. In exchange for specific territories in the Netherlands, Elizabeth provided troops and supplies to help drive the Spanish out of the region. Not surprisingly, Philip saw this commitment as a tacit declaration of war. Finally, in 1587, Elizabeth put Mary on trial and executed her for treason. Mary had been the focal point for numerous conspiracies to overthrow and assassinate Elizabeth. Queen Elizabeth's ministers finally convinced her that Mary must be eliminated. When the ax fell, Philip declared that Elizabeth was making war not only on Spain, but also on Catholicism, for she had killed one of God's anointed.

Philip's response to the events of the 1580s was to assemble an enormous armada of ships and troops to invade England, oust Elizabeth from the throne, and stamp out Protestantism in England. As preparations began and the sound of shipbuilding filled the air along the coast of Spain and Portugal, intelligence filtered back to England about the size of the planned invasion. England prepared for the invasion, daunted by the prospect of a military engagement with Europe's wealthiest and most powerful Catholic nation.

The king of Spain increasingly saw the battle not as one between Spain and England, but as one between good and evil, Catholic and Protestant. As such, he believed that he was waging a just and holy war against heresy and an illegitimate monarch. When his fleet took

The Armada Portrait of Queen Elizabeth I Elizabeth is empress and ruler of the seas in this portrait. She rests her right hand on a globe, her hand taking possession of the Americas, and above her hand rests the imperial crown. Behind her are scenes of the English fireships ready to attack the Spanish Armada on the left and Spanish ships driven by the divine wind onto the English coast on the right.

INVESTIGATING THE PAST

The Mystery of the Unloaded Cannons

To better understand why the Spanish scheme to invade England failed in 1588, historians and archaeologists have investigated the artifacts recovered from the sunken Spanish ships. When the Spanish Armada began to falter against the English navy, part of the Spanish fleet tried to sail the long way home around Scotland and Ireland. In the process, many ships were wrecked along the Scottish and Irish coasts. Treasure-hunters in pursuit of Spanish gold and other artifacts have over the years violated many of these sunken remains. The Spanish ship *San Juan de Sicilia,* for instance, sank in muddy waters off the coast of Scotland and would have been preserved perfectly had not treasure-seeking divers ripped open what remained of the hull looking for doubloons and other valuable antiquities. A Neapolitan ship, the *Girona,* remained undetected off the Irish coast near Antrim until 1967, when divers began to bring up jewelry and gold that had fallen from the hull to the ocean floor.

Still, some Armada wrecks have provided historians and archaeologists with unexpected insights into why the Spanish may have lost their naval encounter with the English. One such ship, *La Trinidad Valencera,* was a Venetian merchant vessel that had been requisitioned by the Spanish navy and outfitted to transport soldiers, horses, and guns between Spain and England. One of the Armada's largest ships, *La Trinidad* carried twenty-eight enormous bronze guns into battle, making it one of the Armada's most heavily armed ships. Along with its great bronze guns, the ship had four more cannons on board, and carried just under eighty mariners and around three hundred Neapolitan and Spanish soldiers. After engaging with the English off the southern coast, *La Trinidad* sailed around northern Scotland and was shipwrecked in a storm off the north coast of Ireland. Most of the men on board made it to the Irish coast before the boat split and sank. The majority of the soldiers were killed, but thirty-two survivors made it to Scotland and from there set sail for France.

The ship's hull was not discovered until 1971. Although few items of value were found on the sunken ship, the ship's guns were still intact. The remains of *La Trinidad* reveal that the historical belief that the Spanish had been beaten despite their superior guns was a myth. When the ship's bronze guns were recovered, they were found unloaded despite Philip's orders that all guns should be kept ready for action at all times. Why the twenty-eight large bronze cannons on board were not ready for use remained a mystery, and that mystery deepened when a set of large wooden wheels unattached to any other equipment were also found in the wrecked ship.

Historians and archaeologists went back to the archives with their findings, reexamining the detailed lists of what was put on each ship and the instructions Philip gave regarding the use of the guns. What they discovered was that the magnificent cannons placed on *La Trinidad* were not meant for use at sea. They were there to support the land invasion of England. *La Trinidad* may have been one of the Armada's largest and most heavily armed ships, but its vast store of weapons was cargo rather than weapons to be used in the sea battle.

QUESTIONS | ***What were Philip's many motives for attacking England? Why were England and Elizabeth lucky to survive the onslaught? Why did England's success in the encounter matter?***

to the seas in 1588, it was neither as large nor as well equipped as he had hoped, but Philip felt that God was on his side and victory certain. A combination of mismanagement, unforeseen bad weather, and the inherent disadvantage that heavy, Spanish warships had when sailing in unfamiliar, coastal waters against smaller, more maneuverable English vessels proved to be disastrous for the Spanish Armada. Many Spanish ships fell victim to English cannons and fire-ships (old fishing and merchant vessels that were set on fire and rammed into the Spanish fleet) before a powerful storm struck. They simply could not turn quickly enough to avoid the oncoming fire-ships. The duke of Parma failed to meet up with the Spanish fleet and then the storm hit, dashing many of the Spanish ships against the English coastline.

After the Armada's spectacular and unexpected loss, England emerged as a powerful naval power in the Atlantic. Medals were struck to celebrate the victory, many of them bearing the inscription "Jehovah blew with His wind and they were scattered." The medals also depict English people kneeling and praying to God for his intervention and divine guidance. Protestants in Europe hailed the English victory as proof that a "Protestant wind" was blowing so fiercely that the old Catholic powers such as Spain would be swept away. Philip made the best of things by blaming the weather, saying that he had sent his ships against the English, not the elements. Spain recovered economically and militarily from the events of 1588, and Philip continued to dream of launching other invasion attempts in the 1590s.

Conclusion

Chapters 11–13 explored how the many different Europes left the Middle Ages and began to fashion an early modern world. The Italian and European Renaissances developed a form of critical thinking about texts and history that undermined the great weight of authority that had lain so heavily on traditional Europe. Overseas exploration ended the economic and geographic isolation of Europeans, for there were other worlds out there beyond Europe, Africa, and Asia, worlds unknown to the ancients and the Bible, facts and economic chances beyond the long accepted ones. Finally, religious re-formation broke the fragile block of religious unity that had dominated the west for a millennium. The early modern world that emerged in the sixteenth century was the result of these crises of authority, knowledge, and religious uniformity, each crisis necessitating a rethinking of European assumptions about the world. Europe's new outlook was not so much a matter of fresh confidence as it was a product of competing certainties, political divisions, and European instabilities.

Though we have separated out these great unburdenings of tradition and authority (textual, geographic, and religious), we need to remember that they were happening at the same time and probably seemed utterly entangled and bewildering to contemporaries. A woman living in Cologne in 1519 might in the same year have seen a map showing Amerigo Vespucci's outlandish claim of the existence of new continents in the west; have first read some passages of Erasmus's *Praise of Folly,* illustrated with funny pictures by Holbein; and heard her husband mention something about an upstart monk somewhere up north challenging the pope and the Catholic Church. She would most likely have felt queasy by the sudden shock to her intellectual assumptions. Early modernity brought not just an awareness of change, but also the unsettling realization that nothing would ever be quite the same again, that change was the new normal condition for all, and that Europe's peculiarity was internal division and fierce competitiveness between its parts.

What separated Europe from the great empires of the Ottoman Turks and the Ming Dynasty in China was precisely the failure of empires in the Middle Ages (Carolingian, Ottonian, Holy Roman, and Byzantine) to dominate Europe. Medieval empires in the West were fractured, limited enterprises, never able to control either big or little Europe. Europeans shared a common culture but were politically, religiously, and linguistically divided. The passing of the Middle Ages and the arrival of intellectual instability, religious difference, and entrenched political divisions made Europe an energetic and aggressive force in the early modern world.

With the Catholic Church already changing by the Late Middle Ages and early sixteenth centuries, few would have predicted that the actions of an Augustinian monk in a small university town in Germany might be enough to threaten its survival. Yet the ideas of Martin Luther, spread with the assistance of the printing press, regional religious fervor, and political divisions, changed European political and religious life profoundly. Many people in the many Europes were ready for Luther or someone very much like him to appear and shake the old establishment. Luther loosened the bonds that had fastened Europe to the official church, freeing up religious objectors across northern Europe to experiment with the creation and institution of new forms of Christianity. By 1600, Europe was no longer a single religious landmass, but a swamp punctuated by islands of different beliefs. Religion still mattered, but it mattered in different ways and within a century it would matter even less.

The cost of religious change was considerable. In 1556, the emperor Charles V, worn out by thirty years of religious and political controversy, resigned his high office in some despair. By the late sixteenth century, the lines drawn by the Protestants and a resurgent Catholic Church had hardened, doctrine had become dogma at Trent, and kings and princes were prepared to send their armies to defend whatever religion they preferred. Europe was divided further into fixed religious and political positions. The emperor Charles paid the price of that great fracturing and might be seen, in his divided commitments and varied regional powers, as every inch the much compromised and confused early modern European ruler. The great achievement of the religious re-formation of Europe in the sixteenth century remains the introduction into Europe of religious diversity and institutional change. The Catholic Church could no longer dominate the life and thought of Europe, if it ever had. The cost of religious revolution was so great that some observers have wondered if it was worth the calamities of spiritual division and anxiety, the blood spilled, and the wars that followed Luther's stubborn stand against the established church.[2] But something was gained: dramatic religious change had come to the many Europes. The imperial papacy was finished; Europe's incorporation under the papal banner had been broken. The age of the monks was over, the papacy reduced to a regional power, and the many Europes were, for better or worse, shaping an early modern world. As such, Europe's sixteenth-century experience intellectually, geographically, and religiously was not just one of religious re-formation, but of the re-formation of Europe into something more modern and familiar, *modern* and *familiar* because we still live with its economic, intellectual, religious, and political consequences.

Critical Thinking Questions

1. What was the tipping point that tumbled Luther's protest into a full-blown European religious revolution?
2. Which of the so-called Reformations was a genuine reformation of established religion, and why?
3. Had religion become a matter of free choice for most Europeans in the sixteenth century, and why did they make the choices they did?
4. What did the religious turmoil of the sixteenth century cost Europe? What did Europe gain? Was it worth it?

Key Terms

Purgatory **(p. 390)**
indulgence **(p. 392)**
Protestant **(p. 399)**
Act of Supremacy **(p. 402)**
Peace of Augsburg **(p. 404)**
Anabaptists **(p. 405)**
millenarianism **(p. 405)**
Society of Jesus (Jesuits) **(p. 407)**
Baroque **(p. 409)**
Huguenots **(p. 411)**
Edict of Nantes **(p. 412)**

Primary Sources in connect

For information on Connect and the online resources available, go to **http://connect.mcgraw-hill.com**.

1. **The Confrontation of Luther and Charles V at Worms**
2. **Martin Luther on the Good Estate of Marriage**
3. **The Twelve Demands of the Peasants**
4. **Policing Calvin's Church**
5. **Queen Elizabeth I's Act of Supremacy**
6. **Charles V's Abdication**

BACK TO THE SOURCE

A Call to Debate: The Ninety-Five Theses

Luther released the Ninety-Five Theses on October 31, 1517. How he did so is a subject of some controversy. No formal debate followed, though that was the stated intention of issuing such a list of contentions. Instead, the Ninety-Five Theses were soon circulating in published form in Latin and German and set off a firestorm of opinion.

Out of love and zeal for truth and the desire to bring it to light, the following theses will be publicly discussed at Wittenberg under the chairmanship of the reverend father Martin Luther, master of arts and sacred theology and regularly appointed lecturer on these subjects at that place. He requests that those who cannot be present to debate orally with us will do so by letter.

In the name of our Lord Jesus Christ. Amen.

1. When our lord and master Jesus Christ said, "Repent" (Matt. 4:17), he willed the entire life of believers to be one of repentance.

2. This word cannot be understood as referring to the sacrament of penance, that is, confession and satisfaction as administered by the clergy.

3. Yet it does not mean solely inner repentance; such inner repentance is worthless unless it produces various outward mortifications of the flesh.

4. The penalty of sin remains as long as the hatred of self, that is, true inner repentance, until our entrance into the kingdom of heaven.

5. The pope neither desires nor is able to remit any penalties except those imposed by his own authority or that of the canons.

6. The pope cannot remit any guilt except by declaring and showing that it has been remitted by God; or, to be sure, by remitting guilt in cases reserved to his judgment. If his right to grant remission in these cases were disregarded, the guilt would certainly remain unforgiven.

7. The penitential canons are imposed only on the living, and, according to the canons themselves, nothing should be imposed on the dying.

8. Therefore the Holy Spirit through the pope is kind to us insofar as the pope in his decrees always makes exception of the article of death and of necessity.

18. Furthermore, it does not seem proved, either by reason or Scripture, that souls in purgatory are outside the state of merit, that is, unable to grow in love.

19. Nor does it seem proved that souls in purgatory, at least not all of them, are certain and assured of their own salvation, even if we ourselves may be entirely certain of it.

20. Therefore the pope, when he uses the words "plenary remission of all penalties," does not actually mean "all penalties," but only those imposed by himself.

21. Those indulgence preachers are in error who say that a man is absolved from every penalty and saved by papal indulgences.

22. As a matter of fact, the pope remits to souls in purgatory no penalty which, according to canon law, they should have paid in life.

23. If remission of all penalties whatsoever could be granted to anyone at all, certainly it would be granted only to the most perfect, that is, to very few.

24. For this reason most people are necessarily deceived by that indiscriminate and high-sounding promise of release from penalty.

25. That power which the pope has in general over purgatory corresponds to the power which any bishop or curate has in a particular way in his own diocese or parish.

26. The pope does very well when he grants remission to souls in purgatory, not by the power of the keys, which he does not have, but by way of intercession for them.

27. They preach only human doctrines who say that as soon as the money clinks into the money chest, the soul flies out of purgatory.

28. It is certain that when money clinks in the money chest, greed and avarice can be increased; but when the church intercedes, the result is in the hands of God alone.

32. Those who believe that they are certain of their salvation because they have indulgence letters will be eternally damned, together with their teachers.

33. Men must especially be on their guard against those who say that the pope's pardons are that inestimable gift of God by which man is reconciled to him.

36. Any truly repentant Christian has a right to full remission of penalty and guilt, even without indulgence letters.

42. Christians are to be taught that the pope does not intend that the buying of indulgences should in any way be compared with works of mercy.

43. Christians are to be taught that he who gives to the poor or lends money to the needy does a better deed than he who buys indulgences.

46. Christians are to be taught that unless they have more than they need, they must reserve enough for their family needs and by no means squander it on indulgences.

50. Christians are to be taught that if the pope knew the exactions of the indulgence preachers, he would rather that the basilica of St. Peter were burned to ashes than built up with the skin, flesh, and bones of his sheep.

51. Christians are to be taught that the pope would and should wish to give of his own money, even though he had to sell the basilica of St. Peter, to many of those from whom certain hawkers of indulgences cajole money.

69. Bishops and curates are bound to admit the commissaries of papal indulgences with all reverence.

70. But they are much more bound to strain their eyes and ears lest these men preach their own dreams instead of what the pope has commissioned.

71. Let him who speaks against the truth concerning papal indulgences be anathema and accursed;

72. But let him who guards against the lust and license of the indulgence preachers be blessed.

81. This unbridled preaching of indulgences makes it difficult even for learned men to rescue the reverence which is due the pope from slander or from the shrewd questions of the laity.

82. Such as: "Why does not the pope empty purgatory for the sake of holy love and dire need of the souls that are there if he redeems an infinite number of souls for the sake of miserable money with which to build a church?"

86. Again, "Why does not the pope, whose wealth is today greater than the wealth of the richest Crassus, build this one basilica of St. Peter with his own money rather than with the money of poor believers?"

90. To repress these very sharp arguments of the laity by force alone, and not to resolve them by giving reasons, is to expose the church and the pope to the ridicule of their enemies and to make Christians unhappy.

91. If, therefore, indulgences were preached according to the spirit and intention of the pope, all these doubts would be readily resolved. Indeed, they would not exist.

94. Christians should be exhorted to be diligent in following Christ their head through penalties, death, and hell;

95. And thus be confident entering into heaven through many tribulations rather than through the false security of peace (Acts 14:22).

QUESTIONS | *Into what categories might the theses be separated? How does Luther define and, therefore, limit papal power? At this point, did Luther still subscribe to the fundamentals of Catholic belief? What are his specific complaints against indulgences?*

Source: Career of the Reformer: I, Luther's Works, XXXI, ed. Harold J. Grimm (Philadelphia: Fortress Press, 1957), 25–33.

14

Perspective View of Louis XIV's Grand Palace Complex at Versailles

ABSOLUTISM AND WAR IN THE SEVENTEENTH CENTURY

LOUIS XIV, SUN KING AND STATE-BUILDER Louis XIV of the house of Bourbon was a man of large appetites. Indeed, the autopsy after the French king's death in 1715 found that his stomach was twice normal size. Louis had a taste not only for rich food, but also for war, work, and glory—and he firmly believed himself to be the man whom God had appointed to rule France and to make it great. His subjects, too, believed him virtually all-powerful; every day hundreds of people lined up to tell the king their troubles, or to petition him for favors. His mere touch was thought to cure the skin infection known as scrofula. Having taken the throne during a period of religious, economic, and political turmoil in France, Louis never wavered in his belief that France's greatness depended on his taking complete command of his kingdom. Throughout his life, he exulted in and cultivated his semi-divine status; but at the same time he devoted his enormous energies into making himself the embodiment of a new kind of state, one with its own increasing appetite for power.

This new state would be one with a centralized army and bureaucracy, one that respected and defended the Catholic Church, but ultimately set limits on its power and would not go to war over religion alone. It would be one in which the monarch collected his own taxes and chose his own advisors—even if most of them remained nobles—rather than one in which the king had to depend on powerful aristocrats to fill his coffers and provide him with soldiers. And above all, it would be a state that kept order. Louis would never forget the terrifying and chaotic world of his childhood, as France itself nearly collapsed in the wake of the horrific Thirty Years' War and the ensuing civil conflict known as the Fronde. He would do his all to be sure that his kingdom never fell prey to such disorder again.

During his long life, Louis pursued the aim of state-building. He worked hard to prevent the spread of Protestantism, believing religious disunity to be an offense against God and an incitement to civil war. Louis worked very hard, often rising early and retiring late to hear petitions and to attend to paperwork, by no means responsibilities a modern-minded monarch could ignore. He waged wars to advance France's interests and sent out surveyors and spies to find out what was happening in the provinces; he spent a great deal of time hunting, attending masses, and giving parties at his fabulous palace complex at Versailles—but such public appearances, too, were political acts, essential to demonstrating the grandeur and graciousness of the king. He may never have uttered the famous phrase, *"L'état c'est moi!"* ("The state? That's me!"), but on his deathbed in 1715, he did say, perhaps with more hope than confidence: "I am going, but the state will remain forever. . . ." Crowned in an era of chaos, it was the quest for permanent security and order that defined the absolute reign of Louis XIV.

The Warrior King Louis XIV loved to see himself depicted in classical garb. Here the king—mounted to demonstrate his suitability for military leadership—is crowned by the winged goddess of fame.

Louis liked to portray himself as the Sun King, around which all of France revolved, but he was eager for Europe,

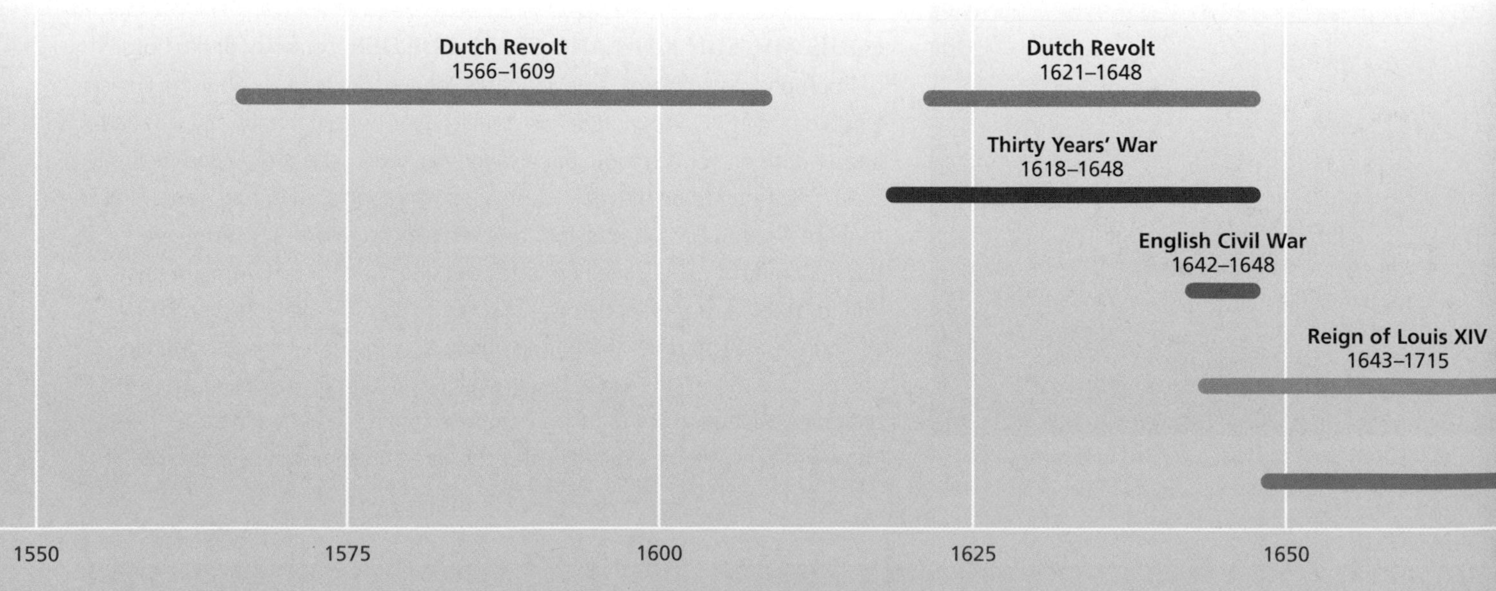

or indeed the world, to revolve around him as well. From the 1670s on, he regularly made war with neighboring states and succeeded in adding some territory to France, though at the cost of hundreds of thousands of lives and a mounting state debt. He set about formalizing French colonial domination over areas in North America, the Caribbean, and Southeast Asia where French traders had established toeholds. Louis's brand of absolute monarchy succeeded, by and large, in stabilizing and modernizing France. But this form of modernization also had its costs, and not just in money and soldiers' lives. During his reign, some two hundred men and women were imprisoned in the Paris prison and armory known as the Bastille for writing, printing, or selling books critical of the church or of royal tyranny, and he allowed church officials to persecute heretics, witches, Protestants, and even nonconformist Catholics known as Jansenists. Louis would leave an absolutist state, but also a troubled legacy, to his heirs.

❊❊❊❊

Louis was by no means alone in perceiving his age as one teetering on the brink of chaos. The seventeenth century—and especially the period before about 1675—was characterized by political upheaval and by intense human misery, in which extreme weather, war, famine, and disease took the lives of millions, and religious passions and prophecies drove people to persecute their neighbors or flee their neighborhoods. In the midst of this misery, however, some Europeans were also finding new opportunities. The Ottoman threat in the East declined at last after the Turks made one last attempt to take Vienna in 1683; this opened up new opportunities for Austrian, Swedish, and Russian enlargement. The older trading networks of the Baltic and Mediterranean Seas, such as the Hanseatic League and the Venetian Empire, were forced to make way for new sea powers, such as the Dutch and the English. The opening up of Spanish and Portuguese, and then Dutch, French, and English trade with Asia and with the Atlantic world expanded the merchant elite and brought new wealth into urban trading centers. The Dutch and English proved particularly adept at developing small industries to refine new products like sugar, tobacco, and copper. In these places, too, landowners began to produce goods for market rather than for consumption at home. Controlling the dynamic forces of increasing commerce, specialized manufacturing, and a widening market became yet another challenge for Europe's rulers.

Europe's kings and kingdoms dealt with these crises and opportunities in different ways, and their choices mattered. Louis XIV's absolutist solution to the crises of the seventeenth century was not the only one available. The Dutch and the English, to give two important exceptions, chose other routes, resulting in the development of crucial models of religious toleration and republican citizenship in the Dutch Republic, and of parliamentary governance and the protection of individual rights in England. But building a modern, centralized state would prove essential in the face of the seventeenth century's new challenges. Those who wanted to retain their power would need large armies, extensive and well-tapped tax

Great Northern War
1700–1721

War of Spanish Succession
1701–1714

Triumph of absolutism in Europe
c. 1648–1789

1700 | 1725 | 1750 | 1775 | 1800

bases, and stomachs strong enough to endure and overcome the sufferings and the often-violent discontents of their peoples. The seventeenth century saw the birth of many modern institutions, including the centralized state, but we cannot forget that these transformations were not inevitable and that they arrived in the midst of religious chaos and political upheaval. Building stable states in such an age—whether absolutist monarchies, republics, or constitutional monarchies—as Louis XIV well knew, was a gigantic task—and one that even he feared might never be done.

The Many Torments of the Seventeenth Century

If we were to attempt to catalogue the torments seventeenth-century Europeans suffered, we would have to start with the Thirty Years' War (1618–1648). Even if we take the lowest estimates of its disastrous consequences—the reduction of 20 percent of the population of central Europe—this still makes the Thirty Years' War the most murderous of Europe's conflicts ever. By no means was it the century's only war; there were multiple civil wars, and conflict over royal succession led to several grand-scale wars both in the seventeenth and in the eighteenth century.

What forms of hardship and conflict did Europeans endure in the seventeenth entury?

Then there were the more generalized forms of misery. The large influx of Spanish New World silver made for serious, continuing inflation, which reduced peasants' real incomes below subsistence levels and spread hunger throughout the continent. There were disastrous harvests in 1660–1663, 1675–1679, 1693–1694, and 1708–1709; in France in 1692–1694, some 2.8 million people, or about 15 percent of the population, died of starvation and malnutrition. Disease cut down those who managed to find enough to eat. In 1665–1666, the plague rampaged through London, killing more than 80,000 of the city's 500,000 inhabitants. The suffering of Londoners was increased the next year by a devastating fire, which destroyed much of the medieval city center. But plague struck elsewhere, too, as did cholera, typhus, and smallpox.

Disaster and chaos were so widespread that many Europeans concluded the world was coming to an end. During the height of the Fronde, a Parisian judge wrote: "If one ever had to believe in the Last Judgment, I believe it is happening right now."[1] In 1666 (calculated by Bible readers to be the year of the Anti-Christ), several would-be Messiahs gathered large followings. Some Europeans blamed witches for crop failures and epidemics, and witch-burning became commonplace, especially in central Europe. In some places, peasants and townspeople turned their anger on tax collectors, exploitative landowners, or hoarders, making for a series of rebellions throughout the continent—though virtually all of these ended with the massacring of rebels, rather than with reforms.

Unquestionably, the combination of hunger, anger, war, political instability, disease, and religious extremism justifies historians speaking of a "crisis of the seventeenth century" for Europe. But the fact that the century brought famines, droughts, and terrible epidemics to places such as Egypt, Mexico, and China has spurred some scholars to wonder if the chaos had at least some of its roots in something more universal: the weather. Whatever the causes of this crisis, the suffering and conflict it entailed contributed greatly to the elaboration of a new form of kingship: **absolutism.**

The Origins of Absolutism

In the medieval world, to be a king was in theory to be raised above the other nobles of the realm by divine sanction. In practice, however, a medieval king remained merely the top-ranking noble in his kingdom. When one king died, his heir needed to be formally elected or at least acclaimed by the other nobles before he could sit comfortably on his throne. In some cases, when a royal line was broken, the nobles chose a new monarch from among their number. Kings depended on their fellow nobles to see that the laws were carried out and the taxes collected, and to raise armies for them when they wanted to go to war. The king was supposed to consult his people, and especially his fellow nobles, about matters of importance to the realm. For that purpose, medieval states had developed various sorts of advisory assemblies, made up mostly of nobles, which met from time to time, at the king's pleasure. In Poland, this body was called the Sejm; in France, it was the Estates General. Spain had several assemblies, the most important of which was called the Cortes. These assemblies had various rights, but they did not have the right to overrule the king. Only in England did Parliament really have the power to resist the king's will, especially in matters of taxation.

How did absolutism differ from previous forms of kingship in Europe?

In the sixteenth century, kings began to see assemblies as obstructions and well-armed nobles as threats, and they began a series of moves designed to centralize power and to ensure the succession of their direct heirs to Europe's many thrones. Some kings claimed that God alone—and *not* the kingdom's other nobles or advisory assemblies—had given them the **divine right** to rule. In the seventeenth century, in the wake of the grueling Thirty Years' War, many kings moved to do away with the assemblies and disarm nobles in favor of state-funded, standing armies. Kings also cut into noble power by allowing wealthy men of lower rank to buy offices that came with titles, or by appointing bureaucrats and foreigners to help them run the kingdom. These innovations distributed power upward, to the king, making him less

Weather and the Seventeenth-Century Crisis

Historians have long described the seventeenth century as a century of crisis. Not only did it see an unprecedented number of bloody wars and civil conflicts, but it was also a century of famines and epidemic diseases, in Europe and across the world. All in all, the century saw levels of mortality of epic proportions.

What caused all this misery? Contemporaries identified a series of very cold winters and crop-destroying droughts as part of the problem, but scholars have recently acquired more comprehensive and accurate means by which to measure the extent to which climate change afflicted the people of the seventeenth century. Combining studies of ice cores, tree rings, pollens, and glacial debris with reports from contemporaries, scientists are now able to show that the seventeenth century was abnormally cold and dry in many places, while floods raged in others. They discovered that the era saw the lowest level of solar activity in two millennia, and that a series of eruptions threw volcanic dust into the atmosphere, further reducing the amount of solar energy that reached the earth. The result was that Europe was, on average, two degrees colder during the seventeenth century than it had been in the sixteenth century, and the growing season was shortened by three to four weeks. In addition, the El Niño effect—which brings floods to Central and South America, and drought to Asia and Europe, on average every five years—struck more frequently in the middle years of the seventeenth century. The result was severe climatic instability, summers blighted by freak frosts, and winters so cold that even the Egyptians took to wearing fur coats. Weather conditions were undoubtedly responsible for many of the famines and contributed to the numbers of plague deaths, but did weather *cause* the political turmoil of the seventeenth century?

That, of course, is quite a different question, and it is the one that the highly respected historian of the era, Geoffrey Parker, is now asking. In a recent essay, Parker suggests that we take more seriously than before the linkages between bad weather and rebellion. We can, he argues, be sure that rising bread or rice prices sparked rebellions in Portugal in 1637, in Catalonia in 1640, in Ireland in 1641, and in Japan in 1642. Other revolts, such as that of the Scots in 1637, were certainly couched in religious terms, but were given urgency by a preceding series of terrible harvests and the resulting scarcity of food. The intransigence of absolutist rulers and the circulation of pamphlets complaining about both political and economic conditions or prophesying imminent apocalypse added the fuel necessary to turn complaints into rebellions. It is instructive, Parker points out, that many of these rebellions began in early summer, the period before the new harvest when the stores from the last year's crop typically ran low. Parker believes that the increases in atmospheric volcanic ash and in El Niño effects "triggered or fatally exacerbated major political upheavals,"[2] and he argues that it is about time historians take climate change seriously in explaining why the seventeenth century saw such pervasive and widespread challenges to authority.

Parker's work is clearly shaped by recent discussion of climate change, but it poses important questions about how we see the past, and about the kinds of sources historians use. Even if some historians will not accept causal linkages between weather and political crises, Parker has put together convincing evidence that environmental factors did play an important part in destabilizing regimes across the world.

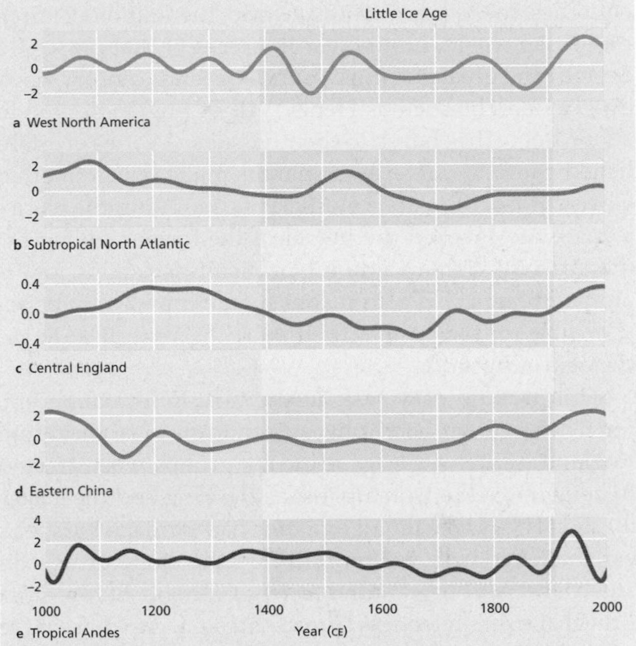

FIGURE 14.1 | Estimated Relative Temperature Variations during the Past Thousand Years

Note the dip in temperature in the middle of the seventeenth century in all regions. ***Does this evidence support Geoffrey Parker's theory that the weather was a major factor in causing the crises of the seventeenth century?***

Source: Adapted from Michael E. Mann, "Little Ice Age," in *Encyclopedia of Global Environmental Change,* Vol. 1: *The Earth System,* ed. Michael C. MacCracken and John S. Perry (Chichester, U.K.: Wiley, 2002), 504–509.

QUESTIONS | ***How did weather affect European societies in the seventeenth century? Do you think weather can have an effect on politics?***

responsive and less beholden to his nobles, who were no longer able to check his "absolute" power. As we will see, England—where Parliament's powers were protected in law—was one of very few European kingdoms able to resist the advent of absolutism.

Another means by which kings sought to establish absolute power was by claiming state dominance over the churches. In the late medieval world, the Catholic Church possessed wealth and power in excess of that possessed even by the greatest kings. In the sixteenth century, however, monarchs such as Henry VIII of England opted to subordinate the church to their dictates. A series of established churches arose as monarchs made one or another Christian sect the state's official faith. Tying the clergy to the state checked the power of the former, giving the monarch the right to appoint (or dismiss) bishops, for example, though this also meant monarchs were to be responsible for seeing that their subjects conformed to the dictates of the faith.

This was no easy task in the post-Reformation era, for Christendom had split, and many states, including England, contained large minority groups who objected to being forced to worship just as the king and the majority did. The Holy Roman emperor had perhaps the greatest challenge here, for by tradition the emperor was an Austrian Habsburg and an ardent Catholic. But by 1600, Protestantism's relentless spread threatened to make it the religion of the majority of the empire's inhabitants. Both the Austrian Habsburgs and their Spanish relatives (for a Habsburg also ruled in Spain after Charles V divided his kingdom in 1556) already believed Protestantism to be a loathsome heresy; now they began to fear that it would undermine the already precarious stability of the empire, and of its semiautonomous kingdoms. Their attempt to reverse the Reformation and to move in the direction of absolutism sparked the greatest war of the seventeenth century.

The Thirty Years' War

The series of conflicts that historians have dubbed the Thirty Years' War were sparked by several sources of intra-European hostility: the unfinished business of religious re-formation; the monarchs' drift toward absolutism; and a changing balance of power, which raised some rulers' hopes that they might use the opportunity to seize someone else's spoils. Among the causes, too, was a long smoldering dispute in one corner of the Spanish Habsburg Empire: the Netherlands.

What factors led to the Thirty Years' War? What were the political, diplomatic, and religious results of the war?

The Habsburg Empire Reacts to Protestantism's Spread

As we saw in Chapter 13, the Spanish Habsburg king Philip II, heir to the western and New World domains possessed by Charles V, had tried his best to suppress what became both a religious revolt and a trade war in the Netherlands. From the 1570s through the 1590s, Philip sent army after army up the Spanish Road, the land route to the Netherlands that passed along the French border (Map 14.1). But the Dutch opened their dikes and flooded the fields and sent well-trained militiamen to beat down waterlogged Spanish troops.

While Philip II and his successor Philip III (r. 1598–1621) struggled to deal with the Dutch Revolt, the Austrian Habsburgs dealt with the Reformation's fallout in their domains. They had some success; in the decades after the Council of Trent, Catholic reformers managed to bring most Poles back to the Catholic fold. But in other places, Protestantism was making serious gains: by the end of the sixteenth century, the majority of the nobles in Hungary, Saxony, Brandenburg, Bohemia, and the Habsburgs' home province, Austria, had become Protestants. Terrified, the Habsburg emperors ennobled Catholic state servants and gave them land, enlarging the Catholic nobility. Pioneering their own absolutist methods, they began also to build a centralized, stable Catholic bureaucracy, which some believed was designed to spy on and undermine the Protestant nobility.

By the 1610s, the Peace of Augsburg had come to seem fragile or outdated, in part because everyone continued to believe that there was only one true church—and that was the one to which the believer adhered. Large numbers of Catholics believed Protestantism to be the work of the devil, and most Protestants believed the pope to be the Anti-Christ. No one wanted to compromise, and the result was war without mercy and seemingly without end.

The Defenestration of Prague

Frederick V (r. 1610–1623), a Calvinist and prince of a western German state called the Palatinate, was one of those who feared that the Reformation might be overturned. He also believed that imperial, Catholic conspirators were out to take away the autonomy and traditional privileges of German noblemen like himself. That is to say, he feared both the reinstatement of Catholicism and absolutism—and he believed he was divinely appointed to stop both of these trains before they left the station. Others shared those fears, most notably Bohemian Protestant nobles, who were forced to accept the Catholic Habsburg prince Ferdinand as king of Bohemia in 1617. After his coronation, rather than working to reconcile the Protestant nobles, Ferdinand returned to the imperial capital of Vienna, and left Bohemia in the hands of hard-line Catholic regents. In response, on May 23, 1618, some passionately Protestant nobles staged a confrontation at the royal palace in Prague and threw two of Ferdinand's regents out an upper-story window. The men survived, thanks to having landed in a huge dung heap. But the incident, known as the Defenestration of Prague, incited both Frederick V and Ferdinand II (who became Holy Roman Emperor Ferdinand II in 1619) to action, touching off what

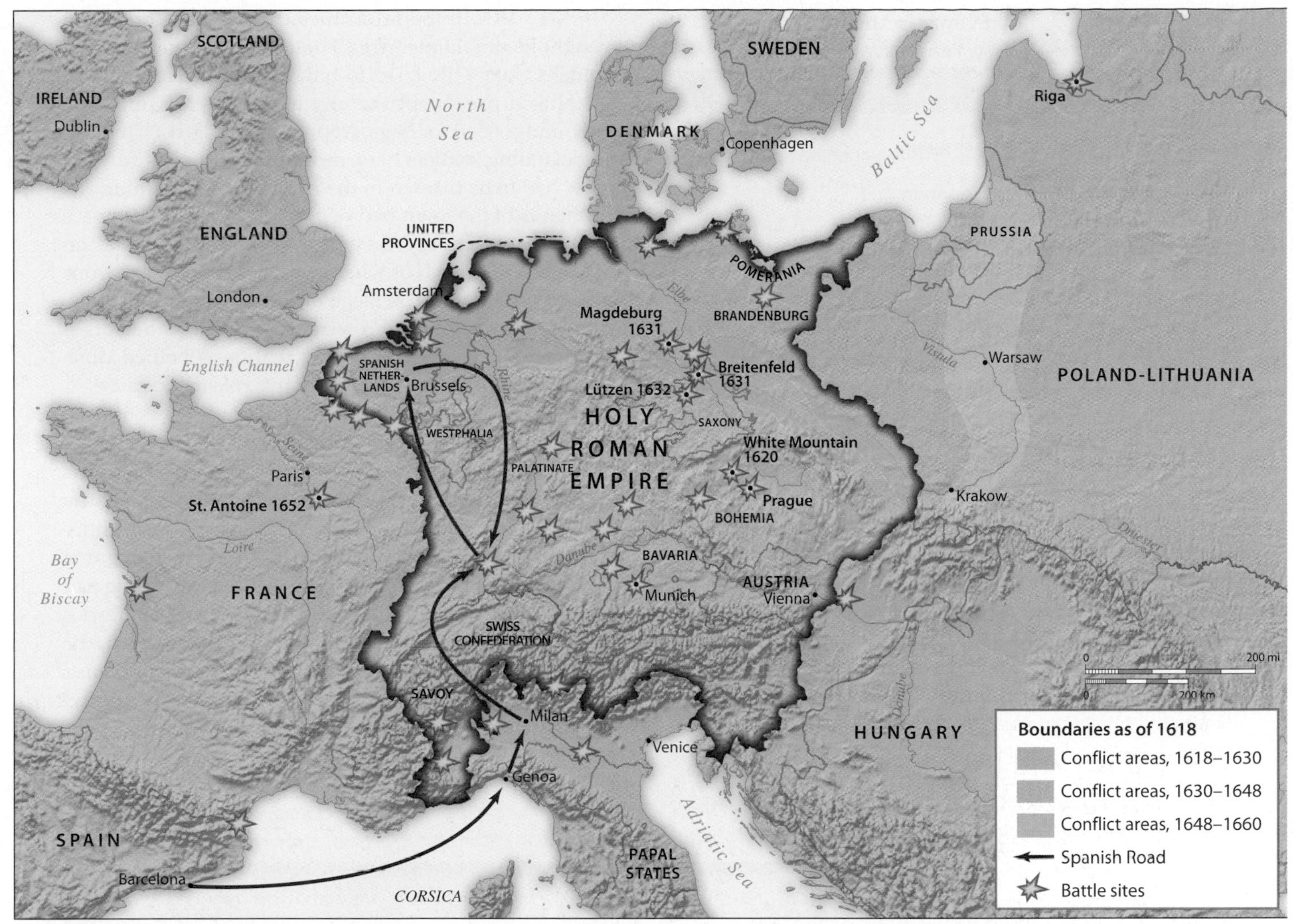

MAP 14.1 | **The Thirty Years' War**

The Thirty Years' War was fought primarily on the territory of the Holy Roman Empire. ***Study the patterns of conflict on this map. Why was France able to recover from these wars so much more quickly than the German states?***

is known as the Bohemian Phase of the Thirty Years' War. Not for the first, nor for the last time in European history, a confrontation between a handful of hardcore believers provoked a world-altering conflict.

The Bohemian Phase

The Bohemian militants moved to form an independent government and conscripted every tenth peasant and every eighth town dweller to form a makeshift army. They rejected Ferdinand as king and elected Frederick V of the Palatinate instead, hoping that Frederick's marriage to the daughter of James I of England would bring England and perhaps other enemies of the empire into the fight on their side. The Bohemian army gained support from Austrian and Hungarian Protestants, though James I remained unmoved. In 1619, 42,000 Protestant troops laid siege to Vienna, but could not sustain it, as their ranks were decimated by disease and lack of food. With his back against the wall, Emperor Ferdinand II bribed Austrian nobles and negotiated for support from the Poles, Bavarians, and Spanish to muster a formidable army.

In early November 1620, a force of 27,000 imperial troops routed a Bohemian army of about 15,000 at White Mountain. They drove the Protestants back to Prague, where stragglers were put to the sword. Imperial officers rounded up rebels, including as many of the defenestrators as could be found, seized their property, and executed twenty-eight of them in Prague's Town Square. Twelve heads, two hands, and one tongue were posted on the city gates, where they remained for more than a decade. Known as the Blood Court, this was in fact one of the *least* bloody reprisals in this grisly war, but it deeply angered the Bohemians, who immediately turned the barbaric acts into propaganda for the Protestant cause.

Of greater general significance for the history of central Europe was what happened next: determined to stamp out religious disunity, in 1621 Ferdinand II ordered all Calvinists (those who were not serfs bound to the land) to leave Bohemia; the serfs he forced to convert to

CHRONOLOGY Key Events in the Thirty Years' War

DATE	EVENT
1618	Defenestration of Prague
1620	Battle of White Mountain
1631	Siege of Magdeburg
1631	Battle of Breitenfeld
1632	Battle of Lützen
1635	France entered war
1648	Peace of Westphalia

Catholicism in mass ceremonies. About 20 percent of the population fled, including most of the nobility. Austrian, Bavarian, and Hungarian Lutherans were treated more leniently, but they too were bullied or bribed to convert. In effect, the Bohemian war reversed the course of the Reformation in eastern central Europe.

The Danish and the Siege of Magdeburg

Emboldened by the Habsburgs' victory in central Europe, the Spanish monarchy renewed its war against the Dutch, seizing Frederick's former kingdom, the strategically important Palatinate, in 1624. Fearing Protestantism would be wiped off the map, Denmark entered the conflict, promising to lead and fund the fragmented Protestant cause. After 1625, England, now under Charles I, also began to funnel money to the Protestants, and sent a few troops as well. Meanwhile, the Catholic Bohemian general Albrecht von Wallenstein took over the rebuilding of the imperial army, creating an effective fighting force of 110,000 men by 1628. The soldiers, for the most part mercenaries or conscripts, received little in the way of supplies and were expected to live chiefly off booty and provisions provided by local populations. More accurately stated, the soldiers were invited to plunder—and plunder they did, especially when they were hungry or their salaries were long overdue.

In May 1631, imperial armies overran the Protestant stronghold of Magdeburg. Though the imperial commander Count Tilly tried to halt the plundering, he lost control as a fire swept the city and soldiers rampaged, raped, and robbed for days. Approximately 20,000 civilians and defending soldiers died, most of them in the fire; their bodies had to be thrown in the river, as the remaining 450 inhabitants of the town had neither the strength nor space to bury them. Nor did they have sufficient wealth to rebuild the town, much of which was still rubble nearly one hundred years later. The Siege of Magdeburg made excellent propaganda for the Protestant side, and its horrors—inflated even beyond the grisly realities—helped push more Protestant allies to take an active role in the cause.

The victories of the imperial armies and events like the Siege of Magdeburg alarmed the Swedish king Gustavus Adolphus (r. 1611–1632), a pious Protestant, as well as Louis XIII of France, who, despite being a Catholic king, had no desire to see the Holy Roman Empire dominate the entire continent. Gustavus Adolphus II was already in Pomerania (see Map 14.1) with his formidable Swedish troops; he had arrived in 1630, intending to protect his own territories and perhaps to acquire new ones. After Magdeburg, the French agreed to a large subsidy for Gustavus Adolphus's army, thereby avoiding sending in troops themselves, and in 1631, the Swedes entered the war on the Protestant side. The Swedish king's energy in recruiting allies and his brilliant battlefield tactics helped turn the tide of the war

Massacre at Magdeburg In May 1631, imperial troops (here depicted bearing the double-headed eagle banner of the Habsburg's monarchy) overran the Protestant stronghold of Magdeburg. Hungry, unpaid, and frustrated by the long siege, Habsburg troops pillaged and burned the city, killing most of its inhabitants and creating useful propaganda for the Protestant cause.

WHAT A DIFFERENCE A YEAR MAKES

1631–1632: The Lion of the North and the Turning of the Tide

For the Protestant side, prospects in the war were poor when Gustavus Adolphus II of Sweden led his troops into the conflict in early 1631. Many Protestant leaders had tried to take command of the Protestant side, including Frederick V and Christian IV of Denmark. Gustavus Adolphus outshone them all, in part because his victories turned the tide dramatically in 1631–1632, and in part because the tactics he employed would provide models for the military revolution to come (see Chapter 15).

Gustavus Adolphus was an ambitious ruler, but so were many of his contemporaries and rivals. More important, he was a savvy military strategist. He had studied Roman and Dutch tactics, and he knew how to use the mobility of his troops to his best advantage. He had been involved in previous conflicts, and he knew the value of motivated and well-trained soldiers. He was also a good propagandist, using the horrors of Magdeburg and his own swagger to convince some neutral German princes to enter the war on his side, though others hesitated, unwilling to commit themselves to war against the powerful empire. At the Battle of Breitenfeld in 1631, the Swedish king decisively defeated an imperial army of about 37,000 men, killing more than 7,000. The empire's military leader, Count Tilly, was wounded and his army diminished to nearly 13,000 after his troops fled the field in disarray. In an era of mercenary soldiers and no prisoner of war camps, Gustavus Adolphus simply forced the more than nine thousand prisoners he had taken to join his army instead.

Gustavus Adolphus II This image commemorates the Swedish king's victory at the Battle of Breitenfeld, 1631.

After the battle was over, Protestant propagandists claimed that the Swede's victory at Breitenfeld was divine retribution for Magdeburg. To some, Gustavus Adolphus, now sweeping down into southern Germany, was a Goth who would sack Rome and restore German liberties; others simply called him the Lion of the North. His charisma counted for much, but the enhanced skills and firepower of his army actually delivered the victory. While the armies of the previous century had relied on pikes and swords, Swedish forces bristled with muskets and cannons, and yet demonstrated far greater mobility than the much larger imperial armies arrayed against them. The Swedish commander trained his musketeers so that they could reload and replace one another to fire a continuous barrage. Though his cannons fired standard-sized balls, state-of-the-art engineering made them lightweight and easier to move. Following the battle at Breitenfeld, the Swedish commander marched with what was, for his day, lightning speed, establishing strategic bases and linking together German allies. He swept across the German states to the Rhine and invaded Bavaria, covering nearly one thousand miles in one year.

In the chaos of the Battle of Lützen in 1632, Gustavus Adolphus strayed from his command post into a fierce cavalry battle and was shot. He fell from his horse and was stabbed repeatedly. Looters eager for trophies unceremoniously stripped the king's body. His Protestant forces fought on, losing thousands in the battle, but the imperial armies retreated first, and the Protestants claimed the field. But the Swedish king's death left the Protestant cause without an effective leader and it lost momentum; the Protestants badly needed the French support they received after 1635. Had the Lion of the North not joined the war in 1631, the imperial cause might have been victorious, and all of continental Europe might have been returned to the Catholic fold.

QUESTION | ***How did Gustavus Adolphus's brief participation in the Thirty Years' War make a difference?***

at a moment when the empire seemed poised to win the war and wipe out Protestantism's remaining strongholds on the continent.

The French Phase and the War's Bitter End

Gustavus Adolphus's victories at Breitenfeld and Lützen prevented a Protestant defeat in 1631, but by 1635 the empire again appeared to be winning, although it too had lost its most charismatic leader. In 1634, Wallenstein was accused of treason and murdered by Austrian agents. Once again alarmed at the prospect of being encircled by the Spanish and Austrian Habsburgs, the French now applied all their resources to the conflict. Louis XIII and his chief minister, Cardinal Richelieu, opened a new round of office-selling and tax levies to enlarge and modernize the French army, and these troops were launched against the imperial armies in the Rhine region while the Swedes fought on in the east and the Dutch harried Spanish ships at sea.

This phase of the war, in particular, was rife with atrocities, committed by both sides, as ravenous and rapacious armies crisscrossed the countryside. Soldiers hanged children and elderly people from trees and roasted peasants over fires until they divulged the hiding places of their valuables. Women were raped, and men had their genitals cut off; horrible forms of torture were invented such as the "Swedish draught," in which robbers forced wood, sand, and feces down the throats of their victims. The war's savagery was worst in central Europe, where the main battlefields lay, but the spinoff civil wars that followed brought horrors to Ireland, Spain, and France, as well. Famine and disease, even more deadly than the conflicts themselves, took a terrible toll. In central Europe and in Spain, the population declined by 20 percent overall, and some places lost 40 percent or more of their prewar inhabitants.

By 1644, Europe's kingdoms were collapsing under the strains of war. The Portuguese and the Catalonians revolted against their greatly weakened Spanish overlords. The Portuguese took back their independence relatively quickly, but bloody fighting in Catalonia continued for some time. The Scots and then the Irish staged their own revolts against Charles I's policies, plunging the British Isles into civil war in 1642. After the death of Louis XIII in 1643, France too, as we have seen, faced internal crisis as well as bankruptcy. It remained only for the exhausted parties to work out a settlement. Negotiations between the various parties were finally concluded in the Peace of Westphalia in 1648.

The Consequences of the Thirty Years' War

The Peace of Westphalia did little to change the outward shape of Europe's states. Sweden gained some new territory and the Dutch Republic was guaranteed its independence, but otherwise, borders changed little. What mattered most were the *religious* provisions of the Peace, which in turn had major political consequences, especially for the Habsburgs. The Peace reiterated the right of the princes of the Holy Roman Empire to choose the religion of their states—and Calvinism was finally recognized alongside Catholicism and Lutheranism. Thus, although the Habsburgs moved toward absolutism in their Austrian lands and succeeded in reconverting Bohemia and parts of Hungary, the Holy Roman Empire remained a federation with a relatively weak emperor nominally in charge of a religiously disunited patchwork of more than three hundred mutually suspicious states. Religious and political disunity would make economic recovery in central Europe even more difficult in the decades to follow.

The Thirty Years' War also bankrupted and dramatically weakened Spain, the greatest power of the sixteenth century. Although the Spanish retained control of the southern Netherlands and its vast empire in the Americas, most of the once formidable Spanish army had died or deserted. Its ranks were now staffed by foreign mercenaries, drunks, and severely wounded men. Civil wars and rule by incompetent kings further damaged Spain in the second half of the seventeenth century.

The Thirty Years' War persuaded statesmen that the quest to impose one true faith on all of Europe was fruitless,

The Horrors of War Mercenary soldiers on both sides of the Thirty Years' War committed atrocities against civilians, often in the process of stealing their horses, livestock, and valuables. Hanging a few villagers (of all ages) from centrally positioned trees was a popular means to scare others into handing over their property.

and after 1648, European states would never again go to war for primarily religious reasons. But the Peace of Westphalia also established another important principle: Christians who belonged to denominations other than that of their prince or king would be allowed to practice their faith in public (according to local restrictions) and in private as they wished.

The High Baroque No building so exemplified the Baroque as did Gian Lorenzo Bernini's new St. Peter's Basilica in Rome, completed in 1626. The Baroque style used shafts of light, heavy ornamentation, and grand-scale, symbolic sculptures to give religious and royal spaces a feeling of sacred presence and historical grandeur.

Although rulers and clerics did not always honor this principle—Louis XIV, for example, officially outlawed Protestantism in France in 1685—it laid the foundations for embryonic forms of religious toleration. Instead of killing "heretics" or driving out Christian minorities, kings began to use other means to coerce their subjects into attending the established church. People did not give up their dislike, or even hatred, toward those who practiced other faiths—and the Peace did not apply at all to Jews, Muslims, individuals accused of being witches, or nonbelievers. But rulers themselves largely stopped using violent means to enforce religious uniformity, especially after some realized that toning down religious strife contributed to political stability and helped the state to attract skilled dissenters to settle inside its borders. They turned their attention, instead, to protecting their domains by building up large and well-equipped armies and by cultivating sufficient splendor to distract at least some of their subjects from the misery around them.

The Culture of the High Baroque

The cultural world of the seventeenth century reflected both apocalyptic sentiments and absolutist aspirations. The early Baroque culture of the later sixteenth century continued, characterized by sensuous extravagance on the one hand and gruesome portrayals of human suffering on the other. Writers and artists continued to draw on stories from the classical and Christian traditions even when they wanted to say new things. In ornate Catholic masterworks such as St. Peter's Basilica in Rome or the Cathedral of St. Gallen in Switzerland, architects, sculptors, and painters created colorful frescoes, gilded rays of light, and row upon row of marble saints and cherubs to remind church-goers of the majesty of the divine—and the terrible suffering of even the saintly on earth. Calvinist sermons, similarly, featured dramatic depictions of earthly torments and warnings about the coming end of the world. Calvinist church interiors, however, were whitewashed to prevent parishioners from committing the sin of idolatry. In both Catholic and Protestant Europe, the late Baroque culture continued to revolve around religious themes. But over the course of the seventeenth century, absolutist state patronage and new commercial wealth began to expand Europeans' cultural portfolio, and to focus at least some attention on more worldly concerns.

How did artists and writers deal with the political, religious, and social strife of the seventeenth century?

The transformations under way in cultural life over the course of the seventeenth century reflect the shifting of power and wealth from south to north and from a predominately church-centered to a predominately court-centered world. At the beginning of the sixteenth century, the global cultural power was the Catholic Church. For theologians, scholars and poets, Latin works remained central at least until the mid-seventeenth century. But over the course of the seventeenth century, more and more works were being published in vernacular languages. Of these, at first Italian and then Spanish dominated, the former the language of the Renaissance, the latter spoken by officials and commercial tradespeople in the Netherlands, the Americas, and the Philippines. The Italian states continued to produce great painters, such as the widely revered Bolognese cousins Annibale, Ludovico, and Agostino Carracci; scientists and scholars, such as Galileo Galilei (see Chapter 15); and architects, such as Gian Lorenzo Bernini, who designed the new St. Peter's Basilica in Rome. And wealthy Spaniards, especially the Spanish kings, poured their New World silver

Diego Velázquez, Portrait of Pope Innocent X (c. 1650) This beautiful painting of a wily and powerful pope is one of the most acclaimed portraits of all time. Like his Dutch contemporary Rembrandt van Rijn, Velázquez frequently used dark backgrounds to focus viewers' attention on the psychological complexity of his subjects' faces.

into patronizing both Italian and Spanish artists, scholars, and churches. Spanish devotionals such as Luis de Granada's *Book of Prayer and Meditation* animated Catholic culture. The poetry and plays of Félix Arturo Lope de Vega treated historical, mythological, and humble subjects and were widely read and imitated. Spanish painters such as Diego Velázquez produced psychologically insightful portraits of Spanish courtiers, including in his depictions their pet dogs and the dwarves they kept for their entertainment.

The late Baroque period also saw the flourishing of eastern European cultures. The Holy Roman Emperor Rudolf II (r. 1576–1612) created an extravagant collection of paintings, gemstones, live animals, and scientific devices, housing them in his huge palace in Prague. He collected scholars, too, paying them to do their work at his court and if possible to help him in occult pursuits, such as finding the philosopher's stone. Even after the Thirty Years' War, the Habsburgs continued to build and furnish lavish Baroque residences and places of worship in the major cities of their grand empire. In Poland-Lithuania, Krakow, one of the great Gothic cities, continued to be renowned for its beauty and wealth even though King Sigismund III of the house of Vasa moved the capital to Warsaw in 1596.

But as economic and military power began to shift from south to north, and from east to west, so too did cultural supremacy. As urban populations and literacy grew in northern Europe, English and especially French works began to attract attention. Willing and able to invest large sums in patronizing artists, dramatists, scholars, and architects, the French monarchy and aristocracy, by the seventeenth century's close, made French culture *the* model for sophistication, elegance, and good taste.

Theater

Throughout Europe, the development of court cultures made possible the expansion of the repertoire of medieval sacred dramas. Princes hired actors to play for themselves and their noble friends, and some localities agreed to allow street performances or even the building of public playhouses. Writers began to compose a rich variety of plays, usually taking their subjects from either classical antiquity or from the Middle Ages, but infusing their work with the powerful and often violent emotions of their day. It was not unusual for Baroque plays to end with piles of dead bodies on the stage or with the sudden intervention of angels, devils, or God himself, though humble people also made their way into the plays of Lope de Vega and the great English writer and actor William Shakespeare (1564–1616). Like Shakespeare and Lope de Vega, many playwrights were accomplished poets and used intricately crafted language to depict these dramatic events. This was particularly true of the great French playwrights of the age, Jean Racine and Pierre Corneille; their work set the standards for beautiful writing in French for centuries to come.

For English speakers, Shakespeare was undoubtedly the master playwright of the seventeenth century, though he died not long after its opening, in 1616. His magnificent tragedies, comedies, and history plays continue to be performed and reinterpreted today, but in his day, Shakespeare was addressing on stage some of his age's greatest anxieties. Would there be a stable succession to the throne, and would the monarch be both brave and honorable? These questions were posed, for example, in *Hamlet* and *King Lear,* and in his sequence of plays on the Wars of the Roses and the Tudor monarchs, *Richard II, Henry IV* (two plays), *Henry V, Henry VI* (three plays), and *Richard III.* Several of the plays deal with Scottish subjects or with the difficulties faced by English kings in uniting the nobility, issues highly relevant to both Elizabeth I and her successor, James I. Shakespeare's plays also reveal much about the problems of lesser people of the period, from the struggle of servants to be treated with human dignity in *The Tempest* to the torments suffered by young lovers seeking to cross political lines in *Romeo and Juliet*. Similarly, the prejudices of the age are reflected in the subjugation of headstrong women in *The Taming of the Shrew* and the humbling of greedy Jews in *The Merchant of Venice*. Of course, Shakespeare's reach extended far beyond political commentary. His insight into the human condition derives in part from the fact that he inhabited a dangerous and uncertain world full of dramatic political and private tragedies but one also characterized by new opportunities and experiences.

Numerous seventeenth-century writers made their mark by composing epic poems or the first novels since Roman times. The earliest of these novels were Spanish, the most famous being Miguel de Cervantes's *Don Quixote*, published serially between 1607 and 1615. The story tracks the adventures of Don Quixote, a would-be conquistador, whose imagination far outstrips his abilities. Instead of crusading against the Moors or conquering the peoples of the Americas, he tilts against windmills. Cervantes presents the Spanish noble knight (hidalgo) as a man of great aspirations, but no practical sense. Quixote, like his fellow Spanish nobles, is too haughty to engage in any sort of labor and survives only thanks to his able and jovial servant, Sancho Panza. In many ways, *Don Quixote* predicts the decline of Spain as its nobles continue to live in the dream world of sixteenth-century conquests and fritter away their riches in pursuit of antiquated ideals.

Another of the period's great novels, *The Adventures of Simplicius Simplicissimus* (1668), by the German writer H. J. C. von Grimmelshausen, comments even more directly on current events. The novel follows the career of another sort of simpleton, not a nobleman like Don Quixote, but an ordinary peasant, during the Thirty Years' War. In the first pages, Simplicius's farm is overrun by marauding soldiers who rape and kill his mother and sister. The peasant survives by hiding with a hermit in a forest until he is nearly murdered by another group of soldiers and forced to join the army. Simplicius learns what it is to be a mercenary—to be a merciless thief and an unprincipled man who works for whomever pays best—and learns that there is no justice, and perhaps no rhyme or reason, in this world.

In his great epic poem *Paradise Lost* (1667), the blind Puritan poet John Milton recast events in the book of Genesis in ways that reflected the moral anguish experienced by many of his contemporaries. In the poem, Satan, the fallen angel, denounces God for rejecting him and for allowing terrible evils to torment humankind. Adam accepts his expulsion from Eden and the inevitable toil and suffering that will now be humankind's lot. *Paradise Lost* demonstrates the extent to which Milton and his contemporaries worried about God's responsibility for the evils and hardships experienced by his earthly children. Readers of the poem often came away convinced not of God's ultimate justice, as Milton wished them to, but resentful of God's cruelty toward both of his creatures, Satan and Adam.

Art and Architecture

The Baroque was an age of enormous canvases and cavernous churches, of dramatic frescoes and gargantuan sculptures of monarchs, religious figures, and historical heroes—but also of new depictions of everyday life and of Europe's new commodities. It was an age of great court painters, as monarchs commissioned portraits that depicted their power and wealth. The Flemish painters Peter Paul Rubens and Anthony Van Dyck, for example, composed hundreds of canvases to be hung in French, Spanish, Italian, and British palaces. These often oversized and dramatically colored paintings frequently employed mythological and religious symbolism to enhance the splendor of the monarchies or to depict the painful agonies of the human condition.

Baroque artists also created vast numbers of religious pieces. They produced sculpted tombs and jewel-studded chalices by the hundreds of thousands. Southern European and Flemish Catholic painters such as Rubens tended to stick with a highly colorful palette and with fleshy renderings of biblical scenes. Protestant artists in the north, notably Rembrandt van Rijn, favored a more somber style, but still produced painting after painting depicting the crucifixion and scenes from the Old Testament.

Some Dutch painters, such as Jan Vermeer, began to paint scenes of ordinary people, illustrating that non-nobles, too, like Vermeer's *Girl Reading a Letter by an Open Window* (c. 1659), could be beautiful to contemplate. Many of these images also came with a moral message. *The Dissolute Household* (1664) by Dutch artist Jan Steen shows what happens to family life when the elders give in to drink and neglect their work. Still-life painting also became fashionable, and the art market teemed with depictions of breakfast tables groaning with fish, wine, fruit, and flowers.

Baroque architecture appealed greatly to royal and clerical patrons, for its theatrical spaces and rich decoration offered ideal settings for hierarchical court rituals and religious services in an era in which monarchs and the clergy were eager to display their wealth and power. There are magnificent examples of such architecture not only in Bernini's Rome, and in Austria, where the court architect Johann Bernhard Fischer von Erlach built his ornate and eclectic masterpieces, but also in the colonies, in Spanish Mexico and Peru, and in Portuguese-dominated Goa. The more humble urban dwellings of Amsterdam and London, such as those depicted in the works of Vermeer and Steen, remind us that there was a new, non-noble architecture evolving as well, one whose inhabitants happily did without Baroque splendor and put their money into private comfort rather than into display.

Music

While Europeans continued, as they always had, to sing and make music in the streets, at village festivals, and in their homes, the polished compositions of the Baroque era remained tied to the church or the court. Music in this era was not meant to make the composer famous, but rather to glorify God or the royal patron. In central Europe's German-speaking states, for example, musicians composed mostly sacred music, as did the great organist Dieter Buxtehude and the late Baroque sensation, Johann Sebastian Bach. Bach was famed for his complicated fugues and his exquisite organ music. As monarchs expanded their courts, chamber music, or music made by small groups of well-trained musicians, came into fashion, and kings hired court composers to compose new chamber pieces. As court composer for Louis XIV of France, Jean-Baptiste Lully produced numerous ballets, operas, and pastorals, as well as church music.

The real center of innovation, however, was Italy. Here in 1607 Claudio Monteverdi composed the first opera, *Orpheus*. By rewriting the myth of the Greek god of music, Orpheus, Monteverdi demonstrated the power and beauty of music itself. Another great Italian musician, Antonio Vivaldi was born a generation after Monteverdi's death. Vivaldi, a virtuoso violinist and composer, worked to develop harmony and counterpoint, in so doing laying the foundations of polyphonic music. Vivaldi produced more than seven hundred works, including operas, concertos, sonatas, and cantatas. Among his best-known works is the violin concerto "The Four Seasons" (1725).

Jan Steen, The Dissolute Household (1665) This humorous Dutch painting teaches middle-class virtues by depicting improper behavior. Here, the (probably inebriated) parents sleep while the children run the household, the dog eats off the table, and valuable books, musical instruments, and dishes, including a spilled glass of wine, are strewn carelessly across the floor. The only intelligent creature in the picture is the monkey, who seems to be recording the scene with a quill pen.

Political Philosophy in the Age of Absolutism

If music and art reflected the rising importance of secular society, political and moral philosophers in the age of absolutism also gradually began to move away from theology and to develop new ideas about the proper nature and practice of statecraft. Most of those who wrote on politics or law in this era continued to be close readers of traditional texts, the works of classical antiquity and the Bible, but some began to read these in new ways. Speculating on the right way to run a state was a dangerous business in most places, especially when intellectuals called into question traditional practices or the privileges of the king, aristocracy, or church. Thus, most of the new ideas came from places where individuals were able to discuss proper governance with relative freedom: the Netherlands and England. Discussions of citizenship, natural law, religious freedom, and what would be called "the social contract" emerged primarily from these relatively free centers. But as the examples here demonstrate, by no means did even these thinkers agree on how the states of the present and future should be ruled.

In the Dutch Republic, the humanist Hugo Grotius found in the work of the Roman orator Cicero a basis for arguing that humans could discover a series of **natural laws** that defined the good society. These laws preserved what Cicero called "the tranquility and happiness of human life" and ensured the safety of the states' citizens. Natural laws stood above laws made by humans and by religious authorities. Drawing on these ideas, Grotius argued for limitations on the power of human laws (that is, those made by particular kings and states). These, he said, should only ensure safety and order and should not coerce citizens in matters of religious belief. Grotius also argued that universally valid natural laws governed warfare and established the freedom of the seas. Again, the laws of nature were more permanent and persuasive than those made by any particular king or state.

The arguments from nature that Grotius used laid the foundations for what would later be called human rights and international law. A few, more radical thinkers found in Roman republican texts an appreciation for the idea of the freedom and equality of citizens within the state, something that contrasted directly with absolutist ideas. With the help of Jewish scholars, some Protestant Bible-readers also concluded that God disapproved of worldly kings. Both of these streams fed an attack on absolutist tyranny that helped launch the English Civil Wars and would be most clearly articulated in the work of the English champion of popular sovereignty and individual liberty, John Locke (see Chapter 16).

But these were dangerous and heretical lines of inquiry, even in England and the Dutch Republic. The ideas of the Englishman Thomas Hobbes (1588–1679) were closer to the ways in which the monarchs of the day thought about proper governance. Horrified by England's political turmoil and the brutality of the Thirty Years' War, Hobbes plunged backward to humankind's beginnings, asking what human societies looked like before monarchs had emerged as rulers. In his masterwork, *Leviathan* (1651), Hobbes argued that in humans' original state of nature, there had been nothing but ceaseless warfare. In Hobbes's pessimistic view, the human condition, human nature itself, was endless selfishness, "a war of all against all." Desperate for peace, humans had agreed to a "social contract," according to which they would obey an absolute ruler, one who could end this conflict and impose order. Hobbes valued order above all, and *Leviathan* was frequently used to justify absolutism as the only means to establish peace. His work, however, contained subtleties and insights that ranged well beyond such political uses and initiated a long series of conversations about human nature and the origins and nature of the social contract between rulers and the ruled.

Popular Culture in the Baroque Era

The cultural world beyond the court and the church was necessarily limited by the fact that for most people life remained, as Hobbes put it, "nasty, brutish and short." There were ceaseless burials and outpourings of religious invective. For readers—of which there were an increasing number, especially in urban areas in the north and west—there were an increasing number of books, some of them inexpensive and adorned with woodcuts. Many of the bestsellers were older religious works; by 1700, Granada's *Book of Prayer and Meditation* (1564) had gone through more than one hundred editions. John Foxe's *Book of Martyrs* (1563) continued to attract large numbers of Protestant readers who found in it lurid stories about Catholic persecutions of religious reformers. In 1678 the English preacher and writer John Bunyan published *Pilgrim's Progress*, an allegorical tale tracing the sufferings of a Christian Everyman as he searches for deliverance, loaded down with his heavy burden of human sin. Not all popular reading, however, was religious. There were joke books, including *Six Varieties of Fart* in French, and books describing how to play games or tell fortunes. Peasants purchased almanacs that advised them on when to plant as well as when to make love; early newssheets and pamphlets circulated widely, describing—usually in highly partisan ways—the latest Catholic or Protestant atrocities, or giving humble people instructions on how to recognize one of the scariest threats to their well being: witchcraft.

Living the Witch Craze

A central feature of both popular and elite culture in the Baroque era was simultaneous fear of and fascination with witchcraft. Since antiquity, many Europeans had believed in some sort of magic or sorcery; this was a convenient way to explain accidents, coincidences, or bad luck. In an age of radical religious conflict, a veritable witch craze seized Europe, and between about 1550 and 1750, hundreds of thousands of people were tried as witches and as many as 50,000 executed in Europe and the Americas. The means to identify the heresy of witchcraft came from a handbook composed by two Dominican priests, *The Malleus Maleficarum* (*The Hammer of Witches*). Printed in 1486, the book's influence spread, especially as the religious warfare and economic disasters of the sixteenth and seventeenth centuries tore apart communities. By 1669, when *The Hammer of Witches* was in its twenty-ninth edition, most Europeans had come to believe that witchcraft was a real and dangerous social and religious problem.

What was it like to live through this witch craze? Suspicions that a witch was at work usually began with a frightening and inexplicable event—a freak hailstorm or the sudden death of an infant. Evildoers were charged with everything from desecrating the host to raising armies of mice, from cursing cows that then sickened and died to causing sudden storms that destroyed crops. A large majority of the accused were women, especially midwives, healers, and those burdensome to the community such as elderly widows. Children and male misfits, including religious nonconformists, were also accused of witchcraft. The accused were handed over to local religious or regional officials, who used *The Hammer of Witches* or other manuals to identify suspects and try them—often using various means of torture. There were some standard accusations: witches consorted with the devil, participated in satanic and sacrilegious rituals, or sold their souls in order to obtain special powers. Sometimes local officials hired "witch-smellers," but usually they could rely on villagers to denounce their neighbors. Some of the accused began to confess that they had participated in nocturnal rides with Satan; Sabbath-eve orgies; black masses; and the cursing of crops, cows, and children. Often open to the public, trials of witches were high drama and could excite both participants and spectators to frenzy. Fearful of allowing the devil's servants to inflict more damage and mindful of the Bible's commandments ("Thou shalt not suffer a witch to live"; Exodus 22:18), both the elite and the peasantry were eager to rid their communities of witches: a single witch endangered everyone. Most Europeans were not revolted by watching witches hanged, drowned, strangled, or burned at the stake, but felt justified in protecting their property, their families, and their souls from Satan's power.

What was it like to be accused of practicing witchcraft or sorcery? Undoubtedly it was terrifying and personally devastating. Most of the accusers were one's neighbors, or in the case of the midwives, one's employers. Establishing innocence was next to impossible when the crime was one committed at a distance: how could a person show that he or she had not cursed a baby or caused lightning to strike? Some accused witches believed in magical powers themselves and feared they had caused the evils with which they were charged. Many confessed at trial, under torture or in hopes of a lighter sentence. Some named accomplices, which could lead to mass accusations and executions. Catharina Schmid, a seventy-four-year-old widow from a small village in southern Germany, tried to resist. Accused first of inflicting madness upon a young girl and of killing a neighbor and her six children, Catharina was subsequently charged with every other misfortune her town had suffered and of sharing her bed with both her daughter and the devil. Catharina tried to tell the court that her neighbor's husband was a violent drunkard, that his children died of abuse and hunger, and that the animals she was accused of killing were struck down by God, in punishment for their owners' sinfulness. But the court persisted, interrogating her twelve times over eight months. Her torturers applied thumbscrews and cut out a "devil's mark" (probably a mole) on her thigh; she was whipped and vinegar poured into her wounds. She maintained her innocence until she finally broke, and confessed that she had been seduced by the devil and inflicted harm on her neighbors and their property. She insisted on her daughter's innocence, but both were executed anyway. Catharina was strangled, then her body was burned at the stake, with bags of gunpowder tied around her neck as an additional, symbolic punishment for having been so stubborn.[3]

Executing Witches This image from a seventeenth-century book depicts the hanging of four witches in England in 1649. The individual marked "D" is said to be a witch-finder, who is being paid for his services.

Of course, trying and executing supposed witches did nothing to ward off the plague or to prevent hailstorms. In some regions, the witch craze itself caused instability as well as injustice. Gradually, in different places at different times, higher-level courts began to intervene to end torture and decriminalize witchcraft, establishing noncapital penalties. The end to witchcraft persecution tended to follow increases in prosperity and in feelings of security. Accordingly, it both started and ended later in central and eastern Europe, where effective state structures and rising incomes arrived more slowly. Executions ended as early as 1603 in the Netherlands and were largely over in France by 1670, but large numbers of witches continued to be burned in central Europe. Catharina Schmid died in 1746; in Poland, the last witch was executed as late as 1776.

Absolutism Triumphant

Where did Absolutism prevail, and where was it less successful?

If trying and executing witches was a popular means to explain and eradicate the evils of the day, European monarchs recognized that it would take more than this to deal with the period's dangers and opportunities. To prevent renewed civil war, to protect themselves against expansionist neighboring states, and to invest in overseas adventures, they would need more power and more money, and more latitude to use both as they wished. Thus, after 1648, monarchs from Spain to Russia with quite different personalities and quite different kingdoms continued early absolutist attempts to stabilize their houses—and in doing so built family dynasties: the Bourbons in France, the Vasas in Sweden and Poland-Lithuania, the Stuarts in England, the Hohenzollerns in Brandenburg, the Romanovs in Russia, and the Habsburgs in Austria and Spain. All also sought to guarantee the succession of their heirs and to develop centralized bureaucracies, standing armies, efficient systems of taxation, and established churches, in the process taking away (to a greater or lesser degree) the independent power and wealth of the kingdom's nobility and the clergy.

Of course, kings and queens needed help to turn Europe's decentralized, rural economies into centralized and efficient providers of income for the state. So they turned to well-educated, hard-working ministers, men whose job it was to impose some sort of uniform system on the kingdom in order to move power and money from the provinces to the capital. Favorite ministers such as the duke of Olivares in Spain or Cardinal Richelieu in France appointed their friends and family members—whom Richelieu aptly called his "creatures"—to important offices. Kings rewarded loyal supporters or members of their own religions with titles, creating a group of new nobles and bureaucrats who depended on royal or ministerial favor. Kings in need of cash also began to tax more extensively and to sell privileges, such as the right to collect taxes in a particular locality, or offices, such as sheriff of a certain town. The older nobility despised both the selling of offices and the ennobling of ministers and loyal bureaucrats, as they saw both as means by which their own privileges and clout were threatened.

As this suggests, not everyone in the kingdom liked absolutist innovations, and in some places, nobles had considerable powers of resistance. In fact, despite monarchs' best efforts, nobles everywhere retained most of their privileges and most of the kingdom's wealth down to 1789. By establishing state churches, monarchs exerted new control over the clergy, but the churches continued to extract the tithe, to censor publications, and to exert independent dominion over enormous tracts of land.

Local conditions shaped the kind of absolute power each king acquired—and the degree to which the nobility was able to protect its traditional powers. In western states such as the Netherlands, England, and France, medieval law codes gave nobles an unimaginable variety of special privileges and rights to sue over them. In France, Louis XIII refused to call his representative assembly, the **Estates General,** into session after 1613, and his son Louis XIV continued the practice of ruling without such a council. But the French kings could not disband the local law courts known as **parlements,** some of which continued to voice their objections to royal policies. By contrast, in eastern Europe, Prussian and Russian monarchs had fewer legal limitations on their power. They used more force to consolidate their states and gave their nobles more control over their serfs. Louis XIV's France may have been the archetypical absolutist state, but absolutism was *more* absolute in the East.

France under Louis XIV and Louis XV

France's gains in the Peace of Westphalia were minimal, especially in view of the enormous costs of the war. Land taxes, for example, had tripled between 1635 and 1648. France's nobles had long chafed under the rule of Louis XIII (who died in 1643) and his chief minister Cardinal Richelieu, whom they blamed for raising taxes without calling an Estates General. They despised Louis's practice of appointing **intendants,** officials who fanned out across France to see that taxes were collected properly and that nobles did as the Crown instructed. Not surprisingly, local nobles who wanted to protect their privileges and their local power bases despised the intendants, who epitomized the king's absolutist leanings. In 1648, a civil war known as the **Fronde** (for the *frondeurs,* or those who slung mud at officials' carriages) terrified the young and as yet uncrowned Louis XIV, who afterward made it his mission to ensure that such a challenge to the house of Bourbon never happened again. He expanded the number of intendants, widened their powers, and took to heart the advice of his chief minister Cardinal Mazarin: "it is up to you to become the most glorious king that has ever been." He pursued this goal partly through the expansion and use of his army; partly through building a centralized, religiously united state; and partly through seeking to extend French power in the world (see Map 15.2, p. 473).

In 1663, Louis made New France—all French holdings in North America—into a province of France. The next year, he claimed the Caribbean island of Hispaniola and established a French East India Company to monopolize what would prove to be a very rich trade in Caribbean sugar. He oversaw the founding of the first French outposts in India, at Chandernagore and Pondicherry, and in general pushed forward the extension of French trade down the African coast, along the Atlantic seaboard, and into the Indian Ocean. Acting as his own chief minister after the death of Mazarin in 1661, Louis instituted a census so that he could better survey and more efficiently tax his subjects. To show that he was just as forward-thinking and generous a king as was Britain's Charles II, he founded a French Academy of Sciences on the model of Britain's Royal Society. Determined to ensure France's stability as well as to enhance his own glory, Louis seized every opportunity to build state power and prosperity.

The great palace complex at **Versailles,** just eleven miles outside of Paris, is the quintessential embodiment of Louis's ambitions for France, and for himself. Building began on the site of Louis XIII's hunting lodge in 1661 and continued for decades thereafter. Louis XIV added lavish buildings to the complex after the conclusion of each of his wars, hiring the most modern architects and artists to create spectacular surroundings for himself and his court. In 1682, he made Versailles the monarchy's official place of business, meaning that all petitioners and nobles who wanted to influence high politics would have to make their way to a palace that reflected Louis's power in every possible way. Visitors could not avoid seeing their king endlessly represented as the Greek sun god Apollo or the Roman god of war Mars. The carefully manicured gardens of Versailles, complete with trick fountains, became world famous, as did the ornate decoration of vast rooms such as the Hall of Mirrors.

LOUIS XIV, ABSOLUTIST WARRIOR. By the 1670s, Louis had established absolutist rule at home, but he was eager to add luster to his image by conquering new territories. For this monarch, true glory was won the old-fashioned way: through victory on the battlefield. Moving in 1672 to push the Spanish back from the French border by attacking the Spanish Netherlands, Louis threw himself into a series of wars with Spain, Sweden, England, and the Dutch Republic, all of which tried to prevent France from making a bid for continental hegemony. Fighting continued periodically from the 1670s through the 1690s, during which time Louis's huge army frequently behaved badly, burning and plundering Dutch and German towns along the Rhine, and creating lasting hatred for the French in both the Netherlands and the German states.

At first, Louis was victorious. He conquered and annexed a number of Rhine basin cities and the provinces of Alsace and Lorraine, incorporating the many German-speakers of this rich region into his empire (Map 14.2). Churches that had been converted for Protestant use, such as the cathedral in Strasbourg, reverted to offering Catholic mass. Evidently Louis cared little that his campaigns plunged France into debt or that the new taxes he imposed generated deep resentment among his subjects. For soon afterward he initiated a new war, one that would prove even more debilitating than the last.

The cause of Louis's next war was the succession to the Spanish throne of a Bourbon prince (as the Habsburg king Charles II had died childless), who in 1700 took the title Philip V of Spain. On his ascension, Philip renounced his right to inherit the French crown as well, but then Louis XIV, worried about his own succession, began to talk of revoking this promise. Outraged, the Austrians took up arms, and the English and the Dutch, equally concerned about the prospect of a single ruler uniting the kingdoms of France and Spain, joined the Habsburg side. Together they fought Louis XIV in the long-lasting War of the Spanish Succession (1701–1714). The army arrayed against the French featured colorful, brilliant commanders such as John Churchill, duke of Marlborough, and Prince Eugene of Savoy, but even they had trouble with Louis's now formidable forces. Marlborough's efforts at the Battle of Blenheim in 1704 and at Malplaquet in 1709 kept the French from marching into the Spanish Netherlands, but at a horrific cost. At Malplaquet alone more than 20,000 of Marlborough's soldiers were killed or wounded, whereas the French casualties were half as great.

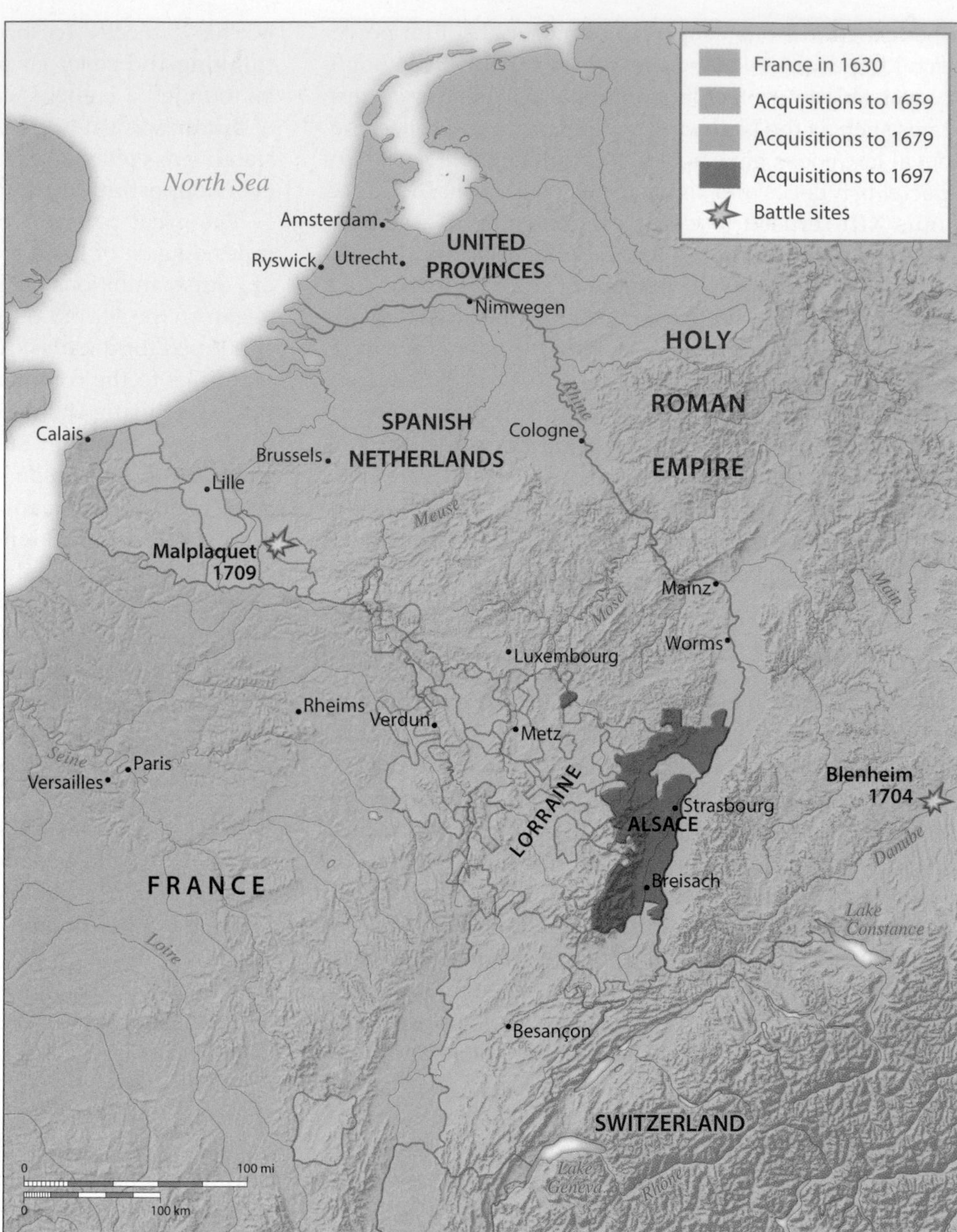

MAP 14.2 | Louis XIV's Annexations

Louis XIV spent much of his reign waging war to extend France's borders and to demonstrate his glory. ***Why was Louis XIV able to seize this territory after 1648?***

In 1713–1714, three peace treaties (the Treaty of Utrecht, the Treaty of Rastatt, and the Treaty of Baden) ended the war, giving the French a partial victory. They were permitted to put a Bourbon king, who took the title Philip V, on the Spanish throne. But they were not permitted to unite the crowns or to take control of Spain's overseas colonies. The real winners in the war were the Austrians and the English. The Austrians obtained Spanish possessions in the Netherlands and Italy, and the English received Gibraltar and Minorca. French hopes of expanding further east were dashed. Louis XIV died two years later, in 1715, proud of the glorious state he had built and seemingly untroubled by the debts and difficulties he was passing on to his heirs.

By the time of Louis's death, France had plenty of problems, some of them brought on by Louis's wars, others by his religious policies. To fund the wars, the king had imposed direct taxes on both nobles and commoners. His relentless conscription of soldiers had made him greatly unpopular with the commoners, and the nobles resented his selling of offices to wealthy members of the middle class and his refusal to listen to noble counselors. His religious policies also drew criticism, within France and beyond. Under the influence of his pious second wife, Madame de Maintenon, Louis had grown less open minded; the court's lavish parties became fewer and more sedate; and the classical nude statues in the gardens of Versailles received fig leaves. More important, in 1685 Louis made Protestantism illegal in France by issuing the Revocation of the Edict of Nantes, thereby defying pledges France had made in the Peace of Westphalia to permit the peaceful practice of Protestantism. Louis's action, meant to shore up Catholic unity, made him unpopular among intellectuals who had come to value religious freedom in the wake of the Thirty Years' War. It also proved an economic blunder, for revoking the Edict drove many skilled and well-educated Protestants to leave France and to settle instead in the Dutch Republic, in Protestant Prussia, or in Britain's North American colonies.

The Ottomans Besiege Vienna, 1683 In what turned out to be the Ottomans' last attempt to seize the Habsburg capital city, troops surrounded Vienna. The intervention of Bavarian and Polish troops, commanded by Jan Sobieski, as well as Ottoman mistakes, saved the city. Depicted on the left is the war tent of Ottoman commander Kara Mustapha, which Sobieski, after the battle, took back to Krakow as one of his prizes.

LOUIS XV. When the Sun King finally died, his only remaining heir was his five-year-old great-grandson. Control of the kingdom was given to a cousin, the duke of Orléans, whose irresponsible investments caused enormous economic turmoil. The regency lasted until 1723, when the thirteen-year-old Louis XV took the throne, but by that time complaints about the court's corruption and the weakness of the state were rife. Louis XV continued the domestic policies of his great-grandfather, selling offices to favorites and spending lavishly on his court; he embroiled France in the Seven Years' War (1756–1763; see Chapter 15), which resulted in the loss of most of France's overseas possessions. Louis's subjects generally disapproved of the company he kept. Everyone knew that his beautiful mistress, Madame de Pompadour, had been a courtesan, and rumor had it that she wasted all the kingdom's money and told the king how to run the state. Throughout his long reign (1715–1774), Louis did not call the Estates General into session, and he had a series of confrontations with the regional parlements. Louis XV did nothing about the nation's debt, which continued to grow. He did not have the Sun King's interest in building the state or his taste for battle. Thus, he did not increase French absolutist rule so much as give it an increasingly bad name.

Absolutism and the Austrian Habsburgs

To France's southeast lay the Holy Roman Empire, where, as we have seen, the Thirty Years' War broke the Habsburgs' attempts to overturn religious pluralism. But the Habsburgs did not break the emperors' desire to consolidate power, at least in Austria, Slovenia, and pieces of what are today Italy and southern Germany—lands where the Habsburgs were hereditary, as opposed to elected rulers. The Habsburgs were successful in large part; in the course of a series of wars with the Ottoman Empire, they gradually built up a modern army and won back all of Hungary. Although the emperors' religious policies were erratic—sometimes Catholicism was forcibly imposed, sometimes Protestants left in peace—the state did manage to claim a considerable amount of power over the church. Although economic modernization was halting—serfdom continued on the land, and the late-arriving idea of becoming an overseas trading power never bore fruit—during the long reign of Maria Theresa (r. 1740–1780), the Habsburg monarchy had largely succeeded in creating an absolutist state.

Crucial in creating backing for Habsburg absolutism were the wars against the "infidel" Turks, who had conquered large swathes of central Europe in the sixteenth century. The Habsburgs tried to push them back in 1663, but failed; in 1683, a huge Turkish army took the offensive, advancing rapidly to the gates of Vienna. The Ottoman commander Kara Mustapha set siege to the city—cannon balls struck the great St. Matthias Church (and can still be seen there today). After two months of fierce fighting, the Austrian army was relieved by the arrival of forces commanded by the charismatic Polish king Jan Sobieski, who later claimed that he had saved central European Christendom. Sobieski did assist in forcing the retreat of the Turkish forces, and he took back to Poland numerous reminders of his victory, including the stirrup of Mustapha, which today hangs at the foot of a revered Gothic crucifix in Krakow's main cathedral.

The defeat of the Turks in 1683 became a boasting point not only for Sobieski but also for the Austrians, especially in light of the wars that followed, in which first the city of Buda and then the rest of Hungary was conquered. By 1718, the eastern Habsburgs had conquered far more territory than had Louis XIV (compare Map 14.1 on p. 427 and Map 15.1 on p. 469). But swallowing Hungary, a nation with a powerful and proud aristocracy of its own, put Austria's digestion to the test, and the Habsburgs never managed to bring this territory fully under absolutist control. The same could be said, to a lesser extent, of the Italian, Flemish, and Croatian nobles. Austria's position between the powerful French in the west and the Turks and increasingly powerful Russians in the east also meant that the empire had to negotiate with others. When Emperor Charles VI (r. 1711–1740) sought to ensure the succession of his daughter, Maria Theresa, he was compelled to make a series of compromises, including giving up an Austrian East India Company based in the Austrian Netherlands. The modernizing policies of Maria Theresa and her son Joseph II (see Chapter 16) would have to go forward without the extra income and influence other states procured by promoting commerce and colonization overseas.

The Consolidation of Prussia

In 1640, when Frederick William, prince of the house of Hohenzollern, became ruler of Brandenburg, his small, land-locked state was occupied by the Swedes and in chaos. Frederick William was an elector—that is, he possessed one of the seven votes required to confirm the appointment of a Holy Roman emperor—but otherwise he was hardly a powerful man. Brandenburg suffered much in the Thirty Years' War, though officially it fought on the Protestant side for only a few years during the conflict. Much more devastating than the battles were the troops quartered there, who robbed, murdered, and spread disease throughout the territory. Perhaps half of the population died during the wars, and marauders burned and pillaged thousands of farmsteads and small towns.

The experience convinced Frederick William that only a powerful military of his own could secure his state, and he began raising taxes and building one as soon as possible. From 3,000 men at arms in 1641–1642, he built a standing army of 38,000 by the 1670s, a force big enough to allow him to push back the Swedes and the Poles on his borders. He built fortifications and founded a cadet school to train his officers in the latest tactics, and he supplied his troops with modern, standardized weaponry. Because his reforms were expensive and usurped some of the powers of the nobility, he created a General War Commissariat to collect taxes and recruit soldiers for the state. During his reign, he also increased the size of his state, adding noncontiguous territory in the west as well as a chunk of Poland-Lithuania. These acquisitions gave his heirs both a window on the west and a foothold in the east.

To manage this transformation, Frederick William, subsequently known as the Great Elector, had to battle his nobles, and in this struggle he scored his greatest successes. As elsewhere, there were terrific battles over taxes, but he prevailed, compelling his nobles to submit to new taxes without the consent of representative assemblies. A Calvinist in a state populated largely by Lutherans, he put many of his co-religionists into the administration and began hiring talented commoners. As compensation, he gave landowning nobles a free hand to exploit their serfs.

The Great Elector died in 1688, leaving to his son and successor, Frederick, the second-largest territory in the Holy Roman Empire (after Austria) and a large modernized army. When the Habsburgs needed allies to fight Louis XIV, Frederick's price was that the emperor should allow Prussia to become a kingdom, and in 1701 he got his wish. As king in Prussia, Frederick I (r. 1701–1713) continued his father's military build-up and administrative reforms, but also tried his hand at emulating the French monarch. He spent twice the annual revenue on his coronation and brought famous painters, musicians, scholars, and cooks to the Prussian court.

Frederick I's son, Frederick William I (r. 1713–1740), was revolted by his father's fancy tastes and the corruption in the court. Immediately upon his accession to the throne, Frederick William I dismissed the musicians and the chocolatier, diverting the money to his first love, the army. He embarked on a vigorous new expansion of the military, and he saw that all officers and men were well drilled. He loved nothing more than to watch their drills from his palace windows.

Frederick William I was a man of many contradictions. A devoted Calvinist, he prayed fervently but showed no mercy to soldiers or state officials, who could be publicly garroted for dereliction of duty. He instituted rigorous examinations for state bureaucrats but chose as friends heavy-drinking, uneducated Prussian aristocrats known as **Junkers.** His son, the future Frederick II ("the Great"), like Peter the Great's son Alexei (see below), also tried to run away from a father whose idea of preparing his heir for kingship amounted to psychological and physical torture. Frederick, unlike Alexei, survived and once again overhauled Prussian court culture. But he too would continue what had now become a Prussian tradition of putting the army at the core of state-building.

Russia: From Ivan the Terrible to Peter the Great

Russian absolutism began with Ivan III ("the Great"; r. 1462–1505), a Muscovite prince who, with the backing of the powerful monasteries, established hegemony over the medieval center of Novgorod. Ivan brought Italian artists to Moscow to rebuild the monastery-fortress-palace complex known as the Kremlin, to which they added a bell-tower whose bells were to mimic the music of the heavens and to warn Muscovites when invaders approached.

Ivan the Great's successor Ivan IV ("the Terrible"; r. 1533–1584) built a standing army, made war in all directions, and extended Muscovy's holdings further than any other prince of his day (Map 14.3). He combined

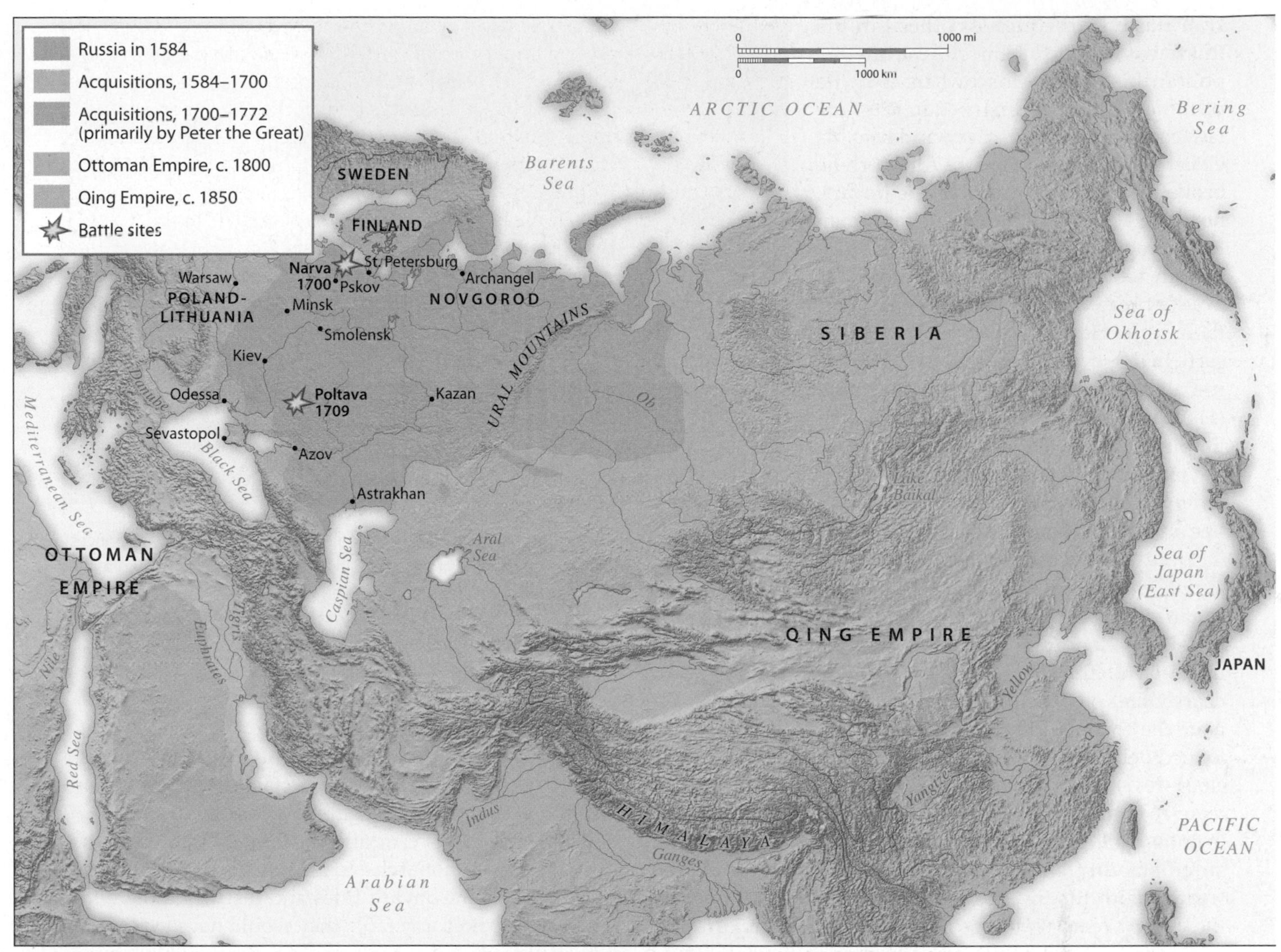

MAP 14.3 | Russian Expansion, Ivan the Terrible to Peter the Great
After 1584, Russia's czars expanded the size of their empire to make it the largest on earth. ***Compare the size of absolutist Russia's annexations to those of France (see Map 14.2). Why were the Russians able to take so much more land than the French?***

Byzantine and absolutist ideas to proclaim Moscow a third Rome and himself czar ("Caesar") of a grand new Russian empire.

Ivan the Terrible made grand plans for modernizing his state, though some of this modernization was also strongly inflected by Ivan's Russian Orthodox piety, by having been beaten as a child, and by his belief that he was divinely appointed to rule. To celebrate his victory over the (Muslim) Khanate of Kazan in 1556, he patronized the building of St. Basil's Cathedral in the Kremlin, which featured a new, Russian style, characterized by elaborate wood-carving and onion-shaped domes. He extended special trading privileges to the Dutch, the Prussians, and the English, though he did so mostly to have friends on the borders of his longtime Lutheran and Catholic enemies, the Swedes and the Poles. He hired many Germans from the Baltic region to staff his military and bureaucracy and rewarded them handsomely. In 1566, Ivan created a national representative assembly, the Zemsky Sobor, not because the czar wanted more advice from delegates, but because he needed help in extracting taxes from his subjects. In the main, he relied on monks and priests to help him formulate policies, and remained suspicious of his nobles, known as boyars. In the 1570s, Ivan set about breaking the boyars' power in ways much more violent than, but parallel to, Louis XIV's attempts to curb noble privileges a century later.

Ivan's modernizing plans entailed such enormous amounts of violence and so much warfare that eventually his kingdom was thrown into chaos. His wars with Poland-Lithuania lasted for decades and devastated the western sector of his kingdom. His hired thugs oversaw forced recruitments and mass murders in areas thought to be potentially disloyal. Novgorod in particular suffered, and Ivan reputedly had some of his boyar enemies roasted to death in a huge frying pan. In a fit of pique,

Ivan executed the highest official in the Russian Orthodox Church, the metropolitan bishop of Moscow. In 1581, he pummeled his pregnant daughter-in-law, causing her to miscarry, and beat his eldest son and heir to death. Although he broke the political power of the boyars, he gave Muscovites and military men huge tracts of land in the newly conquered east and south, and he allowed landowners unchecked power over their serfs. He took away what mobility serfs had previously possessed, instituting a more exploitative second serfdom (see Chapter 15) throughout the Russian Empire. He allowed Moscow's one printing press to be destroyed a year after it arrived, a symbol of his desire to be Russia's one and only modernizer—and master.

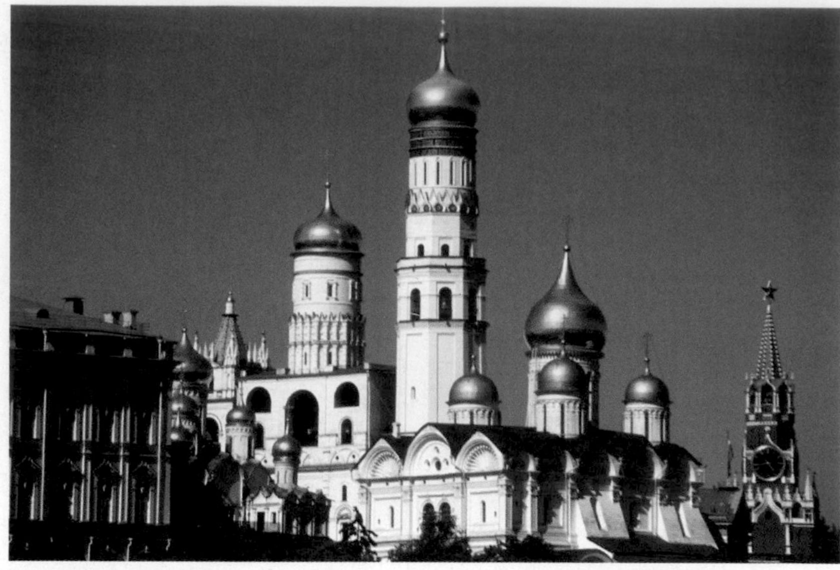

The Splendor of the Kremlin Already by the fourteenth century, the Muscovite princes were adding their residences and churches to the medieval fortress complex known as the Kremlin. This image shows Ivan the Great's Bell Tower, completed in 1508 and long Russia's tallest building, and to the right, the Cathedral of the Assumption, where Russian czars were crowned. Note the distinctive onion-shaped domes, one of the signature features of Russian Orthodox architecture.

Ivan was succeeded by his son, the simple-minded Fyodor I, who left governance in the hands of his brother-in-law, Boris Godonuv. When Fyodor died in 1598, the Zemsky Sobor elected Boris czar, but his election did not end disputes over the throne. Russia suffered a prolonged period of civil war known as the Time of Troubles (1604–1613), during which the Swedes and Poles sought to seize chunks of the czarist empire. Michael Romanov (r. 1613–1645), who was crowned czar in 1613, finally ensured stability but only by signing unfavorable peace treaties with the Swedes and Poles in 1618–1619, just as the Thirty Years' War was beginning in central Europe.

Russia endured another period of crisis between 1682 and 1689, the result of uncertainty about the succession, a revolt by the nobles, and renewed threats from neighboring Swedes and Poles. This was the context in which one of Russia's most powerful czars, Peter I ("the Great"; r. 1689–1725) took the throne. Peter was the first of Russia's rulers to visit western Europe, and he modeled himself partly after Louis XIV—but there was much of Ivan IV in his behavior, as well. During his travels, Peter learned Dutch, which allowed him to communicate with the commercial men of the Baltic rim and spurred his desire to modernize his empire along western lines. He recognized the need to speed up modernization after Russia was humiliated by Sweden in the first battles of the Great Northern War (1700–1721). Acting, as was his wont, quickly and without consulting his boyars, Peter imported English, German, Italian, and Dutch experts to help him reform shipbuilding and arms manufacture. In 1703 he also began building a new Russian capital, St. Petersburg, on boggy but strategically important land seized from the Swedes. Building his "window on the west" required massive amounts of serf labor and suffering—tens of thousands of whom died in the disease-ridden climate—and the importation of hundreds of western architects and craftsmen. But Peter wanted St. Petersburg to be a modern capital and Baltic commercial port for Russia, and as absolute ruler, he made sure that he got his wish.

Peter's powers as czar allowed him to subdue his nobles as western monarchs could not. In 1722, Peter simply eliminated the boyars' titles and instructed them that henceforth, to hold any rank, they would have to serve the state in some fashion. Male children from noble families were sent to cadet schools and then assigned to jobs in the military or bureaucracy. Peter's introduction of the Table of Ranks not only broke the independent power of the nobility, but also provided the czar with the much-needed educated personnel he needed to modernize his state. Nor did Peter spare his family. Peter treated his son, Alexei, with such cruelty that he tried to run away. On his return, Alexei was tortured, probably at Peter's orders, and died.

Peter's cultural policy was a violent parody of that of the Sun King. Rather than simply bribing his nobles to come to his new capital, Peter compelled a thousand nobles to move to St. Petersburg, where they were to build homes at their own expense but designed by Peter's architects. He ordered them to come to his court and to drink with him as long as he desired, and he insisted that all his nobles wear western dress and cut off their beards. The consolation for his nobles was that those who remained on their land were allowed to act as absolute rulers with respect to their own serfs—and that the distances between St. Petersburg and many parts of the empire were enormous, and communications slow. Peter was the most successful of all Europe's monarchs in establishing his absolute rule, but his subjects paid a heavy price for his brand of modernization.

Incomplete Absolutisms: Spain, Poland, and Sweden

In Spain, Poland, and Sweden, for different reasons, monarchs were not as successful in establishing absolutist regimes.

SPAIN. Spain, in many ways, had had its absolutist era too early, during the reign of Philip II (r. 1556–1598). Philip had tried to overrule the Cortes and to subdue nobles unhappy with Habsburg overlordship. He had seen his share of warfare—against the Ottomans, against the French, against the Dutch, and disastrously, against the English, who destroyed his Armada in 1588. He presided over the golden age of Spanish cultural production, patronizing great religious painters such as the Greek painter known as El Greco and the Italian master of color, Titian. In some ways anticipating Louis XIV, he built an enormous palace for himself outside of Madrid—though Philip's El Escorial, finished in 1584, was built according to descriptions of Solomon's Temple, and intended to be a center for Catholic Reformation learning rather than an aristocratic playground. Its austere furnishings and enormous collection of religious art and manuscripts reflected its housing of a monarch who compared himself to the biblical king David, and not to the sun. Philip II was a king who devoted himself to serving and patronizing the church in Rome, rather than one, like Louis XIV, who insisted on keeping the church under his own, secular, control.

Already saddled with debt when he inherited his kingdom in 1556, Philip II was happy to promote silver mining in the Americas, but this early silver rush promoted inflation in Europe and hardships for peasants who could not afford to pay higher food prices. By the time Philip's reign ended, his many wars had further bankrupted the kingdom. The Thirty Years' War completed the eclipse of Spain's Golden Age. Once again, the kingdom declared bankruptcy and now also faced demographic decline—disease and endless conscriptions had decimated the population, and in 1640, civil war broke out in the province of Catalonia, a response to the high-handedness of the court in Madrid.

After 1648, Spain did not recover as rapidly or thoroughly as the French. A problematic succession to the throne and a powerful and deeply conservative landowning elite hampered attempts at reinstituting absolutist rule. The Catholic Church remained more powerful in Spain than elsewhere and nimbly resisted attempts to curb its influence. When the Bourbon king Philip V (r. 1700–1724) took the throne, he attempted to implement French absolutist models with some success, but by this time, Spain had already lost the Spanish Netherlands and southern Italy to Austria. It still held huge territories in the Americas, but its silver mines were playing out, and gradually its trading routes fell into the hands of the Dutch, English, and French. Without money or new military conquests, the Spanish Bourbons never managed to fully break the resistance of the church and the landed nobles to their modernizing projects or their attempts to institute absolutist rule.

POLAND. Polish nobles, similarly, worked hard to protect their privileges and their tax revenues from centralizing forces. When called on to fight—as they often were in this era—the Poles did so effectively, but once the threat to their lands or enticement to conquer more territory was over, the Polish nobles resumed squabbling with one another. The situation was made worse by the fact that the king was, according to tradition, elected by Poland's representative assembly, the Sejm, and had to be an outsider. These conditions meant that the king was beholden to the great nobles in the Sejm and could not force them to agree to new taxes.

Kings elected from the Swedish house of Vasa (such as Sigismund III, r. 1587–1632; and Wladyslaw IV, r. 1632–1648) were patrons of the arts and successful military leaders, but after Wladyslaw's death in 1648, the kingdom suffered a series of invasions—most notably by the Swedes—and internal crises. As we have seen, a heroic moment came in 1683 when Jan Sobieski (r. 1674–1696) helped defeat the Ottomans before the gates of Vienna. But Sobieski's army could not be held together. The troops went home, and the Sejm refused to raise taxes to fund improvements, meaning that Poland could not build a powerful standing army or efficient centralized bureaucracy. Without an absolutist monarch, Poland could not modernize and eventually fell prey to its stronger neighbors. By 1720 it was living under the shadow of Peter the Great's expanding realm to its east, and the rising power of the Prussians to the north and west.

SWEDEN. At the time he took the Swedish throne, the Vasa king Charles XI (r. 1660–1697) could boast a large empire, stretching from Norway (then ruled by the Danes) to the Estonian city of Riga. Charles wrestled with large landowners to force them to hand over some of their huge estates and built an effective bureaucracy and a modernized army on the proceeds. In 1700, just after Charles's death, a united Polish, Danish, and Russian army attacked Sweden in the hopes of divvying up this rich kingdom. But the would-be partitioning powers ran into a buzzsaw in the form of the seventeen-year-old Charles XII (r. 1697–1718), who built on his father's absolutist achievements to create a Swedish military machine. With Dutch and English help, he defeated the Danes and then turned on the Russians, inflicting a humiliating defeat on the army of Peter the Great at the Battle of Narva in November 1700. In 1706 he compelled the Poles, too, to stand down. In this first stage of the long-lasting Great Northern War (1700–1721), Charles XII displayed his bravery, charisma, and stamina—but also his extravagant ambitions. In 1707 he invaded Russia, boasting that he would drive Peter the Great from his throne, and chop up the czar's empire into "petty princedoms."

Horrified by his army's failure at Narva, Peter I had begun rebuilding his own army, borrowing western European expertise. By 1709, when the Russians met Charles XII's Swedish troops at Poltava (see Map 14.3), the Russians were ready. Charles, for the first time, suffered a major defeat. After escaping to the Ottoman Empire, he tried, unsuccessfully, to get the Turks to help him battle the Russians. He returned home in 1714, riding more than nine hundred miles in two weeks' time, to find his war-weary nation broke and his nobility angry. But Charles, whose identity as a king and a man had been forged by ceaseless warfare, could not resist going to war once more, this time against the Danes in Norway. Here he was shot in 1718, perhaps by one of his own soldiers.[4]

After Charles XII's death, the Swedes made a series of peace agreements with their enemies, the result of which was the demise of Sweden as a great power. Weary of war and of charismatic absolutism, Swedish nobles compelled Queen Ulrika, who succeeded her brother Charles, to adopt a constitution that gave Sweden's representative assembly, the Riksdag, power almost equivalent to that of Parliament in England. If Polish absolutism was thwarted by the state's failure to build an army and produce a charismatic king, Swedish absolutism was killed by a flamboyant king who cared about nothing but military glory and was willing to squander the kingdom's resources on battles that, in the end, he could not win.

The Non-absolutist Exceptions: The Venetian and the Dutch Republics

What role did commerce play in the Dutch and Venetian Republics?

Some of Europe's smaller states were never tempted to make themselves into absolutist monarchies. These included Swiss states, such as Geneva, where John Calvin had established a Calvinist republic, and several Italian and Dalmatian city-states, such as Florence and Dubrovnik. The most prominent, however, were two states that used their extensive commercial networks to make possible, at least for a time, their survival in an increasingly absolutist world: the Venetian and the Dutch republics. The differing fates of these two commercial republics demonstrate that adapting to the seventeenth century's challenges was not just a matter of choosing one or another form of government, but of developing the state as such.

Venice, City of Commerce This painting of St. Mark's Square by Antonio Canaletto depicts an ordinary day in the life of this cosmopolitan city, as residents hang out laundry and well-dressed men and women meet to discuss business or to exchange gossip in the square. Close inspection of the image would also reveal a series of stalls lined up in front of the cathedral, some of them tended by turban-wearing Ottoman silk merchants.

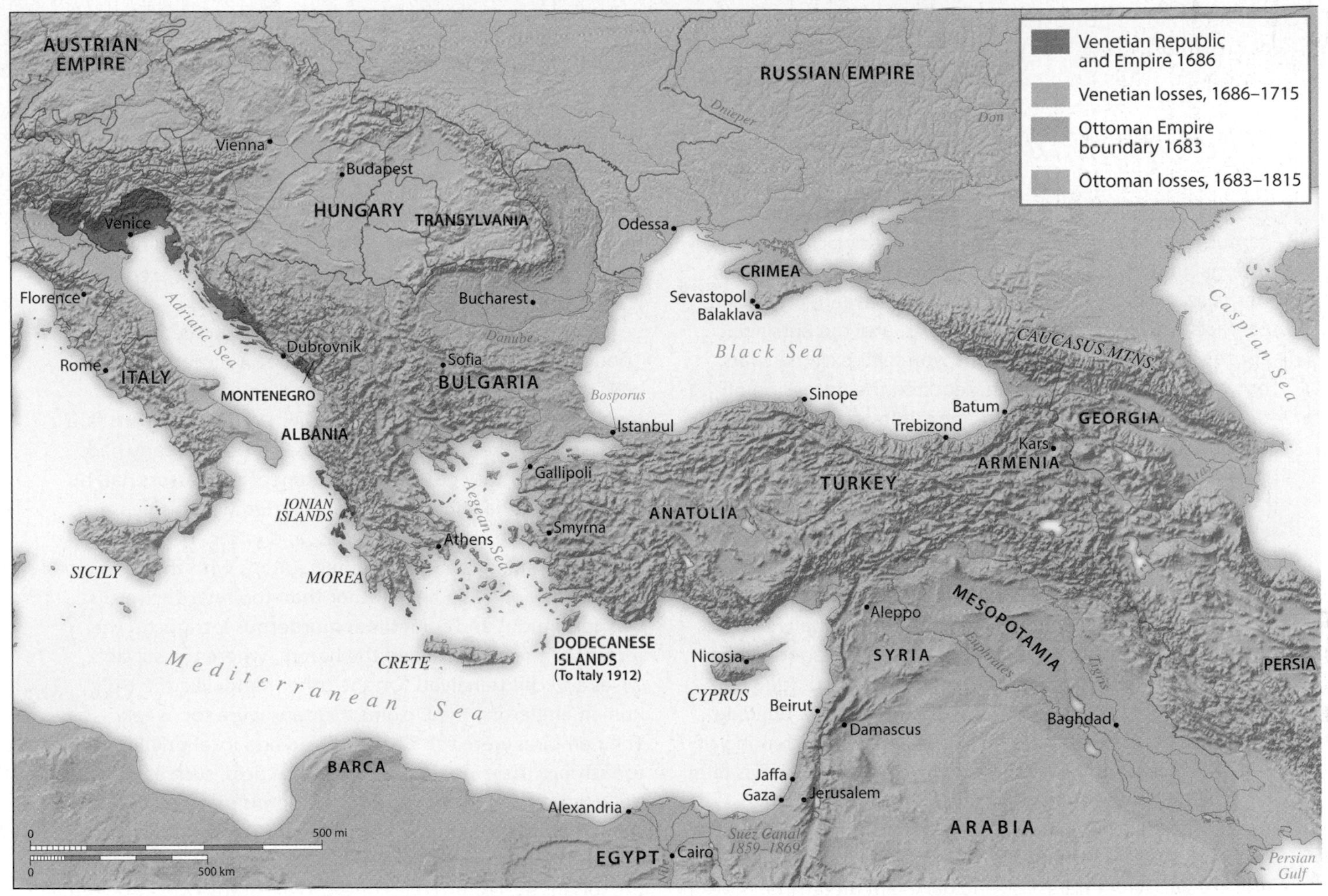

MAP 14.4 | The Ottoman and Venetian Empires, c. 1700

After 1683 the Ottoman and Venetian Empires began to decrease in size, though the Ottomans remained powerful until 1918. The orange shading here indicates areas that belonged to the Venetians but were lost to the Ottomans between 1686 and 1715; the green shading indicates areas that were once Ottoman territory but were lost to the Habsburgs and Russians between 1683 and 1815. ***How did the Ottoman losses of territory suggest that the balance of power in Europe had begun to shift away from the Mediterranean Sea?***

The Venetians

Venice entered the seventeenth century as an already formidable trading empire and exited it still powerful, but in decline. Though the Venetians continued to battle the Ottomans in the Mediterranean throughout the century, they stayed out of the Thirty Years' War and avoided the civil wars that devastated their neighbors. Thus Venice weathered the seventeenth century with its medieval institutions intact. These included its quasi-republican government, with its Great Council and an elected Doge as head of state. Its prosperity allowed the city to support a large number of painters, musicians, and architects, as well as skilled shipbuilders and craftsmen. In its famous St. Mark's Square, vendors of luxury goods—including Ottoman traders—congregated to sell their wares.

Yet infighting among the great families and the prosperity that allowed them to resist change prevented the Venetians from making timely reforms. The Venetians did not venture into the Atlantic or modernize their navy. They did not build an army, found a stock exchange, or create a state bank. Venice remained a Mediterranean power in an era in which influence and wealth was shifting to the Atlantic and the North Sea. Enjoying relatively good times while others suffered repeated crises and then falling off the pace as the absolutist states recovered, the Venetians experienced the seventeenth century in ways that paralleled the experience of their much-differently governed rivals, the Ottomans.

In 1660 the Venetians lost the important island of Crete to the Ottomans; they took part of the Greek mainland in 1699, but lost it again a few years later (see Map 14.4). By the 1720s, Venice itself was still wealthy and its culture rich, but its empire had receded and it no longer posed an expansionary threat.

The Dutch

In the 1579 split of the provinces of the Spanish Netherlands, the southern, largely Catholic Union of Arras got most of the large estates and most of the landowning nobility. The northern, officially Calvinist United

OTHER VOICES, OTHER VIEWS

The Ottoman Empire in the Seventeenth Century

For the Ottomans, as for their neighbors, the seventeenth century was one of virtually uninterrupted warfare and internal unrest. The century opened and closed with a series of wars against the Habsburgs. In between, there were conflicts with the Venetians, the Poles, and the Russians. For the most part, the Ottomans won their external wars, but waging them, once again, required the increasing of taxes, something local leaders and landowners resented. Waging wars also increased Ottoman dependence on the class of warriors known as the Janissaries. Janissaries were Christian boys, forced or bribed to convert to Islam and to serve the state. This was the sultan's way of getting around arming his nobles, and of creating an elite loyal only to the central state. But the Janissaries had to be paid, and when, in the seventeenth century, the sultans occasionally tried to debase the currency to raise extra cash, they staged a series of destabilizing revolts. Thus, the Ottomans had good reason to think that a move toward absolutism—the building of a centralized bureaucracy and army and the increasing of central-state control over the economy—might be advisable.

In 1656, factional fighting and a Janissary uprising threw Istanbul into a state of anarchy. In response, Sultan Mehmed IV (r. 1648–1687) appointed Koprülü Mehmed as grand vizier (chief minister) and gave him dictatorial powers. Over the next fifty years, the Koprülü family would monopolize the office of grand vizier and use it to subdue the Janissaries and take territory for the sultan in both the Mediterranean and central Europe. By 1683 the Ottoman Empire reached the summit of its territorial influence. Although the Ottomans were pushed back from Vienna for the last time that year, it still took several decades before Ottoman decline was noticeable to anyone but Ottoman intellectuals, some of whom had been predicting it since the mid-sixteenth century.

The Sultan's Court Just as in western Europe, the Ottoman sultan daily received visitors and petitioners, some of whom had traveled very long distances to seek his assistance or patronage, or to bring him tribute and gifts.

Ottoman absolutist reforms never fully succeeded. Though the Koprülü reforms helped defuse internal threats, over the next centuries the Ottomans' external enemies multiplied and gained in strength. Why did the reforms fail? In some ways the sultan, like the Russian czar, already had too much arbitrary power, and Mehmed's successors had no qualms about having anyone assassinated who displeased them, including viziers, Janissaries, and wives. The custom of retaining many wives presented sultans with the problem of too many possible heirs rather than too few. The result was continuous and sometimes murderous intrigue in the section of the palace called the harem, where the sultan's wives and children lived. On the other hand, like the Holy Roman emperors, the Ottoman sultans were too weak. Their empires were too decentralized and local privileges too strong; there were some older practices, such as provincial governors' power over local economic matters, that no sultan had the will or power to change. The combination of Russian-style arbitrariness and Habsburg-style weakness put the sultans at risk. In 1703, for example, Sultan Mustafa II (r. 1695–1703) was deposed by Janissaries who disapproved of a peace treaty he had signed with the infidel Habsburgs.

Ottoman absolutism, on the French, Russian, or Prussian model, did not take hold, but the Ottomans' decentralization actually gave them flexibility in dealing with internal factions. They did not found overseas colonies, but older forms of trade and tributary arrangements continued to provide relative prosperity to their subjects. Though battered by the long war with the Habsburgs that ended the century (1683–1699) and the even longer wars with their Persian rivals to the east, the Ottomans in 1700 still controlled an empire that embraced the eastern Mediterranean. Although they did not undertake long sea voyages, such as around the Horn of Africa or across the Atlantic to the New World, they were making a tidy profit on the luxury trades in the Mediterranean. Before his toppling, Mustafa II reigned over a population of some 30 million people and lodged in one of the finest palaces in the world, the Topkapi Palace in Istanbul. The Ottoman Empire did not follow the state-building model of some of its neighbors to the west, but it would prove longer lasting than many of Europe's absolutist kingdoms.

QUESTION | ***What characteristics of the Ottoman Empire prevented the development here of French-style absolutism?***

Provinces of the Netherlands got many centers of trade, including the increasingly important port of Amsterdam. As a small, densely urbanized, and heavily commercial state more similar to Venice or Genoa than to France or Poland, the United Provinces had no need for a monarch to break down traditional privileges or to raise taxes in order to form a modern army and build a modern state bureaucracy. Thus, the United Provinces modernized in another way, one that fit the state's unique geographic and demographic profile.

Clamoring for independence and unwilling to bend to Spanish rule, the United Provinces began to call itself the Dutch Republic. It adopted a novel form of governance in which each of the seven provinces elected delegates to a federal States General. Each province also elected an executive officer, but in times of war, these executive officers were subordinate to a single military commander called a *stadtholder.* Often the *stadtholder* came from the house of Orange-Nassau, as had the great sixteenth-century hero, William of Orange. But Dutch republicans resisted attempts to make the office hereditary. Only the provinces' wealthiest men were permitted to vote, but still, this right made the United Provinces a republic, a somewhat singular form of government in the seventeenth century. After the Peace of Westphalia gave the United Provinces full independence, the Dutch retained this form of governance along with a tradition of religious toleration they had developed in response to the persecutions going on in their neighboring states. This policy of toleration, though far from perfect, meant that exiles and heretics from elsewhere streamed into the Dutch Republic. Eager to work and to live comfortably, the newcomers were also willing to contribute to their new communities by serving in local militias or by donating to new civic institutions such as orphanages and workhouses for the unemployed. The Dutch were notoriously intolerant toward people who broke God's laws, such as prostitutes and gamblers, because they did not perform what the Dutch called honest work.

Modernization in the United Provinces was driven chiefly by geographic circumstances: proximity to the sea and a shortage of arable land. Centuries earlier the Dutch had pioneered the draining of marshes and the building of canals. In the seventeenth century, state-backed loans allowed ordinary citizens to pour more capital into these projects, yielding new land for cultivation and accelerating the transport of goods. The Dutch built on Italian innovations to develop investment tools such as banks and joint stock companies, which provided ordinary citizens sufficient means to expand these activities and to make themselves Europe's richest citizens in the seventeenth century (see also Chapter 15).

The republican political system of the United Provinces did not prevent the Dutch from seeking to establish colonies of their own. On founding the Dutch East India Company in 1602, Dutch merchants quickly pushed their Portuguese rivals out of the islands that now form Indonesia (then known as the Dutch East Indies) and off the African coast. Setting up shop in new places, the Dutch quickly became the dominant traders in nutmeg, cloves, cinnamon, pepper, and salt. They soon added a lively trade in Caribbean sugar and African slaves, as well. And they established trading relationships with the Chinese and the Japanese and set up colonies in South Africa, New Amsterdam (now New York), the West Indies, and throughout Southeast Asia (see Map 15.2, p. 473). The Dutch Republic survived as a formidable military power into the eighteenth century despite growing rivalry with another up-and-coming commercial empire, England, where the struggle to stave off absolutism ended with the establishment of history-changing models of parliamentary governance and the protection of individual rights.

The Defeat of Absolutism in England

When Elizabeth I of England died in 1603, still wearing rouge and pearls, the crown passed to a man who was already a king, James VI of Scotland, son of Mary Stuart, queen of Scots. Known as the union of the crowns, this coupling of Scotland and England resulted in a double title for James. He would hereafter be James I and VI. In addition, the union of crowns put on the English throne a man who was a staunch Anglican and who had already produced two sons and a daughter, heirs who would secure the continuation of the Stuart line now that the Tudors had died out. James was nothing like his vain cousin Elizabeth. He drooled, wore threadbare clothes, and was terrified of water, which meant he rarely washed. If he was shabby, however, James was also endowed with a formidable intellect, and he took his mission to unite England and Scotland very seriously. He once leapt off his horse at the Scottish-English border and laid his body across it, hoping to prove that one king could indeed span two kingdoms.

Why did absolutism fail in England?

Like Holy Roman Emperor Ferdinand II, James, as ruler of England, Scotland, and Ireland, had to try to build a state in a period in which Protestantism, and especially radical new forms of it, were spreading like wildfire. Scotland was already heavily Presbyterian; in London, many merchants and skilled workers had become nonconformists, choosing not to conform to the rituals and beliefs of England's only legal religious institution, the Anglican Church. Some "godly" Anglicans—called Puritans by their critics—demanded the stripping away of the rituals and rich church furnishings that reminded them of Catholicism. James believed that God had appointed him to rule his domains and to protect his church, and he was not about to let Presbyterians or Puritans call the shots. But James did not, like Ferdinand, provoke a showdown with the firebrands, nor simply murder his opponents, as did Ivan the Terrible. Nor did he, like Louis XIII and XIV, refuse to consult his representative assembly. According to English

The King James Bible

Particularly eager to gain the king's favor were those Anglicans who wanted to strip the church of rituals and corruptions that reminded them all too much of Catholicism. They called themselves the godly; critics dubbed them Puritans. In pamphlets and public debates, they attacked "pomp-fed" and "dumb dog" priests as well as the 1552 *Book of Common Prayer,* the manual that prescribed the rituals of the Anglican Church. In 1603 they circulated a petition, in which they demanded reform and asked James to convene a council to discuss religious matters. James resented their attacks on his church, but instead of instead of locking them up, he opted for an unusual approach to peacemaking: he commissioned a new translation of the Bible.

The Bible project began with a conference in December 1603, attended, at James's request, not by "brainsick and heady preachers," but by serious scholars representing both Puritan and orthodox Anglican points of view.[5] At the conference, James denounced the Geneva Bible, the English translation made by Calvinist exiles in the 1550s. Favored by Presbyterians and Puritans, the Geneva Bible was antiroyalist and anticlerical. It made scathing references to tyrants and provided extensive marginal notes so that individual readers could understand the text without needing clergymen to interpret it for them. Of course, the Bible translation used in the Anglican Church, the Bishops' Bible of 1568, was also partisan. It featured a frontispiece depicting Elizabeth and her bishops as the source of religious authority in the kingdom; its language was awkward and frequently obscure.

James was no Puritan, but he recognized that the Bishops' Bible did nothing to bring discerning Christians into the Anglican fold. Thus, his company of fifty-four scholars spent years stitching together and reworking existing translations to produce a Bible worthy of their king. Subsequently known as the King James Version, this Bible combined the clarity of the Geneva translation—without the footnotes—with poetic phrasings intended to highlight God's majesty and authority. This was a Bible meant to defang Puritan critics, but also to unify James's subjects in common reverence for the majesty of God and the poetic power of the scriptures. By examining a short passage from Psalm 23, we can see how much James's translators depended on the Geneva Bible—and how much less elegant the Bishop's Bible sounds to the ear. We can also see how subtle changes in the King James Version make it the most poetic of the three:

> *King James Bible*
> The Lord is my shepherd; I shall not want. He maketh me to lie down in green pastures: he leadeth me beside the still waters. He restoreth my soul: he leadeth me in the paths of righteousness for his name's sake.
>
> *Geneva Bible*
> The Lord is my shepherd, I shall not want. He maketh me to rest in green pasture and leadeth me by the still waters. He restoreth my soul, and leadeth me in the paths of righteousness for his name's sake.
>
> *Bishops' Bible*
> God is my shepheard; therefore I can lack nothing. He will cause myself to repose me in a pasture full of grass, and he will lead me unto calm waters. He will convert my soul and will bring me forth into the paths of righteousness for his name's sake.

Completed in 1611, the King James Bible did not become every Englishman's Bible; even after James prohibited the publishing of the Geneva Bible in 1616 and made the King James Version the only Authorized Version of the Bible in English, Puritans and Presbyterians continued to smuggle the Genevan version in from Holland and Switzerland. But the King James Bible was used for centuries in the Church of England and by generations of English-speaking writers, poets, politicians, and theologians throughout the world. It is the source for numerous idioms still used in everyday conversation, including "by the skin of his teeth," "no rest for the wicked," and "a fly in the ointment." The King James Bible has become a nearly invisible part of the language and heritage of English speakers, in England and abroad. We forget too easily that for King James, this synthetic, poetic translation of the scriptures was a political act, meant to shore up the king's authority—and to make peace.

Episode 7. Part II. THE TRANSLATORS PRESENTING BIBLE TO JAMES I.

King James Gets His Bible In 1611, the scholars charged by King James I of England with the task of producing a new, authorized Bible in English completed their work and presented to their patron what would now be known as the King James Version of the Scriptures. This version of the Bible would thereafter exert an enormous impact on the English language and on English literature.

QUESTIONS | ***Why did King James order a new version of the Bible? How did it differ from its predecessors?***

law, he *had* to get Parliament's consent in matters of taxation. Instead, James chose a moderate course, mollifying moderate and peaceful nonconformists and persecuting or forcing into exile only the most radical critics of the church. Thus, in the very first year of his reign, he took as his motto "blessed are the peacemakers," a motto he would try to employ in the religious as well as the political realm.

Wily and hardworking, James kept the peace even as war exploded on the continent, and political and religious tensions mounted at home. By the 1620s, however, it was clear that James's ambivalent policies had both emboldened and further radicalized critics of the church and king. On his ascent to the throne, James's son Charles I (r. 1625–1649) would learn that his father's peacemaking had not wiped out differences between Scots and Englishmen, between Puritans and Anglicans, or between parliamentarians and the crown. In fact, all now claimed the right to be consulted about how the kingdom should be run.

Charles I and the English Civil War

The year 1625, Charles I's first as king, was a rough one. He ascended the throne during an outbreak of plague, and, having immediately plunged the country into war against Spain, he saw the army's first campaign fail miserably. He married the same year, but his queen, the Catholic sister of Louis XIII, Henrietta Marie, proved hugely unpopular. The next years were equally rocky. Each time he asked for a war subsidy, Parliament protested bitterly before finally giving in. During one standoff, Charles lectured them: "Remember that Parliaments are altogether in my power for their calling, sitting, and dissolution. Therefore, as I find the fruits of them good or evil, they are to continue or not. . . ."[6] Members of the House of Commons, in particular, balked at Charles's high-handed manner, as well as his imprisonment of those who refused to pay the new taxes. In 1628 the House of Commons issued a Petition of Right, insisting on its traditional privilege to approve taxes and objecting to Charles's imposition of something akin to martial law. Charles accepted the Petition with ill grace and in 1629 decided that he would no longer do battle with Parliament, but rule alone.

The period of Charles I's so-called Personal Rule lasted from 1629 until 1641 and was marked by religious as well as political strife. Charles's attempt to reform local government seemed intrusive to rural nobles; his ship tax—England's first yearly tax on income—outraged city dwellers. His appointment of William Laud, a high church Anglican, as archbishop of Canterbury in 1633, provoked further outrage. Laud liked stained glass, candles, and rich vestments, proof to some of the "godly" that he was in league with the Anti-Christ, the pope. The real problem was not only that Laud liked these things, but also that he moved to force all Anglican communities in England, Scotland, and Ireland to worship in the way he did. The reaction was fierce, but even more violent was Presbyterian reaction to Laud's attempt to impose a new, Anglican prayer book on Scotland in 1637. When the Scottish archbishop tried to hold mass according to the new book at St. Giles Cathedral in Edinburgh, a riot erupted, and the archbishop narrowly escaped with his life. The Scots banded together and in 1638 signed a National Covenant, swearing to defend the Presbyterian Church to the death—some signed with their own blood. In 1639 they marched to the English border.

Charles called out an army, which, though badly paid, managed to halt the Scots and convince them to call a truce. The king feared the truce would not last and desperately needed money. Finally, in April 1640 he was forced to call Parliament to fund the raising of a new army. Parliament refused, insisting that reforms come first. After only three weeks in session, Charles dissolved what became known as the short Parliament and called another. The next batch of deputies proved equally intent on reform and demanded that Charles ensure the regular meeting of Parliaments, remove his evil councilors, and end Laud's reforms. At first Charles seemed amenable to these demands, even allowing Laud to be imprisoned in the Tower of London. Emboldened, Puritans demanded even more reform; some sought to purify the churches by shattering their stained glass and painting over Baroque murals.

Reacting to this militant Protestantism and centuries of Anglican persecution, the Irish rose in rebellion in March 1641. Releasing pent-up hostilities, Irish rioters savagely set upon their Protestant overlords, massacring an estimated 12,000 people; rumors circulated that 500,000 were dead. Fear of a Catholic invasion swept England, causing townsfolk to hide in caves and women to suffer miscarriages. In the chaos, Charles moved to head off a supposed plot to imprison his Catholic wife, Henrietta. He charged five key figures of Parliament with treason and sought to lock them up. These actions convinced the reformers that the king was about to reverse course and destroy Parliament's newly won power. As London turned against him, the king found he had to flee his own capital city. Leading Puritan parliamentarians seized control of the army, and Charles was left to raise his own troops among conformist Anglicans and nobles loyal to the throne.

Civil war between the parliamentary and the royalist or "cavalier" armies erupted in the summer of 1642. The royalists long held sway in the north and west, while the parliamentarians commanded the south and east, including the city of London (Map 14.5). The parliamentary army was better organized and in command of more resources than the king's forces, and boasted skillful and charismatic leaders, the most important of whom was a country gentleman named Oliver Cromwell (1599–1658). As in the Thirty Years' War, soldiers on both sides often relied on looting and pillaging for survival and spent a great deal of time laying siege to one another's cities, but also fought with swords, poleaxes, and matchlocks at close range. By 1644 the tide was turning in Parliament's favor. The queen, with her sons Charles and James, escaped to France. In 1646, after the battle of Naseby, Cromwell's army captured the king.

Trial and Regicide

Parliamentary forces were now faced with a dilemma: what should be done with the king? Charles, they believed, had become a tyrant, rather than a benevolent father, to his people. But he would not admit that that was so. As a captive, he continued to insist on his right to rule, and for two years, royalists tried numerous tricks to rescue him. Many members of Parliament hoped to compel the king to negotiate a settlement, but Cromwell and the army wanted to secure their achievements. For them, the only option was regicide, the killing of the king. But the trick was to do it without drawing sympathy for his cause. "This is not a thing done in a corner," Cromwell insisted. There would have to be a trial.

The trial of King Charles I was a first in European history. Never before had a people made their ruler subordinate to the law, nor was it easy to get Parliament to vote to try His Majesty (see Back to the Source at the end of the chapter). The military had to surround the chambers and allow in only the delegates who would be sure to vote their way. Charles never admitted Parliament's right to try him, and in the end, only twenty-six members condemned him to death and signed his death warrant.

Absolutism on Trial This contemporary image of the trial of Charles I depicts the courtroom, with the judges facing the viewer (the chief judge in the center). The king faces the court, still wearing his hat, which he refuses to remove.

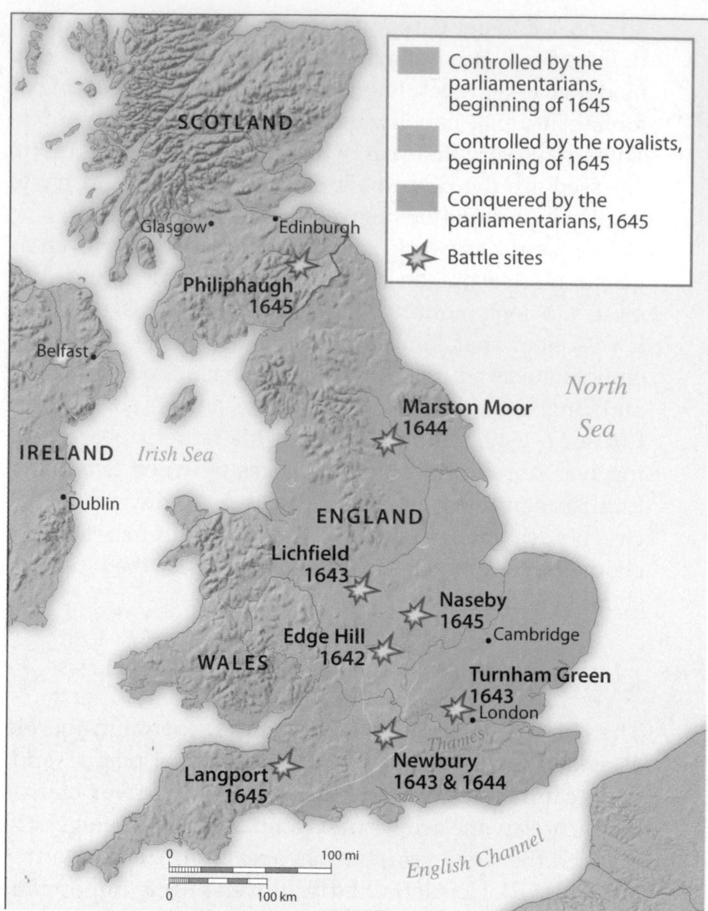

MAP 14.5 | English Civil Wars

This map shows the areas of parliamentary strength as the war began to turn in its favor in 1645. Note that London, by far the richest and most populated city, is easily inside parliamentary territory. ***Why did Charles I look to the more rural west of England and Wales for supporters?***

On the morning of January 30, 1649, Charles was marched from the chambers in which he had been imprisoned to his execution. As it was a very cold day, Charles wore an extra shirt so that he would not shiver before the crowds that gathered to watch in front of Whitehall Palace, the king's major residence. With drums beating, Charles stepped onto the scaffold. Pushing his long hair under a nightcap, he lay his head on the block. One blow of the executioner's heavy axe sufficed to sever the king's head from his body. As was customary, the executioner held up the severed head for the spectators to see it. By most accounts, the crowd greeted the sight with a mighty groan. Parliament, acting in the name of the people of England, had killed their king. Absolutism, to the degree it existed in seventeenth-century England, was dead, and England was declared a republic, or commonwealth.

CHRONOLOGY	Key Events in England, 1629–1689
DATE	EVENT
1629–1641	Personal Rule
1642–1648	English Civil War
1649	Charles I executed
1660	Charles II restored
1685–1689	Rule of James II
1688–1689	Glorious Revolution

The Commonwealth

In the wake of Charles's death, the parliamentarians had to deal with schisms in their own ranks, with renewed violence in Ireland, and with royalists on the Scottish border. Cromwell, who emerged as leader of the movement, dealt with the trouble in Ireland by force. His army massacred thousands, and he kept the peace by settling demobilized troops there, much to the cost of Irish Catholics. Eventually, he cleared the royalists from Scotland, too, sending Charles I's son—who was already calling himself Charles II—into exile in France.

Cromwell found schism within his own ranks harder to deal with. He abolished the monarchy—assuming the role of Lord Protector of the Commonwealth in 1653—and ended Anglicanism's dominance as the established religion. He allowed for a certain amount of religious toleration and even invited Jews to settle in England for the first time in four hundred years. But some of his supporters wanted more radical religious and political reform. Some wanted to make England a grand-scale Geneva, under the rule of the godly. Others, called Levelers, wanted to abolish property qualifications and give all men the vote. Some went so far as to support the redistribution of all property to make all Englishmen truly equal. Cromwell managed to crush the Levelers, but the godly proved more intractable. Parliament enacted a series of godly provisions: immoral acts, such as playing cards or celebrating Christmas, were banned, and adultery and blasphemy were to be punished with death (though few were actually sentenced). But new and more radical sects—such as the Adamites, who insisted on going naked, as Adam did—seemed to appear daily, and to find backers in Parliament. When Cromwell and the army could take no more, they locked the House of Commons and Cromwell pocketed the key, announcing that God made him do it.

England's Colonies

Cromwell and his backers were concerned not only about religion, but also about the English economy, and in 1651 the Commonwealth passed the Navigation Acts, which required that all goods imported from Europe or the Americas arrive in the British Isles on English ships. This legislation was targeted at the Dutch, who were profiting greatly from the carrying trade, and it resulted in a great windfall for English shippers, who now had a monopoly on the increasingly lucrative trade in sugar, slaves, and other commodities (see Chapter 15). Not surprisingly, the Navigation Acts incited a series of trade wars between the English and the Dutch between 1652 and 1674, during which the English seized New Amsterdam and renamed it New York.

Beginning in 1620, Puritan settlers had founded English colonies along North America's Atlantic seaboard, and other English and Scots settlers gradually followed them. Both England's kings and its Lord Protector saw colonial expansion as a good idea, and over the course of the seventeenth century, England's rulers provided the financial backing and occasional military assistance that allowed its traders and planters to lay claim to more and more territory in present-day New England, Canada, and the Caribbean. Increasingly these colonies become neo-Englands, sharing the language, religion, and culture of the mother country, but without enjoying the right to representation in Parliament. Although in terms of domestic policies Cromwell's Commonwealth could not have been more different from the absolute monarchy of Louis XIV, both regimes recognized that long-distance trade and colonization would be fundamental to building powerful new states for the future.

In 1658, Oliver Cromwell died. Parliament honored the Lord Protector's desire to have his son Richard succeed him, but Richard proved an ineffectual leader. Moreover, he could not find a lender to finance the enormous debts incurred in the course of the civil wars. In spring 1660, a group of leading figures decided that restoring the Stuart Dynasty was the only practical option, and they invited Charles I's eldest son (also named Charles) to return from French exile and make England a monarchy once more.

The Restoration

On May 8, 1660, cheering crowds greeted Charles II and his younger brother James as they paraded through the streets of London on their way to Whitehall Palace. Charles moved quickly to assure those hostile to his return that he would forgive and forget past differences if he could have their loyalty in the future, and he avenged himself only on the regicides, who were rounded up and executed. Oliver Cromwell had already died, but his body was symbolically hanged and his severed head displayed over the entrance to the House of Parliament. Charles II (r. 1660–1685) reestablished the Church of England and called a new Parliament, this one well stocked with cavaliers. Unwilling to unleash a new civil war, he did not, however, try to impose religious uniformity or political absolutism, as had his father. He filled his court with his mistresses rather than with Bible-translators, but ominously, too, with Catholics, including his brother James, next in line for the throne. This would not have mattered had Charles II sired a legitimate, Protestant heir. But he did not, and by the later 1670s the succession question began to disturb the restoration settlement.

Charles understood that the nation was dead set against having another Catholic king. The memory of the siege of Magdeburg was still fresh, and his subjects, especially the Puritans and Presbyterians, were terrified that a Catholic ruler might undo the English Reformation. But he believed his Stuart line had been appointed by God to take the throne, and thus he refused to go along with Parliament's desire to exclude James from the succession.

In the course of the raging debates over this question, known as the Exclusion Crisis, the first real political parties developed. Those who opposed James and wished to have Parliament choose a new king were called **Whigs.** Those who made the case for James's legitimate succession were called **Tories.** Both terms were derogatory, but telling. *Tory* was a term originally used to describe Irish bandits, who were of course Catholic. Tories were staunch backers of the king and the Anglican Church, whom opponents wanted to portray as closet Catholics. The term *Whig* was also originally a derogatory term, used for Scottish bandits, especially those of fanatical Presbyterian beliefs. Whigs were in many ways the descendants of the moderate parliamentarians of the civil war era and were usually proponents of parliamentary sovereignty. Most despised Catholicism and thought Anglicanism dangerously "popish." A combination of political and religious allegiances, then, laid the foundations for the party politics of England long after the English Civil War had ended.

The Glorious Revolution

After dissolving several pro-exclusion Parliaments, Charles prevailed and James did succeed to the throne in 1685, in part on the expectation that one of his Protestant daughters (Mary and Anne) would take the throne when he died. But his succession was not without violence. Soon after his coronation, James had to use his army to crush an attempted Protestant coup, and in the aftermath ordered three hundred gentry executed and eight hundred conspirators sent to the West Indies as serfs. Then, worried about the stability of his regime, he began to promote Catholics to positions of power in the army, judiciary, and Parliament. Both Tories and Whigs resented these actions, but the breaking point came when James's second wife, who was Catholic, produced a male heir

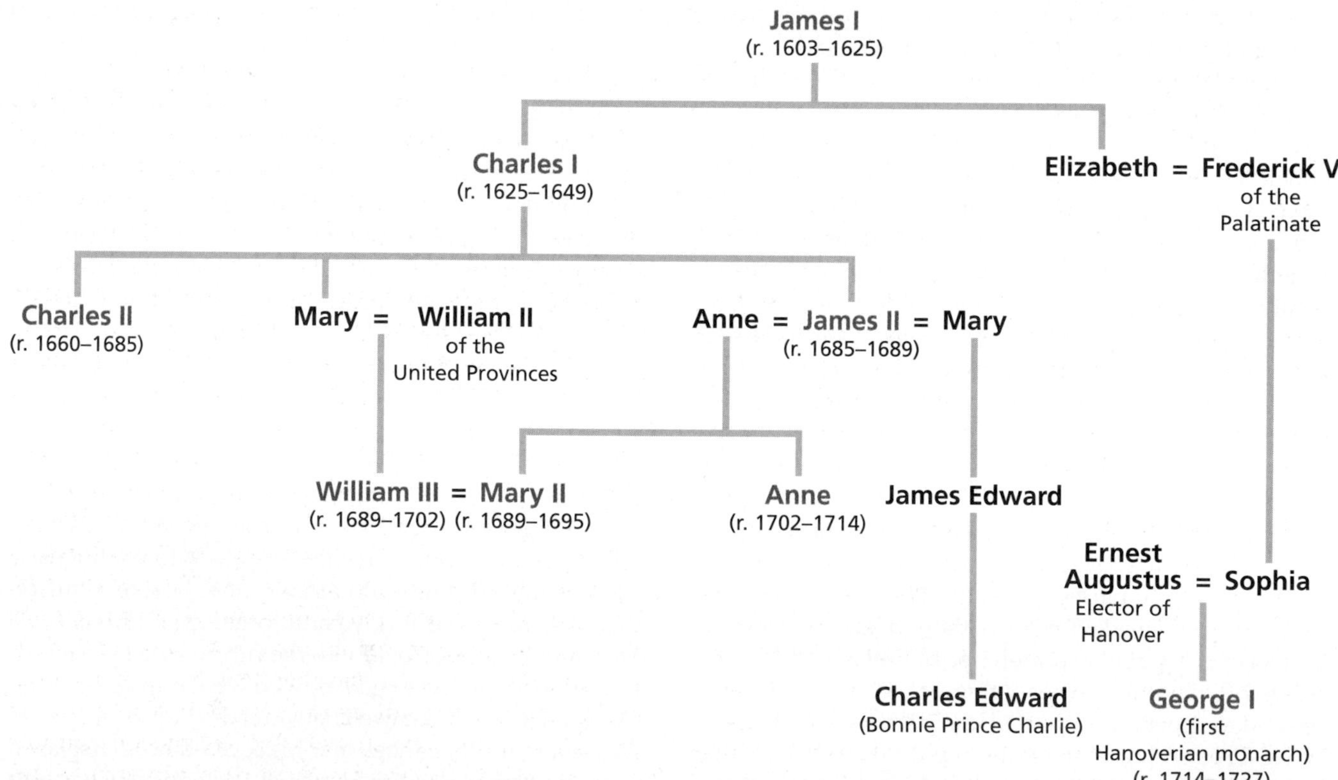

FIGURE 14.2 | The House of Stuart

This figure shows how the English crown descended through the Stuart line, and finally passed to the Hanoverians after the death of Queen Anne in 1714. ***Which of these monarchs did not die in office?***

in 1688. The baby, James Edward Stuart, signaled that a line of Catholic kings would now rule England, a situation both Tories and Whigs found intolerable. Leaders in Parliament sent out feelers to the Dutch prince William of Orange and his wife Mary, James's eldest daughter and a Protestant, both of whom could claim to be next in line for the English throne. They were willing to seize the moment, and in late 1688, William landed in England, commencing the largely bloodless coup known as the Glorious Revolution.

James II and his supporters fled first to Scotland, his grandfather's homeland, and then to France. William and Mary agreed to a Bill of Rights in which they consented to call elections for Parliament regularly and to allow their subjects to petition them without fearing persecution for their opinions. Hereafter, they promised, the English king or queen would not interfere with the operation of the law, nor impose taxes without Parliament's assent. The provisions of the English Bill of Rights amounted to an agreement on the part of the monarchy to share power with Parliament—a move diametrically opposed to absolutist doctrine. Moreover, the monarchs agreed to tie the hands of their heirs in religious matters. At Parliament's insistence, Catholics were banned from the succession. The Church of England remained the established church, and its members retained privileged status in society, but Puritans and Presbyterians were allowed to worship as they pleased.

Under William and Mary, political stability was established without resort to absolutist measures. The monarchs allowed a virtually free press to flourish. They agreed to abide by laws made by Parliament and refrained from persecuting their political opponents—with the exception of Irish or colonial subjects who demanded home rule. All these measures gave English subjects—especially those who were Protestant, male, and middle class or above—a much greater measure of individual liberty and prosperity than could be enjoyed by other Europeans at the time. Stabilization achieved by sharing power with Parliament was so successful that even though neither William and Mary, nor Mary's sister Anne I (r. 1702–1714), produced children to inherit the throne, the crown passed to a German (Protestant) descendant of James I, George I of the house of Hanover (r. 1714–1727), without any whisper of a new rebellion. Absolutism was defeated, though monarchy, the Church of England, and the aristocracy remained firmly in control.

Conclusion

The seventeenth century was an era of terrible wars and catastrophes, of witch hunts, civil wars, and famines. At the center of the century, responsible for much of the chaos, was the disastrous Thirty Years' War, which carried away perhaps a quarter of the population of central Europe and Spain and bankrupted governments across the continent. It destabilized regimes, generating civil wars in England, Spain, and France. Although the Peace of Westphalia of 1648 resulted in few territorial changes, it marked a great change in the attitude of European sovereigns toward the re-formation of the church. The war proved that Europeans would have to live in a Christendom divided among Catholics, Lutherans, Calvinists, and other sects. Never again would Europeans engage in grand-scale warfare for primarily religious ends.

In response to the Thirty Years' War, and to the other crises of the century, many monarchs attempted to consolidate and centralize their states; their successes and failure contributed much to changes in the continent's balance of power. Though often brutal, these absolutist regimes were often modernizing ones, able to raise armies and taxes more efficiently. France, for example, by 1700 could boast Europe's largest army and a network of overseas colonies, and Louis XIV's Versailles, whose elaborately patterned gardens and glittering Hall of Mirrors reflected the glory and orderly kingdom of the Sun King, had begun to eclipse even Baroque Rome. Those who aspired to establish absolutism but lacked the economic power or will to modernize, as in Spain, fell off the pace, as did formerly powerful kingdoms such as Sweden and Poland-Lithuania, both battered, like Spain, by long periods of warfare. Meanwhile, absolutist Russia and Prussia began to build their own empires in the east. But lacking access to Atlantic ports, neither developed the commercial and colonial economies that, by 1700, had begun to yield rich profits to the Dutch, the English, and the French.

A few states managed to both modernize and avoid absolutism, as did England, which quickly became an economic powerhouse and a political model for reform-minded people on the continent. On the whole, Europe's states in the north and west, especially the Netherlands, England, and France, ended the century with a greater share of European power, influence, and prosperity than they had had in 1600, in part because they had begun to exploit their opportunities to trade and colonize in the rest of the world. The crises of the seventeenth century had changed Europe's balance of power internally and globally and opened the way for new opportunities as well as new tensions in the decades ahead.

Critical Thinking Questions

1. What challenges and opportunities did European monarchs face in the seventeenth century?
2. In what ways did the Thirty Years' War alter the course of European history? Did it resolve any dilemmas or disputes? Could you pick a winner, or is it more accurate to say that all sides lost more than they gained?
3. Compare and contrast the absolutist regimes of Louis XIV in France and Charles I in England with the regimes of Fredrick William II of Prussia and Peter the Great of Russia. Where was absolutism more "absolute"?

Key Terms

absolutism **(p. 424)**
divine right **(p. 424)**
natural law **(p. 434)**
Estates General **(p. 437)**
parlements **(p. 437)**
intendants **(p. 437)**
Fronde **(p. 437)**
Versailles **(p. 437)**
Junkers **(p. 440)**
Whig **(p. 452)**
Tory **(p. 452)**

Primary Sources in Connect

1. **James I Defends Absolutism**
2. **Luis Granada,"Meditations for Monday Morning"**
3. **The Trial of Jean Williford for Witchcraft in Faversham, Kent, in 1645**
4. **Hugo Grotius, *The Freedom of the Seas***
5. **Thomas Hobbes, *Leviathan***
6. **Jacques Bossuet Defends Divine Right**
7. **The Absolutism of Peter the Great of Russia**

BACK TO THE SOURCE

The Trial of King Charles I, 1649

In January 1649, the remaining members of the Long Parliament accused Charles I of treason. Even before the outbreak of the civil wars, they argued, he had put himself above the law and had become a tyrant, and in so doing, he had provoked cruel and bloody wars. Not willing to make Charles a martyr, the parliamentarians decided that they would try the king before Parliament, sitting as the kingdom's highest court of justice. Brought before them, Charles denied that Parliament, or any earthly court, had the right to try him. On being seated the king refused to take off his hat (signifying he had no respect for the court or his prosecutor, Parliament's lord president, John Bradshaw) or to enter a plea to the charges against him.[7]

King: I would know by what power I am called hither . . . and when I know what lawful authority, I shall answer. Remember I am your king, your lawful king, and what sins you bring upon your heads, and the judgment of God upon this land; think well upon it, I say, think well upon it, before you go further from one sin to a greater; therefore let me know by what lawful authority I am seated here, and I shall not be unwilling to answer. In the meantime, I shall not betray my trust; I have a trust committed to me by God, by old and lawful descent; I will not betray it, to answer to a new unlawful authority. . . .

Lord President: If you had been pleased to have observed what was hinted to you by the Court, at your first coming hither, you would have known by what authority; which authority requires you, in the name of the people of England, of which you are elected king, to answer them.

King: No. Sir, I deny that.

Lord President: If you acknowledge not the authority of the Court, they must proceed.

King: I do tell them so: England was never an elective kingdom, but an hereditary kingdom, for near these thousand years; therefore let me know by what authority I am called hither. I do stand for more the Liberty of my people, than any here that come to be my pretended Judges; and therefore let me know by what lawful authority I am seated here, and I will answer it: otherwise I will not answer it. . . .

For the rest of that day, and the one following, the king refused to enter a plea. On January 27 the king entered the chambers to cries of "Execution! Justice! Execution!" but still declined to acknowledge the court's jurisdiction. The weary lord president offered a long speech before reading the sentence. Here is a segment of that speech:

Lord President: Sir, you have held yourself, and let fall such language, as if you had been in no way subject to the law, or that the law had not been your superior. Sir, the Court is very sensible of it, and I hope so are all the understanding people of England, that the law is your superior; that you ought to have ruled according to the law; you ought to have [done] so. Sir, I know very well your pretence hath been that you have done so; but, Sir, the difference hath been who shall be the expositors of this law: Sir, whether you and your party, out of courts of justice, shall take upon them to expound law, or the courts of justice, who are the expounders? Nay, the Sovereign and the High Court of Justice, the Parliament of England, that are not only the highest expounders, but the sole makers of the law? Sir, for you to set yourself with your single judgment, and those that adhere unto you, to set yourself against the highest Court of Justice, that is not law. Sir, as the law is your Superior, so truly, Sir, there is something that is superior to the law, and that is indeed the Parent or Author of the Law, and that is the people of England. . . . Sir, the Charge hath called you Tyrant, a Traitor, a Murderer, and a Public Enemy to the Commonwealth of England. . . .

King: Ha!

Lord President: Truly Sir, We have been told "Rex est dum bene regit, Tyrannus qui populum opprimit":* And if that be the definition of a Tyrant, then see how you come short of it in your actions. . . .

Charles still refused to acknowledge either Parliament's right to try him or the truth of the charges—how could a divinely appointed monarch be charged with treason by his people? Thus, the high court simply silenced him, and sentenced him to death.

QUESTIONS | *How does Charles in this episode reveal his pretentions to be an absolute monarch? On what grounds did the lord president claim Charles could be tried by this court?*

Source: State Trials, ed. H. L. Stephens (London, 1899), 371–380.

*He is a king while he rules well, and a tyrant if he oppresses the people.

GLOSSARY

absolutism A form of government in the seventeenth and eighteenth centuries, in which the monarch had the right to rule without legal opposition to his or her authority.

acropolis The common defensible high spot or hilly area of a polis.

Act of Supremacy An English law passed by Parliament in 1534 that established the monarch as the supreme religious authority in the realm with the right to determine church doctrine and practice.

ad fontes The Italian Renaissance humanist drive to return to primary sources and to treat them critically.

aedile Magistrate of the people, guardian of public property.

agon The ancient Greek belief that life was a constant struggle or competition.

agora The marketplace of a polis.

Agricultural Revolution of Prehistory The birth and spread of agriculture 8000–5000 BCE.

alchemy The medieval study of chemistry, concerned primarily with turning base metals into gold.

Allied Powers The alliance of countries opposed to the Axis Powers during WWII, including the Soviet Union, Great Britain, and the United States.

Americanization The influence and presence of American products and practices, most notably mass consumerism, mass production, fast food, Coca-Cola, and Hollywood movies.

Anabaptists Members of a sectarian movement that emerged in the sixteenth century who believed in adult baptism.

anarchism A nineteenth- and early-twentieth-century ideology that viewed the state as a tool of bourgeois interests and thus rejected participation in parliamentary politics in favor of revolutionary action.

anomie The term used by sociologist Emile Durkheim to indicate alienation felt in impersonal modern industrial societies.

anti-pope One elected in opposition to a pope duly elected by church law and custom.

apostate One who lapses from the faith.

apotheosis The transformation of a man into a god.

appeasement The foreign policy of making concessions to satisfy an aggressor; used most notably by Great Britain and France in the late 1930s to avoid war with Nazi Germany.

Archaic Age The Greek period running from 800 BCE to 500 BCE.

arête The pursuit of individual excellence in ancient Greece.

Arianism The doctrine of Arius, a priest from Alexandria and his followers called Arians, who claimed that Christ was subsequent (since his human nature was created) to God the Father and therefore less divine.

Arsenal Located at the mouth of Venice's Grand Canal, the Arsenal equipped and repaired the republic's warships and its merchant vessels.

art nouveau Literally meaning "new art"; a movement in art, architecture, and design from the 1890s to 1914 that incorporated stylized natural forms.

assignat Paper money issued by the French Revolutionary government; replaced by the franc.

astrolabe A device used to measure the angle of the Pole Star relative to the horizon while at sea.

augury Reading the will of the gods and signs of the future by studying the flight of birds.

avant-garde Term meaning "ahead of the rest"; used by movements at the end of the nineteenth century celebrating art considered ahead of its time; associated with elitism and social radicalism.

Axis Powers World War II alliance among Germany, Italy, and Japan and other countries.

balkanize To divide an area such as the landmass of Europe into many rival powers, none able to dominate the others.

barbarian A term used by late Romans to describe the Germans as an uncivilized people who spoke an incomprehensible language and were uncivilized.

Baroque An art movement associated with the reformed Catholic Church that emphasized sumptuous, richly decorated churches and dramatic paintings and sculptures.

basilica A Christian church with a longitudinal axis formed by a nave and side aisles leading from an entranceway in the west to a choir and apse structure in the east.

Bauhaus School of architecture and industrial design that emerged in Germany in the 1920s. This new style insisted that modern buildings and furnishings should be both beautiful and useful.

benefice The land granted by a lord in exchange for the service and oath-bound loyalty of a vassal.

Black Death A term not used until the sixteenth century to describe the outbreak of the bubonic plague that struck Europe in the mid-fourteenth century.

Blitzkrieg A German term meaning "lightning war"; offensive military tactic used by Germany in World War II consisting of overwhelming a certain point in the enemy's defense with dive bombers, tanks, and motorized infantry, making it difficult for the enemy to repel the subsequent mass infantry attack.

Boers A Dutch word meaning farmers; used to describe settlers of Dutch extraction in South Africa.

Bolsheviks Russian communists led by Vladimir Lenin, who advocated a violent, immediate revolution to overthrow capitalism. The Bolsheviks toppled the provisional government in 1917 and became the founders of communism in the Soviet Union.

Bonfire of the Vanities In 1494 in Florence, the burning of books, paintings, cosmetics, and other material trifles as encouraged by Savonarola.

bourgeois Well-to-do members of the third estate, who usually resided in market towns (*bourgs*).

Bretton Woods system The economic framework signed in 1944 and put into effect after World War II in which the U.S. dollar served as the world's reserve currency, allowing international trade without extreme currency fluctuation. The World Bank and the International Monetary Fund were also established to facilitate economic growth and grant loans to countries for currency stabilization.

Brezhnev Doctrine Policy promulgated by Soviet premier Leonid Brezhnev stating that the Soviet Union had the right to intervene in its eastern European satellite states. It was used to justify Soviet suppression of the Prague Spring and other attempts at liberalization in the Eastern bloc.

British East India Company (BEIC) Founded in 1602, this state-chartered company was given monopoly trading rights in India. Between 1757 and 1858, the BEIC acted as a colonizing power in India.

bull A public letter or official proclamation issued by the pope.

Caesarian (or Consular) Faction Sometimes mistakenly called the First Triumvirate. Three magnates, Caesar, Pompey, and Crassus, joined together in an alliance without state sanction to seek power and advantage when one of them was consul, as occurred in 59 BCE when Caesar became consul.

capitularies Carolingian royal laws (pronouncements) issued in chapters (*capitula*) or itemized form by the king.

caravel A three-masted vessel that required a small crew and could hold 50–70 tons of cargo.

Caroline Minuscule A small, regular script that emerged during the reign of Charlemagne and was common in Europe until the twelfth century.

carrack A three-masted ship that was rigged with both square and triangular sails to catch any available wind; generally served as merchant vessels.

cartel An agreement among producers to coordinate prices, marketing, and production.

Central Powers The military alliance in World War I consisting of Germany, Austria-Hungary, Bulgaria, and the Ottoman Empire and opposed to the Entente.

chartered (joint-stock) companies Companies possessing a monopoly by the government and issuing stock to investors; established in the early seventeenth century by several nations (especially the English and Dutch) for the purpose of trade and exploration.

Chartism A reform movement among English workers and radicals that demanded universal suffrage and other political and social rights for the working classes.

Cheka The first of many Soviet secret police forces, charged with eliminating suspected enemies of the Bolsheviks through execution, internment in forced labor camps, and torture.

chiaroscuro The use of contrasting light and shadow in Italian Renaissance paintings to shade figures and give them an impression of three-dimensionality.

chivalry The code of conduct held by the elite warrior class or horsemen of medieval Europe.

Christian socialism A nineteenth-century mass political movement that sought to curb the excesses and inequalities of liberal capitalism, but opposed the idea of socialist revolution.

civic humanism The application of humanist thought to political and social problems, especially as humanists gained confidence that ancient ideals might be used to reform and enlighten their communities.

Civil Constitution of the Clergy Law passed by the National Assembly in 1790 turning the clergy into state employees and requiring the clergy to swear loyalty to the state.

civilization A higher organized form of historical and cultural life, often based on cities, and associated with settlements, a critical mass of people, agriculture, trade, government, law, writing, and abstract thought.

Classical Age Of ancient Greece, stretching from c. 500 to 404 BCE or the end of the Peloponnesian War.

clientage A Roman practice or institution under which an inferior citizen became the dependent or client of a superior. The patron expected loyal service from the client and provided the client with land, gifts, and money.

Code of Hammurabi A law code with nearly three hundred judgments issued by Hammurabi before 1750 BCE.

codex A book with pages bound between two covers as opposed to the papyrus roll.

Cold War Sustained ideological, economic, political, and military tension between the West, led by the United States, and the Communist bloc, led by the Soviet Union, from approximately 1945 to 1989.

collectivization Soviet policy starting in the late 1920s of replacing private farms with large cooperatives under state management.

Columbian Exchange The long-term, two-way transfer of peoples, goods, diseases, and ideas between Europe and the Americas.

Comintern International organization of communist parties directed from Moscow from 1919 to 1943.

Committee of Public Safety Board appointed by the convention to oversee the war effort and to choose members of the Revolutionary Tribunal, which tried suspected traitors; the *de facto* government in France during the Reign of Terror.

Commonwealth of Independent States (CIS) A loose association of former Soviet republics with the goal of coordinating trade and law enforcement.

commune In twelfth-century northern European towns, an association generally of burghers who agreed on local government, tolls, taxes, and the rights of townspeople. In the twelfth and thirteenth centuries in Italy, a form of government or city organization run by groups of citizens, at first by local, powerful, wealthy men and later with some degree of participation by middling landowners, merchants, shopkeepers, and members of trade guilds.

communism A revolutionary form of socialism, formulated by Karl Marx, that advocated overthrowing the bourgeoisie and industrial capitalism in order to give the proletariat ownership of the means of production.

Concert of Europe The intermittent efforts by Austria, Prussia, Russia, and France after the Congress of Vienna to cooperate in order to suppress revolution and keep peace in Europe.

conciliar movement A movement of high churchmen that held that a general council of the church, not the pope, had the authority to set the standards for proper governance for the church and Christian behavior.

Concordat A formal agreement between the papacy and a government regulating the affairs of the church.

Congress of Vienna The peace conference held in Vienna in 1814 and 1815 after Napoleon's defeat, at which the victorious powers (Britain, Austria, Russia, and Prussia) agreed to restore monarchies and cooperate to prevent future revolutions.

conquistador A term that refers to soldiers of fortune; conquerors, particularly of the Mexica and Inca Empires; or the leader of the forces leading those campaigns.

conservative (conservatism) An ideology that stressed order, traditional values, and the maintenance of aristocratic and clerical privileges; and opposed revolution and the implementation of liberal policies.

consuls Chief magistrates, a pair of whom were elected in the Roman Senate to hold office for a single year.

contact vulnerabilities The weak points (political, physical, cultural, etc.) exposed when alien peoples (e.g., native Americans and Europeans) came into contact for the first time in the fifteenth and sixteenth centuries.

Continental System Napoleon's embargo on British products from 1806 to 1814.

Convention Revolutionary government that followed the overthrow of Louis XVI. Ruling from September 1792 to November 1795, it was elected by universal manhood suffrage and marked by radical measures and excesses such as the Reign of Terror and de-Christianization.

converso A convert to Catholicism.

corvée The obligation of peasants to their lords to spend a few days making improvements, such as building roads.

cottage industries Sites of the in-home production of goods, often in villages.

covenant The binding agreement the ancient Hebrews made with God to abandon polytheism and follow but one god.

creoles People of mixed European and non-European ancestry.

cuneiform Wedge-shaped writing inscribed on wet clay tablets, stone, and other surfaces by the Mesopotamian peoples and others.

curule A throne or official chair of the Roman magistrate, adopted from the Etruscans.

Cynics Practitioners of Cynicism, a Hellenistic philosophy that rejected the conventional Hellenistic world and spurned religious piety, reverence for kings and kingdoms, and all hypocrisy.

Dada Artistic movement that emerged out of World War I, emphasizing silly forms and mirroring chaotic conditions in postwar society.

Dark Age The Greek period running from 1100 BCE to 800 BCE in which the Greeks left behind few material remains (buildings or artifacts).

Dayton Accords Peace agreement in 1995 ending the three-year-long war in the former Yugoslavia.

D-Day June 6, 1944; the opening day of the Allies' invasion of Nazi-occupied France.

deism Religious belief of the seventeenth and eighteenth centuries stating that God created the universe and established its laws of operation but did not subsequently intervene in its affairs or those of humans.

Delian League A league located initially on the island of Delos that was formed by Athens to resist any further aggression toward Greece by the Persian Empire.

demos Masses, or people; free male native residents, non-noble, but of some standing and wealth in the Greek polis.

détente Term meaning "relaxation"; refers to the period of easing of tensions between the western powers and the Communist bloc in the 1970s.

devolution The process of passing power to regional assemblies, as practiced particularly by Great Britain in 1997–1998.

devotio moderna Emerging in late-fourteenth-century Europe, the new or modern form of devotion that emphasized individual education, piety, and commitment to God, rather than the sacraments and other standards of the Catholic Church.

diaspora The emigration or spread of the Hebrews from Israel to other lands.

digital revolution The rapid change in communications since the 1980s involving computers, cell phones, the Internet, and information storage, allowing unprecedented access to information and discourse among the world's peoples.

diocese The area of the bishop's jurisdiction.

Directory French government from November 1795 to November 1799 that replaced the Convention with a board of five directors to rule France. The Directory pulled back from the radicalism of the Convention and ended the Terror, but kept France at war, refused to restore the monarchy, and persecuted rebellious clergymen.

divine right The theory that rulers, usually monarchs, received their right to rule from God.

doge The chief official of the Venetian republic; served for his lifetime.

Domesday Book The record ordered by King William the Conqueror of all his royal property in England.

Donation of Pepin A gift of lands in central Italy to the Roman church by Pepin the Short.

Donatism The movement begun by Donatus, a bishop of Carthage, who had led the northern African resistance to restoring lapsed churchmen.

Eastern bloc Term used to describe the Soviet Union and its satellite communist regimes of eastern Europe.

Eastern Question Nineteenth-century discussion among the great powers about what to do about the Ottoman Empire, which seemed on the point of collapse.

Edict of Milan An edict of universal religious toleration proclaimed by the co-emperors Constantine and Licinius, by which Christians and others could now practice their religions openly and without state restraint, and receive back the properties seized by the Roman state.

Edict of Nantes King Henry IV's measure of 1598 that established the terms upon which the Huguenots (Protestants) and Catholics could coexist within France.

Einsatzgruppen A German term meaning "task forces"; German units of the SS assigned to go into occupied areas of the Soviet Union and kill Jews, communists, and partisans.

émigré One who has left the country, usually for political reasons. In the French Revolution, the term applied to nobles, clergymen, and other opponents of the Revolution who fled to foreign countries to organize a counterrevolution.

empiricism In science, the use of observation and experiments to draw conclusions.

encomienda system A system used by the Spanish in the Americas in which a Spanish settler was given, in the name of the king, trusteeship over a piece of land and its native residents in exchange for the military enforcement of Spanish rule and a promise that the colonist would teach the indigenous peoples in his charge about Catholicism.

enlightened absolutism The attempt by absolutist rulers in central and eastern Europe to impose some of the ideals of the Enlightenment on their populations.

Enlightenment Intellectual movement in the eighteenth century emphasizing reason and applying the laws of nature discovered in the scientific revolution to human societies.

Entente An informal "understanding" between Britain, France, and Russia before World War I. Used to describe the forces allied against the Central Powers in the war.

Epicureans Followers of the Hellenistic philosopher Epicurus of Athens, who thought that the world was a product of random combinations of atoms and without an underlying purpose or goodness. The Epicureans renounced simple hedonism, treasured friendship, and sought emotional tranquility.

equestrians In the Early Roman Republic, the name of men in the cavalry; later used to refer to the class of Romans below that of the senators.

Estates General The medieval representative assembly of France, dismissed in 1614 and recalled only in 1788. It consisted of three estates: (1) the clergy, (2) nobility, and (3) the rest. Such assemblies existed in various forms throughout Europe; known as Diets in the Holy Roman Empire, the Sejm in Poland, Zemsky Sobor in Russia, the Riksdag in Sweden, and Parliament in England.

ethnic cleansing The policy of murder, deportation, and violence against members of an ethnic group in order to clear a territory of its members.

European Economic Community (EEC) Association of western European states founded in 1957 to eliminate tariffs and take steps toward economic integration with the goal of economic prosperity and international peace.

European Union (EU) A confederation of twenty-seven European states with a single market; the successor organization to the European Economic Community.

Eurozone Currency union of seventeen states in the European Union that use the euro as its currency.

existentialism Twentieth-century philosophy that emerged out of World War I and remained popular until the 1960s. It asserted that individuals were responsible for finding meaning in a world that was meaningless and incoherent.

extraterritoriality The state of being exempted from local laws. Applied to Europeans in Asia in the nineteenth and early twentieth centuries, this provision extended the jurisdiction of European home laws to Europeans overseas.

fasces A Roman political symbol, an ax and rods joined together to signify the magistrate's right to enforce physical punishment.

Fascism A twentieth-century ideology, marked by dictatorship and militant nationalism, that rejected communism, conservatism, liberalism, and democracy. Fascists stressed the primacy of the nation and directed all resources to strengthening it.

fin de siècle French term meaning "end of the century." Refers to the cultural crisis at the end of the nineteenth century marked by increased mobility, mass politics, and the decline of certainty, positivism, and liberalism.

First Triumvirate See Caesarian (or Consular) Faction.

Flagellants After the outbreak of plague in fourteenth-century Europe, a movement of people who scourged or whipped themselves to appease the anger of God.

the Forty-Five The failed Jacobite Uprising of 1745, in which Charles Edward Stuart ("Bonnie Prince Charlie") landed in the Scottish Highlands and sparked an uprising to restore the Stuart Monarchy in Great Britain.

Fourteen Points Peace plans formulated by U.S. president Wilson as the basis for a new world order after World War I. Called for free trade, German evacuation of occupied territory, national self-determination, and the end of secret treaties.

Freikorps Right-wing paramilitary groups in Germany after World War I consisting of veterans pledging to fight Communist uprisings in Germany; formed the vanguard of the Nazi movement.

Fronde A series of rebellions by nobles from 1648 to 1653 against the French monarch and the development of a fully absolutist state. It ended with the victory of Louis XIV.

galley A Venetian vessel that could be propelled forward either by oars or by wind-filled sails.

General Maximum Law passed in 1793 by the French Convention establishing price controls on food.

Genetic Adam The common male ancestor of human males, who lived in Africa about 75,000–60,000 years ago.

ghetto An area segregated by race or religion; the term was coined after an area of Venice called the *geto nuovo*, where in 1516 Jews were segregated. Prior to implementation of the final solution in World War II, the Nazis concentrated Jews in ghettoes before deporting survivors to extermination camps.

glasnost Term meaning "openness"; part of Soviet premier Mikhail Gorbachev's reform program in the late 1980s to break the tradition of secrecy that had characterized Soviet political culture.

globalization A process, involving the rapid movement of capital, people, and technologies, in which the world's peoples, especially their market economies, are increasingly tied together in the global economy.

Gnostics Those who know; elitist early Christians who thought that they had secret knowledge of God and the ways of the universe.

Golden Bull Issued in 1356 by the emperor Charles IV, recognizing the right of the seven German prince-electors to elect the emperor (so-called because of its golden seal).

Grande Armée Napoleon's highly advanced army, which grew to almost 600,000 men before suffering heavy losses in Russia in 1812.

Great (East-West) Schism The rupture or division between the Christian churches east and west that occurred in 1054.

Great Famine The devastating famine that struck northern Europe between 1315 and 1322.

great powers The five European powers that fielded the largest armies during the Seven Years' War—Britain, France, Russia, Prussia, and Austria; these nations would dominate European politics until at least 1918.

guild An association of craftsmen that controlled production, divided workers into masters and apprentices, and set the prices and terms of trade for goods.

gulag Russian acronym for the system of forced-labor camps used in the Soviet Union to hold criminals, prisoners of war, and political prisoners until the Khrushchev era.

gymnasium A Greek institution of recreation, exercise, education, and cultural exchange.

haruspicy Reading the will of the gods and signs of the future by studying the entrails, particularly the livers, of animals.

Hejira Muhammad's flight in 622 from Mecca to Medina, an event that marks the beginning of Islamic chronology.

heliocentric theory The theory that the planets circle the sun, as proposed by Aristarchus of Samos in the third century BCE.

Hellenistic Those Greek-like traits, tendencies, and cultures of the period after the Classical Age, particularly as they appeared in the wider Greek world shaped by Philip II and his son Alexander the Great.

Hellenization The promotion and spread of the Greek language and the civilized customs associated with Greek culture.

helots Agricultural slaves of the Spartans.

henge Typically, a Neolithic earthenwork having a ditch and ring-shaped bank. Stonehenge, without a ditch, is atypical.

henotheism A preference for one god while still allowing for the existence of other gods.

hieroglyphics The oldest of three forms of ancient Egyptian writing, which the Greeks named "sacred carvings." Hieroglyphics, which were not understood in modern times until the nineteenth century, are a complex system of over seven hundred signs, including pictographic, phonographic, and ideographic elements.

Highlanders Residents of the Highlands in northern Scotland whose Celtic language, clan system, and Catholic religion made them distinct from the Presbyterian, commercially oriented Lowland Scots who inhabited regions closer to the English border.

Holocaust The systematic extermination of about six million Jews by Nazi Germany during World War II.

hoplite The soldier who served in the phalanx formation of infantry for a Greek polis.

hubris A Greek term for exaggerated or dangerous pride.

Huguenots French Protestants or Calvinists.

humanist In the Middle Ages, one with an interest in the classics, Latin eloquence, and human affairs.

Hundred Years' War Between 1337 and 1453, the war waged between France and England over England's claims on the kingdom of France.

hyperinflation Catastrophic rate of inflation, resulting in enormous price increases, such as that which occurred in Germany in 1923.

iconoclasm Icon breaking; the iconoclasts of the Byzantine world denied the veneration of images and sought to destroy icons.

imperator The title of a Roman military commander in the Republican period; used in the Roman Empire to refer to the general commander of the empire.

imperial exchange The exchange, between Europe and its colonies, of goods and ideas such as Christianity, weapons and industrial machinery, and diamonds, tea, rubber, and oriental carpets, resulting in cheap commodities for European consumers.

Impressionism The nineteenth-century school of painting that used thick brushstrokes and stressed the depiction of light.

incunabula The books printed in the first fifty years of printing, thus approximately between 1450 and 1500; *incunabula* means "from the cradle" or "beginning."

indulgence A Catholic device for the remission (through penance or its equivalent) of eternal punishments incurred through sin.

Industrial Revolution The cascade of economic and technological changes since the late eighteenth century that resulted in dramatically increased production using centralized facto ries, usually powered by machinery.

inquisition In the mid-thirteenth century, a process formalized by the papacy to investigate heretics and heretical belief.

intendants French officials, usually nonnobles, sent out to assert the will of the monarch in the provinces of France in the seventeenth and eighteenth centuries.

interdict The exclusion by the pope or a high ecclesiastic such as a bishop of a person, city, or kingdom from participating in or receiving the benefits of the Catholic religion.

Investiture Controversy The dispute that broke out during the pontificate of Gregory VII over the lay investiture of ecclesiastical officeholders, specifically bishops.

Iron Curtain Term first used by Winston Churchill in 1946 to describe the hardening divisions between the Soviet Union and the western powers after World War II. It became a metaphor to describe the division of western and eastern Europe during the Cold War.

Italian Renaissance The term *renaissance* literally means a "rebirth"; when applied to the Italian cultural movement of the fifteenth century, it means the rebirth or, more vaguely, the recovery of the glories of the classical world.

Jacobin Club Parisian political club that grew increasingly radical after 1789. The Jacobins dominated French politics in 1793 and 1794.

Jacquerie The peasants' revolt that broke out in France in 1358; named after the caricature of a good peasant, Jacques Bonhomme.

Jansenism A religious movement among seventeenth- and eighteenth-century Catholics that stressed salvation through faith and simpler, more emotional forms of worship.

jihad Holy war or an individual's personal calling to strive to conform to God's will.

Junkers Traditional landowning nobility in Prussia that exercised substantial political influence on the Prussian, and later German, monarchs.

keep A stone tower erected on an elevated site as part of a castle; it served as the lord's residence and the most defensible and sturdy part of the castle.

Kharijites "Those who walked out," a group that withdrew their support from the caliph Ali.

koine The grammatically simpler form of Greek that became the standard Greek of the Hellenistic Age.

Kulturkampf A German term meaning "culture war"; refers to Bismarck's battle against Catholicism in the 1870s in the newly unified Germany.

laissez-faire Literally, "let it be." An economic theory, developed during the Enlightenment, by which governments should not regulate or intervene in the economy, except to protect property and maintain public order.

Lateran Accords Agreement in 1929 between the papacy and Italy establishing Vatican City as a state and providing state support to Catholicism in Italy.

lay investiture The act by which laymen (lords, kings, emperors) invested bishops with the symbols of their religious offices.

League of Nations Organization of states established after World War I with the goal of resolving disputes through arbitration and maintaining peace.

Lebensraum A German term meaning "living space"; idea conceived before World War I and adopted by the Nazis, stating that Germans needed living space in the east and requiring that the racially inferior inhabitants living there should be killed, enslaved, or forced off the land.

Lend-Lease Agreement American program to supply the Allies in World War II from 1941 to 1945.

liberal (liberalism) An ideology, beginning in the nineteenth century, that stressed the freedom of individuals to use their natural rights. In economic terms, this meant little governmental interference. In the political sphere, liberals usually preferred monarchs constrained by written constitutions.

Linear B A script characterized by straight lines that was employed to write a form of archaic Greek on late Minoan Crete as well as in Mycenaean Greece.

linear perspective A system, based on geometry, used by Italian Renaissance artists to give painted figures a sense of depth.

Little Ice Age A period beginning around 1275–1300 in Europe, in which temperatures dropped and ice fields and glaciers advanced.

Lollards (idlers) A name used by Catholic critics to characterize the supporters of John Wyclif and his teachings on the nature of the church and Christian belief.

long peace The period between 1815 (Napoleonic Wars) and 1914 (First World War) in European history in which no large, general wars encompassing all of Europe broke out.

ma'at An ancient Egyptian principle embodying justice, truth, wisdom, and harmony.

magistrate A representative of the Roman people given the right to hold executive power.

Magna Carta A great charter issued in England in 1215 by King John that provided a series of guarantees to the magnates and people of England, delimiting what the king could demand of his people and powerful lords.

mandates (mandate system) Legal mechanism established in the post-1918 peace treaties by which the administrative functions of the former territories of the Ottoman and German Empires were transferred to the League of Nations, who then entrusted them to be ruled by Britain and France.

Manhattan Project Code name for the research project led by the United States to develop an atomic bomb during World War II.

manorialism An economic and social system in which the holder of the land lives in a manor house and supervises land farmed by dependent laborers.

Marshall Plan American aid package offered to Europe and accepted by western Europeans in 1948 to help rebuild Europe, establish free trade and stability, and combat the appeal of communism.

materfamilias The mother or mistress of the Roman household, who managed the family's children, servants, slaves, and daily resources.

Medieval Warm Period A period of warmer temperatures that stretched from 775 to 1275, reaching its peak in the late eleventh and early twelfth centuries.

mendicants Begging friars such as the Franciscans and Dominicans who devoted themselves to the Roman Catholic Church, the papacy, the poor, and the sick; preached and begged in the cities of Europe; and practiced absolute poverty.

meritocracy The practice of promoting or appointing individuals in government based on merits—such as skill, credentials, and ability—rather than on social status.

Methodism A Protestant sect, emerging out of Anglicanism in the eighteenth century, that stressed piety and preaching the gospel to the common people.

metic A resident foreigner of Athens.

millenarianism The belief that the end of the world is near and a new time of peace and prosperity at hand.

missi dominici Carolingian royal officials (agents of the lord) who were sent into the kingdom to administer the king's justice (traveling judges).

Mitochondrial Eve The common matrilineal (descending from the mother) ancestor of all living humans, who lived approximately 170,000 years ago in Africa.

modernism An umbrella term used to describe cultural and artistic developments from the late nineteenth century until the middle of the twentieth century. Stressed abstraction and universality but also uncertainty and the workings of the unconsciousness.

monophysite The view that God the Father had one, divine nature, and so was unique and omnipotent.

monotheism The religious belief that there is only one god.

Monroe Doctrine Proclamation by U.S. president James Monroe's administration and backed by Britain saying that the Western Hemisphere was off limits to colonization.

mystery religions Those religions that emerged in the Hellenistic world with secret practices and rites of initiation.

Nansen passport Travel papers issued by the League of Nations to refugees who had no homeland after World War I and the Russian Revolution, allowing them to settle in a country that accepted the passport.

Napoleonic Code The name used for the legal codes introduced by Napoleon in 1804, 1806, 1807, and 1808, which imposed a single civil law on France and French-occupied territories. The code outlawed privileges based on birth, allowed freedom of religion, mandated meritocracy, and protected private property.

National Assembly Transitional body established after the Tennis Court Oath in 1789 to replace the Estates General, act as a legislature, and write a new constitution. Replaced by the Constituent Assembly in 1791.

national self-determination The policy articulated by American president Wilson after World War I, which stated that a group considering itself a nation has the right to be ruled only by members of that nation.

nationalism An ideology, originating during the era of the French Revolution and the Napoleonic Wars, that stressed the importance of national identity and the nation-state.

nation-state The dominant form of political organization since the nineteenth century, consisting of a community of people who have a sense of unity based on belief in a common culture and shared interests.

natural law Understandable, rational laws believed to be inherent in nature rather than established by humans.

natural selection A key element in Darwin's theory of evolution, stating that forms of life with traits better suited to survival will reproduce in larger numbers, leading to the extinction of weaker ones.

nave From the Latin *navis* for ship, so named because the central space of a basilica-style or longitudinal church resembles the upside-down hull of a ship.

Nazism German variety of fascism led by Adolf Hitler and the National Socialist Party from the 1920s until 1945; stressed the supremacy of the Aryan race and preached fierce anti-Semitism.

neoclassicism Eighteenth-century artistic movement that drew inspiration from the classical art and architecture of ancient Greece and Rome.

neo-Europes Areas of the world settled and dominated by Europeans and their descendants, such as North America and Australia.

New Economic Policy (NEP) Lenin's economic policy after the Russian civil wars intended to stabilize the economy of the USSR. The NEP allowed Soviet citizens to own land and to sell goods in the private marketplace.

Night of the Broken Glass The anti-Semitic pogrom of November 9, 1938; a series of coordinated attacks on Jews and Jewish property backed by the Nazi government.

nominalism A scholastic philosophy that maintained that universals are mere names and have no real existence, held in particular by William of Ockham.

North Atlantic Treaty Organization (NATO) Alliance of western European states, the United States, Canada, and Turkey during the Cold War, founded in 1949. NATO began to include a few eastern European states after the fall of communism.

numina The vague divine forces that Iron Age Romans believed animated their world.

Nuremberg Trials Trial of high-ranking Nazis after World War II, resulting in the execution of twelve officials for crimes against humanity.

Old Regime(s) European society before the French Revolution; marked by absolutism and privileges for the nobles and the clergy.

oligarchy A form of government in which power lies with the powerful few, often propertied aristocrats or the wealthy.

Orange Revolution The successful protest movement in late 2004 in Ukraine, which resulted in the overturning of rigged election results.

ostracism An institution in classical Athens to expel dangerous individuals from Athens for up to ten years. The procedure was so called because citizens cast ostraka, broken pieces of pottery (shards) or prepared ceramic pieces, with the name of the person they wished to ostracize into a large urn.

Ottonian system The practice of the Ottonian rulers of Germany of treating the churches of the realm and their property (lands, buildings, and worldly revenues) as part of its royal or imperial operation.

pandemic An outbreak of communicable disease extending over many regions and involving high mortality.

papal plenitude of power The doctrine by which the high medieval papacy claimed that the pope had unlimited or absolute power.

parlements Provincial French law courts that acted as legal checks to the absolutist monarch's power.

paterfamilias The powerful head of the large Roman family was the extended family's nominal father or master of the house. He was generally the senior male member of the family, perhaps a grandfather or an uncle, and his powers and responsibilities were far reaching.

patria potestas The extensive paternal power exercised by the *paterfamilias* of the Roman family unit.

patricians Men from the oldest, most well-established, and distinguished Roman families.

Pax Romana The Roman peace fashioned by Augustus and extending over the Roman Empire between approximately 27 BCE and 180 CE.

Peace of Augsburg The 1555 treaty between Protestant and Catholic powers in the Holy Roman Empire that acknowledged that there were two permissible forms of religious observance, Protestant and Catholic.

Peace of God The injunction, formulated by tenth-century churchmen, to curb the violence of local lords against innocents (farmers, women, and children) by threatening to excommunicate violators.

Peloponnesian League A group of poleis committed to the interests of the Peloponnesus of Greece.

perestroika Term meaning "restructuring"; part of Soviet premier Mikhail Gorbachev's unsuccessful reform program in the late 1980s to decentralize and reform the Soviet economy.

Petrine authority Resting its authority in part on Christ's appointment of Peter as the rock upon which he would build his church, the church of Rome claimed that Peter, the first bishop of Rome, and his successors (the popes), had the right and obligation to govern the whole of the church.

phalanx A rectangular formation of infantry.

philosophes Leading French writers and thinkers of the Enlightenment.

Pietism A movement among Protestants that stressed simplicity, reading the Bible, and more emotional forms of worship.

plebeians Lower-class Roman citizens who can be divided roughly into two groups, the farmers and merchants, both of whom held a subordinate position within the Roman Republic.

pluralism The holding of several ecclesiastical offices at once as, for instance, when one man was bishop over several episcopal sees at the same time.

pogrom Organized persecution of the helpless, particularly Jews; often involving beatings and burning of Jewish property; more common in eastern Europe, especially in the Pale of Settlement.

polis (plural, poleis) The Greek city-state, which contained a surrounding territory.

Polish Home Army The main resistance group to German rule in Poland during World War II; loyal to the pro-western Polish government in exile in London.

polytheism The religious belief that many gods exist.

Pontifex Maximus High priest of Roman religion who controlled the calendar and exercised authority over the various colleges of priests.

pontiffs High priests of the Roman Republic and Empire.

Popular Front An alliance of leftist political parties forged in the 1930s, particularly in France, to defeat fascists on the right.

Portolan chart A chart showing navigable ports, landmarks, geographical features, and compass headings so that a pilot could plot his course with respect to the shoreline and his ship's present position.

positivism A nineteenth-century philosophy developed by Auguste Comte that held that scientific investigation and accumulation of data could enable thinkers to discover the laws of mankind and improve society.

postmodernism Umbrella term for artistic styles that reject objective reality, embrace relativism, and stress fragmentation.

praetor Magistrate dealing with military and foreign affairs.

Praetorian Guard A band of soldiers created by the emperor Augustus as his own imperial bodyguard. This guard continued throughout the imperial period.

prehistory The long period (200,000–3300 BCE) before the birth of writing in Mesopotamia, when humans lived in wandering groups that hunted and foraged.

primogeniture The practice, particularly in France, by which land and title passed to the eldest son, not to all heirs.

proletariat The industrial working class described by Marx.

Protestant One who adheres to one of the churches that emerged in the sixteenth century in opposition to the Catholic Church, its teachings, and its practices.

provisional government The interim government set up in Russia after the czar abdicated in spring 1917 and lasting until November 1917; headed by the democratic socialist Alexander Kerensky.

public sphere The virtual world in which individuals from different regions, status groups, and religious backgrounds speak to one another, and to society at large (often in print), on subjects of mutual interest.

purgatory A Catholic doctrine of an intermediate place or station between heaven and hell where after death humans await the Last Judgment.

Pyrrhic Victory Named after the experience of King Pyrrhus of Epirus, who waged a series of successful battles against Rome but found them too costly and withdrew. Hence, such a victory is one that comes at too great a cost.

quadrivium Mathematics, geometry, astronomy, and music; the material component of the seven liberal arts.

quaestor Magistrate and investigator of the Roman Republic.

rationalism The theory that the mind can ascertain truth through thinking, rather than through experimentation and observation; also, more generally, the idea that, through reason, humans can understand the world.

realism A nineteenth-century artistic movement that depicted contemporary objects and people as they appeared in objective reality.

Realpolitik The pragmatic practice of power politics based on realistic chances of success rather than ideals; associated with Bismarck's foreign policy.

Reign of Terror ("the Terror") The attempt to purge enemies of the revolution in 1793 and 1794, leading to arbitrary executions and general chaos as tens of thousands were executed.

relics The remains left behind by the saints such as their bones and objects they touched, which are called contact relics.

Renaissance humanism A set of beliefs and educational standards based on and formed by the mastery of ancient languages; the close, unmediated reading of ancient texts; and the emulation of ancient literary, artistic, and philosophical models.

Renaissance individualism The belief that human beings occupy a special place in the created world and are capable of extraordinary achievements.

revisionism (socialist) A moderate form of socialism, according to which increased equality and better working conditions could be obtained peacefully through parliamentary politics rather than through revolution.

Risorgimento An Italian term for "revival"; refers to the Italian unification movement in the nineteenth century.

robot The obligation of serfs to work the landlord's land for several days a week.

romanticism A cultural and literary movement in the first half of the nineteenth century that stressed feeling over reason.

salons Private gatherings in the Enlightenment, run mostly by aristocratic women, in which discussions of science, politics, economics, and literature took place.

sans-culottes Literally, "without breeches." Radical urban Parisians who demanded legislation such as the General Maximum, which would benefit Parisian workers.

satrap The governor of a satrapy or incorporated part of the Persian Empire who was directly subject to the great king.

Schengen Agreements Treaty signed in European Community nations in 1985 to eliminate internal border controls.

Schlieffen Plan The war plan designed in the German military by Count Alfred von Schlieffen that called for a swift defeat of France in six weeks before committing full forces against Russia; implemented by the Germans in 1914.

scholasticism The general term for the intellectual movement of university thinkers (the schoolmen) of the period between 1150 and 1350.

scramble for Africa The rapid imposition of European rule in Africa beginning in the 1870s and lasting until 1914.

Sea Raiders Unknown peoples who raided in the eastern Mediterranean Sea during the last centuries of the second millennium BCE.

second industrial revolution A new phase of industrialization beginning in the 1870s with breakthroughs in chemistry, electricity, and steel production.

second serfdom The gradual reimposition of serfdom in eastern Europe from the end of the sixteenth century until the middle of the nineteenth century.

Second Vatican Council (Vatican II) High-level meeting (1962–1965) of leaders of the Catholic Church, which resulted in reforms, including interfaith dialogue and the use of vernacular languages in the mass.

sedentism The settling of humans in communities, villages, and cities.

seigneurial dues Payments or services owed by the peasant to the landlord. In some places it continued until the nineteenth century.

Senate Technically a body of seniors or patricians, the Senate was made up of men from the oldest, most well-established, and distinguished Roman families, and represented the aristocratic or oligarchic element in Roman government. In the Republic it exercised control over foreign affairs and war, domestic peace and order, state finance, and religion.

separate spheres The theory that men were fit for the public world of business and politics and women were fit for the domestic sphere of raising children and managing the household.

sepoys South Asian soldiers serving in the armies of European powers and companies in India.

serfdom The legal condition of peasants in Europe beginning in the late Middle Ages, in which the peasant serfs were tied to the land, required to do work on the landlord's property, and needed permission to move or marry; serfdom lasted until the middle of the nineteenth century in portions of eastern Europe.

Shari'ah A code of sacred law determined by legal scholars based on the Qur'an, the traditions of Muhammad, community standards, and precedents.

shock therapy The rapid privatization of previously state-owned enterprises, withdrawal of state subsidies, and relinquishment of price controls. Attempted most notably in Russia and other former communist states in the early 1990s to engineer the rapid transition from a communist to a market economy.

show trial Highly publicized trial in which the outcome has been decided beforehand. Most prominently used in Stalin's regime in the 1930s and in eastern European satellite states in the late 1940s and early 1950s.

simony Named after Simon Magus; the buying or selling of church offices.

Skeptics Practitioners of Skepticism, a form of Hellenistic philosophy that doubted all knowledge.

social contract The idea that humans in their original state of nature agreed to give up some of their natural rights to a ruler in exchange for order and stability.

social Darwinism The late nineteenth- and twentieth-century application of Darwin's theory of evolution to human societies with an emphasis on "survival of the fittest."

social market economy Set of social and economic policies that embraced the capitalist marketplace but also tempered it with provisions guaranteeing social welfare. Characteristic of Western Europe after 1945.

socialist (socialism) An ideology that, in response to industrial capitalism, called for ownership of the means of production by the community, with the purpose of distributing wealth equally.

Society of Jesus (Jesuits) A Catholic holy order founded in the sixteenth century by Ignatius Loyola to convert Muslims and others to Christianity, and to teach.

society of orders The social hierarchy of the Old Regimes, based on birth and fixed in law; usually composed of three basic groups: the nobility, the clergy, and everyone else.

Socratic method A system of teaching named after Socrates that was based on asking students questions on the assumption that the questioned individuals already had the knowledge needed but by discovering it in this way, they would truly know the thing being taught and it would become part of their being.

Solidarity Polish trade union and political party established in 1980 that became the core around which resistance to the communist government formed.

sovereign debt crisis (Euro crisis) Financial crisis among European states since 2009 involving dangerously high levels of national debt accumulation, most notably in Greece and southern European countries.

soviets Workers' councils formed in factories, first during the 1905 revolution in Russia and then in the 1917 revolution; became the basis for government in the Soviet Union.

SPD (*Sozialdemokratische Partei Deutschlands*) Germany's socialist party; founded in the 1870s and banned until 1890.

spheres of influence The informal quasi-colonial division of a country such that others may exert significant political, economic, and cultural influence. Refers to the European division of China into various European zones (British, French, German, for example) in order to gain special privileges without having to take on the burden of administration.

"stab in the back" myth The false rumor circulating in Germany (Weimar Republic) after World War I that Germany had not lost the war but rather was betrayed, especially by Communists, Jews, and republicans operating on the home front.

Stakhanovite Heroicized model worker in the Soviet Union, based on the example of coal worker Alexei Stakhanov. Stakhanovites received perks such as telephones, apartments, or bicycles in exchange for their hard work and enthusiasm.

Stoics Practitioners of Stoicism, a form of Hellenistic philosophy that held that the material world and possessions were worthless, that all men should strive to do their best in all the things that they did or were forced to do, that it was virtuous activity that mattered, and that all should live in harmony with Nature.

stylites Pillar saints, such as Saint Simeon the Stylite (390–459), who lived atop poles or columns.

subsistence economy An agricultural economy that produces only enough food each year to meet its annual needs.

Sudetenland German name for the mountainous border lands of Czechoslovakia in the 1920s and 1930s containing a mostly German population; Nazi Germany demanded and received this territory in 1938.

suffragette Feminist movement in Britain in the early twentieth century seeking to obtain voting rights for women.

symbolism Artistic style of the late nineteenth century that rejected realism in favor of invoking symbols and mythological figures to represent and stir inner emotions.

syncretism The tendency to combine gods, religious beliefs, and practices.

T-4 Program Stands for Tiergarten 4, the address of the Berlin headquarters of the Nazi euthanasia program. Under the T-4 program, the Nazis began murdering mentally and physically handicapped people in 1939; officially stopped in Germany as a result of public pressure (though continued unofficially to 1945).

tabula rasa Literally, "blank slate." A theory favored by English intellectuals, such as John Locke, stating that individuals are born without innate knowledge and learn primarily through observation and experience.

taille The basic land tax imposed on peasants and nonnobles in France.

Tennis Court Oath A pledge by delegates of the Estates General, mostly the third estate, on June 20, 1789, not to disband until they had written a constitution for France. This declaration led to the formation of the National Assembly.

Tetrarchy The system of four rulers of the Roman Empire created by the emperor Diocletian, who appointed two Caesars to serve under the two emperors (Augusti).

Thermidorian reaction The overthrow of Robespierre and other radicals in 1794 as a reaction to the excesses of the Revolution, ending the Reign of Terror. The term refers to the month this occurred on the revolutionary calendar (July 1794).

third world Term used to describe countries not aligned with either the western (first world) or communist (second world) powers in the Cold War. The term has evolved to describe poorer countries.

tithe An obligatory contribution to the church, usually amounting to about 10 percent of earnings; a variety of taxes contained portions paid to the church as tithes.

Torah That part of the Hebrew Bible or Tanakh that contains Genesis, Exodus, Leviticus, Numbers, and Deuteronomy.

Tory Originally a derogatory term used to describe Catholic Irish bandits. It was applied to the faction supporting the king and the Anglican Church in the 1670s. This term stuck and the faction developed into a political party later known as the Conservatives.

total war A form of warfare in which all segments of society are mobilized for war and the distinction between soldier and civilian is blurred.

totalitarianism Authoritarian rule in which the state establishes and exercises complete domination over economic, political, cultural, and private matters, including religion.

Treaty of Brest-Litovsk Treaty between Germany and Bolshevik-controlled Russia in March 1918, in which most of the western Russian empire was ceded to Germany. These territories were taken away when Germany lost the war later that year.

Treaty of Versailles Peace treaty between Germany and the Allied powers that ended World War I.

treaty ports Certain ports in East Asia in which Europeans determined the trade and custom regulations and exempted themselves from local laws (see *extraterritoriality*).

tribune A representative of the Roman people or plebeians; one of ten such elected officers who presided over the Assembly of the People and had certain veto rights.

tribunes Leading magistrates of the Assembly of the People.

the Triumvirate Sometimes mistakenly called the Second Triumvirate; an alliance between Octavian (later Augustus), Marc Antony, and Lepidus that was officially sanctioned by the Roman Senate.

trivium Grammar, rhetoric, and logic; the language component of the seven liberal arts.

Truce of God Tenth-century churchmen extended the Peace of God to cover the violence done by knights and vassals to each other, forbidding violence on certain days of the week or times of the year.

Truman Doctrine U.S. president Harry Truman's policy initiated in 1947 stating that the United States would contain communism and offering military assistance to countries threatened by a communist takeover.

tympanum The curved space, often sculpted or painted, below an arch and above a lintel.

tyrants Autocrats in the Archaic Age of Greece who seized power by force.

Ummah In Islam the community of believers, the people of God.

Unam sanctam A bull issued by Pope Boniface VIII that declared the absolute supremacy of the papacy over all Christendom.

Ustasha Croatian fascists backed by Nazi Germany after the Germans conquered Yugoslavia; committed mass murder of Serbs and Jews during the war.

usury Charging interest on loans, a practice forbidden by the Catholic Church.

utilitarianism A nineteenth-century liberal philosophy that evaluated institutions on their social usefulness in order to achieve "the greatest good for the greatest number."

vassalage The institution or state of being a vassal, the sworn man of a more powerful individual.

velvet divorce The peaceful breakup of Czechoslovakia into the Czech Republic and the Republic of Slovakia in 1992.

velvet revolution Term for the nonviolent demonstrations at the end of 1989 that toppled the communist government of Czechoslovakia.

Versailles Palace built outside Paris and inhabited by Louis XIV. Its luxury and orderly design symbolized absolutism.

Vichy France French state established after France was defeated by Germany in 1940. It collaborated with the Germans until the Allies liberated France in 1944.

Victorian The era in Britain during which Queen Victoria reigned (1837–1901); associated with strict middle-class morality and values, such as patriarchal dominance, self-denial, self-improvement, deference, hard work, and separate spheres for women and men.

Vikings (or Northmen) Scandinavian (generally, Norse, Swedish, or Danish) raiders or pirates, so called from *vik*, meaning a bay or creek, from which their ships set out.

virtus A Latin term, meaning virtue or strength, which was part of the moral code of Rome's aristocratic elite.

volley-firing A military tactic developed during the military revolution, in which infantry would mass in lines, fire their muskets row by row, and repeat, allowing for a continuous line of fire.

war communism Economic system of the Bolsheviks during the Russian civil wars, involving nationalization of industry, state control of trade, collective farms, food rationing, and strict labor obligations.

war guilt clause Article in the Treaty of Versailles that placed the blame for World War I on Germany, creating bitter resentment among Germans.

Warsaw Pact Military alliance of eastern European communist regimes, led by the Soviet Union. It was founded in 1955 and disbanded after the fall of communism in eastern Europe.

welfare state Concept of the state as an institution responsible for the economic and social well-being of its citizens through governmental payments to the unemployed or disabled. Welfare states were also to provide public services such as health care and education.

Western (Papal) Schism A division, lasting from 1379 to 1449, between rival claimants as to who was the rightful pope.

Whig Originally a derogatory term used to describe fanatical Presbyterian Scottish bandits. This term was applied to the faction supporting parliamentary sovereignty and greater religious toleration. The Whigs became a major political faction in the eighteenth and nineteenth centuries, when they became known as the Liberals.

Ziggurat An elaborate temple structure erected by Ur-Nammu.

Zionism The Jewish nationalist movement started in the 1890s by Theodore Herzl; sought to establish an independent Jewish state in Palestine.

Zollverein The German customs union led by Prussia, which by 1834 contained the states that would make up the united Germany in 1871; it excluded Austria.

REFERENCES AND READINGS

Chapter 1

Anthony, David W. *The Horse, the Wheel, and Language: How Bronze-Age Riders from the Eurasian Steppes Shaped the Modern World.* Princeton, N.J.: Princeton University Press, 2007.

Kurht, A. *The Ancient Near East, c. 3000–330 BC,* 2 vols. London: Routledge, 1997.

Renfrew, Colin. *Prehistory: The Making of the Human Mind.* London: Weidenfeld & Nicolson, 2007.

Chapter 2

Bakker, Egbert J., Irene J. F. de Jong, and Hans van Wees, eds. *Brill's Companion to Herodotus.* Leiden/Boston: Brill, 2002.

Fontenrose, Joseph. *The Delphic Oracle: Its Responses and Operations with a Catalogue of Responses.* Berkeley: University of California Press, 1978.

Hornblower, Simon. *The Greek World, 479–323 BC.* London/New York: Methuen, 1983.

Osborne, Robin. *Greece in the Making, 1200–479 BC.* London/New York: Routledge, 1996.

Podlecki, A. J. *The Life of Themistocles: A Critical Survey of the Literary and Archaeological Evidence.* Montreal: McGill-Queen's University Press, 1975.

Samons II, Loren J., ed. *The Cambridge Companion to the Age of Pericles.* Cambridge/New York: Cambridge University Press, 2007.

Chapter 3

Archibald, Zofia H., John K. Davies, and Vincent Gabrielsen, eds. *Making, Moving and Managing: The New World of Ancient Economies, 323–31 BC.* Oxford: Oxbow Books, 2005.

Charboneaux, Jean, Roland Martin, and François Villard. *Hellenistic Art (330–50 B.C.),* Vol. 18: *Arts of Mankind.* New York: Braziller, 1973.

Havelock, Christine Mitchell. *Hellenistic Art: The Art from the Death of Alexander the Great to the Battle of Actium.* New York: Norton, 1981.

Walbank, F. W. *Cambridge Ancient History,* 2nd ed., Vol. 7.1: *The Hellenistic World.* Cambridge: Cambridge University Press, 2008.

Worthington, Ian. *Alexander the Great: Man and God.* Harlow, England/New York: Pearson/Longman, 2004.

Chapter 4

Bringmann, Klaus. *A History of the Roman Republic,* trans. W. J. Smyth. Cambridge: Polity, 2007.

Flower, Harriet I., ed. *The Cambridge Companion to the Roman Republic.* Cambridge: Cambridge University Press, 2004.

Scullard, H. H. *Festivals and Ceremonies of the Roman Republic.* London: Thames and Hudson, 1981.

Chapter 5

Galinsky, Karl, ed. *The Cambridge Companion to the Age of Augustus.* Cambridge: Cambridge University Press, 2005.

Hadot, Pierre. *The Inner Citadel: The Meditations of Marcus Aurelius,* trans. Michael Chase. Cambridge, Mass.: Harvard University Press, 1998.

Knapp, Robert. *Invisible Romans.* Cambridge, Mass.: Harvard University Press, 2011.

Polter, David S., ed. *A Companion to the Roman Empire.* Oxford: Blackwell, 2006.

Shelton, Jo-Ann. *As the Romans Did: A Sourcebook in Roman Social History,* 2nd ed. Oxford: Oxford University Press, 1998.

Zanker, Paul. *The Power of Images in the Age of Augustus,* trans. Alan Shapiro. Ann Arbor: University of Michigan Press, 1988.

Chapter 6

Bandinelli, Ranucci Binchi. *Rome: The Late Empire. Roman Art A.D. 200–400,* trans. Peter Green. New York: George Braziller, 1971.

Barnes, Timothy David. *The New Empire of Diocletian and Constantine.* Cambridge, Mass.: Harvard University Press, 1982.

Brown, Peter. *The World of Late Antiquity from Marcus Aurelius to Muhammad.* London: Thames and Hudson, 1971.

Ehrman, Bart D. *Lost Christianities: The Battle for Scripture and the Faiths We Never Knew.* Oxford: Oxford University Press, 2003.

MacMullen, Ramsay. *Corruption and the Decline of Rome.* New Haven and London: Yale University Press, 1988.

Ward-Perkins, Bryan. *The Fall of Rome and the End of Civilization.* Oxford: Oxford University Press, 2005.

Chapter 7

Brown, Peter. *The Cult of the Saints: Its Rise and Function in Latin Christianity.* Chicago: University of Chicago Press, 1981.

Cameron, Averil. *The Byzantines.* Malden, Mass.: Blackwell, 2006.

Donner, Fred M. *Muhammad and the Believers at the Origins of Islam.* Cambridge, Mass.: Harvard University Press, 2010.

Garver, Valerie L. *Women and Aristocratic Culture in the Carolingian World.* Ithaca, N.Y.: Cornell University Press, 2009.

Lapidus, Ira M. *A History of Islamic Societies.* Cambridge: Cambridge University Press, 2002.

McCormick, Michael. *Origins of the European Economy: Communications and Commerce, AD 300–900.* Cambridge: Cambridge University Press, 2001.

Treadgold, Warren T. *A Concise History of Byzantium.* New York: Palgrave, 2001.

Verhulst, Adriaan. *The Carolingian Economy.* Cambridge: Cambridge University Press, 2002.

Chapter 8

Abels, Richard. *Alfred the Great: War, Kingship, and Cultures in Anglo-Saxon England.* London and New York: Longman, 1998.

Allen, S. J., and Amt, Emilie, eds. *The Crusades: A Reader.* Toronto: University of Toronto Press, 2003.

The Complete Works of Liudprand of Cremona, trans. Paolo Squatriti. Washington, D.C.: The Catholic University of America Press, 2007.

Duby, Georges. *The Three Orders: Feudal Society Imagined*, trans. Arthur Goldhammer. Chicago: University of Chicago Press, 1980.

Chapter 9

Archambault, Paul J., trans. *A Monk's Confession: The Memoirs of Guibert of Nogent*. University Park: Pennsylvania State University Press, 1996.

Fichtenau, Heinrich. *Heretics and Scholars in the High Middle Ages, 1000–1200*, trans. Denise A. Kaiser. University Park: Pennsylvania State University Press, 1998.

Haskins, Charles Homer. *The Rise of Universities* (1923). Ithaca and London: Cornell University Press, 1957.

Kowaleski, Maryanne, ed. *Medieval Towns: A Reader*. Toronto: University of Toronto Press, 2006.

Moore, R. I. *The Formation of a Persecuting Society: Power and Deviance in Western Europe, 950–1250*. Oxford: Blackwell, 1990.

Mundy, John Hine. *Europe in the High Middle Ages*, 3rd ed. Harlow, England: Longman, 2000.

Southern, R. W. *Scholastic Humanism and the Unification of Europe*, Vol. 1: *Foundations*. Oxford: Blackwell, 1995.

Chapter 10

Brown, Neville. *History and Climate: A Eurocentric Perspective*. London: Routlege, 2001.

Fagan, Brian M. *The Little Ice Age: How Climate Made History, 1300–1850*. New York: Basic Books, 2000.

Herlihy, David. *The Black Death and the Transformation of the West*, ed. Samuel K. Cohn Jr. Cambridge, Mass.: Harvard University Press, 1997.

Jordan, William Chester. *The Great Famine: Northern Europe in the Early Fourteenth Century*. Princeton, N.J.: Princeton University Press, 1996.

Reyerson, Kathryn L. *Jacques Coeur: Entrepreneur and King's Bursar*. New York: Pearson Longman, 2005.

Waley, Daniel, and Peter Denley. *Later Medieval Europe, 1250–1520*, 3rd ed. New York: Pearson Longman, 2001.

Chapter 11

Burke, Peter. *The European Renaissance: Centres and Peripheries*. Oxford: Blackwell, 1998.

De Grazia, Sebastian. *Machiavelli in Hell*. Princeton, N.J.: Princeton University Press, 1989.

Pettegree, Andrew. *The Book in the Renaissance*. New Haven, Conn.: Yale University Press, 2010.

Ruggiero, Guido, ed. *A Companion to the Worlds of the Renaissance*. Malden, Mass.: Blackwell, 2002.

Schiffman, Zachary S. *Humanism and the Renaissance*. Boston and New York: Houghton Mifflin, 2002.

Snow, Edward. *Inside Bruegel: The Play of Images in "Children's Games."* New York: North Point Press, 1997.

Vasari, Giorgio. *Lives of the Artists*, 2 vols., trans. Geroge Bull. London: Penguin, 1987.

Chapter 12

Abulafia, David. *The Discovery of Mankind: Atlantic Encounters in the Age of Columbus*. New Haven and London: Yale University Press, 2008.

Bethencourt, Francisco, and Diego Ramada Curto, eds. *Portuguese Oceanic Expansion, 1400–1800*. Cambridge: Cambridge University Press, 2007.

Chiappelli, F., ed., with Michael J. B. Allen and Robert L. Benson. *First Images of America: The Impact of the New World on the Old*. Berkeley: University of California Press, 1976.

Elliott, J. H. *Empires of the Atlantic World: Britain and Spain in America, 1492–1830*. New Haven and London: Yale University Press, 2006.

Elliott, J. H. *The Old World and the New 1492–1650*. Cambridge: Cambridge University Press, 1970.

Newitt, M. D. D. *A History of Portuguese Overseas Expansion, 1400–1686*. London: Routledge, 2005.

Chapter 13

Collinson, Patrick. *The Reformation: A History*. New York: The Modern Library, 2004.

Goldstone, Lawrence, and Nancy Goldstone. *Out of the Flames: The Remarkable Story of a Fearless Scholar, a Fatal Heresy, and One of the Rarest Books in the World*. New York: Broadway Books, 2002.

Hsia, R. Po-chia, ed. *A Companion to the Reformation World*. Malden, Mass.: Blackwell, 2004.

MacCulloch, Diarmaid. *The Reformation*. New York: Viking, 2003.

O'Malley, John W. *Trent and All That: Reforming Catholicism in the Early Modern Era*. Cambridge, Mass.: Harvard University Press, 2000.

Rice, Eugene F., Jr., and Anthony Grafton. *The Foundations of Early Modern Europe, 1460-1559*, 2nd ed. New York: Norton, 1994.

Chapter 14

Blanning, Tim. *The Pursuit of Glory: The Five Revolutions That Made Modern Europe, 1648–1815*. New York: Penguin Books, 2007.

Clark, Christopher. *Iron Kingdom: The Rise and Downfall of Prussia, 1600–1947*. Cambridge, Mass.: Belknap/Harvard University Press, 2006.

Inalcik, Halil, and Donald Quataert, eds. *An Economic and Social History of the Ottoman Empire*, Vol. 2, 1600–1914. Cambridge: Cambridge University Press, 1994.

Kann, Robert A. *A History of the Habsburg Empire, 1526–1918*. Berkeley: University of California Press, 1974.

Kishlansky, Mark. *Monarchy Transformed: Britain 1603–1714*. New York: Penguin Books, 1997.

Parker, Geoffrey. *Europe in Crisis, 1598–1648*, 2nd ed. Oxford: Oxford University Press, 2001.

Roper, Lyndal. *Witch Craze: Terror and Fantasy in Baroque Germany*. New Haven, Conn.: Yale University Press, 2004.

Wilson, Peter H. *The Thirty Years' War; Europe's Tragedy*. Cambridge, Mass.: Belknap/Harvard University Press, 2009.

NOTES

Chapter 1

1. See Andrew Robinson, *The Story of Writing: Alphabets, Hieroglyphs & Pictograms,* 2nd ed. (New York: Thames & Hudson, 2007), 72–79.

Chapter 2

1. M. H. Hasen and T. H. Nielsen, eds. *An Inventory of Archaic and Classical Poleis* (Oxford: Oxford University Press, 2004).

Chapter 4

1. See Ingrid D. Rowland, *The Scarith of Scornello: A Tale of Renaissance Forgery* (Chicago: University of Chicago Press, 2004).

Chapter 5

1. Walter Scheidel, "Quantifying the Source of Slaves in the Early Roman Empire," *Journal of Roman Studies* 87 (1997), 156–169; "The Slave Population of Roman Italy: Speculation and Constraints," *Topoi* 9.1 (1999), 129–144; "The Roman Slave Supply," in *The Cambridge History of Slavery,* Vol. 1: *The Ancient Mediterranean World,* ed. K. Bradley and P. Cartledge (Cambridge: Cambridge University Press, 2011), 287–310.
2. See Ramsay MacMullen, *Romanization in the Time of Augustus* (New Haven and London: Yale University Press, 2000), 124–137.

Chapter 6

1. See *The Nag Hammadi Scriptures: The International Edition,* ed. Marvin Miller (New York: HarperOne, 2007).

Chapter 7

1. See Michael McCormick, Paul Edward Dutton, and Paul A. Mayewski, "Volcanoes and the Climate Forcing of Carolingian Europe, A.D. 750–950," *Speculum* 82 (2007), 865–895.

Chapter 8

1. Elizabeth A. R. Brown, "The Tyranny of a Construct: Feudalism and Historians of Medieval Europe," *American Historical Review* 79:4 (1974), 1063–1088; Susan Reynolds, *Fiefs and Vassals: The Medieval Evidence Reinterpreted* (New York: Oxford University Press, 1994).
2. See Jean Claude Schmitt, *The Holy Greyhound: Guinefort, Healer of Children since the Thirteenth Century* (Cambridge and New York: Cambridge University Press, 1983).
3. See R. Howard Bloch, *A Needle in the Right Hand of God: The Norman Conquest of 1066 and the Making of the Bayeux Tapestry* (New York: Random House, 2006).

Chapter 9

1. Constant Mews, *The Lost Love Letters of Heloise and Abelard: Perceptions of Dialogue in the Twelfth Century,* trans. Neville Chiavaroli and Constant Mews, revised and updated ed. (New York: Palgrave Macmillan, 2008); Jan M. Ziolkowski, "Lost and Not Yet Found: Heloise, Abelard, and the *Epistolae duorum amantium, Journal of Medieval Latin* 14 (2004), 171–202; Constant J. Mews, "Discussing Love: The *Epistolae duorum amantium* and Abelard's *Sic et Non,*" *Journal of Medieval Latin* 19 (2009), 130–147.
2. See Ivan Illich, *In the Vineyard of the Text: A Commentary to Hugh's Didascalicon* (Chicago: The University of Chicago Press, 1993).
3. See Reviel Netz and William Noel, *The Archimedes Codex* (London: Weidenfeld and Nicolson, 2007).

Chapter 10

1. See Eric Jager, *The Last Duel: A True Story of Crime, Scandal, and Trial by Combat in Medieval France* (New York: Broadway Books, 2004).
2. See Caroline Walker Bynum, *Wonderful Blood: Theology and Practice in Late Medieval Northern Germany* (Philadelphia: University of Pennsylvania Press, 2007).
3. See Marilyn Yalom, *Birth of the Chess Queen: A History* (New York: HarperCollins, 2004).

Chapter 11

1. See Peter Burke, *The Italian Renaissance: Culture and Society in Italy* (London: Polity Press, 1987).

Chapter 12

1. See Alfred W. Crosby Jr., *The Columbian Exchange: Biological and Cultural Consequences of 1492* (Westport, Conn.: Praeger, 2003).

Chapter 13

1. See R. W. Scribner, "The Printed Image as Historical Evidence," *German Life and Letters* 48.3 (1995), 324–337.
2. See Richard Marius, *Martin Luther: The Christian between God and Death* (Cambridge, Mass.: Harvard University Press, 1998), xii.

Chapter 14

1. Geoffrey Parker, "Crisis and Catastrophe: The World Crisis of the Seventeenth Century Reconsidered," in *The American Historical Review,* 113 (2008), 1053–1079.
2. Ibid., 1073.
3. Lyndal Roper, *Witch Craze: Terror and Fantasy in Baroque Germany* (New Haven, Conn.: Yale University Press, 2006), 222–246.
4. Tim Blanning, *The Pursuit of Glory: The Five Revolutions That Made Modern Europe, 1648–1815* (New York: Penguin Books, 2007), 559.
5. Quoted in Adam Nicolson, *God's Secretaries: The Making of the King James Bible* (New York: HarperCollins, 2003), 47.
6. Anon., *Conversations on the English Constitution* (London: 1828), Google ebooks, 180.
7. Mark Kishlansky, ed., *University of Chicago Readings in Western Civilization,* Vol. 6: *Early Modern Europe: Crisis of Authority* (Chicago: Chicago University Press, 1987), 371–380.

CREDITS

PHOTO CREDITS

Front Matter © Grant Faint/Photodisc/Getty Images.

Chapter 1 Opener: © ZUMA Press/Newscom; p. 4 (top): © South Tyrol Museum of Archaeology/EURAC/Marco Samadelli-Gregor Staschitz; p. 4 (bottom): © Leemage/Universal Images Group/Getty Images; p. 5: © De Agostini Picture Library/Getty Images; p. 10 (top): © Çatalhöyük Research Project. Photo by John G. Swogger.; p. 10 (bottom): © Photographer's Choice/Getty Images; p. 14: © Alfredo Dagli Orti/The Art Archive/Corbis; p. 15: © ECHO/Max Planck Institute for the History of Science; p. 16, p. 17: © De Agostini Picture Library/Getty Images; p. 21 (both): © S. Vannini/De Agostini Picture Library/Getty Images; p. 22: © De Agostini Picture Library/Getty Images; p. 24 (left): © Chris Hill/Getty Images; p. 24 (right): © Leemage/Universal Images Group/Getty Images; p. 26: © G. Dagli Orti/De Agostini Picture Library/Getty Images; p. 31: © Clara Amit/AFP/Getty Images/Newscom; p. 35: © H. Jensen/AFP/Getty Images/Newscom.

Chapter 2 Opener: © Heritage Images/Corbis; p. 38: © G. Nimatallah/De Agostini Picture Library/Getty Images; p. 40: Image copyright © The Metropolitan Museum of Art. Image source: Art Resource, NY; p. 41 (left): © Antikensammlung, Staatliche Museen, Berlin, Germany/Art Resource, NY; p. 41 (right): © The Gallery Collection/Corbis; p. 42: © Antikensammlung, Staatliche Museen, Berlin, Germany/Art Resource, NY; p. 43: © The Gallery Collection/Corbis; p. 45: © Michael Nicholson/Corbis; p. 47: © Gianni Dagli Orti/The Art Archive at Art Resource, NY; p. 48: © Leemage/Universal Images Group/Getty Images; p. 49: © Marie Mauzy/Art Resource, NY; p. 50: © Erich Lessing/Art Resource, NY; p. 52: © Gianni Dagli Orti/Corbis; p. 55: © Gianni Dagli Orti/The Art Archive at Art Resource, NY; p. 60: Image copyright © The Metropolitan Museum of Art. Image source: Art Resource, NY; p. 61: © Liam White/Alamy; p. 64 (top): © Neil Beer/Getty Images; p. 64 (bottom): © Gianni Dagli Orti/Corbis.

Chapter 3 Opener: © Ulli Seer/AGE Fotostock; p. 72: © David Lees/Corbis; p. 73: © Fernando G. Baptista/National Geographic Stock; p. 76: Courtesy of the University of Manchester; p. 78: © Antikensammlung, Staatliche Museen, Berlin, Germany/Art Resource, NY; p. 79: © Danita Delimont/Gallo Images/Getty Images; p. 81: © De Agostini Editore/G. Nimatallah/AGE Fotostock; p. 85: © David Lees/Corbis; p. 87: © The Art Gallery Collection/Alamy; p. 90: © The Granger Collection, New York; p. 92: © Burke/Triolo/Brand X Pictures/Jupiter Images; p. 93: © Gianni Dagli Orti/The Art Archive at Art Resource, NY; p. 95: © asisi GmbH; p. 96: © North Wind Picture Archives/Alamy; p. 98 (top): © The Metropolitan Museum of Art. Image source: Art Resource, NY; p. 98 (bottom): © G. Dagli Orti/De Agostini Picture Library/Getty Images.

Chapter 4 Opener: © Jeremy Horner/Corbis; p. 104 (top): © Alinari/Art Resource, NY; p. 104 (bottom left): © De Agostini Picture Library/Getty Images; p. 104 (bottom right): © Photoservice Electa/SuperStock; p. 106: © G. Dagli Orti/De Agostini Picture Library/Getty Images; p. 107 (left): © G. Nimatallah/De Agostini Picture Library/Getty Images; p. 107 (right): © Photoservice Electa/SuperStock; p. 108: © Araldo de Luca/Corbis; p. 109: © Scala/Art Resource, NY; p. 113: © Gianni Dagli Orti/Corbis; p. 117: © Araldo de Luca/Corbis; p. 121: © De Agostini Picture Library/Getty Images; p. 124: © Ancient Art & Architecture Collection Ltd/Alamy; p. 126: © Leemage/Universal Images Group/Getty Images; p. 127: © Scala/Art Resource, NY.

Chapter 5 Opener: © Jose Antonio Moreno/AGE Fotostock/Getty Images; p. 134 (top): © Araldo de Luca/Corbis; p. 134 (bottom): © G. Nimatallah/De Agostini Picture Library/Getty Images; p. 135: © Scala/Art Resource, NY; p. 137: © Vanni/Art Resource, NY; p. 139: © The Trustees of the British Museum/Art Resource, NY; p. 145: © Gjon Mili/Time & Life Pictures/Getty Images; p. 146: © The Metropolitan Museum of Art. Image source: Art Resource, NY; p. 148: © Axiom Photographic Limited/SuperStock; p. 149 (top): © Scala/Art Resource, NY; p. 149 (bottom): © B&Y Photography Inc./AGE Fotostock; p. 151: © De Agostini Editore/G. Dagli Orti/AGE Fotostock; p. 152: © Prisma Archivo/Alamy; p. 153: © G. Dagli Orti/De Agostini Picture Library/Getty Images; p. 154: © Bettmann/Corbis; p. 155 (top): © G. Nimatallah/De Agostini Picture Library/Getty Images; p. 155 (bottom): © The Granger Collection, New York; p. 156: AP Photo/Thanassis Stavrakis; p. 158: © Adam Eastland Rome/Alamy.

Chapter 6 Opener: © Guido Baviera/Grand Tour/Corbis; p. 164 (top): © Ashmolean Museum/The Art Archive at Art Resource, NY; p. 164 (bottom left), p. 164 (bottom right): © De Agostini Editore/G. Dagli Orti/AGE Fotostock; p. 165: © The Granger Collection, New York; p. 167 (top): © De Agostini Editore/G. Dagli Orti/AGE Fotostock; p. 167 (bottom): © Demetrio Carrasco/AGE Fotostock; p. 169: © www.BibleLandPictures.com/Alamy; p. 172: © SuperStock; p. 173: © SuperStock/AGE Fotostock; p. 174: © De Agostini Picture Library/Getty Images; p. 177: © Scala/Art Resource, NY; p. 178: © De Agostini Editore/G. Dagli Orti/AGE Fotostock; p. 182: © De Agostini Editore/AGE Fotostock; p. 186: © The Granger Collection, New York; p. 188: © Photoservice Electa/SuperStock; p. 189: © David Madison/Photodisc/Getty Images; p. 191: © Gérard Degeorge/Corbis.

Chapter 7 Opener: © The Granger Collection, New York; p. 198 (top): © Staatliche Museen/Art Resource, NY; p. 198 (bottom): © Harper Collins Publishers/The Art Archive at Art Resource, NY; p. 199: © Peter Willi/SuperStock/Getty Images; p. 201: © The Art Gallery Collection/Alamy; p. 203: © Marco Secchi/Getty Images; p. 205: © Réunion des Musées Nationaux/Art Resource, NY; p. 208: © Michele Falzone/Photographer's Choice/Getty Images; p. 210: © The Print Collector/Alamy; p. 213: © Peter Willi/SuperStock/Getty Images; p. 216: © Digital Vision/Punchstock; p. 217 (top): © akg/Bildarchiv Steffens/Newscom; p. 217 (bottom): © Bibliotheque Municipale, Boulogne-sur-Mer, France/Giraudon/The Bridgeman Art Library; p. 218: © Scala/White Images/Art Resource, NY; p. 220: © Harper Collins Publishers/The Art Archive at Art Resource, NY; p. 223: © The Granger Collection, New York; p. 224: © Werner Forman/Corbis; p. 226: © J. E. Bulloz/De Agostini Picture Library/Getty Images.

Chapter 8 Opener: © Scala/Art Resource, NY; p. 232 (top): © Champollion/akg-images/Newscom; p. 232 (bottom): © Cro

Magnon/Alamy; p. 235 (top): © Album/Oronoz/Newscom; p. 235 (bottom): © Alinari/Art Resource, NY; p. 237: © Archives Larousse, Paris, France/Giraudon/The Bridgeman Art Library; p. 238: © Marc Charmet/The Art Archive at Art Resource, NY; p. 239: © Erich Lessing/Art Resource, NY; p. 240: © The Bridgeman Art Library/Getty Images; p. 243 (all): © Corpus Christi College, Oxford, UK/The Bridgeman Art Library; p. 244: © Foto Marburg/Art Resource, NY; p. 246: © Alinari/Art Resource, NY; p. 249: © Gianni Dagli Orti/The Art Archive at Art Resource, NY; p. 251: © Ancient Art & Architecture Collection Ltd/Alamy; p. 252: © Alfredo Dagli Orti/The Art Archive/Corbis; p. 256: © Gianni Dagli Orti/Corbis.

Chapter 9 Opener: © Sylvain Sonnet/Corbis; p. 262: © HIP/Art Resource, NY; p. 263 (top): © G. Dagli Orti/De Agostini Picture Library/Getty Images; p. 263 (bottom): © Uwe Dettmar/Artedia/View Pictures/Newscom; p. 266: © Gianni Dagli Orti/The Art Archive at Art Resource, NY; p. 268: © Adam Woolfitt/Corbis; p. 269: © National Geographic Image Collection/The Bridgeman Art Library; p. 270: © HIP/Art Resource, NY; p. 271: © Alfredo Dagli Orti/The Art Archive/Corbis; p. 272: © Gianni Dagli Orti/The Art Archive at Art Resource, NY; p. 274: © Erich Lessing/Art Resource, NY; p. 277: © Paul Almasy/Corbis; p. 279: © De Agostini Picture Library/Getty Images; p. 281: © Gianni Dagli Orti/The Art Archive at Art Resource, NY; p. 284: © George Steinmetz/Corbis; p. 286: © Staatliche Museen/Art Resource, NY; p. 287: © Kharbine-Tapabor/The Art Archive at Art Resource, NY; p. 289: © Uwe Dettmar/Artedia/View Pictures/Newscom.

Chapter 10 Opener: © Stan Honda/AFP/Getty Images; p. 294 (top): © Dennis Kunkel Microscopy, Inc./Visuals Unlimited/Corbis; p. 294 (bottom): © Erich Lessing/Art Resource, NY; p. 295 (top): © Réunion des Musées Nationaux/Art Resource, NY; p. 295 (bottom): © The Gallery Collection/Corbis; p. 300: © C. Sappa/De Agostini/Getty Images; p. 302: © Bibliothèque Nationale, Paris, France/The Bridgeman Art Library; p. 303: © Museo Nazionale del Bargello, Florence, Italy/The Bridgeman Art Library; p. 305: © Bridgeman-Giraudon/Art Resource, NY; p. 307: © The Granger Collection, New York; p. 309: © Scala/White Images/Art Resource, NY; p. 311: © Eileen Tweedy/The Art Archive at Art Resource, NY; p. 312: © Erich Lessing/Art Resource, NY; p. 314: © Alfredo Dagli Orti/The Art Archive/Corbis; p. 316: © Bridgeman-Giraudon/Art Resource, NY; p. 317: © Capilla Real Cathedral, Granada, Spain/Art Resource, NY; p. 320: © The Gallery Collection/Corbis.

Chapter 11 Opener: © Erich Lessing/Art Resource, NY; p. 326 (top): © Veneranda Biblioteca Ambrosiana/De Agostini/Getty Images; p. 326 (bottom): © Mark Harris/The Image Bank/Getty Images; p. 330: © Gianni Dagli Orti/The Art Archive at Art Resource, NY; p. 333: © Sandro Botticelli/The Bridgeman Art Library/Getty Images; p. 335 (top): © Universal History Archive/Getty Images; p. 335 (bottom): © Imagno/Hulton Archive/Getty Images; p. 337: © Erich Lessing/Art Resource, NY; p. 341: © Bilderbox/AGE Fotostock; p. 344: © Scala/Art Resource, NY; p. 346: © Alinari/Art Resource, NY; p. 347: © The Bridgeman Art Library; p. 348: © Mark Harris/The Image Bank/Getty Images; p. 350: © Corbis; p. 352: © Private Collection/The Bridgeman Art Library; p. 353: © Corbis.

Chapter 12 Opener: © Gianni Dagli Orti/The Art Archive at Art Resource, NY; p. 358 (top): Ibero-Amerikanisches Institut, Stiftung Preussischer Kulturbesitz, Berlin/Art Resource, NY; p. 358 (bottom): © Diego Duran/The Bridgeman Art Library/Getty Images; p. 359: © The Metropolitan Museum of Art. Image source: Art Resource, NY; p. 360: © Abraham Cresques/The Bridgeman Art Library/Getty Images; p. 362: Courtesy of The New York Public Library; p. 364: © The Metropolitan Museum of Art. Image source: Art Resource, NY; p. 367: © Eric SA House/SuperStock/Getty Images; p. 369: © The Art Archive at Art Resource, NY; p. 371: Library of Congress [ea0146]; p. 374 (left): © The Granger Collection, New York; p. 374 (right): © Gianni Dagli Orti/The Art Archive at Art Resource, NY; p. 377: © Diego Duran/The Bridgeman Art Library/Getty Images; p. 379: © Gianni Dagli Orti/The Art Archive at Art Resource, NY; p. 385 (top left): © Art Resource, NY; p. 385 (top right): © The New York Public Library/Art Resource, NY; p. 385 (bottom): Courtesy of Gilberto Tommasi.

Chapter 13 Opener: © Gianni Dagli Orti/The Art Archive at Art Resource, NY; p. 388 (top left): © De Agostini/SuperStock; p. 388 (top right): © SuperStock; p. 388 (bottom): © akg-images/Newscom; p. 389 (top): © Image Asset Management Ltd./SuperStock; p. 389 (bottom): © The Gallery Collection/Corbis; p. 391: © Erich Lessing/Art Resource, NY; p. 393: Art Resource, NY; p. 398: © akg-images/Newscom; p. 400 (left): © Staatliche Museen, Berlin, Germany/Art Resource, NY; p. 400 (right): © The Art Archive at Art Resource, NY; p. 402: © akg-images/British Library/Newscom; p. 404: © Imagno/Hulton Archive/Getty Images; p. 406: © Roger-Viollet, Paris/The Bridgeman Art Library; p. 407: © The Bridgeman Art Library/Getty Images; p. 409: © akg-images/Pietro Baguzzi/Newscom; p. 410: © Gianni Dagli Orti/Corbis; p. 412: © Image Asset Management Ltd./SuperStock; p. 414: © The Gallery Collection/Corbis.

Chapter 14 Opener: © The Gallery Collection/Corbis; p. 422: © Scala/Art Resource, NY; p. 423, p. 428: © Staatsbibliothek zu Berlin, Stiftung Preussischer Kulturbesitz, Berlin, Germany/Art Resource, NY; p. 429: © akg-images/Newscom; p. 430: © Bridgeman-Giraudon/Art Resource, NY; p. 431: © Matt Propert/National Geographic Society/Corbis; p. 432: © Alinari Archives/Corbis; p. 434: © Sotheby's/akg-images/Newscom; p. 436: © akg-images/British Library/Newscom; p. 439: © Alfredo Dagli Orti/The Art Archive/Corbis; p. 441: © Michel Setboun/Corbis; p. 444: © The Metropolitan Museum of Art. Image source: Art Resource, NY; p. 446: © Gianni Dagli Orti/The Art Archive at Art Resource, NY; p. 448: © Hulton Archive/Getty Images; p. 450: © Mansell/Time & Life Pictures/Getty Images.

TEXT CREDITS

Chapter 1 p. 11: Jerry H. Bentley, Herbert F. Ziegler, and Heather E. Streets-Salter, *Traditions and Encounters: A Brief Global History*, 2nd ed., Table 1.1, p. 23. Copyright © 2010 by The McGraw-Hill Companies, Inc. Reprinted with permission.

Chapter 4 p. 111: Dennis Sherman and Joyce Salisbury, *The West in the World*, 4th ed., p. 112, Figure 4.3. Copyright © 2011 by The McGraw-Hill Companies, Inc. Reprinted with permission.

Chapter 5 p. 148: Dennis Sherman and Joyce Salisbury, *The West in the World*, 4th ed., Map 5.1, p. 144. Copyright © 2011 by The McGraw-Hill Companies, Inc. Reprinted with permission; p. 161: *Roman Civilization. Sourcebook II: The Empire*, ed. Naphtali Lewis and Meyer Reinhold (New York: Columbia University Press, 1955), pp. 9–11, 13–17, 19. Copyright 1955 Columbia University Press, copyright renewed 1983 by Naphtali Lewis and Meyer Reinhold. Reprinted with permission of Columbia University Press.

Chapter 7 p. 221: Dennis Sherman and Joyce Salisbury, *The West in the World*, 4th ed., Figure 7.8, p. 235. Copyright © 2011 by The McGraw-Hill Companies, Inc. Reprinted with permission; p. 229: Einhard, *The Life of Charlemagne* 18–19, trans. Paul Edward Dutton, in *Charlemagne's Courtier: The Complete Einhard* (Toronto: University of Toronto Press, 1998), pp. 27–29. © 1998 Paul Edward Dutton. Reprinted by permission of the University of Toronto Press.

Chapter 9 p. 291: Thomas Aquinas, *Summa Theologica* from *Basic Writings of Saint Thomas Aquinas,* ed. Anton C. Pegis, Vol. 1 (Indianapolis, IN: Hackett, 1997), pp. 21–24. Copyright © 1945 by Random House, Inc. Copyright renewed 1973 by Random House, Inc. Reprinted 1997 by Hackett Publishing Company, Inc. Reprinted by permission of Hackett Publishing Company, Inc. All rights reserved.

Chapter 13 p. 418: Translated by C. M. Jacobs and revised by Harold J. Grimm, from *Luther's Works,* Volume 31: *Career of the Reformer: I* by Martin Luther, edited by Grimm and Lehmann, pp. 25–33, copyright © 1957 Fortress Press, admin. Augsburg Fortress. Reproduced by permission. All rights reserved.

INDEX